W9-BSV-082

Rick Steves'®

BEST OF
EUROPE

2014

CONTENTS

Germany, Austria & Switzerland

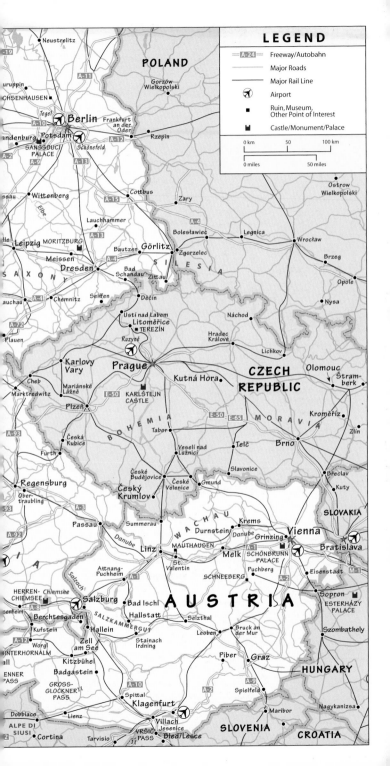

LEGEND

〓A-24〓 Freeway/Autobahn

Major Roads

Major Rail Line

✈ Airport

■ Ruin, Museum, Other Point of Interest

🏰 Castle/Monument/Palace

0 km · 50 · 100 km

0 miles · 50 miles

POLAND

Neustrelitz

uruppin

CHSENHAUSEN ■

Tegel

A-10 ✈ Berlin · Frankfurt an der Oder

andenburg · Potsdam ✈ Schönefeld · Rzepin

A-9 · SANSSOUCI PALACE

A-2

A-13

Gorzów Wielkopolski

Ostrow Wielkopolski

ssau · Wittenberg · Cottbus · Zary

Elbe · Lauchhammer · A-13 · A-15

A-4 · Bolesławiec · Legnica · Wrocław

lle · Leipzig · MORITZBURG

Meissen · Bautzen · Görlitz · Zgorzelec

SAXONY · Dresden · A-4 · Bad Schandau · Zittau

SILESIA · Brzeg

Opole

auchau · A-4 · Chemnitz · Seiffen · Děčín · Nysa

A-72 · Plauen · Ústí nad Labem · Litoměřice · TEREZÍN · Náchod

Ruzyně ✈ · Hradec Králové · Lichkov

Karlovy Vary · Prague · CZECH · Olomouc · Stram-berk

Cheb · Mariánské Lázně · Kutná Hora · REPUBLIC

Marktredwitz · KARLŠTEJN CASTLE · E-50 · Kroměříž

A-93 · Plzeň · E-50 · E-65 · MORAVIA · Zlín

Česká Kubice · BOHEMIA · Tabor · Telč · Brno

Furth · Veselí nad Lužnicí · Břeclav

Regensburg · Slavonice · Kuty

Ober-traubling · České Budějovice · České Velenice · Gmünd

93 · Český Krumlov · SLOVAKIA

A-92 · Passau · Summerau · WACHAU · Krems

Danube · Durnstein · Danube · Grinzing · Vienna

IA · Linz · MAUTHAUSEN · Melk · SCHÖNBRUNN PALACE · Bratislava

A-3 · St. Valentin · A-1 · Puchberg · Eisenstadt · M-1

Salzach · Attnang-Puchheim · SCHNEEBERG · A-2

HERREN- CHIEMSEE ■ · Chiemsee · Salzburg · Bad Ischl · A-1 · Sopron

senheim · SALZKAMMERGUT · ESTERHÁZY PALACE

Berchtesgaden · Hallstatt · Selzthal · AUSTRIA

Kufstein · Hallein · Stainach Irdning · Bruck an der Mur · Szombathely

A-12 · Worgl · Zell am See · Piber · Graz

INTERHORNALM · Kitzbühel · Badgastein · HUNGARY

ENNER · PASS · GROSS-GLOCKNER PASS · A-10 · Spittal · A-2 · Spielfeld

Dobbiaco · Lienz · Klagenfurt ✈ · Maribor · Nagykanizsa

ALPE DI SIUSI · Cortina · Tarvisio · Villach ✈ · Jesenice · SLOVENIA · CROATIA

2 · VRŠIČ PASS · Bled/Lesce

Leoben · Selztal · Piber

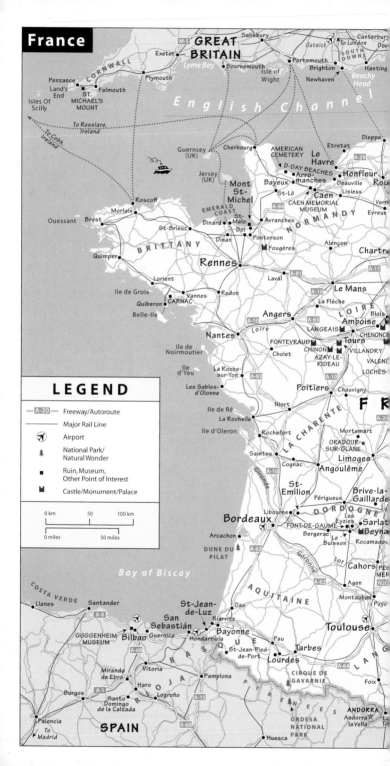

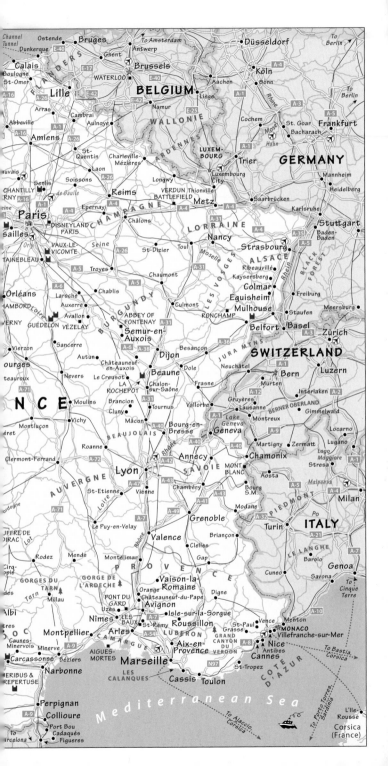

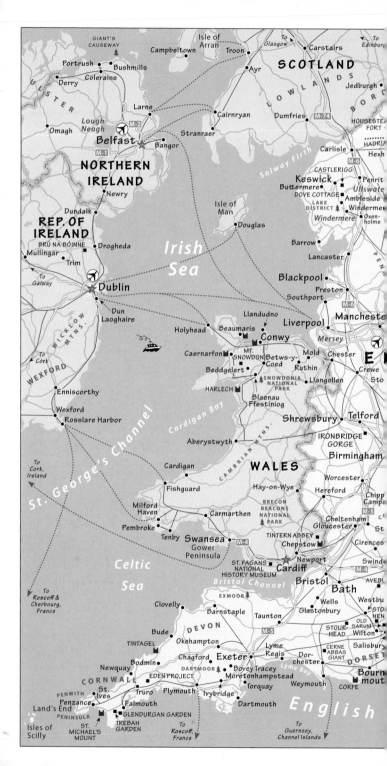

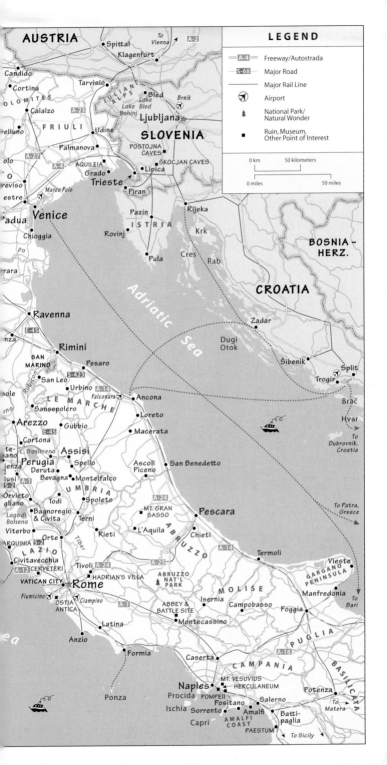

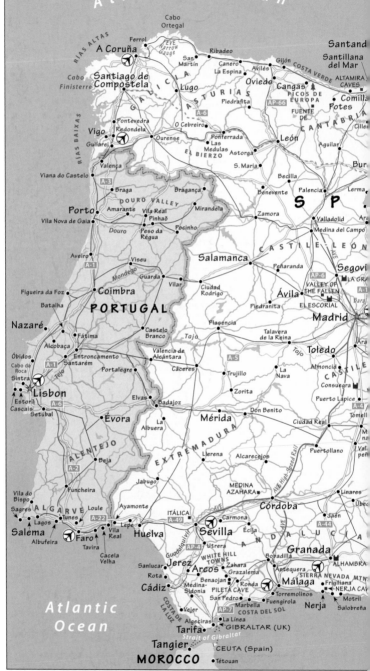

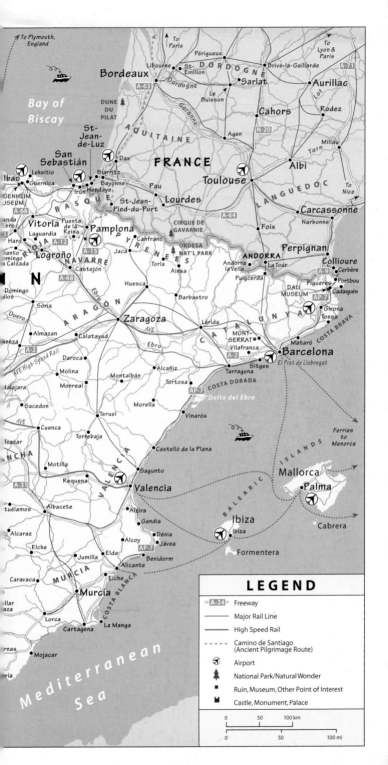

Rick Steves'

BEST OF
EUROPE
2014

500 Kilometers
300 Miles

N

HAARLEM
AMST. BERLIN
LONDON
BRUGES
RHINE
ROTH. SALZBURG
PARIS
BAVARIA
VIENNA
BERNER
HALLSTATT
OBERLAND
(GIMMELWALD)
VENICE
CINQUE
TERRE
PROVENCE
NICE
FLORENCE
BARCELONA
ROME

INTRODUCTION

Big Ben, the Eiffel Tower, and the Roman Colosseum. Yodeling in the Alps, biking down cobblestone paths, and taking a canal ride under the stars. Michelangelo's *David* and "Mad" King Ludwig's castles. Sunny Riviera beaches, medieval German towns, and Spanish streets that teem with people at night. Pasta and bratwurst, strudel and scones, Parisian crêpes and Tuscan grapes....

Europe offers a rich smorgasbord of cultures. To wrestle it down to a manageable size, this book breaks Europe into its top destinations. It then gives you all the information and opinions necessary to wring the maximum value out of your limited time and money in each location. If you plan to stay for two months or less in Europe, this book is all you need for a blitz trip.

Experiencing Europe's culture, people, and natural wonders economically and hassle-free has been my goal for more than 30 years of traveling, tour guiding, and travel writing. With this book, I pass on to you the lessons I've learned, updated for 2014.

Rick Steves' Best of Europe is the crème de la crème of places featured in my country guidebooks. It's balanced to include a comfortable mix of exciting cities and cozy towns: from Paris, London, and Rome to traffic-free Italian Riviera ports, alpine villages, and mom-and-pop châteaux. It covers the predictable biggies and mixes in a healthy dose of Back Door intimacy. Along with Leonardo in the Louvre, you'll enjoy Caterina in her cantina. I've been selective. For example, rather than listing countless medieval towns, I recommend only the best.

The best is, of course, only my opinion. But after three decades of travel research, I've developed a sixth sense for what travelers enjoy.

Key to This Book

Updates

This book is updated every year, but things change. For the latest, visit www.ricksteves.com/update. For a valuable list of reports and experiences—good and bad—from fellow travelers, check www.ricksteves.com/feedback.

Abbreviations and Times

I use the following symbols and abbreviations in this book:
Sights are rated:

▲▲▲   Don't miss
▲▲   Try hard to see
▲   Worthwhile if you can make it
No rating   Worth knowing about

Tourist information offices are abbreviated as **TI**, and bathrooms are WCs. To categorize accommodations, I use a **Sleep Code** (described on page 16).

Like Europe, this book uses the **24-hour clock**. It's the same through 12:00 noon, then keep going: 13:00, 14:00, and so on. For anything over 12, subtract 12 and add p.m. (14:00 is 2:00 p.m.).

When giving **opening times**, I include both peak season and off-season hours if they differ. So, if a museum is listed as "May–Oct daily 9:00–16:00," it should be open from 9 a.m. until 4 p.m. from the first day of May until the last day of October (but expect exceptions).

For **transit** or **tour departures**, I first list the frequency, then the duration. So, a train connection listed as "2/hour, 1.5 hours" departs twice each hour, and the journey lasts an hour and a half.

About This Book

This book is organized by destinations. Each destination is a mini-vacation on its own, filled with exciting sights, strollable neighborhoods, affordable places to stay, and memorable places to eat. In the following chapters, you'll find these sections:

Planning Your Time suggests a schedule for how to best use your limited time.

Orientation includes specifics on public transportation, helpful hints, local tour options, easy-to-read maps, and tourist information.

Sights describes the top attractions and includes their cost and hours.

Sleeping describes my favorite hotels, from good-value deals to cushy splurges.

Eating serves up a range of options, from inexpensive eateries to fancy restaurants.

Map Legend

⅃ʑ	Viewpoint	Ⓣ	Taxi Stand	) (	Tunnel
✦	Entrance	🅃	Tram Stop		Pedestrian Zone
❶	Tourist Info	🄼	Metro Stop		Railway
🆆🅲	Restroom	⊖	Tube		Ferry/Boat Route
🏰	Castle	🅄	U-Bahn	⊢┼┼┤	Tram
▪	Statue/Point of Interest	Ⓢ	S-Bahn		Stairs
🏠	Church	🅅	Vaporetto Stop	‧‧‧‧‧	Walk/Tour Route
	Mosque	🅃	Traghetto Crossing		Trail
	Synagogue	🄶	Gondola Station	○⊞⊞⊞○	Funicular
◎	Fountain	🄰	Alilaguna Stop	●━●●●━●	Mtn. Lift
▲	Mountain Peak	Ⓑ	Bus Stop	●⊞⊞⊞●	Mtn. Rail
	Park	🄿	Parking		Cable Car
)(	Mtn. Pass	Ⓢ	S-Tog Station		
✈	Airport	🄱	Harbor Bus		Gondola
		⛴	Boat Stop		

Use this legend to help you navigate the maps in this book.

Connections outlines your options for traveling to destinations by train, bus, and plane.

The **appendix** has transportation basics, a calling chart, a hotel reservation form, and information on US embassies for the countries in this book.

Browse through this book, choose your favorite destinations, and link them up. Then have a great trip! Traveling like a temporary local and taking advantage of the information here, you'll get the absolute most out of every mile, minute, and dollar. I'm happy you'll be visiting places I know and love, and meeting some of my favorite people.

Planning

This section will help you get started on planning your trip—with advice on trip costs, when to go, and what you should know before you take off.

Travel Smart

Your trip to Europe is like a complex play—easier to follow and to really appreciate on a second viewing. While no one does the same trip twice to gain that advantage, reading this book's chapters on your intended destinations before your trip accomplishes much the same thing.

Design an itinerary that enables you to visit sights at the best possible times. Note holidays, festivals, specifics on sights, and days when sights are closed or most crowded (all covered in this book). For example, many sights in Florence are closed on Mondays; Tuesdays are bad in Paris. Museums and sights, especially large ones, usually stop admitting people 30-60 minutes before closing time.

Be sure to mix intense and relaxed periods in your itinerary. To maximize rootedness, minimize one-night stands. It's worth taking a long drive after dinner (or a train ride with a dinner picnic) to get settled in a town for two nights. Every trip—and every traveler—needs at least a few slack days (for picnics, laundry, people-watching, and so on). Pace yourself. Assume you will return.

Reread this book as you travel, and visit local tourist information offices (abbreviated as TI in this book). Upon arrival in a new town, lay the groundwork for a smooth departure; get the schedule for the train, bus, or boat that you'll take when you depart.

Get online at Internet cafés or your hotel, and carry a mobile phone (or use a phone card) to make travel plans: You can find out tourist information, learn the latest on sights (special events, tour schedule, etc.), book tickets and tours, make reservations, reconfirm hotels, research transportation connections, and keep in touch with your loved ones.

Enjoy the friendliness of the local people. Connect with the culture. Slow down and be open to unexpected experiences. Ask questions—most locals are eager to point you in their idea of the right direction. Keep a notepad in your pocket to organize your thoughts, note directions, and confirm prices with vendors. Wear your money belt, learn the currency, and figure out how to estimate prices in dollars. Those who expect to travel smart, do.

Trip Costs

Five components make up your trip cost: airfare, surface transportation, room and board, sightseeing and entertainment, and shopping and miscellany.

Airfare: A basic round-trip flight from the US to Europe can cost, on average, about $1,000-1,800 total, depending on where you fly from and when (cheaper in winter), plus another $300–500 in taxes, fuel surcharges, and other fees. Consider saving time and money in Europe by flying into one city and out of another—for example, into London and out of Rome.

Surface Transportation: Your best mode of travel depends on the length and scope of your trip. Train passes normally must be

Best of Europe Itinerary

500 Kilometers
300 Miles

START — London
Amst. — Berlin
Bruges — END
RHINE
Salzburg
Roth.
BAVARIA — Vienna
Paris
SWISS ALPS
Venice
PROVENCE
CINQUE TERRE
Florence
Barcelona — Nice
Rome

purchased outside of Europe, but aren't necessarily your best option—you may save money by simply buying tickets as you go (for more information, see page 1420 of the appendix).

Drivers can figure about $400 per person per week (based on two people splitting the cost of the car, tolls, gas, and insurance). Car rental is cheapest to arrange from the US; for trips of three weeks or more, look into leasing.

Room and Board: You can easily manage in Europe in 2014 on an overall average of $120 a day per person for room and board (more for cities, less for towns). A $120-a-day budget allows an average of $15 for lunch, $5 for a snack, $25 for dinner, and $75 for lodging (based on two people splitting the cost of a $150 double room that includes breakfast). Students and tightwads can enjoy Europe for as little as $60 a day ($30 per hostel bed, $30 for meals and snacks).

Sightseeing and Entertainment: In big cities, figure $10–20 per major sight, $5–10 for minor ones, and $30 for splurge experiences (such as walking tours, concerts, or gelato binges). An overall average of $30 a day works for most. Don't skimp here. After all, this category is the driving force behind your trip—you came to sightsee, enjoy, and experience Europe.

Shopping and Miscellany: Figure $2 per postcard, $3 per

coffee and ice-cream cone, and $6 per beer. Shopping can vary in cost from nearly nothing to a small fortune. Good budget travelers find that this category has little to do with assembling a trip full of lifelong and wonderful memories.

Sightseeing Priorities

Only have a week to "see" Europe? You can't, of course, but if you're organized and energetic, you can see the two art-filled cultural capitals of London and Paris plus Europe's most magnificent landscape—the Swiss Alps.

Whether you have just a week, or longer, here are my recommended priorities. These itineraries are fast-paced, but doable by car or train, and each allows about two nights in each spot (I've taken geographical proximity into account). Most work best if you begin and end your trip by flying in and out of different cities (e.g., into London and out of Vienna).

If you have...

5 days:	Paris, Swiss Alps
7 days, add:	London
10 days, add:	Rome
14 days, add:	Rhine, Amsterdam, Haarlem
18 days, add:	Venice, Florence
24 days, add:	Cinque Terre, Rothenburg, Bavaria
27 days, add:	Salzburg, Hallstatt
33 days, add:	Nice, Provence, Barcelona
38 days, add:	Vienna, Berlin
40 days, add:	Bruges

When to Go

May, June, September, and October are the best travel months. Peak season, July and August, offers the sunniest weather and the most exciting slate of activities—but the worst crowds. During this busy time, it's best to reserve rooms well in advance, particularly in big cities.

During the off-season, October through April, expect generally shorter hours at attractions, more closures for lunchtime (especially at smaller sights), fewer activities, and fewer—if any—guided tours in English. Especially off-season, be sure to confirm opening hours for sights at local tourist information offices.

As a general rule any time of year, the climate north of the Alps is mild (like Seattle), while south of the Alps it's like Arizona. For specifics, see www.worldclimate.com. If you wilt in the heat, avoid the Mediterranean in summer. If you want blue skies in the Alps and Britain, travel during the height of summer.

Plan your itinerary to meet your needs. To beat the heat, start

Rick Steves' Audio Europe

If you're bringing a mobile device, be sure to check out **Rick Steves Audio Europe**, where you can download free audio tours and hours of travel interviews (via the Rick Steves Audio Europe smartphone app, www.ricksteves.com/audioeurope, iTunes, or Google Play).

My self-guided **audio tours** are user-friendly, easy-to-follow, fun, and informative and cover the major sights and neighborhoods in:

Vienna: St. Stephen's Cathedral, Vienna City Walk, and Ringstrasse Tram Tour

Salzburg: Salzburg Town Walk

Rhine: Best of the Rhine

Paris: Historic Paris Walk, Louvre, Orsay, and Versailles Palace

London: Westminster Walk, British Museum, British Library, St. Paul's Cathedral, and The City of London Walk

Rome: Colosseum, Forum, Pantheon, St. Peter's Basilica, Sistine Chapel, Trastevere, Jewish Ghetto, and Ostia Antica

Venice: Grand Canal Cruise, St. Mark's Square, St. Mark's Basilica, and Frari Church

Florence: Renaissance Walk, Uffizi Gallery, and Accademia

Amsterdam: Amsterdam City Walk, Red Light District Walk, Jordaan Walk

Compared to live tours, my audio tours are hard to beat: Nobody will stand you up, the quality is reliable, you can take the tour exactly when you like, and they're free.

Rick Steves Audio Europe also offers a far-reaching library of intriguing travel interviews with experts from around the globe.

in the south in the spring and work your way north. To moderate culture shock, start in Britain and travel south and east.

Know Before You Go

Your trip is more likely to go smoothly if you plan ahead. Check this list of things to arrange while you're still at home.

You need a **passport**—but no visa or shots—to travel to any of the countries in this book. You may be denied entry into certain European countries if your passport is due to expire within three to six months of your ticketed date of return. Get it renewed if you'll be cutting it close. It can take up to six weeks to get or renew a passport (for more on passports, see www.travel.state.gov). Pack a photocopy of your passport in your luggage in case the original is lost or stolen.

Book your rooms well in advance if you'll be traveling during peak season or any major **holidays** (the lists at www.ricksteves.com/festivals include most national holidays and major festivals).

Call your **debit- and credit-card companies** to let them know the countries you'll be visiting, to ask about fees, request your PIN code (it will be mailed to you), and more. See page 11 for details.

Do your homework if you want to buy **travel insurance.** Compare the cost of the insurance to the likelihood of your using it and your potential loss if something goes wrong. Also, check whether your existing insurance (health, homeowners, or renters) covers you and your possessions overseas. For more tips, see www.ricksteves.com/insurance.

Consider buying a **railpass** after researching your options (see page 1420 and www.ricksteves.com/rail for all the specifics).

If you're planning on **renting a car** in Europe, bring your driver's license. In addition, an International Driving Permit is required in Austria, Italy, and Spain. They're available at your local AAA office ($15 plus the cost of two passport-type photos, see www.aaa.com). For information on car-rental insurance, check www.ricksteves.com/cdw. Confirm pick-up hours—many car-rental offices close Saturday afternoon and all day Sunday.

If you're bringing a **mobile device,** download any apps you might want to use on the road, such as translators, maps, and transit schedules. Check out **Rick Steves Audio Europe,** featuring audio tours of major sights, hours of travel interviews, and more (via www.ricksteves.com/audioeurope, iTunes, Google Play, or the Rick Steves Audio Europe smartphone app; for details, see page 7).

Check the **Rick Steves guidebook updates** page for any recent changes to this book (www.ricksteves.com/update).

Because **airline carry-on restrictions** are always changing, visit the Transportation Security Administration's website (www.tsa.gov) for an up-to-date list of what you can bring on the plane with you...and what you must check. Some airlines may restrict you to only one carry-on (no extras like a purse or daypack); check with your airline.

Practicalities

Emergency and Medical Help: If you get sick, do as many Europeans do and go to a pharmacist for advice. Or ask at your hotel for help—they'll know the nearest medical and emergency services.

Theft or Loss: To replace a passport, you'll need to go in person to an embassy or consulate (see page 1417). If your credit and debit cards disappear, cancel and replace them (see "Damage Control for Lost Cards" on page 12). File a police report, either on the spot or within a day or two; you'll need it to submit an insurance claim for lost or stolen railpasses or travel gear, and it can help with replacing your passport or credit and debit cards. For more infor-

INTRODUCTION

mation, see www.ricksteves.com/help. Precautionary measures can minimize the effects of loss—back up your photos and other files frequently.

Time Zones: Most of continental Europe is generally six/nine hours ahead of the East/West Coasts of the US. Britain, which is one hour earlier than most of continental Europe, is five/eight hours ahead of the East/West Coasts. For a handy online time converter, try www.timeanddate.com/worldclock.

Watt's Up? Europe's electrical system is 220 volts, instead of North America's 110 volts. Most newer electronics (such as laptops, battery chargers, and hair dryers) convert automatically, so you won't need a converter, but you will need an adapter plug with two round prongs (or three square prongs in Britain), sold inexpensively at travel stores in the US. Avoid bringing older appliances that don't automatically convert voltage; instead, buy a cheap replacement in Europe.

Discounts: While discounts are not listed in this book, seniors (age 60 and over), students with International Student Identification Cards, teachers with proper identification, and youths under 18 often get discounts—but you have to ask. To get a teacher or student ID card, visit www.statravel.com or www.isic.org.

Additional Online Resources: Shoppers can check on VAT refunds (www.ricksteves.com/vat) and custom rules and duty rates (www.cbp.gov; click on "Travel," then "Know Before You Go"). For information on making calls, see www.ricksteves.com/phoning. For sightseeing tips and museum strategies, check www.ricksteves.com/sights.

Money

This section offers advice on how to pay for purchases on your trip (including getting cash from ATMs and paying with plastic), dealing with lost or stolen cards, and tipping.

What to Bring

Bring both a credit card and a debit card. You'll use the debit card at cash machines (ATMs) to withdraw cash for most purchases, and the credit card to pay for larger items. Some travelers carry a third card, in case one gets demagnetized or eaten by a temperamental machine.

For an emergency stash, bring several hundred dollars in hard cash in easy-to-exchange $20 bills. Avoid using currency exchange booths because of their lousy rates and/or outrageous fees. But if you're in France, you'll have to use currency booths—banks won't take dollars.

INTRODUCTION

Exchange Rates

1 euro (€) = about $1.30. To roughly convert prices in euros to dollars, add 30 percent: €20 is about $26.

1 British pound (£1) = about $1.60. To convert prices in pounds to dollars, add 60 percent.

1 Swiss franc (SF) = about $1.10. To easily convert prices in Swiss francs to dollars, add 10 percent.

Cash

Cash is just as desirable in Europe as it is at home. Small businesses (hotels, restaurants, and shops) prefer that you pay your bills with cash. Some vendors will charge you extra for using a credit card, and some won't take credit cards at all. Cash is the best—and sometimes only—way to pay for bus fares, taxis, and local guides.

Throughout Europe, ATMs are the standard way for travelers to get cash. Stay away from "independent" ATMs such as Travelex, Euronet, and Forex, which charge huge commissions and have terrible exchange rates.

To withdraw money from an ATM, you'll need a debit card (ideally with a Visa or MasterCard logo for maximum usability), plus a PIN code. Know your PIN code in numbers; there are only numbers—no letters—on European keypads. Although you can use a credit card for ATM transactions, it's generally more expensive (and only makes sense in an emergency) because it's considered a cash advance rather than a withdrawal. Try to withdraw large sums of money to reduce the number of per-transaction bank fees you'll pay.

Pickpockets target tourists. To safeguard your cash, wear a money belt—a pouch with a strap that you buckle around your waist like a belt and tuck under your clothes. Keep your cash, credit cards, and passport secure in your money belt, and carry only a day's spending money in your front pocket.

Credit and Debit Cards

For purchases, Visa and MasterCard are more commonly accepted than American Express. Just like at home, credit or debit cards work easily at larger hotels, restaurants, and shops. I typically use my debit card to withdraw cash to pay for most purchases. I use my credit card only in a few specific situations: to book hotel reservations by phone, to cover major expenses (such as car rentals, plane tickets, and hotel stays), and to pay for things near the end of my trip (to avoid another visit to the ATM). While you could use a debit card to make most large purchases, using a credit card offers a

INTRODUCTION

greater degree of fraud protection (because debit cards draw funds directly from your account).

Ask Your Credit- or Debit-Card Company: Before your trip, contact the company that issued your debit or credit cards.

• Confirm that your card will work overseas, and alert them that you'll be using it in Europe; otherwise, they may deny transactions if they perceive unusual spending patterns.

• Ask for the specifics on transaction **fees.** When you use your credit or debit card—either for purchases or ATM withdrawals—you'll often be charged additional "international transaction" fees of up to 3 percent (1 percent is normal) plus $5 per transaction. If your card's fees seem high, consider getting a different card just for your trip: Capital One (www.capitalone.com) and most credit unions have low-to-no international fees.

• If you plan to withdraw cash from ATMs, confirm your daily **withdrawal limit,** and if necessary, ask your bank to adjust it. Some travelers prefer a high limit that allows them to take out more cash at each ATM stop (saving on bank fees), while others prefer to set a lower limit in case their card is stolen. Note that foreign banks also set maximum withdrawal amounts for their ATMs.

• Get your bank's emergency **phone number** in the US (but not its 800 number, which isn't accessible from overseas) to call collect if you have a problem.

• Ask for your credit card's **PIN** in case you need to make an emergency cash withdrawal or encounter Europe's chip-and-PIN system; the bank won't tell you your PIN over the phone, so allow time for it to be mailed to you.

Chip and PIN: If your card is declined for a purchase in Europe, it may be because Europeans are increasingly using chip-and-PIN cards, which are embedded with an electronic chip (in addition to the magnetic stripe used on our American-style cards). Much of Europe is adopting this system, and some merchants rely on it exclusively. You're most likely to encounter chip-and-PIN problems at automated payment machines, such as those at train and subway stations, toll roads, parking garages, luggage lockers, and self-serve gas pumps. If a machine won't take your card, find a cashier who can make your card work (they can print a receipt for you to sign), or find a machine that takes cash.

But don't panic. Most travelers who are carrying only magnetic-stripe cards never encounter any problems. Still, it pays to carry plenty of euros (you can always use an ATM with your magnetic-stripe debit card). Memorizing the PIN lets you use it at some chip-and-PIN machines—just enter your PIN when prompted.

If you're still concerned, you can apply for a chip card in the

INTRODUCTION

US (though I think it's overkill). While big US banks offer these cards with high annual fees, a better option is the no-annual-fee GlobeTrek Visa, offered by Andrews Federal Credit Union in Maryland (open to all US residents; see www.andrewsfcu.org).

Dynamic Currency Conversion: If merchants offer to convert your purchase price into dollars (called dynamic currency conversion, or "DCC"), refuse this "service." You'll pay even more in fees for the expensive convenience of seeing your charge in dollars.

Damage Control for Lost Cards

If you lose your credit, debit, or ATM card, you can stop people from using it by reporting the loss immediately to the respective global customer-assistance centers. Call these 24-hour US numbers collect: Visa (tel. 303/967-1096), MasterCard (tel. 636/722-7111), and American Express (tel. 336/393-1111). European toll-free numbers (listed by country) can be found at the websites for Visa and MasterCard.

At a minimum, you'll need to know the name of the financial institution that issued you the card, along with the type of card (classic, platinum, or whatever). Providing the following information will allow for a quicker cancellation of your missing card: full card number, whether you are the primary or secondary cardholder, the cardholder's name exactly as printed on the card, billing address, home phone number, circumstances of the loss or theft, and identification verification (your birth date, your mother's maiden name, or your Social Security number—memorize this, don't carry a copy). If you are the secondary cardholder, you'll also need to provide the primary cardholder's identification-verification details. You can generally receive a temporary card within two or three business days in Europe.

If you report your loss within two days, you typically won't be responsible for any unauthorized transactions on your account, although many banks charge a liability fee of $50.

Tipping

Tipping in Europe isn't as automatic and generous as it is in the US—but for special service, tips are appreciated, if not expected. As in the US, the proper amount depends on your resources, tipping philosophy, and the circumstances, but some general guidelines apply.

Restaurants: Virtually anywhere in Europe, you can do as the Europeans do, and if you're pleased with the service, round up a euro or two. In most places, 5 percent is adequate and 10 percent is considered a big tip. Please believe me—tipping 15–20 percent in Europe is unnecessary, if not culturally insensitive. Tipping is expected only at restaurants with wait staff; skip the tip if you order food at a counter (in a pub, for example). Servers prefer to be tipped in cash even if you pay with your credit card (otherwise the tip may never reach your server).

Taxis: To tip a cabbie, round up. For a typical ride, round up about 5–10 percent (to pay a €4.50 fare, give €5; for a €28 fare, give €30). If the cabbie hauls your bags and zips you to the airport to help you catch your flight, you might want to toss in a little more. But if you feel like you're being driven in circles or otherwise ripped off, skip the tip.

Services: In general, if someone in the service industry does a super job for you, a tip of a euro or two is appropriate...but not required.

If you're not sure whether (or how much) to tip for a service, ask your hotelier or the TI; they'll fill you in on how it's done on their turf.

Sleeping

I favor accommodations (and restaurants) that are handy to your sightseeing activities. Rather than list lodgings scattered throughout a city, I choose my favorite neighborhoods and recommend the best accommodations values in each, from dorm beds to fancy doubles with all of the comforts.

A major feature of this book is its extensive listing of good-value rooms. I like places that are clean, central, relatively quiet at night, reasonably priced, friendly, small enough to have a hands-on owner and stable staff, run with a respect for European traditions, and not listed in other guidebooks. (In Europe, for me, six out of these eight criteria means it's a keeper.) I'm more impressed by a convenient location and a fun-loving philosophy than flat-screen TVs and shoeshine machines.

Book your accommodations well in advance if you'll be traveling during busy times. For tips on making reservations, see page 15.

Rates and Deals

I've described my recommended accommodations using a Sleep Code (see the sidebar). Prices listed are for one-night stays in peak season, include breakfast unless otherwise noted, and assume you're booking directly (not through a TI or online hotel-booking engine). Using an online booking service costs the hotel about 20 percent and logically closes the door on special deals. Book direct.

As you look over the listings, you'll notice that some accommodations promise special discounts to my readers who book direct (without using a room-finding service or hotel-booking website, which take a commission). To get these discounts, you must mention this book when you reserve, and then show the book upon arrival. Rick Steves discounts apply to readers with ebooks as well as printed books. Discounts may not apply to promotional rates.

In general, prices can soften if you do any of the following: offer to pay cash, stay at least three nights, or mention this book. You can also try asking for a cheaper room or a discount, or offer to skip breakfast.

Types of Accommodations

Hotels

Double rooms in hotels listed in this book will range from about $50 (very simple, toilet and shower down the hall) to $450 (maximum plumbing and more), with most clustering at about $150 (with private bathrooms). Prices are higher in big cities and heavily touristed cities, and lower off the beaten path. In general, a triple room is cheaper than the cost of a double and a single. Traveling alone can be expensive: A single room can be close to the cost of a double. Breakfast is generally included (sometimes continental, but often buffet).

If you're arriving early in the morning, your room probably won't be ready. You can drop your bag safely at the hotel and dive right into sightseeing.

Hoteliers can be a great help and source of advice. Most know their city well and can assist you with everything from public transit and airport connections to finding a good restaurant, the nearest Internet launderette, or an Internet café.

Even at the best places, mechanical breakdowns occur: Air-conditioning malfunctions, sinks leak, hot water turns cold, and toilets gurgle and smell. Report your concerns clearly and calmly at the front desk. For more complicated problems, don't expect instant results.

If you suspect night noise will be a problem (if, for instance, the hotel is located above a nightclub), ask for a quiet room in the back or on an upper floor. To guard against theft in your room, keep valuables out of sight. Some rooms come with a safe, and others have safes at the front desk. I've never bothered using one.

Checkout can pose problems if surprise charges pop up on your bill. If you settle your bill the afternoon before you leave, you'll have time to discuss and address any points of contention (before 19:00, when the night shift usually arrives).

Above all, keep a positive attitude. Remember, you're on vacation. If your hotel is a disappointment, spend more time out enjoying the city you came to see.

Bed-and-Breakfasts and Pensions

Between hotels and hostels in price and style is a special class of accommodations: bed-and-breakfasts (B&Bs) and pensions. These are small, warm, and family-run, and offer a personal touch at a budget price—about $40–60 per person. Each country has these friendly accommodations in varying degrees of abundance, facilities, and service. Some include breakfast; some don't. They have different names from country to country—they're called *Gasthäuser* in Germany, *chambre d'hôte* in France, *affitta camere* in Italy, and *casa particulare* in Spain—but all have one thing in common: They satisfy the need for a place to stay that gives you the privacy of a hotel and the comforts of home at an affordable price.

Hostels

You'll pay about $25–30 per bed to stay at a hostel. Travelers of any age are welcome if they don't mind dorm-style accommodations or meeting other travelers. Most hostels offer kitchen facilities, Internet access, Wi-Fi, and a self-service laundry. Nowadays, concerned about bedbugs, hostels are likely to provide all bedding, including sheets. Family and private rooms may be available on request.

Independent hostels tend to be easygoing, colorful, and informal (no membership required); see www.hostelz.com, www.hostelseurope.com, www.hostels.com, and www.hostelbookers.com. **Official hostels** are part of Hostelling International (HI) and share an online booking site (www.hihostels.com). HI hostels typically require that you either have a membership card or pay extra per night.

Making Hotel Reservations

Given the good value of the accommodations I've found for this book, reserve your rooms several weeks in advance—or as soon as you've pinned down your travel dates—particularly if you'll be traveling during peak times. Note that some national holidays jam things up and merit your making reservations far in advance.

Requesting a Reservation: It's usually easiest to book your room through the hotel's website; many have a reservation-request form built right in. (For the best rates, be sure to use the hotel's official site and not a booking agency's site.) Just type in your preferred dates and the website will automatically display a list of available rooms and prices. Simpler websites will generate an email to the hotelier with your request. If there's no reservation form, or for complicated requests, send an email. Other options include calling (see "Phoning" below, and be mindful of time zones) or faxing.

Sleep Code

Price Rankings

To help you easily sort through my hotel listings, I've divided the accommodations into three categories based on the price for a standard double room with bath during high season:

$$$	Higher Priced
$$	Moderately Priced
$	Lower Priced

I always rate hostels as $, whether or not they have double rooms, because they have the cheapest beds in town.

Prices can change without notice; verify the hotel's current rates online or by email.

Abbreviations

To give maximum information in a minimum of space, I use the following code to describe accommodations in this book. Prices are listed per room, not per person. When a price range is given for a type of room, it means the price fluctuates with the season, size of room, or length of stay; expect to pay the upper end for peak-season stays.

S = Single room (or price for one person in a double).

D = Double or twin room. "Double beds" can be two twins sheeted together and are usually big enough for nonromantic couples.

T = Triple (generally a double bed with a single).

Q = Quad (usually two double beds; adding an extra child's bed to a T is usually cheaper).

b = Private bathroom with toilet and shower or tub.

s = Private shower or tub only (the toilet is down the hall).

According to this code, a couple staying at a "Db-€140" hotel in would pay a total of €140 (about $180) for a double room with a private bathroom. Unless otherwise noted, breakfast is included, hotel staff speak basic English, and credit cards are accepted.

There's almost always Wi-Fi and/or Internet access available, either free or for a fee.

The hotelier wants to know these key pieces of information (also included in the sample request form in the appendix):

- number and type of rooms
- number of nights
- date of arrival
- date of departure
- any special needs (such as bathroom in the room or down the hall, twin beds vs. double bed, air-conditioning, quiet, view, ground floor, etc.)

When you request a room, use the European style for writing dates: day/month/year. For example, for a two-night stay in July of 2014, I would request "1 double room for 2 nights, arrive 16/07/14, depart 18/07/14." Consider carefully how long you'll stay; don't just assume you can tack on extra days once you arrive. Make sure you mention any discounts—for Rick Steves readers or otherwise—when you make the reservation.

If you don't get a response to your email, it usually means the hotel is already fully booked—but try sending the message again or call to follow up.

Confirming a Reservation: Most places will request your credit-card number to hold the room. To confirm a room using a hotel's secure online reservation form, enter your contact information and credit-card number; the hotel will email a confirmation.

If you sent an email to request a reservation, the hotel will reply with its room availability and rates. This is not a confirmation. You must email back to say that you want the room at the given rate. While you can email your credit-card information (I do), it's safer to share that confidential info via phone call, two emails (splitting your number between them), or the hotel's secure online reservation form.

Canceling a Reservation: If you must cancel your reservation, it's courteous to do so with as much notice as possible. Simply make a quick phone call or send an email. Family-run places lose money if they turn away customers while holding a room for someone who doesn't show up. Understandably, many hoteliers bill no-shows for one night.

Cancellation policies can be strict: For example, you might lose a deposit if you cancel within two weeks of your reserved stay, or you might be billed for the entire visit if you leave early. Internet deals may require prepayment, with no refunds for cancellations. Ask about cancellation policies before you book.

If canceling via email, request confirmation that your cancellation was received to avoid being accidentally billed.

Reconfirming a Reservation: Always call to reconfirm your room reservation a few days in advance. Smaller hotels and B&Bs

> ## How Was Your Trip?
>
> Were your travels fun, smooth, and meaningful? If you'd like to share your tips, concerns, and discoveries, please fill out the survey at www.ricksteves.com/feedback. I value your feedback. Thanks in advance—it helps a lot.

appreciate knowing your estimated time of arrival. If you'll be arriving late (after 17:00), let them know. On the small chance that a hotel loses track of your reservation, bring along a hard copy of their confirmation.

Reserving Rooms as You Travel: You can make reservations as you travel, calling hotels a few days to a week before your arrival. If everything's full, don't despair. Call a day or two in advance and fill in a cancellation. If you'd rather travel without any reservations at all, you'll have greater success snaring rooms if you arrive at your destination early in the day. When you anticipate crowds (weekends are worst), call hotels at about 9:00 or 10:00 on the day you plan to arrive, when the receptionist knows who'll be checking out and which rooms will be available. If you encounter a language barrier, ask the fluent receptionist at your current hotel to call for you.

Traveling As a Temporary Local

We travel all the way to Europe to enjoy differences—to become temporary locals. You'll experience frustrations. Certain truths that we find "God-given" or "self-evident," like cold beer, ice in drinks, bottomless cups of coffee, hot showers, and bigger being better, are suddenly not so true. One of the benefits of travel is the eye-opening realization that there are logical, civil, and even better alternatives. A willingness to go local ensures that you'll enjoy a full dose of European hospitality.

Europeans generally like Americans. But if there is a negative aspect to their image of Americans, it's that we are loud, wasteful, ethnocentric, too informal (which can seem disrespectful), and a bit naive. While Europeans look bemusedly at some of our Yankee excesses—and worriedly at others—they nearly always afford us individual travelers all the warmth we deserve.

Judging from all the positive comments I receive from travelers who have used this book, it's safe to assume you'll enjoy a great, affordable vacation—with the finesse of an experienced, independent traveler. Thanks, and happy travels!

Back Door Travel Philosophy
From *Rick Steves' Europe Through the Back Door*

Travel is intensified living—maximum thrills per minute and one of the last great sources of legal adventure. Travel is freedom. It's recess, and we need it.

Experiencing the real Europe requires catching it by surprise, going casual..."through the Back Door."

Affording travel is a matter of priorities. (Make do with the old car.) You can eat and sleep—simply, safely, and enjoyably—anywhere in Europe for $120 a day plus transportation costs. In many ways, spending more money only builds a thicker wall between you and what you traveled so far to see. Europe is a cultural carnival, and time after time, you'll find that its best acts are free and the best seats are the cheap ones.

A tight budget forces you to travel close to the ground, meeting and communicating with the people. Never sacrifice sleep, nutrition, safety, or cleanliness to save money. Simply enjoy the local-style alternatives to expensive hotels and restaurants.

Connecting with people carbonates your experience. Extroverts have more fun. If your trip is low on magic moments, kick yourself and make things happen. If you don't enjoy a place, maybe you don't know enough about it. Seek the truth. Recognize tourist traps. Give a culture the benefit of your open mind. See things as different, but not better or worse. Any culture has plenty to share.

Of course, travel, like the world, is a series of hills and valleys. Be fanatically positive and militantly optimistic. If something's not to your liking, change your liking.

Travel can make you a happier American, as well as a citizen of the world. Our Earth is home to seven billion equally precious people. It's humbling to travel and find that other people don't have the "American Dream"—they have their own dreams. Europeans like us, but with all due respect, they wouldn't trade passports.

Thoughtful travel engages us with the world. In tough economic times, it reminds us what is truly important. By broadening perspectives, travel teaches new ways to measure quality of life.

Globetrotting destroys ethnocentricity, helping us understand and appreciate other cultures. Rather than fear the diversity on this planet, celebrate it. Among your most prized souvenirs will be the strands of different cultures you choose to knit into your own character. The world is a cultural yarn shop, and Back Door travelers are weaving the ultimate tapestry. Join in!

AUSTRIA

VIENNA

Wien

Vienna is the capital of Austria, the cradle of classical music, the home of the rich Habsburg heritage, and one of Europe's most livable cities. The city center is skyscraper-free, pedestrian-friendly, dotted with quiet parks, and traversed by electric trams. Many buildings still reflect 18th- and 19th-century elegance, when the city was at the forefront of the arts and sciences. Compared with most modern European urban centers, the pace of life is slow.

Vienna (*Wien* in German—pronounced "veen") has always been considered the easternmost city of the West. For 640 years, Vienna was the capital of the enormous Austrian Empire (a.k.a. the Austro-Hungarian Empire, a.k.a. the Habsburg Empire). Stretching from the Alps of northern Italy to the rugged Carpathians of Romania, and from the banks of the Danube to sunny Dubrovnik, this multiethnic empire was arguably the most powerful European entity since Rome. And yet, of its 60 million people, only eight million were Austrian; Vienna was a kind of Eastern European melting pot. Today, the truly Viennese person is not Austrian, but a second-generation Habsburg cocktail, with grandparents from the distant corners of the old empire—Hungary, the Czech Republic, Slovakia, Poland, Slovenia, Croatia, Bosnia-Herzegovina, Serbia, Romania, and Italy.

Vienna reached its peak in the 19th century. Politically, it hosted European diplomats at the 1814 Congress of Vienna, which reaffirmed Europe's conservative monarchy after the French Revolution and Napoleon. Vienna became one of Europe's cultural capitals, home to groundbreaking composers (Beethoven, Mozart,

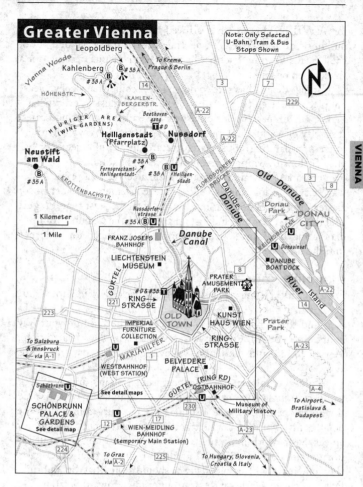

Brahms, Strauss), scientists (Doppler, Boltzmann), philosophers (Freud, Husserl, Schlick, Gödel, Steiner), architects (Wagner, Loos), and painters (Klimt, Schiele, Kokoschka). In 1900, Vienna's 2.2 million inhabitants made it the world's fifth-largest city—after New York, London, Paris, and Berlin. By the turn of the 20th century, Vienna sat on the cusp between stuffy Old World monarchism and subversive modern trends.

However, after starting and losing World War I, the Habsburgs lost their far-flung holdings. Then came World War II: While Vienna's old walls had long held out would-be invaders—Germanic barbarians (in Roman times), marauding Magyars (today's Hungarians, 10th century), Mongol hordes (13th century), Ottoman Turks (the sieges of 1529 and 1683)—they were no match for WWII bombs, which destroyed nearly a quarter of the city's buildings. In the Cold War, neutral Austria took a big bite out of the USSR's Warsaw Pact buffer zone—and Vienna became, for a time, a den of spies.

Today Vienna has settled down into a somewhat sleepy, pleasant place where culture is still king. Classical music is everywhere. People nurse a pastry and coffee over the daily paper at small cafés. It's a city of world-class museums, big and small. Anyone with an interest in painting, music, architecture, beautiful objects, or Sacher-Torte with whipped cream will feel right at home.

From a practical standpoint, Vienna serves as a prime "gateway" city. The location is central and convenient to most major Eastern European destinations. Actually farther east than Prague, Ljubljana, and Zagreb, and just upstream on the Danube from Budapest and Bratislava, Vienna is an ideal launchpad for a journey into the East.

Planning Your Time

For a big city, Vienna is pleasant and laid-back. Packed with sights, it's worth two days and two nights on even the speediest trip. To be grand-tour efficient, you could sleep on the train on your way in and out—Berlin, Prague, Kraków, the Swiss Alps (via Zürich), Venice, Rome, and the Rhine Valley are each handy night trains away.

Palace Choices: The Hofburg and Schönbrunn are both world-class **palaces,** but seeing both is redundant—with limited time or money, I'd choose just one. The Hofburg comes with the popular Sisi Museum and is right in the town center, making for an easy visit. With more time, a visit to Schönbrunn—set outside town amid a grand and regal garden—is also a great experience. (For efficient sightseeing, drivers should note that Schönbrunn Palace is conveniently on the way out of town toward Salzburg.)

Vienna in One to Four Days

Below is a suggested itinerary for how to spend your time. I've left the **evenings** open for your choice of activities. The best options are taking in a concert, opera, or other musical event; enjoying a leisurely dinner (and people-watching) in the stately old town or atmospheric Spittelberg Quarter; heading out to the *Heuriger* wine pubs in the foothills of the Vienna Woods; or touring the Haus der Musik interactive music museum (open nightly until 22:00). Plan your evenings based on the schedule of musical events while you're in town. If you've downloaded my audio tours (see "Rick Steves Audio Europe" sidebar, page 7), the Vienna City Walk works wonderfully in the evening. Whenever you need a break, linger in a classic Viennese café.

VIENNA

Day 1

9:00	Take the 1.5-hour Red Bus City Tour, or circle the Ringstrasse by tram, to get your bearings.
10:30	Drop by the TI for planning and ticket needs.
11:00	Take the Opera House tour.
14:00	Follow my Vienna City Walk, including Kaisergruft visit and St. Stephen's Cathedral self-guided tour (nave closes at 16:30, or 17:30 June-Aug).

Day 2

9:00	Browse the colorful Naschmarkt.
11:00	Tour the Kunsthistorisches Museum.
14:00	Tour the Hofburg Palace Imperial Apartments and Treasury.

Day 3

10:00	Visit Belvedere Palace, with its fine collection of Viennese art and great city views.
15:00	Tour Schönbrunn Palace to enjoy the royal apartments and grounds.

Day 4

10:00	Enjoy (depending on your interest) the engaging Karlsplatz sights (Karlskirche, Wien Museum, Academy of Fine Arts, and The Secession).
12:00	Tour the Albertina Museum.
15:00	Shoppers can stroll Mariahilfer Strasse. Non-shoppers can rent a bike and head out to the modern Donau City "downtown" sector, Danube Island (for fun people-watching), and the Prater amusement park.

Orientation to Vienna

Vienna sits between the Vienna Woods (Wienerwald) and the Danube (Donau). To the southeast is industrial sprawl. The Alps, which arc across Europe from Marseille, end at Vienna's wooded hills, providing a popular playground for walking and sipping new wine. This greenery's momentum carries on into the city. More than half of Vienna is parkland, filled with ponds, gardens, trees, and statue-maker memories of Austria's glory days.

Think of the city map as a target with concentric sections: The bull's-eye is St. Stephen's Cathedral, the towering cathedral south of the Danube. Surrounding that is the old town, bound tightly by the circular road known as the Ringstrasse, marking what used to be the city wall. The Gürtel, a broader ring road, contains the rest

VIENNA

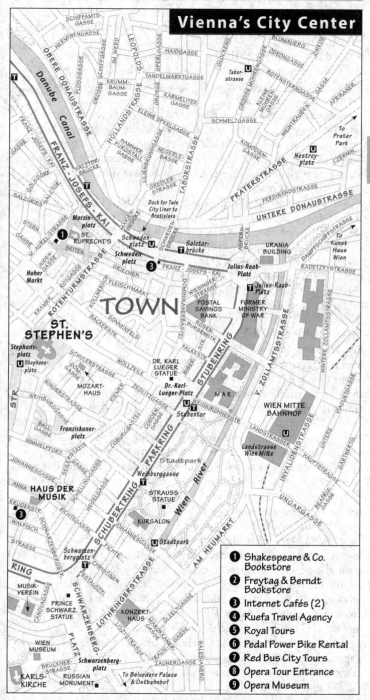

Vienna's City Center

VIENNA

1 Shakespeare & Co. Bookstore
2 Freytag & Berndt Bookstore
3 Internet Cafés (2)
4 Ruefa Travel Agency
5 Royal Tours
6 Pedal Power Bike Rental
7 Red Bus City Tours
8 Opera Tour Entrance
9 Opera Museum

of downtown. Outside the Gürtel lies the uninteresting sprawl of modern Vienna.

Addresses start with the *Bezirk* (district), followed by the street and building number. The Ringstrasse (a.k.a. the Ring) circles the first *Bezirk*. Any address higher than the ninth *Bezirk* is beyond the Gürtel, far from the center.

Much of Vienna's sightseeing—and most of my recommended restaurants—are located in the old town (inside the Ringstrasse). Walking across this circular district takes about 30 minutes. St. Stephen's Cathedral sits in the center, at the intersection of the two main (pedestrian-only) streets: Kärntner Strasse runs north-south and Graben runs east-west.

Several sights sit along, or just beyond, the Ringstrasse: To the southwest are the Hofburg and related Habsburg sights, and the Kunsthistorisches Museum; to the south is a cluster of intriguing sights near Karlsplatz; to the southeast is Belvedere Palace. A branch of the Danube River (*Donau* in German, DOH-now) borders the Ring to the north. As a tourist, concern yourself only with this compact old center. When you do, sprawling Vienna suddenly becomes manageable.

Arrival in Vienna
By Train
Vienna's train stations will be in disarray for the next few years, as the city builds a central train station in the former Südbahnhof location to handle most traffic. Until this is done (likely in 2014), trains to different destinations depart from various stations around the city. As these departure points are prone to change, confirm carefully which station your train uses. As the stations themselves are also in flux (the main ones are all being renovated), the details I've listed below for each one are also subject to change. From most stations, the handiest connection to the center is usually the U-Bahn (subway) system; line numbers and stop names are noted below. For some stations, there's also a handy tram connection.

Westbahnhof (West Station): This wonderful station (at the west end of Mariahilfer Strasse, on the U-3 and U-6 U-Bahn lines) has been beautifully renovated. The old 1950s shell is now filled with a modern, user-friendly mall of services, shops, and eateries (including the recommended Buffet Trześniewski—near the tracks—with €1.10 finger sandwiches). From here trains run to/from many points in **Austria** (including Hallstatt and Salzburg), as well as **Germany (Munich)** and **Switzerland.** You'll find travel agencies, grocery stores, ATMs, change offices, a post office, luggage lockers, and a left-luggage desk (€3, daily 10:00-22:00, near track 1). To reach airport buses and taxis, from the platforms, head outside and to the left.

For the city center, just follow orange *U-3* signs to the subway (direction: Simmering; buy your ticket or transit pass from a machine). If your hotel is along Mariahilfer Strasse, your stop is on this line. If you're sleeping in the center—or just can't wait to start sightseeing—ride five stops to Stephansplatz, at the very center of town.

Wien-Meidling Bahnhof: This temporary "main station" (a mile and a half southeast of Schönbrunn Palace, at the Philadelphiabrücke stop on the U-6 subway line and tram #62) serves many international trains, including southbound trains to/from **Italy, Slovenia,** and **Croatia,** as well as northbound trains to/from the **Czech Republic** and **Poland.** The once-small suburban station has been souped up to accommodate the traffic that formerly passed through the Südbahnhof. It has a train info desk (near track 1 and underground, near track 4), ATMs (near tracks 1 and 6), luggage lockers (underground, near track 7), and airport bus services. To reach the hotels on Mariahilfer Strasse, or to head to Stephansplatz, take the U-Bahn on the U-6 line (direction: Floridsdorf) to the Westbahnhof, then change to the U-3 line (see "Westbahnhof," earlier). If you're staying near the Opera, catch the direct tram #62 (direction: Karlsplatz). For Schwedenplatz, take the U-6 (direction: Floridsdorf) two stops to Längenfeldgasse, then change to the U-4 (direction: Heiligenstadt).

Ostbahnhof (East Station), a.k.a. Südbahnhof (South Station): The temporary Ostbahnhof (just south of Belvedere Palace) is near the former Südbahnhof, and is in the midst of the massive construction zone for the brand-new Hauptbahnhof (Main Station), which is slated to be operational in 2014. Confusingly, during this period of construction, this station goes by any of these three names. For now, this station serves trains to/from **Bratislava,** Slovakia. To reach the city center, take tram #D to the Ring; to reach Mariahilfer Strasse, hop on bus #13A (U-1: Südtiroler Platz is also nearby).

By Plane

For information on nearby airports, see "Vienna Connections," at the end of this chapter.

Tourist Information

Vienna's main TI is a block behind the Opera at Albertinaplatz (daily 9:00-19:00, tel. 01/211-140, www.vienna.info). There's also an airport TI (daily 6:00-23:00). At either TI, confirm your sightseeing plans, and pick up two copies of the free and essential city map with a list of museums and hours (also available at most hotels). Rip up one copy of the Vienna map—reducing it down to just the city-center inset—and keep it in your pocket for ready reference.

(Stuff the other copy in your backpack in case you need it.) Also look for the monthly program of concerts (called *Wien-Programm*) and the *Vienna from A to Z* booklet (both described below), and the annual city guide (called *Vienna Journal*). Ask about their program of guided walks (€14 each). While hotel and ticket-booking agencies at the train station and airport can answer questions and give out maps and brochures, I'd rely on the official TI.

Wien-Programm: This monthly entertainment guide is particularly important, listing all sorts of events, including music, theater, walks, expositions, and museum exhibits. Note the key for abbreviations on the inside cover, which helps make this dense booklet useful even for non-German speakers.

Vienna from A to Z: Consider this handy booklet, sold by the TI for €3.60. Every major building in Vienna sports a numbered flag banner that keys into this booklet and into the TI's city map—handy for finding your way if you get turned around.

Vienna Card: The much-promoted €20 Vienna Card is not worth the mental overhead for most travelers. It gives you a 72-hour transit pass (worth €13.60) and discounts of 10-40 percent at the city's museums. It might save the busy sightseer a few euros (though seniors and students will do better with their own discounts).

Helpful Hints

Sisi Ticket: This €23.50 ticket covers the Royal Imperial Apartments at the Hofburg (including the Sisi Museum and Imperial Porcelain and Silver Collection—but *not* the Hofburg Treasury), Schönbrunn Palace's Grand Tour, and the Imperial Furniture Collection; the ticket saves €0.50 off the combined cost of the Hofburg apartments and Schönbrunn, making the good Furniture Collection effectively free (sold at any participating sight).

Teens Sightsee Free: Those under 19 get in free to state-run museums and sights.

Music Sightseeing Priorities: Be wary of Vienna's various music sights. Many "homes of composers" are pretty disappointing. My advice to music lovers is to concentrate on these activities: Take in a concert, tour the Opera House, snare cheap standing-room tickets to see an opera there (even just part of a performance), enjoy the Haus der Musik, and scour the wonderful Collection of Ancient Musical Instruments in the Hofburg's New Palace. If in town on a Sunday, don't miss the glorious music at the Augustinian Church Mass (see page 66).

Skip This: The highly advertised experience called Time Travel

Vienna (just off the Graben on Habsburgergasse) promises "history, fun, and action." In reality, it's €18 and 45 minutes wasted in a tacky succession of amusement-park history vignettes with much of the information in German only.

Internet Access: The TI has a list of Internet cafés. **Netcafe** is near the Danube Canal (€4/hour with drink, daily 9:00-22:00, Schwedenplatz 3); **Surfland Internet Café** is near the Opera (€6/hour, daily 10:00-23:00, Krugerstrasse 10, tel. 01/512-7701); and **Netcafe-Refill** is close to many of my recommended hotels (€4.50/hour, daily 9:00-22:00, Mariahilfer Strasse 103, tel. 01/595-5558). See map on page 27 for first two locations and page 109 for last location.

Post Offices: The main post office is near Schwedenplatz at Fleischmarkt 19 (Mon-Fri 7:00-22:00, Sat-Sun 9:00-22:00). Branch offices are at the Westbahnhof (Mon-Fri 7:00-22:00, Sat-Sun 9:00-20:00), near the Opera (Mon-Fri 7:00-19:00, closed Sat-Sun, Krugerstrasse 13), and scattered throughout town.

English Bookstore: Stop by the woody and cool **Shakespeare & Co.,** in the historic and atmospheric Ruprechtsviertel district near the Danube Canal (Mon-Sat 9:00-21:00, closed Sun, north of Hoher Markt at Sterngasse 2, tel. 01/535-5053, www.shakespeare.co.at). **Freytag & Berndt** travel bookstore (Mon-Sat 9:30-18:30, Kohlmarkt 9, tel. 01/533-8685, www.freytagberndt.at) is a great place if you need a map or book in English or one of my guidebooks for the next leg of your journey. See map on page 27 for locations.

Keeping Up with the News: Don't buy newspapers. Read them for free in Vienna's marvelous coffeehouses. It's much classier.

Travel Agency: Conveniently located just off the Graben, **Ruefa** sells tickets for flights, trains, and boats to Bratislava. They'll waive the service charge for train tickets for my readers (Mon-Fri 9:00-18:00, Sat 10:00-13:00, closed Sun, Spiegelgasse 15—see map on page 27, tel. 01/513-4000, Gertrude speaks English).

Drinking Water: Vienna, in response to—and anticipation of—global warming, is creating shady spots with benches and installing shiny public water fountains with signs reminding people to stay hydrated. These are especially useful for older travelers and elderly locals, who'll suffer the most as scorching summers become the norm.

The Viennese are proud of their perfectly drinkable tap water from Alpine springs. "Leitungswasser" is happily served in any restaurant. You'll spot locals refilling their little bottles at fountains all over town.

Getting Around Vienna

By Public Transportation: Take full advantage of Vienna's simple, cheap, and super-efficient transit system, which includes trams (a.k.a. streetcars), buses, U-Bahn (subway), and S-Bahn (faster suburban trains). The smooth, modern trams are Porsche-designed, with "backpack technology" that locates the engines and mechanical hardware on the roofs for a lower ride and easier entry. I generally stick to the tram to zip around the Ring and take the U-Bahn to outlying sights or hotels. Trams #1, #2, and #D all travel partway around the Ring.

The free Vienna map, available at TIs and hotels, includes a smaller schematic map of the major public transit lines, making the too-big €2.50 transit map unnecessary. (Transit maps are also posted conveniently on U-Bahn station walls.) As you study the map, note that tram lines are marked with numbers or letters (such as #38 or #D). Buses have numbers followed by an *A* or *B* (such as #38A); three-digit numbers are for buses into the outskirts. Night buses, which start with *N* (such as #N38), operate after other public transit stops running. U-Bahn lines begin with U (e.g., U-1), and the directions are designated by the end-of-the-line stops. Blue lines are the speedier S-Bahns. Transit info: tel. 01/790-9100, www.wienerlinien.at.

Trams, buses, the U-Bahn, and the S-Bahn all use the same tickets. Buy tickets from *Tabak-Trafik* shops, station machines, marked *Vorverkauf* offices in the station, or—for trams or buses only—on board (tickets only, more expensive). You have lots of choices:

- Single tickets (€2, €2.40 if bought on tram or bus, good for one journey with necessary transfers)
- 24-hour transit pass (€6.70)
- 48-hour transit pass (€11.70)
- 72-hour transit pass (€14.50)
- 7-day transit pass (*Wochenkarte*, €15—the catch is that the pass runs from Monday to Monday, so you may get less than seven days of use)
- 8-day "Climate Ticket" (*Acht-Tage-Klimakarte*, €34, can be shared—for example, four people for two days each). With a per-person cost of €4.24/day (compared to €6.70/day for a 24-hour pass), this can be a real saver for groups.

Kids under 15 travel free on Sundays and holidays; kids under 6 always travel free.

Stamp a time on your ticket as you enter the Metro system, tram, or bus (stamp it only the first time for a multiple-use pass). Cheaters pay a stiff €70 fine, plus the cost of the ticket.

Rookies miss stops because they fail to open the door. Push buttons, pull latches—do whatever it takes. Before you exit a U-

Bahn station, study the wall-mounted street map. Choosing the right exit—signposted from the moment you step off the train—saves lots of walking.

Cute little electric buses wind through the tangled old center (from Schottentor to Stubentor). Bus #1A is best for a joyride—hop on and see where it takes you.

By Car: Vienna's comfortable, civilized, and easy-to-flag-down taxis start at €2.50. You'll pay about €10 to go from the Opera to the Westbahnhof. Pay only what's on the meter—any surcharges (other than the €2 fee for calling a cab or €11 fee for the airport) are just crude cabbie rip-offs. Rates are legitimately higher at night.

Consider the luxury of having your own **car and driver.** Johann (a.k.a. John) Lichtl is a kind, honest, English-speaking cabbie who can take up to four passengers in his car (€27/1 hour, €22/hour for 2 hours or more, €27 to or from airport, mobile 0676-670-6750). Consider hiring gentle Johann for a day trip to the Danube Valley (€160, up to 8 hours) or to drive you to Salzburg with Danube sightseeing en route (€350, up to 14 hours; other trips can be arranged). These special prices are valid with this book in 2014.

By Bike: With more than 600 miles of bike lanes, Vienna is a great city on two wheels. With the inability of any single party to get a clear majority, Vienna's government is ruled by a coalition—that gives the Green Party more clout than it might otherwise have. Consequently, life is good for the city's bikers; for one thing, bikes ride the U-Bahn for free (but they aren't allowed during weekday rush hours).

The bike path along the Ring is wonderfully entertaining—you'll enjoy the shady park-like ambience of the boulevard while rolling by many of the city's top sights. Besides the Ring, your best sightseeing by bike is through Stadtpark (City Park), across Danube Island, and out to the modern Donau City business district (for more on biking on Danube Island and to Donau City, see page 91). These routes are easy to follow on the free tourist city map available from the TI.

Borrowing a Free/Cheap Bike: **Citybike Wien** lets you borrow bikes from public racks all over town (toll tel. 0810-500-500, www.citybikewien.at). The three-speed bikes are heavy and clunky—and come with a basket, built-in lock, and ads on the side—but they're perfect for a short, practical joyride in the center (such as around the Ringstrasse).

While bike programs in other European cities are difficult for tourists to take advantage of, Vienna's system is easy to use. Bikes are locked into more than 50 stalls scattered through the city center. To borrow a bike, use the computer terminal at any rack: Press the credit card button, insert and pull out your card, register your name and address, and select a username and password for future rentals (you can also register online at www.citybikewien.at). Then, unlock the bike you want by punching in its number. Registration costs €1 (first time only), and they'll place a refundable €20 hold on your card while you're using the bike (only one bike per credit card—couples must use two different cards). Since the bikes are designed for short-term use, it costs more per hour the longer you keep it (first hour-free, second hour-€1, third hour-€2, €4/hour after that). To avoid registering at a machine, you can instead get a Citybike Tourist Card (sold for €2/day at Royal Tours, near the Hofburg at Herrengasse 1-3—see map on page 27), but this extra step isn't worth the trouble. When you're done, drop off your bike at any stall, and make sure it's fully locked into the rack to avoid being charged for more time.

Renting a Higher-Quality Bike: If you want to ride beyond the town center—or you simply want a better set of wheels—check out **Pedal Power,** with a handy central location near the Opera House. The local authority on bike touring in town and to points along the Danube, Pedal Power rents bikes and provides good biking info (€5/hour, €17/4 hours, €27/24 hours, daily May-Sept 8:30-18:00, Elisabethstrasse 13 at the corner of Eschenbachgasse—see map on page 27, tel. 01/729-7234, www.pedalpower.at). For a better selection and better gear, it's smart to use their main office by Prater Park. While less central, it's very easy to get to (U-1 or U-2: Praterstern, then walk 100 yards to Ausstellungsstr 3). They can also deliver a bike to your hotel and pick it up when you're done (€32/day including delivery, service available year-round), and they organize bike tours (described later). Pedal Power offers a 10 percent discount to anyone with this book.

Tours in Vienna

To sightsee on your own, download my series of free audio tours that illuminate some of Vienna's top sights and neighborhoods (see sidebar on page 7 for details).

Walking Tours
The *Walks in Vienna* brochure (available at the TI) describes the city's many guided walks. The basic 1.5-hour "Vienna at First Glance" introductory walk is offered daily throughout the summer (€14, leaves at 14:00 from the main TI just behind the Opera, in both English and German, just show up, tel. 01/774-8901, mobile 0664-260-4388, www.wienguide.at). Various specialized tours go once a week and are listed on the website.

Bike Tours
Pedal Power runs two different three-hour tours daily from May to September. The morning tour covers the central district, while the

afternoon tour crosses the Danube (€29/tour includes bike, €49 for both tours, €14 extra to keep the bike for the day, departs at 10:00 and 14:30 from the statue in Schillerplatz in front of the Academy of Fine Arts, across the Ring from the Opera, tel. 01/729-7234, www.pedalpower.at). They also rents bikes and offer Segway tours daily in summer (www.segway-vienna.at).

For a private bike tour, contact guide **Wolfgang Höfler** (€140/3 hours, mobile 0676-304-4940, www.vienna-aktivtours.com, office@vienna-aktivtours.com; also leads walking tours—see listing, later, under "Local Guides").

Bus Tours

Red Bus City Tours' convertible buses do a 1.5-hour loop, hitting the highlights of the city with a 20-minute shopping break in the middle. They cover the main first-district attractions as well as a big bus can, along with the entire Ringstrasse. But the most interesting part of the tour is outside the center—zipping through Prater Park, over the Danube for a glimpse of the city's Danube Island playground, and into the "Donau City" skyscraper zone. If the weather's good, the bus goes topless and offers great opportunities for photos. Tours start one block behind the Opera at the main TI—see the map on page 27 for the location (€14 ticket from driver, €2 discount with this book if purchased from office at Lobkowitzplatz 1—100 yards from where the tour begins; departs hourly April-Oct 10:00-18:00, less frequently off-season, pretty good recorded narration in any language, your own earbuds are better than the beat-up headphones they provide, tel. 01/512-4030, www.redbuscitytours.at, Gabriel).

Vienna Sightseeing offers a three-hour city tour, including a tour of Schönbrunn Palace (€39, 3/day April-Oct, 2/day Nov-March). They also run hop-on, hop-off bus tours with recorded commentary. The schedule is posted curbside (three different one-hour routes, €13/1 route, €16/2 routes, €20/all day, departs from the Opera 4/hour July-Aug 10:00-20:00, runs less frequently and stops earlier off-season, tel. 01/7124-6830, www.viennasightseeing.at). Given the city's excellent public transportation and mostly walkable sights, I'd skip this tour; if you just want a quick guided city tour, take the Red Bus tours recommended above.

Ring Tram Tour

One of Europe's great streets, the Ringstrasse is lined with many of the city's top sights. Take a tram ride around the ring with my free audio tour (see page 7), which gives you a fun orientation and a ridiculously quick glimpse of some major sights as you glide by. Neither tram #1 nor #2 makes the entire loop around the Ring, but you can see it all by making one transfer between them (at the Schwedenplatz stop). You can use a single transit ticket to cover the whole route, including the transfer (though you're not allowed to

VIENNA

interrupt your trip, except to transfer). For more on riding Vienna's trams, see page 32.

The **Vienna Ring Tram,** a yellow made-for-tourists streetcar, is an easier though pricier option, running clockwise along the entire Ringstrasse (€7 for 30-minute loop, €9 for 24-hour hop-on, hop-off privileges, 2/hour 10:00-18:00, July-Aug until 19:00, recorded narration, includes a good set of earbuds you can keep and reuse). The tour starts at the top and bottom of each hour on the Opera side of the Ring at Kärntner Ring. At each stop, you'll see an ad for this tram tour (look for *VRT Ring-Rund Sightseeing*). The schedule clearly notes the next departure time.

Horse-and-Buggy Tour

These traditional horse-and-buggies, called *Fiakers,* take rich romantics on clip-clop tours lasting 20 minutes (€55-old town), 40 minutes (€80-old town and the Ring), or one hour (€110-all the above, but more thorough). You can share the ride and cost with up to five people. Because it's a kind of guided tour, talk to a few drivers before choosing a carriage, and pick someone who's fun and speaks English (tel. 01/401-060).

Local Guides

You'll pay about €140 for two hours. Get a group of six or more together and call it a party. The tourist board's website (www.vienna.info) has a long list of local guides with their specialties and contact information. My favorite private Vienna guides are: **Lisa Zeiler** (mobile 0699-120-37550, lisa.zeiler@gmx.at); **Wolfgang Höfler** (a generalist with a knack for having psychoanalytical fun with history, enjoys the big changes of the 19th and 20th centuries, €150/2 hours, mobile 0676-304-4940, www.vienna-aktivtours.com, office@vienna-aktivtours.com, also leads bike tours—described earlier); **Adrienn Bartek-Rhomberg** (€140/half-day, see website for tour topics, mobile 0650-826-6965, www.experience-vienna.at, bartek-rhomberg@chello.at); and **Gerhard Strassgschwandtner** (who runs the Third Man Museum—see page 103—and is passionate about history in all its marvelous complexity, €65/hour, mobile 0676-475-7818, www.special-vienna.com, gerhard@special-vienna.com). If these folks are booked, any of them can set you up with another good guide.

Self-Guided Walk

Vienna City Walk

This walk connects the top three sights in Vienna's old center: the Opera House, St. Stephen's Cathedral, and Hofburg Palace. Along the way, you'll see sights covered elsewhere in this chapter (to find the full descriptions, flip to "Sights in Vienna," later) and get an overview of Vienna's past and present. Allow one hour, and more

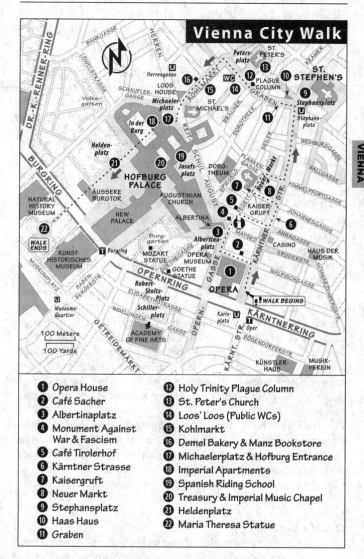

Vienna City Walk

1 Opera House
2 Café Sacher
3 Albertinaplatz
4 Monument Against War & Fascism
5 Café Tirolerhof
6 Kärntner Strasse
7 Kaisergruft
8 Neuer Markt
9 Stephansplatz
10 Haas Haus
11 Graben
12 Holy Trinity Plague Column
13 St. Peter's Church
14 Loos' Loos (Public WCs)
15 Kohlmarkt
16 Demel Bakery & Manz Bookstore
17 Michaelerplatz & Hofburg Entrance
18 Imperial Apartments
19 Spanish Riding School
20 Treasury & Imperial Music Chapel
21 Heldenplatz
22 Maria Theresa Statue

time if you plan to step into any of the major sights along the way. You can download a free Rick Steves **audio tour** of this walk; see page 7.

• *Begin at the square outside Vienna's landmark Opera House. (The entrance faces the Ringstrasse; we're starting at the busy pedestrian square that's to the right of the entrance as you're facing it.)*

1 Opera House

If Vienna is the world capital of classical music, this building is its throne room, one of the planet's premier houses of music. It's typical of Vienna's 19th-century buildings in that it features a revival style—Neo-Renaissance—with arched windows, half-columns, and the sloping, copper mansard roof typical of French Renaissance *châteaux*.

Since the structure was built in 1869, almost all of the opera world's luminaries have passed through here. Its former musical directors include Gustav Mahler, Herbert von Karajan, and Richard Strauss. Luciano Pavarotti, Maria Callas, Placido Domingo, and many other greats have sung from its stage.

In the pavement along the side of the Opera (and all along Kärntner Strasse, the bustling shopping street we'll visit shortly), you'll find star plaques forming a Hollywood-style walk of fame. These represent the stars of classical music—famous composers, singers, musicians, and conductors.

Looking up at the Opera, notice the giant outdoor screen onto which some live performances are projected (as noted in the posted schedules).

If you're a fan, take a guided tour of the Opera. If you're not, you still might consider springing for an evening performance (standing-room tickets are surprisingly cheap; see page 98). Regular opera tickets are sold at various points near here: The closest ticket office is the small one just below the screen, while the main one is on the other side of the building, across the street on Operngasse. For information about other entertainment options during your visit, check in at the Wien Ticket kiosk in the booth on this square.

The Opera House marks a busy intersection in Vienna, where Kärntner Strasse meets the Ring. The Karlsplatz U-Bahn station in front of the Opera is an underground shopping mall with fast food, newsstands, and lots of pickpockets.

• *Walk behind the Opera and across the street toward the dark-red awning to find the famous...*

❷ Café Sacher

This is the home of the world's classiest chocolate cake, the Sacher-Torte: two layers of cake separated by apricot jam and covered in dark-chocolate icing, usually served with whipped cream. It was invented in a fit of improvisation in 1832 by Franz Sacher, dessert chef to Prince Metternich (the mastermind diplomat who redrew the map of post-Napoleonic Europe). The cake became world famous when the inventor's son served it next door at his hotel (you may have noticed the fancy doormen). Many locals complain that the cakes here have gone downhill, and many tourists are surprised by how dry they are—you really need that dollop of *Schlagobers*. Still, coffee and a slice of cake here can be €8 well invested for the historic ambience alone. While the café itself is grotesquely touristy, the adjacent Sacher Stube has ambience and natives to spare (same prices). For maximum elegance, sit inside.

• *Continue past Hotel Sacher. At the end of the street is a small, triangular, cobbled square adorned with modern sculptures.*

❸ Albertinaplatz

As you enter the square, to the right you'll find the **TI**.

On your left, the tan-and-white Neoclassical building with the statue alcoves marks the tip of the Hofburg Palace—the sprawling complex of buildings that was long the seat of Habsburg power (we'll end this walk at the palace's center). The balustraded terrace up top was originally part of Vienna's defensive rampart. Later, it was the balcony of Empress Maria Theresa's daughter Maria Christina, who lived at this end of the palace. Today, her home houses the **Albertina Museum,** topped by a sleek, controversial titanium canopy (called the "diving board" by critics). The museum's plush, 19th-century staterooms are hung with facsimiles from its choice collection of prints, watercolors, and drawings (the originals are too light-sensitive to be displayed continuously). An entire floor is dedicated to the Batliner collection of classical modern art, covering each artistic stage from Impressionism to the present day.

Albertinaplatz itself is filled with statues that make up the powerful, thought-provoking ❹ **Monument Against War and Fascism,** which commemorates the dark years when Austria came under Nazi rule (1938-1945).

The statue group has four parts. The split white monument, *The Gates of Violence,* remembers victims of all wars and violence. Standing directly in front of it, you're at the gates of a concentration camp. Then, as you explore the statues, you step into a montage of wartime images: clubs and WWI gas masks, a dying woman birthing a future soldier, and chained slave laborers sitting on a pedestal of granite cut from the infamous quarry at Mauthausen concentration camp (located not far up the Danube from here). The hunched-over figure on the ground behind is a Jew forced to scrub anti-Nazi graffiti off a street with a toothbrush. Of Vienna's 200,000 Jews, more than 65,000 died in Nazi concentration camps. The statue with its head buried in the stone is Orpheus entering the underworld, meant to remind Austrians (and the rest of us) of the victims of Nazism...and the consequences of not keeping our governments on track. Behind that, the 1945 declaration that established Austria's second republic—and enshrined human rights—is cut into the stone.

Viewing this monument gains even more emotional impact when you realize what happened on this spot: During a WWII bombing attack, several hundred people were buried alive when the cellar they were using as shelter was demolished.

Austria was led into World War II by Germany, which annexed the country in 1938, saying Austrians were wannabe Germans anyway. But Austrians are not Germans—never were, never will be. They're quick to proudly tell you that Austria was founded in the 10th century, whereas Germany wasn't born until 1870. For seven years just before and during World War II (1938-1945), there was no Austria. In 1955, after 10 years of joint occupation by the victorious Allies, Austria regained total independence on the condition that it would be forever neutral (and never join NATO or the Warsaw Pact). To this day, Austria is outside of NATO (and Germany).

Behind the monument is ❺ **Café Tirolerhof**, a classic Viennese café full of things that time has passed by: chandeliers, marble tables, upholstered booths, waiters in tuxes, and newspapers. For more on Vienna's cafés, see page 93.

Often parked nearby are the Red Bus City Tour buses, offering a handy way to get a quick overview of the city (see "Tours in Vienna," earlier).

• *From the café, turn right on Führichsgasse, passing the cafeteria-style Rosenberger Markt Restaurant. Walk one block until you hit...*

❻ Kärntner Strasse

This grand, traffic-free street is the people-watching delight of this in-love-with-life city. Today's Kärntner Strasse (KAYRNT-ner SHTRAH-seh) is mostly a crass commercial pedestrian mall—its famed elegant shops long gone. But locals know it's the same road Crusaders marched down as they headed off from St. Stephen's Cathedral for the Holy Land in the 12th century. Its name indicates that it leads south, toward the region of Kärnten (Carinthia, a province divided between Austria and Slovenia). Today it's full of shoppers and street musicians.

Where Führichsgasse meets Kärntner Strasse, note the city **Casino** (across the street and a half-block to your right, at #41)—once venerable, now tacky, it exemplifies the worst of the street's evolution. Turn left to head up Kärntner Strasse, going away from the Opera. As you walk along, be sure to look up, above the modern storefronts, for glimpses of the street's former glory. Near the end of the block, on the left at #26, **J & L Lobmeyr Crystal** ("Founded in 1823") still has its impressive brown storefront with gold trim, statues, and the Habsburg double-eagle. In the market for some $400 napkin rings? Lobmeyr's your place. Inside, breathe in the classic Old World ambience as you climb up to the glass museum (free entry, Mon-Fri 10:00-19:00, Sat 10:00-18:00, closed Sun).

• *At the end of the block, turn left on Marco d'Aviano Gasse (passing the fragrant flower stall) to make a short detour to the square called Neuer Markt. Straight ahead is an orange-ish church with a triangular roof and cross, the Capuchin Church. In its basement is the...*

❼ Kaisergruft

Under the church sits the Imperial Crypt, filled with what's left of Austria's emperors, empresses, and other Habsburg royalty. For centuries, Vienna was the heart of a vast empire ruled by the Habsburg family, and here is where they lie buried in their fancy pewter coffins. You'll find all the Habsburg greats, including Maria Theresa, her son Josef II (Mozart's patron), Franz Josef, and Empress Sisi. Before moving on, consider paying your respects here.

• *Stretching north from the Kaisergruft is the square called...*

❽ Neuer Markt

A block farther down, in the center of Neuer Markt, is the **four rivers fountain** showing Lady Providence surrounded by figures symbolizing the rivers that flow into the Danube. The sexy statues offended Empress Maria Theresa, who actually organized "Chastity Commissions" to defend her capital city's moral standards. The modern buildings around you were rebuilt after World War II. Half of the city's inner center was intentionally destroyed by Churchill to demoralize the Viennese, who were disconcertingly enthusiastic about the Nazis.

• *Lady Providence's one bare breast points back to Kärntner Strasse (50 yards away). Before you head back to the busy shopping street, you could stop for a sweet treat at the heavenly, recommended Kurkonditorei Oberlaa (to get there, disobey the McDonald's arrows—it's at the far-left corner of the square).*

Leave the square and return to Kärntner Strasse. Turn left and continue down Kärntner Strasse. As you approach the cathedral, you're likely to first see it as a reflection in the round-glass windows of the postmodern Haas Haus. Pass the U-Bahn station (which has WCs) where the street spills into Vienna's main square...

❾ Stephansplatz

The cathedral's frilly spire looms overhead, worshippers and tourists pour inside the church, and shoppers and top-notch street entertainers buzz around the outside. You're at the center of Vienna.

The Gothic **St. Stephen's Cathedral** (c. 1300-1450) is known for its 450-foot south tower, its colorful roof, and its place in Viennese history. When it was built, it was a huge church for what was then a tiny town, and it helped put the fledgling city on the map. At this point, you may want to take a break from the walk to tour the church (see my self-guided tour on page 53).

Where Kärntner Strasse hits Stephansplatz, the grand, soot-covered building with red columns is the **Equitable Building** (filled with lawyers, bankers, and insurance brokers). It's a fine example of Neoclassicism from the turn of the 20th century—look up and imagine how slick Vienna must have felt in 1900.

Facing St. Stephen's is the sleek concrete-and-glass ❿ **Haas Haus,** a postmodern building by noted Austrian architect Hans Hollein (finished in 1990). The curved facade is supposed to echo the Roman fortress of Vindobona (its ruins were found near here). Although the Viennese initially protested having this stark modern tower right next to their beloved cathedral, since then, it's become a fixture of Vienna's main square. Notice how the smooth, rounded glass reflects St. Stephen's pointy architecture, providing a great photo opportunity—especially at twilight.

• Exit the square with your back to the cathedral. Walk past the Haas Haus, and bear right down the street called...

⓫ Graben

This was once a *Graben,* or ditch—originally the moat for the Roman military camp. Back during Vienna's 19th-century heyday, there were nearly 200,000 people packed into the city's inner center (inside the Ringstrasse), walking through dirt streets. Today this area houses 20,000. Graben was a busy street with three lanes of traffic until the 1970s, when it was turned into one of Europe's first pedestrian-only zones. Take a moment to absorb the scene—you're standing in an area surrounded by history, postwar rebuilding, grand architecture, fine cafés, and people enjoying life...for me, quintessential Europe.

As you stroll down the Graben from Stephansplatz, after about 50 yards, you'll reach a modern water dispenser. Vienna has suffered fiercely hot summers lately, leading the city government to install watering stations and shady benches for its citizens and visitors.

In another fifty yards, you reach Dorotheergasse, on your left, which leads (after two more long blocks) to the **Dorotheum** auction house. Consider poking your nose in here later for some fancy window-shopping. Also along this street are two recommended eateries: the sandwich shop Buffet Trześniewski—one of my favorite places for lunch—and the classic Café Hawelka (both described later).

In the middle of the Graben pedestrian zone is the extravagantly blobby ⓬ **Holy Trinity plague column** *(Pestsäule).* The 60-foot pillar of clouds sprouts angels and cherubs, with the wonderfully gilded Father, Son, and Holy Ghost at the top (all protected by an anti-pigeon net).

In 1679, Vienna was hit by a massive epidemic of bubonic plague. Around 75,000 Viennese died—about a third of the city.

Emperor Leopold I dropped to his knees (something emperors never did in public) and begged God to save the city. (Find Leopold about a quarter of the way up the monument, just above the brown banner. Hint: The typical inbreeding of royal families left him with a gaping underbite.) His prayer was heard by Lady Faith (the statue below Leopold, carrying a cross). With the help of a heartless little cupid, she tosses an old naked woman—symbolizing the plague—into the abyss and saves the city. In gratitude, Leopold vowed to erect this monument, which became a model for other cities ravaged by the same plague.

VIENNA

• *Thirty yards past the plague monument, look down the short street to the right, which frames a Baroque church with a stately green dome.*

⓭ St. Peter's Church
Leopold I ordered this church to be built as a thank-you for surviving the 1679 plague. The church stands on the site of a much older church that may have been Vienna's first (or second) Christian church. Inside, St. Peter's shows Vienna at its Baroque best. Note that the church offers free organ concerts (Mon-Fri at 15:00, Sat-Sun at 20:00).

• *Continue west on Graben, where you'll immediately find some stairs leading underground to...*

⓮ Loos' Loos
In about 1900, a local chemical-maker needed a publicity stunt to prove that his chemicals really got things clean. He purchased two wine cellars under Graben and had them turned into classy WCs in the Modernist style (designed by Adolf Loos—Vienna's answer to Frank Lloyd Wright), complete with chandeliers and finely crafted mahogany. While the chandeliers are gone, the restrooms remain a relatively appealing place to do your business—in fact, they're so inviting that they're used for poetry readings. Locals and tourists happily pay €0.50 for a quick visit.

• *Graben dead-ends at the aristocratic supermarket Julius Meinl am Graben. From here, turn left. In the distance is the big green-and-gold dome of the Hofburg, where we'll head soon. The street leading up to the Hofburg is...*

⓯ Kohlmarkt
This is Vienna's most elegant and unaffordable shopping street, lined with Cartier, Armani, Gucci, Tiffany, and the emperor's palace at the end. Strolling Kohlmarkt, daydream about the edible window displays at ⓰ **Demel,** the ultimate Viennese chocolate shop (#14, daily 10:00-19:00). The room is filled with Art Nouveau boxes of Empress Sisi's choco-dreams come true: *Kandierte Veilchen* (candied violet petals), *Katzenzungen* (cats' tongues), and so on.

The cakes here are moist (compared to the dry Sacher-Tortes). The enticing window displays change monthly, reflecting current happenings in Vienna. Wander inside. There's an impressive cancan of Vienna's most beloved cakes—displayed to tempt visitors into springing for the €10 cake-and-coffee deal (point to the cake you want). Farther in, you can see the bakery in action. Sit inside, with a view of the cake-making, or outside, with the street action (upstairs is less crowded). Shops like this boast "K.u.K."—signifying that during the Habsburgs' heyday, it was patronized by the *König und Kaiser* (king and emperor—same guy). If you happen to be looking through Demel's window at exactly 19:01, just after closing, you can witness one of the great tragedies of modern Europe: the daily dumping of its unsold cakes.

Next to Demel, the **Manz Bookstore** has a Loos-designed facade. By the way, across the street (and back a few steps) is a fine travel book and map shop (Freytag & Berndt, which carries most of my guidebooks).

• *Kohlmarkt ends at the square called...*

⑰ Michaelerplatz

This square is dominated by the **Hofburg Palace.** Study the grand Neo-Baroque facade, dating from about 1900. The four heroic giants illustrate Hercules wrestling with his great challenges (Emperor Franz Josef, who commissioned the gate, felt he could relate).

In the center of this square, a scant bit of **Roman Vienna** lies exposed just beneath street level.

Spin Tour: Do a slow, clockwise pan to get your bearings, starting (over your left shoulder as you face the Hofburg) with **St. Michael's Church,** which offers fascinating tours of its crypt. To the right of that is the fancy **Loden-Plankl shop,** with traditional Austrian formalwear, including dirndls. Farther to the right, across Augustinerstrasse, is the wing of the palace that houses the **Spanish Riding School** and its famous white Lipizzaner stallions. Farther down this street lies **Josefsplatz,** with the Augustinian Church, and the Dorotheum auction house. At the end of the street are Albertinaplatz and the Opera (where we started this walk).

Continue your spin: Two buildings over from the Hofburg (to the right), the modern **Loos House** (now a bank) has a facade featuring a perfectly geometrical grid of square columns and windows. Compared to the Neo-Rococo facade of the Hofburg, the stern Modernism of the Loos House appears to be from an entirely different age. And yet, both of these—as well as the Eiffel Tower and Mad Ludwig's fairy-tale Neuschwanstein Castle—were built in the same generation, roughly around 1900. In many ways, this jarring juxtaposition exemplifies the architectural turmoil of the turn of the 20th century, and represents the passing of the torch from Europe's age of divine monarchs to the modern era.

• *Let's take a look at where Austria's glorious history began—at the...*

Hofburg Palace

This is the complex of palaces where the Habsburg emperors lived (except in summer, when they lived out at Schönbrunn Palace). Enter the Hofburg through the gate, where you immediately find yourself beneath a big rotunda (the netting is there to keep birds from perching). The doorway on the right is the entrance to the ⓭ **Imperial Apartments,** where the Habsburg emperors once lived in chandeliered elegance. Today you can tour its lavish rooms, as well as a museum about Empress Sisi, and a porcelain and silver collection. To the left is the ticket office for the ⓮ **Spanish Riding School**.

Continuing on, you emerge from the rotunda into the main courtyard of the Hofburg, called **In der Burg.** The Caesar-like statue is of Habsburg Emperor Franz II (1768-1835), grandson of Maria Theresa, grandfather of Franz Josef, and father-in-law of Napoleon. Behind him is a tower with three kinds of clocks (the yellow disc shows the phase of the moon tonight). To the right of Franz are the Imperial Apartments, and to the left are the offices of Austria's mostly ceremonial president (the more powerful chancellor lives in a building just behind this courtyard).

Franz Josef faces the oldest part of the palace. The colorful red, black, and gold gateway (behind you), which used to have a drawbridge, leads over the moat and into the 13th-century Swiss Court (Schweizerhof), named for the Swiss mercenary guards once stationed there. Study the gate. Imagine the drawbridge and the chain. Notice the Habsburg coat of arms with the imperial eagle above and the Renaissance painting on the ceiling of the passageway.

As you enter the Gothic courtyard, you're passing into the historic core of the palace, the site of the first fortress, and, historically, the place of last refuge. Here you'll find the ⓴ **Treasury** (Schatzkammer) and the **Imperial Music Chapel** (Hofmusikkapelle), where the Boys' Choir sings Mass. Ever since Joseph Hayden and Franz Schubert were choirboys here, visitors have gathered like groupies on Sundays to hear the famed choir sing.

Returning to the bigger In der Burg courtyard, face Franz and turn left, passing through the **tunnel,** with a few tourist shops and restaurants, to spill out into spacious ㉑ **Heldenplatz** (Heroes' Square). On the left is the impressive curved facade of the **New Palace** (Neue Burg). This vast wing was built in the early 1900s to be the new Habsburg living quarters (and was meant to have a matching building facing it). But in 1914, the heir to the throne,

VIENNA

Archduke Franz Ferdinand—while waiting politely for his long-lived uncle, Emperor Franz Josef, to die—was assassinated in Sarajevo. The archduke's death sparked World War I and the eventual end of eight centuries of Habsburg rule.

Today the building houses the **New Palace museums,** an eclectic collection of weaponry, suits of armor, musical instruments, and ancient Greek statues. The two equestrian statues depict Prince Eugene of Savoy (1663-1736), who battled the Ottoman Turks, and Archduke Charles (1771-1847), who battled Napoleon. Eugene gazes toward the far distance at the prickly spires of Vienna's City Hall.

Spin Tour: Make a slow 360-degree turn, and imagine this huge square filled with people.

In 1938, over 200,000 Viennese gathered here on Heldenplatz, entirely filling vast Heroes' Square, to welcome Adolf Hitler and celebrate their annexation with Germany—the *"Anschluss."* The Nazi tyrant stood on the balcony of the New Palace and declared, "Before the face of German history, I declare my former homeland now a part of the Third Reich. One of the pearls of the Third Reich will be Vienna." He never mentioned "Austria," and from that moment on, it was forbidden to say the word.

Many wonder how Austria could so eagerly embrace Hitler and the *Anschluss* (although the notion of annexation with Germany had been batted around even before Hitler's rise). Let me hazard an explanation: Imagine post-WWI Austria. One of the mightiest empires on earth had started—and lost—a great war. In a few bloody years, it went from being a grand empire of 55 million people to a relatively insignificant landlocked state of six million. Treaty stipulations required the republic to remain unaligned with any other power. The capital, Vienna, was left with little to rule. The city alone comprised a third of the entire country's population. In the global economic crisis we know as the Great Depression (which swept the Nazis to power in Germany in 1933), Austria found itself ruled by a fascist government, complete with a dictator named Engelbert Dollfuss. He was as right-wing and anti-Semitic as Hitler, but also anti-Nazi (he was pro-Roman Catholic Church and pro-Habsburg). Under Dollfuss, the Austrian fascists eliminated any leftist opposition. When an Austrian Nazi assassinated Dollfuss in 1934, it created a power vacuum, paving the way for the German Nazis to easily take over four years later. The German Nazis just took over their Austrian counterparts' file cabinets. And, Hitler promised greatness again, and jobs—something that has driven voters to support crazy political notions to this day.

• *Walk on through the Greek-columned passageway (the Äussere Burgtor, an old castle gate), cross the Ringstrasse, and stand in the square between the twin museums, near the...*

㉒ Maria Theresa Monument

Vienna's biggest monument shows the empress holding a scroll from her father granting the right of a woman to inherit his throne. The statues and reliefs surrounding her speak volumes about her reign: Her four top generals sit on horseback while her four top advisors stand. Behind them, reliefs celebrate cultural leaders of her day, including little Wolfie Mozart with mentor "Papa" Joseph Haydn (with his hand on Mozart's shoulder, facing the Natural History Museum). The moral of this propaganda: a strong military and a wise rule are prerequisites for a thriving culture—attributes that characterized the 40-year rule of the woman who was perhaps Austria's greatest monarch.

Standing here, it's fascinating to consider Austrian aspirations for greatness through the ages. Had World War I not messed things up for them, the Habsburgs would have created a vast cultural forum stretching from here across the Ringstrasse. While they never fully realized their vision, the ensemble that was completed is impressive. Two awe-inspiring buildings, purpose-built in the 1880s, house the private art and history collections of the empire, and celebrate its culture and power. The giant Kunsthistorisches and Natural History Museums face each other across the square with the towering monument to Maria Theresa in the center of it all.

• *Our walk is finished. You're in the heart of Viennese sightseeing. Surrounding this square are some of the city's top museums. And the Hofburg Palace itself contains many of Vienna's best sights and museums. From the Opera to the Hofburg, from chocolate to churches, from St. Stephen's to Sacher-Tortes—Vienna waits for you.*

Sights in Vienna

In the Old Town, Within the Ring

These sights are listed roughly from south to north. For a self-guided walk connecting many of central Vienna's top sights—including some of the ones below—see my "Vienna City Walk," earlier.

▲▲▲Opera (Wiener Staatsoper)

The Opera House, facing the Ring and near the TI, is a central point for any visitor. Vienna remains one of the world's great cities for classical music, and this building still belts out some of the finest opera, both classic and cutting-edge. While the critical reception of the building 130 years ago led the architect to commit suicide, and though it's been rebuilt since its destruction by WWII bombs, it's still a sumptuous place. The interior has a chandeliered lobby and carpeted staircases perfect for making the scene. The theater itself features five wraparound balconies, gold-and-red decor, and a bracelet-like chandelier.

Depending on your level of tolerance for opera, you can simply admire the Neo-Renaissance building from the outside, take a guided tour of the lavish interior, visit the Opera Museum, or attend a performance of Vienna's opera company.

Tours: You can only enter the Opera if you're attending a performance or joining a guided 45-minute tour in English (€6.50, ticket covers modest Opera Museum, described below; tours run July-Aug generally daily at the top of each hour 10:00-16:00; Sept-June fewer tours, afternoons only, none on Sun; buy tickets 20 minutes before tour departs—ticket office is around the left side, as you face the main entrance; tel. 01/514-442-606, www.wiener-staatsoper.at). Tour times are often changed or canceled due to rehearsals and performances. Schedules with daily listings for each month (including tour times) are posted all around the building. A list of today's tours in each language is posted to the right of the entry door; you can also pick up the monthly *Prolog* program, which includes the schedule. The entry door opens 30 minutes before each tour and closes when it starts.

Opera Museum (Staatsopernmuseum): This permanent exhibit chronologically traces the illustrious history of the Vienna State Opera, highlighting the most famous singers, directors (including Gustav Mahler and Herbert von Karajan), and performances. It also features old posters, costumes, and lots of photographs (€3, included in Opera tour ticket; Tue-Sun 10:00-18:00, closed Mon; across the street and a block away from the Opera toward the Hofburg, tucked down a courtyard at Hanuschgasse 3, near Albertina Museum, tel. 01/514-442-100).

Performances: For information on buying tickets and attending a performance, see page 98.

▲▲Haus der Musik

Vienna's "House of Music" is a high-tech experience that celebrates this hometown specialty. The museum, spread over five floors and well-described in English, is unique for its effective use of interactive touch-screen computers and headphones to explore the physics of sound. Really experiencing the place takes time. It's open late and makes a good evening activity.

Cost and Hours: €11, includes audioguide for third floor only, half-price after 20:00, €17 combo-ticket with Mozarthaus, daily 10:00-22:00, last entry one hour before closing, two blocks from the Opera at Seilerstätte 30, tel. 01/513-4850, www.hdm.at.

Visiting the Museum: The first floor features a small exhibit on the Vienna Philharmonic Orchestra, including the batons of prominent conductors and Leonard Bernstein's tux. On the second floor, wander through the "sonosphere" and marvel at the amazing acoustics. Spend some time at the well-presented, interactive head-phone stations to learn about the nature of sound and music; I could actually hear what I thought only a piano tuner could discern. The third floor features fine audiovisual exhibits on each of the famous hometown boys (Haydn, Mozart, Beethoven, Schubert, Strauss, and Mahler). Before leaving, pick up a virtual baton to conduct the Vienna Philharmonic. Each time you screw up, the musicians put their instruments down and ridicule you; make it through the piece, and you'll get a rousing round of applause.

VIENNA

▲Dorotheum Auction House (Palais Dorotheum)

For an aristocrat's flea market, drop by Austria's answer to Sotheby's. The ground floor has shops, an info desk with a schedule of upcoming auctions, and a few auction items. Some pieces are available for immediate sale (marked *VKP*, for *Verkaufpreis*—"sales price"), while others are up for auction (marked *DIFF. RUF*). Labels on each item predict the auction value.

The upstairs floors have antique furniture and fancy knick-knacks (some for immediate sale, others for auction), many brought in by people who've inherited old things and don't have room. The top floor has a fancy antique gallery with fixed prices. Wandering through here, you feel like you're touring a museum with exhibits you can buy. Afterward, you can continue your hunt for the perfect curio on the streets around the Dorotheum, lined with many fine antique shops.

Cost and Hours: Free, Mon-Fri 10:00-18:00, Sat 9:00-17:00, closed Sun, classy little café on second floor, between the Graben pedestrian street and Hofburg at Dorotheergasse 17, tel. 01/51560, www.dorotheum.com.

▲St. Peter's Church (Peterskirche)

Baroque Vienna is at its best in this gem, tucked away a few steps from the Graben.

Cost and Hours: Free, Mon-Fri 7:00-20:00, Sat-Sun 9:00-21:00; free organ concerts Mon-Fri at 15:00, Sat-Sun at 20:00; just off the Graben between the Plague Monument and Kohlmarkt, tel. 01/533-6433.

Visiting the Church: Admire the rose-and-gold, oval-shaped Baroque interior, topped with a ceiling fresco of Mary kneeling to be crowned by Jesus and the Father, while the dove of the Holy Spirit floats way up in the lantern. Taken together, the church's elements—especially the organ, altar painting, pulpit, and coat of arms (in the base of the dome) of church founder Leopold I—make St. Peter's one of the city's most beautiful and ornate churches.

To the right of the altar, a dramatic golden statue shows the martyrdom of St. John Nepomuk (c. 1340-1393). The Czech saint defied the heretical King Wenceslas, so he was tossed to his death off the Charles Bridge in Prague. In true Baroque style, we see the

VIENNA

Vienna at a Glance

▲▲▲Opera House Dazzling, world-famous opera house. **Hours:** By guided tour only, July-Aug generally daily at the top of each hour 10:00-16:00; Sept-June fewer tours, afternoon only, none on Sun. See page 47.

▲▲▲St. Stephen's Cathedral Enormous, historic Gothic cathedral in the center of Vienna. **Hours:** Church—daily 6:00-22:00; main nave—Mon-Sat 9:00-11:30 & 13:30-16:30, Sun 13:00-16:30, until 17:30 June-Aug. See page 53.

▲▲▲Hofburg Imperial Apartments Lavish main residence of the Habsburgs. **Hours:** Daily July-Aug 9:00-18:00, Sept-June 9:00-17:30. See page 58.

▲▲▲Hofburg Treasury The Habsburgs' collection of jewels, crowns, and other valuables—the best on the Continent. **Hours:** Wed-Mon 9:00-17:30, closed Tue. See page 62.

▲▲▲Kunsthistorisches Museum World-class exhibit of the Habsburgs' art collection, including works by Raphael, Titian, Caravaggio, Bosch, and Bruegel. **Hours:** Tue-Sun 10:00-18:00, Thu until 21:00, closed Mon. See page 69.

▲▲▲Schönbrunn Palace Spectacular summer residence of the Habsburgs, rivaling the grandeur of Versailles. **Hours:** Daily July-Aug 8:30-18:30, April-June and Sept-Oct 8:30-17:30, Nov-March 8:30-17:00. See page 88.

▲▲Haus der Musik Modern museum with interactive exhibits on Vienna's favorite pastime. **Hours:** Daily 10:00-22:00. See page 48.

▲▲Hofburg New Palace Museums Uncrowded collection of armor, musical instruments, and ancient Greek statues, in the elegant halls of a Habsburg palace. **Hours:** Wed-Sun 10:00-18:00, closed Mon-Tue. See page 64.

▲▲Albertina Museum Habsburg residence with decent apartments and world-class temporary exhibits. **Hours:** Daily 10:00-18:00, Wed until 21:00. See page 67.

▲▲Kaisergruft Crypt for the Habsburg royalty. **Hours:** Daily 10:00-18:00. See page 67.

▲▲Belvedere Palace Elegant palace of Prince Eugene of Savoy, with a collection of 19th- and 20th-century Austrian art (including

Klimt). **Hours:** Daily 10:00-18:00, Lower Palace only until 21:00 on Wed. See page 82.

▲**St. Peter's Church** Beautiful Baroque church in the old center. **Hours:** Mon-Fri 7:00-20:00, Sat-Sun 9:00-21:00. See page 49.

▲**Spanish Riding School** Prancing white Lipizzaner stallions. **Hours:** Spring (Feb-June) and fall (Sept-Dec) only, performances Sun at 11:00 and either Sat at 11:00 or Fri at 19:00, plus less-impressive training sessions generally Tue-Fri and many Sat 10:00-12:00. See page 65.

▲**St. Michael's Church Crypt** Final resting place of about 100 wealthy 18th-century Viennese. **Hours:** By tour Mon-Sat at 11:00 and 13:30. See page 68.

▲**Natural History Museum** Big building facing the Kunsthistorisches, featuring the ancient *Venus of Willendorf*. **Hours:** Wed-Mon 9:00-18:30, Wed until 21:00, closed Tue. See page 73.

▲**Karlskirche** Baroque church offering the unique (and temporary) chance to ride an elevator up into the dome. **Hours:** Mon-Sat 9:00-18:00, Sun 13:00-18:00. See page 75.

▲**Academy of Fine Arts** Small but exciting collection by 15th- to 18th-century masters. **Hours:** Tue-Sun 10:00-18:00, closed Mon. See page 76.

▲**The Secession** Art Nouveau exterior and Klimt paintings *in situ*. **Hours:** Tue-Sun 10:00-18:00, closed Mon. See page 78.

▲**Naschmarkt** Sprawling, lively outdoor market. **Hours:** Mon-Fri 6:00-18:30, Sat 6:00-17:00, closed Sun, closes earlier in winter. See page 79.

▲**Museum of Military History** Huge collection of artifacts tracing the military history of the Habsburg Empire. **Hours**: Tues-Sun, 10:00-17:00, closed Mon. See page 85.

▲**Kunst Haus Wien Museum** Modern art museum dedicated to zany local artist/environmentalist Hundertwasser. **Hours:** Daily 10:00-19:00. See page 86.

▲**Imperial Furniture Collection** Eclectic collection of Habsburg furniture. **Hours:** Tue-Sun 10:00-18:00, closed Mon. See page 87.

dramatic peak of his fall, when John has just passed the point of no return. The Virgin Mary floats overhead in a silver cloud.

The present church (from 1733) stands atop earlier churches dating back 1,600 years. On either side of the nave are glass cases containing skeletons of Christian martyrs from Roman times. Above the relic on the left is a painting of the modern saint Josemaría Escrivá, founder of the conservative Catholic organization Opus Dei, of *Da Vinci Code* notoriety.

VIENNA

Mozarthaus Vienna

Exhibits fill the only surviving Mozart residence in Vienna, where he lived from 1784 to 1787, when he had lots of money (and produced some of his most famous works, including *The Marriage of Figaro* and *Don Giovanni*). Opened in 2006 to commemorate Wolfgang's 250th birthday, this museum is easy to get excited about, but it disappoints. While the museum might be worth the time and money for enthusiasts, I much prefer the Haus der Musik (described earlier).

Cost and Hours: €10, includes audioguide, €17 combo-ticket with Haus der Musik, daily 10:00-19:00, last entry 30 minutes before closing, a block behind the cathedral, go through arcade at #5a and walk 50 yards to Domgasse 5, tel. 01/512-1791, www.mozarthausvienna.at.

Judenplatz Memorial

The classy square called Judenplatz marks the location of Vienna's 15th-century Jewish community, one of Europe's largest at the time. Once filled with a long-gone synagogue, the square is now dominated by a blocky **memorial** to the 65,000 Viennese Jews killed by the Nazis. The memorial—a library turned inside out—invokes Jewish identity as a "people of the book" and asks viewers to ponder the huge loss of culture, knowledge, and humanity that took place between 1938 and 1945.

Jewish Museum Vienna (Jüdisches Museum Wien)

The museum operates two buildings, one on Judenplatz and another on Dorotheergasse, a block south of the Graben.

Cost and Hours: €10 ticket includes both museums; Judenplatz location, at #8—Sun-Thu 10:00-18:00, Fri 10:00-14:00, closed Sat; Dorotheergasse location, at #11—Sun-Fri 10:00-18:00, closed Sat; tel. 01/535-0431, www.jmw.at.

Visiting the Museums: The **Museum Judenplatz,** while sparse, has displays on medieval Jewish life and a well-done video re-creating the ghetto as it looked five centuries ago. Wander the scant remains of the medieval synagogue below street level—discovered during the construction of the Holocaust memorial. This was the scene of a medieval massacre. Since Christians weren't allowed to lend money, Jews were Europe's moneylenders. As so often happened in Europe, when Viennese Christians fell too deeply into debt, they found a convenient excuse to wipe out the local ghetto—and their debts at the same time. In 1421, the synagogue was destroyed, and Jews who refused a forced conversion were expelled from the city or murdered.

The **Jewish Museum Dorotheergasse** is small and modern. Its exhibits document the Viennese Jewish community before 1938 and in recent decades. Its evocative third floor is a "visible storage" archive with stacks of Judaica and works of art that once ornamented synagogues. The collection is well described in English and by the €2 audioguide.

▲▲▲St. Stephen's Cathedral (Stephansdom)

This massive church is the Gothic needle around which Vienna spins. According to the medieval vision of its creators, it stands like a giant jeweled reliquary, offering praise to God from the center of the city. The church and its towers, especially the 450-foot south tower, give the city its most iconic image. (Check your pockets for €0.10 coins; those minted in Austria feature the south tower on the back.) The cathedral has survived Vienna's many wars and today symbolizes the city's spirit and love of freedom.

Cost: It's free to enter the foyer and north aisle of the church, but it costs €3.50 to get into the main nave, where most of the interesting items are located (more for special exhibits). Going up the towers costs €3.50 (by stairs, south tower) or €4.50 (by elevator, north tower). You'll pay €4.50 to visit the catacombs and €4 to see the treasury (for more on the towers, catacombs, and treasury, see the end of this tour). The €16 combo-ticket—covering entry, both towers, catacombs, treasury, and audioguide—is overkill for most visitors.

Hours: The church doors are open daily 6:00-22:00, but the main nave is open for tourists Mon-Sat 9:00-11:30 & 13:30-16:30, Sun 13:00-16:30, until 17:30 June-Aug. During services, you can't enter the main nave (unless you're attending Mass) or access the north tower elevator or catacombs, but you can go into the back of the church.

Information: Tel. 01/515-523-526, www.stephanskirche.at.

Tours: The €4.50 tours in English are entertaining (daily at 15:45, check information board inside entry to confirm schedule; price includes main nave entry). The €1 audioguide is helpful. You can download a free Rick Steves **audio tour** of St. Stephen's; see page 7.

◔ Self-Guided Tour: This tour will give you a good look at the cathedral, inside and out.

Cathedral Exterior: Before we go inside, let's circle around the cathedral for a look at its impressive exterior.

• As you face the church's main entry, go to the right across the little square, and find the old-time photos next to the door marked 3a Stephansplatz. *From here, you can take in the sheer magnitude of this massive church, with its skyscraping spire.*

The church we see today is the third one on this spot. It dates mainly from 1300 to 1450, when builders expanded on an earlier structure and added two huge **towers** at the end of each transept. The impressive 450-foot **south tower**—capped with a golden orb and cross—took two generations to build (65 years) and was finished in 1433. The tower is a rarity among medieval churches in that it was completed before the Gothic style—and the age of faith—petered out.

The half-size **north tower** (223 feet), around the other side of the church, was meant to be a matching steeple. But around 1500, it was abandoned in mid-construction, when the money was needed to defend the country against the Ottomans rather than to build church towers. You can ascend both towers (stairs to the south tower, an elevator to the north tower); for details, see the end of this tour.

The cathedral was heavily damaged at the end of World War II. Near where you are standing are **old photos** showing the destruction. In 1945, Vienna was caught in the chaos between the occupying Nazis and the approaching Soviets. Allied bombs sparked fires in nearby buildings, and the embers leapt to the cathedral rooftop. The original timbered Gothic roof burned, the cathedral's huge bell crashed to the ground, and the fire raged for two days. Civic pride prompted a financial outpouring, and the roof was rebuilt to its original splendor by 1952—doubly impressive considering the bombed-out state of the country at that time.

• Circle the church exterior counterclockwise, passing the entrance to the **south tower.** *If you're up for climbing the 343 stairs to the top, you could do it now, but it's better to wait until the end of this tour (tower climb described at the end of this tour).*

As you hook around behind the church, look for the cathedral bookshop (Dombuchhandlung) at the end of the block. Pause in front of that shop and look toward the cathedral.

Just above street level, notice the marble **pulpit** under the golden starburst. The priest would stand here, stoking public opinion against the Ottomans, in front of crowds far bigger than could fit into the church. Above the pulpit (in a scene from around 1700), a saint stands victoriously atop a vanquished Turk.

• Continue circling the church, passing a line of horse carriages waiting to take tourists for a ride. Go all the way around to the west facade.

The Romanesque-style **main entrance** is the oldest part of the church (c. 1240—part of a church that stood here before). Right behind you is the site of Vindobona, a Roman garrison town. Before the Romans converted to Christianity, there was a pagan temple here, and this entrance pays homage to that ancient heritage. Roman-era statues are embedded in the facade, and the two **octagonal towers** flanking the main doorway are dubbed the "heathen towers" because they're built with a few recycled Roman stones (flipped over to hide the pagan inscriptions and expose the smooth sides).

• *Enter the church.*

Cathedral Interior: Find a spot to peer through the gate down the immense **nave**—more than a football field long and nine stories tall. It's lined with clusters of slender pillars that soar upward to support the ribbed crisscross arches of the ceiling. Stylistically, the nave is Gothic with a Baroque overlay. It's a spacious, glorious venue that's often used for high-profile concerts (there's a ticket office outside the church, to the right as you face the main doorway).

To the right as you enter, in a gold-and-silver sunburst frame, is a crude Byzantine-style **Maria Pócs Icon** (Pötscher Madonna), brought here from a humble Hungarian village church. The picture of Mary and Child is said to have wept real tears in 1697, as Central Europe was once again being threatened by the Turks.

Along the left wall is the **gift shop.** Step in to marvel at the 14th-century statuary decorating its wall—some of the finest carvings in the church.

To the left of the gift shop is the gated entrance to the **Chapel of Prince Eugene of Savoy.** Prince Eugene (1663-1736), a teenage seminary student from France, arrived in Vienna in 1683 as the city was about to be overrun by the Ottoman Turks. He volunteered for the army and helped save the city, launching a brilliant career as a military man for the Habsburgs. His specialty was conquering the Ottomans. When he died, the grateful Austrians buried him here, under this chapel, marked by a tomb hatch in the floor.

• *Nearby is the entrance to the main nave. Buy a ticket and start down the nave toward the altar.*

At the second pillar on the left is the Gothic sandstone pulpit (c. 1500), a masterpiece carved from three separate blocks (see if you can find the seams). A spiral stairway winds up to the lectern, surrounded and supported by the four church "fathers," whose writings influenced early Catholic dogma. The pulpit is as crammed with religious meaning as it is with beautifully realistic carvings. The top of the stairway's railing swarms with lizards (animals of light) and toads (animals of darkness). The "Dog of the Lord" stands at the top, making sure none of those toads pollutes the sermon. Below the toads, wheels with three parts (the Trinity) roll up, while wheels with four spokes (the four seasons and four cardinal directions, symbolizing mortal life on earth) roll down.

Find the guy peeking out from under the stairs. This may be

a **self-portrait** of the sculptor. In medieval times, art was done for the glory of God, and artists worked anonymously. But this pulpit was carved as humanist Renaissance ideals were creeping in from Italy—and individual artists were becoming famous. So the artist included what may be a rare self-portrait bust in his work.

• *Continue up toward the main altar. When you reach the gate that cuts off the front of the nave, turn right and enter the south transept. Go all the way to the doors.*

Look to the left to find a **plaque** commemorating Wolfgang Amadeus Mozart (1756-1791), who spent most of his adult life in Vienna. He attended Mass and was married in St. Stephen's, and had two of his children baptized here. He set up house in a lavish apartment a block east of the church (this house is now the lackluster Mozarthaus museum, described earlier). Mozart lived at the epicenter of Viennese society—among musicians, actors, and aristocrats. He played in a string quartet with Joseph Haydn. At church, he would have heard Beethoven's teacher playing the organ. (Mozart may have met the star-struck young Beethoven in Vienna—or maybe not; accounts vary.)

After his early success, Mozart fell on hard times. When he died at age 35 (in 1791), he was not buried at St. Stephen's, because the cemetery that once surrounded the church had been cleared out a decade earlier as an anti-plague measure. Instead, his remains (along with most Viennese of his day) were dumped into a mass grave outside of town. But he was honored with a funeral service in St. Stephen's—held in the Prince Eugene of Savoy Chapel, where they played his famous (unfinished) *Requiem*.

• *Now head to the chapel at the front-right corner of the church.*

This imposing, red-marble **tomb of Frederick III** is like a big king-size-bed coffin with an effigy of Frederick lying on top (not visible—but there's a photo of the effigy on the left). The top of the tomb is decorated with his coats of arms, representing the many territories he ruled over. Frederick III (1415-1493) is considered the "father" of Vienna for turning the small village into a royal town with a cosmopolitan feel.

• *Walk to the middle of the church.*

The tall, ornate, black marble **high altar** (1641, by Tobias and Johann Pock) is topped with a statue of Mary that barely fits under the towering vaults of the ceiling. It frames a large painting of the stoning of St. Stephen, painted on copper. Stephen (at the bottom), having refused to stop professing his faith, is pelted with rocks by angry pagans. As he kneels, ready to die, he gazes up to see a vision of Christ, the cross, and the angels of heaven.

During World War II, many of the city's top art treasures were stowed safely in cellars and salt mines—hidden by both the Nazi occupiers (to protect against war damage) and by citizens (to protect against Nazi looters). The **stained-glass windows** behind the high altar were meticulously dismantled and packed away. The pulpit was encased in a shell of brick. As the war was drawing to a close, it appeared St. Stephen's would escape major damage. But as the Nazis were fleeing, the bitter Nazi commander in charge of the city ordered that the church be destroyed. Fortunately, his underlings disobeyed. Unfortunately, the church accidentally caught fire during Allied bombing shortly thereafter, and the wooden roof collapsed onto the stone vaults of the ceiling. The Tupperware-colored glass on either side of the nave dates from the 1950s. Before the fire, the church was lit mostly with clear Baroque-era windows.

• *After exploring the nave, consider touring the catacombs or the treasury, or ascending either one of the two towers.*

Catacombs (Katakomben): The catacombs (viewable by guided tour only) hold the bodies—or at least the innards—of 72 Habsburgs, including that of Rudolf IV, the man who began building the south tower. This is where Austria's rulers were buried before the Kaisergruft was built (see page 67), and where later Habsburgs' entrails were entombed. The copper urns preserve the imperial organs in alcohol. I touched Maria Theresa's urn, and it wobbled. (€4.50, daily 10:00-11:30 & 13:30-16:30, tours depart on the half-hour and are in German and English). Just be at the stairs in the left/north transept to meet the guide.

Treasury: Tucked away in a loft in the oldest part of the church, the treasury offers precious relics, dazzling church art, a portrait of Rudolf IV (considered the earliest German portrait), and wonderful views down on the nave (€4 admission includes audioguide, daily 10:00-18:00, look for elevator just inside the cathedral's entry).

Ascending the North Tower: This tower, reached from inside the church (look for the *Aufzug zur Pummerin* sign), holds the famous "Pummerin" bell. Cast from captured Ottoman cannons, this bell rings in the New Year. This tower is easier to ascend than the south tower (described next), but it's much shorter and not as exciting, with lesser views (€4.50, daily 9:00-11:30 & 13:00-16:30, until 17:30 in June-Aug, entrance inside the church on the left/north side of the nave; you can access this elevator without buying a ticket for the main nave).

Climbing the South Tower: The iconic south tower offers a far better view than the north one, but you'll earn it by climbing 343 tightly wound steps up the spiral staircase (€3.50, daily 9:00-17:30; this hike burns about one Sacher-Torte of calories). To reach the entrance, exit the church and make a U-turn to the left. This tower, once key to the city's defense as a lookout point, is still dear to Viennese hearts. (It's long been affectionately nicknamed "Steffl," Viennese for "Stevie.") No church spire in (what was) the

Austro-Hungarian Empire is taller—by Habsburg decree. From the top, use your city map to locate the famous sights.

Hofburg Palace

The complex, confusing, and imposing imperial palace, with 640 years of architecture, demands your attention. This first Habsburg residence grew with the family empire from the 13th century until 1913, when the last "new wing" opened. The winter residence of the Habsburg rulers until 1918, it's still the home of the Austrian president's office, 5,000 government workers, and several important museums. For an overview of the palace layout, see map above.

Planning Your Time: Don't get confused by the Hofburg's myriad courtyards and many museums. Focus on three sights: the Imperial Apartments, Treasury, and the museums at the New Palace (Neue Burg). With more time, consider the Hofburg's many other sights, covering virtually all facets of the imperial lifestyle.

Eating at the Hofburg: Down the tunnel to Heldenplatz is a tiny but handy sandwich bar called **Hofburg Stüberl.** It's ideal for a cool, quiet sit and a drink or snack (same €3 sandwich price whether you sit or go, Mon-Fri 7:00-18:00, Sat-Sun 10:00-16:00). The recommended **Soho Kantine,** in the basement of the National Library, is a cheap-but-not-cheery option (described on page 120).

▲▲▲Hofburg Imperial Apartments (Kaiserappartements)

These lavish, Versailles-type, "wish-I-were-God" royal rooms are the downtown version of the grander Schönbrunn Palace. If you're rushed and have time for only one palace, make it this one. Palace visits are a one-way romp through three exhibits: a porcelain and silver collection, a museum dedicated to the enigmatic and troubled Empress Sisi, and the luxurious apartments themselves.

The Imperial Apartments are a mix of Old World luxury and modern 19th-century conveniences. Here, Emperor Franz Josef I lived and worked along with his wife Elisabeth, known as Sisi. The Sisi Museum traces the development of her legend, analyzing how her fabulous but tragic life created a 19th-century Princess Diana. You'll read bits of her poetic writing, see exact copies of her now-lost jewelry, and learn about her escapes, dieting mania, and chocolate bills.

Cost and Hours: €10.50, includes well-done audioguide, covered by Sisi Ticket (see page 48), daily July-Aug 9:00-18:00, Sept-June 9:00-17:30, last entry one hour before closing; enter from under the rotunda just off Michaelerplatz, through the Michaelertor gate; tel. 01/533-7570, www.hofburg-wien.at.

Information: With the included audioguide and the self-guided tour below, you won't need the €8 *Imperial Apartments/Sisi*

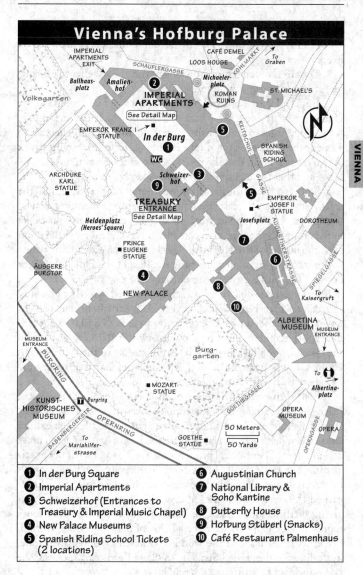

Vienna's Hofburg Palace

1 In der Burg Square
2 Imperial Apartments
3 Schweizerhof (Entrances to Treasury & Imperial Music Chapel)
4 New Palace Museums
5 Spanish Riding School Tickets (2 locations)
6 Augustinian Church
7 National Library & Soho Kantine
8 Butterfly House
9 Hofburg Stüberl (Snacks)
10 Café Restaurant Palmenhaus

VIENNA

Museum/Silver Collection guidebook. If you listen to the entire audioguide, allow 40 minutes for the silver collection, 30 minutes for the Sisi Museum, and 40 minutes for the apartments.

Your ticket grants you admission to three separate exhibits, which you'll visit on a pretty straightforward one-way route. The first floor holds a collection of precious porcelain and silver knickknacks *(Silberkammer)*. You then go upstairs to the Sisi Museum, which has displays about her life. This leads into the 20-odd rooms of Imperial Apartments *(Kaiserappartements)*, starting in Franz Josef's rooms, then heading into the dozen rooms where his wife Sisi lived.

⊘ Self-Guided Tour: Your visit (and the excellent audioguide) starts on the ground floor.

Imperial Porcelain and Silver Collection: Here you'll see the Habsburg court's vast tableware collection, which the audioguide actually manages to make fairly interesting. Browse the collection to gawk at the opulence and to take in some colorful Habsburg trivia. (Who'd have thunk that the court had an official way to fold a napkin—and that the technique remains a closely guarded secret?)

Once you're through all those rooms of dishes, climb the stairs—the same staircase used by the emperors and empresses who lived here. At the top is a timeline of Sisi's life. Swipe your ticket to pass through the turnstile, consider the WC, and enter the room with the **model of the Hofburg.** Circle to the far side to find where you're standing right now, near the smallest of the Hofburg's three domes. The Hofburg was the epicenter of one of Europe's great political powers—600 years of Habsburgs lived here. The Hofburg started as a 13th-century medieval castle (near where you are right now) and expanded over the centuries to today's 240,000-square-meter (60-acre) complex, now owned by the state. To the left of the dome (as you face the facade) is the steeple of the Augustinian Church. It was there, in 1854, that Franz Josef married 16-year-old Elisabeth of Bavaria, and their story began.

Sisi Museum: Empress Elisabeth (1837-1898)—a.k.a. "Sisi"—was Franz Josef's mysterious, beautiful, and narcissistic wife. This museum traces her fabulous but tragic life. The exhibit starts when her life ended and her legend began (see her death mask and pictures of her funeral procession). You'll read bits of her poetic writing, see exact copies of her now-lost jewelry, and learn about her escapes, dieting mania, and chocolate bills. Admire Sisi's hard-earned thin waist (20 inches at age 16, 21 inches at age 50...after giving birth to four children). The black statue in the dark room represents the empress after the suicide of her son—aloof, thin, in black, with her back to the world. At the end, ponder the crude, knife-like file that killed Sisi. (In 1898, while visiting Geneva, she was murdered by an Italian anarchist.)

Imperial Apartments: After the Sisi Museum, a one-way route takes you through a series of royal rooms. The first room—as if to make clear that there was more to the Habsburgs than Sisi—shows a family tree tracing the Habsburgs from 1273 to their messy WWI demise. From here, enter the private apartments of the royal family (Franz Josef's first, then Sisi's).

Franz Josef's apartments illustrate the lifestyle of the last great Habsburg ruler. In these rooms, he presided over defeats and liberal inroads as the world was changing and the monarchy becoming obsolete. Here he met with advisors and welcomed foreign dignitaries, hosted lavish, white-gloved balls and stuffy formal dinners, and raised three children. He slept (alone) on his austere bed while his beloved wife Sisi retreated to her own rooms. He suffered through the assassination of his brother, the suicide of his son and heir, the murder of his wife, and the assassination of his nephew, Archduke Ferdinand, which sparked World War I and spelled the end of the Habsburg monarchy.

Among the rooms you'll see is the **audience room** where Franz Josef received commoners from around the empire. They came from far and wide to show gratitude or to make a request. Imagine you've traveled for days to have your say before the emperor. You're wearing your new fancy suit—Franz Josef required that men coming before him wear a tailcoat, women a black gown with a train. You've rehearsed what you want to say. You hope your hair looks good. Suddenly, you're face-to-face with the emp himself. (The **portrait** on the easel shows Franz Josef in 1915, when he was more than 80 years old.) Despite your efforts, you probably weren't in this room long. He'd stand at the **high table** (far left) as the visiting commoners had their say. (Standing kept things moving.) You'd hear a brief response from him (quite likely the same he'd given all day), and then you'd back out of the room while bowing (also required). On the table is a partial **list** of 56 appointments he had on January 3, 1910 (three columns: family name, meeting topic, and *Anmerkung*—the emperor's "action log").

Franz Josef's **bedroom** shows off his spartan lifestyle. Notice his no-frills **iron bed**. He typically rose at 3:30 and started his day in prayer, kneeling at the **prayer stool** against the far wall. While he had a typical emperor's share of mistresses, his dresser was always well-stocked with **photos** of Sisi.

Sisi's Rooms include her exercise/dressing room, where servants worked three hours a day on the empress' famous hair. She'd exercise on the **wooden structure** and on the **rings** suspended from the doorway to the left. Afterward, she'd get a massage on the red-covered **bed.** In Sisi's main bathroom, you'll see her huge copper tub (with the original wall coverings behind it), where servants washed her hair—an all-day affair. Sisi was the first Habsburg to have running water in her bathroom (notice the hot and cold faucets). In the **small salon,** the portrait is of Crown Prince Rudolf, Franz Josef's and Sisi's only son. On the morning of January 30, 1889, the 30-year-old Rudolf and a beautiful baroness were found shot dead in an apparent murder-suicide in his hunting lodge in Mayerling. The scandal shocked the empire and tainted the Habsburgs; Sisi retreated further into her fantasy world, and Franz Josef carried on stoically with a broken heart.

The tour ends in the **dining room.** It's dinnertime, and Franz Josef has called his extended family together. The settings are modest...just silver. Gold was saved for formal state dinners. Next to each name card was a menu listing the chef responsible for each dish. (Talk about pressure.) While the Hofburg had tableware for 4,000, feeding 3,000 was a typical day. The cellar was stocked with 60,000 bottles of wine. The kitchen was huge—50 birds could be roasted at once on the hand-driven spits.

Franz Josef enforced strict protocol at mealtime: No one could speak without being spoken to by the emperor, and no one could eat after he was done. While the rest of Europe was growing democracy and expanding personal freedoms, the Habsburgs preserved their ossified worldview to the bitter end.

In 1918, World War I ended, Austria was created as a modern nation-state, the Habsburgs were tossed out...and Hofburg Palace was destined to become a museum.

▲▲▲Hofburg Treasury (Weltliche und Geistliche Schatzkammer)

One of the world's most stunning collections of royal regalia, the Hofburg Treasury shows off sparkling crowns, jewels, gowns, and assorted Habsburg bling in 21 darkened rooms. The treasures, well-explained by an audioguide, include the crown of the Holy Roman Emperor, Charlemagne's saber, a unicorn horn, and more precious gems than you can shake a scepter at.

Cost and Hours: €12, €18 combo-ticket with Kunsthistorisches Museum and New Palace museums, Wed-Mon 9:00-17:30, closed Tue; from the Hofburg's central courtyard pass through the black, red, and gold gate, then follow *Schatzkammer* signs to the Schweizerhof; tel. 01/525-240, www.khm.at.

Audioguides: A basic audioguide covering the top 11 jewels is included with your ticket. Or, for €2, you can rent an audioguide programmed to describe the top 100 stops—well worth it to get the most out of this dazzling collection.

❂ Self-Guided Tour: Here's a rundown of the highlights (the audioguide is much more complete).

Room 2: The personal **crown of Rudolf II** (1602) occupies the center of the room along with its accompanying scepter and orb; a bust of Rudolf II (1552-1612) sits nearby. The crown's design symbolically merges a bishop's miter ("Holy"), the arch across the top of a Roman emperor's helmet ("Roman"), and the typical medieval king's crown ("Emperor").

Two centuries later (1806), this crown and scepter became the official regalia of Austria's rulers, as seen in the large **portrait of Franz I** (the one behind you). Napoleon Bonaparte had just conquered Austria and dissolved the Holy Roman Empire. Franz (ruled 1792-1835) was allowed to remain in power, but he had to downgrade his title from "Franz II, Holy Roman Emperor" to "Franz I, Emperor of Austria."

Rooms 3 and 4: These rooms contain some of the **coronation vestments and regalia** needed for the new Austrian (not Holy Roman) Emperor. There was a different one for each of the emperor's subsidiary titles, e.g., King of Hungary or King of Lombardy. So many crowns and kingdoms in the Habsburgs' vast empire!

Room 5: Ponder the **Cradle of the King of Rome,** once occupied by Napoleon's son, who was born in 1811 and made King of Rome. While pledging allegiance to democracy, Napoleon in fact crowned himself Emperor of France and hobnobbed with Europe's royalty. When his wife Josephine could not bear him a male heir, Napoleon divorced her and married into the Habsburg family.

Room 6: For Divine Right kings, even child-rearing was a sacred ritual that needed elaborate regalia for public ceremonies. The 23-pound **gold basin and pitcher** were used to baptize noble children, who were dressed in the **hooded baptismal dresses** displayed nearby.

Room 7: These jewels are the true "treasures," a cabinet of wonders used by Habsburgs to impress their relatives (or to hock when funds got low).

Room 8: The eight-foot-tall, 500-year-old **"unicorn horn"** (a narwhal tusk), was considered to have magical healing powers bestowed from on high. This one was owned by the Holy Roman Emperor—clearly a divine monarch.

Religious Rooms: The next several rooms of **religious objects**—crucifixes, chalices, mini-altarpieces, reliquaries, and bishops' vestments. Habsburg rulers mixed the institutions of church and state, so these precious religious accoutrements were also part of their display of secular power.

Room 10: The big red-silk and gold-thread **mantle,** nearly 900 years old, was worn by Holy Roman Emperors at their coronations.

Room 11: The collection's highlight is the 10th-century **crown of the Holy Roman Emperor.** It was probably made for Otto I (c. 960), the first king to call himself Holy Roman Emperor. The Imperial Crown swirls with symbolism "proving" that the emperor was both holy and Roman: The cross on top says the HRE ruled as Christ's representative on earth, and the jeweled arch over the top is reminiscent of the parade helmet of ancient Romans. The jewels themselves allude to the wearer's kinghood in the here and now. Imagine the impression this priceless, glittering crown must have made on the emperor's medieval subjects.

Nearby is the 11th-century **Imperial Cross** that preceded the emperor in ceremonies. Encrusted with jewels, it had a hollow compartment (its core is wood) that carried substantial chunks thought to be from *the* **cross** on which Jesus was crucified and the **Holy Lance** used to pierce his side (both pieces are displayed in the same glass case). Holy Roman Emperors actually carried the lance into battle in the 10th century. Look behind the cross to see how it was a box that could be clipped open and shut, used for holding holy relics. You can see bits of the "true cross" anywhere, but this is a prime piece—with the actual nail hole.

Room 12: Now picture all this regalia used together. The **painting** shows the coronation of Maria Theresa's son Josef II as Holy Roman Emperor in 1764. Set in a church in Frankfurt (filled with the bigwigs—literally—of the day), Josef is wearing the same crown and royal garb that you've just seen.

Room 12 also displays the **leather cases** used to store and transport the crowns, crosses, and other objects. Another glass case contains **relics**—such as a fragment of Jesus' manger, a piece of Christ's loincloth, and a shred of the Last Supper tablecloth.

The Rest of the Treasury: Rooms 13-15 have (among other things) **portraits of important Habsburgs,** such as Maximilian I and Mary of Burgundy. Room 16 contains the **royal vestments** (15th century), which display perhaps the most exquisite workmanship in the entire Treasury. Look closely—they're "painted" with gold and silver threads. But after seeing so much bling, by the time you view these vestments, they can seem downright understated— just another example of the pomp and circumstance of the majestic Habsburgs.

More Hofburg Sights

▲▲Hofburg New Palace Museums

The New Palace (Neue Burg) houses three separate collections (covered by a single ticket). The **Arms and Armor Collection** displays weaponry and body armor from all over the vast Habsburg Empire, including exotic Turkish suits of armor. The **Ancient Musical Instruments Collection** shows instruments through the ages, including Beethoven's (supposed) clarinet, Leopold Mozart's violin, a keyboard perhaps played by Wolfgang Mozart, and Brahms' piano. The **Ephesus Museum** has artifacts and classical statuary from that bustling ancient Roman city of 300,000 people (located in modern-day Turkey, near Kuşadası on the southwestern coast). The included audioguide brings the exhibits to life and lets you hear the collection's fascinating old instruments being played. An added bonus is the chance to wander alone among the royal Habsburg halls, stairways, and painted ceilings.

Cost and Hours: €12, ticket covers all three collections and the Kunsthistorisches Museum across the Ring, €18 combo-ticket with the Hofburg Treasury, Wed-Sun 10:00-18:00, closed Mon-

Tue, last entry 30 minutes before closing, almost no tourists, tel. 01/525-240, www.khm.at.

▲Spanish Riding School (Spanische Hofreitschule)

This stately 300-year-old Baroque hall at the Hofburg Palace is the home of the renowned Lipizzaner stallions. The magnificent building was an impressive expanse in its day. Built without central pillars, it offers clear views of the prancing horses under lavish chandeliers, with a grand statue of Emperor Charles VI on horseback at the head of the hall.

Lipizzaner stallions were a creation of horse-loving Habsburg Archduke Charles, who wanted to breed the perfect animal. He imported Andalusian horses from his homeland of Spain, then mated them with a local line to produce an extremely intelligent and easily trainable breed. Italian and Arabian bloodlines were later added to tweak various characteristics. Lipizzaner stallions are known for their noble gait and Baroque profile. These regal horses have changed shape with the tenor of the times: They were bred strong and stout during wars, and frilly and slender in more cultured eras. But they're always born black, fade to gray, and turn a distinctive white in adulthood.

Visiting the Riding School: The school offers three options for seeing the horses (tel. 01/533-9031, www.srs.at).

Performances: The Lipizzaner stallions put on great 80-minute shows in spring and fall. The pricey seats book up months in advance, but standing room is usually available the same day, and there's not a bad view in the house (seats-€47-173, standing room-€23-31, prices vary depending on the show; Feb-June and Sept-Dec Sun at 11:00 and either Sat at 11:00 or Fri at 19:00, no shows in Jan or July-Aug; box office opens at 9:00 and is located inside the Hofburg—go through the main Hofburg entryway from Michaelerplatz, then turn left into the first passage).

Training Sessions: Luckily for the masses, training sessions with music take place in the same hall and are open to the public. Don't have high expectations, as the horses often do little more than trot and warm up. Tourists line up early at Josefsplatz (the large courtyard between Michaelerplatz and Albertinaplatz), at the door marked *Spanische Hofreitschule*. But there's no need to show up when the doors open at 10:00, since tickets never really "sell out." Only the horses stay for the full two hours. As people leave, new tickets are printed, so you can just prance in with no wait at all. You can also buy tickets for the training sessions at the box office (€14 at the door, roughly March-June and mid-Aug-Dec Tue-Fri and many Sat 10:00-12:00—but only when the horses are in town; check schedule at www.srs.at).

Stables: Any time of day, you can see the horses in their stalls and view videos of them prancing in the Reitschulgasse corri-

VIENNA

dor. Guided one-hour tours of stalls are given daily (€16; tours at 14:00, 15:00, and 16:00; in English and German, reserve by calling 01/533-9031).

▲Augustinian Church (Augustinerkirche)

This is the Gothic and Neo-Gothic church where the Habsburgs got latched (weddings took place here), then dispatched (the royal hearts are in the vault).

Cost and Hours: Church—free, open long hours daily; Vault—€2.50, usually open to the public immediately after 11:00 Sun Mass only; Augustinerstrasse 3—facing Josefsplatz, with its statue of the great reform emperor Josef II and the imperial library next door.

Visiting the Church: In the front, notice the windows above on the right, from where royals witnessed the Mass in private. Don't miss the exquisite, tomb-like Canova memorial (Neoclassical, 1805) to Maria Theresa's favorite daughter, Maria Christina, with its incredibly sad white-marble procession. The church's 11:00 Sunday Mass is a hit with music lovers—both a Mass and a concert, often with an orchestra accompanying the choir (acoustics are best in front). Pay by contributing to the offering plate and buying a CD afterwards. Programs are posted by the entry.

Austrian National Library (Österreichische Nationalbibliothek)

Next to the Augustinian Church, this Baroque building was once the library of the Habsburgs. Wandering through this impressive temple of learning—with a statue of Charles VI in the center—you find yourself whispering. The setting takes you back to 1730 and gives you the sense that, in imperial times, knowledge of the world was for the elite—and with that knowledge, the elite had power. There are four specialized museums within the library: the State Hall (Baroque heart of the library), the Papyrus Museum (all things papyrus), the Globe Museum (250 terrestrial and celestial globes), and the Esperanto Museum (who knew?). The recommended Soho Kantine in the basement is good for a cheap lunch.

Cost and Hours: Library—free, main reading room open daily 9:00-21:00; museums—€3-7, open Tue-Sun 10:00-18:00, Thu until 21:00, closed Mon; www.onb.ac.at.

Burggarten (Palace Garden) and Butterfly House

This greenbelt, once the backyard of the Hofburg and now a people's park, welcomes visitors to loiter on the grass. On nice days, it's lively with office workers enjoying a break. The statue of Mozart facing the Ringstrasse is popular. The iron-and-glass pavilion (c. 1910 with playful Art Nouveau touches) now houses the recommended Café Restaurant Palmenhaus and a small but fluttery butterfly exhibit (€5.50; April-Oct Mon-Fri 10:00-16:45, Sat-Sun 10:00-18:15; Nov-March daily 10:00-15:45).

▲▲Albertina Museum

This building, at the southern tip of the Hofburg complex (near the Opera), was the residence of Maria Theresa's favorite daughter, Maria Christina, who was the only one allowed to marry for love rather than political strategy. Her many sisters were jealous. (Marie-Antoinette had to marry the French king...and lost her head over it.) Maria Christina's husband, Albert of Saxony, was a great collector of original drawings and amassed an enormous assortment of works by Dürer, Rembrandt, Rubens, and others. As it's Albert and Christina's gallery, it's cleverly called the "Albertina."

VIENNA

Cost and Hours: €11, generally meaningless without €4 audioguide, daily 10:00-18:00, Wed until 21:00, overlooking Albertinaplatz across from the TI and Opera, tel. 01/534-830, www.albertina.at.

Visiting the Museum: To understand both the imperial apartments and the wonderful artworks, invest in the audioguide, which makes this collection a luxurious lesson in modern art appreciation—from Monet to today. Head first to the Albertina's elegant French-Classicist-style **state rooms** (*Prunkräume*) for a great opportunity to wander freely under the chandeliers of a Habsburg palace, with its pure 19th-century imperial splendor unconstrained by velvet ropes. (Because the original drawings and prints that once hung here are so light-sensitive, you'll see only reproductions of some works.) Then follow signs for *Meisterwerke der Moderne* (*Die Sammlung Batliner,* on the top floor). These modern galleries hold a wonderful rotating exhibit from the museum's **Batliner collection** of modern art (from Impressionism to Abstract Expressionism, with minor works by major artists—Monet, Picasso, Chagall, Matisse), along with temporary exhibits.

Church Crypts near the Hofburg

Two churches near the Hofburg offer starkly different looks at dearly departed Viennese: the Habsburg coffins in the Kaisergruft, and the commoners' graves in St. Michael's Church.

▲▲Kaisergruft (Imperial Crypt)

Visiting the imperial remains is not as easy as you might imagine. These original organ donors left their bodies—about 150 in all—in the unassuming Kaisergruft, their hearts in the Augustinian Church (vaults open to public Sun after mass), and their entrails in the crypt below St. Stephen's Cathedral (described on page 53). Don't tripe.

Cost and Hours: €5, daily 10:00-18:00, last entry at 17:40; crypt is in the Capuchin Church at Tegetthoffstrasse 2 at Neuer Markt; tel. 01/512-6853, www.kaisergruft.at.

Visiting the Kaisergruft: As you enter, buy the €0.50 map with a Habsburg family tree and a chart locating each coffin.

Find the pewter double-coffin under the dome. This tomb of **Maria Theresa** (1717-1780) and her husband, **Franz I** (1708-1765), is worth a close look for its artwork. Maria Theresa outlived her husband by 15 years—which she spent in mourning. Old and fat, she installed a special lift enabling her to get down into the crypt to be with her dear, departed Franz (even though he had been far from faithful). The couple recline—Etruscan-style—atop their fancy lead coffin. At each corner are the crowns of the Habsburgs—the Holy Roman Empire, Hungary, Bohemia, and Jerusalem. Notice the contrast between the Rococo splendor of Maria Theresa's tomb and the simple box holding her more modest son, **Josef II** (at his parents' feet). This understated tomb is in keeping with his enlightened politics.

Nearby, find the appropriately austere military tomb of **Franz Josef** (1830-1916) in the more brightly lit modern section. Flanking Franz Josef are the tombs of his son, the archduke **Rudolf,** and Empress Elisabeth. Rudolf and his teenage mistress supposedly committed suicide together in 1889 at Mayerling hunting lodge and—since the Church figured he forced her to take her own life and was therefore a murderer—it took considerable legal hair-splitting to win Rudolf this spot (after examining his brain, it was determined that he was mentally disabled and therefore incapable of knowingly killing himself and his girl). *Kaiserin* Elisabeth (1837-1898), a.k.a. **Sisi,** always gets the "Most Flowers" award.

In front of those three are the two most recent Habsburg tombs. **Empress Zita** was laid to rest here in 1989, followed by her son, **Karl Ludwig,** in 2007. The funeral procession for Karl, the fourth son of the last Austrian emperor, was probably the last such Old Regime event in European history. The monarchy died hard in Austria. Today there are about 700 living Habsburg royals, mostly living in exile. When they die, they get buried in their countries of exile.

Body parts and ornate tombs aside, the real legacy of the Habsburgs is the magnificence of this city. Step outside. Pan up. Watch the clouds glide by the ornate gables of Vienna.

▲St. Michael's Church Crypt (Michaelerkirche)

St. Michael's Church, which faces the Hofburg on Michaelerplatz, offers a striking contrast to the imperial crypt. Regular tours take visitors underground to see a typical church crypt—filled with the rotting wooden coffins of well-to-do commoners.

Cost and Hours: €5 for 45-minute tour, Mon-Sat at 11:00 and 13:30, mostly in German but with enough English, wait at the sign that advertises the tour at the church entrance and pay the guide directly.

Visiting the Crypt: Climbing below the church, you'll see about a hundred 18th-century coffins and stand on three feet of debris, surrounded by niches filled with stacked lumber from decayed coffins and countless bones. You'll meet a 1769 mummy in lederhosen and a wig, along with a woman who is clutching a cross and has flowers painted on her high heels. You'll learn about death in those times—from how the wealthy didn't want to end up in standard shallow graves, instead paying to be laid to rest below the church, to how, in 1780, the enlightened emperor Josef II ended the practice of cemetery burials in cities but allowed the rich to become the stinking rich in crypts under churches. You'll also discover why many were buried with their chin strapped shut (because when the muscles rot, your jaw falls open and you get that ghostly skeleton look that nobody wants).

St. Michael's Church itself has an interesting history. In 1791, a few days after Mozart's death, his *Requiem* was performed here for the first time. (See the small monument just inside the door on the right.) In the rear of the nave, to the right as you enter, is a small memorial to Austrian victims of the concentration camp at Dachau. The cross was made in 1945 at Dachau by newly freed inmates and is dedicated to Austrian martyrs.

Kunsthistorisches Museum and Nearby

In the 19th century, the Habsburgs planned to create a series of triumphal arches spanning the Ringstrasse to connect their museum buildings and the Hofburg Palace in an awe-inspiring ensemble. The vision died with the empire, but today their great museums face off across Maria Theresienplatz, where a huge monument to perhaps the greatest of the Habsburgs, Maria Theresa, sits above it all (for more on this monument, see page 47 of the Vienna City Walk).

▲▲▲Kunsthistorisches Museum

This exciting museum, across the Ring from the Hofburg Palace, showcases the grandeur and opulence of the Habsburgs' collected artwork in a grand building (built in 1888 to display these works). While there's little Viennese art here, you will find world-class European masterpieces galore (including canvases by Raphael, Caravaggio, Velázquez, Dürer, Rubens, Vermeer, Rembrandt, and a particularly exquisite roomful of Bruegels), all well-hung on one glorious floor, plus a fine display of Egyptian, classical, and applied arts. Another highlight, filling a wing of the ground floor, is the Habsburg "Chamber of Wonders" *(Kunstkammer)*, showing off the imperial collection of exquisite fine-art objects and exotic curios.

Cost and Hours: €12 (free for kids under 18), ticket also covers New Palace museums across the Ring, €18 combo-ticket also includes the Hofburg Treasury, Tue-Sun 10:00-18:00, Thu until 21:00, closed Mon, on the Ringstrasse at Maria-Theresien-Platz,

Kunsthistorisches Museum—First Floor

ROOM 17 VERMEER
ROOM 16
ROOM 15 BOSCH & VAN DER WEYDEN
ROOM 14 VAN EYCK
SAAL TEMPORARY
ROOM 18
SAAL XI
SAAL X
SAAL IX
WC
STAIRS TO SECOND FLOOR
BRUEGEL
ROOM 19
SAAL XII
THESEUS STATUE
NORTHERN EUROPEAN ART
SNYDERS
STAIRS FROM GROUND FLOOR
SAAL XIII RUBENS
SAAL XIV RUBENS
SAAL XV DÜRER & HOLBEIN
SHOP
ROOM 20
ROOM 21 REMBRANDT TOUR ENDS
ROOM 22 BRUEGHEL
ROOM 23
ROOM 24 CRANACH & ALTDORFER
MAIN

Maria-Theresien-

U-2 or U-3: Volkstheater/Museumsplatz (exit toward *Burgring*), tel. 01/525-240, www.khm.at.

Audioguide: An excellent €4 audioguide is available at the desk in the atrium, just before the main staircase. Covering nearly 600 items, the audioguide is worthwhile if you want an in-depth tour.

⊖ **Self-Guided Tour:** The Kunsthistorwhateveritis Museum—let's just say "Koonst"—houses the family collection of Austria's luxury-loving Habsburg rulers. Their *joie de vivre* is reflected in this collection—some of the most beautiful, sexy, and fun art from two centuries (c. 1450-1650). At their peak of power in the 1500s, the Habsburgs ruled Austria, Germany, northern Italy, the Netherlands, and Spain—and you'll see a wide variety of art from all these places and beyond.

The building itself is worth notice—a lavish textbook example

of Historicism. Despite its palatial feel, it was originally designed for the same purpose it serves today: to showcase its treasures in an inviting space while impressing visitors with the grandeur of the empire.

Of the museum's many exhibits, we'll tour only the Painting Gallery (Gemäldegalerie) on the first floor. Climb the main staircase, featuring Antonio Canova's statue of *Theseus Clubbing the Centaur.* Italian, Spanish, and French art is in the right half of the building (as you face Theseus), and Northern European art is to the left. Notice that the museum labels the largest rooms with Roman numerals (Saal I, II, III) and the smaller rooms around the perimeter with Arabic (Rooms 1, 2, 3). The museum is reorganizing its paintings, and the locations of some works (especially from the Italian Renaissance) may have shifted by the time you visit.

Venetian Renaissance: The first gallery (Saal 1) spans the long career of **Titian,** who painted portraits, Christian Madonnas, and sexy Venuses with equal ease. Next (Saal 2) comes Paolo **Veronese,** whose colorful works reflect the wealth of Venice, the funnel through which luxury goods from the exotic East flowed into northern Europe. And **Tintoretto**'s many portraits (Saal 3) give us a peek at the movers and shakers of the Venetian Empire.

Italian Renaissance and Mannerism: Rooms 1-4 hold some of the museum's most important works: **Mantegna**'s *St. Sebastian,* **Correggio**'s *Jupiter and Io,* and **Raphael**'s *Madonna of the Meadow (Die Madonna im Grünen),* a geometrically perfect masterpiece of the High Renaissance, painted when Raphael was just 22.

Farther along, through the small rooms along the far end of this wing (likely Room 7), find the cleverly deceptive portraits by Giuseppe **Arcimboldo.** With a pickle nose, pear chin, and cornhusk ears, Arcimboldo's subject literally is what he eats.

Caravaggio and Velázquez: Caravaggio (in Saal V) shocked the art world with brutally honest reality. Compared with Raphael's super-sweet *Madonna of the Meadow,* Caravaggio's *Madonna of the Rosary (Die Rosenkranzmadonna,* the biggest canvas in the room) looks perfectly ordinary, and the saints kneeling around her have dirty feet. In *David with the Head of Goliath (David mit dem Haupt des Goliath)*—in the corner near the window—Caravaggio turns a third-degree-interrogation light on a familiar Bible story. David shoves the dripping head of the slain giant right in our noses.

When the Habsburgs ruled both Austria and Spain, cousins kept in touch through portraits of themselves and their kids. Diego **Velázquez** (in Room 10) was the greatest of Spain's "photojournalist" painters—heavily influenced by Caravaggio's realism, capturing his subjects without passing judgment, flattering, or glorifying them.

Northern European Art: The other half of this floor features works of the "Northern Renaissance." This movement, brought on by the economic boom of Dutch and Flemish trading, was more secular and Protestant than Catholic-funded Italian art. We'll see fewer Madonnas, saints, and Greek gods and more peasants, landscapes, and food. Paintings are smaller and darker, full of down-to-earth objects. Northern artists sweated the details, encouraging the patient viewer to appreciate the beauty in everyday things.

The undisputed master of the slice-of-life village scene was **Pieter Bruegel the Elder** (c. 1525-1569)—think of him as the Norman Rockwell of the 16th century. Saal X contains the largest collection of Bruegels in captivity. Despite his many rural paintings, Bruegel was actually a cultivated urbanite who liked to wear peasants' clothing to observe country folk at play (a trans-fest-ite?). He celebrated their simple life, but he also skewered their weaknesses—not to single them out as hicks, but as universal examples of human folly. *The Peasant Wedding (Bauernhochzeit)*, Bruegel's most famous work, is less about the wedding than the food. It's a farmers' feeding frenzy, as the barnful of wedding guests scrambles to get their share of free eats. Bruegel's *Peasant Dance (Bauerntanz)* shows a celebration at the consecration of a village church. The three Bruegel landscape paintings are part of an original series of six "calendar" paintings, depicting the seasons of the year.

Also on this floor of the museum, don't miss **Rubens'** large, lush canvases (including, in Saal XIII, *The Little Fur/Das Pelzchen*, depicting his much younger, dimpled bride); **Vermeer's** *The Art of Painting (Die Malkunst)*, showing the painter at work in his studio, with a painstaking attention to detail (Room 17); and **Rembrandt's** frank self-portraits—one as a defiant young artist, the other as a broken old man (Room 21).

The Rest of the Kunst: The museum's ground floor has several world-class collections of Greek, Roman, Egyptian, and Near Eastern antiquities. You can see a statue of the Egyptian pharaoh Thutmosis III and the Gemma Augustea, a Roman cameo thought to be kept by Augustus on his private desk. Or view the *Kunstkammer*—the personal collections of the House of Habsburg. Amassed by 17 emperors over the centuries, the *Kunstkammer* ("art cabinet") is a dazzling display of 2,000 ancient treasures, medieval curios, and *objets d'art* from 800 B.C. to 1891.

▲Natural History Museum (Naturhistorisches Museum)

In the twin building facing the Kunsthistorisches Museum, you'll find moon rocks, dinosaur stuff, and the fist-sized *Venus of Willendorf*—at 25,000 years old, the world's oldest sex symbol. This four-inch-tall, chubby stone statuette, found in the Danube Valley, is a generic female (no face or feet) resting her hands on her ample breasts. The statue's purpose is unknown, but she may have been a symbol of fertility for our mammoth-hunting ancestors. Even though the museum is not glitzy or high-tech, it's a hit with children and scientifically curious grown-ups. Of the museum's 20 million objects, you're sure to find something interesting. The collection's presentation is almost charming in its old school-ness.

Cost and Hours: €10, Wed-Mon 9:00-18:30, Wed until 21:00, closed Tue, on the Ringstrasse at Maria-Theresien-Platz, U-2 or U-3: Volkstheater/Museumsplatz, tel. 01/521-770, www. nhm-wien.ac.at.

MuseumsQuartier

The vast grounds of the former imperial stables now corral a cutting-edge cultural center for contemporary arts and design, including several impressive museums; the best are the Leopold Museum and the Museum of Modern Art. For many, the MuseumsQuartier is most enjoyable not for its galleries but as a youthful gathering spot in the evening for light, fun meals and cocktails.

VIENNA

VIENNA

Visiting the MuseumsQuartier: Walk into the complex from the Hofburg side, where the main entrance (with visitors center, shop, and ticket office) leads to a big courtyard with cafés, fountains, and ever-changing "installation lounge furniture," all surrounded by the quarter's various museums. At the visitors center, various **combo-tickets** are available for those interested in more than just the Leopold and Modern Art museums. You can also rent a €4 **audioguide** that explains the complex (behind Kunsthistorisches Museum, U-2 or U-3: Volkstheater/Museumsplatz, tel. 01/525-5881, www.mqw.at).

The **Leopold Museum** features several temporary exhibits of modern Austrian art. The top floor holds the largest collection of works by Egon Schiele (1890-1918; these works make some people uncomfortable—Schiele's nudes are *really* nude) and a few paintings by Gustav Klimt, Kolo Moser, and Oskar Kokoschka. While this is a great collection, you can see even better works from these artists in the Belvedere Palace, described later (€12, €3 audioguide—worth it only for enthusiasts; June-Aug daily 10:00-18:00, Thu until 21:00; Sept-May Wed-Mon 10:00-18:00, Thu until 21:00, closed Tue; tel. 01/525-700, www.leopoldmuseum.org).

The **Museum of Modern Art** (Museum Moderner Kunst Stiftung Ludwig, a.k.a. "MUMOK") is Austria's leading gallery for international modern and contemporary art. It's the striking lava-paneled building—three stories tall and four stories deep, offering seven floors of far-out art that's hard for most visitors to appreciate. This state-of-the-art museum shows off its huge and rotating collection of works by "classical" modernists (Paul Klee, Pablo Picasso, Pop artists) and more contemporary art (€9, good €3 audioguide, Mon 14:00-19:00, Tue-Sun 10:00-19:00, Thu until 21:00, tel. 01/52500, www.mumok.at).

Rounding out the sprawling MuseumsQuartier are an architecture center, Electronic Avenue, design forum, children's museum, "Quartier 21" (with gallery space and shops), and the **Kunsthalle Wien**—an exhibition center for contemporary art (two halls with different exhibitions, €8.50 for one, €7 for the other, €11.50 for both; daily 10:00-19:00, Thu until 21:00, tel. 01/521-8933, www.kunsthallewien.at).

Karlsplatz and Nearby

These sights cluster around Karlsplatz, just southeast of the Ringstrasse (U-1, U-2, or U-4: Karlsplatz). From the U-Bahn station's passageway, it's a 30-minute walk around the sights on Karlsplatz: the Karlskirche, Secession, and Naschmarkt.

Karlsplatz

This picnic-friendly square, with its Henry Moore sculpture in the pond, is ringed with sights. The massive, domed Karlskirche and its twin spiral columns dominates the square. The small green, white, and gold pavilions that line the street across the square from the church are from the late 19th-century municipal train system *(Stadtbahn)*. One of Europe's first subway systems, this precursor to today's U-Bahn was built with a military purpose in mind: to move troops quickly in time of civil unrest—specifically, out to Schönbrunn Palace. With curvy iron frames, decorative marble slabs, and painted gold trim, these are pioneering works in the *Jugendstil* (Art Nouveau) style, designed by Otto Wagner, who influenced Klimt and the Secessionists. One of the pavilions has a sweet little exhibit on **Otto Wagner** which illustrates the Art Nouveau lifestyle around 1900. It also shows models for his never-built dreams and the grand expansion of Vienna (€4, described in English, April-Oct Tue-Sun 10:00-18:00, closed Mon and Nov-March, near the Ringstrasse, tel. 01/5058-7478-5177, www.wienmuseum.at).

▲Karlskirche (St. Charles' Church)

Charles Borromeo, a 16th-century bishop from Milan, inspired his parishioners during plague times. This "votive church" was dedicated to him in 1713, when an epidemic spared Vienna. The church offers the best Baroque in the city, with a unique combination of columns (showing scenes from the life of Charles Borromeo, à la Trajan's Column in Rome), a classic pediment, and an elliptical dome.

Cost and Hours: €6, ticket covers church interior, elevator ride, and skippable one-room museum; audioguide-€2; Mon-Sat 9:00-18:00, Sun 13:00-18:00, last entry 30 minutes before closing; elevator runs until 17:30, last ascent at 17:00. The entry fee may seem steep, but remember that it helps to fund ongoing restoration.

Visiting the Church: The dome's colorful 13,500-square-foot fresco—painted in the 1730s by Johann Michael Rottmayr—shows Signor Borromeo (in red-and-white bishops' robes) gazing up into heaven, spreading his arms wide, and pleading with Christ to spare Vienna from the plague.

The church is especially worthwhile for the chance to ride an **elevator** (installed for renovation work) up into the cupola. The industrial lift takes you to a platform at the base of the 235-foot dome (if you're even slightly afraid of heights, skip this trip). Consider that the church was built and decorated with a scaffolding system essentially the same as this one. Once up top, you'll climb stairs to the steamy lantern at the extreme top of the church.

At that dizzying height, you're in the clouds with cupids and angels. Many details that appear smooth and beautiful from ground level—such as gold leaf, paintings, and fake marble—look rough and sloppy up close. It's surreal to observe the 3-D figures from an unintended angle—check out Christ's leg, which looks dwarf-sized up close. Give yourself a minute to take it in: Faith, Hope, and Charity triumph and inspire. Borromeo lobbies heaven for plague relief. Meanwhile, a Protestant's Lutheran Bible is put to the torch by angels. At the very top, you'll see the tiny dove representing the Holy Ghost, surrounded by a cheering squad of nipple-lipped cupids.

Wien Museum Karlsplatz

This underappreciated city history museum, worth ▲ for those intrigued by Vienna's illustrious past, walks you through the story of Vienna with well-presented artifacts.

Cost and Hours: €10, free first Sun of the month, open Tue-Sun 10:00-18:00, closed Mon, Karlsplatz 8, tel. 01/505-8747, www.wienmuseum.at.

Visiting the Museum: Work your way up chronologically. The ground floor exhibits prehistoric and Roman fragments, along with some original statues from St. Stephen's Cathedral (c. 1350). You'll also enjoy a rare close-up look at original stained class (circa 1500) from the cathedral.

The first floor focuses on the Renaissance and Baroque eras, including suits of armor, old city maps, booty from an Ottoman siege, and an 1850 city model showing the town just before the wall was replaced by the Ring. Finally, the second floor displays a city model from 1898 showing off the new Ringstrasse, sentimental Biedermeier paintings and objets d'art, and early 20th-century paintings (including four by Klimt, as well as works by Schiele, Kokoschka, and other Secessionists).

▲Academy of Fine Arts (Akademie der Bildenden Künste)

This museum—in a grand Neo-Renaissance building—features a small but impressive collection of works by Bosch, Botticelli, Guardi, Rubens, Van Dyck, and other great masters. It's housed upstairs in a working art academy, giving it a certain sense of realness.

Cost and Hours: €8 includes permanent collection and special exhibits, audioguide-€2; Tue-Sun 10:00-18:00, closed Mon, 3 blocks from the Opera at Schillerplatz 3, tel. 01/588-162-222, www.akademiegalerie.at.

◑ Self-Guided Tour: Head into the academy building and go up two floors to the museum (follow signs for *Gemäldegalerie*). Upon entering, the contemporary art collection is on your right and the painting gallery *(Gemäldegalerie)* is on your left. Between them are statues celebrating the body, whose exposed musculature is a reminder that to realistically portray the human form you must first study it.

Walk into the painting gallery, which (confusingly) runs in reverse chronological order. Bear left into the first, smaller room, dedicated to the Academy of Fine Arts itself. At the end of this room is a portrait of the school's founder, Empress Maria Theresa. This portrait, from 1750, is considered one of the best. It's by the Swedish painter Martin Meytens, whose self-portrait looks on approvingly from the right. Also nearby you'll see (pictured in the fine gold frame) one of the major donors of the collection, and early professors painting, drawing, and sculpting a nude model.

Go through the door to the right of Maria Theresa, and work your way counterclockwise through the exhibit. The section of 18th-century Italian works includes a Venice series by **Francesco Guardi.** In the long hall are typically Dutch and Flemish 17th-century still lifes and landscapes, as well as one **Rembrandt** *(Portrait of a Young Woman,* c. 1632). A group of paintings by **Peter Paul Rubens** includes his typical fleshy nudes, as well as quick, sketchy cartoons used to create giant canvases that once decorated a Jesuit church in Antwerp, Belgium (it later burned down, leaving only these rough plans). Don't miss his voluptuous *Three Graces.* Nearby, in an oversized frame, Rubens' talented protégé, **Anthony van Dyck,** shows his prowess in a famous self-portrait painted at the age of 15.

The Italian and Spanish Renaissance are well-represented by the likes of Titian and Murillo. At the end of the hall is one of the museum's prize pieces, a round **Botticelli** canvas (recently cleaned to show off its vivid colors) depicting the Madonna tenderly embracing the Baby Jesus while angels look on.

At the end of the hall is the collection's grand finale, the captivating, harrowing *Last Judgment* triptych by **Hieronymus Bosch** (c. 1482, with some details added by Lucas Cranach). This is the polar opposite of Bosch's other most famous work, *The Garden of Earthly Delights* (in Madrid's El Prado). Read the altarpiece from left to right, following the pessimistically medieval narrative about humankind's fall from God's graces: In the left panel, at the bottom, God pulls Eve from Adam's rib in the Garden of Eden. Just above that, we see a female representing the serpent hold out the forbidden fruit to tempt Eve. Above that, Adam and Eve are being shooed away by an angel. At the top of this panel, God sits on his cloud, evicting the fallen angels (who turn into insect-like monsters). In the middle panel, Christ holds court over the living and the dead. Notice the jarring contrast between Christ's serene expression and the grotesque scene playing out beneath him. These disturbing images crescendo in the final (right) panel, showing an unspeakably horrific vision of hell that few artists have managed to top in the more than half-millennium since Bosch.

On your way out of the academy, ponder how history might have been different if Adolf Hitler—who applied to study architecture here six years in a row but was rejected each time—had been accepted as a student. Before leaving, peek into the ground floor's

Neo-Renaissance central hall: It's textbook Historicism, the Ring-strasse style of the late 1800s.

▲The Secession

This little building, strategically located behind the Academy of Fine Arts, was created by the Vienna Secession movement, a group of nonconformist artists led by Gustav Klimt, Otto Wagner, and friends.

The young trees carved into the walls and the building's bushy "golden cabbage" rooftop are symbolic of a renewal cycle. Today, the Secession continues to showcase cutting-edge art, as well as one of Gustav Klimt's most famous works, the *Beethoven Frieze*.

Cost and Hours: €8.50 includes special exhibits, Tue-Sun 10:00-18:00, closed Mon, Friedrichstrasse 12, tel. 01/587-5307, www.secession.at.

❂ Self-Guided Tour: The staff hopes you take a look at the temporary exhibits here, designed to illustrate how the spirit of the Secession survives a century after its founding. An association of 350 members chooses a dozen or so special exhibits each year to highlight local art happenings (and they're included in the ticket price whether you like it or not).

Understandably—but unfortunately—most tourists head directly for the basement, home to the museum's highlight: Gustav Klimt's classic *Beethoven Frieze*. One of the masterpieces of Viennese Art Nouveau, this 105-foot-long fresco was the multimedia centerpiece of a 1902 exhibition honoring Ludwig van Beethoven. Read the free flier, which explains Klimt's still-powerful work, inspired by Beethoven's *Ninth Symphony*. Klimt embellished the work with painted-on gold (his brother, and colleague, was a goldsmith) and by gluing on reflective glass and mother-of-pearl for the ladies' dresses and jewelry. Working clockwise around the room, follow Klimt's story:

Left Wall: Floating female figures drift and weave and search—like we all do—for happiness. Unfortunately, their aspirations are dashed and brought to earth, leaving them kneeling and humble. They plead for help from heroes stronger than themselves—represented by the firm knight in gold, who revives their hopes and helps them carry on.

Center Wall: The women encounter many obstacles in their pursuit of happiness—the three dangerous Gorgons (naked ladies with snake hair), the gorilla-faced monster of fear, and the three seductive women of temptation. These obstacles can leave us bent over with grief (like the woman on the right) while our hopes pass by overhead.

Right Wall: But we can still find happiness through art, thanks to Lady Poetry (with the lyre) and the great hero of the arts: Beethoven. In the original 1902 exhibition, a statue of Beethoven appeared at this crucial turning point in the narrative, where the blank space is today.

Beethoven's presence inspires the yearning souls to carry on, and they finally reach true happiness. At the climax of the frieze, a naked couple embraces in ecstasy as a heavenly choir sings the "Ode to Joy" from the Ninth Symphony: "Joy, you beautiful spark of the gods...under thy gentle wings, all men shall become brothers."

▲Naschmarkt

In 1898, the city decided to cover up its Vienna River. The long, wide square they created was filled with a lively produce market that still bustles most days (closed Sun). It's long been known as *the* place to get exotic faraway foods. In fact, locals say, "From here start the Balkans."

Hours and Location: Mon-Fri 6:00-18:30, Sat 6:00-17:00, closed Sun, closes earlier in winter; between Linke Wienzeile and Rechte Wienzeile, U-1, U-2, or U-4: Karlsplatz.

Visiting the Naschmarkt: From near the Opera, the Naschmarkt (roughly, "Munchies Market") stretches along Wienzeile street. This "Belly of Vienna" comes with two parallel lanes—one lined with fun and reasonable eateries, and the other featuring the town's top-end produce and gourmet goodies. This is where top chefs like to get their ingredients. At the gourmet vinegar stall, you can sample the vinegar—like perfume—with a drop on your wrist. Farther from the center, the Naschmarkt becomes likeably seedy and surrounded by sausage stands, Turkish *Döner Kebab* stalls, cafés, and theaters. At the market's far end is a line of buildings with fine Art Nouveau facades. Each Saturday, the Naschmarkt is infested by a huge flea market where, in olden days, locals would come to hire a monkey to pick little critters out of their hair (flea market sets up west of the Kettenbrückengasse U-Bahn station).

Picnickers can pick up their grub in the market and head over to Karlsplatz (described earlier) or the Burggarten. In recent years, some stalls have been taken over by hip new eateries and bars, bringing a youthful vibe and fun new tastes to the market scene.

Mariahilfer Strasse

While there are more stately and elegant streets in the central district, the best opportunity to simply feel the pulse of workaday Viennese life is a little farther out, along Mariahilfer Strasse. An easy plan is to ride the U-3 to the Zieglergasse stop, then stroll and browse your way downhill to the MuseumsQuartier U-Bahn station. If you're interested in how Austria handles its people's appetite for marijuana, search out two interesting stores along the way: Bushplanet Headshop (at Esterhazygasse 32, near the Neubaugasse U-Bahn stop) and Bushplanet Growshop (set back in a

VIENNA

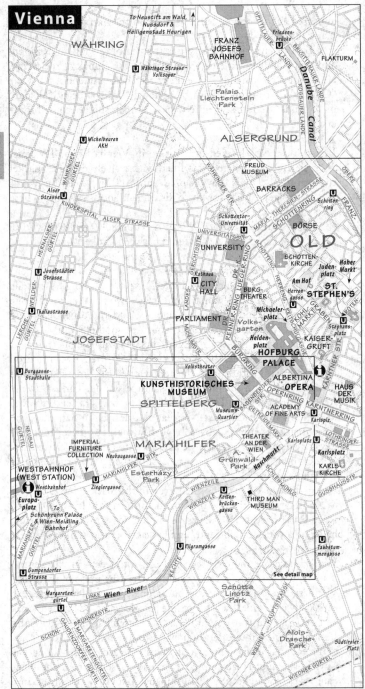

Vienna

WÄHRING

To Neustift am Wald,
Nussdorf &
Heiligenstadt Heurigen

FRANZ
JOSEFS
BAHNHOF

FLAKTURM

Währinger Strasse-
Volksoper

Palais
Liechtenstein
Park

ALSERGRUND

Danube Canal

Friedens-
brücke

Michelbeuren
AKH

FREUD
MUSEUM

BARRACKS

Alser
Strasse

KINDERSPITAL ALSER STRASSE

Schottentor-
Universität

BÖRSE

OLD

Schotten-
ring

Josefstädter
Strasse

UNIVERSITÄTSSTR.

UNIVERSITY

SCHOTTEN-
KIRCHE

Juden-
platz

Hoher
Markt

Thaliastrasse

Rathaus

CITY
HALL

BURG-
THEATER

Am Hof

Herren-
gasse

ST.
STEPHEN'S

JOSEFSTADT

PARLIAMENT

Michaeler-
platz

Volks-
garten

Stephans-
platz

Helden-
platz

HOFBURG
PALACE

KAISER-
GRUFT

Burggasse-
Stadthalle

Volkstheater

ALBERTINA

OPERA

KUNSTHISTORISCHES
MUSEUM

SPITTELBERG

Museums-
Quartier

ACADEMY
OF FINE ARTS

HAUS
DER
MUSIK

Karlsplz.

IMPERIAL
FURNITURE
COLLECTION

Neubaugasse

MARIAHILFER

THEATER
AN DER
WIEN

Karlsplatz

Karlsplatz

KARLS
KIRCHE

WESTBAHNHOF
(WEST STATION)

Zieglergasse

Esterházy
Park

A.
Grünwald-
Park

Naschmarkt

Westbahnhof

Europa-
platz

To
Schönbrunn Palace
& Wien-Meidling
Bahnhof

WIENZEILE

WIENZEILE

Ketten-
brücken-
gasse

THIRD MAN
MUSEUM

Pilgramgasse

Taubstum-
mengasse

Gumpendorfer
Strasse

See detail map

Margareten-
gürtel

LINKE   Wien River

Schütta
Linotz
Park

Alois-
Drasche-
Park

Südtiroler
Platz

WIENER GÜRTEL

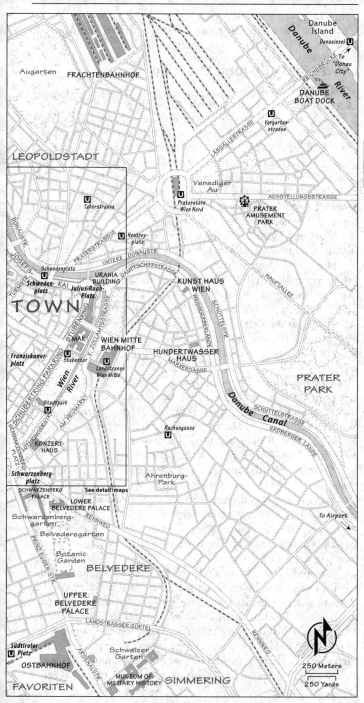

VIENNA

courtyard off Mariahilfer Strasse at #115, both locations Mon-Sat 10:00-19:00, closed Sun, www.bushplanet.at).

More Sights Beyond the Ring
South of the Ring
▲▲Belvedere Palace (Schloss Belvedere)

This is the elegant palace of Prince Eugene of Savoy (1663-1736), the still-much-appreciated conqueror of the Ottomans. Today you can tour Eugene's lavish palace, see sweeping views of the gardens and the Vienna skyline, and enjoy world-class art starring Gustav Klimt, French Impressionism, and a grab bag of other 19th- and early-20th-century artists. While Vienna's other art collections show off works by masters from around Europe, this has the city's best collection of homegrown artists.

Cost and Hours: €11 for Upper Belvedere Palace only, €16 for Upper and Lower palaces (generally not worth it), gardens free except for the Orangerie (included in big ticket), audioguide-€4 or €6/2 people, daily 10:00-18:00, Lower Palace only until 21:00 on Wed, grounds open until dusk, no photos allowed inside, entrance at Prinz-Eugen-Strasse 27, tel. 01/7955-7134, www.belvedere.at.

Eating at the Belvedere: There's a charming little café on the ground floor of the Upper Palace, where you can dine with portraits of the emperor and empress looking down upon you; in summer you can sit outdoors in the garden.

Getting There: The palace is a 15-minute walk south of the Ring. To get there from the center, catch tram #D at the Opera (direction: Südbahnhof). Get off at the Schloss Belvedere stop (just below the Upper Palace gate), cross the street, walk uphill one block, go through the gate (on left), and look immediately to the right for the small building with the ticket office.

❷ Self-Guided Tour: The Belvedere Palace is actually two grand buildings—the Upper Palace and Lower Palace—separated by a fine garden. For our purposes, the **Upper Palace** is what matters. Buy your ticket at the office behind the palace, then go around to the front to enter. Once inside, the palace's eclectic collection is tailor-made for browsing. There are two grand floors, set around impressive middle halls.

Ground Floor: The main floor displays a collection of Austrian Baroque (on the left) and medieval art (on the right). The Baroque section includes a fascinating room of grotesquely grimacing heads by **Franz Xaver Messerschmidt** (1736-1783), a quirky 18th-century Habsburg court sculptor who left the imperial life to follow his own, somewhat deranged muse. After his promising career was cut short by mental illness, Messerschmidt relocated to Bratislava and spent the rest of his days sculpting a series of eerily lifelike "character heads" *(Kopfstücke)*. Their most unusual faces are contorted by extreme emotions.

• *From the entrance, climb the staircase to the **first floor** and enter the grand red-and-gold, chandeliered...*

Marble Hall: This was Prince Eugene's party room. *Belvedere* means "beautiful view," and the **view from the Marble Hall** is especially spectacular.

• *Facing the garden, to the right is the...*

East Wing: Alongside Renoir's ladies, Monet's landscapes, and Van Gogh's rough brushstrokes are similar works by their lesser-known Austrian counterparts. Around 1900, Austrian artists come to the fore, soaking up Symbolism, Expressionism, and other Modernist trends.

In the two rooms full of sumptuous paintings by **Gustav Klimt,** you can get caught up in his fascination with the beauty and danger he saw in women. To Klimt, all art was erotic art. He painted during the turn of the century, when Vienna was a splendid laboratory of hedonism.

The famous painting of *Judith I* (1901) shows no biblical heroine—Klimt paints her as a high-society Vienna woman with an ostentatious dog-collar necklace. With half-closed eyes and slightly parted lips, she's dismissive...yet mysterious and bewitching. Holding the head of her biblical victim, she's the modern femme fatale.

In what is perhaps Klimt's best-known painting, *The Kiss*, two lovers are wrapped up in the colorful gold-and-jeweled cloak of bliss. Klimt's woman is no longer dominating, but submissive, abandoning herself to her man in a fertile field and a vast universe. In a glow emanating from a radiance of desire, the body she presses against is a self-portrait of the artist himself.

Klimt nurtured the next generation of artists, especially **Egon Schiele.** While Klimt's works are mystical and otherworldly, Schiele's tend to be darker and more introspective. One of Schiele's most recognizable works, *The Embrace*, shows a couple engaged in an erotically charged, rippling moment of passion. Striking a darker tone is *The Family*, which depicts a crouching couple. This family portrait from 1918 is especially poignant because his wife died while he was still working on it.

The Rest of the Upper Palace: The Belvedere's collection goes through the whole range of 19th- and 20th-century art: Historicism, Romanticism, Impressionism, Realism, tired tourism, Expressionism, Art Nouveau, and early Modernism.

Grounds and Gardens: The delightfully manicured grounds are free and fun to explore. The only area with an entry fee is the **Orangerie garden,** along the west side of the Lower Palace (and accessed through that palace).

Lower Palace: Covered by a separate ticket, this is the home where Prince Eugene actually hung his helmet. Today it contains a small stretch of three of his private apartments (relatively uninteresting compared to the sumptuous Habsburg apartments elsewhere in town). The Lower Palace also houses some generally good special exhibits, as well as the entrance to the Orangerie, privy garden, and stables (until 12:00). If the special exhibits intrigue you, it's worth buying the combo-ticket to get in here; otherwise, I wouldn't bother to visit.

VIENNA

East of the Ring

Museum of Applied Art
(Österreichisches Museum für Angewandte Kunst)

Facing the old town from across the Ring, the MAK, as it's called, is Vienna's answer to London's Victoria and Albert Museum.

Cost and Hours: €8, €10 includes a hefty English guidebook, free Tue after 18:00; open Wed-Sun 10:00-18:00, Tue 10:00-22:00, closed Mon, Stubenring 5, tel. 01/711-360, www.mak.at.

Visiting the Museum: The MAK is more than just another grand building on the Ringstrasse. It was built to provide models of historic design for Ringstrasse architects and is a delightful space in itself (many locals stop in to enjoy a coffee on the plush couches in the main lobby). The collection of furniture, ceramics, textiles, metalwork, and more shows off the fancies of local aristocratic society, including fine Biedermeier and *Jugendstil* pieces (among them, Klimt designs for a palace in Brussels).

Each wing is dedicated to a different era. Exhibits, well-described in English (borrow the captions in each room), come with a playful modern flair—notable modern designers were assigned various spaces. An interesting section covers the Vienna Workshop project (Wiener Werkstätte). Inspired by England's Arts and Crafts movement, it was born about 1903 to keep craftspeople (cabinetmakers, bookbinders, metalworkers, and so on) competitive in the Industrial Age. While the workshop lasted a decade, it had more idealism than business savvy. Mass production eventually won out, and its products faded into oblivion.

The unique gift shop also makes for a fun diversion.

Eating at the MAK: The beautiful lobby hosts an inviting **café.** The **Restaurant Österreicher im MAK,** in the same building, is named for Chef Helmut Österreicher, who's renowned for his classic and modern Viennese cuisine. Classy and mod, it's trendy for locals (€9-23 plates, daily 10:00-1:00 in the morning, reserve for evening, tel. 01/714-0121).

Austrian Postal Savings Bank
(Die Österreichische Postsparkasse)

Built between 1904 and 1912, Vienna's Postal Savings Bank offers a fascinating look into the society, as well as the architecture, of that age. The main part of the building, which still functions as a bank, is open to the public.

Cost and Hours: Bank foyer—free, museum—€6, Mon-Sat 9:00-17:00, closed Sun, just off the Ringstrasse at Georg-Coch-Platz 2, www.ottowagner.com.

Visiting the Postal Savings Bank: The postal savings system was intended for working-class people, who did not have access to the palatial banks of the 19th century. Secessionist architect Otto Wagner believed "necessity is the master of art," and he declared that "what is impractical can never be beautiful." Everything about his design—so gray, white, and efficient—is practical. It's so clean that the service provided here feels almost sacred. This is a textbook example of form following function, and the form is beautiful.

The product of an age giddy with advancement, the building dignifies the technological and celebrates it as cultural. Study the sleek, yet elegantly modern exterior: Angles high above—made of an exciting new material, aluminum—seem to proclaim the modern age. The facade and its unadorned marble siding panels, secured by aluminum bolts, give the impression that the entire building is a safe-deposit box. The interior is similarly functionalist. The glass roof lets in light; the glass floor helps illuminate the basement. Fixtures, vents, and even the furniture fit right in—all bold, geometrical, and modern. In the back, the fine little **Museum Postsparkasse** is dedicated to Wagner and provides a visual review of his work.

▲Museum of Military History (Heeresgeschichtliches Museum)

While much of the Habsburg Empire was built on strategic marriages rather than the spoils of war, a big part of Habsburg history is military. And this huge place, built about 1860 as an arsenal by Franz Josef, tells the story well with a thoughtful motto (apparently learned from the school of hard knocks): "War belongs to museums."

Cost and Hours: €5 includes good audioguide, daily 9:00-17:00, on Arsenalstrasse near the Ostbahnhof (a.k.a. Südbahnhof), tel. 01/795-610, www.hgm.or.at. It's a 10-minute walk behind the Belevedere Palace.

Visiting the Museum: Located inconveniently outside the Ring, you'll wander the wings of this vast museum nearly all alone. Its two floors hold a rich collection of artifacts and historic treasures from the times of Maria Theresa to Prince Eugene to Franz Joseph. The particularly interesting 20th-century section includes exhibits devoted to Sarajevo in 1914 (with the car Franz Ferdinand rode in and the uniform he wore when he was assassinated), Chancellor Dolfuss and the pre-Hitler Austrian Fascist party, the *Anschluss*, and World War II.

▲Kunst Haus Wien Museum and Hundertwasser Haus

This "make yourself at home" museum and nearby apartment complex are a hit with lovers of modern art, mixing the work and philosophy of local painter/environmentalist Friedensreich Hundertwasser (1928-2000).

Cost and Hours: €10 for Hundertwasser Museum, €12 combo-ticket includes special exhibitions, half-price on Mon, open daily 10:00-19:00, extremely fragrant and colorful garden café, tel. 01/712-0491, www.kunsthauswien.com.

Getting There: It's located at Untere Weissgerberstrasse 13 (tram #1: Radetzkyplatz or U-3: Landstrasse). Note that the tram stop is much closer than the U-Bahn stop. From the Landstrasse U-Bahn stop, walk 10 minutes downhill (north) along Untere Viaduktgasse (a block east of the station), or ride tram #0 three stops to Radetzkyplatz; from there signs point to the museum.

Visiting the Museum and Apartments: Stand in front of the colorful checkerboard building that houses the **Kunst Haus Wien Museum.** Consider Hundertwasser's style. He was against "window racism": Neighboring houses allow only one kind of window, but $100H_2O$'s windows are each different—and he encouraged residents in the Hundertwasserhaus (a 5-10 minute walk away, described below) to personalize them. He recognized "tree tenants" as well as human tenants. His buildings are spritzed with a forest and topped with dirt and grassy little parks—close to nature and good for the soul.

Floors and sidewalks are irregular—to "stimulate the brain" (although current residents complain it just causes wobbly furniture and sprained ankles). Thus $100H_2O$ waged a one-man fight—during the 1950s and 1960s, when concrete and glass ruled—to save the human soul from the city. (Hundertwasser claimed that "straight lines are godless.")

Inside the museum, start with his interesting biography. His fun paintings are half psychedelic *Jugendstil* and half just kids' stuff. Notice the photographs from his 1950s days as part of Vienna's bohemian scene. Throughout the museum, keep an eye out for the fun philosophical quotes from an artist who believed, "If man is creative, he comes nearer to his creator."

The Kunst Haus Wien provides by far the best look at Hundertwasser, but for an actual lived-in apartment complex by the green master, walk 5-10 minutes to the one-with-nature **Hundertwasserhaus Haus** (at Löwengasse and Kegelgasse). This complex of 50 apartments, subsidized by the government to provide affordable housing, was built in the 1980s as a breath of architectural fresh air in a city of boring, blocky apartment complexes. While not open to visitors, it's worth visiting for its fun and colorful patchwork exterior and the Hundertwasser festival of shops across the street.

Don't miss the view from Kegelgasse to see the "tree tenants" and the internal winter garden that residents enjoy.

Hundertwasser detractors—of which there are many—remind visitors that $100H_2O$ was a painter, not an architect. They describe the Hundertwasserhaus as a "1950s house built in the 1980s" that was colorfully painted with no real concern for the environment, communal living, or even practical comfort. Almost all of the original inhabitants got fed up with the novelty and moved out.

North of the Ring
Sigmund Freud Museum
Freud enthusiasts enjoy seeing the humble apartment and work-place of the man who fundamentally changed our understanding of the human psyche. Dr. Sigmund Freud (1856-1939), a graduate of Vienna University, established his practice here in 1891. For the next 47 years, he received troubled patients who hoped to find peace by telling him their dreams, life traumas, and secret urges. It was here that he wrote his influential works, including the landmark *Interpretation of Dreams* (1899).

Cost and Hours: €8 includes audioguide, daily 9:00-18:00, cool shop, half a block downhill from the Schlickgasse tram #D stop, Berggasse 19, tel. 01/319-1596, www.freud-museum.at.

Visiting the Museum: Today, you can walk through his three-room office (but not the apartments next door, where Freud lived with his large family). The rooms are tiny and disappointingly bare. Freud, who was Jewish, fled Vienna when the Nazis came to power. He took most of his furniture with him, including the famous couch that patients reclined on (now in a London museum).

All in all, the museum is quite old-fashioned—tediously described in a three-ring binder loaned to visitors, which complements the more general audioguide.

West of the Ring, on Mariahilfer Strasse
▲Imperial Furniture Collection (Hofmobiliendepot)
Bizarre, sensuous, eccentric, or precious, this collection (on four fascinating floors) is your peek at the Habsburgs' furniture—from the empress's wheelchair ("to increase her fertility she was put on a rich diet and became corpulent") to the emperor's spittoon—all thoughtfully described in English. Evocative paintings help bring the furniture to life. The Habsburgs had many palaces, but only the Hofburg was permanently furnished. The rest were done on the fly—set up and taken down by a gang of royal roadies called the "Depot of Court Movables" (Hofmobiliendepot). When the monarchy was dissolved in 1918, the state of Austria took possession of the Hofmobiliendepot's inventory—165,000 items. Now this royal storehouse is open to the public in a fine and sprawling museum.

Don't go here for the *Jugendstil* furnishings. The older Baroque, Rococo, and Biedermeier pieces are the most impressive and tied most intimately to the royals. Combine a visit to this museum with a stroll down the lively shopping boulevard, Mariahilfer Strasse.

Cost and Hours: €8, covered by Sisi Ticket (see page 30), Tue-Sun 10:00-18:00, closed Mon, Mariahilfer Strasse 88, main entrance around the corner at Andreasgasse 7, U-3: Zieglergasse, tel. 01/5243-3570, www.hofmobiliendepot.at.

▲▲▲Schönbrunn Palace (Schloss Schönbrunn)

Among Europe's palaces, only Schönbrunn rivals Versailles. This former summer residence of the Habsburgs is big, with 1,441 rooms. But don't worry—only 40 rooms are shown to the public. Of the plethora of sights at the palace, the highlight is a tour of the Royal Apartments—the chandeliered rooms where the Habsburg nobles lived. You can also stroll the gardens, tour the coach museum, and visit a handful of lesser sights nearby.

Getting There: While on the outskirts of Vienna, Schönbrunn is an easy 10-minute subway ride from downtown. Take U-4 to Schönbrunn and follow signs for *Schloss Schönbrunn*. Exit bearing right, then cross the busy road and continue to the right along the yellow building to the main entry courtyard, which will be on your left. Tickets are sold at the visitors center, just left of the main entrance to the palace grounds (well before you get to the actual palace).

▲▲▲Royal Apartments

Although the palace's exterior is Baroque, the interior was finished under Maria Theresa in let-them-eat-cake Rococo. As with the similar apartments at the Hofburg (the Habsburgs' winter home), these apartments give you a sense of the quirky, larger-than-life personalities who lived here—especially Franz Josef (r. 1848-1916) and Sisi. Your tour of the apartments, accompanied by an audioguide, covers one small section of the palace's grand interior on a clearly signed route. You have two tour options: Imperial (shorter and cheaper) or Grand (longer and more expensive). Both follow the same route at first, but after a certain point the Imperial group is politely excused while the Grand gang continues on to see a few more rooms.

Cost: The 22-room **Imperial Tour** is €10.50 (35 minutes, includes audioguide, Grand Palace rooms plus apartments of Franz Josef and Sisi—mostly 19th-century and therefore least interesting). The much better 40-room **Grand Tour** costs €13.50 (50 minutes, includes audioguide, everything on Imperial Tour plus Maria Theresa's apartments—18th-century Rococo). If venturing beyond the apartments, consider one of two combo-tickets: The **Classic Pass** includes the Grand Tour, as well as other sights on the grounds—the Gloriette viewing terrace, maze, and privy garden (€16.50, available April-Oct only). The **Classic Pass Plus** includes all the above, plus the court bakery (complete with *Apfelstrudel* demo and tasting; €19.50, available April-Oct only). However, none of the extra sights covered by either pass is really worth the cost of entry, so I'd skip them and just do the Grand Tour, followed by a mosey through the impressive grounds (which are free).

Hours: Daily July-Aug 8:30-18:30, April-June and Sept-Oct 8:30-17:30, Nov-March 8:30-17:00.

Information: Tel. 01/8111-3239, www.schoenbrunn.at.

Reservations: To avoid getting stuck in the ticket-buying line, book advance tickets online at the palace website. You'll reserve an entry time and date, then print your tickets before you come (ask at your hotel if you need access to a printer). Tickets can also be reserved by phone and picked up at the visitors center (tel. 01/81113-239).

Crowd-Beating Tips: Schönbrunn suffers from crowds. It can be a jam-packed sauna in the summer. It's busiest from 9:30 to 11:30, especially on weekends and in July and August; it's least crowded after 14:00, when there are no groups. To avoid the long delays in summer, make a reservation online or by phone (see above).

Visiting the Royal Apartments: Moving from room to room, you're immersed in imperial splendor. The chandeliers are made either of Bohemian crystal or hand-carved wood with gold-leaf gilding. Highlights include Franz Josef's study and bedroom (and the bed he actually died in). The Mirrored Room was where six-year-old Wolfie Mozart performed his first concert. The opulent, chandeliered Great Gallery—with its mirrored walls and dramatically frescoed ceilings—was the site of a famous 1961 summit between John F. Kennedy and Nikita Khrushchev.

Fortunately, the palace managed to escape destruction when WWII bombs rained on the city and the palace grounds. The palace itself took only one direct hit. Thankfully, that bomb, which crashed through three floors—including the sumptuous central ballroom—was a dud. Most of the public rooms are decorated in Neo-Baroque, as they were under Franz Josef and Sisi. The rest of the palace was converted to simple apartments and rented to the families of 260 civil servants, who enjoy rent control and governmental protections so they can't be evicted.

▲▲Palace Gardens

Unlike the gardens of Versailles, meant to shut out the real world, Schönbrunn's park was opened to the public in 1779 while the monarchy was in full swing. It was part of Maria Theresa's reform policy, making the garden a celebration of the evolution of civilization from autocracy into real democracy.

Today it's a delightful, sprawling place to wander—especially on a sunny day. You can spend hours here, enjoying the views and the people-watching. And most of the park is free, as it has been for more than two centuries (open daily sunrise to dusk, entrance on either side of the palace).

Getting Around the Gardens: A **tourist train** makes the rounds all day, connecting Schönbrunn's many attractions (€6, 2/hour in peak season, none Nov-mid-March, one-hour circuit). Unfortunately, there's no bike rental nearby.

Visiting the Gardens: The large, manicured grounds are laid out on angled, tree-lined axes that gradually incline, offering dramatic views back to the palace. The small side gardens flanking the palace are the most elaborate. As you face the back of the palace, to the right is the **privy garden** (*Kronprinzengarten*, €2.50); to the left are the free **Sisi Gardens.** Better yet, just explore, using a map (pick one up at the palace) to locate several whimsical **fountains;** a kid-friendly **maze** *(Irrgarten)* and playground area (€3.50); and the **Gloriette,** a purely decorative monument celebrating an obscure Austrian military victory and offering a fine city view (pay for a pricey drink in the café, shell out €2.50 to hike up to the viewing terrace, or skip the whole thing, as views are about as good from the lawn in front; included in Schönbrunn passes described earlier, daily April-Sept 9:00-18:00, July-Aug until 19:00, Oct 9:00-17:00, closed Nov-March).

At the west end of the grounds is Europe's oldest **zoo** *(Tiergarten),* built by Maria Theresa's husband for the entertainment and education of the court in 1752 (€15, €20 combo-ticket with palm and desert houses, daily April-Sept 9:00-18:30, closes earlier off-season, tel. 01/877-9294, www.zoovienna.at). Nearby are two skippable sights: The **palm house** *(Palmenhaus;* €4, €6 combo-ticket with desert house, €20 combo-ticket also includes zoo, daily May-Sept 9:30-18:00, Oct-April 9:30-17:00, last entry 30 minutes before closing) and the **Desert Experience House** *(Wüstenhaus;* (€4, same combo-tickets and hours as palm house).

▲Coach Museum Wagenburg

The Schönbrunn coach museum is a 19th-century traffic jam of 50 impressive royal carriages and sleighs. Highlights include silly sedan chairs, the death-black hearse carriage (used for Franz Josef in 1916, and most recently for Empress Zita in 1989), and an extravagantly gilded imperial carriage pulled by eight Cinderella horses. This was rarely used other than for the coronation of Holy Roman Emperors, when it was disassembled and taken to Frankfurt for the big event. You'll also get a look at one of Sisi's impossibly narrow-waisted gowns, and (upstairs) Sisi's "Riding Chapel," with portraits of her 25 favorite horses.

Cost and Hours: €6, audioguide-€2, daily April-Oct 9:00-

18:00, Nov-March 10:00-16:00, 200 yards from palace, walk through right arch as you face palace, tel. 01/525-24-3470.

East of the Danube Canal

▲Prater Park (Wiener Prater)

Since the 1780s, when the reformist Emperor Josef II gave his hunting grounds to the people of Vienna as a public park, this place has been Vienna's playground. For the tourist, the "Prater" is the sugary-smelling, tired, and sprawling amusement park (Wurstelprater). For locals, the "Prater" is the vast, adjacent green park with its three-mile-long, tree-lined main boulevard (Hauptallee). The park still tempts visitors with its huge 220-foot-tall, famous, and lazy Ferris wheel *(Riesenrad)*, roller coaster, bumper cars, Lilliputian railroad, and endless eateries. Especially if you're traveling with kids, this is a fun, goofy place to share the evening with thousands of Viennese.

Cost and Hours: Rides run May-Sept 9:00-24:00—but quiet after 22:00, March-April and Oct 10:00-22:00, Nov-Dec 10:00-20:00, grounds always open, U-1: Praterstern, www.prater.at. For a local-style family dinner, eat at Schweizerhaus (good food, great Czech Budvar—the original "Budweiser"—beer, classic conviviality).

Danube Island (Donauinsel)

In the 1970s, as part of a flood protection program, the city dug a channel (the so-called Neue Donau—New Danube) parallel to the Danube River. With the dredged-out dirt, the engineers formed 12-mile-long Danube Island. Originally just an industrial site, it's evolved into a much-loved idyllic escape from the city (easy U-Bahn access on U-1: Donauinsel).

The skinny island provides a natural wonderland. All along the pedestrianized, grassy park, you'll find locals—both Viennese and especially immigrants and those who can't afford their own cabin or fancy vacation—at play. The swimming comes tough, though, with rocky entries rather than sand. The best activity here is a bike ride. If you venture far from the crowds, you're likely to encounter nudists on inline skates.

Biking Danube Island: For a simple, breezy joyride, bike up and down the traffic-free and people-filled island. Weather permitting, you can rent a bike from the shop at the **Reichsbrücke**, the bridge spanning the island (€6/hour, €25/day, March-Oct daily 9:00-21:00, closed off-season, 70 yards from U-1: Donauinsel, tel. 01/263-5242, www.fahrradverleih.at).

Donau City (Danaustadt)

This modern part of town, just beyond Danube Island, is the sky-scraping "Manhattan" of Austria. It was laid out as a potential Vienna-Budapest expo site in the 1990s. But Austrians voted down the fair idea, and eventually the real estate became today's modern planned city: It's quiet and traffic-free, with inviting plazas and a small church dwarfed by towering places of business. The high-rise DC Towers are the tallest office buildings in Austria. With business, residential, and shopping zones surrounded by inviting parkland, this corner of the city is likely to grow as Vienna expands. Its centerpiece is the futuristic UNO City, one of four United Nations headquarters worldwide. While it lacks the Old World character, charm, and elegance of the rest of Vienna, Donau City may interest travelers who are into contemporary glass-and-steel architecture (U-1: Kaisermühlen VIC).

Biking to Donau City and Beyond: Sightseers on bike can cross the Danube to Donau City. From the Opera, it's pretty much a straight pedal around the center via the Ringstrasse, past Prater Park, and across the river. The way is easy enough to find with the help of the basic tourist map from the TI. (Recommended local guide Wolfgang Höfler leads tours along this route, which he shared with me; see page 36.)

The route will take you over four stretches of water: the Danube Canal, the actual Danube, the New Danube, and the Old Danube. Along the way, you'll gain a better understanding of the massive engineering done over the years to contain and tame the river.

As you leave the city center, you'll first pedal over the Danube Canal, an arm of the river that brings river traffic into the city; then you hit the main part of the river and the man-made Danube Island (itself a part of the city's flood barriers). From the Reichsbrücke bridge over the island, survey the river's traffic. The cruise industry is booming, and Vienna's river cruise port is hosting more boats than ever. Many of them sail from here all the way to Romania and the Black Sea coast. You may also be inspired by the entire Austrian navy: Look for the two tiny camouflaged gunboats moored in the shade of the bridge.

In the distance, across the river, are the skyscrapers of Donau City. To reach it, continue across the bridge over Danube Island and cross the New Danube. From Donau City, the bike path leads across the Old Danube (Alte Donau), an old arm of the river but now a lake, which hosts a frolicking park with all the water fun a hot-and-tired city could hope for, including lakeside cafés and boat rentals. From here you can simply retrace your route, or you can make a big circle by following the delightful bike path southeast along the Old Danube to the next bridge (Praterbrücke). This leads to the vast Prater Park, where you'll follow the breezy main boulevard (Hauptallee) back to the big Ferris wheel and ultimately to downtown.

Experiences in Vienna

Vienna's Café Culture

In Vienna, the living room is down the street at the neighborhood coffeehouse. This tradition is just another example of Viennese expertise in good living. Each of Vienna's many long-established (and sometimes even legendary) coffeehouses has its individual character (and characters). These classic cafés can be a bit tired, with a shabby patina and famously grumpy waiters who treat you like an uninvited guest invading their living room. Yet these spaces somehow also feel welcoming, offering newspapers, pastries, sofas, quick and light workers' lunches, elegant ambience, and "take all the time you want" charm for the price of a cup of coffee. Rather than buy the *International Herald Tribune* ahead of time, spend the money on a cup of coffee and read the paper for free, Vienna-style, in a café.

As in Italy and France, Viennese coffee drinks are espresso-based. Obviously, *Kaffee* means coffee and *Milch* is milk; *Obers* is cream, while *Schlagobers* is whipped cream. Americans who ask for a "latte" are mistaken for Italians and given a cup of hot milk.

Cafés

These are some of my favorite Viennese cafés. All of them, except for Café Sperl, are located inside the Ring (see map on page 117).

Café Hawelka has a dark, "brooding Trotsky" atmosphere, paintings by struggling artists who couldn't pay for coffee, a saloon-wood flavor, chalkboard menu, smoked velvet couches, an international selection of newspapers, and a phone that rings for regulars. Frau Hawelka died just a couple weeks after Pope John Paul II. Locals suspect the pontiff wanted her much-loved *Buchteln* (marmalade-filled doughnuts) in heaven. The café remains family-run (Wed-Mon 8:00-21:00, closed Tue, just off the Graben, Dorotheergasse 6, U-1 or U-3: Stephansplatz, tel. 01/512-8230).

Café Central, while a bit touristy, remains a classic place, lavish under Neo-Gothic columns. They serve fancy coffees (€4-6) and two-course daily specials (€10), and entertain guests with live piano—schmaltzy tunes on a fine, Vienna-made Bösendorfer each evening from 17:00-22:00 (daily 7:30-22:00, corner of Herrengasse and Strauchgasse, U-3: Herrengasse, tel. 01/533-3764).

Café Sperl dates from 1880 and is still furnished identically to the day it opened—from the coat tree to the chairs (Mon-Sat 7:00-23:00, Sun 11:00-20:00 except closed Sun July-Aug, just off Naschmarkt near Mariahilfer Strasse, Gumpendorfer 11, U-2: MuseumsQuartier, tel. 01/586-4158; see map on page 109).

Café Bräunerhof, between the Hofburg and the Graben, offers classic ambience with no tourists and live music on weekends (light classics, no cover, Sat-Sun 15:00-18:00), along with a practical menu with daily lunch specials (daily 8:00-20:00, Stallburgasse 2, U-1 or U-3: Stephansplatz, tel. 01/512-3893).

Other Classics in the Old Center: All of these places are open long hours daily: **Café Pruckel** (at Dr.-Karl-Lueger-Platz, across from Stadtpark at Stubenring 24); **Café Tirolerhof** (2 blocks from the Opera, behind the TI on Tegetthoffstrasse, at Führichgasse 8); and **Café Landtmann** (directly across from the City Hall on the Ringstrasse at Dr.-Karl-Lueger-Ring 4). The Landtmann is unique, as it's the only grand café built along the Ring with all the other grand buildings. **Café Sacher** (see page 38) and **Demel** (see page 43) are famous for their cakes, but they also serve good coffee drinks.

Wein in Wien: Vienna's Wine Gardens

The *Heuriger* (HOY-rih-gur) is a uniquely Viennese institution. When the Habsburgs let Vienna's vintners sell their own new wine (called *Sturm*) tax-free, several hundred families opened *Heurigen*—wine-garden restaurants clustered around the edge of town. A tradition was born. Today, they do their best to maintain the old-village atmosphere, serving their homemade wine (the most recent vintage, until November 11, when a new vintage year begins) with small meals and strolling musicians. Most *Heurigen* are decorated with enormous antique presses from their vineyards. (For a near-*Heuriger* experience in downtown Vienna, drop by Gigerl Stadtheuriger—see page 114.)

Many places close one day a week and in winter, so call first. Several employ gypsy-type strolling musicians (accordionists and violinists who add ambience for tips). Most *Heurigen* have play zones for kids. And, depending on the weather, it's either all outside or all inside.

I've listed three good *Heuriger* neighborhoods, all on the outskirts of Vienna. To reach the neighborhoods from downtown Vienna, it's best to use public transportation (cheap, 30 minutes, runs late in the evening, directions given per listing below), or you can take a 15-minute taxi ride from the Ring (about €15-20).

While there are some "destination" *Heurigen*, it can be disappointing to seek out a particular place, because the ambience can change depending on that evening's clientele (locals vs. tour groups). Each neighborhood I've described is a square or hub with two or three recommended spots and many other wine gardens worth considering. Wander around, then choose the *Heuriger* with the best atmosphere.

Neustift am Walde

This district is farthest from the city but is still easy to reach by public transit. It feels a little less touristy than other places.

Fuhrgassl Huber, which brags it's the biggest *Heuriger* in Vienna, can accommodate 1,000 people inside and just as many outside. You can lose yourself in its sprawling backyard, with vineyards streaking up the hill from terraced tables. Musicians stroll most nights (Tue-Sat after 19:00; open daily 14:00-24:00, Neustift am Walde 68, tel. 01/440-1405, www.fuhrgassl-huber.at, family Huber).

Das Schreiberhaus Heurigen-Restaurant is another popular, family-owned place with creaky old-time dining rooms papered with celebrity photos, with 600 spaces inside and another 600 outside, music nightly after 19:00, and a backyard reaching deep into its vineyards (open daily 11:00-24:00, Rathstrasse 54, tel. 01/440-3844, www.dasschreiberhaus.at).

Weinhof Zimmermann, while a bit of a walk from the bus stop, is my favorite. It's a sprawling farmhouse where the green tables on patios echo the terraced fields all around. While dining, you'll feel like you're actually right in the vineyard. The idyllic setting comes with rabbits in petting cages, great food, no city views but fine hillside vistas, and wonderful peace (Mon-Sat 15:00-24:00, closed Sun, tel. 01/440-1207, www.weinhof-zimmermann.at). Ride bus #35A to the Agnesgasse stop (at the corner of Rathstrasse and Agnesgasse, just before the Neustift am Walde stop), then hike uphill on Agnesgasse to the farm at Mitterwurzergasse 20.

Getting to the Neustift am Walde **Heurigen:** Simply ride bus #35A to the stop in Neustift am Walde (catch the bus from the Nussdorfer Strasse stop on the U-6).

Nussdorf

An untouristy district, characteristic and popular with the Viennese, Nussdorf has plenty of *Heuriger* ambience. This area feels very real with a working-class vibe, streets lined with local shops, and characteristic *Heurigen* that feel a little bit rougher around the edges.

Schübel-Auer Heuriger is my favorite here—with a big and user-friendly buffet (many dishes are labeled and the patient staff speaks English). Its rustic ambience can be enjoyed indoors or out (Tue-Sat 16:00-24:00, closed Sun-Mon, Kahlenberger Strasse 22, tel. 01/370-2222, www.schuebel-auer.at).

Heuriger Kierlinger, next door, is also good, with a particularly rollicking, woody room around its buffet (daily 15:30-24:00, Kahlenberger Strasse 20, tel. 01/370-2264, www.kierlinger.at).

Bamkraxler ("Tree-Climber") is the only *Biergarten* amid all these vineyards. It's a fun-loving, youthful place with fine keg beer and a regular menu—traditional, ribs, veggie, kids' menu—rather than the *Heuriger* cafeteria line (€7-13 meals, kids' playground, Tue-Sat 16:00-24:00, Sun 11:00-24:00, closed Mon, Kahlenberger Strasse 17, tel. 01/318-8800, www.bamkraxler.at). To get here, walk all the way through the others, pop out on Kahlenberger Strasse, and walk 20 yards uphill.

Getting to the Nussdorf **Heurigen:** Take tram #D from the Ringstrasse (stops include the Opera, Hofburg/Kunsthistorisches Museum, and City Hall) to its endpoint (the stop labeled *Nussdorf* isn't the end—stay on for one more stop to Beethovengang). Exit the tram, cross the tracks, go uphill 40 yards, and look for the *Heurigen* on your left.

VIENNA

Heiligenstadt (Pfarrplatz)

Not far from Nussdorf, hiding just above the unappealing main road, is Pfarrplatz, which feels like a charming village square watched over by a church. Beethoven lived—and began work on his Ninth Symphony—here in 1817; he'd previously written his Sixth Symphony *(Pastorale)* while staying in this then-rural district. He hoped the local spa would cure his worsening deafness. (Confusingly, the name "Heiligenstadt" is used for two different locations: this little neighborhood, and the big train and U-Bahn station near the river.)

Mayer am Pfarrplatz (a.k.a. Beethovenhaus), right next to the church, is famous, touristy, and feels more polished—almost trendy—compared to the other *Heurigen* I list. This place has a charming inner courtyard under cozy vines with an accordion player, along with a sprawling backyard with a big children's play zone (Mon-Fri 16:00-24:00, Sat-Sun 12:00-24:00, Pfarrplatz 2, tel. 01/370-1287, www.pfarrplatz.at).

Weingut and Heuriger Werner Welser is a block uphill (go up Probusgasse). It's big (serving large tour groups) and traditional, with dirndled waitresses and lederhosened waiters. It feels a bit crank-'em-out, but it's still lots of fun, with music nightly from 19:00 (open daily 15:30-24:00, Probusgasse 12, tel. 01/318-9797, www.werner-welser.at).

Getting to the Heiligenstadt **Heurigen:** Take the U-4 line to its last station, Heiligenstadt, then transfer to bus #38A. Get off at Fernsprechamt/Heiligenstadt, walk uphill, and take the first right onto Nestelbachgasse, which leads to Pfarrplatz and the Beethovenhaus.

Entertainment in Vienna

Vienna—the birthplace of what we call classical music—still thrives as Europe's music capital. On any given evening, you'll have your choice of opera, Strauss waltzes, Mozart chamber concerts, and lighthearted musicals. The Vienna Boys' Choir lives up to its worldwide reputation.

Besides music, you can spend an evening enjoying art, watching a classic film, or sipping Viennese wine in a village wine garden. Save some energy for Vienna after dark.

Music

As far back as the 12th century, Vienna was a mecca for musicians—both sacred and secular (troubadours). The Habsburg emperors of the 17th and 18th centuries were not only generous supporters of music, but fine musicians and composers themselves. (Maria Theresa played a mean double bass.) Composers such as Haydn, Mozart, Beethoven, Schubert, Brahms, and Mahler gravitated to this music-friendly environment. They taught each other, jammed together, and spent a lot of time in Habsburg palaces. Beethoven was a famous figure, walking—lost in musical thought—through the Vienna Woods. In the city's 19th-century belle époque, "Waltz King" Johann Strauss and his brothers kept Vienna's 300 ballrooms spinning.

This musical tradition continues into modern times, leaving many prestigious Viennese institutions for today's tourists to enjoy: the Opera, the Boys' Choir, and the great Baroque halls and churches, all busy with classical and waltz concerts. As you poke into churches and palaces, you may hear groups practicing. You're welcome to sit and listen.

For music lovers, Vienna is also an opportunity to make pilgrimages to the homes (now mostly small museums) of favorite composers. If you're a fan of Schubert, Brahms, Haydn, Beethoven, or Mozart, there's a sight for you. But I find these homes inconveniently located and generally underwhelming. The centrally located Haus der Musik (see page 48) is my favorite setting for celebrating the great musicians and composers who called Vienna home.

Vienna remains the music capital of Europe, with 10,000 seats in various venues around town mostly booked with classical performances. The best-known entertainment venues are the Staatsoper (a.k.a., "the Opera"), the Volksoper (for musicals and operettas), the Theater an der Wien (opera and other performances), the Wiener Musikverein (home of the Vienna Philharmonic Orchestra), and the Wiener Konzerthaus (various events). The events held in these places are listed in the monthly *Wien-Programm* (available at TI).

In Vienna, it's music *con brio* from October through June, reaching a symphonic climax during the Vienna Festival each May and June. Sadly, in summer (generally July and August), the Boys' Choir, Opera, and many other serious music companies are—like you—on vacation. But Vienna hums year-round with live classical music; touristy, crowd-pleasing shows are always available.

Buying Tickets: Most tickets run from €40 to €55 (plus a stiff booking fee when bought in advance or through a box office like the one at the TI). A few venues charge as little as €25; look around if you're not set on any particular concert. While it's easy to book tickets online long in advance, spontaneity is also workable, as there are invariably people selling their extra tickets at face value or less outside the door before concert time. If you call a concert hall directly, they can advise you on the availability of (cheaper) tickets at the door. Vienna takes care of its starving artists (and tourists) by offering cheap standing-room tickets to top-notch music and opera (generally an hour before each performance).

Vienna Boys' Choir (Wiener Sängerknaben)

The boys sing (from a high balcony, heard but not seen) at the 9:15 Sunday Mass from September through June in the Hofburg's Imperial Music Chapel (Hofmusikkapelle). The entrance is at Schweizerhof; you can get there from In der Burg square or go through the tunnel from Josefsplatz.

Reserved seats must be booked two months in advance (€5-29; reserve by fax, email, or mail: fax from the US 011-431-533-992-775, send email to office@hofburgkapelle.at, or write Wiener Hofmusikkapelle, Hofburg-Schweizerhof, 1010 Wien; call 01/533-9927 for information only—they can't book tickets at this number; www.hofburgkapelle.at).

Much easier, standing room inside is free and open to the first 60 who line up. Even better, rather than line up early, you can simply swing by and stand in the narthex just outside, where you can hear the boys and see the Mass on a TV monitor.

Boys' Choir concerts are also given Fridays at 16:00 in late April, May, June, September, and October on stage at the Musikverein, near the Opera and Karlsplatz (€36-56, around 30 standing-room tickets go on sale at 15:30 for €15, Karlsplatz 6; U-1, U-2, or U-4: Karlsplatz; tel. 01/5880-4173).

They're talented kids, but, for my taste, not worth all the commotion. Remember, many churches have great music during Sunday Mass. Just 200 yards from the Boys' Choir chapel, the Augustinian Church has a glorious 11:00 service each Sunday (see page 66).

The Opera

The Vienna State Opera (Staatsoper) puts on 300 performances a year, featuring the "Orchestra of the Opera" in the pit. (Any musician aspiring to join the Vienna Philharmonic Orchestra must put in three years here before even being considered.) In July and August the singers rest their voices (or go on tour). Since there are different operas nearly nightly, you'll see big trucks out back and constant action backstage—all the sets need to be switched each day. Even though the expensive seats normally sell out long in advance, the opera is perpetually in the red and subsidized by the state. The excellent "electronic libretto" translation screens help make the experience worthwhile for opera newbies. (Press the button to turn yours on; press again for English.)

Opera Tickets: Seats range from €8 to €168. You can book tickets in advance by phone (tel. 01/513-1513, phone answered daily 10:00-21:00) or online (www.wiener-staatsoper.at); you'll give them your credit-card number, then pick up your tickets at the box office just before show time. If you want to inquire about tickets in person, head to the theater's box office, which is open from 9:00 until one hour before each performance. The Opera has two ticket offices. The main one is on the west side of the building, across Operngasse and facing the Opera. A smaller one is just under the big screen on the east side of the Opera (facing Kärntner Strasse).

Unless Placido Domingo is in town, it's easy to get one of 567 **standing-room tickets** (*Stehplätze*, €3 up top or €4 downstairs). While the front doors open one hour before the show starts, a side door (middle of building, on the Operngasse side) opens 80 minutes before curtain time, giving those in the know an early grab at standing-room tickets (tickets sold until 20 minutes after curtain time). Just walk straight in, then head right until you see the ticket booth marked *Stehplätze*. If fewer than 567 people are in line, there's no need to line up early. If you're one of the first 160 in line, try for the "Parterre" section and you'll end up dead-center at stage level, directly under the Emperor's Box (otherwise, you can choose between the third floor—*Balkon*, or the fourth floor—*Galerie*). Dress is casual (but do your best) at the standing-room bar. Locals save their spot along the rail by tying a scarf to it.

Rick's Crude Tips: For me, three hours is a lot of opera. But just to see and hear the Opera in action for half an hour is a treat. You can buy a standing-room spot and just drop in for part of the show. Ending time is posted in the lobby—you could stop by for just the finale. If you go at the start or finish, you'll get the added entertainment of seeing Vienna all dressed up. Of the 567 people with cheap standing-room tickets, invariably many will not stand through the entire performance. If you drop by after showtime, you can wait for people to leave and bum their tickets off them—be sure to ask them for clear directions to your spot. (While it's perfectly legal to swap standing-room spots, be discreet if finding your spot

VIENNA

VIENNA

mid-performance—try to look like you know where you're going.) Even those with standing-room tickets are considered "ticket holders," and are welcome to explore the building. As you leave, wander around the first floor (fun if skipping out early, when halls are empty) to enjoy the sumptuous halls (with prints of famous stage sets and performers) and the grand entry staircase. The last resort (and worst option) is to drop into the Café Oper Vienna and watch the performance live on TV screens (inside the Opera, reasonable menu and drinks).

"Live Opera on the Square": Demonstrating its commitment to bringing opera to the masses, each spring and fall the Vienna Opera projects several performances live on a huge screen on its building, puts out chairs for the public to enjoy...and it's all free. (These projected performances are noted as *Oper live am Platz* in the official Opera schedule—posted all around the Opera building; they are also listed in the *Wien-Programm* brochure.)

Vienna Volksoper
For less-serious operettas and musicals, try Vienna's other opera house, located along the Gürtel, west of the city center (see *Wien-Programm* brochure or ask at TI for schedule, Währinger Strasse 78, tel. 01/5144-43670, www.volksoper.at).

Theater an der Wien
Considered the oldest theater in Vienna, this venue was designed in 1801 for Mozart operas—intimate, with just a thousand seats. It treats Vienna's music lovers to a different opera every month—generally Mozart with a contemporary setting and modern interpretation. Although Vienna now supports three opera companies, this is the only company playing through the summer (facing the Naschmarkt at Linke Wienzeile 6, tel. 01/5883-0200 for information, tickets available at www.theater-wien.at).

Touristy Mozart and Strauss Concerts
If the music comes to you, it's touristy—designed for flash-in-the-pan Mozart fans. Powdered-wig orchestra performances are given almost nightly in grand traditional settings (€25-50). Pesky wigged-and-powdered Mozarts peddle tickets in the streets. They rave about the quality of the musicians, but you'll get second-rate chamber orchestras, clad in historic costumes, performing the greatest hits of Mozart and Strauss. These are casual, easygoing concerts with lots of tour groups. While there's not a Viennese person in the audience, the tourists generally enjoy the evening.

To sort through your options, check with the ticket office in the TI (same price as on the street, but with all venues to choose from). Savvy locals suggest getting the cheapest tickets, as no one seems to care if cheapskates move up to fill unsold pricier seats. Critics explain that the musicians are actually very good (often Hungarians, Poles, and Russians working a season here to fund an entire year of music studies back home), but that they haven't performed much together so aren't "tight."

Of the many fine venues, the **Mozarthaus** might be my favorite. Intimate chamber-music concerts take place in a small room richly decorated in Venetian Renaissance style (€35-42, Thu-Fri at 19:30, Sat at 18:00, near St. Stephen's Cathedral at Singerstrasse 7, tel. 01/911-9077, www.mozarthaus.at).

Strauss Concerts in the Kursalon

For years, Strauss concerts have been held in the Kursalon, the hall where the "Waltz King" himself directed wildly popular concerts 100 years ago (€40-60, concerts generally nightly at 20:15, tel. 01/512-5790 to check on availability—generally no problem to reserve—or buy online at www.soundofvienna.at). Shows last two hours and are a mix of ballet, waltzes, and a 15-piece orchestra. It's touristy—tour guides holding up banners with group numbers wait out front after the show. Even so, the performance is playful, visually fun, fine quality for most, and with a tried-and-tested, crowd-pleasing format. The conductor welcomes the crowd in German (with a wink) and English; after that...it's English only.

Musicals

The Wien Ticket pavilion next to the Opera (near Kärntner Strasse) sells tickets to contemporary American and British musicals performed in German (€10-109). Same-day tickets are available at a 24 percent discount from 14:00 until 18:00 (ticket pavilion open daily 10:00-19:00). Or you can reserve (full-price) tickets for the musicals by phone (call Wien Ticket at tel. 01/58885).

Films of Concerts

To see free films of great concerts in a lively, outdoor setting near City Hall, see "Nightlife in Vienna," next.

Ballroom Dancing

If you like to dance (waltz and ballroom), or watch people who are really good at it, consider the Dance Evening at the Tanz Café in the Volksgarten (€5-6, May-Aug Sun from 18:00, www.volksgarten.at).

Organ Concerts

St. Peter's Church puts on free organ concerts weekdays at 15:00 and weekends at 20:00 (see page 49).

Classical Music to Go

To bring home Beethoven, Strauss, or the Wiener Philharmonic on a top-quality CD, shop at Gramola on the Graben or EMI on Kärntner Strasse. The Arcadia shop at the Opera is also good.

Nightlife in Vienna

If powdered wigs and opera singers in Viking helmets aren't your thing, Vienna has plenty of alternatives. For an up-to-date rundown on fun after dark, check www.viennahype.at.

The Evening Scene

More than ever, Vienna has become a great place to just be out and about on a balmy evening. While tourists are attracted to the historic central district and its charming, floodlit corners, locals go elsewhere. Depending on your mood and taste, you can join them. Survey and then enjoy lively scenes with bars, cafés, trendy restaurants, and theaters in these areas: **Donaukanal** (the Danube Canal, especially popular in the summer for its imported beaches); **Naschmarkt** (after the produce stalls close up, the bars and eateries bring new life to the place through the evening; see page 79); **MuseumsQuartier** (surrounded by far-out museums, a young scene of bars with local students filling the courtyard; see page 73); and **City Hall** (on the park-like Rathausplatz, where in summer free concerts and a food circus of eateries attract huge local crowds—described next).

City Hall Open-Air Classical-Music Cinema and Food Circus

A thriving people scene erupts each evening in summer (July-Aug) at the park in front of City Hall (Rathaus, on the Ringstrasse). Thousands of people keep a food circus of 24 simple stalls busy. There's not a plastic cup anywhere, just real plates and glasses— Vienna wants the quality of eating to be as high as the music that's about to begin. About 2,000 folding chairs face a 60-foot-wide screen up against the City Hall's Neo-Gothic facade. When darkness falls, an announcer explains the program, and then the music starts. The program is different every night—mostly movies of opera and classical concerts, with some films. The TI has the schedule (programs generally last about 2 hours, starting when it's dark—between 21:30 in July and 20:30 in Aug).

Since 1991, the city has paid for 60 of these summer event nights each year. Why? To promote culture. Officials know that the City Hall Music Festival is mostly a "meat market" where young people come to hook up. But they believe many of these people will develop a little appreciation of classical music and high culture on the side.

English Cinema

Several great theaters offer three or four screens of English movies nightly (€6-9): **Burg Kino,** a block from the Opera, facing the Ring (see below), tapes its weekly schedule to the door—box office opens 30 minutes before each showing; **English Cinema Haydn,** near my recommended hotels on Mariahilfer Strasse (Mariahilfer

VIENNA

Strasse 57, tel. 01/587-2262, www.haydnkino.at); and **Artis International Cinema,** right in the town center a few minutes from the cathedral (Schultergasse 5, tel. 01/535-6570).

The Third Man at Burg Kino

This movie is set in 1949 Vienna—when it was divided, like Berlin, between the four victorious Allies. Reliving the cinematic tale of a divided city about to fall under Soviet rule and rife with smuggling is an enjoyable two-hour experience while in Vienna (€8, in English; 3-4 showings weekly—usually Friday evening, Sunday afternoon, and Tuesday early evening; Opernring 19, tel. 01/587-8406, www.burgkino.at).

Fans of the movie will enjoy a visit to the **Third Man Museum** (Dritte Mann Museum), the life's work of two enthusiasts who have lovingly collected a vast collection of artifacts about the film, postwar Vienna, and the movie's popularity around the world (€7.50, Sat only 14:00-18:00, or by appointment for *Third Man* nuts, private showings for groups, U4: Kettenbrückengasse, a long block south of the Naschmarkt at Pressgasse 25, tel. 01/586-4872, www.3mpc.net).

Sleeping in Vienna

As you move out from the middle of the city, hotel prices drop. My listings are in the old center (figure at least €100 for a decent double), along the likeable Mariahilfer Strasse (about €90), and near the Westbahnhof (about €70).

Book ahead for Vienna if you can, particularly for holidays. Business hotels have their highest rates in September and October, when it's peak convention time. Prices are also high right around New Year's Eve.

While few accommodations in Vienna are air-conditioned, you can generally get fans on request. Places with elevators often have a few stairs to climb, too. Viennese elevators can be confusing: In most of Europe, 0 is the ground floor, and 1 is the first floor up (our "second floor"). But in Vienna, elevators can also have floors P, U, M, and A before getting to 1—so floor 1 can actually be what we'd call the fifth floor.

For more tips on accommodations, see the "Sleeping" section in the Introduction.

Within the Ring, in the Old City Center

You'll pay extra to sleep in the atmospheric old center, but if you can afford it, staying here gives you the best classy Vienna experience.

$$$ Hotel am Stephansplatz is a four-star business hotel with 56 rooms. It's plush but not over-the-top, and reasonably priced for

Sleep Code

(€1 = about $1.30, country code: 43, area code: 01)
S = Single, **D** = Double/Twin, **T** = Triple, **Q** = Quad, **b** = bathroom, **s** = shower only, **t** = toilet only. English is spoken at each place. Unless otherwise noted, credit cards are accepted, rooms have no air conditioning, and breakfast is included.

To help you easily sort through these listings, I've divided the accommodations into three categories, based on the price for a double room with bath:

$$$ Higher Priced—Most rooms €130 or more.
$$ Moderately Priced—Most rooms between €75-130.
$ Lower Priced—Most rooms €75 or less.

Prices can change without notice; verify the hotel's current rates online or by email.

its sleek comfort and incredible location facing the cathedral. Every detail is modern and quality; breakfast is superb, with a view of the city waking up around the cathedral; and the staff is always ready with a friendly welcome (Sb-€180, Db-€210-250, prices vary with season and room size, prices shoot up during conventions—most often in Sept-Oct; generally less Fri-Sun, July-Aug, and in winter; extra bed-€50, children stay for free or very cheap, air-con, elevator, free Internet access and Wi-Fi, gym and sauna, Stephansplatz 9, U-1 or U-3: Stephansplatz, tel. 01/534-050, fax 01/5340-5710, www.hotelamstephansplatz.at, office@hotelamstephansplatz.at).

$$$ Hotel Pertschy, circling an old courtyard, is big and hotelesque. Its 56 huge rooms are elegantly creaky, with chandeliers and Baroque touches. Those on the courtyard are quietest (Sb-€95-114, Db-€140-170 depending on size, €20-30 cheaper off-season, extra bed-€36, non-smoking rooms, elevator, free Internet access and Wi-Fi, Habsburgergasse 5, U-1 or U-3: Stephansplatz, tel. 01/534-490, fax 01/534-4949, www.pertschy.com, pertschy@pertschy.com).

$$$ Pension Aviano is a peaceful, family-run place. It has 17 comfortable rooms with flowery carpet and other Baroque frills, all on the fourth floor above lots of old-center action (Sb-€104, Db-€148-169 depending on size, roughly €20-30 cheaper per room in July-Aug and Nov-March, ask about discount if you book direct and mention Rick Steves, extra bed-€25-33, non-smoking, fans, elevator, free Internet access and Wi-Fi, between Neuer Markt and Kärntner Strasse at Marco d'Avianogasse 1, tel. 01/512-8330, fax 01/5128-3306, www.secrethomes.at, aviano@secrethomes.at).

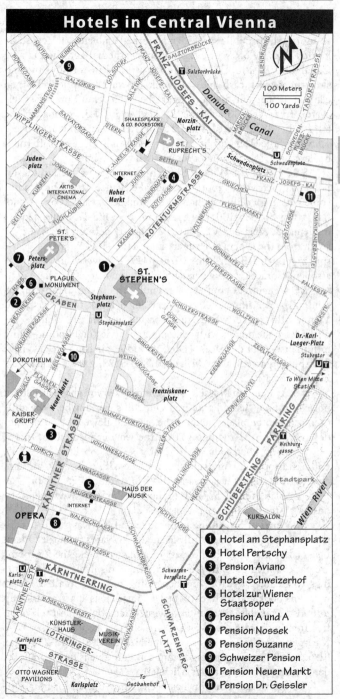

Hotels in Central Vienna

1. Hotel am Stephansplatz
2. Hotel Pertschy
3. Pension Aviano
4. Hotel Schweizerhof
5. Hotel zur Wiener Staatsoper
6. Pension A und A
7. Pension Nossek
8. Pension Suzanne
9. Schweizer Pension
10. Pension Neuer Markt
11. Pension Dr. Geissler

VIENNA

$$$ Hotel Schweizerhof is classy, with 55 big rooms, all the comforts, shiny public spaces, and a formal ambience. It's centrally located midway between St. Stephen's Cathedral and the Danube Canal (Sb-€85-100, Db-€120-160, low prices are for July-Aug and slow times, with cash and this book get your best price and then claim a 10 percent discount, extra bed-€35, grand breakfast, elevator, free Wi-Fi, Bauernmarkt 22, U-1 or U-3: Stephansplatz, tel. 01/533-1931, fax 01/533-0214, www.schweizerhof.at, office@schweizerhof.at). It can be noisy on weekends (Thu-Sat). If you'll be here then, ask for a quiet room when you reserve.

$$$ Hotel zur Wiener Staatsoper, the Schweizerhof's sister hotel, is quiet, with a more traditional elegance. Its 22 tidy rooms come with high ceilings, chandeliers, and fancy carpets on parquet floors (tiny Sb-€85-100, Db-€120-150, Tb-€135-175, rates depend on demand, extra bed-€25, fans on request, elevator, free Wi-Fi, a block from the Opera at Krugerstrasse 11; U-1, U-2, or U-4: Karlsplatz; tel. 01/513-1274, fax 01/513-127-415, www.zurwienerstaatsoper.at, office@zurwienerstaatsoper.at, manager Claudia).

$$ Pension A und A, a friendly nine-room B&B run by Andreas and Andrea, offers a sleek, mod break from crusty old Vienna. This place, wonderfully located just off the Graben, replaces Baroque doilies with contemporary style and blinding-white minimalist public spaces (Db-€100-150, air-con, free Wi-Fi, Habsburgergasse 3, floor M, tel. 01/890-5128, www.aunda.at, office@aunda.at).

$$ At Pension Nossek, an elevator takes you above any street noise into Frau Bernad and Frau Gundolf's world, where the children seem to be placed among the lace and flowers by an interior designer. With 32 rooms right on the wonderful Graben, this is a particularly good value (S-€52-60, Ss-€65, Sb-€85, Db-€125, €30 extra for sprawling suites, extra bed-€35, cash only, air-con, elevator, pay Internet access and Wi-Fi, Graben 17, U-1 or U-3: Stephansplatz, tel. 01/5337-0410, fax 01/535-3646, www.pension-nossek.at, reservation@pension-nossek.at).

$$ Pension Suzanne, as Baroque and doily as you'll find in this price range, is wonderfully located a few yards from the Opera. It's small, but run with the class of a bigger hotel. The 25 rooms are packed with properly Viennese antique furnishings and paintings (Sb-€88, Db-€106-136 depending on size, small discount with this book and cash, extra bed-€25, spacious apartment for up to 6 also available, discounts in winter, fans on request, elevator, free Internet access and Wi-Fi, Walfischgasse 4; U-1, U-2, or U-4: Karlsplatz and follow signs for Opera exit; tel. 01/513-2507, fax 01/513-2500, www.pension-suzanne.at, info@pension-suzanne.at, delightfully run by manager Michael).

$$ Schweizer Pension has been family-owned for four generations. Anita and her son Gerald offer lots of tourist info and 11 homey rooms for a great price, with parquet floors. True to its name, it feels very Swiss—tidy and well-run (S-€46-55, big Sb-€68-81, D-€68-79, Db-€89-98, Tb-€109-125, prices depend on season and room size, cash only, entirely non-smoking, elevator, free Wi-Fi, laundry-€18/load, Heinrichsgasse 2, U-2 or U-4: Schottenring, tel. 01/533-8156, fax 01/535-6469, www.schweizer-pension.com, schweizer.pension@chello.at). They also rent a quad with bath (€129-139—too small for 4 adults but great for a family of 2 adults/2 kids under age 15).

$$ Pension Neuer Markt is family-run, with 37 comfy but faded rooms in a perfectly central locale. Its hallways have the ambience of a cheap cruise ship (Ss-€70-80, Sb-€90-100, smaller Ds-€80-90, Db-€90-135, prices vary with season and room size, extra bed-€20, request a quiet room when you reserve, fans, elevator, free Internet access and Wi-Fi, Seilergasse 9, tel. 01/512-2316, fax 01/513-9105, www.hotelpension.at/neuermarkt, neuermarkt@hotelpension.at, Wolfgang).

$$ Pension Dr. Geissler has 23 plain-but-comfortable rooms in a modern, nondescript apartment building about 10 blocks northeast of St. Stephen's, near the canal (S-€48, Ss-€68, Sb-€76, D-€65, Ds-€77, Db-€95, 20 percent less in winter, elevator, Postgasse 14, U-1 or U-4: Schwedenplatz—Postgasse is to the left as you face Hotel Capricorno, tel. 01/533-2803, fax 01/533-2635, www.hotelpension.at/dr-geissler, dr.geissler@hotelpension.at).

On or near Mariahilfer Strasse

Lively Mariahilfer Strasse connects the Westbahnhof (West Station) and the city center. The U-3 line, starting at the Westbahnhof, goes down Mariahilfer Strasse to the cathedral. This tourist-friendly, vibrant area is filled with shopping malls, simpler storefronts, and cafés. Its smaller hotels and private rooms are generally run by people from the non-German-speaking part of the former Habsburg Empire (i.e., Eastern Europe). Most hotels are within a few steps of a U-Bahn stop, just one or two stops from the Westbahnhof (direction from the station: Simmering). The nearest place to do laundry is **Schnell & Sauber Waschcenter** (€4.50 to wash a small load or €9 for a large load, plus a few euros to dry, daily 6:00-23:00, a few blocks north of Westbahnhof on the east side of Urban-Loritz-Platz).

$$$ NH Atterseehaus Suites, part of a Spanish chain, is a stern, stylish-but-passionless business hotel on Mariahilfer Strasse. It rents ideal-for-families suites, each with a living room, two TVs, bathroom, desk, and kitchenette (rack rate: Db suite-€99-200, going rate usually closer to €110-125, €17/person for optional breakfast, apartments for 2-3 adults, 1 kid under 12 free,

VIENNA

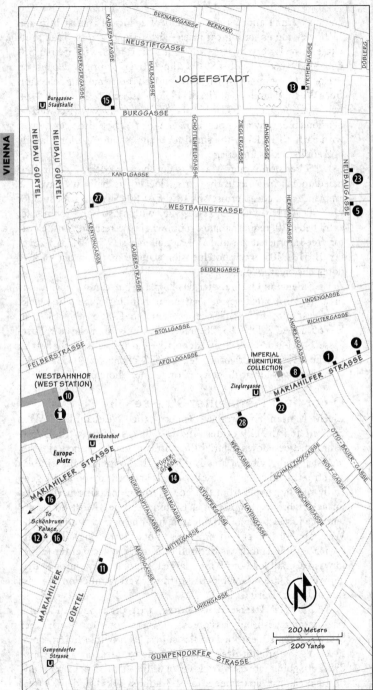

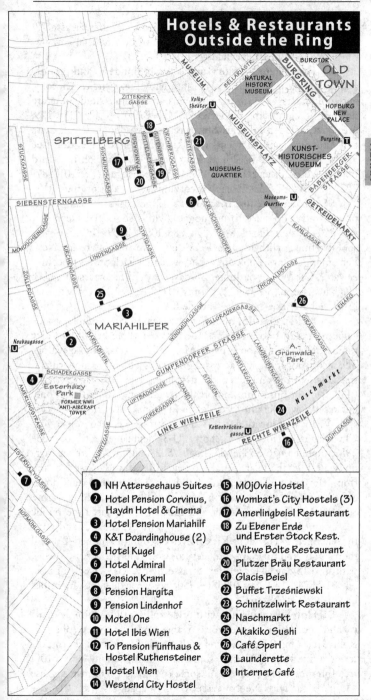

VIENNA

Hotels & Restaurants Outside the Ring

1. NH Atterseehaus Suites
2. Hotel Pension Corvinus, Haydn Hotel & Cinema
3. Hotel Pension Mariahilf
4. K&T Boardinghouse (2)
5. Hotel Kugel
6. Hotel Admiral
7. Pension Kraml
8. Pension Hargita
9. Pension Lindenhof
10. Motel One
11. Hotel Ibis Wien
12. To Pension Fünfhaus & Hostel Ruthensteiner
13. Hostel Wien
14. Westend City Hostel
15. MOjOvie Hostel
16. Wombat's City Hostels (3)
17. Amerlingbeisl Restaurant
18. Zu Ebener Erde und Erster Stock Rest.
19. Witwe Bolte Restaurant
20. Plutzer Bräu Restaurant
21. Glacis Beisl
22. Buffet Trześniewski
23. Schnitzelwirt Restaurant
24. Naschmarkt
25. Akakiko Sushi
26. Café Sperl
27. Launderette
28. Internet Café

non-smoking rooms, elevator, free Wi-Fi, Mariahilfer Strasse 78, U-3: Zieglergasse, tel. 01/524-5600, fax 01/524-560-015, www. nh-hotels.com, nhatterseehaus@nh-hotels.com).

VIENNA

$$ Hotel Pension Corvinus is bright, modern, and proudly and warmly run by a Hungarian family: Miklós, Judit, Anthony, and Zoltan. Its 12 comfortable rooms are spacious, and some are downright sumptuous (Sb-€69-79, Db-€99-109, Tb-€119-129, breakfast included for Rick Steves readers who book direct, extra bed-€26, also has apartments with kitchens, air-con, elevator, free Internet access and Wi-Fi, parking garage-€17/day, on the third floor at Mariahilfer Strasse 57-59, U-3: Neubaugasse, tel. 01/587-7239, fax 01/587-723-920, www.corvinus.at, hotel@corvinus.at).

$$ Hotel Pension Mariahilf's 12 rooms are clean, well-priced, and good-sized (if outmoded), with a slight Art Deco flair (Sb-€60-75, twin Db-€78-98, Db-€88-109, Tb-€99-139, 5-6-person apartment with kitchen-€129-169, lower prices are for Nov-Feb or longer stays, book direct and ask about Rick Steves discount, elevator, free Wi-Fi, parking-€18/day, Mariahilfer Strasse 49, U-3: Neubaugasse, tel. 01/586-1781, fax 01/586-178-122, www.maria-hilf-hotel.at, info@mariahilf-hotel.at.

$$ K&T Boardinghouse rents spacious, comfortable, good-value rooms in two locations. The first has three bright and airy rooms three flights above lively Mariahilfer Strasse (no elevator). The second location, just across the street, is a bit more modern and spacious, with five units on the first floor (Db-€79, Tb-€99, Qb-€119, 2-night minimum, no breakfast, air-con-€10/day, cash only but reserve with credit card, coffee in rooms, free Internet access and Wi-Fi; first location: Mariahilfer Strasse 72, second location: Chwallagasse 2; for either, get off at U-3: Neubaugasse; tel. 01/523-2989, mobile 0676-553-6063, fax 01/522-0345, www.ktboarding-house.at, k.t@chello.at, Tina). To reach the Chwallagasse location from Mariahilfer Strasse, turn left at Café Ritter and walk down Schadekgasse one short block; tiny Chwallagasse is the first right.

$$ Haydn Hotel is big and formal, with masculine public spaces and 50 spacious rooms (Sb-€90, Db-€120, suites and family apartments, ask about Rick Steves discount, extra bed-€30, all rooms non-smoking, air-con, elevator, free Internet access, Wi-Fi, parking-€15/day, Mariahilfer Strasse 57-59, U-3: Neubaugasse, tel. 01/5874-4140, fax 01/586-1950, www.haydn-hotel.at, info@haydn-hotel.at, Nouri).

$$ Hotel Kugel is run with pride and attitude. "Simple quality and good value" is the motto of the hands-on owner, Johannes Roller. It's a big 32-room hotel with simple Old World charm, offering a fine value (Db-€90, supreme Db with canopy beds-€100, free Internet access and Wi-Fi, some tram noise, Siebensterngasse 43, at corner with Neubaugasse, U-3: Neubaugasse, tel. 01/523-

3355, fax 01/5233-3555, www.hotelkugel.at, office@hotelkugel.at).
Herr Roller also offers several cheaper basic rooms for backpackers.

$$ Hotel Admiral is huge and practical, with 80 large, workable rooms. This last resort is on a dreary street across from a rowdy nightclub (request a quiet room), and lacks the charm and personality of my other listings (Sb-€70, Db-€94, mention this book for these special prices, cheaper in winter, extra bed-€25, breakfast-€6/person, free Internet access and Wi-Fi; limited free parking is first-come, first-served—otherwise €12/day; a block off Mariahilfer Strasse at Karl-Schweighofer-Gasse 7, U-2 or U-3: Volkstheater, tel. 01/521-410, fax 01/521-4116, www.admiral.co.at, hotel@admiral.co.at).

$ Pension Kraml is a charming, 17-room place tucked away on a small street between Mariahilfer Strasse and the Naschmarkt. It's family-run and old school, with a typical 1950s-style Viennese breakfast room, no elevator, lots of stairs, big quiet homey rooms, and an Old-World elegance (D-€56, Ds or Dt-€66, Db-€76, extra bed-€23, family apartment available, free Wi-Fi, midway between U-3: Zieglergasse and U-4: Pilgramgasse at Brauergasse 5, tel. 01/587-8588, www.pensionkraml.at, pension.kraml@chello.at).

$ Pension Hargita rents 19 generally small, bright, and tidy rooms (mostly twins) with Hungarian woody-village decor. While the pension is directly on bustling Mariahilfer Strasse, its windows block noise well. This spick-and-span, well-located place is a great value (S-€40, Ss-€47, Sb-€57, D-€54, Ds-€60, tiny Db-€65, Db-€68, Ts-€75, Tb-€82, Qb-€114, reserve with credit card but pay with cash to get these rates, extra bed-€12, breakfast-€5, completely non-smoking, lots of stairs and no elevator, free Internet access, Wi-Fi, corner of Mariahilfer Strasse at Andreasgasse 1, U-3: Zieglergasse, tel. 01/526-1928, fax 01/526-0492, www.hargita.at, pension@hargita.at, Erika and Tibor).

$ Pension Lindenhof rents 19 very basic, very worn but clean rooms. It's a dark and mysteriously dated time warp filled with plants (and a fun guest-generated postcard wall); the stark rooms have outrageously high ceilings and teeny bathrooms (S-€30, Sb-€35, D-€54, Db-€72, T-€81, Tb-€100, Q-€108, Qb-€144, cheaper during slow times, hall shower-€3, cash only, elevator, next door to a harmless strip bar at Lindengasse 4, U-3: Neubaugasse, tel. 01/523-0498, fax 01/523-7362, www.pensionlindenhof.at, pensionlindenhof@yahoo.com, run by Gebrael family).

Near the Westbahnhof (West Station)

$$ Motel One, a German chain that seems ready to take on the hotel world, surveyed business customers and offers only what they want to pay for. The result is what the chain calls a "low-budget design hotel": 440 sleek and modern rooms, built cruise-ship tight with quality materials but no frills, 24-hour reception but minimal service, and refreshingly straightforward pricing (Sb-€72, Db-€87, no triples but you can slip in a child up to age 15 for free, breakfast-€7.50, free Wi-Fi in lounge and in room if you buy breakfast, air-con, attached to the Westbahnhof at Europaplatz 3, tel. 01/359-350, www.motel-one.com, wein-westbahnhof@motel-one.com).

$$ Hotel Ibis Wien, a modern high-rise hotel with American charm, is ideal for anyone tired of quaint old Europe. Its 340 cookie-cutter rooms are bright, comfortable, and modern, with all the conveniences (Sb-€69-75, Db-€87-93, Tb-€106, breakfast-€11, air-con, elevator, free Internet access and Wi-Fi, parking garage-€13/day; exit Westbahnhof to the right and walk 400 yards, Mariahilfer Gürtel 22-24, U-3: Westbahnhof; tel. 01/59998, fax 01/597-9090, www.ibishotel.com, h0796@accor.com).

$ Pension Fünfhaus is big, plain, clean, and bare-bones—almost institutional—with tile floors. The neighborhood is run-down (with a few ladies loitering late at night), but this 47-room pension offers the best doubles you'll find for the price (S-€34, Sb-€43, D-€49, Db-€60, Tb-€84-92, 4-person apartment-€104, cash only, closed mid-Nov-Feb, includes basic breakfast, Sperrgasse 12, U-3: Westbahnhof, tel. 01/892-3545 or 01/892-0286, fax 01/892-0460, www.pension5haus.at, vienna@pension5haus.at, Frau Susi Tersch). Half the rooms are in the main building and half are in the annex, which has good rooms but is near the train tracks and a bit scary on the street at night. From the station, ride tram #52 or #58 two stops down Mariahilfer Strasse away from center, and ask for Sperrgasse.

Cheap Dorms and Hostels near Mariahilfer Strasse

$ Hostel Wien is your classic huge and well-run youth hostel, with 260 beds (€17-21/person in 2- to 6-bed rooms, price depends on season, includes sheets and breakfast, nonmembers pay €3.50 extra, pay Internet access, free Wi-Fi in lobby, always open, no curfew, lockers and lots of facilities, coin-op laundry, Myrthengasse 7, tel. 01/523-6316, fax 01/523-5849, hostel@chello.at).

$ Westend City Hostel, just a block from the Westbahnhof and Mariahilfer Strasse, is well-run and well-located in a residential neighborhood, so it's quiet after 20:00. It has a small lounge and 180 beds in 4- to 12-bed dorms (€22-29/person depending on season and how many in the room, Db-€66-92, cheaper Nov-mid-March—except around New Year's; includes sheets and locker, breakfast included when you book direct, cash only, pay Internet access, free Wi-Fi, laundry-€7, Fügergasse 3, tel. 01/597-6729, fax 01/597-672-927, www.westendhostel.at, info@westendhostel.at).

$ MOjOvie is a creative "little neighbourette," combining a residential apartment feel with a hostel vibe. This network of apartments offers dorm beds as well as private units sleeping two to four (dorm bed–€20, €23-26/person in a private room with shared bathroom, €35-45/person for apartment with private bathroom, includes sheets and towels, cash only for charges under €100, free Wi-Fi, laundry service, shared kitchen, reception open 8:00-23:00, Kaiserstrasse 77, tram #5 or a 10-minute walk from Westbahnhof, mobile 0676-551-1155, www.mymojovie.at, accommodation@mymojovie.at).

$ More Hostels: Other hostels with €18-22 beds and €60-70 doubles near Mariahilfer Strasse are **Wombat's City Hostel** (3 well-run locations—each with about 250 beds, 4-6 beds/room, lockers, bar, free Wi-Fi, and generous public spaces: one near tracks behind the station at Grangasse 6, another even closer to station at Mariahilfer Strasse 137, and one near the Naschmarkt at Rechte Wienzeile 35; tel. 01/897-2336, www.wombats-hostels.com, office@wombats-vienna.at) and **Hostel Ruthensteiner** (smoke-free; leave the Westbahnhof to the right and follow Mariahilfer Strasse behind the station, then left on Haidmannsgasse for a block, then turn right and find Robert-Hamerling-Gasse 24; tel. 01/893-4202, www.hostelruthensteiner.com, info@hostelruthensteiner.com).

Eating in Vienna

The Viennese appreciate the fine points of life, and right up there with waltzing is eating. The city has many atmospheric restaurants (and many offer a *"menu,"* a fixed-price bargain meal, at lunchtime). As you ponder the Eastern European specialties on menus, remember that Vienna's diverse empire may be no more, but its flavors linger.

While cuisines are routinely named for countries, Vienna claims to be the only *city* with a cuisine of its own: Vienna soups come with fillings (semolina dumpling, liver dumpling, or pancake slices). *Gulasch* is a beef ragout based on a traditional Hungarian shepherd's soup (spiced with onion and paprika). Of course, Wiener schnitzel is traditionally a breaded and fried veal cutlet (though pork is more common these days). Another meat specialty is boiled beef *(Tafelspitz)*. While you're sure to have *Apfelstrudel,* try *Topfenstrudel,* too (wafer-thin strudel-pastry filled with sweet cheese and raisins). The *dag* you see in some prices stands for "decigram" (10 grams). Therefore, *10 dag* is 100 grams, or about a quarter-pound.

On nearly every corner, you can find a colorful *Beisl* (BYE-zul). These uniquely Viennese taverns are a characteristic cross between an English pub and a French brasserie—filled with poetry teachers and their students, couples loving without touching, housewives on their way home from cello lessons, and waiters who enjoy serving hearty food and drinks at an affordable price. Ask at your hotel for a good *Beisl*. (Beware: Despite non-smoking laws, *Beisls* may still be quite smoky; fortunately, most have outdoor seating.

For hardcore Viennese cuisine, drop by a *Würstelstand*. The local hot-dog stand is a fixture on city squares throughout the old center, serving a variety of hot dogs and pickled side dishes with a warm corner-meeting-place atmosphere. Be adventurous: Generally, the darker the weenie, the spicier it is. Key words: Key words: *Weisswurst*—boiled white sausage; *Bosna*—with onions and curry; *Käsekrainer*—with melted cheese inside; *Debreziner*—spicy Hungarian; *Frankfurter*—our weenie; *frische*—fresh; *Kren*—horseradish; and *Senf*—mustard (ask for *süss*—sweet, or *scharf*—sharp). Only a tourist puts the sausage in a bun like a hot dog. Munch alternately between the meat and the bread ("that's why you have two hands"), and you'll look like a native.

Two other don't-miss Viennese institutions, its cafés and wine gardens, are covered under "Experiences in Vienna" on page 93.

Near St. Stephen's Cathedral

Each of these eateries is within about a five-minute walk of the cathedral (U-1 or U-3: Stephansplatz).

Gigerl Stadtheuriger offers a fun, near-*Heuriger* wine cellar experience without leaving the city center. Just point to what looks good. Food is sold by the piece or weight; 100 grams *(10 dag)* is about a quarter-pound (cheese and cold meats cost about €3 per 100 grams, salads are about €2 per 100 grams; price sheet posted on wall to right of buffet line). The *Karree* pork with herbs is particularly tasty and tender. They also have entrées, spinach strudel, quiche, *Apfelstrudel*, and, of course, casks of new and local wines (sold by the *Achtel*, about 4 oz). Meals run €7-12 (daily 15:00-24:00, indoor/outdoor seating, behind cathedral, a block off Kärntner Strasse, a few cobbles off Rauhensteingasse on Blumenstock, tel. 01/513-4431).

Zu den Drei Hacken, another fun and typical *Weinstube*, is famous for its local specialties (€10 plates, Mon-Sat 11:00-23:00, closed Sun, indoor/outdoor seating, Singerstrasse 28, tel. 01/512-5895).

Buffet Trześniewski is an institution—justly famous for its elegant and cheap finger sandwiches and small beers (€1 each). Three different sandwiches and a *kleines Bier (Pfiff)* make a fun, light lunch. Point to whichever delights look tasty (or grab the English translation sheet and take time to study your 22 sandwich options). The classic favorites are *Geflügelleber* (chicken liver), *Matjes mit Zwiebel* (herring with onions), and *Speck mit Ei* (bacon and eggs). Pay for your sandwiches and a drink. Take your drink tokens to the lady on the right. Sit on the bench and scoot over to a tiny table when a spot opens up. Trześniewski has been a Vienna favorite for more than a century...and many of its regulars seem to have been here for the grand opening. You can grab an early quick dinner here, but the selection can get paltry by the end of the day (Mon-Fri 8:30-19:30, Sat 9:00-17:00, closed Sun; 50 yards off the Graben, nearly across from brooding Café Hawelka, Dorotheergasse 2; tel. 01/512-3291). In the fall, this is a good opportunity to try the fancy grape juices—*Most* or *Traubenmost*. Their other locations—at Mariahilfer Strasse 95 (near many recommended hotels, Mon-Fri 8:30-19:00, Sat 9:00-18:00, closed Sun, U-3: Zieglergasse, tel. 01/596-4291) and in the Westbahnhof train station (near the tracks, Mon-Fri 7:00-23:00, Sat-Sun 8:00-23:00, U-3: Westbahnhof, tel. 01/982-2975)—serve the same sandwiches with the same menu but without the historic ambience.

Reinthaler's Beisl is a time warp that serves simple, traditional *Beisl* fare all day. It's handy for its location (a block off the Graben, across the street from Buffet Trześniewski) and because it's a rare restaurant in the center that's open on Sunday. Its fun, classic interior winds way back, and it also has a few tables on the quiet street outside (use the handwritten daily menu rather than the printed English one, €6-12 plates, daily 11:00-22:30, at Dorotheergasse 4, tel. 01/513-1249).

Cantinetta La Norma, a short walk from the cathedral, serves fresh, excellent Italian dishes amid a cozy, yet energetic ambience. Even on weeknights the small dining area is abuzz with friendly chatter among its multinational, loyal regulars (€8 pizzas and pastas, €7-18 entrées, lunch specials, daily 11:00-24:00, outdoor seating, Franziskaner Platz 3, tel. 01/512-8665, run by friendly Paco and Hany).

Gyros is a humble little Greek/Turkish joint run by Yilmaz, a fun-loving Turk from Izmir. He simply loves to feed people—the food is great, the prices are decent, and you almost feel like you took a quick trip to Istanbul (€8-12 plates, Mon-Sat 10:00-23:00, closed Sun, a long block off Kärntner Strasse at corner of Fichtegasse and Seilerstätte, mobile 0699-1016-3726).

Akakiko Sushi is a small chain of Japanese restaurants with an easy pan-Asian menu that's worth considering if you're just schnitzeled out. They serve sushi, of course, but also noodles, stir-fry, and other meals. The €11 bento box meals are a decent value. There are several convenient locations: Singerstrasse 4 (a block off Kärntner Strasse near the cathedral), Rotenturmgasse 6 (also near the cathedral), Heidenschuss 3 (near other recommended eateries just off Am Hof, U-3: Herrengasse), and Mariahilfer Strasse 42-48 (fifth floor of Kaufhaus Gerngross, near many recommended ho-

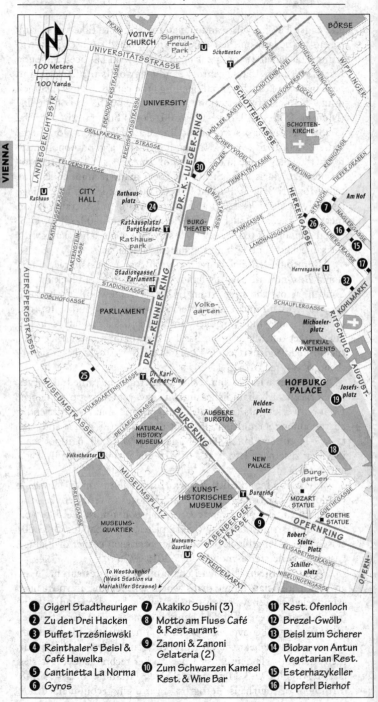

1 Gigerl Stadtheuriger
2 Zu den Drei Hacken
3 Buffet Trześniewski
4 Reinthaler's Beisl & Café Hawelka
5 Cantinetta La Norma
6 Gyros
7 Akakiko Sushi (3)
8 Motto am Fluss Café & Restaurant
9 Zanoni & Zanoni Gelateria (2)
10 Zum Schwarzen Kameel Rest. & Wine Bar
11 Rest. Ofenloch
12 Brezel-Gwölb
13 Beisl zum Scherer
14 Biobar von Antun Vegetarian Rest.
15 Esterhazykeller
16 Hopferl Bierhof

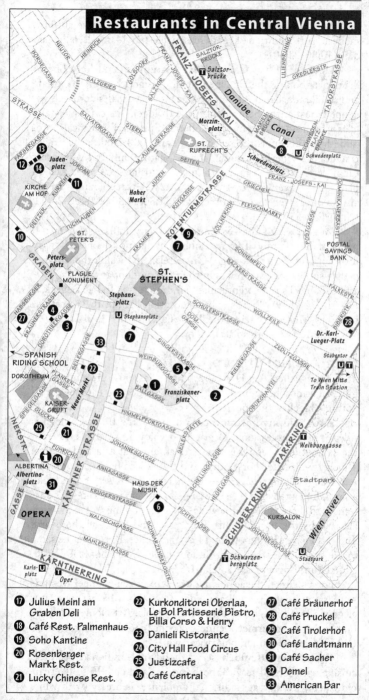

Restaurants in Central Vienna

VIENNA

17 Julius Meinl am Graben Deli
18 Café Rest. Palmenhaus
19 Soho Kantine
20 Rosenberger Markt Rest.
21 Lucky Chinese Rest.

22 Kurkonditorei Oberlaa, Le Bol Patisserie Bistro, Billa Corso & Henry
23 Danieli Ristorante
24 City Hall Food Circus
25 Justizcafe
26 Café Central

27 Café Bräunerhof
28 Café Pruckel
29 Café Tirolerhof
30 Café Landtmann
31 Café Sacher
32 Demel
33 American Bar

tels, U-3: Neubaugasse). Though they lack charm, these are fast, modern, air-conditioned, and reasonable (€8-14 meals, all open daily 10:30-23:30).

Motto am Fluss Café and Restaurant is good for a bite or drink overlooking the Danube Canal. The modern, shipshape café and restaurant share space on a barge moored canal-side at Schwedenplatz just at the Schwedenbrücke (bridge). The café is upstairs (classy on the deck and inside, moderately priced simple meals from same fine kitchen as the restaurant, daily 8:00-24:00); the pricier restaurant is one floor down (indoor seating only but with great canal-perch tables, elegant with modern cuisine—€3 cover, €15-20 plates, extensive wine-by-the-glass list, €21-three-course specials always offer a vegetarian entrée, daily 11:30-14:30 & 18:00-24:00, tel. 01/252-5510).

Ice Cream!: **Zanoni & Zanoni** is a very Italian *gelateria* run by an Italian family. They're mobbed by happy Viennese hungry for their huge €2 cones to go. Or, to relax and watch the thriving people scene, lick your gelato in their fun outdoor area (daily 7:00-24:00, 2 blocks up Rotenturmstrasse from cathedral at Lugeck 7, tel. 01/512-7979). There's another location behind the Kunsthistorisches Museum, facing the Ring (at Burgring 1, U-2 or U-3: Volkstheater/Museumsplatz).

Near Am Hof Square

The square called Am Hof (U-3: Herrengasse) is surrounded by a maze of atmospheric medieval lanes; the following eateries are all within a block of the square.

Zum Schwarzen Kameel Wine Bar ("The Black Camel") is filled with a professional local crowd enjoying small plates from the same kitchen as their fancy restaurant, but at a better price. This is *the* place for horseradish and thin-sliced ham (*Beinschinken mit Kren,* €10/plate, *Achtung*—the horseradish is *hot*). Stand, grab a stool, find a table on the street, or sit anywhere you can—it's customary to share tables in the wine-bar section. Fine Austrian wines are sold by the *Achtel* (eighth-liter glass) and listed on the board. They also have a buffet of tiny €1-2 sandwiches. Prices are the same inside or at their street-side outdoor tables (Mon-Sat 8:30-24:00, closed Sun, Bognergasse 5, tel. 01/533-8125).

For a splurge, the adjacent **Zum Schwarzen Kameel Restaurant** (same hours, phone, and address as the wine bar) is a tiny, elegant alternative. The dark-wood, 12-table, Art Nouveau restaurant serves fine gourmet Viennese cuisine (€36 three-course lunch, €80 four-course dinner, plus pricey wine.

Restaurant Ofenloch serves good, old-fashioned Viennese cuisine with formal service, both indoors and out. This 300-year-old eatery, with great traditional ambience, is dressy (with white tablecloths) but intimate and woodsy (€14 lunch specials; €15-19 main courses—meat, fish, and vegetarian; Mon-Sat 11:00-22:30, closed Sun, Kurrentgasse 8, tel. 01/533-8844).

Brezel-Gwölb, a Tolkienesque wine cellar with outdoor dining on a quiet square, serves forgettable food in an unforgettable atmosphere. It's ideal for a romantic late-night glass of wine (daily 11:30-23:30; leave Am Hof on Drahtgasse, then take first left to Ledererhof 9; tel. 01/533-8811).

Beisl zum Scherer, around the corner, is untouristy and serves traditional plates for €8-20. Sitting outside, you'll face a stern Holocaust memorial. Inside comes with a soothing woody atmosphere and intriguing decor. It's named for a pre-World War I satirical newspaper that was published here. Let friendly Sakis explain the daily specials—which don't show up on the English menu (Mon-Sat 11:30-22:00, closed Sun, Judenplatz 7, tel. 01/533-5164).

Biobar von Antun Vegetarian Restaurant is a cheery and earthy little place with an €8 or €11 lunch special and hearty €10 salads, plenty of vegan options, and the fancy juices you'd expect (daily 12:00-23:00, on Judenplatz at Drahtgasse 3, tel. 01/968-9351).

Esterhazykeller, both ancient and popular, has traditional fare deep underground. For a cheap and sloppy buffet, climb down to the lowest level. This wine cellar, which dates back to 1683, comes with a hearty deli counter. While the food is self-serve (a meal-sized plate costs around €10), you'll order drinks at your table. For table service from a pricier menu on a pleasant square, sit outside (Mon-Sat 11:00-23:00, Sun 16:00-23:00, may close for lunch in Aug-Sept and/or in bad weather, just below Am Hof at Haarhof 1, tel. 01/533-3482).

The outdoor seating at **Hopferl Bierhof** on the same square might be a better option if it's hot and you're in the mood for a beer. It can offer a heartier value and nicer ambience (daily 11:30-24:00, Naglergasse 13, tel. 01/533-2641).

Julius Meinl am Graben, a posh supermarket with two floors of temptations right on the Graben, has been famous since 1862 as a top-end delicatessen with all the gourmet fancies. Assemble a meal from the picnic fixings on the shelves. There's also a café, with light meals and great outdoor seating; a stuffy and pricey restaurant upstairs; and a take-out counter with good benches for people-watching while you munch (shop open Mon-Fri 8:00-19:30, Sat 9:00-18:00, closed Sun; restaurant open Mon-Sat until 24:00, closed Sun; Am Graben 19, tel. 01/532-3334).

Near the Opera

These eateries are within easy walking distance of the Opera (U-1, U-2, or U-4: Karlsplatz).

VIENNA

Café Restaurant Palmenhaus overlooks the Palace Garden (Burggarten—see page 66). Tucked away in a green and peaceful corner two blocks behind the Opera in the Hofburg's backyard, this is a world apart. If you want to eat modern Austrian cuisine surrounded by palm trees rather than tourists, this is the place. And, since it's at the edge of a huge park, it's great for families. Their fresh fish with generous vegetables specials are on the board (€9 lunch plates available Mon-Fri, €15-18 entrées, open daily 10:00-24:00, serious vegetarian dishes, fish, extensive fine-wine list, indoors in greenhouse or outdoors, Burggarten 1, tel. 01/533-1033).

Soho Kantine is a grim, government-subsidized cantina serving the National Library and offering the best cheap, sit-down lunches in the Hofburg. Pay for your meal—your choice of bland meat or bland vegetarian—and a drink at the bar, take your token to the kitchen, and then sit down and eat with the locals (€6 two-course lunch, Mon-Fri 11:30-15:00, closed Sat-Sun and Aug, hard to find on ground floor of library—opposite the butterflies in a forlorn little square with no sign, Burggarten, Josefsplatz 1, tel. 01/532-8566, mobile 0676-309-5161).

Rosenberger Markt Restaurant is mobbed with tour groups. Still, if you don't mind a freeway-cafeteria ambience in the center of the German-speaking world's classiest city, this self-service eatery is fast and easy. It's just a block toward the cathedral from the Opera. The best cheap meal here is a small salad or veggie plate stacked high (daily 10:30-23:00, lots of fruits, veggies, fresh-squeezed juices, addictive banana milk, ride the glass elevator downstairs, Maysedergasse 2, tel. 01/512-3458).

Lucky Chinese Restaurant is simply a good, modern, and well-located option for Chinese food. The inside is fresh and air-conditioned, the outside seating is on a great square, and the service is friendly (€10-15 plates, daily 11:30-23:00, Neuer Markt 8, tel. 01/512-3428). While this spot is handy, you'll enjoy better Chinese and Asian food at the Naschmarkt (described later).

Kurkonditorei Oberlaa may not have the royal and plush fame of Demel (see page 43), but this is where Viennese connoisseurs serious about the quality of their pastries go to get fat. With outdoor seating on Neuer Markt, it's particularly nice on a hot summer day. Upstairs has more temptations and good seating (€10 daily three-course lunches, great selection of cakes, daily 8:00-20:00, Neuer Markt 16, other locations about town, including the Naschmarkt, tel. 01/5132-9360).

Le Bol Patisserie Bistro (next to Oberlaa) satisfies your need for something French. The staff speaks to you in French, serving fine €8 salads, baguette sandwiches, and fresh croissants (Mon-Sat 8:00-22:00, Sun 10:00-20:00, Neuer Markt 14).

Billa Corso is a top-end member of the Billa supermarket chain. This location sells hot gourmet ready-made foods (by weight) with its restaurant partner called **Henry.** You're welcome to sit and enjoy whatever you've purchased in either eating area: inside (air-conditioned) and out on the square. They also have a great deli selection of salads, soups, and picnic items (warm food €1.80/100 grams, WC on ground floor, Mon-Sat 8:00-20:00, closed Sun, Neuer Markt 17, on the corner where Seilergasse hits Neuer Markt, tel. 01/961-2133).

Danieli Ristorante is your best classy Italian bet in the old town. White-tablecloth dressy, but not stuffy, it has reasonable prices. Dine in their elegant back room or on the street (€13-18 pizzas and pastas, €18-25 main courses, fresh fish specialties, daily 10:00-24:00, 30 yards off Kärntner Strasse opposite Neuer Markt at Himmelpfortgasse 3, tel. 01/513-7913).

City Hall Food Circus

During the summer, scores of outdoor food stands and hundreds of picnic tables are set up in the park in front of the City Hall (Rathausplatz). Local mobs enjoy mostly ethnic meals for decent-but-not-cheap prices and classical entertainment on a big screen. The fun thing here is the energy of the crowd and a feeling that you're truly eating as the Viennese do...not schnitzel and quaint traditions, but trendy "world food" with young people out having fun in a fine Vienna park setting (July-Aug daily from 11:00 until late, in front of City Hall on the Ringstrasse, U-2: Rathaus).

Just West of the Ring

Justizcafe, the cafeteria serving Austria's Supreme Court of Justice, offers a fine view, great prices, and a memorable lunchtime experience—even if the food is somewhat bland. Enter the Palace of Justice through its grand front door, pass through tight security (no guns), say "wow" to the Historicist architecture in the courtyard, and ride the elevator to the rooftop. You can sit behind the windows inside or dine outside on the roof, enjoying one of the best views of Vienna while surrounded by legal beagles—go early or late to miss the crush (€8-12 main dishes, Mon-Fri 11:00-14:30, closed Sat-Sun, Schmerlingplatz 10, U-2 or U-3: Volkstheater/Museumsplatz, mobile 0676-755-6100).

Spittelberg Quarter

Spittelberg has a rare-in-Vienna Prague-like ambiance. Most of the city's architecture dates from 1880 to 1910, when the population exploded. But the Spittelberg quarter dates from before 1880. This charming cobbled grid of traffic-free lanes and Biedermeier apartments has become a favorite neighborhood for Viennese wanting

VIENNA

a little dining charm between the MuseumsQuartier and Maria-hilfer Strasse (handy to many recommended hotels; take Stiftgasse from Mariahilfer Strasse, or wander over here after you close down the Kunsthistorisches Museum; U-2 or U-3: Volkstheater/Museumsplatz). Tables tumble down sidewalks and into breezy courtyards filled with appreciative natives enjoying dinner or a relaxing drink. It's only worth the trip on a balmy summer evening, as it's dead in bad weather. Stroll Spittelberggasse, Schrankgasse, and Gutenberggasse, then pick your favorite. Don't miss the vine-strewn wine garden at Schrankgasse 1. To locate these restaurants, see the map on page 109.

Amerlingbeisl, with a charming, casual atmosphere both on the cobbled street and in its vine-covered courtyard, is a great value, serving a mix of traditional Austrian and international dishes (always a €7 vegetarian daily special, other specials for €6-10, €9-14 dinners, daily 9:00-2:00 in the morning, Stiftgasse 8, tel. 01/526-1660).

Zu Ebener Erde und Erster Stock ("Downstairs, Upstairs") is a charming little restaurant with a near-gourmet menu. True to its name, it has two distinct eating zones (with the same menu): a casual, woody bistro downstairs (traditionally the quarters of the poor); and a fancy Biedermeier-style dining room with red-velvet chairs and violet tablecloths upstairs (where the wealthy convened). There are also a few al fresco tables out front. Reservations are smart (€10-19 main dishes, €25 traditional three-course fixed-price meal, seasonal specials, Mon-Fri 7:30-21:30, last seating at 20:00, closed Sat-Sun, Burggasse 13, tel. 01/523-6254).

Witwe Bolte is classy and a good choice for uninspired Viennese cuisine with tablecloths. The interior is tight, but its tiny square has wonderful leafy ambience (€11-17 main dishes, daily 11:30-23:30 except closed 15:00-17:30 mid-Jan-mid-March, Gutenberggasse 13, tel. 01/523-1450).

Plutzer Bräu, next door to Amerlingbeisl, feels a bit more touristy. It's a big, sprawling, impersonal brewpub serving stick-to-your-ribs pub grub (€7-9 vegetarian dishes, €9-20 meals, ribs, burgers, traditional dishes, Tirolean beer from the keg, also brew their own, daily 11:00-2:00 in the morning, food until 24:00, Schrankgasse 4, tel. 01/526-1215).

Glacis Beisl, located at the top edge of the MuseumsQuartier just before Spittelberg, is popular with locals. Tucked away in a gravelly wine garden atop a city fortification, it's particularly appealing on a balmy evening, when locals fill the rickety outdoor tables to enjoy good €15 plates and the breezy ambience (daily 11:00-24:00, Breitegasse 4, tel. 01/526-5660).

Mariahilfer Strasse and the Naschmarkt

Mariahilfer Strasse (see map on page 109) is filled with reasonable cafés serving all types of cuisine. For a quick yet traditional bite, consider the venerable **Buffet Trześniewski** sandwich bar at Mariahilfer Strasse 95.

Schnitzelwirt is an old classic with a 1950s patina and a clientele to match. In this smoky, working-class place, no one finishes their schnitzel ("to-go" for the dog is wrapped in newspaper, "to-go" for you is wrapped in foil). You'll find no tourists, just cheap €6-11 schnitzel meals (Mon-Sat 10:00-23:00, closed Sun, Neubaugasse 52, U-3: Neubaugasse, tel. 01/523-3771).

For a picnic or a trendy dinner, try the **Naschmarkt,** Vienna's sprawling produce market. This thriving Old World scene comes with plenty of fresh produce, cheap local-style eateries, cafés, kebab and sausage stands, and the best-value sushi in town (Mon-Fri 6:00-18:30, Sat 6:00-17:00, closed Sun, closes earlier in winter; U-1, U-2, or U-4: Karlsplatz, follow *Karlsplatz* signs out of the station). Picnickers can buy supplies at the market and eat on nearby Karlsplatz (plenty of chairs facing the Karlskirche) or pop into the Burggarten behind the famous Mozart statue.

In recent years, the Naschmarkt has become fashionable for dinner (or cocktails), with an amazing variety of local and ethnic eateries to choose from. Prices are great, the produce is certainly fresh, and the dinners are as local as can be. The best plan: Stroll through the entire market to survey the many options, and then pick the place that appeals. For more on the Naschmarkt, see page 79.

Vienna Connections

By Train

Remember, Vienna has several train stations, the biggest of which are undergoing an extensive renovation. Be sure you know which station your train departs from; see page 28 for the basic rundown, but always confirm locally. For general train information in Austria, call 051-717 (to get an operator, dial 2, then 2), or visit www.oebb.at.

From Vienna by Train to: Salzburg (3/hour, 2.5-3 hours), **Hallstatt** (hourly, 4 hours, change in Attnang-Puchheim), **Innsbruck** (almost hourly, 5 hours), **Budapest** (every 2 hours direct, 3 hours; more with transfers; may be cheaper by Orange Ways bus: 3-4/day, 3 hours, www.orangeways.com), **Prague** (6/day direct, 4.75 hours; more with 1 change, 5-6 hours; 1 night train, 6 hours), **Munich** (6/day direct, 4.25 hours; otherwise about hourly, 5-5.75 hours, transfer in Salzburg or Plattling), **Berlin** (9/day, most with 1 change, 9.5 hours, some via Czech Republic; longer on night train), **Zürich** (nearly hourly, 9-10 hours, 1 with changes in Innsbruck and Feldkirch, night train), **Ljubljana** (1 convenient early-morning train, 6 hours; otherwise 7/day with change in Villach, Maribor, or Graz, 6-7 hours), **Kraków** (5/day, 8—10.5 hours with 1-3 changes, plus a night train), **Rome** (3/day, 12-13 hours, plus several overnight options), **Venice** (3/day, 8-9.5 hours with changes—some may involve bus connection; plus 1 direct night train, 12 hours), **Frankfurt** (6/day direct, 7 hours; plus 1 direct night train, 10 hours), **Paris** (7/day, 12-13 hours, 1-3 changes), **Amsterdam** (2/day, 11-12 hours, 1-2 changes).

To Prague and Budapest: Vienna is the springboard for a quick trip to these two magnificent cities—it's three hours by train to Budapest and about five hours to Prague (including a Prague night train, leaves Westbahnhof around 22:00). Americans and Canadians do not need visas to enter the Czech Republic or Hungary. Purchase tickets at the station or at most travel agencies.

By Plane
Vienna International Airport, 12 miles from the center, has easy connections to Vienna's various train stations (airport code: VIE, airport tel. 01/700-722-233, www.viennaairport.com).

Two different trains transport airport passengers into Vienna. Both go to the same point in the city center: the Wien-Mitte Bahnhof, on the east side of the Ring (adjacent to the Landstrasse U-Bahn stop, with a handy connection to Mariahilfer Strasse hotels and other accommodations neighborhoods). The main differences between them are time and cost. The **S-Bahn** commuter train (S-7 yellow line) works just fine and is plenty fast (€4, 2/hour, 24 minutes, buy 2-zone ticket from machines on the platform, price includes any bus or S- or U-Bahn transfers). The fast **CAT** (City Airport Train) takes a third less time but costs triple (€12, €13.50 includes a ride to your final destination on Vienna's transit system, 2/hour, usually departs at :05 and :35, 16 minutes, www.cityairporttrain.com).

Convenient express airport **buses** go to various points in Vienna: Morzinplatz/Schwedenplatz U-Bahn station (for city-center hotels), Westbahnhof (for Mariahilfer Strasse hotels), and Wien-Meidling Bahnhof. To reach these buses from the arrivals hall, go outside and to your left (note destination and times on curbside TV monitors; €8, 2/hour, generally 30 minutes, buy ticket from driver, tel. 0810-222-333 for timetable info, www.postbus.at).

The 30-minute ride into town by **taxi** costs about €35-40 (including the €11 airport surcharge).

Bratislava Airport (Letisko Bratislava)
Bratislava Airport is six miles northeast of downtown Bratislava

(www.letiskobratislava.sk). The airport offers budget flights on low-cost carriers Ryanair (www.ryanair.com) and Danube Wings (www.danubewings.eu). Some airlines market it as "Vienna-Bratislava," thanks to its proximity to both capitals. To reach Vienna, you can take a Eurolines bus to the Erdberg stop of Vienna's U-3 subway line. A taxi directly to Vienna costs €60-90 (depending on whether you use a cheaper Slovak or more expensive Austrian cab).

SALZBURG

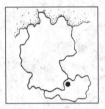

Salzburg and its residents—or at least its tourism industry—are forever smiling to the tunes of Mozart and *The Sound of Music*. Thanks to its charmingly preserved old town, splendid gardens, Baroque churches, and Europe's largest intact medieval fortress, Salzburg feels made for visitors. As a musical mecca, the city puts on a huge annual festival, as well as constant concerts. It's a city with class. Vagabonds wish they had nicer clothes.

Even without Mozart and the Von Trapps, Salzburg is steeped in history. In about A.D. 700, Bavaria gave Salzburg to Bishop Rupert in return for his promise to Christianize the area. Salzburg remained an independent city (belonging to no state) until Napoleon came in the early 1800s. Thanks in part to its formidable fortress, Salzburg managed to avoid the ravages of war for 1,200 years...until World War II. Much of the city was destroyed by WWII bombs (mostly around the train station), but the historic old town survived.

Eight million tourists crawl its cobbles each year. That's a lot of Mozart balls—and all that popularity has led to a glut of businesses hoping to catch the tourist dollar. Still, Salzburg is both a must and a joy.

Planning Your Time

While Salzburg's sights are, frankly, mediocre, the town itself is a Baroque museum of cobbled streets and elegant buildings—simply a touristy stroller's delight. Even if your time is short, consider allowing half a day for the *Sound of Music* tour. The *S.O.M.* bus tour kills a nest of sightseeing birds with one ticket (city overview, *S.O.M.* sights, and a fine drive by the lakes).

You'd probably enjoy at least two nights in Salzburg—nights

are important for swilling beer in atmospheric gardens and attending concerts in Baroque halls and chapels. Seriously consider one of Salzburg's many evening musical events (a few are free, some are as cheap as €12, and most average €40).

To get away from it all, bike down the river or hike across the Mönchsberg cliffs that rise directly from the middle of town.

Orientation to Salzburg

Salzburg, a city of 150,000 (Austria's fourth-largest), is divided into old and new. The old town, sitting between the Salzach River and its mini-mountain (Mönchsberg), holds nearly all the charm and most of the tourists. The new town, across the river, has the train station, a few sights and museums, and some good accommodations.

Tourist Information

Salzburg has three helpful TIs (main tel. 0662/889-870, www.salzburg.info): at the **train station** (daily June-Aug 8:30-19:00, Sept-May 9:00-18:00, tel. 0662/8898-7340); on **Mozartplatz** in the old center (daily 9:00-18:00, July-Aug until 19:00, closed Sun mid-Jan-Easter and Oct-mid-Nov, tel. 0662/889-870); and at the **Salzburg Süd park-and-ride** (April-Sept generally Tue-Sat 10:00-16:30 but sometimes longer hours, closed Sun-Mon and all of Oct-March, tel. 0662/8898-7360).

At any TI, you can pick up a free city-center map (the €0.70 map has a broader coverage and more information on sights, and is particularly worthwhile if biking out of town), the Salzburg Card brochure (listing sights with current hours and prices), and a bimonthly events guide. The TIs also book rooms (€2.20 fee and 10 percent deposit). Inside the Mozartplatz TI is the privately run Salzburg Ticket Service counter, where you can book concert tickets (see "Music in Salzburg," page 159).

Salzburg Card: The TIs sell the Salzburg Card, which covers all your public transportation (including the Mönchsberg elevator and funicular to the fortress) and admission to all the city sights (including Hellbrunn Castle and a river cruise). The card is pricey, but if you'd like to pop into all the sights, it can save money and enhance your experience (€25/24 hours, €34/48 hours, €40/72 hours). To analyze your potential savings, here are the major sights and what you'd pay without the card: Hohensalzburg Fortress and funicular-€11; Mozart's Birthplace and Residence-€17; Hellbrunn Castle-€9.50; Salzburg Panorama 1829-€3; Salzach River cruise-€14; 24-hour transit pass-€4.20. Busy sightseers can save plenty. Get this card, feel the financial pain once, and the city will be all yours.

Arrival in Salzburg

By Train: The Salzburg station is a gleaming commercial center with all the services you need: train information, tourist information, luggage lockers, and a handy SPAR supermarket (daily 6:00-23:00)—plus a popular shopping mall that's open on weekends. The transit info desk down the stairs from bus platform C has information on local buses.

Getting downtown from the station is a snap. Simply step outside, find **bus platform C** (labeled *Zentrum-Altstadt*), and hop on the next bus. Buses #1, #3, #5, #6, and #25 all do the same route into the city center before diverging at the far end of town. For most sights and city-center hotels, get off just after the bridge, at the fifth stop. For my recommended new town hotels, get off at Makartplatz (the fourth stop), just before the bridge.

Taxis don't make much sense to get from the train station into town, as they're expensive for short rides (€2.50 drop charge, about €8 for most rides in town).

To **walk** downtown (15 minutes), turn left as you leave the station, and walk straight down Rainerstrasse, which leads under the tracks past Mirabellplatz, turning into Dreifaltigkeitsgasse. From here, you can turn left onto Linzergasse for many of my recommended hotels, or cross the river to the old town. For a slightly longer but more dramatic approach, leave the station the same way but follow the tracks to the river, turn left, and walk the riverside path toward the fortress.

By Car: Mozart never drove in the old town, and neither should you. The best place to park is the **Salzburg Süd park-and-ride** lot. Coming on A-1 from Vienna or Munich, take A-10 toward Hallein, and then take the next exit (Salzburg Süd) in the direction of Anif. First, you'll pass Hellbrunn Castle (and zoo), then the Salzburg Süd TI, before arriving at the parking lot. Park your car (€5/24 hours), get sightseeing information and transit tickets from the TI, and catch bus #3 or #8 into town (€1.90 single-ride ticket or €4.20 *Tageskarte* 24-hour pass, more expensive if you buy tickets on board, every 5 minutes). If traveling with more than one other person, take advantage of a park-and-ride combo-ticket: For €13 (€10 July-Aug), you get 24 hours of parking and a 24-hour bus pass for up to five people.

If you don't believe in park-and-rides, head to the easiest, cheapest, most central parking lot—the 1,500-car Altstadtgarage, in the tunnel under the Mönchsberg (€14/day, note your slot number and which of the twin lots you're in, tel. 0662/846-434). Your hotel may provide discounted parking passes. If staying in the new town, the Mirabell-Congress garage makes more sense than the Altstadtgarage (see page 162 for directions).

Helpful Hints

Recommendations Skewed by Kickbacks: Salzburg is addicted to the tourist dollar, and it can never get enough. Virtually all hotels are on the take when it comes to concert and tour recommendations, influenced more by their potential kickback than by what's best for you. Take any tour or concert advice with a grain of salt.

Music Festival: The Salzburg Festival (Salzburger Festspiele) runs each year from late July to the end of August (see page 159).

Internet Access: A small Internet café is next to the base of the Mönchsberg elevator (€2/hour, daily 10:00-22:00, Gstättengasse 11). The city has several free Wi-Fi hotspots (one is in the Mirabell Gardens; info at www.salzburg-surft.at). Travelers with this book can get free Wi-Fi or use a computer for a few minutes (long enough to check email) at the Panorama Tours terminal on Mirabellplatz (daily 8:00-18:00).

Post Office: A full-service post office is located in the heart of town, in the New Residenz (Mon-Fri 8:00-18:00, Sat 9:00-12:00, closed Sun).

Laundry: A handy launderette is at Paris-Lodron-Strasse 16, at the corner of Wolf-Dietrich-Strasse, near my recommended Linzergasse hotels (€10 self-service, €15 same-day full-service, Mon-Fri 7:30-18:00, Sat 8:00-12:00, closed Sun, tel. 0662/876-381).

Cinema: Das Kino is an art-house movie theater that plays films in their original language (a block off the river and Linzergasse on Steingasse, tel. 0662/873-100, www.daskino.at).

Smoking Policies: Conservative Austria has been slow to embrace the smoke-free movement. By law, big restaurants must offer smoke-free zones (and smoking zones, if they choose). Smaller places choose to be either smoking or non-smoking, indicated by red or green stickers on the door.

Market Days: Popular farmer's markets pop up in the old town on Saturdays and in the new town on Thursdays. On summer weekends, a string of craft booths with fun goodies for sale stretches along the river.

Morning Joggers: Salzburg is a great place for running. Within minutes you can be huffing and puffing "The hills are alive..." in green meadows outside of town. The obvious best bets in town are through the Mirabell Gardens along its riverbank pedestrian lanes.

Updates to this Book: For news about changes to this book's coverage since it was published, see www.ricksteves.com/update.

Getting Around Salzburg

By Bus: At machines and *Tabak/Trafik* shops, you can buy €1.90 single-ride tickets or a €4.20 day pass (*Tageskarte*) good for 24 hours (€2.30 and €5.20 from the driver, respectively). To get from the old town to the train station, catch bus #1 from the inland side of Hanuschplatz. From the other side of the river, find the Makartplatz/Theatergasse stop and catch bus #1, #3, #5, or #6. Bus info: www.svv-info.at, tel. 800-660-660.

By Bike: Salzburg is great fun for cyclists. The following two bike-rental shops offer 20 percent off to anyone with this book—ask for it: **Top Bike** rents bikes on the river next to the Staatsbrücke (€6/2 hours, €10/4 hours, €15/24 hours, usually daily April-June and Sept-Oct 10:00-17:00, July-Aug 9:00-19:00, closed Nov-March, easy return available 24/7, free helmets with this book, mobile 0676-476-7259, www.topbike.at, Sabine). **A'Velo Radladen** rents bikes in the old town, just outside the TI on Mozartplatz (€4.50/1 hour, €10/4 hours, €16/24 hours, more for electric or mountain bikes; daily 9:00-18:00, until 19:00 July-Aug, but hours unreliable, shorter hours off-season and in bad weather; passport number for security deposit, mobile 0676-435-5950, www.a-velo.at). Some of my recommended hotels and pensions also rent bikes, and several of the B&Bs on Moosstrasse have free loaner bikes for guests.

By Funicular and Elevator: The old town is connected to the top of the Mönchsberg mountain (and great views) via funicular and elevator. The **funicular** *(Festungsbahn)* whisks you up into the imposing Hohensalzburg Fortress (included in castle admission, goes every few minutes—for details, see page 147). The **elevator** (Mönchsberg Aufzug) on the west side of the old town lifts you to the recommended Gasthaus Stadtalm café and hostel, the Museum of Modern Art and its chic café, wooded paths, and more great views (€2 one-way, €3.20 round-trip, normally Mon 8:00-19:00, Tue-Sun 8:00-24:00).

By Buggy: The horse buggies *(Fiaker)* that congregate at Residenzplatz charge €36 for a 25-minute trot around the old town (www.fiaker-salzburg.at).

Tours in Salzburg

Walking Tours

Any day of the week, you can take a one-hour guided walk of the old town without a reservation—just show up at the TI on Mozartplatz and pay the guide. The tours are informative. While generally in English only, on slow days you may be listening to everything in both German and English (€9, daily at 12:15, Mon-Sat also at 14:00, tel. 0662/8898-7330). To save money, you can easily do it on

your own using this chapter's self-guided walk (or download a free
Rick Steves **audio tour** of my walk—see page 7).

Local Guides

Salzburg is home to over a hundred licensed guides. I have worked
with three who are art historians and well worth recommending:
Christiana Schneeweiss ("Snow White") has been instrumental
in both my guidebook research and my TV production in Salzburg, and has her own minibus for private tours outside of town
(on foot: €135/2 hours, €160/3 hours; with minibus: €220/4 hours,
€350-400/day, up to 6 people; mobile 0664-340-1757, other options explained at www.kultur-tourismus.com, info@kultur-tour-
ismus.com). Both **Sabine Rath** (mobile 0664-201-6492, www.
tourguide-salzburg.com, info@tourguide-salzburg.com) and **Anna
Stellnberger** (mobile 0664-787-5177, anna.stellnberger@aon.at)
are excellent guides and a joy to learn from; they charge similar
rates (€145/2 hours, €185/4 hours, €275/8 hours). Salzburg has
many other good guides (to book, call 0662/840-406).

Boat Tours

City Cruise Line (a.k.a. Stadt Schiff-Fahrt) runs a basic 40-min-
ute round-trip river cruise with recorded commentary (€14, 9/day
July-Aug, 7/day May-June, fewer Sept-Oct and March-April, no
boats Nov-Feb). For a longer cruise, ride to Hellbrunn and return
by bus (€17, 1-2/day April-Oct). Boats leave from the old town
side of the river just downstream of the Makartsteg bridge (tel.
0662/825-858, www.salzburghighlights.at). While views can be
cramped, passengers are treated to a fun finale just before docking,
when the captain twirls a fun "waltz."

▲▲*The Sound of Music* Tours

I took one of these tours skeptically (as part of my research)—and
had a great time. The bus tour version includes a quick but good
general city tour, hits the *S.O.M.* spots (including the stately home
used in the movie, flirtatious gazebo, and grand wedding church),
and shows you a lovely stretch of the Salzkammergut Lake District. This is worthwhile for *S.O.M.* fans and those who won't otherwise be going into the Salzkammergut. Warning: Many think
rolling through the Austrian countryside with 30 Americans singing "Doe, a deer..." is pretty schmaltzy. Local Austrians don't understand all the commotion.

You have plenty of *S.O.M.* options: big buses (heavy on the
countryside around Salzburg, cannot go into old town), minibuses
(a mix of town and countryside), and bike (best for the town and
meadows nearby but doesn't get you into the foothills of the Alps).
Guides are generally native English-speakers—young, fun-loving,
and entertaining.

Of the many companies doing the tour by bus, consider Bob's
Special Tours (usually uses a minibus) and Panorama Tours (big

Salzburg

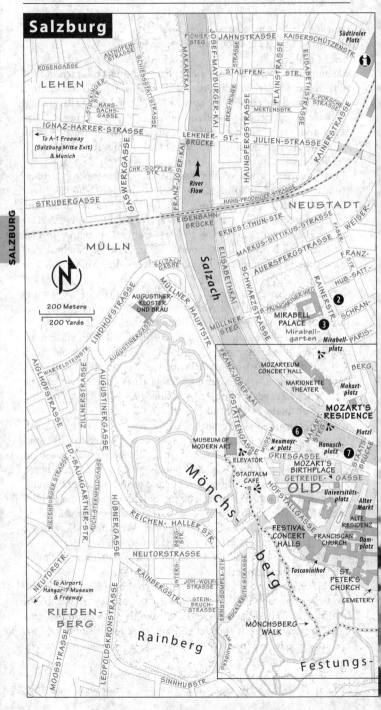

SALZBURG

N

200 Meters
200 Yards

To A-1 Freeway
(Salzburg Mitte Exit)
& Munich

To Airport,
Hangar-7 Museum
& Freeway

River
Flow

SÜDTIROLER
PLATZ

ROSENGASSE

LEHEN

IGNAZ-HARRER-STRASSE

STRUBERGASSE

MÜLLN

JAHNSTRASSE   KAISERSCHÜTZENSTR.

PIONIER-
STEG

ALTHOFEN-
STRASSE

STAUFFEN-
STR.

MERTENSSTR.

JULIEN-STRASSE

NEUSTADT

ERNEST-THUN-STR.

MARKUS-SITTIKUS-STRASSE

AUERSPERGSTRASSE

MIRABELL
PALACE

Mirabell-
garten

Mirabell-
platz

MOZARTEUM
CONCERT HALL

MARIONETTE
THEATER

BERG

Makart-
platz

MOZART'S
RESIDENCE

Platzl

Hanusch-
platz

MOZART'S
BIRTHPLACE

MUSEUM OF
MODERN ART

ELEVATOR

STADTALM
CAFÉ

Neumayr-
platz

GRIESGASSE

GETREIDE- GASSE

Universitäts-
platz

OLD

Alter
Markt

ALTE
RESIDENZ

Dom-
platz

FESTIVAL
CONCERT
HALLS

FRANCISCAN
CHURCH

Toscaninihof

ST.
PETER'S
CHURCH

CEMETERY

MÖNCHSBERG →
WALK

Festungs-

AUGUSTINER-
KLOSTER
UND BRÄU

Salzach

Mönchs-

berg

RIEDEN-
BERG

Rainberg

NEUTORSTRASSE

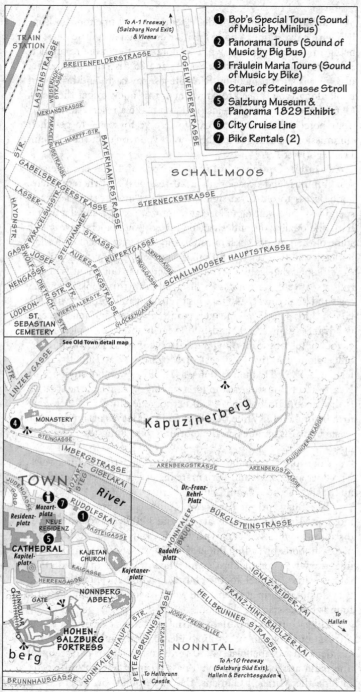

1. Bob's Special Tours (Sound of Music by Minibus)
2. Panorama Tours (Sound of Music by Big Bus)
3. Fräulein Maria Tours (Sound of Music by Bike)
4. Start of Steingasse Stroll
5. Salzburg Museum & Panorama 1829 Exhibit
6. City Cruise Line
7. Bike Rentals (2)

SALZBURG

50-seat bus). Each one provides essentially the same tour (in English with a live guide, 4 hours); with Bob's you pay a little more for being in a smaller group, while Panorama offers a more predictable, professional experience. You'll get a €5 discount from either if you book direct, mention Rick Steves, pay cash, and bring this book along (you'll need to show them this book to get the deal). Getting a spot is simple—just call and make a reservation. Note: Your hotel will be eager to call to reserve for you—to get their commission—but if you let them do it, you won't get the discount I've negotiated.

Minibus Option: Most of **Bob's Special Tours** use an eight-seat minibus (and occasionally a 20-seat bus) and therefore have good access to old town sights, promote a more casual feel, and spend less time waiting to load and unload. As it's a smaller operation, the quality of guides can be mixed (my readers have found some of their guides gruff or rude), and they may cancel with short notice if the tour doesn't fill up. Conversely, during busy times it can fill up early—calling in advance increases your chances of getting a seat (€45 for adults, €5 discount with this book if you pay cash and book direct, €40 for kids over age 6 and students with ID, €35 for kids ages 0-6—includes required car seat but must reserve in advance, daily at 9:00 and 14:00 year-round, they'll pick you up at your hotel for the morning tour, afternoon tours leave from Bob's office along the river just east of Mozartplatz at Rudolfskai 38, tel. 0662/849-511, mobile 0664-541-7492, www.bobstours.com). Nearly all of Bob's tours stop for a fun luge ride when the weather is dry (mountain bobsled-€4.50 extra, generally April-Oct, confirm beforehand). While the afternoon tour leaves promptly, you'll waste up to 30 minutes on the morning tour doing the hotel pick-ups.

For a private minibus tour consider **Christina Schneeweiss,** who does an *S.O.M.* tour with more history and fewer jokes (€220, up to 6 people, see "Local Guides," earlier).

Big-Bus Option: Panorama Tours depart from their smart kiosk at Mirabellplatz daily at 9:30 and 14:00 year-round (€37, €5 discount for *S.O.M.* tours with this book if you book direct and pay cash, book by calling 0662/874-029 or 0662/883-2110, or online at www.panoramatours.com). Many travelers appreciate their more businesslike feel, roomier buses, and higher vantage point. As they do not pick up at hotels, you won't waste any time making the rounds before starting the tour.

Bike Tours by "Fräulein Maria": For some exercise with your *S.O.M.* tour, you can meet your guide (likely a man) at the Mirabell Gardens (at Mirabellplatz 4, 50 yards to the left of palace entry). The main attractions that you'll pass during the eight-mile pedal include the Mirabell Gardens, the horse pond, St. Peter's Cemetery, Nonnberg Abbey, Leopoldskron Palace, and, of course, the gazebo. The tour is very family-friendly, and you'll get lots of stops for goofy photo ops (€26 includes bike, €18 for kids ages 11-16, €12 for kids under age 11, discount for adults and kids with this book, daily May-Sept at 9:30, June-Aug also at 16:30, allow 3.5 hours, reservations required only for afternoon tours, tel. 0650/342-6297, www.mariasbicycletours.com). For €8 extra (€20 per family), you're welcome to keep the bike all day.

Beyond Salzburg

Both Bob's and Panorama Tours also offer an extensive array of other day trips from Salzburg (e.g., Berchtesgaden/Eagle's Nest, salt mines, Hallstatt, and Salzkammergut lakes and mountains).

Bob's Special Tours offers two particularly well-designed day tours (both depart daily at 9:00; either one costs €90 with a €10 discount if you show this book and book direct, does not include entrance fees). Their *Sound of Music*/**Hallstatt Tour** first covers everything in the standard four-hour *Sound of Music* tour, then continues for a four-hour look at the scenic, lake-speckled Salzkammergut (with free time to explore charming Hallstatt). Bob's **Bavarian Mountain Tour** covers the main things you'd want to do in and around Berchtesgaden (Königssee, Hitler's mountaintop Eagle's Nest, Obersalzberg Documentation Center, salt mine tour).

Self-Guided Walk

▲▲▲Salzburg's Old Town

I've linked the best sights in the old town into this handy self-guided orientation walk. You can download a free Rick Steves **audio tour** of this walk to your mobile device; see page 7.

• *Begin in the heart of town, just up from the river, near the TI on...*

❶ Mozartplatz

All the happy tourists around you probably wouldn't be here if not for the man honored by this statue—Wolfgang Amadeus Mozart. (Many consider this to be a terrible likeness.) The statue was erected in 1842 on the 50th anniversary of Mozart's death, during a music festival that included his two sons (making this event, in a sense, the first Salzburg Festival). Mozart spent much of his first 25 years (1756-1777) in Salzburg, the greatest Baroque city north of the Alps. But the city itself is much older: The Mozart statue sits on bits of Roman Salzburg, and the pink Church of St. Michael that overlooks the square dates from A.D. 800. The first Salzburgers settled right around here. Near you is the TI (with a concert box office), and just around the downhill corner is a pedestrian bridge

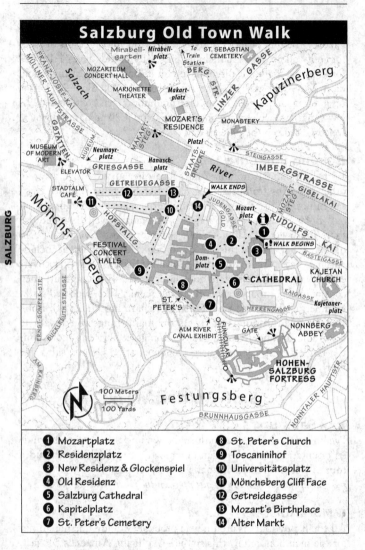

Salzburg Old Town Walk

1. Mozartplatz
2. Residenzplatz
3. New Residenz & Glockenspiel
4. Old Residenz
5. Salzburg Cathedral
6. Kapitelplatz
7. St. Peter's Cemetery
8. St. Peter's Church
9. Toscaninihof
10. Universitätsplatz
11. Mönchsberg Cliff Face
12. Getreidegasse
13. Mozart's Birthplace
14. Alter Markt

leading over the Salzach River to the quiet and most medieval street in town, Steingasse (described on page 155).

You may see lots of conservative Muslim families vacationing in Salzburg. While there are plenty of Muslims in Austria, most of the conservatively dressed women you'll see here are generally from the United Arab Emirates. Lots of wealthy families from the Middle East come here in the summer to escape the heat back home, to enjoy a break from their very controlled societies, or for medical treatment. Nearby Munich is a popular destination for hospital visits, and the entire family usually joins in for sightseeing and shopping.

• *Walk toward the cathedral and into the big square with the huge fountain.*

❷ Residenzplatz

Important buildings have long ringed this square. Salzburg's energetic Prince Archbishop Wolf Dietrich von Raitenau (who ruled 1587-1612) was raised in Rome, was a cousin of the influential Florentine Medici family, and had grandiose Italian ambitions for Salzburg. After a convenient fire destroyed the town's cathedral, Wolf Dietrich set about building the "Rome of the North." This square, with his new cathedral and palace, was the centerpiece of his Baroque dream city. A series of interconnecting squares—like you'll see nowhere else—make a grand processional way, leading from here through the old town. As we stroll through this heart and soul of historic Salzburg, notice how easily we slip from noisy commercial streets to peaceful, reflective courtyards. Also notice the two dominant kinds of stone around town: a creamy red marble and a chunky conglomerate (see the cathedral's exterior wall). The conglomerate was cheap—actually cut right out of the town's little mountain. As you wander, enjoy the pedestrian-friendly peace and quiet. After 11:00 each morning, barrier stumps go up around the perimeter of the old town, keeping traffic out.

For centuries, Salzburg's leaders were both important church officials *and* princes of the Holy Roman Empire, hence the title "prince archbishop"—mixing sacred and secular authority. But Wolf Dietrich misplayed his hand, losing power and spending his last five years imprisoned in the Hohensalzburg Fortress. (It's a complicated story—basically, the pope counted on Salzburg to hold the line against the Protestants for several generations following the Reformation. Wolf Dietrich was a good Catholic, as were most Salzburgers. But the town's important businessmen and the region's salt miners were Protestant, and for Salzburg's financial good, Wolf Dietrich dealt with them in a tolerant and pragmatic way. So the pope—who allowed zero tolerance for Protestants in those heady Counter-Reformation days—had Wolf Dietrich locked up and replaced.)

The fountain (completed in 1661) is as Italian as can be, with a Triton matching Bernini's famous Triton Fountain in Rome. During the Baroque era, skilled Italian artists and architects were in high demand in central European cities such as Salzburg and Prague. Local artists even Italianized their names in order to raise their rates.

• *Along the left side of Residenzplatz (as you face the cathedral) is the...*

❸ New (Neue) Residenz and Glockenspiel

This former palace, long a government administration building, now houses the central post office, the **Heimatwerk** (a fine shop showing off all the best local handicrafts, Mon-Sat 9:00-18:00, closed Sun), and two worthwhile sights: the fascinating **Salzburg Panorama 1829** exhibit; and the **Salzburg Museum,** which offers the best peek at the history of this one-of-a-kind city (both sights described on pages 145-146).

The famous **glockenspiel** rings atop the New Residenz. This bell tower has a carillon of 35 17th-century bells (cast in Antwerp) that chimes throughout the day and plays tunes (appropriate to the month) at 7:00, 11:00, and 18:00. A big barrel with adjustable tabs turns like a giant music-box mechanism, pulling the right bells in the appropriate rhythm. Notice the ornamental top: an upside-down heart in flames surrounding the solar system (symbolizing that God loves all of creation). Twice-weekly tours let you get up close to watch the glockenspiel action (€3, April-Oct Thu at 17:30 and Fri at 10:30, no tours Nov-March, meet in Salzburg Panorama 1829, just show up).

Look back, past Mozart's statue, to the 4,220-foot-high **Gaisberg**—the forested hill with the television tower. A road leads to the top for a commanding view. Its summit is a favorite destination for local nature-lovers and strong bikers.

• *Head to the opposite end of the square. This building is the...*

❹ Old (Alte) Residenz

Across from the New Residenz is Wolf Dietrich's palace, the Old Residenz, which is connected to the cathedral by an arched bridge. Its series of ornately decorated "stately rooms" *(Prunkräume)* is well-described in an included audioguide, which gives you a good feel for the wealth and power of the prince archbishop. Walking through 15 fancy rooms (all on one floor), you'll see Renaissance, Baroque, and Classicist styles—200 years of let-them-eat-cake splendor.

Cost and Hours: €9, daily 10:00-17:00, tel. 0662/8042-2690, www.residenz-salzburg.at.

• *Walk under the prince archbishop's skyway and step into Domplatz (Cathedral Square), where you'll find...*

❺ Salzburg Cathedral (Salzburger Dom)

This cathedral, rated ▲▲, was one of the first Baroque buildings north of the Alps. It was consecrated in 1628, during the Thirty Years' War. (Pitting Roman Catholics against Protestants, this war devastated much of Europe and brought most grand construction projects to a halt.) Experts differ on what motivated the determined builders: emphasizing Salzburg's commitment to the Roman Catholic cause and the power of the Church here, or showing that there could be a peaceful alternative to the religious strife that was racking Europe at the time. Salzburg's archbishop was technically the top papal official north of the Alps, but the city managed to steer clear of the war. With its rich salt production, it had enough money to stay out of the conflict and carefully maintain its independence from the warring sides, earning it the nickname "Fortified Island of Peace."

Domplatz, the square in front of the cathedral, is surrounded by the prince archbishop's secular administration buildings. The **statue of Mary** (from 1771) is looking away from the church, welcoming visitors. If you stand in the rear of the square, immediately under the middle arch, you'll see that she's positioned to be crowned by the two angels on the church facade.

The dates on the cathedral's iron gates refer to milestones in the church's history: In 774, the previous church (long since destroyed) was founded by St. Virgil, to be replaced in 1628 by the church you see today. In 1959, a partial reconstruction was completed, made necessary by a WWII bomb that had blown through the dome.

Cost and Hours: Free, but donation prominently requested; May-Sept Mon-Sat 9:00-19:00, Sun 13:00-19:00; March-April, Oct, and Dec closes at 18:00; Jan-Feb and Nov closes at 17:00; www.salzburger-dom.at.

Visiting the Cathedral: Enter the cathedral as if part of a festival procession—drawn toward the resurrected Christ by the brightly lit area under the dome, and cheered on by ceiling paintings of the Passion.

Built in just 14 years (1614-1628), the church boasts harmonious architecture. When Pope John Paul II visited in 1998, some 5,000 people filled the cathedral (330 feet long and 230 feet tall). The baptismal font (dark bronze, left of the entry) is from the previous cathedral (basin from about 1320, although the lid is modern). Mozart was baptized here (Amadeus means "beloved by God"). Concert and Mass schedules are posted at the entrance; the Sunday Mass at 10:00 is famous for its music (usually choral; more info at www.kirchen.net/dommusik).

The **paintings** lining the nave, showing events leading up to Christ's death, are relatively dark. But the Old Testament themes that foreshadow Jesus' resurrection, and the Resurrection scene painted at the altar, are well-lit. The church has never had stained glass—just clear windows to let light power the message.

The stucco, by a Milanese artist, is exceptional. Sit under the **dome**—surrounded by the tombs of 10 archbishops from the 17th century—and imagine all four organs playing, each balcony filled with musicians...glorious surround-sound. Mozart, who was the organist here for two years, would advise you that the acoustics are best in pews immediately under the dome. Study the symbolism of the decor all around you—intellectual, complex, and cohesive. Think of the altar in Baroque terms, as the center of a stage, with sunrays as spotlights in this dramatic and sacred theater.

In the left transept, stairs lead down into the **crypt** *(Krypta),* where you can see foundations of the earlier church, more tombs, and a tourist-free chapel (reserved for prayer) directly under the dome.

Other Cathedral Sights: The **Cathedral Excavations Museum** (Domgrabungsmuseum, outside the church on Residenz-platz and down the stairs) offers a chance to see the foundations of the medieval church, some Roman engineering, and a few Roman mosaics from Roman street level. It has the charm of an old basement garage; unless you've never seen anything Roman, I'd skip it (€2.50, July-Aug daily 9:00-17:00, closed Sept-June, www.salz-burgmuseum.at).

The **Cathedral Museum** (Dom Museum) has a rich collection of church art (entry at portico, €6, mid-May-Oct and Dec Mon-Sat 10:00-17:00, Sun 11:00-18:00, closed Nov and Jan-mid-May, tel. 0662/8047-1870), www.kirchen.net/dommuseum.

• *From the cathedral, exit left and walk toward the fortress into the next square.*

❻ Kapitelplatz

Head past the underground public WCs (€0.50) to the giant **chessboard.** It's just under the golden orb topped by a man gazing up at the castle, trying to decide whether to walk up or shell out €11 for the funicular. Every year since 2002, a foundation has commissioned a different artist to create a new work of public art somewhere in the city; this is the piece from 2007.

Detour across the square to the fountain. This was a **horse bath,** the 18th-century equivalent of a car wash. Notice the puzzle above it—the artist wove the date of the structure into a phrase. It says, "Leopold the Prince Built Me," using the letters LLDVIC-MXVXI, which total 1732 (add it up...it works)—the year it was built. Return to the chessboard and face away from the cathedral. Look for the arrow pointing to the *Stieglkeller;* here a small road leads uphill to the fortress (and fortress funicular). To the right is a gate with a sign that reads *zum Peterskeller.* Walk through this gate, which leads to a waterwheel and St. Peter's Cemetery.

It's fair to say that Salzburg is glorious in great part because of its clever use of its water. The **waterwheel** is part of a canal system that has brought water into Salzburg from Berchtesgaden, 15 miles away, since the 13th century. Climb up the steps to watch the inflow and imagine the thrill felt by medieval engineers harnessing this raw power. The stream was divided into smaller canals and channeled through town to provide fire protection, to flush out the streets (Thursday morning was flood-the-streets day), and to power factories. As late as the 19th century there were still more than 100 watermill-powered firms in Salzburg. Because of its water-powered hygiene (relatively good for the standards of the time), Salzburg never suffered from a plague—it's probably the only Austrian town you'll see with no plague monument. For more on the canal system, check out the **Alm River Canal exhibit** (at the exit of the funicular, described on page 152).

Before leaving, drop into the fragrant and traditional **bakery** at the waterfall, which sells various fresh rolls—both sweet and not, explained on the wall—for less than €1 (Mon-Tue 8:00-17:30, Thu-Fri 7:00-17:30, Sat 7:00-13:00, closed Wed and Sun). From here there's a good view of the funicular climbing up to the castle.
• *Now find the* Katakomben *sign and step into...*

❼ St. Peter's Cemetery

This collection of lovingly tended mini-gardens abuts the Mönchberg's rock wall.

Cost and Hours: Cemetery—free, silence is requested, daily April-Sept 6:30-19:00, Oct-March 6:30-18:00; www.stift-stpeter.at.

Visiting the Cemetery: Walk in about 50 yards to the intersection of lanes at the base of the cliff marked by a stone ball. You're surrounded by three churches, each founded in the early Middle Ages atop a pagan Celtic holy site. St. Peter's Church is closest to the stone ball. Notice the fine Romanesque stonework on the apse of the chapel nearest you, and the rich guys' fancy Renaissance-style tombs decorating its walls. Wealthy as those guys were, they ran out of caring relatives. The graves surrounding you are tended by descendants of the deceased. In Austria, gravesites are rented, not owned. Rent bills are sent out every 10 years. If no one cares enough to make the payment, your tombstone is removed.

While the cemetery where the Von Trapp family hid out in *The Sound of Music* was a Hollywood set, it was inspired by this one. Look up the cliff. Legendary medieval hermit monks are said to have lived in the hillside—but "catacombs" they're not. You can climb lots of steps to see a few old caves, a chapel, and some fine views (€1.50, entrance at far end of cemetery, visit takes 10 minutes).

Stroll past the stark Gothic funeral chapel (c. 1491) to the uphill corner of the cemetery, and follow the high lane back to see the finer tombs in the arcade. Tomb #XXXI belongs to the cathedral's architect—forever facing his creation. Tomb #LIV, at the catacomb entry, is a chapel carved into the hillside, holding the tombs of Mozart's sister and Joseph Haydn's younger brother Michael, also a composer of note.

SALZBURG

• *Continue downhill through the cemetery and out the opposite end. Just outside, hook right and drop into...*

❽ St. Peter's Church (Stiftskirche St. Peter)

Just inside, enjoy a carved Romanesque welcome. Over the inner doorway, a fine tympanum shows Jesus on a rainbow flanked by Peter and Paul over a stylized Tree of Life and under a Latin inscription reading, "I am the door to life, and only through me can you find eternal life." Enter the nave and notice how the once purely Romanesque vaulting has since been iced with a sugary Rococo finish. Salzburg's only Rococo interior feels Bavarian (because it is—the fancy stucco work was done by Bavarian artists). Up the right side aisle is the tomb of St. Rupert, with a painting showing Salzburg in 1750 (one bridge, salt ships sailing the river, and angels hoisting barrels of salt to heaven as St. Rupert prays for his city). Salt was Salzburg's white gold, granting the city enough wealth to maintain its independence as a prince-archbishopric for an entire millennium (798-1803). On pillars farther up the aisle are faded bits of 13th-century Romanesque frescoes. Similar frescoes hide under Rococo whitewash throughout the church.

Cost and Hours: Free, daily April-Oct 8:00-21:00, Nov-March 8:00-19:00, www.stift-stpeter.at.

• *Leaving the church, notice on the left the **Stiftskeller St. Peter** restaurant—known for its Mozart Dinner Concert. Charlemagne ate here in the year 803, allowing locals to claim that it's the oldest restaurant in Europe. Opposite where you entered the square (look through the arch), you'll see St. Rupert holding his staff and waving you into the next square. Once there, you're surrounded by early 20th-century Bauhaus-style dorms for student monks. Notice the modern crucifix (1926) painted on the far wall. Here's a good place to see the two locally quarried stones (marble and conglomerate) so prevalent in all the town's buildings.*

Walk through the archway under the crucifix into...

❾ Toscaninihof

This small courtyard is wedged behind the 1925 **Festival Hall.** The hall's three theaters seat 5,000 (see a photo of the main theater ahead on the wall, at the base of the stairs). This is where, in *The Sound of Music*, Captain von Trapp nervously waits before walking onstage to sing "Edelweiss," just before he escapes with his family. On the left is an entrance to the city's 1,500-space, inside-the-mountain parking lot; ahead, behind the *Felsenkeller* sign, is a tunnel (generally closed) leading to the actual concert hall; and to the right is the backstage of a smaller hall where carpenters are often building stage sets (door open on hot days). The stairway leads a few flights up to a picnic perch with a fine view, and then up to the top of the cliff and the recommended Gasthaus Stadtalm café and hostel.

Walk downhill through the archway onto **Max-Reinhardt-Platz.** Pause here to survey the line of Salzburg Festival concert halls to your left. As the festival was started in the austere 1920s, the city remodeled existing buildings (e.g., the prince archbishop's stables and riding school) for venues.

• *Continue straight—passing the big church on your left, along with popular wurst stands and a public WC—into...*

⑩ Universitätsplatz

This square hosts an **open-air produce market**—Salzburg's liveliest, though it's pricey (mornings Mon-Sat, best on Sat). The market really bustles on Saturday mornings, when the farmers are in town.

Public marketplaces have fountains for washing fruit and vegetables. Bear left around the church and you'll find the one here—a part of the medieval water system. The sundial (over the fountain's drain) is accurate (except for the daylight savings hour) and two-dimensional, showing both the time (obvious) and the date (less obvious). The fanciest facade overlooking the square (the yellow one) is the backside of Mozart's Birthplace (we'll see the front soon).

• *Continue past the fountain to the far end of the square. Most of the houses on your right have nicely arcaded medieval passages that connect the square to Getreidegasse, which runs parallel to Universitätsplatz. Just for fun, you could weave between this street and Getreidegasse several times, following these "through houses" as you work your way toward the cliff face ahead.*

⑪ Mönchsberg Cliff Face

Look up—200 feet above you is the Mönchsberg, Salzburg's mountain. Today you see the remains of an aborted attempt in the 1600s to cut through the Mönchsberg. It proved too big a job, and when new tunneling technology arrived, the project was abandoned. The stones cut did serve as a quarry for the city's 17th-century growth spurt—the bulk of the cathedral, for example, is built of this economic and local conglomerate stone.

Early one morning in 1669, a huge landslide killed more than 200 townspeople who lived close to where the elevator is now (to the right). Since then the cliffs have been carefully checked each spring and fall. Even today, you might see crews on the cliff, monitoring its stability.

Across the busy road are giant horse troughs. Cross the street (looking left at the string of Salzburg Festival halls again) for a closer look. Paintings show the various breeds and temperaments of horses in the prince's stable. Like Vienna, Salzburg had a passion for the equestrian arts.

• *Turn right (passing a courtyard on your left that once housed a hospital for the poor, and now houses a toy museum and a museum of historic musical instruments), and then right again, which brings you to the start of a long and colorful pedestrian street. (At this point you could take a short side-trip up the mountain via the elevator—Mönchsberg Aufzug—described on page 152.)*

⑫ Getreidegasse

This street, rated ▲▲, was old Salzburg's busy, colorful main drag. It's been a center of trade since Roman times (third century). It's lined with *Schmuck* (jewelry) shops and other businesses. This is the burgher's (secular) Salzburg. The buildings, most of which date from the 15th century, are tall for that age, and narrow, and densely packed. Space was tight here because such little land was available between the natural fortifications provided by the mountain and the river, and so much of what was available was used up by the Church. Famous for its old wrought-iron signs, the architecture on the street still looks much as it did in Mozart's day—though much of its former elegance is now gone, replaced by chain outlets.

As you walk away from the cliffs, look up and enjoy the traditional signs indicating what each shop made or sold: Watch for spirits, bookmakers, a horn (indicating a place for the postal coach), brewery (the star for the name of the beer, Sternbräu—"Star Brew"), glazier (window-maker), locksmith, hamburgers, pastries, tailor, baker (the pretzel), pharmacy, and a hatter.

On the right at #39, **Sporer** serves up homemade spirits (€1.60/shot, Mon-Sat 9:30-17:00, closed Sun). This has been a family-run show for a century—fun-loving, proud, and English-speaking. *Nuss* is nut, *Marille* is apricot (typical of this region), the *Kletzen* cocktail is like a super-thick Baileys with pear, and *Edle Brande* are the stronger schnapps. The many homemade firewaters are in jugs at the end of the bar.

After noticing the building's old doorbells—one per floor—continue down Getreidegasse. At #40, **Eisgrotte** serves good ice cream (€1/scoop). Across from Eisgrotte, a tunnel leads to the recommended **Balkan Grill** (signed as *Bosna Grill*), the local choice for the very best wurst in town. At #28, Herr Wieber, the iron- and locksmith, welcomes the curious. Farther along, you'll pass McDonald's (required to keep its arches Baroque and low-key).

The knot of excited tourists and salesmen hawking goofy gimmicks by #9 marks the home of Salzburg's most famous resident: ⑬ **Mozart's Birthplace** *(Geburtshaus)*—the house where Mozart was born, and where he composed many of his early works (described on page 146).

At #3, dip into the passage and walk under a whalebone, likely once used to advertise the wares of an exotic import shop. Look up at the arcaded interior. On the right, at the venerable **Schatz Konditorei,** you can enjoy coffee under the vaults with your choice of top-end cakes and pastries.

With your back to the pastry shop, go straight ahead through the passage to Sigmund-Haffner-Gasse. Before heading right, look left to see the tower of the old City Hall at the end. The blue-and-white ball halfway up is an 18th-century moon clock. It still tells the phase of the moon.

• *Go right, then take your first left to....*

⑩ Alter Markt

Here in Salzburg's old marketplace, you'll find the recommended **Café Tomaselli.** On the other side of the fountain, look for the fun **Josef Holzermayr candy shop,** and, next door, the beautifully old-fashioned **Alte F.E. Hofapotheke** pharmacy—duck in discreetly to peek at the Baroque shelves and containers (be polite—the people in line are here for medicine; no photography). Even in our fast-changing, modern age, the traditional soul of Salzburg—embraced by its citizens—lives on.

• *Our walk is finished. From here, you can circle back to some of the old town sights (such as those in the New Residenz, described next); head up to the Hohensalzburg Fortress on the cliffs over the old town (see page 147); or continue to some of the sights across the river. To reach those new town sights, head for the river, jog left (past the fast-food fish restaurant and free WCs), climb to the top of the Makartsteg pedestrian bridge, and follow my walking directions (see page 153).*

Sights in Salzburg

In the Old Town

In the New (Neue) Residenz

▲▲Salzburg Museum

This two-floor exhibit is the best in town for history. The included audioguide wonderfully describes the great artifacts in the lavish prince archbishop's residence.

Cost and Hours: €7, €8.50 combo-ticket with Salzburg Panorama, includes audioguide, Tue-Sun 9:00-17:00, closed Mon, tel. 0662/620-8080, www.salzburgmuseum.at.

Visiting the Museum: The Salzburg Personalities exhibit fills the first floor with a charming look at Salzburg's greatest historic characters—mostly artists, scientists, musicians, and writers who would otherwise be forgotten. The *Kunsthalle* in the basement shows off special exhibits.

But upstairs is the real reason to come. Here you'll see lavish ceremonial rooms filled with an exhibit called The Salzburg Myth, which traces the city's proud history, art, and culture since early modern times. The focus is on its quirky absolutist prince archbishop and its long-standing reputation as a fairy-tale "Alpine Arcadia."

From the Salzburg Museum, the Panorama Passage (clearly marked from the entry) leads underground to the Salzburg Panorama (described next). This passage is lined with archaeological finds (Roman and early medieval), helping you trace the development of Salzburg from its Roman roots until today.

▲Salzburg Panorama 1829

In the early 19th century, before the advent of photography, 360-degree "panorama" paintings of great cities or events were popular. These creations were even taken on extended road trips. When this one was created, the 1815 Treaty of Vienna had just divvied up post-Napoleonic Europe, and Salzburg had become part of the Habsburg realm. This photo-realistic painting served as a town portrait done at the emperor's request. The circular view, painted by Johann Michael Sattler, shows the city as seen from the top of its castle. When complete, it spent 10 years touring the great cities of Europe, showing off Salzburg's breathtaking setting.

Today, the exquisitely restored painting, hung in a circular room, offers a fascinating look at the city in 1829. The river was slower and had beaches. The old town looks essentially as it does today, and Moosstrasse still leads into idyllic farm country. Your ticket also lets you see the temporary exhibitions in the room that surrounds the Panorama, which is part of the Salzburg Museum, but with a separate entrance and ticket counter.

Cost and Hours: €3, €8.50 combo-ticket with Salzburg Museum, open daily 9:00-17:00, Residenzplatz 9, tel. 0662/620-808-730, www.salzburgmuseum.at.

▲▲Mozart's Birthplace (Geburtshaus)

The Mozart family lived here for 26 years. Of the seven Mozart children born here, two survived. Wolfgang was born here in 1756. It was in this building that he composed most of his boy-genius works. Today it's the most popular Mozart sight in town—for fans, it's almost a pilgrimage. Shuffling through with all the crowds, you'll peruse three floors of rooms with exhibits displaying paintings, letters, personal items, and lots of facsimiles, all attempting to bring life to the Mozart story. There's no audioguide, but everything's described in English.

Cost and Hours: €10, €17 combo-ticket includes Mozart's Residence in the new town—see page 154, daily 9:00-17:30, July-Aug until 20:00, Getreidegasse 9, tel. 0662/844-313, www.mozarteum.at.

Visiting Mozart's Birthplace: Start by walking to the top floor, where you enter the Mozart family apartment—furnished only with the violin given to him at age six. This section introduces Mozart's family, shows you the room where he was born, tells of his wife's and children's fates after his death, and tries to explain his enduring fame. Next is an exhibition on his life in Vienna, and a room of computer terminals with a wonderful program allowing you to see his handwritten scores and hear them performed at the same time (Mozart's Residence, across town, has the same terminals). The middle floor includes a room of dioramas showing stage sets for Mozart's operas and an old clavichord he supposedly composed on. (A predecessor of the more complicated piano, the clavichord's keys hit the strings with a simple teeter-totter motion that allows you to play very softly—ideal for composers living in tight apartment quarters.) The lower-floor exhibit takes you on the road with the child prodigy, and gives a slice-of-life portrait of Salzburg during Mozart's time, including a bourgeois living room furnished much as the Mozart family's would have been.

If I had to choose between Mozart's birthplace *(Geburtshaus)* and his residence *(Wohnhaus),* I'd go with the birthplace, since its exhibits are more extensive and educational. If you're truly interested in Mozart and his times, take advantage of the combi-ticket and see both. If Mozart isn't important to you, skip both museums and concentrate on the city's other sights and glorious natural surroundings.

Atop the Cliffs Above the Old Town

Atop the Mönchsberg—the mini-mountain that rises behind the old town—is a tangle of paved walking paths with great views, a hostel with a pleasant café/restaurant, a modern art museum, a neighborhood of very fancy homes, and one major sight (the Hohensalzburg Fortress, perched on the Festungsberg, the Mönchsberg's southern arm). You can walk up from several points in town, including Festungsgasse (behind the cathedral), Toscaninihof, and the Augustiner Bräustübl beer garden. At the west end of the old town, the Mönchsberg elevator whisks you up to the top for a couple euros. The funicular directly up to the fortress is expensive, and worthwhile only if you plan to visit the fortress, which is included in the funicular ticket.

▲▲Hohensalzburg Fortress (Festung)

Construction of Hohensalzburg Fortress was begun by Archbishop Gebhard of Salzburg as a show of the Catholic Church's power. Built on a rock (called Festungsberg) 400 feet above the Salzach River, this fortress was never really used. That's the idea. It was a good investment—so foreboding, nobody attacked the town for nearly a thousand years. The city was never taken by force, but when Napoleon stopped by, Salzburg wisely surrendered. After a

Salzburg at a Glance

▲▲▲**Salzburg's Old Town Walk** Old town's best sights in handy orientation walk. **Hours:** Always open. See page 135.

▲▲**Salzburg Cathedral** Glorious, harmonious Baroque main church of Salzburg. **Hours:** May-Sept Mon-Sat 9:00-19:00, Sun 13:00-19:00; March-April, Oct, and Dec closes at 18:00; Jan-Feb and Nov closes at 17:00. See page 138.

▲▲**Getreidegasse** Picturesque old shopping lane with characteristic wrought-iron signs. **Hours:** Always open. See page 144.

▲▲**Hohensalzburg Fortress** Imposing castle capping the mountain overlooking town, with tourable grounds, several mini-museums, commanding views, and good evening concerts. **Hours:** Fortress museums open daily May-Sept 9:00-19:00, Oct-April 9:30-17:00. Concerts nearly nightly. See page 147.

▲▲**Salzburg Museum** Best place to learn more about the city's history. **Hours:** Tue-Sun 9:00-17:00, closed Mon. See page 145.

▲▲*The Sound of Music* **Tour** Cheesy but fun tour through the S.O.M. sights of Salzburg and the surrounding Salzkammergut Lake District, by minibus, big bus, or bike. **Hours:** Various options daily at 9:00, 9:30, 14:00, and 16:30. See page 131.

▲▲**Mozart's Birthplace** House where Mozart was born in 1756, featuring his instruments and other exhibits. **Hours:** Daily 9:00-17:30, July-Aug until 20:00. See page 146.

▲**Old Residenz** Prince Archbishop Wolf Dietrich's palace, with ornate rooms and good included audioguide. **Hours:** Daily 10:00-17:00. See page 138.

▲**Salzburg Panorama 1829** A vivid peek at the city in 1829. **Hours:** Daily 9:00-17:00. See page 146.

stint as a military barracks, the fortress was opened to the public in the 1860s by Habsburg Emperor Franz Josef. Today, it remains one of Europe's mightiest castles, dominating Salzburg's skyline and offering incredible views, as well as a couple mediocre museums.

Cost: You'll pay to enter the castle, whether you reach the castle on foot (the walk is easier than it looks), or, for a couple euros more, by funicular.

On Foot: If you walk up to the fortress (or walk over from the Mönchsberg, reachable either by stairs from Toscaninihof or the

▲**Mozart's Residence** Restored house where the composer lived. **Hours:** Daily 9:00-17:30, July-Aug until 20:00. See page 154.

▲**Mönchsberg Walk** "The hills are alive" stroll you can enjoy right in downtown Salzburg. **Hours:** Doable anytime during daylight hours. See page 152.

▲**Mirabell Gardens and Palace** Beautiful palace complex with fine views, Salzburg's best concert venue, and *Sound of Music* memories. **Hours:** Gardens—always open; concerts—free in the park May-Aug Sun at 10:30, in the palace nearly nightly. See page 153.

▲**Steingasse** Historic cobbled lane with trendy pubs—a tranquil, tourist-free section of old Salzburg. **Hours:** Always open. See page 155.

▲**St. Sebastian Cemetery** Baroque cemetery with graves of Mozart's wife and father, and other Salzburg VIPs. **Hours:** Daily April-Oct 9:00-18:30, Nov-March 9:00-16:00. See page 156.

▲▲**Hellbrunn Castle** Palace on the outskirts of town featuring gardens with trick fountains. **Hours:** Daily May-Sept 9:00-17:30, July-Aug until 21:00, April and Oct-Nov 9:00-16:30, closed Dec-March. See page 157.

St. Peter's Cemetery Atmospheric old cemetery with mini-gardens overlooked by cliff face with monks' caves. **Hours:** Cemetery—daily April-Sept 6:30-19:00, Oct-March 6:30-18:00. See page 141.

St. Peter's Church Romanesque church with Rococo decor. **Hours:** Daily April-Oct 8:00-21:00, Nov-March 8:00-19:00. See page 142.

SALZBURG

elevator from the west end of Griesgasse/southern end of Gstättengasse), you'll pay €7.80 to enter (at the fortress gate), which includes entry to the fortress grounds, all the museums inside, and your funicular ride down—whether you want it or not. Within one hour of the museums' closing time, the entry price is reduced to €4.

Via Funicular: Most visitors enter the fortress by taking a one-minute trip on the funicular (Festungsbahn). The lower station is on Festungsgasse, which is just off Kapitelplatz, behind Salzburg's cathedral. The top end of the funicular is inside the fortress complex. Your round-trip funicular ticket includes admission to the fortress grounds and all the museums inside—whether you want to see them or not (€11, €25.50 family ticket). If you board the funicular within one hour of the museums' closing time (i.e., May-Sept after 18:00 or Oct-April after 16:00), you pay only €7.80, or €6.40 if you don't want to take the funicular down; this is a good deal if you only want a glimpse of the museums. After the museums have closed, the funicular continues to run until about 21:30 (later if there's a concert) and costs €3.80 round-trip, or €2.40 one-way.

Hours: The museums in the fortress are open daily May-Sept 9:00-19:00, Oct-April 9:30-17:00, tel. 0662/8424-3011. The grounds of the fortress stay open and the funicular continues to run even after the museums close—usually until about 21:30 or 22:00, especially when there's a concert (300 nights a year).

Concerts: The fortress serves as a venue for evening concerts (the Festungskonzerte), which are held in the old banquet rooms on the upper floor of the palace museum. A concert is a good way to see the fortress at its quietest. For details, see "Music in Salzburg" on page 159.

Eating: The cafés to either side of the upper funicular station are a great place to nibble on apple strudel while taking in the jaw-dropping view.

◑ Self-Guided Tour: At the top of the funicular, most visitors turn left. Instead, head right and down the stairs to bask in the **view** to the south (away from town) toward the Alps, either from the café or the view terrace a little farther along. (You'll enjoy superb city views later on this tour.)

• *Once you're done snapping photos, walk through the arches into the fortress courtyard. Your ticket lets you into two exhibits: The first is a tour of the fortifications, while the second is a historical museum inside the "palace" in the fortress courtyard. The courtyards themselves offer a few other things to see, as well as great views in several directions. Go left (uphill). From here, you'll make a clockwise circuit around the courtyard. The first sight you'll come to, labeled #1, is the...*

Fortress Interior: Here you get to see a few rooms in the outer fortifications. Only 40 people are allowed in at a time, usually with an escort who gives a 30-minute commentary. While the interior furnishings are mostly gone—taken by Napoleon—the rooms themselves survived fairly well (no one wanted to live here after 1500, so the building was never modernized). Your tour includes a room dedicated to the art of "enhanced interrogation" (to use American military jargon)—filled with tools of that gruesome trade. The highlight is the commanding city view from the top of a tower. In summer, there can be a long wait to get in.

• *Continue uphill to sight #2—the fortress's "palace" (labeled* Inneres Schloß*). Immediately inside, visit the...*

Marionette Exhibit: Two fun rooms show off this local tradition. Three videos play continuously: two with peeks at Salzburg's ever-enchanting Marionette Theater performances of Mozart classics (described under "Music in Salzburg," later) and one with a behind-the-scenes look at the action. Give the hands-on marionette a whirl.

• *Head down the hall and up the stairs following* Festungsmuseum *signs to the...*

Fortress Museum (Festungsmuseum): The lower floor of this spacious museum has exhibits on the history of the fortress, from music to torture. One room explains how they got all this stuff up here, while another has copies of the pencil sketches for the Salzburg Panorama (described earlier). On the top floor are three pretty ceremonial rooms, including the one where the evening concerts are held. (Check out the colorfully painted tile stove in the far room.) The rest of the top floor is given over to the Rainer Regiments Museum, dedicated to the Salzburg soldiers who fought mountain-to-mountain on the Italian front during World War I.

• *Exit the museum and continue on out into the...*

Fortress Courtyard: The courtyard was the main square for the medieval fortress's 1,000-some residents, who could be self-sufficient when necessary. The square was ringed by the shops of craftsmen, blacksmiths, bakers, and so on. The well dipped into a rain-fed cistern. As you enter, look to your left to see the well-described remains of a recently excavated Romanesque chapel. The current church is dedicated to St. George, the protector of horses (logical for an army church) and decorated by fine red marble reliefs (c. 1502). Behind the church is the top of the old lift (still in use) that helped supply the fortress. Under the archway next to it are the steps that lead back into the city, or to the paths across the Mönchsberg.

• *Near the chapel, turn left into the Kuenburg Bastion (once a garden) for fine city views.*

Kuenburg Bastion: Notice how the fortress has three parts: the original section inside the courtyard, the vast whitewashed walls (built when the fortress was a residence), and the lower, beefed-up fortifications (added for extra defense against the expected Ottoman invasion). Survey Salzburg from here and think about fortifying an important city by using nature. The Mönchsberg (the cliffs to the left) and Festungsberg (the little mountain you're on) naturally cradle the old town, with just a small gate between the ridge and the river needed to bottle up the place. The new town across the river needed a bit of a wall arcing from the river to its hill. Back then, only one bridge crossed the Salzach into town, and it had a fortified gate.

• *Go back inside the fortress courtyard. Our tour is over. Either circle back to where you entered and ride the funicular down, or go through the archway and down the stairs if you prefer to hike back to town or along the top of the Mönchsberg (see "Mönchsberg Walk," below). If you take the funicular down, don't miss (at the bottom of the lift) the...*

Alm River Canal Exhibit: At the base of the funicular, below the fortress, is this fine little exhibit on how the river was broken into five smaller streams—powering the city until steam took up the energy-supply baton. Pretend it's the year 1200 and follow (by video) the flow of the water from the river through the canals, into the mills, and as it's finally dumped into the Salzach River. (The exhibit technically requires a funicular ticket—but you can see it by slipping through the exit at the back of the amber shop, just uphill from the funicular terminal.)

Mönchsberg Sights

▲Mönchsberg Walk

The paved, wooded walking path between the Mönchsberg elevator and the fortress is less than a mile long and makes for a great 30-minute hike. The mountain is small, and frequent signposts direct you between all the key points, so it's hard to get lost. The views of Salzburg are the main draw, but there's also a modern art museum, mansions to ogle, and a couple of places to eat or enjoy a scenic drink.

You can do this walk in either direction. (To save a few euros—and the climb—visit the fortress last: Take the Mönchsberg elevator, walk across to the fortress, pay the reduced entry price at the fortress gate, see the fortress, then take the funicular down—included in your fortress ticket.) The Mönchsberg **elevator** *(Aufzug)* starts from Gstättengasse/Griesgasse on the west side of the old town (€2 one-way, €3.20 round-trip, normally Mon 8:00-19:00, Tue-Sun 8:00-24:00).

You can also **climb** up and down under your own power; this saves a few more euros (no matter which direction you go). Paths or stairs lead up from the Augustiner beer hall (see page 175), Toscaninihof (near the Salzburg Festival concert halls), and Festungsgasse (at the base of the fortress).

Cafés: The elevator deposits you right at Mönchsberg 32, a sleek modern café/bar/restaurant adjacent to the modern art museum and a fine place for a drink or bite (they serve breakfast until 16:00). From there, it's a five-minute walk to the rustic Gasthaus Stadtalm café, with wooden picnic tables and a one-with-nature allure. Next to the Stadtalm is a surviving section of Salzburg's medieval wall; pass under the wall and walk left along it to a tableau showing how the wall once looked.

Museum of Modern Art on Mönchsberg

The modern-art museum, which features temporary exhibits, is right at the top of the Mönchsberg elevator.

Cost and Hours: €8, Tue-Sun 10:00-18:00, closed Mon.

In the New Town, North of the River

The following sights are across the river from the old town. I've connected them with walking instructions.

• *Begin at the Makartsteg pedestrian bridge, where you can survey the...*

Salzach River

Salzburg's river is called "salt river" not because it's salty, but because of the precious cargo it once carried—the salt mines of Hallein are just nine miles upstream. Salt could be transported from here all the way to the Danube, and on to the Mediterranean via the Black Sea. The riverbanks and roads were built when the river was regulated in the 1850s. Before that, the Salzach was much wider and slower moving. Houses opposite the old town fronted the river with docks and "garages" for boats. The grand buildings just past the bridge (with their elegant promenades and cafés) were built on reclaimed land in the late 19th century in the historicist style of Vienna's Ringstrasse.

Scan the cityscape. Notice all the churches. Salzburg, nicknamed the "Rome of the North," has 38 Catholic churches (plus two Protestant churches and a synagogue). Find the five streams gushing into the river. These date from the 13th century, when the river was split into five canals running through the town to power its mills. The Stein Hotel (upstream, just left of next bridge) has a popular roof-terrace café (see page 156). Downstream, notice the Museum of Modern Art atop the Mönchsberg, with a view restaurant and a faux castle (actually a water reservoir). The Romanesque bell tower with the green copper dome in the distance is the Augustine church, site of the best beer hall in town (the Augustiner Bräustübl).

• *Cross the bridge, pass the recommended Café Bazar (a fine place for a drink), walk two blocks inland, and take a left past the heroic statues into...*

▲Mirabell Gardens and Palace (Schloss)

The bubbly gardens laid out in 1730 for the prince archbishop have been open to the public since 1850 (thanks to Emperor Franz Josef, who was rattled by the popular revolutions of 1848). The gardens are free and open until dusk. The palace is open only as a concert venue (explained later). The statues and the arbor (far left) were featured in *The Sound of Music*. Walk through the gardens to the palace. Look back, enjoy the garden/cathedral/castle view, and imagine how the prince archbishop must have reveled in a vista

SALZBURG

that reminded him of all his secular and religious power. Then go around to the river side of the palace and find the horse.

The rearing **Pegasus statue** (rare and very well-balanced) is the site of a famous *Sound of Music* scene where the kids all danced before lining up on the stairs with Maria (30 yards farther along). The steps lead to a small mound in the park (made of rubble from a former theater).

Nearest the horse, stairs lead between two lions to a pair of tough dwarfs (early volleyball players with spiked mittens) welcoming you to Salzburg's **Dwarf Park.** Cross the elevated walk (noticing the city's fortified walls) to meet statues of a dozen dwarfs who served the prince archbishop—modeled after real people with real fashions in about 1600. This was Mannerist art, from the hyper-realistic age that followed the Renaissance.

There's plenty of **music** here, both in the park and in the palace. A brass band plays free park concerts (May-Aug Sun at 10:30). To properly enjoy the lavish Mirabell Palace—once the prince archbishop's summer palace and now the seat of the mayor—get a ticket to a Schlosskonzerte (my favorite venue for a classical concert—see page 160).

• *Now go a long block southeast to Makartplatz, where, opposite the big and bright Hotel Bristol, you'll find...*

▲Mozart's Residence (Wohnhaus)

Mozart's second home (his family moved here when he was 17) is less interesting than the house where he was born, but it's also roomier, less crowded, and comes with an informative audioguide and a 30-minute narrated slideshow. The building, bombed in World War II, is a reconstruction.

Cost and Hours: €10, €17 combo-ticket includes Mozart's Birthplace in the old town—see page 146, daily 9:00-17:30, July-Aug until 20:00, allow at least one hour for visit, Makartplatz 8, tel. 0662/8742-2740, www.mozarteum.at. Behind the ticket desk is the free Ton und Filmsammlung, an archive of historic concerts on video (Mon-Tue and Fri 9:00-13:00, Wed-Thu 13:00-17:00, closed Sat-Sun).

Visiting Mozart's Residence: The exhibit—seven rooms on one floor—starts in the main hall, which was used by the Mozarts to entertain Salzburg's high society. Here, you can see the museum's prize possession, Mozart's very own piano. Notice the family portrait (c. 1780) on the wall, showing Mozart with his sister Nannerl, their father, and their mother—who'd died two years earlier in Paris. Mozart also had silly crude bull's-eyes made for the pop-gun game popular at the time (licking an "arse," Wolfgang showed his disdain for the rigors of high society).

The rest of the seven rooms feature real artifacts that explore his loves, his intellectual pursuits, his travels, and his family life. At the end, the 30-minute slideshow runs twice an hour, with alternating German/English narration (confirm times when you enter, English usually starts around :40 after the hour).

This museum offers the same computer program as Mozart's Birthplace does, allowing you to see handwritten scores scroll along while actually listening to the same music.

• *From here, you can walk a few blocks back to the main bridge (Staats-brücke), where you'll find the Platzl, a square once used as a hay market. Pause to enjoy the kid-pleasing little fountain. Near the fountain (with your back to the river), Steingasse leads darkly to the right.*

▲Steingasse Stroll

This street, a block in from the river, is wonderfully tranquil and free of Salzburg's touristy crush. Inviting cocktail bars along here come alive at night (see "Steingasse Pub Crawl" on page 176).

The kid-pleasing fountain where Linzgasse meets Steingasse marks an important intersection: where the road to Vienna (Linzgasse) hit the road to Italy (Steingasse). From here traders and pilgrims would look across the river and see the impressive domed University Church (modeled after Vienna's Karlskirche) and know they were entering an important place. Heading up dank, narrow Steingasse, you get a rare glimpse of medieval Salzburg. It's not the church's Salzburg of grand squares and Baroque facades, but the people's Salzburg, of cramped quarters and humble cobbled lanes.

Stop at #9 and look across the river into the old town; this is where the city's original bridge once connected Salzburg's two halves. According to the plaque (of questionable veracity) at #9, this is where Joseph Mohr, who wrote the words to "Silent Night," was born—poor and illegitimate—in 1792. There is no doubt, however, that the popular Christmas carol was composed and first sung in the village of Oberndorf, just outside of Salzburg, in 1818. Stairs lead from near here up to a 17th-century Capuchin monastery.

On the next corner, the wall is gouged out. This scar was left even after the building was restored, to serve as a reminder of the American GI who tried to get a tank down this road during a visit to the town brothel—two blocks farther up Steingasse. Within steps of here is the art cinema (showing movies in their original language) and four recommended bars (described on page 177).

At #19, find the carvings on the old door. Some say these are notices from beggars to the begging community (more numerous after post-Reformation religious wars, which forced many people out of their homes and towns)—a kind of "hobo code" indicating whether the residents would give or not. Trace the wires of the old-fashioned doorbells to the highest floors.

Farther on, you step through the old fortified gate (at #20) and find a commanding Salzburg view across the river. Notice the red dome marking the oldest nunnery in the German-speaking world (established in 712) under the fortress and to the left. The real Maria, who inspired *The Sound of Music*, taught in this nunnery's school. In 1927, she and Captain von Trapp were married in the church you see here (not the church filmed in the movie). He was 47. She was 22. Hmmmm.

From here look back, above the arch you just passed through, and up at part of the town's medieval fortification. The coat of arms on the arch is of the prince archbishop who paid Bavaria a huge ransom to stay out of the Thirty Years' War (smart move). He then built this fortification (in 1634) in anticipation of rampaging armies from both sides.

Today, this street is for making love, not war. The Maison de Plaisir (a few doors down, at #24) has for centuries been a Salzburg brothel. But the climax of this walk is more touristic.

• *For a grand view, head back to the Platzl and the bridge, enter the Stein Hotel (left corner, overlooking the river), and ride the elevator to...*

Stein Terrasse

This café offers one of the best views in town. Hidden from the tourist crush, it's a trendy, professional, local scene. You can discreetly peek at the view, enjoy a drink or light meal, or come back later to gaze into the eyes of your travel partner as you sip a nightcap (small snacks, indoor/outdoor seating, daily 9:00-24:00).

• *Back at the Platzl and the bridge, you can head straight up Linzergasse (away from the river) into a neighborhood packed with recommended accommodations, as well as our final new town sight, the...*

▲St. Sebastian Cemetery

Wander through this quiet oasis. Mozart is buried in Vienna, his mom's in Paris, and his sister is in Salzburg's old town (St. Peter's)—but Wolfgang's wife Constanze ("Constantia") and his father Leopold are buried here (from the black iron gate entrance on Linzergasse, walk 17 paces and look left). When Prince Archbishop Wolf Dietrich had the cemetery moved from around the cathedral and put here, across the river, people didn't like it. To help popularize it, he had his own mausoleum built as its centerpiece. Continue straight past the Mozart tomb to this circular building (English description at door). In the corner to the left of the entrance is the tomb of the Renaissance scientist and physician Paracelsus, best known for developing laudanum as a pain-killer.

Cost and Hours: Free, daily April-Oct 9:00-18:30, Nov-March 9:00-16:00, entry at Linzergasse 43 in summer; in winter go around the corner to the right, through the arch at #37, and around the building to the doorway under the blue seal.

Near Salzburg
▲▲Hellbrunn Castle and Gardens

In about 1610, Prince Archbishop Sittikus decided he needed a lavish palace with a vast and ornate garden purely for pleasure (I imagine after meditating on stewardship and Christ-like values). He built this summer palace and hunting lodge, and just loved inviting his VIP guests from throughout Europe for fun with his trick fountains. Today, Hellbrunn is a popular sight for its palace, formal garden (one of the oldest in Europe, with a gazebo made famous by *The Sound of Music*), amazing fountains, and the excuse it offers to simply get out of the city.

Cost and Hours: €9.50 ticket includes fountain tour and palace audioguide, daily May-Sept 9:00-17:30, July-Aug until 21:00—but tours from 18:00 on don't include the castle (which closes in the evening), April and Oct-Nov 9:00-16:30, these are last tour times, closed Dec-March, tel. 0662/820-3720, www.hellbrunn.at.

Getting There: Hellbrunn is nearly four miles south of Salzburg.

By Bus: Bus #25 leaves from the train station and from the Staatsbrücke bridge (2-3/hour, 20 minutes).

By Bike: In good weather, the trip out to Hellbrunn makes for a pleasant 30-minute bike excursion (see "Riverside or Meadow Bike Ride," later, and ask for a map when you rent your bike).

Visiting the Castle: Upon arrival, buy your **fountain tour** ticket and get a tour time. Tours generally go on the half-hour. The 40-minute English/German tours take you laughing and scrambling through a series of amazing 17th-century garden settings with lots of splashy fun and a guide who seems almost sadistic in the joy he has in soaking his group. (Hint: When you see a wet place, cover your camera.) If there's a wait until your tour, you can see the palace first.

With the help of the included audioguide, wander through the **palace** exhibit to the sounds of shrieking fountain-taunted tourists below. The palace was built in a style inspired by the Venetian architect Palladio, who was particularly popular around 1600, and quickly became a cultural destination. This was the era when the aristocratic ritual was to go hunting in the morning (hence the decor's theme) and enjoy an opera in the evening. The first opera north of the Alps, imported from Italy, was performed here. The decor is Mannerist (between Renaissance and Baroque), with faux antiquities and lots of surprising moments—intentional irregularities were in vogue after the strict logic, balance, and Greek-inspired symmetry of the Renaissance. (For example, the main hall is not in the palace's center, but at the far end.) The palace exhibit also explains the impressive 17th-century hydraulic engineering that let gravity power the intricate fountains.

SALZBURG

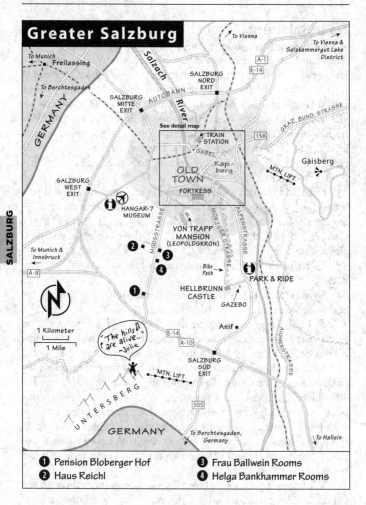

Greater Salzburg

To Munich
Freilassing
To Berchtesgaden
GERMANY
To Vienna
To Vienna &
Salzkammergut Lake
District
Salzach River
SALZBURG NORD EXIT
A-1
E-14
AUTOBAHN
SALZBURG MITTE EXIT
GRAZ. BUND. STRASSE
See detail map
TRAIN STATION
158
GABEL
OLD TOWN
Kap.-berg
MTN. LIFT
Gaisberg
SALZBURG WEST EXIT
FORTRESS
HANGAR-7 MUSEUM
MOOSSTRASSE
VON TRAPP MANSION (LEOPOLDSKRON)
MORZGER STRASSE
ALPENSTRASSE
To Munich & Innsbruck
A-8
❷
❸
❹
Bike Path
PARK & RIDE
❶
HELLBRUNN CASTLE
GAZEBO
AIGNERSTRASSE
1 Kilometer
1 Mile
N
"The hills are alive..." -Julie
E-14
Anif
A-10
SALZBURG SÜD EXIT
MTN. LIFT
UNTERSBERG
305
GERMANY
To Berchtesgaden, Germany
To Hallein

❶ Pension Bloberger Hof   ❸ Frau Ballwein Rooms
❷ Haus Reichl   ❹ Helga Bankhammer Rooms

After the fountain tour you're free to wander the delightful **garden** and pop out to see the **gazebo** made famous by the "Sixteen Going On Seventeen" song from *The Sound of Music*.

▲▲Riverside or Meadow Bike Ride

The Salzach River has smooth, flat, and scenic bike lanes along each side (thanks to medieval tow paths—cargo boats would float downstream and be dragged back up by horses). On a sunny day, I can think of no more shout-worthy escape from the city.

Perhaps the most pristine, meadow-filled farm-country route is the nearly four-mile path along Hellbrunner Allee; it's an easy ride with a worthy destination (Hellbrunn Castle, listed above): From the middle of town, head along the river on Rudolfskai, with the river on your left and the fortress on your right. After passing the last bridge at the edge of the old town (Nonntaler Brücke), cut inland along Petersbrunnstrasse, until you reach the university and Akademiestrasse. Beyond it find the start of Freisaalweg, which becomes the delightful Hellbrunner Allee bike path...which leads directly to the palace (paralleling Morzgerstrasse; see map on page 158).

Even a quickie ride across town is a great Salzburg experience. In the evening, the riverbanks are a world of floodlit spires. For bike rental information, see "Getting Around Salzburg—By Bike," earlier.

Hangar-7

This purpose-built hangar at the Salzburg airport houses the car-and-aircraft collection of Dietrich Mateschitz, the flamboyant founder of the Red Bull energy-drink empire. Under the hangar's modern steel-and-glass dome are 20 or so glittering planes and racecars, plus several pretentious bars, cafés, and restaurants, all designed to brandish the Red Bull "culture." To learn about what's on display you can borrow an iPod Touch with English information, or get information on the iPads posted by each exhibit.

Mateschitz is Salzburg's big personality these days: He has a mysterious mansion at the edge of town, sponsors the local "Red Bull" soccer and hockey teams, owns several chic Salzburg eateries and cocktail bars, and employs 6,000 mostly good-looking people. He seems much like the energy drink that made him rich and powerful—a high-energy, anything's-possible cultural Terminator.

Cost and Hours: Free, daily 9:00-22:00, bus #8 from Hanuschplatz to the Salzburg airport, www.hangar-7.com.

Eating: At the hangar, the Mayday Bar serves experimental food, and Restaurant Ikarus features a different well-known chef each month. (Mateschitz's recommended Carpe Diem cocktail bar, in the old town, is also Red Bullish.)

Music in Salzburg

▲▲Salzburg Festival (Salzburger Festspiele)

Each summer, from late July to the end of August, Salzburg hosts its famous Salzburg Festival, founded in 1920 to employ Vienna's musicians in the summer. This fun and festive time is crowded—a total of 200,000 tickets are sold to festival events annually—but there are usually plenty of beds (except for a few August weekends). Events take place primarily in three big halls: the Opera and Orchestra venues in the Festival House, and the Landes Theater, where German-language plays are performed. Tickets for the big festival events are generally expensive (€50-600) and sell out well in advance (bookable from January). Most tourists think they're "going to the Salzburg Festival" by seeing smaller non-festival events that go on during the festival weeks. For these lesser events, same-day tickets are normally available (the ticket office on Mozartplatz, in the TI, prints a daily list of concerts and charges a 30 percent fee to book them). For specifics on this year's festival schedule and tickets, visit www.salzburgfestival.at.

Music lovers in town during the festival who don't have tickets (or money) can still enjoy **Festival Nights,** a free series showing videos of previous festival performances, projected on a big screen on Kapitelplatz (behind the cathedral). It's a fun scene, with plenty of folding chairs and a food circus of temporary eateries; schedules are posted next to the screen.

▲▲Musical Events Year-Round

Salzburg is busy throughout the year, with 2,000 classical performances in its palaces and churches annually. Pick up the events calendar at the TI (free, bimonthly). I've never planned in advance, and I've enjoyed great concerts with every visit. Whenever you visit, you'll have a number of concerts (generally small chamber groups) to choose from. Here are some of the more accessible events:

Concerts at Hohensalzburg Fortress (Festungskonzerte)

Nearly nightly concerts—Mozart's greatest hits for beginners—are held atop Festungsberg, in the "prince's chamber" of the fortress, featuring small chamber groups (open seating after the first six more expensive rows, €31 or €38 plus €3.80 for the funicular; at 19:30, 20:00, or 20:30; doors open 30 minutes early, reserve at tel. 0662/825-858 or via www.salzburghighlights.at, pick up tickets at the door). The medieval-feeling chamber has windows overlooking the city, and the concert gives you a chance to enjoy the grand city view and a stroll through the castle courtyard. For €51, you can combine the concert with a four-course dinner (starts 2 hours before concert). The downside: Hearing Baroque music in an incongruously Gothic setting is not ideal.

Concerts at the Mirabell Palace (Schlosskonzerte)

The nearly nightly chamber music concerts at the Mirabell Palace are performed in a lavish Baroque setting. They come with more sophisticated programs and better musicians than the fortress concerts... and Baroque music flying around a Baroque hall is a happy bird in the right cage (open seating after the first five pricier rows, €29-35, usually at 20:00—but check flier for times, doors open one hour ahead, tel. 0662/848-586, www.salzburger-schlosskonzerte.at).

"Five O'Clock Concerts" (5-Uhr-Konzerte)

These concerts are cheaper, since they feature young artists. While the series is formally named after the brother of Joseph Haydn, it offers music from various masters. Performances are generally chamber music with a string trio playing original 18th-century instruments. On my last visit, the concerts were still being held next to St. Peter's Church in the old town—but they may relocate in

2014 (€12-15, mid-June-mid-Sept Tue and Thu at 17:00, no concerts in off-season, 45-60 minutes, tel. 0662/8445-7619, www.5-uhr-konzerte.com).

Mozart Piano Sonatas

St. Peter's Abbey hosts these concerts each weekend. This short (45-minute) and inexpensive concert is ideal for families (€18, €9 for children, €45 for a family of four, Fri and Sat at 19:00 year-round, in the abbey's Romanesque Hall—a.k.a. Romanischer Saal, mobile 0664-423-5645).

Marionette Theater

Salzburg's much-loved marionette theater offers operas with spell-binding marionettes and recorded music. A troupe of 10 puppeteers—actors themselves—brings the artfully created puppets at the end of their five-foot strings to life. The 180 performances a year alternate between *The Sound of Music* and various German-language operas (with handy superscripts in English). While the 300-plus-seat venue is forgettable, the art of the marionettes enchants adults and children alike (€24-35, May-Sept nearly nightly at 17:00 or 19:30, near Mozart's Residence at Schwarzstrasse 24, tel. 0662/872-406, www.marionetten.at). For a sneak preview, check out the videos playing at the marionette exhibit up in the fortress.

Mozart Dinner Concert

For those who'd like some classical music but would rather not sit through a concert, the recommended Stiftskeller St. Peter restaurant offers a traditional candlelit meal with Mozart's greatest hits performed by a string quartet and singers in historic costumes gavotting among the tables. In this elegant Baroque setting, tourists clap between movements and get three courses of food (from Mozart-era recipes) mixed with three 20-minute courses of crowd-pleasing music—structured much as such evenings were in Baroque-era times (€54, €9 discount for Mozart-lovers who book direct with this book, nightly at 20:00, dress is "smart casual," call to reserve at 0662/828-695, www.mozartdinnerconcert.com.

Music at Mass

Each Sunday morning, three great churches offer a Mass, generally with glorious music. The **Salzburg Cathedral** is likely your best bet for fine music to worship by, and many Masses are followed by a free organ concert (10:00 Mass, music program at www.kirchen.net/dommusik). Nearby (just outside Domplatz, with the pointy green spire), the **Franciscan church** is the locals' choice and is enthusiastic about its musical Masses (at 9:00, www.franziskanerkirche-salzburg.at—click on "Programm"). **St. Peter's Church** sometimes has music (at 10:15, www.stift-stpeter.at—click on "Kirchenmusik"). For more, see the Salzburg events guide (available at TIs) for details.

Free Brass Band Concert
A traditional brass band plays in the Mirabell Gardens (May-Aug Sun at 10:30).

Sleeping in Salzburg

Finding a room in Salzburg, even during its music festival (mid-July-Aug), is usually easy. Rates always rise significantly (20-30 percent) during the music festival, during Advent (four weeks leading up to Christmas, when street markets are at full blast) and usually around Easter. Unless otherwise noted, these higher "festival" prices do not appear in the ranges I've listed. Many places charge 10 percent extra for a one-night stay.

In the New Town, North of the River

These listings, clustering around Linzergasse, are in a pleasant neighborhood a 15-minute walk from the train station (for directions, see "Arrival in Salzburg," earlier) and a 10-minute walk to the old town. If you're coming from the old town, simply cross the main bridge (Staatsbrücke) to the mostly traffic-free Linzergasse. If driving, exit the highway at Salzburg-Nord, follow Vogelweiderstrasse straight to its end, and turn right. Parking is easy at the nearby Mirabell-Congress garage (€15/day, your hotel may be able to get you a €1-2 discount, Mirabellplatz).

$$$ Altstadthotel Wolf-Dietrich, around the corner from Linzergasse on pedestrians-only Wolf-Dietrich-Strasse, is well-located (half its rooms overlook St. Sebastian Cemetery). With 40 tastefully plush rooms—a third of them in an annex across the street—it projects a big-hotel feeling, but has small-hotel prices (roughly Sb-€80, Db-€120, rates vary with demand, family deals, readers of this book get a discount on prevailing price, non-smoking, elevator, free Internet access and Wi-Fi, annex rooms have air-con, pool with loaner swimsuits, sauna, free DVD library, Wolf-Dietrich-Strasse 7, tel. 0662/871-275, fax 0662/871-2759, www.salzburg-hotel.at, office@salzburg-hotel.at).

$$ Hotel Trumer Stube, well-located three blocks from the river just off Linzergasse, has 20 clean rooms and is run by the Hirschbichler family (Sb-€65, Db-€105, Tb-€128, Qb-€147; for best prices, email and ask for the best Rick Steves cash-only rate; breakfast with a personal touch-€7.50 extra, non-smoking, elevator, free Wi-Fi, look for the flower boxes at Bergstrasse 6, tel. 0662/874-776, fax 0662/874-326, www.trumer-stube.at, info@trumer-stube.at; mom and daughter are both named Marianne).

$$ Hotel Krone1512, about five blocks from the river, is plain and basic, with 20 big, creaky, and well-kept rooms. Back-

Sleep Code

(€1 = about $1.30, country code: 43, area code: 0662)
S = Single, **D** = Double/Twin, **T** = Triple, **Q** = Quad, **b** = bathroom, **s** = shower only. Unless otherwise noted, credit cards are accepted and breakfast is included. All of these places speak English.

To help you sort easily through these listings, I've divided the accommodations into three categories, based on the price for a standard double room with bath:

  $$$ **Higher Priced**—Most rooms €120 or more.
  $$ **Moderately Priced**—Most rooms between €60-120.
  $ **Lower Priced**—Most rooms €60 or less.

Prices can change without notice; verify the hotel's current rates online or by email.

---

facing rooms are quieter than the streetside ones. Stay a while in their pleasant cliffside garden (Sb-€69, Db-€119, Tb-€159, Qb-€189, ask for discount off these prices with this book, elevator, free Wi-Fi in common areas, Linzergasse 48, tel. 0662/872-300, fax 0662/8723-0066, www.krone1512.at, hotel@krone1512.at, Günther Hausknost). Günther also offers tours (€10/person, 2 hours, 5 people minimum).

$$ Hotel Schwarzes Rössl is a university dorm that becomes a student-run hotel each July, August, and September. The location couldn't be handier. It looks like a normal hotel from the outside, and its 50 rooms, while a bit spartan, are as comfortable as a hotel on the inside (S-€46, Sb-€60, D-€76, Db-€92, Tb-€120, ask for Rick Steves discount, good breakfast, free Internet access and Wi-Fi in common areas, no rooms rented Oct-June, just off Linzergasse at Priesterhausgasse 6, tel. 0662/874-426, www.academiahotels.at, schwarzes.roessl@academiahotels.at).

$$ Institute St. Sebastian is in a somewhat sterile but very clean historic building next to St. Sebastian Cemetery. From October through June, the institute houses female students from various Salzburg colleges and also rents 40 beds for travelers (men and women). From July through September, the students are gone, and they rent all 100 beds (including 20 twin rooms) to travelers. The building has spacious public areas, a roof garden, a piano that guests are welcome to play, and some of the best rooms and dorm beds in town for the money. The immaculate doubles come with modern baths and head-to-toe twin beds (S-€37, Sb-€45, D-€58,

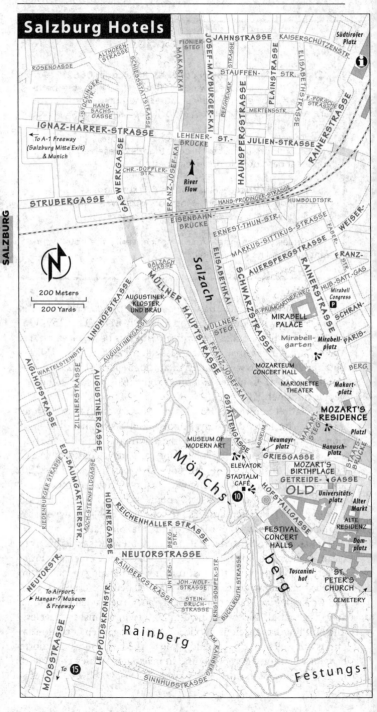

Salzburg Hotels

SALZBURG

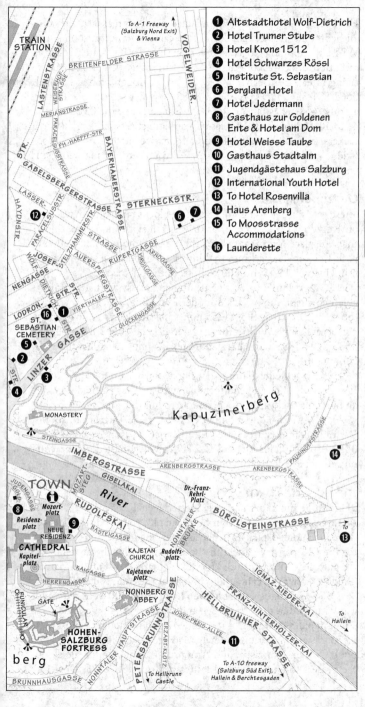

1. Altstadthotel Wolf-Dietrich
2. Hotel Trumer Stube
3. Hotel Krone 1512
4. Hotel Schwarzes Rössl
5. Institute St. Sebastian
6. Bergland Hotel
7. Hotel Jedermann
8. Gasthaus zur Goldenen Ente & Hotel am Dom
9. Hotel Weisse Taube
10. Gasthaus Stadtalm
11. Jugendgästehaus Salzburg
12. International Youth Hotel
13. To Hotel Rosenvilla
14. Haus Arenberg
15. To Moosstrasse Accommodations
16. Launderette

SALZBURG

Db-€72, Tb-€87, Qb-€98, includes simple breakfast, elevator, all bedrooms are non-smoking, free cable Internet in rooms, pay Wi-Fi in common areas, self-service laundry-€4/load, Oct-June reception closed 12:00-16:00—call to arrange key pickup if arriving after 21:00, Linzergasse 41, enter through arch at #37, tel. 0662/871-386, fax 0662/8713-8685, www.st-sebastian-salzburg.at, office@st-sebastian-salzburg.at). Students like the €21 bunks in 4- to 10-bed dorms (€1.50 less if you have sheets, no lockout, free lockers, free showers). You'll find self-service kitchens on each floor (fridge space is free; request a key). If you need parking, request it well in advance.

On Rupertgasse

These two similar hotels are about five blocks farther from the river on Rupertgasse—a breeze for drivers but with more street noise than the places on Linzergasse. They're both modern and well-run, with free on-site parking, making them good values if you don't mind being a 15-20-minute walk from the old town.

$$ Bergland Hotel is charming and classy, with 18 comfortable neo-rustic rooms. It's a modern building, spacious and solid (Sb-€65, Db-€105, Tb-€125, non-smoking, elevator, pay Internet access, free Wi-Fi, Rupertgasse 15, tel. 0662/872-318, fax 0662/872-3188, www.berglandhotel.at, office@berglandhotel.at, Kuhn family).

$$ Hotel Jedermann, a few doors down, is simpler and larger. It's tastefully done and comfortable, with an artsy painted-concrete ambience, a backyard garden, and 30 rooms (Sb-€65, Db-€95, Tb-€120, Qb-€160, non-smoking, elevator, cable Internet in rooms, Wi-Fi in common areas, free Internet access, Rupertgasse 25, tel. 0662/873-2410, fax 0662/873-2419, www.hotel-jedermann.com, office@hotel-jedermann.com, Herr und Frau Gmachl).

In the Old Town

These three hotels are perfectly located near Residenzplatz. While this area is car-restricted, your hotel can give you a code that lets you drive in to unload, pick up a map and parking instructions, and head for the €14-per-day garage in the mountain (punch the code into the gate near Mozartplatz). You can't actually drive into the narrow Goldgasse, but you can park to unload at the end of the street.

$$$ Gasthaus zur Goldenen Ente is in a 600-year-old building with medieval stone arches and narrow stairs on a pedestrian street in old Salzburg. Located above a good restaurant, most of its 22 rooms are modern and newly renovated—ask for one when you book. Ulrike, Franziska, and Anita run a tight ship for the absentee owners (Sb-€100, Db-€125; festival rates Sb-€125, Db-€160;

extra person-€40, non-smoking, elevator, free Internet access and Wi-Fi, Goldgasse 10, tel. 0662/845-622, fax 0662/845-6229, www.ente.at, hotel@ente.at).

$$$ Hotel am Dom, across from the Goldenen Ente, offers 15 chic, upscale rooms, some with their original wood-beam ceilings (Sb-€100-180, standard Db-€120-260, "superior" Db-€140-280, rates vary with demand, air-con, non-smoking, elevator, free Internet access, cable Internet and Wi-Fi available, Goldgasse 17, tel. 0662/842-765, fax 0662/8427-6555, www.hotelamdom.at, office@hotelamdom.at).

$$ Hotel Weisse Taube has 30 comfortable rooms in a quiet dark-wood 14th-century building, well-located about a block off Mozartplatz (Sb-€69-94, Db with shower-€104-139, bigger Db with bath-€119-185, higher prices are during festival, ask for discount with this book if you reserve direct and pay cash, elevator, pay Internet access and Wi-Fi, tel. 0662/842-404, fax 0662/841-783, Kaigasse 9, www.weissetaube.at, hotel@weissetaube.at).

Hostels

The Institute St. Sebastian, listed earlier, also has cheap dorm beds.

$ Gasthaus Stadtalm (a.k.a. the *Naturfreundehaus*) is a local version of a mountaineers' hut and a great budget alternative. Snuggled in a forest on the remains of a 15th-century castle wall atop the little mountain overlooking Salzburg, it has magnificent town and mountain views. While the 22 beds are designed-for-backpackers basic, the price and view are the best in town—with the right attitude, it's a fine experience (€19/person in 4- and 6-bed dorms, one double-bedded D-€43; includes breakfast, sheets, and shower; non-smoking, free Wi-Fi, recommended café, lockers, 2 minutes from top of Mönchsberg elevator, Mönchsberg 19C, tel. & fax 0662/841-729, www.stadtalm.at, info@diestadtalm.com, Peter). Once you've dropped your bags here, it's a five-minute walk down the cliffside stairs into Toscaninihof, in the middle of the old town (path always lit).

$ Jugendgästehaus Salzburg, just steps from the center of the old town, is nevertheless removed from the bustle. While its dorm rooms are the standard crammed-with-beds variety—and the hallways will bring back high-school memories—the doubles and family rooms are modern, roomy, and bright, and the public spaces are quite pleasant (bed in 8-person dorm-€24; Db-€80-120; includes breakfast and sheets, free Internet access and Wi-Fi, *The Sound of Music* plays daily, bike rental-€10/day or €6/half-day, parking-€5/day, just around the east side of the castle hill at Josef-Preis-Allee 18; from train station, take bus #5 or #25 to the Justizgebäude stop, then head left one block along the bushy wall, cross Petersbrunnstrasse, find shady Josef-Preis-Allee, and walk a few minutes to the end—the hostel is the big orange/green building on the right; tel. 05/708-3613, fax 05/708-3611, www.jufa.eu/salzburg, salzburg@jufa.eu).

$ International Youth Hotel, a.k.a. the "Yo-Ho," is the most lively, handy, and American of Salzburg's hostels. This backpacker haven is a youthful and easygoing place that speaks English first; has cheap meals, 186 beds, lockers, tour discounts, and no curfew; plays *The Sound of Music* free daily at 19:00; runs a lively bar; and welcomes anyone of any age. The noisy atmosphere and lack of a curfew can make it hard to sleep (€18-21/person in 4- to 8-bed dorms, €21-22 in dorms with bathrooms, D-€60, Ds-€75, T-€66, Q-€75, Qs-€87, includes sheets, breakfast-€3.50, pay Internet access, free Wi-Fi, laundry-€4 wash and dry, 6 blocks from station toward Linzergasse and 6 blocks from river at Paracelsusstrasse 9, tel. 0662/879-649, www.yoho.at, office@yoho.at).

Four-Star Hotels in Residential Neighborhoods away from the Center

If you want plush furnishings, spacious public spaces, generous balconies, gardens, and free parking, consider the following places. These two modern hotels in nondescript residential neighborhoods are a fine value if you don't mind the 15-minute walk from the old town. While not ideal for train travelers, drivers in need of no-stress comfort for a home base should consider these (see map on page 164).

$$$ Hotel Rosenvilla, close to the river, offers 15 rooms with bright furnishings, surrounded by a leafy garden (Sb-€79-108, Db-€135-165, bigger Db-€145-199, Db suite-€168-255, higher prices are during festival, no elevator, free Wi-Fi, Höfelgasse 4, tel. 0662/621-765, fax 0662/625-2308, www.rosenvilla.com, hotel@rosenvilla.com).

$$$ Haus Arenberg, higher up opposite the old town, rents 17 big, breezy rooms—most with generous balconies—in a quiet garden setting (Sb-€85-104, Db-€135-159, Tb-€159-175, Qb-€165-185, higher prices are during festival, no elevator, free Wi-Fi, electric bikes-€12/day, Blumensteinstrasse 8, tel. 0662/640-097, fax 0662/640-0973, www.arenberg-salzburg.at, info@arenberg-salzburg.at, family Leobacher).

Pensions on Moosstrasse

These are generally roomy and comfortable, and come with a good breakfast, easy parking, and tourist information. Off-season, competition softens prices. While they are a bus ride from town, with a €4.20 transit day pass *(Tageskarte)* and the frequent service, this shouldn't keep you away (see map on page 158). In fact, many homeowners will happily pick you up at the train station if you simply telephone them and ask. Most will also do laundry for a small fee for those staying at least two nights. I've listed prices for two nights or more—if staying only one night, expect a 10 percent surcharge. Most push tours and concerts to make money on the side. As they are earning a commission, if you go through them, you'll probably lose the discount I've negotiated for my readers who go direct.

The busy street called Moosstrasse, which runs southwest of the Mönchsberg (behind the mountain and away from the center old town), is lined with farmhouses offering rooms. Handy bus #21 connects Moosstrasse to the center frequently (Mon-Fri 4/ hour until 19:00, Sat 4/hour until 17:00, evenings and Sun 2/hour, 20 minutes). To get to these pensions from the train station, take any bus heading toward the center to Makartplatz, where you'll change to #21. If you're coming from the old town, catch bus #21 from Hanuschplatz, just downstream of the Staatsbrücke bridge near the *Tabak* kiosk. Buy a €1.90 *Einzelkarte-Kernzone* ticket (for one trip) or a €4.20 *Tageskarte* (day pass, good for 24 hours) from the streetside machine and punch it when you board the bus. The bus stop you use for each place is included in the following listings. If you're driving from the center, go through the tunnel, continue straight on Neutorstrasse, and take the fourth left onto Moosstrasse. Drivers exit the autobahn at *Süd* and then head in the direction of *Grödig*. Each place can recommend a favorite Moosstrasse eatery (Reiterhof, at #151, is particularly popular).

$$ Pension Bloberger Hof, while more a hotel than a pension, is comfortable and friendly, with a peaceful, rural location and 20 farmer-plush, good-value rooms. It's the farthest out, but reached by the same bus #21 from the center. Inge and her daughter Sylvia offer a discount to those who have this book, reserve direct, and pay cash (Sb-€60-75, Db-€75, big new Db with balcony-€100-110, Db suite-€120-130, higher prices are during festival, extra bed-€20, 10 percent extra for one-night stays, family apartment with kitchen, non-smoking, free Internet access and Wi-Fi, restaurant for guests, free loaner bikes, free station pickup if staying 3 nights, Hammerauer Strasse 4, bus stop: Hammerauer Strasse, tel. 0662/830-227, fax 0662/827-061, www.blobergerhof.at, office@blobergerhof.at).

$$ Haus Reichl, with two good rooms at the end of a long lane, feels peaceful and remote, but may close in 2013. Franziska offers free loaner bikes for guests (20-minute pedal to the center) and bakes fresh cakes most days (Db-€60-64, Tb-€75-84, Qb-€92-104, higher prices are during festival, cash preferred, in-room tea/coffee, non-smoking, no Internet access, between Ballwein and

Bankhammer B&Bs, 200 yards down Reiterweg to #52, bus stop: Gsengerweg, tel. & fax 0662/826-248, www.privatzimmer.at/ haus-reichl, haus.reichl@telering.at).

$ Frau Ballwein offers eleven cozy, charming, and fresh rooms in a delightful, family-friendly farmhouse. Some rooms come with intoxicating-view balconies (Sb-€38-45, Db-€55-65, Tb-€75-85, Qb-€85-95, 2-bedroom apartment for up to 5 people-€95-110, higher prices are during festival, no surcharge for one-night stays, cash only, farm-fresh breakfasts amid her hanging teapot collection, non-smoking, free Wi-Fi, 2 free loaner bikes, free parking, Moosstrasse 69a, bus stop: Gsengerweg, tel. & fax 0662/824-029, www.haus-ballwein.at, haus.ballwein@gmx.net).

$ Helga Bankhammer rents four nondescript rooms in a farmhouse, with a real dairy farm out back (D-€48, Db-€52, no surcharge for one-night stays, family deals, non-smoking, no Internet access, laundry-about €7/load, Moosstrasse 77, bus stop: Marienbad, tel. & fax 0662/830-067, www.privatzimmer.at/helga. bankhammer, bankhammer@aon.at).

Eating in Salzburg

In the Old Town

Salzburg boasts many inexpensive, fun, and atmospheric eateries. Most of these restaurants are centrally located in the old town, famous with visitors but also enjoyed by locals.

Gasthaus zum Wilden Mann is *the* place if the weather's bad and you're in the mood for a hearty, cheap meal at a shared table in one well-antlered (and non-smoking) room. Notice the century-old flood photos on the wall. For a quick lunch, get the *Bauernschmaus*, a mountain of dumplings, kraut, and peasant's meats (€12). While they have a few outdoor tables, the atmosphere is all indoors, and the menu is not great for hot-weather food. Owner Robert—who runs the restaurant with Schwarzenegger-like energy—enjoys fostering a convivial ambience, encouraging strangers to share tables, and serving fresh traditional cuisine at great prices. I simply love this place (€8.50 two-course lunch specials, €9-13 daily specials posted on the wall, kitchen open Mon-Sat 11:00-21:00, closed Sun, 2 minutes from Mozart's Birthplace, enter from Getreidegasse 22 or Griesgasse 17, tel. 0662/841-787).

Stiftskeller St. Peter has been in business for more than 1,000 years—it was mentioned in the biography of Charlemagne. It's classy and high-end touristy, serving uninspired traditional Austrian cuisine (€14-26 main courses, daily 11:30-22:30, indoor/outdoor seating, next to St. Peter's Church at foot of Mönchsberg, tel. 0662/841-268). They host the Mozart Dinner Concert described on page 161.

St. Paul's Stub'n Beer Garden is tucked secretly away under the fortress with a decidedly untouristy atmosphere. The food is better than at beer halls, and a young, bohemian-chic clientele fills its two troll-like rooms and its idyllic tree-shaded garden. *Kasnock'n* is a tasty mountaineers' pasta with cheese served in an iron pan with a side salad for €9—it's enough for two. Reservations are smart (€9-17 main courses, Mon-Sat 17:00-22:00, open later for drinks only, closed Sun, Herrengasse 16, tel. 0662/843-220, Bernard).

Zirkelwirt serves cheese dumplings and modern Mediterranean, Italian, and Austrian dishes, and always has a daily special (chalked on the board). It's an old *Gasthaus* dining room with a medieval tiki-hut terrace a block off Mozartplatz, yet a world away from the tourism of the old town. While the waitstaff, music, and vibe feel young, it attracts Salzburgers of all ages (€9-14 main courses, nightly 17:00-24:00, Pfeifergasse 14, tel. 0662/843-472).

Café Tomaselli (with its Kiosk annex and terrace seating across the way) has long been Salzburg's top place to see and be seen. While pricey, it is good for lingering and people-watching. Tomaselli serves light meals and lots of drinks, keeps long hours daily, and has fine seating on the square, a view terrace upstairs, and indoor tables. Despite its fancy inlaid wood paneling, 19th-century portraits, and chandeliers, it's surprisingly low-key (€3-7 light meals, daily 7:00-21:00, until 22:00 during music festival, until 20:00 Nov-March, Alter Markt 9, tel. 0662/844-488).

Saran Essbar is the product of hardworking Mr. Saran (from the Punjab), who cooks and serves with his heart. This delightful little eatery casts a rich orange glow under medieval vaults. Its fun menu is small (Mr. Saran is committed to both freshness and value), mixing Austrian (great schnitzel and strudel), Italian, and Asian vegetarian, and always offering salads (€10-16 main courses, daily 11:00-15:00 & 17:00-22:00, often open later, a block off Mozartplatz at Judengasse 10, tel. 0662/846-628).

Vietnam Pho 18, fragrant with fresh cilantro, is where the Nguyen family dishes up Vietnamese noodle soups and other Asian standards in a six-table restaurant a long block from the cathedral (€8 main courses, eat in or take out, Sat-Thu 11:30-15:00 & 17:00-20:00, Fri 11:30-15:00, Kapitelgasse 11, mobile 0660-257-5588).

Youthful Cafés at the West End of the Old Town

Bar Club Café Republic, a hip hangout for local young people opposite the base of the Mönchsberg elevator, feels like a theater lobby during intermission. It serves good food both outdoors and in (with both smoking- and non-smoking rooms inside). It's ideal if you want something mod, untouristy, and un-wursty (Asian and

SALZBURG

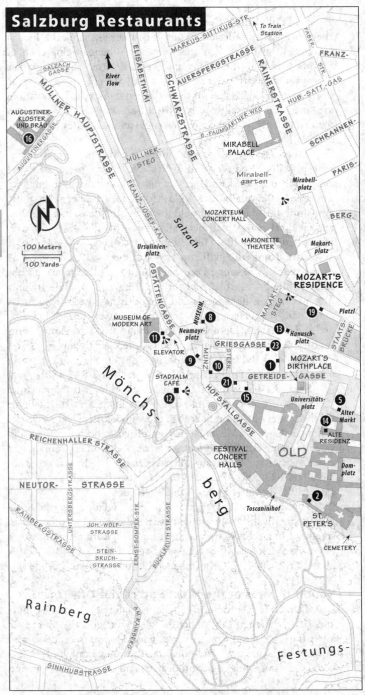

Salzburg Restaurants

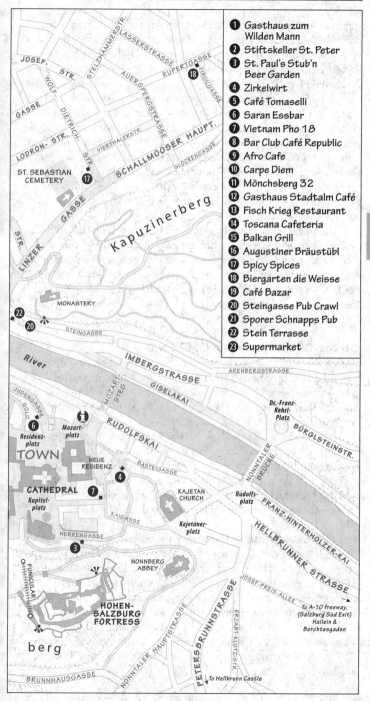

1. Gasthaus zum Wilden Mann
2. Stiftskeller St. Peter
3. St. Paul's Stub'n Beer Garden
4. Zirkelwirt
5. Café Tomaselli
6. Saran Essbar
7. Vietnam Pho 18
8. Bar Club Café Republic
9. Afro Cafe
10. Carpe Diem
11. Mönchsberg 32
12. Gasthaus Stadtalm Café
13. Fisch Krieg Restaurant
14. Toscana Cafeteria
15. Balkan Grill
16. Augustiner Bräustübl
17. Spicy Spices
18. Biergarten die Weisse
19. Café Bazar
20. Steingasse Pub Crawl
21. Sporer Schnapps Pub
22. Stein Terrasse
23. Supermarket

SALZBURG

international menu, €9-15 main courses, lots of hard drinks, open daily 8:00-late, trendy breakfasts served 8:00-18:00, Sun brunch with live music 10:00-14:00, music with a DJ Fri and Sat from 23:00, salsa dance club Tue night from 21:00—no cover, Anton-Neumayr-Platz 2, tel. 0662/841-613).

Afro Cafe, between Getreidegasse and the Mönchsberg elevator, is a hit with local students. Its agenda: to put a fun spin on African cuisine (adapted to European tastes). It serves tea, coffee, cocktails, and tasty food with a dose of '70s funk and a healthy sense of humor. The menu includes pan-African specialties—try the spicy chicken couscous—as well as standard salads (€7 weekday lunch specials, €10-15 main courses, Mon-Sat 9:00-24:00, closed Sun, between Getreidegasse and cliff face at Bürgerspitalplatz 5, tel. 0662/844-888).

Carpe Diem is a project by the local Donald Trump, Red Bull tycoon Dietrich Mateschitz. Salzburg's beautiful people, fueled by Red Bull, present themselves here in the chic ground-floor café and trendy "lifestyle bar," which serves quality cocktails and fine finger food in cones. Upstairs is a restaurant boasting a Michelin star (restaurant closed Sun, otherwise whole place open daily 8:30-late, Getreidegasse 50, tel. 0662/848-800).

On the Cliffs Above the Old Town

Riding the Mönchsberg elevator from the west end of the old town up to the clifftop deposits you near two very different eateries: the chic Mönchsberg 32 at the modern art museum, and the Gasthaus Stadtalm Café at the funky old mountaineers' hut—each with commanding city views.

Mönchsberg 32 is a sleek, modern café/bar/restaurant overlooking Salzburg from the top of the Mönchsberg elevator. Even if you're not hiking anywhere, this makes for a great place to enjoy a drink and the view (daily 9:00-24:00, closed Mon off-season, popular breakfast place daily 9:00-16:00, buy a one-way elevator ticket—they give customers a free pass to descend, tel. 0662/841-000).

Gasthaus Stadtalm Café, in Salzburg's mountaineers' hut, sits high above the old town on the edge of the cliff with cheap prices, good traditional food, and great views. If hiking across the Mönchsberg, make this a stop (€10-12 main dishes, €9-10 salads, cliff-side garden seating or cozy-mountain-hut indoor seating—one indoor view table is booked for a decade of New Year's celebrations, daily 10:00-18:00, June-Aug until 23:00, hours are weather-dependent, 5 minutes from top of Mönchsberg elevator, also reachable by stairs from Toscaninihof, Mönchsberg 19C, tel. 0662/841-729, Peter).

Eating Cheaply in the Old Town

Fisch Krieg Restaurant, on the river where the fishermen used to sell their catch, is a great value. They serve fast, fresh, and inexpensive fish in a casual dining room—where trees grow through the ceiling—as well as great riverside seating (€2.30 fishwiches to go, €7.50 self-serve main courses, salad bar, Mon-Fri 8:30-18:30, Sat 8:30-13:00, closed Sun, Hanuschplatz 4, tel. 0662/843-732).

Toscana Cafeteria Mensa is the students' lunch canteen, fast and cheap—with indoor seating and a great courtyard for sitting outside with students and teachers instead of tourists. Choose between two daily soup-and-main course specials, each around €5 (Mon-Thu 8:30-17:00, Fri 8:30-15:00, hot meals served 11:00-13:30 only, closed Sat-Sun, behind the Old Residenz, in the courtyard opposite Sigmund-Haffner-Gasse 16).

Sausage stands *(Würstelstände)* serve the town's favorite "fast food." The best stands (like those on Universitätsplatz) use the same boiling water all day, which gives the weenies more flavor. The Salzburgers' favorite spicy sausage is sold at the 60-year-old **Balkan Grill,** run by chatty Frau Ebner (€3; survey the five spicy options—described in English—and choose a number; takeaway only, steady and sturdy local crowd, daily 11:00-19:00, hours vary with demand, hiding down the tunnel at Getreidegasse 33 across from Eisgrotte).

Picnics: Picnickers will appreciate the well-stocked **Billa supermarket** at Griesgasse 19a, just across the street from the recommended Fisch Krieg Restaurant (Mon-Fri 7:15-19:30, Sat 7:15-18:00, closed Sun). The bustling morning **produce market** (Mon-Sat, closed Sun) on Universitätsplatz, behind Mozart's Birthplace, is fun, but expensive.

Away from the Center

Augustiner Bräustübl, a huge 1,000-seat beer garden within a monk-run brewery in the Kloster Mülln, is rustic and raw. On busy nights, it's like a Munich beer hall with no music but the volume turned up. When it's cool outside, you'll enjoy a historic setting inside beer-sloshed and smoke-stained halls. On balmy evenings, it's like a Renoir painting—but with beer breath—under chestnut trees. Local students mix with tourists eating hearty slabs of schnitzel with their fingers or cold meals from the self-serve picnic counter, while children frolic on the playground kegs. For your beer: Pick up a half-liter or full-liter mug, pay the lady (*schank* means self-serve price, *bedienung* is the price with waiter service), wash your mug, give Mr. Keg your receipt and empty mug, and you will be made happy. Waiters only bring beer; they don't bring food—instead, go up the stairs, survey the hallway of deli counters, and assemble your own meal (or, as long as you buy a drink, you can bring in a picnic). Classic pretzels from the bakery and spiraled, salty radishes make great beer even better. For dessert—after a visit to the strudel kiosk—enjoy the incomparable floodlit view of old Salzburg from the nearby Müllnersteg pedestrian bridge and a riverside stroll home (open daily 15:00-23:00, Augustinergasse 4, tel. 0662/431-246).

Getting There: It's about a 15-minute walk along the river (with the river on your right) from the Staatsbrücke bridge. After passing the Müllnersteg pedestrian bridge, just after Café am Kai, follow the stairs up to a busy street, and cross it. From here, either continue up more stairs into the trees and around the small church (for a scenic approach to the monastery), or stick to the sidewalk as it curves around to Augustinergasse. Either way, your goal is the huge yellow building. Don't be fooled by second-rate gardens serving the same beer nearby.

North of the River, near Recommended Linzergasse Hotels

Spicy Spices is a trippy vegetarian-Indian restaurant where Suresh Syal (a.k.a. "Mr. Spicy") serves tasty curry and rice, samosas, organic salads, vegan soups, and fresh juices. It's a *namaste* kind of place, where everything's proudly organic (€6.50 specials served all day, €8 with soup or salad, Mon-Fri 10:30-21:30, Sat-Sun 12:00-21:30, takeout available, Wolf-Dietrich-Strasse 1, tel. 0662/870-712).

Biergarten die Weisse, close to the hotels on Rupertgasse and away from the tourists, is a longtime hit with the natives. If a beer hall can be happening, this one—modern yet with antlers—is it. Their famously good beer is made right there; favorites include their fizzy wheat beer *(Weisse)* and their seasonal beers (on request). Enjoy the beer with their good, cheap traditional food in the great garden seating, or in the wide variety of indoor rooms—sports bar, young and noisy, or older and more elegant (€10-13 main courses, Mon-Sat 10:00-24:00, closed Sun, Rupertgasse 10, east of Bayerhamerstrasse, tel. 0662/872-246).

Café Bazar, overlooking the river between the Mirabell Gardens and the Staatsbrücke bridge, is as close as you'll get to a Vienna coffee house in Salzburg. Their outdoor terrace is a venerable spot for a classy drink with an Old-Town-and-castle view (light meals, Mon-Sat 7:30-23:00, Sun 9:00-18:00, Schwarzstrasse 3, tel. 0662/874-278).

Steingasse Pub Crawl

For a fun post-concert activity, drop in on a couple of atmospheric bars along medieval Steingasse (described on page 155). This is a local and hip scene—yet is accessible to older tourists: dark bars filled with well-dressed Salzburgers lazily smoking cigarettes and talking philosophy to laid-back tunes (no hip-hop). These four places are all within about 100 yards of each other. Start at the Linzergasse end of Steingasse. As they are quite different, survey all before choosing your spot (all open until the wee hours).

Pepe Cocktail Bar, with Mexican decor and Latin music, serves Mexican snacks *con* cocktails (nightly 19:00-3:00 in the morning, live DJs Fri-Sat from 19:00, Steingasse 3, tel. 0662/873-662).

Saiten Sprung wins the "Best Atmosphere" award. After midnight, the door is kept closed to keep out the crude and rowdy. Just ring the bell and enter its hellish interior—lots of stone and red decor, with mountains of melted wax beneath age-old candlesticks and an ambience of classic 70s and 80s music. Stelios, who speaks English with Greek charm, serves cocktails and fine wine, though no food (nightly 21:00-4:00 in the morning, Steingasse 11, tel. 0662/881-377).

Fridrich, just next door, is an intimate little place under an 11th-century vault, with lots of mirrors and a silver ceiling fan. Bernd Fridrich is famous for his martinis and passionate about Austrian wines, and has a tattered collection of vinyl that seems hell-bent on keeping the 1970s alive. Their Yolanda cocktail (grapefruit and vodka) is a favorite. He and his partner Ferdinand serve little dishes designed to complement the focus on socializing and drinking, though their €12 "little of everything dish" can be a meal for two (€5-12 plates, Thu-Mon from 18:00 in summer, from 17:00 in winter, closed Wed, Steingasse 15, tel. 0662/876-218).

Selim's Bar, with cozy seating both inside and out, has a cool, conversation-friendly atmosphere with mellow music (Mon-Sat 17:00-late, also open Sun in summer and during festival, across street from cinema at Steingasse 10, mobile 0664-433-844).

Salzburg Connections

By Train
Salzburg's train station, located so close to the German border, is covered not just by Austrian railpasses, but German ones as well.

From Salzburg by Train to: Reutte (every two hours, 4.5-5.5 hours, quickest with changes in Garmisch and Munich), **Hallstatt** (hourly, 50 minutes to Attnang-Puchheim, 20-minute wait, then 1.5 hours to Hallstatt), **Vienna** (3/hour, 2.75-3 hours), **Nürnberg,** Germany (hourly with change in Munich, 3 hours),

Ljubljana (6/day, 4.25-5 hours, some with change in Villach), **Interlaken** (9/day, 7.5-8 hours, 2-3 changes), **Florence** (4/day, 8.5-9 hours, 2 changes, overnight options), **Venice** (7/day, 7-8 hours, 2-3 changes). Train info: Tel. 051-717 (to get an operator, dial 2, then 2), www.oebb.at.

SALZBURG

HALLSTATT AND THE SALZKAMMERGUT

Commune with nature in the Salzkammergut, Austria's Lake District. "The hills are alive," and you're surrounded by the loveliness that has turned on everyone from Emperor Franz Josef to Julie Andrews. This is *Sound of Music* country. Idyllic and majestic, but not rugged, it's a gentle land of lakes, forested mountains, and storybook villages, rich in hiking opportunities and inexpensive lodging. Settle down in the postcard-pretty, lake-cuddling town of Hallstatt. While there are plenty of lakes and charming villages in the Salzkammergut, Hallstatt is really the only one that matters.

Planning Your Time

Hallstatt serves as a relaxing break between Vienna and Salzburg. One night and a few hours to browse are all you'll need to fall in love. To relax or take a hike in the surroundings, give it two nights and a day.

Orientation to Hallstatt

Lovable Hallstatt (HAHL-shtaht) is a tiny town bullied onto a ledge between a selfish mountain and a swan-ruled lake, with a waterfall ripping furiously through its middle. It can be toured on foot in about 15 minutes. Salt veins in the mountain rock drew people here centuries before Christ. The symbol of Hallstatt, which you'll see all over town, consists of two adjacent spirals—a design based on jewelry found in Bronze Age Celtic graves high in the nearby mountains.

Hallstatt has two parts: the tightly packed medieval town center (which locals call the Markt) and the newer, more car-friendly Lahn, a few minutes' walk to the south. A lakeside promenade connects the old center to the Lahn. The tiny "main" boat dock (a.k.a. Market Dock), where boats from the train station arrive, is in the old center of town. Another boat dock is in the Lahn, next to Hallstatt's bus stop and grocery store.

The charms of Hallstatt are the village and its lakeside setting. Come here to relax, nibble, wander, and paddle. While tourist crowds can trample much of Hallstatt's charm in August, the place is almost dead in the off-season. The lake is famous for its good fishing and pure water.

Tourist Information

At the helpful TI, Teresa and the other staff can explain hikes and excursions, and find you a room (July-Aug Mon-Fri 9:00-18:00, Sat-Sun 9:00-15:00; Sept-June Mon-Fri 9:00-13:00 & 14:00-17:00, closed Sat-Sun; one block from Market Square, across from museum at Seestrasse 169, tel. 06134/8208, www.dachstein-salzkammergut.at).

In the summer, the TI offers 1.5-hour **walking tours** of the town in English and German (€4, mid-May-Sept Sat at 10:00). They can also arrange private tours (€95), or you can use an audioguide to explore (€5, €50 deposit).

Arrival in Hallstatt

By Train: If you're coming on the main train line that runs between Salzburg and Vienna, you'll change trains at Attnang-Puchheim to get to Hallstatt (you won't see Hallstatt on the schedules, but any train to Ebensee and Bad Ischl will stop at Hallstatt). Day-trippers can check their bags at the Attnang-Puchheim station (follow signs for *Schliessfächer*, coin-op lockers are at the street, curbside near track 1, €2-3.50/24 hours). Note: Connections can be fast—check the TV monitor.

Hallstatt's train station is a wide spot on the tracks across the lake from town. *Stefanie* (a boat) meets you at the station and glides scenically across the lake to the old town center (€2.40, meets each train until 18:50—don't arrive after that, www.hallstattschifffahrt.at). The last departing boat-train connection leaves Hallstatt at 18:15, and the first boat goes in the morning at 6:50 (8:50 Sat-Sun).

Once in Hallstatt, walk left from the boat dock for the TI; you're steps away from the hotels in the old center and a 15-minute walk from accommodations in the Lahn.

By Bus: Hallstatt's bus stop is by the boat dock in the Lahn. It takes 15 minutes to walk from the bus stop into the old center along the lakeside path.

By Car: The main road skirts Hallstatt via a long tunnel above the town. Gates close off traffic to the old center during the daytime. As you approach town, electronic signs direct you to available spots in three parking areas. If you are staying at a hotel in the old town, drive to lot P1 (€9/day, reserved for hotel guests). Choose "Hotelt-icket" at the gate when you enter and hang onto your ticket—you'll need it when you leave. To reach your hotel, go to the Hotel-Shuttle Info-Point in the lot, tell the attendant (or the intercom) where you're staying, and hop on the free shuttle, which will drop you at or near your hotel. You can also use this shuttle when you depart; ask your hotelier for details. When you leave the lot, pay at the machine. (If you're staying at one of my recommended accommodations in the Lahn, you can park right at the hotel—all have free parking.)

If you're day-tripping, head to one of the other parking areas. P2 is a shorter walk to the old town center (€7/3-12 hours; www.hallstatt.net/parking-in-hallstatt/cars).

Helpful Hints

Internet Access: Try **Hallstatt Umbrella Bar** (€4/hour, summers only, weather permitting—since it's literally under a big um-brella, halfway between the old center and the Lahn along the lake at Seestrasse 145). For free Wi-Fi, drop by the café at the recommended **Heritage Hotel.**

Laundry: The staff of the **campground** in the Lahn will wash and dry (but not fold) your clothes for €8/load (drop off mid-April-mid-Oct daily 8:00-10:00 & 16:00-18:00, pick up in after-noon or next morning, closed off-season, tel. 06134/83224). In the center, the recommended **Hotel Grüner Baum** does laundry for non-guests (€13/load, on Market Square).

Boat Rental: Two places rent electric boats; both rent from two locations in high season. **Riedler** is next to the main boat dock and 75 yards past Bräugasthof (€13/hour, tel. 06134/20619). **Hemetsberger** is near Gasthof Simony and by the Lahn boat dock (€12/hour, tel. 06134/8228). Both are open daily until 19:00 in peak season and in good weather. Boats have two speeds: slow and stop. Spending an extra €3/hour gets you a faster, 500-watt boat. Both places also rent rowboats and paddleboats (slightly cheaper).

Dirndl Rental: If you feel compelled to re-enact the *Sound of Music,* **Dirndl to Go** rents authentic versions of these tradi-tional dresses by the hour (€22/first hour, €6/hour after that, May-Oct Wed-Sun 13:00-18:00, closed Mon-Tue and Nov-April, Badergraben 189, tel. 06503/666503, www.dirndl-to-go.at, Claudia).

Parks and Swimming: Green and peaceful lakeside parks line the south end of Lake Hallstatt. If you walk 15 minutes south of

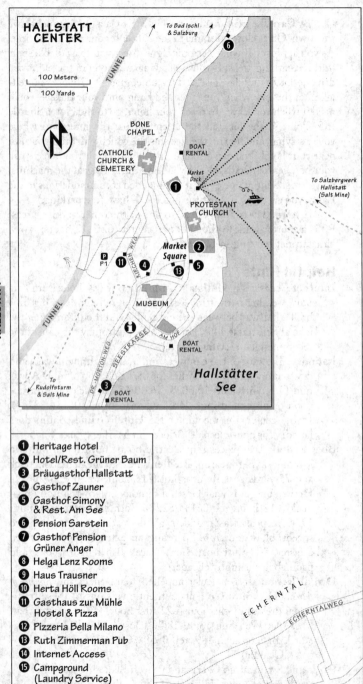

HALLSTATT

HALLSTATT CENTER

100 Meters
100 Yards

TUNNEL

To Bad Ischl & Salzburg

BONE CHAPEL

CATHOLIC CHURCH & CEMETERY

BOAT RENTAL

Market Dock

PROTESTANT CHURCH

To Salzbergwerk Hallstatt (Salt Mine)

KIRCHEN WEG

P P1

Market Square

MUSEUM

DR. MORTON-WEG

SEESTRASSE

AM HOF

BOAT RENTAL

To Rudolfsturm & Salt Mine

BOAT RENTAL

Hallstätter See

ECHERNTAL

ECHERNTALWEG

1 Heritage Hotel
2 Hotel/Rest. Grüner Baum
3 Bräugasthof Hallstatt
4 Gasthof Zauner
5 Gasthof Simony & Rest. Am See
6 Pension Sarstein
7 Gasthof Pension Grüner Anger
8 Helga Lenz Rooms
9 Haus Trausner
10 Herta Höll Rooms
11 Gasthaus zur Mühle Hostel & Pizza
12 Pizzeria Bella Milano
13 Ruth Zimmerman Pub
14 Internet Access
15 Campground (Laundry Service)

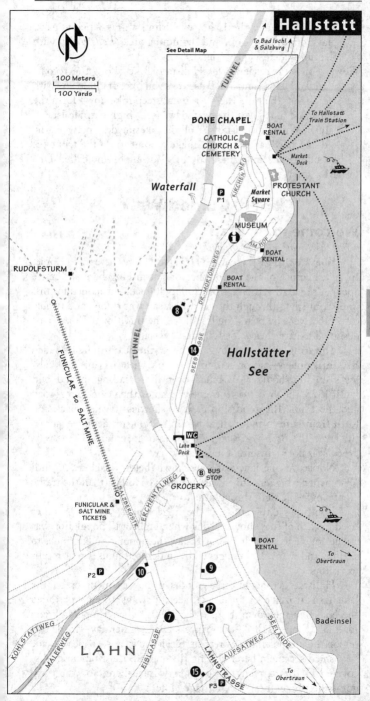

the old center to the Lahn, you'll find a grassy public park, playground, mini-golf, and swimming area *(Badestrand)* with the fun Badeinsel play-island.

Views: For a great view over Hallstatt, hike above the recommended Helga Lenz B&B as far as you like, or climb any path leading up the hill. The 40-minute steep hike down from the salt-mine tour gives the best views (see "Sights in Hallstatt," later). While most visitors stroll the lakeside drag between the old and new parts of town, make a point to do the trip once by taking the more higgledy-piggledy high lane called Dr.-Morton-Weg.

Self-Guided Walk

Welcome to Hallstatt

• *This short walk starts at the dock.*

Boat Landing: There was a Hallstatt before there was a Rome. In fact, because of the importance of salt mining here, an entire epoch—the Hallstatt Era, from 800 to 400 B.C.—is named for this important spot. Through the centuries, salt was traded and people came and went by boat. You'll still see the traditional *Fuhr* boats, designed to carry heavy loads in shallow water.

Towering above the town is the **Catholic church.** Its faded St. Christopher—patron saint of travelers, with his cane and baby Jesus on his shoulder—watched over those sailing in and out. Until 1875, the town was extremely remote...then came a real road and the train. The good ship *Stefanie* shuttles travelers back and forth from here to the Hallstatt train station, immediately across the lake. The *Bootverleih* sign advertises boat rentals. By the way, *Schmuck* is not an insult...it means jewelry.

Notice the one-lane road out of town (below the church). Until 1966, when a bigger tunnel was built above Hallstatt, all the traffic crept single-file right through the town.

Look down the shore at the huge homes. Several families lived in each of these houses, back when Hallstatt's population was about double its present 1,000. Today, the population continues to shrink, and many of these generally underused houses rent rooms to visitors.

Hallstatt gets about three months of snow each winter, but the lake hasn't frozen over since 1981. See any swans? They've patrolled the lake like they own it since the 1860s, when Emperor Franz Josef and Empress Sisi—the Princess Diana of her day—made this region their annual holiday retreat. Sisi loved swans, so locals made sure she'd see them here. During this period, the Romantics discovered Hallstatt, many top painters worked here, and the town got its first hotel (now the Heritage Hotel).

Tiny Hallstatt has two big churches: Protestant (bordering the square on the left, with a grassy lakeside playground) and Catholic (up above, with its fascinating bone chapel).

• *Walk over the town's stream, and pop into the...*

Protestant Church: The Catholic Counter-Reformation was very strong in Austria, but pockets of Protestantism survived, especially in mining towns like Hallstatt. In 1860, Emperor Franz Josef finally allowed non-Catholic Christians to build churches. Before that, they were allowed to worship only in low-key "houses of prayer." In 1863, Hallstatt's miners pooled their humble resources and built this fine church. Step inside (free and often open). It's very plain, emphasizing the pulpit and organ rather than fancy art and saints. Check out the portraits: Martin Luther (left of altar), the town in about 1865 with its new church (left wall), and a century of pastors.

• *Continue past the church to the...*

Market Square (Marktplatz): In 1750, a fire leveled this part of town. The buildings you see now are all late 18th-century structures built of stone rather than flammable wood. The three big buildings on the left are government-subsidized housing (mostly for seniors and people with health problems). Take a close look at the two-dimensional, up-against-the-wall pear tree (it likes the sun-warmed wall). The statue features the Holy Trinity.

• *Continue a block past Gasthof Simony. At the first corner, just before the* Gemeindeamt *(City Hall), jog left across the little square and then right down the tiny lane marked* Am Hof, *which leads through an intimate bit of domestic town architecture, boat houses, lots of firewood, and maybe a couple of swans hanging out. The lane circles back to the main drag and the...*

Museum Square: Because 20th-century Hallstatt was of no industrial importance, it was untouched by World War II. But once upon a time, its salt was worth defending. High above, peeking out of the trees, is Rudolfsturm (Rudolf's Tower). Originally a 13th-century watchtower protecting the salt mines, and later the mansion of a salt-mine boss, it's now a restaurant with a great view. A zigzag trail connects the town with Rudolfsturm and the salt mines just beyond. The big, white houses by the waterfall were water-powered mills that once ground Hallstatt's grain. (If you hike up a few blocks, you'll see the river raging through town.)

Around you are the town's TI, post office, museum, City Hall, and Dachstein Sport Shop (described later). A statue recalls the mine manager who excavated prehistoric graves in about 1850. Much of the *Schmuck* sold locally is inspired by the jewelry found in the area's Bronze Age tombs.

The memorial wooden stairs in front of the museum are a copy of those found in Hallstatt's prehistoric mine—the original stairs

HALLSTATT

are more than 2,500 years old. For thousands of years, people have been leaching salt out of this mountain. A brine spring sprung here, attracting Bronze Age people in about 1600 B.C. Later, they dug tunnels to mine the rock (which was 70 percent salt), dissolved it into a brine, and distilled out the salt—precious for preserving meat. For a look at early salt-mining implements and the town's story, visit the museum (described later).

Across from the TI, Pension Hallberg has a quirky hallway full of Nazi paraphernalia and other stuff found on the lake bed (€1). Only recently did local divers realize that, for centuries, the lake had been Hallstatt's garbage can. If something was *kaputt*, locals would just toss it into the lake. In 1945, Nazi medals decorating German and Austrian war heroes suddenly became dangerous to own. Throughout the former Third Reich, hard-earned medals floated down to lonely lake beds, including Hallstatt's.

Under the TI is the "Post Partner"—a government-funded attempt to turn inefficient post offices into something more viable (selling souvenirs, renting bikes, and employing people with disabilities who otherwise wouldn't work). The *Fischerei* provides the town with its cherished fresh lake fish. The county allows two commercial fishermen on the lake. They spread their nets each morning and sell their catch here to town restaurants, or to any locals cooking up a special dinner (Mon-Fri 9:00-12:00, closed Sat-Sun).

• *Nearby, still on Museum Square, find the...*

Dachstein Sport Shop: During a renovation project, the builders dug down and hit a Celtic and ancient Roman settlement. Peek through the glass pavement on the covered porch to see where the Roman street level was. If the shop is open, pop in and go downstairs (free). You'll walk on Roman flagstones and see the small gutter that channeled water to power an ancient hammer mill (used to pound iron into usable shapes). In prehistoric times, people lived near the mines. Romans were the first Hallstatt lakeside settlers. The store's owners are committed to sharing Hallstatt's fascinating history, and often display old town paintings and folk art.

• *From this square, the first right (after the bank) leads up a few stairs to...*

Dr.-Morton-Weg: House #26A dates from 1597. Follow the lane uphill to the left past more old houses. Until 1890, this was the town's main drag, and the lake lapped at the lower doors of these houses. Therefore, many main entrances were via the attic, from this level. Enjoy this back-street view of town. Just after the arch, near #133, check out the old tools hanging outside the workshop, and the piece of wooden piping. It's a section taken from the 25-mile wooden pipeline that carried salt brine from Hallstatt to Ebensee. This was in place from 1595 until the last generation, when the last stretch of wood was replaced by plastic piping. At the pipe,

HALLSTATT

enjoy the lake view and climb down the stairs. From lake level, look back up at the striking traditional architecture (the fine woodwork on the left was recently rebuilt after a fire; parts of the old house on the right date to medieval times).

• *Your tour is finished. From here, you have boat rentals, the salt-mine tour, the town museum, and the Catholic church (with its bone chapel) all within a few minutes' walk.*

Sights in Hallstatt

▲▲Catholic Church and Bone Chapel

Hallstatt's Catholic church overlooks the town from above. The lovely church has twin altars. The one on the left was made by town artists in 1897. The one on the right is more historic—dedicated in 1515 to Mary, who's flanked by St. Barbara (on right, patron of miners) and St. Catherine (on left, patron of foresters—a lot of wood was needed to fortify the many miles of tunnels, and to boil the brine to distill the salt).

Behind the church, in the well-tended graveyard, is the 12th-century Chapel of St. Michael (even older than the church). Its bone chapel—or charnel house *(Beinhaus)*—contains more than 600 painted skulls. Each skull has been lovingly named, dated, and decorated (skulls with dark, thick garlands are oldest—18th century; those with flowers are more recent—19th century). Space was so limited in this cemetery that bones had only 12 peaceful, buried years here before making way for the freshly dead. Many of the dug-up bones and skulls ended up in this chapel. They stopped this practice in the 1960s, about the same time the Catholic Church began permitting cremation. But one woman (who died in 1983) managed to sneak her skull in later (dated 1995, under the cross, with the gold tooth). The skulls on the books are those of priests.

Cost and Hours: €1.50, free English flier, daily May-Sept 10:00-18:00, Oct 10:00-16:00, closed Nov-April, tel. 06134/8279.

Getting There: From near the main boat dock, hike up the covered wooden stairway and follow the *Kath. Kirche* signs.

▲Hallstatt Museum

This pricey but high-quality museum tells the story of Hallstatt. It focuses on the Hallstatt Era (800-400 B.C.), when this village was the salt-mining hub of a culture that spread from France to the Balkans. Back then, Celtic tribes dug for precious salt, and Hallstatt was, as its name means, the "place of salt." The highlight of the museum is the countless number of artifacts excavated from prehistoric gravesites around the mine. The museum also offers a five-minute 3-D movie and 26 displays on everything from the region's flora and fauna to local artists and the surge in Hallstatt tourism

Salzkammergut

during the Romantic Age. Everything is labeled in English, and the ring binders have translations of the longer texts.

Cost and Hours: €7.50, May-Sept daily 10:00-18:00, shorter hours off-season, closed Mon-Tue Nov-March, adjacent to TI at Seestrasse 56, tel. 06134/828-015, www.museum-hallstatt.at. On Thursdays in summer, when candlelit boats run, the museum stays open until 20:00 (see "Nightlife in Hallstatt," later).

HALLSTATT

▲Lake Trip

For a quick boat trip, you can ride the *Stefanie* across the lake and back for €4.80. It stops at the tiny Hallstatt train station for 30 minutes (note return time in the boat's window), giving you time to walk to a hanging bridge (ask the captain to point you to the *Hängebrücke*—HENG-eh-brick-eh—a 10-minute lakeside stroll to the left). Longer lake tours are also available (€9/50 minutes,

€10/75 minutes, sporadic schedules—especially off-season—so check chalkboards by boat docks for today's times). Those into relaxation can rent a sleepy electric motorboat to enjoy town views from the water.

▲Salt-Mine Tour

If you have yet to tour a salt mine, consider visiting Hallstatt's, which claims to be the oldest in the world. The presentation is very low-tech, as the mining company owns all three mine tours in the area and sees little reason to invest in the experience when they can simply mine the tourists. Still, it gives an interesting look at mining through the centuries and culminates with a fun banister slide.

Cost and Hours: €24 combo-ticket includes mine and funicular round-trip, €18 for mine tour only, €2 audioguide (leave ID as deposit), buy all tickets at funicular station—note the time and tour number on your ticket, daily May-mid-Sept 9:00-16:00, mid-Sept-Oct 9:00-14:30, later funicular departures miss the last tour of the day, closed Nov-April, no children under age 4, arrive early or late to avoid summer crowds, tel. 06132/200-2400, www.salzwelten.at.

Funicular: You can also just take the funicular without going on the mine tour (€7 one-way, €12 round-trip, 4/hour, daily May-mid-Sept 9:00-18:00, mid-Sept-Oct 9:00-16:30, closed Nov-April). The funicular starts in the Lahn, close to the bus stop and Lahn boat dock.

Visiting the Mine: After riding the funicular above town, you'll hike 10 minutes to the mine (past excavation sites of many prehistoric tombs and a glass case with 2,500-year-old bones—but there's little to actually see). Report to the mine 10 minutes before the tour time on your ticket, check your bag, and put on old miners' clothes. Then hike 200 yards higher in your funny outfit to meet your guide, who escorts your group down a tunnel dug in 1719.

Inside the mountain, you'll watch a slide show, follow your guide through several caverns as you learn about mining techniques over the last 7,000 years, see a silly laser show on a glassy subterranean lake, peek at a few waxy cavemen with pickaxes, and ride the train out. The highlight for most is sliding down two banisters (the second one is longer and ends with a flash for an automatic souvenir photo that clocks your speed—see how you did compared to the rest of your group after the tour).

While the tour is mostly in German, the guide is required to speak English if you ask...so ask. Be sure to dress for the constant 47-degree temperature.

Returning to Hallstatt: If you skip the funicular down, the steep and scenic 40-minute hike back into town is (with strong knees) a joy. At the base of the funicular, notice the train tracks leading to the Erbstollen tunnel entrance. This lowest of the salt tunnels goes many miles into the mountain, where a shaft connects it to the tunnels you just explored. Today, the salty brine from these tunnels flows 25 miles through the world's oldest pipeline—made of wood until quite recently—to the huge modern salt works (next to the highway) at Ebensee.

▲**Local Hikes**

Mountain-lovers, hikers, and spelunkers who use Hallstatt as their home base keep busy for days (ask the TI for ideas). A good, short, and easy walk is the two-hour round-trip up the Echern Valley to the Waldbachstrub waterfall and back: From the parking lot, follow signs to the salt mines, then follow the little wooden signs marked *Echerntalweg*. With a car, consider hiking around nearby Altaussee (flat, 3-hour hike) or along Grundlsee to Toplitzsee. Regular buses connect Hallstatt with Gosausee for a pleasant hour-long walk around that lake. Or consider walking nine miles halfway around Lake Hallstatt via the town of Steeg (boat to train station, walk left along lake and past idyllic farmsteads, returning to Hallstatt along the old salt trail, *Soleleitungsweg*); for a shorter hike, walk to Steeg along either side of the lake, and catch the train from Steeg back to Hallstatt's station. The TI can also recommend a great two-day hike with an overnight in a nearby mountain hut.

Biking

The best two bike rides take nearly the same routes as the hikes listed previously: up the Echern Valley and around the lake (bikers do better going via Obertraun along the lakeside bike path—start with a ride on the *Stefanie*). There's no public bike rental in Hallstatt, but some hotels have loaner bikes for guests.

Near Hallstatt

▲▲**Dachstein Mountain Cable Car and Caves**

From Obertraun, three miles beyond Hallstatt on the main road (or directly across the lake as the crow flies), a cable car glides up to the Dachstein Plateau. Along the way, you can hop off to tour two different caves: the refreshingly chilly Giant Ice Caves and the less-impressive Mammoth Caves.

Getting to Obertraun: The cable car to Dachstein leaves from the outskirts of Obertraun. To reach the cable car from Hallstatt, the handiest and cheapest option is the bus (€1.70, 5-6/day, leaves from Lahn boat dock, drops you directly at cable-car station). Romantics can take the boat from Hallstatt's main boat dock to Obertraun (€5.50, 5/day July-Aug, 3/day in June and Sept, 30 minutes, www.hallstattschifffahrt.at)—but it's a 40-minute hike from there to the lift station. The impatient can consider hitching a ride—virtually all cars leaving Hallstatt to the south will pass through Obertraun in a few minutes.

Returning to Hallstatt: Plan to leave by mid-afternoon. The last bus from the cable-car station back to Hallstatt (at 17:05 in summer) inconveniently leaves before the last cable car down—if you miss the bus, try getting a ride from a fellow cable-car passenger. Otherwise, you can either call a taxi (€13, ask cable-car staff for help) or walk back along the lakefront (about one hour).

Dachstein Cable Car

From Obertraun, this mighty gondola goes in three stages high up the Dachstein Plateau—crowned by Dachstein, the highest mountain in the Salzkammergut (9,800 ft). The first segment stops at **Schönbergalm** (4,500 ft, runs May-late Oct), which has a mountain restaurant and two huge caves (described next). The second segment goes to the summit of **Krippenstein** (6,600 ft, runs mid-May-late Oct). The third segment descends to **Gjaidalm** (5,800 ft, runs mid-June-late Oct), where several hikes begin.

For a quick high-country experience, Krippenstein is better than Gjaidalm. Its "five-fingers" viewpoint features metal walkways that extend out from the mountain (not for the faint of heart). From Krippenstein, you get 360-degree views of the surrounding mountains and a good look at the scrubby, limestone, karstic landscape (which absorbs, through its many cracks, the rainfall that ultimately carves all those caves).

Cost and Hours: €26, last cable car back down usually at about 17:00, tel. 06131/50140, www.dachstein-salzkammergut. com.

Cable Car and Caves Combo-Tickets: Several combo-tickets are available for the cable car and caves. The round-trip cable-car ride to Schönbergalm, including entrance to one of the caves, is €27. The €33 combo-ticket includes the cable car and entry to both caves. If you're gung-ho enough to want to visit both caves and ride the cable car farther up the mountain, the €39 same-day, all-inclusive ticket makes sense (covers the cable car all the way to Gjaidalm and back, as well as entry to both caves). Cheaper family rates are available.

Giant Ice Caves (Riesen-Eishöhle)

Located near the Schönbergalm cable-car stop (4,500 ft), these caves were discovered in 1910. Today, guides lead tours in German and English on an hour-long, half-mile hike through an eerie, icy, subterranean world, passing limestone canyons the size of subway stations.

At the Schönbergalm lift station, report to the ticket window to get your cave appointment. Drop by the little free museum near the lift station—in a local-style wood cabin designed to support 200 tons of snow—to see the cave-system model, exhibits about its exploration, and info about life in the caves. Then hike 10 minutes from the station up to the cave entry. The temperature is just above freezing, and although the 700 steps help keep you warm, you'll want to bring a sweater. The limestone caverns, carved by rushing water, are named for scenes from Wagner's operas—the favorite of the mountaineers who first came here. If you're nervous, note that the iron oxide covering the ceiling takes 5,000 years to form. Things are very stable. Allow 1.5 hours total from the station.

Cost and Hours: €27 includes cable car, various combo-tickets available (described earlier), open May-late Oct, hour-long tours start at 9:20, last tour at 15:30, stay in front and assert yourself to get English information, tel. 06131/50140.

Mammoth Caves (Mammuthöhle)

While huge and well-promoted, these are much less interesting than the ice caves and—for most—not worth the time. Of the 30-mile limestone labyrinth excavated so far, you'll walk a half-mile with a German-speaking guide.

Cost and Hours: €27 includes cable car, various combo-tickets available (described earlier), open May-late Oct, hour-long tours in English and German 10:15-14:30, entrance a 10-minute hike from lift station.

Summer Luge Rides (Sommerrodelbahnen) on the Hallstatt-Salzburg Road

If you're driving between Salzburg and Hallstatt, you'll pass two luge rides operated by the same company (www.rodelbahnen.at). Each is a ski lift that drags you backward up the hill as you sit on your go-cart. At the top, you ride the cart down the winding metal course. It's easy: Push to go, pull to stop, take your hands off your stick and you get hurt.

Each course is just off the road with easy parking. The ride up and down takes about 15 minutes. The one in **Fuschl am See** (closest to Salzburg, look for *Sommerrodelbahn* sign) is half as long and cheaper (1,970 ft). The one in **Strobl** near Wolfgangsee (look for *Riesenschutzbahn* sign) is a double course, and more scenic with grand lake views (4,265 ft, each track is the same speed).

Cost and Hours: Fuschl am See—4.30/ride, €30/10 rides, tel. 06226/8452; Strobl—€6.40/ride, €45/10 rides, tel. 06137/7085; courses open May-Oct 10:00-18:00 but generally close in bad weather.

Nightlife in Hallstatt

Locals would laugh at the thought. But if you want some action after dinner, you do have a few options: **Gasthaus zur Mühle** is a youth hostel with a rustic sports-bar ambience in its restaurant when drinks replace the food (open late, closed Tue Sept-mid-May, run by Ferdinand). Or, for your late-night drink, savor the Market Square from the trendy little pub called **Ruth Zimmermann,** where locals congregate with soft music, a good selection of drinks, two small rooms, and tables on the square (daily May-Sept 10:00-2:00 in the morning, Oct-April 11:00-2:00, mobile 0664/501-5631). From late July to late August, **candlelit boat rides** leave at 20:30 on Thursday evenings (€13.50, €16 combo-ticket with Hallstatt Museum).

Sleeping in Hallstatt

Hallstatt's TI can almost always find you a room (either in town or at B&Bs and small hotels outside of town—which are more likely to have rooms available and come with easy parking). If you are arriving by car and have a reservation for a place in the old town, head directly to parking lot P1, where you'll catch a shuttle to your hotel (see page 181).

Mid-July and August can be tight. Early August is worst. Hallstatt is not the place to splurge—some of the best rooms are in *Gästezimmer*, just as nice and modern as rooms in bigger hotels, at half the cost. In summer, a double bed in a private home costs about €50 with breakfast. It's hard to get a one-night advance reservation (try calling the TI for help). But if you drop in and they have a spot, one-nighters are welcome. Prices include breakfast, lots of stairs, and a silent night. *"Zimmer mit Aussicht?"* (TSIM-mer mit OWS-zeekt) means "Room with view?"—worth asking for. Unlike many businesses in town, the cheaper places don't take credit cards.

As most rooms here are in old buildings with well-cared-for wooden interiors, dripping laundry is a no-no at Hallstatt pensions. Be especially considerate when hanging laundry over anything but tile—if you must wash larger clothing items here, ask your host about using their clothesline.

$$$ Heritage Hotel, next to the main boat dock, is the town's fanciest place to stay. It has 34 rooms with modern furnishings in a lakeside main building with an elevator; uphill are another 20 rooms in two separate buildings for those willing to climb stairs for better views (Sb-€150, Db-€209, free sauna, free cable Internet in rooms and Wi-Fi in lobby, laundry service-€13, Landingsplatz 120, tel. 06134/20036, fax 06134/20042, www.hotel-hallstatt.com, info@hotel-hallstatt.com).

$$$ Hotel Grüner Baum, on the other side of the church from the main boat dock, has a great location, fronting Market Square and overlooking the lake in back. The owner, Monika, moved here from Vienna and renovated this stately—but still a bit creaky—old hotel with urban taste. Its 22 rooms are huge, each with a separate living area and ancient hardwood floors, but you may not need so much space and the high price that comes with it (suite-like Db-€140-210, price depends on view, 8 percent dis-

Sleep Code

(€1 = about $1.30, country code: 43, area code: 06134)
S = Single, **D** = Double/Twin, **T** = Triple, **Q** = Quad, **b** = bathroom, **s** = shower only. Unless otherwise noted, credit cards are accepted, English is spoken, and breakfast is included.

To help you sort easily through these listings, I've divided the rooms into three categories, based on the price for a standard double room with bath:

$$$ Higher Priced—Most rooms €100 or more.
$$ Moderately Priced—Most rooms between €70-100.
$ Lower Priced—Most rooms €70 or less.

Prices can change without notice; verify the hotel's current rates online or by email.

count with this book, family rooms, Internet access in restaurant, laundry service-€13, closed in Nov, 20 yards from boat dock, tel. 06134/82630, fax 06134/826-344, www.gruenerbaum.cc, contact@gruenerbaum.cc).

$$$ Bräugasthof Hallstatt is like a museum filled with antique furniture and ancient family portraits. This former brewery, now a good restaurant, rents eight clean, cozy upstairs rooms. It's run by Virena and her daughter, Virena. Six of the rooms have gorgeous little lakeview balconies (Sb-€65, Db-€105, Tb-€155, just past TI along lake at Seestrasse 120, tel. 06134/8221, fax 06134/82214, www.brauhaus-lobisser.com, info@brauhaus-lobisser.com, Lobisser family).

$$$ Gasthof Zauner is run by a friendly mountaineer, Herr Zauner, whose family has owned it since 1893. The 13 pricey, pine-flavored rooms near the inland end of Market Square are decorated with sturdy alpine-inspired furniture (sealed not with lacquer but with beeswax, to let the wood breathe out its calming scent). Lederhosen-clad Herr Zauner recounts tales of local mountaineering lore, including his own impressive ascents (Sb-€63, Db-€108, lakeview Db-€116, cheaper mid-Oct-April, Internet access in office, closed Nov-early Dec, Marktplatz 51, tel. 06134/8246, fax 06134/82468, www.zauner.hallstatt.net, zauner@hallstatt.at).

$$$ Gasthof Simony is a well-worn, grandmotherly, 12-room place on the square, with a lake view, balconies, ancient beds, creaky wood floors, slippery rag rugs, antique furniture, and a lakefront garden for swimming. Reserve in advance, and call if arriving late (S-€45, D-€65, Ds-€70, Db-€105, third person-€20 extra, cash only, free Wi-Fi in lobby, kayaks for guests, Marktplatz 105, tel. & fax 06134/8231, www.gasthof-simony.at, info@gasthof-simony.at, Susanna Scheutz and family).

$$ Pension Sarstein is a big, flower-bedecked house right on the water on the edge of the old center. Its seven renovated rooms are bright, and all have lakeview balconies. You can swim from its plush and inviting lakeside garden (D-€55, Db-€70, Tb-€90; apartments with kitchen: Db-€65, Tb-€90, Qb-€100, apartment prices don't include breakfast; €3 extra per person for 1-night stay, cash only, free Wi-Fi in lobby, 200 yards to the right of the main boat dock at Gosaumühlstrasse 83, tel. 06134/8217, www.pension-sarstein.at.tf, pension.sarstein@aon.at, helpful Isabelle and Klaus Fischer).

$$ Gasthof Pension Grüner Anger, in the Lahn near the bus station and base of the funicular, is practical and modern. It's big and quiet, with 11 rooms and no creaks or squeaks. There are mountain views, but none of the lake (Sb-€43-48, Db-€76-90, third person-€20, price depends on season, non-smoking, free Internet access and Wi-Fi, free loaner bikes, free parking, Lahn 10, tel. 06134/8397, fax 06134/83974, www.anger.hallstatt.net, anger@aon.at, Sulzbacher family). If arriving by train, have the boat captain call Herr Sulzbacher, who will pick you up at the dock. They run a good-value restaurant, too, with discounts for guests.

$ Helga Lenz rents two fine *Zimmer* a steep five-minute climb above Dr.-Morton-Weg (look for the green *Zimmer* sign). This large, sprawling, woodsy house has a nifty garden perch, wins the "Best View" award, and is ideal for those who sleep well in tree houses and don't mind the steps up from town (Db-€52, Tb-€78, €2 more per person for one-night stay, cash only, family room, closed Nov-March, Hallberg 17, tel. 06134/8508, www.hallstatt.net/lenz, haus-lenz@aon.at).

$ Two *Gästezimmer* are a few minutes' stroll south of the center, just past the bus stop/parking lot and over the bridge. **Haus Trausner** has three clean, bright, new-feeling rooms adjacent to the Trausner family home (Ds/Db-€50, 2-night minimum for reservations, cash only, breakfast comes to your room, free parking, Lahnstrasse 27, tel. 06134/8710, trausner1@aon.at, charming Maria Trausner makes you want to settle right in). **Herta Höll** rents out three spacious, modern rooms on the ground floor of her riverside house crawling with kids (Db-€50, apartment for up to five-€60-90, €2 more per person for one-night stay, cash only, free parking, free cable Internet, Salzbergstrasse 45, tel. 06134/8531, fax 06134/825-533, frank.hoell@aon.at).

$ *Hostel:* **Gasthaus zur Mühle Jugendherberge,** below the waterfall and along the gushing town stream, has 46 of the cheapest good beds in town (bed in 3- to 8-bed coed dorms-€16, twin

D-€32, family quads, sheets-€4 extra, breakfast-€6, big lockers with a €15 deposit, free Wi-Fi, closed Nov, reception closed Tue Sept-mid-May—so arrange in advance if arriving on Tue, below P1 tunnel parking lot, Kirchenweg 36, tel. & fax 06134/8318, to-eroe-f@hallstatturlaub.at, Ferdinand Törö). It's also popular for its great, inexpensive pizza (described later).

Eating in Hallstatt

In this town, when someone is happy to see you, they'll often say, "Can I cook you a fish?" While everyone cooks the typical Austrian fare, fish is your best bet here. *Reinanke* (whitefish) is caught wild out of Lake Hallstatt and served the same day. *Saibling* (lake trout) is also tasty and costs less. You can enjoy good food inexpensively, with delightful lakeside settings. Restaurants in Hallstatt tend to have unreliable hours and close early on slow nights, so don't wait too long to get dinner. Most of the eateries listed here are run by recommended hotels.

Restaurant Bräugasthof, on the edge of the old center, is a good value. The indoor dining room is cozy in cool weather. On a balmy evening, its great lakeside tables offer the best ambience in town—you can feed the swans while your trout is being cooked (€10-20 main courses, daily May-Oct 11:30-late, closed Nov-April, Seestrasse 120, tel. 06134/8221).

Hotel Grüner Baum is a more upscale option, with elegant (and often slow) service at tables overlooking the lake inside and out (€15-25 main courses, daily Dec-Oct 8:00-22:00, closed Nov, at bottom of Market Square, tel. 06134/8263).

Gasthof Simony's Restaurant am See serves Austrian cuisine on yet another gorgeous lakeside terrace, as well as indoors (€12-16 main courses, Thu-Tue 11:30-20:00, until 21:00 June-Sept and on winter weekends, closed Wed, tel. 06134/20646).

Gasthaus zur Mühle serves the best pizza in town. Chow down cheap and hearty here with fun-loving locals and the youth-hostel crowd. Note that smoking is allowed here (€8 pizza, lots of Italian, some Austrian, Wed-Mon in summer 16:00-21:00, closed Tue, Kirchenweg 36, tel. 06134/8318, Ferdinand).

Pizzeria Bella Milano, in the Lahn area, is a local favorite and a good option after visiting the salt mines or going swimming. To-go meals are available if you want to eat by the lake. They serve mainly pizzas and Italian dishes, along with some Austrian options (€7-10 main courses, daily 11:00-22:00, Lahn 41, tel. 06134/20037).

Picnics and Cheap Eats: The **Zauner** bakery/butcher/grocer, great for picnickers, makes fresh sandwiches to go (Tue-Fri 7:00-12:00 & 15:00-18:00, Sat and Mon 7:00-12:00, closed Sun, uphill to the left from Market Square). The only **supermarket** is Konsum, in the Lahn at the bus stop (Mon-Fri 7:30-12:00 & 15:00-18:00, Sat 7:30-12:00, closed Sun, July-Aug no midday break and until 17:00 on Sat, Sept-April closed Wed). **Snack stands** near the main boat dock and the Lahn boat dock sell *Döner Kebab* and so on for €3 (tables and fine lakeside picnic options nearby).

Hallstatt Connections

From Hallstatt by Train: Most travelers leaving Hallstatt are going to Salzburg or Vienna. In either case, you need to catch the shuttle boat (€2.40, departs 15 minutes before every train) to the little Hallstatt train station across the lake, and then ride 1.5 hours to **Attnang-Puchheim** (hourly from about 7:00 to 18:00). Trains are synchronized, so after a short wait in Attnang-Puchheim, you'll catch your onward connection to **Salzburg** (50 minutes) or **Vienna** (2.5 hours). The Hallstatt station has no staff or ticket machines, but you can buy tickets from the conductor without a penalty. In town, your hotel or the TI can help you find schedule information, or check www.oebb.at. Train info: tel. 051-717 (to get an operator, dial 2, then 2).

By Bus to Salzburg: The bus ride from Hallstatt to Salzburg is cheaper and more scenic than the train, and only slightly slower. You can still start off from Hallstatt by rail, taking the boat across the lake to the station and then the train toward Attnang-Puchheim—but get off after about 20 minutes in **Bad Ischl,** where you catch bus #150 to Salzburg (€8.80, Mon-Fri almost hourly, less Sat-Sun).

Alternatively, you can reach Bad Ischl by bus from the Hallstatt bus stop (€4.20, change in Gosaumühle) and then catch bus #150 to Salzburg. The Hallstatt TI has a schedule. In Salzburg, bus #150 stops at Hofwirt and Mirabellplatz (convenient to Linzergasse hotels) before ending at the Salzburg train station.

BELGIUM

BRUGES

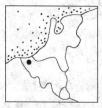

With pointy gilded architecture, stay-a-while cafés, vivid time-tunnel art, and dreamy canals dotted with swans, Bruges is a heavyweight sightseeing destination, as well as a joy. Where else can you ride a bike along a canal, munch mussels and wash them down with the world's best beer, savor heavenly chocolate, and see Flemish Primitives and a Michelangelo, all within 300 yards of a bell tower that jingles every 15 minutes? And do it all without worrying about a language barrier?

The town is Brugge (BROO-ghah) in Dutch, and Bruges (broozh) in French and English. Its name comes from the Viking word for wharf. Right from the start, Bruges was a trading center. In the 11th century, the city grew wealthy on the cloth trade.

By the 14th century, Bruges' population was 35,000, as large as London's. As the middleman in the sea trade between northern and southern Europe, it was one of the biggest cities in the world and an economic powerhouse. In addition, Bruges had become the most important cloth market in northern Europe.

In the 15th century, while England and France were slugging it out in the Hundred Years' War, Bruges was the favored residence of the powerful Dukes of Burgundy—and at peace. Commerce and the arts boomed. The artists Jan van Eyck and Hans Memling had studios here.

But by the 16th century, the harbor had silted up and the economy had collapsed. The Burgundian court left, Belgium became a minor Habsburg possession, and Bruges' Golden Age abruptly ended. For generations, Bruges was known as a mysterious and dead city. In the 19th century, a new port, Zeebrugge, brought renewed vitality to the area. And in the 20th century, tourists discovered the town.

Today, Bruges prospers because of tourism: It's a uniquely well-preserved Gothic city and a handy gateway to Europe. It's no secret, but even with the crowds, it's the kind of place where you don't mind being a tourist.

Bruges' ultimate sight is the town itself, and the best way to enjoy it is to get lost on the back streets, away from the lace shops and ice-cream stands.

Planning Your Time

Bruges needs at least two nights and a full, well-organized day. Even nonshoppers enjoy browsing here, and the Belgian love of life makes a hectic itinerary seem a little senseless. With one day—other than a Monday, when the Groeninge and Memling museums are closed—a speedy visitor could do the Bruges blitz described below:

9:30   Climb the bell tower on the Markt (Market Square).
10:00 Tour the sights on Burg Square.
11:30 Tour the Groeninge Museum.
13:00 Eat lunch and buy chocolates.
14:00 Take a short canal cruise.
14:30 Visit the Church of Our Lady and see Michelangelo's *Madonna and Child*.
15:00 Tour the Memling Museum.
16:00 Catch the De Halve Maan Brewery tour (note that on winter weekdays, their last tour runs at 15:00).
17:00 Relax in the Begijnhof courtyard.
18:00 Ride a bike around the quiet back streets of town or take a horse-and-buggy tour.
20:00 Enjoy the low light of magic hour on the Markt, then lose the tourists and find dinner elsewhere.

If this schedule seems insane, skip the bell tower and the brewery—or stay another day.

Orientation to Bruges

The tourist's Bruges—and you'll be sharing it—is less than one square mile, contained within a canal (the former moat). Nearly everything of interest and importance is within a convenient cobbled swath between the train station and the Markt (Market Square; a 20-minute walk). Many of my quiet, charming, recommended accommodations lie just beyond the Markt.

Bruges

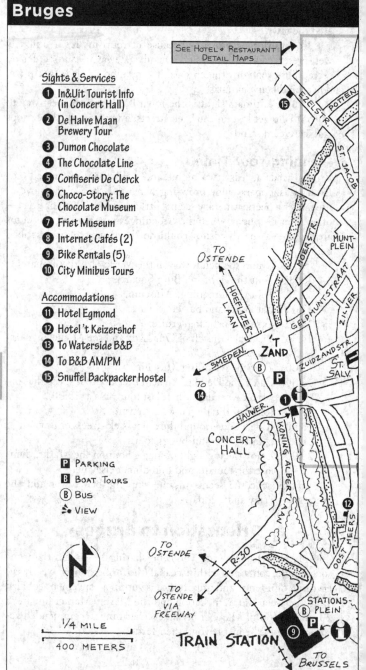

See Hotel + Restaurant Detail Maps

Sights & Services

1 In&Uit Tourist Info (in Concert Hall)
2 De Halve Maan Brewery Tour
3 Dumon Chocolate
4 The Chocolate Line
5 Confiserie De Clerck
6 Choco-Story: The Chocolate Museum
7 Friet Museum
8 Internet Cafés (2)
9 Bike Rentals (5)
10 City Minibus Tours

Accommodations

11 Hotel Egmond
12 Hotel 't Keizershof
13 To Waterside B&B
14 To B&B AM/PM
15 Snuffel Backpacker Hostel

P PARKING
B BOAT TOURS
B BUS
View

1/4 MILE
400 METERS

TO OSTENDE
TO OSTENDE
TO OSTENDE VIA FREEWAY
TO BRUSSELS

'T ZAND
CONCERT HALL
STATIONS-PLEIN
TRAIN STATION

R-30

BRUGES

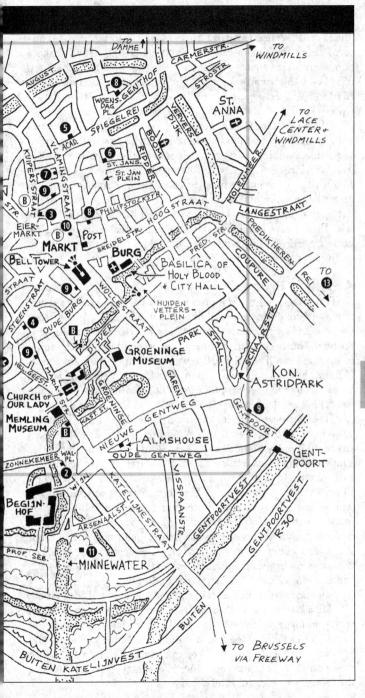

BRUGES

Tourist Information

The main TI, called **In&Uit** ("In and Out"), is in the big, red concert hall on the square called 't Zand (daily 10:00-18:00, take a number from the touch-screen machines and wait, 't Zand 34, tel. 050-444-646, www.brugge.be). They have three terminals with free Internet access and printers. The other TI is at the train station (Mon-Fri 10:00-17:00, Sat-Sun 10:00-14:00).

The TIs sell the €2.50 *Love Bruges Visitors' Guide*, which comes with a map (costs €0.50 if bought separately), a few well-described self-guided walking tours, and listings of all the sights and services (free with Brugge City Card). You can also pick up a free monthly English-language program called *events@brugge*, and information on train schedules and tours (see "Tours in Bruges," later). Many hotels give out free maps with more detail than the map the TIs sell. The TI also has a free "Use-It" map available for young-at-heart travelers—filled with tips for backpackers and well worth asking for.

Arrival in Bruges

By Train: Bruges' train station is what all stations under construction aspire to: in a clean, park-like setting, where travelers step out the door and are greeted by a taxi stand and a roundabout with center-bound buses circulating through every couple minutes. Coming in by train, you'll see the bell tower that marks the main square (Markt, the center of town). Upon arrival, stop by the train station TI to pick up the *Love Bruges Visitors' Guide* (with map). The station has ATMs and lockers (€3-4).

The best way to get to the town center is by **bus.** Buses #1, #3, #4, #6, #11, #13, #14, and #16 go to the Markt (all marked *Centrum*). Simply hop on, pay €2 (€1.20 if you buy in advance at Lijnwinkel shop just outside the train station), and you're there in four minutes (get off at third stop—either Markt or Wollestraat). Buses #4 and #14 continue to the northeast part of town (to the windmills and recommended accommodations on and near Carmersstraat, stop: Gouden Handstraat). If you arrive after 20:30, when the daytime bus routes end, you can still take the bus, but the "evening line" buses run much less frequently (buses marked *Avondlijn Centrum, Avondlijn Noord*—#91, *Avondlijn Oost*—#92, and *Avondlijn Zuid*—#93 all go to the Markt).

The **taxi** fare from the train station to most hotels is about €8.

It's a 20-minute **walk** from the station to the center—no fun with your luggage. If you want to walk to the Markt, cross the busy street and canal in front of the station, head up Oostmeers, and turn right on Zwidzandstraat. You can rent a **bike** at the station for the duration of your stay, but other bike-rental shops are closer to the center (see "Helpful Hints," below).

By Car: Park in front of the train station in the handy two-story garage for just €3.50 for 24 hours. The parking fee includes a round-trip bus ticket into town and back for everyone in your car. There are pricier underground parking garages at the square called 't Zand and around town (€9/day, all of them well-marked). Paid parking on the street in Bruges is limited to four hours. Driving in town is very complicated because of the one-way system. The best plan for drivers: Park at the train station, visit the TI at the station, and rent a bike or catch a bus into town.

Helpful Hints

Blue Monday: In Bruges, nearly all museums are open Tuesday through Sunday year-round from 9:30 to 17:00 and are closed on Monday. If you're in Bruges on a Monday, the following attractions are open: bell-tower climb on the Markt, Begijnhof, De Halve Maan Brewery Tour, Basilica of the Holy Blood, City Hall's Gothic Room, chocolate shops and museum, and Church of Our Lady. You can also join a boat, bus, or walking tour, or rent a bike and pedal into the countryside.

Museum Passes: The 't Zand TI and city museums sell a "Museumpas" **combo-ticket** (any five museums for €20, valid for 3 days). Because the Groeninge and Memling museums cost €8 each, art lovers will save money with this pass.

The **Brugge City Card** is a more extensive pass covering entry to 26 museums, including all the major sights (€35/48 hours, €40/72 hours, sold at TIs and many hotels). If you'll be doing some serious sightseeing, this card can save you money. Its long list of bonuses and discounts includes a free canal boat ride (March-Nov), a visitors' guide, and discounts on bike rental, parking, and some performances.

Market Days: Bruges hosts markets on Wednesday morning (on the Markt) and Saturday morning ('t Zand). On good-weather Saturdays, Sundays, and public holidays, a flea market hops along Dijver in front of the Groeninge Museum. The Fish Market sells souvenirs daily and seafood Wednesday through Saturday mornings until 13:00.

Shopping: Shops are generally open from 10:00 to 18:00 and closed Sundays. Grocery stores usually are closed on Sunday. The main shopping street, Steenstraat, stretches from the Markt to 't Zand Square. The **Hema** department store is at Steenstraat 73. **FNAC,** the electronics/department store for all your needs, is on the Markt. There's a good travel bookstore (which carries my guidebooks) at #12 on the Markt.

Internet Access: There are three free terminals at the **TI** on 't Zand. **Call Shop,** just a block off the Markt, is the most central of the city's many "telephone shops" offering Internet access (€1.50/30 minutes, €2.50/hour, daily 9:00-20:00, Philip-stockstraat 4). **Bean Around the World** is a cozy coffeehouse with imported Yankee snacks and free Wi-Fi for customers (€1/15 minutes on their computers, Thu-Mon 10:00-19:00, Wed 11:30-19:00, closed Tue, Genthof 5, tel. 050-703-572, run by American expat Olene).

Post Office: It's on the Markt near the bell tower (Mon-Fri 9:00-18:00, Sat 9:30-15:00, closed Sun, tel. 050-331-411).

Laundry: Bruges has three self-service launderettes, each a five-minute walk from the center; ask your hotelier for the nearest one.

Bike Rental: Bruges Bike Rental is central and cheap, with friendly service and long hours (€3.50/hour, €5/2 hours, €7/4 hours, €10/day, show this book to get student rate—€8/day, no deposit required—just ID, daily 10:00-22:00, free city maps and child seats, behind the far-out iron facade at Niklaas Desparsstraat 17, tel. 050-616-108, Bilal). **Fietsen Popelier Bike Rental** is also good (€4/hour, €8/4 hours, €12/day, 24-hour day is OK if your hotel has a safe place to store bike, no deposit required, daily 10:00-19:00, sometimes open later in summer, free Damme map, Mariastraat 26, tel. 050-343-262). **Koffieboontje Bike Rental** is just under the bell tower on the Markt (€4/hour, €9/day, €20/day for tandem, these prices for Rick Steves readers, daily 9:00-22:00, free city maps and child seats, Hallestraat 4, tel. 050-338-027). **De Ketting** is less central, but cheap (€6/day, Mon-Fri 9:00-12:15 & 13:30-18:30 except Mon opens at 10:00, Sat 9:30-12:15, closed Sun, Gentpoortstraat 23, tel. 050-344-196, www.deketting.be). **Fietspunt Brugge** is a huge outfit at the train station (7-speed bikes, €12/24-hours, €7/4 hours, free maps, Mon-Fri 7:00-19:30, Sat-Sun 9:00-21:30, just outside the station and to the right as you exit, tel. 050-396-826).

Best Town View: The bell tower overlooking the Markt rewards those who climb it with the ultimate town view.

Updates to this Book: Check www.ricksteves.com/update for any significant changes that have occurred since this book was printed.

Getting Around Bruges

Most of the city is easily walkable, but you may want to take the bus or taxi between the train station and the city center at the Markt (especially if you have heavy luggage).

By Bus: A bus ticket is good for an hour (€1.20 if you buy in advance at Lijnwinkel shop just outside the train station, or €2 on the bus). And though you can buy various day passes, there's really no need to buy one for your visit. Nearly all city buses go directly from the train station to the Markt and fan out from there; they then return to the Markt and go back to the train station. Note that buses returning to the train station from the Markt also leave from the library bus stop, a block off the square on nearby Kuiperstraat (every 5 minutes). Your key: Use buses that say either *Station* or *Centrum*.

By Taxi: You'll find taxi stands at the station and on the Markt (€8/first 2 km; to get a cab in the center, call 050-334-444 or 050-333-881).

Tours in Bruges

Bruges by Boat

The most relaxing and scenic (though not informative) way to see this city of canals is by boat, with the captain narrating. The city carefully controls this standard tourist activity, so the many companies all offer essentially the same thing: a 30-minute route (roughly 4/hour, daily 10:00-17:00), a price of €7.60 (cash only), and narration in three or four languages. Qualitative differences are because of individual guides, not companies. Always let them know you speak English to ensure you'll understand the spiel. Two companies give the group-rate discount to individuals with this book: Boten Stael (just over the canal from Memling Museum at Katelijnestraat 4, tel. 050-332-771) and Gruuthuse (Nieuwstraat 11, opposite Groeninge Museum, tel. 050-333-393).

Bruges by Bike

QuasiMundo Bike Tours leads daily five-mile English-language bike tours around the city (€25, €3 discount with this book, 2.5 hours, departs March-Oct at 10:00, in Nov only with good weather, no tours Dec-Feb). For more details and contact info, see their listing under "Near Bruges," later.

City Minibus Tour

City Tour Bruges gives a rolling overview of the town in an 18-seat, two-skylight minibus with dial-a-language headsets and video support (€16, 50 minutes, pay driver). The tour leaves hourly from the Markt (10:00-19:00, until 18:00 in fall, less in winter, tel. 050-355-024, www.citytour.be). The narration, though clear, is slow-moving and a bit boring. But the tour is a lazy way to cruise past virtually every sight in Bruges.

Walking Tour

Local guides walk small groups through the core of town (€9, 2 hours, daily July-Aug, Sat-Sun only mid-April-June and Sept-Oct, depart from TI on 't Zand Square at 14:30—just drop in a few minutes early and buy tickets at the TI desk). Though earnest, the tours are heavy on history and given in two languages, so they may be less than peppy. Still, to propel you beyond the pretty gables and canal swans of Bruges, they're good medicine. In the off-season, "winter walks" leave from the same TI four evenings a week (€9, Nov-Feb Sat-Mon and Wed at 17:00).

Local Guide

A private two-hour guided tour costs €70 (reserve at least one week in advance through TI, tel. 050-448-686). Or contact Christian Scharlé and Daniëlle Janssens, who give two-hour walks for €80, three-hour walks for €120, and full-day tours of Bruges and Brussels for €210 (Christian's mobile 0475-659-507, Daniëlle's mobile 0476-493-203, www.tourmanagementbelgium.be, tmb@skynet. be).

Horse-and-Buggy Tour

The buggies around town can take you on a clip-clop tour (€36, 35 minutes; price is per carriage, not per person; buggies gather in Minnewater, near entrance to Begijnhof, and on the Markt). When divided among four or five people, this can be a good value.

Near Bruges

Popular tour destinations from Bruges are Flanders Fields (famous WWI sites about 40 miles to the southwest) and the picturesque town of Damme (4 easy-to-bike miles to the northeast).

Quasimodo Countryside Tours

This company offers those with extra time two entertaining, all-day, English-only bus tours through the rarely visited Flemish countryside. The "Flanders Fields" tour concentrates on WWI battlefields, trenches, memorials, and poppy-splattered fields (Tue-Sun at 9:15, no tours Mon or in Jan, 8 hours, visit to In Flanders Fields Museum not included). The other tour, "Triple Treat," focuses on Flanders' medieval past and rich culture, with tastes of chocolate, waffles, and beer (departs Mon, Wed, and Fri at 9:15, 8 hours). Be ready for lots of walking.

Tours cost €63, or €53 if you're under 26 (cash preferred, €10 discount on second tour if you've taken the other, includes sandwich lunch, 9- or 30-seat bus depending on demand, non-smoking, reservations required—call 050-370-470, www.quasimodo.be). After making a few big-hotel pickups, the buses leave town from the Park Hotel on 't Zand Square (arrange for pickup when you reserve).

Bike Tours

QuasiMundo Bike Tours, which runs bike tours around Bruges (listed earlier), also offers a daily "Border by Bike" tour through the nearby countryside to Damme (€25, €3 discount with this book, March-Oct, departs at 13:00, 15 miles, 4 hours, tel. 050-330-775, www.quasimundo.com). Both their city and border tours include bike rental, a light raincoat (if necessary), water, and a drink in a local café. Meet at the metal "car wash" fountain on Burg Square 10 minutes before departure. If you already have a bike, you're welcome to join either tour for €15. Jos, who leads most departures, is a high-energy and entertaining guide.

Charming Mieke of **Pink Bear Bike Tours** takes small groups on an easy and delightful 3.5-hour guided pedal along a canal to the historic town of Damme and back, finishing with a brief tour of Bruges. English tours go daily through peak season and nearly daily the rest of the year (€23, €2 discount with this book, €16 if you already have a bike, meet at 10:25 under bell tower on the Markt, tel. 050-616-686, mobile 0476-744-525, www.pinkbear. freeservers.com).

For bike rental shops in Bruges, see page 206.

Sights in Bruges

These sights are listed in walking order, from the Markt (Market Square), to Burg Square, to the cluster of museums around the Church of Our Lady, to the Begijnhof (10-minute walk from beginning to end, without stops). Be aware that many sights stop admitting visitors 30 minutes before closing.

▲Markt (Market Square)

Ringed by a bank, the post office, lots of restaurant terraces, great old gabled buildings, and the iconic bell tower, this square is the modern heart of the city (most city buses run from near here to the train station—use the library bus stop, a block down Kuiperstraat from the Markt). Under the bell tower are two great Belgian-style french-fry stands, a quadrilingual Braille description of the old town, and a metal model of the tower. In Bruges' heyday as a trading center, a canal came right up to this square. Geldmuntstraat, just off the square, is a delightful street with many fun and practical shops and eateries.

▲▲Bell Tower (Belfort)

Most of this bell tower has presided over the Markt since 1300, serenading passersby with carillon music. The octagonal lantern was added in 1486, making it 290 feet high—that's 366 steps. The view is worth the climb and probably even the pricey admission.

Cost and Hours: €8, daily 9:30-17:00, 16:15 last-entry time strictly enforced—best to show up before 16:00, €0.30 WC in courtyard.

▲▲Burg Square

This opulent square is Bruges' civic center, the historic birthplace of Bruges, and the site of the ninth-century castle of the first count of Flanders. Today, it's an atmospheric place to take in an outdoor concert while surrounded by six centuries of architecture.

▲Basilica of the Holy Blood

Originally the Chapel of Saint Basil, this church is famous for its relic of the blood of Christ, which, according to tradition, was brought to Bruges in 1150 after the Second Crusade. The lower chapel is dark and solid—a fine example of Romanesque style. The upper chapel (separate entrance, climb the stairs) is decorated Gothic. An interesting treasury museum is next to the upper chapel.

Cost and Hours: April-Sept daily 9:30-12:00 & 14:00-18:00; Oct-March daily 10:00-12:00 & 14:00-16:00 except closed Wed afternoon; Burg Square, tel. 050-336-792, www.holyblood.com.

▲City Hall

This complex houses several interesting sights. Your €2 ticket includes an audioguide; access to a room full of old town maps and paintings; the grand, beautifully restored **Gothic Room** from 1400, starring a painted and carved wooden ceiling adorned with hanging arches (daily 9:30-17:00, last entry 30 minutes before closing, Burg 12); and the less impressive **Renaissance Hall** (Brugse Vrije), basically just one ornate room with a Renaissance chimney (same hours, separate entrance—in corner of square at Burg 11a).

▲▲Groeninge Museum

This museum has one of the world's best collections of the art produced in the city and surrounding area, from Memling to Magritte. In the 1400s, Bruges was northern Europe's richest, most cosmopolitan, and most cultured city. New ideas, fads, and painting techniques were imported and exported with each shipload. Beautiful paintings were soon an affordable luxury, like fancy clothes or furniture. Internationally known artists set up studios in Bruges, producing portraits and altarpieces for wealthy merchants from all over Europe.

While there's plenty of worthwhile modern art, the Groeninge's highlights are the vivid and pristine Flemish Primitives. ("Primitive" here means "before the Renaissance.") This early Flemish style, though less appreciated and understood today than the Italian Renaissance art produced a century later, is subtle, technically advanced, and beautiful. Flemish art is shaped by its love of detail, its merchant patrons' egos, and the power of the Church. Lose yourself in the halls of Groeninge: Gaze across 15th-century canals, into the eyes of reassuring Marys, and through town squares littered with leotards, lace, and lopped-off heads.

Cost and Hours: €8, Tue-Sun 9:30-17:00, closed Mon, Dijver 12, tel. 050-448-743, www.brugge.be.

▲▲Church of Our Lady (Onze-Lieve-Vrouwekerk)

The church stands as a memorial to the power and wealth of Bruges in its heyday. A delicate *Madonna and Child* by Michelangelo is near the apse (to the right if you're facing the altar). It's said to be the only Michelangelo statue to leave Italy in his lifetime (thanks to the wealth generated by Bruges' cloth trade). If you like tombs and church art, pay to wander through the apse.

Cost and Hours: The rear of the church is free to the public. To get into the main section costs €4; church open Mon-Sat 9:30-17:00, Sun 13:30-17:00, Mariastraat, www.brugge.be.

▲▲Memling Museum/St. John's Hospital (Sint Janshospitaal)

The former monastery/hospital complex has a fine museum in what was once the monks' church. The museum offers a glimpse into medieval medicine, displaying surgical instruments, documents, and visual aids as you work your way to the museum's climax: several of Hans Memling's glowing masterpieces. Memling's art was the culmination of Bruges' Flemish Primitive style. His serene, soft-focus, motionless scenes capture a medieval piety that was quickly fading. The popular style made Memling (c. 1430-1494) one of Bruges' wealthiest citizens, and his work was gobbled up by visiting Italian merchants, who took it home with them, cross-pollinating European art. His *Mystical Wedding of St. Catherine* triptych is a highlight, as is the miniature, gilded-oak shrine to St. Ursula.

Cost and Hours: €8, includes good audioguide, Tue-Sun 9:30-17:00, closed Mon, last entry 30 minutes before closing, across the street from the Church of Our Lady, Mariastraat 38, Bruges museums tel. 050-448-713, www.brugge.be.

▲▲Begijnhof

Inhabited by Benedictine nuns, the Begijnhof courtyard (free, daily 6:30-18:30) almost makes you want to don a habit and fold your hands as you walk under its wispy trees and whisper past its frugal little homes. For a good slice of Begijnhof life, walk through the simple Beguine's House museum.

Cost and Hours: €2, Mon-Sat 10:00-17:00, Sun 14:30-17:00, shorter hours off-season, English explanations, museum is left of entry gate.

Minnewater

Just south of the Begijnhof is Minnewater, an idyllic world of flower boxes, canals, and swans.

Almshouses

As you walk from the Begijnhof back to the town center, you might detour along Nieuwe Gentweg to visit one of about 20 almshouses in the city. At #8, go through the door marked *Godshuis de Meulenaere 1613* into the peaceful courtyard (free). This was a medieval form of housing for the poor. The rich would pay for someone's tiny room here in return for lots of prayers.

Bruges Experiences: Beer, Chocolate, Windmills, and Biking

▲▲De Halve Maan Brewery Tour

Belgians are Europe's beer connoisseurs, and this handy tour is a great way to pay your respects. The brewery makes the only beers

Bruges at a Glance

▲▲**Groeninge Museum** Top-notch collection of mainly Flemish art. **Hours:** Tue-Sun 9:30-17:00, closed Mon. See page 210.

▲▲**Bell Tower** Overlooking the Markt, with 366 steps to a worthwhile view and a carillon close-up. **Hours:** Daily 9:30-17:00. See page 209.

▲▲**Burg Square** Historic square with sights and impressive architecture. **Hours:** Always open. See page 209.

▲▲**Memling Museum/St. John's Hospital** Art by the greatest of the Flemish Primitives. **Hours:** Tue-Sun 9:30-17:00, closed Mon. See page 211.

▲▲**Church of Our Lady** Tombs and church art, including Michelangelo's *Madonna and Child*. **Hours:** Church open Mon-Sat 9:30-17:00, Sun 13:30-17:00. See page 210.

▲▲**Begijnhof** Benedictine nuns' peaceful courtyard and Beguine's House museum. **Hours:** Courtyard open daily 6:30-18:30; museum open Mon-Sat 10:00-17:00, Sun 14:30-17:00, shorter hours off-season. See page 211.

▲▲**De Halve Maan Brewery Tour** Fun tour that includes beer. **Hours:** April-Oct daily on the hour 11:00-16:00, Sat until 18:00;

brewed in Bruges: Brugse Zot ("Fool from Bruges") and Straffe Hendrik ("Strong Henry"). The happy gang at this working-family brewery gives entertaining and informative 45-minute tours in two languages. Avoid crowds by visiting at 11:00.

Cost and Hours: €6.50 includes a beer, lots of very steep steps, great rooftop panorama; tours run April-Oct daily on the hour 11:00-16:00, Sat until 18:00; Nov-March Mon-Fri 11:00 and 15:00 only, Sat-Sun on the hour 11:00-17:00; Walplein 26, tel. 050-444-223, www.halvemaan.be.

▲Chocolate Shops

Bruggians are connoisseurs of fine chocolate. You'll be tempted by chocolate-filled display windows all over town. While Godiva is the best big-factory/high-price/high-quality brand, there are plenty of smaller family-run places in Bruges that offer exquisite handmade chocolates. All three of the following chocolatiers are proud of their creative varieties, generous with their samples, and welcome you to assemble a 100-gram assortment of five or six chocolates.

Nov-March Mon-Fri at 11:00 and 15:00 only, Sat-Sun on the hour 11:00-17:00. See page 211.

▲▲**Biking** Exploring the countryside and pedaling to nearby Damme. **Hours:** Rental shops generally open daily 10:00-19:00. See page 215.

▲**Markt** Main square that is the modern heart of the city, with carillon bell tower (described on opposite page) . **Hours:** Always open. See page 209.

▲**Basilica of the Holy Blood** Romanesque and Gothic church housing a relic of the blood of Christ. **Hours:** April-Sept daily 9:30-12:00 & 14:00-18:00; Oct-March daily 10:00-12:00 & 14:00-16:00 except closed Wed afternoon. See page 209.

▲**City Hall** Beautifully restored Gothic Room from 1400, plus the Renaissance Hall. **Hours:** Daily 9:30-17:00. See page 210.

▲**Chocolate Shops** Bruges' specialty, sold at Dumon, The Chocolate Line, Confiserie De Clerck, and on and on. **Hours:** Shops generally open 10:00-18:00. See page 212.

▲**Choco-Story: The Chocolate Museum** The whole delicious story of Belgium's favorite treat. **Hours:** Daily 10:00-17:00. See page 214.

BRUGES

Dumon: Perhaps Bruges' smoothest, creamiest chocolates are at Dumon, just off the Markt (a selection of 5 or 6 chocolates are a deal at €2.30/100 grams). Nathalie Dumon runs the store with Madame Dumon still dropping by to help make their top-notch chocolate daily and sell it fresh (Wed-Mon 10:00-18:00, closed Tue, old chocolate molds on display in basement, Eiermarkt 6, tel. 050-346-282). The Dumons don't provide English labels because they believe it's best to describe their chocolates in person—and they do it with an evangelical fervor. Try a small mix-and-match box to sample a few out-of-this-world flavors, and come back for more of your favorites.

The Chocolate Line: Locals and tourists alike flock to The Chocolate Line (pricey at €5.60/100 grams) to taste the *gastronomique* varieties concocted by Dominique Person—the mad scientist of chocolate. His unique creations mix chocolate with various, mostly savory, flavors. Even those that sound gross can be surprisingly good (be adventurous). Options include Havana cigar (marinated in rum, cognac, and Cuban tobacco leaves—so, therefore, technically illegal in the US), lemongrass, lavender, ginger (shaped like a Buddha), saffron curry, spicy chili, Moroccan mint, Pop Rocks/cola chocolate, wine vinegar, fried onions, bay leaf, sake, lime/vodka/passion fruit, wasabi, and tomatoes/olives/basil. The kitchen—busy whipping up 80 varieties—is on display in the back. Enjoy the window display, refreshed monthly (daily 9:30-18:00 except Sun-Mon opens at 10:30, between Church of Our Lady and the Markt at Simon Stevinplein 19, tel. 050-341-090).

Confiserie De Clerck: Third-generation chocolate maker Jan sells his handmade chocolates for just €1.20/100 grams, making this one of the best deals in town. Some locals claim his chocolate's just as good as at pricier places—taste it and decide for yourself. The time-warp candy shop itself is so delightfully old-school, you'll want to visit no matter what (Mon-Wed and Fri-Sat 10:00-19:00, closed Sun and Thu, Academiestraat 19, tel. 050-345-338).

▲Choco-Story: The Chocolate Museum

The Chocolate Fairy leads you through 2,600 years of chocolate history—explaining why, in the ancient Mexican world of the Mayas and the Aztecs, chocolate was considered the drink of the gods, and cocoa beans were used as a means of payment. With lots of artifacts well-described in English, this kid-friendly museum fills you in on the production of truffles, bonbons, hollow figures, and solid bars of chocolate. You'll view a delicious little video (8 minutes long, runs continuously, English subtitles). Your finale is in the "demonstration room," where—after a 10-minute cooking demo—you get a taste.

Cost and Hours: €7, €11 combo-ticket includes nearby Friet Museum, daily 10:00-17:00; where Wijnzakstraat meets Sint Jansstraat at Sint Jansplein, 3-minute walk from the Markt; tel. 050-612-237, www.choco-story.be.

Nearby: The Chocolate Museum owner's wife got tired of his ancient lamp collection...so he opened a **Lamp Museum** next door (€11 combo-ticket with Chocolate Museum). While obscure, it's an impressive and well-described collection showing lamps through the ages.

Friet Museum

While this fun-loving and kid-friendly place tries hard to elevate the story of the potato, this is—for most—one museum too many. Still, it's the only place in the world that enthusiastically tells the story of french fries, which, of course, aren't even French—they're Belgian.

Cost and Hours: €6, €11 combo-ticket includes Chocolate Museum, daily 10:00-17:00, Vlamingstraat 33, tel. 050-340-150, www.frietmuseum.be.

Windmills and Lace by the Moat

A 15-minute walk from the center to the northeast end of town (faster by bike) brings you to four windmills strung along a pleasant grassy setting on the "big moat" canal. The St. Janshuys **windmill** is open to visitors (€2; May-Aug Tue-Sun 9:30-12:30 & 13:30-17:00, closed Mon, last entry at 16:30; Sept same hours but open Sat-Sun only; closed Oct-April; go to the end of Carmersstraat and hang a right).

The **Folklore Museum,** in the same neighborhood, is cute but forgettable (€2, Tue-Sun 9:30-17:00, last entry at 16:30, closed Mon, Balstraat 43, tel. 050-448-764). To find it, ask for the Jerusalem Church. On the same street is a lace shop with a good reputation, **'t Apostelientje** (Tue 13:00-17:00, Wed-Sat 9:30-12:15 & 13:15-17:00, Sun 10:00-13:00, closed Mon, Balstraat 11, tel. 050-337-860, mobile 0495-562-420).

▲▲Biking

The Dutch word for bike is *fiets* (pronounced "feets"). And though Bruges' sights are close enough for easy walking, the town is a treat for bikers, and a bike quickly gets you into dreamy back lanes without a hint of tourism. Take a peaceful evening ride through the town's nooks and crannies and around the outer canal. Consider keeping a bike for the duration of your stay—it's the way the locals get around. Along the canal that circles the town is a park with a delightful bike lane. Rental shops have maps and ideas (see "Bike Rental" on page 206 for more info).

BRUGES

Nightlife in Bruges

Herberg Vlissinghe and **De Garre** (both listed later, under "Eating in Bruges") are great places to just nurse a beer and enjoy new friends.

Charlie Rockets is an American-style bar—lively and central—with foosball games, darts, and five pool tables (€9/hour) in the inviting back room. It also runs a youth hostel upstairs and therefore is filled with a young, international crowd who take full advantage of the guest-only happy hour prices (a block off the Markt at Hoogstraat 19). It's open nightly until 4:00 in the morning with nonstop rock 'n' roll.

Nighttime Bike Ride: Great as these pubs are, my favorite way to spend a late-summer evening in Bruges is in the twilight on a rental bike, savoring the cobbled wonders of its back streets, far from the touristic commotion.

Evening Carillon Concerts: The tiny courtyard behind the bell tower has a few benches where people can enjoy the free carillon concerts (generally Mon, Wed, and Sat at 21:00 in the summer; schedule posted on courtyard wall).

Sleeping in Bruges

Bruges is a great place to sleep, with Gothic spires out your window, little traffic noise, and the cheerily out-of-tune carillon heralding each new day at 8:00 sharp. (Thankfully, the bell tower is silent from 22:00 to 8:00.) Most Bruges accommodations are located between the train station and the old center, with the most distant (and best) being a few blocks to the north and east of the Markt (Market Square).

B&Bs offer the best value (listed on page 220), but hoteliers have lobbied City Hall to make it harder to have more than two "official" rooms. Creative B&B owners have found ways to get around the new restrictions. All are on quiet streets and (with a few exceptions) keep the same prices throughout the year.

Bruges is most crowded Friday and Saturday evenings from Easter through October—July and August weekends are the worst. Many hotels charge a bit more on Friday and Saturday, and won't let you stay just one night if it's a Saturday.

Hotels

$$$ Hotel Heritage offers 24 rooms, with chandeliers that seem hung especially for you, in a solid and completely modernized old building with luxurious public spaces. Tastefully decorated and offering all the amenities, it's one of those places that does everything just right yet still feels warm and inviting—if you can afford it (Db-€178, superior Db-€229, deluxe Db-€283, extra bed-€60, wonderful buffet breakfast-€24, continental breakfast-€12, iPad in every room, air-con, elevator, free Internet access and Wi-Fi, sauna, tanning bed, fitness room, bike rental, free 2-hour guided city tour, parking-€35/day, Niklaas Desparsstraat 11, a block north of the Markt, tel. 050-444-444, fax 050-444-440, www.hotel-heritage.com, info@hotel-heritage.com). It's run by cheery and hardworking Johan and Isabelle Creytens.

$$$ Hotel Adornes is small and classy—a great value situated in the most charming part of town. This 17th-century canalside house has 20 rooms with full modern bathrooms, free parking (reserve in advance), free loaner bikes, and a cellar lounge with games and videos (small Db-€125, larger Db-€145-155, Tb-€175, Qb-€185, elevator, free Wi-Fi in lobby, some street noise, near Carmersstraat at St. Annarei 26, tel. 050-341-336, fax 050-342-085, www.adornes.be, info@adornes.be). Nathalie runs the family business with the help of courteous Rik.

$$ Hotel Patritius, family-run and centrally located, is a grand, circa-1830 Neoclassical mansion with hardwood oak floors in its 16 stately, high-ceilinged rooms. It features a plush lounge, a chandeliered breakfast room, and a courtyard garden. If you get a

Sleep Code

(€1 = about $1.30, country code: 32)
S = Single, **D** = Double/Twin, **T** = Triple, **Q** = Quad, **b** = bathroom, **s** = shower only. Everyone speaks English. Unless otherwise noted, breakfast is included and credit cards are accepted.

To help you easily sort through these listings, I've divided the accommodations into three categories, based on the price for a standard double room with bath:

$$$ **Higher Priced**—Most rooms €125 or more.
$$ **Moderately Priced**—Most rooms between €80-125.
$ **Lower Priced**—Most rooms €80 or less.

Prices can change without notice; verify the hotel's current rates online or by email.

room at the lower end of the price range, this can be a great value (Db-€100-140, Tb-€140-165, Qb-€165-200, cheaper in off-season, rates depend on room size and demand—check site for best price, extra bed-€25, air-con, elevator, free Internet access and Wi-Fi, coin-op laundry, parking-€9/day, garage parking-€15/day, Riddersstraat 11, tel. 050-338-454, fax 050-339-634, www.hotelpatritius.be, info@hotelpatritius.be, cordial Garrett and Elvi Spaey).

$$ Hotel Egmond is a creaky mansion located in the middle of the quietly idyllic Minnewater. Its eight 18th-century rooms are plain, with small modern baths shoehorned in, and the guests-only garden is just waiting for a tea party. This hotel is ideal for romantics who want a countryside setting—where you sleep surrounded by a park, not a city (Sb-€95, small twin Db-€105, larger Db-€115, Tb-€150, cheaper in winter, free Wi-Fi, parking-€10/day, Minnewater 15, for location see map on page 202, tel. 050-341-445, fax 050-342-940, www.egmond.be, info@egmond.be, Steven).

$$ Hotel Botaniek, quietly located a block from Astrid Park, is a pint-sized hotel with a comfy lounge, renting nine slightly worn rooms—some of them quite big (Db-€95 weekday special for my readers, €99 Fri-Sat; Qb-€145, €149 Fri-Sat; less for longer and off-season stays, elevator, Waalsestraat 23, tel. 050-341-424, fax 050-345-939, www.botaniek.be, info@botaniek.be, Andy).

$$ Hotel ter Reien is big and basic, with 26 rooms overlooking a canal in the town center (Db-€70-110, Tb-€95-130, Qb-€140-160, rates vary widely with demand—check their website for best prices; cheapest rates for weekdays, stays of at least 3 nights, or rooms without canal views; extra bed-€24-29, pay Internet access

Bruges Accommodations near the Center

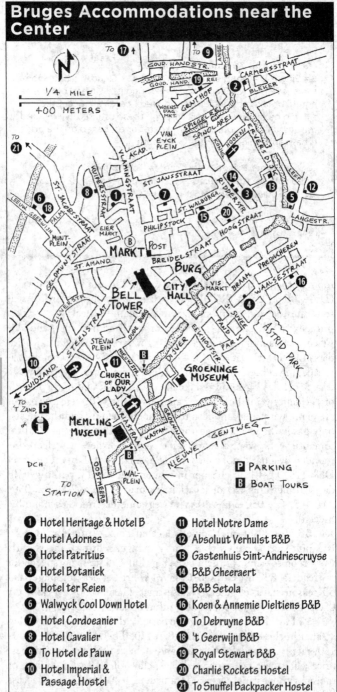

1. Hotel Heritage & Hotel B
2. Hotel Adornes
3. Hotel Patritius
4. Hotel Botaniek
5. Hotel ter Reien
6. Walwyck Cool Down Hotel
7. Hotel Cordoeanier
8. Hotel Cavalier
9. To Hotel de Pauw
10. Hotel Imperial & Passage Hostel
11. Hotel Notre Dame
12. Absoluut Verhulst B&B
13. Gastenhuis Sint-Andriescruyse
14. B&B Gheeraert
15. B&B Setola
16. Koen & Annemie Dieltiens B&B
17. To Debruyne B&B
18. 't Geerwijn B&B
19. Royal Stewart B&B
20. Charlie Rockets Hostel
21. To Snuffel Backpacker Hostel

and Wi-Fi, Langestraat 1, tel. 050-349-100, fax 050-340-048, www.hotelterreien.be, info@hotelterreien.be, owned by Diederik and Stephanie Pille-Maes).

$$ Walwyck Cool Down Hotel—a bit of modern comfort, chic design, and English verbiage in a medieval shell—is a nicely located hotel with 21 spacious rooms. If you're getting tired of Bruges cute, this is the place (small Db-€100, standard Db-€110, "superior" Db-€120, Tb-€150, family room-€155, "superior" family room-€180, free Wi-Fi, Leeuwstraat 8, tel. 050-616-360, fax 050-616-560, www.walwyck.com, rooms@walwyck.com).

$$ Hotel Cordoeanier, a charming family-run hotel, rents 22 simple, compact, hardwood-floor rooms on a quiet street two blocks off the Markt. It's one of the best deals in town (Sb-€75-105, Db-€80-110, twin Db-€90-120, Tb-€110-150, Qb-€135, cheaper with cash if you show this book, breakfast buffet served in their pleasant Café Rose Red, no elevator, pay Internet access, free Wi-Fi, patio, Cordoeanierstraat 16-18, tel. 050-339-051, fax 050-346-111, www.cordoeanier.be, info@cordoeanier.be, Kris).

$$ Hotel B (formerly the Hotel Nicolas) recently underwent a complete makeover, so expect its 20 big rooms to have all the amenities—and higher prices. The location is ideal—on a quiet street a block off the Markt (Db-€90-130, elevator, Niklaas Desparsstraat 9, tel. 050-335-502, fax 050-343-544, www.hotel-b.be, info@hotel-b.be, Sophie).

$ Hotel Cavalier, with lots of stairs and lots of character, rents eight rooms decorated with quirky knickknacks; some units have remodeled bathrooms. The staff serves a hearty buffet breakfast in a once-royal setting (Sb-€60, Db-€73, Tb-€95, Qb-€105, 2 lofty en-suite "backpackers' doubles" on fourth floor-€45-50, book direct and mention this book for special Rick Steves price, free Wi-Fi, Kuipersstraat 25, tel. 050-330-207, fax 050-347-199, www.hotelcavalier.be, info@hotelcavalier.be, run by friendly Viviane De Clerck).

$ Hotel de Pauw is tall, skinny, flower-bedecked, and family-run, with eight straightforward rooms on a quiet street next to a church (Sb-€70-75, Db-€85-95, no elevator, free and easy street parking, Sint Gilliskerkhof 8, tel. 050-337-118, fax 050-345-140, www.hoteldepauw.be, info@hoteldepauw.be, Philippe and Hilde).

$ Hotel 't Keizershof is a dollhouse of a hotel that lives by its motto, "Spend a night...not a fortune." (Its other motto: "When you're asleep, we look just like those big fancy hotels.") It's simple and tidy, with seven small, cheery, old-time rooms split between two floors, with a shower and toilet on each (S-€30-45, D-€45, T-€66, Q-€84, cash only, free Wi-Fi, free and easy parking, laundry service-€7.50, Oostmeers 126, a block in front of station, for location see map on page 202, tel. 050-338-728, www.hotelkeizershof.be, info@hotelkeizershof.be). The hotel is run by Stefaan and

Hilde, with decor by their children, Lorie and Fien; it's situated in a pleasant area near the train station and Minnewater, a 15-minute walk from the Markt.

$ Hotel Imperial is an old-school hotel with seven old-school rooms. It's simple and well-run in a charming building on a handy, quiet street (Db-€70-90, cash only, no elevator, free Wi-Fi, Dweersstraat 24, tel. 050-339-014, www.hotelimperial.be, info@hotelimperial.be, Paul Bernolet and Hilde).

$ Hotel Notre Dame has seen better days, but new owner Gauthier is renovating its 12 well-worn rooms. Since this place is in the thick of things, it's worth considering, but stay in the renovated rooms only (Db-€70-75, free Internet access and Wi-Fi, Mariastraat 3, tel. 050-333-193, fax 050-337-608, www.hotelnotredame.be, info@hotelnotredame.be).

Bed-and-Breakfasts

These B&Bs, run by people who enjoy their work, offer a better value than hotels. Most families rent out their entire top floor—several rooms and a small sitting area. And most are mod and stylish—they're just in medieval shells. Each is central, with lots of stairs and €70 doubles you'd pay €100 for in a hotel. Many places charge €10-15 extra for one-night stays. It's possible to find parking on the street in the evening (pay 9:00-19:00, 2-hour maximum for metered parking during the day, free overnight).

$$ Absoluut Verhulst is a great, modern-feeling B&B with three rooms in a 400-year-old house, run by friendly Frieda and Benno (Db-€95; huge and lofty suite-€130 for 2, €160 for 3, €180 for 4; €10 more for one-night stays, cash only, free Wi-Fi, 5-minute walk east of the Markt at Verbrand Nieuwland 1, tel. 050-334-515, www.b-bverhulst.com, b-b.verhulst@pandora.be).

$$ Gastenhuis Sint-Andriescruyse offers warmly decorated rooms with high ceilings in a spacious, cheerfully red canalside house a short walk from the Old Town action. Owners Luc and Christiane treat guests like long-lost family, and proudly share their photo albums with pictures of previous guests (S-€75, D/Db-€100, T-€125, Q-€150, family room for up to 5 comes with board games, cash only, free soft drinks, free Internet access, free pick-up at station, Verversdijk 15A, tel. 050-789-168, mobile 0477-973-933, www.gastenhuisst-andriescruyse.be, luc.cloet@telenet.be).

$$ B&B Gheeraert is a Neoclassical mansion where Inne rents three huge, bright, comfy rooms (Sb-€75, Db-€85, Tb-€95, two-night minimum stay required, cash only but credit card required to hold reservation, strictly non-smoking, fridges in rooms, free Internet access and Wi-Fi, Ridderstraat 9, 5-minute walk east of the Markt, tel. 050-335-627, fax 050-345-201, www.bb-bruges.be, bb-bruges@skynet.be).

$ B&B Setola, run by Lut and Bruno Setola, offers three expansive rooms and a spacious breakfast/living room on the top floor of their house. Wooden ceiling beams give the modern rooms a touch of Old World flair, and the family room has a fun loft for the kids (Sb-€65, Db-€75, extra person-€25, add €15 for one-night stays, free Wi-Fi, 5-minute walk from the Markt, Sint Walburgas- straat 12, tel. 050-334-977, fax 050-332-551, www.bedandbreak- fast-bruges.com, setola@bedandbreakfast-bruges.com).

$ Koen and Annemie Dieltiens are a friendly couple who enjoy getting to know their guests while sharing a wealth of in- formation on Bruges. You'll eat a hearty breakfast around a big table in their comfortable house (Sb-€60, Db-€70, Tb-€90, €10 more for one-night stays, cash only, free Internet access and Wi- Fi, Waalsestraat 40, three blocks southeast of Burg Square, tel. 050-334-294, www.bedandbreakfastbruges.be, dieltiens@bedan- dbreakfastbruges.be).

$ Debruyne B&B, run by Marie-Rose and her architect hus- band, Ronny, offers three rooms with artsy, modern decor (check out the elephant-size yellow doors—Ronny's design). The glass walls in the breakfast room open to a cloister-like garden. The ar- chitecture is cool but the hosts have genuine warmth (Sb-€65, Db- €70, Tb-€90, €10 more for one-night stays, cash only, Internet ac- cess, free Wi-Fi, 7-minute walk north of the Markt, 2 blocks from the little church at Lange Raamstraat 18, tel. 050-347-606, www. bedandbreakfastbruges.com, mietjedebruyne@yahoo.co.uk).

$ 't Geerwijn B&B, run by Chris de Loof, offers homey rooms in the old center. Check out the fun, lofty A-frame room upstairs (Ds/Db-€75-80 depending on season, Tb-€85-90, cash only, pleasant breakfast room and royal lounge, free Wi-Fi, Geer- wijnstraat 14, tel. 050-340-544, fax 050-343-721, www.geerwijn. be, info@geerwijn.be). Chris also rents an apartment that sleeps five.

$ Royal Stewart B&B, run by Scottish Maggie and her hus- band, Gilbert, has three thoughtfully decorated rooms in a quiet, convent-style 17th-century house that was inhabited by nuns until 1953 (S-€48, D/Db-€65, Tb-€85, cash only, pleasant breakfast room, Genthof 25-27, 5-minute walk from the Markt, tel. 050- 337-918, fax 050-337-918, www.royalstewart.be, r.stewart@pan- dora.be).

$ Waterside B&B has two fresh, Zen-like rooms, one floor above a peaceful canal south of the town center (D-€80, €5 more on Sat, continental breakfast, free Wi-Fi, 15-minute walk from Burg Square at Kazernevest 88, for location see map on page 202, tel. & fax 050-616-686, mobile 0476-744-525, www.waterside.be, waterside@telenet.be, run by Mieke of recommended Pink Bear Bike Tours).

BRUGES

$ B&B AM/PM sports three ultra-modern rooms in a residential neighborhood just west of the old town (Db-€70, Tb-€90, €10 more for one-night stay, cash only, free Internet access—mornings only, free Wi-Fi, 5-minute walk from 't Zand at Singel 10, for location see map on page 202, mobile 0485-071-003, www.bruges-bedandbreakfast.com, info@bruges-bedandbreakfast.com, artsy young couple Tiny and Kevin). From the train station, head left down busy Buiten Begijnevest to the roundabout. Stay to the left, take the pedestrian underpass, then follow the busy road (now on your left). Just before the next bridge, turn right onto the footpath called Buiten Boeverievest, then turn left onto Singel; the B&B is at #10.

Hostels

Bruges has several good hostels offering beds for around €16 in 4- to 12-bed rooms. Breakfast is about €3 extra. The American-style **$ Charlie Rockets** hostel (and bar), a backpacker dive, is the liveliest and most central. The ground floor feels like a 19th-century sports bar, with a foosball-and-movie-posters party ambience. Upstairs is an industrial-strength pile of hostel dorms (90 beds, €18/bed with sheets, €22/bed with sheets and breakfast, 4-6 beds/ room, D-€55 includes breakfast, lockers, free Wi-Fi, Hoogstraat 19, tel. 050-330-660, www.charlierockets.com). Other small and loose places are the minimal, funky, and central **$ Passage** (€16/ bed with sheets, 4-7 beds/room, D-€52, Db-€67, Dweerstraat 26, tel. 050-340-232, www.passagebruges.com, info@passagebruges. com) and **$ Snuffel Backpacker Hostel,** which is less central and pretty grungy, but friendly and laid-back (60 beds, €16-18/bed includes sheets and breakfast, 4-12 beds/room, Ezelstraat 47, tel. 050-333-133, www.snuffel.be).

Eating in Bruges

Bruges' specialties include mussels cooked a variety of ways (one order can feed two), fish dishes, grilled meats, and french fries. The town's two indigenous beers are the prizewinning Brugse Zot (Bruges Fool), a golden ale, and Straffe Hendrik, a potent, bitter triple ale.

You'll find plenty of affordable, touristy restaurants on floodlit squares and along dreamy canals. Bruges feeds 3.5 million tourists a year, and most are seduced by a high-profile location. These can be great experiences for the magical setting and views, but the quality of food and service will likely be mediocre. I wouldn't blame you for eating at one of these places, but I won't recommend any. I prefer the candle-cool bistros that flicker on back streets.

Restaurants

Rock Fort is a chic spot with a modern, fresh coziness and a high-powered respect for good food. Two young chefs, Peter Laloo and Hermes Vanliefde, give their French cuisine a creative, gourmet twist. At the bar they serve a separate tapas menu. Reservations recommended. This place is a winner (€6-12 tapas, great pastas and salads, €15 lunch special, beautifully presented €19-34 dinner plates, €40 five-tapas special, fancy €50 fixed-price four-course meal, open Mon-Fri 12:00-14:30 & 18:30-23:00, closed Sat-Sun, Langestraat 15, tel. 050-334-113).

Bistro in den Wittenkop, very Flemish, is a stylishly small, laid-back, old-time place specializing in local favorites, where Lindsey serves while Patrick cooks. It's a classy spot to enjoy hand-cut fries, which go particularly well with Straffe Hendrik beer (€37 three-course meal, €20-25 plates, Tue-Sat 18:00-21:30, closed Sun-Mon, reserve ahead, terrace in back in summer, Sint Jakobsstraat 14, tel. 050-332-059).

Bistro den Amand, with a plain interior and a few outdoor tables, exudes unpretentious quality the moment you step in. In this mussels-free zone, Chef An is enthusiastic about stir-fry and vegetables, as her busy wok and fun salads prove. Portions are splittable and there are always good vegetarian options. The creative dishes—some with a hint of Asian influence—are a welcome departure from Bruges' mostly predictable traditional restaurants. It's on a bustling pedestrian lane a half-block off the Markt (€35 three-course meal, €20-25 plates; Mon-Tue and Thu-Sat 12:00-14:00 & 18:00-21:00, closed Wed and Sun; Sint-Amandstraat 4, tel. 050-340-122, An Vissers and Arnout Beyaert). Reservations are smart for dinner.

The Flemish Pot is a busy eatery where enthusiastic chefs Mario and Rik cook up a traditional menu of vintage Flemish specialties—from beef and rabbit stew to eel—served in little iron pots and skillets. Seating is tight and cluttered, and service can be spotty. But you'll enjoy huge portions, refills from the hovering "fries angel," and a good selection of local beers (€26-30 three-course meals, €16-24 plates, daily 12:00-22:00, reservations smart, just off Geldmuntstraat at Helmstraat 3, tel. 050-340-086).

Lotus Vegetarian Restaurant serves serious lunch plates (€10 *plat du jour* offered daily), salads, and homemade chocolate cake in a pleasantly small, bustling, and upscale setting. To keep carnivorous companions happy, they also serve several very good, organic meat dishes (Mon-Fri from 11:45, last orders at 14:00, closed Sat-Sun, just north of Burg Square at Wapenmakersstraat 5, tel. 050-331-078).

De Hobbit, featuring an entertaining menu, is always busy

Bruges Restaurants

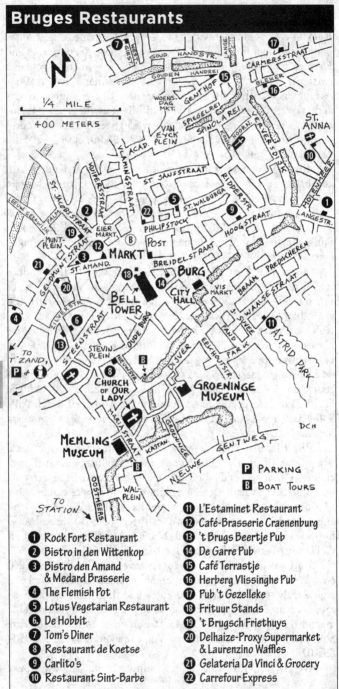

1/4 MILE
400 METERS

P PARKING
B BOAT TOURS

1. Rock Fort Restaurant
2. Bistro in den Wittenkop
3. Bistro den Amand & Medard Brasserie
4. The Flemish Pot
5. Lotus Vegetarian Restaurant
6. De Hobbit
7. Tom's Diner
8. Restaurant de Koetse
9. Carlito's
10. Restaurant Sint-Barbe
11. L'Estaminet Restaurant
12. Café-Brasserie Craenenburg
13. 't Brugs Beertje Pub
14. De Garre Pub
15. Café Terrastje
16. Herberg Vlissinghe Pub
17. Pub 't Gezelleke
18. Frituur Stands
19. 't Brugsch Friethuys
20. Delhaize-Proxy Supermarket & Laurenzino Waffles
21. Gelateria Da Vinci & Grocery
22. Carrefour Express

with happy eaters. For a swinging deal, try the all-you-can-eat spareribs with bread and salad for €18.50. It's nothing fancy, just good, basic food served in a fun, crowded, traditional grill house (daily 18:00-23:00, family-friendly, Kemelstraat 8-10, reservations smart, tel. 050-335-520).

Tom's Diner is a trendy, cozy little candlelit bistro in a quiet, cobbled residential area a 10-minute walk from the center. Young chef Tom gives traditional dishes a delightful modern twist, such as his signature Flemish meat loaf with rhubarb sauce. If you want to flee the tourists and experience a popular neighborhood joint, this is it—the locals love it (€15-20 plates, Tue-Sat 12:00-14:00 & 18:00-23:00, closed Sun-Mon, north of the Markt near Sint-Gilliskerk at West-Gistelhof 23, tel. 050-333-382).

Restaurant de Koetse is handy for central, good-quality, local-style food. The feeling is traditional, a bit formal (stuffy even), and dressy, yet accessible. The cuisine is Belgian and French, with an emphasis on grilled meat, seafood, and mussels (€30 three-course meals, €20-30 plates include vegetables and a salad, Fri-Wed 12:00-14:30 & 18:00-22:00, closed Thu, non-smoking section, Oude Burg 31, tel. 050-337-680, Piet).

Carlito's is a good choice for basic Italian fare. Their informal space, with whitewashed walls and tea-light candles, is two blocks from Burg Square (€8-13 pizzas and pastas, daily 12:00-14:00 & 18:00-22:30, patio seating in back, Hoogstraat 21, tel. 050-490-075).

Restaurant Sint-Barbe, on the eastern edge of town, is a homey little neighborhood place where Evi serves classy Flemish dishes made from local ingredients in a fresh, modern space on two floors (€12 soup-and-main lunch, €14-25 main courses, Thu-Mon 11:30-14:30 & 18:00-22:00, closed Tue-Wed, food served until 21:00, St. Annaplein 29, tel. 050-330-999).

L'Estaminet is a youthful, jazz-filled eatery, similar to one of Amsterdam's brown cafés. Don't be intimidated by its lack of tourists. Local students flock here for the Tolkien-chic ambience, hearty €9 spaghetti, and big dinner salads. This is Belgium—it serves more beer than wine. For outdoor dining under an all-weather canopy, enjoy the relaxed patio facing peaceful Astrid Park (Fri-Wed 11:30-24:00, Thu 16:00-24:00, Park 5, tel. 050-330-916).

Restaurants on the Markt: Most tourists seem to be eating on the Markt with the bell tower high overhead and horse carriages clip-clopping by. The square is ringed by tourist traps with aggressive waiters expert at getting you to consume more than you intended. Still, if you order smartly, you can have a memorable meal or drink here on one of the finest squares in Europe at a reasonable price. Consider **Café-Brasserie Craenenburg,** with a straightforward menu, where you can get pasta and beer for €15 and spend all the time you want ogling the magic of Bruges (daily 7:30-23:00, Markt 16, tel. 050-333-402). While it's overpriced for dining, it can be a fine place to savor a before- or after-meal drink with the view.

Cheap Eats: **Medard Brasserie,** just a block off the Markt, serves the cheapest hot meal in town—hearty meat spaghetti (big plate-€3, huge plate-€5.50, sit inside or out, Fri-Wed 11:00-20:30, closed Thu, Sint Amandstraat 18, tel. 050-348-684).

Bars Offering Light Meals, Beer, and Ambience

My best budget-eating tip for Bruges: Stop into one of the city's bars for a simple meal and a couple of world-class beers with great Bruges ambience. The last three pubs listed are in the wonderfully *gezellig* (cozy) quarter, northeast of the Markt. Just walking out here is a treat as it gets you away from the tourists.

The **'t Brugs Beertje** is young and convivial. Although any pub or restaurant carries the basic beers, you'll find a selection here of more than 300 types, including seasonal brews. They serve light meals, including pâté, spaghetti, toasted sandwiches, and a traditional cheese plate. You're welcome to sit at the bar and talk with the staff (€12 for splittable plate with 5 cheeses, bread, and salad; Thu-Tue 16:00-24:00, closed Wed, Kemelstraat 5, tel. 050-339-616, run by fun-loving manager Daisy). Daisy's on a mission to sell the world on the wonders of beer and cheese rather than wine and cheese.

De Garre (deh-HHHHAHR-rah) is another good place to gain an appreciation of the Belgian beer culture. Rather than a noisy pub scene, it has a dressy, sit-down-and-focus-on-your-friend-and-the-fine-beer vibe. It's mature and cozy with tables, light meals (cold cuts, pâtés, and toasted sandwiches), and a huge selection of beers, with heavy beers being the forte (Tue-Sun 12:00-24:00, closed Mon, additional seating up tiny staircase, off Breidelstraat between Burg and the Markt, on tiny Garre alley, tel. 050-341-029).

Café Terrastje is a cozy pub serving light meals. Enjoy the subdued ambience inside, or relax on the front terrace overlooking the canal and heart of the *gezellig* district (€6-8 sandwiches, €10-18 dishes; food served Fri-Mon 12:00-21:00, open until 23:30; Tue 12:00-18:00; closed Wed-Thu; corner of Genthof and Langerei, tel. 050-330-919, Ian and Patricia).

Herberg Vlissinghe is the oldest pub in town (1515). Bruno keeps things basic and laid-back, serving simple plates (lasagna, grilled cheese sandwiches, and famous €8 angel-hair spaghetti) and great beer in the best old-time tavern atmosphere in town. This must have been the Dutch Masters' rec room. The garden outside comes with a *boules* court—free for guests to watch or play (Wed-Sat 11:00-24:00, Sun 11:00-19:00, closed Mon-Tue, Blekersstraat 2, tel. 050-343-737).

Pub 't Gezelleke lacks the mystique of the Vlissinghe, but it's a true neighborhood pub offering spaghetti and a few basic plates and a good chance to drink with locals (if you sit at the bar). Its name is an appropriate play on the word for *cozy* and the name of a great local poet (daily 11:00-24:00, but closed Sun and Wed, Carmersstraat 15, tel. 050-338-381, Jean de Bruges). Don't come here to eat outdoors.

Fries, Fast Food, and Picnics

Local french fries *(friets)* are a treat. Proud and traditional *frituurs* serve tubs of fries and various local-style shish kebabs. Belgians dip their *friets* in mayonnaise, but ketchup is there for the Yankees (along with spicier sauces). For a quick, cheap, hot, and scenic snack, hit a *frituur* and sit on the steps or benches overlooking the Markt (convenience benches are about 50 yards past the post office).

Markt *Frituurs*: Twin take-away fry carts are on the Markt at the base of the bell tower (daily 10:00-24:00). Skip the ketchup and have a sauce adventure. I find the cart on the left more user-friendly.

't Brugsch Friethuys, a block off the Markt, is handy for fries you can sit down and enjoy. Its forte is greasy, deep-fried Flemish fast food. The €12 "Big Hunger menu" comes with all the traditional gut bombs: shrimp, *frikandel* minced-meat sausage, and "gypsy stick" sausage (daily 11:00-late, at the corner of Geldmuntstraat and Sint Jakobstraat, Luc will explain your options).

Delhaize-Proxy Supermarket is ideal for picnics. Its push-button produce pricer lets you buy as little as one mushroom (Mon-Sat 9:00-19:00, closed Sun, 3 blocks off the Markt on Geldmuntstraat). For midnight snacks, you'll find Indian-run corner grocery stores scattered around town.

Carrefour Express is handy for picnics and stocking your hotel room pantry. It's just off the Markt on Vlamingstraat (daily 8:00-19:00).

Belgian Waffles and Ice Cream

You'll see waffles sold at restaurants and take-away stands. **Laurenzino** is particularly good, and a favorite with Bruges' teens when they get the waffle munchies. Their classic waffle with chocolate costs €3 (daily in summer 10:00-22:00, until 23:00 Fri-Sat; winter 10:00-20:00, until 22:00 Fri-Sat; across from Gelateria Da Vinci at Noordzandstraat 1, tel. 050-333-213).

BRUGES

Gelateria Da Vinci, the local favorite for homemade ice cream, has creative flavors and a lively atmosphere. As you approach, you'll see a line of happy lickers. Before ordering, ask to sample the Ferrero Rocher (chocolate, nuts, and crunchy cookie) and plain yogurt (daily 11:00-23:00, later in summer, Geldmuntstraat 34, run by Sylvia from Austria).

Bruges Connections

From Bruges by Train to: Brussels (2/hour, usually at :31 and :58, 1 hour), **Brussels Airport** (2/hour, 1.5 hours, transfer at Brussels Nord), **Delft** (hourly, 3 hours, change in Ghent, Antwerp, and Rotterdam), **Paris** (roughly hourly via Brussels, 2.5 hours on fast Thalys trains—it's best to book by 20:00 the day before), **Amsterdam** (hourly, 3 hours, transfer at Antwerp Central or Brussels Midi; transfer can be tight—be alert and check with conductor; some trips via Thalys train, which requires supplement), **Amsterdam's Schiphol Airport** (10/day, 2.75 hours, change in Antwerp), **Haarlem** (hourly, 3.5 hours, 2-3 changes—avoid Thalys if traveling with a railpass).

Trains from London: Bruges is an ideal "Welcome to Europe" stop after London. Take the Eurostar train from London to Brussels (10/day, 2.5 hours), then transfer, backtracking to Bruges (2/hour, 1 hour, entire trip just a few dollars more with Eurostar ticket).

Trains to London: Eurostar trains to London leave from tracks 1 and 2 at Brussels' Midi/Zuid/South Station. Arrive 30 minutes early to get your ticket validated and your luggage and passport checked by British authorities (similar to airport check-in for an international flight).

By Bus to: London (generally €43 one-way, €72 round-trip, 1/day direct, about 5 hours, Eurolines tel. 02-274-1350 in Brussels, www.eurolines.be).

FRANCE

PARIS

Paris—the City of Light—has been a beacon of culture for centuries. As a world capital of art, fashion, food, literature, and ideas, it stands as a symbol of all the fine things human civilization can offer. Come prepared to celebrate this, rather than judge our cultural differences, and you'll capture the romance and *joie de vivre* this city exudes.

Paris offers sweeping boulevards, chatty crêpe stands, chic boutiques, and world-class art galleries. Sip decaf with deconstructionists at a sidewalk café, then step into an Impressionist painting in a tree-lined park. Climb Notre-Dame and rub shoulders with the gargoyles. Cruise the Seine, zip to the top of the Eiffel Tower, and saunter down Avenue des Champs-Elysées. Master the Louvre and Orsay museums. Save some after-dark energy for one of the world's most romantic cities.

Planning Your Time

I've listed sights in descending order of importance, filling up to five very busy but doable days in Paris. Therefore, if you have only one day, just do Day 1; for two days, add Day 2; and so on. When planning where to plug in Versailles, keep in mind that the Château is closed on Mondays and especially crowded on Sundays and Tuesdays—try to avoid these days.

Day 1
Morning: Follow my Historic Paris Walk, featuring Ile de la Cité, Notre-Dame, the Latin Quarter, and Sainte-Chapelle.
Afternoon: Tour the Louvre.

Evening: Enjoy the Trocadéro scene and a twilight ride up the Eiffel Tower.

Day 2
Morning: Wander the Champs-Elysées from the Arc de Triomphe down the grand Avenue des Champs-Elysées to the Tuileries Garden.
Afternoon: Cross the pedestrian bridge from the Tuileries Garden, then tour the Orsay Museum.
Evening: Take one of the tours by bus, taxi, or retro-chic Deux Chevaux car (see page 311). (If you're staying more than two days, save this for your last-night finale.)

Day 3
Morning: Catch the RER suburban train by 8:00 to arrive early at Versailles (before it opens at 9:00) and tour the palace's interior. (If you get a later start, reverse today's plan by doing the gardens first and the château's interior later in the afternoon.)
Midday: Have lunch in the gardens at Versailles.
Afternoon: Spend the afternoon touring the gardens, the Trianon Palaces, and Domaine de Marie-Antoinette.
Evening: Have dinner in Versailles town or return to Paris. For dessert, cruise the Seine River.

Day 4
Morning: Visit Montmartre (one-time stomping ground of Impressionist painters) and the Sacré-Cœur Basilica. Have lunch on Montmartre.
Afternoon: Continue your Impressionist theme by touring the Orangerie and the Rodin Museum, or switch gears and tour the Army Museum and Napoleon's Tomb.
Evening: Enjoy dinner on Ile St. Louis, then a floodlit walk by Notre-Dame.

Day 5
Morning: Ride scenic bus #69 to the Marais and tour this neighborhood, including the Pompidou Center.
Afternoon: Tour the Opéra Garnier, and end your day enjoying the glorious rooftop views at the Galeries Lafayette and Printemps department stores.
Evening: Stroll the Champs-Elysées at night.

Orientation to Paris

Paris (population of city center: 2,234,000) is split in half by the Seine River, divided into 20 arrondissements (proud and independent governmental jurisdictions), circled by a ring-road freeway (the *périphérique*), and speckled with Métro stations. You'll find Paris easier to navigate if you know which side of the river you're on, which arrondissement you're in, and which Métro stop you're closest to. If you're north of the river (the top half of any city map), you're on the Right Bank (Rive Droite). If you're south of it, you're on the Left Bank (Rive Gauche). The bull's-eye of your Paris map is Notre-Dame, which sits on an island in the middle of the Seine. Most of your sightseeing will take place within five blocks of the river.

Arrondissements are numbered, starting at the Louvre and moving in a clockwise spiral out to the ring road. The last two digits in a Parisian zip code indicate the arrondissement number. The abbreviation for "Métro stop" is "Mo." In Parisian jargon, the Eiffel Tower is on *la Rive Gauche* (the Left Bank) in the *7ème* (7th arrondissement), zip code 75007, Mo: Trocadéro.

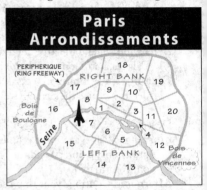

Paris Arrondissements

Paris Métro stops are used as a standard aid in giving directions, even for those not taking the Métro. As you're tracking down addresses, these words and pronunciations will help: Métro (may-troh), *place* (plahs; square), *rue* (roo; road), *avenue* (ah-vuh-noo), *boulevard* (boo-luh-var), and *pont* (pohn; bridge).

Tourist Information

Paris TIs can provide useful information but may have long lines. Pick up the free *Paris for You!* booklet. If you're looking for a map, they may charge you for it (all you really need are the freebie maps available at any hotel). TIs also sell individual tickets to sights (see "Avoiding Lines with Advance Tickets" on page 235), as well as Paris Museum Passes (see page 261). If you plan to get a Museum Pass, it's quicker to buy these at participating sights (except major museums, where lines can be long).

Paris has several TI locations, including **Pyramides** (daily May-Oct 9:00-19:00, Nov-April 10:00-19:00, at Pyramides Métro stop between the Louvre and Opéra), **Gare du Nord** (daily 8:00-

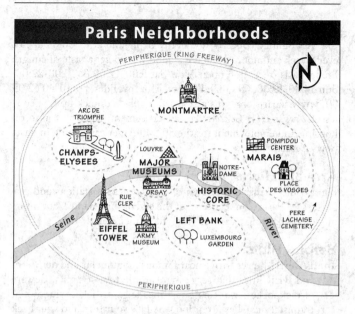

Paris Neighborhoods

PERIPHERIQUE (RING FREEWAY)

MONTMARTRE

ARC DE
TRIOMPHE

CHAMPS-
ELYSEES

LOUVRE

MAJOR
MUSEUMS

ORSAY

POMPIDOU
CENTER

MARAIS

PLACE
DES VOSGES

NOTRE-
DAME

HISTORIC
CORE

RUE
CLER

Seine

EIFFEL
TOWER

ARMY
MUSEUM

LEFT BANK

LUXEMBOURG
GARDEN

River

PERE
LACHAISE
CEMETERY

PERIPHERIQUE

18:00), and two in **Montmartre,** both with a focus on their neighborhood (one on Place du Tertre, daily 10:00-18:00, tel. 01 42 62 21 21, and the other above the Anvers Métro stop, daily 10:00-18:00). In summer, TI kiosks may pop up in the squares in front of Notre-Dame and Hôtel de Ville. The official website for Paris' TIs is www.parisinfo.com. Both **airports** have handy information offices with long hours and short lines.

Pariscope: The weekly €0.40 *Pariscope* magazine (or one of its clones, available at any newsstand) lists museum hours, art exhibits, concerts, festivals, plays, movies, and nightclubs. Smart sightseers rely on this for the latest listings.

Other Publications: *L'Officiel des Spectacles* (€0.35), which is similar to *Pariscope,* also lists goings-on around town (in French). The *Paris Voice,* with snappy reviews of concerts, plays, and current events, is available only online at www.parisvoice.com. For a schedule of museum hours and English museum tours, get the free *Musées, Monuments Historiques, et Expositions* booklet at any museum.

Helpful Websites: These websites come highly recommended for local information and events: www.gogoparis.com, www.secretsofparis.com, and www.bonjourparis.com.

American Church and Franco-American Center: This interdenominational church—in the Rue Cler neighborhood, facing the river between the Eiffel Tower and Orsay Museum—is a nerve center for the American expat community. Worship services are held every Sunday (traditional services at 9:00 and 11:00, contemporary service at 13:30). The coffee hour after the 11:00 service and the free Sunday concerts (generally Sept-June at 17:00—but not every week and not in Dec) are a good way to get a taste of émigré life in Paris (reception open Mon-Sat 9:00-12:00 & 13:00-22:00, Sun 14:30-19:00, 65 Quai d'Orsay, Mo: Invalides, tel. 01 40 62 05 00, www.acparis.org). It's also a handy place to pick up free copies of *France-USA Contacts*, an advertisement paper with info on housing and employment for the 50,000 Americans living in Paris (www.fusac.fr).

Arrival in Paris

For a comprehensive rundown of the city's train stations and airports, see "Paris Connections," at the end of this chapter. For information on parking a car, see "Helpful Hints," next.

Helpful Hints

Theft Alert: Thieves thrive near famous monuments and on Métro and RER lines that serve high-profile tourist sights. Beware of pickpockets working busy lines (e.g., at ticket windows at train stations). Pay attention when it's your turn and your back is to the crowd—keep your bag firmly gripped in front of you. In general, it's smart to wear a money belt, put your wallet in your front pocket, loop your day bag over your shoulders, and keep a tight grip on your purse or shopping bag. Muggings are rare, but they do occur. If you're out late, avoid the dark riverfront embankments and any place where the lighting is dim and pedestrian activity is minimal.

    Paris is taking action to combat crime by stationing police at monuments, on streets, and on the Métro, as well as security cameras at key sights. You'll go through quick and reassuring airport-like security checks at many major attractions.

ATM Alert: When withdrawing money from a cash machine, use your hand to shield your PIN number from prying eyes. Don't engage with anyone who offers to "help" you use an ATM (which works just like ours do) or warns you that it isn't working properly. If that happens, cancel your operation and find a different machine.

Tourist Scams: Be aware of the latest scams, including these current favorites. The "found ring" scam involves an innocent-looking person who picks up a ring off the ground and asks if you dropped it. When you say no, the person examines the ring more closely, then shows you a mark "proving" that it's pure gold. He offers to sell it to you for a good price—several times more than he paid for it before dropping it on the sidewalk.

    In the "friendship bracelet" scam, a vendor approaches

you and asks if you'll help him with a demonstration. He proceeds to make a friendship bracelet right on your arm. When finished, he asks you to pay for the bracelet he created just for you. And since you can't easily take it off on the spot, he counts on your feeling obliged to pay up.

Distractions by a stranger—often a "salesman," someone asking you to sign a petition, or someone posing as a deaf person to show you a small note to read—can all be tricks that function as a smokescreen for theft. As you try to wriggle away from the pushy stranger, an accomplice picks your pocket.

In popular tourist spots (such as in front of Notre-Dame) young ladies ask if you speak English, then pretend to beg for money while actually angling to get your wallet.

To all these scammers, simply say "no" firmly, don't apologize, don't smile, and step away purposefully.

Pedestrian Safety: Parisian drivers are notorious for ignoring pedestrians. Look both ways (many streets are one-way) and be careful of seemingly quiet bus/taxi lanes. Don't assume you have the right of way, even in a crosswalk. When crossing a street, keep your pace constant and don't stop suddenly. By law, drivers are allowed to miss pedestrians by up to just one meter—a little more than three feet (1.5 meters in the countryside). Drivers calculate your speed so they won't hit you, provided you don't alter your route or pace.

Watch out for bicyclists. This popular and silent transportation may come at you from unexpected places and directions—cyclists ride in specially marked bike lanes on wide sidewalks and also have a right to use lanes reserved for buses and taxis. Bikes commonly go against traffic, as many bike paths are on one-way streets. Always look both ways.

Busy Parisian sidewalks are much like freeways, so conduct yourself as if you were a foot-fueled-car: Stick to your lane, look to the left before passing a slow-moving pedestrian, and if you need to stop, look for a safe place to pull over.

Medical Help: The American Hospital, established by a group of expat doctors, provides medical attention from English-speaking staff (63 Boulevard Victor Hugo, in Neuilly suburb, Mo: Porte Maillot, then bus #82, tel. 01 46 41 25 25, www. american-hospital.org).

Museum Strategies: The worthwhile Paris Museum Pass, covering most sights in the city, is sold at museums and monuments, as well as TIs and FNAC stores (no surcharge). For detailed information, see page 261.

Avoiding Lines with Advance Tickets: If a Museum Pass does not fit your needs, you do have other line-skipping options. TIs and FNAC stores sell individual fast-track *coupe-file* tickets,

PARIS

letting you use the Museum Pass entrance at sights. TIs sell these tickets for no extra fee, but FNACs add a surcharge of 10-20 percent—often worth it, as these stores are everywhere, even on the Champs-Elysées (ask your hotelier for the nearest one). For sights that can otherwise have long waits (such as the Arc de Triomphe, Opéra Garnier, and Versailles), these tickets are a good idea. (Note that Versailles and the Arc de Triomphe are covered by the Paris Museum Pass.)

For some sights, you can book tickets online and print a receipt (either from home or at your hotel) that serves as your entry pass. This works great at the Eiffel Tower (though you must choose an entry time) and the Jacquemart-André Museum, as well as for activities like the Bateaux-Mouches cruises and Sainte-Chapelle concerts. Increasingly, other sights are adding this helpful service. However, buying Paris Museum Passes and certain tickets online is not worth the cost or hassle because you have to either pay dearly to have them shipped to you or print vouchers and redeem them in person at a Paris TI.

Bookstores: Paris has many English-language bookstores, where you can pick up guidebooks (at nearly double their American prices). Most carry Rick Steves titles. My favorites include:

• **Shakespeare and Company** (some used travel books, Mon-Fri 10:00-23:00, Sat-Sun 11:00-23:00, 37 Rue de la Bûcherie, across the river from Notre-Dame, Mo: St. Michel, tel. 01 43 25 40 93).

• **W. H. Smith** (Mon-Sat 9:00-19:00, Sun 12:30-19:00, 248 Rue de Rivoli, Mo: Concorde, tel. 01 44 77 88 99).

• **San Francisco Book Company** (Mon-Sat 11:00-21:00, Sun 14:00-19:30, 17 Rue Monsieur le Prince, Mo: Odéon, tel. 01 43 29 15 70).

Public WCs: Most public toilets are free. If it's a pay toilet, the price will be clearly indicated. If the toilet is free but there's an attendant, it's polite (but not necessary) to leave a tip of €0.20-0.50. Booth-like pay toilets on the sidewalks provide both relief and a memory (don't leave small children inside unattended). The restrooms in museums are free and the best you'll find. Or walk into any sidewalk café like you own the place, and find the toilet in the back. If you have to buy something, your cheapest option is to order a shot of espresso *(un café)* standing at the bar. Keep toilet paper or tissues with you, as some WCs are poorly stocked.

Parking: Street parking is generally free at night (19:00 to 9:00), all day Sunday, and anytime in August, when many Parisians are on vacation. To pay for streetside parking, you must go to a tabac and buy a parking card *(une carte de stationnement)*, sold in €10, €20, and €30 denominations. Insert the card into the meter (chip-side in) and punch the desired amount of time (generally €1-2/hour), then take the receipt and display it in your windshield. Meters limit street parking to a maximum of two hours. For a longer stay, park for less at an airport (about €10/day) and take public transport or a taxi into the city. Underground lots are numerous in Paris—you'll find them under Ecole Militaire, St. Sulpice Church, Les Invalides, the Bastille, and the Panthéon; all charge about €30-40/day (€60/3 days, €10/day more after that, for locations see www.vincipark.com). Some hotels offer parking for less—ask your hotelier.

Tobacco Stands *(Tabacs):* These little kiosks—usually just a counter inside a café—are handy and very local. They sell public-transit tickets, cards for parking meters, postage stamps (though not all sell international postage—to mail something home, use two domestic stamps, or go to a post office), prepaid phone cards, and...oh yeah, cigarettes. To find one of these kiosks, just look for a *Tabac* sign and the red cylinder-shaped symbol above certain cafés. A *tabac* can be a godsend for avoiding long ticket lines at the Métro, especially at the end of the month when ticket booths get crowded with locals buying next month's pass.

Winter Activities: The City of Light sparkles year-round. For background on what to do and see here in winter months, see www.ricksteves.com/pariswinter.

Updates to this Book: For news about changes to this book's coverage since it was published, see www.ricksteves.com/update.

Getting Around Paris

Paris is easy to navigate. Your basic choices are Métro (in-city subway), RER (suburban rail tied into the Métro system), public bus, and taxi. (Also consider the hop-on, hop-off bus and boat tours, described under "Tours in Paris," later.)

You can buy tickets and passes at Métro stations and at many *tabacs*. Staffed ticket windows in stations are gradually being phased out in favor of ticket machines, so expect some stations to have machines only—be sure to carry coins or small bills of €20 or less (not all machines take bills and none takes American credit cards). If a ticket machine is out of order or if you're out of change, buy tickets at a *tabac*.

Public-Transit Tickets: The Métro, RER, and buses all work on the same tickets. You can make as many transfers as you need on a single ticket, except when transferring between the Métro/RER system and the bus system, which requires using an additional ticket. A **single ticket** costs €1.70. To save money, buy a *carnet* (kar-nay) of 10 tickets for €12.70 (cheaper for ages 4-10). *Carnets* can be shared among travelers.

Passe Navigo: You can buy a chip-embedded card, called the Passe Navigo (though for most tourists, *carnets* are a better deal). You pay a one-time €5 fee for the Navigo card itself (which also requires a postage-stamp-size photo of yourself—bring your own, print a color photo, or use the €4 photo booths in major Métro stations). For a weekly *(hebdomadaire)* version good for travel in central Paris (zones 1-2), you'll pay €19.15, which gives you free run of the bus, Métro, and non-suburban RER system from Monday to Sunday (expiring on Sunday, even if you buy it on, say, a Thursday). A monthly version is also available.

To use the Navigo, whether at a Métro turnstile or on the bus, touch the card to the purple pad, wait for the green validation light and the "ding," and you're on your way. The basic pass covers only central Paris, not regional destinations such as Versailles.

Navigo or *Carnet*? It's hard to beat the *carnet*. Two 10-packs of *carnets*—enough for most travelers staying a week—cost €25.40, are shareable, and don't expire. Though similar in price, the Passe Navigo is more of a hassle to buy, cannot be shared, and only becomes worthwhile for visitors who stay a full week (or more), start their trip early in the week (on a Monday or Tuesday), and use the system a lot.

Other Passes: A handy one-day bus/Métro pass (called **Mobilis**) is available for €6.40. The overpriced **Paris Visite** passes are poorly designed for tourists and offer minor reductions at minor sights (1 day/€9.75, 2 days/€15.85, 3 days/€21.60, 5 days/€31.15).

By Métro

In Paris, you're never more than a 10-minute walk from a Métro station. Europe's best subway system allows you to hop from sight to sight quickly and cheaply (runs daily 5:30-24:30, Fri-Sat until 2:00 in the morning, www.ratp.fr). Learn to use it. Color Métro maps are free at Métro stations and included on freebie Paris maps at your hotel.

Using the Métro System: To get to your destination, determine the closest "Mo" stop and which line or lines will get you there. The lines are color-coded and numbered, and you can tell their direction by their end-of-the-line stops. For example, the La Défense/Château de Vincennes line, also known as line 1 (yellow), runs between La Défense, on its west end, and Vincennes on its east end. Once in the Métro station, you'll see the color-coded line numbers and/or blue-and-white signs directing you to the train going in your direction (e.g., *direction: La Défense*). Insert your ticket in the automatic turnstile, reclaim your ticket, pass through, and keep it until you exit the system (some stations require you to pass your ticket through a turnstile to exit). The smallest stations are unstaffed and have ticket machines (coins are essential). Be warned that fare inspectors regularly check for cheaters and accept absolutely no excuses—keep that ticket or pay a minimum fine of €25.

Be prepared to walk significant distances within Métro stations (especially when you transfer). Transfers are free and can be made wherever lines cross, provided you do so within 1.5 hours. When you transfer, follow the appropriately colored line number for your next train, or find orange *correspondance* (connection) signs that lead to your next line.

When you reach your destination, look for the blue-and-white *sortie* signs pointing you to the exit. Before leaving the station, check the helpful *plan du quartier* (map of the neighborhood) to get your bearings. At stops with several *sorties*, you can save time by choosing the best exit.

After you exit the system, toss or tear your used ticket so you don't confuse it with unused tickets—they look almost identical.

Beware of Pickpockets: Thieves dig the Métro and RER. Be on guard. If your pocket is picked as you pass through a turnstile, you end up stuck on the wrong side (after the turnstile bar has closed behind you) while the thief gets away. Stand away from Métro doors to avoid being a target for a theft-and-run just before the doors close. Any jostling or commotion—especially when boarding or leaving trains—is likely the sign of a thief or a team of thieves in action. See page 234 for tips on keeping your bag close. Make any fare inspector show proof of identity (ask locals for help if you're not certain). Never show anyone your wallet.

By RER

The RER (Réseau Express Régionale; air-ay-air) is the suburban arm of the Métro, serving outlying destinations such as Versailles, Disneyland Paris, and the airports. These routes are indicated by thick lines on your subway map and identified by the letters A, B, C, and so on.

Within the city center, the RER works like the Métro and can be speedier if it serves your destination directly, because it makes fewer stops. Métro tickets and the Passe Navigo card are good on the RER when traveling in the city center. You can transfer between the Métro and RER systems with the same ticket. But to travel outside the city (to Versailles or the airport, for example), you'll need a separate, more expensive ticket. Unlike the Métro, not every train stops at every station along the way; check the sign or screen over the platform to see if your destination is listed as a stop (*"toutes les gares"* means it makes all stops along the way), or confirm with a local before you board. For RER trains, you may need to insert your ticket in a turnstile to exit the system.

PARIS

By City Bus

Paris' excellent bus system is worth figuring out. Buses don't seem as romantic as the famous Métro and are subject to traffic jams, but savvy travelers know that buses can have you swinging through the city like Tarzan in an urban jungle.

Buses require less walking and fewer stairways than the Métro, and you can see Paris unfold as you travel. Bus stops are everywhere, and every stop comes with all the information you need: a good city bus map, route maps showing exactly where each bus that uses this stop goes, a frequency chart and schedule, a *plan du quartier* map of the immediate neighborhood, and a *soirées* map explaining night service, if available (www.ratp.fr). Bus-system maps are also available in any Métro station (and in the €6.50 *Paris Pratique* map book sold at newsstands). For longer stays, consider buying the €6 *Le Bus* book of bus routes.

Using the Bus System: Buses use the same tickets and passes as the Métro and RER. One Zone 1 ticket buys you a bus ride anywhere in central Paris within the freeway ring road *(le périphérique)*. Use your Métro ticket or buy one on board for €0.20 more. (The ticket system has a few quirks—see "More Bus Tips," later.)

Just like the Métro, every bus stop has a name, and every bus is headed to one end-of-the-line stop or the other. First, find your stop on the chart, then find your destination stop. Now, find out exactly where to catch the bus going in that direction. (On the maps showing the bus route, notice the triangle-shaped arrows pointing in the direction the bus is headed. With so many one-way streets in Paris, it's easy to get on the bus in the wrong direction.) When the bus pulls up, double-check that the sign on the front of the bus has the end-of-the-line stop going in your direction.

Board your bus through the front door. (Families with strollers can use any doors—the ones in the center are wider. To open the middle or back doors on long buses, push the green button located by those doors.) Validate your ticket in the machine and reclaim it. With a Passe Navigo, scan it on the purple touchpad. Keep track of what stop is coming up next by following the on-board diagram or listening to recorded announcements. When you're ready to get off, push the red button to signal you want a stop, then exit through the central or rear door. Even if you're not certain you've figured out the system, do some joyriding.

More Bus Tips: Avoid rush hour (Mon-Fri 8:00-9:30 & 17:30-19:30), when buses are jammed and traffic doesn't move. While the Métro shuts down at about 24:30, some buses continue much later (called *Noctilien* lines, www.noctilien.fr). Not all city buses are air-conditioned, so they can become rolling greenhouses on summer days. You can transfer from one bus to another on the same ticket (within 1.5 hours, revalidate your ticket on the next bus), but you can't do a round-trip or hop on and off on the same line. You also can't transfer between the bus and the Métro/RER systems using the same ticket, or between buses with a ticket bought on board (go figure).

I've listed the handiest bus routes for each recommended hotel neighborhood under "Sleeping in Paris," later.

By Taxi

Parisian taxis are reasonable, especially for couples and families. The meters are tamper-proof. Fares and supplements (described in English on the rear windows) are straightforward and tightly regulated.

A taxi can fit three people comfortably. Cabbies are legally required to accept four passengers, though they don't always like it. If you have five in your group, you can book a larger taxi in advance (your hotelier can call), or try your luck at a taxi stand. Beyond three passengers, expect to pay €3 extra per person. For a sample taxi tour of the city at night, see page 312.

Rates: All Parisian taxis start with €2.40 on the meter and have a minimum charge of €6.40. A 20-minute ride (e.g., Bastille to the Eiffel Tower) costs about €20 (versus €1.27/person to get anywhere in town using a *carnet* ticket on the Métro or bus). Drivers charge higher rates at rush hour, at night, all day Sunday, for extra passengers (see above), and to any of the airports. Each piece of luggage you put in the trunk is €1 extra (though it won't appear on the meter, it is a legitimate charge). To tip, round up to the next euro (at least €0.50).

How to Catch *un Taxi:* You can try waving down a taxi, but it's often easier to ask someone for the nearest taxi stand (*"Où est une station de taxi?"*; oo ay ewn stah-see-ohn duh "taxi"). Taxi stands are indicated by a circled "T" on good city maps, and on many maps in this chapter. To order a taxi in English, call 01 41 27 66 99, or ask your hotelier for help. When you summon a taxi by phone, the meter starts running as soon as the call is received, often adding €6 or more to the bill.

Taxis are tough to find during rush hour, when it's raining, on weekend nights, or on any night after the Métro closes (Sun-Thu at 24:30, Fri-Sat at 2:00 in the morning). If you need to catch a train or flight early in the morning, book a taxi the day before (especially for weekday departures). Some taxi companies require a €5 reservation fee by credit card for weekday morning rush-hour departures (7:00-10:00) and only have a limited number of reservation spots.

PARIS

By Bike

Paris is surprisingly easy by bicycle. The city is flat, and riders have access to more than 370 miles of bike lanes and the many priority lanes for buses and taxis (though be careful on these). I biked along the river from Notre-Dame to the Eiffel Tower in 15 wonderfully scenic minutes.

Urban bikers will find Paris a breeze. First-timers will get the hang of it quickly enough by following some simple rules. Always stay to the right in your lane, bike single-file, stay off sidewalks, watch out for opening doors on parked cars, signal with your arm before making turns, and use bike paths when available. Obey the traffic laws as if you were driving a car. Parisians use the same road rules as Americans, with two exceptions: When passing vehicles or other bikes, always pass on the left (it's illegal to pass on the right); and where there is no stoplight, always yield to traffic merging from the right, even if you're on a major road and the merging driver is on a side street. You'll find a bell on your bike; use it like a horn to warn pedestrians who don't see you.

The TIs have a helpful "Paris à Vélo" map, which shows all the dedicated bike paths. Many other versions are available for sale at newsstand kiosks, some bookstores, and department stores.

Renting a Bike: The following rental companies offer organized bike tours as well (see "Tours in Paris—Tour by Bike, Segway, or Pedicab" later). **Bike About Tours** is your best bet for bike rental. Some of their units are foldable, which allows you to collapse your bike and jump on the Métro if the weather turns bad or if you get tired (€15/day during office hours, €20/24 hours; includes locks, helmets, and comfy gel seats; daily mid-Feb-Dec 9:00-18:00, closed Dec-mid-Feb; shop located near Hôtel de Ville in Vinci parking garage—see map on page 324, Mo: Hôtel de Ville, www.bikeabouttours.com, info@bikeabouttours.com). **Fat Tire Bike Tours** has a limited supply of bikes for rent, so call ahead to check availability (€4/hour, €25/24 hours, includes helmets and locks, credit-card imprint required for deposit, ask about rental discount with this book; office open daily 9:00-18:30, May-Aug bike rental only after 11:30 as priority is given to those taking a tour, 24 Rue Edgar Faure—see map on page 279, Mo: Dupleix, tel. 01 56 58 10 54, www.fattirebiketoursparis.com).

You'll see many bike-rack stations throughout Paris. The city's **Vélib'** program (from *vélo* + *liberté* or *libre* = "bike freedom" or "free bike") gives residents access to more than 20,000 bikes, which they can unlock from the nearly 1,500 stations scattered around the city. You can use the Vélib' system, too, but only if you have a certain kind of credit card (American Express or a chip-and-PIN card— see page 11) or if you buy a subscription online (€1.70/1 day, €8/7 days, http://en.velib.paris.fr—click on "Subscriptions and Fees," tel. 01 30 79 79 30). The first 30 minutes of any trip are included with your subscription; after that there's a fee for each additional 30 minutes.

By Rollerblade

Inline skaters take to the streets Sunday afternoons and Friday evenings. It's serious skaters only on Fridays (they meet at 21:30 and are ready to roll at 22:00), but anyone can join in on Sundays (at 14:30). Police close off different routes each week to keep locals engaged, but the starting points are always the same. On Sunday, skaters leave from the south side of Place de la Bastille (for the route, see www.rollers-coquillages.org); on Fridays it's from Place Raoul Dautry (Mo: Montparnasse; see route at www.pari-roller.com). You can rent skates near Sunday's starting point at Nomades (€5/half-day, €9/day, Tue-Fri 11:00-13:30 & 14:30-19:30, Sat 10:00-19:00, Sun 12:00-18:00, closed Mon, 37 Boulevard Bourdon, near Place de la Bastille, Mo: Bastille, tel. 01 44 54 07 44, www.nomadeshop.com).

By Scooter

Left Bank Scooters will deliver and pick-up rental scooters to daring travelers over 20 years old with a valid driver's license (€80-100/day, price depends on size of the scooter and how long you keep it, mobile 06 78 12 04 24, www.leftbankscooters.com).

Tours in Paris

To sightsee on your own, download my series of free audio tours that illuminate some of Paris' top sights and neighborhoods, including the Historic Paris Walk, Louvre, Orsay, and Versailles Palace (see page 7 for details).

By Bus

Bus Tours

Paris Vision (also called Cityrama) offers bus tours of Paris, day and night (advertised in hotel lobbies). I'd consider a Paris Vision tour only for their nighttime tour (see page 312). During the day, you'll get a better value and more versatility by taking a hop-on, hop-off tour by bus (described next) or Batobus boat (see "By Boat," later), which provide transportation between sights.

Hop-on, Hop-off Bus Tours

Double-decker buses connect Paris' main sights, allowing you to hop on and off along the way. You get a disposable set of earbuds to listen to a basic running commentary (dial English for the so-so narration). You can get off at any stop, tour a sight, then catch a later bus. These are best in good weather, when you can sit up top. There are two companies: L'Open Tours and Les Cars Rouges

PARIS

(pick up their brochures showing routes and stops from any TI or on their buses). You can start either tour at just about any of the major sights, such as the Eiffel Tower.

L'Open Tours uses bright yellow buses and provides more extensive coverage (and slightly better commentary) on four different routes, rolling by most of the important sights in Paris. Their Paris Grand Tour (the green route) offers the best introduction. The same ticket gets you on any of their routes within the validity period. Buy your tickets from the driver (1 day-€31, 2 days-€34, kids 4-11 pay €15 for 1 or 2 days, allow 2 hours per tour). Two to four buses depart hourly from about 10:00 to 18:00; expect to wait 10-15 minutes at each stop (stops can be tricky to find—look for yellow signs; tel. 01 42 66 56 56, www.parislopentour.com). A combo-ticket includes the Batobus boats, too (2 days-€43, 3 days-€46, kids 4-11 pay €20 for 2 or 3 days; described later).

Les Cars Rouges' bright red buses offer one route with just nine stops and recorded narration, but for a little less (adult-€29, kids 4-12 pay €15, good for 2 days, 10 percent cheaper if you book online, tel. 01 53 95 39 53, www.carsrouges.com).

Tours by Boat

Seine Cruises

Several companies run one-hour boat cruises on the Seine. For the best experience, cruise at twilight or after dark. (To dine while you cruise, see "Dinner Cruises" on page 368.) Two of the companies—Bateaux-Mouches and Bateaux Parisiens—are convenient to the Rue Cler hotels, and both run daily year-round (April-Oct 10:00-22:30, 2-3/hour; Nov-March shorter hours, runs hourly). Some offer discounts for early online bookings.

Bateaux-Mouches, the oldest boat company in Paris, departs from Pont de l'Alma's right bank and has the biggest open-top, double-decker boats (higher up means better views). But this company caters to tour groups, making their boats jammed and noisy (€11.50, kids 4-12 pay €5.50, tel. 01 42 25 96 10, www.bateaux-mouches.fr).

Bateaux Parisiens has smaller covered boats with handheld audioguides, fewer crowds, and only one deck. It leaves from right in front of the Eiffel Tower (€12, kids 3-12 pay €5, tel. 01 76 64 14 45, www.bateauxparisiens.com).

Vedettes du Pont Neuf offers essentially the same one-hour tour as the other companies, but starts and ends at Pont Neuf, closer to recommended hotels in the Marais and Luxembourg Garden neighborhoods. The boats feature a live guide whose delivery (in English and French) is as stiff as a recorded narration—and as hard to understand, given the quality of their sound system (€13, ask about discount if you book direct with this book, online booking costs just €9, kids 4-12 pay €7, tip requested, nearly 2/hour, daily 10:30-22:30, tel. 01 46 33 98 38, www.vedettesdupontneuf.com).

Hop-on, Hop-off Boat Tour

Batobus allows you to get on and off as often as you like at any of eight popular stops along the Seine. The boats, which make a continuous circuit, stop in this order: Eiffel Tower, Orsay Museum, St. Germain-des-Prés, Notre-Dame, Jardin des Plantes, Hôtel de Ville, the Louvre, and Pont Alexandre III, near the Champs-Elysées (1 day-€15, 2 days-€18, 5 days-€21, April-Aug boats run every 20 minutes 10:00-21:30, Sept-March every 25 minutes 10:00-19:00, 45 minutes one-way, 1.5-hour round-trip, worthless narration, www.batobus.com). If you use this for getting around—sort of a scenic, floating alternative to the Métro—it can be worthwhile, especially with a five-day pass. But if you just want a guided boat tour, the Seine cruises are a better choice (described above).

Low-Key Cruise on a Tranquil Canal

Canauxrama runs a lazy 2.5-hour cruise on a peaceful canal out of sight of the Seine. Tours start from Place de la Bastille and end at Bassin de la Villette (near Mo: Stalingrad). During the first segment of your trip, you'll pass through a long tunnel (built by order of Napoleon in the early 19th century, when canal boats were vital for industrial transport). Once outside, you glide—not much faster than you can walk—through sleepy Parisian neighborhoods and slowly climb through four double locks as a guide narrates the trip in French and English (adults-€16, kids 12 and under-€8.50, check online for discounts for advance booking, departs at 9:45 and 14:30 across from Opéra Bastille, just below Boulevard de la Bastille, opposite #50—where the canal meets Place de la Bastille, tel. 01 42 39 15 00, www.canauxrama.com). The same tour also goes in the opposite direction, from Bassin de la Villette to Place de la Bastille (departs at 9:45 and 14:45). It's OK to bring a picnic on board.

On Foot

Paris Walks

This company offers a variety of two-hour walks, led by British and American guides. Tours are thoughtfully prepared and entertaining. Don't hesitate to stand close to the guide to hear (€12-15, generally 2/day—morning and afternoon, private tours available, family guides and Louvre tours a specialty, call 01 48 09 21 40 for schedule in English or check printable online schedule at www.paris-walks.com). Tours focus on the Marais (4/week), Montmartre (3/week), medieval Latin Quarter (Mon), Ile de la Cité/Notre-Dame (Mon), the "Two Islands" (Ile de la Cité and Ile St. Louis, Wed), the Revolution (Tue), and Hemingway's Paris (Fri). They also run less-regular tours of Paris' **Puces St. Ouen** flea market and of the Catacombs, plus a themed walk on the Occupation and Resistance in Paris during the 1940s. Call a day or two ahead to hear the current schedule and starting point. Most tours don't require reservations, but specialty tours—such as the Louvre, fashion, or chocolate tours—require advance reservations and prepayment with credit card (deposits aren't refundable).

Context Paris

These "intellectual by design" walking tours, geared for serious learners, are led by docents (historians, architects, and academics). They cover both museums and specific neighborhoods, and range from traditional topics such as French art history in the Louvre and the Gothic architecture of Notre-Dame to more thematic explorations like immigration and the changing face of Paris, jazz in the Latin Quarter, and the history of the baguette. It's best to book in advance—groups are limited to six participants and can fill up fast (€40-90/person, admission to sights extra, generally 3 hours, tel. 01 72 81 36 35, US tel. 800-691-6036, www.contextparis.com). They also offer private tours and excursions outside Paris.

Classic Walks

The antithesis of Context Paris' walks, these lowbrow, lighter-on-information but high-fun walking tours are run by Fat Tire Bike Tours. Their 3.5-hour Classic Walk covers most major sights (€20, departs May-Sept daily at 10:00; Mon, Wed, Fri and Sun only March-April and Oct; meet at their office at 24 Rue Edgar Faure, Mo: Dupleix, tel. 01 56 58 10 54, www.classicwalksparis.com). They also offer neighborhood walks of Montmartre, the Marais, and Latin Quarter, as well as themed walks on the French Revolution and World War II (€20, tours leave several times a week—see website for details). Their Easy Pass tours are designed to allow you to skip the lines at major sights. They run tours of the Louvre, Catacombs, Eiffel Tower, Pompidou, Orsay, and Versailles (€45-85/person, includes entry and guided tour, www.easypasstours.com) and sell skip-the-line tickets to key sights. Ask about discounts with this book.

Local Guides

For many, Paris merits hiring a Parisian as a personal guide. **Arnaud Servignat** is an excellent licensed guide (€190/half-day, also does car tours of the countryside around Paris for a little more, mobile 06 68 80 29 05, www.french-guide.com, arnotour@me.com). **Thierry Gauduchon** is a terrific guide well worth his fee (€200/half-day, €400/day, tel. 01 56 98 10 82, mobile 06 19 07 30 77, tgauduchon@aol.com). **Elisabeth Van Hest** is another likable and capable guide (€190/half-day, tel. 01 43 41 47 31, elisa.guide@gmail.com).

Food Tours

Friendly Canadian **Rosa Jackson** designs personalized "Edible Paris" itineraries based on your interests and three-hour "food-guru" tours of Paris led by her or one of her two colleagues (unguided itineraries from €125, €300 guided tours for up to 3, mobile 06 81 67 41 22, www.edible-paris.com, rosa@rosajackson.com).

By Bike, Segway, or Pedicab

A bike tour is a fun way to see Paris. Two companies—Bike About Tours and Fat Tire Bike Tours—offer tours, sell bottled water and bike maps of Paris, and give advice on cycling routes in the city. Their tour routes cover different areas of the city, so avid cyclists could do both without much repetition.

Bike About Tours

Run by Christian (American) and Paul (New Zealander), this company offers easygoing tours with a focus on the eastern half of the city. Their four-hour tours run daily year-round at 10:00 (also at 15:00 June-Sept). You'll meet at the statue of Charlemagne in front of Notre-Dame, then walk to the nearby rental office to get bikes. The tour includes a good back-street visit of the Marais, Rive Gauche outdoor sculpture park, Ile de la Cité, heart of the Latin Quarter (with a lunch break), Louvre, Les Halles, and Pompidou Center. Group tours have a 12-person maximum—reserve online to guarantee a spot, or show up and take your chances (€30, ask about discount with this book, maximum 2 discounts per book, 15 percent discount for families, includes helmets upon request, private tours available, see listing on page 242 for contact info).

Fat Tire Bike Tours

A hardworking gang of young anglophone expats runs an extensive program of bike, Segway, and walking tours (see Classic Walks listing, earlier). Their high-energy guides run four-hour bike tours of Paris, by day and by night (adults-€30, kids-€28, show this book and ask for a discount, maximum 2 discounts per book, reservations not necessary—just show up). Kid-sized bikes are available, as are nifty tandem attachments that hook on to a parent's bike.

On the day tour, you'll pedal with a pack of 10-20 riders, mostly in parks and along bike lanes, with a lunch stop in the Tuileries Garden (tours leave daily rain or shine at 11:00, April-Oct at 15:00 as well, no minimum number of participants required). Livelier night tours follow a route past floodlit monuments and include a boat cruise on the Seine (April-Oct daily at 19:00, March daily at 18:00, end of Feb and all of Nov Tue, Thu, and Sat-Sun at 18:00, no night tours Dec-mid-Feb). Both tours meet at the south pillar of the Eiffel Tower, where you'll get a short history lesson, then walk six minutes to the Fat Tire office to pick up bikes (helmets available upon request at no extra charge, for contact info see listing on page

242). They also run bike tours to Versailles and Giverny (reservations required, see website for details). Their office has Internet access with English keyboards.

Fat Tire's pricey four-hour **City Segway Tours**—on stand-up motorized scooters—are novel in that you learn to ride a Segway while exploring Paris (you'll get the hang of it after about half an hour). These tours take no more than eight people at a time, so reservations are required (€85, daily at 9:30, April-Oct also at 14:00 and 18:30, March and Nov also at 14:00, tel. 01 56 58 10 54, www.citysegwaytours.com).

TripUp Pedicab Tours

You'll see these space-age pedicabs *(cyclopolitains)* everywhere in central Paris. The hard-pedaling, free-spirited drivers (who get some electrical assistance) are happy to either transport you from point A to B or give you a tour at a snail's pace—which is a lovely way to experience Paris (€40-50/hour, www.tripup.fr).

Weekend Tour Packages for Students

Andy Steves (my son) runs **Weekend Student Adventures,** offering experiential and active three-day weekend tours for €199 designed for American students studying abroad (see www.wsaeurope.com for details on tours of Paris and other great European cities).

Excursions from Paris

Most of the local guides listed earlier will do excursion tours from Paris using your rental car. Or consider these companies, which provide transportation:

Paris Webservices, a reliable outfit, offers many services, including day trips with English-speaking chauffeur-guides in cushy minivans for private groups (price depends on tour, use promo code "PWS52K13" and show current edition of this book for a discount on tours and airport transfers—discount not valid on services they book for you through other companies; see contact info in listing on page 371).

Many companies offer bus tours to regional sights. **Paris Vision** runs uninspired minivan and bus tours to several popular regional destinations, including the Loire Valley, Champagne region, D-Day beaches, and Mont St-Michel (tel. 01 42 60 30 01, www.parisvision.com). Their minivan tours are pricier, but more personal and given in English, and most offer convenient pickup at your hotel (half-day tour about €80/person, day tour about €190/person). Their full-size bus tours (operated by their Cityrama subsidiary, www.pariscityrama.fr) are multilingual, mass-marketed, and mediocre at best, but cheaper than the minivan tours—worthwhile for some travelers simply for the ease of transportation to the sights (about €70-150, destinations include Versailles, Giverny, and more).

Self-Guided Walk

Historic Paris

(This information is distilled from the Historic Paris Walk chapter in *Rick Steves' Paris,* by Rick Steves, Steve Smith, and Gene Openshaw. You can download a free audio version of this walk; see page 7.)

Allow four hours to do justice to this three-mile walk; just follow the dotted line on the "Historic Paris Walk" map. Start where the city did—on the Ile de la Cité, the island in the Seine River and the physical and historic bull's-eye of your Paris map. The closest Métro stops are Cité, Hôtel de Ville, and St. Michel, each a short walk away.

• *On the square in front of Notre-Dame Cathedral, view the facade from the bronze plaque on the ground marked "Point Zero" (30 yards from the central doorway). You're standing at the center of the country, the point from which all distances in France are measured. Find the circular window in the center of the cathedral's facade.*

▲▲▲Notre-Dame Cathedral

This 700-year-old cathedral is packed with history and tourists. Study its sculpture and windows, take in a Mass, eavesdrop on guides, and walk all around the outside.

Cost and Hours: Cathedral—free, Mon-Fri 8:00-18:45, Sat-Sun 8:00-19:15; Treasury—€4, not covered by Museum Pass, Mon-Fri 9:30-17:40, Sat-Sun 9:30-18:10; audioguide—€5, free English tours—normally Wed-Thu at 14:15, Sat-Sun at 14:30. The cathedral hosts several Masses every morning, plus Vespers at 17:45. The international Mass is held Sun at 11:30, with an organ concert at 16:30. Call or check the website for a full schedule. On Good Friday and the first Friday of the month at 15:00, the (visually underwhelming) relic known as Jesus' Crown of Thorns goes on display (Mo: Cité, Hôtel de Ville, or St. Michel; tel. 01 42 34 56 10, www.notredamedeparis.fr).

Tower Climb: The entrance for Notre-Dame's towers is outside the cathedral, along the left side. It's 400 steps up, but it's worth it for the gargoyle's-eye view of the cathedral, Seine, and city (€8.50, covered by Museum Pass but no bypass line for passholders; daily April-Sept 10:00-18:30, Sat-Sun until 23:00 in July-Aug, Oct-March 10:00-17:30, last entry 45 minutes before closing; to avoid long lines arrive before 10:00 or after 17:00—after 16:00 in winter; tel. 01 53 10 07 00, www.notre-dame-de-paris.monuments-nationaux.fr).

PARIS

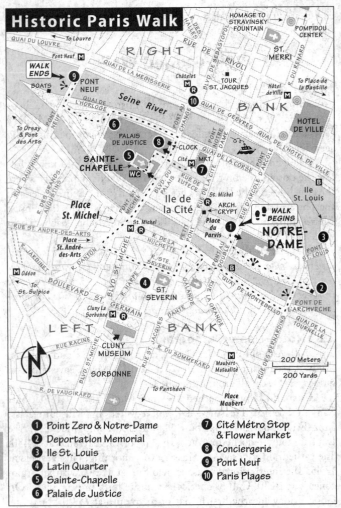

Historic Paris Walk

1. Point Zero & Notre-Dame
2. Deportation Memorial
3. Ile St. Louis
4. Latin Quarter
5. Sainte-Chapelle
6. Palais de Justice
7. Cité Métro Stop & Flower Market
8. Conciergerie
9. Pont Neuf
10. Paris Plages

⊙ **Self-Guided Tour:** The **cathedral facade** is worth a close look. The church is dedicated to "Our Lady" *(Notre Dame)*. Mary is center stage—cradling God, right in the heart of the facade, surrounded by the halo of the rose window. Adam is on the left and Eve is on the right.

Below Mary and above the arches is a row of 28 statues known as the Kings of Judah. During the French Revolution, these biblical kings were mistaken for the hated French kings, and Notre-Dame represented the oppressive Catholic hierarchy. The citizens stormed the church, crying, "Off with their heads!" All were decapitated, but have since been recapitated.

Speaking of decapitation, look at the carving to the left of the doorway on the left. The man with his head in his hands is St. Denis. Back when there was a Roman temple on this spot, Christianity began making converts. The fourth-century bishop of Roman Paris, Denis was beheaded as a warning to those forsaking the Roman gods. But those early Christians were hard to keep down. The man who would become St. Denis got up, tucked his head under his arm, headed north, paused at a fountain to wash it off, and continued until he found just the right place to meet his maker: Montmartre. (Although the name "Montmartre" comes from the Roman "Mount of Mars," later generations—thinking of their beheaded patron, St. Denis—preferred a less pagan version, "Mount of Martyrs.") The Parisians were convinced by this miracle, Christianity gained ground, and a church soon replaced the pagan temple.

Medieval art was OK if it embellished the house of God and told biblical stories. For a fine example, move to the base of the central column (at the foot of Mary, about where the head of St. Denis could spit if he were really good). Working around from the left, find God telling a barely created Eve, "Have fun, but no apples." Next, the sexiest serpent I've ever seen makes apples à la mode. Finally, Adam and Eve, now ashamed of their nakedness, are expelled by an angel. This is a tiny example in a church covered with meaning.

Enter the church at the right doorway (the line moves quickly). You'll be routed around the ambulatory, in much the same way medieval pilgrims were. Notre-Dame has the typical basilica floor plan shared by so many Catholic churches: a long central nave lined with columns and flanked by side aisles. It's designed in the shape of a cross, with the altar placed where the crossbeam intersects. The church can hold up to 10,000 faithful, and it's probably buzzing with visitors now, just as it was 600 years ago. The quiet, deserted churches we see elsewhere are in stark contrast to the busy, center-of-life places they were in the Middle Ages.

Don't miss the **rose windows** that fill each of the transepts. Just past the altar is the **choir,** enclosed with carved-wood walls, where more intimate services can be held in this spacious building. Circle the choir—the back side of the choir walls features **scenes of the resurrected Jesus** (c. 1350). Just ahead on the right is the **Treasury.** It contains lavish robes, golden reliquaries, and the humble tunic of King (and St.) Louis IX, but it probably isn't worth the entry fee.

Back outside, walk around the church through the park on the riverside for a close look at the **flying buttresses.** The Neo-Gothic 300-foot **spire** is a product of the 1860 reconstruction of the dilapidated old church. Around its base (visible as you approach the back

Affording Paris' Sights

Paris is an expensive city for tourists, with lots of pricey sights, but—fortunately—lots of freebies, too. Smart, budget-minded travelers begin by buying and getting the most out of a **Paris Museum Pass** (see page 261), then considering these frugal sight-seeing options.

Free (or Almost Free) Museums: Some museums are always free (with the possible exception of special exhibits), including the Carnavalet, Petit Palais, Victor Hugo's House, and Fragonard Perfume Museum. Many of Paris' most famous museums offer free entry on the first Sunday of the month, including the Louvre, Orsay, Rodin, Cluny, Pompidou Center, Quai Branly, and Delacroix museums. These sights are free on the first Sunday of off-season months: the Arc de Triomphe (Oct-March) and Versailles (Nov-March). Expect big crowds on free days. You can also visit the Orsay Museum for free at 17:00 (or Thu at 21:00), an hour before the museum closes. One of the best everyday values is the Rodin Museum's garden, where it costs just €1 to experience many of Rodin's finest works in a lovely outdoor setting.

Other Freebies: Many worthwhile sights don't charge entry, including the Notre-Dame Cathedral, Père Lachaise Cemetery, Deportation Memorial, Holocaust Memorial, Paris Plages (summers only), Sacré-Cœur Basilica, St. Sulpice Church (with organ recital), and La Défense mall.

Paris' glorious, entertaining parks are free, of course. These include Luxembourg Garden, Champ de Mars (under the Eiffel Tower), Tuileries Garden (between the Louvre and Place de la Concorde), Palais Royal Courtyards, Jardin des Plantes, Parc Monceau, the Promenade Plantée walk, and Versailles' gardens (except when the fountains perform on Tue late May-late June and weekends April-Oct).

Reduced Prices: Several sights offer a discount if you enter later in the day, including the Orsay (Fri-Wed after 16:15 and Thu after 18:00), the Orangerie (after 17:00), and the Army Museum and Napoleon's Tomb (after 17:00). The Eiffel Tower costs less if

end of the church) are apostles and evangelists (the green men) as well as Eugène-Emmanuel Viollet-le-Duc, the architect in charge of the work. The apostles look outward, blessing the city, while the architect (at top) looks up the spire, marveling at his fine work.

Nearby: The **archaeological crypt** is a worthwhile 15-minute stop if you have a Paris Museum Pass (€4 without Museum Pass, Tue-Sun 10:00-18:00, closed Mon, last entry 30 minutes before closing, enter 100 yards in front of the cathedral, tel. 01 55 42 50 10). You'll see remains of the many structures that have stood on this spot in the center of Paris: Roman buildings that surrounded a temple of Jupiter; a wall that didn't keep the Franks out; the main you're willing to restrict your visit to the two lower levels—and even less if you're willing to use the stairs.

Free Concerts: Venues offering free or cheap (€6-8) concerts include the American Church, Hôtel des Invalides, St. Sulpice Church, La Madeleine Church, and Notre-Dame Cathedral. For a listing of free concerts, check *Pariscope* magazine (under the "Musique" section) and look for events marked *entrée libre*.

Self-Guided Bus Tours: Instead of paying €25 for a tour company to give you an overview of Paris, ride bus #69 for the cost of a Métro ticket. This scenic route crosses the city east-west, running between the Eiffel Tower and Père Lachaise Cemetery, and passing these great monuments and neighborhoods: Eiffel Tower, Ecole Militaire, Rue Cler, Les Invalides (Army Museum and Napoleon's Tomb), Louvre Museum, Ile de la Cité, Ile St. Louis, Hôtel de Ville, Pompidou Center, Marais, Bastille, and Père Lachaise.

You can board daily until 22:30 (last departure from Eiffel Tower stop). It's best to avoid weekday rush hours (8:00-9:30 & 17:30-19:30) and hot days (no air-conditioning). Sundays are quietest, and it's easy to get a window seat. Evening bus rides are magical from fall through spring (roughly Sept-April), when it gets dark early enough to see the floodlit monuments before the bus stops running. In the Rue Cler area, eastbound line #69 leaves from the Eiffel Tower on Avenue Joseph Bouvard. The first stop is at the southwestern end of the avenue; the second stop is at the eastern end (just before Avenue de la Bourdonnais).

Good-Value Tours: At €12-15, Paris Walks' tours are a good value. The €11-13 Seine River cruises, best after dark, are also worthwhile.

Pricey...but worth it? Certain big-ticket items—primarily the top of the Eiffel Tower, the Louvre, and Versailles—are expensive and crowded, but offer once-in-a-lifetime experiences. All together they amount to less than a ticket to Disneyland—only these are real.

medieval road that once led grandly up the square to Notre-Dame; and even (wow) a 19th-century sewer.

• *Behind Notre-Dame, cross the street and enter through the iron gate into the park at the tip of the island. Look for the stairs and head down to reach the...*

▲Deportation Memorial
(Mémorial de la Déportation)

This memorial to the 200,000 French victims of the Nazi concentration camps (1940-1945) draws you into their experience. France was quickly overrun by Nazi Germany, and Paris spent the war years under Nazi occupation. Jews and dissidents were rounded up and deported—many never returned.

As you descend the steps, the city around you disappears. Surrounded by walls, you have become a prisoner. Your only freedom is your view of the sky and the tiny glimpse of the river below. Enter the dark, single-file chamber up ahead. Inside, the circular plaque in the floor reads, "They went to the end of the earth and did not return."

The hallway stretching in front of you is lined with 200,000 lighted crystals, one for each French citizen who died. Flickering at the far end is the eternal flame of hope. The tomb of the unknown deportee lies at your feet. Above, the inscription reads, "Dedicated to the living memory of the 200,000 French deportees shrouded by the night and the fog, exterminated in the Nazi concentration camps." The side rooms are filled with triangles—reminiscent of the identification patches inmates were forced to wear—each bearing the name of a concentration camp. Above the exit as you leave is the message you'll find at many other Holocaust sites: "Forgive, but never forget."

Cost and Hours: Free, April-Sept Tue-Sun 10:00-19:00, Oct-March Tue-Sun 10:00-18:00, closed Mon year-round, may randomly close at other times; at the east tip of the island named Ile de la Cité, behind Notre-Dame and near Ile St. Louis (Mo: Cité); tel. 06 14 67 54 98.

• *Back on street level, look across the river (north) to the island called...*

Ile St. Louis

If Ile de la Cité is a tugboat laden with the history of Paris, it's towing this classy little residential dinghy, laden only with high-rent apartments, boutiques, characteristic restaurants (see page 359), and famous ice cream shops.

Ile St. Louis wasn't developed until much later than Ile de la Cité (17th century). What was a swampy mess is now harmonious Parisian architecture and one of Paris' most exclusive neighborhoods. If you won't have time to return here for an evening stroll (see page 310), consider taking a brief detour across the pedestrian bridge, Pont St. Louis. It connects the two islands, leading right to Rue St. Louis-en-l'Ile. This spine of the island is lined with appealing shops and reasonably priced restaurants. A short stroll takes you to the famous Berthillon ice cream parlor at #31. Gelato-lovers head instead to Amorino Gelati at 47 Rue St. Louis-en-l'Ile. When you're finished exploring, loop back to the pedestrian bridge along the parklike quays (walk north to the river and turn left). This walk is about as peaceful and romantic as Paris gets.

• *From the Deportation Memorial, cross the bridge to the Left Bank. All those* **padlocks** *adorning the railing are akin to lighting candles in a*

1 Berthillon Ice Cream
2 Amorino Gelati
3 Good Picnic Spot
4 Grocery Store

church. Locals and tourists alike honor loved ones by writing a brief message on the lock and attaching it to the railing. You can buy a lock (called cadenas, €5) at a nearby bookseller's stall along the river.

Turn right after crossing the bridge and walk along the river, toward the front end of Notre-Dame. Stairs detour down to the riverbank if you need a place to picnic. This side view of the church from across the river is one of Europe's great sights and is best from river level. For the best view and the sweetest crêpes you've ever had, look for the old river barge Daphné and see if Valeria is open (€2.50-3.50). If the sun is out, he should be there.

After passing the Pont au Double (the bridge leading to the facade of Notre-Dame), watch on your left for **Shakespeare and Company,** an atmospheric reincarnation of the original 1920s bookshop and a good spot to page through books (37 Rue de la Bûcherie; see page 236). Before returning to the island, walk a block behind Shakespeare and Company, and take a spin through the...

▲Latin Quarter

This area's touristy fame relates to its intriguing, artsy, bohemian character. This was perhaps Europe's leading university district in the Middle Ages, when Latin was the language of higher education.

The neighborhood's main boulevards (St. Michel and St. Germain) are lined with cafés—once the haunts of great poets and philosophers, now the hangouts of tired tourists. Though still youth-

PARIS

ful and artsy, much of this area has become a tourist ghetto filled with cheap North African eateries. Exploring a few blocks up- or downriver from here gives you a better chance of feeling the pulse of what survives of Paris' classic Left Bank. For colorful wandering and café-sitting, afternoons and evenings are best.

Walking along Rue St. Séverin, you can still see the shadow of the medieval sewer system. The street slopes into a central channel of bricks. In the days before plumbing and toilets, when people still went to the river or neighborhood wells for their water, flushing meant throwing it out the window. At certain times of day, maids on the fourth floor would holler, *"Garde de l'eau!"* ("Watch out for the water!") and heave it into the streets, where it would eventually wash down into the Seine.

Consider a visit to the **Cluny Museum** for its medieval art and unicorn tapestries (see page 285). The **Sorbonne**—the University of Paris' humanities department—is also nearby; visitors can ogle at the famous dome, but they are not allowed to enter the building (two blocks south of the river on Boulevard St. Michel).

Be sure to see **Place St. Michel.** This square (facing the Pont St. Michel) is the traditional core of the Left Bank's artsy, liberal, hippie, bohemian district of poets, philosophers, and winos. In less commercial times, Place St. Michel was a gathering point for the city's malcontents and misfits. In 1830, 1848, and again in 1871, the citizens took the streets from the government troops, set up barricades *Les Miz*-style, and fought against royalist oppression. During World War II, the locals rose up against their Nazi oppressors (read the plaques under the dragons at the foot of the St. Michel fountain). Even today, whenever there's a student demonstration, it starts here.

• *From Place St. Michel, look across the river and find the prickly steeple of the Sainte-Chapelle church. Head toward it. Cross the river on Pont St. Michel and continue north along the Boulevard du Palais. On your left, you'll see the doorway to Sainte-Chapelle (usually with a line of people).*

You'll need to pass through a strict security checkpoint to get into the Sainte-Chapelle complex (this is more than a tourist attraction: France's Supreme Court meets to the right of Sainte-Chapelle in the Palais de Justice). Expect a long wait unless you arrive before it opens. (The Annexe Café across the street sells €1 coffee to-go—perfect for sipping while you wait in line.) First comes the security line (all sharp objects are confiscated). No one can skip this line. Security lines are shortest on weekday mornings and on weekends (when the courts are closed). Once past security, you'll enter the courtyard outside Sainte-Chapelle, where you'll find WCs and information about upcoming church concerts (for concert details, see page 308). You'll also encounter another line to buy tickets to go into the church. Those with combo-tickets or Museum Passes can skip the ticket-buying line.

▲▲▲Sainte-Chapelle

This triumph of Gothic church architecture is a cathedral of glass like no other. It was speedily built between 1242 and 1248 for King Louis IX—the only French king who is now a saint—to house the supposed Crown of Thorns. Its architectural harmony is due to the fact that it was completed under the direction of one architect and in only six years—unheard of in Gothic times. In contrast, Notre-Dame took over 200 years.

Cost and Hours: €8.50, €12.50 combo-ticket with Conciergerie, under 18 free, covered by Museum Pass, audioguide-€4.50; daily March-Oct 9:30-18:00, Wed until 21:30 mid-May-mid-Sept, Nov-Feb 9:00-17:00; last entry 30 minutes before closing, be prepared for long lines, evening concerts—see page 308, 4 Boulevard du Palais, Mo: Cité, tel. 01 53 40 60 80, www.sainte-chapelle.monuments-nationaux.fr.

Visiting the Church: Though the inside is beautiful, the exterior is basically functional. The muscular buttresses hold up the stone roof, so the walls are essentially there to display stained glass. The lacy spire is Neo-Gothic—added in the 19th century.

Inside, the layout clearly shows an *ancien régime* approach to worship. The low-ceilinged basement was for staff and other common folks—worshipping under a sky filled with painted fleurs-de-lis, a symbol of the king. Royal Christians worshipped upstairs. The paint job, a 19th-century restoration, helps you imagine how grand this small, painted, jeweled chapel was. (Imagine Notre-Dame painted like this...) Each capital is playfully carved with a different plant's leaves.

Climb the spiral staircase to the **Chapelle Haute.** Fill the place with choral music, crank up the sunshine, face the top of the altar, and really believe that the Crown of Thorns is there, and this becomes one awesome space.

Fiat lux. "Let there be light." From the first page of the Bible, it's clear: Light is divine. Light shines through stained glass like God's grace shining down to earth. Gothic architects used their new technology to turn dark stone buildings into lanterns of light. The glory of Gothic shines brighter here than in any other church.

There are 15 separate panels of **stained glass** (6,500 square feet—two thirds of it 13th-century original), with more than 1,100 different scenes, mostly from the Bible. These cover the entire Christian history of the world, from the Creation in Genesis (first window on the left, as you face the altar), to the coming of Christ (over the altar), to the end of the world (the round "rose"-shaped

PARIS

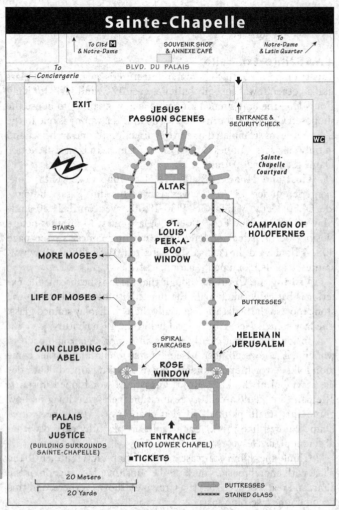

Sainte-Chapelle

To Cité M & Notre-Dame
SOUVENIR SHOP & ANNEXE CAFÉ
To Notre-Dame & Latin Quarter

BLVD. DU PALAIS

To Conciergerie

EXIT

JESUS' PASSION SCENES

ENTRANCE & SECURITY CHECK

WC

Sainte-Chapelle Courtyard

ALTAR

STAIRS

ST. LOUIS' PEEK-A-BOO WINDOW

CAMPAIGN OF HOLOFERNES

MORE MOSES

LIFE OF MOSES

BUTTRESSES

CAIN CLUBBING ABEL

SPIRAL STAIRCASES

HELENA IN JERUSALEM

ROSE WINDOW

PALAIS DE JUSTICE (BUILDING SURROUNDS SAINTE-CHAPELLE)

ENTRANCE (INTO LOWER CHAPEL)
■TICKETS

20 Meters
20 Yards

BUTTRESSES
STAINED GLASS

window at the rear of the church). Each individual scene is interesting, and the whole effect is overwhelming.

The **altar** was raised up high to better display the Crown of Thorns, the relic around which this chapel was built. The supposed crown cost King Louis more than three times as much as this church. Today it is kept by the Notre-Dame Treasury (though it's occasionally brought out for display).

• *Exit Sainte-Chapelle. Back outside, as you walk around the church exterior, look down to see the foundation and take note of how much Paris has risen in the 750 years since Sainte-Chapelle was built. Next door to Sainte-Chapelle is the...*

Palais de Justice

Sainte-Chapelle sits within a huge complex of buildings that has housed the local government since ancient Roman times. It was the site of the original Gothic palace of the early kings of France. The only surviving medieval parts are Sainte-Chapelle and the Conciergerie prison.

Most of the site is now covered by the giant Palais de Justice, built in 1776, home of the French Supreme Court. The motto *Liberté, Egalité, Fraternité* over the doors is a reminder that this was also the headquarters of the Revolutionary government. Here they doled out justice, condemning many to imprisonment in the Conciergerie downstairs or to the guillotine.

• *Now pass through the big iron gate to the noisy Boulevard du Palais. Cross the street to the wide, pedestrian-only Rue de Lutèce and walk about halfway down.*

Cité "Metropolitain" Métro Stop

Of the 141 original early-20th-century subway entrances, this is one of only a few survivors—now preserved as a national art treasure. (New York's Museum of Modern Art even exhibits one.) It marks Paris at its peak in 1900—on the cutting edge of Modernism, but with an eye for beauty. The curvy, plantlike ironwork is a textbook example of Art Nouveau, the style that rebelled against the erector-set squareness of the Industrial Age. Other similar Métro stations in Paris are Abbesses and Porte Dauphine.

The flower and plant market on Place Louis Lépine is a pleasant detour. On Sundays this square flutters with a busy bird market. And across the way is the Préfecture de Police, where Inspector Clouseau of *Pink Panther* fame used to work, and where the local resistance fighters took the first building from the Nazis in August of 1944, leading to the Allied liberation of Paris a week later.

• *Pause here to admire the view. Sainte-Chapelle is a pearl in an ugly architectural oyster. Double back to the Palais de Justice, turn right onto Boulevard du Palais, and enter the...*

▲Conciergerie

Though pretty barren inside, this former prison echoes with history (and is free with the Museum Pass—remember that passholders can skip the ticket-buying line). Positioned next to the courthouse, the Conciergerie was the gloomy prison famous as the last stop for 2,780 victims of the guillotine, including France's last *ancien régime* queen, Marie-Antoinette. Before then, kings had used the building to torture and execute failed assassins. (One of its towers along the river was called "The Babbler," named for the pain-induced sounds that leaked from it.) When the Revolution (1789) toppled the king, the building kept its same function, but without torture. The progressive Revolutionaries proudly unveiled a modern and more humane way to execute people—the guillotine.

Inside, pick up a free map and breeze through the one-way circuit. It's well-described in English. See the spacious, low-ceilinged Hall of Men-at-Arms (Room 1), used as the guards' dining room, with four large fireplaces (look up the chimneys). This big room gives a feel for the grandeur of the Great Hall (upstairs, not open to visitors), where the Revolutionary tribunals grilled scared prisoners on their political correctness.

You'll also see a re-creation of Marie-Antoinette's cell, which houses a collection of her mementos. In another room, a list of those made "a foot shorter at the top" by the "national razor" includes ex-King Louis XVI, Charlotte Corday (who murdered the Revolutionary writer Jean-Paul Marat in his bathtub), and—oh, the irony—Maximilien de Robespierre, the head of the Revolution, the man who sent so many to the guillotine.

Cost and Hours: €8.50, €12.50 combo-ticket with Sainte-Chapelle, covered by Museum Pass, daily March-Oct 9:30-18:00, Nov-Feb 9:00-17:00, last entry 30 minutes before closing, 2 Boulevard du Palais, Mo: Cité, tel. 01 53 40 60 80, www.conciergerie.monuments-nationaux.fr.

• *Back outside, turn left on Boulevard du Palais and head north. On the corner is the city's oldest public clock. The mechanism of the present clock is from 1334, and even though the case is Baroque, it keeps on ticking.*

Turn left onto Quai de l'Horloge and walk west along the river, past "The Babbler" tower. The bridge up ahead is the Pont Neuf, where we'll end this walk. At the first corner, veer left into a sleepy triangular square called Place Dauphine. Marvel at how such coziness could be lodged in the midst of such greatness. At the equestrian statue of Henry IV (at the other end of Place Dauphine), turn right onto the old bridge and take refuge in one of the nooks halfway across, on the Eiffel Tower side.

Pont Neuf

This "new bridge" is now Paris' oldest. Built during Henry IV's reign (about 1600), its arches span the widest part of the river. Unlike other bridges, this one never had houses or buildings growing on it. The turrets were originally for vendors and street entertainers. In the days of Henry IV, who promised his peasants "a chicken in every pot every Sunday," this would have been a lively scene. From the bridge, look downstream (west) to see the next bridge, the pedestrian-only Pont des Arts. Ahead on the Right Bank is the long Louvre Museum. Beyond that, on the Left Bank, is the Orsay. And what's that tall black tower in the distance?

• *Our walk is finished. From here, you can tour the Seine by boat (the departure point for Seine river cruises offered by Vedettes du Pont Neuf is through the park at the end of the island—see page 244), continue to the Louvre, or (if it's summer) head to the...*

▲Paris Plages (Paris Beaches)

The Riviera it's not, but this string of fanciful faux beaches—assembled in summer along a one-mile stretch of the Right Bank of the Seine—is a fun place to stroll, play, and people-watch on a sunny day. Each summer, the Paris city government closes the embankment's highway and trucks in potted palm trees, hammocks, lounge chairs, and 2,000 tons of sand to create colorful urban beaches. You'll also find "beach cafés," climbing walls, prefab pools, trampolines, *boules*, a library, beach volleyball, badminton, and Frisbee areas.

Cost and Hours: Free, mid-July–mid-Aug daily 8:00–24:00, no beach off-season; on Right Bank of Seine, just north of Ile de la Cité, between Pont des Arts and Pont de Sully; for information, go to www.paris.fr, click on "English," then "Visit," then "Highlights."

Sights in Paris

Paris Museum Pass

In Paris there are two classes of sightseers—those with a Paris Museum Pass, and those who stand in line. The pass admits you to many of Paris' most popular sights, allowing you to skip ticket-buying lines. You'll save time and money by getting this pass.

Buying the Pass

The pass pays for itself with four key admissions in two days (for example, the Louvre, Orsay, Sainte-Chapelle, and Versailles), and it lets you skip the ticket line at most sights (2 days/€39, 4 days/€54, 6 days/€69, no youth or senior discount). It's sold at participating museums, monuments, FNAC department stores, and TIs (even at airports). Try to avoid buying the pass at a major museum (such as the Louvre), where the supply can be spotty and lines long. For more info, visit www.parismuseumpass.com or call 01 44 61 96 60.

To see if the pass is a good value for your trip, tally up what you want to see from the list on the facing page. And remember, an advantage of the pass is that you skip to the front of most (but not all) lines, which can save hours of waiting, especially in summer. Another benefit of the pass is that you can pop into lesser sights that otherwise might not be worth the expense.

Families: The pass isn't worth buying for children and teens, as most museums are free or discounted for those under 18 (teenagers may need to show ID as proof of age). If parents have a Museum Pass, kids can usually skip the ticket lines as well. A few places,

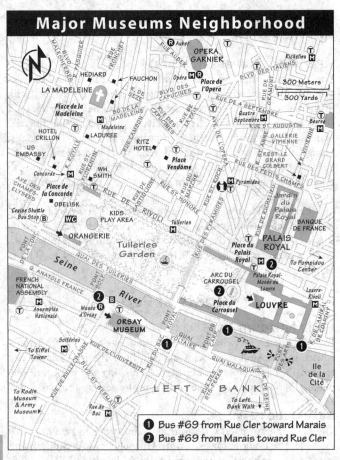

Major Museums Neighborhood

① Bus #69 from Rue Cler toward Marais
② Bus #69 from Marais toward Rue Cler

such as the Arc de Triomphe and Army Museum, require every-one—even passholders—to stand in line to collect your child's free ticket.

What the Paris Museum Pass Covers

Most of the sights listed in this chapter are covered by the pass. It even covers Versailles' two major sights—worth €25 alone. No-table exceptions that are *not* covered by the pass include: the Eiffel Tower, Montparnasse Tower, Marmottan Museum, Opéra Gar-nier, Notre-Dame Treasury, Jacquemart-André Museum, Grand Palais, Catacombs, Montmartre Museum, Sacré-Cœur's dome, Dalí Museum, Museum of Erotic Art, and the ladies of Pigalle.

Here's a list of key included sights and their admission prices without the pass:

Louvre (€11)   Notre-Dame Tower (€8.50)

Orsay Museum (€9)	Paris Archaeological Crypt (€4)
Orangerie Museum (€7.50)	Paris Sewer Tour (€4.30)
Sainte-Chapelle (€8.50)	Cluny Museum (€8)
Arc de Triomphe (€9.50)	Pompidou Center (€11-13)
Rodin Museum (€9)	Jewish Art and History Museum (€7)
Army Museum (€9)	National Maritime Museum (€7)
Conciergerie (€8.50)	Delacroix Museum (€5)
Panthéon (€8.50)	Quai Branly Museum (€8.50)
Picasso Museum (€10)	

Architecture and Monuments Museum (€8)

Versailles (€25 total—€15 for Château, €10 for Trianon Palaces and Domaine de Marie-Antoinette)

Activating and Using the Pass

The pass is activated the first time you use it—you must write the starting date on the pass. Validate it only when you're ready to tackle the covered sights on consecutive days. Plan carefully to make the most of your pass. First, make sure the sights you want to visit will be open (many museums are closed Mondays or Tuesdays). The pass provides the best value on days when sights close later, letting you extend your sightseeing day. Take advantage of these late hours. For instance, the Arc de Triomphe and Pompidou Center are always open later, while the Notre-Dame Tower, Sainte-Chapelle, Louvre, Orsay, and Army Museum and Napoleon's Tomb have late hours on selected evenings (or at certain times of year). On days that you don't have pass coverage, plan to visit free sights and those not covered by the pass (see page 252 for a list of free sights).

To use your pass at sights, boldly walk to the front of the ticket line (after going through security if necessary), hold up your pass, and ask the ticket-taker: *Entrez, pass?* (ahn-tray pahs). You'll either be allowed to enter at that point, or you'll be directed to a special entrance. For major sights, such as the Louvre and Orsay museums, I've identified passholder entrances on the maps in this chapter. Don't be shy—some places (Sainte-Chapelle and the Arc de Triomphe, in particular) have long lines where passholders wait needlessly. At a few sights (including the Louvre, Sainte-Chapelle, Notre-Dame Tower, and Château de Versailles), everyone has to shuffle through the slow-moving baggage-check lines for security—but you still save time by avoiding the ticket line.

Major Museums Neighborhood

Paris' grandest park, the Tuileries Garden, was once the private property of kings and queens. Today it links the Louvre, Orangerie, Jeu de Paume, and Orsay museums. And across from the Louvre are the tranquil, historic courtyards of the Palais Royal.

▲▲▲Louvre (Musée du Louvre)

This is Europe's oldest, biggest, greatest, and second-most-crowded museum (after the Vatican). Housed in a U-shaped, 16th-century palace (accentuated by a 20th-century glass pyramid), the Louvre is Paris' top museum and one of its key landmarks. It's home to *Mona Lisa, Venus de Milo,* and hall after hall of Greek and Roman masterpieces, medieval jewels, Michelangelo statues, and paintings by the greatest artists from the Renaissance to the Romantics (mid-1800s).

Touring the Louvre can be overwhelming, so be selective. Focus on the Denon wing (south, along the river), with Greek sculptures, Italian paintings (by Raphael and da Vinci), and—of course—French paintings (Neoclassical and Romantic), and the adjoining Sully wing, with Egyptian artifacts and more French paintings. For extra credit, tackle the Richelieu wing (north, away from the river), displaying works from ancient Mesopotamia (today's Iraq), as well as French, Dutch, and Northern art.

Expect changes—the sprawling Louvre is constantly shuffling its collection. Rooms are periodically closed for renovation, and pieces are removed from display if they're being restored or loaned to other museums. The new Islamic art space—with its glass roof modeled on a head scarf (visible in the Cour de Visconti courtyard of the Denon wing) may be open by the time you visit, but various galleries devoted to decorative arts may still be in flux. If you don't find the artwork you're looking for, ask the nearest guard for its new location.

Cost and Hours: €11, free on first Sun of month, covered by Museum Pass, tickets good all day, reentry allowed; Wed-Mon 9:00-18:00, Wed and Fri until 21:45 (except on holidays), closed Tue, galleries start shutting 30 minutes before closing, last entry 45 minutes before closing; crowds worst in the morning (arrive 30 minutes before opening) and all day Sun, Mon, and Wed; several cafés, tel. 01 40 20 53 17, recorded info tel. 01 40 20 51 51, www.louvre.fr.

Getting There: It's at the Palais Royal-Musée du Louvre Métro stop. (The old Louvre Métro stop, called Louvre-Rivoli, is farther from the entrance.) Bus #69 also runs past the Louvre.

Getting In: There is no grander entry than through the main entrance at the **pyramid** in the central courtyard, but metal detectors (not ticket-buyers) can create a long line. Museum Pass holders can use the **group entrance** in the pedestrian passageway (labeled *Pavilion Richelieu*) between the pyramid and Rue de Rivoli. It's under the arches, a few steps north of the pyramid; find the uniformed guard at the security checkpoint entrance, at the down escalator. Anyone can enter the Louvre from its less crowded **underground entrance,** accessed through the Carrousel du Louvre

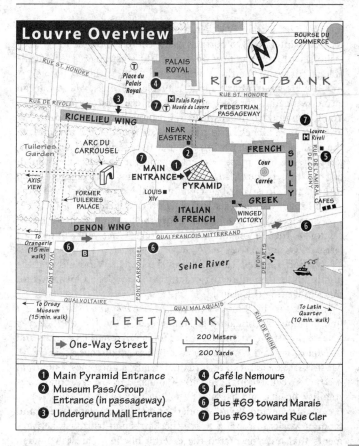

Louvre Overview

BOURSE DU COMMERCE

RUE ST. HONORE

Place du Palais Royal ⓣ

PALAIS ROYAL ④

R I G H T   B A N K

RUE ST. HONORE

RUE DE RIVOLI

③

Ⓜ Palais Royal-Musée du Louvre ⑦ ⓣ

PEDESTRIAN PASSAGEWAY

RICHELIEU WING

Louvre- Ⓜ Rivoli ⑦

NEAR EASTERN

Tuileries Garden

ARC DU CARROUSEL

② FRENCH

S U L L Y

RUE DE L'AMIRAL DE COLIGNY

⑤

⑦

Cour Carrée

MAIN ENTRANCE➔ ① PYRAMID

AXIS VIEW

FORMER TUILERIES PALACE

LOUIS XIV

GREEK

CAFÉS ▪▪▪

To Orangerie (15 min walk)

ITALIAN & FRENCH

WINGED VICTORY

DENON WING

QUAI FRANÇOIS MITTERRAND

⑥ Ⓑ

⑥

PONT ROYAL

PONT CARROUSEL

PONT DES ARTS

Seine River

To Orsay Museum (15 min. walk)

QUAI VOLTAIRE

QUAI MALAQUAIS

RUE DE SEINE

To Latin Quarter (10 min. walk)

L E F T   B A N K

➔ One-Way Street

200 Meters
200 Yards

① Main Pyramid Entrance
② Museum Pass/Group Entrance (in passageway)
③ Underground Mall Entrance
④ Café le Nemours
⑤ Le Fumoir
⑥ Bus #69 toward Marais
⑦ Bus #69 toward Rue Cler

shopping mall. Enter the mall at 99 Rue de Rivoli (the door with the red awning) or directly from the Métro stop Palais Royal-Musée du Louvre (stepping off the train, take the exit to *Musée du Louvre-Le Carrousel du Louvre*). Once inside the underground mall, continue toward the inverted pyramid and the Louvre's security entrance. Museum Pass holders can skip to the head of the security line.

Buying Tickets: Self-serve ticket machines located under the pyramid are faster to use than the ticket windows (machines accept euro bills, coins, and chip-and-PIN Visa cards). The *tabac* in the underground mall (near the Carrousel du Louvre entrance) sells tickets to the Louvre, Orsay, and Versailles, plus Museum Passes, for no extra charge (cash only).

Tours: Ninety-minute English-language **guided tours** leave twice daily (except the first Sunday of the month) from the *Accueil des Groupes* area, under the pyramid between the Sully and Denon wings (normally at 11:00 and 14:00, sometimes more often in sum-

PARIS

mer; €9 plus your entry ticket, tour tel. 01 40 20 52 63). **Videoguides** on Nintendo 3DS portable game consoles provide tech-savvy visitors with commentary on about 700 masterpieces (€5, available at entries to the three wings, at the top of the escalators). A free Louvre **smartphone app** is available at iTunes, where you can also download my free self-guided Louvre **audio tour** (see page 7). You'll also find English explanations throughout the museum.

Baggage Check: The free *bagagerie* is under the pyramid, to the right of the Denon wing entrance (it is signed *visiteurs individuels*). Large bags must be checked, and you can also check small bags to lighten your load. The baggage-claim clerk might ask you in French, "Does your bag contain anything of value?" You can't check cameras, money, passports, or other valuables.

Services: WCs are located under the pyramid, behind the escalators to the Denon and Richelieu wings. Once you're in the galleries, WCs are scarce.

◐ Self-Guided Tour: Start in the Denon Wing and visit the highlights, in the following order (thanks to Gene Openshaw for his help writing this tour).

Look for the famous ***Venus de Milo (Aphrodite)*** statue. You'll find her not far from another famous statue, the *Winged Victory of Samothrace.* This goddess of love (c. 100 B.C., from the Greek island of Melos) created a sensation when she was discovered in 1820. Most "Greek" statues are actually later Roman copies, but *Venus* is a rare Greek original. She, like Golden Age Greeks, epitomizes stability, beauty, and balance.

After viewing *Venus,* wander through the **ancient Greek and Roman works** to room 6 to see the Parthenon frieze (stone fragments that once decorated the exterior of the greatest Athenian temple), mosaics from the ancient city of Antioch, Etruscan sarcophagi, and Roman portrait busts.

Later Greek art was Hellenistic, adding motion and drama. For a good example, see the exciting ***Winged Victory of Samothrace*** (*Victoire de Samothrace,* on the landing). This statue of a woman with wings, poised on the prow of a ship, once stood on a hilltop to commemorate a naval victory. This is the *Venus de Milo* gone Hellenistic.

The **Italian collection**—including the *Mona Lisa*—is scattered throughout the rooms of the long Grand Gallery, to the right (as you face her) of *Winged Victory* (look for **two Botticelli frescoes** as you enter). In painting, the Renaissance meant realism, and for the Italians, realism was spelled "3-D." Painters were inspired by the realism and balanced beauty of Greek sculpture. Painting a 3-D world on a 2-D surface is tough, and after a millennium of Dark Ages, artists were rusty. Living in a religious age, they painted mostly altarpieces full of saints, angels, Madonnas-and-

PARIS

bambinos, and crucifixes floating in an ethereal gold-leaf heaven. Gradually, though, they brought these otherworldly scenes down to earth.

Two masters of the Italian High Renaissance (1500-1600) were Raphael (see his *La Belle Jardinière*, showing the Madonna, Child, and John the Baptist) and Leonardo da Vinci. The Louvre has the greatest collection of Leonardos in the world—five of them, including the exquisite *Virgin and Child with St. Anne;* the neighboring *Virgin of the Rocks;* and the androgynous *John the Baptist*.

But his most famous, of course, is the **Mona Lisa** (*La Joconde* in French), located in the Salle des Etats, midway down the Grand Gallery, on the right. After several years and a €5 million renovation, Mona is alone behind glass on her own false wall. Leonardo was already an old man when François I invited him to France. Determined to pack light, he took only a few paintings with him. One was a portrait of Lisa del Giocondo, the wife of a wealthy Florentine merchant. When Leonardo arrived, François immediately fell in love with the painting, making it the centerpiece of the small collection of Italian masterpieces that would, in three centuries, become the Louvre museum. He called it *La Gioconda* (*La Joconde* in French)—a play on both her last name and the Italian word for "happiness." We know it as the *Mona Lisa*—a contraction of the Italian for "my lady Lisa." Warning: François was impressed, but *Mona* may disappoint you. She's smaller than you'd expect, darker, engulfed in a huge room, and hidden behind a glaring pane of glass.

The huge canvas opposite *Mona* is Paolo Veronese's **The Marriage at Cana,** showing the Renaissance love of beautiful things gone hog-wild. Venetian artists like Veronese painted the good life of rich, happy-go-lucky Venetian merchants.

Now for something **Neoclassical.** Exit behind *Mona Lisa* and turn right into the Salle Daru to find **The Coronation of Emperor Napoleon** by Jacques-Louis David. Neoclassicism, once the rage in France (1780-1850), usually features Greek subjects, patriotic sentiment, and a clean, simple style. After Napoleon quickly conquered most of Europe, he insisted on being made emperor (not merely king) of this "New Rome." He staged an elaborate coronation ceremony in Paris, and rather than let the pope crown him, he crowned himself. The setting was Notre-Dame Cathedral, with Greek columns and Roman arches thrown in for effect. Napoleon's mom was also added, since she couldn't make it to the ceremony. A key on the frame describes who's who in the picture.

The **Romantic** collection, in an adjacent room (Salle Mollien), has works by Théodore Géricault (*The Raft of the Medusa*—one of my favorites) and Eugène Delacroix *(Liberty Leading the People)*. Romanticism, with an emphasis on motion and emotion, is the flip

Paris at a Glance

▲▲▲**Notre-Dame Cathedral** Paris' most beloved church, with towers and gargoyles. **Hours:** Cathedral Mon-Fri 8:00-18:45, Sat-Sun 8:00-19:15; tower daily April-Sept 10:00-18:30, Sat-Sun until 23:00 in July-Aug, Oct-March 10:00-17:30; Treasury Mon-Fri 9:30-17:40, Sat-Sun 9:30-18:10. See page 249.

▲▲▲**Sainte-Chapelle** Gothic cathedral with peerless stained glass. **Hours:** Daily March-Oct 9:30-18:00, Wed until 21:30 mid-May-mid-Sept, Nov-Feb 9:00-17:00. See page 257.

▲▲▲**Louvre** Europe's oldest and greatest museum, starring *Mona Lisa* and *Venus de Milo*. **Hours:** Wed-Mon 9:00-18:00, Wed and Fri until 21:45, closed Tue. See page 264.

▲▲▲**Orsay Museum** Nineteenth-century art, including Europe's greatest Impressionist collection. **Hours:** Tue-Sun 9:30-18:00, Thu until 21:45, closed Mon. See page 272.

▲▲▲**Eiffel Tower** Paris' soaring exclamation point. **Hours:** Daily mid-June-Aug 9:00-24:00, Sept-mid-June 9:30-23:00. See page 277.

▲▲▲**Champs-Elysées** Paris' grand boulevard. **Hours:** Always open. See page 290.

▲▲▲**Versailles** The ultimate royal palace (Château), with a Hall of Mirrors, vast gardens, a grand canal, plus a queen's playground (Trianon Palaces and Domaine de Marie-Antoinette). **Hours:** Château April-Oct Tue-Sun 9:00-18:30, Nov-March Tue-Sun 9:00-17:30, closed Mon year-round. Trianon/Domaine April-Oct Tue-Sun 12:00-18:30, Nov-March Tue-Sun 12:00-17:30, closed Mon year-round; in winter only the two Trianon Palaces are open. Gardens generally open April-Oct daily 9:00-20:30, Nov-March Tue-Sun 8:00-18:00, closed Mon. See page 377.

▲▲**Orangerie Museum** Monet's water lilies, plus works by Utrillo, Cézanne, Renoir, Matisse, and Picasso, in a lovely setting. **Hours:** Wed-Mon 9:00-18:00, closed Tue. See page 272.

▲▲**Army Museum and Napoleon's Tomb** The emperor's imposing tomb, flanked by museums of France's wars. **Hours:** Museum—daily April-Sept 10:00-18:00, may be open Tue until 21:00, Oct-March 10:00-17:00, closed first Mon of month year-round. Tomb—daily April-June and Sept 10:00-18:00, may be open Tue until 21:00; July-Aug 10:00-19:00, may be open Tue until 21:00; Oct-March 10:00-17:00, closed first Mon of month Sept-May. See page 283.

▲▲**Rodin Museum** Works by the greatest sculptor since Michelangelo, with many statues in a peaceful garden. **Hours:** Tue-Sun 10:00-17:45, Wed until 20:45, closed Mon. See page 284.

▲▲**Marmottan Museum** Untouristy art museum focusing on Monet. **Hours:** Tue-Sun 10:00-18:00, Thu until 20:00, closed Mon. See page 285.

▲▲**Cluny Museum** Medieval art with unicorn tapestries. **Hours:** Wed-Mon 9:15-17:45, closed Tue. See page 285.

▲▲**Arc de Triomphe** Triumphal arch with viewpoint, marking start of Champs-Elysées. **Hours:** Interior—daily April-Sept 10:00-23:00, Oct-March 10:00-22:30. See page 292.

▲▲**Jacquemart-André Museum** Art-strewn mansion. **Hours:** Daily 10:00-18:00, Mon and Sat until 21:00 during special exhibits. See page 294.

▲▲**Pompidou Center** Modern art in colorful building with city views. **Hours:** Wed-Mon 11:00-21:00, closed Tue. See page 300.

▲▲**Sacré-Cœur and Montmartre** White basilica atop Montmartre with super views. **Hours:** Daily 6:00-22:30; dome climb daily May-Sept 9:00-19:00, Oct-April 9:00-17:00. See page 303.

▲**Panthéon** Neoclassical monument celebrating the struggles of the French. **Hours:** Daily 10:00-18:30 in summer, until 18:00 in winter. See page 288.

▲**Opéra Garnier** Grand belle époque theater with a modern ceiling by Chagall. **Hours:** Generally daily 10:00-17:00, mid-July-Aug until 18:00. See page 293.

▲**La Défense and La Grande Arche** The city's own "little Manhattan" business district and its colossal modern arch. **Hours:** Always open. See page 295.

▲**Jewish Art and History Museum** Displays history of Judaism in Europe. **Hours:** Sun-Fri 11:00-18:00, closed Sat. See page 299.

▲**Carnavalet Museum** Paris' history wrapped up in a 16th-century mansion. **Hours:** Tue-Sun 10:00-18:00, closed Mon. See page 298.

▲**Père Lachaise Cemetery** Final home of Paris' illustrious dead. **Hours:** Mon-Fri 8:00-18:00, Sat 8:30-18:00, Sun 9:00-18:00, closes at 17:30 in winter. See page 302.

PARIS

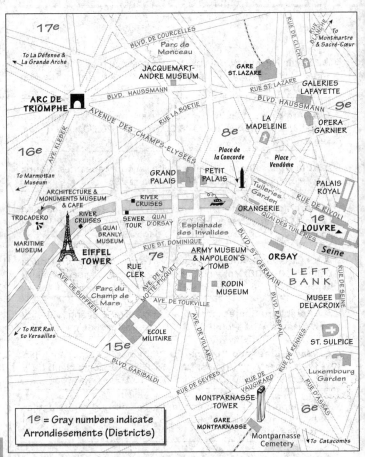

To La Défense &
La Grande Arche

To Montmartre
& Sacré-Cœur

JACQUEMART-
ANDRE MUSEUM

GARE
ST. LAZARE

GALERIES
LAFAYETTE

ARC DE
TRIOMPHE

OPERA
GARNIER

LA
MADELEINE

To Marmottan
Museum

Place de
la Concorde

Place
Vendôme

GRAND
PALAIS

PETIT
PALAIS

PALAIS
ROYAL

ARCHITECTURE &
MONUMENTS MUSEUM
& CAFE

Tuileries
Garden

RIVER
CRUISES

ORANGERIE

TROCADERO

RIVER
CRUISES

SEWER
TOUR

QUAI
D'ORSAY

LOUVRE

MARITIME
MUSEUM

QUAI
BRANLY
MUSEUM

EIFFEL
TOWER

Esplanade
des Invalides

ORSAY

Seine

ARMY MUSEUM
& NAPOLEON'S
TOMB

LEFT
BANK

RUE
CLER

MUSEE
DELACROIX

RODIN
MUSEUM

Parc du
Champ de
Mars

To RER Rail
to Versailles

ST. SULPICE

ECOLE
MILITAIRE

Luxembourg
Garden

MONTPARNASSE
TOWER

GARE
MONTPARNASSE

Montparnasse
Cemetery

To Catacombs

1e = Gray numbers indicate
Arrondissements (Districts)

PARIS

side of cool, balanced Neoclassicism, though they both flourished
in the early 1800s. Delacroix's *Liberty*, commemorating the stir-
rings of democracy in France, is also an appropriate tribute to the
Louvre, the first museum ever opened to the common rabble of
humanity. The good things in life don't belong only to a small,
wealthy part of society, but to everyone. The motto of France is
Liberté, Egalité, Fraternité—liberty, equality, and the brotherhood
of all.

Exit the room at the far end (past Café Mollien) and go downstairs, where you'll bump into the bum of a large, twisting male
nude looking like he's just waking up after a thousand-year nap.
The two *Slaves* (1513-1515) by Michelangelo are a fitting end to
this museum—works that bridge the ancient and modern worlds.
Michelangelo, like his fellow Renaissance artists, learned from the
Greeks. The perfect anatomy, twisting poses, and idealized faces

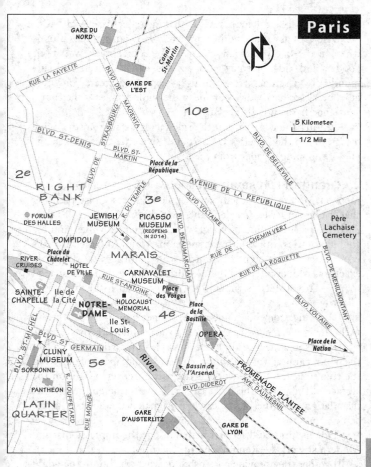

appear as if they could have been created 2,000 years earlier. Michelangelo said that his purpose was to carve away the marble to reveal the figures God put inside. The *Rebellious Slave*, fighting against his bondage, shows the agony of that process and the ecstasy of the result.

Although this makes for a good first tour, there's so much more. After a break (or on a second visit), consider a stroll through a few rooms of the Richelieu wing, which contain some of the Louvre's most ancient pieces. Bible students, amateur archaeologists, and Iraq War vets may find the collection especially interesting.

Nearby: Across from the Louvre are the lovely **Palais Royal courtyards.** Although the palace is closed to the public, the courtyards are always open and free (directly north of the Louvre on Rue de Rivoli, Mo: Palais Royal-Musée du Louvre). Enter through a whimsical (locals say tacky) courtyard filled with stubby, striped columns and playful fountains (with fun, reflective metal balls). Next, you'll pass into another, perfectly Parisian garden. This is where in-the-know Parisians come to take a quiet break, walk their poodles and kids, or enjoy a rendezvous—amid flowers and surrounded by a serene arcade. Bring a picnic and create your own quiet break, or have a drink at one of the outdoor cafés at the courtyard's northern end. This is Paris.

Exiting the courtyard at the side facing away from the Seine brings you to the Galeries Colbert and Vivienne, attractive examples of shopping arcades from the early 1900s.

▲▲Orangerie Museum (Musée de l'Orangerie)

Step out of the tree-lined, sun-dappled Impressionist painting that is the Tuileries Garden, and into the Orangerie (oh-rahn-zheh-ree), a little bijou of select works by Claude Monet and his contemporaries. Start with the museum's claim to fame: Monet's water lilies. These eight mammoth-scale paintings are displayed exactly as Monet intended them—surrounding you in oval-shaped rooms—so you feel as though you're immersed in his garden at Giverny.

Working from his home there, Monet built a special studio with skylights and wheeled easels to accommodate the canvases—1,950 square feet in all. Each canvas features a different part of the pond, painted from varying angles at distinct times of day—but the true subject of these works is the play of reflected light off the surface of the pond. The Monet rooms are considered the first art installation, and the blurry canvases signaled the abstract art to come.

Downstairs you'll see artists that bridge the Impressionist and Modernist worlds—Renoir, Cézanne, Utrillo, Matisse, and Picasso. Together they provide a snapshot of what was hot in the world of art collecting, circa 1920.

Cost and Hours: €7.50, €5 after 17:00, under 18 free, €14 combo-ticket with Orsay Museum (valid for four days, one visit per sight), covered by Museum Pass; Wed-Mon 9:00-18:00, closed Tue, galleries shut down 15 minutes before closing time; audioguide-€5, €6 English tours usually offered Mon and Thu at 14:30; located in Tuileries Garden near Place de la Concorde (Mo: Concorde), 15-minute stroll from the Orsay, tel. 01 44 77 80 07, www.musee-orangerie.fr.

▲▲▲Orsay Museum (Musée d'Orsay)

The Musée d'Orsay (mew-zay dor-say) houses French art of the 1800s and early 1900s (specifically, 1848-1914), picking up where the Louvre's art collection leaves off. For us, that means Impressionism, the art of sun-dappled fields, bright colors, and crowded

Parisian cafés. The Orsay houses the best general collection any-where of Manet, Monet, Renoir, Degas, Van Gogh, Cézanne, and Gauguin.

Cost and Hours: €9, €6.50 Tues-Wed and Fri-Sun after 16:15 and Thu after 18:00, free on first Sun of month and right when the ticket booth stops selling tickets (Tue-Wed and Fri-Sun at 17:00, Thu at 21:00; they won't let you in much after that), covered by Museum Pass, €14 combo-ticket with Orangerie Museum (valid for four days, one visit per sight); Tue-Sun 9:30-18:00, Thu until 21:45, closed Mon, Impressionist galleries start shutting 45 min-utes before closing, last entry one hour before closing (45 minutes before on Thu); crowded on Tue, when Louvre is closed; cafés and restaurant, tel. 01 40 49 48 14, www.musee-orsay.fr.

Getting There: The museum, at 1 Rue de la Légion d'Honneur, sits above the RER-C stop called Musée d'Orsay; the nearest Métro stop is Solférino, three blocks southeast of the Orsay. Bus #69 also stops at the Orsay. From the Louvre, it's a lovely 15-min-ute walk through the Tuileries Garden and across the pedestrian bridge to the Orsay.

Getting In: As you face the museum from Rue de la Légion d'Honneur (with the river on your left), passholders and ticket-holders enter on the right (Entrance C). Ticket purchasers enter closer to the river (Entrance A).

Tours: Audioguides cost €5. English guided tours usually run daily at 11:30 (€7.50/1.5 hours, none on Sun, may run at other times—inquire when you arrive). Or you can download my free self-guided Orsay **audio tour** (see page 7).

Background: The Impressionist painters rejected camera-like detail for a quick style more suited to capturing the passing mo-ment. Feeling stifled by the rigid rules and stuffy atmosphere of the Academy (the state-funded art school), the Impressionists took as their motto, "Out of the studio, into the open air." They grabbed their berets and scarves and went on excursions to the country, where they set up their easels (and newly invented tubes of pre-mixed paint) on riverbanks and hillsides, or they sketched in cafés and dance halls. Gods, goddesses, nymphs, and fantasy scenes were out; common people and rural landscapes were in.

The quick style and everyday subjects were ridiculed and called childish by the "experts." Rejected by the Salon (where works were exhibited to the buying public), the Impressionists staged their own exhibition in 1874. They brashly took their name from an insult thrown at them by a critic who laughed at one of Monet's "impres-sions" of a sunrise. During the next decade, they exhibited their own work independently. The public, opposed at first, was slowly won over by the simplicity, the color, and the vibrancy of Impres-sionist art.

PARIS

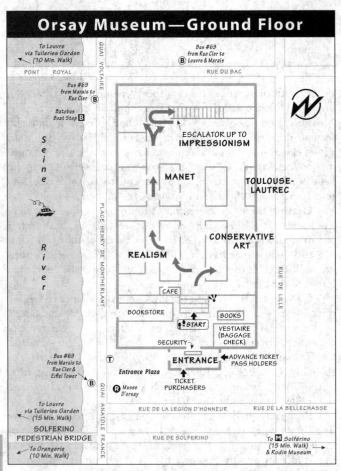

Orsay Museum—Ground Floor

To Louvre
via Tuileries Garden
(10 Min. Walk)

Bus #69
from Rue Cler to
🅑 Louvre & Marais

QUAI VOLTAIRE

PONT ROYAL

RUE DU BAC

Bus #69
from Marais to
Rue Cler 🅑

Batobus
Boat Stop 🅑

Seine River

ESCALATOR UP TO
IMPRESSIONISM

PLACE HENRY DE MONTHERLANT

MANET

**TOULOUSE-
LAUTREC**

**CONSERVATIVE
ART**

REALISM

RUE DE LILLE

CAFE

BOOKSTORE

BOOKS

🚻 START

VESTIAIRE
(BAGGAGE
CHECK)

SECURITY

Bus #69
from Marais to
Rue Cler &
Eiffel Tower 🅑

Ⓣ

Entrance Plaza

Ⓡ Musee
D'orsay

ENTRANCE

← ADVANCE TICKET
PASS HOLDERS

TICKET
PURCHASERS

QUAI ANATOLE FRANCE

RUE DE LA LEGION D'HONNEUR

RUE DE LA BELLECHASSE

SOLFERINO
PEDESTRIAN BRIDGE

RUE DE SOLFERINO

To Ⓜ Solférino
(15 Min. Walk)
& Rodin Museum

To Louvre
via Tuileries Garden
(15 Min. Walk)

→ To Orangerie
(10 Min. Walk)

PARIS

⊙ **Self-Guided Tour:** This former train station, or *gare*, barely escaped the wrecking ball in the 1970s, when the French realized it'd be a great place to exhibit the enormous collections of 19th-century art scattered throughout the city. The ground floor (level 0) houses early 19th-century art, mainly conservative art of the Academy and Salon, plus Realism. On the top floor is the core of the collection—the Impressionist rooms. If you're pressed for time, go directly there. Keep in mind that the collection is always on the move—paintings on loan, in restoration, or displayed in different rooms. The museum updates its website daily with the latest layout (www.musee-orsay.fr).

Conservative Art to Realism: In the Orsay's first few rooms, you're surrounded by visions of idealized beauty—nude women in languid poses, Greek mythological figures, and anatomically perfect statues. This was the art adored by French academics and the middle-class *(bourgeois)* public.

Farther along on the ground floor, you'll witness the shift to Realism. **Jean-François Millet's** *The Gleaners* (*Les Glaneuses*, 1867) depicts the poor women who pick up the meager leftovers after a field has already been harvested by the wealthy. This is "Realism" in two senses. It's painted "realistically," not prettified. And it's the "real" world—not the fantasy world of Greek myth, but the harsh life of the working poor.

Alexandre Cabanel's *The Birth of Venus* (*La Naissance de Vénus*, 1863) and **Edouard Manet's** *Olympia* (1863) offer two opposing visions of Venus. Cabanel's Venus is a perfect fantasy, an orgasm of beauty. Manet's nude is a Realist's take on the traditional Venus. Manet doesn't gloss over anything. The pose is classic, but the sharp outlines and harsh, contrasting colors are new and shocking. Manet replaced soft-core porn with hard-core art.

Impressionism: The Impressionist collection is scattered somewhat randomly through rooms 29-36 of the top floor. You'll see Monet hanging next to Renoir, Manet sprinkled among Pissarro, and a few Degas here and a few Cézannes there. Shadows dance and the displays mingle. Where they're hung is a lot like their brushwork...delightfully sloppy.

In **Manet's** *Luncheon on the Grass* (*Le Déjeuner sur l'Herbe*, 1863), a new revolutionary movement is starting to bud—Impressionism. Notice the background: the messy brushwork of trees and leaves, the play of light on the pond, and the light that filters through the trees onto the woman who stoops in the haze. Also note the strong contrast of colors (white skin, black clothes, green grass). This is a true out-of-doors painting, not a studio production.

Edgar Degas blended classical lines with Impressionist color, spontaneity, and everyday subjects from urban Paris. He loved the unposed "snapshot" effect, catching his models off guard. In *The Dance Class* (*La Classe de Danse*, c. 1873-1875), bored, tired dancers scratch their backs restlessly at the end of a long rehearsal. *In a Café*, or *Absinthe* (*Au Café, dit L'Absinthe*, 1876) captures a weary lady of the evening meeting morning with a last, lonely, nail-in-the-coffin drink in the glaring light of a four-in-the-morning café. Degas approaches his dance students, women at work, and café scenes from odd angles that aren't always ideal, but that make the scenes seem more real.

To paint common Parisians living and loving in the afternoon sun, **Pierre-Auguste Renoir** headed for the fields on Butte Montmartre (near the Sacré-Cœur basilica) on Sunday afternoons, when working-class folk would dress up and dance, drink, and eat little crêpes (galettes) till dark. In *Dance at the Moulin de la Galette* (*Bal du Moulin de la Galette*, 1876), the sunlight filtering through the

PARIS

trees creates a kaleidoscope of colors—the 19th-century equivalent of a mirror ball throwing darts of light onto the dancers. Like a photographer who uses a slow shutter speed to show motion, Renoir paints a waltzing blur.

Next, it's the father of Impressionism, **Claude Monet.** Look for paintings from his garden at Giverny and *The Cathedral of Rouen* (*La Cathédrale de Rouen*, 1893), "a series of differing impressions" of the cathedral facade at various times of day and year. In all, he did 30 paintings of the cathedral, and each is unique. The time-lapse series shows the sun passing slowly across the sky, creating different-colored light and shadows.

Post-Impressionism: It was **Paul Cézanne** who brought Impressionism into the 20th century. Compared with the color of Monet, the warmth of Renoir, and Van Gogh's passion, Cézanne's rather impersonal canvases can be difficult to appreciate. Bowls of fruit, landscapes, and a few portraits were Cézanne's passion. Because of his style (not his content), he is often called the first modern painter.

Find his paintings in room 36. In *Landscape* (*Rochers près des Grottes au-dessus de Château-Noir,* 1904), Cézanne uses chunks of green, tan, and blue paint as building blocks to construct this rocky brown cliff. These chunks are like little "cubes" (a style that later influenced the...Cubists). The subjects of Cézanne's *The Card Players* (*Les Joueurs de Cartes*, c. 1890-1895) aren't people—they're studies in color and pattern. The subject matter—two guys playing cards—is less important than the pleasingly balanced pattern they make on the canvas, two sloping forms framing a cylinder (a bottle) in the center. Later, abstract artists would focus solely on shapes and colors.

Like Michelangelo, Beethoven, Rembrandt, Wayne Newton, and a select handful of others, **Vincent van Gogh** put so much of himself into his work that art and life became one. In the Orsay's collection of Van Goghs (level 2), you'll see both the artist's painting style and his life unfold.

Encouraged by his art-dealer brother, Van Gogh moved to Paris, and *voilà!* The color! He met Monet, drank with Paul Gauguin and Henri de Toulouse-Lautrec, and soaked up the Impressionist style. In his *Self-Portrait, Paris* (*Portrait de l'Artiste*, 1887), you can see how he built a bristling brown beard with thick, side-by-side strokes of red, yellow, and green.

The social life of Paris became too much for the solitary Van Gogh, and he moved to southern France. At first, in the glow of the bright spring sunshine, he had a period of incredible creativity and happiness, as he was overwhelmed by the bright colors, landscape vistas, and common people—an Impressionist's dream. But being alone in a strange country began to wear on him. An ugly man, he found it hard to get a date. The close-up perspective of *Van Gogh's Room at Arles* (*La Chambre de van Gogh à Arles*, 1889) makes his tiny rented room look even more cramped.

Van Gogh wavered between happiness and madness, even mutilating his own ear at one point. He despaired of ever being sane enough to continue painting. His *Self-Portrait, St. Rémy* (1889) shows a man engulfed in a confused background of brushstrokes that swirl and rave, setting in motion the waves of the jacket. But in the midst of this rippling sea of mystery floats a still, detached island of a face with probing, questioning, yet wise eyes. Do his troubled eyes know that only a few months on, he will take a pistol and put a bullet through his chest? Vincent van Gone.

Nearby are the paintings of **Paul Gauguin,** who got the travel bug early in childhood and grew up wanting to be a sailor. He traveled to the South Seas in search of the exotic, finally settling on Tahiti. There he found his Garden of Eden. *Arearea*, or *Joyousness* (*Joyeusetés*, 1892) shows native women and a dog. In the "distance" (there's no attempt at traditional 3-D here), a procession goes by with a large pagan idol.

Pointillism, as illustrated by many paintings in the next rooms, brings Impressionism to its logical conclusion. Little dabs of pure colors are placed side by side to blend in the viewer's eye. In works such as *The Circus* (*Le Cirque,* 1891), **Georges Seurat** (1859-1891) used only red, yellow, blue, and green points of paint to create a mosaic of colors that shimmers at a distance, capturing the wonder of the dawn of electric light.

The Rest of the Orsay: The open-air mezzanine of level 2 is lined with statues. Stroll the mezzanine, enjoying the works of great French sculptors, including **Auguste Rodin,** who combined classical solidity with Impressionist surfaces. Look for *The Walking Man* (*L'Homme Qui Marche,* c. 1900) by room 71. Like this statue, Rodin had one foot in the past, while the other was stepping into the future. With no mouth or hands, the subject speaks with his body. The rough, "unfinished" surface reflects light in the same way the rough Impressionist brushwork does, making the statue come alive, never quite at rest in the viewer's eye. Rodin's powerful, haunting works are a good place to end this tour. With a stable base of 19th-century stone, he launched art into the 20th century.

Eiffel Tower Area
▲▲▲Eiffel Tower (La Tour Eiffel)

It's crowded, expensive, and there are probably better views in Paris, but visiting this 1,000-foot-tall ornament is worth the trouble. Visitors to Paris may find *Mona Lisa* to be less than expected, but the Eiffel Tower rarely disappoints, even in an era of skyscrapers.

Cost: €14 for an elevator ride all the way to the top, €8.50 if you're only going up to the two lower levels, not covered by Museum Pass; save some time in line by climbing the stairs to the first and second levels for €5 (€3.50 if you're under 25); once inside the tower, you can buy your way to the top with no penalty—ticket booths and machines on the first and second levels sell supplements for €5.50.

Hours: Daily mid-June-Aug 9:00-24:00, last ascent to top at 23:00 and to lower levels at 23:30; Sept-mid-June 9:30-23:00, last ascent to top at 22:00 and to lower levels at 22:30, stairs close at 18:00 in off-season.

Reservations: Frankly, you'd be crazy to show up without a reservation. At www.tour-eiffel.fr, you can book an entry time and skip the initial line (the longest)—at no extra cost. Book well in advance, as soon as you know when you'll be in Paris. Just pay online with a credit card and print your own ticket. When buying tickets online, make sure you select "Lift entrance ticket with access to the summit" in order to go all the way to the top. For "Type of ticket," it doesn't really matter whether you pick "Group" or "Individual"; a "Group" ticket just gives you one piece of paper covering everyone in your party. You must enter a mobile phone number for identification purposes, so if you don't have one, make one up—and jot it down so you won't forget it (French mobile phone numbers begin with 06 or 07 and have 10 digits). Arrive at the tower 10 minutes before your entry time and look for either of the two entrances marked *Visiteurs avec Reservation (Visitors with Reservation)*, where attendants scan your ticket and put you on the first available elevator. Alternatively, Classic Walks may have tickets with reservations (see page 246).

When to Go: For the best of all worlds, arrive with enough light to see the views, then stay as it gets dark to see the lights. The views are grand whether you ascend or not. At the top of the hour, a five-minute display features thousands of sparkling lights (best viewed from Place du Trocadéro or the grassy park below).

Avoiding Lines: Crowds overwhelm this place much of the year, with one- to two-hour waits to get in (unless it's rainy, when lines can evaporate). Weekends and holidays are worst, but prepare for ridiculous crowds almost any time. The best solution is to make an online reservation (see above) and to take the stairs down (from first or second levels). If you don't have a reservation, go early; get in line 30 minutes before the tower opens. Going later is the next-best bet (after 19:00 May-Aug, after 17:00 off-season, a bit earlier in winter as it gets dark by 17:00). When you buy tickets, all members of your party must be with you. You can bypass some (but not all) lines if you have a reservation at either of the tower's view restaurants or hike the stairs.

Getting There: The tower is about a 10-minute walk from the

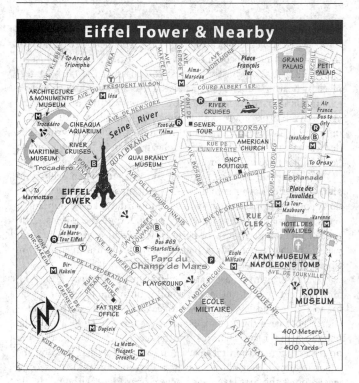

Eiffel Tower & Nearby

Métro (Bir-Hakeim or Trocadéro stops) or train (Champ de Mars-Tour Eiffel RER stop). The Ecole Militaire Métro stop in the Rue Cler area is 20 minutes away. Buses #69 and #87 stop nearby on Avenue Joseph Bouvard in the Champ de Mars park.

Pickpockets: Beware. Street thieves plunder awestruck visitors gawking below the tower. And tourists in crowded elevators are like fish in a barrel for predatory pickpockets. *En garde.* There's a police station at the Jules Verne pillar.

Security Check: Bags larger than 19" × 8" × 12" are not allowed, but there is no baggage check. All bags are subject to a security search. No knives, glass bottles, or cans are permitted.

Services: Free WCs are at the base of the tower, behind the east pillar. Inside the tower itself, WCs are on all levels, but they're small, with long lines.

Best Views of the Tower: The best place to view the tower is from Place du Trocadéro to the north. It's a 10-minute walk across the river, a happening scene at night, and especially fun for kids. Consider arriving at the Trocadéro Métro stop for the view, then walking toward the tower. Another delightful viewpoint is from the Champ de Mars park to the south.

Background: Built on the 100th anniversary of the French

Revolution (and in the spirit of the Industrial Revolution), the tower was the centerpiece of a World Expo designed simply to show off what people could build in 1889. Bridge-builder Gustave Eiffel (1832-1923) won the contest to construct the fair's centerpiece by beating out rival proposals such as a giant guillotine. To a generation hooked on technology, the tower was the marvel of the age, a symbol of progress and human ingenuity. Not all were so impressed, however; many found it a monstrosity. The writer Guy de Maupassant (1850-1893) routinely ate lunch in the tower just so he wouldn't have to look at it.

Visiting the Tower: Delicate and graceful when seen from afar, the Eiffel Tower is massive—even a bit scary—close up. You don't appreciate its size until you walk toward it; like a mountain, it seems so close but takes forever to reach. Despite the tower's 7,300 tons of metal and 60 tons of paint, it is so well-engineered that it weighs no more per square inch at its base than a linebacker on tiptoes.

There are three observation platforms, at roughly 200, 400, and 900 feet. To get to the top, you'll wait in line to ride an elevator to the second level. A separate elevator—with another line—shuttles between the second level and the top. (Note: Whether you have a ticket for the top or just for the second level, elevators going up do not stop at the first level. You can see the first level on the way back down, but not all elevators descending from the second level stop at the first level—ask before boarding.) Although being on the windy top of the Eiffel Tower is a thrill you'll never forget, the view is better from the second level, where you can actually see Paris' monuments.

The stairs—yes, you can walk up to the first and second levels—are next to the entrance to the pricey Jules Verne restaurant. As you ascend through the metal beams, imagine being a worker, perched high above nothing, riveting this thing together.

The **top level,** called *le sommet,* is tiny. (It can close temporarily without warning when it reaches capacity or in windy conditions.) All you'll find here are wind and grand, sweeping views. The city lies before you (pick out sights with the help of the panoramic maps). On a good day, you can see for 40 miles.

The **second level** has the best views because you're closer to the sights, and the monuments are more recognizable. (While the best views are up the short stairway, on the platform without the wire-cage barriers, at busy times much of that zone is taken up by people waiting for the elevator to the top.) This level has souvenir shops, public telephones to call home, and a small stand-up café. While you'll save no money, consider taking the elevator up and the stairs down (5 minutes from second level to first, 5 minutes more to ground) for good exercise and views.

The **first level** has more great views, all well-described by the tower's panoramic displays. There are a number of photo exhibits on the tower's history, WCs, a conference hall (closed to tourists), an ATM, and souvenirs. A small café sells pizza and sandwiches (outdoor tables in summer). This level also has two fine restaurants run by famous French chef Alain Ducasse: 58 Tour Eiffel (listed on page 349) has more accessible prices than the Jules Verne Restaurant (€90 weekday lunch *menu*, €170-220 weekend lunch *menus*, €220 dinner *menu*, reserve 2-3 months in advance, tel. 01 45 55 61 44, www.lejulesverne-paris.com). In winter, part of the first level is set up for winter activities (most recently as an ice-skating rink). Climb the stairs to Cineiffel for a small gallery and theater. A tired eight-minute video that continuously features clips of the tower's construction, its paint job, its place in pop culture, and the millennium fireworks.

After Your Visit: Descend back to earth. From here, consider catching the Bateaux Parisiens boat for a Seine cruise (see page 244) or visiting one of the following nearby sights: the Quai Branly Museum (page 282), Rue Cler market street, Army Museum and Napoleon's Tomb (page 283), or Rodin Museum (page 284).

For a final peek at the tower, stroll across the river to Place du Trocadéro or to the end of the Champ de Mars and look back for great views. However impressive it may be by day, the tower is an awesome thing to see at twilight, when it becomes engorged with light, and virile Paris lies back and lets night be on top. When darkness fully envelops the city, the tower seems to climax with a spectacular light show at the top of each hour...for five minutes.

Near the Eiffel Tower

▲Architecture and Monuments Museum
(Cité de l'Architecture et du Patrimoine)

This museum, on the east side of Place du Trocadéro, takes you through 1,000 years of French architecture, brilliantly displaying casts and models of some of France's most cherished monuments from the 11th to 21st centuries. Gaze into the eyes of medieval statues and wander under doorways, tympanums, and arches from the abbey of Cluny, Chartres Cathedral, Château de Chambord, and much more. You'll see how colorfully painted the chapels were in Romanesque churches and discover a vast array of models from modern projects, along with thought-provoking designs for low-income housing. The views from the upper rooms to the Eiffel Tower are sensational, as are those from the terrace of the on-site café, Café Carlu.

Cost and Hours: €8, covered by Museum Pass, audioguide-€3; Wed-Mon 11:00-19:00, Thu until 21:00, closed Tue; excellent English explanations, great view café (reasonable prices, open same hours as museum and does not require entry into the museum), 1 Place du Trocadéro, Mo: Trocadéro, RER: Champ de Mars-Tour Eiffel, tel. 01 58 51 52 00, www.citechaillot.fr.

Quai Branly Museum (Musée du Quai Branly)

This is the best collection I've seen anywhere of so-called Primitive Art from Africa, Polynesia, Asia, and America. It's presented in a wild, organic, and strikingly modern building that caused a stir in Paris when it opened in 2006. Masks, statuettes, musical instruments, clothes, voodoo dolls, and a variety of temporary exhibitions and activities are artfully presented and exquisitely lit. It's not, however, accompanied by much printed English information—to really appreciate the exhibit, you need to rent the audioguide. Even if you skip the museum, drop by its peaceful garden café for fine Eiffel Tower views (closes 30 minutes before museum) and enjoy the intriguing gardens. The pedestrian bridge that crosses the river and runs up to the museum has terrific views of the Eiffel Tower.

Cost and Hours: €8.50, free on first Sun of the month, covered by Museum Pass, audioguide-€5; museum—Tue-Sun 11:00-19:00, Thu-Sat until 21:00, closed Mon, ticket office closes one hour before closing; gardens—Tue-Sun 9:15-19:30, Thu-Sat until 21:15, closed Mon; 37 Quai Branly, 10-minute walk east (upriver) of Eiffel Tower, along the river (RER: Champ de Mars-Tour Eiffel or Pont de l'Alma), tel. 01 56 61 70 00, www.quaibranly.fr.

National Maritime Museum (Musée National de la Marine)

This extensive museum houses an amazing collection of ship models, submarines, torpedoes, cannonballs, *beaucoup* bowsprits, and naval you-name-it, including a small boat made for Napoleon. Don't miss the model and story of how the obelisk on Place de la Concorde was delivered from Egypt to Paris entirely by waterways (behind stairs leading down to special exhibits space). Take advantage of the audioguide that explains key exhibits and adds important context to your visit. Kids love it, too.

Cost and Hours: €7, 26 and under free, includes audioguide, covered by Museum Pass; Mon and Wed-Fri 11:00-18:00, Sat-Sun 11:00-19:00, closed Tue; on left side of Place du Trocadéro with your back to Eiffel Tower, tel. 01 53 65 69 69, www.musee-marine.fr.

▲Paris Sewer Tour (Les Egouts de Paris)

Discover what happens after you flush. This quick, interesting, and slightly stinky visit (a perfumed hanky helps) takes you along a few hundred yards of water tunnels in the world's first underground sewer system. Pick up the helpful English self-guided tour, then drop down into Jean Valjean's world of tunnels, rats, and manhole covers. (Victor Hugo was friends with the sewer inspector when he wrote *Les Misérables*.) You'll pass well-organized displays with helpful English information explaining the history of water distribution in Paris, from Roman times to the present. The evolution of this amazing network of sewers is surprisingly fascinating. More than 1,500 miles of tunnels carry 317 million gallons of water daily through this underworld. It's the world's longest sewer system—so long, they say, that if it was laid out straight, it would stretch from Paris all the way to Istanbul.

In the gift shop, you can ask about the slideshow and occasional tours in English. The WCs are just beyond the gift shop.

Cost and Hours: €4.30, covered by Museum Pass, May-Sept Sat-Wed 11:00-17:00, Oct-April Sat-Wed 11:00-16:00, closed Thu-Fri, located where Pont de l'Alma greets the Left Bank—on the right side of the bridge as you face the river, Mo: Alma-Marceau, RER: Pont de l'Alma, tel. 01 53 68 27 81.

▲▲Army Museum and Napoleon's Tomb (Musée de l'Armée)

The Hôtel des Invalides, a former veterans' hospital topped by a golden dome, houses Napoleon's over-the-top-ornate tomb, as well as Europe's greatest military museum. Visiting the Army Museum's different sections, you can watch the art of war unfold from stone axes to Axis powers.

At the center of the complex, Napoleon Bonaparte lies majestically dead inside several coffins under a grand dome—a goose-bumping pilgrimage for historians. Your visit continues through an impressive range of museums filled with medieval armor, cannons and muskets, Louis XIV-era uniforms and weapons, and Napoleon's horse—stuffed and mounted.

The best section is dedicated to the two World Wars. Walk chronologically through displays on the trench warfare of World War I, the victory parades, France's horrendous loss of life, and the humiliating Treaty of Versailles that led to World War II. The WWII rooms use black-and-white photos, maps, videos, and a few artifacts to trace Hitler's rise, the Blitzkrieg that overran France, America's entry into the war, D-Day, concentration camps, the atomic bomb, and the eventual Allied victory. There's special insight into France's role (the French Resistance) and how it was Charles de Gaulle who actually won the war.

Cost and Hours: €9, €7 after 17:00, free for military personnel in uniform, free for kids but they must wait in line for ticket, covered by Museum Pass, audioguide-€6; museum—daily April-Sept 10:00-18:00, may be open Tue until 21:00, Oct-March 10:00-17:00, closed first Mon of month year-round; tomb—daily April-June and Sept 10:00-18:00, may be open Tue until 21:00; July-Aug 10:00-19:00, may be open Tue until 21:00; Oct-March 10:00-17:00, closed first Mon of month Sept-May, last tickets sold 30 minutes before closing, cafeteria, tel. 01 44 42 38 77 or 08 10 11 33 99, www.invalides.org.

Getting There: The Hôtel des Invalides is at 129 Rue de Grenelle; Mo: La Tour Maubourg, Varenne, or Invalides. Bus #69 from the Marais and Rue Cler area also takes you there, or it's a 10-minute walk from Rue Cler.

▲▲Rodin Museum (Musée Rodin)

This user-friendly museum is filled with passionate works by the greatest sculptor since Michelangelo. Note that the museum will likely be undergoing a major renovation during your visit. Expect some statues to be moved around and some rooms to be closed altogether. The gardens remain open. To compensate for the closures, the museum has added a few rarely displayed pieces to its exhibits.

Auguste Rodin (1840-1917) sculpted human figures on an epic scale, revealing through their bodies his deepest thoughts and feelings. Like many of Michelangelo's unfinished works, Rodin's statues rise from the raw stone around them, driven by the life force. With missing limbs and scarred skin, these are prefab classics, making ugliness noble. Rodin's people are always moving restlessly. Even the famous *Thinker* is moving. While he's plopped down solidly, his mind is a million miles away.

Rodin worked with many materials—he chiseled marble (though not often), modeled clay, cast bronze, worked plaster, painted on canvas, and sketched on paper. He often created different versions of the same subject in different media.

Rodin lived and worked in this mansion, renting rooms alongside Henri Matisse, the poet Rainer Maria Rilke (Rodin's secretary), and the dancer Isadora Duncan. The well-displayed exhibits trace Rodin's artistic development, explain how his bronze statues were cast, and show some of the studies he created to work up to his masterpiece (the unfinished *Gates of Hell*). Learn about Rodin's tumultuous relationship with his apprentice and lover, Camille Claudel. Mull over what makes his sculptures some of the most evocative since the Renaissance. And stroll the gardens, packed with many of his greatest works (including *The Thinker, Balzac,* the *Burghers of Calais,* and the *Gates of Hell*). The beautiful gardens are ideal for artistic reflection.

Cost and Hours: €9, under 18 free, free on first Sun of the month, €1 for garden only (possibly Paris' best deal, as many works are on display there), both museum and garden covered by Museum Pass, audioguide-€6; Tue-Sun 10:00-17:45, Wed until 20:45, closed Mon; gardens close at 18:00, Oct-March at 17:00; last entry 30 minutes before closing, mandatory baggage check, self-service café in garden, near the Army Museum and Napoleon's Tomb at 79 Rue de Varenne, Mo: Varenne, tel. 01 44 18 61 10, www.musee-rodin.fr.

▲▲Marmottan Museum (Musée Marmottan Monet)

This intimate, less-touristed mansion on the southwest fringe of urban Paris has the best collection of works by the father of Impressionism, Claude Monet (1840-1926). Fiercely independent and dedicated to his craft, Monet gave courage to the other Impressionists in the face of harsh criticism.

Though the museum is not arranged chronologically, you can trace his life. You'll see black-and-white sketches from his youth, his discovery of open-air painting, and the canvas—*Impression: Sunrise*—that gave Impressionism its name. There are portraits of his wives and kids, and his well-known "series" paintings (done at different times of day) of London, Gare St. Lazare, and the Cathedral of Rouen. The museum's highlight is scenes from his garden at Giverny—the rose trellis, the Japanese bridge, and the larger-than-life water lilies.

In addition, the Marmottan features a world-class collection of works by Berthe Morisot and other Impressionists; an eclectic collection of non-Monet objects (furniture, illuminated manuscript drawings); and temporary exhibits.

Cost and Hours: €10, not covered by Museum Pass, audioguide-€3, Tue-Sun 10:00-18:00, Thu until 20:00, closed Mon, last entry 30 minutes before closing, 2 Rue Louis-Boilly, Mo: La Muette, tel. 01 44 96 50 33, www.marmottan.com.

Left Bank

Opposite Notre-Dame, on the left bank of the Seine, is the Latin Quarter.

▲▲Cluny Museum (Musée National du Moyen Age)

This treasure trove of Middle Ages (Moyen Age) art fills old Roman baths, offering close-up looks at stained glass, Notre-Dame carvings, fine goldsmithing and jewelry, and rooms of tapestries. The highlights are several original stained-glass windows from Sainte-Chapelle and the exquisite Lady and the Unicorn series of six tapestries: A delicate, as-medieval-as-can-be noble lady introduces a delighted unicorn to the senses of taste, hearing, sight, smell, and touch. This museum helps put the Middle Ages in perspective, reflecting a time when Europe was awakening from a thousand-year slumber and Paris was emerging on the world stage. Trade was booming, people actually owned chairs, and the Renaissance was moving in like a warm front from Italy.

Cost and Hours: €8, free on first Sun of month, covered by Museum Pass, ticket includes audioguide though passholders must pay €1; Wed-Mon 9:15-17:45, closed Tue, ticket office closes at 17:15; near corner of Boulevards St. Michel and St. Germain at 6 Place Paul Painlevé; Mo: Cluny-La Sorbonne, St. Michel, or Odéon; tel. 01 53 73 78 16, www.musee-moyenage.fr.

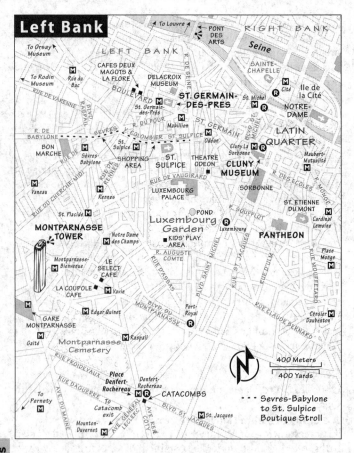

Left Bank

To Louvre
PONT DES ARTS
RIGHT BANK
Seine
To Orsay Museum
LEFT BANK
SAINTE-CHAPELLE
To Rodin Museum
Rue du Bac
CAFES DEUX MAGOTS & LA FLORE
DELACROIX MUSEUM
St. Germain-des-Prés
BOULEVARD
ST. GERMAIN-DES-PRES
St. Michel
Cité
Ile de la Cité
NOTRE-DAME
RUE DE VARENNE
BLVD. RASPAIL
R. DE SEINE
R. DU FOUR
ST. GERMAIN
LATIN QUARTER
R. DE BABYLONE
SEVRES
R. DE RENNES
V. COLOMBIER
Mabillon
ST. SULPICE
Odéon
Cluny La Sorbonne
BLVD. ST. MICHEL
BON MARCHE
Sèvres-Babylone
St. Sulpice
SHOPPING AREA
ST. SULPICE
THEATRE ODEON
CLUNY MUSEUM
Maubert-Mutualité
RUE DU CHERCHE-MIDI
Vaneau
Rennes
RUE DE VAUGIRARD
LUXEMBOURG PALACE
SORBONNE
R. DES ECOLES
R. MONGE
St. Placide
Luxembourg Garden
POND
Luxembourg
R. SOUFFLOT
ST. ETIENNE DU MONT
PANTHEON
Cardinal Lemoine
MONTPARNASSE TOWER
Notre Dame des Champs
KIDS' PLAY AREA
R. AUGUSTE COMTE
BLVD. SAINT MICHEL
R. D'ULM
Place Monge
RUE MOUFFETARD
Montparnasse-Bienvenue
LE SELECT CAFE
RUE D'ASSAS
R. ST. JACQUES
LA COUPOLE CAFE
Vavin
BLVD. DU MONTPARNASSE
Port-Royal
RUE CLAUDE BERNARD
Censier Daubenton
GARE MONTPARNASSE
Edgar Quinet
Gaité
Montparnasse Cemetery
Raspail
RUE FROIDEVAUX
RUE DAGUERRE
AVE. DU MAINE
Place Denfert-Rochereau
Denfert-Rochereau
CATACOMBS
AVE. GENERAL LECLERC
AVE. RENE COTY
BLVD. ST. JACQUES
St. Jacques
400 Meters
400 Yards
To Pernety
To Catacomb exit
Mouston-Duvernet
- - - Sevres-Babylone to St. Sulpice Boutique Stroll

PARIS

St. Germain-des-Prés

A church was first built on this site in A.D. 558. The church you see today was constructed in 1163 and is all that's left of a once sprawling and influential monastery. The colorful interior reminds us that medieval churches were originally painted in bright colors. The surrounding area hops at night with venerable cafés, fire-eaters, mimes, and scads of artists.

Cost and Hours: Free, daily 8:00-20:00, Mo: St. Germain-des-Prés.

▲St. Sulpice Church

Since it was featured in *The Da Vinci Code,* this grand church has become a trendy stop for the book's many fans. But the real reason to visit is to see and hear its intimately accessible organ. For pipe-organ enthusiasts, this is one of Europe's great musical treats. The Grand Orgue at St. Sulpice Church has a rich history, with a succession of 12 world-class organists—including Charles-Marie Widor and Marcel Dupré—that goes back 300 years. Widor started the tradition of opening the loft to visitors after the Sunday morning service. Daniel Roth (or his understudy) continues to welcome guests in three languages while playing five keyboards.

Cost and Hours: Free, church open daily 7:30-19:30, Mo: St. Sulpice or Mabillon. See www.stsulpice.com for special concerts.

Sunday Organ Visits: The 10:30-11:30 Sunday Mass (come appropriately dressed) is followed by a high-powered 25-minute recital. Then, at noon, the small, unmarked door is opened (left of entry as you face the rear). Visitors scamper like 16th notes up spiral stairs, past the 19th-century StairMasters that five men once pumped to fill the bellows, into a world of 7,000 pipes. You can see the organ and visit with Daniel (or his substitute, who might not speak English). Space is tight—only 15 people are allowed in at a time, and only a few can gather around the organist at once—you need to be quick to allow others a chance to meet him. You'll likely have about 20 minutes to kill before watching the master play during the next Mass (church views are great, and there's a small lounge to wait in); you can leave at any time. If you're late or rushed, show up around 12:30 and wait at the little door (last entry is at 13:00). As someone leaves, you can slip in, climb up, and catch the rest of the performance.

Nearby: Tempting boutiques surround the church, and Luxembourg Garden is nearby.

Delacroix Museum (Musée National Eugène Delacroix)

This museum for Eugène Delacroix (1798-1863) was once his home and studio. A friend of bohemian artistic greats—including George Sand and Frédéric Chopin—Delacroix is most famous for the flag-waving painting *Liberty Leading the People*, which is displayed at the Louvre, not here.

Cost and Hours: €5, free on first Sun of the month, covered by Museum Pass, Wed-Mon 9:30-17:00, closed Tue, last entry 30 minutes before closing, 6 Rue de Furstenberg, Mo: St. Germain-des-Prés, tel. 01 44 41 86 50, www.musee-delacroix.fr.

▲Luxembourg Garden (Jardin du Luxembourg)

Paris' most beautiful, interesting, and enjoyable garden/park/recreational area, le Jardin du Luxembourg, is a great place to watch Parisians at rest and play. This 60-acre garden, dotted with fountains and statues, is the property of the French Senate, which meets here in the Luxembourg Palace.

Luxembourg Garden has special rules governing its use (for example, where cards can be played, where dogs can be walked, where joggers can run, and when and where music can be played). The brilliant flower beds are changed three times a year, and the boxed trees are brought out of the *orangerie* in May. Children enjoy the rentable toy sailboats. The park hosts marionette shows several times weekly (Les Guignols, Wed 15:30, Sat-Sun 11:00 and 15:30). Pony rides are available from April through October. (Meanwhile, the French CIA plots espionage in their underground offices beneath the park.)

Challenge the card and chess players to a game (near the tennis courts), or find a free chair near the main pond and take a well-deserved break.

Cost and Hours: Free, daily dawn until dusk, Mo: Odéon, RER: Luxembourg.

Nearby: The grand Neoclassical-domed Panthéon, now a mausoleum housing the tombs of great French notables, is three blocks away (see below).

Other Parks: If you enjoy Luxembourg Garden and want to see more green spaces, you could visit the more elegant **Parc Monceau** (Mo: Monceau), the colorful **Jardin des Plantes** (Mo: Jussieu or Gare d'Austerlitz, RER: Gare d'Austerlitz), or the hilly and bigger **Parc des Buttes-Chaumont** (Mo: Buttes-Chaumont).

▲Panthéon

This state-capitol-style Neoclassical monument celebrates France's illustrious history and people, balances Foucault's pendulum, and is the final home of many French VIPs.

Cost and Hours: €8.50, under 18 free, covered by Museum Pass, daily 10:00-18:30 in summer, until 18:00 in winter, last entry 45 minutes before closing, Mo: Cardinal Lemoine. Ask about occasional English tours or call ahead for schedule; tel. 01 44 32 18 00, www.pantheon.monuments-nationaux.fr.

Visiting the Panthéon: Inside the vast building (360' by 280' by 270') are monuments tracing the celebrated struggles of the French people: a beheaded St. Denis (painting on left wall of nave), St. Geneviève saving the fledgling city from Attila the Hun, and scenes of Joan of Arc (left transept).

Foucault's pendulum swings gracefully at the end of a 220-foot cable suspended from the towering dome. It was here in 1851 that the scientist Léon Foucault first demonstrated the rotation of the earth. Stand a few minutes and watch the pendulum's arc (appear to) shift as you and the earth rotate beneath it.

Stairs in the back lead down to the crypt, where a pantheon of greats is buried. Rousseau is along the right wall as you enter, Voltaire faces him across the hall. Also buried here are scientist Marie Curie, Victor Hugo (*Les Misérables*, *The Hunchback of Notre-Dame*), Alexandre Dumas (*The Three Musketeers*, *The Count of Monte Cristo*), and Louis Braille, who invented the script for the blind.

Dome Climb: For fine views, climb 206 steps to the dome gallery. Visits are by escort only and leave every hour until 17:30 from the bookshop near the entry—see schedule as you go in. Note that dome access may be closed for renovation during your visit.

Montparnasse Tower (La Tour Montparnasse)

This sadly out-of-place 59-story superscraper has one virtue: Its sensational views are cheaper and far easier to access than the Eiffel Tower's. Come early in the day for clearest skies and be treated to views from a comfortable interior and from up on the rooftop. (Some say it's the very best view in Paris, as you can see the Eiffel Tower clearly...and you can't see the Montparnasse Tower at all.)

Exit the elevator at the 56th floor, passing the eager photographer (they'll superimpose your group's image with the view) to views of *tout Paris*. Here you can have a drink or a light lunch (OK prices), peruse the gift shop, or use the good WCs. Take time to explore every corner of the floor. Dioramas identify highlights of the star-studded vista. From here it's easy to admire Georges-Eugène Haussmann's grand-boulevard scheme. Notice the lush courtyards hiding behind grand street fronts. The exhibits change often, but you'll likely see historic photos and enjoy a plush little theater playing a continuous video.

For more views, climb to the open terrace on the 59th floor to enjoy the surreal scene of a lonely man in a box and a helipad surrounded by the window-cleaner track. Here, 690 feet above Paris, you can scan the city with the wind in your hair.

Cost and Hours: €13, not covered by Museum Pass; April-Sept daily 9:30-23:30; Oct-March Sun-Thu 9:30-22:30, Fri-Sat 9:30-23:00; last entry 30 minutes before closing, sunset is great, but views are disappointing after dark, entrance on Rue de l'Arrivée, Mo: Montparnasse-Bienvenüe—from the Métro stay inside the station and follow the signs for *La Tour*; tel. 01 45 38 52 56, www.tourmontparnasse56.com.

▲Catacombs

Descend 60 feet below the street and walk a one-mile (one-hour) route through tunnels containing the anonymous bones of six million permanent Parisians.

In 1786, health-conscious Parisians looking to relieve congestion and improve the city's sanitary conditions emptied the church cemeteries and moved the bones here, to former limestone quarries. For decades, priests led ceremonial processions of black-veiled, bone-laden carts into the quarries, where the bones were stacked in piles five feet high and as much as 80 feet deep. Ignore the sign announcing, "Halt, this is the empire of the dead," and walk through passageways of skull-studded tibiae, past more cheery signs: "Happy is he who is forever faced with the hour of his death and prepares himself for the end every day." You emerge far from where you entered, with white-limestone-covered toes, telling everyone you've been underground gawking at bones. Note to wannabe Hamlets: An attendant checks your bag at the exit for stolen souvenirs.

Cost and Hours: €8, not covered by Museum Pass, Tue-Sun 10:00-17:00, closed Mon, ticket booth closes at 16:00; tel. 01 43 22 47 63, www.catacombes-de-paris.fr.

Warning: Lines are long (figure an hour wait) and hard to avoid. Arrive no later than 14:30 or risk not getting in.

Getting There: 1 Place Denfert-Rochereau. Take the Métro to Denfert-Rochereau, then find the lion in the big traffic circle; if he looked left rather than right, he'd stare right at the green entrance to the Catacombs.

After Your Visit: You'll exit at 36 Rue Rémy Dumoncel, far from where you started. Turn right out of the exit and walk to Avenue du Général Leclerc, where you'll be equidistant from Métro stops Alésia (walk left) and Mouton Duvernet (walk right).

Champs-Elysées and Nearby

▲▲▲Champs-Elysées

This famous boulevard is Paris' backbone, with its greatest concentration of traffic. From the Arc de Triomphe down Avenue des Champs-Elysées, all of France seems to converge on Place de la Concorde, the city's largest square. And though the Champs-Elysées has become as international as it is Parisian, a walk here is still a must.

Background: In 1667, Louis XIV opened the first section of the street as a short extension of the Tuileries Garden. This year is considered the birth of Paris as a grand city. The Champs-Elysées soon became *the* place to cruise in your carriage. (It still is today; traffic can be gridlocked even at midnight.) One hundred years later, the café scene arrived. From the 1920s until the 1960s, this boulevard was pure elegance; Parisians actually dressed up to come here. It was mainly residences, rich hotels, and cafés. Then, in 1963, the government pumped up the neighborhood's commercial metabolism by bringing in the RER (commuter train). Suburbanites had easy access, and *pfft*—there went the neighborhood.

The *nouveau* Champs-Elysées, revitalized in 1994, has newer benches and lamps, broader sidewalks, all-underground parking, and a fleet of green-suited workers who drive motorized street cleaners. Blink away the modern elements, and it's not hard to imagine the boulevard pre-1963, with only the finest structures lining both sides all the way to the palace gardens.

○ Self-Guided Walk: To reach the top of the Champs-Elysées, take the Métro to the Arc de Triomphe (Mo: Charles de Gaulle-Etoile), then saunter down the grand boulevard (Métro stops every few blocks, including George V and Franklin D. Roosevelt). If you plan to tour the Arc de Triomphe (see next listing), do it before starting this walk.

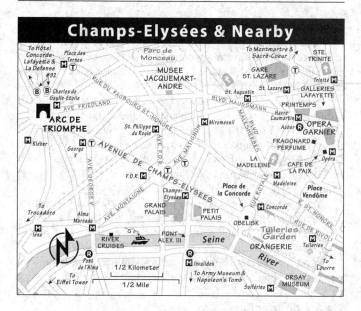

Champs-Elysées & Nearby

Fancy car dealerships include **Peugeot,** at #136 (showing off its futuristic concept cars, often alongside the classic models), and **Mercedes-Benz,** a block down at #118, where you can pick up a Mercedes watch and cufflinks to go with your new car. In the 19th century this was an area for horse stables; today, it's the district of garages, limo companies, and car dealerships. If you're serious about selling cars in France, you must have a showroom on the Champs-Elysées.

Next to Mercedes is the famous **Lido,** Paris' largest cabaret (and a multiplex cinema). You can walk all the way into the lobby. Paris still offers the kind of burlesque-type spectacles that have been performed here since the 19th century, combining music, comedy, and scantily clad women. Movie-going on the Champs-Elysées provides another kind of fun, with theaters showing the very latest releases. Check to see if there are films you recognize, then look for the showings *(séances)*. A "v.o." *(version originale)* next to the time indicates the film will be shown in its original language; a "v.f." stands for *version française.*

The flagship store of leather-bag maker **Louis Vuitton** may be the largest single-brand luxury store in the world. Step inside. The store insists on providing enough salespeople to treat each customer royally—if there's a line, it means shoppers have overwhelmed the place.

Fouquet's café-restaurant (#99), under the red awning, is a popular spot among French celebrities, serving the most expensive shot of espresso I've found in downtown Paris (€8). Opened in 1899 as a coachman's bistro, Fouquet's gained fame as the hangout of France's WWI biplane fighter pilots—those who weren't shot down by Germany's infamous "Red Baron." It also served as James Joyce's dining room.

Since the early 1900s, Fouquet's has been a favorite of French actors and actresses. The golden plaques at the entrance honor winners of France's Oscar-like film awards, the Césars (one is cut into the ground at the end of the carpet). There are plaques for Gérard Depardieu, Catherine Deneuve, Roman Polanski, Juliette Binoche, and several famous Americans (but not Jerry Lewis). More recent winners are shown on the floor just inside.

Ladurée (two blocks downhill at #75) is a classic 19th-century tea salon/restaurant/*pâtisserie*. Non-patrons can discreetly wander around the place, though photos are not allowed. A coffee here is *très élégant* (only €3.50).

From posh cafés to stylish shops, monumental sidewalks to glimmering showrooms, the Champs-Elysées is Paris at its most Parisian.

▲▲Arc de Triomphe

Napoleon had the magnificent Arc de Triomphe commissioned to commemorate his victory at the battle of Austerlitz. There's no triumphal arch bigger (165 feet high, 130 feet wide). And, with 12 converging boulevards, there's no traffic circle more thrilling to experience—either from behind the wheel or on foot (take the underpass).

The foot of the arch is a stage on which the last two centuries of Parisian history have played out—from the funeral of Napoleon to the goose-stepping arrival of the Nazis to the triumphant return of Charles de Gaulle after the Allied liberation. Examine the carvings on the pillars, featuring a mighty Napoleon and excitable Lady Liberty. Pay your respects at the Tomb of the Unknown Soldier. Then climb the 284 steps to the observation deck up top, with sweeping skyline panoramas and a mesmerizing view down onto the traffic that swirls around the arch.

Cost and Hours: Outside and at the base—free, always viewable; steps to rooftop—€9.50, under 18 free, free on first Sun of month Oct-March, covered by Museum Pass; daily April-Sept 10:00-23:00, Oct-March 10:00-22:30, last entry 45 minutes before closing; Place Charles de Gaulle, use underpass to reach arch, Mo: Charles de Gaulle-Etoile, tel. 01 55 37 73 77, www.arc-de-triomphe.monuments-nationaux.fr.

Avoiding Lines: Bypass the slooow ticket line with your Museum Pass (though if you have kids, you'll need to line up to get the free tickets for children). There may be another line (that you can't skip) at the entrance to the stairway up the arch. Lines disappear after 17:00—come for sunset.

▲Opéra Garnier

This gleaming grand theater of the belle époque was built for Napoleon III and finished in 1875. (For the best view, stand in front of the Opéra Métro stop.) From Avenue de l'Opéra, once lined with Paris' most fashionable haunts, the facade suggests "all power to the wealthy." And a shimmering Apollo, holding his lyre high above the building, seems to declare, "This is a temple of the highest arts."

Cost and Hours: €9, not covered by Museum Pass, erratic hours due to performances and rehearsals, but generally daily 10:00-17:00, mid-July-Aug until 18:00, last entry 30 minutes before closing, 8 Rue Scribe, Mo: Opéra, RER: Auber.

Tours: English tours of the building run during summer and off-season on weekends and Wed, usually at 11:30 and 14:30—call to confirm schedule (€13.50, includes entry, 1.5 hours, tel. 01 40 01 17 89 or 08 25 05 44 05, press 2 for tours).

Visiting the Theater: You'll enter around the left side of the building—as you face the front, find the red carpet across from American Express on Rue Scribe. As you pass the bust of the architect, Monsieur Garnier, pay your respects and check out the bronze floor plan of the complex etched below. Notice how little space is given to seating.

The building is huge—though the auditorium itself seats only 2,000. The real show was before and after the performance, when the elite of Paris—out to see and be seen—strutted their elegant stuff in the extravagant lobbies. Think of the grand marble stairway as a theater. As you wander the halls and gawk at the decor, imagine this place in its heyday, filled with beautiful people. The massive foundations straddle an underground lake (inspiring the mysterious world of the *Phantom of the Opera*). Visitors can peek from two boxes into the actual red-velvet performance hall to view Marc Chagall's colorful ceiling (1964) playfully dancing around the eight-ton chandelier (guided tours take you into the performance hall; you can't enter when they're changing out the stage). Note the box seats next to the stage—the most expensive in the house, with an obstructed view of the stage...but just right if you're here only to be seen.

The elitism of this place prompted former President François Mitterrand to have an opera house built for the people in the 1980s, situated symbolically on Place de la Bastille, where the French Revolution started in 1789. This left the Opéra Garnier home only to ballet and occasional concerts. The library/museum will interest opera buffs, but anyone will enjoy the second-floor grand foyer and Salon du Glacier, iced with decor typical of 1900.

PARIS

Nearby: The Fragonard Perfume Museum (described next) is on the left side of the Opéra, and the venerable Galeries Lafayette department store (marvelous views from roof terrace) is just behind. Across the street, the illustrious Café de la Paix has been a meeting spot for the local glitterati for generations. If you can afford the coffee, this spot offers a delightful break.

Fragonard Perfume Museum

Near Opéra Garnier, this perfume shop masquerades as a museum. Housed in a beautiful 19th-century mansion, it's the best-smelling museum in Paris—and you'll learn a little about how perfume is made, too (ask for the English handout).

Cost and Hours: Free, Mon-Sat 9:00-18:00, Sun 9:00-17:00, 9 Rue Scribe, Mo: Opéra, RER: Auber, tel. 01 47 42 04 56, www.fragonard.com.

▲▲Jacquemart-André Museum (Musée Jacquemart-André)

This thoroughly enjoyable museum (with an elegant café) showcases the lavish home of a wealthy, art-loving, 19th-century Parisian couple. After wandering the grand boulevards, get inside for an intimate look at the lifestyles of the Parisian rich and fabulous. Edouard André and his wife Nélie Jacquemart—who had no children—spent their lives and fortunes designing, building, and then decorating this sumptuous mansion. What makes the visit so rewarding is the excellent audioguide tour (in English, included with admission—plan on spending an hour with the audioguide). The place is strewn with paintings by Rembrandt, Botticelli, Uccello, Mantegna, Bellini, Boucher, and Fragonard—enough to make a painting gallery famous.

Cost and Hours: €11, includes audioguide, not covered by Museum Pass; daily 10:00-18:00, Mon and Sat until 21:00 during special exhibits; can avoid lines by purchasing tickets online (€2 fee) and printing receipt, 158 Boulevard Haussmann, Mo: Miromesnil or St. Philippe-du-Roule, bus #80 makes a convenient connection to Ecole Militaire; tel. 01 45 62 11 59, www.musee-jacquemart-andre.com.

After Your Visit: Consider a break in the sumptuous museum tearoom, with delicious cakes and tea (daily 11:45-17:30). From here walk north on Rue de Courcelles to see Paris' most beautiful park, Parc Monceau.

▲Petit Palais (and its Musée des Beaux-Arts)

This free museum displays a broad collection of paintings and sculpture from the 1600s to the 1900s. It's a museum of second-choice art, but the building itself is impressive, and there are a few 19th-century diamonds in the rough, including pieces by Courbet, Monet, the American painter Mary Cassatt, and other Impressionists. The Palais also has a pleasant garden courtyard and café.

Cost and Hours: Free, Tue-Sun 10:00-18:00, Thu until 20:00 for temporary exhibitions, closed Mon; across from Grand Palais on Avenue Winston Churchill, a looooong block west of Place de la Concorde; tel. 01 53 43 40 00, www.petitpalais.paris.fr.

Grand Palais

This grand exhibition hall, built for the 1900 World's Fair, is used for temporary exhibits. The building's Industrial Age, erector-set, iron-and-glass exterior is striking, but the steep entry price is only worthwhile if you're interested in any of the several different exhibitions (each with different hours and costs, located in various parts of the building). Many areas are undergoing renovations, which may still be under way during your visit. Get details on the current schedule from a TI, in *Pariscope,* or from the website.

Cost and Hours: Admission prices and hours vary with each exhibition; major exhibitions usually €11, not covered by Museum Pass; generally open daily 10:00-20:00, Wed until 22:00, some parts of building closed Mon, other parts closed Tue, closed between exhibitions; Avenue Winston Churchill, Mo: Rond Point or Champs-Elysées, tel. 01 44 13 17 17, www.grandpalais.fr.

▲La Défense and La Grande Arche

Though Paris keeps its historic center classic and skyscraper-free, this district, nicknamed "le petit Manhattan," offers an impressive excursion into a side of Paris few tourists see: that of a modern-day economic superpower. La Défense was first conceived more than 60 years ago as a US-style forest of skyscrapers that would accommodate the business needs of the modern world. Today La Défense is a thriving commercial and shopping center, home to 150,000 employees and 55,000 residents.

For an interesting visit, take the Métro to the La Défense Grande Arche stop, follow *Sortie Grande Arche* signs, and climb the steps of La Grande Arche for distant city views. Then stroll gradually downhill among the glass buildings to the Esplanade de la Défense Métro station, and return home from there.

La Grande Arche de la Fraternité: This is the centerpiece of this ambitious complex. Inaugurated in 1989 on the 200th anniversary of the French Revolution, it was, like the Revolution, dedicated to human rights and brotherhood. The place is big—Notre-Dame Cathedral could fit under its arch. The "cloud"—a huge canvas canopy under the arch—is an attempt to cut down on the wind-tunnel effect this gigantic building creates.

Lunch on the Steps: Join the locals and picnic on the arch steps; good to-go places are plentiful (and cafés are nearby).

The Esplanade: La Défense is much more than its eye-catching arch. Survey the skyscraping scene from the top of the steps. Wander from the arch back toward the city center (and to the next

PARIS

Métro stop) along the Esplanade (a.k.a. "le Parvis"). The Esplanade is a virtual open-air modern art gallery, sporting pieces by Joan Miró (blue, red, and yellow), Alexander Calder (red), and Yaacov Agam (the fountain with colorful stripes and rhythmically dancing spouts), among others. *La Défense de Paris*, the statue that gave the area its name, recalls the 1871 Franco-Prussian war—it's a rare bit of old Paris out here in the 'burbs.

As you descend the Esplanade, notice how the small gardens and *boules* courts (reddish dirt areas) are designed to integrate tradition into this celebration of modern commerce. Note also how the buildings decrease in height and increase in age—the Nexity Tower (closest to central Paris) looks old compared to the other skyscrapers. Dating from the 1960s, it was one of the first buildings at La Défense. Your walk ends at the amusing fountain of Bassin Takis, where you'll find the Esplanade de la Défense Métro station that zips you out of all this modernity and directly back into town.

Marais Neighborhood and Nearby

The Marais neighborhood extends along the Right Bank of the Seine, from the Pompidou Center to the Bastille, the prison of Revolution fame. But don't waste time looking for the Bastille; the building is long gone, and just the square remains. With more pre-Revolutionary lanes and buildings than anywhere else in town, the Marais is more atmospheric than touristy. It's medieval Paris, and the haunt of the old nobility. During the reign of Henry IV, this area—originally a swamp *(marais)*—became the hometown of the French aristocracy. In the 17th century, big shots built their private mansions *(hôtels)* close to Henry's stylish Place des Vosges.

With the Revolution, the aristocratic splendor of this quarter passed, and the Marais became a dumpy bohemian quarter so sordid it was nearly slated for destruction. In the mid-1800s, the wrecking ball was poised over the Marais: Napoleon III had ordered Baron Georges-Eugène Haussmann to modernize Paris by blasting out narrow streets to construct broad boulevards (wide enough for the big guns of the army, too wide for revolutionary barricades). By 1910, the renovation was almost complete, and a big boulevard was planned to slice right through the Marais. But then the march of "progress" was halted by one tiny little event—World War I.

Today the Marais is a thriving, trendy, real community—home to fashion boutiques, quiet cafés, Jewish bakeries, nightlife, and actual Parisians. When strolling the Marais, stick to the west-east axis formed by Rue Ste. Croix de la Bretonnerie, Rue des Rosiers (heart of Paris' Jewish community), and Rue St. Antoine. On

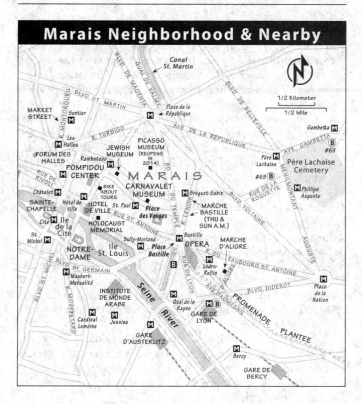

Marais Neighborhood & Nearby

Sunday afternoons, this trendy area pulses with shoppers and café crowds.

Place des Vosges and West

The following sights are listed roughly in geographical order from east to west, starting at the heart of the Marais.

▲Place des Vosges

Henry IV (r. 1589-1610) built this centerpiece of the Marais in 1605 and called it "Place Royal." As he'd hoped, it turned the Marais into Paris' most exclusive neighborhood. Walk to the center, where Louis XIII, on horseback, gestures, "Look at this wonderful square my dad built." He's surrounded by locals enjoying their community park. You'll see children frolicking in the sandbox, lovers warming benches, and pigeons guarding their fountains while trees shade this escape from the glare of the big city (you can refill your water bottle in the center of the square).

Study the architecture: nine pavilions (houses) per side. The two highest—at the front and back—were for the king and queen (but were never used). Warm red brickwork—some real, some fake—is topped with sloped slate roofs, chimneys, and another quaint relic of a bygone era: TV antennas. The insightful writer **Victor Hugo** lived at #6—at the southeast corner of the square, marked by the French flag—from 1832 to 1848. This was when he wrote much of his most important work, including his biggest hit, *Les Misérables*. Inside you'll wander through eight plush rooms and enjoy a fine view of the square (free, fee for optional exhibits—usually about €7, and usually not worth paying for, audioguide-€5, Tue-Sun 10:00-18:00, closed Mon, last entry at 17:40, 6 Place des Vosges; Mo: Bastille, St. Paul, or Chemin Vert; tel. 01 42 72 10 16, www.musee-hugo.paris.fr).

Sample the upscale art galleries ringing the square, then exit the square at its northwest corner, and head west on Rue des Francs-Bourgeois.

▲Carnavalet Museum (Musée Carnavalet)

At the Carnavalet Museum, French history unfolds in a series of stills—like a Ken Burns documentary, except you have to walk. The Revolution is the highlight, but you get a good overview of everything—from Louis XIV-period rooms to Napoleon to the belle époque. Though explanations are in French only, many displays are fairly self-explanatory.

The Revolution section is the best. No period of history is as charged with the full range of human drama: bloodshed, martyrdom, daring speeches, murdered priests, emancipated women, backstabbing former friends—all in the name of government "by, for, and of the people."

You'll see paintings of the Estates-General assembly that planted the seeds of democracy and a model of the Bastille, the hated prison that was the symbol of oppression. Read the "Declaration of the Rights of Man." See pictures of the ill-fated King Louis XVI and Queen Marie-Antoinette, and the fate that awaited them—the guillotine. You'll see portraits of all the major players in the Revolutionary spectacle—Maximilien de Robespierre, Georges Danton, Charlotte Corday—as well as the dashing general who would inherit democracy and turn it into dictatorship...Napoleon Bonaparte.

Cost and Hours: Free, fee for some temporary (but optional) exhibits, audioguide-€5, Tue-Sun 10:00-18:00, closed Mon; avoid lunchtime (12:30-14:30), when many rooms may be closed; 23 Rue de Sévigné, Mo: St. Paul, tel. 01 44 59 58 58, www.carnavalet.paris.fr.

▲▲Picasso Museum (Musée Picasso)

This museum has been closed for a major renovation but should reopen in time for your visit. It contains the world's largest collection of Picasso's paintings, sculptures, sketches, and ceramics, along with his small collection of Impressionist art. Tucked into a corner of the Marais, it's worth ▲▲▲ if you're a Picasso fan. When the museum reopens, its exhibition space will be much larger; more than 500 of Picasso's works will be on view over four floors. Room-by-room English introductions will help make sense of Picasso's artwork—from the Toulouse-Lautrec-like portraits at the beginning of his career to his gray-brown Cubist period to his return-to-childhood, Salvador Dalí-like finish.

Cost and Hours: Entry about €10, likely covered by Museum Pass, additional fees for temporary exhibits, hours likely Wed-Mon 9:30-18:00, may be closed Tue, confirm cost and hours prior to your visit; 5 rue de Thorigny, Mo: St. Paul or Chemin Vert, tel. 01 42 71 25 21, www.musee-picasso.fr.

Rue des Rosiers: Paris' Jewish Quarter

This tiny yet colorful Jewish district of the Marais was once considered the largest in Western Europe. Today, Rue des Rosiers is lined with Jewish shops and kosher eateries, and the district is being squeezed by the trendy boutiques of modern Paris. Visit any day but Saturday, when most businesses are closed—it's best on Sunday. The intersection of Rue des Rosiers and Rue des Ecouffes marks the heart of the small neighborhood that Jews call the Pletzl ("little square"). Lively Rue des Ecouffes, named for a bird of prey, is a derogatory nod to the moneychangers' shops that once lined this lane.

Eating: If you're visiting at lunchtime, you'll be tempted by kosher pizza and plenty of cheap fast-food joints selling falafel "to go" *(emporter)*. **L'As du Falafel,** with its bustling New York deli atmosphere, is terrific (at #34, sit-down or to go). The **Sacha Finkelsztajn** Yiddish bakery at #27 is also good (Polish and Russian cuisine, pop in for a tempting treat, sit for the same price as takeaway). Nearby, the recommended **Chez Marianne** cooks up traditional Jewish meals and serves excellent falafel to go (at corner of Rue des Rosiers and Rue des Hospitalières-St-Gervais).

▲Jewish Art and History Museum
(Musée d'Art et Histoire du Judaïsme)

This fine museum, located in a beautifully restored Marais mansion, tells the story of Judaism in France and throughout Europe, from the Roman destruction of Jerusalem to the theft of famous artworks during World War II. Displays illustrate the cultural unity maintained by this continually dispersed population. You'll learn about the history of Jewish traditions, from bar mitzvahs to menorahs, and see the exquisite traditional costumes and objects central to daily life. The museum also displays paintings by famous Jewish artists, including Marc Chagall, Amedeo Modigliani, and Chaim Soutine. The English explanations posted in many rooms

PARIS

provide sufficient explanation for most; the included audioguide provides greater detail.

Cost and Hours: €7, includes audioguide, covered by Museum Pass, Sun-Fri 11:00-18:00, closed Sat, last entry 45 minutes before closing, 71 Rue du Temple; Mo: Rambuteau or Hôtel de Ville a few blocks farther away, RER: Châtelet-Les Halles; tel. 01 53 01 86 60, www.mahj.org.

Holocaust Memorial (Mémorial de la Shoah)

This sight commemorates the lives of the more than 76,000 Jews deported from France in World War II. It has several facets: a WWII deportation memorial, a museum on the Holocaust, and a Jewish resource center. Displaying original deportation records, the museum takes you through the history of Jews in Europe and France, from medieval pogroms to the Nazi era. But its focal point is underground, where victims' ashes are buried.

Cost and Hours: Free, Sun-Fri 10:00-18:00, Thu until 22:00, closed Sat and certain Jewish holidays, south of Rue de Rivoli at 17 Rue Geoffroy l'Asnier, tel. 01 42 77 44 72, www.memorialdelashoah.org.

▲▲Pompidou Center (Centre Pompidou)

One of Europe's greatest collections of far-out modern art is housed in the Musée National d'Art Moderne, on the fourth and fifth floors of this colorful exhibition hall. The building itself is "exoskeletal" (like Notre-Dame or a crab), with its functional parts—the pipes, heating ducts, and escalator—on the outside and the meaty art inside. It's the epitome of Modern architecture, where "form follows function." Created ahead of its time, the 20th-century art in this collection is still waiting for the world to catch up.

Cost and Hours: €11-13 depending on current exhibits, free on first Sun of month, Museum Pass covers permanent collection and view escalators, €3 Panorama Ticket lets you ride to the top for the view (doesn't include museum entry); Wed-Mon 11:00-21:00, closed Tue, ticket counters close at 20:00, arrive after 17:00 to avoid crowds (mainly for special exhibits); café on mezzanine, pricey view restaurant on Level 6, Mo: Rambuteau or farther-away Hôtel de Ville, tel. 01 44 78 12 33, www.centrepompidou.fr.

Visiting the Museum: Buy your ticket on the ground floor, then ride up the escalator (or run up the down escalator to get in the proper mood). When you see the view, your opinion of the Pompidou's exterior should improve a good 15 percent. Find the permanent collection—the entrance is either on the fourth or fifth floor (it varies). Enter, show your ticket, and get the current floor plan *(plan du musée)*.

The 20th century—accelerated by technology and fragmented by war—was exciting and chaotic, and the art reflects the turbulence of that century of change. In this free-flowing and airy museum, you'll come face-to-face with works from the first half of the 20th century, including pieces by Pablo Picasso, Marc Chagall, Henri Matisse, Wassily Kandinsky, Piet Mondrian, Paul Klee, Salvador Dalí, Max Ernst, Jackson Pollock, and many more.

The contemporary collection highlights post-1960 works, including Andy Warhol's pop art. You'll also see fewer traditional canvases or sculptures and lots of mixed-media work, combining painting, sculpture, welding, photography, video, computer programming, new resins, plastics, industrial techniques, and lighting and sound systems. Even skeptics of modern art will find that after so many Madonnas-and-children, a piano smashed to bits and glued to the wall is refreshing.

View from the Pompidou: Ride the escalator for a great city view from the top (ticket or Museum Pass required).

Nearby: The Pompidou Center and the square that fronts it are lively, with lots of people, street theater, and activity inside and out—a perpetual street fair. Kids of any age enjoy the fun, colorful fountain (called *Homage to Stravinsky*) next to the Pompidou Center.

Hôtel de Ville

Looking more like a grand château than a public building, Paris' city hall stands proudly on the river (a few blocks south of the Pompidou Center). The Renaissance-style building (built 1533-1628, and reconstructed after a 19th-century fire) displays hundreds of statues of famous Parisians on its facade. Peek through the doors to see elaborate spiral stairways reminiscent of Château de Chambord in the Loire. Playful fountains energize the big, lively square in front.

This spacious stage has seen much of Paris' history. On July 14, 1789, Revolutionaries rallied here on their way to the Bastille. In 1870, it was home to the radical Paris Commune. During World War II, General Charles de Gaulle appeared at the windows to proclaim Paris' liberation from the Nazis. And in 1950, Robert Doisneau snapped a famous black-and-white photo of a kissing couple, with Hôtel de Ville as a romantic backdrop.

Today, this is the symbolic heart of the city of Paris. Demonstrators gather here to speak their minds. Crowds cheer during big soccer games shown on huge TV screens. In summer, the square hosts sand volleyball courts; in winter, a big ice-skating rink. And year-round, the place is always beautifully lit after dark.

PARIS

East of Place des Vosges

Promenade Plantée Park (Viaduc des Arts)

This two-mile-long, narrow garden walk on an elevated viaduct was once used for train tracks and is now a fine place for a refreshing stroll or run. Botanists appreciate the well-maintained and varying vegetation. From west (near Opéra) to east, the first half of the path is elevated until the midway point, the pleasant Jardin de Reuilly (a good stopping point for most, near Mo: Dugommier), then it continues on street level—with separate paths for pedestrians and cyclists—out to Paris' ring road, the *périphérique*.

Cost and Hours: Free, opens Mon-Fri at 8:00, Sat-Sun at 9:00, closes at sunset (17:30 in winter, 20:30 in summer). It runs from Place de la Bastille (Mo: Bastille) along Avenue Daumesnil to St. Mandé (Mo: Michel Bizot) or Porte Dorée, passing within a block of Gare de Lyon.

Getting There: To get to the park from Place de la Bastille (exit the Métro following *Sortie Rue de Lyon* signs), walk a looooong block down Rue de Lyon hugging the Opéra on your left. Find the low-key entry and steps up the red-brick wall a block after the Opéra.

▲**Père Lachaise Cemetery (Cimetière du Père Lachaise)**
Littered with the tombstones of many of the city's most illustrious dead, this is your best one-stop look at Paris' fascinating, romantic past residents. Enclosed by a massive wall and lined with 5,000 trees, the peaceful, car-free lanes and dirt paths of Père Lachaise cemetery encourage park-like meandering. Named for Father *(Père)* La Chaise, whose job was listening to Louis XIV's sins, the cemetery is relatively new, having opened in 1804 to accommodate Paris' expansion. Today, this city of the dead (pop. 70,000) still accepts new residents, but real estate prices are sky high (a 21-square-foot plot costs more than €11,000).

The 100-acre cemetery is big and confusing, with thousands of graves and tombs crammed every which way, and only a few pedestrian pathways to help you navigate. The maps available from any of the nearby florists help direct you to the graves of Frédéric Chopin, Molière, Edith Piaf, Oscar Wilde, Gertrude Stein, Jim Morrison, Héloïse and Abélard, and many more.

Cost and Hours: Free, Mon-Fri 8:00-18:00, Sat 8:30-18:00, Sun 9:00-18:00, closes at 17:30 in winter, last entry 15 minutes before closing; two blocks from Mo: Gambetta (not Mo: Père Lachaise) and two blocks from bus #69's last stop; tel. 01 55 25 82 10, searchable map available at non-official website: www.pere-lachaise.com.

Montmartre

Stroll along Paris' highest hilltop (420 feet) for a different perspective on the City of Light. Walk in the footsteps of the people who've lived here—monks stomping grapes (1200s), farmers grinding grain in windmills (1600s), dust-coated gypsum miners (1700s), Parisian liberals (1800s), Modernist painters (1900s), and all the struggling artists, poets, dreamers, and drunkards who came here for cheap rent, untaxed booze, rustic landscapes, and cabaret nightlife. With vineyards, wheat fields, windmills, animals, and a village tempo of life, it was the perfect escape from grimy Paris.

For restaurant recommendations in this area, see page 367.

▲▲Sacré-Cœur

The Sacré-Cœur (Sacred Heart) Basilica's exterior, with its onion domes and bleached-bone pallor, looks ancient, but was finished only a century ago by Parisians humiliated by German invaders. Otto von Bismarck's Prussian army laid siege to Paris for more than four months in 1870. Things got so bad for residents that urban hunting for dinner (to cook up dogs, cats, and finally rats) became accepted behavior. Convinced they were being punished for the country's liberal sins, France's Catholics raised money to build the church as a "praise the Lord anyway" gesture.

The five-domed, Roman-Byzantine-looking basilica took 44 years to build (1875-1919). It stands on a foundation of 83 pillars sunk 130 feet deep, necessary because the ground beneath was honeycombed with gypsum mines. The exterior is laced with gypsum, which whitens with age.

Take a clockwise spin around the crowded interior to see impressive mosaics, and to give St. Peter's bronze foot a rub. For an unobstructed panoramic view of Paris, climb 260 feet (300 steps) up the tight and claustrophobic spiral stairs to the top of the dome (especially worthwhile if you have kids with excess energy).

Cost and Hours: Church—free, daily 6:00-22:30, last entry at 22:15; dome—€6, not covered by Museum Pass, daily May-Sept 9:00-19:00, Oct-April 9:00-17:00; tel. 01 53 41 89 00, www.sacre-coeur-montmartre.com.

Getting There: You have several options. You can take the Métro to the Anvers stop (to avoid the stairs up to Sacré-Cœur, buy one more Métro ticket and ride the funicular, though it's sometimes closed for maintenance). The Abbesses stop is closer but less scenic. Or you can go to Place Pigalle, then take the tiny electric Montmartrobus, which drops you right by Place du Tertre, near Sacré-Cœur (costs one Métro ticket, 4/hour). A taxi to the top of the hill saves time and avoids sweat (about €13, €20 at night).

The Heart of Montmartre

Montmartre's main square **(Place du Tertre),** one block from the church, was once the haunt of Henri de Toulouse-Lautrec and the original bohemians. Today, it's mobbed with tourists and unoriginal bohemians, but it's still fun (to beat the crowds, go on a weekday or early on weekend mornings). From here, head up Rue des Saules to find Paris' lone vineyard and the **Montmartre Museum** (described later). Return uphill, then follow Rue Lepic down to the old windmill, **Moulin de la Galette,** which once pressed monks'

PARIS

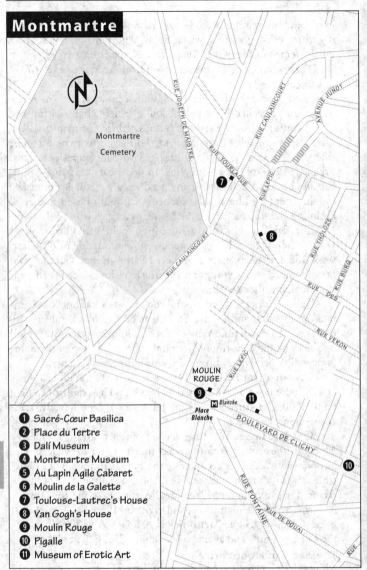

Montmartre

Montmartre Cemetery

MOULIN ROUGE

Place Blanche

Blanche

BOULEVARD DE CLICHY

1 Sacré-Cœur Basilica
2 Place du Tertre
3 Dalí Museum
4 Montmartre Museum
5 Au Lapin Agile Cabaret
6 Moulin de la Galette
7 Toulouse-Lautrec's House
8 Van Gogh's House
9 Moulin Rouge
10 Pigalle
11 Museum of Erotic Art

PARIS

grapes and farmers' grain, and crushed gypsum rocks into powdery plaster of Paris (there were once 30 windmills on Montmartre). When the gypsum mines closed (c. 1850) and the vineyards sprouted apartments, this windmill turned into the ceremonial centerpiece of a popular outdoor dance hall. Farther down Rue Lepic, you'll pass near the former homes of **Toulouse-Lautrec** (at Rue Tourlaque—look for the brick-framed art-studio windows under the heavy mansard roof) and **Vincent van Gogh** (54 Rue Lepic).

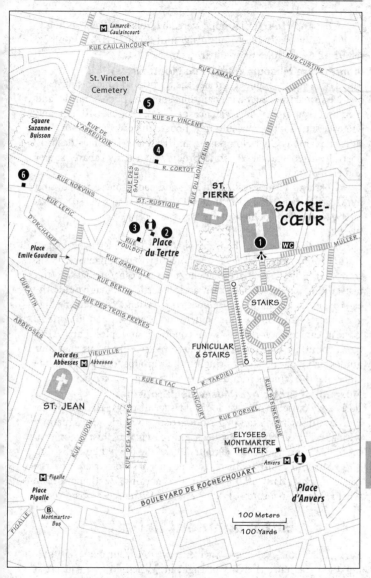

Dalí Museum (L'Espace Dalí)

This beautifully lit black gallery (well-described in English) offers a walk through statues, etchings, and paintings by the master of Surrealism. The Spaniard found fame in Paris in the 1920s and '30s. He lived in Montmartre for a while, hung with the Surrealist crowd in Montparnasse, and shocked the world with his dreamscape paintings and experimental films. Don't miss the printed interview on the exit stairs.

Cost and Hours: €11, not covered by Museum Pass, audioguide-€3, daily 10:00-18:00, July-Aug until 20:00, 11 Rue Poulbot, tel. 01 42 64 40 10, www.daliparis.com.

Montmartre Museum (Musée de Montmartre)

This 17th-century home re-creates the traditional cancan-and-cabaret Montmartre scene, with paintings, posters, photos, music, and memorabilia. Once the residence of Pierre-Auguste Renoir and Maurice Utrillo, the museum now houses the original *Lapin Agile* sign, the famous Chat Noir poster, and Toulouse-Lautrec's dashing portrait of red-scarved Aristide Bruant, the earthy cabaret singer and club owner.

Cost and Hours: €8, includes good audioguide, not covered by Museum Pass, daily 10:00-18:00, 12 Rue Cortot, tel. 01 49 25 89 39, www.museedemontmartre.fr.

Pigalle

Paris' red light district, the infamous "Pig Alley," is at the foot of Butte Montmartre. *Ooh la la.* It's more racy than dangerous. Walk from Place Pigalle to Place Blanche, teasing desperate barkers and fast-talking temptresses. In bars, a €150 bottle of (what would otherwise be) cheap champagne comes with a friend. Stick to the bigger streets, hang on to your wallet, and exercise good judgment. Cancan can cost a fortune, as can con artists in topless bars. After dark, countless tour buses line the streets, reminding us that tour guides make big bucks by bringing their groups to touristy nightclubs like the famous Moulin Rouge (Mo: Pigalle or Abbesses).

Museum of Erotic Art (Musée de l'Erotisme)

Paris' sexy museum has five floors of risqué displays—mostly paintings and drawings—ranging from artistic to erotic to disgusting, with a few circa-1920 porn videos and a fascinating history of local brothels tossed in. It's in the center of the Pigalle red light district.

Cost and Hours: €10, €7 online, no...it's not covered by the Museum Pass, daily 10:00-2:00 in the morning, 72 Boulevard de Clichy, Mo: Blanche, tel. 01 42 58 28 73, www.musee-erotisme.com.

Entertainment in Paris

Paris is brilliant after dark. Save energy from your day's sightseeing and experience the City of Light lit. Whether it's a concert at Sainte-Chapelle, a boat ride on the Seine, a walk in Montmartre, a hike up the Arc de Triomphe, or a late-night café, you'll see Paris at its best. Night walks in Paris are wonderful.

Adjust your expectations to the changing times. Paris will always be the City of Light, but it shines a little dimmer these days. In an effort to go green and save money, Paris has toned down the lighting on several monuments, including the Arc de Triomphe and the Louvre's glass pyramid.

Music
Jazz and Blues Clubs

With a lively mix of American, French, and international musicians, Paris has been an internationally acclaimed jazz capital since World War II. You'll pay €12-25 to enter a jazz club (may include one drink; if not, expect to pay €5-10 per drink; beer is cheapest). See *Pariscope* magazine under "Musique" for listings, or, even better, the *Paris Voice* website for a good monthly review (www.parisvoice.com). You can also check Time Out's website (www.timeout.fr/paris) or each club's website (all have English versions), or drop by the clubs to check out the calendars posted on their front doors. Music starts after 21:00 in most clubs. Some offer dinner concerts from about 20:30 on. Here are several good bets:

Caveau de la Huchette, a characteristic old jazz/dance club, fills an ancient Latin Quarter cellar with live jazz and frenzied dancing every night (admission about €12 on weekdays, €14 on weekends, €6-8 drinks, daily 21:30-2:30 in the morning or later, 5 Rue de la Huchette, Mo: St. Michel, recorded info tel. 01 43 26 65 05, www.caveaudelahuchette.fr).

Autour de Midi et Minuit is a an Old World bistro at the foot of Montmartre, sitting above a *cave à jazz*. Eat upstairs if you like (see page 368 for details), then make your way down to the basement to find bubbling jam sessions on Tuesday and Wednesday and concerts on Thursday, Friday, and Saturday (no cover, €5 minimum Tue-Wed; €16 cover Thu-Sat includes one drink; jam sessions at 21:30, concerts usually at 22:00; no music Sun-Mon; 11 Rue Lepic, Mo: Blanche or Abbesses, tel. 01 55 79 16 48, www.autourdemidi.fr).

For a spot teeming with late-night activity and jazz, go to the two-block-long Rue des Lombards, at Boulevard Sébastopol, midway between the river and the Pompidou Center (Mo: Châtelet). **Au Duc des Lombards** is one of the most popular and respected jazz clubs in Paris, with concerts nightly in a great, plush, 110-seat theater-like setting (admission €20-30, buy online and arrive early for best seats, cheap drinks, shows at 20:00 and 22:00, 42 Rue des Lombards, tel. 01 42 33 22 88, www.ducdeslombards.fr). **Le Sunside,** run for 18 years by Stephane Portet, is just a block away. The club offers two little stages (ground floor and downstairs): "le Sunset" stage tends toward contemporary world jazz; "le Sunside" stage features more traditional and acoustic jazz (concerts range from free to €25, check their website; generally at 20:00, 21:00, and 22:00; 60 Rue des Lombards, tel. 01 40 26 46 60, www.sunset-sunside.com).

For a less pricey—and less central—concert club, try **Utopia.** From the outside it's a hole in the wall, but inside it's filled with devoted fans of rock and folk blues. Though Utopia is officially a private club (and one that permits smoking), you can pay €3 to join

PARIS

for an evening, then pay a reasonable charge for the concert (usually €10 or under, concerts start about 22:00). It's located in the Montparnasse area (79 Rue de l'Ouest, Mo: Pernety, tel. 01 43 22 79 66, www.utopia-cafeconcert.fr).

Old-Time Parisian Cabaret on Montmartre: Au Lapin Agile

This historic little cabaret tries its best to maintain the atmosphere of the heady days when bohemians would gather here to enjoy wine, song, and sexy jokes. Today, you'll mix in with a few locals and many tourists (the Japanese love the place) for a drink and as many as 10 different performers—mostly singers with a piano. Performers range from sweet and innocent Amélie types to naughty Maurice Chevalier types. And though tourists are welcome, there's no accommodation for English speakers (except on their website), so non-French-speakers will be lost. You sit at carved wooden tables in a dimly lit room, taste the traditional drink (a small brandy with cherries), and are immersed in an old-time Parisian ambience. The soirée covers traditional French standards, love ballads, sea chanteys, and more (€24, €7 drinks, Tue-Sun 21:00-2:00 in the morning, closed Mon, best to reserve ahead, 22 Rue des Saules, tel. 01 46 06 85 87, www.au-lapin-agile.com).

Classical Concerts

For classical music on any night, consult *Pariscope* magazine (check "Concerts Classiques" under "Musique" for listings), and look for posters at tourist-oriented churches.

From March through November, these churches regularly host concerts: St. Sulpice, St. Germain-des-Prés, La Madeleine, St. Eustache, St. Julien-le-Pauvre, and Sainte-Chapelle.

Sainte-Chapelle: Enjoy the pleasure of hearing Mozart, Bach, or Vivaldi, surrounded by 800 years of stained glass (unheated—bring a sweater). The acoustical quality is surprisingly good. There are usually two concerts per evening, at 19:00 and 20:30; specify which one you want when you buy or reserve your ticket. VIP tickets get you a seat in the first eight rows (€40), Prestige tickets cover the next 15 rows (€30) and Normal tickets are the last five rows (€16). Seats are unassigned within each section, so arrive at least 30 minutes early to get through the security line and snare a good view.

You can book at the box office, by phone, or online. Two different companies present concerts, but the schedule will tell you who to contact for tickets to a particular performance. The small box office (with schedules and tickets) is to the left of the chapel entrance gate (4 Boulevard du Palais, Mo: Cité), or call 01 42 77 65 65 or 06 67 30 65 65 for schedules and reservations. You can leave your message in English—just speak clearly and spell your name. You can check schedules at www.archetspf.asso.fr, but if you want to book online, visit www.classictic.com, which lets you con-

PARIS

veniently print out your email confirmation as your ticket. Flavien from Euromusic offers last-minute discounts with this book when seats are available (limit 2 tickets per book). VIP tickets are discounted to €30 and Prestige tickets to €25. The offer applies only to Euromusic concerts and must be purchased with cash only at the Sainte-Chapelle ticket booth close to concert time.

The evening entrance is at 4 Boulevard du Palais, between the gilded gate of the Palais de Justice and the Conciergerie. You'll enter through the law courts hall, directly into the royal upper chapel, just as St. Louis once did.

Salle Pleyel: This concert hall on the Right Bank hosts world-class artists, from string quartets and visiting orchestras to international opera stars. Tickets range from €10 to €150, depending on the artist and seats you choose, and are usually hard to come by, so it's best to order online in advance (252 Rue du Faubourg St. Honoré, Mo: Ternes, tel. 01 42 56 13 13, www.sallepleyel.fr).

Other Venues: Look also for daytime concerts in parks, such as the Luxembourg Garden. Even the Galeries Lafayette department store offers concerts. Many of these concerts are free *(entrée libre)*, such as the Sunday atelier concert sponsored by the American Church (generally Sept-June at 17:00 but not every week and not in Dec, 65 Quai d'Orsay, Mo: Invalides, RER: Pont de l'Alma, tel. 01 40 62 05 00, www.acparis.org).

Opera

Paris is home to two well-respected opera venues. The **Opéra Bastille** is the massive modern opera house that dominates Place de la Bastille. Come here for state-of-the-art special effects and modern interpretations of classic ballets and operas. In the spirit of this everyman's opera, unsold seats are available at a big discount to seniors and students 15 minutes before the show. Standing-room-only tickets for €15 are also sold for some performances (Mo: Bastille). The **Opéra Garnier,** Paris' first opera house, hosts opera and ballet performances. Come here for less expensive tickets and grand belle époque decor (Mo: Opéra). To get tickets for either opera house, it's easiest to reserve online at www.operadeparis.fr, or call 01 71 25 24 23 outside France or toll tel. 08 92 89 90 90 inside France. You can also go directly to the Opéra Bastille's ticket office (open daily 11:00-18:00).

Evening Museum Visits

Various **museums** are open late on different evenings—called *visites nocturnes*—offering the opportunity for more relaxed, less crowded visits: the Louvre (Wed and Fri until 21:45), Orsay (Thu until 21:45), Pompidou Center (Wed-Mon until 21:00), Grand Palais (Wed until 22:00), Holocaust Memorial (Thu until 22:00), Quai Branly (Thu-Sat until 21:00), Rodin Museum (Wed until

20:45), and Marmottan Museum (Thu until 20:00). The Army Museum may be open Tuesdays until 21:00 (April-Sept).

Summer Night Spectacle: An elaborate sound-and-light show (Grandes Eaux Nocturnes) takes place at the Château in Versailles on Saturdays (€23, mid-June-Aug at 21:00, www.chateau-versailles.fr).

Night Walks

Go for an evening walk to best appreciate the City of Light. Break for ice cream, pause at a café, and enjoy the sidewalk entertainers as you join the post-dinner Parisian parade. Remember to avoid poorly lit areas and stick to main thoroughfares. Consider the following suggestions.

▲▲▲Trocadéro and Eiffel Tower

This is one of Paris' most spectacular views at night. Take the Métro to the Trocadéro stop and join the party on Place du Trocadéro for a magnificent view of the glowing Eiffel Tower. It's a festival of hawkers, gawkers, drummers, and entertainers.

Walk down the stairs, passing the fountains and rollerbladers, then cross the river to the base of the tower, well worth the effort even if you don't go up (tower open daily mid-June-Aug until 24:00, Sept-mid-June until 23:00).

From the Eiffel Tower you can stroll through the Champ de Mars park past tourists and romantic couples, and take the Métro home (Ecole Militaire stop, across Avenue de la Motte-Picquet from far southeast corner of park). Or there's a handy RER stop (Champ de Mars-Tour Eiffel) two blocks west of the Eiffel Tower on the river.

▲▲Champs-Elysées and the Arc de Triomphe

The Avenue des Champs-Elysées glows after dark. Start at the Arc de Triomphe (observation deck open daily, April-Sept until 23:00, Oct-March until 22:30), then stroll down Paris' lively grand promenade. A right turn on Avenue George V leads to the Bateaux-Mouches river cruises. A movie on the Champs-Elysées is a fun experience (weekly listings in *Pariscope* under "Cinéma"), and a drink or snack at Renault's futuristic car café is a kick (at #53, toll tel. 08 11 88 28 11).

▲Ile St. Louis and Notre-Dame

This stroll features floodlit views of Notre-Dame and a taste of the Latin Quarter. Take the Métro (line 7) to the Pont Marie stop, then cross Pont Marie to Ile St. Louis. Turn right up Rue St. Louis-en-l'Ile, stopping for dinner—or at least a Berthillon ice cream (at #31) or Amorino Gelati (at #47). At the end of Ile St. Louis, cross Pont St. Louis to Ile de la Cité, with a great view of Notre-Dame. Wander to the Left Bank on Quai de l'Archevêché, and drop down to the river for the best floodlit views. From May through September you'll find several permanently moored barges *(péniches)* that operate as bars. Although I wouldn't eat dinner on one of these barges, the atmosphere is great for a drink, often including live music on weekends (daily until 2:00 in the morning, closed Oct-April, live music often Thu-Sun from 21:00). End your walk on Place du Parvis Notre-Dame in front of Notre-Dame (tower open Sat-Sun until 23:00 in July-Aug), or go back across the river to the Latin Quarter.

Open-Air Sculpture Garden

Day or night, this skinny riverfront park dotted with modern art makes for a pleasant walk, but it's especially fun on balmy evenings in the summer, when you may encounter rock and salsa dancing. It's on the Left Bank across from Ile St. Louis, running between the Arab World Institute and Jardin des Plantes (free, music around 20:00, very weather-dependent, Quai St. Bernard, Mo: Cardinal Lemoine plus an eight-minute walk up Rue Cardinal Lemoine toward the river).

After-Dark Tours

Several companies offer evening tours of Paris. You can take a traditional, mass-produced bus tour for €25 per person, or for a little more (around €100 per couple), take an hour-long, vintage-car tour with a student guide. A pedicab will take you around for €40-50 per hour. Do-it-yourself-ers can save money by hiring a cab for a private tour (€50 for one hour). All options are described below.

▲▲▲Deux Chevaux Car Tours

If rumbling around Paris and sticking your head out of the rolled-back top of a funky old 2CV car *à la* Inspector Clouseau sounds like your kind of fun, do this. Two enterprising companies have assembled a veritable fleet of these "tin-can" cars (France's version of the VW "bug," which hasn't been made since 1985) for giving tourists tours of Paris day and night (Paris Authentic and 4 Roues Sous 1 Parapluie). Night is best. The student-guides are informal, speak English, and are passionate about showing you their city. Appreciate the simplicity of the vehicle you're in. Notice the bare-bones dashboard. Ask your guide to honk the horn, to run the silly little wipers, and to open and close the air vent—*c'est magnifique!* They'll pick you up and drop you at your hotel or wherever you choose. Paris Authentic offers many options (€45/person for 2 people for a 1-hour tour, €33/person for 3 people; €160/couple for a 2-hour tour that includes Montmartre and a bottle of champagne, 10 percent tip is appropriate, 23 Rue Jean-Jacques Rousseau, mobile 06 64 50 44 19, www.parisauthentic.com, infos@parisauthentic.com). 4 Roues Sous 1 Parapluie, which translates to "4 wheels under 1 umbrella," offers comparable tours with candy-colored cars and drivers dressed in striped shirts and berets. Evening tours last 1.5 hours and cost €90 per person for two, €60 per person if you fit three pas-

PARIS

sengers, and €180 if you want the whole backseat to yourself (tel. 08 00 80 06 31, mobile 06 67 32 26 68, www.4roues-sous-1parapluie. com, info@4roues-sous-1parapluie.com)

Pedicab Tours

Experience the City of Light at an escargot's pace with your private chauffeur pedaling a sleek, human-powered tricycle from TripUp Pedicab Tours. Call ahead, book online, or flag one down; they usually work until about 22:00 (€40-50/hour, mobile 06 98 80 69 33, www.tripup.fr, contact@tripup.fr).

▲Nighttime Bus Tours

Below I've listed two different night tours run by the same parent company (Paris Vision). Tickets are sold through your hotel (no booking fee, brochures in lobby) or directly at the Paris Vision office at 214 Rue de Rivoli, across the street from the Tuileries Métro stop.

The nightly **Paris Illuminations** tour is run by Cityrama and connects all the great illuminated sights of Paris with a 100-minute bus tour in 12 languages. The double-decker buses have huge windows, but the most desirable front seats are sometimes reserved for customers who've bought tickets for the overrated Moulin Rouge. Left-side seats are better. Visibility is fine in the rain.

These tours are not for everyone. You'll stampede on with a United Nations of tourists, get a set of headphones, dial up your language, and listen to a tape-recorded spiel (which is interesting, but includes an annoyingly bright TV screen and a pitch for the other, more expensive excursions). Uninspired as it is, the ride provides an entertaining overview of the city at its floodlit and scenic best. Bring your city map to stay oriented as you go. You're always on the bus, but the driver slows for photos at viewpoints (€25, kids-€12.50, 1.75 hours, departs from 2 Rue des Pyramides at 20:00 Nov-March, at 22:00 April-Oct, reserve one day in advance, arrive 30 minutes early to wait in line for best seats, Mo: Pyramides, tel. 01 42 60 30 01, www.pariscityvision.com/en/cityrama/paris-illuminations).

Paris Vision also offers **Paris Illuminations-By Minibus,** which are minivan night tours following a similar route to the bus tours. They will pick you up and drop you off at your hotel (€55, kids-€40, 2 hours, tel. 01 42 60 30 01, www.parisvision.com).

▲▲▲Do-It-Yourself Floodlit Paris Taxi Tour

I recommend a loop trip that takes about an hour and connects these sights: Notre-Dame, Hôtel de Ville, Ile St. Louis, the Orsay Museum, Esplanade des Invalides, Champ de Mars park at Place Jacques Rueff (five-minute stop), Eiffel Tower from Place du Trocadéro (five-minute stop), Arc de Triomphe, Champs-Elysées, Place de la Concorde, and the Louvre. The trip should cost about €45 (taxis have a strict meter of €33/hour plus about €1/kilometer).

Sleeping in Paris

I've focused most of my recommendations in four safe, handy, and colorful neighborhoods: the village-like Rue Cler (near the Eiffel Tower), the artsy and trendy Marais (near Place de la Bastille), the historic island of Ile St. Louis (next door to Notre-Dame), and the lively and Latin yet classy Luxembourg Garden neighborhood (on the Left Bank). Before choosing a hotel, read the descriptions of the neighborhoods closely. Each offers different pros and cons: Your neighborhood is as important as your hotel for the success of your trip.

You'll also find recommendations for good budget accommodations in two more neighborhoods—Montmartre and along lively Rue Mouffetard—plus a few bed-and-breakfast and apartment-rental agencies, and suggestions for sleeping near Paris' airports.

Reserve ahead for Paris—the sooner, the better. In August and at other times when business is slower, some hotels offer lower rates to fill their rooms. Check hotel websites for the best deals.

Old, characteristic, budget Parisian hotels have always been cramped. Retrofitted with toilets, private showers, and elevators (as most are today), they are even more cramped. Get suggestions from your hotelier for safe parking (for parking basics, see page 236).

In the Rue Cler Neighborhood
(7th arrondissement, Mo: Ecole Militaire, La Tour Maubourg, or Invalides)

Rue Cler, lined with open-air produce stands six days a week, is a safe, tidy, village-like pedestrian street. It's so French that when I step out of my hotel in the morning, I feel like I must have been a poodle in a previous life. How such coziness lodged itself between the high-powered government district, the Eiffel Tower, and Les Invalides, I'll never know. This is a neighborhood of wide, tree-lined boulevards, stately apartment buildings, and lots of Americans. The American Church (see page 233), American Library, American University, and many of my readers call this area home. Hotels here are a relatively good value, considering the elegance of the neighborhood and the higher prices of the more cramped hotels in other central areas. And for sightseeing, you're within walking distance of the Eiffel Tower, Army Museum, Quai Branly Museum, Seine River, Champs-Elysées, and Orsay and Rodin museums.

Become a local at a Rue Cler café for breakfast, or join the afternoon crowd for *une bière pression* (a draft beer). On Rue Cler you can eat and browse your way through a street full of cafés, pastry shops, delis, cheese shops, and colorful outdoor produce stalls. Afternoon *boules* (outdoor bowling) on the Esplanade des Invalides is a relaxing spectator sport (look for the dirt area to the upper right

Sleep Code

(€1 = about $1.30, country code: 33)
S = Single, **D** = Double/Twin, **T** = Triple, **Q** = Quad, **b** = bathroom, **s** = shower only, ***** = French hotel rating system (0-5 stars).

Unless otherwise noted, hotel staff speak basic English, credit cards are accepted, and breakfast is not included (but is usually optional). All hotels in these listings have elevators, air-conditioning, Internet access (a public terminal in the lobby for guests to use), and Wi-Fi, unless otherwise noted. "Wi-Fi only" means there's no public computer available.

To help you easily sort through my listings, I've divided the accommodations into three categories based on the price for a standard double room with bath during high season:

$$$ **Higher Priced**—Most rooms €200 or more.
$$ **Moderately Priced**—Most rooms between €150-200.
$ **Lower Priced**—Most rooms €150 or less.

Prices can change without notice; verify the hotel's current rates online or by email.

---

as you face the front of Les Invalides). The manicured gardens behind the golden dome of the Army Museum are free, peaceful, and filled with flowers (at southwest corner of grounds, closes at about 19:00).

Though hardly a happening nightlife spot, Rue Cler offers many low-impact after-dark activities. Take an evening stroll above the river through the parkway between Pont de l'Alma and Pont des Invalides. For an after-dinner cruise on the Seine, it's a 15-minute walk to the river and the Bateaux-Mouches (see page 244). For a post-dinner cruise on foot, saunter into the Champ de Mars park to admire the glowing Eiffel Tower. For more ideas on Paris after hours, see "Entertainment in Paris," earlier.

Services: There's a large **post office** at the end of Rue Cler on Avenue de la Motte-Picquet and a handy **SNCF Boutique** at 80 Rue St. Dominique (Mon-Sat 8:30-19:30, closed Sun, get there when it opens to avoid a long wait). At both of these offices, take a number and wait your turn. A smaller post office is closer to the Eiffel Tower on Avenue Rapp, one block past Rue St. Dominique toward the river. You can buy your Paris Museum Pass at **Tabac La Cave à Cigares** on Avenue de la Motte-Picquet, across from where the Rue Cler ends.

Markets: Cross the Champ de Mars park to mix it up with bargain-hunters at the twice-weekly open-air market, **Marché**

Boulevard de Grenelle, under the Métro, a few blocks southwest of the Champ de Mars park (Wed and Sun 7:00-12:30, between Mo: Dupleix and Mo: La Motte-Picquet-Grenelle). Two minuscule grocery stores, both on Rue de Grenelle, are open until midnight: **Epicerie de la Tour** (at #197) and **Alimentation** (at corner with Rue Cler). **Rue St. Dominique** is the area's boutique-browsing street and well worth a visit if shopping for clothes.

Internet Access: Com Avenue is good (about €5/hour, shareable and multi-use accounts, Mon-Sat 10:00-20:00, closed Sun, 24 Rue du Champ de Mars, tel. 01 45 55 00 07).

Laundry: Launderettes are omnipresent; ask your hotel for the nearest. Here are three handy locations: on Rue Augereau, on Rue Amélie (both between Rue St. Dominique and Rue de Grenelle), and at the southeast corner of Rue Valadon and Rue de Grenelle.

Booking Agency: To book tickets for key sights, or for assistance with hotels, transportation, or excursions, contact the helpful staff at **Paris Webservices** (Mon-Fri 9:00-21:00, Sat-Sun 9:00-18:00, 12 Rue de l'Exposition, Mo: Ecole Militaire, RER: Pont de l'Alma, tel. 09 52 06 02 59, www.pariswebservices.com, contactpws@pariswebservices.com).

Métro Connections: Key Métro stops are Ecole Militaire, La Tour Maubourg, and Invalides. The useful RER-C line runs from the Pont de l'Alma and Invalides stations, serving Versailles to the southwest; the Marmottan Museum to the northwest; and the Orsay Museum, Latin Quarter (St. Michel stop), and Austerlitz train station to the east.

Bus Routes: Smart travelers take advantage of these bus routes (see map on page 70 for stop locations):

Line #69 runs east-west along Rue St. Dominique and serves Les Invalides, Orsay, Louvre, Marais, and Père Lachaise Cemetery.

Line #63 runs along the river (the Quai d'Orsay), serving the Latin Quarter along Boulevard St. Germain to the east (ending at Gare de Lyon), and Trocadéro and areas near the Marmottan Museum to the west.

Line #92 runs along Avenue Bosquet, north to the Champs-Elysées and Arc de Triomphe (faster than the Métro) and south to the Montparnasse Tower and Gare Montparnasse.

Line #87 runs from Avenue Joseph Bouvard in the Champ de Mars park up Avenue de la Bourdonnais and serves the Sèvres-Babylone shopping area, St. Sulpice Church, Luxembourg Garden, the Bastille, and Gare de Lyon (also more convenient than Métro for these destinations).

Line #80 runs on Avenue Bosquet, crosses the Champs-Elysées, and serves Gare St. Lazare.

Rue Cler Hotels

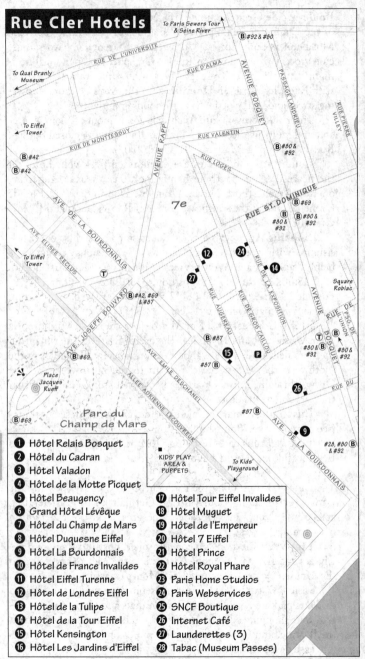

PARIS

1. Hôtel Relais Bosquet
2. Hôtel du Cadran
3. Hôtel Valadon
4. Hôtel de la Motte Picquet
5. Hôtel Beaugency
6. Grand Hôtel Lévêque
7. Hôtel du Champ de Mars
8. Hôtel Duquesne Eiffel
9. Hôtel La Bourdonnais
10. Hôtel de France Invalides
11. Hôtel Eiffel Turenne
12. Hôtel de Londres Eiffel
13. Hôtel de la Tulipe
14. Hôtel de la Tour Eiffel
15. Hôtel Kensington
16. Hôtel Les Jardins d'Eiffel
17. Hôtel Tour Eiffel Invalides
18. Hôtel Muguet
19. Hôtel de l'Empereur
20. Hôtel 7 Eiffel
21. Hôtel Prince
22. Hôtel Royal Phare
23. Paris Home Studios
24. Paris Webservices
25. SNCF Boutique
26. Internet Café
27. Launderettes (3)
28. Tabac (Museum Passes)

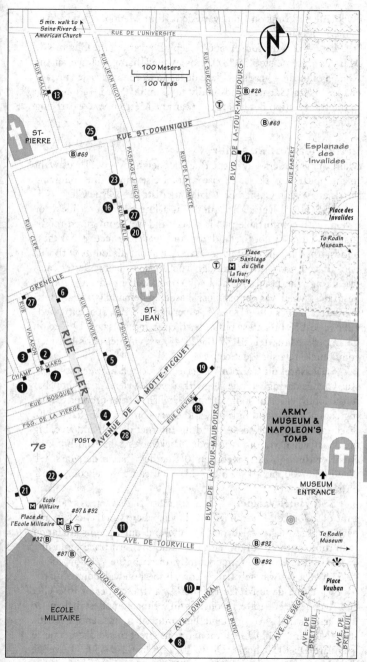

PARIS

Line #28 runs on Boulevard de la Tour Maubourg and serves Gare St. Lazare.

Line #42 runs from Avenue Joseph Bouvard in the Champs de Mars park (same stop as #87), crosses the Champs-Elysées at the Rond-Point, then heads to Place de la Concorde, Place de la Madeleine, Opéra Garnier, and finally to Gare du Nord—a long ride to the train station but less tiring than the Métro if you're carrying suitcases.

In the Heart of Rue Cler

Many of my readers stay in the Rue Cler neighborhood. If you want to disappear into Paris, choose a hotel elsewhere. The following hotels are within Camembert-smelling distance of Rue Cler.

$$$ Hôtel Relais Bosquet*** is a fine hotel in an ideal location, with comfortable public spaces and well-configured rooms that are large by local standards and feature effective darkness blinds. The staff are politely formal. Ask about discounts with this book if you book direct, though you'll often get far better rates by "liking" the hotel on Facebook. Book well in advance for the best rates, which vary enormously based on demand (standard Db-€150-235, bigger Db-€175-275, superior Db-€190-305, extra bed-€29, good €15 breakfast buffet with eggs and sausage, 19 Rue du Champ de Mars, tel. 01 47 05 25 45, www.hotel-paris-bosquet.com, hotel@relaisbosquet.com).

$$$ Hôtel du Cadran***, perfectly located a *boule* toss from Rue Cler, is daringly modern—with a *chocolat-et-macaron* shop/bar in the lobby, efficient staff, and über-stylish yet tight rooms featuring cool colors, mood lighting, and every comfort (Db-€250-290; discount off lowest rates—including Internet deals—and free, big breakfast when you use the code "RickSteves rate" and book by email or through their website; 10 Rue du Champ de Mars, tel. 01 40 62 67 00, fax 01 40 62 67 13, www.cadranhotel.com, resa@cadranhotel.com).

$$$ Hôtel Valadon***, almost across the street, is really an annex of Hôtel du Cadran (listed above), where you'll check in and have breakfast. The Valadron's 12 cute-and-quiet rooms are larger than those at the Cadran, with the same comfort, prices, and discounts (Tb available, one good family suite, 16 Rue Valadon, tel. 01 47 53 89 85, www.hotelvaladon.com, info@hotelvaladon.com).

$$ Hôtel de la Motte Picquet***, at the corner of Rue Cler and Avenue de la Motte-Picquet, is an intimate, modest little place with narrow halls, comfortable but compact rooms, and a terrific staff (Moe and Tina). Get a room off the street to avoid street noise (standard Db-€150, bigger Db-€230, Tb/Qb-€270-350, 30 Avenue de la Motte-Picquet, tel. 01 47 05 09 57, fax 01 47 05 74 36, www.hotelmottepicquetparis.com, book@hotelmottepicquetparis.com).

$$ Hôtel Beaugency*,** a good value on a quieter street a short block off Rue Cler, has 30 smallish rooms with standard furnishings and a lobby that you can stretch out in (Sb-€120, Db-€155, twin Db-€165, occasional discounts for Rick Steves readers—ask when you book, 21 Rue Duvivier, tel. 01 47 05 01 63, fax 01 45 51 04 96, www.hotel-beaugency.com, infos@hotel-beaugency.com).

Warning: The next two hotels are very busy with my readers (reserve long in advance).

$$ Grand Hôtel Lévêque,** ideally located on Rue Cler, is all about location. It's a busy place with a sliver-size elevator, a sleek breakfast room that doubles as a lounge, impersonal service, and so-so accommodations (some rooms are fine, while others feel neglected). Rooms on Rue Cler come with fun views but morning noise as the market sets up (S-€75-120, Db-€140-170, Tb-€200, don't let them talk you into a pricier room than the one you booked, 29 Rue Cler, tel. 01 47 05 49 15, fax 01 45 50 49 36, www.hotel-leveque.com, info@hotel-leveque.com).

$ Hôtel du Champ de Mars,** with adorable rooms and serious owners Françoise and Stephane, is a cozy Rue Cler option. This plush little hotel has a small-town feel from top to bottom. The rooms are snug but lovingly kept, and single rooms can work as tiny doubles. It's an excellent value despite the lack of air-conditioning (Sb-€100, Db-€120, 30 yards off Rue Cler at 7 Rue du Champ de Mars, tel. 01 45 51 52 30, fax 01 45 51 64 36, www.hotelduchampdemars.com, reservation@hotelduchampdemars.com).

Near Rue Cler, Close to Ecole Militaire Métro Stop

The following listings are a five-minute walk from Rue Cler, near Métro stop Ecole Militaire or RER: Pont de l'Alma.

$$$ Hôtel Duquesne Eiffel*,** a few blocks farther from the action, is calm, hospitable, and very comfortable. It features handsome rooms (some with terrific Eiffel Tower views for only €20 more), a welcoming lobby, and a big, hot breakfast for €13 (Db-€190-250, price grows with room size, Tb-€270, ask about discount with this book, 23 Avenue Duquesne, tel. 01 44 42 09 09, fax 01 44 42 09 08, www.hotel-duquesne-eiffel-paris.com, contact@hde.fr).

$$$ Hôtel La Bourdonnais*** is *très* Parisian, mixing an Old World feel with creaky, comfortable rooms and generous public spaces. Its mostly spacious rooms are traditionally decorated, and its bathrooms are due for an upgrade (Db-€200-300, Tb-€240-320, Qb-€280-350, ask about free breakfast with this book, closed for renovation through March 2014, 111-113 Avenue de la Bourdonnais, tel. 01 47 05 45 42, fax 01 45 55 75 54, www.hotellabourdonnais.fr, hlb@hotellabourdonnais.fr).

$$ Hôtel de France Invalides** is an OK mid-range option

PARIS

away from most other hotels I list. It's run by a brother-sister team (Alain and Marie-Hélène) with a small bar/lounge and 60 well-maintained rooms, some with knockout views of Invalides' golden dome. Rooms on the courtyard are very quiet, while those facing Les Invalides face a large street (Sb-€115, standard Db-€140-250, ask about discount with this book, connecting rooms possible for families, no air-con, 102 Boulevard de la Tour Maubourg, tel. 01 47 05 40 49, fax 01 45 56 96 78, www.hoteldefrance.com, contact@hoteldefrance.com).

$$ Hôtel Eiffel Turenne** has comfortable rooms at OK rates and a lobby with windows on the world. There are five true singles and several connecting rooms good for families (Sb-€130, Db-€150-200, Tb-€190-230, Wi-Fi only, 20 Avenue de Tourville, tel. 01 47 05 99 92, fax 01 45 56 06 04, www.hotel-turenne.com, reservation@hoteleiffelturenne.com).

Near Rue Cler, Closer to Rue St. Dominique (and the Seine)

$$$ Hôtel de Londres Eiffel*** is my closest listing to the Eiffel Tower and the Champ de Mars park. Here you get immaculate, warmly decorated rooms (several are connecting for families), snazzy public spaces, and a service-oriented staff. Some rooms are pretty small—request a bigger room. It's less convenient to the Métro (10-minute walk), but very handy to buses #69, #80, #87, and #92, and to RER-C: Pont de l'Alma (Sb-€175, small Db-€190, bigger Db-€205, Db with Eiffel Tower view-€230, Tb-€270, 1 Rue Augereau, tel. 01 45 51 63 02, fax 01 47 05 28 96, www.hotel-paris-londres-eiffel.com, info@londres-eiffel.com, helpful Cédric and Arnaud). The owners also run a good two-star hotel with similar comfort in the cheaper Montparnasse area, **$$ Hôtel Apollon Montparnasse** (Db-€140-170, look for Web deals, 91 Rue de l'Ouest, Mo: Pernety, tel. 01 43 95 62 00, fax 01 43 95 62 10, www.apollon-montparnasse.com, info@apollon-montparnasse.com).

$$ Hôtel de la Tulipe***, three blocks from Rue Cler toward the river, feels pricey but unique. The 20 small and simple rooms surround a seductive, wood-beamed lounge and a peaceful, leafy courtyard. Ask about discount when you book direct with this book (Sb-€160, Db-€182, Tb-€224, 4-person apartment-€335, 2-room suite for up to 5 people-€365, no air-con, no elevator, 33 Rue Malar, tel. 01 45 51 67 21, fax 01 47 53 96 37, www.paris-hotel-tulipe.com, hoteldelatulipe@wanadoo.fr).

$ Hôtel de la Tour Eiffel** is a good two-star value on a quiet street near several of my favorite restaurants. The rooms are well-designed and comfortable, but some have thin walls and none have air-conditioning (snug Db-€110, bigger Db-€120-140, no breakfast offered, Wi-Fi only, 17 Rue de l'Exposition, tel. 01 47 05 14 75, fax 01 47 53 99 46, www.hotel-toureiffel.com, hte7@wanadoo.fr).

$ Hôtel Kensington** is a good budget value close to the Eiffel Tower and run by elegant, though formal, Daniele. It's an unpretentious place with mostly small, basic, but well-kept rooms (Sb-€65-74, Db-€80-97, big Db on back side-€98-117, Eiffel Tower views for those who ask, no air-con, pay Internet access, 79 Avenue de la Bourdonnais, tel. 01 47 05 74 00, fax 01 47 05 25 81, www.hotel-kensington.com, hk@hotel-kensington.com).

Near La Tour Maubourg Métro Stop

The next four listings are within three blocks of the intersection of Avenue de la Motte-Picquet and Boulevard de la Tour Maubourg.

$$$ Hôtel Les Jardins d'Eiffel***, on a quiet street, feels like the modern motel it is, with professional service, its own parking garage (€24/day), and a spacious lobby. Most rooms are big and quiet by Parisian standards (standard Db-€180-210, renovated Db-€215-240, ask about Rick Steves discount when you book direct, check website for special discounts, 8 Rue Amélie, tel. 01 47 05 46 21, fax 01 45 55 28 08, www.hoteljardinseiffel.com, reservations@hoteljardinseiffel.com).

$$$ Hôtel Tour Eiffel Invalides*** advertises its Best Western status proudly and offers a generous-size lobby with a small courtyard and good, traditionally decorated rooms with big beds but no firm prices (the Internet decides). Allow about €220-280 for a double but look for better rates on their website. Ask for a non-smoking room (35 Boulevard de la Tour Maubourg, tel. 01 45 56 10 78, fax 01 47 05 65 08, www.timhotel.fr, invalides@timhotel.fr).

$$$ Hôtel Muguet***, a peaceful, stylish, immaculate refuge, gives you three-star comfort for a two-star price. This delightful spot offers 43 tasteful rooms, a greenhouse lounge, and a small garden courtyard. The hands-on owner, Catherine, gives her guests a restful and secure home in Paris (Sb-€140-175, Db-€195-245—more with view, Tb-€195-245, strict cancellation policy: cancel 7 days before arrival or lose deposit, 11 Rue Chevert, tel. 01 47 05 05 93, fax 01 45 50 25 37, www.hotelparismuguet.com, muguet@wanadoo.fr).

$$$ Hôtel de l'Empereur** is well-run and offers good service. It delivers smashing views of Invalides from most of its very comfortable and tastefully designed rooms. Fifth-floor rooms have small balconies, and all rooms have queen-size beds (Sb-€140-175, Db-€195-245—more with view, Tb-€195-245, two-room Qb-€370, strict cancellation policy: cancel 7 days before arrival or lose deposit, 2 Rue Chevert, tel. 01 45 55 88 02, fax 01 45 51 88 54, www.hotelempereurparis.com, contact@hotelempereur.com).

PARIS

Lesser Values in the Rue Cler Area

Given how fine this area is, these are acceptable last choices.

$$$ Hôtel 7 Eiffel**** is an ultra-modern, high-design, four-star splurge, complete with bar and fireplace lounge in lobby, colorful rooftop terrace, room service, and all the usual comforts of a business hotel (Db-€270-370, check Web for deals, 17 bis Rue Amélie, tel. 01 45 55 10 01, fax 01 47 05 28 68, www.7eiffel.com, reservation@7eiffel.com).

$ Hôtel Prince**,** across from the Ecole Militaire Métro stop, has a spartan lobby, drab halls, and plain-but-acceptable rooms for the price (Sb-€109, Db-€130, Tb-€150, ask about free breakfast with this book, Wi-Fi only, 66 Avenue Bosquet, tel. 01 47 05 40 90, fax 01 47 53 06 62, www.hotel-paris-prince.com, paris@hotel-prince.com).

$ Hôtel Royal Phare**,** facing the busy Ecole Militaire Métro stop, is a humble place. The 34 basic, pastel rooms are unimaginative but sleepable. Rooms on the courtyard are quietest, with peek-a-boo views of the Eiffel Tower from the fifth floor up (Sb-€84, Db with shower-€98, Db with tub-€108, Tb-€120, fridges in rooms, no air-con but fans, no Wi-Fi, 40 Avenue de la Motte-Picquet, tel. 01 47 05 57 30, fax 01 45 51 64 41, www.hotel-royalphare-paris.com, hotel-royalphare@wanadoo.fr, friendly manager Hocin).

In the Marais Neighborhood
(4th arrondissement, Mo: Bastille, St. Paul, and Hôtel de Ville)

Those interested in a more SoHo/Greenwich Village-type locale should make the Marais their Parisian home. Once a forgotten Parisian backwater, the Marais—which runs from the Pompidou Center east to the Bastille (a 15-minute walk)—is now one of Paris' most popular residential, tourist, and shopping areas. This is jumbled, medieval Paris at its finest, where classy stone mansions sit alongside trendy bars, antiques shops, and fashion-conscious boutiques. The streets are a fascinating parade of artists, students, tourists, immigrants, and baguette-munching babies in strollers. The Marais is also known as a hub of the Parisian gay and lesbian scene. This area is *sans doute* livelier (and louder) than the Rue Cler area.

In the Marais you have these major sights close at hand: the Carnavalet Museum, Victor Hugo's House, the Jewish Art and History Museum, the Pompidou Center, and the Picasso Museum. You're also a manageable walk from Paris' two islands (Ile St. Louis and Ile de la Cité), home to Notre-Dame and Sainte-Chapelle. The Opéra Bastille, Promenade Plantée park, Place des Vosges (Paris' oldest square), Jewish Quarter (Rue des Rosiers), the Latin Quarter, and nightlife-packed Rue de Lappe are also walkable. Strolling home (day or night) from Notre-Dame along Ile St. Louis is marvelous.

Most of my recommended hotels are located a few blocks north of the Marais' main east-west drag, Rue St. Antoine/Rue de Rivoli.

Tourist Information: The nearest TI is at the Pyramides Métro stop (daily May-Oct 9:00-19:00, Nov-April 10:00-19:00).

Services: Most banks and other services are on the main street, Rue de Rivoli, which becomes Rue St. Antoine. Marais **post offices** are on Rue Castex and at the corner of Rue Pavée and Rue des Francs Bourgeois. There's a busy **SNCF Boutique** where you can take care of all train needs on Rue St. Antoine at Rue de Turenne (Mon-Fri 8:00-20:30, Sat 10:00-20:30, closed Sun). A quieter SNCF Boutique is nearer Gare de Lyon at 5 Rue de Lyon (Mon-Sat 8:30-18:00, closed Sun).

Markets: The Marais has two good open-air markets: the sprawling **Marché de la Bastille,** along Boulevard Richard Lenoir, on the north side of Place de la Bastille (Thu and Sun until 14:30); and the more intimate, untouristy **Marché d'Aligre** (Tue-Sat 9:00-14, closed Mon, cross Place de la Bastille and walk about 10 blocks down Rue du Faubourg St. Antoine, turn right at Rue de Cotte to Place d'Aligre; or, take Métro line 8 from Bastille in the direction of Créteil-Préfecture, get off at the Ledru-Rollin stop, and walk a few blocks southeast). A small **grocery** is open until 23:00 on Rue St. Antoine (near intersection with Rue Castex). To shop at a Parisian Sears, find the **BHV** department store next to Hôtel de Ville. Paris' oldest covered market, **Marché des Enfants Rouges,** lies a 10-minute walk north of Rue de Rivoli.

Internet Access: Try **Paris CY** (Mon-Sat 10:00-20:00, Sun 13:00-20:00, 8 Rue de Jouy, Mo: St. Paul, tel. 01 42 71 37 37).

Laundry: There are many launderettes; ask your hotelier for the nearest. Here are three you can count on: on Impasse Guéménée (north of Rue St. Antoine), on Rue Ste. Croix de la Bretonnerie (just east of Rue du Temple), and on Rue du Petit Musc (south of Rue St. Antoine).

Métro Connections: Key Métro stops in the Marais are, from east to west: Bastille, St. Paul, and Hôtel de Ville (Sully-Morland, Pont Marie, and Rambuteau stops are also handy). Métro connections are excellent, with direct service to the Louvre, Champs-Elysées, Arc de Triomphe, and La Défense (all on line 1); the Rue Cler area and Opéra Garnier (line 8 from Bastille stop); and four major train stations: Gare de Lyon, Gare du Nord, Gare de l'Est, and Gare d'Austerlitz (all accessible from Bastille stop).

Bus Routes: For stop locations, see the "Marais Hotels" map.

Line #69 on Rue St. Antoine takes you eastbound to Père Lachaise Cemetery and westbound to the Louvre, Orsay, and Rodin museums, plus the Army Museum, ending at the Eiffel Tower.

Line #87 runs down Boulevard Henri IV, crossing Ile St.

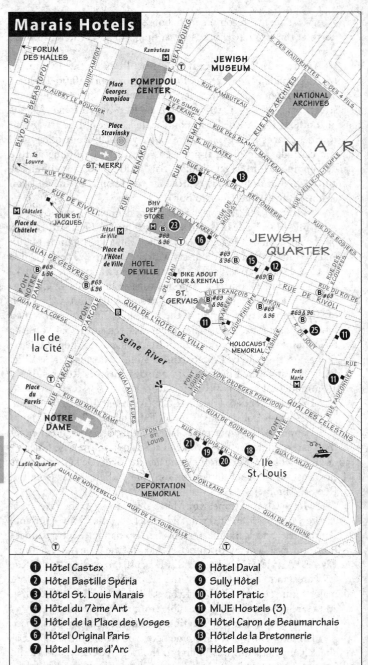

Marais Hotels

FORUM DES HALLES

R. QUINCAMPOIX

R. AUBRY LE BOUCHER

BLVD. DE SEBASTOPOL

Rambuteau

R. BEAUBOURG

R. DES HAUDRIETTES

R. DES 4 FILS

R. DES ARCHIVES

JEWISH MUSEUM

NATIONAL ARCHIVES

Place Georges Pompidou

POMPIDOU CENTER

RUE RAMBUTEAU

RUE DU TEMPLE

RUE SIMON LE FRANC

⑭

Place Stravinsky

RUE DES BLANCS MANTEAUX

M A R

To Louvre

RUE PERNELLE

ST. MERRI

RUE DU RENARD

R. DU PLATRE

R. DU TEMPLE

RUE STE. CROIX DE LA BRETONNERIE

⑬

RUE VIEILLE-DU-TEMPLE

RUE DE RIVOLI

㉖

RUE DE MOUSSY

Châtelet

M Châtelet

Place du Châtelet

TOUR ST. JACQUES

Hôtel de Ville

BHV DEP'T STORE

B ㉓ #69 & 96

RUE DE LA VERRERIE

RUE DES ROSIERS

JEWISH QUARTER

M

⑯

B ⑮ #69 & 96

㉒ B

RUE DES ECOUFFES

QUAI DE GESVRES

Place de l'Hôtel de Ville

HOTEL DE VILLE

R. DE LOBAU

#69 B & 96

RUE DE RIVOLI

RUE DU ROI DE

B #69 & 96

B #69 & 96

B #69 & 96

BIKE ABOUT TOUR & RENTALS

RUE FRANÇOIS

B #69 & 96

ST. GERVAIS

MIRON

RUE LOUIS PHILIPPE

B #69 & 96

B #69 & 96 ㉕

R. DE JOUY

PONT NOTRE DAME

PONT D'ARCOLE

QUAI DE L'HOTEL DE VILLE

R. DES BARRES

⑪

⑪

QUAI DE LA CORSE

HOLOCAUST MEMORIAL

RUE G. L'ASNIER

Ile de la Cité

Seine River

PONT LOUIS PHILIPPE

VOIE GEORGES POMPIDOU

QUAI DES CELESTINS

RUE FAUCONNIER

Pont Marie

M

⑪

Place du Parvis

QUAI D'ARCOLE

RUE DU NOTRE DAME

QUAI AUX FLEURS

NOTRE DAME

PONT ST. LOUIS

QUAI DE BOURBON

QUAI D'ANJOU

PONT MARIE

To Latin Quarter

QUAI DE MONTEBELLO

RUE ST. LOUIS-EN-L'ILE

㉑ ⑲ ⑱

⑳

Ile St. Louis

DEPORTATION MEMORIAL

QUAI D'ORLEANS

QUAI DE LA TOURNELLE

QUAI DE BETHUNE

T

T

① Hôtel Castex	⑧ Hôtel Daval
② Hôtel Bastille Spéria	⑨ Sully Hôtel
③ Hôtel St. Louis Marais	⑩ Hôtel Pratic
④ Hôtel du 7ème Art	⑪ MIJE Hostels (3)
⑤ Hôtel de la Place des Vosges	⑫ Hôtel Caron de Beaumarchais
⑥ Hôtel Original Paris	⑬ Hôtel de la Bretonnerie
⑦ Hôtel Jeanne d'Arc	⑭ Hôtel Beaubourg

PARIS

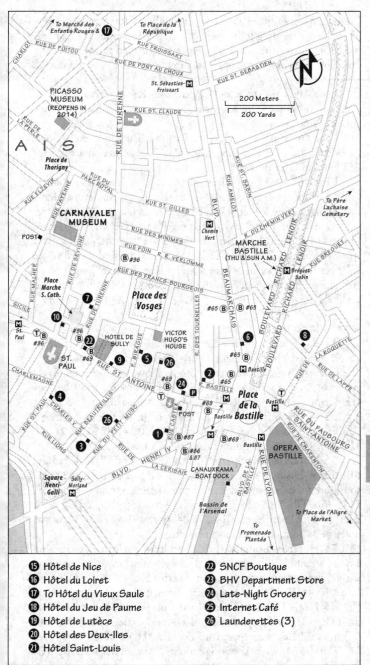

To Marché des Enfants Rouges & ❶

To Place de la République

RUE FROISSART

RUE DE PONT AU CHOUX

RUE DE POITOU

RUE ST. SÉBASTIEN

CHARLOT

St. Sébastien-Froissart Ⓜ

PICASSO MUSEUM (REOPENS IN 2014)

RUE DE LA PERLE

RUE ST. CLAUDE

RUE DE TURENNE

AIS

Place de Thorigny

RUE ELZEVIR

RUE DU PARC ROYAL

RUE PAYENNE

RUE ST. GILLES

RUE ST. SABIN

200 Meters

200 Yards

To Père Lachaise Cemetery

CARNAVALET MUSEUM

RUE DES MINIMES

BLVD.

Ⓜ Chemin Vert

R. DU CHEMIN VERT

R. DU CHEMIN VERT

RUE DE SÉVIGNÉ

RUE MALHER

POST

RUE DES FRANCS-BOURGEOIS

RUE FOIN   R. R. VERLOMME

Ⓑ #96

MARCHE BASTILLE (THU & SUN A.M.)

BOULEVARD RICHARD LENOIR

RUE DE BRÉGUET

Bréguet-Sabin Ⓜ

Place Marche S. Cath.

❼

RUE DE TURENNE

Place des Vosges

#65 Ⓑ   Ⓑ #65

SICILE

❿

Ⓜ St. Paul

ⓉⒷ

#96

#96

ⒷⒷ

#69

HOTEL DE SULLY

㉒

ST. PAUL

❾

RUE ST. ANTOINE

VICTOR HUGO'S HOUSE

R. DES TOURNELLES

BEAUMARCHAIS

❻

#65 Ⓑ

Ⓜ Bastille

❽

LA ROQUETTE

RUE DE

CHARLEMAGNE

R. K. BIRAGUE

❺

㉖

#69

❷

#65

RUE DE LAPPE

Ⓣ Bastille

RUE ST. PAUL

CHARLES V.

❹

㉔

Ⓣ

P

R. BASTILLE

Place de la Bastille

RUE DU FAUBOURG SAINT-ANTOINE

RUE BEAUTREILLIS

㉖

RUE DU PETIT MUSC

POST

#69

Ⓑ

Ⓜ

Bastille

Ⓜ

Bastille

RUE DE CHARENTON

RUE LIONS

❸

RUE CASTEX

❶

Ⓑ #87

Ⓜ

Bastille

OPERA BASTILLE

BLVD. HENRI IV

Ⓑ #86 & #87

Ⓑ #69

RUE DE LYON

Square Henri-Galli Ⓜ

Sully-Morland

CANAUXRAMA BOAT DOCK

LA CERISAIE

BLVD. DE LA BASTILLE

To Place de l'Aligre Market

Bassin de l'Arsenal

To Promenade Plantée

PARIS

⓯ Hôtel de Nice
⓰ Hôtel du Loiret
⓱ To Hôtel du Vieux Saule
⓲ Hôtel du Jeu de Paume
⓳ Hôtel de Lutèce
⓴ Hôtel des Deux-Iles
㉑ Hôtel Saint-Louis

㉒ SNCF Boutique
㉓ BHV Department Store
㉔ Late-Night Grocery
㉕ Internet Café
㉖ Launderettes (3)

Louis and serving the Latin Quarter along Boulevard St. Germain, before heading to St. Sulpice Church/Luxembourg Garden, the Eiffel Tower, and the Rue Cler neighborhood to the west. The same line, running in the opposite direction, brings you to Gare de Lyon.

Line #96 runs on Rues Turenne and Rivoli, serves Ile de la Cité and St. Sulpice Church (near Luxembourg Garden), and ends at Gare Montparnasse.

Line #65 runs from Gare de Lyon up Rue de Lyon, around Place de la Bastille, and then up Boulevard Beaumarchais to Gare de l'Est and Gare du Nord.

Line #67 runs from Place d'Italie to the Jardin des Plantes (just south of the Seine), across Ile St. Louis (on Boulevard Henri IV), along Rue de Rivoli past the Louvre, then up to Montmartre.

Taxis: You'll find taxi stands on Place de la Bastille (where Boulevard Richard Lenoir meets the square), on the south side of Rue St. Antoine (in front of St. Paul Church), behind the Hôtel de Ville on Rue du Lobau (where it meets Rue de Rivoli), and a quieter one on the north side of Rue St. Antoine (where it meets Rue Castex).

Near Place des Vosges

$$ Hôtel Castex*,** on a quiet street near Place de la Bastille, is a well-located place with tile-floored rooms (that amplify noise). Their clever system of connecting rooms allows families total privacy between two rooms, each with its own bathroom. The 30 rooms are narrow (Sb-€145, Db-€175, Tb-€220, ask about free buffet breakfast with this book, just off Place de la Bastille and Rue St. Antoine at 5 Rue Castex, Mo: Bastille, tel. 01 42 72 31 52, fax 01 42 72 57 91, www.castexhotel.com, info@castexhotel.com).

$$ Hôtel Bastille Spéria*,** a short block off Place de la Bastille, offers business-type service in a great location. The 42 well-configured rooms are modern and comfortable, with big beds (Sb-€135-150, Db-€165-185, good buffet breakfast-€13, 1 Rue de la Bastille, Mo: Bastille, tel. 01 42 72 04 01, fax 01 42 72 56 38, www.hotelsperia.com, info@hotelsperia.com).

$$ Hôtel St. Louis Marais*,** an intimate little hotel, lies on a quiet street closer to the river. The well-maintained rooms come with character and reasonable rates (Db-€175-195, 1 Rue Charles V, tel. 01 48 87 87 04, www.saintlouismarais.com).

$$ Hôtel Original Paris*,** on a busy street barely off Place de la Bastille, has artsy rooms and a good location (Db-€155-190, 8 Boulevard Beaumarchais, Mo: Bastille, tel. 01 47 00 91 50, fax 01 47 00 06 31, www.hoteloriginalparis.com, info@hoteloriginalparis.com).

$ Hôtel du 7ème Art**, two blocks south of Rue St. Antoine toward the river, is a young, carefree, Hollywood-nostalgia place with a full-service café-bar and Charlie Chaplin murals. Its 23 good-value rooms have brown 1970s decor, but are comfortable enough. Sadly, smoking is allowed in all rooms, so you might detect an odor. The large rooms are American-spacious (small Db-€100, standard Db-€115, large Db-€130-160, Tb-€150-180, extra bed-€20, no elevator, 20 Rue St. Paul, Mo: St. Paul, tel. 01 44 54 85 00, fax 01 42 77 69 10, www.paris-hotel-7art.com, hotel7art@ wanadoo.fr).

$ Hôtel de la Place des Vosges** has simple, chic rooms and is brilliantly located between Rue St. Antoine and Place des Vosges. Amenities are sparse, there's no air-conditioning, and the elevator skips floors five and six, but the price is right (Db-€95-140, 12 Rue de Biraque, Mo: St. Paul, tel. 01 42 72 60 46, fax 01 42 72 02 64, www.hotelplacedesvosges.com, contact@hpdv.net).

$ Hôtel Jeanne d'Arc**, a lovely little hotel with a stylish lobby and thoughtfully appointed rooms, is ideally located for (and very popular with) connoisseurs of the Marais. It's a fine value and worth booking way ahead (three months in advance, if possible). Sixth-floor rooms have views, and corner rooms are wonderfully bright in the City of Light. Rooms on the street can be noisy until the bars close (Sb-€65-96, Db-€96, larger twin Db-€119, Tb-€149, good Qb-€164, no air-con, Wi-Fi only—in lobby, 3 Rue de Jarente, Mo: St. Paul, tel. 01 48 87 62 11, fax 01 70 24 83 38, www. hoteljeannedarc.com, information@hoteljeannedarc.com).

$ Hôtel Daval**, an unassuming place on the wild side of Place de la Bastille, is ideal for night owls. The rooms are tiny and the halls are narrow, but the rates are good for an air-conditioned place. Ask for a quieter room on the courtyard side if sleep matters (Sb-€86, Db-€92-101, Tb-€112, Qb-€131, Wi-Fi only, 21 Rue Daval, Mo: Bastille, tel. 01 47 00 51 23, fax 01 40 21 80 26, www. hoteldaval.com, info@hoteldaval.com).

$ Sully Hôtel, sitting right on Rue St. Antoine, is a basic, cheap dive run by no-nonsense Monsieur Zeroual. The rooms are frumpy, dimly lit, and can smell of smoke, and the entry is narrow, but the price fits (Db-€80, Tb-€90, Qb-€110, no elevator, no air-con, Wi-Fi only, 48 Rue St. Antoine, Mo: St. Paul, tel. 01 42 78 49 32, fax 01 44 61 76 50, www.sullyhotelparis.com, sullyhotel@ orange.fr).

$ Hôtel Pratic, just off the quiet and charming Place du Sainte Catherine, works for travelers who don't mind squeezing sideways to make it past the bed into the bathroom. The half-timbered interior gives this hotel a modest level of charm, but also makes for dark rooms and hallways (Sb-€69, Db-€69-119, Tb-€119-159, more for rooms with view of square, no elevator, no air-con, 9 Rue d'Ormesson, tel. 01 48 87 80 47, fax 01 48 87 40 04, www.pratichotelparis.com, pratic.hotel@wanadoo.fr).

$ *MIJE Youth Hostels:* The Maison Internationale de la Jeunesse et des Etudiants (MIJE) runs three classy old residences, ideal for budget travelers. Each is well-maintained, with simple, clean, single-sex (unless your group takes a whole room), one- to four-bed rooms for travelers of any age. The hostels are **MIJE Fourcy** (biggest and loudest, €11 dinners available with a membership card, 6 Rue de Fourcy, just south of Rue de Rivoli), **MIJE Fauconnier** (no elevator, 11 Rue du Fauconnier), and **MIJE Maubisson** (smallest and quietest, no outdoor terrace, 12 Rue des Barres). None have double beds or air-conditioning; all have private showers in every room (all prices per person: Sb-€51, Db-€38, Tb-€33, Qb-€31, credit cards accepted, includes breakfast but not towels, required membership card-€2.50 extra/person, 7-day maximum stay, rooms locked 12:00-15:00, curfew at 1:00 in the morning). They all share the same contact information (tel. 01 42 74 23 45, fax 01 40 27 81 64, www.mije.com, info@mije.com) and Métro stop (St. Paul). Reservations are accepted (six weeks ahead online, 10 days ahead by phone)—though you must show up by noon, or call the morning of arrival to confirm a later arrival time.

Near the Pompidou Center

These hotels are farther west, closer to the Pompidou Center than to Place de la Bastille. The Hôtel de Ville Métro stop works well for all of these hotels, unless a closer stop is noted.

$$ Hôtel Caron de Beaumarchais*,** on a busy corner, feels like a fluffy folk museum, with 20 pricey but cared-for and character-filled rooms. Its small lobby is cluttered with bits from an elegant 18th-century Marais house (small Db in back-€165, larger Db facing the front-€195, Wi-Fi only, 12 Rue Vieille du Temple, tel. 01 42 72 34 12, fax 01 42 72 34 63, www.carondebeaumarchais. com).

$$ Hôtel de la Bretonnerie*,** three blocks from the Hôtel de Ville, makes a fine Marais home. It has a warm, welcoming lobby and 29 well-appointed, good-value rooms with an antique, open-beam warmth but no air-conditioning (standard "classic" Db-€145, bigger "charming" Db-€175, Db suite-€200, Tb/Qb-€225, between Rue Vieille du Temple and Rue des Archives at 22 Rue Ste. Croix de la Bretonnerie, tel. 01 48 87 77 63, fax 01 42 77 26 78, www.bretonnerie.com, hotel@bretonnerie.com).

$$ Hôtel Beaubourg*** is a solid three-star value on a small street in the shadow of the Pompidou Center. The lounge is inviting, and the 28 rooms are comfy, well-appointed, and quiet (standard Db-€140, bigger twin or king-size Db-€160 and worth the extra cost, rates vary wildly with availability, 11 Rue Simon Le Franc, Mo: Rambuteau, tel. 01 42 74 34 24, fax 01 42 78 68 11, www.beaubourg-paris-hotel.com, reservation@hotelbeaubourg. com).

$ Hôtel de Nice**, on the Marais' busy main drag, features a turquoise-and-fuchsia "Marie-Antoinette-does-tie-dye" decor. Its narrow halls are littered with paintings and layered with carpets, and its 23 Old World rooms have thoughtful touches and tight bathrooms. Twin rooms, which cost the same as doubles, are larger and on the street side—but have effective double-paned windows (Sb-€80-130, Db-€110-160, Tb-€135-170, reception on second floor, 42 bis Rue de Rivoli, tel. 01 42 78 55 29, fax 01 42 78 36 07, www.hoteldenice.com, contact@hoteldenice.com, laissez-faire management).

$ Hôtel du Loiret* is a centrally located and rare Marais budget hotel. It's basic, but the rooms are surprisingly sharp, considering the price and location (Db-€80-100, Tb-€130, no air-con, expect some noise, 8 Rue des Mauvais Garçons, tel. 01 48 87 77 00, fax 01 48 04 96 56, www.hotel-du-loiret.fr, hotelduloiret@hotmail. com).

Near the Marché des Enfants Rouges

$$ Hôtel du Vieux Saule*** has 27 simple rooms with little character in a great location. Rooms are tight and modern. Avoid the smoking rooms on the first floor (Sb-€95-140, Db-€110-160, *supérieure* Db-€145-190, deluxe Db-€180-250, rates vary greatly with season, check online for best deals, small sauna free for guests, 6 Rue de Picardie, Mo: Filles du Calvaire or Temple, tel. 01 42 72 01 14, fax 01 40 27 88 21, www.hotelvieuxsaule.com, reserv@ hotelvieuxsaule.com).

On Ile St. Louis

(4th arrondissement; Mo: Pont Marie and Sully-Morland)
The peaceful, residential character of this river-wrapped island, with its brilliant location and homemade ice cream, has drawn Americans for decades. There are no budget values here—all of the hotels are three-star or more—though prices are reasonable for the level of comfort. The island's village ambience and proximity to the Marais, Notre-Dame, and the Latin Quarter make this area well worth considering. All of the following hotels are on the island's main drag, Rue St. Louis-en-l'Ile, where I list several restaurants (see page 359). For nearby services, see the Marais neighborhood section; for locations, see the Marais Hotels map, earlier.

$$$ Hôtel du Jeu de Paume****, occupying a 17th-century tennis center, is the most expensive hotel I list in Paris. When you enter its magnificent lobby, you'll understand why. Greet Scoop, *le chien*, then take a spin in the glass elevator for a half-timbered-tree-house experience. The 30 rooms are carefully designed and tasteful, though not particularly spacious (you're paying for the location and public areas). Most rooms face a small garden; all are pin-drop peaceful (standard Db-€290-330, deluxe Db-€400-560, €18 breakfast, 54 Rue St. Louis-en-l'Ile, tel. 01 43 26 14 18, fax 01 40 46 02 76, www.jeudepaumehotel.com, info@jeudepaumehotel.com).

$$$ **Hôtel de Lutèce*** comes with a sit-awhile wood-paneled lobby and a real fireplace. Rooms at this appealing hotel are handsome, and those on lower floors have high ceilings. Twin rooms are larger and the same price as double rooms. Rooms with bathtubs are on the louder street-side, while those with showers are on the courtyard (Db-€220, Tb-€255, 65 Rue St. Louis-en-l'Ile, tel. 01 43 26 23 52, fax 01 43 29 60 25, www.hoteldelutece.com, info@hoteldelutece.com).

$$$ **Hôtel des Deux-Iles*** has the same owners and same prices as the Lutèce (listed above), with a tad less personality (59 Rue St. Louis-en-l'Ile, tel. 01 43 26 13 35, fax 01 43 29 60 25, www.hoteldesdeuxiles.com, info@hoteldesdeuxiles.com).

$$ **Hôtel Saint-Louis*** blends character with modern comforts. The well-maintained rooms come with cool stone floors and exposed beams. Rates are reasonable...for the location (Db-€175-195, top-floor Db with micro-balcony-€245, Tb-€289, iPads available for guest in-room use, 75 Rue St. Louis-en-l'Ile, tel. 01 46 34 04 80, fax 01 46 34 02 13, www.hotelsaintlouis.com, slouis@noos.fr).

In the Luxembourg Garden Area (St. Sulpice to Panthéon)

(5th and 6th arrondissements, Mo: St. Sulpice, Mabillon, Odéon, and Cluny-La Sorbonne; RER: Luxembourg)

This neighborhood revolves around Paris' loveliest park and offers quick access to the city's best shopping streets and grandest café-hopping. Hotels in this central area are more expensive than those in the Rue Cler area or Marais neighborhood, but a better value than accommodations on Ile St. Louis. Sleeping in the Luxembourg area offers a true Left Bank experience without a hint of the low-end commotion of the nearby Latin Quarter tourist ghetto. The Luxembourg Garden, Boulevard St. Germain, Cluny Museum, and Latin Quarter are all at your doorstep. Here you get the best of both worlds: youthful Left Bank energy and the classic trappings that surround the monumental Panthéon and St. Sulpice Church.

Having the Luxembourg Garden as your backyard allows strolls through meticulously cared-for flowers, a great kids' play area, and a purifying escape from city traffic. Place St. Sulpice presents an elegant, pedestrian-friendly square and quick access to some of Paris' best boutiques. Sleeping in the Luxembourg area also puts several movie theaters at your fingertips (at Métro stop: Odéon), as well as lively cafés on Boulevard St. Germain, Rue de Buci, Rue des Canettes, Place de la Sorbonne, and Place de la Contrescarpe, all of which buzz with action until late.

While it takes only 15 minutes to walk from one end of this neighborhood to the other, I've located the hotels by the key monument they are close to (St. Sulpice Church, the Odéon Theater, and the Panthéon). Most hotels are within a five-minute walk of the Luxembourg Garden (and none is more than 15 minutes away).

Services: The nearest **TI** is across the river at the Pyramides Métro stop (daily May-Oct 9:00-19:00, Nov-April 10:00-19:00). There are two useful **SNCF Boutiques** for easy train reservations and ticket purchase: at 79 Rue de Rennes (Mon-Sat 10:00-19:00, closed Sun) and at 54 Boulevard St. Michel (Tue-Sat 8:15-19:45, Mon 13:00-19:45, closed Sun).

Markets: The colorful street market at the south end of Rue Mouffetard is a worthwhile 10- to 15-minute walk from these hotels (Tue-Sat 10:00-13:00 & 16:00-19:00, Sun 10:00-13:00, closed Mon, five blocks south of Place de la Contrescarpe, Mo: Place Monge).

Bookstore: San Francisco Book Company is a welcoming bookstore with a full selection of English-language books, including mine (Mon-Sat 11:00-21:00, Sun 14:00-19:30, 17 Rue Monsieur le Prince, tel. 01 43 29 15 70).

Internet Access: Try **Cyber Cube** at 5 Rue Mignon (Mon-Sat 10:00-10:00, closed Sun).

Métro Connections: Métro lines 10 and 4 serve this area (10 connects to the Austerlitz train station, and 4 runs to the Montparnasse, Est, and Nord train stations). Neighborhood stops are Cluny-La Sorbonne, Mabillon, Odéon, and St. Sulpice. RER-B (Luxembourg station is handiest) provides direct service to Charles de Gaulle airport and Gare du Nord trains, and access to Orly airport via the Orlybus (transfer at Denfert-Rochereau).

Bus Routes: Buses #86 and #87 run eastbound through this area on or near Boulevard St. Germain, and westbound along Rue des Ecoles, stopping on Place St. Sulpice. Lines #63 and #87 provide a direct connection west to the Rue Cler area. Line #63 also serves the Orsay and Marmottan museums to the west and Gare de Lyon to the east. Lines #86 and #87 run east to the Marais, and #87 continues to Gare de Lyon. Line #96 stops at Place St. Sulpice

Hotels near Luxembourg Garden

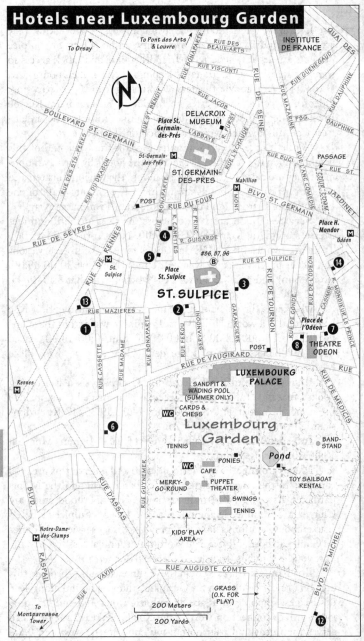

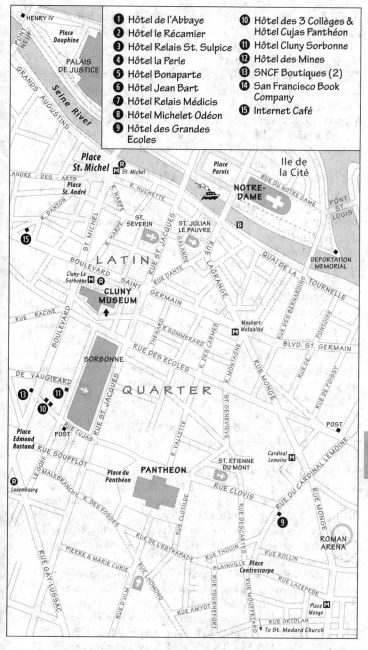

1. Hôtel de l'Abbaye
2. Hôtel le Récamier
3. Hôtel Relais St. Sulpice
4. Hôtel la Perle
5. Hôtel Bonaparte
6. Hôtel Jean Bart
7. Hôtel Relais Médicis
8. Hôtel Michelet Odéon
9. Hôtel des Grandes Ecoles
10. Hôtel des 3 Collèges & Hôtel Cujas Panthéon
11. Hôtel Cluny Sorbonne
12. Hôtel des Mines
13. SNCF Boutiques (2)
14. San Francisco Book Company
15. Internet Café

southbound en route to Gare Montparnasse and runs north along Rue de Rennes and Boulevard St. Germain into the Marais.

Near St. Sulpice Church

These hotels are all within a block of St. Sulpice Church and two blocks from famous Boulevard St. Germain. This is nirvana for boutique-minded shoppers—and you'll pay extra for the location. Métro stops St. Sulpice and Mabillon are equally close.

$$$ **Hôtel de l'Abbaye****** is a lovely refuge just west of Luxembourg Garden; it's a find for well-heeled connoisseurs of this area. The hotel's four-star luxury includes refined lounges inside and out, with 44 sumptuous rooms and every amenity (standard Db-€265-285, bigger Db-€385-415, suites and apartments available for €480-580, includes breakfast, 10 Rue Cassette, tel. 01 45 44 38 11, fax 01 45 48 07 86, www.hotelabbayeparis.com, hotel. abbaye@wanadoo.fr).

$$$ **Hôtel le Récamier****, romantically tucked in the corner of Place St. Sulpice, is high-end defined, with designer public spaces, elaborately appointed rooms, a courtyard tea salon, and professional service (classic Db-€260, deluxe Db-€300, traditional Db-€330, deluxe rooms offer best value, 3 bis Place St. Sulpice, tel. 01 43 26 04 89, fax 01 43 26 35 76, www.hotelrecamier.com, contact@hotelrecamier.com).

$$$ **Hôtel Relais St. Sulpice*****, burrowed on the small street just behind St. Sulpice Church, is a high-priced boutique hotel with a cozy lounge and 26 dark, stylish rooms, most surrounding a leafy glass atrium. Top-floor rooms get more light and are worth requesting (Db-€222-270 depending on size, much less off-season, sauna free for guests, 3 Rue Garancière, tel. 01 46 33 99 00, fax 01 46 33 00 10, www.relais-saint-sulpice.com, relaisstsulpice@wanadoo.fr).

$$$ **Hôtel la Perle***** is a spendy pearl in the thick of the lively Rue des Canettes, a block off Place St. Sulpice. This modern, business-class hotel is built around a central bar and atrium (standard Db-€210, bigger Db-€225, luxury Db-€250, check website or call for last-minute deals within 5 days of your stay, 14 Rue des Canettes, tel. 01 43 29 10 10, fax 01 46 34 51 04, www.hotellaperle. com, frontdesk@hotellaperle.com).

$ **Hôtel Bonaparte****, an unpretentious and welcoming place wedged between boutiques, is a few steps from Place St. Sulpice. Although the 29 Old World rooms don't live up to the handsome entry, they're plenty comfortable and spacious by Paris standards, with big bathrooms, traditional decor, and molded ceilings (Sb-€104-128, Db-€130-169, Tb-€171, 61 Rue Bonaparte, tel. 01 43 26 97 37, fax 01 46 33 57 67, www.hotelbonaparte.fr, reservation@hotelbonaparte.fr; helpful Fréderic and owner Eric at reception).

West of Luxembourg Garden

$ Hôtel Jean Bart** feels like it's from another era—prices included. Run by smiling Madame Lechopier, it's a rare budget hotel find in this neighborhood, one block from Luxembourg Garden. Beyond the dark, retirement home-like lobby, you'll find 33 spotless rooms with creaking floors and tight bathrooms. The cheapest rooms share one shower on the first floor (S-€57, Sb-€70, D-€57, Db-€78-82, cash only, no air-con, 9 Rue Jean-Bart, tel. 01 45 48 29 13, fax 01 45 48 10 79, hotel.jean.bart@gmail.com).

Near the Odéon Theater

These two hotels are between the Odéon Métro stop and Luxembourg Garden (five blocks east of St. Sulpice) and may have rooms when others don't. In addition to the Odéon Métro stop, the RER-B Luxembourg stop is a short walk away.

$$$ Hôtel Relais Médicis*** is ideal if you've always wanted to live in a Monet painting and can afford it. A glassy entry hides 17 rooms surrounding a fragrant little garden courtyard and fountain, giving you a countryside break fit for a Medici in the heart of Paris. This delightful refuge is tastefully decorated with floral Old World charm and permeated with thoughtfulness (Sb-€172, Db-€208-228, deluxe Db-€258, Tb-€298, Qb-€348, €30 cheaper mid-July-Aug and Nov-March, includes extravagant continental breakfast, faces the Odéon Theater at 5 Place de l'Odéon, tel. 01 43 26 00 60, fax 01 40 46 83 39, www.relaismedicis.com, reservation@relaismedicis.com, kind Marie at reception).

$ Hôtel Michelet Odéon** sits in a corner of Place de l'Odéon with big windows on the square. Though it lacks personality, it's a fair value in this pricey area, with 24 simple rooms with modern decor and views of the square (Db-€120-140, Tb-€170, Qb-€190, no air-con, 6 Place de l'Odéon, tel. 01 53 10 05 60, fax 01 46 34 55 35, www.hotelmicheletodeon.com, hotel@micheletodeon.com).

PARIS

Near the Panthéon and Rue Mouffetard

$ Hôtel des Grandes Ecoles*** is idyllic. A private cobbled lane leads to three buildings that protect a flower-filled garden courtyard, preserving a sense of tranquility rare in this city. Its 51 rooms are French-countryside-pretty and reasonably spacious, but have no air-conditioning. This romantic spot is deservedly popular, so book ahead. Reservations are not accepted more than four months in advance; new openings become available on the 15th of each month (Db-€120-150 depending on size, extra bed-€20, no TVs in rooms, parking garage-€30/day, 75 Rue du Cardinal Lemoine, Mo: Cardinal Lemoine, tel. 01 43 26 79 23, fax 01 43 25 28 15, www.hotel-grandes-ecoles.com, hotel.grandes.ecoles@free.fr; mellow Marie speaks English, Mama does not).

$ Hôtel des 3 Collèges** greets clients with a bright lobby, narrow hallways, and unimaginative rooms. Rates are fair and the smiling staff is eager to please (Sb-€89-114, Db-€111-160, Tb-€160-180, 16 Rue Cujas, tel. 01 43 54 67 30, fax 01 46 34 02 99, www.3colleges.com, hotel@3colleges.com).

$ Hôtel Cujas Panthéon** gives boring, standard two-star comfort with air-conditioning at fair prices (Db-€130-145, Tb-€170-180, free Wi-Fi, 18 Rue Cujas, tel. 01 43 54 58 10, fax 01 43 25 88 02, www.cujas-pantheon-paris-hotel.com, hotel-cujas-pantheon@wanadoo.fr).

$ Hôtel Cluny Sorbonne** is a modest place located in the thick of things across from the famous university and below the Panthéon. Rooms are well-worn with thin walls (small Db-€105-110, really big Db/Tb/Qb-€160, check website for deals, no air-con, Wi-Fi only, 8 Rue Victor Cousin, tel. 01 43 54 66 66, fax 01 43 29 68 07, www.hotel-cluny.fr, cluny@club-internet.fr).

South of Luxembourg Garden
$$ Hôtel des Mines** is less central, but its 50 well-maintained rooms are a fair value and come with updated bathrooms and an inviting lobby (Sb-€125, Db-€160, Tb-€190, Qb-€220, less for last-minute bookings and stays of 3 nights or more, frequent Web deals, between Luxembourg and Port-Royal stations on the RER-B line, a 10-minute walk from Panthéon, one block past Luxembourg Garden at 125 Boulevard St. Michel, tel. 01 43 54 32 78, fax 01 46 33 72 52, www.hoteldesminesparis.com, hotel@hoteldesmines-paris.com).

Budget Accommodations Away from the Center

Acceptable budget accommodations in central neighborhoods are few and far between in Paris. I've listed the best I could find in the neighborhoods described previously, most at about €100 for a double room. These are great (moderate) budget options, but if you want even lower rates or greater selection, you need to look farther away from the river (prices drop proportionately with distance from the Seine). Below you'll find more budget listings in less-central, but still-appealing neighborhoods. You'll spend more time on the Métro or bus getting to sights but save money by sleeping in these areas.

At the Bottom of Rue Mouffetard
These accommodations, away from the Seine and other tourists in an appealing workaday area, offer more room for your euro. Rue Mouffetard is the bohemian soul of this area. Two thousand years

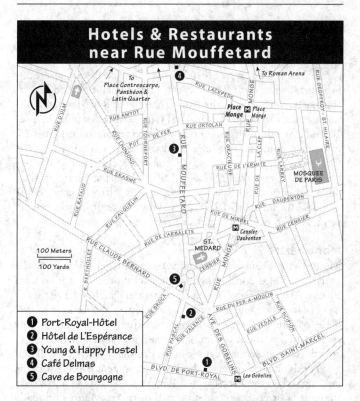

Hotels & Restaurants near Rue Mouffetard

❶ Port-Royal-Hôtel
❷ Hôtel de L'Espérance
❸ Young & Happy Hostel
❹ Café Delmas
❺ Cave de Bourgogne

ago, it was the principal Roman road south to Italy. Today, this small, meandering street has a split personality. The lower half thrives in the daytime as a pedestrian shopping street. The upper half sleeps during the day, but comes alive after dark. Use Métro stop Censier Daubenton or Les Gobelins. A terrific Saturday market sprawls along Boulevard Port Royal, just east of the Port Royal Métro stop.

$ Port-Royal-Hôtel* has only one star, but don't let that fool you. Its 46 rooms are polished top to bottom and have been well-run by the same proud family for 81 years. You could eat off the floors of its spotless, comfy rooms...but you won't find air-conditioning, Internet access, or Wi-Fi. Ask for a room away from the street (S-€49-60, D-€60, Db-€86-96 depending on size, big shower down the hall-€3, cash only, nonrefundable cash deposit required, on busy Boulevard de Port-Royal at #8, Mo: Les Gobelins, tel. 01 43 31 70 06, fax 01 43 31 33 67, www.hotelportroyal.fr, portroyalhotel@wanadoo.fr).

$ Hôtel de L'Espérance** is simply a terrific two-star value. It's quiet and cushy, with soft rooms, canopy beds, and nice public spaces (Sb-€85, Db-€85-100, Tb-€120, 15 Rue Pascal, Mo: Censier Daubenton, tel. 01 47 07 10 99, fax 01 43 37 56 19, www.hoteldelesperance.fr, hotel.esperance@wanadoo.fr).

$ Young & Happy Hostel is easygoing, well-run, and English-speaking, with Internet access, kitchen facilities, and acceptable hostel conditions. It sits dead-center in the Rue Mouffetard action...which can be good or bad (all rates per person: bunk in 4- to 10-bed co-ed dorm-€24-32, in 3- to 5-bed female-only dorm-€28, in double room-€35, includes breakfast, sheet deposit-€5, towel-€1, credit cards accepted, no air-con, no lockers but safety box at reception, pay Wi-Fi, 11:00-16:00 lockout but reception stays open, no curfew, 80 Rue Mouffetard, Mo: Place Monge, tel. 01 47 07 47 07, fax 01 47 07 22 24, www.youngandhappy.fr, smile@youngandhappy.fr, friendly Alex at the helm).

Montmartre

Montmartre is surprisingly quiet once you get away from the touristy top of the hill. Ditch the flow of visitors streaming from Place d'Anvers to Sacré-Cœur Basilica, and you'll find a charming neighborhood happily living in the shadow of the hulking monument. Montmartre is a mix of young families, artists, and sprightly senior citizens, and is becoming increasingly popular with the *bobo* crowd (*bourgeois bohemian*, French for "hipster"). Travelers will find good deals on hotel rooms and a lively atmosphere, especially in the evenings when the terraces are full and tiny bars spill crowds onto the narrow streets. There's a TI at the Anvers Métro stop (daily 10:00-18:00, 72 Boulevard Rochechouart).

Most of the action is centered around Rue des Abbesses, starting at Place des Abbesses, and stretching several blocks to Rue Lepic. Rue Lepic is also lively, but the lower you go the seedier it gets: Scammers and shady characters swarm the base of the hill after hours (along Boulevard Clichy and Boulevard Rochechouart, where you'll find what's left of Paris' red light district). For fun nightlife, explore the narrow streets uphill from Rue des Abbesses around Rue Durantin and Rue des Trois Frères. For restaurant suggestions, see page 367.

Métro and Bus Connections: Métro line 12 is the handiest (use the Abbesses stop). Line 2 is also close, using the Blanche, Pigalle, or Anvers stops, but requires a four-block uphill walk to reach my recommended hotels. There's only one bus line on the hill—the Montmartrobus electric bus—which connects Pigalle, Abbesses, and Place du Tertre in 10 minutes (4/hour). At the base of the hill you can catch bus #67 (next to the Pigalle Métro station) and ride straight to the Louvre, along the Seine, across Ile St. Louis, and eventually to the Jardin des Plantes.

PARIS

$$$ Le Relais Montmartre is a spotless hotel with cushy public spaces, pastel paint, and 26 cozy rooms sporting floral curtains. There are lots of guest-centered amenities, including a shared iPad, fireplace, and quiet central courtyard (Db-€185-240 depending on room size, 6 Rue Constance, tel. 01 70 64 25 25, fax 01 70 64 25 00, www.relaismontmartre.fr, contact@relaismontmartre.fr).

$ Hôtel Regyn's Montmartre** is located directly on the lively Abbesses square, with 22 small but adequate rooms, no air-conditioning, and mediocre bathrooms. Rooms in the front come with pleasant views and noise from the square. Guests in fourth- and fifth-floor rooms can see all the way to the Eiffel Tower (Sb-€91-110, Db-€122-142, check website for specials, 18 Place des Abbesses, tel. 01 42 54 45 21, fax 01 42 59 08 85, www.hotel-regyns-paris.com, info@hotel-regyns-montmartre.net).

$ Hôtel André Gill ** makes me smile. It's a family affair: The front desk is run by two lovely sisters, two lap dogs, and two fat cats. Breakfast is included and served in a living room filled with plastic flowers and photos of the sisters' grandchildren. The hallways and elevator are alarmingly dark and narrow, but the rooms themselves are bright and clean (Sb-€45, Db-€63-89, Tb-€105, large double with Eiffel Tower view-€120-150, 4 Rue André Gill, tel. 01 42 62 48 48, fax 01 42 62 77 92, andregill@hotmail.com).

$ My Hôtel in France Montmartre, a chain hotel, has 41 small, basic-but-good-value rooms on six floors, with no elevator or air-conditioning. Twin rooms are larger than doubles for the same price. Continental breakfast and a sandwich lunch-box are included (Sb-€80-89, Db-€90-99, prices vary greatly depending on occupancy, 57 Rue des Abbesses, tel. 01 42 51 50 00, fax 01 42 51 08 68, www.myhotelinfrance-montmartre.com, montmartre@my-hotel-in-france.com).

$ Plug-Inn Boutique Hostel is part hotel and part hostel, but with a hotel vibe. Half a block off Rue des Abbesses, it has a young clientele, bathrooms in all 30 rooms, free Wi-Fi, and several public computer terminals. Early arrivals can leave their luggage and take a shower. Not all rooms are available online, so book by phone or email (all prices per person: bunk in dorm-€29-36, private Db room-€49-52, female-only rooms available, includes breakfast, kitchen facilities, elevator, 24-hour front desk staff, no curfew, 7 Rue Aristide Bruant, tel. 01 42 58 42 58, fax 01 42 23 93 88, www.plug-inn.fr, bonjour@plug-inn.fr).

$ Hôtel Bonséjour Montmartre, run by eager Michel and his family, is an old, worn, hostelesque place with dirt-cheap prices. All rooms have sinks, but share a hallway toilet. Some rooms share one public shower on main floor, and others have small, oddly

Hotels & Restaurants in Montmartre

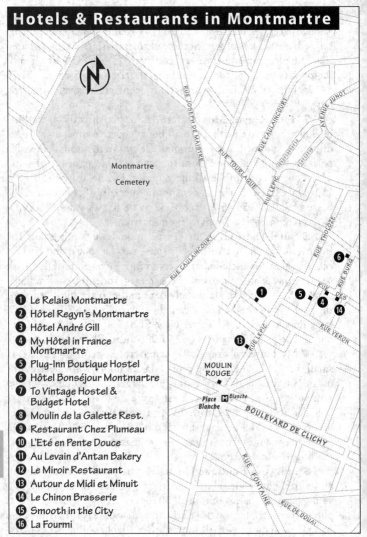

Montmartre Cemetery

1 Le Relais Montmartre
2 Hôtel Regyn's Montmartre
3 Hôtel André Gill
4 My Hôtel in France Montmartre
5 Plug-Inn Boutique Hostel
6 Hôtel Bonséjour Montmartre
7 To Vintage Hostel & Budget Hotel
8 Moulin de la Galette Rest.
9 Restaurant Chez Plumeau
10 L'Eté en Pente Douce
11 Au Levain d'Antan Bakery
12 Le Miroir Restaurant
13 Autour de Midi et Minuit
14 Le Chinon Brasserie
15 Smooth in the City
16 La Fourmi

MOULIN ROUGE

Place Blanche

BOULEVARD DE CLICHY

PARIS

placed shower cabins right next to the bed (S-€35-50, D-€56-69, Tb-€80, higher price for private shower, no elevator, no air-con, 11 Rue Burq, tel. 01 42 54 22 53, fax 01 42 54 25 92, www.hotel-bonsejour-montmartre.fr, hotel-bonsejour-montmartre@wanadoo.fr).

$ The Vintage Hostel & Budget Hotel sits halfway between the hill of Montmartre and Gare du Nord (both destinations are a 10-minute walk away). This hostel/hotel hybrid appeals to young-sters and oldsters alike. Private double rooms—an especially good

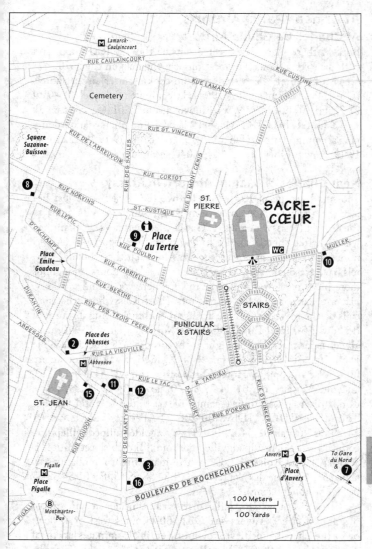

value—are on the top two floors, and most come with romantic balconies just big enough for a table and two chairs (bunk in dorm room with private toilet and shower-€35-45, Sb-€75-85, Db-€90-120, includes breakfast, towel-€1, Wi-Fi only—in lobby, 73 Rue de Dunkerque, tel. 01 40 16 16 40, www.vintage-hostel.com, contact@vintage-hostel.com).

At or near Paris' Airports

At Charles de Gaulle Airport

Both of these places are located outside the T-3 RER stop, and both have restaurants. For locations, see the map on page 370.

$$ Novotel*** is a step up from cookie-cutter airport hotels (Db-€145-200, can rise to €290 for last-minute rooms, tel. 01 49 19 27 27, fax 01 49 19 27 99, www.novotel.com, h1014@accor.com).

$ Hôtel Ibis CDG Airport** is huge and offers standard airport accommodations (Db-€115-155, tel. 01 49 19 19 19, fax 01 49 19 19 21, www.ibishotel.com, h1404@accor.com).

Near Charles de Gaulle Airport, in Roissy

The small village of **Roissy-en-France** (you'll see signs just before the airport as you come from Paris), which gave its name to the airport (Roissy Charles de Gaulle), has better-value chain hotels with free shuttle service to and from the airport (4/hour, 15 minutes, look for *navettes hôtels* signs to reach these hotels). Hotels have reasonably priced restaurants with long hours, though it's more pleasant to walk into the town, where you'll find a bakery, pizzeria, cafés, and a few restaurants. Most Roissy hotels list specials on their websites. These hotels are within walking distance of the town: **$ Hôtel Ibis CDG Paris Nord 2**** (Db-€90-110, usually cheaper than the Ibis right at the airport, 335 Rue de la Belle Etoile, tel. 01 48 17 56 56, fax 01 48 17 56 51, www.ibishotel.com, h0815@accor.com), **$ Hôtel Campanile Roissy***** (Db-€90-120, allée des Vergers, tel. 01 34 29 80 40, fax 01 34 29 80 39, www.campanile-roissy.fr, roissy@campanile.fr), and **$$ Hôtel Golden Tulip Paris CDG***** (Db-€130-200, 11 Allée des Vergers, tel. 01 34 29 00 00, fax 01 34 29 00 11, www.goldentulipcdgvillepinte.com, info@goldentulipcdgvillepinte.com). The cheapest option is **$ B&B Hôtel Roissy CDG***, where many flight attendants stay (Db-€55, 17 Allée des Vergers, tel. 01 34 38 55 55, fax 01 34 38 55 00, www.hotelbb.com).

To avoid rush-hour traffic, drivers can consider sleeping north of Paris in either **Auvers-sur-Oise** (30 minutes west of airport) or in the pleasant medieval town of **Senlis** (15 minutes north of airport). In Auvers, **$$ Hostellerie du Nord***** is small, friendly, and polished—a treat for those who want to sleep in luxury. It has modern, spacious rooms and a seriously good restaurant that requires reservations (Db-€100-130, suites-€190, *menus* from €60, a block from train station at 6 Rue du Général de Gaulle, tel. 01 30 36 70 74, fax 01 30 36 72 75, www.hostelleriedunord.fr). In Senlis, **$ Hôtel Ibis Senlis**** is a few minutes from town (Db-€80-110, Route Nationale A1, tel. 03 44 53 70 50, fax 03 44 53 51 93, www.ibishotel.com, h0709@accor.com). If you don't have a car, sleep elsewhere.

Near Orly Airport

Two chain hotels, owned by the same company and very close to the Sud terminal, are your best options near Orly. Both have free shuttles *(navettes)* to the terminal.

$$$ Hôtel Mercure Paris Orly* provides high comfort for a high price; check their website for discounts (Db-€140-220, book early for better rate, tel. 01 49 75 15 51, fax 01 49 75 15 51, www.accorhotel.com, h1246@accor.com).

$ Hôtel Ibis Orly Aéroport* is reasonable and basic (Db-€85-110, tel. 01 56 70 50 60, fax 01 56 70 50 70, www.ibishotel.com, h1413@accor.com).

Apartment Rentals

Among the many English-speaking organizations renting apartments in Paris, the following have proven most reliable. Their websites are good and essential to understanding your options. Read the rental conditions very carefully.

Paris Perfect has offices in Paris with English-speaking staff who seek the "perfect apartment" for their clients and are selective about what they offer. Their service gets rave reviews. Many units have Eiffel Tower views, and most include free Internet, free local and international phone calls, satellite TV, air-conditioning, and washers and dryers (studio-€125/night, one-bedroom apartment-€199/night, two-bedroom apartment-€285/night, discount off regular rates for Rick Steves readers, US toll-free tel. 888-520-2087, www.parisperfect.com).

Cobblestone Paris Rentals is a small, American-run outfit offering furnished rentals with a focus on the Marais and central Paris. All apartments offer free Wi-Fi, free international phone calls, and free cable TV. Apartments come stocked with English-language DVDs, coffee, tea, cooking spices, and basic bathroom amenities (two free river cruises for Rick Steves readers who book a stay of five nights or more, www.cobblestoneparis.com, reservations@cobblestoneparis.com).

Paris Appartements Services rents studios (€100-170/night) and one-bedroom apartments (€150-230/night) in central neighborhoods (20 Rue Bachaumont, tel. 01 40 28 01 28, fax 01 40 28 92 01, www.paris-appartements-services.com, info@paris-apts.com).

Home Rental Service has been in business for 18 years and offers a big selection of apartments throughout Paris with no agency fees (120 Champs-Elysées, tel. 01 42 25 65 40, fax 01 42 25 65 45, www.homerental.fr, info@homerental.fr).

Locaflat offers accommodations ranging from studios to five-room apartments, with occasional specials online (63 Avenue de la Motte-Picquet, tel. 01 43 06 78 79, fax 01 40 56 99 69, www. locaflat.com, locaflat@gmail.com).

Paris Home is a small outfit with only two small studios, but both are located on Rue Amélie in the heart of the Rue Cler area (see map on page 316). Each has modern furnishings and laundry facilities. Friendly Slim, the owner, is the best part (€590/week, no minimum stay, special rates for longer stays, credit cards accepted, free Internet access and US or France telephone calls, free maid service, airport/train station transfers possible, mobile 06 19 03 17 55, www.parishome2000.com, parishome2000@yahoo.fr).

Paris for Rent, a San Francisco-based group, has been renting top-end apartments in Paris for more than a decade (US tel. 866-4-FRANCE, www.parisforrent.com).

Tournights, run by Frederick and Mayra, rents several apartments around Paris (www.tournights.com).

Cross-Pollinate is a reputable online booking agency representing B&Bs and apartments in a handful of European cities. Paris listings range from a Bastille B&B room for two for €90 per night to a two-bedroom Montmartre apartment sleeping six for €160 per night. Minimum stays vary from one to five nights (US tel. 800-270-1190, France tel. 09-75-18-11-10, www.cross-pollinate.com, info@cross-pollinate.com).

Eating in Paris

The Parisian eating scene is kept at a rolling boil. Entire books (and lives) are dedicated to the subject. Paris is France's wine-and-cuisine melting pot. Though it lacks a style of its own (only French onion soup is truly Parisian; otherwise, there is no "Parisian cuisine" to speak of), it draws from the best of France. Paris could hold a gourmet Olympics and import nothing.

My recommendations are centered on the same great neighborhoods listed earlier, under "Sleeping in Paris"; you can come home exhausted after a busy day of sightseeing and find a good selection of restaurants right around the corner. And evening is a fine time to explore any of these delightful neighborhoods, even if you're sleeping elsewhere.

Linger longer over dinner—restaurants expect you to enjoy a full meal. Most restaurants I've listed have set-price *menus* between €20 and €35. In most cases, the few extra euros you pay are well-spent, and open up a variety of better choices. Remember that a service charge is included in the prices (so little or no tipping is expected). Eat early with tourists or late with locals. Before choosing a seat outside, remember that smokers love outdoor tables.

Budget Tips: To save piles of euros, go to a bakery for takeout,

---

Restaurant Price Code

To help you choose among these listings, I've divided the restaurants into three categories, based on the price for a typical main course.

  \$\$\$ **Higher Priced**—Most main courses €25 or more.
    \$\$ **Moderately Priced**—Most main courses between €15-25.
     \$ **Lower Priced**—Most main courses €15 or less.

---

or stop at a café for lunch. Cafés and brasseries are happy to serve a *plat du jour* (garnished plate of the day, about €12-18) or a chef-like salad (about €10-13) day or night.

To save even more, consider picnics (tasty take-out dishes are available at charcuteries). The Palais Royal (across place du Palais Royal from the Louvre) and place des Vosges in the Marais make exquisite spots for peaceful, royal picnics. For great river views, try the little triangular Henry IV park on the west tip of Ile de la Cité, the bench-equipped pedestrian pont des Arts bridge (across from the Louvre), or the grass parkway running along the Seine between Les Invalides and pont de l'Alma (near rue Cler). Parks, such as the Tuileries and Luxembourg Garden, make for ideal picnics—as do the gardens behind Les Invalides and the Champ de Mars park below the Eiffel Tower (eat at the sides of the park; the central area is off-limits). Be aware that parks, including the grassy area on place des Vosges, close at dusk. For an urban setting and terrific people-watching, try the Pompidou Center (by the *Homage to Stravinsky* fountains) or the courtyard around the pyramid of the Louvre. Hoteliers frown on in-room picnics.

In the Rue Cler Neighborhood

The Rue Cler neighborhood caters to its residents. Its eateries, while not destination places, have an intimate charm. I've provided a full range of choices—from cozy ma-and-pa diners to small and trendy boutique restaurants to classic, big, boisterous bistros. For all restaurants listed in this area, use the Ecole Militaire Métro stop (unless another station is listed).

On Rue Cler

\$ Café du Marché boasts the best seats, coffee, and prices on Rue Cler. The owner's philosophy: Brasserie on speed—crank out good food at great prices to chic locals and savvy tourists. It's high-energy, with young waiters who barely have time to smile...*très* Pa-

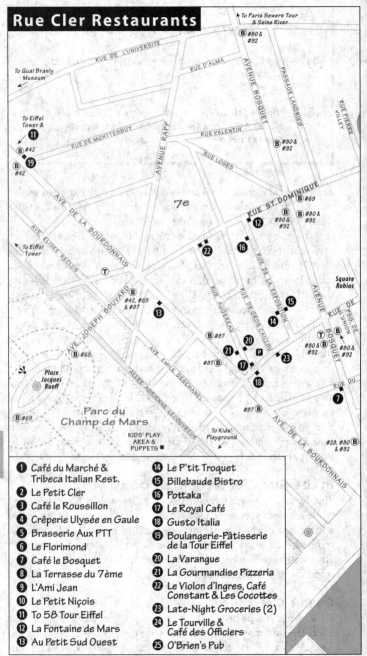

Rue Cler Restaurants

To Paris Sewers Tour & Seine River

Ⓑ #80 & #92

RUE DE L'UNIVERSITÉ

RUE D'ALMA

AVENUE BOSQUET

PASSAGE LANDRIEU

RUE PIERRE VILLEY

To Quai Branly Museum

RUE DE MONTTESSUY

AVENUE RAPP

RUE VALENTIN

RUE LOGES

Ⓑ #80 & #92

To Eiffel Tower &

⑪

Ⓑ #42

⑲ Ⓑ #42

RUE ST. DOMINIQUE

Ⓑ #69

7e

Ⓑ #69

AVE. DE LA BOURDONNAIS

⑫

Ⓑ #80 & #92

Ⓑ #80 & #92

AVE. ELISÉE RECLUS

To Eiffel Tower

Ⓣ

㉒

⑯

RUE DE LA TEXPOSITION

AVENUE BOSQUET

Square Robiac

RUE DE PSG. D'UNION

AVE. JOSEPH BOUVARD

Ⓑ #42, #69 & #87

⑬

RUE AUGEREAU

RUE DE GROS CAILLOU

⑮

⑭

Ⓣ Ⓑ

Ⓑ #80 & #92

Ⓑ #80 & #92

Ⓑ #87

Ⓑ #69

AVE. ÉMILE DESCHANEL

㉑ ⑳

Ⓑ #87

⑰ P ㉓

⑱

Place Jacques Rueff

ALLÉE ADRIENNE LECOUVREUR

#87 Ⓑ

RUE DU

⑦

Ⓑ #69

Parc du Champ de Mars

AVE. DE LA BOURDONNAIS

KIDS' PLAY AREA & PUPPETS ■

To Kids' Playground

Ⓑ #28, #80 & #92

① Café du Marché & Tribeca Italian Rest.
② Le Petit Cler
③ Café le Roussillon
④ Crêperie Ulysée en Gaule
⑤ Brasserie Aux PTT
⑥ Le Florimond
⑦ Café le Bosquet
⑧ La Terrasse du 7ème
⑨ L'Ami Jean
⑩ Le Petit Niçois
⑪ To 58 Tour Eiffel
⑫ La Fontaine de Mars
⑬ Au Petit Sud Ouest

⑭ Le P'tit Troquet
⑮ Billebaude Bistro
⑯ Pottaka
⑰ Le Royal Café
⑱ Gusto Italia
⑲ Boulangerie-Pâtisserie de la Tour Eiffel
⑳ La Varangue
㉑ La Gourmandise Pizzeria
㉒ Le Violon d'Ingres, Café Constant & Les Cocottes
㉓ Late-Night Groceries (2)
㉔ Le Tourville & Café des Officiers
㉕ O'Brien's Pub

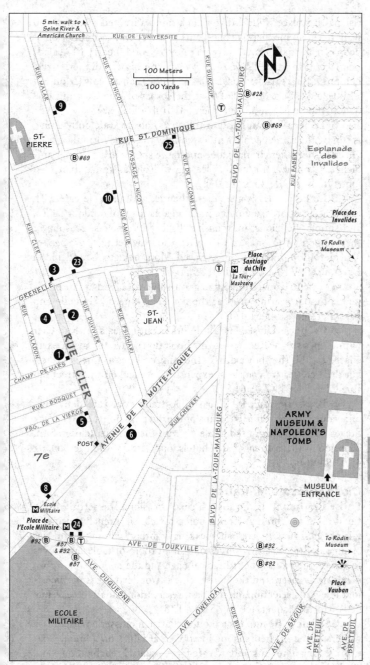

5 min. walk to
Seine River &
American Church

RUE DE L'UNIVERSITE

RUE MALAR

RUE JEAN NICOT

RUE SURCOUF

BLVD. DE LA TOUR-MAUBOURG

B #28

9

ST-
PIERRE

B #69

RUE ST. DOMINIQUE

25

RUE DE LA COMETE

B #69

Esplanade
des
Invalides

RUE FABERT

100 Meters

100 Yards

PASSAGE J. NICOT

10

RUE AMELIE

RUE CLER

Place des
Invalides

To Rodin
Museum

3

23

Place
Santiago
du Chile

T

M

La Tour-
Maubourg

GRENELLE

RUE DUVIVIER

RUE PSICHARI

ST-
JEAN

4

2

RUE VALADON

RUE CLER

1

AVENUE DE LA MOTTE-PICQUET

BLVD. DE LA-TOUR-MAUBOURG

CHAMP DE MARS

RUE BOSQUET

RUE CHEVERT

ARMY
MUSEUM &
NAPOLEON'S
TOMB

PSG. DE LA VIERGE

5

6

POST

7e

MUSEUM
ENTRANCE

8

Ecole
Militaire

M

Place de
l'Ecole Militaire

M

24

B #92

B #87
& #92

B

T

AVE. DE TOURVILLE

B #92

To Rodin
Museum

B #87

AVE. DUQUESNE

ECOLE
MILITAIRE

AVE. LOWENDAL

RUE BIXIO

AVE. DE SEGUR

B #92

Place
Vauban

AVE. DE
BRETEUIL

AVE. DE
BRETEUIL

PARIS

risian. This place is ideal if you don't mind a limited selection and want to eat an inexpensive one-course meal among a commotion of people. The chalkboard lists your choices: good, hearty €10 salads or more filling €10-12 *plats du jour*. If coming for dinner, arrive before 19:30; it's packed at 21:00, and service can be slow (Mon-Sat 11:00-23:00, Sun 11:00-17:00, at the corner of Rue Cler and Rue du Champ de Mars, 38 Rue Cler, tel. 01 47 05 51 27).

$ Tribeca Italian Restaurant, next door to Café du Marché, is run by the same people with essentially the same formula *à la italienne*. They offer similar value and more space with a calmer ambience. Choose from family-pleasing €13 pizzas and Italian *plats* (open daily, tel. 01 45 55 12 01).

$ Le Petit Cler is a small, authentic, and adorable café with long leather booths, a vintage interior, a handful of outdoor tables, and simple, delicious, inexpensive dishes (€9 omelets, €7 soup of the moment, €12 salads, €13 *plats*, mouthwatering *petit pots* of chocolate or vanilla pudding, closed Mon, next to Grand Hôtel Lévêque at 29 Rue Cler, tel. 01 45 50 17 50).

$ Café le Roussillon offers good-value café food at fair prices (daily, indoor seating only, at the corner of Rue de Grenelle and Rue Cler, tel. 01 45 51 47 53).

$ Crêperie Ulysée en Gaule offers cheap seats on Rue Cler with crêpes to go. Readers of this book don't have to pay an extra charge to sit if they buy a drink. The family adores its Greek dishes, but their crêpes are your least expensive hot meal on this street (28 Rue Cler, tel. 01 47 05 61 82).

$ Brasserie Aux PTT, a simple traditional café delivering fair-value fare, reminds Parisians of the old days on Rue Cler. Rick Steves diners are promised a free *kir* with their dinner (closed Sun, 2-minute walk from most area hotels, opposite 53 Rue Cler, tel. 01 45 51 94 96).

Close to Ecole Militaire

$$ Le Florimond is fun for a special occasion. The setting is intimate and welcoming. Locals come for classic French cuisine at fair prices. Friendly English-speaking Laurent, whose playful ties change daily, gracefully serves one small room of tables and loves to give suggestions. The stuffed cabbage and the *confit de canard* are particularly tasty, and the house wine is wonderful (€36 *menu*, affordable wine selection, closed Sun, reservations smart, 19 Avenue de la Motte-Picquet, tel. 01 45 55 40 38).

$$ Café le Bosquet is a modern Parisian brasserie with dressy waiters. Dine in their snappy interior or at tables on a broad sidewalk. Come here for standard café fare—salad, French onion soup, steak, or a *plat du jour* for about €14-19. The escargots are tasty, and the house red wine is plenty good (continental breakfast for €6, free Wi-Fi, closed Sun, reservations smart Fri-Sat, corner of Rue du Champ de Mars and Avenue Bosquet, 46 Avenue Bosquet, tel. 01 45 51 38 13).

$$ La Terrasse du 7ème is a sprawling, happening café with grand outdoor seating and a living room-like interior with comfy love seats. Located on a corner, it overlooks a busy intersection with a constant parade of people. Chairs are set up facing the street, as a meal here is like dinner theater—and the show is slice-of-life Paris (€16-22 *plats*, good €13 *salade niçoise*, no fixed-price *menu*, daily until at least 24:00 and sometimes until 2:00 in the morning, at Ecole Militaire Métro stop, tel. 01 45 55 00 02).

Between Rue de Grenelle and the River, East of Avenue Bosquet

$$$ L'Ami Jean offers top Basque specialties. You'll get hearty portions at palatable prices (considering the quality), while sitting in snug-but-fun, get-to-know-your-neighbor spaces. Parisians detour long distances to savor the gregarious chef's special cuisine and convivial atmosphere. Arrive by 19:30 or call ahead (€43 *menu*, closed Sun-Mon, 27 Rue Malar, Mo: La Tour-Maubourg, tel. 01 47 05 86 89).

$$ Le Petit Niçois celebrates fish from southern France. Come here for everything from bouillabaisse to bass to paella to mussels, and enjoy the area's top seafood at decent prices (a few meat dishes are available). Start with the delectable *escargot à la provençale*, dive into the *marmite du pêcheur*—a delicious version of bouillabaisse, sample the sinful puréed potatoes, and finish yourself off with the lemon twist finale *(citron confit givré aux frais)* or *café gourmand* desserts. The atmosphere is contemporary—warm though formal—and the welcome is genuine (€22 two-course *menu*, €32 three-course *menu*; better yet, ask the owner, caring Carlos, to give you the royal treatment—matching three courses with wine and apéritifs for €50; daily, 10 Rue Amélie, Mo: La Tour Maubourg, tel. 01 45 51 83 65).

Between Rue de Grenelle and the River, West of Avenue Bosquet

Some of these places line peaceful Rue de l'Exposition (a few blocks west of Rue Cler), allowing you to comparison shop *sans* stress.

$$$ 58 Tour Eiffel, on the tower's first level, is popular both for its incredible views and the cuisine of its famed French chef, Alain Ducasse. Dinner here is pricey (you must order a complete *menu*—€70-85) and requires a reservation (two seatings: 18:30 and 21:00; reserve long in advance, especially if you want a view, either

PARIS

by calling or going online; within France, dial toll tel. 08 25 56 66 62; from outside France, dial 01 76 64 14 64; www.restaurants-toureiffel.com). Lunch is easier (€20 *menu*, daily 11:30-16:00, no reservations possible, Mo: Bir-Hakeim or Trocadéro, RER: Champ de Mars-Tour Eiffel).

$$$ La Fontaine de Mars, a longtime favorite and neighborhood institution, draws Parisians who want to be seen. It's charmingly situated on a tiny, jumbled square with tables jammed together for the serious business of eating. Reserve in advance for a table on the ground floor or on the square, and enjoy the same meal Barack Obama did. Street-level seats come with the best ambience (€20-30 *plats du jour,* superb foie gras, superb-er desserts, 129 Rue St. Dominique, tel. 01 47 05 46 44).

$$ Au Petit Sud Ouest has stone walls and wood beams, making it a cozy place to sample fine cuisine from southwestern France. Duck, goose, foie gras, *cassoulet,* and truffles are among its specialties. Tables come with toasters to heat your bread—it enhances the flavors of the foie gras (closed Sun-Mon, 46 Avenue de la Bourdonnais, tel. 01 45 55 59 59).

$$ Le P'tit Troquet is a petite eatery taking you back to the Paris of the 1920s. Marie welcomes you warmly, and chef José cooks a delicious three-course €33 *menu* with a range of traditional choices prepared creatively. The homey charm and gourmet quality make this restaurant a favorite of connoisseurs (opens at 18:30, closed Sun, reservations smart, 28 Rue de l'Exposition, tel. 01 47 05 80 39).

$$ Billebaude, run by patient Pascal, is a small, authentic Parisian bistro popular with locals. The focus is on what's fresh, including catch-of-the-day fish and meats from the hunt (available in the fall and winter). Chef Sylvain, an avid hunter (as the decor will remind you), is determined to deliver quality at a fair price—and he succeeds. Try *filet de bar* (sea bass) for your main course and *œufs à la neige* for dessert (€33 *menu*, closed Sun-Mon, 29 Rue de l'Exposition, tel. 01 45 55 20 96).

$$ Pottaka is a snug eatery where in-the-know locals go for delicious Basque cuisine at reasonable prices (€34 *menu*, €19 *plats*, reservations smart for Wed-Sat nights, 4 Rue de l'Exposition, tel. 01 45 51 88 38).

$ Le Royal is a tiny neighborhood fixture. This humble time-warp place, with prices and decor from another era, comes from an age when cafés sold firewood and served food as an afterthought. Parisians dine here because "it's like eating at home." Gentle Michele runs the counter while hustling Giles tends to the tables (€5 omelets, €9 *plats*, filling three-course *menu*-€13, closed Sat-Sun, 212 Rue de Grenelle, tel. 01 47 53 92 90).

PARIS

$ Gusto Italia serves up tasty, good-value Italian cuisine in a shoebox-size place with a few tables outside. Arrive early or plan to wait (€12 salads, €14 pasta, daily, 199 Rue de Grenelle, tel. 01 45 55 00 43).

$ Boulangerie-Pâtisserie de la Tour Eiffel delivers inexpensive salads, quiches, and sandwiches. Enjoy the views of the Eiffel Tower (daily, outdoor and indoor seating, one block southeast of the tower at 21 Avenue de la Bourdonnais, tel. 01 47 05 59 81).

$ La Varangue is an entertaining one-man show featuring English-speaking Philippe, who once ran a catering business in Pennsylvania. He now lives upstairs and has found his niche serving a mostly American clientele. The food is cheap and basic, the tables are few, and he opens at 17:30. Norman Rockwell would dig his minuscule dining room—with the traditional kitchen sizzling just over the counter. Try his snails and chocolate cake—but not together (€12 *plats*, €18 *menu*, always a vegetarian option, closed Sun, 27 Rue Augereau, tel. 01 47 05 51 22).

$ La Gourmandise Pizzeria is a kid-friendly, cheap pizzeria across from La Varangue (closed Sun, eat in or take out, 28 Rue Augereau, tel. 01 45 55 45 16).

The Constant Lineup: Ever since leaving the venerable Hôtel Crillon, famed chef Christian Constant has made a career of taking the "snoot" out of French cuisine—and making it accessible to people like us. Today you'll find three of his restaurants strung along one block of Rue St. Dominique between Rue Augereau and Rue de l'Exposition. Each is distinct, and each offers a different experience and price range. None of these places is cheap, but they all deliver top-quality cuisine.

$$$ Le Violon d'Ingres, where Christian won his first Michelin star, makes for a good excuse to dress up and really dine finely in Paris. Glass doors open onto a lively and chic eating scene, service is formal yet helpful, and the cuisine is what made this restaurateur's reputation (€60-80 *menus*, daily, reservations essential, 135 Rue St. Dominique, tel. 01 45 55 15 05).

$$ Les Cocottes is a trendy, bar-stool-only place serving simple dishes in small iron pots to yuppie Parisians (daily, no reservations taken, 135 Rue St. Dominique).

$$ Café Constant is a cool, two-level place that feels more like a small bistro-wine bar than a café. Delicious and fairly priced dishes are served in a fun setting to a dedicated clientele. Arrive early to get a table (downstairs seating is better); the friendly staff speak English (€11 *entrées*, €16 *plats*, €7 desserts, closed Sun-Mon, no reservations taken, corner of Rue Augereau and Rue St. Dominique, next to recommended Hôtel Londres Eiffel, tel. 01 47 53 73 34).

PARIS

Picnicking near Rue Cler

Rue Cler is a festival of food. The street is lined with businesses run by people whose lives seem to be devoted to their specialty: polished produce, rotisserie chicken, freshly made crêpes, or deliciously stinky cheese.

For a magical picnic dinner at the Eiffel Tower, assemble it in no fewer than five shops on Rue Cler. Then lounge on the best grass in Paris, with the dogs, Frisbees, a floodlit tower, and a cool breeze in the Champ de Mars park (picnics are allowed off to the sides, but not in the central area, which is off-limits).

Asian delis (generically called *traiteurs asiatique*) provide low-stress, low-price take-out treats (€8 dinner plates; the one on Rue Cler near Rue du Champ de Mars has tables). **Crêperie Ulysée en Gaule,** the Greek restaurant on Rue Cler across from Grand Hôtel Lévêque, sells take-away crêpes (see page 348). For the cheapest, easiest meals, consider getting sandwiches or kebabs, just beyond the cute zone a few steps past the Ecole Militaire Métro stop on Avenue de Tourville.

Small, **late-night groceries** are at 197 Rue de Grenelle (open daily until midnight), as well as where Rues Cler and Grenelle cross.

Breakfast on Rue Cler

Hotel breakfasts, though convenient, are generally not a good value. For a great Rue Cler start to your day, drop by **Brasserie Aux PTT,** where Rick Steves readers are promised a *deux pour douze* breakfast special (two "American" breakfasts—juice, a big coffee, croissant, bread, ham, and eggs—for €12; closed Sun, 53 Rue Cler). For a continental breakfast for about €6, try nearby **Café le Bosquet** (closed Sun, 46 Avenue Bosquet).

Nightlife in Rue Cler

This sleepy neighborhood was not made for night owls, but there are a few notable exceptions. The focal point of before- and after-dinner posing occurs along the broad sidewalk at the intersection of Avenues de la Motte-Picquet and Tourville (Mo: Ecole Militaire). **Le Tourville** and **Café des Officiers** gather a sea of outward-facing seats for the important business of people-watching—and fashion-model recruiting.

La Terrasse du 7ème, across the avenue, has a less-pretentious clientele (see listing, earlier). Nearby, **Café du Marché** (listed earlier) attracts a Franco-American crowd until at least midnight, as does the younger **Café Roussillon** (good French pub atmosphere, corner of Rue de Grenelle and Rue Cler). **O'Brien's Pub** is a relaxed Parisian rendition of an Irish pub, full of Anglophones (77 Rue St. Dominique, Mo: La Tour Maubourg).

In the Marais Neighborhood

The trendy Marais is filled with diners enjoying good food in colorful and atmospheric eateries. The scene is competitive and changes all the time. I've listed an assortment of eateries—all handy to recommended hotels—that offer good food at decent prices, plus a memorable experience.

On Romantic Place des Vosges

This square offers Old World Marais elegance, a handful of eateries, and an ideal picnic site until dusk, when the park closes (use Bastille or St. Paul Métro stops). Strolling around the arcade after dark is more important than dining here—fanciful art galleries alternate with restaurants and cafés. Choose a restaurant that best fits your mood and budget; most have arcade seating and provide big space heaters to make outdoor dining during colder months an option. Also consider a drink or dessert on the square at Café Hugo or Carette after eating elsewhere.

$$$ **Ma Bourgogne** is a vintage eatery where you'll sit under warm arcades in a whirlpool of Frenchness, as bow-tied and black-aproned waiters serve you traditional French specialties: blood-red steak (try the *brochette de bœuf*), piles of fries, escargot, and good red wine. Monsieur Cougoureux (koo-goo-ruh) has commanded this ship since de Gaulle was sniveling at Americans. He offers anyone with this book a free *amuse-bouche* ("amusement for your mouth") of his homemade *steak tartare*—but you may need to remind him (show him my picture in this book). This is your chance to try this "raw spiced hamburger" delicacy without dedicating an entire meal to it (€40 *menu*, daily, cash only, at northwest corner at #19, tel. 01 42 78 44 64).

$$ **La Place Royale** offers a fine location on the square; there's comfortable seating inside or you can sit outside under the arches. The cuisine is traditional, well-priced, and served nonstop all day (€23-39 *menus*, daily, 2 bis Place des Vosges, tel. 01 42 78 58 16).

$$ **Café Hugo,** named for the square's most famous resident, is best for drinks only, as the cuisine does not live up to its setting (daily, 22 Place des Vosges, tel. 01 42 72 64 04).

Near Place des Vosges

$$ **Les Bonnes Soeurs,** a block from the square, blends modern and traditional fare with simple, contemporary ambience. Portions are big and inventive. The delicious and filling *pressé de chèvre* starter (a hunk of goat cheese topped with tapenade and tomatoes) begs to be shared. Their hearty French hamburger comes with a salad and the best fries I've tasted in Paris (*plats* from €16, no *menu*, daily, 8 Rue du Pas de la Mule, tel. 01 42 74 55 80).

$$ **Chez Janou,** a Provençal bistro, tumbles out of its corner

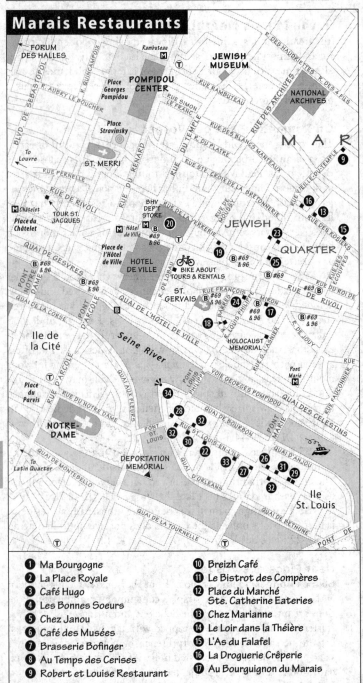

Marais Restaurants

FORUM DES HALLES

Rambuteau

JEWISH MUSEUM

R. DES HAUDRIETTES   R. DES 3 FILS

R. QUINCAMPOIX

R. AUBRY LE BOUCHER

Place Georges Pompidou

POMPIDOU CENTER

RUE SIMON LE FRANC

RUE RAMBUTEAU

RUE DES ARCHIVES

NATIONAL ARCHIVES

BLVD. DE SÉBASTOPOL

RUE DU TEMPLE

RUE DES BLANCS MANTEAUX

M A R

Place Stravinsky

ST. MERRI

RUE DU PLATRE

RUE STE. CROIX DE LA BRETONNERIE

RUE VIEILLE DU TEMPLE

❾

RUE PERNELLE

RUE DE RIVOLI

Châtelet   M

Place du Châtelet

TOUR ST. JACQUES

BHV DEP'T STORE

RUE DE LA VERRERIE

RUE DE MOUSSY

JEWISH

RUE DES ROSIERS

❶❻
❶❸
❶❺

Hôtel de Ville   #69 & 96

⑳

M

Place de l'Hôtel de Ville

②③

QUARTER

QUAI DE GESVRES

PONT NOTRE-DAME   B #69 & 96

B #69 & 96

HOTEL DE VILLE

R. DE LOBAU

BIKE ABOUT TOURS & RENTALS

❶❾   #69 & 96

②⑤

B #69

RUE DU ROI DE

RUE DES ÉCOUFFES

RUE DE RIVOLI

QUAI DE LA CORSE

B

QUAI DE L'HOTEL DE VILLE

ST. GERVAIS

RUE FRANÇOIS

#69 & 96

②④

RUE PAVÉE

MIKON

❶❼

B #69 & 96

Île de la Cité

Seine River

❶❽

R. LOUIS PHILIPPE

HOLOCAUST MEMORIAL

RUE E.G. GASNIER

R. DE JOUY

RUE FAUCONNIER

Place du Parvis   T

RUE D'ARCOLE

RUE DU NOTRE DAME

③④

PONT LOUIS PHILIPPE

VOIE GEORGES POMPIDOU

QUAI DES CÉLESTINS

Pont Marie   M

NOTRE-DAME

QUAI AUX FLEURS

②⑧

QUAI DE BOURBON

PONT MARIE

RUE

To Latin Quarter

QUAI DE MONTEBELLO

PONT ST. LOUIS

DEPORTATION MEMORIAL

③②
③②
③⓪

RUE ST. LOUIS-EN-L'ILE

②②

③③

QUAI D'ANJOU

②⑥   ③①   ②⑨

②⑦

③②

Île St. Louis

QUAI D'ORLEANS

QUAI DE LA TOURNELLE

QUAI DE BETHUNE

PONT DE

PARIS

❶ Ma Bourgogne
❷ La Place Royale
❸ Café Hugo
❹ Les Bonnes Soeurs
❺ Chez Janou
❻ Café des Musées
❼ Brasserie Bofinger
❽ Au Temps des Cerises
❾ Robert et Louise Restaurant

❿ Breizh Café
⓫ Le Bistrot des Compères
⓬ Place du Marché Ste. Catherine Eateries
⓭ Chez Marianne
⓮ Le Loir dans la Théière
⓯ L'As du Falafel
⓰ La Droguerie Crêperie
⓱ Au Bourguignon du Marais

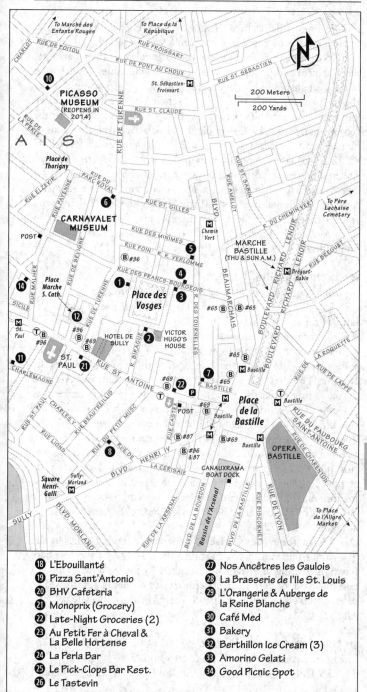

PARIS

18 L'Ebouillanté
19 Pizza Sant'Antonio
20 BHV Cafeteria
21 Monoprix (Grocery)
22 Late-Night Groceries (2)
23 Au Petit Fer à Cheval &
   La Belle Hortense
24 La Perla Bar
25 Le Pick-Clops Bar Rest.
26 Le Tastevin

27 Nos Ancêtres les Gaulois
28 La Brasserie de l'Ile St. Louis
29 L'Orangerie & Auberge de
   la Reine Blanche
30 Café Med
31 Bakery
32 Berthillon Ice Cream (3)
33 Amorino Gelati
34 Good Picnic Spot

building and fills its broad sidewalk with happy eaters. At first glance, you know this place has a following. Don't let the trendy and youthful crowd intimidate you: It's relaxed and charming, with helpful and patient service. The curbside tables are inviting, but I'd sit inside (with very tight seating) to immerse myself in the happy commotion. The style is French Mediterranean, with an emphasis on vegetables (€16-20 *plats du jour* that change with the season, daily from 19:45—book ahead or arrive when it opens, 2 blocks beyond Place des Vosges at 2 Rue Roger Verlomme, tel. 01 42 72 28 41). They're proud of their 81 varieties of *pastis* (licorice-flavored liqueur, €3.50 each, browse the list above the bar).

   $ Café des Musées is an unspoiled, zinc-countered bistro serving traditional dishes with little fanfare and a €22 daily *menu* special that's hard to beat. The place is just far enough away to be overlooked by tourists but packed with locals, so arrive early or book ahead (daily, 49 Rue de Turenne, tel. 01 42 72 96 17).

Near the Bastille

To reach these restaurants, use the Bastille Métro stop.

   $$$ Brasserie Bofinger, an institution for over a century, is famous for fish and traditional cuisine with Alsatian flair. You'll eat in a sprawling interior, surrounded by brisk, black-and-white-attired waiters. It's a high-energy feast for all the senses. Downstairs rooms are elaborately decorated and reminiscent of the Roaring Twenties, while upstairs rooms have traditional Alsatian decor. Eating under the grand 1919 *coupole* is a memorable treat (as is using the "historic" 1919 WC downstairs). Check out the boys shucking and stacking seafood platters out front before you enter. Their €29 two-course and €34 three-course *menus,* while not top cuisine, are a good value. If you've always wanted one of those picturesque seafood platters, this is a good place—you can take the standard platter or create one à la carte (open daily for lunch and for dinner, fun kids' menu, reasonably priced wines, 5 Rue de la Bastille, don't be confused by the lesser "Petite" Bofinger across the street, tel. 01 42 72 87 82).

   $$ Au Temps des Cerises is a cozy place serving wines by the glass and simple meals with a smile. The woody 1950s atmosphere has tight seating and wads of character. Come for a glass of wine and move on, or better yet, stay for a tasty dinner (€9 starters, €18 *plats*, cheap wine, daily, at Rue du Petit Musc and Rue de la Cerisaie, tel. 01 42 72 08 63).

In the Heart of the Marais

These are closest to the St. Paul Métro stop.

   $$ Robert et Louise (now run by Pascal *et* François) crams tables into a tiny, rustic-as-it-gets interior, warmed by a fireplace grill. The food is red-meat good, well-priced, and popular with tourists (€7 starters, €18 *plats*, €6 desserts, closed Mon, 64 Rue du Vieille du Temple, tel. 01 42 78 55 89).

$ Breizh (Brittany) Café is worth the walk. It's a simple Breton joint serving organic crêpes and small rolls made for dipping in rich sauces and salted butter. The crêpes are the best in Paris and run the gamut from traditional andouille (pork sausage) to Asian fusion (buckwheat crêpe topped with seaweed butter). They also serve oysters, have a fantastic list of sweet crêpes, and talk about cider like a sommelier would talk about wine. Try a sparkling cider, a Breton cola, or my favorite—*lait ribot*, a buttermilk-like drink (€7-12 dinner crêpes and *plats*, serves nonstop from 12:00 to late, closed Mon-Tue, 109 Rue du Vieille du Temple, tel. 01 42 72 13 77).

$ Le Bistrot des Compères has a privileged location on a quiet corner in the thick of the Marais; there's a warm and welcoming feel whether you sit inside or out. The cuisine is traditional with creative twists, the staff is relaxed, and the prices are very fair (€7 starters, €15 *plats*, €7 desserts, closed Sun-Mon, 16 Rue Charlemagne, tel. 01 42 72 14 16).

$ *On Place du Marché Ste. Catherine:* This small, romantic square, just off Rue St. Antoine, is an international food festival cloaked in extremely Parisian, leafy-square ambience. On a balmy evening, this is clearly a neighborhood favorite, with a handful of restaurants offering €20-30 three-course meals. Study the square, and you'll find three popular French bistros with similar features: **La Terrasse Ste. Catherine**, **Le Marché**, and **Au Bistrot de la Place** (all open daily with €24 three-course *menus* on weekdays, must order à la carte on weekends, tight seating on flimsy chairs indoors and out). Other inviting eateries nearby serve a variety of international food. You'll eat under the trees, surrounded by a futuristic-in-1800 planned residential quarter.

$ Several hardworking **Asian fast-food eateries,** great for an €8 meal, line Rue St. Antoine.

On Rue des Rosiers in the Jewish Quarter: These places line up along the same street in the heart of the Jewish Quarter.

$ Chez Marianne is a neighborhood fixture that blends delicious Jewish cuisine with Parisian *élan* and wonderful atmosphere. Choose from several indoor zones with a cluttered wine shop/deli feeling, or sit outside. You'll select from two dozen *Zakouski* elements to assemble your €12-16 *plat*. Vegetarians will find great options (€8 falafel sandwich—only €6 if you order it to go, long hours daily, corner of Rue des Rosiers and Rue des Hospitalières-St.-Gervais, tel. 01 42 72 18 86). For takeout, pay inside first and get a ticket before you order outside.

$ Le Loir dans la Théière ("The Dormouse in the Teapot") is a cozy, mellow teahouse offering a welcoming ambience for tired travelers. It's ideal for lunch and popular for weekend brunch. They offer a daily assortment of creatively filled quiches, and bake up an impressive array of homemade desserts that are proudly displayed in the dining room. Try the mile-high lemon meringue "pie" or the oversized *mille-feuille* (Mon-Fri 12:00-19:00, Sat-Sun 10:00-19:00, 3 Rue des Rosiers, tel. 01 42 72 90 61).

$ L'As du Falafel rules the falafel scene in the Jewish quarter. Monsieur Isaac, the "Ace of Falafel" here since 1979, brags, "I've got the biggest pita on the street...and I fill it up." (Apparently it's Lenny Kravitz's favorite, too.) Your inexpensive meal comes on plastic plates, in a bustling setting that seems to prove he's earned his success. The €7 "special falafel" is the big hit (€6 to go), but many Americans enjoy his lighter chicken version *(poulet grillé)* or the tasty and massive *assiette de falafel* (€9). Wash it down it a cold Maccabee beer. Their take-out service draws a constant crowd (long hours daily except closed Fri evening and all day Sat, air-con, 34 Rue des Rosiers, tel. 01 48 87 63 60).

$ La Droguerie, an outdoor crêpe stand a few blocks farther down Rue des Rosiers, is an option if falafels don't work for you, but cheap does (€5 dinner crêpes, closed Mon, 56 Rue des Rosiers).

Near Hôtel de Ville
To reach these eateries, use the Hôtel de Ville Métro stop.

$$ Au Bourguignon du Marais is a handsome wine bar/bistro for Burgundy lovers, where excellent wines (Burgundian only, available by the glass) blend with a good selection of well-designed dishes and efficient service. The *œufs en meurette* are mouthwatering, and the *bœuf bourguignon* could feed two (€10-14 starters, €20-26 *plats*, closed Sun-Mon, pleasing indoor and outdoor seating, 52 Rue François Miron, tel. 01 48 87 15 40).

$ L'Ebouillanté is a breezy crêperie-café, romantically situated near the river on a broad, cobbled pedestrian lane behind a church. With great outdoor seating and an artsy, cozy interior, it's perfect for an inexpensive and relaxing tea, snack, or lunch—or for dinner on a warm evening. Their *Brick,* a Tunisian-inspired dish that looks like a stuffed omelet, has several filling options and comes with a small salad (€15); it left me stuffed (*plats* and big salads-€13, daily 12:00-21:30 except closed Mon Nov-March, a block off the river at 6 Rue des Barres, tel. 01 42 71 09 69).

$ Pizza Sant'Antonio is bustling and cheap, serving up €11 pizzas and salads on a fun Marais square (daily, barely off Rue de Rivoli at 1 Rue de la Verrerie, tel. 01 42 77 78 47).

$ BHV Department Store's fifth-floor cafeteria provides nice views, good prices, and no-brainer, point-and-shoot cafeteria cuisine (Mon-Sat 11:30-18:00, closed Sun, at intersection of Rue du Temple and Rue de la Verrerie, one block from Hôtel de Ville).

Picnicking in the Marais

Picnic at peaceful Place des Vosges (closes at dusk) or on the *quai* on Ile St. Louis (described later). Stretch your euros at the basement supermarket of the **Monoprix** department store (closed Sun, near Place des Vosges on Rue St. Antoine). You'll find small **groceries** open until 23:00 at 48 Rue St. Antoine and on Ile St. Louis.

Nightlife in the Marais

Trendy cafés and bars—popular with gay men—cluster on Rue des Archives and Rue Ste. Croix de la Bretonnerie (closing at about 2:00 in the morning). There's also a line of bars and cafés providing front-row seats for the buff parade on Rue Vieille du Temple, a block north of Rue de Rivoli (the horseshoe-shaped **Au Petit Fer à Cheval** bar-restaurant and the atmospheric **La Belle Hortense** bookstore/wine bar are the focal points of the action). Nearby, Rue des Rosiers bustles with youthful energy, but there are no cafés to observe from. **La Perla** dishes up inexpensive Tex-Mex and is stuffed with Parisian yuppies in search of the perfect margarita (26 Rue François Miron, tel. 01 42 77 59 40).

$ Le Pick-Clops bar-restaurant is a happy peanuts-and-lots-of-cocktails diner with bright neon, loud colors, and a garish local crowd. It's perfect for immersing yourself in today's Marais world—a little boisterous, a little edgy, a little gay, fun-loving, easygoing...and no tourists. Sit inside on old-fashioned diner stools, or streetside to watch the constant Marais parade. The name means "Steal the Cigarettes"—but you'll pay €11 for your big salad (daily 7:00-24:00, 16 Rue Vieille du Temple, tel. 01 40 29 02 18).

More Options: The best scene for hard-core clubbers is the dizzying array of wacky eateries, bars, and dance halls on **Rue de Lappe.** Just east of the stately Place de la Bastille, it's one of the wildest nightspots in Paris and not for everyone.

The most enjoyable peaceful evening may be simply mentally donning your floppy "three musketeers" hat and slowly strolling Place des Vosges, window-shopping the art galleries.

On Ile St. Louis

This romantic and peaceful neighborhood is filled with promising and surprisingly inexpensive possibilities; it merits a trip for dinner even if your hotel is elsewhere. Cruise the island's main street for a variety of options, from cozy *crêperies* to Italian eateries to Alsatian brasseries and romantic bistros. After dinner, sample Paris' best ice cream and stroll across to Ile de la Cité to see a floodlit Notre-Dame. These recommended spots line the island's main drag, Rue St. Louis-en-l'Ile (see map on page 354; to get here use the Pont Marie Métro stop).

$$$ Le Tastevin is an intimate mother-and-son-run restaurant serving top-notch traditional French cuisine with white-tablecloth, candlelit, gourmet elegance under heavy wooden beams. The romantic setting (and the elegantly romantic Parisian couples enjoying the place) naturally makes you whisper. The *menus*, which start at €31 (two courses) and rise to €40-54 (three courses), offer a handful of classic choices that change with the season (daily, reserve for late-evening dining, fine wine list, 46 Rue St. Louis-en-l'Ile, tel. 01 43 54 17 31, owner Madame Puisieux and her gentle son speak just enough English).

$$$ Nos Ancêtres les Gaulois ("Our Ancestors the Gauls"), famous for its rowdy, medieval-cellar atmosphere, is made for hungry warriors and wenches who like to swill hearty wine. They serve up a rustic all-you-can-eat buffet with straw baskets of raw veggies and bundles of sausage (cut whatever you like with your dagger), massive plates of pâté, a meat course, and all the wine you can stomach for €41. The food is just food; burping is encouraged. If you want to overeat, drink too much wine, be surrounded with tourists (mostly French), and holler at your friends while receiving smart-aleck buccaneer service, you're home (daily, 39 Rue St. Louis-en-l'Ile, tel. 01 46 33 66 07).

$$ La Brasserie de l'Ile St. Louis is situated at the prow of the island's ship as it faces Ile de la Cité, offering purely Alsatian cuisine (try the *choucroute garnie* or *coq au riesling* for €19), served in a vigorous, Teutonic setting with no-nonsense, slap-it-down service on wine-stained paper tablecloths. This is a good, balmy-evening perch for watching the Ile St. Louis promenade. If it's chilly, the interior is fun for a memorable night out (closed Wed, no reservations, 55 Quai de Bourbon, tel. 01 43 54 02 59).

$$ L'Orangerie is an inviting place with soft lighting and comfortable seating where diners speak in hushed voices so that everyone can appreciate the delicious cuisine and tasteful setting (€35 three-course *menu*, €27 two-course *menu*, Tue-Sun from 19:00, closed Mon, 28 Rue St. Louis-en-l'Ile, tel. 01 46 33 93 98).

$ Auberge de la Reine Blanche welcomes diners willing to rub elbows with their neighbors under heaving beams. Earnest owner Michel serves traditional cuisine at reasonable prices. The giant goat-cheese salad is a beefy meal in itself (€20 two-course *menu*, €25 three-course *menu*, daily from 18:00, 30 Rue St. Louis-en-l'Ile, tel. 01 46 33 07 87).

$ Café Med, near the pedestrian bridge to Notre-Dame, is a tiny, cheery *crêperie* with good-value salads, crêpes, and €11 *plats* (€14 and €20 *menus*, daily, limited wine list, 77 Rue St. Louis-en-l'Ile, tel. 01 43 29 73 17). Two similar *crêperies* are just across the street.

Riverside Picnic for Impoverished Romantics

On sunny lunchtimes and balmy evenings, the *quai* on the Left Bank side of Ile St. Louis is lined with locals who have more class than money, spreading out tablecloths and even lighting candles for elegant picnics. And tourists can enjoy the same budget meal. A handy grocery store at #67 on the main drag (open until 22:00, closed Tue) has tabouli and other simple, cheap take-away dishes for your picnicking pleasure. The bakery a few blocks down at #40 serves quiche and pizza (open until 20:00, closed Sun-Mon).

Ice-Cream Dessert

Half the people strolling Ile St. Louis are licking an ice-cream cone, because this is the home of *les glaces Berthillon* (now sold throughout Paris). The original **Berthillon** shop, at 31 Rue St. Louis-en-l'Ile, is marked by the line of salivating customers (closed Mon-Tue). For a less famous but at least as satisfying treat, the homemade Italian gelato a block away at **Amorino Gelati** is giving Berthillon competition (no line, bigger portions, easier to see what you want, and they offer little tastes—Berthillon doesn't need to, 47 Rue St. Louis-en-l'Ile, tel. 01 44 07 48 08). Having some of each is not a bad thing.

In the Luxembourg Garden Area

Sleeping in the Luxembourg neighborhood puts you near many appealing dining and after-hours options. Because my hotels in this area cluster near St. Sulpice Church and the Panthéon, I've organized restaurant listings the same way. Restaurants around St. Sulpice tend to be boisterous; those near the Panthéon are calmer; it's a short walk from one area to the other. Anyone sleeping in this area is close to the inexpensive eateries that line the always-bustling Rue Mouffetard. You're also within a 15-minute walk of the *grands cafés* of St. Germain and Montparnasse (with Paris' first café and famous artist haunts).

Near St. Sulpice Church

The eateries in this section are served by the St. Sulpice, Mabillon, and St. Germain-des-Prés Métro stops. The streets between St. Sulpice Church and Boulevard St. Germain abound with restaurants, *crêperies*, wine bars, and jazz haunts (for this area, use Mo: St. Sulpice). Find Rue des Canettes and Rue Guisarde, and win-

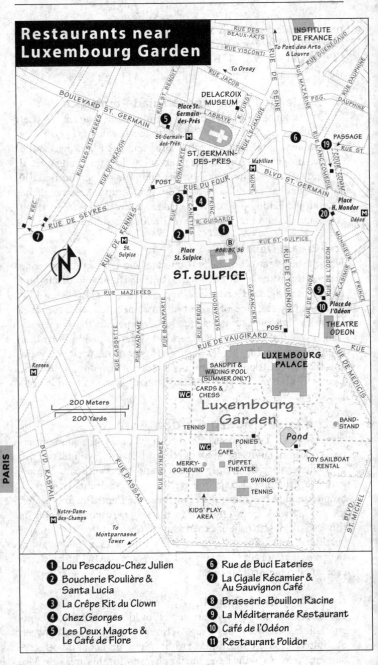

Restaurants near Luxembourg Garden

1 Lou Pescadou–Chez Julien
2 Boucherie Roulière & Santa Lucia
3 La Crêpe Rit du Clown
4 Chez Georges
5 Les Deux Magots & Le Café de Flore
6 Rue de Buci Eateries
7 La Cigale Récamier & Au Sauvignon Café
8 Brasserie Bouillon Racine
9 La Méditerranée Restaurant
10 Café de l'Odéon
11 Restaurant Polidor

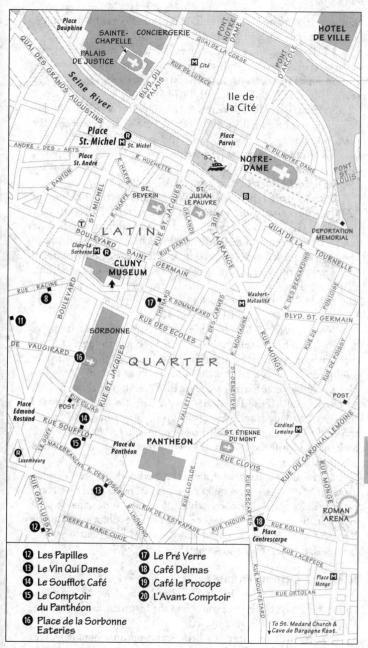

Legend:

12 Les Papilles
13 Le Vin Qui Danse
14 Le Soufflot Café
15 Le Comptoir du Panthéon
16 Place de la Sorbonne Eateries
17 Le Pré Verre
18 Café Delmas
19 Café le Procope
20 L'Avant Comptoir

PARIS

dow-shop the many French and Italian eateries—most with similar prices, but each with a slightly different feel.

$$ Lou Pescadou-Chez Julien offers a comfortable atmosphere and above-average bistro fare in a zone where every restaurant looks the same (€9 starters, €18 *plats*, daily, some outdoor seating, 16 Rue Mabillon, tel. 01 43 54 56 08).

$$ Boucherie Roulière has a dark interior crammed with locals in search of a thick steak or other meat dish (€9 *entrées*, €19 *plats*, closed Mon, 24 Rue des Canettes, tel. 01 43 26 25 70).

$$ Santa Lucia draws positive reviews with wood-fired pizza, good pasta, and killer tiramisu (€12-14 pizza and pastas, €22 *plats*, closed Mon, 22 Rue des Canettes, tel. 01 43 26 42 68).

$ La Crêpe Rit du Clown cooks up yummy crêpes (Mon-Sat 12:00-23:00, closed Sun, 6 Rue des Canettes, tel. 01 46 34 01 02).

Chez Georges is a bohemian pub lined with black-and-white photos of the artsy and revolutionary French '60s. Have a drink as you sit in a cool little streetside table nook, or venture downstairs to find a hazy, drippy-candle, traditionally French world in the Edith Piaf-style dance cellar (cheap drinks from old-fashioned menu, Tue-Sat 14:00-2:00 in the morning, closed Sun-Mon and in Aug, 11 Rue des Canettes, tel. 01 43 26 79 15).

Near Boulevard St. Germain: A five-minute walk from St. Sulpice Church, this venerable boulevard is home to some of Paris' most famous cafés and best pre- or post-dinner strolling. Consider a light dinner with a table facing the action at Hemingway's **Les Deux Magots** or at Sartre's **Le Café de Flore** (figure about €12 for an omelet and €18-28 for a salad or *plat*). A block north (toward the river), **Rue de Buci** offers a lineup of bars, cafés, and bistros targeted to a young clientele who are more interested in how they look than how the food tastes. It's terrific theater for passersby from 18:00 until late.

$$ La Cigale Récamier, near the Sèvres-Babylone shopping area, is a classy place for a quiet meal at reasonable prices with appealing indoor and outdoor seating. It's about 10 minutes west of Place St. Sulpice, on a short pedestrian square a block off Rue de Sèvres (€20 *plats*, à la carte only, closed Sun, 4 Rue Récamier, Mo: Sèvres-Babylone, tel. 01 46 48 86 58).

Near the Odéon Theater

To reach these, use the Odéon or Cluny-la Sorbonne Métro stops. In this same neighborhood, you'll find the historic Café le Procope, Paris' more-than-300-year-old café.

$ L'Avant Comptoir is a little stand-up-only hors d'oeuvres bar serving up a delightful array of French-Basque tapas for €3-6 on a sleek zinc counter. The menu is fun and accessible; it has a good list of wines by the glass; and crêpes are made fresh to go (daily 12:00-23:00, 9 Carrefour de l'Odéon, tel. 01 44 27 07 97).

$$ Brasserie Bouillon Racine takes you back to 1906 with an Art Nouveau carnival of carved wood, stained glass, and old-time lights reflected in beveled mirrors. The over-the-top decor and energetic waiters give it an inviting conviviality. Check upstairs before choosing a table. Their roast suckling pig (€19) is a house favorite. There's Belgian beer on tap and a fascinating history on the menu (€18-23 *plats*, €31 *menu*, a few fish options and lots of meat, daily, 3 Rue Racine, tel. 01 44 32 15 60).

$$ La Méditerranée is all about seafood from the south served in a pastel and dressy setting...with similar clientele. The scene and the cuisine are sophisticated yet accessible, and the view of the Odéon is *formidable*. The sky-blue tablecloths and the lovingly presented dishes add to the romance (€28 two-course *menus*, €33 three-course *menus*, daily, reservations smart, facing the Odéon at 2 Place de l'Odéon, tel. 01 43 26 02 30).

$$ Café de l'Odéon offers a great chance to savor light meals with a classy crowd on a peaceful and elegant square in front of a venerable theater. Though limited, the menu is accessible and decently priced, and you'll feel like a winner eating so well and so reasonably in such a Parisian setting. From May to October, the café is outdoors-only and serves lunch and dinner—or just go for drinks (good €14 salads, €17 *plats* such as salmon and *steak tartare*; May-Oct daily 12:00-23:00—weather permitting, no reservations, Place de l'Odéon, tel. 01 44 85 41 30). In the winter (Nov-April) they serve lunch only inside the palatial theater lobby.

$ Restaurant Polidor, a bare-bones neighborhood fixture since the 19th century, is much loved for its unpretentious quality cooking, fun old-Paris atmosphere, and fair value. Stepping inside, you know this is a winner—noisy, happy diners sit tightly at shared tables as waiters chop and serve fresh bread. The selection features classic bourgeois *plats* from every corner of France; their *menu fraicheur* is designed for lighter summer eating (€12-17 *plats*, €25-35 three-course *menus*, daily 12:00-14:30 & 19:00-23:00, cash only, no reservations, 41 Rue Monsieur-le-Prince, tel. 01 43 26 95 34).

Between the Panthéon and the Cluny Museum

To reach these restaurants, use the Cluny-La Sorbonne Métro stop or the Luxembourg RER stop.

$$ At Les Papilles you just eat what's offered...and you won't complain. It's a foodie's dream come true—one *menu*, no choices, and no regrets. Choose your wine from the shelf or ask for advice from the burly rugby-playing owner, then relax and let the food arrive. Book this place ahead (€34 *menu*, €16 daily *marmite du marché*—a.k.a. market stew, closed Sun-Mon, 30 Rue Gay Lussac, tel. 01 43 25 20 79).

$$ Le Vin Qui Danse is a warm little place serving a good selection of tasty dishes and well-matched wines to appreciative clients (€27 two-course *menu*, add €15 for three wines selected to complement your meal, daily, 4 Rue des Fossés St. Jacques, tel. 01 43 54 80 81).

$ *On Rue Soufflot with Panthéon Views:* Facing each other are two cafés—**Le Soufflot** and **Le Comptoir du Panthéon**—that are well-positioned for afternoon sun and soft evening light. A block in front of the Panthéon, they deliver dynamite views of the inspiring dome. Both serve classic café food all day until late and are great for a pensive drink or a light meal—simply choose the one that appeals.

$ *Place de la Sorbonne:* This appealing little square surrounds a gurgling fountain and faces Sorbonne University, just a block from the Cluny Museum. It offers several opportunities for a good outdoor lunch or a pleasant dining experience. At amiable Carole's tiny **Baker's Dozen,** you'll pay take-away prices for light fare you can sit down to eat (€5 salads and sandwiches, Mon-Sat until 15:30, closed Sun, tel. 01 44 07 08 09). **Café de l'Ecritoire** is a typical brasserie with salads, *plats du jour,* and good seating inside and out (daily, tel. 01 43 54 60 02). **Patios** serves basic Italian cuisine, including pizza, at decent prices (daily until late, tel. 01 45 38 71 19). **Le Bac de la Sorbonne** is a tad cheaper, but you get what you pay for.

$$ Le Pré Verre, a block from the Cluny Museum, is a chic wine bistro—a refreshing alternative in a part of the Latin Quarter mostly known for low-quality, tourist-trapping eateries. Offering imaginative, modern cuisine at fair prices, the place is packed. The bargain lunch *menu* includes a starter, main course, glass of wine, and coffee for €14. The three-course dinner *menu* at €30 is worth every *centime.* They pride themselves equally on their small-producers' wine list, so follow your server's advice (closed Sun-Mon, 8 Rue Thénard, reservations necessary, tel. 01 43 54 59 47).

On Rue Mouffetard

Several blocks behind the Panthéon, Rue Mouffetard is a conveyor belt of comparison-shopping eaters with wall-to-wall budget options (fondue, crêpes, Italian, falafel, and Greek). Come here to sift through the crowds and eat cheaply. This street stays up late and likes to party (particularly around Place de la Contrescarpe). The gauntlet begins on top, at thriving Place de la Contrescarpe, and ends below where Rue Mouffetard stops at St. Médard Church.

Both ends offer fun cafés where you can watch the action. The upper stretch is pedestrian and touristy; the bottom stretch is purely Parisian. Anywhere between is no-man's land for consistent quality. Still, strolling with so many fun-seekers is enjoyable, whether you eat or not. To get here, use the Censier Daubenton or Place Monge Métro stop.

$$ Café Delmas, at the top of Rue Mouffetard on picturesque Place de la Contrescarpe, is *the* place to see and be seen. Come here for a before- or after-dinner drink on the terrace, typical but pricey café cuisine, or great chocolate ice cream (open daily).

$ Cave de Bourgogne, a young and local hangout, has reasonably priced café fare at the bottom of Rue Mouffetard. The outside has picture-perfect tables on a raised terrace; the interior is warm and lively (€13-16 *plats*, specials listed on chalkboards, daily, 144 Rue Mouffetard—see map on page 337).

In Montmartre

Much of Montmartre is extremely touristy, with mindless mobs following guides to cancan shows. But the ambience is undeniably fun, so either join in the touristic fray or walk a few blocks away and find a quieter, more authentic meal at one of the places I've listed below. For locations, see map on page 340.

Near Sacré-Cœur

The steps in front of Sacré-Cœur are perfect for a picnic with a view, though the spot comes with lots of company. For a quieter setting, consider the park directly behind the church. Along the touristy main drag (near Place du Tertre and just off it), several fun piano bars serve mediocre crêpes but offer great people-watching. The options become less touristy and far more tasty as you get away from the top of the hill (skip any place on Place du Tertre). The Anvers Métro stop works well if you're visiting Sacré-Cœur. The Abbesses Métro stop will land you in the heart of the residential Montmartre neighborhood.

$$$ Moulin de la Galette lets you dine with Renoir under the historic windmill in a comfortable setting with good prices. Find the old photos scattered about the place (€23 two-course and €29 three-course *menus* at lunch only; €15 starters and €28 *plats* for dinner, daily, 83 Rue Lepic, Mo: Abbesses, tel. 01 46 06 84 77).

$$ Restaurant Chez Plumeau, just off jam-packed Place du Tertre, is touristy yet moderately priced, with formal service but great seating on a tiny, characteristic square (elaborate €17 salads, €18-22 *plats*, closed Tue Oct-April and Wed year-round, 4 Place du Calvaire, Mo: Abbesses, tel. 01 46 06 26 29).

$ L'Eté en Pente Douce is a good Montmartre choice, hiding

PARIS

under the generous branches of street trees. Just downhill from the crowds on a classic neighborhood corner, it features cheery indoor and outdoor seating, €10 *plats du jour* and salads, vegetarian options, and good wines (daily, many steps below Sacré-Cœur to the left as you leave, down the stairs below the WC, 23 Rue Muller, Mo: Anvers, tel. 01 42 64 02 67).

Near Place des Abbesses

At the bottom of Montmartre, residents pile into a long lineup of brasseries and cafés near Place des Abbesses, especially along Rue des Abbesses and Rue des Martyrs. The food is average; the atmosphere is anything but. Come here for a lively, tourist-free scene. Rue des Abbesses is perfect for a picnic-gathering stroll with cheese shops, delis, wine stores, and bakeries. In fact, the baker at **Au Levain d'Antan** won the award for the best baguette in Paris in 2011 (Mon-Fri 7:30-20:00, closed Sat-Sun, 6 Rue des Abbesses). Unless another Métro stop is listed, use the Abbesses stop.

$$ Le Miroir's kitchen is run by a young and enthusiastic chef cooking up seasonal French fare. Go for high-quality ingredients served to a locals-only crowd. If you enjoyed the wine you had with your meal, cross the street to their wine shop and pick up a bottle to go (€26-33 two or three-course *menus,* Tue-Sat lunch and dinner, Sun lunch only, closed Mon, 94 Rue des Martyrs, tel. 01 46 06 50 73).

$$ Autour de Midi et Minuit is a classic French bistro sitting on top of a jazz cellar (see page 307). Hot food served upstairs; cool jazz served downstairs (lunch €15, dinner €26-33, closed Mon, 11 Rue Lepic, Mo: Blanche or Abbesses, tel. 01 55 79 16 48).

$ Le Chinon Brasserie offers good seating inside and out and is the best bet for café/wine bar ambience and food (daily, 49 Rue des Abbesses, tel. 01 42 62 07 17).

$ Smooth in the City provides a much-needed break from rich French fare. For €8.50 you get a fresh fruit smoothie, a healthy salad or veggie-packed sandwich, and a homemade dessert. Order it to go for your walk up the hill, or sit at one of their three outdoor tables (daily 10:00-19:00, 11 Rue des Abbesses, tel. 01 83 56 56 55).

$ La Fourmi sits at the bottom of the hill. Open all day, they offer the cheapest coffee and croissants in Montmartre, and simple, affordable lunches (€8-12). In the evening, the place is taken over by hilltop hipsters who come for the inexpensive beer and generous cheese plates (daily, 74 Rue des Martyrs, Mo: Anvers or Pigalle, tel. 01 42 64 70 35).

Dinner Cruises

The following companies all offer dinner cruises (reservations required). Bateaux-Mouches and Bateaux Parisiens have the best reputations and the highest prices. They offer multicourse meals

PARIS

and music in aircraft-carrier-size dining rooms with glass tops and good views. For both, proper dress is required—no denim, shorts, or sport shoes; Bateaux-Mouches requires a jacket and tie for men. The main difference between these companies is the music: Bateaux-Mouches offers violin and piano to entertain your romantic evening, whereas Bateaux Parisiens boasts a lively atmosphere with a singer, band, and dance floor.

Bateaux-Mouches, started in 1949, is hands-down the most famous. You can't miss its sparkling port on the north side of the river at Pont de l'Alma. The boats usually board 19:30-20:15, depart at 20:30, and return at 22:45 (€100-155/person, RER: Pont de l'Alma, tel. 01 42 25 96 10, www.bateaux-mouches.fr).

Bateaux Parisiens leaves from Port de la Bourdonnais, just east of the bridge under the Eiffel Tower. Begin boarding at 19:45, leave at 20:30, and return at 23:00 (€66-165/person, price depends on departure time, view seating, and *menu* option; tel. 01 76 64 14 45, www.bateauxparisiens.com). The middle level is best. Pay the few extra euros to get seats next to the windows—it's more romantic and private, with sensational views.

Le Capitaine Fracasse offers the budget option (€50/person, €80 with wine or champagne; reserve ahead—easy online—or get there early to secure a table; boarding times vary by season and day of week, walk down stairs in the middle of Bir-Hakeim bridge near the Eiffel Tower to Iles aux Cygne, Mo: Bir-Hakeim or RER: Champ de Mars-Tour Eiffel, tel. 01 46 21 48 15, www.croisiere-paris.com).

Paris Connections

Whether you're aiming to catch a train or plane, budget plenty of time to reach your departure point. Paris is a big, crowded city, and getting across town on time is a goal you'll share with millions of other harried people. Factor in traffic delays and walking time through huge stations and vast terminals. At the airport, expect lines at ticketing, check-in, baggage check, and security points. Always keep your luggage safely near you. Pickpockets prey on jet-lagged and confused tourists on public transportation.

By Plane
Charles de Gaulle Airport
Paris' main airport has three terminals: T-1, T-2, and T-3. Most flights from the US use T-1 or T-2 (check your ticket, or contact your airline). All three terminals have ATMs *(distributeurs)*, shops, bars, and access to ground transportation into Paris. You can travel between terminals on the free CDGVAL automated shuttle train (departs every 5 minutes, 24/7). Allow 30 minutes to travel between terminals and an hour for total travel time between your gates at T-1 and T-2.

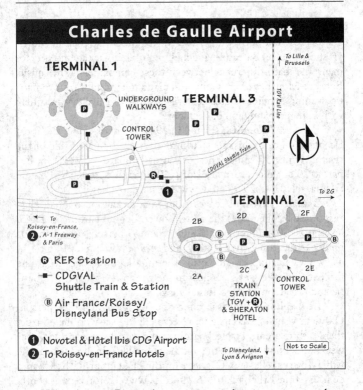

Charles de Gaulle Airport

TERMINAL 1

UNDERGROUND WALKWAYS

TERMINAL 3

CONTROL TOWER

To Lille & Brussels

TGV Rail Line

CDGVAL Shuttle Train

To 2G

TERMINAL 2

2B   2D   2F

2A   2C   2E

TRAIN STATION (TGV + ®) & SHERATON HOTEL

CONTROL TOWER

To Roissy-en-France, A-1 Freeway & Paris

® RER Station

▪— CDGVAL Shuttle Train & Station

® Air France/Roissy/ Disneyland Bus Stop

❶ Novotel & Hôtel Ibis CDG Airport

❷ To Roissy-en-France Hotels

To Disneyland, Lyon & Avignon

Not to Scale

When leaving Paris, plan to arrive at the airport two to three hours early for an overseas flight, or one to two hours for flights within Europe (particularly on budget airlines, which can have especially long check-in lines). For flight info, dial either 3950 from French landlines (€0.35/minute) or, from the US, dial 011 33 1 70 36 39 50, or visit www.adp.fr (airport code: CDG).

Transportation Between Charles de Gaulle Airport and Paris

Buses, airport vans, commuter trains, and taxis link the airport's terminals with central Paris. If you're traveling with two or more companions, carrying lots of baggage, or are just plain tired, taxis are worth the extra cost. If you're arriving on a weekday morning, however, taxis are much less appealing, as traffic into Paris can be bad—in that case, the train is likely to be a better option.

By Bus: **Roissy-Buses** make the 50-minute trip to the Opéra Métro stop in central Paris, arriving on Rue Scribe. From there, it's an easy Métro ride to anywhere in the city. To get to the Métro entrance or nearest taxi stand, turn left as you exit the bus and walk counterclockwise around the lavish Opéra building to its front

(€10, runs 6:00-23:00, 4/hour until 20:45, 3/hour after that, 50 minutes, buy ticket on bus).

"Les Cars" Air France buses run at least twice hourly from 5:45 until 23:00 (tel. 08 92 35 08 20). **Bus #2** goes to the Etoile stop on Rue Carnot, near the Arc de Triomphe (€16.50, 45 minutes) and Porte Maillot (with connections to Beauvais Airport, described later). Once at the Arc de Triomphe, catch city bus #92 (one block away; see map on page 291) to the Rue Cler area. **Bus #4** runs to Gare de Lyon (45 minutes) and the Montparnasse Tower/train station (€16.50, 1 hour). **Bus #3** goes to Orly airport (€19, 1 hour). Buy tickets from the driver (round-trip tickets or 2 persons traveling together save 20 percent) or online, which saves you an additional 10 percent (www.lescarsairfrance.com).

From Paris to the airport, catch Air France buses at Etoile/Arc de Triomphe (on Avenue Carnot—the non-Champs-Elysées side), Porte Maillot (on Boulevard Gouvion-St-Cyr—right side of the Palais des Congres), Gare Montparnasse (on Rue du Commandant Mouchotte—facing the station with the tower behind you, it's around the left side), or Gare de Lyon (follow the Rue Diderot exit, then turn right when you hit the street and find the bus stall with the tiny *Les Cars Air France* sign).

By Airport Van: The shuttle vans from Charles de Gaulle work like those at home, carrying passengers directly to and from their hotels, with stops along the way to pick up other passengers. Shuttles work best for trips from your hotel to the airport, since they require you to book a precise pickup time in advance—even though you can't ever know exactly when your flight will actually arrive. Airport vans cost about €32 for one person, €46 for two, and €58 for three. While these vans take longer to reach the airport than a taxi does, compared to taxis they're a good value for single travelers and big families. Have your hotelier book at least a day in advance.

Several companies offer shuttle service; I usually just go with the one my hotel normally uses. Otherwise, try **Paris Shuttles Network** (tel. 01 45 26 01 58, www.shuttlesnetwork.com) or **Airport Connection** (tel. 01 43 65 55 55, www.supershuttle.fr).

Paris Webservices actually works well from the airport to Paris, because they meet you inside the terminal and will wait for you if you're late (tel. 01 53 62 02 29, fax 01 53 01 35 84, www.parisweb-services.com, contactpws@pariswebservices.com). For a one-way trip they charge about €30 for one person, or €44 for 2 people. Booking a round trip costs about €160-180 for up to 4 people. Claim a 10 percent discount by mentioning promo code "PWS52K13" when you book, then showing your driver a current edition of this book. They also sell Museum Passes with no extra fee (order ahead) and offer excursions (see page 248).

PARIS

By Commuter Train: The RER, Paris's suburban commuter train, is your cheapest (though not most convenient) option for getting between the airport and the city center (€9.30, runs 5:00-24:00, 4/hour, 30 minutes to Gare du Nord). It runs directly to well-located RER/Métro stations (including Gare du Nord, Châtelet-Les Halles, St. Michel, and Luxembourg); from there, you can hop the Métro to get exactly where you need to go. It's handy and cheap, but it can require walking with your luggage through big, crowded stations.

From the airport terminal, follow *Paris by Train* signs, then *RER* signs. (If you're landing at Terminals 1 or 3, you'll need to take the CDGVAL shuttle to reach the RER station.) The RER station at T-2 is also a crowded train station, with long ticket-window lines. It's faster to buy tickets from the machines (use the green-colored machines that read *Paris/Ile de France,* coins required, break your bills at an airport shop). Beware of pickpockets; wear your money belt, and keep your bags close.

By Taxi: The 50-minute trip costs about €65 (more if traffic is bad). Taxis can carry three people with bags comfortably, and are legally required to accept a fourth passenger for €3 extra (though they may not like it). Larger parties can wait for a larger vehicle. Expect to pay €1/bag handling fee. Don't take an unauthorized taxi from cabbies greeting you on arrival. Official taxi stands are well-signed.

For trips from Paris to the airport, have your hotel arrange it. Specify that you want a real taxi *(un taxi normal),* not a limo service that costs €20 more (and gives your hotel a kickback). For weekday morning departures (7:00-10:00), reserve at least a day ahead (€5 reservation fee payable by credit card). For more on taxis in Paris, see page 241.

By Car: Car-rental desks are well-signed from the arrival halls. When returning your car, allow ample time to reach the check-in desks, especially if flying out of Terminal 2—its imperfect signage can make it especially confusing to navigate.

Orly Airport

This easy-to-navigate airport feels small, but is good for rental-car pickup and drop-off, as it's closer to Paris and far easier to navigate than Charles de Gaulle Airport (for flight info from French land-lines dial 3950, from the US dial 011 33 1 70 36 39 50, www.adp.fr, airport code: ORY).

Transportation Between Orly Airport and Paris

Shuttle buses *(navettes),* the RER, taxis, and airport vans connect Paris with either terminal.

By Bus: "Les Cars" Air France bus #1 runs to Gare Montparnasse, Invalides, and Etoile Métro stops, all of which have connections to several Métro lines. Upon request, drivers will also stop at the Porte d'Orléans Métro stop. For the Rue Cler neighborhood, take the bus to Invalides, then the Métro to La Tour Maubourg or Ecole Militaire. Buses depart from Ouest arrival level exit B-C or Sud exit L: Look for signs to *navettes* (€12 one-way, 4/hour, 40 minutes to Invalides, buy ticket from driver or save 10 percent by booking online, round-trip tickets or 2 persons traveling together save 20 percent, www.lescarsairfrance.com).

The **Orlybus** goes directly to the Denfert-Rochereau Métro stop. From there, you can catch the Métro or RER-B to central Paris, including the Luxembourg Garden area, Notre-Dame Cathedral, and Gare du Nord. The Orlybus departs from Ouest arrival level exit D and Sud exit H (€7, 3/hour, 30 minutes).

A different bus called **"Paris par le train"** takes you to the Pont d'Orly RER station, where you can catch the RER-C to Gare d'Austerlitz, St. Michel/Notre-Dame, Musée d'Orsay, Invalides (change here for Rue Cler hotels), and Pont de l'Alma. Catch this bus at Ouest arrival level exit G or Sud exit F (€7 total, 4/hour, 40 minutes).

The **Orlyval shuttle train** takes you to the Antony RER station, where you can catch RER-B (direction: Mitry-Claye or Aéroport Charles de Gaulle) to Luxembourg and many recommended hotels, Châtelet-Les Halles, St. Michel, and Gare du Nord. Catch the Orlyval at Ouest arrival level exit A or Sud exit K (€11 total, 6/hour, 40 minutes).

By Taxi: Taxis are outside Ouest arrival level exit B, and to the far right as you leave terminal Sud, at exit M. Allow €40-50 with bags for a taxi into central Paris.

By Airport Van: Airport vans are a good means of getting from Paris to the airport, especially for single travelers or families of four or more (too many for most taxis; see page 372). From Orly, figure about €23 for one person or €30 for two people (less per person for larger groups and kids).

Beauvais Airport

Budget airlines such as Ryanair use this small airport, offering dirt-cheap airfares but leaving you 50 miles north of Paris. Still, this airport has direct buses to Paris (see below) and is handy for travelers heading to Normandy or Belgium (car rental available). The airport is basic, waiting areas are crowded, and services are sparse, but improvements are gradually on the way (airport code: BVA, airport tel. 08 92 68 20 66—lines open daily 8:00-20:00, www.aeroport-beauvais.com; Ryanair tel. 08 92 78 02 10—lines open Mon-Fri 9:00-19:00, Sat 10:00-17:00, Sun 11:00-17:00; www.ryanair.com).

Transportation Between Beauvais Airport and Paris

By Bus: Buses depart from the airport when they're full (about 20 minutes after flights arrive) and take 1.5 hours to reach Paris. Buy your ticket (€15 one-way) at the little kiosk to the right as you exit the airport. Buses arrive at Porte Maillot on the west edge of Paris (on Métro line 1 and RER-C). The closest taxi stand is at Hôtel Concorde-Lafayette.

Buses heading to Beauvais Airport leave from Porte Maillot about 3.25 hours before scheduled flight departures. Catch the bus in the parking lot on Boulevard Pershing next to Hôtel Concorde-Lafayette. Arrive with enough time to purchase your bus ticket before boarding (*parking* Pershing ticket booth tel. 01 58 05 08 45, airport ticket booth tel. 03 44 11 46 86).

By Train: Trains connect Beauvais' city center and Paris' Gare du Nord (20/day, 1.25 hours). To reach Beauvais' train station, take the Beauvais *navette* (€4, 6/day, 30 minutes) or local bus #12 (€1, 12/day, 30 minutes).

By Taxi: You can take a taxi from Beauvais Airport to Beauvais' train station or city center (€14) or to central Paris (allow €130 and 1.25 hours).

By Train

Paris is Europe's rail hub, with six major stations and one minor one, with trains heading in different directions:

- Gare du Nord (northbound trains)
- Gare Montparnasse (west- and southwest-bound trains)
- Gare de Lyon (southeast-bound trains)
- Gare de l'Est (eastbound trains)
- Gare St. Lazare (northwest-bound trains)
- Gare d'Austerlitz (southwest-bound trains)
- Gare de Bercy (smaller station with non-TGV southbound trains)

All six main train stations have banks or currency exchanges, ATMs, train information desks, telephones, cafés, newsstands, and clever pickpockets (pay attention in ticket lines—keep your bag firmly gripped in front of you). Because of security concerns, not all have baggage checks.

Any train station has schedule information, can make reservations, and can sell tickets for any destination. Or you can save time and stress by buying train tickets or making train reservations at an SNCF Boutique. These small branch offices of the French national rail company are conveniently located throughout Paris, with offices near most of my recommended hotels and museums and at Charles de Gaulle and Orly Airports. Arrive when they open to avoid lines (generally open Mon-Sat 8:30-19:00 or 20:00, closed

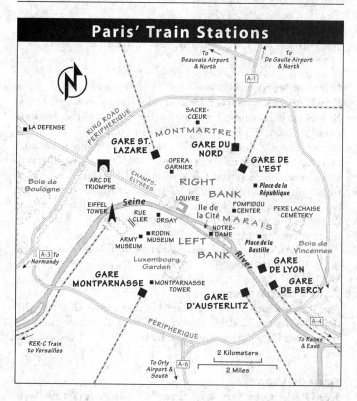

Paris' Train Stations

To Beauvais Airport & North

To De Gaulle Airport & North

A-1

RING ROAD PÉRIPHÉRIQUE

LA DEFENSE

SACRE-CŒUR

MONTMARTRE

GARE ST. LAZARE

GARE DU NORD

GARE DE L'EST

OPERA GARNIER

Place de la République

ARC DE TRIOMPHE

CHAMPS-ELYSEES

RIGHT BANK

Bois de Boulogne

LOUVRE

EIFFEL TOWER

Seine

RUE CLER

ORSAY

Ile de la Cité

POMPIDOU CENTER

PERE LACHAISE CEMETERY

MARAIS

NOTRE-DAME

ARMY MUSEUM

RODIN MUSEUM

LEFT BANK

A-3 To Normandy

Luxembourg Garden

River

Place de la Bastille

Bois de Vincennes

GARE DE LYON

GARE MONTPARNASSE

MONTPARNASSE TOWER

GARE DE BERCY

GARE D'AUSTERLITZ

A-4

PERIPHERIQUE

To Reims & East

RER-C Train to Versailles

2 Kilometers

2 Miles

To Orly Airport & South

A-6

Sun). For a complete list of SNCF Boutiques, see www.mega-comik.info/boutiquesncf.htm.

Each station offers two types of rail service: long distance to other cities, called Grandes Lignes (major lines); and suburban service to nearby areas, called Banlieue, Transilien, or RER. You also may see ticket windows identified as *Ile de France*. These are for Transilien trains serving destinations outside Paris in the Ile de France region (usually no more than an hour from Paris). When arriving by Métro, follow signs for *Grandes Lignes-SNCF* to find the main tracks. Métro and RER trains, as well as buses and taxis, are well-marked at every station.

Budget plenty of time before your departure to factor in ticket lines and making your way through large, crowded stations. Paris train stations can be intimidating, but if you slow down, take a deep breath, and ask for help, you'll find them manageable and efficient. Bring a pad of paper for clear communication at ticket/info windows. All stations have helpful information booths *(accueil)*; the bigger stations have roving helpers, usually wearing red or blue vests. They're capable of answering rail questions more quickly than

PARIS

the staff at the information desks or ticket windows. I make a habit of confirming my track number and departure time with these helpers.

Gare du Nord

Key Destinations Served by Gare du Nord Grandes Lignes: **Bruges** (at least hourly, 2.5-3 hours, change in Brussels), **Amsterdam** (8-10/day, 3.5 hours direct), **Berlin** (4/day, 8.25 hours, 1-2 changes, via Belgium, non-Belgium-traversing trains leave from Gare de l'Est), **Copenhagen** (7/day, 14-18 hours, 1 night train), and **London** via Eurostar Chunnel train (12-15/day, 2.5-3 hours; for details, see "To Paris or Brussels via Eurostar Train" on page 807. Routes via **Brussels** (e.g., to Amsterdam and Bruges) require taking the pricey Thalys train; for details and tips, see "Amsterdam Connections" on page 1235.

By Banlieue/RER Lines: **Charles de Gaulle Airport** (4/hour, 45 minutes, runs 5:00-24:00, track 4).

Gare Montparnasse

Key Destinations Served by Gare Montparnasse: Chartres (10/day, 65 minutes), **Madrid** (3/day, 12-14 hours, expensive overnight trains from Gare d'Austerlitz), and **Lisbon** (2/day, 21-24 hours via Irun).

Gare de Lyon

Key Destinations Served by Gare de Lyon: Avignon (9/day in 2.5 hours to Avignon TGV Station, 5/day in 3.5 hours to Avignon Centre-Ville station, more connections with change—3-4 hours), **Arles** (11/day, 2 direct TGVs—4 hours, 9 with change in Avignon—5 hours), **Nice** (hourly, 5.75 hours, may require change, 11.5-hour night train possible out of Gare d'Austerlitz), **Venice** (5/day, 10-12 hours with 1-3 changes; 1 direct overnight, 14 hours, operated by private company Thello—which doesn't accept railpasses, important to reserve ahead at www.thello.com; 4 more night trains with changes), **Rome** (3/day, 11-16 hours; 1 night train, 14 hours, may transfer in Milan, operated by private company Thello—which doesn't accept railpasses, important to reserve ahead at www.thello.com), **Interlaken** (7/day, 5-6.5 hours, 1-3 changes, 2 more from Gare de l'Est), and **Barcelona** (2/day, 7.5 hours, change in Figueres; night train possible from Gare d'Austerlitz).

Gare de l'Est

Key Destinations Served by Gare de l'Est: Interlaken (2/day, 6.5 hours, 2-3 changes, 7 more from Gare de Lyon), **Frankfurt** (5 direct/day, 4 hours; 4 more/day with change in Karlsruhe, 4.5 hours), **Vienna** (7/day, 12-17 hours, 1-3 changes, night train via Munich or

Frankfurt), **Prague** (5/day, 12-18 hours, night train via Mannheim or Berlin), **Munich** (6/day, 6 hours, most with 1 change, 1 direct night train), and **Berlin** (5/day, 8.5 hours, 1-2 changes; 1 direct night train, 12.5 hours).

Gare St. Lazare

Key Destinations Served by Gare St. Lazare: Bayeux (9/day, 2.5 hours, some change in Caen), **Caen** (14/day, 2 hours), and **Pontorson/Mont St-Michel** (2/day, 4-5.5 hours, via Caen; more trains from Gare Montparnasse).

Gare d'Austerlitz

Key Destinations Served by Gare d'Austerlitz: Versailles (via RER line C, 4/hour, 35 minutes), **Barcelona** (1/night, 12.5 hours, make mandatory reservation at least 2 weeks ahead; day trains from Gare de Lyon), and **Madrid** (1 direct night train, 13-14 hours, make mandatory reservation at least 2 weeks ahead, 16 hours via Irun; day trains from Gare Montparnasse).

Gare de Bercy

This smaller station handles southbound non-TGV trains (Mo: Bercy, one stop east of Gare de Lyon on line 14, exit the Métro station and it's across the street). Facilities are limited—just a WC and a sandwich-fare take-out café.

Versailles

Every king's dream, Versailles (vehr-"sigh") was the residence of French monarchs and the cultural heartbeat of Europe for about 100 years—until the Revolution of 1789 changed all that. The Sun King (Louis XIV) created Versailles, spending freely from the public treasury to turn his dad's hunting lodge into a palace fit for the gods (among whom he counted himself). Louis XV and Louis XVI spent much of the 18th century gilding Louis XIV's lily. In 1837, about 50 years after the royal family was evicted by citizen-protesters, King Louis-Philippe opened the palace as a museum. Today you can visit parts of the huge palace and wander through acres of manicured gardens sprinkled with fountains and studded with statues. Europe's next-best palaces are just Versailles wannabes.

Worth ▲▲▲, Versailles offers three blockbuster sights. The main attraction is the palace itself, called the **Château.** Here you walk through dozens of lavish, chandeliered rooms once inhabited by Louis XIV and his successors. Next come the expansive **Gardens** behind the palace, a landscaped wonderland dotted with

PARIS

statues and fountains. Finally, at the far end of the Gardens, is the pastoral area called the **Trianon Palaces and Domaine de Marie-Antoinette** (a.k.a. Trianon/Domaine), designed for frolicking blue bloods and featuring several small palaces and Marie's Hamlet—perfect for getting away from the mobs at the Château.

In general, allow 1.5 hours each for the Château, the Gardens, and the Trianon/Domaine. Add another two hours for round-trip transit, plus another hour for lunch, and you're looking at an eight-hour day—at the very least.

Visiting Versailles can seem daunting because of its size and hordes of visitors. But if you follow my tips, a trip here during even the busiest times is manageable.

Getting There

By Train: The town of Versailles is 35 minutes southwest of Paris. Take the **RER-C train** (4/hour, 35 minutes one-way, €6.50 round-trip) from any of these Paris RER stops: Gare d'Austerlitz, St. Michel, Musée d'Orsay, Invalides, Pont de l'Alma, or Champ de Mars. You can buy your train tickets at any Métro ticket window in Paris—for no extra cost it will include the connection from that Métro stop to the RER. At the RER station, catch any train listed as "Versailles R.G." or "Versailles Rive Gauche" (Rive Gauche is the Versailles station closest to the Château—there are two others). Ride to the last stop.

At the Versailles R.G. train station, exit through the turnstiles by inserting your ticket. Ignore the hawkers peddling guided Versailles tours and tickets. To reach the **palace,** just follow the crowds: Turn right out of the station, then left at the first boulevard, and walk 10 minutes. To return to Paris, all trains serve all downtown Paris RER stops on the C line.

A Phébus shuttle bus links the Versailles R.G. train station to the **Trianon/Domaine,** but doesn't go to the palace. It's ideal if you are visiting the Trianon/Domaine first, before the Château—or if you want to return to the train station from the Trianon/Domaine (1-2/hour, runs mid-April-Oct only, €1.70 or one Métro ticket, check current schedule for "Ligne TRI" at www.phebus.tm.fr).

By Taxi: The 30-minute ride (without traffic) between Versailles and Paris costs about €60.

By Car: Get on the *périphérique* freeway that circles Paris, and take the toll-free A-13 autoroute toward Rouen. Exit at Versailles, follow signs to *Versailles Château,* and park in the huge pay lot at Place d'Armes (€5.50/2 hours, €10/4 hours, €15/8 hours).

Orientation to Versailles

Cost: Buy either a Paris Museum Pass or a Versailles Le Passeport Pass, both of which give you access to the most important parts of the complex (see "Passes" below).

If you don't get a pass, buy individual tickets for each of the three different sections.

The Château: €15, includes audioguide, under 18 free. Covers the famous Hall of Mirrors, the king and queen's living quarters, many lesser rooms, and any temporary exhibitions. For €1 more, you can get a guided tour of the Château—a great deal (see "Guided Tours," later). Free on the first Sunday of off-season months (Nov-March).

The Trianon Palaces and Domaine de Marie-Antoinette: €10, no audioguide available, under 18 free. Covers the Grand Trianon and its gardens, the Petit Trianon, the queen's Hamlet, and a smattering of nearby buildings. Free on the first Sunday of off-season months (Nov-March).

The Gardens: Free, except on Fountain Spectacle days, when admission is €8.50 (weekends April-Oct plus Tue late May-late June; see "Fountain Spectacles in the Gardens," later).

Passes: The following passes can save money and allow you to skip the long ticket-buying lines (but not security checks before entering the palaces). Both passes include the Château audioguide.

The **Paris Museum Pass** (see page 261) covers the Château and the Trianon/Domaine area (a €25 value) and is the best solution for most. It doesn't include the Gardens on Fountain Spectacle days.

The **Le Passeport** one-day pass costs €18 and covers the Château and the Trianon/Domaine area. The price bumps up to €25 on Fountain Spectacle days.

Buying Passes and Tickets: It's best to buy tickets or passes in advance. They're available at any Paris TI or FNAC department store (small fee), or online at www.chateauversailles.fr (print out your pass/ticket or pick it up near the entrance).

In Versailles, passes are sold at the city TI (€2 fee; for TI details, see "Information," later).

Your last option is to buy your pass or ticket at the Château ticket-sales office (to the left as you face the palace). Ticket windows accept American credit cards but have long lines in the morning—avoid the wait by using the ticket machines at the back of the room (you'll need a chip-and-PIN card or bills—which half the machines accept).

Hours: The **Château** is open April-Oct Tue-Sun 9:00-18:30, Nov-March Tue-Sun 9:00-17:30; closed Mon year-round.

The **Trianon Palaces and Domaine de Marie-Antoinette** are open April-Oct Tue-Sun 12:00-18:30, Nov-March Tue-Sun 12:00-17:30; closed Mon year-round (off-season only the two Trianon Palaces are open, not the Hamlet or other outlying buildings).

The **Gardens** are open April-Oct daily 9:00-20:30, but may close earlier for special events; Nov-March Tue-Sun 8:00-18:00, closed Mon.

Last entry to all areas is 30 minutes before closing.

Crowd-Beating Strategies: Versailles can be packed May-Sept 10:00-13:00. Avoid Tuesdays and Sundays, when the place is jammed with a slow shuffle of tourists from open to close. Ticket and security lines can be long: To skip the ticket-buying line, use a Paris Museum Pass or Le Passeport, buy tickets in advance, or book a guided tour (below). Everyone—including holders of advance tickets and passes—must go through security (longest lines 10:00-12:00). Before queuing up at the security entrance, check for signs that they might have opened up a special, shorter line for passholders (but don't count on it).

Pickpockets: Assume pickpockets are working the tourist crowds.

Information: Before you go, check the excellent website for updates and special events—www.chateauversailles.fr. The palace's general contact number is tel. 01 30 83 78 00. Versailles has two information offices. You'll pass the city TI on your walk from the RER station to the palace—it's just past the Pullman Hôtel (daily 9:00-19:00, tel. 01 39 24 88 88). The information office at the Château is on the left side of the courtyard as you face the Château (WCs, toll tel. 08 10 81 16 14). Pick up the free, useful map just inside the Château.

Guided Tours: The 1.5-hour English guided tour gives you access to a few extra rooms (the lineup varies) and lets you skip ticket-buying lines if you came *sans* pass. Ignore the tours hawked as you leave the train station. Book at the guided-tours office in the Château courtyard—it's to your right as you approach the palace (look for *Visites Conferences* signs). You can book a tour online on the palace's website or reserve immediately upon arrival—tours can sell out by 13:00 (€16 includes palace entry—just €1 more than entry alone, €7 if you have pass, tours run about hourly from 9:00-15:00).

Audioguide Tours: A free audioguide to the Château is included in your admission (pick up just inside the palace, return as you leave).

You can download a free Rick Steves audio tour of Versailles; see page 7. Other podcasts and digital tours are available in the "multimedia" section at www.chateauversailles.fr.

The palace audioguide and my audio tour complement one another: Eager students can easily transfer earbuds between devices and listen to both tours as you shuffle through the lavish rooms.

Baggage Check: Large bags and baby strollers are not allowed in the Château and the two Trianons (use a baby backpack or hire a babysitter for the day); you must use the free baggage check and retrieve your items one hour before closing.

Services: There are WCs on either side of the Château courtyard (in the ticket-sales office and in the guided-tours office), immediately upon entering the Château (Entrance H), and near the exit from the Dauphin's Apartments. You'll also find WCs near the Grand Café d'Orléans, in the Gardens near the Latona Basin, at the Grand Canal, in the Grand Trianon and Petit Trianon, and at several other places scattered around the grounds. Any café generally has a WC.

Photography: Allowed, but no flash indoors.

Eating: To the left of the Château's golden Royal Gate entrance, the Grand Café d'Orléans offers good value self-service meals (€5 sandwiches and small salads, great for picnicking in the Gardens). In the Gardens, you'll find several restaurants, cafés, and snack stands. Most are located near the Latona Fountain (less crowded) and in a delightful cluster at the Grand Canal (more crowds and more choices, including two restaurants).

In **town,** restaurants are on the street to the right of the parking lot (as you face the Château). Handy McDonald's and Starbucks (both with WCs) are across from the train station. The best choices are on the lively Place du Marché Notre-Dame in the town center.

Fountain Spectacles in the Gardens: On spring and summer weekends, the Gardens charge a mandatory admission fee for these spectacles. Loud classical music fills the king's backyard, and the Gardens' fountains are in full squirt. Louis XIV had his engineers literally reroute a river to fuel these gushers. Even by today's standards, they are impressive.

The fountains run on Saturdays and Sundays from April through October (11:00-12:00 & 15:30-17:30; finale starts at 17:20). They also perform on Tuesdays from late May until late June at the same times. On these "spray days," the Gardens cost €8.50. (Pay at the Gardens entrance; covered by Le Passeport but not Paris Museum Pass.) The calendar of spectacles also includes a few music-only days (on the rare Tue, €8.50) and elaborate sound-and-light displays (Sat mid-June-Aug at

PARIS

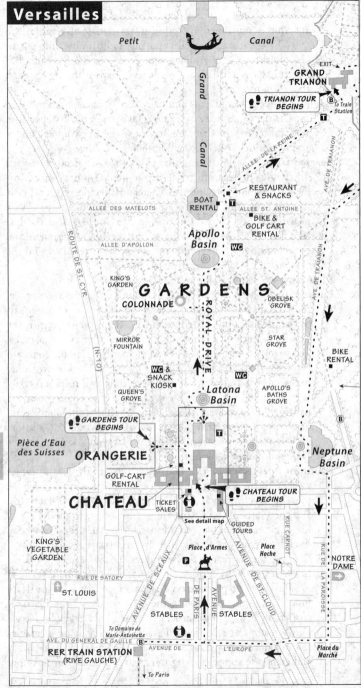

Versailles

Petit Canal

Grand Canal

EXIT

GRAND TRIANON

To Train Station

TRIANON TOUR BEGINS

ALLÉE DE LA REINE

AVE. DE TRIANON

RESTAURANT & SNACKS

ALLÉE DES MATELOTS

BOAT RENTAL

ALLÉE ST. ANTOINE

BIKE & GOLF CART RENTAL

Apollo Basin

ALLÉE D'APOLLON

WC

ROUTE DE ST. CYR

KING'S GARDEN

G A R D E N S

COLONNADE

OBELISK GROVE

ROYAL DRIVE

(N-10)

MIRROR FOUNTAIN

STAR GROVE

BIKE RENTAL

WC & SNACK KIOSK

WC

QUEEN'S GROVE

APOLLO'S BATHS GROVE

Latona Basin

B

Pièce d'Eau des Suisses

GARDENS TOUR BEGINS

Neptune Basin

ORANGERIE

GOLF-CART RENTAL

T

CHATEAU

TICKET SALES

CHATEAU TOUR BEGINS

RUE CARNOT

RUE DE LA PAROISSE

See detail map

GUIDED TOURS

NOTRE DAME

KING'S VEGETABLE GARDEN

Place d'Armes

P

Place Hoche

AVENUE DE SCEAUX

AVENUE DE ST-CLOUD

RUE DE SATORY

ST. LOUIS

STABLES

DE PARIS

AVENUE

STABLES

Place du Marché

To Domaine de Marie-Antoinette

AVE. DU GÉNÉRAL DE GAULLE

B

AVENUE DE

L'EUROPE

RER TRAIN STATION (RIVE GAUCHE)

To Paris

PARIS

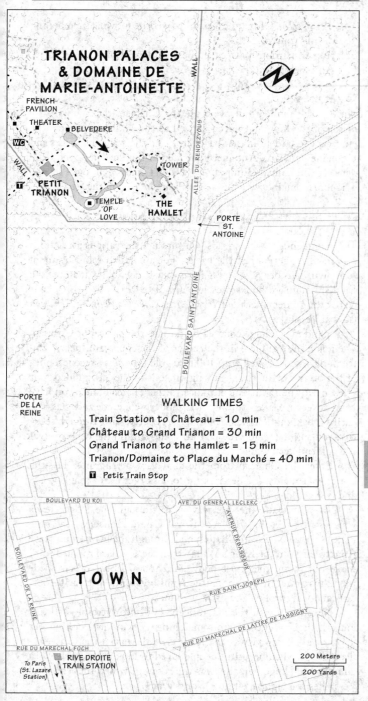

TRIANON PALACES & DOMAINE DE MARIE-ANTOINETTE

FRENCH PAVILION
THEATER
BELVEDERE
WC
WALL
PETIT TRIANON
TOWER
TEMPLE OF LOVE
THE HAMLET

WALL
ALLÉE DU RENDEZVOUS

PORTE ST. ANTOINE

PORTE DE LA REINE

BOULEVARD SAINT-ANTOINE

WALKING TIMES

Train Station to Château = 10 min
Château to Grand Trianon = 30 min
Grand Trianon to the Hamlet = 15 min
Trianon/Domaine to Place du Marché = 40 min

🚋 Petit Train Stop

BOULEVARD DU ROI
AVE. DU GENERAL LECLERC
AVENUE DE BASSEUX

BOULEVARD DE LA REINE

TOWN

RUE SAINT-JOSEPH

RUE DU MARECHAL DE LATTRE DE TASSIGNY

RUE DU MARECHAL FOCH

To Paris (St. Lazare Station)
RIVE DROITE TRAIN STATION

200 Meters
200 Yards

PARIS

21:00, €23). Check the Versailles website for what's happening during your visit.

Starring: Luxurious palaces, endless gardens, Louis XIV, Marie-Antoinette, and the *ancien régime*.

Overview

On this self-guided tour, we'll see the Château (the State Apartments of the king and queen as well as the Hall of Mirrors), the landscaped Gardens in the "backyard," and the Trianon Palaces and Domaine de Marie-Antoinette, located at the far end of the Gardens. If your time is limited or you don't enjoy walking, skip the Trianon/Domaine, which is a 30-minute hike from the Château.

Self-Guided Tour

This commentary, which leads you through the various attractions at Versailles, covers just the basics. For a detailed room-by-room rundown, consider *Rick Steves' Paris* (buy in the US or at any of the English-language bookstores in Paris listed earlier in this chapter) or the guidebook called *The Châteaux, the Gardens, and Trianon* (sold at Versailles).

Stand in the huge courtyard and face the palace, or Château. The golden Royal Gate in the center of the courtyard, nearly 260 feet long and decorated with 100,000 gold leaves, is a recent replica of the original. The ticket-buying office is to the left; guided-tour sales are to the right. The entrance to the Château (once you have your ticket or pass) is through the modern concrete-and-glass security checkpoint, marked *Entrance A*. After passing through security, you spill out into the open-air courtyard on the other side of the golden Royal Gate.

Enter the Château from the courtyard at Entrance H—the State Apartments. Inside are an info desk (get a free map), WCs, and free audioguides.

The Château: The one-way walk through the palace leads you past the dazzling 700-seat **Royal Opera House;** by the intimate, two-tiered **Royal Chapel;** and through the glamorous **State Apartments.** In the **King's Wing** you'll see a billiard room, a royal make-out room, the Swiss bodyguard room, Louis' official bedroom, his grand throne room (the **Apollo Room**—with a 10-foot-tall canopied throne), and his war rooms.

Next you'll visit the magnificent **Hall of Mirrors**—250 feet long, with 17 arched mirrors matching 17 windows looking out upon royal garden views. The mirrors—a luxury at the time—reflect an age when beautiful people loved to look at themselves. In another age altogether, this was the room in which the Treaty of Versailles was signed, ending World War I.

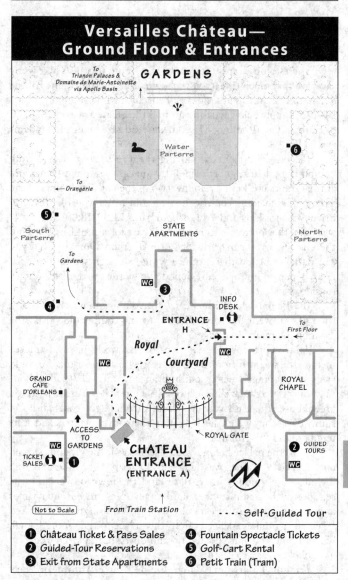

Versailles Château— Ground Floor & Entrances

GARDENS

To Trianon Palaces & Domaine de Marie-Antoinette via Apollo Basin

Water Parterre

6

To ← Orangerie

5
South Parterre

STATE APARTMENTS

North Parterre

To Gardens

WC

3

INFO DESK
i

4

ENTRANCE H

To First Floor

Royal

WC

Courtyard

WC

GRAND CAFE D'ORLEANS

ROYAL CHAPEL

ACCESS TO GARDENS

ROYAL GATE

WC

TICKET SALES **i** **1**

CHATEAU ENTRANCE (ENTRANCE A)

2 GUIDED TOURS

WC

Not to Scale   From Train Station

- - - - Self-Guided Tour

1 Château Ticket & Pass Sales
2 Guided-Tour Reservations
3 Exit from State Apartments
4 Fountain Spectacle Tickets
5 Golf-Cart Rental
6 Petit Train (Tram)

PARIS

You'll finish in the **Queen's Wing,** where you'll visit the Queen's bedchamber, the guard room where Louis XVI and Marie-Antoinette surrendered to the Revolution, and Napoleon's coronation room.

Getting Around the Gardens: It's a 30- to 45-minute **walk** from the palace, down to the Grand Canal, past the two Trianon palaces, to the Hamlet at the far end of Domaine de Marie-Antoinette. Allow more time if you stop along the way. After enduring the slow Château shuffle, stretching your legs out here feels pretty good.

There's a **bike rental** station by the Grand Canal. A bike won't save you that much time (you can't take it inside the grounds of the Trianon/Domaine; park it near an entrance while you tour inside). Instead, simply enjoy pedaling around the greatest royal park in all of Europe (€6.50/hour or €15/half-day, kid-size bikes and tandems available).

The fast-looking, slow-moving **tram** *(petit train)* leaves from behind the Château (north side). It stops at the Grand Canal and at the Grand and Petit Trianons (two of the entrance points to the Trianon/Domaine). You can hop on and off as you like (€7, pay driver, free for kids under 11, 4/hour, runs 11:00-18:00).

Another option is to rent a **golf cart** for a fun drive through the Gardens. You can't drive it in the Trianon/Domaine, but you can park it outside the entrance while you sightsee inside (€30/hour, 4-person limit per cart, rent down by the canal or at Orangerie side of palace).

The Phébus **shuttle bus** can save you 30 minutes of walking time, if you want to return directly to the train station from the Trianon/Domaine (see page 378).

Palace Gardens: The Gardens offer a world of royal amusements. The warmth from the Sun King was so great that he could even grow orange trees in chilly France. Louis XIV had a thousand of these to amaze his visitors. In winter they were kept in the greenhouses (beneath your feet) that surround the courtyard. On sunny days, they were wheeled out in their silver planters and scattered around the grounds.

With the palace behind you, it seems as if the grounds stretch out forever. Versailles was laid out along an eight-mile axis that included the grounds, the palace, and the town of Versailles itself, one of the first instances of urban planning since Roman times and a model for future capitals, such as Washington, D.C., and Brasilia. A promenade leads from the palace to the Grand Canal, where France's royalty floated up and down in imported Venetian gondolas.

Trianon Palaces and Domaine de Marie-Antoinette: Versailles began as an escape from the pressures of kingship. But in a short time, the Château had become as busy as Paris ever was. Louis XIV needed an escape from his escape and built a smaller palace out in the boonies. Later, his successors retreated still farther from the Château and French political life, ignoring the real world that was crumbling all around them. They expanded the Trianon area, building a fantasy world of palaces and pleasure gardens—the enclosure called Marie-Antoinette's Domaine.

The beautifully restored **Grand Trianon Palace** is as sumptuous as the main palace, but much smaller. With its pastel-pink colonnade and more human scale, this is a place you'd like to call home. Nearby are the **French Pavilion,** Marie-Antoinette's **Theater,** and the octagonal **Belvedere** palace.

You can almost see princesses bobbing gaily in the branches as you walk through the enchanting forest, past the white marble **Temple of Love** to the queen's fake-peasant **Hamlet** *(le Hameau).* Marie-Antoinette's happiest days were spent at the Hamlet, under a bonnet, tending her perfumed sheep and manicured gardens in a thatch-happy wonderland.

Despite her bad reputation with the public, Marie-Antoinette was a sweet girl from Vienna who never quite fit in with the fast, sophisticated crowd at Versailles. She made the **Petit Trianon,** a masterpiece of Neoclassical architecture, a place to get away and re-create the simple home life she remembered from her childhood. Here she played, while in the cafés of faraway Paris, revolutionaries plotted the end of the *ancien régime.*

PROVENCE

This magnificent region is shaped like a giant wedge of quiche. From its sunburned crust, fanning out along the Mediterranean coast from the Camargue to Marseille, it stretches north along the Rhône Valley to Orange. The Romans were here in force and left many ruins—some of the best anywhere. Seven popes, artists such as Vincent van Gogh and Paul Cézanne, and author Peter Mayle all enjoyed their years in Provence. This destination features a splendid recipe of arid climate, oceans of vineyards, dramatic scenery, lively cities, and adorable hill-capping villages.

Explore France's greatest Roman ruin, the Pont du Gard aqueduct. Admire the skill of ball-tossing *boules* players in small squares in every Provençal village and city. Spend a few Van Gogh-inspired starry, starry nights in Arles. Youthful but classy Avignon bustles in the shadow of its brooding Palace of the Popes.

Planning Your Time

Make Arles or Avignon your sightseeing base—particularly if you have no car. Italophiles prefer smaller Arles, while poodles pick urban Avignon. Arles has a blue-collar quality; the entire city feels like Van Gogh's bedroom. Avignon—double the size of Arles—feels sophisticated, with more nightlife and shopping, and makes a good base for non-drivers thanks to its convenient public-transit options.

When budgeting your time, you'll want a full day for sightseeing in Arles (best on Wed or Sat, when it's market day); a half-day for Avignon; and a day or two for the villages and sights in the countryside.

Pont du Gard is a 50-minute bus ride west of Avignon.

Getting Around Provence

By Bus or Train: Public transit is good between cities and decent to some towns, but marginal at best to the smaller villages. Frequent trains link Avignon and Arles (no more than 30 minutes between each).

From Avignon, you can bus to Pont du Gard.

By Car: The region is made to order for a car, though travel time between some sights will surprise you—thanks, in part, to narrow roads and endless roundabouts. The yellow Michelin maps #332 (Luberon and Côtes du Rhône) and #340 (Arles area) are worth considering; the larger-scale orange Michelin map #527 also includes the Riviera. Avignon (pop. 110,000) is a headache for drivers. Arles (pop. 52,000) is easier but still challenging. Be wary

Public Transportation in Provence

Rail
TGV Rail
Bus

Not to Scale

To Lyon & Paris

P R O V E N C E

Montelimar

Nyons

Buis Les B.

Vaison la Romaine

Orange

CÔTES DU RHÔNE

Châteauneuf-du-Pape

To Grenoble

Uzès

PONT DU GARD

Avignon

Isle-sur-la-Sorgue

Avignon TGV

Roussillon

Cavaillon

L U B E R O N

Apt

Nîmes

Tarascon

Lourmarin

To Montpellier, Carcassonne & Barcelona (Spain)

Rhône

St-Rémy

Les Baux

Arles

Rhône

Aigues-Mortes

C A M A R G U E

Aix TGV

Aix-en-Provence

Petit Rhône

To Nice

Cassis Stn.

Toulon

Stes-Maries

Marseille

Les Calanques

La Ciotat

Cassis

Mediterranean Sea

of thieves—this is France's worst area for car break-ins. Park only in well-monitored spaces and leave nothing valuable in your car.

Tours of Provence

Wine Safari

Dutchman Mike Rijken runs a one-man show, taking travelers through the region he adopted more than 20 years ago. Mike came to France to train as a chef, later became a wine steward, and has now found his calling as a driver/guide. His English is fluent, and though his focus is on wine and wine villages, Mike knows the region thoroughly and is a good teacher of its history (€60/half-day, €110/day, priced per person, group size varies from 2 to 6; pickups possible in Arles, Avignon, Lyon, Marseille, or Aix-en-Provence;

tel. 04 90 35 59 21, mobile 06 19 29 50 81, www.winesafari.net, mikeswinesafari@orange.fr).

Local Guides

Celine Viany is a retired wine sommelier turned charming tour guide. She's an easy-to-be-with expert on her region and its chief product (tel. 04 90 46 90 80, mobile 06 76 59 56 30, www.levinalabouche.com, contact@degustation-levinalabouche.com).

Avignon Wine Tour

For a playful and distinctly French perspective on wines of the Côtes du Rhône region, contact François Marcou, who runs his tours with passion and energy, offering different itineraries every day (€80/person for all-day wine tours that include 4-5 tastings, €350 for private groups, mobile 06 28 05 33 84, www.avignon-wine-tour.com, avignon.wine.tour@modulonet.fr).

Imagine Tours

Unlike most tour operators, this nonprofit organization focuses on cultural excursions, offering low-key, personalized tours that allow visitors to discover the "true heart of Provence and Occitania." The itineraries are adapted to your interests, and the guides will meet you at your hotel or the departure point of your choice (€170/half-day, €295/day, prices are for up to 4 people starting from the region around Avignon or Arles, mobile 06 89 22 19 87, fax 04 90 24 84 26, www.imagine-tours.net, imagine.tours@gmail.com). They are also happy to help you plan your itinerary, book hotel rooms, or address other travel issues.

Wine Uncovered

Passionate and engaging Englishman Olivier Hickman takes small groups on focused tours of selected wineries in Châteauneuf-du-Pape and in the villages near Vaison la Romaine. Olivier is serious about French wine and knows his subject matter inside and out. His in-depth tastings include a half-day tour of two or three wineries; the Châteauneuf-du-Pape tour is especially popular. He also offers multiday tours with food and wine tastings, and if you need transportation, he can help arrange it (€35-70/person for half-day to full-day tours, prices subject to minimum tour fees, see website for details, mobile 06 75 10 10 01, www.wine-uncovered.com, olivier.hickman@wine-uncovered.com).

Tours du Rhône

American Doug Graves, who owns a small wine domaine in the Côtes du Rhône, shares his passion for his adopted region, its people, and its wines on his guided tours of Châteauneuf-du-Pape, the villages of the Côtes du Rhône, and the Luberon Valley (€100/person, 4-person max, mobile 06 37 16 04 56, www.toursdurhone.com, doug@masdelalionne.com).

PROVENCE

Visit Provence

This company runs day tours from Avignon and Arles. Tours from Avignon run year-round and include a great variety of destinations; tours from Arles run April through September only and are more limited (check their website for current destinations). While these tours provide introductory commentary to what you'll see, there is no guiding at the actual sights. They use eight-seat, air-conditioned minivans (about €60-80/half-day, €100-120/day; they'll pick you up at your hotel in Avignon or at the main TI in Arles). Ask about their cheaper big-bus excursions, or consider hiring a van and driver for your private use (plan on €220/half-day, €490/day, tel. 04 90 14 70 00, www.provence-reservation.com).

Arles

By helping Julius Caesar defeat Marseille, Arles (pronounced "arl") earned the imperial nod and was made an important port city. With the first bridge over the Rhône River, Arles was a key stop on the Roman road from Italy to Spain, the Via Domitia (a model of this bridge is at the Ancient History Museum). After reigning as the seat of an important archbishop and as a trading center for centuries, the city became a sleepy backwater of little importance in the 1700s. Vincent van Gogh settled here in the late 1800s, but left only a chunk of his ear (now long gone). American bombers destroyed much of Arles in World War II as the townsfolk hid out in its underground Roman galleries. But today Arles thrives again, with its evocative Roman ruins, an eclectic assortment of museums, made-for-ice-cream pedestrian zones, and squares that play hide-and-seek with visitors.

The city's unpolished streets and squares are not to everyone's taste. This workaday city has not sold out to tourism, so you won't see dolled-up lanes and perfectly preserved buildings. But to me, that's part of its charm.

Orientation to Arles

Arles faces the Mediterranean, turning its back on Paris. And though the town is built along the Rhône, it largely ignores the river. Landmarks hide in Arles' medieval tangle of narrow, winding streets. Virtually everything is close—but first-timers can walk forever to get there. Hotels have good, free city maps, and Arles provides helpful street-corner signs that point you toward sights and hotels. Speeding cars enjoy Arles' medieval lanes, turning sidewalks into tightropes and pedestrians into leaping targets.

PROVENCE

Tourist Information

The **main TI** is on the ring road Boulevard des Lices, at Esplanade Charles de Gaulle (April-Sept daily 9:00-18:45; Oct-March Mon-Sat 9:00-16:45, Sun 10:00-13:00; tel. 04 90 18 41 20, www. arlestourisme.com). There's also a **train station TI** (Mon-Fri 9:30-13:00 & 14:00-18:00, closed Sat-Sun).

At either TI, pick up the city map, get the bus schedules you need, and ask for English information on nearby destinations such as the Camargue wildlife area. Ask about "bullgames" in Arles and nearby towns (Provence's more humane version of bullfights—see page 404). Skip the useless €1 brochure describing several walks in Arles, including one that locates Van Gogh's "easels". Both TIs can help you reserve hotel rooms (credit card required for deposit).

Arrival in Arles

By Train: The train station is on the river, a 10-minute walk from the town center. Before heading into town, get what you need at the train station TI. There's no baggage storage at the station, but you can walk 10 minutes to stow it at Hôtel Régence (see "Helpful Hints," later).

To reach the town center or Ancient History Museum, wait for the free **Envia minibus** at the glass shelter facing away from the station (cross the street and veer left, 3/hour Mon-Sat 7:00-19:00, none Sun). The bus makes a loop around Arles, stopping near most of my recommended hotels. It's a 15-minute **walk** into town (turn left out of the train station). **Taxis** usually wait in front of the station, but if you don't see any, call the posted telephone numbers, or dial 04 89 73 36 00. If the train station TI is open, you can ask them to call. Taxi rates are fixed—allow about €10 to any of my recommended hotels.

By Bus: All buses stop at the Centre-Ville bus station, a few blocks below the main TI, on the ring road at 16-24 Boulevard Georges Clemenceau. Buses to Avignon's TGV station also stop at the train station.

By Car: Most hotels have parking nearby—ask for detailed directions (€2.80/8 hours at most meters; free 12:00-14:00 & 19:00-9:00, and all day on Sundays; some meters limited to 2.5 hours). For most hotels, first follow signs to *Centre-Ville*, then *Gare SNCF* (train station). You'll come to a big roundabout (Place Lamartine) with a Monoprix department store to the right. You can park along the city wall and find your hotel on foot; the hotels I list are no more than a 10-minute walk away (best not to park here overnight due to theft concerns and markets on Wed and Sat). Fearless drivers can plunge into the narrow streets between the two stumpy towers via Rue de la Calade, and follow signs to their hotel. Again,

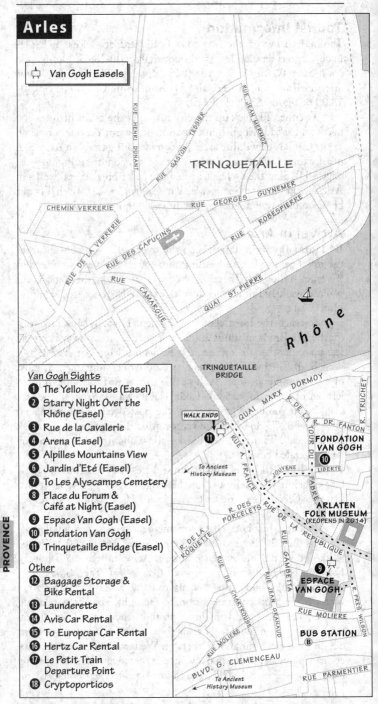

Arles

⌂ Van Gogh Easels

TRINQUETAILLE

RUE HENRI DUNANT

RUE GASTON TESSIER

RUE JEAN VERMOZ

RUE GEORGES GUYNEMER

RUE ROBESPIERRE

CHEMIN VERRERIE

RUE DES CAPUCINS

RUE DE LA VERRERIE

RUE CAMARGUE

RUE

QUAI ST. PIERRE

Rhône

TRINQUETAILLE
BRIDGE

QUAI MARX DORMOY

R. DE LA TOUR DU FABRE

R. DR. FANTON

R. TRUCHET

WALK ENDS

11

To Ancient
History Museum

R. A. FRANCE

R. JOUVENE

LIBERTE

FONDATION
VAN GOGH

10

ARLATEN
FOLK MUSEUM
(REOPENS IN 2014)

R. DES
PORCELETS

RUE DE LA REPUBLIQUE

RUE DE LA
ROQUETTE

RUE GAMBETTA

RUE DE LA CHARTROUSE

RUE JEAN GRANAUD

ESPACE
VAN GOGH

9

RUE MOLIERE

RUE PRES. WILSON

BUS STATION
Ⓑ

RUE MOLIERE

BLVD. G. CLEMENCEAU

To Ancient
History Museum

RUE PARMENTIER

Van Gogh Sights

- ❶ The Yellow House (Easel)
- ❷ Starry Night Over the Rhône (Easel)
- ❸ Rue de la Cavalerie
- ❹ Arena (Easel)
- ❺ Alpilles Mountains View
- ❻ Jardin d'Eté (Easel)
- ❼ To Les Alyscamps Cemetery
- ❽ Place du Forum & Café at Night (Easel)
- ❾ Espace Van Gogh (Easel)
- ❿ Fondation Van Gogh
- ⓫ Trinquetaille Bridge (Easel)

Other

- ⓬ Baggage Storage & Bike Rental
- ⓭ Launderette
- ⓮ Avis Car Rental
- ⓯ To Europcar Car Rental
- ⓰ Hertz Car Rental
- ⓱ Le Petit Train Departure Point
- ⓲ Cryptoporticos

PROVENCE

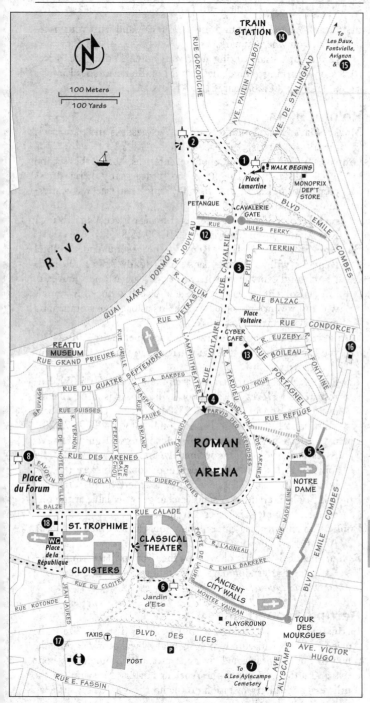

TRAIN STATION 14

To Les Baux, Fontvielle, Avignon & 15

1 WALK BEGINS
Place Lamartine

MONOPRIX DEP'T STORE

PETANQUE
CAVALERIE GATE
2

RUE GORODICHE
AVE. PAULIN TALABOT
AVE. DE STALINGRAD
BLVD. EMILE COMBES

12
RUE CAVALERIE
JULES FERRY
R. TERRIN
R. PUITS
3
RUE BALZAC
Place Voltaire
RUE CONDORCET
CYBER CAFE
13
R. EUZEBY
RUE BOILEAU
RUE PORTAGNEL
16
LA FONTAINE

River

QUAI MARX DORMOY
R. JOUVEAU
RUE METRAS
R. L. BLUM
RUE VOLTAIRE
L'AMPHITHEATRE
R. A TARDIEU
DU FOUR

REATTU MUSEUM
RUE GRAND PRIEURE
RUE DU QUATRE SEPTEMBRE
RUE GRILLE
R. A. BARBES
R. RASPAIL
R. A. FAURE
RUE DE L'HOTEL DE VILLE
R. BRIAND

4
PARVIS DES ARENES
RONDPOINT DES ARENES
ROND-POINT DES ARENOISES
RUE REFUGE

8
Place du Forum
FAVORIN
R. NICOLAI
RUE DES ARENES
R. DIDEROT
R. PERRIAT
R. PERRALE
R. BALZE
R. VERNON
RUE SUISSES

ROMAN ARENA

5
NOTRE DAME
RUE MADELEINE
BLVD. EMILE COMBES

18
ST. TROPHIME
RUE CALADE
CLASSICAL THEATER
R. L'AGNEAU
PORTE DE LAURE
R. EMILE BARRERE

WC
Place de la République
CLOISTERS
RUE DU CLOITRE
6
Jardin d'Ete

ANCIENT CITY WALLS
MONTEE VAUBAN
PLAYGROUND
TOUR DES MOURGUES
AVE. VICTOR HUGO

RUE ROTONDE
RUE JEAN JAURES
17
TAXIS
POST
P
BLVD. DES LICES
7
To & Les Alyscamps Cemetery
AVE. ALYSCAMPS

RUE E. FASSIN

PROVENCE

N
100 Meters
100 Yards

theft is a problem—leave nothing in your car, and trust your hotelier's advice on where to park.

If you can't find parking near your hotel, Parking des Lices (Arles' only parking garage), near the TI on Boulevard des Lices, is a good fallback (€2.20/hour, €15/24 hours).

Helpful Hints

Market Days: The big markets are on Wednesdays and Saturdays. For all the details, see page 404.

Crowds: An international photo event jams hotels the second weekend of July. The let-'er-rip, twice-yearly Féria draws crowds over Easter and in mid-September (see www.arles-tourisme.com for dates).

Internet Access: There's an Internet café near Place Voltaire at 31 Rue Augustin Tardieu (daily, tel. 04 90 18 87 40).

Baggage Storage and Bike Rental: The recommended **Hôtel Régence** will store your bags for €3 (daily 7:30-22:00 mid-March-mid-Nov, closed in winter, 5 Rue Marius Jouveau). They also rent bikes (€7/half-day, €14/day, one-way rentals within Provence possible, same hours as baggage storage) and may have electric bikes—ask.

Laundry: A launderette is at 12 Rue Portagnel (daily 7:00-21:30, you can stay later to finish if you're already inside, English instructions).

Car Rental: Avis is at the train station (tel. 08 20 05 05 05); **Europcar** and **Hertz** are downtown (Europcar is at 61 Avenue de Stalingrad, tel. 04 90 93 23 24; Hertz is closer to Place Voltaire at 10 Boulevard Emile Combes, tel. 04 90 96 75 23).

Local Guide: Charming **Agnes Barrier** is a good guide, knows Arles and nearby sights intimately, and loves her work. Her tours of Arles cover Van Gogh and Roman history (€130/3 hours, mobile 06 11 23 03 73, agnes.barrier@hotmail.fr).

English Book Exchange: A small exchange is available at the recommended **Soleileis** ice-cream shop.

Public Pools: Arles has three public pools (indoor and outdoor). Ask at the TI or your hotel.

Boules: The local "*boul*ing alley" is by the river on Place Lamartine. After their afternoon naps, the old boys congregate here for a game of *pétanque*.

Getting Around Arles

In this flat city, everything's within **walking** distance. Only the Ancient History Museum requires a healthy walk (or you can take a taxi or bus). The elevated riverside promenade provides Rhône views and a direct route to the Ancient History Museum (to the southwest) and the train station (to the northeast). Keep your head up for *Starry Night* memories, but eyes down for decorations by dogs with poorly trained owners.

Arles' **taxis** charge a set fee of about €10, but nothing except the Ancient History Museum is worth a taxi ride. To call a cab, dial 04 89 73 36 00 or 04 90 96 90 03.

The free **Envia minibus** circles the town (3/hour, Mon-Sat 7:00-19:00, none Sun), useful for access to the train station and the Ancient History Museum.

Le Petit Train d'Arles, a typical tourist train, gives you the lay of the land—if you prefer sitting to walking (€7, 35 minutes, stops in front of the main TI and at the Roman Arena).

Sights in Arles

Most sights cost €3.50-7, and though any sight warrants a few minutes, many aren't worth their individual admission price. The TI sells two different monument passes (called "Passeports"). **Le Passeport Avantage** covers almost all of Arles' sights (€13.50, under 18-€12); **Le Passeport Liberté** (€9) lets you choose any five monuments (one must be a museum). Depending on your interests, the €9 Passeport is probably best.

Start at the Ancient History Museum (closed Tue) for a helpful overview (drivers should try to do this museum on their way into Arles), then dive into the city-center sights. Remember, many sights stop selling tickets one hour before closing (both before lunch and at the end of the day).

▲▲Ancient History Museum (Musée de l'Arles et de la Provence Antiques)

Begin your town visit here, for Roman Arles 101. Located on the site of the Roman chariot racecourse (the arc of which is built into the parking lot), this air-conditioned, all-on-one-floor museum is just west of central Arles along the river. Models and original sculptures (with almost no posted English translations but a decent handout) re-create the Roman city, making workaday life and culture easier to imagine.

Cost and Hours: €6, Wed-Mon 10:00-18:00, closed Tue, Presqu'île du Cirque Romain, tel. 04 13 31 51 03, www.arles-antique.cg13.fr. Ask for the English booklet, which provides a helpful if not in-depth background on the collection.

Getting There: To reach the museum, take the free **Envia minibus** (stops at the train station and along Rue du 4 Septembre, then along the river, 3/hour Mon-Sat, none Sun). If you're coming **on foot** from the city center (a 20-minute walk), turn left at the river and take the scruffy riverside path under two bridges to the big, blue, modern building. As you approach the museum, you'll pass the verdant Hortus Garden—designed to recall the Roman circus and chariot racecourse that were located here. A **taxi** ride costs €10 (museum can call a taxi for your return).

◐ Self-Guided Tour: The collection is housed in one large room separated by dividers and exhibits. Tour the room moving basically counterclockwise.

A big **map** of the Roman Arles region greets visitors and shows the key Roman routes accessible to Arles. You'll then pass a model of a small **pre-Roman village** (allowing you to compare pre- and post-Roman life in Arles), and see maps showing Arles' expanding city limits during its Roman era.

Next you'll see **models** of every Roman structure in (and near) Arles. These are the highlight for me, as they breathe life into the buildings, showing them as they looked 2,000 years ago. Start with the model of Roman Arles, and imagine the city's splendor. Find the Forum—still the center of town today, though only two columns survive. Look at the space Romans devoted to their arena and huge racecourse—a reminder that an emphasis on sports is not unique to modern civilizations. The model also illustrates how little Arles seems to have changed over two millennia, with its houses still clustered around the city center, and warehouses still located on the opposite side of the river.

Look for individual models of important buildings shown in the city model: the elegant forum; the floating bridge that gave Arles a strategic advantage (over the widest, and therefore slowest, part of the river); the theater (with its magnificent stage wall); the arena (with its movable stadium cover to shelter spectators from sun or rain); the hydraulic mill of Barbegal (with its 16 waterwheels powered by water cascading down a hillside); and the circus (a.k.a. chariot racecourse). Part of the original racecourse was just outside the windows, and though long gone, it must have resembled Rome's Circus Maximus in its day—its obelisk is now the centerpiece of Arles' Place de la République.

You'll also pass displays of pottery, jewelry, metal and glass artifacts, and well-crafted mosaic floors that illustrate how Roman Arles was a city of art and culture. The many **statues** that you see are all original, except for the greatest—the *Venus of Arles*, which Louis XIV took a liking to and had moved to Versailles. It's now in the Louvre—and, as locals say, "When it's in Paris...bye-bye."

Preparations are well under way for the installation of a **Gallo-Roman vessel** and much of its cargo, to be displayed in a large new room facing the Hortus Garden. This almost 100-foot-long Roman barge was pulled out of the Rhône in 2010, along with some 280 amphorae and 3,000 ceramic artifacts. It was typical of flat-bottomed barges used to shuttle goods between Arles and ports along the Mediterranean (vessels were manually towed upriver).

Just before leaving, you'll pass an impressive row of pagan and early-Christian **sarcophagi** (from the second to fifth centuries A.D.). These would have lined the Via Aurelia outside the town wall. In the early days of the Church, Jesus was often portrayed beardless and as the good shepherd, with a lamb over his shoulder.

In Central Arles
Ideally, visit these sights in the order listed below. I've included some walking directions to connect the dots (see the Arles map on page 394).

▲▲Forum Square (Place du Forum)
Named for the Roman forum that once stood here, Place du Forum was the political and religious center of Roman Arles. Still lively, this café-crammed square is a local watering hole and popular for a *pastis* (anise-based apéritif). The bistros on the square, though no place for a fine dinner, can put together a good-enough salad or *plat du jour*—and when you sprinkle on the ambience, that's €12 well spent.

At the corner of Grand Hôtel Nord-Pinus (a favorite of Pablo Picasso), a plaque shows how the Romans built a foundation of galleries to make the main square level in order to compensate for Arles' slope down to the river. The two columns are all that survive from the upper story of the entry to the Forum. Steps leading to the entrance are buried—the Roman street level was about 20 feet below you (you can get a glimpse of it by peeking through the street-level openings under the Hôtel d'Arlatan, two blocks below Place du Forum on Rue du Sauvage). To see the underground arches, visit the Cryptoporticos (see next page).

The statue on the square is of **Frédéric Mistral** (1830-1914). This popular poet, who wrote in the local dialect rather than in French, was a champion of Provençal culture. After receiving the Nobel Prize in Literature in 1904, Mistral used his prize money to preserve and display the folk identity of Provence. He founded the regional folk museum (the Arlaten Folk Museum, described later) at a time when France was rapidly centralizing. (The local mistral wind—literally "master"—has nothing to do with his name.)

The **bright-yellow café**—called Café la Nuit—was the subject of one of Vincent van Gogh's most famous works in Arles. Although his painting showed the café in a brilliant yellow from the glow of gas lamps, the facade was bare limestone, just like the other cafés on this square. The café's current owners have painted it to match Van Gogh's version...and to cash in on the Vincent-crazed hordes who pay too much to eat or drink here.

• *Facing Café la Nuit, walk right one block (past Grand Hôtel Nord Pinus) and turn left. Walk through the Hôtel de Ville's vaulted entry (or take the next right if it's closed), and pop out onto the big...*

PROVENCE

Republic Square (Place de la République)

This square used to be called "Place Royale"...until the French Revolution. The obelisk was the former centerpiece of Arles' Roman Circus. The lions at its base are the symbol of the city, whose slogan is (roughly) "the gentle lion." Find a seat and watch the peasants—pilgrims, locals, and street musicians. There's nothing new about this scene.

• *Return to the Hôtel de Ville (where you came in) and look for the entrance to...*

Cryptoporticos (Cryptoportiques)

This dark, drippy underworld of Roman arches was constructed to support Forum Square. Two thousand years ago, most of this gallery of arches was at or above street level—modern Arles has buried about 20 feet of its history over the millennia. Pick up the minimalist English flier and read it before you descend into the dark.

Cost and Hours: €3.50, daily May-Sept 9:00-12:00 & 14:00-19:00, March-April and Oct 9:00-12:00 & 14:00-18:00, Nov-Feb 10:00-12:00 & 14:00-17:00.

• *Just outside the Hôtel de Ville, back in Place de la République, find...*

▲▲St. Trophime Church

Named after a third-century bishop of Arles, this church sports the finest Romanesque main entrance I've seen anywhere.

Cost and Hours: Church—free, daily April-Sept 9:00-12:00 & 14:00-18:30, Oct-March 9:00-12:00 & 14:00-17:00; cloisters—€3.50, daily May-Sept 9:00-19:00, March-April and Oct 9:00-18:00, Nov-Feb 10:00-17:00.

◒ Self-Guided Tour: Like a Roman triumphal arch, the church facade trumpets the promise of Judgment Day. The tympanum (the semicircular area above the door) is filled with Christian symbolism. Christ sits in majesty, surrounded by symbols of the four evangelists: Matthew (the winged man), Mark (the winged lion), Luke (the ox), and John (the eagle). The 12 apostles are lined up below Jesus. It's Judgment Day...some are saved, and others aren't. Notice the condemned (on the right)—a chain gang doing a sad bunny-hop over the fires of hell. For them, the tune trumpeted by the three angels above Christ is not a happy one. Below the chain gang, St. Stephen is being stoned to death, with his soul leaving through his mouth and instantly being welcomed by angels. Ride the exquisite detail back to a simpler age. In an illiterate medieval world, long before the vivid images of our Technicolor time, this was a neon billboard over the town square.

Interior: Just inside the door on the right, a chart locates the interior highlights and helps explain the carvings you just saw on the tympanum.

Tour the church counterclockwise. The tall 12th-century Romanesque nave is decorated by a set of tapestries showing scenes from the life of Mary (17th century, from the French town of Aubusson). Amble around the Gothic apse. Two-thirds of the way around, find the relic chapel behind the ornate wrought-iron gate, with its fine golden boxes that hold long-venerated bones of obscure saints. The next chapel houses the skull of St. Anthony of the Desert, with good English explanations of this saint's importance. Several chapels down, look for the early-Christian sarcophagus from Roman Arles (dated about A.D. 300) under the black columns. The heads were lopped off during the French Revolution.

This church is a stop on the ancient pilgrimage route to Santiago de Compostela in northwest Spain. For 800 years pilgrims on their way to Santiago have paused here...and they still do today. Notice the modern-day pilgrimages advertised on the far right near the church's entry.

Cloisters: Leaving the church, turn left, then left again through a courtyard to enter the adjacent cloisters.

The cloisters are worth a look only if you have a pass (enter at the far end of the courtyard). The many small columns were scavenged from the ancient Roman theater. Enjoy the sculpted capitals, the rounded 12th-century Romanesque arches, and the pointed 14th-century Gothic ones. The pretty vaulted hall exhibits 17th-century tapestries showing scenes from the First Crusade to the Holy Land. On the second floor, you'll walk along an angled rooftop designed to catch rainwater—notice the slanted gutter that channeled the water into a cistern and the heavy roof slabs covering the tapestry hall below.

• *Turn right out of the church cloisters, then take the first right on Rue de la Calade to reach the...*

Classical Theater (Théâtre Antique)

This first-century B.C. Roman theater once seated 10,000. This theater was an elegant, three-level structure with 27 arches radiating out to the street level. From the outside, it looked much like a halved version of Arles' Roman Arena. Budget travelers can peek over the fence from Rue du Cloître and see just about everything for free.

Cost and Hours: €6.50, daily May-Sept 9:00-19:00, March-April and Oct 9:00-18:00, Nov-Feb 10:00-17:00.

Visiting the Theater: Start with the video outside, which provides helpful background information and images that make it easier to put the scattered stones back in place (crouch in front to make out the small English subtitles). Next, walk to a center aisle and pull up a stone seat. To appreciate the theater's original size, look left (about 9:00) to the upper-left side of the tower and find the protrusion that supported the highest seating level. The structure required 33 rows of seats covering three levels to accommodate demand. During the Middle Ages, the old theater became a con-

PROVENCE

venient town quarry—St. Trophime Church was built from theater rubble. Precious little of the original theater survives—though it still is used for events, with seating for 3,000 spectators.

Two lonely Corinthian columns are all that remain of a three-story stage wall that once featured more than 100 columns and statues painted in vibrant colors. The orchestra section is defined by a semicircular pattern in the stone in front of you. Stepping up onto the left side of the stage, look down to the slender channel that allowed the brilliant-red curtain to disappear below, like magic. The stage, which was built of wood, was about 160 feet across and 20 feet deep. The actors' changing rooms are backstage, down the steps.

• *A block uphill is the...*

▲▲▲Roman Arena (Amphithéâtre)

Nearly 2,000 years ago, gladiators fought wild animals here to the delight of 20,000 screaming fans. Today local daredevils still fight wild animals here—"bullgame" posters around the arena advertise upcoming spectacles (described later, under "Experiences in Arles"). A lengthy restoration process is almost complete, giving the amphitheater an almost bleached-teeth whiteness. After the ticket kiosk is a helpful English information display that describes the arena's history and renovation.

Cost and Hours: €6.50, daily May-Sept 9:00-19:00, March-April and Oct 9:00-18:00, Nov-Feb 10:00-17:00, Rond-point des Arènes, tel. 08 91 70 03 70, www.arenes-arles.com.

Visiting the Arena: Find a seat in the upper deck. In Roman times, games were free (sponsored by city bigwigs), and fans were seated by social class. Thirty-four rows of stone bleachers extended all the way to the top of those vacant arches that circle the arena. There were no gates, just welcoming arches, numbered to allow entertainment-seekers to come and go freely. The purpose was to create a populace that was thoroughly Roman—enjoying the same activities and entertainment, all thinking as one (not unlike Americans' nationwide obsession with the same reality-TV shows). The many passageways you'll see (called *vomitoires*) allowed for rapid dispersal after the games—fights would break out among frenzied fans if they couldn't leave quickly. Through medieval times and until the early 1800s, the arches were bricked up and the stadium became a fortified town—with 200 humble homes crammed within its circular defenses. Parts of three of the medieval towers survive (the one above the ticket booth is open and rewards those who climb it with terrific views). To see two still-sealed arches—complete with cute medieval window frames—turn right as you leave, walk to the L'Andaluz Restaurant, and look back to the second floor.

• *The next three sights are back across town. The Arlaten Folk Museum (may be closed) and the relocated Fondation Van Gogh are close to Place du Forum, and the Réattu Museum is near the river.*

▲Arlaten Folk Museum (Musée Arlaten/Museon Arlaten)

This museum, which explains the ins and outs of daily Provençal life, was recently under renovation and may not be open in time for your visit. Ask at the TI or check the museum's website for the latest (www.museonarlaten.fr, French only).

▲Fondation Van Gogh

This art gallery recently moved to a new location in the Hôtel Léautaud de Donines, a 15th-century townhouse, and should be open in time for your visit (5 Place Honoré Clair, between Place du Forum and Trinquetaille Bridge). A good variety of Van Gogh souvenirs, prints, and postcards are available in the gift shop. The following description assumes the collection has remained intact (for details, call 04 90 93 08 08 or visit www.fondation-vincentvangogh-arles. org).

The foundation offers a refreshing stop for modern-art lovers and Van Gogh fans (but be warned that the collection contains no Van Gogh originals). Contemporary artists, including Roy Lichtenstein and Robert Rauschenberg, pay homage to Vincent through thought-provoking interpretations of his works). The black-and-white photographs (both art and shots of places that Vincent painted) complement the paintings. Unfortunately, this collection is often on the road from July through September, when material not related to Van Gogh is displayed.

Réattu Museum (Musée Réattu)

Housed in the former Grand Priory of the Knights of Malta, this modern-art collection is always changing. The permanent collection usually includes a series of works by homegrown Neoclassical artist Jacques Réattu, along with at least one Picasso painting and a roomful of his drawings (donated by the artist, some two-sided and all done in a flurry of creativity). The museum shuffles its large Picasso collection around regularly (they have more works than space to display them). Most of the three-floor museum houses temporary exhibits of modern artists—check the website to see who's playing.

Cost and Hours: €7, free first Sun of each month, open July-Sept Tue-Sun 10:00-19:00, Oct-June Tue-Sun 10:00-12:30 & 14:00-18:30, closed Mon year-round, last entry 30 minutes before closing for lunch or at end of day, 10 Rue du Grand Prieuré, tel. 04 90 49 37 58, www.museereattu.arles.fr.

PROVENCE

Experiences in Arles

▲▲Markets

On Wednesday and Saturday mornings, Arles' ring road erupts into an open-air festival of fish, flowers, produce, and you-name-it. The main event is on Saturday, with vendors jamming the ring road from Boulevard Emile Combes to the east, along Boulevard des Lices near the TI (the heart of the market), and continuing down Boulevard Georges Clemenceau to the west. Wednesday's market runs only along Boulevard Emile Combes, between Place Lamartine and bis Avenue Victor Hugo; the segment nearest Place Lamartine is all about food, and the upper half features clothing, tablecloths, purses, and so on. On the first Wednesday of the month, a flea market doubles the size of the usual Wednesday market along Boulevard des Lices near the main TI. Join in: Buy some flowers for your hotelier, try the olives, sample some wine, and swat a pickpocket. Both markets are open until 12:30.

▲▲Bullgames (Courses Camarguaises)

Provençal "bullgames" are held in Arles and in neighboring towns. Those in Arles occupy the same seats that fans have used for nearly 2,000 years, and take in Arles' most memorable experience—the *courses camarguaises* in the ancient arena. The nonviolent bullgames are more sporting than bloody bullfights (though traditional Spanish-style bullfights still take place on occasion). The bulls of Arles (who, locals stress, "die of old age") are promoted in posters even more boldly than their human foes. In the bullgame, a ribbon *(cocarde)* is laced between the bull's horns. The *razeteur*, with a special hook, has 15 minutes to snare the ribbon. Local businessmen encourage a *razeteur* (dressed in white with a red cummerbund) by shouting out how much money they'll pay for the *cocarde*. If the bull pulls a good stunt, the band plays the famous "Toreador" song from *Carmen*. The following day, newspapers report on the games, including how many *Carmens* the bull earned.

Three classes of bullgames—determined by the experience of the *razeteurs*—are advertised in posters: The *course de protection* is for rookies. The *trophée de l'Avenir* comes with more experience. And the *trophée des As* features top professionals. During Easter and the fall rice-harvest festival *(Féria du Riz)*, the arena hosts traditional Spanish bullfights as it has for 150 years (look for *corrida*) with outfits, swords, spikes, and the whole gory shebang.

Don't pass on a chance to see *Toro Piscine*, a silly spectacle for warm summer evenings where the bull ends up in a swimming pool (uh-huh...get more details at TI). Nearby villages stage *courses camarguaises* in small wooden bullrings nearly every weekend; TIs have the latest schedule, or check online at www.ffcc.info.

Cost and Hours: Arles' bullgame tickets usually run €5-15;

Sleep Code

(€1 = about $1.30, country code: 33)
S = Single, **D** = Double/Twin, **T** = Triple, **Q** = Quad, **b** = bathroom, **s** = shower only, * = French hotel rating system (0-5 stars). Unless otherwise noted, credit cards are accepted and English is spoken.

To help you sort easily through these listings, I've divided the accommodations into three categories based on the price for a standard double room with bath:

$$$ **Higher Priced**—Most rooms €90 or more.
$$ **Moderately Priced**—Most rooms between €65-90.
$ **Lower Priced**—Most rooms €65 or less.

Prices can change without notice; verify the hotel's current rates online or by email.

bullfights are pricier (€14-80). Schedules vary (usually July-Aug on Wed and Fri)—ask at the TI or check online at www.arenes-arles. com.

Sleeping in Arles

Hotels are a great value here—many are air-conditioned, though few have elevators. The Calendal, Musée, and Régence hotels offer exceptional value.

$$$ Hôtel le Calendal*** is a seductive place located between the Roman Arena and Classical Theater. Enter an expertly run hotel with airy lounges and a lovely palm-shaded courtyard. Enjoy the elaborate €12 buffet breakfast, have lunch in the courtyard or at the inexpensive sandwich bar (daily 12:00-15:00), and take advantage of their four free laptops for guests. You'll also find a Jacuzzi and a spa with a Turkish bath, hot pool, and massages at good rates. The comfortable rooms sport Provençal decor and come in all shapes and sizes (standard Db-€119, larger or balcony Db-€139, spacious Db-€169, Tb/Qb-€169, air-con, Wi-Fi, reserve ahead for parking-€8, just above arena at 5 Rue Porte de Laure, tel. 04 90 96 11 89, fax 04 90 96 05 84, www.lecalendal.com, contact@lecalendal.com). Ask about their studio apartments. They also run the nearby, budget La Maison du Pelerin, described later.

$$$ Hôtel d'Arlatan***, built on the site of a Roman basilica, offers faded elegance in a classy shell. It has comfy public spaces, a tranquil terrace, a pool, and a range of rooms, many with high, wood-beamed ceilings and stone walls (a newer wing has more

PROVENCE

Arles Hotels & Restaurants

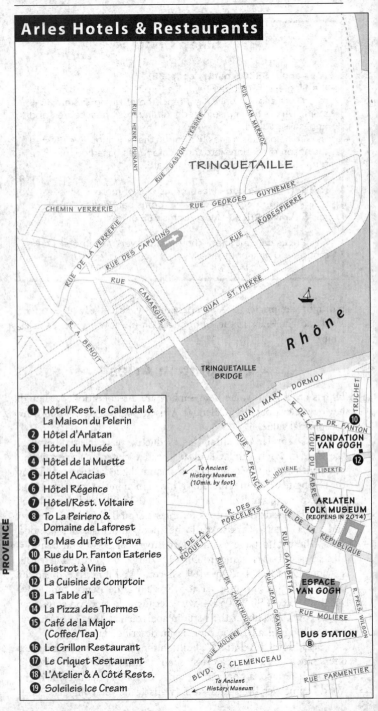

PROVENCE

TRINQUETAILLE

RUE HENRI DUNANT

RUE GASTON TESSIER

RUE JEAN MERMOZ

RUE GEORGES GUYNEMER

CHEMIN VERRERIE

RUE ROBESPIERRE

RUE DES CAPUCINS

RUE

RUE DE LA VERRERIE

RUE CAMARGUE

QUAI ST. PIERRE

R. A. BENOIT

Rhône

TRINQUETAILLE BRIDGE

QUAI MARX DORMOY

R. DE LA TOUR DU FABRE

TRUCHET

R. DR. FANTON

FONDATION VAN GOGH

RUE A. FRANCE

R. JOUVENE

LIBERTE

To Ancient History Museum (10min. by foot)

ARLATEN FOLK MUSEUM (REOPENS IN 2014)

R. DES PORCELETS

RUE DE LA RÉPUBLIQUE

RUE DE LA ROQUETTE

RUE DE CHARTROUSE

RUE JEAN GRANAUD

RUE GAMBETTA

ESPACE VAN GOGH

R. PRES. WILSON

RUE MOLIÈRE

RUE MOLIÈRE

BUS STATION
B

BLVD. G. CLEMENCEAU

RUE PARMENTIER

To Ancient History Museum

1. Hôtel/Rest. le Calendal & La Maison du Pelerin
2. Hôtel d'Arlatan
3. Hôtel du Musée
4. Hôtel de la Muette
5. Hôtel Acacias
6. Hôtel Régence
7. Hôtel/Rest. Voltaire
8. To La Peiriero & Domaine de Laforest
9. To Mas du Petit Grava
10. Rue du Dr. Fanton Eateries
11. Bistrot à Vins
12. La Cuisine de Comptoir
13. La Table d'L
14. La Pizza des Thermes
15. Café de la Major (Coffee/Tea)
16. Le Grillon Restaurant
17. Le Criquet Restaurant
18. L'Atelier & A Côté Rests.
19. Soleileis Ice Cream

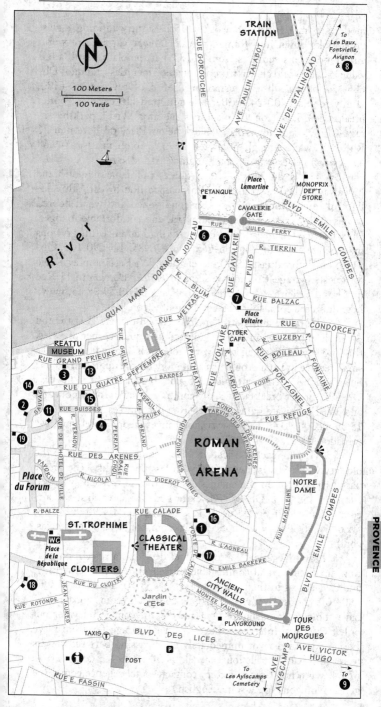

modern rooms). In the lobby of this 15th-century building, a glass floor looks down into Roman ruins. Hallway carpets are worn, and some rooms could use some TLC, but the place is still a fair value if Old World charm trumps updated amenities (standard Db-€85-137, bigger Db with terrace or Tb-€157, Db/Qb suites-€180, family rooms-€200-247, killer last-minute deals, excellent buffet breakfast-€15, air-con, ice machines, elevator, Wi-Fi, parking garage-€15, closed Nov-April, 1 block below Place du Forum at 26 Rue du Sauvage—tough by car, tel. 04 90 93 56 66, fax 04 90 49 68 45, www.hotel-arlatan.fr, hotel-arlatan@wanadoo.fr).

$$ Hôtel du Musée** is a quiet, affordable manor-home hideaway tucked deep in Arles (difficult to find by car). This delightful refuge comes with 28 air-conditioned and wood-floored rooms, a flowery two-tiered courtyard, and comfortable lounges. Lighthearted Claude and English-speaking Laurence, the gracious owners, are eager to help (Sb-€65, Db-€70-85, Tb-€90-100, Qb-€140, buffet breakfast-€8.50, no elevator, Wi-Fi, laptop available for guests, garage-€10, follow signs to *Réattu Museum* to 11 Rue du Grand Prieuré, tel. 04 90 93 88 88, fax 04 90 49 98 15, www.hoteldumusee.com, contact@hoteldumusee.com).

$$ Hôtel de la Muette**, with reserved owners Brigitte and Alain, is another good choice. Located in a quiet corner of Arles, this low-key hotel is well kept, with stone walls, brown tones, and a small terrace in front. You'll pay a bit more for the upgraded rooms, but it's money well spent (most Db-€66, bigger Db-€75, Tb-€77, Qb-€92, buffet breakfast-€8, air-con, no elevator, Internet access and Wi-Fi, private garage-€8, 15 Rue des Suisses, tel. 04 90 96 15 39, fax 04 90 49 73 16, www.hotel-muette.com, hotel.muette@wanadoo.fr).

$$ Hôtel Acacias**, just off Place Lamartine and inside the old city walls, is a modern hotel with less personality. The pretty pastel rooms are on the small side, but they're reasonably priced (standard Sb-€55, Db-€65-74, extra bed-€15, breakfast-€6, air-con, elevator, Wi-Fi, 2 Rue de la Cavalerie, tel. 04 90 96 37 88, fax 04 90 96 32 51, www.hotel-acacias.com, contact@hotel-acacias.com).

$ Hôtel Régence**, a top budget deal, has a riverfront location, immaculate and comfortable Provençal rooms, safe parking, and easy access to the train station (Db-€55-70, Tb-€70-85, Qb-€80-100, choose river view or quieter courtyard rooms, most rooms have showers, good buffet breakfast-€7, air-con, no elevator but only two floors, Internet access and Wi-Fi, garage-€6; from Place Lamartine, turn right immediately after passing between towers to reach 5 Rue Marius Jouveau; tel. 04 90 96 39 85, fax 04 90 96 67 64, www.hotel-regence.com, contact@hotel-regence.com). The gentle Nouvions speak some English.

$ Hôtel Voltaire* rents 12 small, spartan rooms with ceiling fans and nifty balconies overlooking a fun square. A block below the arena, it's good for starving artists who aren't particular about cleanliness. Smiling owner "Mr." Ferran (fur-ran) loves the States, and hopes you'll add to his postcard collection (D-€30, Ds-€35, Db-€40, 1 Place Voltaire, tel. 04 90 96 49 18, fax 04 90 96 45 49, levoltaire13@aol.com). They also serve a good-value lunch and dinner in their recommended restaurant.

$ La Maison du Pelerin offers spotless dorm rooms with three to six beds per room. It's a great value, just above the Roman Arena and Classical Theater, with a shared kitchen and homey living area. Book in advance by phone or email and get the door code. You can also check in next door at the recommended Hôtel le Calendal (they own the place). Sheets are included (€25/person, shared bath, must pay in advance, Wi-Fi, 26 Place Pomme, mobile 06 99 71 11 89, www.arles-pelerins.fr).

Eating in Arles

You can dine well in Arles on a modest budget—in fact, it's hard to blow a lot on dinner here (most of my listings have *menus* for under €25). The bad news is that restaurants change regularly, so double-check my suggestions. Before dinner, go local on Place du Forum and enjoy a *pastis*. This anise-based apéritif is served straight in a glass with ice, plus a carafe of water—dilute to taste. Sunday is a quiet night for restaurants, though most eateries on Place du Forum are open.

For **picnics,** a big, handy Monoprix supermarket/department store is on Place Lamartine (Mon-Thu 8:30-19:30, Fri-Sat 8:30-20:00, closed Sun).

On or near Place du Forum

Great atmosphere and mediocre food at fair prices await on Place du Forum. By all accounts, the garish yellow Café la Nuit is worth avoiding. Most other cafés on the square deliver acceptable quality and terrific ambience. For better cuisine, wander away from the square.

On Rue du Dr. Fanton

A half-block below the Forum, on Rue du Dr. Fanton, lies a terrific lineup of restaurants. Come here to peruse your options side by side. You can't go wrong—all offer good value and have appealing indoor and outdoor seating.

Le 16 is a warm, affordable place to enjoy a fresh salad (€10) or a fine two- or three-course dinner (€20-€25). The choices are limited, so check the selection before sitting down. The goat cheese *croustillant* salad and *taureau* (bull's meat) in a tasty sauce make a fine combination (closed Sat-Sun, 16 Rue du Dr. Fanton, tel. 04 90 93 77 36).

Le Gaboulet is a popular local spot, blending a cozy interior, classic French cuisine, and service with a smile (thanks to owner Frank). It's the most expensive of the places I list on this street, but it's still busy. If it's cold out, the huge chimney should be lit (€27 *menu*, great fries, closed Sun-Mon, 18 Rue du Dr. Fanton, tel. 04 90 93 18 11).

Au Brin du Thym, next door, offers a reliable blend of traditional French and Provençal cuisine at very fair prices. Arrive early for an outdoor table or call ahead, and let hardworking and formal Monsieur and Madame Colombaud and their daughter take care of you. Monsieur does *le cooking* while Madame does *le serving* (€14 lunch *menu*; excellent à la carte choices: €9 starters, €16 *plats*; closed Tue, 22 Rue du Dr. Fanton, tel. 04 90 49 95 96).

Le Plaza, next to Au Brin, features tasty Provençal cuisine served in a fine setting at good prices (€22 *menu*, closed Wed, 28 Rue du Dr. Fanton, tel. 04 90 96 33 15).

Bistrot à Vins suits wine lovers who enjoy pairing food and drink, and those in search of a good glass of *vin*. Sit at a convivial counter or at one of five tables while listening to light jazz (book ahead for a table). Affable Ariane speaks enough English and offers a limited selection of simple, tasty dishes. Her savory tarts and fresh green salad make a great meal (€10-16), and the wines—many available by the glass—are well priced (indoor dining only from 18:30 to 22:00, closed Mon-Tue, 2 Rue du Dr. Fanton, tel. 04 90 52 00 65).

Other Places near Place du Forum

At **La Cuisine de Comptoir,** a cool little bistro, locals of all ages abandon Provençal decor. Welcoming owners Alexandre and Vincent offer light *tartine* dinners—a delicious cross between pizza and bruschetta, served with soup or salad for just €11 (a swinging deal—the *brandada* is tasty and filling). Sit at the counter and watch *le chef* at work as you sip your €2 glass of rosé in fine glassware (closed Sun, mostly indoor dining, just off Place du Forum's lower end at 10 Rue de la Liberté, tel. 04 90 96 86 28).

La Table d'L has mod decor and is warmly run by eager-to-please waitress Ellie and chef Jay. Relatively new to Arles, Jay worked in a restaurant in New York for 17 years. The selection is limited but the quality is not. Jay loves her lamb and fish, and so will you (€8-21 starters, €24-34 *plats*, reasonably priced wine list, closed Mon, 1 bis Rue Réattu, tel. 04 90 96 32 53).

La Pizza des Thermes is a welcoming eatery with comfortable indoor and outdoor seating a few blocks north of Place du Forum.

It serves good pizza and pasta for €9-12 (daily, 6 Rue du Sauvage, tel. 04 90 49 60 64).

Café de la Major is *the* place to go to recharge with some serious coffee or tea (closed Sun, 7 bis Rue Réattu, tel. 04 90 96 14 15).

Near the Roman Arena

For about the same price as on Place du Forum, you can enjoy regional cuisine with a point-blank view of the arena. Because they change regularly, the handful of (mostly) outdoor eateries that overlook the arena are pretty indistinguishable.

Le Grillon, with the best view above the arena, offers friendly service (say *bonjour* to smiling Nordine) and good-enough salads (the *camarguaise* is a riot of color), pizza and tasty *tartines* for €10 (including small salad), and *plats du jour* for €10-14 (closed all day Wed and Sun nights, at the top of the arena on Rond-point des Arènes, tel. 04 90 96 70 97).

Le Criquet is a sweet little place serving Provençal classics with joy at good prices two blocks above the arena. If you're really hungry, try the €25 *bourride*—a creamy fish soup thickened with aioli and garlic and stuffed with mussels, clams, calamari, and more (good €19-26 three-course *menus*, indoor and outdoor dining, 21 Rue Porte de Laure, tel. 04 90 96 80 51).

For details on the next two places, see their listings under "Sleeping in Arles," earlier: **Hôtel le Calendal** serves lunch in its lovely courtyard (€12-18, daily 12:00-15:00) or delicious little sandwiches for €2.50 each at its small café. **Hôtel Voltaire,** well-situated on a pleasing square, serves simple three-course lunches and dinners at honest prices to a loyal clientele (€13 *menus*; hearty *plats* and filling salads for €10—try the *salade fermière*, *salade Latine*, or the filling *assiette Provençale*; closed Sun evening).

A Gastronomic Dining Experience

One of France's most recognized chefs, Jean-Luc Rabanel, has created a sensation with two very different options 50 yards from Place de la République (at 7 Rue des Carmes). They sit side by side, both offering indoor and terrace seating.

L'Atelier is so intriguing that people travel great distances just for the experience. Diners fork over €95 (at lunch, you'll spoon out €55) and trust the chef to create a memorable meal...which he does. There is no menu, just an onslaught of delicious taste sensations served in artsy dishes. Don't plan on a quick dinner, and don't come for the setting—it's a contemporary, shoebox-shaped dining room, but several outdoor tables are also available. The get-to-know-your-neighbor atmosphere means you can't help but join the party. You'll probably spot the famous chef (hint: he has long brown hair), as he is very hands-on with his waitstaff (closed Mon-Tue, best to book

PROVENCE

ahead, friendly servers will hold your hand through this palate-widening experience, tel. 04 90 91 07 69, www.rabanel.com).

A Côté saddles up next door, offering a smart wine bar/bistro ambience and top-quality cuisine for far less. Here you can sample the famous chef's talents for as little as €18 (daily *plat*) or as much as €38 (three-course *menu*, smallish servings, reasonably priced wines, open daily, tel. 04 90 47 61 13).

And for Dessert...

Soleileis has Arles' best ice cream, with all-natural ingredients and unusual flavors such as *fadoli*—olive oil mixed with nougatine. There's also a shelf of English books for exchange (open daily 14:00-18:30, across from recommended Le 16 restaurant at 9 Rue du Dr. Fanton).

Arles Connections

Some trains in and out of Arles require a **reservation**. These include connections with Nice to the east and Bordeaux to the west (including intermediary stops). Ask at the station.

From Arles by Train to: Paris (11/day, 2 direct TGVs—4 hours, 9 with transfer in Avignon—5 hours), **Avignon Centre-Ville** (roughly hourly, 20 minutes, less frequent in the afternoon), **Nîmes** (9/day, 30 minutes), **Marseille** (11/day, 1.5 hours), **Nice** (11/day, 3.75-4.5 hours, most require transfer in Marseille), **Barcelona** (2/day, 6 hours,), **Italy** (3/day transfer in Marseille and Nice; from Arles, it's 4.5-5 hours to Ventimiglia on the border, 8 hours to Milan, 9.5 hours to Cinque Terre, 11-12 hours to Florence, and 13 hours to Venice or Rome).

From Arles Train Station to Avignon TGV Station: If you're going to the TGV station in Avignon, it's easiest to take the SNCF bus directly there from Arles' train station (10/day, 1 hour, €7, included with railpass). Another option—which takes the same amount of time, but adds more walking—is to take the regular train from Arles to Avignon's Centre-Ville Station, then catch the *navette* (shuttle bus) to the TGV Station from there.

From Arles by Bus to: Nîmes (bus #C30, 6/day, 1 hour, €1.50). The bus station is at 16-24 Boulevard Georges Clemenceau (2 blocks below main TI, next to Café le Wilson). Bus info: tel. 04 90 49 38 01 (unlikely to speak English).

Avignon

Famous for its nursery rhyme, medieval bridge, and brooding Palace of the Popes, contemporary Avignon (ah-veen-yohn) bustles and prospers behind its mighty walls. During the 94 years (1309-1403) that Avignon starred as the *Franco Vaticano* (the temporary residence of the popes) and hosted two antipopes, it grew from a quiet village into a thriving city. With its large student population and fashionable shops, today's Avignon is an intriguing blend of medieval history, youthful energy, and urban sophistication. Street performers entertain the international throngs who fill Avignon's ubiquitous cafés and trendy boutiques. If you're here in July, be prepared for big crowds and higher prices, thanks to the rollicking theater festival. (Reserve your hotel far in advance.) Clean, lively, and popular with tourists, Avignon is more impressive for its outdoor ambience than for its museums and monuments.

Orientation to Avignon

Cours Jean Jaurès, which turns into Rue de la République, runs straight from the Centre-Ville train station to Place de l'Horloge and the Palace of the Popes, splitting Avignon in two. The larger eastern half is where the action is. Climb to the Jardin du Rochers des Doms for the town's best view, consider touring the pope's immense palace, lose yourself in Avignon's back streets (you can follow my "Discovering Avignon's Back Streets" self-guided walk), and find a shady square to call home. Avignon's shopping district fills the traffic-free streets near where Rue de la République meets Place de l'Horloge. As you wander, look for signs in Occitan—the language of the Occitania region; you might see the name of the city written as "Avinhon" or "Avignoun."

Tourist Information

The **main TI** is between the Centre-Ville train station and the old town, at 41 Cours Jean Jaurès (April-Oct Mon-Sat 9:00-18:00—until 19:00 in July, Sun 9:45-17:00; Nov-March Mon-Fri 9:00-18:00, Sat 9:00-17:00, Sun 10:00-12:00; tel. 04 32 74 32 74, www.avignon-tourisme.com). From April through mid-October, a branch TI office is open inside **Les Halles market** (Fri-Sun 10:00-13:00, closed Mon-Thu). At any TI, get the helpful map. If you're staying awhile, pick up the free *Guide Pratique* (info on bike rentals, hotels, apartment rentals, events, and museums).

Sightseeing Pass: Everyone should pick up the free **Avignon Passion Pass** (valid 15 days, for up to five family members). Get the pass stamped when you pay full price at your first sight, and then

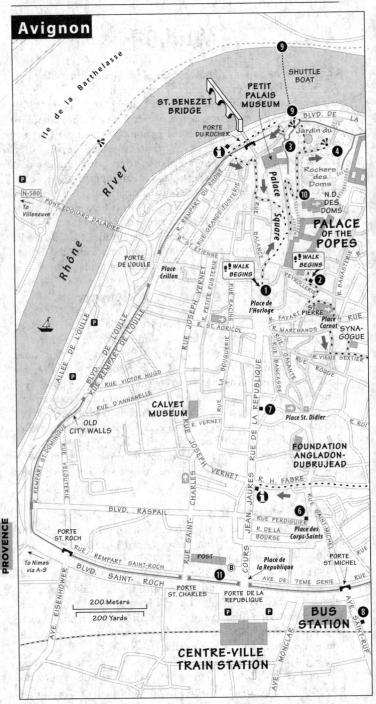

Avignon

Île de la Barthelasse

ST. BENEZET BRIDGE

PETIT PALAIS MUSEUM

SHUTTLE BOAT

PORTE DU ROCHER

Jardin du Rochers des Doms

N.D. DES DOMS

PALACE OF THE POPES

Rhône River

To Villeneuve

N-580

PONT EDOUARD DALADIER

R. REMPART DU RHÔNE

PORTE DE L'OULLE

Place Crillon

Palace Square

WALK BEGINS

WALK BEGINS

Place de l'Horloge

ST. PIERRE

Place Carnot

SYNA-GOGUE

CALVET MUSEUM

OLD CITY WALLS

FOUNDATION ANGLADON-DUBRUJEAD

Place St. Didier

Place des Corps-Saints

POST

Place de la Republique

To Nimes via A-9

PORTE ST. ROCH

BLVD. SAINT-ROCH

PORTE ST. CHARLES

PORTE DE LA REPUBLIQUE

BUS STATION

CENTRE-VILLE TRAIN STATION

200 Meters

200 Yards

PROVENCE

1. Start of Welcome to Avignon Walk
2. Start of Discovering Back Streets Walk (Hôtel La Mirande)
3. Best Views & Stairs to Tower
4. More Views
5. Shakespeare Bookshop
6. Launderette
7. Carrefour City Grocery
8. Bike Rental
9. Shuttle Boat Stops (2)
10. Tourist Train Stop
11. TGV Shuttle Stop & Bus #11 Stop

PROVENCE

receive reductions at the others (for example, €2 less at the Palace of the Popes and €3 less at the Petit Palais). The discounts add up—always show your Passion Pass when buying a ticket. The pass comes with the Avignon "Passion" map and guide, which includes several good (but tricky-to-follow) walking tours.

Arrival in Avignon

By Train

Avignon has two train stations: TGV (linked to downtown by frequent shuttle buses) and Centre-Ville. While most TGV trains serve only the TGV Station, some also stop at Centre-Ville—verify your station in advance.

TGV Station (Gare TGV): This shiny new station, on the outskirts of town, has no baggage storage (bags can be stored only at the Centre-Ville train station).

To get to the city center, take the *navette*/**shuttle bus** (marked *Navette/Avignon Centre;* €1.20, buy ticket from driver, 3/hour, 15 minutes). To find the bus stop, leave the station by the north exit *(sortie nord)*, walk down the stairs, and find the long bus shelter to the left. In downtown Avignon, you'll arrive at a stop just inside the city walls, in front of the post office on Cours Président Kennedy (see map on page 414). From here you're three blocks from the city's main TI and two blocks from the Centre-Ville train station. A **taxi** ride between the TGV Station and downtown Avignon costs about €20 (to find taxis, exit the TGV Station via *sortie nord*).

To pick up a **rental car** at the TGV Station, walk out the south exit *(sortie sud)* to find the *location de voitures* in the parking lot. If you're driving directly to Arles, leave the station, following signs to *Avignon Sud*, then *La Rocade*. You'll soon see exits to Arles.

If you're heading from the Avignon TGV Station to the **Arles train station,** catch the direct SNCF bus from the TGV Station's bus stop (10/day, 1 hour, €7, schedule posted on the shelter and available at any information booth inside the TGV Station).

Centre-Ville Station (Gare Avignon Centre-Ville): All non-TGV trains (and a few TGV trains) serve the central station. You can stash your bags here—exit the station to the left and look for the *consignes* sign (confirm closing time when you leave your bag). To reach the town center, cross the busy street in front of the station and walk through the city walls onto Cours Jean Jaurès. The TI is three blocks down, at #41.

By Bus

The dingy bus station *(gare routière)* is 100 yards to the right as you leave the Centre-Ville train station, beyond and below Hôtel Ibis (info desk open Mon-Sat 8:00-19:30, closed Sun, tel. 04 90 82 07 35, staff speaks a little English).

By Car

Drivers entering Avignon follow *Centre-Ville* and *Gare SNCF* (train station) signs. You'll find central pay lots (about €10/half-day, €15/day) in the garage next to the Centre-Ville train station, at the Parking Jean Jaurès under the ramparts across from the station. Two less pricey options are the Parking Les Halles in the center of town, on Place Pie ("pee"), and the Parking Palais des Papes. Hotels have advice for smart overnight parking, and some offer small discounts in the municipal parking garages.

Free or Cheap Parking: Two free lots have complimentary shuttle buses to the center except on Sunday (follow *P Gratuit* signs): One is just across Daladier Bridge (Pont Daladier) on Ile de la Barthelasse, with shuttles to Place Crillon; the other is along the river east of the Palace of the Popes, with shuttles to Place Carnot (both lots are within walking distance of the city center if need be). Parking on the street is free in the *bleu* zones 12:00-14:00 and 19:00-9:00. It's €2 for about three hours 9:00-12:00 and 14:00-19:00 (hint: if you put €2 in the meter after 19:00, it's good until 14:00 the next day). No matter where you park, leave nothing in your car.

Helpful Hints

Book Ahead for July: During the July theater festival, rooms are sparse—reserve very early, or stay in Arles.

Local Help: David at **Imagine Tours** (a nonprofit group whose goal is to promote this region) can help with hotel emergencies or tickets to special events (mobile 06 89 22 19 87, www. imagine-tours.net, imagine.tours@gmail.com). If you get no answer, leave a message.

Internet Access: The TI has a current list of Internet cafés, or you can ask your hotelier. Many bigger cafés provide free Wi-Fi to anyone who buys a drink.

English Bookstore: Try **Shakespeare Bookshop** (Tue-Sat 9:30-12:00 & 14:00-18:30, closed Sun-Mon, 155 Rue Carreterie, in Avignon's northeast corner, tel. 04 90 27 38 50).

Baggage Storage: You can leave your bags at Centre-Ville train station (see "Arrival in Avignon," earlier).

Laundry: The launderette at 66 Place des Corps-Saints, where Rue Agricol Perdiguier ends, has English instructions and is handy to most hotels (daily 7:00-20:00).

Grocery Store: **Carrefour City** is central and has long hours (Mon-Sat 7:00-22:00, Sun 9:00-12:00, next to McDonald's, 2 blocks from the TI, toward Place de l'Horloge on Rue de la République).

Bike Rental: You can rent bikes and scooters at **Provence Bike** (7

PROVENCE

Avenue St. Ruf, tel. 04 90 27 92 61, www.provence-bike.com)
You'll enjoy riding on the Ile de la Barthelasse.

Car Rental: The TGV Station has car-rental agencies (open long hours daily).

Shuttle Boat: A free shuttle boat, the *Navette Fluviale*, plies back and forth across the river (as it did in the days when the town had no functioning bridge) from near St. Bénezet Bridge (daily July-Aug 11:00-21:00, Sept-June roughly 10:00-12:30 & 14:00-18:00, 3/hour). It drops you on the peaceful Ile de la Barthelasse, with its recommended riverside restaurant, grassy walks, and bike rides with terrific city views. If you stay on the island for dinner, check the schedule for the last return boat—or be prepared for a taxi ride or a pleasant 25-minute walk back to town.

Commanding City Views: For great views of Avignon and the river, walk or drive across Daladier Bridge, or ferry across the Rhône on the *Navette Fluviale* (described above). I'd take the boat across the river, walk the view path to Daladier Bridge, and then cross back over the bridge (45-minute walk over mostly level ground). You can enjoy other impressive vistas from the top of the Jardin du Rochers des Doms, from the tower in the Palace of the Popes, from the end of the famous, broken St. Bénezet Bridge, and from the entrance to Fort St. André, across the river in Villeneuve-lès-Avignon.

Tours in Avignon

Walking Tours

On mid-season Mondays and Saturdays, the TI offers informative English walking tours of Avignon, which include a visit to the Palace of the Popes (€17, discounted with Avignon Passion Pass, April-June and Aug-Oct Mon at 10:30 and Sat at 14:30, no tours in July or Nov-March).

Tourist Trains

The little train leaves regularly from in front of the Palace of the Popes and offers a decent overview of the city, including the Jardin du Rochers des Doms and St. Bénezet Bridge (€7, 2/hour, 40 minutes, mid-March-mid-Oct daily 10:00-18:00, until 19:00 July-Aug, English commentary).

Guided Excursions

Several minivan tour companies based in Avignon offer transportation to destinations around Provence, including Pont du Gard (about €65-80/person for all-day tours). See "Tours of Provence" on page 390 (note that guide François Marcou and Imagine Tours are both based in Avignon).

Self-Guided Walks

For a fine overview of the city, combine these two walks. "Welcome to Avignon" covers the major sights, while "Discovering Avignon's Back Streets" leads you along the lanes less taken, delving beyond the surface of this historic city.

▲▲Welcome to Avignon

Before starting this walk—which connects the city's top sights—be sure to pick up the Avignon Passion Pass at the TI, then show it when entering each attraction to receive discounted admission (explained earlier, under "Tourist Information").

• *Start your tour where the Romans did, on Place de l'Horloge, in front of City Hall (Hôtel de Ville).*

Place de l'Horloge

This café square was the town forum during Roman times and the market square through the Middle Ages. (Restaurants here offer good people-watching, but they also have less ambience and low-quality meals—you'll find better squares elsewhere to hang your beret in.) Named for a medieval clock tower mostly hidden behind City Hall (find plaque in English), this square's present popularity arrived with the trains in 1854. Walk a few steps to the center of the square, and look down the main drag, Rue de la République. When the trains came to Avignon, proud city fathers wanted a direct, impressive way to link the new station to the heart of the city (just like in Paris)—so they plowed over homes to create Rue de la République and widened Place de l'Horloge. This main drag's Parisian feel is intentional—it was built not in the Provençal manner, but in the Haussmann style that is so dominant in Paris (characterized by broad, straight boulevards lined with stately buildings).

• *Walk uphill past the carousel (public WCs behind). Look up and follow the golden statue of Mary, floating high above the buildings. Veer right at the street's end, and continue into...*

Palace Square (Place du Palais)

This grand square is lined with the Palace of the Popes, the Petit Palais, and the cathedral. In the 1300s, the entire headquarters of the Catholic Church was moved to Avignon. The Church bought Avignon and gave it a complete makeover. Along with clearing out vast spaces like this square and building this three-acre palace, the Church erected more than three miles of protective wall (with 39 towers), "appropriate" housing for cardinals (read: mansions), and residences for its entire bureaucracy. The city was Europe's largest construction zone. Avignon's population grew from 6,000 to 25,000 in short order. (Today, 13,000 people live within the walls.)

The limits of pre-papal Avignon are outlined on city maps: Rues Joseph Vernet, Henri Fabre, des Lices, and Philonarde all follow the route of the city's earlier defensive wall.

The Petit Palais (Little Palace) seals the uphill end of the square and was built for a cardinal; today it houses medieval paintings (museum described later). The church just to the left of the Palace of the Popes is Avignon's cathedral. It predates the Church's purchase of Avignon by 200 years. Its small size reflects Avignon's modest, pre-papal population. The gilded Mary was added in 1854, when the Vatican established the doctrine of her Immaculate Conception. Mary is taller than the Palace of the Popes by design: The Vatican never accepted what it called the "Babylonian Captivity" and had a bad attitude about Avignon long after the pope was definitively back in Rome. There hasn't been a French pope since the Holy See returned to Rome—over 600 years ago. That's what I call a grudge.

Directly across the square from the palace's main entry stands a cardinal's residence, built in 1619 (now the Conservatoire National de Musique). Its fancy Baroque facade was a visual counterpoint to the stripped-down Huguenot aesthetic of the age. During this time, Provence was a hotbed of Protestantism—but, buried within this region, Avignon was a Catholic stronghold. Notice the stumps in front and nearby. Nicknamed *bites* (slang for the male anatomy), they effectively keep cars from double-parking in areas designed for people. Many of the metal ones slide up and down by remote control to let privileged cars come and go.

• *You can visit the massive **Palace of the Popes** (described later) now, but it works better to visit that palace at the end of this walk, then continue directly to the "Discovering Avignon's Back Streets" walk, described later.*

   Now is a good time to take in the...

Petit Palais Museum (Musée du Petit Palais)

This former cardinal's palace now displays the Church's collection of mostly medieval Italian painting (including one delightful Botticelli) and sculpture. All 350 paintings deal with Christian themes. A visit here before going to the Palace of the Popes helps furnish and populate that otherwise barren building, and a quick peek into its courtyard (even if you don't tour the museum) shows the importance of cardinal housing.

Cost and Hours: €6, €3 English brochure, some English explanations posted; Wed-Mon 10:00-13:00 & 14:00-18:00, closed Tue; at north end of Palace Square, tel. 04 90 86 44 58.

• *From Palace Square, we'll head up to the rocky hilltop where Avignon was first settled, then drop down to the river. With this short loop, you can enjoy a small park, hike to a grand river view, and visit Avignon's beloved broken bridge—an experience worth ▲▲.*

Start by climbing to the church level (you can fill your bottle with cold water here), then continue up to...

▲▲Jardin du Rochers des Doms

Though the park itself is a delight—with a sweet little café (good prices for food and drinks) and public WCs—don't miss the climax: a panoramic view of the Rhône River Valley and the broken bridge. For the best views (and the favorite make-out spot for local teenagers later in the evening), find the terrace behind the odd zodiac display (across the grass from the pond-side park café, near the statue of Jean Althen). If the green fence is ruining it for you, stand on the short wall behind you, or detour a few minutes through the park (to the right, with the river on your left) to find a bigger terrace.

On a clear day, the tallest peak you see, with its white limestone cap, is Mont Ventoux ("Windy Mountain"). Below and just to the right, you'll spot free passenger ferries shuttling across the river (great views from path on other side of the river), and—tucked amidst the trees on the far side of the river—a fun, recommended restaurant, Le Bercail. The island in the river is the Ile de la Barthelasse, a nature preserve where Avignon can breathe.

Fort St. André (across the river on the hill; see the info plaque to the left) was built by the French in 1360, shortly after the pope moved to Avignon, to counter the papal incursion into this part of Europe. The castle was across the border, in the kingdom of France. Avignon's famous bridge was a key border crossing, with towers on either end—one was French, and the other was the pope's. The French one, across the river, is the Tower of Philip the Fair (described later, under "More Sights in Avignon").

Cost and Hours: Free, park gates open daily April-Sept 7:30-20:00, Oct-March 7:30-18:00.

• From the smaller viewpoint (with the zodiac), take the stairs to the left (closed at night) down to the tower. You'll catch glimpses of the...

Ramparts

The only bit of the rampart you can walk on is accessed from St. Bénezet Bridge (pay to enter—see next). Just after the papacy took control of Avignon, the walls were extended to take in the convents and monasteries that had been outside the city. What you see today was restored in the 19th century.

• When you come out of the tower on street level, take the right-side exit and walk left along the wall to the old bridge. Pass under the bridge to find its entrance shortly after.

▲▲St. Bénezet Bridge (Pont St. Bénezet)

This bridge, whose construction and location were inspired by a shepherd's religious vision, is the "Pont d'Avignon" of nursery-rhyme fame. The ditty (which you've probably been humming all day) dates back to the 15th century: *Sur le Pont d'Avignon, on y danse, on y danse, sur le Pont d'Avignon, on y danse tous en rond* ("On the bridge of Avignon, we will dance, we will dance, on the bridge of Avignon, we will dance all in a circle").

But the bridge was a big deal even outside of its kiddie-tune fame. Built between 1171 and 1185, it was the only bridge crossing the mighty Rhône in the Middle Ages—important to pilgrims, merchants, and armies. It was damaged several times by floods and subsequently rebuilt, until 1668, when most of it was knocked down by a disastrous icy flood. Lacking a government stimulus package, the townsfolk decided not to rebuild this time, and for more than a century, Avignon had no bridge across the Rhône. While only four arches survive today, the original bridge was huge: Imagine a 22-arch, 3,000-foot-long bridge extending from Vatican territory to the lonely Tower of Philip the Fair, which marked the beginning of France (see displays of the bridge's original length).

Cost and Hours: €4.50, includes audioguide, €13 combo-ticket includes Palace of the Popes, same hours as the Palace of the Popes (described next), tel. 04 90 27 51 16.

Visiting the Bridge: The ticket booth is housed in what was a medieval hospital for the poor (funded by bridge tolls). Admission includes a small room dedicated to the song of Avignon's bridge and your only chance to walk a bit of the ramparts (enter both from the tower). A Romanesque chapel on the bridge is dedicated to St. Bénezet. Though there's not much to see on the bridge, the audioguide included with your ticket tells a good enough story. It's also fun to be in the breezy middle of the river with a sweeping city view.

• *To get to the Palace of the Popes from here, exit left, then turn left again back into the walls. Walk to the end of the short street, then turn right following signs to Palais des Papes. Next, look for brown signs leading left under the passageway. After a block of uphill walking, find the stairs to the palace square.*

▲Palace of the Popes (Palais des Papes)

In 1309, a French pope was elected (Pope Clément V). At the urging of the French king, His Holiness decided that dangerous Italy was no place for a pope, so he moved the whole operation to Avignon for a secure rule under a supportive king. The Catholic Church literally bought Avignon (then a two-bit town), and popes resided here until 1403. Meanwhile, Italians demanded a Roman pope, so from 1378 on, there were twin popes—one in Rome and one in Avignon—causing a schism in the Catholic Church that wasn't fully resolved until 1417.

Cost and Hours: €10.50 (more for special exhibits), includes audioguide, €13 combo-ticket includes St. Bénezet Bridge, daily mid-March-Oct 9:00-19:00, until 20:00 in July-Sept, until 21:00 in Aug, Nov-mid-March 9:30-17:45, last entry one hour before closing, tel. 04 90 27 50 74, www.palais-des-papes.com.

Visiting the Palace: A visit to the mighty yet barren papal palace comes with a slick multimedia audioguide that leads you along a one-way route and does a decent job of overcoming the complete lack of furnishings. It teaches the basic history while allowing you to tour at your own pace. A small museum inside the palace also helps add context. Still, touring the palace is pretty anticlimactic, given its historic importance.

As you wander, ponder that this palace—the largest surviving Gothic palace in Europe—was built to accommodate 500 people as the administrative center of the Holy See and home of the pope. This was the most fortified palace of the age (remember, the pope left Rome to be more secure). Nine popes ruled from here, making this the center of Christianity for nearly 100 years. You'll walk through the pope's personal quarters (frescoed with happy hunting scenes), see many models of how the various popes added to the building, and learn about its state-of-the-art plumbing. The rooms are huge. The "pope's chapel" is twice the size of the adjacent Avignon cathedral.

The last pope (or, technically, antipope, since by then Rome also had its own rival pope) checked out in 1403 (escaping a siege), but the Church owned Avignon until the French Revolution in 1789. During this interim period, the pope's "legate" (official representative, normally a nephew) ruled Avignon from this palace. Avignon residents, many of whom had come from Rome, spoke Italian for a century after the pope left, making it a linguistic ghetto within France. In the Napoleonic age, the palace was a barracks, housing 1,800 soldiers. You can see cuts in the wall where high ceilings gave way to floor beams. Climb the tower (Tour de la Gâche) for grand views and a rooftop café with surprisingly good food at very fair prices.

Wine Room: A room at the end of the tour (called *la boutellerie*) is dedicated to the region's wines, of which they claim the pope was a fan. Sniff "Le Nez du Vin"—a black box with 54 tiny bottles designed to develop your "nose." (Blind-test your travel partner.) The nearby village of Châteauneuf-du-Pape is where the pope summered in the 1320s. Its famous wine is a direct descendant of his wine. You're welcome to taste here (€6 for 3-5 fine wines and souvenir tasting cup). If it's only wine you want, go directly to the back entrance of the palace and enter the boutique.

• *You'll exit at the rear of the palace, where my "Back Streets" walking tour begins (described next). Or, to return to Palace Square, make two rights after exiting the palace.*

▲▲Discovering Avignon's Back Streets

Use the map in this chapter or the TI map to navigate this easy, level, 30-minute walk. This self-guided tour begins in the small square (Place de la Mirande) behind the Palace of the Popes. If you've toured the palace, this is where you exit. Otherwise, from the front of the palace, follow the narrow, cobbled Rue de la Peyrollerie—carved out of the rock—around the palace on the right side as you face it.

• *Our walk begins at the...*

Hôtel La Mirande: Located on the square, Avignon's finest hotel welcomes visitors. Find the atrium lounge and consider a coffee break amid the understated luxury (€13 afternoon tea served daily 15:00-18:00, includes a generous selection of pastries). Inspect the royal lounge and recommended dining room; cooking demos are offered in the basement below. Rooms start at about €425 in high season.

• *Turn left out of the hotel and left again on Rue de la Peyrollerie ("Coppersmiths Street"), then take your first right on Rue des Ciseaux d'Or. On the small square ahead you'll find the...*

Church of St. Pierre: The original chestnut doors were carved in 1551, when tales of New World discoveries raced across Europe. (Notice the Indian headdress, top center of left-side door.) The fine Annunciation (eye level on right-side door) shows Gabriel giving Mary the exciting news in impressive Renaissance 3-D. Now take 10 steps back from the door and look way up. The tiny statue breaking the skyline of the church is the pagan god Bacchus, with oodles of grapes. What's he doing sitting atop a Christian church? No one knows. The church's interior holds a beautiful Baroque altar. (For recommended restaurants near the Church of St. Pierre, see "Eating in Avignon," later.)

• *With your back to the church, follow the alley to the right, which was covered and turned into a tunnel during the town's population boom. It leads into...*

Place des Châtaignes: The cloister of St. Pierre is named for the chestnut *(châtaigne)* trees that once stood here (now replaced by plane trees). The practical atheists of the French Revolution destroyed the cloister, leaving only faint traces of the arches along the church side of the square.

• *Continue around the church and cross the busy street to the Banque Chaix. Across little Rue des Fourbisseurs find the classy...*

15th-Century Building: With its original beamed eaves showing, this is a rare vestige from the Middle Ages. Notice how this building widens the higher it gets. A medieval loophole based taxes on ground-floor square footage—everything above was tax-free. Walking down Rue des Fourbisseurs ("Street of the Animal Furriers"), notice how the top floors almost meet. Fire was a constant danger in the Middle Ages, as flames leapt easily from one home to the next. In fact, the lookout guard's primary responsibility was watching for fires, not the enemy. Virtually all of Avignon's medieval homes have been replaced by safer structures.

• *Walk down Rue des Fourbisseurs and turn left onto the traffic-free Rue du Vieux Sextier ("Street of the Old Balance," for weighing items); another left under the first arch leads 10 yards to Avignon's...*

Synagogue: Jews first arrived in Avignon with the Diaspora (exile) of the first century. Avignon's Jews were nicknamed "the Pope's Jews" because of the protection that the Vatican offered to Jews expelled from France. Although the original synagogue dates from the 1220s, in the mid-19th century it was completely rebuilt in a Neoclassical Greek-temple style by a non-Jewish architect. This is the only synagogue under a rotunda that you'll see anywhere. It's an intimate, classy place dressed with white colonnades and walnut furnishings. To enter the synagogue, you'll have to email in advance of your visit (free, closed Sat-Sun, 2 Place Jerusalem, tel. 04 90 55 21 24, rabinacia@hotmail.fr).

• *Retrace your steps to Rue du Vieux Sextier and turn left, then continue to the big square and find the big, boxy...*

Market (Les Halles): In 1970, the town's open-air market was replaced by this modern one. The market's jungle-like green wall reflects the changes of seasons and helps mitigate its otherwise stark exterior (open Tue-Sun until 13:00, closed Mon, small TI inside open Fri-Sun). Step inside for a sensual experience of organic breads, olives, and festival-of-mold cheeses. Rue des Temptations cuts down the center. Cafés and cheese shops are on the right—as far as possible from the stinky fish stalls on the left. Follow your nose away from the fish and have a coffee with the locals.

• *Exit out the back door of Les Halles, turn left on Rue de la Bonneterie ("Street of Hosiery"), and track the street for five minutes to the plane trees, where it becomes...*

Rue des Teinturiers: This "Street of the Dyers" is a tie-dyed, tree- and stream-lined lane, home to earthy cafés and galleries. This was the cloth industry's dyeing and textile center in the 1800s. The stream is a branch of the Sorgue River. Those stylish Provençal fabrics and patterns you see for sale everywhere were first made here, after a pattern imported from India.

About three small bridges down, you'll pass the Grey Penitents chapel on the right. The upper facade shows the GPs, who dressed up in robes and pointy hoods to do their anonymous good

PROVENCE

deeds back in the 13th century (long before the KKK dressed this way). As you stroll on, you'll see the work of amateur sculptors, who have carved whimsical car barriers out of limestone.

Fun restaurants on this atmospheric street are recommended later, under "Eating in Avignon."

• *Farther down Rue des Teinturiers, you'll come to the...*

Waterwheel: Standing here, imagine the Sorgue River—which hits the mighty Rhône in Avignon—being broken into several canals in order to turn 23 such wheels. In about 1800, waterwheels powered the town's industries. The little cogwheel above the big one could be shoved into place, kicking another machine into gear behind the wall.

• *To return to the real world, double back on Rue des Teinturiers and turn left on Rue des Lices, which traces the first medieval wall. (Lice is the no-man's-land along a wall.) After a long block, you'll pass a striking four-story building that was a home for the poor in the 1600s, an army barracks in the 1800s, a fine-arts school in the 1900s, and is a deluxe condominium today (much of this neighborhood is going high-class residential). Eventually you'll return to Rue de la République, Avignon's main drag.*

More Sights in Avignon

Most of Avignon's top sights are covered earlier by my self-guided walks. With more time, consider these options.

Fondation Angladon-Dubrujeaud

Visiting this museum is like being invited into the elegant home of a rich and passionate art collector. It mixes a small but enjoyable collection of art from Post-Impressionists to Cubists (including Paul Cézanne, Vincent van Gogh, Honoré Daumier, Edgar Degas, and Pablo Picasso), with re-created art studios and furnishings from many periods. It's a quiet place with a few superb paintings.

Cost and Hours: €6, Tue-Sun 13:00-18:00, closed Mon, 5 Rue Laboureur, tel. 04 90 82 29 03, www.angladon.com.

Calvet Museum (Musée Calvet)

This fine-arts museum impressively displays its collection, highlighting French Baroque works. This museum goes ignored by most, but you'll find a few diamonds in the rough upstairs: Géricault, Soutine, and one painting each from Manet, Sisley, Bonnard, Dufy, and Vlaminck.

Cost and Hours: €6, includes audioguide, Wed-Mon 10:00-13:00 & 14:00-18:00, closed Tue, in the quieter western half of town at 65 Rue Joseph Vernet, antiquities collection a few blocks away at 27 Rue de la République—same hours and ticket, tel. 04 90 86 33 84, www.musee-calvet.org.

Near Avignon, in Villeneuve-lès-Avignon

▲Tower of Philip the Fair (Tour Philippe-le-Bel)

Built to protect access to St. Bénezet Bridge in 1307, this massive tower offers a terrific view over Avignon and the Rhône basin. It's best late in the day.

Cost and Hours: €2.10; April-Sept daily 10:00-12:30 & 14:00-18:30; Oct-Nov Tue-Sat 10:00-12:30 & 14:00-17:00, closed Sun-Mon; closed Dec-March.

Getting There: To reach the tower from Avignon, drive 5 minutes (cross Daladier Bridge, follow signs to *Villeneuve-lès-Avignon*), or take bus #11 (2/hour, catch bus in front of post office on Cours Président Kennedy—see map on page 414).

Sleeping in Avignon

(€1 = about $1.30, country code: 33)

Hotel values are better in Arles, though I've found some good values in Avignon and have listed them below. Avignon is crazy during its July festival, when you must book long ahead (expect inflated prices). Drivers should ask about parking deals.

Near Avignon's Centre-Ville Station

These listings are a five- to ten-minute walk from the Centre-Ville train station.

$$$ Hôtel Bristol*** is a big, professionally run place on the main drag, offering predictable "American" comforts, including spacious public spaces, large rooms decorated in neutral tones, duvets on the beds, a big elevator, air-conditioning, and a generous buffet breakfast (standard Db-€96-€116, bigger Db-€140, Tb/Qb-€168, breakfast-€12, parking-€12, 44 Cours Jean Jaurès, tel. 04 90 16 48 48, fax 04 90 66 22 72, www.bristol-hotel-avignon.com, contact@bristol-avignon.com).

$$ Hôtel Ibis Centre Gare** offers no surprises—just predictable two-star comfort at the central train and bus stations. This well-priced place offers generous public spaces, a café, an elevator, and a bar (Db-€75-90, Internet access and Wi-Fi, 42 Boulevard St. Roch, tel. 04 90 85 38 38, fax 04 90 86 44 81, www.ibishotel.com, h0944@accor.com).

$$ Hôtel Colbert** is a solid two-star hotel and a good mid-range bet, with richly colored, comfortable rooms in many sizes. Your hardworking hosts—Patrice, Annie, and *le chien* Brittany—care for this restored manor house, with its warm public spaces and sweet little patio. It's a popular place, so it's best to book in advance (Sb-€68, small Db-€78, bigger Db-€90, some tight bathrooms, no triples, rooms off the patio are a bit musty, creative homemade breakfast-€12, air-con, no elevator, Wi-Fi, closed Nov-mid-

PROVENCE

Avignon Hotels & Restaurants

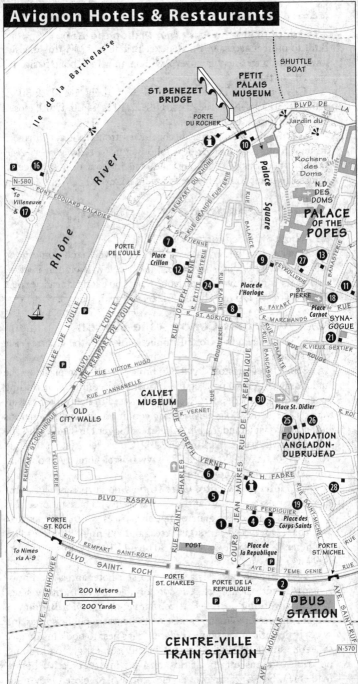

ILE DE LA BARTHELASSE

Rhône River

SHUTTLE BOAT

ST. BENEZET BRIDGE

PETIT PALAIS MUSEUM

PORTE DU ROCHER

BLVD. DE LA

Jardin du

Rochers des Doms

N.D. DES DOMS

Palace Square

PALACE OF THE POPES

N-580
To Villeneuve & **17**

PONT EDOUARD DALADIER

R. REMPART DU RHONE

R. ST. ETIENNE

RUE GRANDE FUSTERIE

PORTE DE L'OULLE

Place Crillon

RUE JOSEPH VERNET

R. PETITE FUSTERIE

RUE RACINE

Place de l'Horloge

PEYROLLERIE

R. BANASTERIE

ST. PIERRE

RUE

Place Carnot

SYNA-GOGUE

Allée de l'Oulle

BLVD. DE L'OULLE

RUE REMPART DE L'OULLE

RUE VICTOR HUGO

RUE D'ANNANELLE

R. ST. AGRICOL

R. LA BOURGRE

R. FAVART

R. MARCHANDS

RUE GALANTE

RUE BANCASSE

RUE VIEUX SEXTIER

ROUGE

OLD CITY WALLS

CALVET MUSEUM

RUE VERNET

RUE JOSEPH VERNET

RUE DE LA REPUBLIQUE

Place St. Didier

R. ROI

FOUNDATION ANGLADON-DUBRUJEAD

R. REMPART ST-DOMINIQUE

RUE VELOUTERIE

BLVD. RASPAIL

RUE SAINT-CHARLES

JEAN JAURES

R. H. FABRE

RUE SAINT-MICHEL

PORTE ST. ROCH

To Nimes via A-9

RUE REMPART SAINT-ROCH

POST

RUE PERDIGUIER

Place des Corps-Saints

PORTE ST. MICHEL

BLVD. SAINT-ROCH

AVE. EISENHOWER

COURS JEAN JAURES

Place de la Republique

AVE. DE 7EME GENIE

PORTE ST. CHARLES

PORTE DE LA REPUBLIQUE

BUS STATION

200 Meters
200 Yards

CENTRE-VILLE TRAIN STATION

AVE. MONCLAR

AVE. SAINT-RUF

N-570

PROVENCE

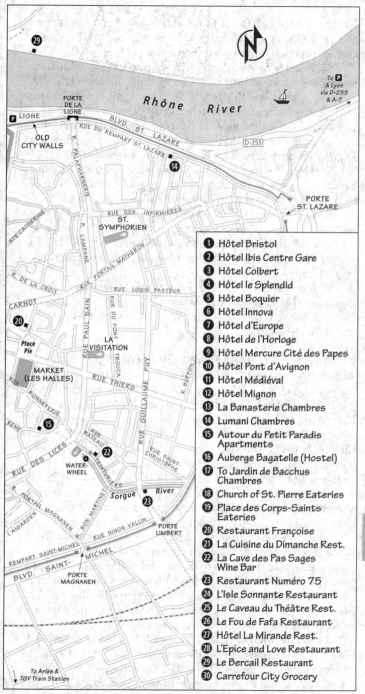

1. Hôtel Bristol
2. Hôtel Ibis Centre Gare
3. Hôtel Colbert
4. Hôtel le Splendid
5. Hôtel Boquier
6. Hôtel Innova
7. Hôtel d'Europe
8. Hôtel de l'Horloge
9. Hôtel Mercure Cité des Papes
10. Hôtel Pont d'Avignon
11. Hôtel Médiéval
12. Hôtel Mignon
13. La Banasterie Chambres
14. Lumani Chambres
15. Autour du Petit Paradis Apartments
16. Auberge Bagatelle (Hostel)
17. To Jardin de Bacchus Chambres
18. Church of St. Pierre Eateries
19. Place des Corps-Saints Eateries
20. Restaurant Françoise
21. La Cuisine du Dimanche Rest.
22. La Cave des Pas Sages Wine Bar
23. Restaurant Numéro 75
24. L'Isle Sonnante Restaurant
25. Le Caveau du Théâtre Rest.
26. Le Fou de Fafa Restaurant
27. Hôtel La Mirande Rest.
28. L'Epice and Love Restaurant
29. Le Bercail Restaurant
30. Carrefour City Grocery

PROVENCE

March, turn right off Cours Jean Jaurès on Rue Agricol Perdiguier to #7, tel. 04 90 86 20 20, fax 04 90 85 97 00, www.lecolbert-hotel. com, contact@avignon-hotel-colbert.com).

$$ Hôtel le Splendid* rents 17 acceptable rooms with faux-wood floors, most of which could use a little attention (Sb-€50, Db-€70, bigger Db with air-con-€80, Tb with air-con-€88, three Db apartments-€95, continental breakfast-€9, no elevator, Internet access and Wi-Fi, turn right off Cours Jean Jaurès on Rue Agricol Perdiguier to #17, tel. 04 90 86 14 46, fax 04 90 85 38 55, www. avignon-splendid-hotel.com, splendidavignon@gmail.com).

$ Hôtel Boquier**, run by engaging managers Madame Sendra and husband Pascal, has 12 quiet, good-value, and homey rooms under wood beams in a central location (small Db-€61, bigger Db-€73, Tb-€81, Qb-€92, air-con, Internet access and Wi-Fi, steep and narrow stairways to some rooms and no elevator, parking-€12, near the TI at 6 Rue du Portail Boquier, tel. 04 90 82 34 43, fax 04 90 86 14 07, www.hotel-boquier.com, contact@hotel-boquier.com).

$ Hôtel Innova is a shy little place with 11 spotless rooms at good rates (Db-€50-60, extra person-€7, no air-con, no elevator, 100 Rue Joseph Vernet, tel. 04 90 82 54 10, www.hotel-innova.fr, innova.hotel@wanadoo.fr).

In the Center, near Place de l'Horloge

$$$ Hôtel d'Europe**, with Avignon's most prestigious address, lets peasants sleep royally without losing their shirts—but only if you land one of the 10 surprisingly reasonable "classique" rooms. Enter a shady courtyard, linger in the lounges, and savor every comfort. The hotel is located on the handsome Place Crillon, near the river (standard Db-€195, superior Db-€365, prestige Db-€550, breakfast-€21, elevator, Internet access, garage-€18, near Daladier Bridge at 12 Place Crillon, tel. 04 90 14 76 76, fax 04 90 14 76 71, www.heurope.com, reservations@heurope.com). The hotel's restaurant is Michelin-rated (one star) and serves an upscale €48 *menu* in its formal dining room or front courtyard.

$$$ Hôtel de l'Horloge**, a top three-star choice, is as central as it gets—right on Place de l'Horloge. It offers 66 fine rooms, some with terraces and views of the city and the Palace of the Popes (standard Db-€100-120, bigger Db with terrace-€150-200, terrace rooms also work as Tb or Qb, buffet breakfast-€14, Rue Félicien David, tel. 04 90 16 42 00, fax 04 90 82 17 32, www.hotel-avignon-horloge.com, hotel.horloge@hotels-ocre-azur.com).

$$$ Hôtel Mercure Cité des Papes** is a modern chain hotel within spitting distance of the Palace of the Popes. It has 89 small, smartly designed rooms (Sb-€135-150, Db-€170-190, breakfast-€13, promotional deals best if booked 15 days ahead, many

PROVENCE

rooms have views over Place de l'Horloge, air-con, elevator, 1 Rue Jean Vilar, tel. 04 90 80 93 00, fax 04 90 80 93 01, www.mercure. com, h1952@accor.com).

$$$ Hôtel Pont d'Avignon***, just inside the walls near St. Bénezet Bridge, is part of the same chain as the Hôtel Mercure Cité des Papes, with the same prices for its 87 rooms (direct access to a garage makes parking easier than at the other Mercure hotel, elevator, on Rue Ferruce, tel. 04 90 80 93 93, fax 04 90 80 93 94, www.mercure.com, h0549@accor.com).

$$ Hôtel Médiéval** is burrowed deep a few blocks from the Church of St. Pierre. Built as a cardinal's home, this massive stone mansion has a small garden and 35 wood-paneled, air-conditioned, unimaginative rooms, with friendly-as-they-get Régis at the helm. Big renovation plans may change the layout—and increase prices (Sb-€51, Db-€65-81, bigger Db or Tb-€90-97, breakfast-€8, kitchenettes available but require 3-night minimum stay, no elevator, Wi-Fi, 5 blocks east of Place de l'Horloge, behind Church of St. Pierre at 15 Rue Petite Saunerie, tel. 04 90 86 11 06, fax 04 90 82 08 64, www.hotelmedieval.com, hotel.medieval@wanadoo.fr).

$$ Hôtel Mignon* is a good-enough, one-star place with basic comfort and tiny bathrooms (Db-€70-75, Tb-€85, Qb-€116, air-con, Internet access and Wi-Fi, 12 Rue Joseph Vernet, tel. 04 90 82 17 30, www.hotel-mignon.com, reservation@hotel-mignon.fr).

Chambres d'Hôtes and Apartments

$$$ La Banasterie, a well-located refuge in a historic building a block behind the Palace of the Popes, has five spacious rooms—two with decks (Db-€100-190, cash only, includes breakfast, air-con, 11 Rue de la Banasterie, mobile 06 87 72 96 36, www.labanasterie. com, labanasterie@labanasterie.com).

$$$ Lumani provides the ultimate urban refuge just inside the city walls, a 15-minute walk from the Palace of the Popes. In this graceful old manor house, gentle Elisabeth and Jean welcome guests to their art-gallery-cum-bed-and-breakfast that surrounds a fountain-filled courtyard with elbow room. She paints, he designs buildings, and both care about your experience in Avignon. The five rooms are decorated with flair; no two are alike, and all overlook the shady garden (small Db-€100, big Db-€140, Db suites-€170, extra person-€30, includes breakfast, Internet access and Wi-Fi, music studio, parking-€10 or easy on street, 37 Rue de Rempart St. Lazare, tel. 04 90 82 94 11, www.avignon-lumani.com, lux@avignon-lumani.com).

$$$ At Autour du Petit Paradis Apartments, owners Sabine and Patrick welcome visitors into their four well-furnished apartments with everything you need. They are conveniently located in

PROVENCE

the city center (€750-1,000/week, 5 Rue Noel Biret, tel. 04 90 81 00 42, www.autourdupetitparadis.com; contact@autourdupetit-paradis.com).

On the Outskirts of Town

$ Auberge Bagatelle's hostel offers dirt-cheap beds, lively atmosphere, café, grocery store, launderette, great views of Avignon, and campers for neighbors (Ds-€44, Ts-€73, Tb-€82, Q-€73, Qb-€100, dorm bed-€18, includes breakfast, across Daladier Bridge on Ile de la Barthelasse, bus #10 from main post office, tel. 04 90 86 71 31, fax 04 90 27 16 23, www.campingbagatelle.fr, auberge.bagatelle@wanadoo.fr).

Near Avignon

$$$ At **Jardin de Bacchus,** just 15 minutes northwest of Avignon and convenient to Pont du Gard, enthusiastic and English-speaking Christine and Erik offer three rooms in their rural farmhouse, which overlooks the famous rosé vineyards of Tavel (Db-€90-120, €30 extra for one-night stays, includes breakfast, fine dinner possible, Wi-Fi, swimming pool, tel. 04 66 90 28 62, www.jardindebacchus.fr, jardindebacchus@free.fr). To learn about their small-group food and wine tours, check their website. For bus connections, see www.edgard-transport.fr.

Eating in Avignon

Dining on a Square

Skip the overpriced, underwhelming restaurants on Place de l'Horloge and find a more intimate location for your dinner. Avignon is riddled with delightful squares filled with tables ready to seat you.

Near the Church of St. Pierre

The church stands between two enchanting squares: Quiet and intimate Place St. Pierre (where L'Epicerie sits alone) and, just under the nearby arch, lively and enchanting Place des Châtaignes, with a fun commotion of tables—peruse your options.

La Vache à Carreaux venerates cheese and wine (while offering a full range of cuisine). The colorful decor is fun, and the wine list is extensive and reasonable. This place is a hit with locals, who gather around outside, sipping €4 glasses of good wine, reluctant to leave (€12-18 *plats*, open daily, just off Place des Châtaignes at 14 Rue de la Peyrollerie, tel. 04 90 80 09 05).

L'Epicerie, homey inside and out, serves top cuisine with a focus on products from the south of France—expect lots of color and a dash of spice (€35 *menu*, €18-25 *plats*, daily, 10 Place St. Pierre, tel. 04 90 82 74 22).

Other Place des Châtaignes Options: The **Crêperie du Cloître** makes mediocre dinner crêpes and salads (daily, cash only). Next door and across from La Vache à Carreaux is the family-run Vietnamese **Restaurant Nem** (*menus* from €12, cash only). **Coin Caché** is lighthearted, with decidedly French fare (€6 starters and desserts, €15 *plats*, closed Tue). **Pause Gourmande** is a small, lunch-only eatery with €9 *plats du jour*, and always has a veggie option (closed Sun, around the corner and behind the church).

Place des Corps-Saints: This untouristy yet welcoming square is my favorite place for simple outdoor dining in Avignon. You'll find several youthful and reasonable eateries with tables sprawling under big plane trees. **Bistrot à Tartines** specializes in—you guessed it—*tartines* (big slices of toast smothered with toppings), and has the coziest interior and best desserts on the square (€8 *tartines* and salads, €10 lunch *menu*, daily, tel. 04 90 85 58 70). **Zeste** is a friendly, modern deli offering fresh soups, pasta salads, wraps, smoothies, and more. Get it to go, or eat inside or on the scenic square—all at unbeatable prices (closed Sun, tel. 09 51 49 05 62). **Boulangerie Olivero** makes a fine setting for a budget breakfast, lunch, or a light (and early) dinner. Monsieur Olivero makes a mean baguette and offers anyone showing this book a free croissant with any purchase. Enjoy your coffee, croissant, sandwich, or quiche at the outside tables (on the square near Rue des Lices, daily until 20:00).

By the Market (Les Halles)

Here you'll find a good selection of eateries with good prices.

Restaurant Françoise is a pleasant café and tea salon, where fresh-baked tarts—savory and sweet—and a variety of salads and soups make a healthful meal, and vegetarian options are plentiful (€7-12 dishes, Mon-Sat 8:00-19:00, closed Sun, free Wi-Fi, 6 Rue Général Leclerc, tel. 04 32 76 24 77).

La Cuisine du Dimanche offers an appealing stone interior with an atrium courtyard. They get rave reviews for the quality of their cuisine—but not for the service (€18-25 *plats*, daily, 31 Rue de la Bonneterie, tel. 04 90 82 99 10).

Rue des Teinturiers

This "Tie-Dye Street" has a wonderful concentration of eateries popular with the natives, and justifies the long walk. It's a trendy, youthful area, spiffed up with a canalside ambience and little hint of tourism.

La Cave des Pas Sages makes a colorful pause before dinner. The owners enjoy serving you a fragrant and cheap glass of regional wine. Choose from the blackboard by the bar that lists all the bottles open today, then join the gang outside by the canal. In

PROVENCE

the evening, this place is a hit with the young local crowd for its wine and weekend concerts (Mon-Sat 10:00-1:00 in the morning, closed Sun, no food in evening, across from waterwheel at 41 Rue des Teinturiers).

Restaurant Numéro 75 is worth the walk (just past where the cobbles end on Rue des Teinturiers). It fills the Pernod mansion (of *pastis* liquor fame) and a large, romantic courtyard with outdoor tables. The selection is limited to Mediterranean cuisine, but everything's *très* tasty. It's best to go with the options offered by your young black-shirted server (€30 lunch *menu*; dinner *menus:* €29/appetizer and main course or main course and dessert, €35/three courses; Mon-Sat 12:00-14:00 & 20:00-22:00, closed Sun, 75 Rue Guillaume Puy, tel. 04 90 27 16 00).

Elsewhere in Avignon

At **L'Isle Sonnante,** join chef Boris and wife Anne to dine intimately in their formal and charming one-room *bistrot*. You'll choose from a small selection offering only fresh products and be served by owners who care (*menus* from €35, closed Sun-Mon, 100 yards from the carousel on Place de l'Horloge at 7 Rue Racine, tel. 04 90 82 56 01, best to book ahead).

Le Caveau du Théâtre is a welcoming place where Richard invites diners to have a glass of wine or dinner at a sidewalk table, or inside in one of two carefree rooms (€15 *plats*, €20-24 *menus*, fun ambience for free, closed for lunch Sat and all day Sun, 16 Rue des Trois Faucons, tel. 04 90 82 60 91).

Le Fou de Fafa sits across from Le Caveau du Théâtre. Its friendly British owners are making a splash with locals, serving top-notch crêpes and inexpensive dishes in a warm setting (closed Mon, 17 Rue des Trois Faucons, tel. 04 32 76 35 13).

Hôtel La Mirande is the ultimate Avignon splurge. Reserve ahead here for understated elegance and Avignon's finest cuisine (€35 lunch *menu*, €105 dinner tasting *menu*; closed Tue-Wed—but for a price break, dine in the kitchen with the chef on these "closed" days for €92 including wine; behind Palace of the Popes, 4 Place de la Mirande, tel. 04 90 14 20 20, www.la-mirande.fr).

At **L'Epice and Love** (the name is a fun French-English play on words, pronounced "lay peace and love"), English-speaking owner Marie creates a playful atmosphere in her inviting restaurant, where the few colorfully decorated tables (inside only) greet the hungry traveler. The limited selection changes daily, and Marie cooks it all: tasty meat, fish, and vegetarian dishes, some with a North African touch, all served at good prices (€16 *menus*, closed Sun, 30 Rue des Lices, tel. 04 90 82 45 96).

Across the River

Le Bercail offers a fun opportunity to get out of town (barely) and take in *le fresh air* with a terrific riverfront view of Avignon, all while enjoying fun Provençal cooking served in big portions (*menus* from €26, serves late, daily April-Oct, tel. 04 90 82 20 22). Take the free shuttle boat (located near St. Bénezet Bridge) to the Ile de la Barthelasse, turn right, and walk five minutes. As the boat usually stops running at about 18:00 (except in July-Aug, when it runs until 21:00), you can either taxi home or walk 25 minutes along the pleasant riverside path and over Daladier Bridge.

Avignon Connections

By Train

Remember, there are two train stations in Avignon: the suburban TGV Station and the Centre-Ville Station in the city center (€1.20 shuttle buses connect to both stations, buy ticket from driver, 3/hour, 15 minutes). TGV trains usually serve the TGV Station only, though a few depart from Centre-Ville Station (check your ticket). Only Centre-Ville has baggage storage (see "Arrival in Avignon," page 416). Car rental is available only at the TGV Station. Some cities are served by slower local trains from Centre-Ville Station as well as by faster TGV trains from the TGV Station; I've listed the most convenient stations for each trip.

From Avignon's Centre-Ville Station to: Arles (roughly hourly, 20 minutes, less frequent in the afternoon), **Lyon** (10/day, 2 hours, also from TGV Station in 1 hour—see below), **Paris'** Gare de Lyon (5/day, 3.5 hours), **Barcelona,** Spain (2/day, 5.75 hours with changes in Nîmes and Figueres-Vilafant; more frequent but slower with a change in Cerbère).

From Avignon's TGV Station to: Nice (20/day, most by TGV, 4 hours, most require transfer in Marseille), **Marseille** (10/day, 35 minutes), **Lyon** (12/day, 1.5 hour, also from Centre-Ville Station—see above), **Paris'** Gare de Lyon (9/day direct, 2.5 hours; more connections with transfer, 3-4 hours), **Paris'** Charles de Gaulle Airport (7/day, 3 hours).

By Bus

The bus station *(gare routière)* is just past and below Hôtel Ibis, to the right as you exit the train station. Nearly all buses leave from this station (a few leave from the ring road outside the station—ask, buy tickets on bus, small bills only). Service is reduced or nonexistent on Sundays and holidays. Check your departure time beforehand, and make sure to verify your destination with the driver.

From Avignon to Pont du Gard: Buses go to this famous old aqueduct (3/day, 50 minutes, departs from bus station, usually from stall #11, also from TGV Station); I'd also consider a taxi one-way and bus back.

From Avignon to Arles: (10/day, 1 hour, leaves from TGV Station).

Pont du Gard

Throughout the ancient world, aqueducts were like flags of stone that heralded the greatness of Rome. A visit to this sight still works to proclaim the wonders of that age. This perfectly preserved Roman aqueduct was built in about 19 B.C. as the critical link of a 30-mile canal that, by dropping one inch for every 350 feet, supplied nine million gallons of water per day (about 100 gallons per second) to Nîmes—one of ancient Europe's largest cities. Though most of the aqueduct is on or below the ground, at Pont du Gard it spans a canyon on a massive bridge—one of the most remarkable surviving Roman ruins anywhere. Wear sturdy shoes if you want to climb around the aqueduct (footing is tricky), and bring swimwear and flip-flops if you plan to backstroke with views of the monument.

Getting to Pont du Gard

The famous aqueduct is between Remoulins and Vers-Pont du Gard on D-981, 13 miles from Avignon.

By Car: Pont du Gard is a 25-minute drive due west of Avignon (follow N-100 from Avignon, tracking signs to *Nîmes* and *Remoulins,* then *Pont du Gard* and *Rive Gauche*), and 45 minutes northwest of Arles (via Tarascon on D-15). If going to Arles from Pont du Gard, follow signs to *Nîmes* (not *Avignon*), then follow D-986 and then D-15 to Arles.

By Bus: Buses run to Pont du Gard (on the Rive Gauche side) from Avignon (3/day, 50 minutes), Nîmes, and Uzès. Consider this plan: Take a morning bus from Avignon's bus or TGV Station (leaves bus station at about 8:45 or 11:40, leaves TGV Station at 8:30 or 11:25). To return to Avignon, the bus leaves Pont du Gard at 13:20 or 17:30. Confirm all of these times at a TI or at www.pontdugard.fr. The 8:45 trip out and 13:20 trip back works best for most. Allow about four or five hours for visiting Pont du Gard, including transportation time from Avignon.

Buses stop at the traffic roundabout 300 yards from the aqueduct (see Pont du Gard map). In summer and on weekends, however, buses usually drive into the Pont du Gard site and stop at the parking lot's ticket booth. Confirm where the bus stops at the parking booth inside the Pont du Gard site.

PROVENCE

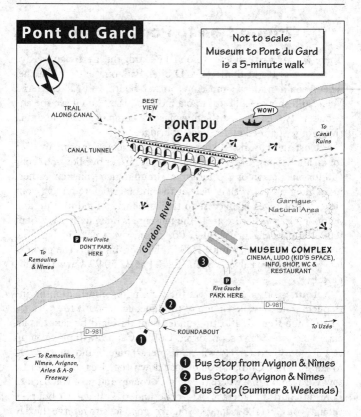

Pont du Gard

Not to scale:
Museum to Pont du Gard
is a 5-minute walk

TRAIL ALONG CANAL HERE

BEST VIEW

PONT DU GARD

WOW!

To Canal Ruins

CANAL TUNNEL

Gardon River

Garrigue Natural Area

P Rive Droite DON'T PARK HERE

To Remoulins & Nîmes

MUSEUM COMPLEX
CINEMA, LUDO (KID'S SPACE), INFO, SHOP, WC & RESTAURANT

❸

P Rive Gauche PARK HERE

D-981

To Uzès

❷

D-981

ROUNDABOUT

❶

To Remoulins, Nîmes, Avignon, Arles & A-9 Freeway

❶ Bus Stop from Avignon & Nîmes
❷ Bus Stop to Avignon & Nîmes
❸ Bus Stop (Summer & Weekends)

At the roundabout, the stop for buses coming from Avignon and Nîmes (and going to Uzès) is on the side opposite Pont du Gard; the stop for buses to Nîmes and to Avignon is on the same side as Pont du Gard (a block to your left as you exit Pont du Gard onto the main road). Make sure you're waiting for the bus on the correct side of the traffic circle (stops have schedules posted), and wave your hand to signal the bus to stop for you (otherwise, it'll chug on by). Buy your ticket when you get on and verify your destination with the driver.

By Taxi: From Avignon, it's about €50 for a taxi to Pont du Gard (allow €64 after 19:00 and on Sun). If you're staying in Avignon and have limited time to see Pont du Gard, take the first bus there, and splurge on a taxi back (arrange in advance or ask the staff at Pont du Gard to call one for you).

Orientation to Pont du Gard

There are two riversides to Pont du Gard: the Left Bank (Rive Gauche) and Right Bank (Rive Droite). Park on the Rive Gauche, where you'll find the museums, ticket booth, ATM, cafeteria, WCs, and shops—all built into a modern plaza. You'll see the aqueduct in two parts: first the fine museum complex, then the actual river gorge spanned by the ancient bridge.

Cost and Hours: €18 per car (no matter how few or many; €23 for an annual pass). If arriving on foot, by bus, or by bike, you'll pay €10 for one person or €15 for groups of up to five (consider gathering a gang of fellow sightseers at the entrance before buying your ticket). This gives you access to the aqueduct, museum, film, and outdoor *garrigue* nature area. The museum is open daily May-Sept 9:00-19:00, Oct-April 9:00-17:00, closed two weeks in Jan. The aqueduct itself is open until 1:00 in the morning, as is the parking lot. The *garrigue* is always open. Tel. 04 66 37 50 99, www.pontdu-gard.fr.

Tours: Call ahead or visit the website for information on infrequent guided walks on top of the aqueduct (about €10).

Canoe Rental: Floating under Pont du Gard by canoe is an experience you won't soon forget. Collias Canoes will pick you up at Pont du Gard (or elsewhere, if pre-arranged) and shuttle you to the town of Collias. You'll float down the river to the nearby town of Remoulins, where they'll pick you up and take you back to Pont du Gard (€21/person, €12/child under 12, usually 2 hours—though you can take as long as you like, good idea to reserve the day before in July-Aug, tel. 04 66 22 85 54).

Plan Ahead for Swimming and Hiking: Pont du Gard is perhaps best enjoyed on your back and in the water—bring along a swimsuit and flip-flops for the rocks. The best Pont du Gard viewpoints are up steep hills with uneven footing—bring good shoes.

Sights at Pont du Gard

▲Museum

In this state-of-the-art museum (well-presented in English), you'll enter to the sound of water and understand the critical role fresh water played in the Roman "art of living." You'll see examples of lead pipes, faucets, and siphons; walk through a mock rock quarry; and learn how they moved those huge rocks into place and how those massive arches were made. While actual artifacts from the aqueduct are few, the exhibit shows the immensity of the undertaking as well as the payoff. Imagine the excitement as this extravagant supply of water finally tumbled into Nîmes. A relaxing highlight is the scenic video of a helicopter ride along the entire

30-mile course of the structure, from its start at Uzès all the way to the Castellum in Nîmes.

Other Activities

Several additional attractions are designed to give the sight more meaning—and they do (but for most visitors, the museum is sufficient). A corny, romancing-the-aqueduct 25-minute film plays in the same building as the museum and offers good information in a flirtatious French-Mediterranean style...and a cool, entertaining, and cushy break. The nearby kids' museum, called *Ludo*, offers a scratch-and-sniff teaching experience (in English) of various aspects of Roman life and the importance of water. The extensive outdoor *garrigue* natural area, closer to the aqueduct, features historic crops and landscapes of the Mediterranean.

▲▲▲Viewing the Aqueduct

A park-like path leads to the aqueduct. Until a few years ago, this was an actual road—adjacent to the aqueduct—that had spanned the river since 1743. Before you cross the bridge, pass under it and hike about 300 feet along the riverbank for a grand viewpoint from which to study the world's second-highest standing Roman structure. (Rome's Colosseum is only 6 feet taller.)

This was the biggest bridge in the whole 30-mile-long aqueduct. It seems exceptional because it is: The arches are twice the width of standard aqueducts, and the main arch is the largest the Romans ever built—80 feet (so it wouldn't get its feet wet). The bridge is about 160 feet high and was originally about 1,100 feet long. Today, 12 arches are missing, reducing the length to 790 feet.

Though the distance from the source (in Uzès) to Nîmes was only 12 miles as the eagle flew, engineers chose the most economical route, winding and zigzagging 30 miles. The water made the trip in 24 hours with a drop of only 40 feet. Ninety percent of the aqueduct is on or under the ground, but a few river canyons like this required bridges. A stone lid hides a four-foot-wide, six-foot-tall chamber lined with waterproof mortar that carried the stream for more than 400 years. For 150 years, this system provided Nîmes with good drinking water. Expert as the Romans were, they miscalculated the backup caused by a downstream corner, and had to add the thin extra layer you can see just under the lid to make the channel deeper.

The bridge and the river below provide great fun for holiday-goers. While parents suntan on rocks, kids splash into the gorge from under the aqueduct. Some daredevils actually jump from the aqueduct's lower bridge—not knowing that crazy winds scrambled by the structure cause painful belly flops (and sometimes even accidental deaths). For the most refreshing view, float flat on your back underneath the structure.

The appearance of the entire gorge changed in 2002, when a

PROVENCE

huge flood flushed lots of greenery downstream. Those floodwaters put Roman provisions to the test. Notice the triangular-shaped buttresses at the lower level—designed to split and divert the force of any flood *around* the feet of the arches rather than *into* them. The 2002 floodwaters reached the top of those buttresses. Anxious park rangers winced at the sounds of trees crashing onto the ancient stones...but the arches stood strong.

The stones that jut out—giving the aqueduct a rough, unfinished appearance—supported the original scaffolding. The protuberances were left, rather than cut off, in anticipation of future repair needs. The lips under the arches supported wooden templates that allowed the stones in the round arches to rest on something until the all-important keystone was dropped into place. Each stone weighs four to six tons. The structure stands with no mortar (except at the very top, where the water flowed)—taking full advantage of the innovative Roman arch, made strong by gravity.

Hike over the bridge for a closer look and the best views. Steps lead up a high trail (marked *panorama*) to a superb viewpoint (go right at the top; best views are soon after the trail starts descending). You'll also see where the aqueduct meets a rock tunnel. Walk through the tunnel and continue for a bit, following a trail that meanders along the canal's path.

Back on the museum side, steps lead up to the Rive Gauche (parking lot) end of the aqueduct, where you can follow the canal path along a trail (marked with red-and-white horizontal lines) to find some remains of the Roman canal. You'll soon reach another *panorama* with great views of the aqueduct. Hikers can continue along the path, following the red-and-white markings that lead through a forest, after which you'll come across more remains of the canal (much of which are covered by vegetation). There's not much left to see because of medieval cannibalization—frugal builders couldn't resist the precut stones as they constructed area churches (stones along the canal were easier to retrieve than those high up on the aqueduct). The path continues for about 15 miles, but there's little reason to go farther. However, there is talk of opening the ancient quarry...someday.

NICE ON THE FRENCH RIVIERA

La Côte d'Azur

A hundred years ago, celebrities from London to Moscow flocked to the French Riviera to socialize, gamble, and escape the dreary weather at home. Today, budget vacationers and heat-seeking Europeans fill belle-époque resorts at France's most sought-after fun-in-the-sun destination.

Some of the Continent's most stunning scenery and intriguing museums lie along this strip of land—as do millions of sun-worshipping tourists. Evenings on the Riviera, a.k.a. La Côte d'Azur, were made for a promenade and outdoor dining.

My favorite (and the most convenient) home base is Nice, the region's capital and France's fifth-largest city. With easy train and bus connections to most regional sights, it's practical for train travelers. Urban Nice has a full palette of world-class museums, a splendid beachfront promenade, a seductive old town, and all the drawbacks of a major city (traffic, crime, pollution, and so on).

Nice also has the best selection of hotels in all price ranges, and good nightlife options. A car is a headache in Nice, though it's easily stored at one of the many pricey parking garages or for free at an outer tram station.

Nice

Nice (sounds like "niece"), with its spectacular Alps-to-Mediterranean surroundings, is an enjoyable big-city highlight of the Riviera. Its traffic-free old city mixes Italian and French flavors to create a spicy Mediterranean dressing, while its big squares, broad seaside

The French Riviera

walkways, and long beaches invite lounging and people-watching. Nice may be nice, but it's hot and jammed in July and August—reserve ahead and get a room with air-conditioning *(une chambre avec climatisation)*. Everything you'll want to see in Nice is either within walking distance or a short bus or tram ride away.

Orientation to Nice

The main points of interest lie between the beach and the train tracks (about 15 blocks apart). The city revolves around its grand Place Masséna, where pedestrian-friendly Avenue Jean Médecin meets Vieux (Old) Nice and the Albert 1er parkway (with quick access to the beaches). It's a 20-minute walk (or a €15 taxi ride) from the train station to the beach, and a 20-minute walk along the promenade from the fancy Hôtel Negresco to the heart of Vieux Nice.

A 10-minute ride on the smooth-as-silk tramway through the center of the city connects the train station, Place Masséna, Vieux Nice, and the port (from nearby Place Garibaldi). The tram and all city and regional buses cost only €1 per trip, making this one of the cheapest and easiest cities in France to get around in (see "Getting Around Nice," later). A new tramway line along the Promenade des Anglais may be under construction—prepare for detours and traffic delays.

Tourist Information

Nice's helpful TIs share a phone number and website (tel. 08 92 70 74 07, www.nicetourisme.com). There are TI branches at the **airport** (desks in both terminals, typically quiet, daily 8:00-21:00, closed Sun off-season); next to the **train station** (busy, summer Mon-Sat 8:00-20:00, Sun 9:00-19:00; rest of year Mon-Sat 9:00-19:00, Sun 10:00-17:00); facing the **beach** at 5 Promenade des Anglais (moderately busy, daily 9:00-18:00, until 20:00 July-Aug, closed Sun off-season); and in a kiosk at the south end of **Place Masséna** (less busy, mid-June-Sept, typically daily 10:00-19:00). Pick up the thorough *Practical Guide to Nice* and a free Nice map (or find a better one at your hotel), but skip the Riviera Pass. You can also get day-trip information at any TI.

Arrival in Nice

By Train: All trains stop at Nice's main station, Nice-Ville (baggage storage at the far right with your back to the tracks, lockers open daily 8:00-21:00). (Don't get off at the suburban Nice-Riquier station, which is one stop east of the main station.) The station area is gritty and busy: Never leave your bags unattended, and don't linger here longer than necessary.

Turn left out of the station to find a **TI** next door. Continue a few more blocks down Avenue Jean Médecin for the Gare Thiers **tram stop** (this will take you to Place Masséna, the old city, and the port). Board the tram heading toward the right (direction: Pont Michel; see "Getting Around Nice," later). You'll find many recommended hotels a 10- to 20-minute walk down the same street (listed under "Between Nice Etoile and the Sea" on page 470), though it's easier to take the tram to Place Masséna and walk from there.

To walk to other recommended hotels (listed under "Between the Train Station and Nice Etoile" on page 466, and "Between Boulevard Victor Hugo and the Sea" on page 472), cross Avenue Thiers in front of the station, go down the steps by Hôtel Interlaken, and continue walking down Avenue Durante. Follow this same route for the fastest path from the station to the beach—Avenue Durante turns into Rue des Congrés. You'll soon reach the heart of Nice's beachfront promenade.

Taxis and **buses to the airport** (#23 and #99) wait in front of the train station. **Car rental** offices are to the right as you exit the station.

NICE

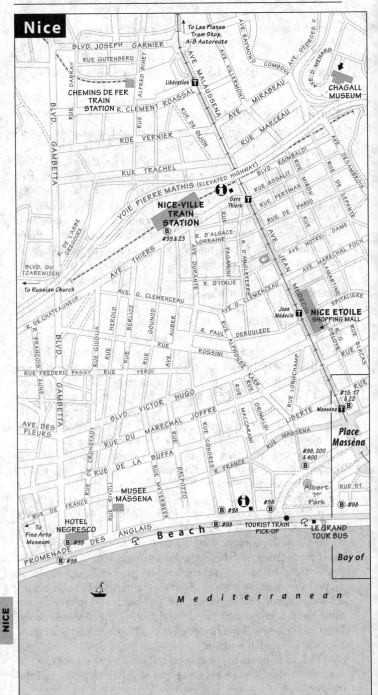

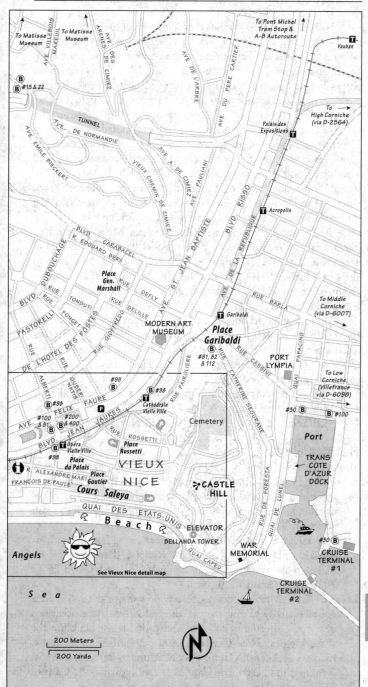

To Matisse Museum

To Matisse Museum

AVE. VILLEBOIS

MARAEUIL

AVE. DES ARENES DE CIMIEZ

AVE. DE L'ARBRE

AVE. DU PÈRE CARTIER

AVE. DE LA REPUBLIQUE

To Pont Michel
Tram Stop &
A-8 Autoroute

Vauban

(B) #15 & 22

AVE. EMILE BIECKERT

TUNNEL
AVE. DE NORMANDIE

VIEUX CHEMIN DE CIMIEZ

AVE. A. DE CIMIEZ

AVE. PAULIANI

Palais des
Expositions

To
High Corniche
(via D-2564)

BLVD. RISSO

Acropolis

BLVD. CARABACEL

R. EDOUARD BÉRI

Place
Gen.
Marshall

RUE DEFLY

RUE DELILLE

AVE. ST. JEAN BAPTISTE

RUE BARLA

To Middle
Corniche
(via D-6007)

BLVD. DUBOUCHAGE

RUE TONDUTI

RUE FONGET

RUE GIOFFREDO

Garibaldi

MODERN ART
MUSEUM

Place
Garibaldi

RUE CASSINI

PORT
LYMPIA

QUAI PAPACINO

To Low
Corniche
(Villefranche
via D-6098)

BLVD. PASTORELLI

RUE DE L'HOTEL DES POSTES

RUE PAIROLIERE

RUE CATHERINE SÉGURANE

#81, 82
& 112

(B)

RUE ALBERTI

RUE GUBER NATIS

RUE MATTIS

FELIX FAURE

#98

(B)

#98

(T) Cathédrale
Vielle Ville

#98

Cemetery

#30 (B)

#100 (B)

AVE. #100
& 81

#98

#200

(B) #400

BLVD. JEAN JAURÈS

RUE JAURÈS

RUE
ROSSETTI

Place
Rossetti

VIEUX

Port

TRANS
COTE
D'AZUR
DOCK

(B)

Opéra
Vielle Ville

#98

Place
du Palais

NICE

CASTLE
HILL

RUE DE FORESTA

QUAI DE LUNEL

R. ALEXANDRE MARI

Place
Gautier

FRANÇOIS DE PAULE

Cours Saleya

QUAI DES ETATS-UNIS

Beach

ELEVATOR
BELLANDA TOWER

WAR
MEMORIAL

#30 (B)

CRUISE
TERMINAL
#1

Angels

QUAI CAPEU

See Vieux Nice detail map

CRUISE
TERMINAL
#2

S e a

200 Meters

200 Yards

NICE

By Bus: Most stops for bus routes important to travelers (those serving Antibes, the airport, Vence, Villefranche-sur-Mer, Monaco, and St-Jean-Cap-Ferrat) are located between Boulevard Jean Jaurès and Avenue Félix Faure, near Place Masséna (see map on page 454). As Nice has been doing a lot of renovation work along its parkway, bus stop locations are subject to change; confirm locally.

By Car: To reach the city center on the autoroute from the west, take the first Nice exit (for the airport—called Côte d'Azur, Central) and follow signs for *Nice Centre* and *Promenade des Anglais* (expect detours if tramway construction is underway). Avoid arriving at rush hour (usually Mon-Fri 8:00-9:30 & 17:00-19:30), when Promenade des Anglais grinds to a halt. Hoteliers know where to park (allow €15-26/day; some hotels offer special deals, but space is limited, so reserve ahead). The parking garage at the Nice Etoile shopping center on Avenue Jean Médecin is pricey but near many recommended hotels (ticket booth on third floor, about €20/day, €12 overnight—20:00-8:00). The garage next to the recommended Hôtel Ibis at the train station has better rates. All on-street parking is metered (9:00-18:00 or 19:00), but usually free all day Sunday.

You can avoid driving in the center—and park for free during the day (no overnight parking)—by ditching your car at a parking lot at a remote tram stop (Las Planas is best) and taking the tram into town (10/hour, 15 minutes, €1, don't leave anything in your car; tramway described later, under "Getting Around Nice"). To find the Las Planas tram station from the A-8 autoroute, take the *Nice Nord* exit.

By Plane: For information on Nice's airport, see page 481.

Helpful Hints

Theft Alert: Nice has its share of pickpockets. Thieves target fanny packs: Have nothing important on or around your waist, unless it's in a money belt tucked out of sight. Don't leave things unattended on the beach while swimming, and stick to main streets in Vieux Nice after dark.

Medical Help: Riviera Medical Services has a list of English-speaking physicians all along the Riviera. They can help you make an appointment or call an ambulance (tel. 04 93 26 12 70, www.rivieramedical.com).

Events: The Riviera is famous for staging major events. Unless you're actually taking part in the festivities, these occasions give you only room shortages and traffic jams. Here are the three biggies: **Nice Carnival** (mid-Feb-early March, www.nicecarnaval.com), **Grand Prix of Monaco** (late May, www.acm.mc), and Festival de Cannes, better known as the **Cannes Film Festival** (mid-May, www.festival-cannes.com).

NICE

Sightseeing Tips: Some Nice museums (Chagall, Matisse, Archaeological) are closed on Tuesdays, while others (Modern and Contemporary Art, Fine Arts) close on Mondays. All of the sights in Nice—except the Chagall Museum and the Russian Cathedral—cost zilch to enter, making rainy-day options a swinging deal here.

Internet Access: There's no shortage of places to get online. Almost all of the hotels I list have free Wi-Fi, and some have computers for guests. For other access points, ask at your hotel or look for one of these establishments, all with free Wi-Fi: Quick Hamburger, Häagen Dazs, and McDonald's (multiple locations), or the Nice Etoile shopping center and Virgin Megastore (on Avenue Jean Médecin).

Laundry: You'll find launderettes everywhere in Nice—ask your hotelier for the nearest one.

Grocery Store: The big **Monoprix** on Avenue Jean Médecin and Rue Biscarra has it all, including deli counter, bakery, and cold drinks (Mon-Sat 8:30-21:00, closed Sun, see map on page 476). You'll also find many small grocery stores (some open Sun and/or until late hours) near my recommended hotels.

Boutique Shopping: The chic streets where Rue Alphonse Karr meets Rue de la Liberté and then Rue de Paradis are known as the "Golden Square." If you need pricey stuff, shop here.

SNCF Boutique: There's a handy French rail ticket office a half-block west of Avenue Jean Médecin at 2 Rue de la Liberté (Mon-Fri 10:00-18:00, closed Sat-Sun).

Renting a Bike (and Other Wheels): Roller Station rents bikes (*vélos*, can be taken on trains, €5/hour, €10/half-day, €15/day), rollerblades, skateboards, and Razor-type scooters (*trotinettes*, €7/half-day, €9/day). You'll need to leave your ID as a deposit (daily March-May and Sept-Oct 10:00-17:00, June-Aug 10:00-22:00, Nov-Feb 10:00-18:00, next to yellow awnings of Pailin's Asian restaurant at 49 Quai des Etats-Unis—see map on page 454, tel. 04 93 62 99 05, owner Eric). If you need more power, the TI has a list of places renting electric scooters.

You'll notice blue bikes **(Vélos Bleu)** stationed at various points in the city. A thousand of these bikes, available for locals to use when running errands, rent cheaply for short-term use (first 30 minutes free, requires European-style chip-and-PIN credit card, American Express cards should work).

Car Rental: Renting a car is easiest at Nice's airport, which has offices for all the major companies. You'll also find most companies represented at Nice's train station and near Albert 1er Park.

English Radio: Tune in to Riviera-Radio at FM 106.5.

Views: For panoramic views, climb Castle Hill (see page 459), or

NICE

take a one-hour boat trip (described later, under "Tours in Nice and the Riviera").

Beach Gear: To make life tolerable on the rocks, swimmers should buy a pair of the cheap plastic beach shoes sold at many shops (flip-flops fall off in the water). **Go Sport** at #13 on Place Masséna sells beach shoes, flip-flops, and cheap sunglasses (daily 10:00-20:00—see map on page 454).

Getting Around Nice

Although you can walk to most attractions in Nice, smart travelers make good use of the buses and tram. Both are covered by the same €1 single-ride ticket (good for 74 minutes in one direction, including transfers between bus and tram; can't be used for a round-trip). The **bus** is particularly handy for reaching the Chagall and Matisse museums and the Russian Cathedral. Pick up timetables at Nice's TIs (or view them online at www.lignesdazur.com) and buy tickets from the driver. Make sure to validate your ticket in the machine just behind the driver—watch locals do it and imitate.

The €4 all-day pass is valid on city buses and trams, as well as buses to some nearby destinations. The all-day ticket makes sense if you plan to take the bus to museums, use the tramway several times, or are going to the airport (you must validate your ticket on every trip). Express buses to and from the airport (#98 and #99) require the €4 all-day ticket, so savvy riders pack in other bus and/or tram rides on the day of their flight.

Nice's **tramway** makes an "L" along Avenue Jean Médecin and Boulevard Jean Jaurès, and connects the main train station (Gare Thiers stop), Place Masséna (Masséna stop, near many regional bus stops and a few blocks' walk from the sea), Vieux Nice (Opéra-Vieille Ville, Cathédrale-Vieille Ville), and the Modern and Contemporary Art Museum and port (Place Garibaldi).

Boarding the tram in the direction of Pont Michel takes you from the train station toward the beach and Vieux Nice (direction: Las Planas goes the other way). Buy tickets at the machines on the platforms (coins only, no credit cards). Choose the English flag to change the display language, turn the round knob and push the green button to select your ticket, press it twice at the end to get your ticket, or press the red button to cancel. Once you're on the tram, validate your ticket by inserting it into the top of the white box, then reclaiming it (http://tramway.nice.fr).

Taxis are useful for getting to Nice's less-central sights, and worth it if you're nowhere near a bus or tram stop (figure €15 from Promenade des Anglais). Cabbies normally only pick up at taxi stands *(tête de station)*, or you can call 04 93 13 78 78.

The hokey **tourist train** gets you up Castle Hill (see "Tours in Nice and the Riviera," later).

NICE

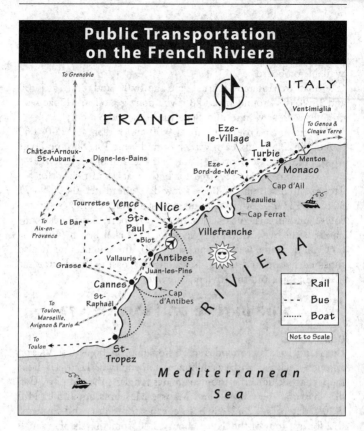

Getting Around the Riviera

By Train and Bus: Nice is perfectly situated for exploring the Riviera by public transport. Monaco, Eze-le-Village, Villefranche-sur-Mer, Antibes, Vence, and St-Paul-de-Vence are all within about a one-hour bus or train ride. The train is pricier (fares range from €2 to nearby Villefranche-sur-Mer to €8.50 to farther-away Grasse) than the bus (€1 for most destinations), but will often save you time. Both modes of transportation work well (see the map on page 444 for key bus locations).

All trains serving Nice arrive at and depart from the Nice-Ville Station. Most regional buses stop near Place Masséna (look for the J.C. Bermond stop, between Boulevard Jean Jaurès and Avenue Félix Faure), along Boulevard Jean Jaurès, or near Place Garibaldi (near Vieux Nice; see map on page 454 for stop locations, www.lignesdazur.com).

For a summary of train and bus connections, see "Nice Connections" on page 480.

By Boat: From June to mid-September, Trans Côte d'Azur of-

NICE

fers scenic trips several days a week from Nice to Monaco and Nice to St-Tropez. Boats leave in the morning and return in the evening, giving you all day to explore your destination. Drinks and WCs are available on board.

Boats to **Monaco** depart at 9:30 and 16:00, and return at 11:00 and 18:00 (€34 round-trip, €28 if you don't get off in Monaco, 45 minutes each way, June-mid-Sept Tue, Thu, and Sat only).

Boats to **St-Tropez** depart at 9:00 and return at 19:00 (€60 round-trip, 2.5 hours each way; July-mid-Sept Tue-Sun, no boats Mon; June and late Sept Tue, Thu, Sat, and Sun only).

Reservations are required for both boats, and tickets for St-Tropez often sell out, so book a few days ahead (tel. 04 92 98 71 30 or 04 92 00 42 30, www.trans-cote-azur.com, croisieres@trans-cote-azur.com). The boats leave from Nice's port, Bassin des Amiraux, just below Castle Hill—look for the ticket booth *(billeterie)* on Quai de Lunel (see map on page 444). The same company also runs one-hour round-trip cruises along the coast to Cap Ferrat (see "Tours in Nice and the Riviera," next).

Tours in Nice and the Riviera

Bus Tour
Le Grand Tour Bus provides an 11-stop, hop-on, hop-off service on an open-deck bus with headphone commentary (2/hour, 1.5-hour loop) that includes the Promenade des Anglais, the old port, Cap de Nice, and the Chagall and Matisse Museums on Cimiez Hill (€20/1-day pass, €23/2-day pass, cheaper for seniors and students, €12 for last tour of the day at about 18:00, some hotels offer small discounts, buy tickets on bus, main stop is near where Promenade des Anglais and Quai des Etats-Unis meet, across from the Plage Beau Rivage lounge, tel. 04 92 29 17 00, www.nicelegrandtour. com). This tour is a pricey way to get to the Chagall and Matisse Museums, but it's an acceptable option if you also want a city over-view. Check the schedule if you plan to use this bus to see the Russian Cathedral, as it may be faster to walk there.

▲Boat Cruise
Here's your chance to view Nice from the water. On this one-hour star-studded tour run by Trans Côte d'Azur, you'll cruise in a comfortable yacht-size vessel to Cap Ferrat and past Villefranche-sur-Mer, then return to Nice with a final lap along Promenade des Anglais. It's a scenic trip; the best views are from the seats on top.

French (and sometimes English-speaking) guides play Robin Leach, pointing out mansions owned by some pretty famous people, including Elton John (just as you leave Nice, it's the soft-yellow square-shaped place right on the water), Sean Connery (on the hill above Elton, with rounded arches and tower), and Microsoft co-founder Paul Allen (in saddle of Cap Ferrat hill, above yellow-umbrella beach with sloping red-tile roof). I wonder if this gang ever hangs out together. Guides also like to point out the mansion (between Villefranche-sur-Mer and Cap Ferrat) where the Rolling Stones recorded *Exile on Main Street* (€16; April-Oct Tue-Sun 2/day, usually at 11:00 and 15:00, no boats Mon or in off-season, call ahead to verify schedule, arrive 30 minutes early to get best seats, drinks and WCs available). For directions to the dock and contact information, see "Getting Around the Riviera—By Boat," earlier.

Tourist Train

For €8 (€4 for children under age 9), you can spend 45 embarrassing minutes on the tourist train tooting along the promenade, through the old city, and up to Castle Hill. This is a sweat-free way to get to the top of the hill—but so is the elevator, which is free (train runs every 30 minutes, daily 10:00-18:00, June-Aug until 19:00, recorded English commentary, meet train near Le Grand Tour Bus stop on Quai des Etats-Unis, next departure posted, tel. 02 99 88 47 07, www.ttdf.com).

Walking Tours

The TI on Promenade des Anglais organizes weekly walking tours of Vieux Nice in French and English (€12, May-Oct only, usually Sat morning at 9:30, 2.5 hours, reservations necessary, depart from TI, tel. 08 92 70 74 07). They also have evening art walks on Fridays at 19:00.

Minivan Tours

The TI and most hotels have information on minivan excursions from Nice (roughly €50/half-day, €80-110/day). **Revelation Tours** takes pride in its guides (tel. 04 93 53 69 85, www.revelation-tours.com). **Med-Tour** is one of many (tel. 04 93 82 92 58, mobile 06 73 82 04 10, www.med-tour.com); **Tour Azur** is another (tel. 04 93 44 88 77, www.tourazur.com). All also offer private tours by the day or half-day (check with them for their outrageous prices, about €90/hour).

Local Guides

Agnès Dumartin, a top guide for the region, is a good teacher who understands Nice particularly well and loves all forms of art (€200/half-day, €295/day, mobile 06 81 82 17 67, fax 04 93 51 48 63, agnes.dumartin@orange.fr). **Sylvie Di Cristo** offers terrific full-day tours throughout the French Riviera in a car or minivan. She adores educating people about this area's culture and history, and loves adapting her tour to your interests, from overlooked hill towns to wine, cuisine, art, or perfume (€250/person for 2-3 people, €150/person for 4-6 people, €90/person for 7-8 people, 2-person minimum, mobile 06 09 88 83 83, www.frenchrivieraguides.net,

NICE

dicristosylvie@gmail.com). Lovely **Sofia Villavicencio** is a pleasant guide with a passion for art (€145/half-day, €200/day, tel. 04 93
32 45 92, mobile 06 68 51 55 52, sofia.villavicencio@laposte.net).

Cooking Tour and Classes

Charming Canadian Francophile Rosa Jackson, a food journalist, Cordon Bleu-trained cook, and longtime resident of France,
runs **Les Petits Farcis,** which offers three-hour "Taste of Nice"
food tours for €90. She also teaches popular cooking classes in
Vieux Nice, which include a morning trip to the open-air market
on Cours Saleya to pick up ingredients, and an afternoon session
spent creating an authentic Niçois meal from your purchases (€195/
person, mobile 06 81 67 41 22, www.petitsfarcis.com).

Self-Guided Walk

▲▲A Scratch-and-Sniff Walk Through Vieux Nice

This approximately hour-long walk leads you through the delights
of Vieux (Old) Nice.

• *See the map on the next page, and start at Nice's main market square...*

Cours Saleya (koor sah-lay-yuh): Named for its broad expo-
sure to the sun *(soleil)*, this commotion of color, sights, smells, and
people has been Nice's main market square since the Middle Ages
(produce market held Tue-Sun until 13:00—on Mon, an antiques
market takes center stage). Amazingly, part of this square was a
parking lot until 1980, when the mayor of Nice had an underground garage built.

The first section is devoted to the Riviera's largest flower market (all day Tue-Sun and in operation since the 19th century). Here
you'll find plants and flowers that grow effortlessly and ubiquitously
in this climate, including the local favorites: carnations, roses, and
jasmine. Not long ago, this region supplied all of France with its
flowers; today, many are imported from Africa (the glorious orchids
are from Kenya). Still, fresh flowers are perhaps the best value in
this city.

The boisterous produce section trumpets the season with
mushrooms, strawberries, white asparagus, zucchini flowers, and
more—whatever's fresh gets top billing. Find your way down the
center and buy something healthy.

The market opens up at Place Pierre Gautier (also called Plassa
dou Gouvernou—bilingual street signs include the old Niçoise language, an Italian dialect). This is where farmers set up stalls to sell
their produce and herbs directly.

Continue down the center of Cours Saleya, stopping when you
see La Cambuse restaurant on your left. In front, hovering over
the black-barrel fire with the paella-like pan on top, is the self-

proclaimed **Queen of the Market,** Thérèse. She's cooking *socca*, Nice's chickpea crêpe specialty (until about 13:00). Spend €3 for a wad (careful—it's hot, but good). If Thérèse doesn't have a pan out, that means it's on its way (watch for the frequent scooter deliveries). Wait in line...or else it'll be all gone when you return.

• *Continue down Cours Saleya. The fine golden building that seals the end of the square is where Henri Matisse spent 17 years with a brilliant view onto Nice's world. The **Café les Ponchettes** is perfectly positioned for a people-watching break. Turn at the café onto...*

Rue de la Poissonnerie: Look up at the first floor of the first building on your right. **Adam and Eve** are squaring off, each holding a zucchini-like gourd. This scene (post-apple) represents the annual rapprochement in Nice to make up for the sins of a too-much-fun Carnival (Mardi Gras, the pre-Lenten festival). Residents of Nice have partied hard during Carnival for more than 700 years.

A few steps ahead, check out the small **Baroque church** (Notre-Dame-de-l'Annonciation) dedicated to St. Rita, the patron saint of desperate causes. She holds a special place in locals' hearts, making this the most popular church in Nice.

• *Turn right on the next street, where you'll pass Vieux Nice's most happening café/bar, **Distilleries Ideales**, with a lively happy hour (18:00-20:00) and a Pirates of the Caribbean-style interior.*

Now turn left on "Right" Street (Rue Droite), and enter an area that feels like a Little Naples.

Rue Droite: In the Middle Ages, this straight, skinny street provided the most direct route from wall to wall, or river to sea. Stop at **Esipuno's bakery** (at Place du Jésus, closed Mon-Tue) and say *bonjour* to the friendly folks. Decades ago, this baker was voted the best in France—the trophies you see were earned for bread-making, not bowling. His son now runs the place. Notice the firewood stacked behind the oven. Try the house specialty, *tourte aux blettes*—a Swiss chard tart. It's traditionally made with jam (a sweet, tasty breakfast treat), but there's also a savory version, stuffed with pine nuts, raisins, and white beets (my favorite for lunch).

Farther along, at #28, Thérèse (whom you met earlier) cooks her *socca* in the wood-fired oven before she carts it to her barrel on Cours Saleya. The balconies of the mansion in the next block mark the **Palais Lascaris** (c. 1647, gorgeous at night), a rare souvenir from one of Nice's most prestigious families. It's worth popping inside (handy WCs) for its Baroque Italian architecture and terrific collection of antique musical instruments—harps, guitars, violins, and violas (good English explanations). You'll also find elaborate tapestries and a few well-furnished rooms. The palace has four levels: The ground floor was used for storage, the first floor was

Vieux Nice Hotels & Restaurants

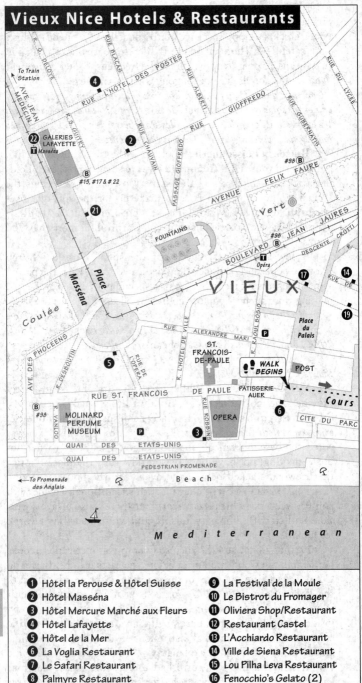

1 Hôtel la Perouse & Hôtel Suisse
2 Hôtel Masséna
3 Hôtel Mercure Marché aux Fleurs
4 Hôtel Lafayette
5 Hôtel de la Mer
6 La Voglia Restaurant
7 Le Safari Restaurant
8 Palmyre Restaurant
9 La Festival de la Moule
10 Le Bistrot du Fromager
11 Oliviera Shop/Restaurant
12 Restaurant Castel
13 L'Acchiardo Restaurant
14 Ville de Siena Restaurant
15 Lou Pilha Leva Restaurant
16 Fenocchio's Gelato (2)

NICE

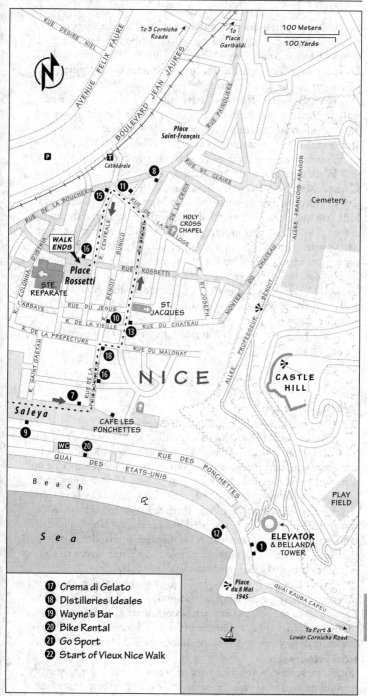

RUE DESIRE NIEL

To 3 Corniche Roads

To Place Garibaldi

100 Meters

100 Yards

AVENUE FELIX FAURE

BOULEVARD JEAN JAURES

RUE PAIROLIÈRE

Place Saint-François

P

T Cathédrale

8

RUE ST. CLAIRE

11

15

RUE DE LA BOUCHERIE

RUE DE LA CROIX

HOLY CROSS CHAPEL

R. CENTRALE

RUE DE LA LOGE

Cemetery

ALLEE FRANÇOIS ARAGON

WALK ENDS

16

R. BUNICO

BENOIT

RUE ROSSETTI

Place Rossetti

COLONNA D'ISTRIA

STE. REPARATE

L'ABBAYE

RUE DU JESUS

10

R. DE LA VIEILLE

ST. JACQUES

R. ST. JOSEPH

RUE DU CHATEAU

13

MONTEE DU CHATEAU

ALLEE PROFESSEUR BENOIT

R. DE LA PREFECTURE

18

RUE DU MALONAT

16

R. DE LA

N I C E

CASTLE HILL

R. SAINT GAETAN

7

Saleya

9

CAFE LES PONCHETTES

WC **20**

QUAI DES ETATS-UNIS

RUE DES PONCHETTES

B e a c h

PLAY FIELD

S e a

12

ELEVATOR & BELLANDA TOWER

1

Place du 8 Mai 1945

QUAI RAUBA CAPEU

To Port & Lower Corniche Road

17 Crema di Gelato
18 Distilleries Ideales
19 Wayne's Bar
20 Bike Rental
21 Go Sport
22 Start of Vieux Nice Walk

NICE

devoted to reception rooms (and musical events), the owners lived a floor above that, and the servants lived at the top—with a good view but lots of stairs (free, Wed-Mon 10:00-18:00, closed Tue). Look up and make faces back at the guys under the balconies.

• *Turn left on Rue de la Loge, then left again on Rue Centrale, to reach...*

Place Rossetti: The most Italian of Nice's piazzas, Place Rossetti feels more like Roma than Nice. Named for the man who donated his land to create this square, Place Rossetti comes alive after dark. The recommended Fenocchio gelato shop is popular for its many flavors, ranging from classic to innovative.

Walk to the fountain and stare back at the church. This is the **Cathedral of St. Réparate**—an unassuming building for a major city's cathedral. It was relocated here in the 1500s, when Castle Hill was temporarily converted to military use only. The name comes from Nice's patron saint, a teenage virgin named Réparate whose martyred body floated to Nice in the fourth century accompanied by angels. The interior of the cathedral gushes Baroque, a response to the Protestant Reformation. With the Catholic Church's Counter-Reformation, the theatrical energy of churches was cranked up with re-energized, high-powered saints and eye-popping decor.

• *Our walk is over. Castle Hill is straight up the stepped lane opposite the cathedral.*

Sights in Nice

Walks and Beach Time

▲▲▲Promenade des Anglais and Beach

Welcome to the Riviera. There's something for everyone along this four-mile-long seafront circus. Watch Europeans at play, admire the azure Mediterranean, anchor yourself on a blue seat, and prop your feet up on the made-to-order guardrail. Later in the day, come back to join the evening parade of tans along the promenade.

The broad sidewalks of the Promenade des Anglais ("walkway of the English") were financed by upper-crust English tourists who wanted a secure and comfortable place to stroll and admire the view. The walk was done in marble in 1822 for aristocrats who didn't want to dirty their shoes or smell the fishy gravel.

Stroll like the belle-époque English aristocrats for whom the promenade was paved. Start at the pink-domed Hôtel Negresco, then cross to the sea and end your promenade at Castle Hill. The following sights are listed in the order you'll pass them. This walk is ideally done at sunset (as a pre-dinner stroll).

Hôtel Negresco

Nice's finest hotel is also a historic monument, offering up the city's most expensive beds (see "Sleeping in Nice," later) and a free "mu-

Nice at a Glance

▲▲▲Chagall Museum The world's largest collection of Marc Chagall's work, popular even with people who don't like modern art. **Hours:** Wed-Mon 10:00-17:00, May-Oct until 18:00, closed Tue year-round. See page 460.

▲▲▲Promenade des Anglais Nice's four-mile sunstruck seafront promenade. **Hours:** Always open. See page 456.

▲▲Vieux Nice Charming old city offering enjoyable atmosphere and a look at Nice's French-Italian cultural blend. **Hours:** Always open. See page 452.

▲Matisse Museum Small but worthwhile collection of Henri Matisse's paintings, sketches, paper cutouts, and more. **Hours:** Wed-Mon 10:00-18:00, closed Tue. See page 461.

▲Modern and Contemporary Art Museum Ultramodern museum with enjoyable collection from the 1960s-1970s, including Warhol and Lichtenstein. **Hours:** Tue-Sun 10:00-18:00, closed Mon. See page 462.

▲Russian Cathedral Finest Orthodox church outside of Russia. **Hours:** Mon-Sat 9:00-12:00 & 14:30-18:00, Sun 14:30-18:00, until 17:00 off-season. See page 463.

▲Castle Hill Site of an ancient fort boasting great views—especially in early mornings and evenings. **Hours:** Park closes at 20:00 in summer, earlier off-season. Free elevator runs daily 10:00-19:00, until 20:00 in summer. See page 459.

Fine Arts Museum Lush villa shows off impressive paintings by Monet, Sisley, Bonnard, and Raoul Dufy. **Hours:** Tue-Sun 10:00-18:00, closed Mon. See page 463.

Molinard Perfume Museum Two-room museum in storefront boutique tracing the history of perfume. **Hours:** Daily April-Sept 10:00-19:00, Oct-March 10:00-13:00 & 14:00-18:30, sometimes closed Sun off-season. See page 463.

seum" interior (always open, provided you're dressed decently—absolutely no beach attire).

March straight through the lobby (as if you're staying here) into the exquisite **Salon Royal,** an elegant place for a drink and a frequent host to modern art exhibits (opens at 11:00). The chandelier hanging from the Eiffel-built dome is made of 16,000 pieces of crystal. It was built in France for the Russian czar's Moscow palace...but thanks to the Bolshevik Revolution in 1917, he couldn't take delivery (portraits of Czar Alexander III and his wife, Maria Feodorovna—who returned to her native Denmark after the revolution—are to the right, under the dome). Saunter around the perimeter counterclockwise. If the bar door is open (after about 15:00), wander up the marble steps for a look. Farther along, nip into the toilets for either an early 20th-century powder room or a Battle of Waterloo experience. The chairs nearby were typical of the age (cones of silence for an afternoon nap sitting up).

Bay of Angels (Baie des Anges)

Grab a blue chair and face the sea. The body of Nice's patron saint, Réparate, was supposedly escorted into this bay by angels in the fourth century. To your right is where you might have been escorted into France—Nice's airport, built on a massive landfill. On that tip of land way beyond the runway is Cap d'Antibes. Until 1860, Antibes and Nice were in different countries—Antibes was French, but Nice was a protectorate of the Italian kingdom of Savoy-Piedmont, a.k.a. the Kingdom of Sardinia. In 1850, the people here spoke Italian and ate pasta. As Italy was uniting, the region was given a choice: Join the new country of Italy or join good old France (which was enjoying good times under the rule of Napoleon III). The vast majority voted in 1860 to go French...and voilà!

The lower green hill to your left is Castle Hill (described later). Farther left lies Villefranche-sur-Mer (marked by the tower at land's end, and home to lots of millionaires), then Monaco (which you can't see, with more millionaires), then Italy (with lots of, uh, Italians). Behind you are the foothills of the Alps (Alpes-Maritimes), which trap threatening clouds, ensuring that the Côte d'Azur enjoys sunshine more than 300 days each year. While half a million people live here, pollution is carefully treated—the water is routinely tested and very clean.

Stroll the promenade with the sea starboard, and contemplate beach time (see next) on your way to the Albert 1er Park.

Beaches

Settle in on the smooth rocks or find a section with imported sand, and consider your options: You can play beach volleyball, table tennis, or *boules;* rent paddleboats, personal watercraft, or windsurfing equipment; explore ways to use your zoom lens for some revealing people-watching; or snooze on a comfy beach bed.

To rent a spot on the beach, compare rates, as prices vary— beaches on the east end of the bay are usually cheaper (chair and mattress—*chaise longue* and *transat*—about €15, umbrella-€5, towel-€4). Some hotels have special deals with certain beaches for discounted rentals (check with your hotel for details). Have lunch in your bathing suit (€12 salads and pizzas in bars and restaurants all along the beach). Or, for a peaceful café au lait on the Mediterranean, stop here first thing in the morning before the crowds hit. *Plage Publique* signs explain the 15 beach no-nos (translated into English).

Albert 1er Park

The park is named for the Belgian king who enjoyed wintering here—these were his private gardens. While the English came first, the Belgians and Russians were also big fans of 19th-century Nice. That tall statue at the edge of the park commemorates the 100-year anniversary of Nice's union with France.

If you detour from the promenade into the park and continue down the center of the grassy strip, you'll be walking over Nice's river, the Paillon (covered since the 1800s). For centuries, this river was Nice's natural defense to the north and west (the sea protected the south, and Castle Hill defended the east). Imagine the fortified wall that ran along its length from the hills behind you to the sea. With the arrival of tourism in the 1800s, Nice expanded over and beyond the river.

▲Castle Hill (Colline du Château)

This hill—in an otherwise flat city center—offers sensational views over Nice, the port (to the east), the foothills of the Alps, and the Mediterranean. The views are best early or at sunset, or whenever the weather's clear (park closes at 20:00 in summer, earlier off-season). The city of Nice was first settled here by Greeks circa 400 B.C. In the Middle Ages, a massive castle stood here, with turrets, high walls, and soldiers at the ready. With the river guarding one side and the sea the other, this mountain fortress seemed strong—until Louis XIV leveled it in 1706. Nice's medieval seawall ran along the lineup of two-story buildings below. Today you'll find a waterfall, a playground, two cafés (with fair prices), and a cemetery—but no castle—on Castle Hill. Nice's port is just below on the east edge of Castle Hill.

Getting There: You can get to the top of Castle Hill by foot, by elevator (free, runs daily 10:00-19:00, until 20:00 in summer, next to beachfront Hôtel Suisse), or by pricey tourist train (described under "Tours in Nice and the Riviera," earlier).

Bike Routes

Meandering along Nice's seafront on foot or by bike is a must. To rev up the pace of your saunter, rent a bike and glide along the coast in either or both directions (about 30 minutes each way; for rental info see "Helpful Hints," earlier). Both of the following paths start along Promenade des Anglais.

The path to the **west** stops just before the airport at perhaps the most scenic *boules* courts in France. Pause here to watch the old-timers while away the afternoon tossing shiny metal balls. If you take the path heading **east,** you'll round the hill—passing a scenic cape and the town's memorial to both world wars—to the harbor of Nice, with a chance to survey some fancy yachts. Pedal around the harbor and follow the coast past the Corsica ferry terminal (you'll need to carry your bike up a flight of steps). From there the path leads to an appealing tree-lined residential district.

Museums and Monuments

To bring culture to the masses, the city of Nice has nixed entry fees to all municipal museums—so it's free to enter all the following sights except the Chagall Museum and the Russian Cathedral. Cool.

The first two museums (Chagall and Matisse) are a long walk northeast of Nice's city center. Because they're in the same direction and served by the same bus line (buses #15 and #22 stop at both museums), it makes sense to visit them on the same trip. From Place Masséna, the Chagall Museum is a 10-minute bus ride or a 30-minute walk, and the Matisse Museum is a 20-minute bus ride or a one-hour walk.

▲▲▲Chagall Museum (Musée National Marc Chagall)

Even if you're suspicious of modern art, this museum—with the world's largest collection of Marc Chagall's work in captivity—is a delight. After World War II, Marc Chagall (1887-1985) returned from the United States to settle in Vence, not far from Nice. Between 1954 and 1967 he painted a cycle of 17 large murals designed for, and donated to, this museum. These paintings, inspired by the biblical books of Genesis, Exodus, and the Song of Songs, make up the "nave," or core, of what Chagall called the "House of Brotherhood."

Each painting is a collage of images that draws from Chagall's Russian folk-village youth, his Jewish heritage, biblical themes, and his feeling that he existed somewhere between heaven and earth. He believed that the Bible was a synonym for nature, and that color and biblical themes were key for understanding God's love for his creation. Chagall's brilliant blues and reds celebrate nature, as do his spiritual and folk themes. Notice the focus on couples. To Chagall, humans loving each other mirrored God's love of creation.

Although Chagall would suggest that you explore his works without help, the free audioguide gives you detailed explanations of his works and covers temporary exhibits. The free *Plan du Musée* helps you locate the rooms, though you can do without, as the museum is pretty simple.

Cost and Hours: €7.50, €1-2 more with (frequent) special exhibits, free first Sun of the month (but crowded), open Wed-Mon 10:00-17:00, May-Oct until 18:00, closed Tue year-round, Avenue Docteur Ménard, tel. 04 93 53 87 20, www.musee-chagall.fr.

NICE

Getting to the Chagall Museum: You can reach the museum, located on Avenue Docteur Ménard, by bus or on foot.

Buses #15 and #22 serve the Chagall Museum from the Masséna Guitry stop, near Place Masséna (5/hour Mon-Sat, 3/hour Sun, €1, immediately behind Galeries Lafayette department store—see map on page 454). The museum's bus stop (called Musée Chagall, shown on the bus shelter) is on Boulevard de Cimiez (walk uphill from the stop to find the museum).

To **walk** from central Nice to the Chagall Museum (30 minutes), go to the train-station end of Avenue Jean Médecin and turn right onto Boulevard Raimbaldi. Walk four long blocks along the elevated road, then turn left onto Avenue Raymond Comboul, and follow *Musée Chagall* signs.

Cuisine Art and WCs: An idyllic café (€10 salads and *plats*) awaits in the corner of the garden. A spick-and-span WC is next to the ticket desk (there's one inside, too).

Leaving the Museum: To take **buses** #15 or #22 back to downtown Nice, turn right out of the museum, then make another right down Boulevard de Cimiez, and catch the bus heading downhill. To continue on to the Matisse Museum, catch buses #15 or #22 using the uphill stop located across the street. **Taxis** usually wait in front of the museum. It's about €12 for a ride to the city center.

To **walk** to the train station area from the museum (20 minutes), turn left out of the museum grounds on Avenue Docteur Ménard, and follow the street to the left at the first intersection, continuing to hug the museum grounds. Where the street curves right (by #32), take the ramps and staircases down on your left, turn left at the bottom, cross under the freeway and the train tracks, then turn right on Boulevard Raimbaldi to reach the station.

▲Matisse Museum (Musée Matisse)

This small museum contains a sampling of works from the various periods of Henri Matisse's long artistic career. The museum offers a painless introduction to the artist's many styles and materials, both shaped by Mediterranean light and by fellow Côte d'Azur artists Pablo Picasso and Pierre-Auguste Renoir. The collection is scattered throughout several rooms with a few worthwhile works, though it lacks a certain *je ne sais quoi* when compared to the Chagall Museum.

Henri Matisse (1869-1954), the master of leaving things out, could suggest a woman's body with a single curvy line—letting the viewer's mind fill in the rest. Ignoring traditional 3-D perspective, he expressed his passion for life through simplified but recognizable scenes in which dark outlines and saturated, bright blocks of color create an overall decorative pattern. You don't look "through" a Matisse canvas, like a window; you look "at" it, like wallpaper.

Matisse understood how colors and shapes affect us emotionally. He could create either shocking, clashing works (early Fauvism) or geometrical, balanced, harmonious ones (later cutouts). Whereas other modern artists reveled in purely abstract design, Matisse (almost) always kept the subject matter at least vaguely recognizable. He used unreal colors and distorted lines not just to portray what an object looks like, but to express its inner nature (even inanimate objects). Meditating on his paintings helps you connect with life—or so Matisse hoped.

Cost and Hours: Free, Wed-Mon 10:00-18:00, closed Tue, 164 Avenue des Arènes de Cimiez, tel. 04 93 81 08 08, www.musee-matisse-nice.org. The museum is housed in a beautiful Mediterranean mansion set in an olive grove amid the ruins of the ancient Roman city of Cemenelum.

Getting to the Matisse Museum: It's a long uphill walk from the city center. Take the bus (details follow) or a cab (€20 from Promenade des Anglais). Once here, walk into the park to find the pink villa. **Buses #15, #17,** and **#22** offer regular service to the Matisse Museum from just off Place Masséna on Rue Sacha Guitry (Masséna Guitry stop, at the east end of the Galeries Lafayette department store—see map on page 454, 20 minutes; note that bus #17 does not stop at the Chagall Museum). **Bus #20** connects the port to the museum. On any bus, get off at the Arènes-Matisse bus stop (look for the crumbling Roman wall).

Leaving the Museum: When leaving the museum, find the stop for buses #15 and #22 (frequent service downtown and stops en route at the Chagall Museum): Turn left from the Matisse Museum into the park and keep straight on Allée Barney Wilen, exiting the park at the Archaeological Museum, then turn right. Pass the bus stop across the street (#17 goes to the city center but not the Chagall Museum, and #20 goes to the port), and walk to the small roundabout. Cross the roundabout to find the shelter (facing downhill) for buses #15 and #22.

▲Modern and Contemporary Art Museum (Musée d'Art Moderne et d'Art Contemporain)

This ultramodern museum features an explosively colorful, far-out, yet manageable collection focused on American and European-American artists from the 1960s and 1970s (Pop Art and New Realism styles are highlighted). The exhibits cover three floors and include a few works by Andy Warhol, Roy Lichtenstein, and Jean Tinguely, and small models of Christo's famous wrappings. You'll find rooms dedicated to Robert Indiana, Yves Klein, and Niki de Saint Phalle (my favorite). The temporary exhibits can be as appealing to modern-art lovers as the permanent collection: Check the museum website for what's playing. Don't leave without exploring the rooftop terrace.

NICE

Cost and Hours: Free, Tue-Sun 10:00-18:00, closed Mon, about a 15-minute walk from Place Masséna, near Vieux Nice on Promenade des Arts, tel. 04 93 62 61 62, www.mamac-nice.org.

Fine Arts Museum (Musée des Beaux-Arts)

Housed in a sumptuous Riviera villa with lovely gardens, this museum holds 6,000 artworks from the 17th to 20th centuries. Start on the first floor and work your way up to experience an appealing array of paintings by Monet, Sisley, Bonnard, and Raoul Dufy, as well as a few sculptures by Rodin and Carpeaux.

Cost and Hours: Free, Tue-Sun 10:00-18:00, closed Mon, inconveniently located at the western end of Nice, take bus #12 or #23 from the train station to the Rosa Bonheur stop and walk to 3 Avenue des Baumettes, tel. 04 92 15 28 28, www.musee-beaux-arts-nice.org.

Molinard Perfume Museum

The Molinard family has been making perfume in Grasse (about an hour's drive from Nice) since 1849. Their Nice store has a small museum in the rear that illustrates the story of their industry. Back when people believed water spread the plague (Louis XIV supposedly bathed less than once a year), doctors advised people to rub fragrances into their skin and then powder their body. At that time, perfume was a necessity of everyday life.

Cost and Hours: Free, daily April-Sept 10:00-19:00, Oct-March 10:00-13:00 & 14:00-18:30, sometimes closed Sun off-season, just between beach and Place Masséna at 20 Rue St. François de Paule, see map on page 454, tel. 04 93 62 90 50, www.molinard.com.

Visiting the Museum: The tiny first room shows photos of the local flowers, roots, and other plant parts used in perfume production. The second, main room explains the earliest (18th-century) production method. Petals were laid out in the sun on a bed of animal fat, which would absorb the essence of the flowers as they baked. For two months, the petals were replaced daily, until the fat was saturated. Models and old photos show the later distillation process (660 pounds of lavender produced only a quarter-gallon of essence). Perfume is "distilled like cognac and then aged like wine." The bottles on the tables demonstrate the role of the "blender" and the perfume mastermind called the "nose" (who knows best); clients are allowed to try their hand at mixing scents. Of the 150 real "noses" in the world, more than 100 are French. Notice the photos of these lab-coat-wearing perfectionists. You are welcome to enjoy the testing bottles.

▲Russian Cathedral (Cathédrale Russe)

Nice's Russian Orthodox church, claimed by some to be the finest outside Russia, is worth a visit.

Cost and Hours: Free, Mon-Sat 9:00-12:00 & 14:30-18:00,

Sun 14:30-18:00, until 17:00 off-season; chanted services Sat at 17:30 or 18:00, Sun at 10:00; no tourist visits during services, no short shorts, 17 Boulevard du Tzarewitch, tel. 04 93 96 88 02, www.acor-nice.com. The park around the church stays open at lunch and makes a fine setting for picnics.

Getting to the Russian Cathedral: It's at 17 Boulevard du Tzarewitch, a 10-minute walk from the train station. Head west on Avenue Thiers, turn right on Avenue Gambetta, go under the freeway, and turn left following *Eglise Russe* signs. Or, from the station, take any bus heading west on Avenue Thiers and get off at Avenue Gambetta (then follow the previous directions).

Background: Five hundred rich Russian families wintered in Nice in the late 19th century, and they needed a worthy Orthodox house of worship. Czar Nicholas I's widow provided the land (which required tearing down her house), and Czar Nicholas II gave this church to the Russian community in 1912. (A few years later, Russian comrades who *didn't* winter on the Riviera assassinated him.) Here in the land of olives and anchovies, these proud onion domes seem odd. But, I imagine, so did those old Russians.

Visiting the Cathedral: The one-room interior is filled with icons and candles, and old Russian music adds to the ambience. The wall of icons (iconostasis) divides things between the spiritual realm and the temporal world of the worshippers. Only the priest can walk between the two worlds, by using the "Royal Door." The items lining the front are interesting (described in order from left corner). The angel with red boots and wings—the protector of the Romanov family—stands over a symbolic tomb of Christ. The tall, black, hammered-copper cross commemorates the massacre of Nicholas II and his family in 1918. A Jesus icon is to the right of the Royal Door. According to a priest here, as worshippers meditate, staring deep into the eyes of Jesus, they enter a lake where they find their soul. Surrounded by incense, chanting, and your entire community...it could happen. Farther to the right, the icon of the unhappy-looking Virgin and Child is decorated with semiprecious stones from the Ural Mountains. Artists worked a triangle into each iconic face—symbolic of the Trinity.

Other Nice Museums

Both of these museums are acceptable rainy-day options, and free of charge.

Archaeological Museum (Musée Archéologique)

This museum displays various objects from the Romans' occupation of this region. It's convenient—just below the Matisse Museum—but has little of interest to anyone but ancient Rome aficionados. You also get access to the Roman bath ruins...which are, sadly, overgrown with weeds.

Cost and Hours: Free, very limited information in English, Wed-Mon 10:00-18:00, closed Tue, near Matisse Museum at 160 Avenue des Arènes de Cimiez, tel. 04 93 81 59 57, www.musee-archeologique-nice.org.

Masséna Museum (Musée Masséna)

Like Nice's main square, this museum was named in honor of Jean-André Masséna, a highly regarded commander during France's Revolutionary and Napoleonic wars. The beachfront mansion is worth a gander for its lavish decor and lovely gardens alone (pick up your free ticket at the boutique just outside; no English information available).

Cost and Hours: Free, Wed-Mon 10:00-18:00, closed Tue, last entrance 30 minutes before closing, 35 Promenade des Anglais, tel. 04 93 91 19 10, www.massena-nice.org.

Visiting the Museum: There are three levels. The elaborate reception rooms on the ground floor host occasional exhibits and give the best feeling for aristocratic Nice at the turn of the 19th century (find Masséna's portrait to the right after entering). The first floor up, offering a folk-museum-like look at Nice through the years, deserves most of your time. Moving counterclockwise around the floor, you'll find Napoleonic paraphernalia, Josephine's impressive cape and tiara, and Napoleon's vest (I'd look good in it). Next, antique posters promote vacations in Nice—look for the model and photos of the long-gone La Jetée Promenade and its casino, Nice's first. You'll see paintings of Russian nobility who appreciated Nice's climate, images of the city before its river was covered over by Place Masséna, and paintings honoring Italian patriot and Nice favorite Giuseppe Garibaldi. The top-floor painting gallery is devoted to the Riviera before World War II, with scenes of rural Villefranche-sur-Mer and other bucolic spots showing how the area looked before the tourist boom.

Nightlife in Nice

Promenade des Anglais, Cours Saleya, and Rue Masséna are all worth an evening walk. Nice's bars play host to a happening late-night scene, filled with jazz, rock, and trolling singles. Most activity focuses on Vieux Nice. Rue de la Préfecture and Place du Palais are ground zero for bar life, though Place Rossetti and Rue Droite are also good targets. **Distilleries Ideales** is a good place to start or end your evening, with a lively international crowd and a fun interior (where Rues de la Poissonnerie and Barillerie meet, happy hour 18:00-20:00). **Wayne's Bar** is a happening spot for the younger, English-speaking backpacker crowd (15 Rue Préfecture). Along the Promenade des Anglais, the plush bar at **Hôtel Negresco** is fancy-cigar old English.

NICE

Plan on a cover charge or expensive drinks where music is involved. If you're out very late, avoid walking alone. Nice is well known for its lively after-dark action.

Sleeping in Nice

Don't look for charm in Nice. Go for modern and clean, with a central location and in summer, air-conditioning. The rates listed here are for April through October. Prices generally drop €15-30 November through March, but go sky-high during the Nice Carnival, the Cannes Film Festival, and Monaco's Grand Prix. Between the film festival and the Grand Prix, the second half of May is very tight every year. Nice is also one of Europe's top convention cities, and June is convention month here. Reserve early if visiting from May through August, especially during these times. For parking, ask your hotelier (several hotels offer deals for stashing your car or have limited private parking; reserve early), or see "Arrival in Nice—By Car" on page 446.

I've divided my sleeping recommendations into three areas: between the train station and Nice Etoile shopping center (easy access to the train station and Vieux Nice via the tramway, 20-minute walk to Promenade des Anglais); between Nice Etoile and the sea (east of Avenue Jean Médecin, good access to Vieux Nice and the sea at Quai des Etats-Unis); and between Boulevard Victor Hugo and the sea (a somewhat classier and quieter area, offering better access to the Promenade des Anglais but longer walks to the train station and Vieux Nice). I've also listed a hostel on the outskirts, and a few hotel-chain options near the airport. Before reserving, check hotel websites for deals (more common at larger hotels).

Between the Train Station and Nice Etoile

This area offers Nice's cheapest sleeps, though most hotels near the station ghetto are overrun, overpriced, and loud. The following hotels are the pleasant exceptions (most are near Avenue Jean Médecin), and are listed in order of proximity to the train station, going toward the beach.

$$ At Hôtel Durante**, you know you're on the Mediterranean as soon as you enter this cheery, way-orange building with rooms wrapped around a flowery courtyard. Every one of its quiet rooms overlooks a spacious, well-maintained patio/garden with an American-style Jacuzzi. The rooms are good enough (mostly big beds), the price is right enough, and the parking (limited spaces) is free (Sb-€85-105, Db-€100-115, Tb-€150-175, Qb-€180-200, breakfast-€10, air-con, Wi-Fi, 16 Avenue Durante, tel. 04 93 88 84 40, fax 04 93 87 77 76, www.hotel-durante.com, info@hotel-durante.com).

NICE

Sleep Code

(€1 = about $1.30, country code: 33)
S = Single, **D** = Double/Twin, **T** = Triple, **Q** = Quad, **b** = bathroom, **s** = shower only, * = French hotel rating (0-5 stars). Hoteliers speak English; the hotels have elevators and accept credit cards unless otherwise noted.

To help you sort easily through these listings, I've divided the accommodations into three categories based on the price for a standard double room with bath:

$$$ **Higher Priced**—Most rooms €200 or more.
 $$ **Moderately Priced**—Most rooms between €100-200.
  $ **Lower Priced**—Most rooms €100 or less.

Prices can change without notice; verify the hotel's current rates online or by email.

$$ Hôtel St. Georges, five blocks from the station toward the sea, is a basic place with reasonably clean, high-ceilinged rooms, orange tones, blue halls, fair rates, a backyard patio, and friendly Houssein at the reception (Sb-€95, Db-€115, Tb with 3 beds-€135, extra bed-€20, breakfast-€9, air-con, free Wi-Fi, 7 Avenue Georges Clemenceau, tel. 04 93 88 79 21, fax 04 93 16 22 85, www.hotelsaintgeorges.fr, contact@hotelsaintgeorges.fr).

$ Hôtel Ibis Nice Centre Gare, 100 yards to the right as you leave the station, gives those in need of train station access a secure refuge in this seedy area. It's big (200 rooms) and modern, but a good value with sharp rooms, a refreshing pool, and cheap €9 parking (Db-€93, big "Club" Db-€125, air-con, Internet access and Wi-Fi, bar, café, 14 Avenue Thiers, tel. 04 93 88 85 85, fax 04 93 88 58 00, www.ibishotel.com, h1396@accor.com).

$ Hôtel Belle Meunière, in a fine old mansion built for Napoleon III's mistress, offers cheap beds and private rooms a block below the train station. Lively and youth hostel-esque, this simple but well-kept place attracts budget-minded travelers of all ages with basic-but-adequate rooms and charismatic Mademoiselle Marie-Pierre presiding (with perfect English). Tables in the front yard greet guests and provide opportunities to meet other travelers (bunk in 4-bed dorm-€28 with private bath, €22 with shared bath; Db-€78, Tb-€93, Qb-€124, includes breakfast, Wi-Fi, laundry service, limited parking-€9, 21 Avenue Durante, tel. 04 93 88 66 15, fax 04 93 82 51 76, www.bellemeuniere.com, hotel.belle. meuniere@cegetel.net).

$ Auberge de Jeunesse les Camélias is a fun, laid-back youth

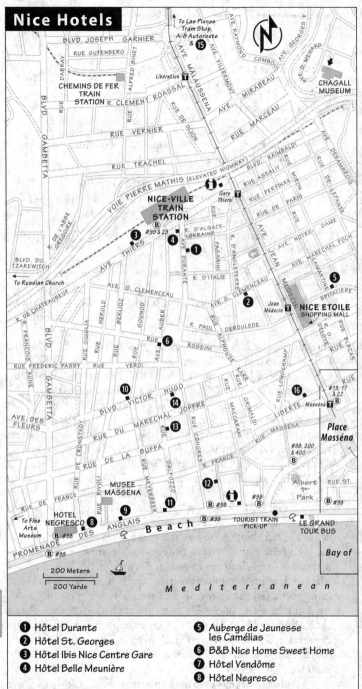

Nice Hotels

1 Hôtel Durante
2 Hôtel St. Georges
3 Hôtel Ibis Nice Centre Gare
4 Hôtel Belle Meunière

5 Auberge de Jeunesse les Camélias
6 B&B Nice Home Sweet Home
7 Hôtel Vendôme
8 Hôtel Negresco

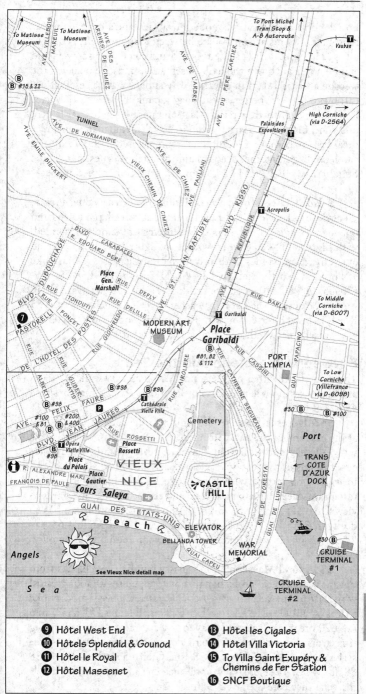

9 Hôtel West End
10 Hôtels Splendid & Gounod
11 Hôtel le Royal
12 Hôtel Massenet

13 Hôtel les Cigales
14 Hôtel Villa Victoria
15 To Villa Saint Exupéry &
   Chemins de Fer Station
16 SNCF Boutique

NICE

hostel with a great location, modern facilities, and a fun evening atmosphere. Rooms accommodate between four and eight people of all ages in bunk beds (136 beds in all) and come with showers and sinks—WCs are down the hall. Reservations must be made on the website at least 3 days in advance. If you don't have a reservation, call by 10:00—or, better, try to snag a bunk in person. The place is popular but worth a try for last-minute availability (€26/bed, one-time €16 extra charge without hostel membership, includes breakfast, maximum 6-night stay, rooms closed 11:00-15:00 but can leave bags, Internet access, laundry, kitchen, safes, bar, 3 Rue Spitalieri, tel. 04 93 62 15 54, www.hihostels.com, nice-camelias@fuaj.org).

$ B&B Nice Home Sweet Home is a great value. Gentle Genevieve (a.k.a. Jennifer) Levert rents out three large rooms and one small single in her home. Her rooms are simply decorated, with high ceilings, big windows, lots of light, and space to spread out. One room comes with private bath; otherwise, it's just like at home...down the hall (S-€35-44, D-€61-75, Db-€65-78, Tb-€75-85, Q-€80-110, includes breakfast, air-con units available in summer, elevator, one floor up, washer/dryer-€6, kitchen access, 35 Rue Rossini at intersection with Rue Auber, mobile 06 19 66 03 63, www.nicehomesweethome.com, glevert@free.fr).

Between Nice Etoile and the Sea

These hotels are either on the sea or within an easy walk of it, and are the closest to Vieux Nice. For locations, see the map on page 454.

$$$ Hôtel la Perouse****, built into the rock of Castle Hill at the east end of the bay, gets my vote for Nice's best splurge. This refuge-hotel is top-to-bottom flawless in every detail—from its elegant rooms (satin curtains, velour headboards) and attentive staff to its rooftop terrace with Jacuzzi, sleek pool, and lovely garden restaurant. Sleep here to be spoiled and escape the big city (garden-view Db-€325, seaview Db-€480, good family options and Web deals, free Wi-Fi, 11 Quai Rauba Capeu, tel. 04 93 62 34 63, fax 04 93 62 59 41, www.hotel-la-perouse.com, lp@hotel-la-perouse.com).

$$$ Hôtel Masséna***, in a classy building two blocks from Place Masséna, is a "professional" hotel (popular with tour groups) with 110 rooms at almost-reasonable rates and way-mod public spaces (small Db-€199, larger Db-€289, still larger Db-€339, skip the €20 breakfast, call same day for special rates—prices drop big time when hotel is not full, sixth-floor rooms have balconies, reserve parking ahead-€30/day, 58 Rue Gioffredo, tel. 04 92 47 88 88, fax 04 92 47 88 89, www.hotel-massena-nice.com, info@hotel-massena-nice.com).

$$$ Hôtel Suisse*, below Castle Hill, has Nice's best sea and city views for the money, and is surprisingly quiet given the busy street below. Rooms are quite comfortable, the decor is tasteful, and the staff helpful. There's no reason to sleep here if you don't land a view, so I've listed prices only for view rooms—many of which have balconies (Db-€175-220, extra bed-€36, breakfast-€15, Wi-Fi, 15 Quai Rauba Capeu, tel. 04 92 17 39 00, fax 04 93 85 30 70, www.hotels-ocre-azur.com, hotel.suisse@hotels-ocre-azur.com).

$$ Hôtel Mercure Marché aux Fleurs**** is ideally situated across from the sea and behind Cours Saleya. Rooms are tastefully designed and well-maintained (some with beds in a loft). Prices are reasonable, though rates vary dramatically depending on demand—check their website for deals. Don't confuse this Mercure with the four other branches in Nice (standard Db-€170, superior Db-€200 and worth the extra euros, sea view-€50 extra, air-con, 91 Quai des Etats-Unis, tel. 04 93 85 74 19, fax 04 93 13 90 94, www.hotelmercure.com, h0962@accor.com).

$$ Hôtel Vendôme* gives you a whiff of the belle époque, with pink pastels, high ceilings, and grand staircases in a mansion set off the street. Its public spaces are delightful. The rooms are modern and come in all sizes; the best have balconies (on floors 4 and 5)—request *une chambre avec balcon* (Sb-€115-130, Db-€150-180, Tb-€180-200, prices vary with demand, check website for deals, breakfast-€15, air-con, Internet access and Wi-Fi, book ahead for limited parking-€15, 26 Rue Pastorelli at the corner of Rue Alberti, tel. 04 93 62 00 77, fax 04 93 13 40 78, www.vendome-hotel-nice.com—useless website except to make reservation, contact@vendome-hotel-nice.com). For location, see map on page 468.

$$ Hôtel Lafayette*, in a handy location a block behind the Galeries Lafayette department store, is a good value. It's comfortable, homey, and modest, with 18 mostly spacious rooms (some with thin walls), all one floor up from the street. It's family-run by Kiril, George, and young Victor. Rooms not overlooking Rue de l'Hôtel des Postes are quieter and worth requesting (standard Db-€105-120, spacious Db-€115-130, preferential rates for Rick Steves readers, coffee service in rooms, breakfast-€10, air-con, no elevator, Internet access and Wi-Fi, 32 Rue de l'Hôtel des Postes, tel. 04 93 85 17 84, fax 04 93 80 47 56, www.hotellafayettenice.com, info@hotellafayettenice.com).

$$ Hôtel de la Mer is a tiny place with an enviable position overlooking Place Masséna, just steps from Vieux Nice (it's among the closest of my listings to the old town). Half of the rooms are smartly renovated and worth the higher price; the other half are "old school" and priced that way (older Db-€110, newer Db-€130,

Tb-€155, air-con, Wi-Fi, 4 Place Masséna, tel. 04 93 92 09 10, fax 04 93 85 00 64, www.hoteldelamernice.com, hotel.mer@wanadoo.fr).

Between Boulevard Victor Hugo and the Sea

These hotels are close to the Promenade des Anglais (and far from Vieux Nice). The Negresco, West End, and le Royal are big, vintage Nice hotels that open onto the sea from the heart of the Promenade des Anglais.

$$$ Hôtel Negresco**** owns Nice's most prestigious address on Promenade des Anglais and knows it. Still, it's the kind of place that if you were to splurge just once in your life.... Rooms are opulent (see page 456 for more description), and tips are expected (viewless Db-€380, seaview Db-€330-680, view suite-€770-2,200, breakfast-€30, Old World bar, 37 Promenade des Anglais, tel. 04 93 16 64 00, fax 04 93 88 35 68, www.hotel-negresco-nice.com, reservations@hotel-negresco.com).

$$$ Hôtel West End*** delivers formal service and decor, polished public spaces, and high prices. Its chic rooms come with effective blinds and all the comforts (viewless Db-€300, seaview Db-€340, check website for deals, Internet access and Wi-Fi, 31 Promenade des Anglais, tel. 04 92 14 44 00, fax 04 93 88 85 07, www.hotel-westend.com, reception@westsend3ahotels.com).

$$$ Hôtel Splendid**** is a worthwhile splurge if you miss your Marriott. The panoramic rooftop pool, bar/restaurant, and breakfast room almost justify the cost...but throw in plush rooms (all six floors are non-smoking), a free gym, spa services, and air-conditioning, and you're as good as home (Db-€235—some with decks, deluxe Db with terrace-€280, suites-€360-410, breakfast-€16, better prices available on website, parking-€24, 50 Boulevard Victor Hugo, tel. 04 93 16 41 00, fax 04 93 16 42 70, www.splendid-nice.com, info@splendid-nice.com).

$$ Hôtel le Royal*** is a relaxed resort hotel with 140 rooms, big lounges, and hallways that stretch forever. But the prices are reasonable considering the reliable air-conditioned comfort and terrific location—and sometimes they have rooms when others don't (viewless Db-€145-189, seaview Db-€180-205, bigger view room-€200-225 and worth it, extra person-€25, 23 Promenade des Anglais, tel. 04 93 16 43 00, fax 04 93 16 43 02, www.hotel-royal-nice.cote.azur.fr, royal@vacancesbleues.com).

$$ Hôtel Massenet*** is tucked away a block off the Promenade des Anglais in a pedestrian zone. It has 29 tidy rooms (love the shag carpet) at good rates (small Db-€95, standard Db-€130-155, larger Db-€160, some rooms with decks, parking-€10, 11 Rue Massenet, tel. 04 93 87 11 31, fax 04 93 16 08 69, www.hotelmassenet.fr, hotelmassenet@wanadoo.fr).

$$ Hôtel les Cigales*, a few blocks from the Promenade des Anglais, is a smart little pastel place with tasteful decor, 19 sharp rooms (those with showers are a tad small, most have tub-showers and are standard size), air-conditioning, and a nifty upstairs terrace, all well managed by friendly Mr. Valentino, with Veronique and Elaine. Rick Steves readers who book directly through the hotel website get a discount by typing this code: RICK (standard Db-€110-160, Tb-€130-180, free Wi-Fi, 16 Rue Dalpozzo, tel. 04 97 03 10 70, fax 04 97 03 10 71, www.hotel-lescigales.com, info@ hotel-lescigales.com).

$$ Hôtel Gounod* is behind Hôtel Splendid. Because the two share the same owners, Gounod's guests are allowed free access to Splendid's pool, Jacuzzi, and other amenities. Don't let the lackluster lobby fool you—most rooms are comfortable, with high ceilings (Db-€170, palatial 4-person suites-€270, air-con, parking-€17, 3 Rue Gounod, tel. 04 93 16 42 00, fax 04 93 88 23 84, www.gounod-nice.com, info@gounod-nice.com).

$$ Hôtel Villa Victoria* is a fine place managed by cheery Marlena, who welcomes travelers into her spotless, classy old building with an open, attractive lobby overlooking a sprawling garden-courtyard. Rooms are traditional and well kept, with space to stretch out (streetside Db-€150, garden-side Db-€180, Tb-€160-185, suites-€210-235, breakfast-€15, air-con, minibar, Wi-Fi, parking-€18, 33 Boulevard Victor Hugo, tel. 04 93 88 39 60, fax 04 93 88 07 98, www.villa-victoria.com, contact@villa-victoria.com).

Barely Beyond Nice

$ Villa Saint Exupéry, a service-oriented hostel (they answer the phone in English) is a haven two miles north of the city center. Its amenities and 60 comfortable, spick-and-span rooms create a friendly climate for budget-minded travelers of any age. Often filled with energetic youth, the place can be noisy. There are units for one, two, and up to six people. Many have private bathrooms and views of the Mediterranean—some come with balconies. You'll also find a laundry room, complete kitchen facilities, and a lively bar. There's easy Internet access with a wall of computers in the lobby and Wi-Fi in all the rooms (bed in dorm-€30/person, S-€50-70, Db-€60-90, Tb-€115, includes big breakfast, no curfew, 22 Avenue Gravier, tel. 04 93 84 42 83, toll-free tel. 08 00 30 74 09—works only within France, fax 04 92 09 82 94, www.villahostels.com, reservations@vsaint.com). From the center of town, ride the tram (direction: Las Planas) to the Compte de Falicon stop, then either walk 10 minutes, or take the free shuttle from the Casino supermarket by the tram stop (no service 12:00-17:00).

NICE

Near the Airport

Several airport hotels offer a handy and cheap port-in-the-storm for those with early flights or who are just stopping in for a single night: Etap Hôtel (the cheapest, www.etaphotel.com), Hôtel Première Classe (www.premiereclasse.com), and Hôtel Ibis Nice Aéroport (www.ibisnice.com). Free shuttles connect these hotels with both airport terminals.

You'll find greater comfort at the airport for a bit more (and free private shuttle vans) at these hotels: Novotel (www.novotel.com), Holiday Inn (www.holidayinn.com), and Campanile (www.campanile.fr).

Eating in Nice

Remember, you're in a resort. Seek ambience and fun, and lower your palate's standards. Italian is a low-risk and regional cuisine. The listed restaurants are concentrated in neighborhoods close to my recommended hotels. Several offer fixed-price, multi-course meals *(menus)*. Promenade des Anglais is ideal for picnic dinners on warm, languid evenings. Vieux Nice has the best and busiest dining atmosphere (and best range of choices), while the Nice Etoile area is more local, convenient, and also offers a good range of choices. To feast cheaply, eat on Rue Droite in Vieux Nice, or explore the area around the train station. Allow yourself one dinner at a beachfront restaurant in Nice, and for terribly touristy trolling, wander the wall-to-wall eateries lining Rue Masséna. Yuck.

In Vieux Nice

Nice's dinner scene converges on Cours Saleya, which is entertaining enough in itself to make the generally mediocre food a good deal. It's a fun, festive spot to compare tans and mussels. Even if you're eating elsewhere, wander through here in the evening. For locations, see the map on page 454.

La Voglia has figured out a winning formula: Good food + ample servings + fair prices = good business. Come here early for top-value Italian cuisine, or plan on waiting for a table. There's fun seating inside and out (€12-14 pizza and pasta, €15-25 *plats*, open daily, at the western edge of Cours Saleya at 2 Rue St. Francois de Paule, tel. 04 93 80 99 16).

Le Safari is a fair option for outdoor dining on Cours Saleya, with a few more locals than tourists. The cuisine is Italo-*niçoise*, and the service is professional (€12-18 *plats*, open daily, 1 Cours Saleya, tel. 04 93 80 18 44).

Palmyre is the place to eat on a budget in the old town. The ambience is rustic but intimate, and the menu changes every two weeks. The three-course *menu* is only €15, and the food could not be more homemade (closed Sun, cash only, 5 Rue Droite, tel. 04 93 85 72 32).

La Festival de la Moule is a simple, touristy place for lovers of mussels (or for just plain hungry folks). For €15 you get all-you-can-eat fries and mussels (3 sauces included, 7 additional for €2.50 each) in a youthful outdoor setting (other bistro fare available, 20 Cours Saleya, tel. 04 93 62 02 12).

Le Bistrot du Fromager's owner, Hugo, is crazy about cheese and wine. Come here to escape the heat and dine in cozy, cool, vaulted cellars surrounded by shelves of wine. All dishes use cheese as their base ingredient, although you'll also find pasta, ham, and salmon (with cheese, of course). This is a good choice for vegetarians (€10-13 starters, €15-21 *plats*, €6 desserts, closed Sun, just off Place du Jésus at 29 Rue Benoît Bunico, tel. 04 93 13 07 83).

Oliviera venerates the French olive. This shop/restaurant sells a variety of oils, offers free tastings, and serves a menu of dishes paired with specific oils (think of a wine pairing). Welcoming owner Nadim, who speaks excellent English, knows all his producers and provides "Olive Oil 101" explanations with his tastings (best if you buy something afterward or have a meal). You'll learn how passionate he is about his products, and once you've had a taste, you'll want to stay and eat—so go early (or reserve ahead), as tables fill fast (allow €40 with wine, €16-24 main dishes, Tue-Sat 10:00-22:00, closed Sun-Mon, indoor seating only, 8 bis Rue du Collet, tel. 04 93 13 06 45).

Restaurant Castel is a fine eat-on-the-beach option, thanks to its location at the very east end of Nice looking over the bay. You almost expect Don Ho to step up and grab a mic. Lose the city hustle and bustle by dropping down the steps below Castle Hill. The views are unforgettable even if the cuisine is not; you can even have lunch at your beach chair if you've rented one here (€15/half-day, €18/day). Dinner here is best: Arrive before sunset and find a waterfront table perfectly positioned to watch evening swimmers get in their last laps as the sky turns pink and city lights flicker on. Linger long enough to justify the few extra euros the place charges (€17 salads and pastas, €20-26 main courses, 8 Quai des Etats-Unis, tel. 04 93 85 22 66).

Dining Cheap *à la Niçoise*

Try at least one of these places—not just because they're terrific budget options, but primarily because they offer authentic *niçoise* cuisine.

L'Acchiardo, hidden away in the heart of Vieux Nice, is a homey eatery that does a good job mixing a loyal clientele with hungry tourists. Its simple, hearty *niçoise* cuisine is served for fair prices by gentle Monsieur Acchiardo. The small plaque under the

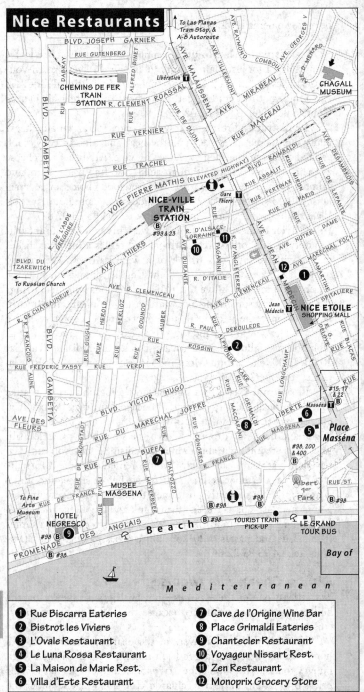

Nice Restaurants

1 Rue Biscarra Eateries
2 Bistrot les Viviers
3 L'Ovale Restaurant
4 Le Luna Rossa Restaurant
5 La Maison de Marie Rest.
6 Villa d'Este Restaurant
7 Cave de l'Origine Wine Bar
8 Place Grimaldi Eateries
9 Chantecler Restaurant
10 Voyageur Nissart Rest.
11 Zen Restaurant
12 Monoprix Grocery Store

NICE

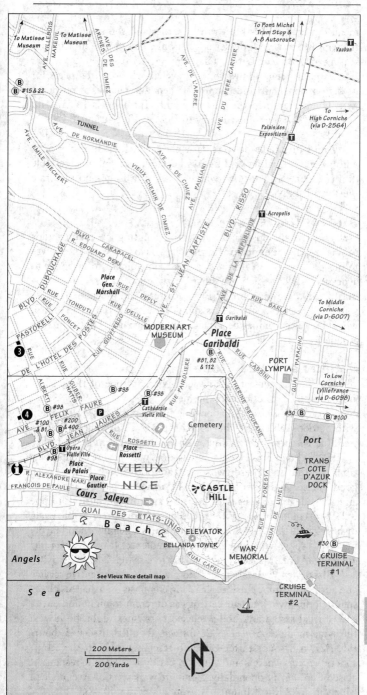

menu outside says it's been run by father and son since 1927 (€8 starters, €15 *plats*, €5 desserts, cash only, closed Sat-Sun, indoor seating only, 38 Rue Droite, tel. 04 93 85 51 16).

Ville de Siena draws young travelers who dig this place for its big portions, fair prices, open kitchen, and raucous atmosphere with tables crammed on a narrow lane. The food is Italian and hearty (€12-17 *plats*, closed Sun, 10 Rue St. Vincent, tel. 04 93 80 12 45).

Lou Pilha Leva delivers basic cheap lunch or dinner options with *niçoise* specialties and always busy outdoor-only picnic-table dining (open daily, located where Rues de la Loge and Centrale meet in Vieux Nice).

And for Dessert...

Gelato lovers should save room for the tempting ice-cream stands in Vieux Nice. **Fenocchio** is the city's favorite, with mouthwatering displays of 86 flavors ranging from tomato to lavender to avocado—all of which are surprisingly good (daily March-Nov until 24:00, two locations: 2 Place Rossetti and 6 Rue de la Poissonnerie). Gelato connoisseurs should head for **Crema di Gelato,** where the selection may be a fraction of Fenocchio's, but the quality is superior (5 Rue de la Préfecture, on Place du Palais).

Eating near Nice Etoile

If you're not up for eating in Vieux Nice, try one of these spots around the Nice Etoile shopping mall.

On Rue Biscarra: An appealing lineup of bistros overflowing with outdoor tables stretches along the broad sidewalk on traffic-free Rue Biscarra (just east of Avenue Jean Médecin behind Nice Etoile, all closed Sun). Come here to dine with area residents away from the tourists. These two places are both good choices, with good interior and exterior seating: **L'Authentic** has the most creative cuisine and comes with a memorable owner, burly Philippe (€23 two-course *menus*, €27 three-course *menus*, reasonable pasta dishes, tel. 04 93 62 48 88). **Le 20 sur Vin** is a neighborhood favorite with a cozy, wine-bar-meets-café ambience. It offers *(bien sûr)* good wines at fair prices, and basic bistro fare (tel. 04 93 92 93 20).

Bistrot les Viviers attracts those who require attentive service and authentic *niçoise* cuisine with a big emphasis on fish. This classy splurge offers two intimate settings as different as night and day: a soft, formal restaurant, and a relaxed *bistrot* next door, both with the same menu (€55 *menu*, €28-38 *plats*, bouillabaisse-€45, bourride-€27, fish soup starter-€10). I'd reserve a table in the atmospheric *bistrot*, where some outdoor seating is available (restaurant closed Sun, *bistrot* open daily, 5-minute walk west of Avenue Jean Médecin at 22 Rue Alphonse Karr, tel. 04 93 16 00 48).

L'Ovale takes its name from the shape of a rugby ball. This welcoming, well-run bistro has quality food at respectable prices, with an emphasis on the cuisine of southwestern France. Dine inside on big *plats* for €10-13; consider their specialty, cassoulet (€17), or the *salade de manchons* (€13), with duck and walnuts (excellent €18 three-course *menu*, €13 big salads, daily, air-con, 29 Rue Pastorelli, tel. 04 93 80 31 65).

Le Luna Rossa is *molto* Italian, with a smart setting inside and out. It's also *molto* popular with locals. Come early or book ahead (€10 starters, €20-27 *plats*, just north of the parkway at 3 Rue Chauvain, tel. 04 93 85 55 66).

La Maison de Marie is a surprisingly good-quality refuge off touristy Rue Masséna, where most other restaurants serve mediocre food to tired travelers. Enter through a deep-red arch to a bougainvillea-draped courtyard, and enjoy the fair prices and excellent cuisine that draw neighborhood regulars and out-of-towners alike. The interior tables are as appealing as those in the courtyard, but expect some smokers outside. The €23 *menu* is a terrific value (€10-15 starters and €15-30 *plats*, great fruit-salad dessert, open daily, look for the square red sign at 5 Rue Masséna, tel. 04 93 82 15 93).

Villa d'Este has the same owners as the recommended La Voglia (listed earlier, under "In Vieux Nice"). The portions are big, the price is right, and the quality is tops (daily, on a busy pedestrian street at 6 Rue Masséna, tel. 04 93 82 47 77).

Near Promenade des Anglais

Worthwhile restaurants are few and far between in this area. Either head for Vieux Nice or try one of these good places.

Cave de l'Origine is a find, and would be even away from the tourist fray. Kind Isabelle and her English-speaking staff welcome you to their cozy wine shop/*bistrot*. Isabelle prepares fresh, homemade dishes and finds the perfect wines to match. She features original cuisine from many areas in France (especially the southwest), made with regional, fresh ingredients (€7-11 starters, €16-21 *plats*, open Tue-Sat for lunch and dinner, reservations smart, indoor seating only; wine shop open Tue-Sat 10:00-20:00, closed Sun-Mon; 3 Rue Dalpozzo, tel. 04 83 50 09 60).

On Place Grimaldi: This square nurtures a lineup of appealing restaurants with good indoor and outdoor seating along a broad sidewalk under tall, leafy sycamore trees. **Crêperie Bretonne** is the only *crêperie* I list in Nice (€8 dinner crêpes, closed Sun, 3 Place Grimaldi, tel. 04 93 82 28 47). **Le Grimaldi** is popular for its café fare (€14 pasta, €15-25 *plats*, closed Sun, 1 Place Grimaldi, tel. 04 93 87 98 13).

Chantecler has Nice's most prestigious address—inside the Hôtel Negresco. This is everything a luxury restaurant should be: elegant, soft, and top quality. If your trip is ending in Nice, call or email for reservations—you've earned this splurge (*menus* from €90, closed Mon-Tue, 37 Promenade des Anglais, tel. 04 93 16 64 00, chantecler@lenegresco.com).

Near the Train Station

Both of the following restaurants, a block below the train station, provide good indoor and outdoor seating as well as excellent value.

Voyageur Nissart has blended good-value cuisine with cool Mediterranean ambience and friendly service since 1908. Current owner Max is a great host, and the quality of his cuisine makes this a good choice for travelers on any budget—try the wonderful €14 *filet de rouget à la niçoise* or the fine €8 *salade niçoise* (€17 three-course *menus*, good *plats* from €11, inexpensive wines, closed Mon, 19 Rue d'Alsace-Lorraine, tel. 04 93 82 19 60).

Zen provides a Japanese break from French cuisine. Interior seating is arranged around the chef's stove, and the tasty specialties draw a strong following (€16 three-course *menu*, €8-13 sushi, open daily, 27 Rue d'Angleterre, tel. 04 93 82 41 20).

Nice Connections

By Train and Bus

Note that most long-distance train connections to other French cities require a change in Marseille. The Grande Ligne train to Bordeaux (serving Antibes, Cannes, Toulon, and Marseille—and connecting from there to Arles, Nîmes, and Carcassonne) requires a reservation. Remember that on regional buses (except on express airport buses), many one-way rides cost €1—regardless of length (the €1 ticket is good for up to 74 minutes of travel in one direction, including transfers).

From Nice by Train to: Cannes (2/hour, 30-40 minutes), **Antibes** (2/hour, 15-30 minutes), **Villefranche-sur-Mer** (2/hour, 10 minutes), **Eze-le-Village** (2/hour, 15 minutes to Eze-Bord-de-Mer, then bus #83 to Eze, 8/day), **Monaco** (2/hour, 20 minutes) **Menton** (2/hour, 25 minutes), **Grasse** (15/day, 1.25 hours), **Marseille** (18/day, 2.5 hours), **Arles** (11/day, 3.75-4.5 hours, most require transfer in Marseille or Avignon), **Avignon** (20/day, most by TGV, 4 hours, most require transfer in Marseille), **Paris'** Gare de Lyon (hourly, 5.75 hours, may require change; 11.5-hour night train goes to Paris' Gare d'Austerlitz), **Munich** (4/day, 12.5-14 hours with 2-4 transfers, longer night trains possible, some via Italy), **Interlaken** (6/day, 9-10 hours, 2-5 transfers), **Florence** (6/day, 7-9 hours, 1-3 transfers), **Venice** (5/day, 8-9 hours, all require transfers), **Barcelona** (1/day via Montpellier, 10 hours, more with multiple changes).

From Nice by Bus to: Cannes (#200, 4/hour Mon-Sat, 2-3/hour Sun, 1.5-1.75 hours), **Antibes** (#200, 4/hour Mon-Sat, 2-3/hour Sun, 1-1.5 hours), **Villefranche-sur-Mer** (#100, 4/hour Mon-Sat, 3/hour Sun, 20 minutes; or #81, 2-4/hour, 20 minutes), **St-Jean-Cap-Ferrat** (#81, 2-4/hour, 35 minutes), **Eze-le-Village** (#82 or #112, 16/day Mon-Sat, 8/day Sun, 40 minutes), **La Turbie** (#116 or #T-66, 5/day Mon-Sat, 7/day Sun, 45 minutes), **Monaco** (#100, 4/hour Mon-Sat, 3/hour Sun, 45 minutes), **Menton** (#100, 4/hour Mon-Sat, 3/hour Sun, 1.25 hours), **St-Paul-de-Vence** (#400, every 30-45 minutes, 45 minutes), **Vence** (#400, every 30-45 minutes, 50 minutes), **Grasse** (#500, every 30-45 minutes, 1.25 hours).

By Plane

Nice's easy-to-navigate airport (Aéroport de Nice Côte d'Azur; airport code: NCE) is on the Mediterranean, a 20- to 30-minute drive west of the city center. Planes leave roughly hourly for Paris (one-hour flight, about the same price as a train ticket, check www.easyjet.com for the cheapest flights to Paris' Orly airport). The two terminals (Terminal 1 and Terminal 2) are connected by frequent shuttle buses *(navettes)*. Both terminals have TIs (and Terminal 1 has an info desk just for Monaco), banks, ATMs, taxis, baggage storage (€6.50/day per piece, open daily 5:45-23:00), and buses to Nice (tel. 04 89 88 98 28, www.nice.aeroport.fr).

Getting from the Airport to the City Center

Taxis into the center are expensive considering the short distance (figure €35 to recommended hotels, 10 percent more 19:00-7:00 and all day Sun). Taxis stop outside door *(Porte)* A-1 at Terminal 1 and outside *Porte* A-3 at Terminal 2. Notorious for overcharging, Nice taxis are not always so nice. If your fare for a ride into town is much higher than €35 (or €40 at night or on Sun), refuse to pay the overage. If this doesn't work, tell the cabbie to call a *gendarme* (police officer). It's always a good idea to ask for a receipt *(reçu)*.

Airport shuttle vans work with some of my recommended hotels, but they only make sense when going *to* the airport, not when arriving on an international flight. Unlike taxis, shuttle vans offer a fixed price that doesn't rise on Sundays, early mornings, or evenings. Prices are best for groups (figure €30 for one person, and only a little more for additional people). **Nice Airport Shuttle** is one option (1-2 people-€32, additional person-€14, mobile 06 60 33 20 54, www.nice-airport-shuttle.com), or ask your hotelier for recommendations.

Three bus lines connect the airport with the city center, offering good alternatives to high-priced taxis. **Bus #99** (airport express) runs from both terminals to Nice's main train station (€4,

NICE

2/hour, 8:00-21:00, 30 minutes, drops you within a 10-minute walk of many recommended hotels). To take this bus *to* the airport, catch it right in front of the train station (departs on the half-hour). If your hotel is within walking distance of the station, #99 is a breeze.

Bus #98 serves both terminals, and runs along Promenade des Anglais to the edge of Vieux Nice (€4, 3/hour, from the airport 6:00-23:00, to the airport until 21:00, 30 minutes, see map on page 476 for stops). The slower, cheaper local **bus #23** serves only Terminal 1, and makes every stop between the airport and train station (€1, 5/hour, runs 6:00-20:00, 40 minutes, direction: St-Maurice).

For all buses, buy tickets in the information office just outside either terminal, or from the driver. To reach the bus information office and stops at Terminal 1, turn left after passing customs and exit the doors at the far end. Buses serving Terminal 2 stop across the street from the airport exit (information kiosk and ticket sales to the right as you exit).

If you take bus #98 or #99, hang on to your €4 ticket—it's good all day on any public bus and the tramway in Nice, and for buses between Nice and some nearby towns.

GERMANY

BAVARIA AND TIROL

Füssen • King's Castles • Reutte, Austria

Two hours south of Munich, in the most picturesque corner of Germany's Bavaria and Austria's Tirol, is a timeless land of fairy-tale castles, painted buildings shared by cows and farmers, and locals who still yodel when they're happy.

In southern Bavaria, tour "Mad" King Ludwig II's ornate Neuschwanstein Castle, Europe's most spectacular. Just over the border in Austria, explore the ruined Ehrenberg Castle.

My favorite home base for exploring Bavaria's castles is actually in Austria, in the Tirolean town of Reutte. Reutte's hotels offer better value to those with a car. Füssen, in Germany, is more touristy, but a handier home base for train travelers.

Planning Your Time and Getting Around Bavaria

While Germans and Austrians vacation here for a week or two at a time, the typical speedy American traveler will find two days' worth of sightseeing. With a car and more time, you could enjoy three or four days.

By Public Transportation

Where you stay determines which sights you can see most easily. Train travelers use **Füssen** as a base, and bus or bike the three miles to Neuschwanstein and the Tegelberg luge or gondola. Although **Reutte** is the least convenient base if you're carless, travelers staying there can easily bike or hike to the Ehrenberg ruins, and can reach Neuschwanstein by bus (via Füssen), bike (1.5 hours), or taxi (€35 one-way); if you stay at the recommended Gutshof zum Schluxen hotel (between Reutte and Füssen, in Pinswang, Austria) it's a 1- to 1.5-hour hike through the woods to Neuschwanstein.

Those staying in **Füssen** can day-trip by bus to Reutte and the Ehrenberg ruins.

By Bike

This is great biking country. Many hotels loan bikes to guests, and shops in Reutte and at the Füssen train station rent bikes for €8-15 per day. The ride from Reutte to Neuschwanstein and the Tegelberg luge (1.5 hours) is a natural.

Füssen

Dramatically situated under a renovated castle on the lively Lech River, Füssen (FEW-sehn) is a handy home base for exploring the region. This town has been a strategic stop since ancient times. Its main street sits on the Via Claudia Augusta, which crossed the Alps (over the Brenner Pass) in Roman times. Going north, early traders could follow the Lech River downstream to the Danube, and then cross over to the Main and Rhine valleys—a route now known to modern travelers as the "Romantic Road." Today, while Füssen is overrun by tourists in the summer, few venture to the back streets...which is where you'll find the real charm. Apart from my self-guided walk and the Füssen Heritage Museum, there's little to do here. It's just a pleasant small town with a big history and lots of hardworking people in the tourist business.

Halfway between Füssen and the border (as you drive, or a woodsy walk from the town) is the **Lechfall,** a thunderous waterfall (with a handy WC).

Orientation to Füssen

Füssen's train station is a few blocks from the TI, the town center (a cobbled shopping mall), and all my hotel listings.

Tourist Information

The TI is in the center of town (July-mid-Sept Mon-Fri 9:00-18:00, Sat 10:00-14:00, Sun 10:00-12:00; mid-Sept-June Mon-Fri 9:00-17:00, Sat 10:00-14:00, closed Sun; one free Internet terminal, 3 blocks down Bahnhofstrasse from station at Kaiser-Maximilian-Platz 1, tel. 08362/93850, www.fuessen.de). If necessary, the TI can help you find a room. After hours, the little self-service info pavilion near the front of the TI features an automated room-finding service with a phone to call hotels.

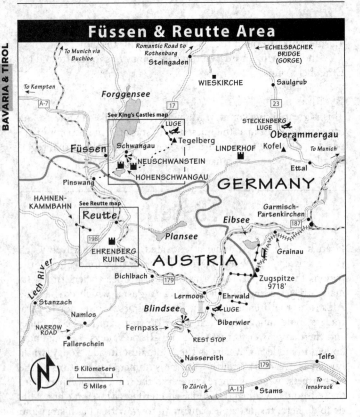

Füssen & Reutte Area

Arrival in Füssen

From the train station (lockers available, €2-3), exit to the left and walk a few blocks to reach the center of town and the TI. Buses to Neuschwanstein, Reutte, and elsewhere leave from a parking lot next to the station.

Helpful Hints

Internet Access: CSI Internet Café has four computers and decent prices (€1.50/hour, daily 9:00-late, Luitpoldstrasse 8, tel. 08362/883-7073).

Bike Rental: Bike Station, sitting right where the train tracks end, outfits sightseers with good bikes and tips on two-wheeled fun in the area (€9-12/24 hours, March-Oct Mon-Fri 9:00-12:00 & 14:00-18:00, Sat 9:00-13:00, Sun 10:00-12:00, closed Nov-Feb, tel. 08362/983-651, mobile 0176-2205-3080, www.ski-sport-luggi.de).

Car Rental: Peter Schlichtling, in the town center, rents cars for reasonable prices (€62/day, includes insurance, Mon-Fri 8:00-18:00, Sat 9:00-12:00, closed Sun, Kemptener Strasse 26, tel.

08362/922-122, www.schlichtling.de). **Auto Osterried/Europcar** rents at similar prices, but is an €8 taxi ride away from the train station. Their cheapest car goes for about €59 per day (daily 8:00-19:00, past waterfall on road to Austria, Tiroler Strasse 65, tel. 08362/6381).

Local Guide: Silvia Beyer speaks English, knows the region very well, and can even drive you to sights that are hard to reach by train (€30/hour, mobile 0160-901-13431, silliby@web.de).

Self-Guided Walk

Welcome to Füssen

For most, Füssen is just a home base for visiting Ludwig's famous castles. But the town has a rich history and hides some evocative corners, as you'll see when you follow this short orientation walk. Throughout the town, "City Tour" information plaques explain points of interest in English (in more detail than I've provided).

• *Begin at the square in front of the TI, three blocks from the train station.*

❶ Kaiser-Maximilian-Platz: The entertaining "Seven Stones" fountain on this square, by sculptor Christian Tobin, was built in 1995 to celebrate Füssen's 700th birthday. The stones symbolize community, groups of people gathering, conviviality...each is different, with "heads" nodding and talking. It's granite on granite. The moving heads are not connected, and nod only with water-power. While frozen in winter, it's a popular and splashy play zone for kids on hot summer days.

• *Just half a block down the busy street stands...*

❷ Hotel Hirsch and Medieval Towers: Recent renovations have restored some of the original Art Nouveau flavor to Hotel Hirsch, which opened in 1904. In those days, aristocratic tourists came here to appreciate the castles and natural wonders of the Alps. Across the busy street stands one of two surviving towers from Füssen's medieval town wall (c. 1515), and next to it is a passageway into the old town.

• *Walk 50 yards farther down the street to another tower. Just before it, you'll see an information plaque and an archway where a small street called Klosterstrasse emerges through a surviving piece of the old town wall. Step through the smaller pedestrian archway, walk along Klosterstrasse for a few yards, and turn left through the gate into the...*

❸ Historic Cemetery of St. Sebastian (Alter Friedhof): This peaceful oasis of Füssen history, established in the 16th century, fills a corner between the town wall and the Franciscan monastery. It's technically full, and only members of great and venerable Füssen families (who already own plots here) can join those who are buried (free, daily April-Sept 7:30-19:00, Oct-March 8:00-17:00).

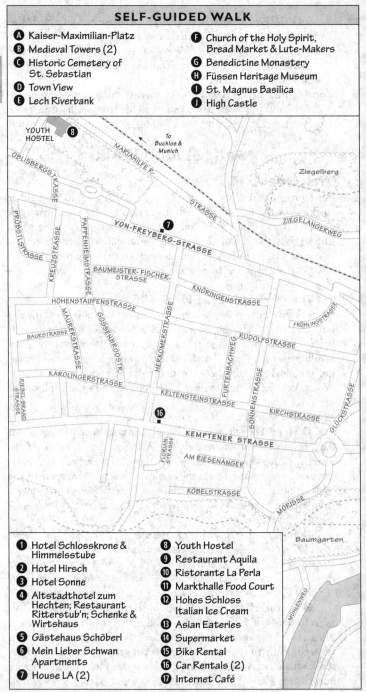

SELF-GUIDED WALK

A Kaiser-Maximilian-Platz
B Medieval Towers (2)
C Historic Cemetery of St. Sebastian
D Town View
E Lech Riverbank
F Church of the Holy Spirit, Bread Market & Lute-Makers
G Benedictine Monastery
H Füssen Heritage Museum
I St. Magnus Basilica
J High Castle

1 Hotel Schlosskrone & Himmelsstube
2 Hotel Hirsch
3 Hotel Sonne
4 Altstadthotel zum Hechten; Restaurant Ritterstub'n; Schenke & Wirtshaus
5 Gästehaus Schöberl
6 Mein Lieber Schwan Apartments
7 House LA (2)
8 Youth Hostel
9 Restaurant Aquila
10 Ristorante La Perla
11 Markthalle Food Court
12 Hohes Schloss Italian Ice Cream
13 Asian Eateries
14 Supermarket
15 Bike Rental
16 Car Rentals (2)
17 Internet Café

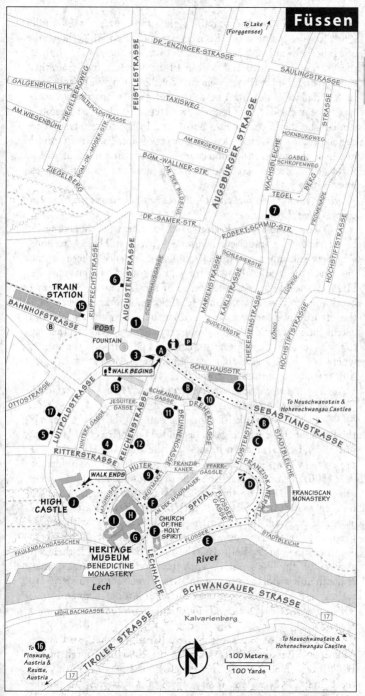

BAVARIA & TIROL

Just inside the gate (on the right) is the tomb of Dominic Quaglio, who painted the Romantic scenes decorating the walls of Hohenschwangau Castle in 1835. Over on the old city wall is the World War I memorial, listing all the names of men from this small town killed in that devastating conflict (along with each one's rank and place of death). A bit to the right, also along the old wall, is a statue of the hand of God holding a fetus—a place to remember babies who died before being born. And in the corner, farther to the right, are the simple wooden crosses of Franciscans who lived just over the wall in the monastery. Note the fine tomb art from many ages collected here, and the loving care this community gives its cemetery.

• *Exit on the far side, just past the dead Franciscans, and continue toward the big church.*

❿ Town View from Franciscan Monastery (Franziskanerkloster): From the Franciscan Monastery (which still has big responsibilities, but only a handful of monks in residence), there's a fine view over the medieval town. The Church of St. Magnus and the High Castle (the summer residence of the Bishops of Augsburg) break the horizon. The chimney (c. 1886) and workers' housing on the left are reminders that when Ludwig built Neuschwanstein, the textile industry (linen and flax) was very big here. Walk all the way to the far end of the monastery chapel and peek around the corner, where you'll see a gate that proclaims the *Ende der romantischen Strasse* (end of the Romantic Road).

• *Now go down the stairway and turn left, through the medieval "Bleachers' Gate," to the riverbank.*

❶ Lech Riverbank: This low end of town, the flood zone, was the home of those whose work depended on the river—bleachers, rafters, and fishermen. In its heyday, the Lech River was an expressway to Augsburg (about 70 miles to the north). Around the year 1500, the rafters established the first professional guild in Füssen. As Füssen was on the Via Claudia, cargo from Italy passed here en route to big German cities farther north. Rafters would assemble rafts and pile them high with goods—or with people needing a lift. If the water was high, they could float all the way to Augsburg in as little as one day. There they'd disassemble their raft and sell off the lumber along with the goods they'd carried, then make their way home to raft again. Today you'll see no modern-day rafters here, as there's a hydroelectric plant just downstream.

• *Walk upstream a bit, and head inland immediately after crossing under the bridge.*

❶ Church of the Holy Spirit, Bread Market, and Lute-Makers: Climbing uphill, you pass the colorful Church of the Holy Spirit (Heilig-Geist-Spitalkirche) on the right. As this was the church of the rafters, their patron, St. Christopher, is prominent on the facade. Today it's the church of Füssen's old folks' home (it's adjacent—notice the easy-access skyway).

Farther up the hill on the right (almost opposite an archway into a big courtyard) is Bread Market Square (Brotmarkt), with a fountain honoring the famous 16th-century lute-making family, the Tieffenbruckers. In its day, Füssen was a huge center of violin- and lute-making, with about 200 workshops. Today only two survive.

• *Backtrack and go through the archway into the courtyard of the former...*

❻ Benedictine Monastery (Kloster St. Mang): From 1717 until secularization in 1802, this was the powerful center of town. Today the courtyard is popular for concerts, and the building houses the City Hall and Füssen Heritage Museum (and a public WC).

❼ Füssen Heritage Museum: This is Füssen's one must-see sight (€6, €7 combo-ticket includes painting gallery and castle tower; April-Oct Tue-Sun 11:00-17:00, closed Mon; Nov-March Fri-Sun 13:00-16:00, closed Mon-Thu; tel. 08362/903-146, www. fuessen.de). Pick up the loaner English translations and follow the one-way route. In the St. Anna Chapel, you'll see the famous *Dance of Death*. This was painted shortly after a plague devastated the community in 1590. It shows 20 social classes, each dancing with the Grim Reaper—starting with the pope and the emperor. The words above say, essentially, "You can say yes or you can say no, but you must ultimately dance with death."

Leaving the chapel, you walk over the metal lid of the crypt. Upstairs, exhibits illustrate the rafting trade and violin- and lute-making (with a complete workshop). The museum also includes an exquisite *Festsaal* (main festival hall), an old library, an exhibition on textile production, and a King Ludwig-style "castle dream room."

• *Leaving the courtyard, hook left around the old monastery and go up-hill. The square tower marks...*

❶ St. Magnus Basilica (Basilika St. Mang): St. Mang (or Magnus) is Füssen's favorite saint. In the eighth century, he worked miracles all over the area with his holy rod. For centuries, pilgrims came from far and wide to enjoy art depicting the great works of St. Magnus. Above the altar dangles a glass cross containing his relics (including that holy stick). Just inside the door is a chapel remembering a much more modern saint—Franz Seelos (1819-1867), the local boy who went to America (Pittsburgh and New Orleans) and lived such a righteous life that in 2000 he was beatified by Pope John Paul II. If you're in need of a miracle, fill out a request card next to the candles.

• *From the church, a lane leads high above, into the courtyard of the...*

❶ High Castle (Hohes Schloss): This castle, long the summer residence of the Bishop of Augsburg, houses a painting gallery (the upper floor is labeled in English) and a tower with a view over the town and lake (included in the €7 Füssen Heritage Museum combo-ticket, otherwise €6, same hours as museum). Its courtyard is interesting for the striking perspective tricks painted onto its flat walls. From below the castle, the city's main drag (once the Roman Via Claudia, and now Reichenstrasse) leads from a grand statue of St. Magnus past lots of shops, cafés, and strolling people to Kaiser-Maximilian-Platz and the TI...where you began.

Sleeping in Füssen

(country code: 49, area code: 08362)

Though I prefer sleeping in Reutte, convenient Füssen is just three miles from Ludwig's castles and offers a cobbled, riverside retreat. It's fairly touristy, but it has plenty of rooms, and is the region's best base for those traveling by train. All recommended accommodations are within a few handy blocks of the train station and the town center. Parking is easy at the station, and some hotels also have their own lot or garage. Prices listed are for one-night stays; most hotels give about 5-10 percent off for two-night stays—always request this discount. Competition is fierce, and off-season prices are soft. High season is mid-June-September. Rooms are generally 10-15 percent less in shoulder season and much cheaper in off-season.

Big, Fancy Hotels in the Center of Town

$$$ Hotel Schlosskrone, with 62 rooms and all the amenities, is just a block from the station. It also runs two restaurants and a fine pastry shop—you'll notice at breakfast (Sb-€99-109, standard Db-€119-139, bigger Db-€129-165, Tb-€145-165, Qb-€159-179, 4-person suite-€240-279, lower prices are for Oct-April, you'll likely save money by booking via their website, great breakfast, air-con in some rooms, elevator, free Wi-Fi and cable Internet, free sauna and fitness center, parking-€9/day, Prinzregentenplatz 2-4, tel. 08362/930-180, fax 08362/930-1850, www.schlosskrone.com, info@schlosskrone.com, Norbert Schöll and family).

$$$ Hotel Hirsch is a romantic, well-maintained, 53-room, old-style hotel on the main street two blocks from the station. Their standard rooms are fine, and their rooms with historical and landscape themes are a fun splurge (Sb-€90, standard Db-€123-133, theme Db-€150-180, lower prices are for Nov-March and during slow times, family rooms, elevator, expensive Internet access, free Wi-Fi, free parking, Kaiser-Maximilian-Platz 7, tel. 08362/93980, fax 08362/939-877, www.hotelfuessen.de, info@hotelhirsch.de).

$$$ Hotel Sonne, in the heart of town, has a modern lobby

Sleep Code

(€1 = about $1.30, Germany country code: 49, Austria country code: 43)

S = Single, **D** = Double/Twin, **T** = Triple, **Q** = Quad, **b** = bathroom, **s** = shower only. Unless otherwise noted, credit cards are accepted, English is spoken, and breakfast is included.

To help you sort easily through these listings, I've divided the accommodations into three categories, based on the price for a standard double room with bath:

$$$ **Higher Priced**—Most rooms €100 or more.
$$ **Moderately Priced**—Most rooms between €60-100.
$ **Lower Priced**—Most rooms €60 or less.

Prices can change without notice; verify the hotel's current rates online or by email.

---

and takes pride in decorating (some would say over-decorating) its 50 stylish rooms (Sb-€89-121, Db-€111-135, bigger Db-€155-185, Tb-€149, bigger Tb-€169-183, Qb-€189-219, lower prices are for Nov-March, discount if you book on their website, elevator, free Internet access and Wi-Fi, free sauna and fitness center, parking-€5-7/day, kitty-corner from TI at Prinzregentenplatz 1, tel. 08362/9080, fax 08362/908-100, www.hotel-sonne.de, info@hotel-sonne.de).

Smaller, Mid-Priced Hotels and Pensions

$$ Altstadthotel zum Hechten offers 35 modern and newly renovated rooms in a friendly, traditional building right under Füssen Castle in the old-town pedestrian zone (Sb-€59-69, Db-€94-108, Tb-€130, Qb-€160, ask for Rick Steves price when you reserve, also mention if you're very tall as most beds can be short, non-smoking, lots of stairs, free Internet access in lounge, free Wi-Fi, parking-€3/day, laundry-€10-20/load, travel resource room with maps and books, fun miniature bowling alley in basement, recommended restaurant, electric-bike rental-€20/day; from TI, walk down pedestrian street and take second right to Ritterstrasse 6; tel. 08362/91600, fax 08362/916-099, www.hotel-hechten.com, info@hotel-hechten.com, Pfeiffer and Tramp families).

$$ Gästehaus Schöberl, run by the head cook at Altstadthotel zum Hechten, rents six attentively furnished, modern rooms a five-minute walk from the train station. One room is in the owners' house, and the rest are in the building next door (Sb-€40-50, Db-€70-75, Tb-€85-95, Qb-€100-120, lower prices are for Jan-

Feb and Nov or for longer stays, cash only, free Wi-Fi, free parking, Luitpoldstrasse 14-16, tel. 08362/922-411, www.schoeberl-fuessen.de, info@schoeberl-fuessen.de, Pia and Georg Schöberl).

$$ Mein Lieber Schwan, a block from the train station, is a former private house with four superbly outfitted apartments, each with a double bed, sofa bed, and kitchen. The catch is the three-night minimum stay (Sb-€68-79, Db-€78-89, Tb-€88-99, Qb-€98-109, price depends on apartment size, slightly cheaper off-season, cash or PayPal only, no breakfast, free Wi-Fi, free parking, laundry facilities, garden, from station turn left at traffic circle to Augustenstrasse 3, tel. 08362/509-980, fax 08362/509-914, www.meinlieberschwan.de, fewo@meinlieberschwan.de, Herr Bletschacher).

Budget Beds

$ House LA, run by energetic mason Lahdo Algül and hardworking Agata, has two branches. The backpacker house has 11 basic, clean four-bed dorm rooms at rock-bottom prices about a 10-minute walk from the station (€18/bed, D-€42, breakfast-€2.50, free Internet access and Wi-Fi, free parking, Wachsbleiche 2). A second building has five family apartments with kitchen and bath, each sleeping 4-6 people (apartment-€60-90, breakfast-€2.50, free Wi-Fi, free parking, 6-minute walk back along tracks from station to von Freybergstrasse 26; contact info for both: tel. 08362/607-366, mobile 0170-624-8610, fax 08362/925-1909, www.housela.de, info@housela.de). Both branches rent bikes (€8/day) and have laundry facilities (€9/load).

$ Füssen Youth Hostel occupies a pleasant modern building in a grassy setting an easy walk from the center. There are ping-pong tables and a basketball net out front (bed in 2- to 6-bed dorm rooms-€22, D-€50, €3 more for nonmembers, includes breakfast and sheets, laundry-€4/load, dinner-€5, office open 8:00-12:00 & 17:00-22:00, free Wi-Fi, free parking, from station backtrack 10 minutes along tracks, Mariahilfer Strasse 5, tel. 08362/7754, fax 08362/2770, www.fuessen.jugendherberge.de, jhfuessen@djh-bayern.de).

Eating in Füssen

Restaurant Aquila serves modern international dishes in a simple, traditional *Gasthaus* setting with great seating outside on the delightful little Brotmarkt square (€10-16 main courses, serious €9-10 salads, Wed-Mon 11:30-14:30 & 17:30-22:00, closed Tue, Brotmarkt 9, tel. 08362/6253).

Restaurant Ritterstub'n offers delicious, reasonably priced fish, salads, veggie plates, gluten-free options, and a fun kids' menu. They have three eating zones: modern decor in front, traditional Bavarian in back, and a courtyard. Demure Gabi serves while her husband cooks standard Bavarian fare (€8-15 main courses, €5.50 lunch specials, €19 three-course fixed-price dinners, Tue-Sun 11:30-14:30 & 17:30-23:00, closed Mon, Ritterstrasse 4, tel. 08362/7759).

Schenke & Wirtshaus (inside the recommended Altstadthotel zum Hechten) dishes up hearty, traditional Bavarian fare. They specialize in pike *(Hecht)* pulled from the Lech River, served with a tasty fresh-herb sauce (€8-14 main courses, salad bar, cafeteria ambience, daily 10:00-22:00, Ritterstrasse 6, tel. 0836/91600).

The **Himmelsstube** ("heaven's lounge," inside Hotel Schlosskrone, right on Füssen's main traffic circle) boasts good weekly specials and live Bavarian zither music most Fridays and Saturdays during dinner. Choose between a traditional dining room and a pastel winter garden. If your pension doesn't offer breakfast, consider their €13 "American-style" breakfast or huge €15 Sunday spread (open daily 7:30-10:30 & 11:30-14:30 & 18:00-22:00, Prinzregentenplatz 2-4, tel. 08362/930-180). The hotel's second restaurant, **Chili,** serves Mediterranean dishes.

Ristorante La Perla is the place to sate your Italian-food cravings, with friendly staff and fair prices. Sit either in the classic interior, or in one of two delightful outside areas: streetside seating, or the more peaceful back courtyard (€5-12 pizzas and pastas, €10-23 meat and fish dishes, daily 11:00-22:00, in winter closed 14:30-17:30 and all day Mon, Drehergasse 44, tel. 08362/7155).

The **Markthalle** is a fun food court offering a wide selection of reasonably priced, wurst-free food. Located in an old warehouse from 1483, it's now home to a fishmonger, deli counters, a fruit stand, a bakery, and a wine bar. Buy your food from one of the vendors, park yourself at any one of the tables, then look up and admire the Renaissance ceiling (Mon-Fri 7:30-18:30, Sat 7:30-14:30, closed Sun, corner of Schrannengasse and Brunnengasse).

Gelato: **Hohes Schloss Italian Ice Cream** is a good *gelateria* on the main drag and has an inviting people-watching perch for coffee or dessert (Reichenstrasse 14).

Asian Food: You'll find inexpensive Thai, Indian, and Chinese restaurants in the Luitpold-Passage at Reichenstrasse 33.

Picnic Supplies: Bakeries and *Metzgers* (butcher shops) abound and frequently have ready-made sandwiches. For groceries, try the underground **Netto** supermarket at Prinzregentenplatz, the roundabout on your way into town from the train station (Mon-Sat 7:00-20:00, closed Sun).

Füssen Connections

From Füssen to: Neuschwanstein (bus #73 or #78, departs from train station, most continue to Tegelberg lift station after castles, 1-2/hour, 10 minutes, €2 one-way, €4 round-trip; taxis cost €10 one-way); **Reutte** (bus #74; Mon-Fri almost hourly, last bus 19:00; Sat-Sun every 3 hours, last bus 19:00; 45 minutes, €4.10 one-way; taxis cost €35 one-way); **Munich** (hourly trains, 2 hours, some change in Buchloe); **Salzburg** (hourly via Munich, 4 hours, 1-2 changes); **Rothenburg ob der Tauber** (hourly, 5 hours, look for connections with only 2-3 changes—often in Augsburg, Treuchtlingen, and Steinach); **Frankfurt** (hourly, 5-6 hours, 1-2 changes). Train info: tel. 0180-599-6633, www.bahn.com.

The King's Castles

The most popular tourist destinations in southern Bavaria are the two "King's Castles" (Königsschlösser) near Füssen. The older Hohenschwangau, King Ludwig's boyhood home, is less touristy but more historic. The more dramatic Neuschwanstein, which inspired Walt Disney, is the one everyone visits. I'd recommend visiting both, and planning some time to hike above Neuschwanstein to Mary's Bridge—and, if you enjoy romantic hikes, down through the gorge below. Reservations are a magic wand to smooth out your visit. With fairy-tale turrets in a fairy-tale alpine setting built by a fairy-tale king, these castles are understandably a huge hit.

Getting There

If arriving by **car,** note that road signs in the region refer to the sight as *Königsschlösser,* not Neuschwanstein. There's plenty of parking (all lots-€5). The first lots require more walking. Drive right through Touristville and past the ticket center, and park in lot #4 by the lake for the same price.

From **Füssen,** those without cars can catch **bus** #73 or #78 (1-2/hour, €2 each way, 10 minutes, catch bus at train station, extra buses often run when crowded), take a **taxi** (€10 one-way), or ride a rental **bike** (two level miles). The bus drops you at the tourist office; it's a one-minute walk from there to the ticket office.

From **Reutte,** take bus #74 to the Füssen train station, then hop on bus #73 or #78 to the castles. Or pay €35 for a taxi right to the castles.

Orientation to the King's Castles

Cost: Neuschwanstein and Hohenschwangau cost €12 apiece. A "Königsticket" combo-ticket for both castles costs €23, and a "Schwanenticket," which also covers the Museum of the Bavarian Kings—described on page 501—costs €28.50. Children under 18 (accompanied by an adult) are admitted free.

Hours: The ticket center, located at street level between the two castles, is open daily April-Sept 8:00-17:00, Oct-March 9:00-15:00. The first and last castle tours of the day depart an hour after the ticket office opens and closes: April-Sept at 9:00 and 18:00, Oct-March at 10:00 and 16:00.

Getting Tickets for the Castles: Every tour bus in Bavaria converges on Neuschwanstein, and tourists flush in each morning from Munich. A handy reservation system sorts out the chaos for smart travelers. Tickets, whether reserved in advance or bought on the spot, come with admission times. If you miss your appointed tour time, you can't get in. To tour both castles, you must do Hohenschwangau first (logical, since this gives a better introduction to King Ludwig's short life). You'll get two tour times: Hohenschwangau and then, two hours later, Neuschwanstein.

Arrival: Make the **ticket center** your first stop. If you have a reservation, stand in the short line for picking up tickets. If you don't have a reservation...welcome to the very long line. Arrive by 8:00 in summer, and you'll likely be touring at 9:00. During August, the busiest month, tickets for English tours usually run out between 16:00 and 17:00.

Reservations: It's smart to reserve in peak season (June-early Oct—especially in July-Aug, when slots can book up several days in advance). Reservations cost €1.80 per person per castle, and must be made no later than 17:00 on the previous day. It works best to book online (www.ticket-center-hohenschwangau.de); you can also reserve by phone (tel. 08362/930-830) or email (info@ticket-center-hohenschwangau.de). You must pick up reserved tickets an hour before the appointed entry time, as it takes a while to walk up to the castles. (It doesn't usually take an hour, though—so this might be a good time to pull out a sandwich or a snack.) Show up late and they may have given your slot to someone else (but then they'll likely help you make another reservation). If you know a couple of hours in advance that you're running late and can call the office, they'll likely rebook you at no charge.

Getting Up to the Castles: From the ticket booth, Hohenschwangau is an easy 10-minute climb, while Neuschwanstein is a steep 30-minute hike in the other direction. To minimize

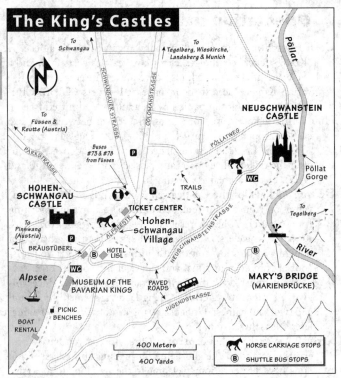

The King's Castles

hiking to Neuschwanstein, you can take a shuttle bus (leaves every few minutes from in front of Hotel Lisl, just above ticket office and to the left) or a horse-drawn carriage (in front of Hotel Müller, just above ticket office and to the right), but neither gets you to the castle doorstep. The shuttle bus drops you off near Mary's Bridge (Marienbrücke), leaving you a steep, 10-minute downhill walk to the castle—so be sure to see the view from Mary's Bridge *before* hiking down (€1.80 one-way, the €2.60 round-trip is not worth it since you have to hike uphill to the bus stop for your return trip; expect a wait in line, especially if it's raining, of up to 45 minutes—plan accordingly). Carriages (€6 up, €3 down) are slower than walking and stop below Neuschwanstein, leaving you a five-minute uphill hike. Here's the most economical and least strenuous plan: Ride the bus to Mary's Bridge for the view, hike down to Neuschwanstein, and then catch the horse carriage from the castle back down to the parking lot. Carriages also run to Hohenschwangau (€4 up, €2 down).

Entry Procedure: For each castle, tourists jumble at the entry, waiting for their ticket number to light up on the board. When it does, power through the mob (most waiting there are holding higher numbers) and go to the turnstile. Warning: You must use your ticket while your number is still on the board. If you space out while waiting for a polite welcome, you'll miss your entry window and never get in.

Services: A helpful TI, bus stop, ATM, WC (€0.30), and telephones cluster around the main intersection a couple hundred yards before you get to the ticket office (TI open daily April-Sept 10:00-18:00, Oct-March 11:00-17:00, tel. 08362/81980, www.schwangau.de).

Eating: Bring a packed lunch. The park by the Alpsee (the nearby lake) is ideal for a picnic, although you're not allowed to sit on the grass—only on the benches (you could also eat out on the lake in one of the old-fashioned rowboats, rented by the hour in summer). There are no grocery shops by the castles, but you can buy sandwiches and hot dogs across from the TI and at the Hotel Alpenstuben. The restaurants in the "village" at the foot of Europe's Disney castle are mediocre, feeding off the endless droves of hungry, shop-happy tourists. The **Bräustüberl cafeteria** serves the cheapest grub, but isn't likely to be a highlight of your visit (€6-7 gut-bomb grill meals, often with live folk music, daily 10:00-18:00, close to end of road and lake).

Sights at the King's Castles

▲▲▲Hohenschwangau Castle

Standing quietly below Neuschwanstein, the big, yellow Hohenschwangau Castle was Ludwig's boyhood home. Originally built in the 12th century, it was ruined by Napoleon. Ludwig's father, King Maximilian II, rebuilt it in 1830. Hohenschwangau (hoh-en-SHVAHN-gow, loosely translated as "High Swanland") was used by the royal family as a summer hunting lodge until 1912.

The interior decor is harmonious, cohesive, and original—all done in 1835, with paintings inspired by Romantic themes. The Wittelsbach family (which ruled Bavaria for nearly seven centuries) still owns the place (and lived in the annex—today's shop—until the 1970s). As you tour the castle, imagine how the paintings must have inspired young Ludwig. For 17 years, he lived here at his dad's place and followed the construction of his dream castle across the way—you'll see the telescope still set up and directed at Neuschwanstein.

The excellent 30-minute tours give a better glimpse of Ludwig's life than the more-visited and famous Neuschwanstein Castle tour. Tours here are smaller (35 people rather than 60) and more relaxed.

▲▲▲Neuschwanstein Castle

Imagine "Mad" King Ludwig as a boy, climbing the hills above his dad's castle, Hohenschwangau, dreaming up the ultimate fairy-tale castle. Inheriting the throne at the young age of 18, he had the power to make his dream concrete and stucco. Neuschwanstein (noy-SHVAHN-shtine, roughly "New Swanstone") was designed first by a theater-set designer...then by an architect. It looks medieval, but it's modern iron-and-brick construction with a sandstone veneer—only about as old as the Eiffel Tower. It feels like something you'd see at a home show for 19th-century royalty. Built from 1869 to 1886, it's the epitome of the Romanticism popular in 19th-century Europe. Construction stopped with Ludwig's death (only a third of the interior was finished), and within six weeks, tourists were paying to go through it.

During World War II, the castle took on a sinister role. The Nazis used Neuschwanstein as one of their primary secret storehouses for stolen art. After the war, Allied authorities spent a year sorting through and redistributing the art, which filled 49 rail cars from this one location alone. It was the only time the unfinished rooms were put to use.

Today, guides herd groups of 60 through the castle, giving an interesting—if rushed—30-minute tour. You'll go up and down more than 300 steps, through lavish rooms based on Wagnerian opera themes, the king's gilded-lily bedroom, and his extravagant throne room. You'll visit 15 rooms with their original furnishings and fanciful wall paintings. After the tour, before you descend to the king's kitchen, see the 20-minute video about the king's life and passions accompanied by Wagner's music (next to the café, alternates between English and German, schedule board at the entry says what's playing and what's on deck). After the kitchen (state of the art for this high-tech king in its day), you'll see a room lined with fascinating drawings (described in English) of the castle plans, construction, and drawings from 1883 of Falkenstein—a whimsical, over-the-top, never-built castle that makes Neuschwanstein look stubby. Falkenstein occupied Ludwig's fantasies the year he died.

Near the Castles

Mary's Bridge (Marienbrücke)

Before or after the Neuschwanstein tour, climb up to Mary's Bridge to marvel at Ludwig's castle, just as Ludwig did. This bridge was quite an engineering accomplishment 100 years ago. From the bridge, the frisky can hike even higher to the *Beware—Danger of Death* signs and an even more glorious castle view. (Access to the bridge is closed in bad winter weather, but many travelers walk around the barriers to get there—at their own risk, of course.) The

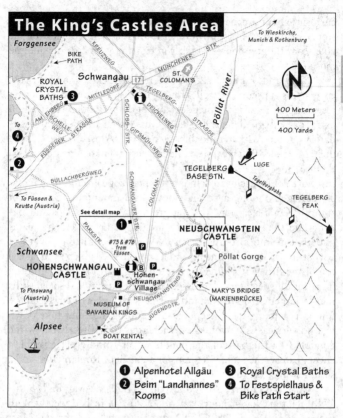

The King's Castles Area

To Wieskirche,
Munich & Rothenburg

Forggensee

BIKE
PATH

KREUZWEG

MÜNCHENER STR.

ST.
COLOMAN'S

Schwangau 17

ROYAL
CRYSTAL
BATHS 3

MITTLEDORF

TEGELBERG-
STR.

DEICHELWEG

SCHLOSS-
STR.

GIPSMÜHLWEG

Pöllat River

To
4

AM EHBERG

SCHELLE-
WEG

FÜSSENER STRASSE

STR.

SCHWANGAUER-
STR.

COLOMAN-
STR.

STRASSE

400 Meters

400 Yards

LUGE

TEGELBERG
BASE STN.

Tegelbergbahn

TEGELBERG
PEAK

2

BULLACHBERGWEG

To Füssen &
Reutte (Austria)

See detail map

1

PARKSTR.

#73 & #78
from Füssen

P

B

P

NEUSCHWANSTEIN
CASTLE

Pöllat Gorge

Schwansee

HOHENSCHWANGAU
CASTLE

i B

Hohen-
schwangau
Village

P

NEUSCHWANSTEINSTR.

JUGENDSTR.

MARY'S BRIDGE
(MARIENBRÜCKE)

To Pinswang
(Austria)

MUSEUM OF
BAVARIAN KINGS

Alpsee

BOAT RENTAL

1 Alpenhotel Allgäu   3 Royal Crystal Baths
2 Beim "Landhannes"   4 To Festspielhaus &
   Rooms   Bike Path Start

most scenic way to descend from Neuschwanstein is to walk up to Mary's Bridge and then follow the signs down the Pöllat Gorge to the TI (*Pöllatschlucht*, 15 minutes longer than walking down the road but worth it, steel walkways and railings make this slippery area safer).

Museum of the Bavarian Kings
(Museum der Bayerischen Könige)

About a five-minute walk from the castles' ticket center, in a former grand hotel on the shore of the Alpsee, this sparkling new exhibit documents the history of the Wittelsbachs, Bavaria's royal family. On display are a handful of paintings, pictures, and treasures, such as Ludwig II's monstrous royal robe and elaborately decorated fairy-tale sword, and the impressive dining set given as a golden-anniversary present to his cousin Ludwig III and his wife, the last reigning Wittelsbachs. A free audioguide lends some context to the family's history—but most of the artifacts and information here are similar to what's displayed inside the two castles. If you have time to kill between your castle reservations and a higher-than-average curiosity about arcane Teutonic dynasties, this might be worth a stop. For most visitors, however, the highlight is the view of the lake from the top floor—which you can enjoy for free outside the museum.

Cost and Hours: €28.50 "Schwanenticket" combo-ticket covers this museum as well as both castles, otherwise €8.50; no reservations required, includes audioguide, guided tour-€1.50 extra, daily April-Sept 9:00-19:00, Oct-March 10:00-18:00, mandatory lockers with refundable €1 deposit, Alpseestrasse 27, tel. 08362/926-4640, www.museumderbayerischenkoenige.de).

▲Tegelberg Gondola

Just north of Neuschwanstein is a fun play zone around the mighty Tegelberg Gondola, a scenic ride to the mountain's 5,500-foot summit. On a clear day, you get great views of the Alps and Bavaria and the vicarious thrill of watching hang gliders and paragliders leap into airborne ecstasy. Weather permitting, scores of adventurous Germans line up and leap from the launch ramp at the top of the lift. With someone leaving every two or three minutes, it's great for spectators. Thrill-seekers with exceptional social skills may talk themselves into a tandem ride with a paraglider. From the top of Tegelberg, it's a steep and demanding 2.5-hour hike down to Ludwig's castle. (Avoid the treacherous trail directly below the gondola.) At the base of the gondola, you'll find a playground, a cheery eatery, the stubby remains of an ancient Roman villa, and a summer luge ride (described next).

Cost and Hours: €18 round-trip, €11.50 one-way, daily 9:00-17:00, closed Nov, 4/hour, last ride at 16:30, in bad weather call first to confirm, tel. 08362/98360, www.tegelbergbahn.de. Most buses #73 and #78 from Füssen continue from the castles to Tegelberg.

▲Tegelberg Luge

Next to the Tegelberg Gondola is a summer luge course *(Sommerrodelbahn)*. A luge is like a bobsled on wheels, with a funky cable system pulling riders (in their sleds) to the top without a ski lift. On your way down, push the stick forward to go faster, pull back to apply brakes, keeping both hands on your stick. To avoid getting into a bumper-to-bumper traffic jam, let the person in front of you get way ahead before you start. You'll emerge from the course with a windblown hairdo and a smile-creased face. This course's stainless-steel track is heated, so it's often dry and open even when drizzly weather shuts down the concrete luges.

Cost and Hours: €3.30/ride, 6-ride shareable card-€11.50, July-Sept daily 10:00-18:00, otherwise same hours as gondola, in winter sometimes opens late if track is wet, in bad weather call first to confirm, waits can be long in good weather, no children under 3, ages 3-8 may ride with an adult, tel. 08362/98360, www.tegelberg-bahn.de.

Sleeping near the King's Castles

(€1 = about $1.30, country code: 49, area code: 08362)
Inexpensive farmhouse B&Bs abound in the Bavarian countryside around Neuschwanstein, offering drivers a decent value. Look for *Zimmer Frei* signs ("room free"/vacancy). The going rate is about €50-65 for a double, including breakfast. Though a bit inconvenient for those without a car, my listings here are a quick taxi ride from the Füssen train station and also close to local bus stops.

$$ Alpenhotel Allgäu is a small, family-run hotel with 18 rooms in a bucolic setting. It's a 15-minute walk from the castle ticket office, not far beyond the humongous parking lot (small Sb without balcony-€48, Sb-€58, perfectly fine older Db-€80, newer Db-€93, Tb-€120, these prices when you book direct, ask about discount with cash and this book, all rooms except one single have porches or balconies—some with castle views, family rooms, free Wi-Fi, elevator, free parking, just before tennis courts at Schwangauer Strasse 37 in the town of Schwangau—don't let your GPS take you to Schwangauer Strasse 37 in Füssen, tel. 08362/81152, fax 08362/987-028, www.alpenhotel-allgaeu.de, info@alpenhotel-allgaeu.de, Frau Reiss).

$ Beim "Landhannes," a 200-year-old working dairy farm run by Conny Schön, rents three creaky but sunny rooms, and keeps flowers on the balconies, big bells and antlers in the halls, and cows in the yard (Sb-€30, Db-€60, €5 less per person for 3 or more nights, also rents apartments with kitchen with a 5-night minimum, cash only, free Wi-Fi, nearby bike rental, poorly signed in the village of Horn on the Füssen side of Schwangau, look for the farm down a tiny lane through the grass 100 yards in front of Hotel Kleiner König, Am Lechrain 22, tel. 08362/8349, www.landhannes.de, info@landhannes.de).

Reutte, Austria

Reutte (ROY-teh, with a rolled *r*), a relaxed Austrian town of 5,700, is located 20 minutes across the border from Füssen. While overlooked by the international tourist crowd, it's popular with Germans and Austrians for its climate. Doctors recommend its "grade 1" air. I like Reutte for the opportunity it offers to simply be in a real community. As an example of how the town is committed to its character, real estate can be sold only to those using it as a primary residence. (Many formerly vibrant alpine towns made a pile of money but lost their sense of community by becoming resorts. They allowed wealthy foreigners—who just drop in for a week or two a year—to buy up all the land, and are now shuttered up and dead most of the time.)

Reutte has one claim to fame among Americans: As Nazi Germany was falling in 1945, Hitler's top rocket scientist, Werner von Braun, joined the Americans (rather than the Russians) in Reutte. You could say that the American space program began here.

Orientation to Reutte

Reutte isn't featured in any other American guidebook. While its generous sidewalks are filled with smart boutiques and lazy coffeehouses, its charms are subtle. It was never rich or important. Its castle is ruined, its buildings have painted-on "carvings," its churches are full, its men yodel for each other on birthdays, and its energy is spent soaking its Austrian and German guests in gemütlichkeit. Most guests stay for a week, so the town's attractions are more time-consuming than thrilling.

Tourist Information

Reutte's TI is a block in front of the train station (Mon-Fri 8:00-12:00 & 14:00-17:00, no midday break July-Aug, Sat 8:30-12:00, closed Sun, Untermarkt 34, tel. 05672/62336, www.reutte.com). Go over your sightseeing plans, ask about a folk evening, pick up city and biking maps, bus schedules, and the *Sommerprogramm* events schedule (in German only), and ask about discounts with the hotel guest cards. Their free informational booklet has a good self-guided town walk.

Ask your hotel to give you an **Aktiv-Card,** which gives free travel on local buses (including the Reutte-Füssen route) as well as small discounts on sights and activities.

Arrival in Reutte

If you're coming by car from Germany, skip the north *(Nord)* exit and take the south *(Süd)* exit into town. For parking in town, blue lines denote pay-and-display spots. There is a free lot (P-1) near the train station on Muhlerstrasse.

While Austria requires a **toll sticker** *(Vignette)* for driving on its expressways (€8/10 days, buy at the border, gas stations, car-rental agencies, or *Tabak* shops), those just dipping into Tirol from Bavaria do not need one—even on the expressway-like bypass around Reutte.

Helpful Hints

Internet Access: Café Alte Post has one expensive terminal in a back room (€7.20/hour, Mon-Fri 7:00-19:00, Sat-Sun 9:00-18:00, Untermarkt 15).

Laundry: There isn't an actual launderette in town, but the recommended Hotel Maximilian lets non-guests use its laundry service (wash, dry, and fold—€16/load).

Bike Rental: Try **Intersport** (€15/day, Mon-Fri 9:00-18:00, Sat 9:00-17:00, closed Sun, Lindenstrasse 25, tel. 05672/62352), or check at the recommended Hotel Maximilian.

Taxi: STM Shuttle Service promises 24-hour service (mobile 0664-113-3277). The car-rental agency listed below also operates taxis.

Car Rental: Reisebüro Köck rents cars at Mühlerstrasse 12 (tel. 05672/62233, www.koeck-tours.com, koeck@koeck-tours.com).

"Nightlife": Reutte is pretty quiet. For any action at all, there's a strip of bars, dance clubs, and Italian restaurants on Lindenstrasse.

Sights in and near Reutte

▲▲Ehrenberg Castle Ensemble (Festungsensemble Ehrenberg)

If Neuschwanstein was the medieval castle dream, Ehrenburg is the medieval castle reality. Once the largest fortification in Tirol, its brooding ruins lie about two miles outside Reutte. Ehrenburg is actually an "ensemble" of four castles, built to defend against the Bavarians and to bottle up the strategic Via Claudia trade route, which cut through the Alps as it connected Italy and Germany. Today, these castles have become a European "castle museum," showing off 500 years of military architecture in one swoop. The European Union is helping fund the project (paying a third of its €9 million cost) because it promotes the heritage of a multinational region—Tirol—rather than a country.

The four parts of the complex are the fortified Klause toll booth on the valley floor, the oldest castle on the first hill above (Ehrenberg), a mighty and more modern castle high above (Schlosskopf, built in the age when cannon positioned there made the original castle vulnerable), and a smaller fourth castle across the valley (Fort Claudia, an hour's hike away). All four were once a single complex connected by walls. Signs posted throughout the site help visitors find their way and explain some background on the region's history, geology, geography, culture, flora, and fauna. (While the castles are free and open all the time, the museum and multimedia show at the fort's parking lot charge admission.)

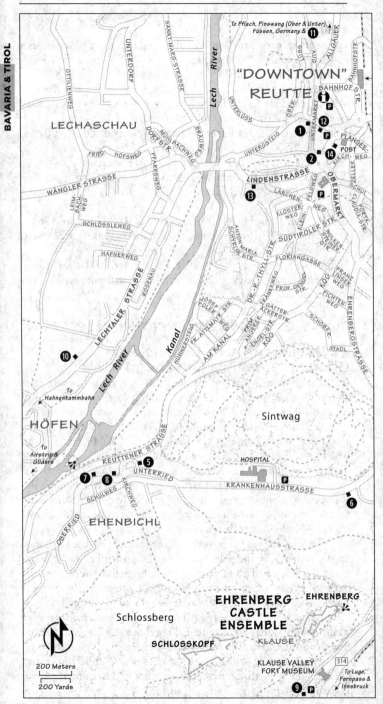

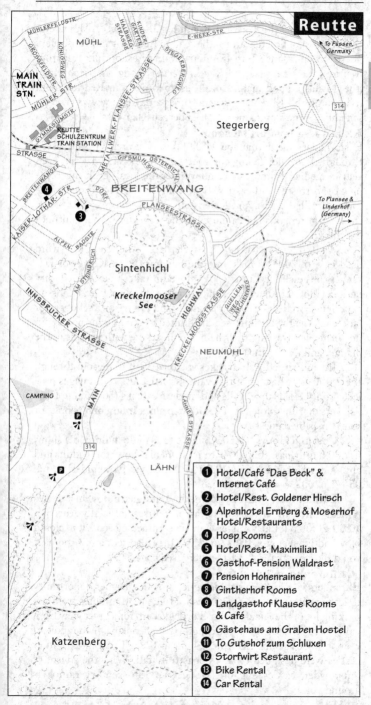

Reutte

MÜHLERFELDSTR.

MÜHL

KINDER-
GARTEN
STRASSE

HALBWEG
STRASSE

E-WERK-STR.

To Füssen,
Germany

MAIN
TRAIN
STN.

GROSSFELDSTR.

KÖNIGSWEG

MÜHLER STR.

GYMNASIUMSTR.

STEGERBERGWEG

314

REUTTE-
SCHULZENTRUM
TRAIN STATION

Stegerberg

STRASSE

BREITENWANGER

METZWERK-PLANSEE-STRASSE

GIPSMÜHLSTR.

OSTERBICHL

DORF

BREITENWANG

PLANSEESTRASSE

To Plansee &
Linderhof
(Germany)

KAISER-LOTHAR-STR.

ALPEN-

BADSEE

Sintenhichl

AM STEINBUCH

*Kreckelmooser
See*

HIGHWAY

KRECKELMOOSSTRASSE

QUELLEN-
WEG
LÄRCHENWEG

INNSBRUCKER STRASSE

NEUMÜHL

CAMPING

P

MAIN

LAHNER STRASSE

314

LÄHN

P

Katzenberg

❶ Hotel/Café "Das Beck" &
Internet Café

❷ Hotel/Rest. Goldener Hirsch

❸ Alpenhotel Ernberg & Moserhof
Hotel/Restaurants

❹ Hosp Rooms

❺ Hotel/Rest. Maximilian

❻ Gasthof-Pension Waldrast

❼ Pension Hohenrainer

❽ Gintherhof Rooms

❾ Landgasthof Klause Rooms
& Café

❿ Gästehaus am Graben Hostel

⓫ To Gutshof zum Schluxen

⓬ Storfwirt Restaurant

⓭ Bike Rental

⓮ Car Rental

Getting to the Castle Ensemble: The Klause, Ehrenberg, and Schlosskopf castles are on the road to Lermoos and Innsbruck. These are a pleasant 30- to 45-minute walk or a short bike ride from Reutte; bikers can use the *Radwanderweg* along the Lech River (the TI has a good map). Local bus #5 runs from Reutte's main train station to Ehrenberg several times a day (see www.vvt.at for schedules—the stop name is "Ehrenberger Klause").

▲Klause Valley Fort Museum

Historians estimate that about 10,000 tons of precious salt passed through this valley (along the route of Rome's Via Claudia) each year in medieval times, so it's no wonder the locals built this complex of fortresses and castles. Beginning in the 14th century, the fort controlled traffic and levied tolls on all who passed. Today, these scant remains hold a museum and a theater with a multimedia show.

While there are no real artifacts here (other than the sword used in A.D. 2008 to make me the honorary First Knight of Ehrenberg), the clever, kid-friendly **museum** takes one 14th-century decade (1360-1370) and attempts to bring it to life. It's a hands-on experience, well-described in English. You can try on a set of armor (and then weigh yourself), see the limited vision knights had to put up with when wearing their helmet, empathize with victims of the plague, and join a Crusade.

The **multimedia show** takes you on a 30-minute spin through the 2,000-year history of this valley's fortresses, with images projected on the old stone walls and modern screens (50-minute English version runs Mon-Fri at 13:00 with a minimum of 5 people, or sometimes by request).

Cost and Hours: €7.50, €3 more to include multimedia show, €17.80 family pass (€20.80 with multimedia show) for 2 adults and any number of kids, daily 10:00-17:00, closed Nov-mid-Dec, tel. 05672/62007, www.ehrenberg.at.

Eating: Next to the museum, the **Landgasthof Klause** serves typical Tirolean meals (€9-15 main courses, officially Tue-Sun 10:00-20:00 but likely longer hours in summer, closed Mon, closed Nov and Jan-Feb, tel. 05672/62213). They also rent a few rooms if you'd like to stay right at Ehrenberg (see page 513).

▲▲Ehrenberg Ruins

Ehrenberg, a 13th-century rock pile, provides a super opportunity to let your imagination off its leash. Hike up 30 minutes from the parking lot of the Klause Valley Fort Museum for a great view from your own private ruins. Ehrenberg (which means "Mountain of Honor") was the first castle here, built in 1296. Thirteenth-century castles were designed to stand boastfully tall. With the advent of gunpowder, castles dug in. (Notice the 18th-century **ramparts** around you.)

Approaching Ehrenberg Castle, look for the small **door** to the left. It's the night entrance (tight and awkward, and therefore safer against a surprise attack). Entering this castle, you go through two doors. Castles allowed step-by-step retreat, giving defenders time to regroup and fight back against invading forces.

Before climbing to the top of the castle, follow the path around to the right to a big, grassy courtyard with commanding views and a fat, restored **turret.** This stored gunpowder and held a big cannon that enjoyed a clear view of the valley below. In medieval times, all the trees approaching the castle were cleared to keep an unobstructed view.

Look out over the valley. The pointy spire marks **Breitenwang,** which was a stop on the ancient Via Claudia. In A.D. 46, there was a Roman camp there. In 1489, after Reutte's bridge crossed the Lech River, Reutte (marked by the onion-domed church) was made a market town and eclipsed Breitenwang in importance. Any gliders circling? They launch from just over the river in Höfen.

For centuries, this castle was the seat of government—ruling an area called the "judgment of Ehrenberg" (roughly the same as today's "district of Reutte"). When the emperor came by, he stayed here. In 1604, the ruler moved downtown into more comfortable quarters, and the castle was no longer a palace.

Now climb to the top of Ehrenberg Castle. Take the high ground. There was no water supply here—just kegs of wine, beer, and a cistern to collect rain.

Ehrenberg repelled 16,000 Swedish soldiers in the defense of Catholicism in 1632. Ehrenberg saw three or four other battles, but its end was not glorious. In the 1780s, a local businessman bought the castle in order to sell off its parts. Later, in the late 19th century, when vagabonds moved in, the roof was removed to make squatting miserable. With the roof gone, deterioration quickened, leaving only this evocative shell and a whiff of history.

▲Schlosskopf

From Ehrenberg, you can hike up another 30 minutes to the mighty Schlosskopf ("Castle Head"). When the Bavarians captured Ehrenberg in 1703, the Tiroleans climbed up to the bluff above it to rain cannonballs down on their former fortress. In 1740, a mighty new castle—designed to defend against modern artillery—was built on this sky-high strategic location. By the end of the 20th century, the castle was completely overgrown with trees—you literally couldn't see it from Reutte. But today the trees have been shaved away, and the castle has been excavated. In 2008, the Castle Ensemble project, led by local architect Armin Walch, opened the site with English descriptions and view platforms. One spot gives spectacular views of the strategic valley. The other looks down on the older Ehrenberg Castle ruins, illustrating the strategic problems presented with the advent of cannon.

In the Town

Reutte Museum (Museum Grünes Haus)

Reutte's cute city museum offers a quick look at the local folk culture and the story of the castles. There are exhibits on Ehrenberg and the Via Claudia, local painters, and more—ask to borrow the English translations.

Cost and Hours: €3; May-Oct Tue-Sat 13:00-17:00, closed Sun-Mon; early Dec-Easter Wed-Sat 14:00-17:00, closed Sun-Tue; closed Easter-end of April and Nov-early Dec; in the bright-green building at Untermarkt 25, around corner from Hotel Goldener Hirsch, tel. 05672/72304, www.museum-reutte.at.

▲▲Tirolean Folk Evening

Ask the TI or your hotel if there's a Tirolean folk evening scheduled. During the summer (July-Aug), nearby towns (such as Höfen on Tuesdays) occasionally put on an evening of yodeling, slap dancing, and Tirolean frolic. These are generally free and worth the short drive. Off-season, you'll have to do your own yodeling. There are also weekly folk concerts featuring the local choir or brass band in Reutte's Zeiller Platz (free, July-Aug only, ask at TI). For listings of these and other local events, pick up a copy of the German-only *Sommerprogramm* schedule at the TI.

Sleeping in and near Reutte

(€1 = about $1.30, country code: 43, area code: 05672)

Reutte is a mellow Füssen with fewer crowds and easygoing locals with a contagious love of life. Come here for a good dose of Austrian ambience and lower prices. While it's not impossible by public transport, staying here makes most sense for those with a car. Reutte is popular with Austrians and Germans, who come here year after year for one- or two-week vacations. The hotels are big, elegant, and full of comfy carved furnishings and creative ways to spend lots of time in one spot. They take great pride in their restaurants, and the owners send their children away to hotel-management schools. All include a great breakfast, but few accept credit cards. Most hotels give a small discount for stays of two nights or longer.

The Reutte TI has a list of 50 private homes that rent out generally good rooms *(Zimmer)* with facilities down the hall, pleasant communal living rooms, and breakfast. Most charge €20 per person per night, and the owners speak little or no English. As these are family-run places, it is especially important to cancel in advance if your plans change. I've listed a few favorites in this section, but the TI can always find you a room when you arrive.

Reutte is surrounded by several distinct "villages" that basically feel like suburbs—many of them, such as Breitenwang, within easy walking distance of the Reutte town center. If you want to hike through the woods Neuschwanstein Castle, stay at Gutshof zum Schluxen. To locate these accommodations, see the Reutte map.

In Central Reutte

These two hotels are the most practical if you're traveling by train or bus.

$$ Hotel "Das Beck" offers 17 clean, sunny rooms (many with balconies) filling a modern building in the heart of town close to the train station. It's a great value, and guests are personally taken care of by Hans, Inge, Tamara, and Birgit. Their small café offers tasty snacks and specializes in Austrian and Italian wines. Expect good conversation overseen by Hans (Sb-€48, Db-€72, Tb suite-€100, Qb suite-€115, ask for Rick Steves price if you book direct, non-smoking, free Internet access and Wi-Fi for Rick Steves readers, free parking, Untermarkt 11, tel. 05672/62522, fax 05672/625-2235, www.hotel-das-beck.at, info@hotel-das-beck.at).

$$ Hotel Goldener Hirsch, also in the center of Reutte just two blocks from the station, is a grand old hotel with 56 rooms and one lonely set of antlers (Sb-€60-64, Db-€90-100, Tb-€135, Qb-€150, less for 2 nights, elevator, free Wi-Fi, restaurant, Mühlerstrasse 1, tel. 05672/62508, fax 05672/625-087, www.goldener-hirsch.at, info@goldener-hirsch.at; Monika, Helmut, and daughters Vanessa and Nina).

In Breitenwang

Now basically a part of Reutte, the older and quieter village of Breitenwang has good *Zimmer* and a fine bakery. It's a 20-minute walk from the Reutte train station: From the post office, follow Planseestrasse past the onion-dome church to the pointy straight-dome church near the two hotels. The Hosps—as well as other B&Bs—are along Kaiser-Lothar-Strasse, the first right past this church. If your train stops at the tiny Reutte-Schulzentrum station, hop out here—you're just a five-minute walk from Breitenwang.

$$ Alpenhotel Ernberg's 26 fresh rooms are run with great care by friendly Hermann, who combines Old World elegance with modern touches. Nestle in for some serious coziness among the carved-wood eating nooks, tiled stoves, and family-friendly backyard (Sb-€55, Db-€90, less for 2 nights, free Wi-Fi, popular restaurant, swimming complex nearby, Planseestrasse 50, tel.

05672/71912, fax 05672/719-1240, www.ernberg.at, info@ern-berg.at).

$$ Moserhof Hotel has 40 new-feeling rooms plus an elegant dining room (Sb-€58, Db-€96, larger Db-€106, confirm you're getting Rick Steves rate when you reserve and pay cash, extra bed-€35, most rooms have balconies, elevator, free Wi-Fi, restaurant, sauna and whirlpool, free parking, Planseestrasse 44, tel. 05672/62020, fax 05672/620-2040, www.hotel-moserhof.at, info@hotel-moserhof.at, Hosp family).

$ Walter and Emilie Hosp rent three rooms in a comfortable, quiet, and modern house two blocks from the Breitenwang church steeple. You'll feel like you're staying at Grandma's (S-€26, D-€42, T-€60, Q-€80, cash only, Kaiser-Lothar-Strasse 29, tel. 05672/65377).

In Ehenbichl, near the Ehrenberg Ruins

The next listings are a bit farther from central Reutte, a couple of miles upriver in the village of Ehenbichl (under the Ehrenberg ruins). From central Reutte, go south on Obermarkt and turn right on Kög, which becomes Reuttener Strasse, following signs to Ehenbichl. These listings are best for car travelers—if you arrive by train you'll need to take a taxi (or brave the infrequent local buses; see www.vvt.at for schedules).

$$ Hotel Maximilian offers 30 rooms at a great value. It includes table tennis, play areas for children (indoors and out), a pool table, and the friendly service of Gabi, Monika, and the rest of the Koch family. They host many special events, and their hotel has lots of wonderful extras such as a sauna and a piano (Sb-€60, Db-€80-90, ask for Rick Steves rate when you book direct, family deals, elevator, free Internet access and Wi-Fi in common areas, pay Wi-Fi in rooms, laundry service-€12/load, good restaurant, Reuttener Strasse 1, tel. 05672/62585, fax 05672/625-8554, www.maxihotel.com, info@hotelmaximilian.at). They rent cars to guests only (€0.72/km, book in advance) and bikes to anyone (€6/half-day, €10/day, more if you're not a guest).

$$ Gasthof-Pension Waldrast, separating a forest and a meadow, is run by the farming Huter family and their dog, Picasso. The place feels hauntingly quiet and has no restaurant, but it's inexpensive and offers 10 nice rooms with generous sitting areas and castle-view balconies (Sb-€39, Db-€66, Tb-€82, Qb-€99; ask about discounts with this book, cash only, non-smoking, free Wi-Fi, free parking; about a mile from Reutte, just off main drag toward Innsbruck, past campground and under castle ruins on Ehrenbergstrasse; tel. & fax 05672/62443, www.waldrasttirol.com, info@waldrasttirol.com, Gerd).

$$ Pension Hohenrainer, a big, quiet, no-frills place, is a good value with 12 modern rooms and some castle-view balconies (Sb-€30-32, Db-€60-64, €1.50/person less for 2 nights, €3/person less for 3 nights, lower prices are for April-June and Sept-Oct, cash only, family rooms, non-smoking rooms, free Internet access and Wi-Fi, swimming pool, restaurant and reception in Gasthof Schlosswirt across the street, follow signs up the road behind Hotel Maximilian into village of Ehenbichl, Unterried 3, tel. 05672/62544 or 05672/63262, fax 05672/62052, www.hohenrainer.at, hohenrainer@aon.at).

$$ Gintherhof is a working farm that provides its guests with fresh milk, butter, and bacon. Annelies Paulweber offers geranium-covered balconies, six nice rooms with carved-wood ceilings, and a Madonna in every corner (Db-€70, Db suite-€75, €3/person less for third night, cash only, free Wi-Fi, Unterried 7, just up the road behind Hotel Maximilian, tel. 05672/67697, www.gintherhof.com, gintherhof@aon.at).

At the Ehrenberg Ruins

$$ Landgasthof Klause café, just below the Ehrenberg ruins and next to the castle museum, rents six non-smoking rooms with balconies on its upper floor. The downside is that the café closes a little early (at 20:00), and you'll need a car to get anywhere besides Ehrenberg (Sb-€40, Db-€80, Tb-€111, ask for Rick Steves discount when you book, discount for 2 or more nights, free Wi-Fi, apartments available, closed Nov and Jan, tel. 05672/62213, www.gasthof-klause.com, gasthof-klause@gmx.at).

A Hostel Across the River

The homey **$ Gästehaus am Graben hostel** has 4-6 beds per room and includes breakfast and sheets. It's lovingly run by the Reyman family—Frau Reyman, Rudi, and Gabi keep the 50-bed place traditional, clean, and friendly. This is a super value less than two miles from Reutte, and the castle views are fantastic. If you've never hosteled and are curious (and have a car or don't mind a bus ride), try it. If traveling with kids, this is a great choice. The double rooms are hotel-grade, and they accept nonmembers of any age (dorm bed-€26, hotel-style Db-€70, cash only, non-smoking, expensive Internet access and Wi-Fi, laundry service-€9, no curfew, closed April and Nov-mid-Dec; from downtown Reutte, cross bridge and follow main road left along river, or take the bus—hourly until 19:30, ask for Graben stop; Graben 1, tel. 05672/626-440, fax 05672/626-444, www.hoefen.at, info@hoefen.at).

In Pinswang

The village of Pinswang is closer to Füssen (and Ludwig's castles), but still in Austria.

$$ Gutshof zum Schluxen gets the "Remote Old Hotel in an Idyllic Setting" award. This family-friendly farm offers rustic elegance draped in goose down and pastels. Its picturesque meadow setting will turn you into a dandelion-picker, and its proximity to Neuschwanstein will turn you into a hiker—the castle is just an hour's walk away (Sb-€52, Db-€90-98, extra person-€29, ask for Rick Steves rate, about 5-10 percent cheaper Nov-March, 5 percent discount for stays of three or more nights, free Wi-Fi in common areas, laundry-€9, mountain-bike rental-€10/day or €5/half-day, restaurant, fun bar, between Reutte and Füssen in village of Pinswang, tel. 05677/89030, fax 05677/890-323, www.schluxen. com, info@schluxen.at). While this hotel works best for drivers, it is reachable by bus from the Füssen train station (every 2 hours, 14 minutes, get off at Pinswang Gemeindeamt stop, verify details with hotel).

To reach Neuschwanstein from this hotel by foot or bike, follow the dirt road up the hill behind the hotel. When the road forks at the top of the hill, go right (downhill), cross the Austria-Germany border (marked by a sign and deserted hut), and follow the narrow paved road to the castles. It's a 1- to 1.5-hour hike or a great circular bike trip (allow 30 minutes; cyclists can return to Schluxen from the castles on a different 30-minute bike route via Füssen).

Eating in Reutte

The hotels here take great pride in serving local cuisine at reasonable prices to their guests and the public. Rather than go to a cheap restaurant, eat at one of the Reutte hotels recommended earlier (**Alpenhotel Ernberg, Moserhof Hotel, Hotel Maximilian,** and **Hotel Goldener Hirsch**). Hotels typically serve €10-15 dinners from 18:00 to 21:00 and are closed one night a week.

Storfwirt is *the* place for a quick and cheap weekday lunch. You can get the usual sausages here, as well as baked potatoes and salads (€5.50-9 daily specials, salad bar, always something for vegetarians, Mon-Fri 9:00-14:30, closed Sat-Sun, Schrettergasse 15, tel. 05672/62640).

Across the street from the Hotel Goldener Hirsch on Mühlerstrasse is a *Bauernladen* (farmer's shop) with rustic sandwiches and meals prepared from local ingredients (Wed-Fri 9:00-18:00, Sat 9:00-12:00, closed Sun-Tue, mobile 0676-575-4588).

Picnic Supplies: **Billa** supermarket has everything you'll need (across from TI, Mon-Fri 7:15-19:30, Sat 7:15-18:00, closed Sun).

Reutte Connections

From Reutte by Train to: Garmisch (every 2 hours, 1 hour), **Munich** (every 2 hours, 2.5 hours, change in Garmisch), **Salzburg** (every 2 hours, 4.5-5.5 hours, quickest with changes in Garmisch and Munich). Train info: tel. 0180-599-6633, www.bahn.com.

By Bus to: Füssen (Mon-Fri almost hourly, Sat-Sun every 3 hours, 45 minutes, €4.10 one-way, buses depart from train station, pay driver).

Taxis cost about €35 one-way to Füssen or the King's Castles.

ROTHENBURG

In the Middle Ages, when Frankfurt and Munich were just wide spots on the road, Rothenburg ob der Tauber was a "free imperial city" beholden only to the Holy Roman Emperor. With a whopping population of 6,000, it was one of Germany's largest. Today, it's the country's best-preserved medieval walled town, enjoying tremendous tourist popularity without losing its charm.

During Rothenburg's heyday, from 1150 to 1400, it was a strategic stop on the trade routes between northern and southern Europe. Now that route is known as the "Romantic Road," linking Frankfurt and Munich through a medieval heartland strewn with picturesque villages, farmhouses, onion-domed churches, and walled cities.

Today, Rothenburg's great trade is tourism: Two-thirds of the townspeople are employed to serve you. While 2.5 million people visit each year, a mere 500,000 spend the night. Rothenburg is yours after dark, when the groups vacate and the town's floodlit cobbles wring some romance out of any travel partner.

Too often, Rothenburg brings out the shopper in visitors before they've had a chance to see the historic town. True, this is a fine place to do your German shopping, but appreciate Rothenburg's great history and sights, too.

Planning Your Time

If time is short, you can make just a two- to three-hour midday stop in Rothenburg, but the town is really best appreciated after the day-trippers have gone home. Spend at least one night in Rothenburg (hotels are cheap and good). With two nights and a day, you'll be able to see more than the essentials and actually relax a little.

Rothenburg in one day is easy, with four essential experiences: the Medieval Crime and Punishment Museum, Tilman Riemenschneider's wood carving in St. Jakob's Church, a walk along the city wall, and the entertaining Night Watchman's Tour. With more time, you could visit several mediocre but entertaining museums, take some scenic hikes and bike rides in the nearby countryside, and enjoy the town's plentiful cafés and shops.

Rothenburg is very busy through the summer and in the Christmas Market month of December. Spring and fall are a joy, but it's pretty bleak from January through March—when most locals are hibernating or on vacation. Many shops stay open on Sundays during the tourist season, but close on Sundays in November and from Christmas to Easter.

There are several Rothenburgs in Germany, so make sure you are going to **Rothenburg ob der Tauber** (not "ob der" any other river); people really do sometimes drive or ride the train to other, nondescript Rothenburgs by accident.

Orientation to Rothenburg

To orient yourself in Rothenburg, think of the town map as a human head. Its nose—the castle garden—sticks out to the left, and the skinny lower part forms a wide-open mouth, with the youth hostel and a recommended hotel in the chin. The town is a delight on foot. No sights or hotels are more than a 15-minute walk from the train station or each other.

Most of the buildings you'll see were in place by 1400. The city was born around its long-gone castle—built in 1142, destroyed in 1356—which was located where the castle garden is now. You can see the shadow of the first town wall, which defines the oldest part of Rothenburg, in its contemporary street plan. Two gates from this wall still survive: the Markus Tower and the White Tower. The richest and biggest houses were in this central part. The commoners built higgledy-piggledy (read: picturesque) houses farther from the center, but still inside the present walls. Rothenburg's classic street scene is the Plönlein ("Little Square"), a picture-perfect tableau of a yellow house wedged between two towers at a diverging road (3 blocks due south of Market Square).

Although Rothenburg is technically in Bavaria, the region around the town is called by its medieval name, Franken (Franconia).

Tourist Information

The TI is on Market Square (May-Oct and Dec Mon-Fri 9:00-18:00, Sat-Sun 10:00-17:00; Nov and Jan-April Mon-Fri 9:00-

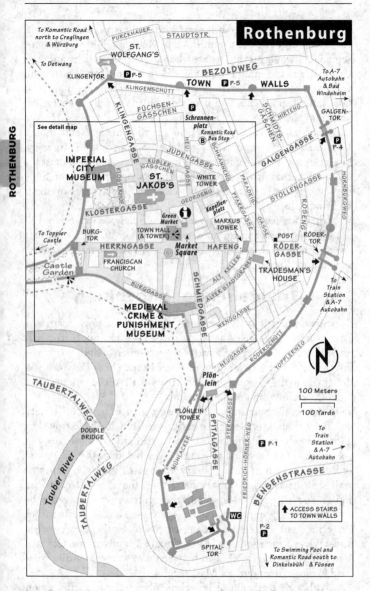

Rothenburg

17:00, Sat 10:00-13:00, closed Sun; Marktplatz 2, tel. 09861/404-800, www.rothenburg.de). If there's a long line, just raid the rack where they keep all the free pamphlets. The free city map comes with a walking guide to the town. The free *RoTour* monthly magazine lists all the events and entertainment (mostly in German); look for current concert listing posters here and at your hotel. Ask about the daily English walking tour at 14:00 (€7, April-Oct and Dec; see "Tours in Rothenburg," later). The TI has one free Internet terminal (15-minute maximum).

Visitors who arrive after closing can check the handy map highlighting which hotels have rooms available, with a free direct phone connection to them; it's just outside the door. A pictorial town map is available for free with this book at the Friese shop, two doors west from the TI (toward St. Jakob's Church; see "Shopping in Rothenburg," later).

Arrival in Rothenburg

By Train: It's a 10-minute walk from the station to Rothenburg's Market Square (following the brown *Altstadt* signs, exit left from station, turn right on Ansbacher Strasse, and head straight into the Middle Ages). Day-trippers can leave luggage in station lockers (€1-2, on platform) or at a local shop (try the Friese shop on Market Square, listed on page 532). Free WCs are behind the snack bar next door to the station. Taxis wait at the station (€5-6 to any hotel).

By Car: You're always allowed to drive into the old town to get to your hotel. Otherwise, driving in the central section around Market Square (roughly, the area within the earlier town walls) is only permitted between 6:00-11:00 and 16:00-19:00. There are no restrictions on driving in the outer parts of the old town (toward the train station and along Spitalgasse). Unless your hotel offers private parking, just plan to park in one of the lots—numbered P-1 through P-5—that line the outside of the town walls (€5/day, buy ticket from *Parkscheinautomat* machines and display, 5-10 minute walk to town). On weekdays, P-5 and a small part of P-4 are free.

Helpful Hints

Festivals: For one weekend each spring, *Biergartens* spill out into the street and Rothenburgers dress up in medieval costumes to celebrate Mayor Nusch's Meistertrunk victory (the story of the draught that saved the town is described under "Meistertrunk Show" on page 523, more info at www.meistertrunk.de). The Reichsstadt festival every September celebrates Rothenburg's history.

Christmas Market: Rothenburg is dead in November, January, and February, but December is its busiest month—the entire town cranks up the medieval cuteness with concerts and costumes, shops with schnapps, stalls filling squares, hot spiced wine, giddy nutcrackers, and mobs of earmuffed Germans. Christmas markets are big all over Germany, and Rothenburg's is considered one of the best. The market takes place each year during Advent. Virtually all sights listed in this chapter are open longer hours during these four weeks. Try to avoid Saturdays and Sundays, when big-city day-trippers really clog the grog.

Internet Access: All of the recommended hotels have Wi-Fi. If you didn't bring a smartphone or laptop, head to the **Nuschhaus Café,** just below Market Square, which has terminals (€3/hour) and Wi-Fi (€2/hour, daily 10:00-20:00, may close earlier in winter, across the street from the Medieval Crime and Punishment Museum at Obere Schmiedgasse 23, tel. 09861/976-838). The **TI** has one free terminal for brief use (maximum 15 minutes).

Laundry: A handy launderette is near the station, off Ansbacher Strasse (€5.50/load, includes soap, English instructions, owner isn't always around to make change so it's smart to bring coins, opens at 8:00, last load Mon-Fri at 18:00, Sat at 14:00, closed Sun, Johannitergasse 9, tel. 09861/2775).

Bike Rental: Consider renting a bike to enjoy the nearby countryside; you can follow the route described on page 531. Two shops, both outside the old town, rent bikes. **Fahrradhaus Krauss** is a little cheaper (€5/6 hours, €10/24 hours, €18/all weekend, no helmets, Mon-Fri 9:00-18:00, Sat 9:00-13:00, closed Sun but ask about arranging return, Ansbacher Strasse 85, tel. 09861/3495, www.fahrradhaus-krauss.de); to reach it from the old town, head toward the train station, then continue along Ansbacher Strasse, bearing right over the train tracks. **Rad & Tat** is a little closer to town (€9/6 hours, €12/24 hours, Mon-Fri 9:00-18:00, Sat 9:00-13:00, closed Sun, Bensenstrasse 17, tel. 09861/87984, www.mietraeder.de); leave the old town toward the train station, but take a right on Erlbacher Strasse, cross the tracks, and look for the shop across the street from the Lidl supermarket.

Taxi: For a taxi, call 09861/2000 or 09861/7227.

Haircuts: At **Salon Wack** (pronounced "vack," not "wack"), Horst and his team speak English and welcome both men and women (wash and cut: €21 for men, €32-39 for women; Tue-Fri 8:00-12:00 & 13:30-18:00, Sat 8:30-14:00, closed Sun-Mon, in the old center just off Wenggasse at Goldene Ringgasse 8, tel. 09861/7834).

Swimming: Rothenburg has a fine swimming complex, with a heated outdoor pool *(Freibad)* from mid-May to mid-September, and an indoor pool and sauna the rest of the year. It's about a 15-minute walk south of the Spitaltor along the main road toward Dinkelsbühl (adults-€4, kids-€2; outdoor pool Fri-Tue 9:00-20:00, Wed 6:30-20:00, Thu 10:00-20:00; indoor pool

Mon 14:00-21:00, Tue-Thu 9:00-21:00, Fri-Sun 9:00-18:00; Nördlinger Strasse 20, tel. 09861/4565).

Tours in Rothenburg

▲▲Night Watchman's Tour

This tour is flat-out the most entertaining hour of medieval wonder anywhere in Germany. The Night Watchman (a.k.a. Hans-Georg Baumgartner) jokes like a medieval Jerry Seinfeld as he lights his lamp and takes tourists on his rounds, telling slice-of-gritty-life tales of medieval Rothenburg (€7, teens-€4, free for kids 12 and under, mid-March-Dec nightly at 20:00, in English, meet at Market Square, www.nightwatchman.de). This is the best evening activity in town. Night Watchman fans can often meet him in person at his wife's store, Kleiderey, during the day (see "Shopping in Rothenburg," later).

Old Town Historic Walk

The TI offers 1.5-hour guided walking tours in English (€7, April-Oct and Dec daily at 14:00, no English tours in Nov or Jan-March, departs from Market Square). Take this tour for the serious side of Rothenburg's history, and to make sense of the town's architecture; you won't get as much of that on the fun—and completely different—Night Watchman's Tour. It would be a shame not to take advantage of this informative tour just because you took the other.

Local Guides

A local historian can really bring the ramparts alive. Prices are standardized (€68/1.5 hours, €86/2 hours). Reserve a guide by emailing the TI (info@rothenburg.de; more info under "Guided Tours" at www.rothenburg.de). I've had good experiences with **Martin Kamphans,** who also works as a potter (tel. 09861/7941, www.stadtfuehrungen-rothenburg.de, post@stadtfuehrungen-rothenburg.de).

Self-Guided Walk

Welcome to Rothenburg

This one-hour circular walk weaves Rothenburg's top sights together.
• *Start the walk on Market Square.*

Market Square Spin-Tour

Stand at the bottom of Market Square (10 feet below the wooden post on the corner) and spin 360 degrees clockwise, starting with the Town Hall tower. Now do it again, this time more slowly, following these notes:

ROTHENBURG

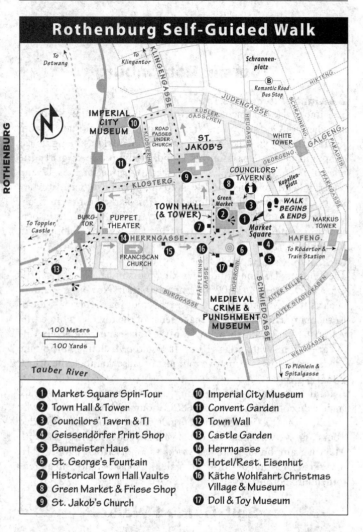

Rothenburg Self-Guided Walk

① Market Square Spin-Tour
② Town Hall & Tower
③ Councilors' Tavern & TI
④ Geissendörfer Print Shop
⑤ Baumeister Haus
⑥ St. George's Fountain
⑦ Historical Town Hall Vaults
⑧ Green Market & Friese Shop
⑨ St. Jakob's Church
⑩ Imperial City Museum
⑪ Convent Garden
⑫ Town Wall
⑬ Castle Garden
⑭ Herrngasse
⑮ Hotel/Rest. Eisenhut
⑯ Käthe Wohlfahrt Christmas Village & Museum
⑰ Doll & Toy Museum

Town Hall and Tower: Rothenburg's tallest spire is the Town Hall tower (Rathausturm). At 200 feet, it stands atop the old Town Hall, a white, Gothic, 13th-century building. Notice the tourists enjoying the best view in town from the black top of the tower (€2 and a rigorous but interesting climb, 214 steps, narrow and steep near the top—watch your head, April-Oct daily 9:30-12:30 & 13:00-17:00, closed Nov-March, enter on Market Square through middle arch of new Town Hall). After a fire in 1501 burned down part of the original building, a new Town Hall was built alongside what survived of the old one (fronting the square). This half of the rebuilt complex is in the Renaissance style from 1570.

Meistertrunk Show: At the top of Market Square stands the proud Councilors' Tavern (clock tower from 1466). In its day, the city council—the rich guys who ran the town government—drank here. Today, it's the TI and the focus of most tourists' attention when the little doors on either side of the clock flip open and the wooden figures (from 1910) do their thing. Be on Market Square at 11:00, 12:00, 13:00, 14:00, 15:00, 20:00, 21:00, or 22:00 for the ritual gathering of the tourists to see the less-than-breathtaking re-enactment of the Meistertrunk ("Master Draught") story:

In 1631, in the middle of the Thirty Years' War, the Catholic army took the Protestant town and was about to do its rape, pillage, and plunder thing. As was the etiquette, the mayor had to give the conquering general a welcoming drink. The general enjoyed a huge tankard of local wine. Feeling really good, he told the mayor, "Hey, if you can drink this entire three-liter tankard of wine in one gulp, I'll spare your town." The mayor amazed everyone by drinking the entire thing, and Rothenburg was saved.

While this is a nice story, it was dreamed up in the late 1800s for a theatrical play designed (effectively) to promote a romantic image of the town. In actuality, if Rothenburg was spared, it happened because it bribed its way out of a jam. It was occupied and ransacked several times in the Thirty Years' War, and it never recovered—which is why it's such a well-preserved time capsule today.

For the best show, don't watch the clock; watch the open-mouthed tourists gasp as the old windows flip open. At the late shows, the square flickers with camera flashes.

Bottom of Market Square: At the bottom end of the square, the cream-colored building on the corner has a fine **print shop** around back (described under "Shopping in Rothenburg," later). Adjoining that is the **Baumeister Haus,** featuring a famous Renaissance facade with statues of the seven virtues and the seven vices—the former supporting the latter. The statues are copies; the originals are in the Imperial City Museum (described later on this walk). The green house below that is the former home of the 15th-century Mayor Toppler (it's now the recommended Gasthof Goldener Greifen).

Keep circling to the big 17th-century **St. George's fountain.** The long metal gutters slid, routing the water into the villagers' buckets. Rothenburg had an ingenious water system. Built on a rock, it had one real source above the town, which was plumbed to serve a series of fountains; water flowed from high to low through Rothenburg. Its many fountains had practical functions beyond providing drinking water (some were stocked with fish on market days and during times of siege). Water was used for fighting fires, and because of its plentiful water supply—and its policy of requiring relatively wide lanes as fire breaks—the town never burned entirely, as so many neighboring villages did.

Two fine buildings behind the fountain show the old-time lofts with warehouse doors and pulleys on top for hoisting. All over town, lofts were filled with grain and corn. A year's supply was required by the city so they could survive any siege. The building behind the fountain is an art gallery showing off work by members of the local artists' association (free, Tue-Sun 14:00-18:00, closed Mon). To the right is Marien Apotheke, an old-time pharmacy mixing old and new in typical Rothenburg style.

The broad street running under the Town Hall tower is **Herrngasse.** The town originated with its castle (built in 1142 but now long gone; only the castle garden remains). Herrngasse connected the castle to Market Square. The last leg of this circular walking tour will take you from the castle garden up Herrngasse and back here. For now, walk a few steps down Herrngasse and stop by the arch under the Town Hall tower (between the new and old town halls). On the left wall are the town's measuring rods—a reminder that medieval Germany was made of 300 independent little countries, each with its own weights and measures. Merchants and shoppers knew that these were the local standards: the rod (4.3 yards), the *Schuh* ("shoe," roughly a foot), and the *Ell* (from elbow to fingertip—four inches longer than mine...try it). Notice the protruding cornerstone. These are all over town—originally to protect buildings from reckless horse carts (and vice versa).

• *Under the arch, you'll find the...*

▲Historical Town Hall Vaults (Historiengewölbe)

This grade-schoolish little museum gives a waxy but interesting look at Rothenburg during the Catholics-vs.-Protestants Thirty Years' War. With helpful English descriptions, it offers a look at "the fateful year 1631," a replica of the mythical Meistertrunk tankard, and a dungeon complete with three dank cells and some torture lore.

Cost and Hours: €2.50, daily May-Oct 9:30-17:30, shorter hours April and Dec, closed Nov and Jan-March, tel. 09861/86751.

• *Leaving the museum, turn left (past a much-sketched-and-photographed venerable door), and walk through the courtyard to a square called...*

Green Market (Grüner Markt)

Once a produce market, this parking lot fills with Christmas shops during December. Notice the clay-tile roofs. These "beaver tail" tiles became standard after thatched roofs were outlawed to prevent fires. Today, all of the town's roofs are made of these. The little fences keep the snow from falling, and catch tiles that blow off during storms. The free public WC is on your left, the recommended Friese shop is on your right, and straight ahead is St. Jakob's Church.

Outside the church, you'll see 14th-century statues (mostly original) showing Jesus praying at Gethsemane, a common feature of Gothic churches. The artist is anonymous, because in the Gothic age (pre-Albrecht Dürer), artists were just nameless craftspeople working only for the glory of God. Five yards to the left (on the wall), notice the nub of a sandstone statue—a rare original, looking pretty bad after 500 years of weather and, more recently, pollution. Most original statues are now in the city museum. The better-preserved statues you see on the church are copies.

• If it's your wedding day, take the first entrance. Otherwise, use the second (downhill) door to enter…

▲▲St. Jakob's Church (St. Jakobskirche)

Rothenburg's main church is home to Tilman Riemenschneider's breathtaking, wood-carved *Altar of the Holy Blood*.

Cost and Hours: €2, worthwhile 45-minute audioguide-€2, daily April-Oct 9:00-17:15, Dec 10:00-16:45, Nov and Christmas-March 10:00-12:00 & 14:00-16:00, on Sun wait to enter until services end at 10:45, free helpful English info sheet, concerts and tour schedule posted on the door; guided tours in English for no extra charge Sat at 15:00 April-Oct.

Visiting the Church: Built in the 14th century, this church has been Lutheran since 1544. The **interior** was "purified" by Romantics in the 19th century—cleaned of everything Baroque or not original and refitted in the Neo-Gothic style. (For example, the baptismal font and the pulpit above the second pew *look* Gothic, but are actually Neo-Gothic.) The stained-glass windows behind the altar, which are most colorful in the morning light, are originals from the 1330s.

At the back of the church, take the stairs that lead up behind the pipe organ. In the loft, you'll find the artistic highlight of Rothenburg and perhaps the most wonderful wood carving in all of Germany: the glorious 500-year-old, 35-foot-high *Altar of the Holy Blood*. Tilman Riemenschneider, the Michelangelo of German woodcarvers, carved this from 1499 to 1504 to hold a precious rock-crystal capsule (set in a cross) that contains a scrap of tablecloth miraculously stained in the shape of a cross by a drop of communion wine. The altar is a realistic commotion, showing that Riemenschneider—while a High Gothic artist—was ahead of his time. Below, in the scene of the Last Supper, Jesus gives Judas a piece of bread, marking him as the traitor, while John lays his head on Christ's lap. Everything is portrayed exactly as described in the Bible. On the left: Jesus enters a walled city. (Historians dispute whether it's Jerusalem, in keeping with the altar's Holy Week theme, or Jericho—notice the man in the tree, who could be Jericho's shy tax collector Zacchaeus.) Notice the fun attention to detail—down to the nails on the horseshoe. On the right: Jesus prays in the Garden of Gethsemane. Judas, with his big bag of cash, could be removed from the scene—illustrated by photos on the wall nearby—as was the tradition for the four days leading up to Easter.

Head back down the stairs to the church's main hall. Go up front to take a close look at the **main altar** (from 1466, by Friedrich Herlin). Below Christ are statues of six saints. St. James (Jakob in German) is the one with the shell. He's the saint of pilgrims, and this church was a stop on the medieval pilgrimage route to Santiago ("St. James" in Spanish) de Compostela in Spain. Study the painted panels—ever see Peter with spectacles? Go around the back of the altarpiece and look at the doors (upper left)—you'll see a painting of Rothenburg's Market Square in the 15th century, looking much like it does today, with the exception of the full-Gothic Town Hall (as it was before the big fire of 1501). Notice Christ's face on the veil of Veronica (center of back side). It follows you as you walk from side to side—this must have given the faithful the religious heebie-jeebies four centuries ago.

The **small altar** to the left is also worth a look. It's a century older than the main altar. Notice the unusual Trinity: the Father and Son are literally bridged by a dove, which represents the Holy Spirit. Stepping back, you can see that Jesus is standing on a skull—clearly "overcoming death."

Before leaving the front of the church, notice the old **medallions** above the carved choir stalls. They feature the coats of arms of Rothenburg's leading families and portraits of city and church leaders.

• *Leave the church and, from its outside steps, walk around the corner to the right and under the chapel (built over the road). Go two blocks down Klingengasse and stop at the corner of the street called Klosterhof. Looking down Klingengasse, you see the...*

Klingentor

This cliff tower was Rothenburg's water reservoir. From 1595 until 1910, a copper tank high in the tower provided clean spring water (pumped up by river power) to the privileged. To the right of the Klingentor is a good stretch of wall rampart to walk. To the left, the wall is low and simple, lacking a rampart because it guards only a cliff. Now find the shell decorating a building on the street corner next to you. That's the symbol of St. James (pilgrims commemorated their visit to Santiago de Compostela with a shell), indicating that this building is associated with the church.

• *Turn left down Klosterhof, passing the shell and, on your right, the colorful, recommended Altfränkische Weinstube am Klosterhof pub, to reach the...*

▲Imperial City Museum (Reichsstadt-Museum)

You'll get a scholarly sweep through Rothenburg's history at this museum, housed in a former Dominican convent. Cloistered nuns used the lazy Susan embedded in the wall (to the right of the museum door) to give food to the poor without being seen.

Just follow the *Rundgang/Tour* signs. Highlights include the *Rothenburg Passion*, a 12-panel series of paintings from 1492 showing scenes leading up to Christ's crucifixion (in the *Konventsaal*); an exhibit of Jewish culture in Rothenburg through the ages *(Judaika)*; a 14th-century convent kitchen *(Klosterküche)* with a working model of the lazy Susan and a massive chimney; romantic paintings of the town *(Gemäldegalerie)*; the fine Baumann collection of weapons and armor; and sandstone statues from the church and Baumeister Haus (the seven vices and seven virtues).

Cost and Hours: €4, daily April-Oct 9:30-17:30, Nov-March 13:00-16:00, English info sheet and descriptions, Klosterhof 5, tel. 09861/939-043, www.reichsstadtmuseum.rothenburg.de.

• *Leaving the museum, go around to the right and into the Convent Garden (when locked at night, continue straight to the T-intersection and see the barn three doors to the right).*

Convent Garden

This spot is a peaceful place to work on your tan...or mix a poisoned potion. Monks and nuns, who were responsible for concocting herbal cures in the olden days, often tended herb gardens. Smell (but don't pick) the *Pfefferminze, Juniper* (gin), *Chamomilla* (disinfectant), and *Origanum*. Don't smell the plants in the poison corner (potency indicated by the number of crosses, like stars indicating spiciness on a restaurant menu).

Cost and Hours: Free, daily April-Oct 9:00-19:30, closed Nov-March.

• *Exit opposite from where you entered, angling left through the nuns' garden (site of the now-gone Dominican church), eventually leaving via an arch at the far end. Turn right and go downhill to the...*

Town Wall

This part of the wall (view through bars, look to far right) takes advantage of the natural fortification provided by the cliff, and is therefore much smaller than the ramparts. Angle left along the wall to the big street (Herrngasse), then right under the Burgtor tower. Notice the tiny "eye of the needle" door cut into the big door. If trying to get into town after curfew, you could bribe the guard to

ROTHENBURG

let you through this door (which was small enough to keep out any fully armed attackers).

• *Step through the gate and outside the wall. Look around and imagine being locked out in the year 1400. This was a wooden drawbridge (see the chain slits above). Notice the "pitch nose" mask—designed to pour boiling Nutella on anyone attacking. High above is the town coat of arms: a red castle (roten Burg).*

Castle Garden (Burggarten)

The garden before you was once that red castle (destroyed in the 14th century). Today, it's a picnic-friendly park. The chapel (50 yards into the park on the left) is the only bit of the original castle to survive. It's now a memorial to local Jews killed in a 1298 slaughter. A few steps beyond that is a grapevine trellis that provides a fine picnic spot. If you walk all the way out to the garden's far end, you'll find a great viewpoint (well past the tourists, and considered the best place to kiss by romantic local teenagers). But the views of the lush Tauber River Valley below are just as good from the top end of the park. Facing the town, on the left, a path leads down to the village of Detwang (you can see the church spire below)—a town even older than Rothenburg (for a walk to Detwang, see "A Walk in the Countryside," page 531). To the right is a fine view of the fortified Rothenburg and the "Tauber Riviera" below.

• *Return to the tower, cross carefully under the pitch nose, and hike back up Herrngasse to your starting point.*

Herrngasse

Many towns have a Herrngasse, where the richest patricians and merchants (the *Herren*) lived. Predictably, it's your best chance to see the town's finest old mansions. Strolling back to Market Square, you'll pass the old-time puppet theater (German only, on left) and the Franciscan church (from 1285, oldest in town, on right). The house at #18 is the biggest patrician house on the street. The family, which has lived here for three centuries, disconnected the four old-time doorbells. Their door—big enough to allow a carriage in (with a human-sized door cut into it)—is typical of the age. The Hotel Eisenhut, with its recommended restaurant, is Rothenburg's fanciest hotel and worth a peek inside. The Käthe Wohlfahrt Christmas shops (at Herrngasse 1 and 2; described later, under "Shopping in Rothenburg") are your last, and perhaps greatest, temptations before reaching your starting and ending point: Market Square.

Sights in Rothenburg

Museums Within a Block of Market Square

▲▲Medieval Crime and Punishment Museum (Mittelalterliches Kriminalmuseum)

This museum is the best of its kind, specializing in everything connected to medieval criminal justice. Learn about medieval police, medieval criminal law, and above all, instruments of punishment and torture—even a special cage complete with a metal gag for nags. The museum is more eclectic than its name, and includes exhibits on general history, superstition, biblical art, and temporary displays in a second building. Follow the yellow arrows—the one-way traffic system makes it hard to double back. Exhibits are tenderly described in English.

Cost and Hours: €4.20, daily May-Oct 10:00-18:00, Nov and Jan-Feb 14:00-16:00, Dec and March 13:00-16:00, April 11:00-17:00, last entry 45 minutes before closing, fun cards and posters, Burggasse 3-5, tel. 09861/5359, www.kriminalmuseum.rothenburg.de.

Nearby: If you insist on trying a *Schneeball*, the museum café (located in the next building down Burggasse) sells mini-*Schneeballen* for €0.40 (open May-Oct and Dec Tue-Thu and Sat-Sun, closed Mon and Fri year-round, closed Nov and Jan-April, no museum admission required for café after 13:00).

▲Doll and Toy Museum (Puppen und Spielzeugmuseum)

These two floors of historic *Kinder* cuteness are a hit with many little kids. Pick up the free English binder (just past the entry curtain) for an extensive description of the exhibits.

Cost and Hours: €4, kids 12 and under-€1.50, family ticket-€10, daily March-Dec 9:30-18:00, Jan-Feb 11:00-17:00, just off Market Square, downhill from the fountain at Hofbronnengasse 11-13, tel. 09861/7330, www.spielzeugmuseum.rothenburg.de.

▲German Christmas Museum (Deutsches Weihnachtsmuseum)

This excellent museum, upstairs in the giant Käthe Wohlfahrt Christmas Village shop, tells the history of Christmas decorations. There's a unique and thoughtfully described collection of Christmas-tree stands, mini-trees sent in boxes to WWI soldiers at the front, early Advent calendars, old-time Christmas cards, and a look at tree decorations through the ages—including the Nazi era and when you were a kid. The museum is not just a ploy to get shoppers to spend more money, but a serious collection managed by professional curator Felicitas Höptner.

Cost and Hours: €4, April-Dec daily 10:00-18:00, Jan-March Sat-Sun 10:00-18:00 and irregularly on weekdays, last entry at

17:00, Herrngasse 1, tel. 09861/409-365, www.germanchristmas-museum.com.

More Sights in Rothenburg

▲▲Walk the Wall

Just longer than a mile and a half around, providing great views and a good orientation, this walk can be done by those under six feet tall in less than an hour (unless your camera can't stop snapping). The hike requires no special sense of balance. This walk is covered and is a great option in the rain. Photographers will stay very busy, especially before breakfast or at sunset, when the lighting is best and the crowds have dissipated. You can enter or exit the ramparts at nearly every tower. The best fortifications are in the Spitaltor (south end). The names you see along the way belong to people who donated money to rebuild the wall after World War II, and those who've more recently donated €1,000 per meter for the maintenance of Rothenburg's heritage.

▲▲The Allergic-to-Tourists Wall and Moat Walk

For a quiet and scenic break from the tourist crowds and a chance to appreciate the marvelous fortifications of Rothenburg, consider this hike: From the Castle Garden, go right and walk outside the wall to the Klingentor. At the Klingentor, climb up to the ramparts and walk on the wall past the Galgentor to the Rödertor. Then descend, leave the old town, and hike through the park (once the moat) down to the Spitaltor. Explore the fortifications here before hiking a block up Spitalgasse, turning left to pass the youth hostel, popping back outside the wall, and heading along the upper scenic reaches of the river valley and above the vineyards back to the Castle Garden.

▲Tradesman's House
(Alt-Rothenburger Handwerkerhaus)

See the everyday life of a Rothenburger in the town's heyday in this restored 700-year-old home.

Cost and Hours: €2.50; Easter-Oct Mon-Fri 11:00-17:00, Sat-Sun 10:00-17:00; Dec daily 14:00-16:00; closed Nov and Jan-Easter; near Markus Tower at Alter Stadtgraben 26, tel. 09861/5810.

St. Wolfgang's Church

This fortified Gothic church is built into the medieval wall at the Klingentor. Its dungeon-like passages and shepherd's-dance exhibit are pretty lame.

Cost and Hours: €1.50, Wed-Mon April-Sept 10:00-13:00 & 14:30-17:00, Oct 10:00-16:00, closed Tue and Nov-March.

Near Rothenburg
▲A Walk in the Countryside

From the *Burggarten* (castle garden), head into the Tauber Valley. With your back to town, go down the hill, exiting the castle garden on your left. Once outside the wall, walk around, keeping the castle and town on your right. The trail becomes really steep, taking you down to the wooden covered bridge on the valley floor. Across the bridge, the road goes left to Toppler Castle and right (downstream, with a pleasant parallel footpath) to Detwang.

Toppler Castle (Topplerschlösschen) is cute, skinny, sky-blue, and 600 years old. It was the castle/summer home of the medieval Mayor Toppler. The tower's top looks like a house—a sort of tree fort for grownups. It's in a farmer's garden, and it's open whenever he's around and willing to let you in (€1.50, normally Fri-Sun 13:00-16:00, closed Mon-Thu and Nov, one mile from town center at Taubertalweg 100, tel. 09861/7358). People say the mayor had this valley-floor escape built to get people to relax about leaving the fortified town...or to hide a mistress.

To extend your stroll, walk back to the bridge and follow the river downstream (passing the recommended Unter den Linden beer garden) to the peaceful village of **Detwang.** One of the oldest villages in Franconia (one of Germany's medieval dukedoms), Detwang dates from 968. Like Rothenburg, it has a Riemenschneider altarpiece in its church.

Franconian Bike Ride

To get a fun, breezy look at the countryside around Rothenburg, rent a bike (see "Helpful Hints" on page 519). For a pleasant half-day pedal, escape the old town through the Rödertor, bike along Topplerweg to the Spitaltor, and follow the curvy road down into the river valley. Turn right at the yellow *Leutzenbronn* sign to cross the double-arcaded bridge. From here a peaceful road follows the river downstream to **Detwang,** passing the cute Toppler Castle (described earlier). From Detwang, follow the main road to the old mill, and turn left to follow the *Liebliches Taubertal* bike path signs as far up the Tauber River (direction: Bettwar) as you like. After 2.5 miles, you'll arrive in the sleepy farming town of **Bettwar,** where you can claim a spot among the chickens and the apple trees for a picnic or have a drink at one of the two restaurants in town.

Franconian Open-Air Museum
(Fränkisches Freilandmuseum)

A 20-minute drive from Rothenburg—in the undiscovered "Rothenburgy" town of Bad Windsheim—is an open-air folk museum that, compared with others in Europe, is a bit humble. But it tries very hard and gives you the best look around at traditional rural Franconia.

Cost and Hours: €6, daily mid-March-Sept 9:00-18:00, Oct-mid-Dec 10:00-16:00, closed mid-Dec-mid-March, last entry one hour before closing, tel. 09841/66800, www.freilandmuseum.de.

Shopping in Rothenburg

Be warned...Rothenburg is one of Germany's best shopping towns. Do it here and be done with it. Lovely prints, carvings, wine glasses, Christmas-tree ornaments, and beer steins are popular. Rödergasse is the old town's everyday shopping street. There's also a modern shopping center across the street from the train station.

Christmas Souvenirs

Rothenburg is the headquarters of the **Käthe Wohlfahrt** Christmas trinkets empire, which is spreading across the half-timbered reaches of Europe. In Rothenburg, tourists flock to two Käthe Wohlfahrt stores (at Herrngasse 1 and 2, just off Market Square). Start with the **Christmas Village** (Weihnachtsdorf) at Herrngasse 1. This Christmas wonderland is filled with enough twinkling lights (196,000—mostly LEDs) to require a special electrical hookup. You're greeted by instant Christmas mood music (best appreciated on a hot day in July) and American and Japanese tourists hungrily filling little woven shopping baskets with €5-8 goodies to hang on their trees. (OK, I admit it, my Christmas tree sports a few KW ornaments.) Let the spinning flocked tree whisk you in, but pause at the wall of Steiff stuffed animals, jerking uncontrollably and mesmerizing little kids. The **Christmas Museum** upstairs is described earlier, under "Sights in Rothenburg." The smaller **Christmas Market** (Weihnachtsmarkt), across the street at Herrngasse 2, specializes in finely crafted wooden ornaments. A third, much smaller store is at Untere Schmiedgasse 19. Käthe started the business in Stuttgart in 1964, and it's now run by her son Harald Wohlfahrt, who lives in Rothenburg (all stores open Mon-Sat 9:00-18:00, May-Dec also most Sun 10:00-17:00, Jan-April closed Sun but museum and museum shop open, show this book and ask about discount on official KW products, tel. 09861/409-150, www.wohlfahrt.com or www.bestofchristmas.com).

German Souvenirs

Cuckoo with friendliness, trinkets, and souvenirs, the **Friese shop** has been welcoming my readers for more than 30 years (on the smaller square just off Market Square, west of TI, on corner across from free public WC). They give shoppers with this book tremendous service: show your book for a discount and a free pictorial map (normally €1.50). Anneliese Friese, who runs the place with her son Bernie (ask him about the plaque on the town wall), charges only her cost for shipping and lets tired travelers leave their bags in her back room for free (Mon-Sat 9:00-17:00, Sun 10:00-16:00, Grüner Markt 8, tel. 09861/7166, fax 09861/936-619, anneliese-friese@ gmx.de).

Romantic Prints and Etchings: The Ernst Geissendörfer print shop has sold fine prints, etchings, and paintings on the corner of Market Square since 1908. To find the shop, walk a few steps down Hafengasse (it's on your right, just before the Bosporus Café). If you're interested in more expensive prints and etchings than those on display, ask Frau Geissendörfer to take you upstairs—she'll offer you a free shot of German brandy while you browse. Show this book and ask about a discount off marked prices (May-Dec daily 11:00-18:00; March-April Mon-Sat 11:00-18:00, closed Sun; closed Jan-Feb; Obere Schmiedgasse 1 at corner of Hafengasse, tel. 09861/2005, www.geissendoerfer.de).

At the **Kleiderey,** an offbeat clothing store, the Night Watchman hangs out during the day (it's run by his wife). He's happy to sign autographs (April-Dec Mon-Sat 10:00-18:00, Sun 11:00-17:00; Jan-March open only Sat 11:00-17:00; just below Market Square at Untere Schmiedgasse 7, tel. 09861/938-633). For details on the Night Watchman's entertaining tour, see "Tours in Rothenburg," earlier.

Wine Stuff: You'll recognize local Franconian wines by the shape of the bottle—short, stubby, and round. For characteristic wine glasses, winemaking gear, and the real thing from the town's oldest winemakers, drop by the **Glocke Weinladen am Plönlein** (daily 10:00-18:00, Untere Schmiedgasse 27—see page 543 for info on wine-tasting).

Books: A good bookstore is **Rothenburger Büchermarkt** at Rödergasse 3, on the corner of Alter Stadtgraben (Mon-Sat 9:00-18:30, Sun 10:30-18:00, Jan-April closed Sun).

Mailing Your Goodies Home: You can get handy yellow €2.50 boxes at the old town **post office** (Mon-Tue and Thu-Fri 9:00-13:00 & 14:00-17:30, Wed 9:00-13:00, Sat 9:00-12:00, closed Sun, inside photo shop at Rödergasse 11). The main post office is in the shopping center across from the train station.

Pastries: Those who prefer to eat their souvenirs browse the *Bäckereien* (bakeries). Their succulent pastries, pies, and cakes are pleasantly distracting...but skip the bad-tasting *Rothenburger Schneeballen*. Unworthy of the heavy promotion they receive, *Schneeballen* are bland pie crusts crumpled into a ball and dusted with powdered sugar or frosted with sticky-sweet glop. There's little reason to waste your appetite on a *Schneeball* when you can enjoy a curvy *Mandelhörnchen* (almond crescent cookie), a triangular *Nussecke* ("nut corner"), a round *Florentiner* cookie, a couple of fresh *Krapfen* (like jelly doughnuts), or even just a soft, warm German pretzel.

Sleeping in Rothenburg

Rothenburg is crowded with visitors, but most are day-trippers. Except for the rare Saturday night and during festivals (see page 519), finding a room is easy throughout the year. Competition keeps quality high. If you want to splurge, you'll snare the best value by paying extra for the biggest and best rooms at the hotels I recommend. In the off-season (Nov and Jan-March), hoteliers may be willing to discount.

Train travelers save steps by staying in the area toward the Rödertor (east end of town). Hotels and guest houses will sometimes pick up tired heavy-packers at the station. If you're driving and unable to find where you're sleeping, stop and give them a call. They will likely come rescue you.

Keep your key when out late. Rothenburg's hotels are small, and they often lock the front entrance at about 22:00, asking you to let yourself in through a side door.

In the Old Town

$$$ **Hotel Kloster-Stüble,** deep in the old town near the castle garden, is my classiest listing. Rudolf does the cooking, while Erika—his fun and energetic first mate—welcomes guests. Twenty-one rooms fill two medieval buildings, connected by a modern atrium. The hotel is just off Herrngasse on a tiny side street (Sb-€58-78, traditional Db-€88-108, bigger and more modern Db-€118-128, Tb-€108-146, see website for suites and family rooms, kids 5 and under free, free Internet access, free Wi-Fi in most rooms, Heringsbronnengasse 5, tel. 09861/938-890, fax 09861/938-829, www.klosterstueble.de, hotel@klosterstueble.de).

$$$ **Hotel Spitzweg** is a rustic-yet-elegant 1536 mansion (never bombed or burned) with 10 big rooms, open beams, and endearing hand-painted antique furniture. It's run by gentle Herr Hocher, whom I suspect is the former Wizard of Oz—now retired and in a very good mood (Sb-€65, Db-€85-95, Tb-€115, Qb apartment-€150, non-smoking, elegant breakfast room, free parking, pay Internet access and Wi-Fi at son-in-law's nearby hotel, Paradeisgasse 2, tel. 09861/94290, fax 09861/1412, www.hotel-spitzweg.de, info@hotel-spitzweg.de).

$$$ **Hotel Gerberhaus** is warmly run by Inge and Kurt and daughter Deborah, who mix modern comforts into 20 bright and airy rooms that still maintain a sense of half-timbered elegance. Enjoy the pleasant garden in back (Sb-€65-75, Db-€79-120, Tb-€139-150, Qb-€145-185, Quint/b-€195-205, prices depend on room size; 2-room suite in separate building-€130/2 people, €195/4 people; discount off the second and subsequent nights and a free *Schneeball* if you book direct and pay cash, non-smoking, 4 rooms

---

Sleep Code

(€1 = about $1.30, country code: 49, area code: 09861)
S = Single, **D** = Double/Twin, **T** = Triple, **Q** = Quad, **b** = bathroom, **s** = shower only. Unless otherwise noted, credit cards are accepted, English is spoken, and breakfast is included.

To help you sort easily through these listings, I've divided the accommodations into three categories, based on the price for a standard double room with bath:

$$$ Higher Priced—Most rooms €80 or more.
$$ Moderately Priced—Most rooms between €60-80.
$ Lower Priced—Most rooms €60 or less.

Prices can change without notice; verify the hotel's current rates online or by email.

---

have canopied 4-poster *Himmel* beds, free Internet access, free Wi-Fi with this book, laundry-€7, close to P-1 parking lot, Spitalgasse 25, tel. 09861/94900, fax 09861/86555, www.gerberhaus. rothenburg.de, gerberhaus@t-online.de). The downstairs café and *Biergarten* serve good soups, salads, and light lunches.

$$$ Gasthof Goldener Greifen, once Mayor Toppler's home, is a big, traditional, 600-year-old place with 14 spacious rooms and all the comforts. It's run by a helpful family staff and creaks with rustic splendor (Sb-€48, small Db-€65, big Db-€85-90, Tb-€105-125, Qb-€125-150, 10 percent less for 3-night stays, non-smoking, pay Wi-Fi, full-service laundry-€8, free and easy parking, half a block downhill from Market Square at Obere Schmiedgasse 5, tel. 09861/2281, fax 09861/86374, www.gasthof-greifen-rothenburg. de, info@gasthof-greifen-rothenburg.de, Brigitte and Klingler family). The family also has a couple of free loaner bikes for guests and runs a good restaurant, serving meals in the back garden or dining room.

$$ Hotel Altfränkische Weinstube am Klosterhof is *the* place for well-heeled bohemians. Mario, Hanne, and their lovely daughter Viktoria rent six cozy rooms above their dark and evocative pub in a 600-year-old building. It's an upscale *Lord of the Rings* atmosphere, with TVs, modern showers, open-beam ceilings, and canopied four-poster beds. They also have two similarly decorated rooms of equal quality in another building a couple of doors away (Sb-€59, Db-€65, bigger Db-€78, Db suite-€89, Tb-€88-98, cash preferred, kid- and dog-friendly, free Wi-Fi, free parking, off Klingengasse at Klosterhof 7, tel. 09861/6404, fax 09861/6410, www. altfraenkische.de, info on second building at www.am-klosterhof.

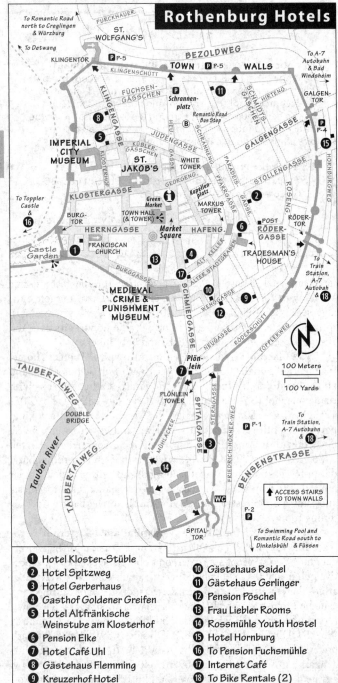

Rothenburg Hotels

1. Hotel Kloster-Stüble
2. Hotel Spitzweg
3. Hotel Gerberhaus
4. Gasthof Goldener Greifen
5. Hotel Altfränkische Weinstube am Klosterhof
6. Pension Elke
7. Hotel Café Uhl
8. Gästehaus Flemming
9. Kreuzerhof Hotel
10. Gästehaus Raidel
11. Gästehaus Gerlinger
12. Pension Pöschel
13. Frau Liebler Rooms
14. Rossmühle Youth Hostel
15. Hotel Hornburg
16. To Pension Fuchsmühle
17. Internet Café
18. To Bike Rentals (2)

ROTHENBURG

de, altfraenkische-weinstube@web.de). Their pub is a candlelit classic—and a favorite with locals, serving hot food to Hobbits until 22:30, and closing at 1:00 in the morning. Drop by on Wednesday evening (19:00-24:00) for the English Conversation Club (see "Meet the Locals" on page 543).

$$ Pension Elke, run by spry Erich Endress and his son Klaus, rents 12 modern and comfy rooms above the family grocery store. Guests who jog are welcome to join Klaus on his half-hour run around the city every evening at 19:30 (S-€32, Sb-€40, D-€45-52, Db-€62-65, price depends on room size, extra bed-€18, ask about discount with this book if you plan to stay at least 2 nights, cash only, free Internet access and Wi-Fi; reception in grocery store until 19:00, otherwise go around corner to back of building and ring bell at top of stairs; near Markus Tower at Rödergasse 6, tel. 09861/2331, fax 09861/935-355, www.pension-elke-rothenburg. de, info@pension-elke-rothenburg.de).

$$ Hotel Café Uhl offers 12 fine rooms over a pastry shop (Sb-€39-59, Db-€69-89, Tb-€89-109, Qb-€119-129, price depends on room size, ask about discount with this book if paying cash and booking direct, reception in café, pay Internet access, free Wi-Fi, parking-€6/day, closed Jan, Plönlein 8, tel. 09861/4895, fax 09861/92820, www.hotel-uhl.de, info@hotel-uhl.de, Paul and Robert the baker).

$$ Gästehaus Flemming has seven tastefully modern, fresh, and comfortable rooms and a peaceful terrace and garden behind St. Jakob's Church (Sb-€49, Db-€64, Tb-€87, family suite, non-smoking, pay Wi-Fi, Klingengasse 21, tel. 09861/92380, fax 09861/976-384, www.gaestehaus-flemming.de, gaestehaus-flemming@t-online.de, Regina).

$$ Kreuzerhof Hotel offers nine pleasant rooms surrounding a courtyard on a quiet side street near the Rödertor (Sb-€48, Db-€72, large Db-€92, Tb-€95, Qb-€119, 6-bed room-€159, family deals, non-smoking, free Internet access and Wi-Fi, laundry-€6/load, parking in courtyard-€3/day, Millergasse 2-6, tel. 09861/3424, fax 09861/936-730, www.kreuzerhof.eu, info@kreuzerhof-rothenburg.de, Heike and Walter Maltz).

$$ Gästehaus Raidel rents eight rooms in a 500-year-old house filled with beds and furniture, all handmade by friendly Norry Raidel himself. The ramshackle ambience makes me want to sing the *Addams Family* theme song—but the place has a rare, time-passed family charm. Norry, who plays in a Dixieland band, has invented a fascinating hybrid saxophone/trombone called the Norryphone...and loves to jam (Sb-€45, Db-€69, Tb-€90, Qb suite-€120, cash only, free Wi-Fi, Wenggasse 3, tel. 09861/3115, Norry asks you to use the reservations form at www.romanticroad. com/raidel).

$ Gästehaus Gerlinger, a fine value, has four comfortable rooms in a pretty 16th-century house with a small terrace for guests (Db-€59, Tb-€75, cash only, non-smoking, free Wi-Fi, easy parking, Schlegeleinsweth 10, tel. 09861/87979, mobile 0171-690-0752, www.pension-gerlinger.de, info@pension-gerlinger.de, Hermann).

$ Pension Pöschel is simple and friendly, with six plain rooms in a concrete but pleasant building, and an inviting garden out back. Only one room has a private shower and toilet (S-€25, D-€45, Db-€50, T-€60, Tb-€65, small kids free, cash only, non-smoking, free Wi-Fi, Wenggasse 22, tel. 09861/3430, mobile 0170-700-7041, www.pensionpoeschel.de, pension.poeschel@t-online.de, Bettina).

$ Frau Liebler rents two large, modern, ground-floor rooms with kitchenettes. They're great for those looking for real privacy—you'll have your own room fronting a quiet cobbled lane just below Market Square. On the top floor is an attractive two-bedroom apartment (Db-€44, apartment-€55, extra bed-€12, show this book and ask about discount for stays of 2 or more nights, breakfast-€6, cash only, non-smoking, free Wi-Fi, laundry-€5, behind Christmas shop at Pfäffleinsgässchen 10, tel. 09861/709-215, fax 09861/709-216, www.gaestehaus-liebler.de). Frau Liebler also has three more apartments on Rödergasse, a couple blocks away.

$ Rossmühle Youth Hostel rents 186 beds in two buildings. While it's mostly four- to six-bed dorms, this charming hostel also has 15 doubles. Reception is in the droopy-eyed building—formerly a horse-powered mill, it was used when the old town was under siege and the river-powered mill was inaccessible (dorm bed-€24, bunk-bed Db-€56, guests over 26 pay €4 extra unless traveling with a family, nonmembers pay €3 extra, includes breakfast and sheets, all-you-can-eat dinner-€6, free Wi-Fi in common areas, self-serve laundry including soap-€5, close to P-1 parking lot, entrance on Rossmühlgasse, tel. 09861/94160, fax 09861/941-620, www.rothenburg.jugendherberge.de, rothenburg@jugendherberge.de).

Outside the Wall

$$$ Hotel Hornburg, a grand 1903 mansion, is close to the train station, a two-minute walk outside the wall. With groomed grounds, gracious sitting areas, and 10 spacious, tastefully decorated rooms, it's a super value (Sb-€61-78, Db-€78-110, Tb-€100-130, non-smoking, family-friendly, dogs welcome—ask for pet-free room if you're allergic, free Internet access and Wi-Fi; if walking, exit station and go straight on Ludwig-Siebert-Strasse, then turn left on Mannstrasse until you're 100 yards from town wall; if driving, the hotel is across from parking lot P-4; Hornburgweg 28, at intersection with Mannstrasse, tel. 09861/8480, fax 09861/5570, www.hotel-hornburg.de, info@hotel-hornburg.de, Gabriele and Martin).

$$ Pension Fuchsmühle is a guest house in a renovated old mill on the river below the castle end of Rothenburg, across from the Toppler Castle. It feels rural, but is a pleasant (though steep) 15-minute hike to Market Square, and a €10 taxi ride from the train station. Alex and Heidi Molitor, a young couple with kids, offer eight bright, modern light-wood rooms. The building's electric power comes from the millwheel by the entrance, with excess sold to the grid (Sb-€52, Db-€74, Tb-€96, Qb-€132, 3-room suite-€165/5 people or €198/6 people, less if you stay at least 3 days, includes healthy farm-fresh breakfasts—or €7 less per person if you don't want breakfast, non-smoking, free Wi-Fi, free parking, laundry facilities, flashlights provided for your walk back after dark, Taubertalweg 101, tel. 09861/92633, fax 09861/933-895, www.fuchsmuehle.de, fuchsmuehle@t-online.de).

Eating in Rothenburg

Many restaurants take a mid-afternoon break, and stop serving lunch at 14:00 and dinner as early as 20:00. My recommendations are all within a five-minute walk of Market Square. While all survive on tourism, many still feel like local hangouts. Your choices are typical German or ethnic. Any bakery will sell you a sandwich for a couple of euros.

Traditional German Restaurants

Gasthof Goldener Greifen is in a historic building just off the main square. The Klingler family serves quality Franconian food at a good price...and with a smile. The wood is ancient and polished from generations of happy use, and the ambience is practical rather than posh—and that's just fine with me (€8-15 main courses, €12 three-course daily specials, €10 one-plate specials include a drink, super-cheap kids' meals, Mon-Sat 11:30-21:00, may open Sun 11:30-14:00, Obere Schmiedgasse 5, tel. 09861/2281).

Hotel Restaurant Kloster-Stüble, on a small street off Herrngasse near the castle garden, is a classy place for delicious and beautifully presented traditional cuisine, including homemade *Maultaschen* (similar to ravioli). Chef Rudy's food is better than his English, so head waitress Erika makes sure communication goes smoothly. The shady terrace is nice on a warm summer evening. I prefer their traditional dining room to the stony, sleek, modern room (€10-16 main courses, Thu-Tue 11:00-14:00 & 18:00-21:00, closed Wed, Heringsbronnengasse 5, tel. 09861/938-890).

Bürgerkeller is a typical European cellar restaurant with a quiet, calming atmosphere, medieval murals, pointy pikes, and a few sidewalk tables for good weather. Without a burger in sight (*Bürger* means "townsman"), English-speaking Harry Terian and his family pride themselves on quality local cuisine, offering a small but inviting menu and reasonable prices. Harry likes oldies, and you're welcome to look over his impressive playlist and request your favorite music (€7-14 main courses, cash only, Thu-Tue 12:00-14:00 & 17:30-20:30, closed Wed, near bottom of Herrngasse at #24, tel. 09861/2126).

Altfränkische Weinstube am Klosterhof seems designed for gnomes to celebrate their anniversaries. At this very dark pub, classically candlelit in a 600-year-old building, Mario whips up gourmet pub grub (€7-14 main courses, hot food served Wed-Mon 18:00-22:30, closes at 1:00 in the morning, closed Tue, off Klingengasse at Klosterhof 7, tel. 09861/6404). If you'd like dinner company, drop by on Wednesday evening, when the English Conversation Club has a big table reserved from 19:00 on (see "Meet the Locals," page 543). You'll eat well and with new friends—both travelers and locals.

Alter Keller is a modest, inexpensive restaurant with outdoor tables on a peaceful square just a couple blocks off Market Square. The menu has German classics at reasonable prices—*Spätzle*, schnitzel, trout, and roasts—as well as steak (€8-14 main dishes, steaks higher-priced, Mon 17:00-22:00, Wed-Sun 11:00-22:00, closed Tue, Alter Keller 8, tel. 09861/2268).

Eisenhut Restaurant, in Hotel Eisenhut, is a fine place for a dress-up splurge with surprisingly reasonable prices. You'll enjoy elegantly presented dishes, both traditional and international, with formal service. Sit in their royal dining room or on their garden sun terrace (€17-27 main courses, fixed-price meals from €28, daily 12:00-14:30 & 18:30-21:30, Herrngasse 3, tel. 09861/7050).

Reichs-Küchenmeister is a forgettable big-hotel restaurant, but on a balmy evening, its pleasant tree-shaded terrace overlooking St. Jakob's Church is hard to beat (€12-23 main courses, €7-10 *Flammkuchen*—German-style pizza, daily 11:00-23:00, Kirchplatz 8, tel. 09861/9700).

Breaks from Pork and Potatoes

Pizzeria Roma is the locals' favorite for €6-7 pizza and pastas, with good Italian wine. The Magrini family moved here from Tuscany in 1970 (many Italians immigrated to Germany in those years), and they've been cooking pasta for Rothenburg ever since (Thu-Tue 11:00-24:00, closed Wed and mid-Aug-mid-Sept, Galgengasse 19, tel. 09861/4540, Ricardo).

China-Restaurant Peking, on the picturesque Plönlein square, has two-course lunch specials (€5-7, Mon-Sat only), and

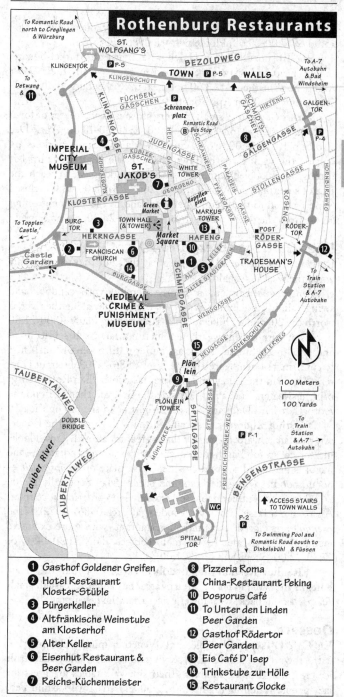

Rothenburg Restaurants

ROTHENBURG

1. Gasthof Goldener Greifen
2. Hotel Restaurant Kloster-Stüble
3. Bürgerkeller
4. Altfränkische Weinstube am Klosterhof
5. Alter Keller
6. Eisenhut Restaurant & Beer Garden
7. Reichs-Küchenmeister
8. Pizzeria Roma
9. China-Restaurant Peking
10. Bosporus Café
11. To Unter den Linden Beer Garden
12. Gasthof Rödertor Beer Garden
13. Eis Café D' Isep
14. Trinkstube zur Hölle
15. Restaurant Glocke

its noisy streetside tables have a fine tower view (open daily 11:00-15:00 & 17:00-23:00, Plönlein 4, tel. 09861/938-738).

The **Bosporus Café** at Hafengasse 2, just off Market Square, serves cheap and tasty Turkish food to go or eat in. Their *Döner Kebabs* must be the best €3.50 hot meal in Rothenburg (daily 9:00-19:00, until 21:00 in April-Sept).

Picnic Goodies: A small **grocery store** is in the center of town at Rödergasse 6 (Mon-Fri 7:30-19:00, Sat 7:30-18:00, April-Dec also Sun 10:00-18:00, closed Sun Jan-March). **Supermarkets** are outside the wall: Exit the town through the Rödertor, turn left through the cobbled gate, and cross the parking lot to reach the Edeka supermarket (Mon-Fri 8:00-20:00, Sat 8:00-18:00, closed Sun); or head to the even bigger Kaufland in the shopping center across from the train station (Mon-Sat 7:00-20:00, closed Sun).

Beer Gardens *(Biergartens)*

Rothenburg's *Biergarten*s can be great fun, but they're open only when the weather is balmy.

Unter den Linden, a family-friendly (with sandbox and swing), slightly bohemian *Biergarten* in the valley along the river, is worth the 20-minute hike on a pleasant evening (daily 10:00-21:00 in season with decent weather, sometimes later, self-service food and good beer, Sunday breakfast buffet until noon-€12, call first to confirm it's open, Kurze Steige 7, tel. 09861/5909, Helmut Dürrer). As it's in the valley on the river, it's cooler than Rothenburg; bring a sweater. Take a right outside the Burgtor, then a left on the footpath toward Detwang; it's at the bottom of the hill on the left.

Gasthof Rödertor, just outside the wall through the Rödertor, runs a backyard *Biergarten* that's great for a rowdy crowd looking for cheap food and good beer. Their passion is potatoes—the menu is dedicated to spud cuisine. Try a plate of *Schupfnudeln*—potato noodles with sauerkraut and bacon (May-Sept daily 17:00-24:00 in good weather, table service only—no ordering at counter, Ansbacher Strasse 7, look for wooden gate, tel. 09861/2022). If the *Biergarten* is closed, their indoor restaurant, with more extensive menu, is a good value (€7-13 main courses, daily 11:30-14:00 & 17:30-22:00 except Sun until 21:00).

Eisenhut Restaurant (described earlier), behind the fancy hotel of the same name on Herrngasse, has a gentle, casual, small *Biergarten* out back, with lower prices than the restaurant.

Dessert

Eis Café D'Isep, with a pleasant "Venetian minimalist" interior, is the town's ice-cream parlor, serving up cakes, drinks, fresh-fruit ice cream, and fancy sundaes. Their sidewalk tables are great for lazy people-watching (daily 9:30-22:30, closed early Oct-mid-Feb,

one block off Market Square at Hafengasse 17, run by Paolo and
Paola D'Isep).

Wine-Drinking in the Old Center

Trinkstube zur Hölle ("Hell") is dark and foreboding, offering a
thick wine-drinking atmosphere, pub food, and a few main courses (€12-20). It's small and can get painfully touristy in summer
(Mon-Sat 17:00-24:00, closed Sun, a block past Medieval Crime
and Punishment Museum on Burggasse, with the devil hanging
out front, tel. 09861/4229).

Mario's **Altfränkische Weinstube am Klosterhof** (listed
earlier) is the liveliest place, and a clear favorite with locals for an
atmospheric drink or late meal. When every other place is asleep,
you're likely to find good food, drink, and energy here.

Restaurant Glocke, a *Weinstube* (wine bar) with a full menu,
is run by Rothenburg's oldest winemakers, the Thürauf family. The
very extensive wine list is in German only because the friendly staff
wants to explain your options in person. Their €4.80 deal, which
lets you sample five Franconian wines, is popular (€8-18 main
courses, Mon-Sat 11:00-23:00, Sun 11:00-14:00, Plönlein 1, tel.
09861/958-990).

Meet the Locals

For a rare chance to mix it up with locals who aren't selling anything, bring your favorite slang and tongue twisters to the **English Conversation Club** at Mario's Altfränkische Weinstube am
Klosterhof (Wed 19:00-24:00, restaurant listed earlier). This group
of intrepid linguists has met more than 1,000 times. Hermann the
German and his sidekick Wolfgang are regulars. Consider arriving
early for dinner, or after 21:00, when the beer starts to sink in, the
crowd grows, and everyone seems to speak that second language a
bit more easily.

Rothenburg Connections

Reaching Rothenburg ob der Tauber by Train: A tiny branch
train line connects Rothenburg to the outside world via **Steinach**
in 14 minutes (generally hourly from Rothenburg at :06 and from
Steinach at :35). Train connections in Steinach are usually quick
and efficient (trains to and from Rothenburg generally use track 5;
use the conveyor belts to haul your bags smartly up and down the
stairs).

If you plan to arrive in Rothenburg in the evening, note that
the last train from Steinach to Rothenburg departs at about 22:30.
All is not lost if you arrive in Steinach after the last train—there's a
subsidized taxi service to Rothenburg (cheaper for the government

than running an almost-empty train). To use this handy service, called AST *(Anrufsammeltaxi)*, make an appointment with a participating taxi service (call 09861/2000 or 09861/7227) at least an hour in advance (2 hours ahead is better), and they'll drive you from Steinach to Rothenburg for the train fare (€4/person) rather than the regular €25 taxi fare.

The Rothenburg station has a touch-screen terminal for fare and schedule information and ticket sales. If you need extra help, visit the combined ticket office and travel agency in the station building (€1-4 surcharge for most tickets, €0.50 charge for questions without ticket purchase, Mon-Fri 9:00-18:00, Sat 9:00-13:00, closed Sun, tel. 09861/7711). The station at Steinach is entirely unstaffed, but also has touch-screen ticket machines. As a last resort, call for train info at tel. 0180-599-6633, or visit www.bahn.com.

From Rothenburg by Train to: Würzburg (hourly, 70 minutes), **Nürnberg** (hourly, 1.25 hours, change in Ansbach), **Munich** (hourly, 2.5-3.5 hours, 2-3 changes), **Füssen** (hourly, 5 hours, often with changes in Treuchtlingen and Augsburg), **Frankfurt** (hourly, 2.5-3 hours, change in Würzburg), **Frankfurt Airport** (hourly, 3-3.25 hours, change in Würzburg), **Berlin** (hourly, 5-6 hours, often via Würzburg and Göttingen). Remember, all destinations also require a change in Steinach.

From Rothenburg by Bus: The Deutsche Touring company (tel. 069/719-126-268, www.romanticroadcoach.de) runs daily tour buses that roughly follow the Romantic Road. The bus stops in Rothenburg once a day (mid-April-late Oct) on its way from Frankfurt to Munich and Füssen (and vice versa). The bus stop is at Schrannenplatz, a short walk north of Market Square.

RHINE VALLEY

The Rhine Valley is storybook Germany, a fairy-tale world of legends and robber-baron castles. Cruise the most castle-studded stretch of the romantic Rhine as you listen for the song of the treacherous Loreley. For hands-on thrills, climb through the Rhineland's greatest castle, Rheinfels, above the town of St. Goar. Spend your nights in a castle-crowned village, either Bacharach or St. Goar.

Planning Your Time

The Rhineland is magical, but doesn't take much time to see. Both Bacharach and St. Goar are an easy 1.5-hour train ride (€15) or a one-hour drive from Frankfurt Airport, and they make a good first or last stop for travelers flying in or out.

Ideally, spend two nights here, sleep in Bacharach, cruise the best hour of the river (from Bacharach to St. Goar), and tour Rheinfels Castle. If rushed, focus on Rheinfels Castle and cruise less.

If possible, visit the Rhine between April and October. The low season is lower here than in some other parts of Germany. Many hotels and restaurants close from November to February or March. Riverboats don't run, sights close or have short hours, and neither Bacharach or St. Goar have much in the way of Christmas markets.

The Best of the Rhine

Ever since Roman times, when this was the empire's northern boundary, the Rhine has been one of the world's busiest shipping rivers. You'll see a steady flow of barges with 1,000- to 2,000-ton loads. Tourist-packed buses, hot train tracks, and highways line both banks.

Many of the castles were "robber-baron" castles, put there by petty rulers (there were 300 independent little countries in medieval Germany, a region about the size of Montana) to levy tolls on passing river traffic. A robber baron would put his castle on, or even in, the river. Then, often with the help of chains and a tower on the opposite bank, he'd stop each ship and get his toll. There were 10 customs stops in the 60-mile stretch between Mainz and Koblenz alone (no wonder merchants were early proponents of the creation of larger nation-states).

Some castles were built to control and protect settlements, and others were the residences of kings. As times changed, so did the lifestyles of the rich and feudal. Many castles were abandoned for more comfortable mansions in the towns.

Most Rhine castles date from the 11th, 12th, and 13th centuries. When the pope successfully asserted his power over the German emperor in 1076, local princes ran wild over the rule of their emperor. The castles saw military action in the 1300s and 1400s, as emperors began reasserting their control over Germany's many silly kingdoms.

The castles were also involved in the Reformation wars, in which Europe's Catholic and Protestant dynasties fought it out using a fragmented Germany as their battleground. The Thirty Years' War (1618-1648) devastated Germany. The outcome: Each ruler got the freedom to decide if his people would be Catholic or Protestant, and one-third of Germans died. (Production of Gummi Bears ceased entirely.)

The French—who feared a strong Germany and felt the Rhine was the logical border between them and Germany—destroyed most of the castles as a preventative measure (Louis XIV in the 1680s, the Revolutionary army in the 1790s, and Napoleon in 1806). Many were rebuilt in Neo-Gothic style in the Romantic Age—the late 1800s—and today are enjoyed as restaurants, hotels, hostels, and museums.

Getting Around the Rhine

The Rhine flows north from Switzerland to Holland, but the scenic stretch from Mainz to Koblenz hoards all the touristic charm. Studded with the crenellated cream of Germany's castles, it bustles

Rhine Overview

Düsseldorf

Rhine

Köln

UNROMANTIC
RHINE

Bonn

•Aachen

Remagen•

BELG.

BURG
ELTZ

Cochem•

Beilstein

BEST OF
THE RHINE
See detail map

•Koblenz

St.
Goar

Bingen

Bacharach

Frankfurt

Wies-
baden

Mainz

Main R.

FRANK-
FURT

Mosel R.

LUX.

Lux.
City

•Trier

HAHN

GERMANY

Neckar R.

Heidelberg

Rhine

FRANCE

30 Miles

50 Kilometers

Berlin•
GERMANY

N

with boats, trains, and highway traffic. Have fun exploring with a mix of big steamers, tiny ferries *(Fähre)*, trains, and bikes.

By Boat: While some travelers do the whole Mainz-Koblenz trip by boat (5.5 hours downstream, 8.5 hours up), I'd just focus on the most scenic hour—from St. Goar to Bacharach. Sit on the boat's top deck with your handy Rhine map-guide (or the kilometer-keyed tour in this chapter) and enjoy the parade of castles, towns, boats, and vineyards.

Two boat companies take travelers along this stretch of the Rhine. Boats run daily in both directions from early April through October, with no boats off-season.

Most travelers sail on the bigger, more expensive, and romantic **Köln-Düsseldorfer (K-D) Line** (free with German railpass or any Eurailpass that covers Germany, but starts the use of a day of any flexipass; recommended Bacharach-St. Goar trip: €12.50 one-way, €15 round-trip, bikes-€2.80/day, €2 extra if paying with credit card; discounts: 30 percent if over 60; 20 percent if you present a connecting train ticket; 50 percent on your birthday; Tue and Thu—2 bicyclists travel for the price of 1; tel. 06741/1634 in St.

Goar, tel. 06743/1322 in Bacharach, www.k-d.com). Complete, up-to-date schedules are posted at any Rhineland station, hotel, TI, and www.k-d.com. Purchase tickets at the dock up to five minutes before departure. (Confirm times at your hotel the night before.) The boat is never full. Romantics will enjoy the old-time paddle-wheeler *Goethe*, which sails each direction once a day (noted on schedule, confirm time locally).

The smaller **Bingen-Rüdesheimer Line** is slightly cheaper than the K-D, isn't covered by railpasses, and makes three trips in each direction daily (St. Goar to Bacharach: €12 one-way, €14 round-trip, buy tickets on boat; departs St. Goar at 11:00, 14:10, and 16:10; departs Bacharach at 10:10, 12:00, and 15:00; no morning departures last two weeks of Oct; tel. 06721/14140, www.bingen-ruedesheimer.de).

By Car: Drivers have these options: 1) skip the boat; 2) take a round-trip cruise from St. Goar or Bacharach; 3) draw pretzels and let the loser drive, prepare the picnic, and meet the boat; 4) rent a bike, bring it on the boat for €2.80, and bike back; or 5) take the boat one-way and return by train. When exploring by car, don't hesitate to pop onto one of the many little ferries that shuttle across the bridgeless-around-here river.

By Ferry: While there are no bridges between Koblenz and Mainz, you'll see car-and-passenger ferries (usually family-run for generations) about every three miles. Bingen-Rüdesheim, Lorch-Niederheimbach, Engelsburg-Kaub, and St. Goar-St. Goarshausen are some of the most useful routes (times vary; St. Goar-St. Goarshausen ferry departs each side every 15-20 minutes, Mon-Sat 5:30-24:00, Sun 6:30-24:00; one-way fares: adult-€1.50, car and driver-€4, pay on the boat; www.faehre-loreley.de). For a fun little jaunt, take a quick round-trip with some time to explore the other side.

By Bike: You can bike on either side of the Rhine, but for a designated bike path, stay on the west side, where a 35-mile path runs between Koblenz and Bingen. The six-mile stretch between St. Goar and Bacharach is smooth and scenic, but mostly along the highway. The bit from Bacharach to Bingen hugs the riverside and is road-free. Either way, biking is a great way to explore the valley. Many hotels provide free or cheap bikes to guests; in Bacharach, anyone can rent bikes at Hotel Hillen (see page 564, €12/day for non-guests).

Consider biking one-way and taking the bike back on the riverboat, or designing a circular trip using the fun and frequent shuttle ferries. A good target might be Kaub (where a tiny boat shuttles sightseers to the better-from-a-distance castle on the island).

By Train: Hourly milk-run trains hit every town along the Rhine (St. Goar-Bacharach, 10 minutes, €3.40; Bacharach-Mainz,

1 hour; Mainz-Koblenz, 1.5 hours). Express trains speed past the small towns, taking only 50 minutes non-stop between Mainz and Koblenz. Some train schedules list St. Goar but not Bacharach as a stop, but any schedule listing St. Goar also stops at Bacharach. Tiny stations are not staffed—buy tickets at the platform machines (user-friendly, take paper money, may not accept US credit cards).

The **Rheinland-Pfalz-Ticket** day pass covers travel on milk-run trains to anywhere in this chapter (1 person-€21, up to 4 additional people-€4/each, buy from station ticket machines, good after 9:00 Mon-Fri and all day Sat-Sun, valid on trains labeled *RB*, *RE*, and *MRB*).

Self-Guided Tour

▲▲▲Rhine Blitz Tour by Train or Boat

One of Europe's great train thrills is zipping along the Rhine enjoying this blitz tour. Or, even better, do it relaxing on the deck of a Rhine steamer, surrounded by the wonders of this romantic and historic gorge. This quick and easy tour (you can cut in anywhere) skips most of the syrupy myths filling normal Rhine guides. You can follow along on a train, boat, bike, or car. By train or boat, sit on the left (river) side going south from Koblenz. While nearly all the castles listed are viewed from this side, train travelers need to clear a path to the right window for the times I yell, "Cross over!"

You'll notice large black-and-white kilometer markers along the riverbank. I erected these years ago to make this tour easier to follow. They tell the distance from the Rhine Falls, where the Rhine leaves Switzerland and becomes navigable. (Today, river-barge pilots also use these markers to navigate.) We're tackling just 36 miles (58 km) of the 820-mile-long (1,320-km) Rhine. Your Rhine Blitz Tour starts at Koblenz and heads upstream to Bingen. If you're going the other direction, it still works. Just hold the book upside-down.

You can download a free Rick Steves **audio tour** of this Rhine sightseeing jaunt—it works in either direction (see page 7).

Km 590—Koblenz: This Rhine blitz starts with Romantic Rhine thrills, at Koblenz. Koblenz is not a nice city (it was hit hard in World War II), but its place as the historic *Deutsches Eck* (German corner)—the tip of land where the Mosel River joins the Rhine—gives it a certain charm. Koblenz, from the Latin for "confluence," has Roman origins. If you stop here, take a walk through the park, noticing the reconstructed memorial to the *Kaiser*. Across the river, the yellow Ehrenbreitstein Castle now houses a hostel. It's a 30-minute hike from the station to the Koblenz boat dock.

Km 586—Lahneck Castle (Burg Lahneck): Above the modern autobahn bridge over the Lahn River, this castle *(Burg)*

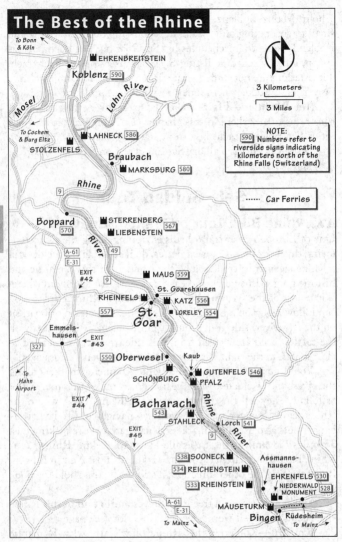

The Best of the Rhine

To Bonn & Köln

EHRENBREITSTEIN

Koblenz [590]

Lahn River

Mosel

To Cochem & Burg Eltz

LAHNECK [586]

STOLZENFELS

Braubach

MARKSBURG [580]

Rhine

9

Boppard [570]

River

STERRENBERG
LIEBENSTEIN [567]

A-61
E-31

EXIT #42

9

49

MAUS [559]

St. Goarshausen

RHEINFELS

KATZ [556]

557

LORELEY [554]

St. Goar

Emmels-hausen

EXIT #43

327

To Hahn Airport

[550] Oberwesel

Kaub

GUTENFELS [546]

SCHÖNBURG

PFALZ

EXIT #44

Bacharach [543]

Rhine

STAHLECK

Lorch [541]

9

River

EXIT #45

[538] SOONECK

[534] REICHENSTEIN

Assmanns-hausen

[533] RHEINSTEIN

EHRENFELS [530]

NIEDERWALD MONUMENT [528]

A-61
E-31

MÄUSETURM

Bingen

Rüdesheim

To Mainz

To Mainz

3 Kilometers

3 Miles

NOTE:
[590] Numbers refer to riverside signs indicating kilometers north of the Rhine Falls (Switzerland)

······ Car Ferries

was built in 1240 to defend local silver mines; the castle was ruined by the French in 1688 and rebuilt in the 1850s in Neo-Gothic style. Burg Lahneck faces another Romantic rebuild, the yellow Schloss Stolzenfels (out of view above the train, a 10-minute climb from tiny parking lot, open for touring, closed Mon). Note that a *Burg* is a defensive fortress, while a *Schloss* is mainly a showy palace.

Km 580—Marksburg Castle: This castle (bold and white, with the three modern chimneys behind it, just before the town of Spay) is the best-looking of all the Rhine castles and the only surviving medieval castle on the Rhine. Because of its commanding position, it was never attacked in the Middle Ages (though it was captured by the US Army in March of 1945). It's now open as a museum with a medieval interior (€6, family card-€15, daily April-Oct 10:00-18:00, Nov-March 11:00-17:00, last tour departs one hour before closing, tel. 02627/206, www.marksburg.de). The three modern smokestacks vent Europe's biggest car-battery recycling plant just up the valley.

Km 570—Boppard: Once a Roman town, Boppard has some impressive remains of fourth-century walls. Look for the Roman towers and the substantial chunk of Roman wall near the train station, just above the main square. You'll notice that a church is a big part of each townscape. Many small towns have two towering churches. Four centuries ago, after enduring a horrific war, each prince or king decided which faith his subjects would follow (more often Protestant to the north and east, Catholic to the south and west). While church attendance in Germany is way down, the towns here, like Germany as a whole, are still divided between Catholic and Protestant church-goers.

If you visit Boppard, head to the fascinating Church of St. Severus below the main square. Find the carved Romanesque crazies at the doorway. Inside, to the right of the entrance, you'll see Christian symbols from Roman times. Also notice the painted arches and vaults (originally, most Romanesque churches were painted this way). Down by the river, look for the high-water *(Hochwasser)* marks on the arches from various flood years. (You'll find these flood marks throughout the Rhine Valley.)

Km 567—Sterrenberg Castle and Liebenstein Castle: These are the "Hostile Brothers" castles across from Bad Salzig. Take the wall between the castles (actually designed to improve the defenses of both castles), add two greedy and jealous brothers and a fair maiden, and create your own legend. Burg Liebenstein is now a fun, friendly, and affordable family-run hotel (9 rooms, Db-€135, suite-€160, giant king-and-the-family room-€235, easy parking, tel. 06773/308 or 06773/251, www.castle-liebenstein.com, info@ burg-liebenstein.de, Nickenig family).

Km 560: While you can see nothing from here, a 19th-century lead mine functioned on both sides of the river, with a shaft actually tunneling completely under the Rhine.

Km 559—Maus Castle (Burg Maus): The Maus (mouse) got its name because the next castle was owned by the Katzenelnbogen family. (*Katz* means "cat.") In the 1300s, it was considered a state-of-the-art fortification...until 1806, when Napoleon had it blown up with then-state-of-the-art explosives. It was rebuilt true to its original plans in about 1900. Today, the castle is open only for concerts and weddings, with occasional guided tours (20-minute walk up, tel. 06771/9100, www.burg-maus.de).

Km 557—St. Goar and Rheinfels Castle: Cross to the other side of the train. The pleasant town of St. Goar was named for a sixth-century hometown monk. It originated in Celtic times (really old) as a place where sailors would stop, catch their breath, send home a postcard, and give thanks after surviving the seductive and treacherous Loreley crossing. St. Goar is worth a stop to explore its mighty Rheinfels Castle. (For a self-guided castle tour and accommodations, see page 570.)

Km 556—Katz Castle (Burg Katz): Burg Katz (Katzenelnbogen) faces St. Goar from across the river. Together, Burg Katz (built in 1371) and Rheinfels Castle had a clear view up and down the river, effectively controlling traffic (there was absolutely no duty-free shopping on the medieval Rhine). Katz got Napoleoned in 1806 and rebuilt in about 1900.

Today, the castle is shrouded by intrigue and controversy. In 1995, a wealthy and eccentric Japanese man bought it for about $4 million. His vision: to make the castle—so close to the Loreley that Japanese tourists are wild about—an exotic escape for his countrymen. But the town wouldn't allow his planned renovation of the historic (and therefore protected) building. Stymied, the frustrated investor abandoned his plans. Today, Burg Katz sits empty...the Japanese ghost castle.

Below the castle, notice the derelict grape terraces—worked since the eighth century, but abandoned in the last generation. The Rhine wine is particularly good because the local slate absorbs the heat of the sun and stays warm all night, resulting in sweeter grapes. Wine from the flat fields above the Rhine gorge is cheaper, and good only as table wine. Wine from the steep side of the Rhine gorge—where grapes are harder to grow and harvest—is tastier and more expensive. Rumor has it that 2011 was an especially good year.

About Km 555: A statue of the Loreley, the beautiful-but-deadly nymph, combs her hair at the end of a long spit—built to give barges protection from vicious ice floes that until recent years raged down the river in the winter. The actual Loreley, a cliff (marked by the flags), is just ahead.

Km 554—The Loreley: Steep a big slate rock in centuries of legend and it becomes a tourist attraction—the ultimate Rhinestone. The Loreley (flags and visitors center on top, name painted near shoreline), rising 450 feet over the narrowest and deepest point of the Rhine, has long been important. It was a holy site in pre-Roman days. The fine echoes here—thought to be ghostly voices—fertilized legend-tellers' imaginations.

Because of the reefs just upstream (at km 552), many ships

never made it to St. Goar. Sailors (after days on the river) blamed their misfortune on a *wunderbares Fräulein,* whose long, blond hair almost covered her body. Heinrich Heine's *Song of Loreley* (the CliffsNotes version is on local postcards) tells the story of a count sending his men to kill or capture this siren after she distracted his horny son, who forgot to watch where he was sailing and drowned. When the soldiers cornered the nymph in her cave, she called her father (Father Rhine) for help. Huge waves, the likes of which you'll never see today, rose from the river and carried Loreley to safety. And she has never been seen since.

But alas, when the moon shines brightly and the tour buses are parked, a soft, playful Rhine whine can still be heard from the Loreley. As you pass, listen carefully ("Sailors...sailors...over my bounding mane").

Km 552—The Seven Maidens: Killer reefs, marked by red-and-green buoys, are called the "Seven Maidens." Okay, one more goofy legend: The prince of Schönburg Castle (*über* Oberwesel—described next) had seven spoiled daughters who always dumped men because of their shortcomings. Fed up, he invited seven of his knights to the castle and demanded that his daughters each choose one to marry. But they complained that each man had too big a nose, was too fat, too stupid, and so on. The rude and teasing girls escaped into a riverboat. Just downstream, God turned them into the seven rocks that form this reef. While this story probably isn't entirely true, there was a lesson in it for medieval children: Don't be hard-hearted.

Km 550—Oberwesel: Cross to the other side of the train. Oberwesel was a Celtic town in 400 B.C., then a Roman military station. It now boasts some of the best Roman-wall and medieval-tower remains on the Rhine, and the commanding Schönburg Castle (now a posh hotel). Notice how many of the train tunnels have entrances designed like medieval turrets—they were actually built in the Romantic 19th century. OK, back to the riverside.

Km 546—Gutenfels Castle and Pfalz Castle, the Classic Rhine View: Burg Gutenfels (now a privately owned hotel) and the shipshape Pfalz Castle (built in the river in the 1300s) worked very effectively to tax medieval river traffic. The town of Kaub grew rich as Pfalz raised its chains when boats came, and lowered them only when the merchants had paid their duty. Those who didn't pay spent time touring its prison, on a raft at the bottom of its well. In 1504, a pope called for the destruction of Pfalz, but the locals withstood a six-week siege, and the castle still stands. Notice the overhanging outhouse (tiny white room between two wooden ones). Pfalz (also known as Pfalzgrafenstein) is tourable but bare and dull (€3 ferry from Kaub, €3 entry, March-Oct Tue-Sun 10:00-18:00, closed Mon; Nov and Jan-Feb Sat-Sun 10:00-17:00, closed Mon-

Fri; completely closed Dec, last entry one hour before closing, mobile 0172-262-2800, www.burg-pfalzgrafenstein.de).

In Kaub, on the riverfront directly below the castles, a green statue (near the waving flags) honors the German general Gebhard von Blücher. He was Napoleon's nemesis. In 1813, as Napoleon fought his way back to Paris after his disastrous Russian campaign, he stopped at Mainz—hoping to fend off the Germans and Russians pursuing him by controlling that strategic bridge. Blücher tricked Napoleon. By building the first major pontoon bridge of its kind here at the Pfalz Castle, he crossed the Rhine and outflanked the French. Two years later, Blücher and Wellington teamed up to defeat Napoleon once and for all at Waterloo.

Immediately opposite Kaub (where the ferry lands, marked by blue roadside flags) is a gaping hole in the mountainside. This marks the last working slate mine on the Rhine.

Km 544—"The Raft Busters": Just before Bacharach, at the top of the island, buoys mark a gang of rocks notorious for busting up rafts. The Black Forest, upstream from here, was once poor, and wood was its best export. Black Foresters would ride log booms down the Rhine to the Ruhr (where their timber fortified coalmine shafts) or to Holland (where logs were sold to shipbuilders). If they could navigate the sweeping bend just before Bacharach and then survive these "raft busters," they'd come home reckless and horny—the German folkloric equivalent of American cowboys after payday.

Km 543—Bacharach and Stahleck Castle (Burg Stahleck): Cross to the other side of the train. The town of Bacharach is a great stop (described on next page). Some of the Rhine's best wine is from this town, whose name likely derives from "altar to Bacchus." Local vintners brag that the medieval Pope Pius II ordered Bacharach wine by the cartload. Perched above the town, the 13th-century Burg Stahleck is now a hostel. Return to the riverside.

Km 541—Lorch: This pathetic stub of a castle is barely visible from the road. Check out the hillside vineyards. These vineyards once blanketed four times as much land as they do today, but modern economics have driven most of them out of business. The vineyards that do survive require government subsidies. Notice the small car ferry, one of several along the bridgeless stretch between Mainz and Koblenz.

Km 538—Sooneck Castle: Cross back to the other side of the train. Built in the 11th century, this castle was twice destroyed by people sick and tired of robber barons.

Km 534—Reichenstein Castle and **Km 533—Rheinstein Castle:** Stay on the other side of the train to see two of the first castles to be rebuilt in the Romantic era. Both are privately owned, tourable, and connected by a pleasant trail. Go back to the river side.

Km 530—Ehrenfels Castle: Opposite Bingerbrück and the Bingen station, you'll see the ghostly Ehrenfels Castle (clobbered by the Swedes in 1636 and by the French in 1689). Since it had no view of the river traffic to the north, the owner built the cute little *Mäuseturm* (mouse tower) on an island (the yellow tower you'll see near the train station today). Rebuilt in the 1800s in Neo-Gothic style, it's now used as a Rhine navigation signal station.

Km 528—Niederwald Monument: Across from the Bingen station on a hilltop is the 120-foot-high Niederwald monument, a memorial built with 32 tons of bronze in 1877 to commemorate "the re-establishment of the German Empire." A lift takes tourists to this statue from the famous and extremely touristy wine town of Rüdesheim.

From here, the Romantic Rhine becomes the industrial Rhine, and our tour is over.

RHINE VALLEY

Bacharach

Once prosperous from the wine and wood trade, charming Bacharach (BAHKH-ah-rahkh, with a guttural *kh* sound) is now just a pleasant half-timbered village of 2,000 people working hard to keep its tourists happy. Businesses that have been "in the family" for eons are dealing with succession challenges, as the allure of big-city jobs and a more cosmopolitan life lure away the town's younger generation. But Bacharach retains its time-capsule quaintness.

Orientation to Bacharach

Bacharach cuddles, long and narrow, along the Rhine. The village is easily strollable—you can walk from one end of town to the other along its main drag, Oberstrasse, in about 10 minutes. Bacharach widens at its stream, where more houses trickle up its small valley (along Blücherstrasse) away from the Rhine. The hillsides above town are occupied by vineyards, scant remains of the former town walls, and a castle-turned-youth hostel.

Tourist Information

The TI, on the main street in the Posthof courtyard next to the church, will store bags for day-trippers (April-Oct Mon-Fri 9:00-17:00, Sat-Sun 10:00-15:00; Nov-March Mon-Fri 9:00-13:00, closed Sat-Sun; from train station, turn right and walk 5 blocks down main street with castle high on your left, Oberstrasse 45; tel.

1 Rhein Hotel & Stüber Rest.
2 Hotel zur Post
3 Hotel/Rest. Kranenturm
4 Pension im Malerwinkel
5 Pension Binz
6 Hotel Hillen & Bike Rental
7 Pension Lettie
8 To Pension Winzerhaus
9 Irmgard Orth B&B
10 Jugendherberge Stahleck Hostel
11 Altes Haus Restaurant
12 Gasthaus Jägerstube
13 Posthof Rest. & Café
14 Bacharacher Kebap Haus
15 Eis Café Italia
16 Zum Kleinen Monning Irish Pub
17 Zur Alt Backstubb
18 Bastian's Weingut zum Grüner Baum
19 Weingut Karl Heidrich
20 Grocery

RHINE VALLEY

06743/919-303, www.bacharach.de or www.rhein-nahe-touristik. de, Herr Kuhn and his team).

Helpful Hints

Shopping: The **Jost** German gift store, across the main square from the church, carries most everything a souvenir-shopper could want—from beer steins to cuckoo clocks—and can ship purchases to the US. This family shop celebrated its centennial in 2011 (find a photo of the great-grandfather on the wall). The Josts offer discounts to my readers: 10 percent with cash, 5 percent with credit card (March-Oct Mon-Fri 8:30-18:00, Sat 8:30-17:00, possibly Sun 10:00-16:00; Nov-Feb shorter hours and closed Sun; Blücherstrasse 4, tel. 06743/1224, phil. jost@t-online.de).

Internet Access: The **TI** has one computer (€0.50/15 minutes).

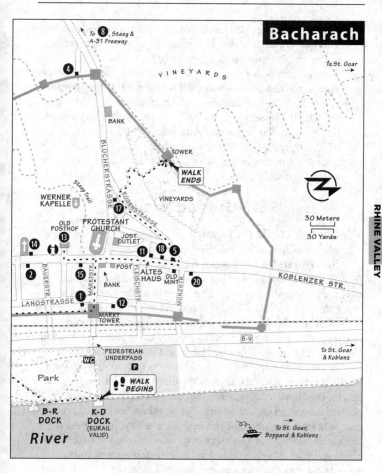

Post Office: It's inside a news agents' shop, across from the church and Altes Haus, at Oberstrasse 56.

Grocery Store: Pick up picnic supplies at **Nahkauf,** a basic grocery store (Mon-Fri 8:00-12:30 & 14:00-18:00, Sat 8:30-12:30, closed Sun, Koblenzer Strasse 2).

Bike Rental: While many hotels loan bikes to guests, the only real bike-rental business in the town center is run by Erich at the recommended **Hotel Hillen** (non-guests-€12/day, guests-€7/day, 35 bikes available, daily 9:00 until dark, Langstrasse 18, tel. 06743/1287).

Parking: It's simple to park along the highway next to the train tracks or, better, in the big lot by the boat dock (€3 from 9:00 to 18:00, pay with coins at *Parkscheinautomat* and put slip on dashboard, free overnight).

Local Guides: Get acquainted with Bacharach by taking a walking tour. These guides enjoy sharing their town with visitors: **Thomas Gundlach** is a charming local who's licensed as a guide and happily gives 1.5-hour town walks to individuals or small groups for €25. He can also drive up to three people around the region in his car (€70/6 hours, €120/long day, mobile 0179-353-6004, thomas_gundlach@gmx.de). Also good are **Birgit Wessels** (tel. 06743/937-514, wessels.birgit@t-online.de) and Aussie **Joanne Augustin** (€30/1.5 hours, mobile 0179-231-1389, jopetit90@yahoo.com). The TI books 1.5-hour tours in English (€70/group). Or take one or both of my self-guided walks, below.

Self-Guided Walks

Welcome to Bacharach

• *Start at the Köln-Düsseldorfer ferry dock (next to a fine picnic park).*

Riverfront: View the town from the parking lot—a modern landfill. The Rhine used to lap against Bacharach's town wall, just over the present-day highway. Every few years the river floods, covering the highway with several feet of water. The **castle** on the hill is now a youth hostel. Two of the town's original 16 towers are visible from here (up to five if you look really hard). The huge roadside keg declares that this town was built on the wine trade.

Reefs farther upstream forced boats to unload upriver and reload here. Consequently, in the Middle Ages, Bacharach became the biggest wine-trading town on the Rhine. A riverfront crane hoisted huge kegs of prestigious "Bacharach" wine (which, in practice, was from anywhere in the region). The tour buses next to the dock and the flags of the biggest spenders along the highway remind you that today's economy is basically founded on tourism.

• *Before entering the town, walk upstream through the...*

Riverside Park: This park was laid out in 1910 in the English style: Notice how the trees were planted to frame fine town views, highlighting the most picturesque bits of architecture. The dark, sad-looking monument—its "eternal" flame long snuffed out—is a **war memorial.** The German psyche is permanently scarred by war memories. Today, many Germans would rather avoid monuments like this, which revisit the dark periods before Germany became a nation of pacifists. Take a close look at the monument. Each panel honors sons of Bacharach who died for the Kaiser: in 1864 against Denmark, in 1866 against Austria, in 1870 against France, in 1914 during World War I. The military Maltese cross—flanked by classic German helmets—has a W at its center, for Kaiser Wilhelm.

• *Look (but don't go) upstream from here to see the...*

Trailer Park and Campground: In Germany, trailer vacationers and campers are two distinct subcultures. Folks who travel in trailers, like many retirees in the US, are a nomadic bunch, cruising around the countryside in their motorhomes and paying a few euros a night to park. Campers, on the other hand, tend to set up camp in one place—complete with comfortable lounge chairs and TVs—and stay put for weeks, even months. They often come back to the same spot year after year, treating it like their own private estate. These camping devotees have made a science out of relaxing.

• *Continue to where the park meets the playground, and then cross the highway to the fortified riverside wall of the Catholic church, decorated with...*

High-Water Marks: These recall various floods. Twenty yards to the left is a metal ring on the medieval slate wall. Before the 1910 reclamation project, the river extended out to here, and boats would use the ring to tie up.

• *From the church, go under the 1858 train tracks and hook right past the yellow floodwater yardstick and up the stairs onto the town wall. Atop the wall, turn left and walk under the long arcade. After 30 meters, on your left, notice a...*

Well: Rebuilt as it appeared in the 17th century, this is one of 40 such wells that provided water to the townsfolk until 1900. Walk 50 yards past the well along the wall to an alcove in the medieval tower with a view of the war memorial in the park. You're under the crane tower *(Kranenturm)*. After barrels of wine were moved overland from Bingen past dangerous stretches of river, the precious cargo could be lowered by cranes from here into ships to continue more safely down the river. The Rhine has long been a major shipping route through Germany. In modern times, it's a bottleneck in Germany's train system. The train company gives hotels and residents along the tracks money for soundproof windows (hotels along here routinely have quadruple-pane windows...and earplugs on the nightstand).

• *Continue walking along the town wall. Pass the recommended Rhein Hotel (hotel is before the Markt tower, which marks one of the town's 15 original 14th-century gates), descend, pass another well, and follow Marktstrasse away from the river toward the town center, the two-tone church, and the town's...*

Main Intersection: From here, Bacharach's main street (Oberstrasse) goes right to the half-timbered red-and-white Altes Haus (from 1368, the oldest house in town) and left 400 yards to the train station. Spin around to enjoy the higgledy-piggledy building styles.

• *To the left (south) of the church, a golden horn hangs over the old...*

Posthof: The postal horn symbolizes the postal service throughout Europe. In olden days, when the postman blew this, traffic stopped and the mail sped through. This post station (now home to the TI) dates from 1724, when stagecoaches ran from

RHINE VALLEY

Köln to Frankfurt and would change horses here, Pony Express-style.

Step past the old oak doors into the courtyard—once a carriage house and inn that accommodated Bacharach's first VIP visitors, and now home to a restaurant. Notice the fascist eagle (from 1936, on the left as you enter; a swastika once filled its center) and the fine view of the church and a ruined chapel above.

Two hundred years ago, Bacharach's main drag was the only road along the Rhine. Napoleon widened it to fit his cannon wagons. The steps alongside the church lead to the castle.

• *Return to the church, passing the recommended Italian ice-cream café (Eis Café Italia), where friendly Mimo serves his special invention: Riesling wine-flavored gelato.*

Protestant Church: Inside the church (daily May-Sept 10:00-18:00, April and Oct 10:00-17:00, closed Nov-March, English info on table near door), you'll find Grotesque capitals, brightly painted in medieval style, and a mix of round Romanesque and pointed Gothic arches. The church was fancier before the Reformation wars, when it (and the region) was Catholic. Bacharach lies on the religious border of Germany and, like the country as a whole, is split between Catholics and Protestants. To the left of the altar, some medieval frescoes survive where an older Romanesque arch was cut by a pointed Gothic one.

• *Continue down Oberstrasse to the...*

Altes Haus: Notice the 14th-century building style—the first floor is made of stone, while upper floors are half-timbered (in the ornate style common in the Rhine Valley). Some of its windows still look medieval, with small, flattened circles as panes (small because that's all that glass-blowing technology of the time would allow), pieced together with molten lead (like medieval stained glass in churches). Frau Weber welcomes visitors to enjoy the fascinating ground floor of the recommended Altes Haus restaurant, with its evocative old photos and etchings (consider eating here later).

• *Keep going down Oberstrasse to the...*

Old Mint (Münze): The old mint is marked by a crude coin in its sign. Across from the mint, the recommended **Bastian** family's wine garden is a lively place after dark. Above you in the vineyards stands a lonely white-and-red tower—your final destination.

• *At the next street, look right and see the mint tower, painted in the medieval style, and then turn left. Wander 30 yards up Rosenstrasse to the well. Notice the sundial and the wall painting of 1632 Bacharach with its walls intact. Climb the tiny-stepped lane behind the well up into the vineyard and to the...*

Tall Tower: The slate steps lead to a small path through the vineyard that deposits you at a viewpoint atop the stubby remains of the old town wall. If the tower's open, hike to its top floor for the best view.

Romantic Rhine View: A grand medieval town spreads before you. For 300 years (1300-1600), Bacharach was big (population 4,000), rich, and politically powerful.

From this perch, you can see the chapel ruins and six surviving **city towers**. Visually trace the wall to the castle. The castle was actually the capital of Germany for a couple of years in the 1200s. When Holy Roman Emperor Frederick Barbarossa went away to fight the Crusades, he left his brother (who lived here) in charge of his vast realm. Bacharach was home to one of seven electors who voted for the Holy Roman Emperor in 1275. To protect their own power, these prince electors did their best to choose the weakest guy on the ballot. The elector from Bacharach helped select a two-bit prince named Rudolf von Habsburg (from a no-name castle in Switzerland). However, the underestimated Rudolf brutally silenced the robber barons along the Rhine and established the mightiest dynasty in European history. His family line, the Habsburgs, ruled much of Central and Eastern Europe from Vienna until 1918.

Plagues, fires, and the Thirty Years' War (1618-1648) finally did in Bacharach. The town, with a population of about 2,000, has slumbered for several centuries. Today, the castle houses commoners—40,000 overnights annually by youth hostelers.

In the mid-19th century, painters such as J. M. W. Turner and writers such as Victor Hugo were charmed by the Rhineland's romantic mix of past glory, present poverty, and rich legend. They put this part of the Rhine on the old Grand Tour map as the "Romantic Rhine." Victor Hugo pondered the ruined 15th-century chapel that you see under the castle. In his 1842 travel book, *Excursions Along the Banks of Rhine*, he wrote, "No doors, no roof or windows, a magnificent skeleton puts its silhouette against the sky. Above it, the ivy-covered castle ruins provide a fitting crown. This is Bacharach, land of fairy tales, covered with legends and sagas." If you're enjoying the Romantic Rhine, thank Victor Hugo and company.

• *To get back into town, take the level path away from the river that leads along the once-mighty wall up the valley past the next tower. Then cross the street into the parking lot. Pass Pension im Malerwinkel on your right, being careful not to damage the old arch with your head. Follow the creek past a delightful little series of half-timbered homes and cheery gardens known as "Painters' Corner" (Malerwinkel). Resist looking into some pervert's peep show (on the right) and continue downhill back to the village center.*

Walk Along the Old Town Walls

A well-maintained and clearly marked walking path follows the remains of Bacharach's old town walls and makes for a good hour's workout. The TI has maps that show the entire route. The path starts near the train station, then climbs up to the youth hostel, descends into the side valley, and then continues up the other side to the tower in the vineyards before returning to town. To start the walk at the train station, find the house at Oberstrasse 2 and climb up the stairway to its left. Then follow the *Stadtmauer-Rundweg* signs. Good bilingual signposts tell the history of each of the towers along the wall—some are intact, one is a private residence, and others are now only stubs.

RHINE VALLEY

Sleeping in Bacharach

(area code: 06743)

None of the hotels listed here have elevators. The only listings with parking are Pension im Malerwinkel, Pension Winzerhaus, and the youth hostel. For the others, you can drive in to unload your bags and then park in the public lot (see "Helpful Hints," earlier).

$$$ Rhein Hotel, overlooking the river with 14 spacious and comfortable rooms, is classy, well-run, and decorated with modern flair. Since it's right on the train tracks, its river- and train-side rooms come with quadruple-paned windows and air-conditioning. This place has been in the Stüber family for six generations (Sb-€55, Db-€94, Tb-€125, Qb-€145, ask for Rick Steves price with this book and direct reservation, cheaper for longer stays and off-season, €18/person half-board includes big three-course dinner, nonsmoking, free loaner bikes, free Wi-Fi, directly inland from the K-D boat dock at Langstrasse 50, tel. 06743/1243, fax 06743/1413, www.rhein-hotel-bacharach.de, info@rhein-hotel-bacharach.de). Their recommended Stüber Restaurant is considered the best in town.

$$ Hotel zur Post, refreshingly clean and quiet, is conveniently located right in the town center with no train noise. It comes with a focus on solid comfort rather than old-fashioned character, and rents 12 good rooms for a good price (Sb-€40-45, Db-€66-70, Qb-€110, Oberstrasse 38, tel. 06743/1277, www.hotel-zur-post-bacharach.de, h.zurpost@t-online.de, Precoma family).

$$ Hotel Kranenturm, offering castle ambience without the climb, combines hotel comfort with *Privatzimmer* funkiness right downtown. Run by hardworking Kurt Engel and his intense but friendly wife, Fatima, this 16-room hotel is part of the medieval town wall. The rooms in its former *Kranenturm* (crane tower) have the best views. When the riverbank was higher, cranes on this tower loaded barrels of wine onto Rhine boats. While just 15 feet

---

Sleep Code

(€1 = about $1.30, country code: 49)
S = Single, **D** = Double/Twin, **T** = Triple, **Q** = Quad, **b** = bathroom, **s** = shower only. Staff at all hotels speak at least some English. Breakfast is included and credit cards are accepted unless otherwise noted.

To help you sort easily through these listings, I've divided the accommodations into three categories, based on the price for a standard double room with bath:

$$$ Higher Priced—Most rooms €80 or more.
$$ Moderately Priced—Most rooms between €55-80.
$ Lower Priced—Most rooms €55 or less.

The Rhine is an easy place for cheap sleeps. B&Bs and *Gasthäuser* with €25-30 beds abound (and normally discount their prices for longer stays). Rhine-area hostels offer €20 beds to travelers of any age. Each town's TI is eager to set you up, and finding a room should be easy any time of year (except for Sept-Oct winefest weekends). Bacharach and St. Goar, the best towns for an overnight stop, are 10 miles apart, connected by milk-run trains, riverboats, and a riverside bike path. Bacharach is a much more interesting town, but St. Goar has the famous castle (for St. Goar recommendations, see that section).

Prices can change without notice; verify current rates online or by email.

from the train tracks, a combination of medieval sturdiness, triple-paned windows, and included earplugs makes the riverside rooms sleepable (Sb-€40-46, small Db-€59-65, regular Db-€64-70, Db in huge tower rooms with castle and river views-€73-80, Tb-€85-95, Qb great for families with small kids-€100-115, lower prices are for 3-night stay, family deals, cash preferred, €2 extra with credit card, Rhine views come with train noise, back rooms are quiet, non-smoking, showers can be temperamental, kid-friendly, good breakfast, free Internet access and Wi-Fi in common areas, laundry service-€13.50, closed Dec-early Feb, Langstrasse 30, tel. 06743/1308, www.kranenturm.com, hotel-kranenturm@t-online. de). Kurt, a good cook, serves €10-16 main courses in their recommended restaurant.

$$ Pension im Malerwinkel sits like a grand gingerbread house that straddles the town wall in a quiet little neighborhood so charming it's called "Painters' Corner" *(Malerwinkel)*. The Vollmer family's 20-room place is super-quiet and comes with a sunny garden on a brook, views of the vineyards, and easy parking

(Sb-€43; Db-€68 for one-night stay, €63/night for 2 nights, €60/night for 3 nights or more; family rooms, cash only, no train noise, non-smoking, free Wi-Fi, bike rental-€6/day, parking; from Oberstrasse, turn left at the church, and stay to the left of the babbling brook until you reach Blücherstrasse 41-45; tel. 06743/1239, www.im-malerwinkel.de, info@im-malerwinkel.de, Armin and Daniela). Several German towns have guesthouses called *Im Malerwinkel*; when reserving, double-check that you're contacting the one in Bacharach.

$$ Pension Binz offers four large, bright, plainly furnished rooms in a good location with no train noise (Sb-€37-40, Db-€60-65, Tb-€78-83, higher price is for one-night stay, cash only, no Internet access, Koblenzer Strasse 1, tel. 06743/1604, fax 06743/937-9916, http://pensionbinz.funpic.de, pension.binz@freenet.de, Carla speaks a little English).

$ Hotel Hillen, a block south of Hotel Kranenturm, has less charm and similar train noise (with the same ultra-thick windows). It offers spacious rooms and friendly owners (S-€30, Sb-€35, D-€40, Ds-€45, Db-€50, Tb-€65, Qb-€80, ask for Rick Steves price when you reserve direct with this book, 10 percent discount for 2-night stay, family rooms, cash only, closed mid-Nov-Easter, Langstrasse 18, tel. 06743/1287, fax 06743/1037, hotel-hillen@web.de, kind Iris speaks some English). The hotel also rents bikes (see page 548).

$ Pension Lettie, run by effervescent and eager-to-please Lettie, rents four bright rooms. Lettie speaks English (she worked for the US Army before they withdrew) and does laundry for €13/load (Sb-€38, Db-€55, Tb-€75, Qb-€90, Quint/b-€105, ask for Rick Steves price with this book when you reserve direct, €5 discount for 2-night stay, 10 percent more if paying with credit card, non-smoking, buffet breakfast with waffles and eggs, no train noise, free Wi-Fi, inland from Hotel Kranenturm, Kranenstrasse 6, tel. 06743/2115, pension.lettie@t-online.de).

$ Pension Winzerhaus, a 10-room place run by friendly Sybille and Stefan, is outside the town walls, 200 yards up the side-valley road from the town gate, directly under the vineyards. The rooms are simple, clean, and modern, and parking is easy (Sb-€33, Db-€49, Tb-€69, Qb-€79, ask about discount when you book direct and show this book at check-in, cash only, non-smoking, free Wi-Fi, free loaner bikes for guests, parking, Blücherstrasse 60, tel. 06743/1294, www.pension-winzerhaus.de, winzerhaus@gmx.de).

$ Irmgard Orth B&B rents three fresh rooms, two of which share a bathroom on the hall. Irmgard speaks almost no English, but is exuberantly cheery and serves homemade honey with breakfast (S-€22-25, D-€36-38, Db-€38-40, higher price is for one-night stay, cash only, non-smoking, no Internet access, Spurgasse

2, look for *Honig* signs with picture of a beehive, tel. 06743/1553, speak slowly).

$ Jugendherberge Stahleck hostel is a 12th-century castle on the hilltop—350 steps above Bacharach—with a royal Rhine view. Open to travelers of any age, this is a gem with 168 beds and a private modern shower and WC in most rooms. The hostel offers hearty €7.50 all-you-can-eat buffet dinners, and in summer its pub serves cheap local wine and snacks until midnight. If you're arriving at the train station with luggage, it's an €8.50 taxi ride to the hostel—call 06743/1653 (€20 dorm beds with breakfast and sheets, nonmembers-€3.10 extra, couples can share one of five €51 Db, non-smoking, pay Internet access and Wi-Fi, laundry-€6; reception open 7:30-20:00, call if arriving later and check in at bar until 21:30; curfew at 22:00, tel. 06743/1266, www.diejugendherbergen. de, bacharach@diejugendherbergen.de). If driving, don't go in the driveway; park on the street and walk 200 yards.

Eating in Bacharach

Restaurants

Bacharach has no shortage of reasonably priced, atmospheric restaurants offering fine indoor and outdoor dining. Two of my recommended hotels—Rhein and Kranenturm—have good restaurants. Non-German options on the main street include a pizzeria and *Döner Kebab* joint (open daily until late) and an Irish pub.

The Rhein Hotel's **Stüber Restaurant** is Bacharach's best top-end choice. Chef Andreas Stüber, his family's sixth-generation chef, prepares regional, seasonal plates, served at river- and track-side seating or indoors with a spacious wood-and-white-tablecloth elegance. Consider his €16 William Turner pâté sampler plate, named after the British painter who liked Bacharach (€12-22 main courses, €27-37 fixed-price meals, always a good vegetarian option, open Wed-Mon 11:30-14:15 & 17:30-21:15, closed Tue and mid-Dec-Feb, call to reserve on weekends or for an outdoor table, facing the K-D boat dock below town center, Langstrasse 50, tel. 06743/1243).

Hotel Kranenturm is another good value, with hearty dinners (Kurt prides himself on his *Sauerbraten*—marinated beef with potato dumplings and red cabbage) and good main-course salads. If you're a trainspotter, sit on their trackside terrace and trade travel stories with new friends over dinner, letting screaming trains punctuate your conversation. If you prefer charming old German decor, sit inside (€10-16 main courses, open 6 days a week 17:00-21:00—closed day varies, restaurant closed Dec-early Feb). Kurt and Fatima are your hosts.

Altes Haus, the oldest building in town (see page 560), serves food with Bacharach's most romantic atmosphere. Find the cozy little dining room with photos of the opera singer who sang about Bacharach, adding to its fame (€9-15 main courses, May-Oct Thu-Tue 12:00-15:30 & 18:00-23:00, closed Wed and Nov-April, dead center by the Protestant church, tel. 06743/1209).

Gasthaus Jägerstube is every local's non-touristy, good-value hangout. It's a no-frills place with no outdoor seating, run by a former East German family determined to keep Bacharach's working class well-fed and watered. Next to the WC is a rare "party cash box." Regulars drop in bits of money throughout the year, Frau Tischmeier banks it, and by year's end...there's plenty in the little savings account for a community party (€9-16 main courses, March-Nov Wed-Mon 11:00-21:30, Dec-Feb Wed-Mon 15:00-23:00, closed Tue year-round, Marktstrasse 3, tel. 06743/1492, Tischmeier family).

The restaurant and café in the **Posthof** courtyard (by the TI) has nice outdoor seating and a medieval feel, with a view of the ruined cathedral above (€12 main courses, daily Easter-Oct 12:00-21:00, closed Nov-Easter, Oberstrasse 45-49, tel. 06743/947-1830).

Bacharacher Kebap Haus, on the main drag in the town center, is the town favorite for €4 *Döner Kebabs,* cheap pizzas, and salads (daily 10:00-23:00, Oberstrasse 43, tel. 06743/3127).

Eis Café Italia, on the main street, is run by friendly Mimo Calabrese, who brought gelato to town in 1976. He's known for his refreshing, not-too-sweet Riesling-flavored gelato. Notice the big sundae bowls on the shelves. To enjoy your *Eis* German-style, sit down and order ice cream off the menu, or just stop by for a cone "to go" for your evening stroll (€0.80/scoop, no tastes offered, April-mid-Oct daily 10:00-22:00, closed mid-Oct-March, Oberstrasse 48).

Pubs

Zum Kleinen Monning Irish Pub, with international beers on tap, provides the liveliest after-dinner scene in town. Bacharach's 2,000 residents hail from more than two dozen different nations, and you'll meet many of them here enjoying the convivial atmosphere created by Martina and Marcus (light meals too, Tue-Fri 12:00-15:00 & 18:00-24:00, Sat-Sun 14:30-24:00, closed Mon, Oberstrasse 35, tel. 06743/947-115).

If the Zum Kleinen Monning is dead, another late-night spot for drinks (and pizza) is **Zur Alt Backstubb** (seating inside and out, €7 pastas and pizzas, nightly until late, Blücherstrasse 16). Also try **Jugendherberge Stahleck**—Bacharach's youth hostel—where the pub serves cheap local wine and snacks until midnight in summer (listed earlier, under "Sleeping in Bacharach").

Wine-Tasting

Bacharach is proud of its wine. Two places in town—Bastian's rowdy and rustic Grüner Baum, and the more sophisticated Weingut Karl Heidrich—offer visitors an inexpensive tasting memory. Each creates carousels of local wines that small groups of travelers (who don't mind sharing a glass) can sample and compare. Both places offer light plates of food if you'd like a rustic meal.

At **Bastian's Weingut zum Grüner Baum,** groups of 2-6 people pay €19.50 for a wine carousel of 15 glasses—14 different white wines and one lonely rosé—and a basket of bread. Your mission: Team up with others who have this book to rendezvous here after dinner. Spin the Lazy Susan, share a common cup, and discuss the taste. Doris Bastian insists: "After each wine, you must talk to each other" (Mon-Wed and Fri from 13:00, Sat-Sun from 12:00, closed Thu and Jan-mid-March, just past Altes Haus, tel. 06743/1208). To make a meal of a carousel, consider the €8 *Käseteller* (seven different cheeses—including *Spundekäse,* the local soft cheese—with bread and butter).

Weingut Karl Heidrich is a fun family-run wine shop and *Stube* in the town center (at Oberstrasse 16), where Markus and daughter Magdalena proudly share their family's centuries-old wine tradition, explaining its fine points to travelers. They offer a variety of carousels with six wines, English descriptions, and bread (€11.80)—ideal for the more sophisticated wine taster—plus light meals (Thu-Tue 11:00-22:00, closed Wed and Nov-Easter, will ship to the US, tel. 06743/93060).

Bacharach Connections

Train Connections from the Rhine

Milk-run trains stop at Rhine towns each hour starting as early as 6:00, connecting at Mainz and Koblenz to trains farther afield. Trains between St. Goar and Bacharach depart at about :20 after the hour in each direction (€3.40, buy tickets from the machine in the unstaffed stations). The ride times listed below are calculated from Bacharach; for St. Goar, the difference is only 10 minutes. Train info: Tel. 0180-599-6633, www.bahn.com.

From Bacharach by Train to: St. Goar (hourly, 10 minutes), **Köln** (hourly, 1.75 hours with change in Koblenz, 2.5 hours direct), **Frankfurt Airport** (hourly, 1-1.5 hours, change in Mainz or Bingen), **Frankfurt** (hourly, 1.25-1.75 hours, change in Mainz or Bingen), **Rothenburg ob der Tauber** (every 2 hours, 4.25 hours, 3-4 changes), **Munich** (hourly, 5 hours, 2 changes), **Berlin** (hourly, 6.5-7.5 hours, 1-3 changes), **Amsterdam** (hourly, 5-6 hours, change in Köln, sometimes 1-2 more changes), **Bruges** (at least every 2 hours, 5.5-6.5 hours, some via Thalys, 2-3 changes).

St. Goar

St. Goar (sahnkt gwahr) is a classic Rhine tourist town. Its hulk of a castle overlooks a half-timbered shopping street and leafy riverside park, busy with sightseeing ships and contented strollers. Rheinfels Castle, once the mightiest on the Rhine, is the single best Rhineland ruin to explore. While the town of St. Goar itself is less interesting than Bacharach, be sure to explore beyond the shops: Thoughtful little placards scattered around town explain factoids (in English) about each street, lane, and square. St. Goar also makes a good base for hiking or biking the region. A tiny car ferry will shuttle you back and forth across the busy Rhine from here. (If you run out of things to see, a great pastime in St. Goar is simply chatting with friendly Heike at the K-D boat kiosk.) For train connections, see "Bacharach Connections," earlier.

Orientation to St. Goar

St. Goar is dominated by its mighty castle, Rheinfels. The village—basically a wide spot in the road at the foot of Rheinfels' hill—isn't much more than a few hotels and restaurants. From the riverboat docks, the main drag—a dull pedestrian mall without history—cuts through town before ending at the road up to the castle.

Tourist Information

The helpful St. Goar TI, which books rooms and stores bags for free, is on the pedestrian street, three blocks from the K-D boat dock and train station (May-Sept Mon-Fri 9:00-18:00, Sat 10:00-13:00, closed Sun; April and Oct Mon-Fri 9:00-12:30 & 13:30-17:00, closed Sat-Sun; Nov-March Mon-Thu 9:00-12:30 & 13:30-17:00, Fri 9:00-14:00, closed Sat-Sun; from train station, go downhill around church and turn left, Heerstrasse 86, tel. 06741/383, www.st-goar.de).

Helpful Hints

Picnics: St. Goar's waterfront park is hungry for picnickers. You can buy picnic fixings at the tiny **St. Goarer Stadtladen** grocery store on the pedestrian street (Mon-Fri 8:00-18:00, Sat 8:00-13:00, closed Sun, Heerstrasse 106).

Shopping: The Montag family runs two shops (one specializes in steins and the other in cuckoo clocks), both at the base of the castle hill road. The stein shop under the hotel has Rhine guides and fine steins. The other shop boasts "the largest free-hanging cuckoo clock in the world" (both open daily 8:30-18:00, shorter hours Nov-April). Montag's shops offer dis-

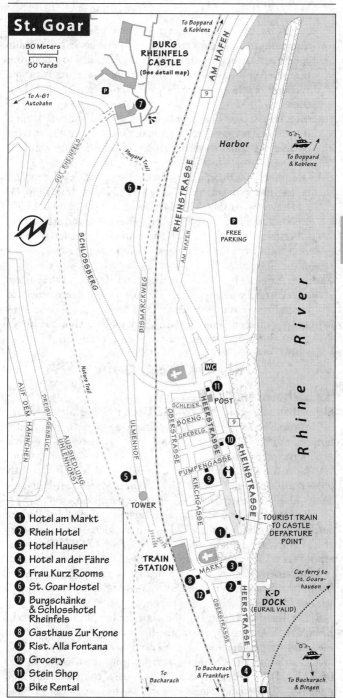

St. Goar

50 Meters
50 Yards

To A-61
Autobahn

BURG
RHEINFELS
CASTLE
(See detail map)

To Boppard
& Koblenz

AM HAFEN

Harbor

To Boppard
& Koblenz

FREE
PARKING

RHINE VALLEY

Vineyard Trail

SCHLOSSBERG

BISMARCKWEG

Nature Trail

RHEINSTRASSE

AM HAFEN

Rhine River

AUF DEM HÄHNCHEN

DREIBURGENBLICK

AUSSIEDLUNG
UHLENHORST

ULMENHOF

TOWER

SCHLEIER

OBERSTRASSE

BORNG.

GREBELG.

PUMPENGASSE

KIRCHGASSE

HEERSTRASSE

WC

POST

RHEINSTRASSE

TOURIST TRAIN
TO CASTLE
DEPARTURE
POINT

TRAIN
STATION

MARKT

OBERSTRASSE

HEERSTRASSE

Car ferry to
St. Goars-
hausen

K-D
DOCK
(EURAIL VALID)

To
Bacharach

To Bacharach
& Frankfurt

To Bacharach
& Bingen

1 Hotel am Markt
2 Rhein Hotel
3 Hotel Hauser
4 Hotel an der Fähre
5 Frau Kurz Rooms
6 St. Goar Hostel
7 Burgschänke
 & Schlosshotel
 Rheinfels
8 Gasthaus Zur Krone
9 Rist. Alla Fontana
10 Grocery
11 Stein Shop
12 Bike Rental

counts on any of their souvenirs (including Hummels; €10 minimum purchase) for travelers with this book. They'll ship your purchase home—or give you a VAT form to claim your tax refund at the airport if you're carrying your items with you. A couple of other souvenir shops are across from the K-D boat dock.

Internet Access: The **TI** is your best bet (€0.50/10 minutes), but if it's crowded or closed, the backup option is the expensive coin-op access (€6/hour, 4 terminals) or Wi-Fi (€5/hour) amid the slot machines at **Hotel Montag** (Heerstrasse 128).

Bike Rental: Goar Bike, run by Richard and Gabriele Langhans, is near the train station (€7/5 hours, €12/day, must show ID and leave €50 deposit, May-Oct Tue-Sun 9:00-13:00 & 15:00-19:00, closed Mon and Nov-April, go right as you exit station, Oberstrasse 44, tel. 06741/1735, goarbike@web.de). Richard, who speaks English, has maps and can suggest routes (or ask at the TI).

Parking: A free lot is at the downstream end of town, by the harbor. For on-street parking by the K-D boat dock and recommended hotels, use coins to get a ticket from the machine *(Parkschein-automat)* and put it on the dashboard (€4/day, Mon-Sat 10:00-18:00, Sun 12:00-18:00, coins only, free overnight).

Sights in St. Goar

▲▲▲Rheinfels Castle

Sitting like a dead pit bull above St. Goar, this mightiest of Rhine castles rumbles with ghosts from its hard-fought past. This hollow but interesting shell offers your single best hands-on ruined-castle experience on the river.

Cost and Hours: €4, family card-€10; mid-March-Oct daily 9:00-18:00, last entry at 17:00; Nov-mid-March Sat-Sun only 11:00-17:00, last entry at 16:00—weather permitting.

Tours and Information: Follow my self-guided tour. The free castle map is helpful, but the €2 English booklet is of no real value. If it's damp, be careful of slippery stones. Tel. 06741/7753, in winter 06741/383, www.st-goar.de. Gaby Loch is the castle manager.

Services: A handy WC is immediately across from the ticket booth (check out the guillotine urinals—stand back when you pull to flush).

Let There Be Light: If planning to explore the castle tunnels, bring a flashlight or buy one at the ticket office (€3.50). For a real medieval atmosphere, they also sell candles with matches (€0.50).

Getting to the Castle: A **taxi** up from town costs €5 (tel. 06741/7011). Or take the kitschy "tschu-tschu" **tourist train** (€2.50 one-way, €3.50 round-trip, 8 minutes to the top, hours vary but

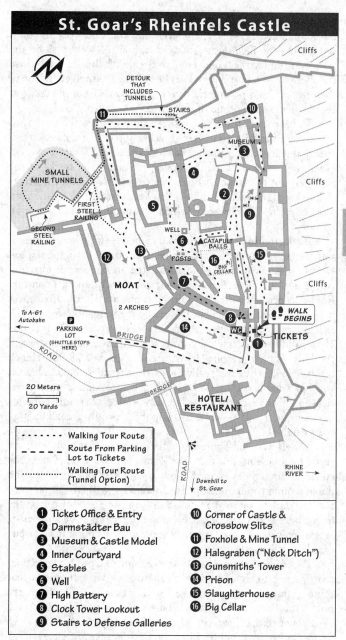

St. Goar's Rheinfels Castle

Cliffs

DETOUR THAT INCLUDES TUNNELS

STAIRS

11

10

MUSEUM

3

SMALL MINE TUNNELS

4

FIRST STEEL RAILING

2

Cliffs

SECOND STEEL RAILING

5

9

RHINE VALLEY

WELL

6

CATAPULT BALLS

15

12

13

POSTS

16

BIG CELLAR

MOAT

7

Cliffs

2 ARCHES

To A-61 Autobahn

P PARKING LOT (SHUTTLE STOPS HERE)

14

8

WC

WALK BEGINS

1

TICKETS

BRIDGE

ROAD

20 Meters
20 Yards

BRIDGE

HOTEL/ RESTAURANT

- - - - - Walking Tour Route

— — — Route From Parking Lot to Tickets

.... Walking Tour Route (Tunnel Option)

ROAD

RHINE RIVER

Downhill to St. Goar

1 Ticket Office & Entry
2 Darmstädter Bau
3 Museum & Castle Model
4 Inner Courtyard
5 Stables
6 Well
7 High Battery
8 Clock Tower Lookout
9 Stairs to Defense Galleries

10 Corner of Castle & Crossbow Slits
11 Foxhole & Mine Tunnel
12 Halsgraben ("Neck Ditch")
13 Gunsmiths' Tower
14 Prison
15 Slaughterhouse
16 Big Cellar

generally April-Oct daily 9:30-17:30, 2/hour, complete with lusty music, mobile 0171-445-1525). The train waits between the train station and the K-D dock. To avoid feeling silly as you sit on the train waiting for the "conductor" to decide it's time to go, browse the shopping street and hop on as he goes by (just wave him down, then pay at the top). The train returns to town from the castle at about the top and bottom of each hour.

To **hike** up to the castle, you can simply follow the main road up through the railroad underpass at the top end of the pedestrian street. But it's more fun to take the nature trail: Start at the St. Goar train station. Take the underpass under the tracks at the north end of the station, climb the steep stairs uphill, turn right (following *Burg Rheinfels* signs), and keep straight along the path just above the old city wall, which takes you to the castle in 10 minutes.

Background: Burg Rheinfels *was* huge—for five centuries, it was the biggest castle on the Rhine. Built in 1245 to guard a toll station, it soon earned the nickname "the unconquerable fortress." In the 1400s, the castle was thickened to withstand cannon fire. Rheinfels became a thriving cultural center and, in the 1520s, was visited by the artist Albrecht Dürer and the religious reformer Ulrich Zwingli. It saw lots of action in the Thirty Years' War (1618-1648), and later became the strongest and most modern fortress in the Holy Roman Empire. It withstood a siege of 28,000 French troops in 1692. But eventually the castle surrendered to the French without a fight, and in 1797, the French Revolutionary army destroyed it. For years, the ruined castle was used as a source of building stone, and today—while still mighty—it's only a small fraction of its original size.

❸ Self-Guided Tour: Rather than wander aimlessly, visit the castle by following this tour. We'll start at the museum, then circulate through the courtyards, up to the highest lookout point, and down around through the fortified ramparts, with an option to go into the dark tunnels. We'll finish in the prison and big cellar. The basic route below can be done without a flashlight or any daring acts of chivalry. (To go through the tunnels, bring a light or buy candles at the castle museum.)

Pick up the free map and use its commentary to navigate from red signpost to signpost through the castle. My self-guided tour route is similar to the one marked on the castle map. That map, the one in this book, and this tour all use the same numbering system. (You'll notice that I've skipped a few stops—just walk on by signs for ❷ *Darmstädter Bau,* ❺ *Stables,* and ❻ *Gunsmiths' Tower.*)

• *The ticket office is under the castle's clock tower, labeled* ❶ *Uhrturm. Walk through the entranceway and continue straight, passing several points of interest (which we'll visit later), until you get to the* ❸ *museum.*

Museum and Castle Model: The pleasant museum, located in the only finished room of the castle, has good English descriptions and comes with Romantic Age etchings that give a sense of the place as it was in the 19th century (daily mid-March-Oct 10:00-12:30 & 13:00-17:30; closed Nov-mid-March).

The seven-foot-tall carved stone immediately inside the door (marked *Flammensäule*)—a tombstone from a nearby Celtic grave—is from 400 years before Christ. There were people here long before the Romans...and this castle.

The sweeping castle history exhibit in the center of the room is well-described in English. The massive fortification was the only Rhineland castle to withstand Louis XIV's assault during the 17th century. At the far end of the room is a model reconstruction of the castle showing how much bigger it was before French Revolutionary troops destroyed it in the 18th century. Study this. Find where you are. (Hint: Look for the tall tower.) This was the living quarters of the original castle, which was only the smallest ring of buildings around the tiny central courtyard (13th century). The ramparts were added in the 14th century. By 1650, the fortress was largely complete. Since its destruction by the French in the late 18th century, it's had no military value. While no WWII bombs were wasted on this ruin, it served St. Goar as a stone quarry for generations. The basement of the museum shows the castle pharmacy and an exhibit of Rhine-region odds and ends, including tools, an 1830 loom, and photos of icebreaking on the Rhine. While once routine, icebreaking hasn't been necessary here since 1963.

• *Exit the museum and walk 30 yards directly out, slightly uphill into the castle courtyard, where you'll see a sign for the inner courtyard (❹ Innenhof).*

Medieval Castle Courtyard: Five hundred years ago, the entire castle encircled this courtyard. The place was self-sufficient and ready for a siege, with a bakery, pharmacy, herb garden, brewery, well (top of yard), and livestock. During peacetime, 300-600 people lived here; during a siege, there would be as many as 4,000. The walls were plastered and painted white. Bits of the original 13th-century plaster survive.

• *Continue through the courtyard under the* Erste Schildmauer *(first shield wall) sign, turn left, and walk straight to the two old wooden upright posts. Find the pyramid of stone catapult balls on your left.*

Castle Garden: Catapult balls like these were too expensive not to recycle—they'd be retrieved after any battle. Across from the balls is a well (❻ *Brunnen*)—essential for any castle during the age of sieges. Look in. Thirsty? The old posts are for the ceremonial baptizing of new members of the local trading league. While this guild goes back centuries, it's now a social club that fills this court with a huge wine party the third weekend of each September.

• *Climb uphill to the castle's highest point by walking along the cobbled path up past the high battery (❼ Hohe Batterie) to the castle's best viewpoint—up where the German flag waves (signed ❽ Uhrturm).*

Highest Castle Tower Lookout: Enjoy a great view of the river, the castle, and the forest. Remember, the fortress once covered five times the land it does today. Notice how the other castles (across the river) don't poke above the top of the Rhine canyon. That would make them easy for invading armies to see.

From this perch, survey the Rhine Valley, cut out of slate over millions of years by the river. The slate absorbs the heat of the sun, making the grapes grown here well-suited for wine. Today the slate is mined to provide roofing. Imagine St. Goar settling here 1,500 years ago, establishing a place where sailors—thankful to have survived the treacherous Loreley—would stop and pray. Imagine the frozen river of years past, when the ice would break up and boats would huddle in manmade harbors like the one below for protection. Consider the history of trade on this busy river—from the days when castles levied tolls on ships, to the days when boats would be hauled upstream with the help of riverside towpaths, to the 21st century when 300 ships a day move their cargo past St. Goar. And imagine this castle before the French destroyed it... when it was the mightiest structure on the river, filled with people and inspiring awe among all who passed.

• *Return to the catapult balls, walk downhill and through the tunnel, veer left through the arch marked ❾ zu den Wehrgängen ("to the defense galleries"), and go down two flights of stairs. Turn left and step into the dark, covered passageway. From here, we'll begin a rectangular walk taking us completely around (counterclockwise) the perimeter of the castle.*

Covered Defense Galleries with "Minutemen" Holes: Soldiers—the castle's "minutemen"—had a short commute: defensive positions on the outside, home in the holes below on the left. Even though these living quarters were padded with straw, life was unpleasant.

• *Continue straight through the dark gallery, up the stairs, and to the corner of the castle, where you'll see a white painted arrow at eye level and a red signpost with the number ❿. Stand with your back to the arrow on the wall.*

Corner of Castle: Gape up. A three-story, half-timbered building originally rose beyond the highest stone fortification. The two stone tongues near the top just around the corner (to the right) supported the toilet. (Insert your own joke here.) Turn around and face the wall. The crossbow slits below the white arrow were once steeper. The bigger hole on the riverside was for hot pitch.

• *Follow that white arrow out along the back side of the castle. Notice the stairs on the right, which lead down to the Small Mine Tunnels—if you'd like to visit them, see the "Optional Detour" on page 576. You'll rejoin this tour at the prison. Otherwise, keep going, and at the corner, turn left.*

Thoop...You're Dead: Look ahead at the smartly placed crossbow slit. While you're lying there, notice the stonework. The little round holes were for scaffolds used as they built up. They indicate this stonework is original. Notice also the fine stonework on the chutes. More boiling pitch...now you're toast, too.

• *Pick yourself up, and walk back a few steps and over to the gray railing. Look up the valley and uphill where the sprawling fort stretched. Below, just outside the wall, is land where attackers would gather. The mine tunnels are under there, waiting to blow up any attackers.*

Now keep going along the perimeter (under three low archways), jog left, go down five steps and into an open field, and walk toward the wooden bridge. The "old" wooden bridge is actually modern.

Dark Tunnel Detour: For a short detour through a castle tunnel—possible only if you have a light—turn your back to the main castle (with the modern bridge to your left) and face the stone structure labeled ⓬ *Halsgraben.* (You'll exit in a few minutes at the high railing above the red *#12* sign.) Go 20 yards to the right, and enter the tunnel at the bottom, following the red *Grosser Minengang* sign. At the end of the short, big tunnel, take two steps up and walk eight level steps, turn left, and follow the long uphill ramp (this is where it's pitch-black, and adults will need to watch their heads). At the end, a spiral staircase takes you up to the high-railing opening you saw earlier, and then back to the courtyard.

• *When ready to leave this courtyard, angle left (under the red zum Verliess sign, before the bridge) through two arches and through the rough entry to the* ⓮ *Verliess (prison) on the left.*

Prison: This is one of six dungeons. You just walked through an entrance prisoners only dreamed of 400 years ago. They came and went through the little square hole in the ceiling. The holes in the walls supported timbers that thoughtfully gave as many as 15 residents something to sit on to keep them out of the filthy slop that gathered on the floor. Twice a day, they were given bread and water. Some prisoners actually survived longer than two years in here. While the town could torture and execute, the castle had permission only to imprison criminals in these dungeons. Consider this: According to town records, the two men who spent the most time down here—2.5 years each—died within three weeks of regaining their freedom. Perhaps after a diet of bread and water, feasting on meat and wine was simply too much.

• *Continue through the next arch, under the white arrow, then turn left and walk 30 yards to the* ⓯ *Schlachthaus.*

Slaughterhouse: Any proper castle was prepared to survive a six-month siege. With 4,000 people, that's a lot of provisions. The cattle that lived within the walls were slaughtered in this room.

The castle's mortar was congealed here (by packing all the organic waste from the kitchen into kegs and sealing it). Notice the drainage gutters. "Running water" came through from drains built into the walls (to keep the mortar dry and therefore strong...and less smelly).

• *Back outside, climb the modern stairs to the left (look for the zum Ausgang sign). A skinny, dark passage leads you into the...*

Big Cellar: This ⓰ *Grosser Keller* was a big pantry. When the castle was smaller, this was the original moat—you can see the rough lower parts of the wall. The original floor was 13 feet deeper. The drawbridge rested upon the stone nubs on the left. When the castle expanded, the moat became this cellar. Halfway up the walls on the entrance side of the room, square holes mark spots where timbers made a storage loft, perhaps filled with grain. In the back, an arch leads to the wine cellar (sometimes blocked off) where finer wine was kept. Part of a soldier's pay was wine...table wine. This wine was kept in a single 180,000-liter stone barrel (that's 47,550 gallons), which generally lasted about 18 months.

The count owned the surrounding farmland. Farmers got to keep 20 percent of their production. Later, in more liberal feudal times, the nobility let them keep 40 percent. Today, the German government leaves the workers with 60 percent...and provides a few more services.

• *You're free. Climb out, turn right, and leave. For coffee on a terrace with a great view, visit Schlosshotel Rheinfels, opposite the entrance.*

Optional Detour—Into the Small Mine Tunnels: Tall people might want to skip this foray into low, cramped tunnels (some only three feet high). In about 1600, to protect their castle, the Rheinfellers cleverly booby-trapped the land just outside their walls by building tunnels topped with thin slate roofs and packed with explosives. By detonating the explosives when under attack, they could kill hundreds of invaders. In 1626, a handful of underground Protestant Germans blew 300 Catholic Spaniards to—they figured—hell. You're welcome to wander through a set of never-blown-up tunnels. But be warned: It's 600 feet long, assuming you make no wrong turns; it's pitch-dark, muddy, and claustrophobic, with confusing dead-ends; and you'll never get higher than a deep crouch. It cannot be done without a light (candles and flashlights available at entrance). Be sure to bring the castle map, which shows the tunnels in detail.

To tour the Small Mine Tunnels, start at the red ❿ signpost at the crossbow slits (described earlier). Follow the modern stairs on the right leading down to the mine (*zu den Minengängen* sign on upper left). The ⓫ *Fuchsloch* (foxhole) sign welcomes you to a covered passageway. Walk level (take no stairs) past the first black-steel railing (where you hope to emerge later) and around a few bends to the second steel railing. Climb down.

The "highway" in this foxhole is three feet high. The ceiling may be painted with a white line indicating the correct path. Don't venture into the narrower side aisles. These were once filled with the gunpowder. After a small decline, take the second right. At the T-intersection, go right (uphill). After about 10 feet, go left. Take the next right and look for a light at the end of the tunnel. Head up a rocky incline under the narrowest part of the tunnel, and you'll emerge at that first steel railing. The stairs on the right lead to freedom. Cross the field, walk under the bigger archway, and continue uphill toward the old wooden bridge. Angle left through two arches (before the bridge) and through the rough entry to the ⓴ *Verliess* (prison) on the left, where you can rejoin the self-guided tour.

Sleeping in St. Goar

(€1 = about $1.30, country code: 49, area code: 06741)
For parking advice, see "Helpful Hints," earlier.

$$ Hotel am Markt, run by Herr and Frau Marx and their friendly staff, is rustic and a good deal, with all the modern comforts. It features a hint of antler with a pastel flair, 17 bright rooms, and a good restaurant. It's a good value and a stone's throw from the boat dock and train station (S-€40, Sb-€50, standard Db-€65, bigger riverview Db-€80, cheaper March-mid-April and Oct, closed Nov-Feb, free Internet access and Wi-Fi, parking-€5, Markt 1, tel. 06741/1689, fax 06741/1721, www.hotel-am-markt-sankt-goar.de, info@hotel-am-markt-sankt-goar.de).

$$ Rhein Hotel, two doors down from Hotel am Markt and run with enthusiasm by young and energetic Gil Velich, has 10 quality rooms in a spacious building (Sb-€50-55, quiet viewless Db-€65-70, river-view balcony Db-€85-90, larger view/balcony Db-€95-100, higher prices are for Fri-Sat nights, non-smoking, free Wi-Fi, laundry-€15/load, closed mid-Nov-Feb, Heerstrasse 71, tel. 06741/981-240, www.rheinhotel-st-goar.de, info@rhein-hotel-st-goar.de).

$ Hotel Hauser, across the square from Hotel am Markt, is a very basic place with ramshackle halls and 12 tidy rooms. It may be closed or have new owners when you visit—call ahead (S-€23, D-€46, Db-€54, Db with Rhine-view balconies-€58, free Wi-Fi, Heerstrasse 77, tel. 06741/333, fax 06741/1464, www.hotelhauser.de, info@hotelhauser.de).

$ Hotel an der Fähre is a simple, well-run place (though the lobby has a slight aroma of cigarette smoke) on the busy road at the end of town, immediately across from the ferry dock. It rents

12 cheap but decent rooms (S-€25, Sb-€30, D-€45, Db-€50, extra bed-€20, cash only, street noise but double-glazed windows, free Wi-Fi, closed Nov-Feb, Heerstrasse 47, tel. 06741/980-577, www.hotel-stgoar.de, anderfaehre@t-online.de, Armin and Svetla Stecher, limited English spoken).

$ Frau Kurz has been housing my readers since 1988. With the help of her daughter, Jeanette, she offers St. Goar's best B&B, renting three delightful rooms (sharing 2.5 bathrooms) with bathrobes, a breakfast terrace, garden, fine three-castle views, and homemade marmalade (S-€30, D-€54, 2-night minimum, D-€50 if you stay at least 4 nights, cash only, non-smoking, free and easy parking, no Internet access, ask about apartment with kitchen if staying at least 5 days, Ulmenhof 11, tel. 06741/459, www.gaestehaus-kurz. de, webmaster@gaestehaus-kurz.de). It's a steep five-minute hike from the train station: Exit left from the station, take an immediate left under the tracks, and go part-way up the zigzag stairs, turning right through an archway onto Ulmenhof; #11 is just past the tower.

$ St. Goar Hostel, the big beige building down the hill from the castle, rents 126 beds, mostly in 4- to 10-bed dorms but also in 18 doubles. The facilities hark back to an earlier age of hosteling, with shared baths down the hall (hence the low price), but it has Rhine views, a nice terrace, and hearty €7 dinners (dorm beds-€15.50, D-€38, includes breakfast, nonmembers-€3.10 extra, non-smoking, open all day, curfew 22:00—but you can borrow the key, closed mid-Nov-mid-March, Bismarckweg 17, tel. 06741/388, fax 06741/2869, www.diejugendherbergen.de, st-goar@diejugendherbergen.de). It's a fairly level 10-minute walk from the train station, following the red *Jugendherberge* signs.

Eating in St. Goar

Hotel am Markt serves tasty traditional meals with plenty of game and fish (specialties include marinated roast beef and homemade cheesecake) at fair prices with good atmosphere and service. Choose cozy indoor seating, or dine outside with a river view (€9-15 main courses, March-Oct daily 8:00-21:00, closed Nov-Feb, Markt 1, tel. 06741/1689).

Burgschänke, on the ground floor of Schlosshotel Rheinfels (the hotel across from the castle ticket office—enter through the souvenir shop) offers the only reasonably priced lunches up at Rheinfels Castle. It's family-friendly and has a Rhine view from its fabulous outdoor terrace (€7-9 pizzas, pastas, and *Flammkuchen;* Sun-Thu 11:00-18:00, Fri-Sat 11:00-21:00, tel. 06741/802-806).

The **Schlosshotel Rheinfels** dining room is your Rhine splurge, with an incredible indoor view terrace in an elegant, dressy setting. Call and reserve if you're coming for breakfast or want a window table (€16 buffet breakfast, €19-24 main courses, €32-36 three-course fixed-price meals, daily 7:00-11:00, 12:00-14:00 & 18:30-21:00, tel. 06741/8020).

Gasthaus Zur Krone is the local choice for traditional German food in a restaurant that has no river view and isn't part of a hotel (€7-10 main courses, Thu-Tue 11:00-14:30 & 18:00-21:00, closed Wed, next to the train station and church at Oberstrasse 38, tel. 06741/1515).

Ristorante Alla Fontana, tucked away on a back lane and busy with locals, serves the best Italian food in town at great prices in a lovely dining room (€7 pizza and pasta, Tue-Sun 11:30-14:00 & 17:30-22:00, closed Mon, reservations smart, Pumpengasse 5, 06741/96117).

Picnics: The grocery store (see "Helpful Hints," earlier) has plenty of goodies. You can assemble a picnic to enjoy at the riverside park or up at the castle.

RHINE VALLEY

BERLIN

No tour of Germany is complete without a look at its historic and reunited capital. Over the last two decades, Berlin has been a construction zone. Standing on ripped-up tracks and under a canopy of cranes, visitors witnessed the rebirth of a great European capital. Although construction continues, today the once-divided city is thoroughly woven back together. Berlin has emerged as one of Europe's top destinations: captivating, lively, fun-loving, all-around enjoyable—and easy on the budget.

As you enjoy the thrill of walking over what was the Wall and through the well-patched Brandenburg Gate, it's clear that history is not contained in some book, but is an exciting story of which we are a part. In Berlin, the fine line between history and current events is excitingly blurry. But even for non-historians, Berlin is a city of fine experiences. Explore the fun and funky neighborhoods emerging in the former East, packed with creative hipster eateries and boutiques trying to one-up each other. Go for a pedal or a cruise along the delightful Spree riverfront. In the city's world-class museums, stroll up the steps of a classical Greek temple amid rough-and-tumble ancient statuary, and peruse canvases by Dürer, Rembrandt, and Vermeer. Nurse a stein of brew in a rollicking beer hall, or dive into a cheap *Currywurst* (grilled bratwurst with curry-infused ketchup, arguably the most beloved food ever to come out of Berlin).

Of course, Berlin is still largely defined by its tumultuous 20th century. The city was Hitler's capital during World War II, and in the postwar years, Berlin became the front line of a new global war—one between Soviet-style communism and American-style capitalism. The East-West division was set in stone in 1961, when

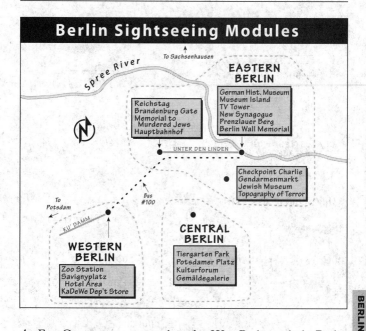

Berlin Sightseeing Modules

To Sachsenhausen

Spree River

EASTERN BERLIN

German Hist. Museum
Museum Island
TV Tower
New Synagogue
Prenzlauer Berg
Berlin Wall Memorial

Reichstag
Brandenburg Gate
Memorial to
 Murdered Jews
Hauptbahnhof

UNTER DEN LINDEN

Checkpoint Charlie
Gendarmenmarkt
Jewish Museum
Topography of Terror

To Potsdam

Bus #100

KU'DAMM

WESTERN BERLIN

Zoo Station
Savignyplatz
Hotel Area
KaDeWe Dep't Store

CENTRAL BERLIN

Tiergarten Park
Potsdamer Platz
Kulturforum
Gemäldegalerie

BERLIN

the East German government boxed in West Berlin with the Berlin Wall. The Wall stood for 28 years. In 1990, less than a year after the Wall fell, the two Germanys—and the two Berlins—officially became one. When the dust settled, Berliners from both sides of the once-divided city faced the monumental challenge of reunification.

Berliners joke that they don't need to travel anywhere because their city's always changing. Spin a postcard rack to see what's new. A 10-year-old guidebook on Berlin covers a different city. City planners have seized on the city's reunification and the return of the national government to make Berlin a great capital once again. When the Wall fell, the East was a decrepit wasteland and the West was a paragon of commerce and materialism. More than 20 years later, the roles are reversed: It's eastern Berlin where you feel the vibrant pulse of the city, while western Berlin seems like yesterday's news.

Today, Berlin is like the nuclear fuel rod of a great nation. It's so vibrant with youth, energy, and an anything-goes-and-anything's-possible buzz that Munich feels spent in comparison. Berlin is both extremely popular and surprisingly affordable. As a booming tourist attraction, Berlin now welcomes more visitors than Rome.

Planning Your Time

I'd give Berlin three nights and at least two full days, and spend them this way:

Day 1: Begin your day getting oriented to this huge city. For a quick and relaxing once-over-lightly tour, jump on one of the many hop-on, hop-off buses that make a two-hour narrated orientation loop through the city. Use the bus as you like, to hop off and on at places of interest (such as Potsdamer Platz). Then walk from the Reichstag (reservations required), under the Brandenburg Gate, and down Unter den Linden. Tour the German History Museum, and cap your sightseeing day by catching the one-hour Spree River boat tour (or pedaling a rented bike) along the parklike banks of the Spree River from Museum Island to the Chancellery.

Day 2: Spend your morning touring the great museums on Museum Island (Pergamon Museum and the Egyptian collection at the Neues Museum—timed-entry tickets required for both, and Romantic German art in the Old National Gallery). Dedicate your afternoon to sights of the Third Reich and Holocaust: After lunch, hike via Potsdamer Platz to the Topography of Terror exhibit and along the surviving Zimmerstrasse stretch of the Wall to Checkpoint Charlie. You could also head up to the Berlin Wall Memorial

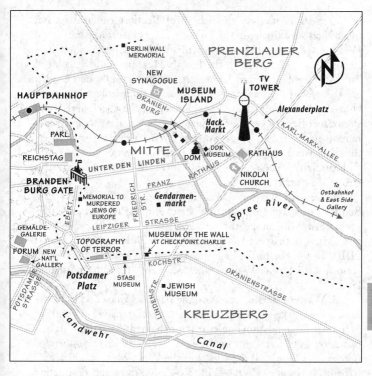

for a more in-depth survey of that infamous barrier, or swing by the Jewish Museum. Finish your day in the lively East—ideally in the once glum, then edgy, now fun-loving and trendy Prenzlauer Berg district.

Orientation to Berlin

Berlin is huge, with 3.4 million people. The city is spread out and its sights numerous, so you'll need to be well-organized to experience the city smartly. The tourist's Berlin can be broken into three main digestible chunks:

1. Eastern Berlin has the highest concentration of notable sights and colorful neighborhoods. Near the landmark Brandenburg Gate, you'll find the Reichstag building, Pariser Platz, and the Memorial to the Murdered Jews of Europe. From Brandenburg Gate, the famous Unter den Linden boulevard runs eastward through former East Berlin, passing the German History Museum (a history lover's favorite) and Museum Island (Pergamon Museum, Neues Museum, and Berlin Cathedral) on the way to Alexanderplatz (TV Tower). The intersection of Unter den Linden and Friedrichstrasse has reclaimed its place as the center of the city. South of Unter den Linden are the delightful Gendarmenmarkt square, most Nazi sites (including the Topography of Terror), some good Wall-related sights (Museum of the Wall at Checkpoint Charlie and East Side Gallery), the Jewish Museum, and the colorful Turkish neighborhood of Kreuzberg. North of Unter den Linden are these worth-a-wander neighborhoods: Oranienburger Strasse (Jewish Quarter and New Synagogue), Hackescher Markt, and Prenzlauer Berg (several recommended hotels and a very lively restaurant/nightlife zone). Just west of Prenzlauer Berg is the Berlin Wall Memorial (with an intact surviving section of the Wall). Eastern Berlin's pedestrian-friendly Spree riverbank is also worth a stroll (or a river cruise).

2. Central Berlin is dominated by the giant Tiergarten park. South of the park are Potsdamer Platz and the Kulturforum museum cluster (including the Gemäldegalerie, New National Gallery, Musical Instruments Museum, and Philharmonic Concert Hall). To the north, the huge Hauptbahnhof (main train station) straddles the former Wall in what was central Berlin's no-man's-land.

3. Western Berlin centers on the Bahnhof Zoo (Zoo train station, often marked "Zoologischer Garten" on transit maps) and the grand Kurfürstendamm boulevard, nicknamed "Ku'damm" (transportation hub, tours, information, shopping, and recommended hotels). The East is all the rage. But the West, while staid in comparison, is bouncing back—with big-name stores and destination restaurants that keep the area buzzing. During the Cold War, this "Western Sector" was the hub for Western visitors. Capitalists visited the West, with a nervous side-trip beyond the Wall into the grim and foreboding East. (Cubans, Russians, Poles, and Angolans stayed behind the Wall and did their sightseeing in the East.) Remnants of this Iron Curtain-era Western focus have left today's visitors with a stronger focus on the Ku'damm and Bahnhof Zoo than the district deserves.

Tourist Information

With any luck, you won't have to use Berlin's TIs—they're for-profit agencies working for the city's big hotels, which colors the information they provide. TI branches, appropriately called "info-stores," are unlikely to have the information you need (tel. 030/250-025, www.visitberlin.de). You'll find them at the **Hauptbahnhof** train station (daily 8:00-22:00, by main entrance on Europaplatz), **Ku'damm** (Kurfürstendamm 22, in the glass-and-steel Neues Kranzler Eck building, Mon-Sat 9:30-20:00, Sun 9:30-18:00), and the **Brandenburg Gate** (daily 9:30-19:00).

Skip the TI's €1 map, and instead pick up any of the walking tour companies' brochures—they include nearly-as-good maps for free (most hotels also provide free city maps). While the TI does sell the three-day Museumspass (described next), it's also available at major museums. If you take a walking tour, your guide is likely a better source of nightlife or shopping tips than the TI.

Museum Passes: The three-day, €19 **Museumspass** is a great value. It gets you into more than 50 museums, including the national museums and most of the recommended biggies, on three consecutive days. As you'll routinely spend €6-10 per admission, this pays for itself in a hurry. And you'll enjoy the ease of popping in and out of museums that you might not otherwise want to pay for. Buy it at the TI or any participating museum. The pass generally lets you skip the line and go directly into the museum (though occasionally you may have to wait in line to get a printed free ticket). The €14 **Museum Island Pass** (Bereichskarte Museumsinsel, price can change with special exhibits) covers all the museums on Museum Island (otherwise €8-13 each) and is a fine value—but for just €5 more, the three-day Museumspass gives you triple the days and many more entries. TIs also sell the **WelcomeCard,** a transportation pass that also includes some museum discounts (described later, under "Getting Around Berlin").

Local Publications: Various magazines can help make your time in Berlin more productive (available at the TI and/or many newsstands). *Berlin Programm* is a comprehensive German-language monthly, especially strong in high culture, that lists upcoming events and museum hours (€2, www.berlin-programm.de). *Exberliner Magazine,* the only English monthly (published mostly by expat Brits who love to poke fun at expat Americans), is very helpful for curious travelers. It has an edgy, somewhat pretentious, youthful focus and gives a fascinating insider's look at this fast-changing city (€3 but often given away at theaters or on the street, www.exberliner.com).

Arrival in Berlin
By Train at Berlin Hauptbahnhof
Berlin's newest and grandest train station is Berlin Hauptbahnhof (main train station, a.k.a. simply "der Bahnhof", abbreviated Hbf). All long-distance trains arrive here, at Europe's biggest, mostly underground train station. This is a "transfer station"—unique for its major lines coming in at right angles—where the national train system meets the city's train system (S-Bahn).

The gigantic station can be intimidating on arrival, but it's laid out logically on five floors (which, confusingly, can be marked in different ways). Escalators and elevators connect the **main floor** (*Erdgeschoss*, EG, a.k.a level 0); the two **lower levels** (*Untergeschoss*, UG1 and UG2, a.k.a. levels -1 and -2); and the two **upper levels** (*Obergeschoss*, OG1 and OG2, a.k.a. levels +1 and +2). Tracks

BERLIN

1-8 are in the lowest underground level (UG2), while tracks 11-16 (along with the S-Bahn) are on the top floor (OG2). Shops and services are concentrated on the three middle levels (EG, OG1, and UG1). The south entrance (toward the Reichstag and downtown, with a taxi stand) is marked *Washingtonplatz*, while the north entrance is marked *Europaplatz*.

Services: The **TI** is on the main floor (EG)—facing the north/*Europaplatz* entrance, look left; a 24-hour **pharmacy** is across the hall on the right (one floor above you, on OG1). The **"Rail & Fresh WC"** facility (public pay toilets) is on the main floor (EG) near the Burger King and food court. You can store your **luggage** at the Gepäck Center, an efficient and secure deposit service (€5/day per bag, daily 6:00-22:00, on upper level OG1 directly under track 14). Luggage lockers (€4) are difficult to find since they're in the parking garage (levels P-1, P-2, and P-3; look for the garage entrance near Kaisers supermarket on the underground shopping level UG1).

Train Information and Tickets: The station has two DeutscheBahn *Reisezentrum* information counters: one on the upper level (OG1/+1, daily 6:00-22:00), and the other on the lower level (UG1/-1, Mon-Fri 8:00-22:00, Sat-Sun 10:00-20:00; this branch also has the EurAide counter described next). If you're staying in western Berlin, keep in mind that the info center at the Bahnhof Zoo station is just as good and much less crowded.

EurAide is an English-speaking information desk with answers to your questions about train travel around Europe. It operates from a single counter in the underground shopping level *Reisezentrum* (follow signs to tracks 5-6 and *Reisezentrum –1*). It's American-run, so communication is simple. This is an especially good place to make fast-train and *couchette* reservations for later in your trip (April-Sept Mon-Fri 11:00-20:00—though May-July opens at 10:00, May-Aug also open Sat 10:00-16:00—otherwise closed on Sat and always closed Sun; off-season Mon-Fri 11:00-18:30 only and closed Jan-Feb; www.euraide.com).

Shopping: In addition to all those trains, the Hauptbahnhof is also the home of 80 shops with long hours—some locals call the station a "shopping mall with trains" (daily 8:00-22:00, only stores selling travel provisions are open Sun). The Kaisers supermarket (on underground shopping level UG1, follow signs for tracks 1-2) is handy for assembling a picnic for your train ride.

Getting into Town: Taxis and buses wait outside the station, but the S-Bahn is probably the best means of connecting to your destination within Berlin. The cross-town express S-Bahn line connects the station with my recommended hotels in a few minutes. It's simple: All S-Bahn trains are on tracks 15 and 16 at the top of the station (level OG2/+2). All trains on track 15 go east, stopping at Friedrichstrasse, Hackescher Markt (with connections to Prenzlauer Berg), Alexanderplatz, and Ostbahnhof; trains on track 16 go west, toward Bahnhof Zoo and Savignyplatz. Your train ticket or railpass into the station covers your connecting S-Bahn ride into town (and your ticket out includes the transfer via S-Bahn to the Hauptbahnhof). U-Bahn rides are not covered by tickets or railpasses.

If you're sleeping at one of my recommended hotels in eastern Berlin's Prenzlauer Berg neighborhood, take any train on track 15 two stops to Hackescher Markt, then catch tram #M1 north (see map on page 660).

If you're sleeping at one of my recommended hotels in western Berlin, catch any train on track 16 to Savignyplatz, and you're a five-minute walk from your hotel (see map on page 666). Savignyplatz is one stop after **Bahnhof Zoo** (rhymes with "toe"; a.k.a. Bahnhof Zoologischer Garten), the once-grand train hub now eclipsed by the Hauptbahnhof. Nowadays Bahnhof Zoo is useful mainly for its shops, uncrowded train-information desk, and BVG transit office (outside the entrance, amid the traffic).

The Berlin Hauptbahnhof is not well-connected to the city's U-Bahn (subway) system—yet. The station's sole U-Bahn line—U55—goes only two stops, to the Brandenburger Tor station, and doesn't really connect to the rest of the system. It's part of a planned extension of the U5 line to Alexanderplatz that's far from completion. But for transit junkies, it is an interesting ride on Europe's shortest subway line.

BERLIN

By Plane

For information on reaching the city center from Berlin's new airport, see "Berlin Connections" at the end of this chapter.

Helpful Hints

Medical Help: "Call a doc" is a nonprofit referral service designed for tourists (tel. 01805-321-303, phone answered 24 hours a day, www.calladoc.com). Payment is arranged between you and the doctor, and is likely far more affordable than similar care in the US. The US Embassy also has a list of local English-speaking doctors (tel. 030/83050, www.usembassy.de).

Museum Tips: Some major Berlin museums are closed on Monday—if you're in town on that day, review hours carefully before making plans. If you plan to see several museums, you'll save money with the Museumspass, which covers nearly all the city sights for three days—including everything covered by the one-day Museum Island Pass (see "Tourist Information—Museum Passes," earlier).

Addresses: Many Berlin streets are numbered with odd and even numbers on the same side of the street, often with no connection to the other side (for example, Ku'damm #212 can be across the street from #14). To save steps, check the white street signs on curb corners; many list the street numbers covered on that side of the block.

Cold War Terminology: Cold War history is important here, so it's helpful to learn a few key terms. What Americans called "East Germany" was technically the German Democratic Republic—known here by its German name, the Deutsche Demokratische Republik. The initials **DDR** (day-day-AIR) are the shorthand you'll still see around what was once East Germany. The formal name for "West Germany" was the Federal Republic of Germany—the Bundesrepublik Deutschland (BRD)—and is the name now shared by all of reunited Germany.

Internet Access: You'll find Internet access in most hotels and hostels, as well as at small Internet cafés all over the city. Near Savignyplatz, **Internet-Terminal** is at Kantstrasse 38. In eastern Berlin, try **Hotdog World** in Prenzlauer Berg (Weinbergsweg 4, just a few steps from U8: Rosenthaler Platz toward Kastanienallee), or **Surf Inn** at Alexanderplatz 9. Bahnhof Zoo, Friedrichstrasse, and Hauptbahnhof train stations have coin-operated Internet terminals (though these unmanned machines can come with greater security risks).

Bookstore: Berlin Story, a big, cluttered, fun bookshop, has a knowledgeable staff and the best selection anywhere in town of English-language books on Berlin. They also stock an amusing mix of knickknacks and East Berlin nostalgia souvenirs (Mon-Sat 10:00-19:00, Sun 10:00-18:00, Unter den Linden 40, tel. 030/2045-3842, www.berlinstory.de). I'd skip the overpriced little museum in the back.

Other Berlin Souvenirs: If you're taken with the city's unofficial mascot, the *Ampelmännchen* (traffic-light man), you'll find a world of souvenirs slathered with his iconic red and green image at **Ampelmann Shops** (various locations, including near Gendarmenmarkt at Markgrafenstrasse 37, near Museum Island inside the DomAquarée mall, in the Hackeschen Höfe, and at Potsdamer Platz).

Laundry: Berlin has several self-service launderettes with long hours (wash and dry—€4-9/load). Near my recommended hotels in Prenzlauer Berg, try **Waschsalon 115** (daily 6:00-23:00, exact change required, free Wi-Fi, Torstrasse 115, around the corner from the recommended Circus hostel) or **Eco-Express Waschsalon** (daily 6:00-23:00, handy pizzeria next door, Danziger Strasse 7). The **Schnell & Sauber Was-**

chcenter chain has a location in Prenzlauer Berg (daily 6:00-23:00, exact change required, Oderberger Strasse 1).

Updates to this Book: For news about changes to this book's coverage since it was published, see www.ricksteves.com/update.

Getting Around Berlin

Berlin's sights spread far and wide. Right from the start, commit yourself to the city's fine public-transit system.

By Public Transit: Subway, Train, Tram, and Bus

Berlin's many modes of transportation are consolidated into one system that uses the same ticket: U-Bahn (*Untergrund-Bahn*, Berlin's subway), S-Bahn (*Stadtschnellbahn*, or "fast urban train," mostly aboveground and with fewer stops), *Strassenbahn* (streetcars, called "trams" by locals), and buses. For all types of transit, there are three lettered zones (A, B, and C); all of the sights listed in this chapter lie within zones A and B (the city proper). If you'll be here for a few days, get and use the excellent *Discover Berlin by Train and Bus* map-guide published by the public transit operator BVG (at subway ticket windows).

Ticket Options: You have several options for tickets.

• The €2.30 **basic** ticket (*Einzelfahrschein*) covers two hours of travel in one direction on buses or subways. It's easy to make this ticket stretch to cover several rides...as long as they're all in the same direction.

• The €1.40 **short-ride** ticket (*Kurzstrecke*) covers a single ride of six bus stops or three subway stations (one transfer allowed).

• The €8.20 **four-trip** ticket (*4-Fahrten-Karte*) is the same as four basic tickets at a small discount.

• The **day pass** (*Tageskarte*) is good until 3:00 the morning after it expires (€6.30 for zones AB). For longer stays, consider a seven-day pass (*Sieben-Tage-Karte*; €27.20 for zones AB), or the WelcomeCard (described below), which is good for up to five days and also includes sightseeing discounts. The *Kleingruppenkarte* lets groups of up to five travel all day (€15 for zones AB).

• If you've already bought a ticket for zones A and B, and later decide that you also want to go to zone C, you can buy an **"extension ticket"** (*Anschlussfahrschein*) for €1.50 per ride in that zone.

• If you plan to cover a lot of ground using public transportation during a two- or three-day visit, the **WelcomeCard** (available at TIs) is usually the best deal. For longer stays, there's even a five-day option. It covers all public transportation and gives you up to 50 percent discounts on lots of minor and a few major museums (including Checkpoint Charlie), sightseeing tours (including 25 percent off the recommended Original Berlin Walks),

BERLIN

and music and theater events (www.visitberlin.de/welcome-card). The Berlin-only option covers transit zones AB (€17.90/48 hours, €23.90/72 hours). If you're a museum junkie, consider the **WelcomeCard+Museumsinsel** (€34/72 hours), which combines travel in zones A and B with unlimited access to the five museums on Museum Island. Families get an extra price break: The ABC version (€36/72 hours) is valid for one adult and up to three kids younger than 15.

Buying Tickets: You can buy U- and S-Bahn tickets from machines at stations. (They are also sold at BVG pavilions at train stations and the TI, and on board trams and buses—drivers give change.) *Erwachsener* means "adult"—anyone 14 or older. Don't be afraid of the automated machines: First select the type of ticket you want, then load the coins or paper bills. As you board the bus or tram, or enter the subway system, punch your ticket in a red or yellow clock machine to validate it (or risk a €40 fine—which may increase to €200 in 2014; for an all-day or multiday pass, stamp it only the first time you ride). Be sure to travel with a valid ticket. Tickets are checked frequently, often by plainclothes inspectors. Within Berlin, Eurailpasses are good only on S-Bahn connections from the train station when you arrive and to the station when you depart.

Transit Tips: The S-Bahn crosstown express is a river of public transit through the heart of the city, in which many lines converge on one basic highway. Get used to this, and you'll leap within a few minutes between key locations: Savignyplatz (hotels in western Berlin), Bahnhof Zoo (Ku'damm, bus #100), Hauptbahnhof (all major trains in and out of Berlin), Friedrichstrasse (a short walk north of the heart of Unter den Linden), Hackescher Markt (Museum Island, restaurants, nightlife, connection to Prenzlauer Berg hotels and eateries), and Alexanderplatz (eastern end of Unter den Linden).

Sections of the U- or S-Bahn sometimes close temporarily for repairs. In this situation, a bus route often replaces the train (*Ersatzverkehr*, or "replacement transportation"; *zwischen* means "between").

Berlin's public transit is operated by BVG (except the S-Bahn, run by the Deutsche Bahn). Schedules, including bus timetables, are available on the helpful BVG website (www.bvg.de).

By Taxi

Taxis are easy to flag down, and taxi stands are common. A typical ride within town costs €8-10, and a crosstown trip (for example, Bahnhof Zoo to Alexanderplatz) will run about €15. Tariff 1 is for a *Kurzstrecke* (see below). All other rides are tariff 2 (€3.20 drop plus €1.65/kilometer). If possible, use cash—paying with a credit card comes with a hefty surcharge (about €4, regardless of the fare).

Money-Saving Taxi Tip: For any ride of less than two kilometers (about a mile), you can save several euros if you take advantage of the *Kurzstrecke* (short-stretch) rate. To get this rate, it's important that you flag the cab down on the street—not at or even near a taxi stand. Also, you must ask for the *Kurzstrecke* rate as soon as you hop in: Confidently say *"Kurzstrecke, bitte"* (KOORTS-shtreh-keh, BIT-teh), and your driver will grumble and flip the meter to a fixed €4 rate (for a ride that would otherwise cost €7).

By Bike

Flat Berlin is a very bike-friendly city, but be careful—Berlin's motorists don't brake for bicyclists (and bicyclists don't brake for pedestrians). Fortunately, some roads and sidewalks have special red-painted bike lanes. Don't ride on the regular sidewalk—it's *verboten*. Good bike shops can suggest a specific route.

Fat Tire Bikes rents good bikes at two handy locations—East (at the base of the TV Tower near Alexanderplatz—facing the entrance to the tower, go around to the right) and West (at Bahnhof Zoo—leaving the station onto Hardenbergplatz, turn left and walk 100 yards to the big bike sign). Both locations have the same hours and rates (€7/4 hours, €12/day, cheaper rate for two or more days, free luggage storage and Internet access, daily May-Sept 9:30-20:00, March-April and Oct-Nov 9:30-18:00, shorter hours or by appointment only Dec-Feb, leave ID, tel. 030/2404-7991, www.berlinbikerental.com).

In eastern Berlin, **Take a Bike** near the Friedrichstrasse S-Bahn station is owned by a lovely Dutch-German couple who know a lot about bikes and have a huge inventory. They can help you find the perfect fit (3-gear bikes: €12.50/day, €19/2 days; more for better bikes, slightly cheaper for longer rentals; electric bikes-€29/day, helmets, daily 9:30-19:00, Neustädtische Kirchstrasse 8, tel. 030/2065-4730, www.takeabike.de). To find it, leave the S-Bahn station via the Friedrichstrasse exit, turn right, go through a triangle-shaped square, and hang a left on Neustädtische Kirchstrasse.

Tours in Berlin

▲▲▲Hop-on, Hop-off Bus Tours

Several companies offer the same routine: a €15 circuit of the city with unlimited hop-on, hop-off privileges all day (about 14 stops at the city's major sights) on buses with cursory narration in English and German by a live (but tired) guide or a boring recorded commentary in whatever language you want to dial up. In season, each company has buses running four times per hour. They are cheap and great for photography—and Berlin really lends itself to this kind of bus-tour orientation. You can hop off at any major tourist spot (Potsdamer Platz, Museum Island, Brandenburg Gate, the Kaiser Wilhelm Memorial Church, and so on). Go with a live guide rather than the recorded spiel (so you get a few current asides). When choosing seats, check the sun/shade situation—some buses are entirely topless, and others are entirely covered. My favorites are topless with a shaded covered section in the back (April-Oct daily 10:00-18:00, last bus leaves all stops at 16:00, 2-hour loop; for specifics, look for brochures in your hotel lobby or at the TI). Keep your ticket so you can hop off and on (with the same company) all day. In winter (Nov-March), buses come only twice an hour, and the last departure is at 15:00. Brochures explain extras offered by each company.

Other Bus Tours

City Bus #100
For do-it-yourselfers, Berlin's city bus #100 is a great alternative to the commercial hop-on, hop-off bus tours—and you can follow along with my self-guided bus tour on page 598.

Full-Blown Bus Tours
BEX Sightseeing Berlin offers a long list of bus tours (not hop-on, hop-off) in and around Berlin; their three-hour "Berlin Classic Live" tour is a good introduction (€20; April-Oct daily at 10:00, Fri-Sun also at 14:00; Nov-March Wed-Sat at 10:00, no tours Sun-Tue; live guides in two languages, interesting historical photos displayed on bus monitors, departs from Ku'damm 216, buy ticket at bus, tel. 030/880-4190, www.berlinerstadtrundfahrten.de).

▲▲▲Walking Tours

Berlin, with a fascinating recent history that can be challenging to appreciate on your own, is an ideal place to explore with a walking tour. The city is a battle zone of extremely competitive and creative walking-tour companies. Unlike many other European countries, Germany has no regulations controlling who can give city tours. This can make guide quality hit-or-miss, ranging from brilliant history buffs who've lived in Berlin for years while pursuing their PhDs, to new arrivals who memorize a script and start leading tours after being in town for just a couple of weeks. A good Berlin tour guide is equal parts historian and entertainer; the best tours make the city's dynamic story come to life. While upstart companies abound, in general you have the best odds of landing a great guide by using one of the more established companies I recommend in this section.

Most outfits offer walks that are variations on the same themes: general **introductory** walk, **Third Reich** walk (Hitler and Nazi sites), and day trips to **Potsdam** and the **Sachsenhausen Concen-**

tration Camp Memorial. Most tours cost about €12-15 and last about three to four hours (longer for the side-trips to Potsdam and Sachsenhausen); public-transit tickets and entrances to sights are extra. I've included some basic descriptions for each company, but for details—including prices and specific schedules—see the various websites or look for brochures in town (widely available at TIs, hotel reception desks, and many cafés and shops).

Vive Berlin
This "guiding collective" was formed by some of the city's most experienced guides. They offer the usual lineup, with an introductory walk (Essential Berlin—Mon, Thu, and Sat at 10:00), plus Third Reich, Cold War, and Sachsenhausen itineraries on other days. All tours meet at Potsdamer Platz 10, in front of Balzac Coffee (U2/S-Bahn: Potsdamer Platz, use Stresemannstrasse exit; tel. 0157/845-46696, www.viveberlintours.de).

Insider Tour
This well-regarded company runs the full gamut of itineraries: introductory walk (daily), Third Reich, Cold War, Jewish Berlin, Sachsenhausen, and Potsdam, as well as bike tours, pub crawls, and a day trip to Dresden. Their tours have two meeting points (some tours convene at both, others at just one—check the schedule): in the West at the McDonald's across from Bahnhof Zoo, and in the East at AMT Coffee at the Hackescher Markt S-Bahn station (tel. 030/692-3149, www.insidertour.com).

Brewer's Berlin Tours
Specializing in longer, more in-depth walks, this company was started by Terry Brewer, who retired from the British diplomatic service in East Berlin. Today Terry's guides lead exhaustive—or, for some, exhausting—tours through the city (their Best of Berlin introductory tour, billed at 6 hours, can last 8 hours or more; daily at 10:30). Terry himself (who can be a bit gruff) leads a "six-hour" tour to some off-the-beaten-path hidden gems of Berlin twice weekly. They also do all-day Potsdam tours. Their tours depart from Bandy Brooks ice cream shop at the Friedrichstrasse S-Bahn station (tel. 030/2248-7435, mobile 0177-388-1537, www.brewers-berlintours.com).

Original Berlin Walks
Aiming at a clientele that's curious about the city's history, their flagship introductory walk, Discover Berlin, offers a good overview in four hours (daily year-round, meet at 10:00 at Bahnhof Zoo, April-Oct also daily at 13:30). They offer a Third Reich walking tour (4/week in summer), tours to Potsdam and Sachsenhausen, and themed Jewish Life in Berlin and Nest of Spies walks (both 1/week April-Oct only). Readers of this book get a €1 discount per tour. You can buy tickets in advance at any S-Bahn service center, or just show up and buy a ticket from the guide. All tours meet

Berlin at a Glance

▲▲▲German History Museum The ultimate swing through Germany's tumultuous story. **Hours:** Daily 10:00-18:00. See page 615.

▲▲▲Pergamon Museum World-class museum of classical antiquities on Museum Island, featuring the fantastic second-century b.c. Greek Pergamon Altar and frieze. **Hours:** Daily 10:00-18:00, Thu until 21:00. See page 618.

▲▲Reichstag Germany's historic parliament building, topped with a striking modern dome you can climb (reservations required). **Hours:** Daily 8:00-24:00, last entry at 23:00. See page 599.

▲▲Brandenburg Gate One of Berlin's most famous landmarks, a massive columned gateway, at the former border of East and West. **Hours:** Always open. See page 606.

▲▲Memorial to the Murdered Jews of Europe Holocaust memorial with almost 3,000 symbolic pillars, plus an exhibition about Hitler's Jewish victims. **Hours:** Memorial always open; information center open Tue-Sun 10:00-20:00, Oct-March until 19:00, closed Mon. See page 607.

▲▲Unter den Linden Leafy boulevard through the heart of former East Berlin, lined with some of the city's top sights. **Hours:** Always open. See page 609.

▲▲Neues Museum and Egyptian Collection Proud home (on Museum Island) of the exquisite 3,000-year-old bust of Queen Nefertiti. **Hours:** Daily 10:00-18:00, Thu-Sat until 20:00. See page 621.

▲▲Gendarmenmarkt Inviting square bounded by twin churches (one with a fine German history exhibit), a chocolate shop, and a concert hall. **Hours:** Always open. See page 628.

▲▲Topography of Terror Chilling exhibit documenting the Nazi perpetrators, built on the site of the former Gestapo/SS headquarters. **Hours:** Daily 10:00-20:00. See page 630.

▲▲Museum of the Wall at Checkpoint Charlie Kitschy but moving museum with stories of brave Cold War escapes, near the former site of the famous East-West border checkpoint; the surrounding street scene is almost as interesting. **Hours:** Daily 9:00-22:00. See page 634.

▲▲Jewish Museum Berlin Engaging, accessible museum celebrating Jewish culture, in a highly conceptual building. **Hours:** Daily 10:00-20:00, Mon until 22:00. See page 635.

▲▲**Gemäldegalerie** Germany's top collection of 13th- through 18th-century European paintings, featuring Holbein, Dürer, Cranach, Van der Weyden, Rubens, Hals, Rembrandt, Vermeer, Velázquez, Raphael, and more. **Hours:** Tue-Sun 10:00-18:00, Thu until 22:00, closed Mon. See page 648.

▲**Old National Gallery** German paintings, mostly from the Romantic Age. **Hours:** Tue-Sun 10:00-18:00, Thu until 22:00, closed Mon. See page 623.

▲**DDR Museum** Quirky collection of communist-era artifacts. **Hours:** Daily 10:00-20:00, Sat until 22:00. See page 626.

▲**New Synagogue** Largest prewar synagogue in Berlin, damaged in World War II, with a rebuilt facade and modest museum. **Hours:** March-Oct Sun-Mon 10:00-20:00, Tue-Thu 10:00-18:00, Fri 10:00-17:00—until 14:00 Oct and March-May, closed Sat; Nov-Feb Sun-Thu 10:00-18:00, Fri 10:00-14:00, closed Sat. See page 639.

▲**Berlin Wall Memorial** A "docu-center" with videos and displays, several outdoor exhibits, and lone surviving stretch of an intact Wall section. **Hours:** Visitor Center April-Oct Tue-Sun 9:30-19:00, Nov-March until 18:00, closed Mon; outdoor areas accessible 24 hours daily. See page 640.

▲**Potsdamer Platz** The "Times Square" of old Berlin, long a postwar wasteland, now rebuilt with huge glass skyscrapers, an underground train station, and—covered with a huge canopy—the Sony Center mall. **Hours:** Always open. See page 645.

▲**Deutsche Kinemathek Film and TV Museum** An entertaining look at German film and TV, from *Metropolis* to Dietrich to Nazi propaganda to the present day. **Hours:** Tue-Sun 10:00-18:00, Thu until 20:00, closed Mon. See page 647.

▲**Kaiser Wilhelm Memorial Church** Evocative destroyed church in the heart of the former West Berlin, with a modern annex. **Hours:** Church—daily 9:00-19:00; Memorial Hall in the bombed tower—Mon-Sat 10:00-18:00, shorter hours Sun. See page 653.

▲**Käthe Kollwitz Museum** The black-and-white art of the Berlin artist who conveyed the suffering of her city's stormiest century. **Hours:** Daily 11:00-18:00. See page 655.

BERLIN

at the taxi stand in front of the Bahnhof Zoo train station; the Discover Berlin, Jewish Life, and Sachsenhausen tours also have a second departure point opposite East Berlin's Hackescher Markt S-Bahn station, outside the Weihenstephaner restaurant (tour info: tel. 030/301-9194, www.berlinwalks.de).

Sandeman's New Europe Berlin "Free" Tours

You'll see this company advertising supposedly "free" introductory tours, plus paid itineraries similar to those offered by competitors. But Sandeman's tours aren't really free—just misleading. Guides for the "free" tours pay the company a cut of €3 per person, so they hustle for tips. They expect to be "tipped in paper" (i.e., €5 minimum tip per person). This business model leads to high guide turnover, meaning that the guides are, overall, less experienced (though some are quite entertaining). They offer the standard Berlin itineraries, but target a younger crowd. Basic introductory city walks leave daily at 9:00, 11:00, 13:00, and 16:00 from outside the Starbucks on Pariser Platz, near the Brandenburg Gate. Paid tours include a wildly popular €12 pub crawl (nightly; for more info, see page 658) and an excellent Alternative Berlin tour, which explores Berlin's gritty counterculture, squats, and urban life (€12, daily at 14:00; tel. 030/5105-0030, www.newberlintours.com).

Berlin Underground Association (Berliner Unterwelten Verein)

Much of Berlin's history lies beneath the surface, and this group has an exclusive agreement with the city to explore and research what is hidden underground. Their one-of-a-kind **Dark Worlds** tour of a WWII air-raid bunker features a chilling explanation of the air war over Berlin (Wed-Mon at 11:00, also Mon at 13:00; Dec-Feb no tours on Wed). The **From Flak Towers to Mountains of Debris** tour enters the Humboldthain air defense tower (April-Oct Thu-Sun at 16:00). The **Subways, Bunkers, Cold War** tour visits a completely stocked and fully functional nuclear emergency bunker in former West Berlin (Tue-Sun at 13:00, March-Nov also Tue at 11:00, Dec-Feb no tours on Wed; each tour costs €10; meet in the hall of the Gesundbrunnen U-Bahn/S-Bahn station, follow signs to *Humboldthain/Brunnenstrasse* exit and walk up the stairs to their office, tel. 030/4991-0517, www.berliner-unterwelten.de).

Local Guides

Both **Nick Jackson** (mobile 0171-537-8768, nick.jackson@berlin.de; also helps with Berlin Underground tours) and **Lee Evans** (my longtime helper in Berlin, mobile 0177-423-5307, lee.evans@berlin.de) enjoy sharing the story of their adopted hometown with visitors. If they're busy, try **Jennifer DeShirley** at Berlin and Beyond—this company has a crew of excellent, professional guides with an academic bent (tel. 030/8733-0584, mobile 0176-633-

55565, info@berlinandbeyond.de). **Bernhard Wagner** is a young, enthusiastic historian with a particular passion for Germany's 20th-century history (mobile 0176-6422-9119, schlegelmilch@gmx.net).

Bike Tours

Fat Tire Bike Tours

Choose among five different tours (each €24, 4-6 hours, 6-10 miles): **City Tour** (March-Nov daily at 11:00, May-Sept also daily at 16:00, Dec-Feb Wed and Sat at 11:00), **Berlin Wall Tour** (April-Oct Mon, Thu, and Sat at 10:30), **Third Reich Tour** (April-Oct Wed, Fri, and Sun at 10:30), "**Raw**" **Tour** (covers counter-cultural, creative aspects of contemporary Berlin, April-Oct Tue, Fri, and Sun at 10:30), and **Gardens and Palaces of Potsdam Tour** (April-Oct Wed, Sat, and Sun at 10:00). For any tour, meet at the TV Tower at Alexanderplatz—but don't get distracted by the Russians pretending to be Fat Tire (reserve ahead for the Wall, Third Reich, Raw, and Potsdam tours, no reservations necessary for City Tour, tel. 030/2404-7991, www.fattirebiketours.com).

Finding Berlin Tours

This small, easygoing company offers tours that take you away from the mainstream sights and focus on Berlin's neighborhoods, people, and street art (€20-25/person, max 8 people, 3-5 hours, meet at Revaler Strasse 99, near intersection with Warschauer Strasse—look for gate with *RAW* sign and walk into courtyard to their shipping-container kiosk, S-Bahn: Warschauer Strasse, mobile 0176-9933-3913, see schedule at www.findingberlin-tours.com).

Boat Tours

Spree River Cruises

Several boat companies offer one-hour, €10 trips up and down the river. A relaxing hour on one of these boats can be time and money well-spent. You'll listen to excellent English audioguides, see lots of wonderful new government-commissioned architecture, and enjoy the lively park action fronting the river. Boats leave from various docks that cluster near the bridge at the Berlin Cathedral (just off Unter den Linden). I enjoyed the Historical Sightseeing Cruise from **Stern und Kreisschiffahrt** (mid-March-Nov daily 10:30-18:30, leaves from Nikolaiviertel Dock—cross bridge from Berlin Cathedral toward Alexanderplatz and look right, tel. 030/536-3600, www.sternundkreis.de). Confirm that the boat you choose comes with English commentary.

BERLIN

Self-Guided Bus Tour

Bus #100 from Bahnhof Zoo to Alexanderplatz

While hop-on, hop-off bus tours are a great value, Berlin's city bus #100 laces together the major sights in a kind of poor man's bus tour. Bus #100 stops at Bahnhof Zoo, the Berlin Zoo, Victory Column, Reichstag, Unter den Linden, Brandenburg Gate, Pergamon Museum, and Alexanderplatz. A reader board inside the bus displays the upcoming stop. A basic €2.30 bus ticket is good for two hours of travel in one direction, and buses leave every few minutes.

Starting in the West from Bahnhof Zoo, here's a quick review of what you'll see: Leaving the train station, on your left and straight ahead, you'll spot the bombed-out hulk of the **Kaiser Wilhelm Memorial Church,** with its postwar sister church (described on page 653). Then, on the left, the elephant gates mark the entrance to the venerable and much-loved **Berlin Zoo** (described on page 655) and its aquarium. After a left turn, you cross the canal and pass Berlin's **embassy row.** The first interesting embassy is Mexico's, with columns that seem to move when you're driving by (how do they do that?). The big turquoise wall marks the communal home of all five Nordic embassies. This building is very "green," run entirely on solar power.

The bus then enters the 400-acre **Tiergarten** park, packed with cycling paths, joggers, and—on hot days—nude sunbathers. Straight ahead, the **Victory Column** (Siegessäule; with the gilded angel, described on page 644), towers above this vast city park that was once a royal hunting grounds. A block beyond the Victory Column (on the left) is the 18th-century late-Rococo **Bellevue Palace.** Formerly the official residence of the Prussian (and later German) crown prince, and at one time a Nazi VIP guest house, it's now the residence of the federal president (whose power is mostly ceremonial—the chancellor wields the real clout). If the flag's out, he's in.

Driving along the Spree River (on the left), you'll see buildings of the **national government.** The huge brick "brown snake" complex (across the river) was built to house government workers—but it didn't sell, so now its apartments are available to anyone. A metal Henry Moore sculpture titled *Butterfly* (a.k.a. "The Drinker's Liver") floats in front of the slope-roofed House of World Cultures (Berliners have nicknamed this building "the pregnant oyster" and "Jimmy Carter's smile"). The modern tower (next, on the left) is a carillon with 68 bells (from 1987). Through the trees on the left you'll see Germany's **Chancellery**—essentially Germany's White House. The big open space is the **Platz der Republik,** where the Victory Column (which you passed earlier) stood until

BERLIN

Hitler moved it. The Hauptbahnhof (Berlin's vast main train station, marked by its tall tower with the *DB* sign) is across the field between the Chancellery and the **Reichstag** (Germany's parliament—the old building with the new dome, described below).

If you get off here, the "Sights in Eastern Berlin" descriptions in the following section cover the next string of attractions, which are best seen on foot. If you stay on the bus, you'll zip by them in this order:

Unter den Linden, the main east-west thoroughfare, stretches from the **Brandenburg Gate** (behind you) through Berlin's historic core (ahead) to the TV Tower in the distance (Alexanderplatz, where this bus finishes). You'll pass the **Russian Embassy** and the Aeroflot airline office (right). Crossing **Friedrichstrasse,** look right for a Fifth Avenue-style conga line of big, glitzy department stores. Later, on the left, are the **German History Museum, Museum Island** (with the **Pergamon Museum**), and the **Berlin Cathedral;** across from these (on the right) is the construction site of the new **Humboldt-Forum** (with the Humboldt-Box visitors center). Then you'll rumble to a final stop at what was the center of East Berlin in communist times: **Alexanderplatz.**

Sights in Eastern Berlin

The following sights are arranged roughly west to east, from the Reichstag down Unter den Linden to Alexanderplatz. It's possible to link these sights as a convenient self-guided orientation walk (I've included walking directions for this purpose)—allow about 1.5 hours without stops for sightseeing. Adding tours of several sights can easily fill a whole day. Remember that reservations are required for the Reichstag dome, and you'll need timed-entry tickets for the Pergamon and Neues Museums.

Also described here are sights to the south and north of Unter den Linden.

▲▲Reichstag

The parliament building—the heart of German democracy—has a short but complicated and emotional history. When it was inaugurated in the 1890s, the last emperor, Kaiser Wilhelm II, disdainfully called it the "chatting home for monkeys" *(Reichsaffenhaus).* It was placed outside of the city's old walls—far from the center of real power, the imperial palace. But it was from the Reichstag that the German Republic was proclaimed in 1918.

In 1933, this symbol of democracy nearly burned down. The Nazis—whose influence on the German political scene was on the rise—blamed a communist plot. A Dutch communist, Marinus van der Lubbe, was eventually convicted and guillotined for the crime. Others believed that Hitler himself planned the fire, using it as a handy excuse to frame the communists and grab power. Even though Van der Lubbe was posthumously pardoned by the German government in 2008, most modern historians concede that he most likely was indeed guilty, and had acted alone—the Nazis were just incredibly lucky to have his deed advance their cause.

The Reichstag was hardly used from 1933 to 1999. Despite the fact that the building had lost its symbolic value, Stalin ordered his troops to take the Reichstag from the Nazis by May 1, 1945 (the date of the workers' May Day parade in Moscow). More than 1,500 Nazi soldiers made their last stand here—extending World War II by two days. On April 30, after fierce fighting on this rooftop, the Reichstag fell to the Red Army.

For the building's 101st birthday in 1995, the Bulgarian-American artist Christo wrapped it in silvery gold cloth. It was then wrapped again—in scaffolding—and rebuilt by British architect Lord Norman Foster into the new parliamentary home of the Bundestag (Germany's lower house, similar to the US House of Representatives). To many Germans, the proud resurrection of the Reichstag symbolizes the end of a terrible chapter in their country's history.

The **glass cupola** rises 155 feet above the ground. Its two sloped ramps spiral 755 feet to the top for a grand view. Inside the dome, a cone of 360 mirrors reflects natural light into the legislative chamber below. Lit from inside at night, this gives Berlin a memorable nightlight. The environmentally friendly cone—with an opening at the top—also helps with air circulation, drawing stale air out of the legislative chamber (no joke) and pulling in cool air from below.

Because of a terrorist plot discovered and thwarted in 2010, the building has tight security; getting in now requires a reservation.

Cost and Hours: Free but reservations highly recommended—see below, daily 8:00-24:00, last entry at 23:00, metal detectors, no big luggage allowed, Platz der Republik 1; S- or U-Bahn: Friedrichstrasse, Brandenburger Tor, or Bundestag; tel. 030/2273-2152, www.bundestag.de.

Reservations: To visit the dome, it's best to make a reservation (free); spots book up several days in advance. If you're in Berlin without a reservation, try dropping by the visitors center (on the Tiergarten side of Scheidemannstrasse, across from Platz der Republik) to ask if they have open slots (whole party must be present, ID required, slots available no less than 2 hours and no more than 2 days out).

Your only way to guarantee a spot is to reserve farther ahead **online.** The website is user-friendly, if (not surprisingly) a bit bureaucratic. Go to www.bundestag.de, click "English" at the top of the screen, and—under the "Visit the Bundestag" menu—select "Online registration." On this page, select "Visit the dome." Fill in the number of people in your party, ignore the "Comments" field, and click "Next." After entering the scrambled captcha code, you can select your preferred visit date and time (you can request up to three different time slots) and fill in your contact information. Once you complete the form and agree to their privacy policy, you'll be sent a confirmation email with a link to a website where you'll enter the name and birthdate for each person in your party and confirm your request. After completing this form, you'll receive a confirmation of your request (not a confirmation of your visit) by email. But you still have to wait for yet another email confirming your visit. If the English page isn't working, you can try using the German version: Go to https://www.bundestag.de/besuche/besucherdienst/index.jsp and call up a German-speaking friend to help you out. Or, if you use Google's Chrome browser, simply click the "Translate" button to see the steps in English.

While they claim it's possible to **email** a reservation request (kuppelbesuch@bundestag.de), you won't receive a confirmation until the day before your visit—which can be stressful. Use the website instead.

Getting In: Once you have a reservation, simply report to the visitors center at the appointed time, and be ready to show ID. Give your name to the attendant, and you'll be let right in.

Tours: Pick up the English **"Outlooks" flier** just after the visitors center. The free GPS-driven **audioguide** explains the building and narrates the view as you wind up the spiral ramp to the top of the dome; the commentary starts automatically as you step onto the bottom of the ramp.

❂ Self-Guided Tour: As you approach the building, look above the door, surrounded by stone patches from WWII bomb damage, to see the motto and promise: *Dem Deutschen Volke* ("To the German People"). The open, airy lobby towers 100 feet high, with 65-foot-tall colors of the German flag. See-through glass doors show the **central legislative chamber.** The message: There will be no secrets in this government. Look inside. Spreading his wings behind the podium is a stylized German eagle: the *Bundestagsadler* (a.k.a. "the fat hen"), representing the Bundestag (each branch of government has its own symbolic eagle). Notice the doors marked *Ja* (Yes), *Nein* (No), and *Enthalten* (Abstain)...an homage to the Bundestag's traditional "sheep jump" way of counting votes by exiting the chamber through the corresponding door (for critical votes, however, all 669 members vote with electronic cards).

Ride the elevator to the base of the glass **dome.** Pick up the free audioguide and take some time to study the photos and read

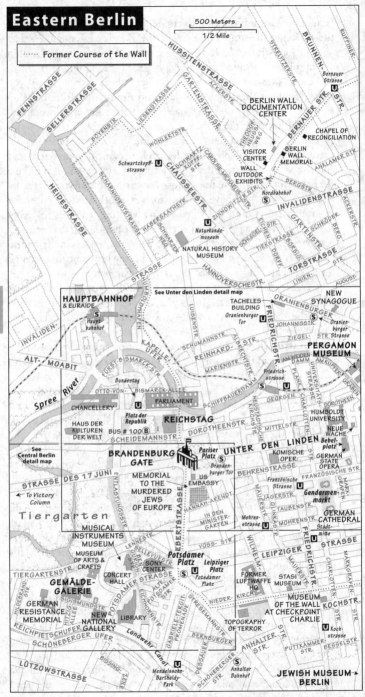

Eastern Berlin

····· Former Course of the Wall

500 Meters
1/2 Mile

BERLIN

HUSSITENSTRASSE

FENNSTRASSE

SELLERSTRASSE

HEIDESTRASSE

POYENSTR.
LIESENSTRASSE

GARTENSTRASSE

WÖHLERTSTR.

ACKERSTR.

THEODOR-HEUSS-WEG

CAROLINE-MICHAELIS-STR.

Schwartzkopff-strasse

SCHWARTZ-KOPFF-STR.

BERNAUER STR.

Bernauer Strasse

BERLIN WALL
DOCUMENTATION
CENTER

CHAPEL OF
RECONCILIATION

VISITOR
CENTER

BERLIN
WALL
MEMORIAL

WALL
OUTDOOR
EXHIBITS

ANKLAMER STR.

BERGSTR.

Nordbahnhof

INVALIDENSTRASSE

GARTENSTRASSE

SCHÖNHAUSER STR.

ACKERSTR.

TORSTRASSE

U CHAUSSEESTR.

SCHARNHORSTSTRASSE

HABERSAATHSTR.

SCHWARZ-WEG

ZINNOWITZER STR.

Naturkünde-museum

NATURAL HISTORY
MUSEUM

U

HANNOVERSCHESTR.

LINIEN-STR.

AUGUST-

HAUPTBAHNHOF
& EURAIDE

Haupt-bahnhof

S

HUMBOLDTHAFEN

KAPELLE-UFER

See Unter den Linden detail map

TACHELES
BUILDING

Oranienburger Tor

ORANIENBURGER STR.

NEW
SYNAGOGUE

S

Oranien-burger
Strasse

JOHANNISSTR.

ZIEGEL-STR.

PERGAMON
MUSEUM

INVALIDEN-

ALT- MOABIT

Spree River

FÜRST-BISMARCK-STR.

OTTO-VON-BISMARCK-ALLEE

Bundestag

CHANCELLERY

Platz der
Republik

HAUS DER
KULTUREN
DER WELT

PARLIAMENT

B BUS # 100

SCHEIDEMANNSTR.

SCHUMANNSTR.

REINHARD-STR.

MARIENSTR.

SCHIFFBAUERDAMM

FRIEDRICHSTR.

AM WEIDEN-DAMM

Friedrich-strasse

GEORGEN-

NEUSTÄDTISCHE KIRCHSTR.

DOROTHEENSTR.

UNIVERSITÄTS STRASSE

PLANK-

CHARLOTTEN-

HANK-

AM KUPFER-

DOROTHEEN-STR.

GRABEN

HUMBOLDT
UNIVERSITY

NEUE
WACHE

Bebel-platz

REICHSTAG

Pariser
Platz

Branden-burger Tor

UNTER DEN LINDEN

KOMISCHE
OPER

GERMAN
STATE
OPERA

See
Central Berlin
detail map

STRASSE DES 17 JUNI

← To Victory
Column

Tiergarten

ENTLASTUNGSTR.

BRANDENBURG
GATE

MEMORIAL
TO THE
MURDERED JEWS
OF EUROPE

US EMBASSY

HANNAH-ARENDT-STR.

IN DEN
MINISTER-GÄRTEN

EBERTSTRASSE

BEHRENSTRASSE

Französische
Strasse

JÄGERSTR.

TAUBENSTR.

MAUERSTR.

GLINKA-

MOHRENSTR.

Mohren-strasse

Gendarmenmarkt

FRANZÖSISCHE STR.

GERMAN
CATHEDRAL

Stadt-mitte

FRIEDRICHSTR.

MUSICAL
INSTRUMENTS
MUSEUM

MUSEUM
OF ARTS &
CRAFTS

GEMÄLDE-
GALERIE

GERMAN
RESISTANCE
MEMORIAL

TIERGARTENSTR.

HILDEBRAND-STR.

HITZIG-

SIGISMUND-STR.

REICHPIETSCHUFER

SCHÖNEBERGER UFER

LÜTZOWSTRASSE

BELLEVUE-STR.

LENNÉSTR.

CONCERT
HALL

NEW
NATIONAL
GALLERY

LIBRARY

POTSDAMER STRASSE

ALTE
POTSDAMER STR.

EICHHORN-STR.

SONY
CENTER

Potsdamer
Platz

Leipziger
Platz

S Potsdamer
Platz

VOSS- STR.

LEIPZIGER STR.

WILHELM-

STR.

FORMER
LUFTWAFFE
HQ

STASI
MUSEUM

MUSEUM
OF THE WALL
AT CHECKPOINT
CHARLIE

U Koch-strasse

KOCHSTR.

SCHÖNEBERGER STR.

GABRIELE-TERGIT-PROMENADE

STRESEMANNSTR.

BERNBURGER STR.

NIEDER-

KIRCH-

TOPOGRAPHY
OF TERROR

ANHALTER STR.

PUTTKAMER
STR.

CHARLOTTEN-

BESSELSTR.

Landwehr Canal

BISSING-

Mendelssohn-Bartholdy-Park

U

DESSAUER STR.

SCHÖNEBERGER-STR.

Anhalter
Bahnhof

JEWISH MUSEUM →
BERLIN

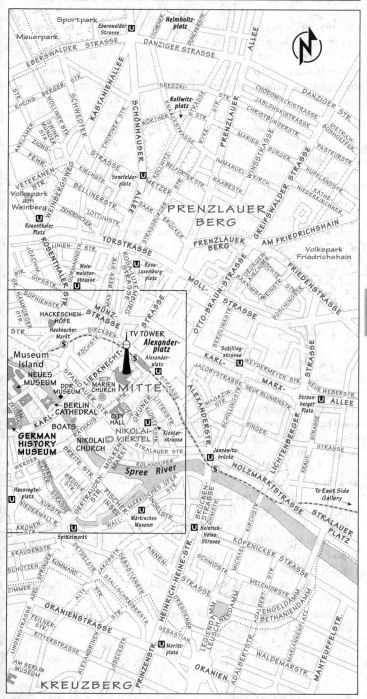

the circle of captions—around the base of the central funnel—for an excellent exhibit telling the Reichstag story. Then study the surrounding architecture: a broken collage of new on old, torn between antiquity and modernity, like Germany's history. Notice the dome's giant and unobtrusive sunscreen that moves as necessary with the sun. Peer down through the skylight to look over the shoulders of the elected representatives at work. For Germans, the best view from here is down—keeping a close eye on their government.

Start at the ramp nearest the elevator and wind up to the top of the **double ramp.** Take a 360-degree survey of the city as you hike: The big park is the **Tiergarten,** the "green lungs of Berlin." Beyond that is the **Teufelsberg** ("Devil's Hill"): Built of rubble from the destroyed city in the late 1940s, it was famous during the Cold War as a powerful ear of the West—notice the telecommunications tower on top. Knowing the bombed-out and bulldozed story of their city, locals say, "You have to be suspicious when you see the nice, green park."

Find the **Victory Column** (Siegessäule), glimmering in the middle of the park. This was moved by Hitler in the 1930s from in front of the Reichstag to its present position in the Tiergarten, as the first step in creating a grandiose axis he envisioned for postwar Berlin. Next, scenes of the new Berlin spiral into your view—**Potsdamer Platz,** marked by the conical glass tower that houses Sony's European headquarters. Continue circling left, and find the green chariot atop the **Brandenburg Gate.** Just to its left is the curving fish-like roof of the **DK Bank** building, designed by the unconventional American architect, Frank Gehry. The **Memorial to the Murdered Jews of Europe** stretches south of the Brandenburg Gate. Next, you'll see **former East Berlin** and the city's next huge construction zone, with a forest of 300-foot-tall skyscrapers in the works. Notice the TV Tower, the Berlin Cathedral's massive dome, and the golden dome of the New Synagogue.

Follow the train tracks in the distance to the left toward Berlin's huge main train station, the **Hauptbahnhof.** Complete your spin-tour with the blocky **Chancellery,** nicknamed by Berliners "the washing machine." It may look like a pharaoh's tomb, but it's the office and home of Germany's most powerful person, the chancellor (currently Angela Merkel). To remind the chancellor who he or she works for, the Reichstag, at about 130 feet, is about six feet taller than the Chancellery.

Continue spiraling up. You'll pass all the same sights again, twice, from a higher vantage point.

Near the Reichstag
Memorial to Politicians Who Opposed Hitler

Near the road in front of the Reichstag, enmeshed in all the security apparatus, is a memorial of slate stones embedded in the ground. This row of slate slabs (which looks like a fancy slate bicycle rack) is a memorial to the 96 members of the Reichstag (the equivalent of our members of Congress) who were persecuted and murdered because their politics didn't agree with Chancellor Hitler's. They were part of the Weimar Republic, the weak and ill-fated attempt at post-WWI democracy in Germany. These were the people who could have stopped Hitler...so they became his first victims. Each slate slab remembers one man—his name, party (mostly KPD—Communists, and SPD—Social Democrats), and the date and location of his death—generally in concentration camps. (*KZ* stands for "concentration camp.") They are honored here, in front of the building in which they worked.

• *Facing the Reichstag, you can take a short side-trip to the river by circling around to the left of the building.*

Spree Riverfront

Admire the wonderful architecture incorporating the Spree River into the people's world. It's a poignant spot because this river was once a symbol of division—the East German regime put nets underwater to stymie those desperate enough for freedom to swim to the West. When kings ruled Prussia, government buildings went right up to the water. But today, the city is incorporating the river thoughtfully into a people-friendly cityscape. From the Reichstag, a delightful riverside path leads around the curve, past "beach cafés," to the Chancellery. For a slow, low-impact glide past this zone, consider a river cruise (see page 597; we'll pass the starting point—on Museum Island—later on this walk). The fine bridges symbolize the connection of East and West.

• *Leaving the Reichstag, return to the busy road, and cross the street at your first opportunity, to the big park. Walk (with the park on your right) to the corner. Along the railing at the corner of Scheidemannstrasse and Ebertstrasse is a small memorial of white crosses. This is the...*

Berlin Wall Victims Memorial

This monument—now largely usurped by business promos and impromptu wacko book stalls—commemorates some of the East Berliners who died trying to cross the Wall. This 96-mile-long "Anti-Fascist Protective Rampart," as it was called by the East German government, was erected almost overnight in 1961 to stop the outward flow of people from East to West (3 million had leaked out between 1949 and 1961). Of these people, many perished within months of the wall's construction on August 13, 1961. Most died trying to swim the river to freedom. The monument used to stand right on the Berlin Wall behind the Reichstag. Notice that the last person killed while trying to escape was 20-year-old Chris Gueffroy, who died nine months before the Wall fell in 1989. (He was shot through the heart in no-man's-land.)

In the park just behind the monument, another memorial is planned. It will remember the Roma (Gypsy) victims of the Holocaust. The Roma, as persecuted by the Nazis as the Jews were, lost the same percentage of their population to Hitler. Unfortunately, the project is stalled for lack of a well-funded individual or group to finance it.

• *From here, head to the Brandenburg Gate. Stay on the park side of the street for a better view of the gate ahead. As you cross at the light, notice the double row of* **cobblestones**—*it goes around the city, marking where the Wall used to stand.*

Brandenburg Gate and Nearby
▲▲Brandenburg Gate (Brandenburger Tor)

The historic Brandenburg Gate (1791) was the grandest—and is the last survivor—of 14 gates in Berlin's old city wall (this one led to the neighboring city of Brandenburg). The gate was the symbol of Prussian Berlin—and later the symbol of a divided Berlin. It's crowned by a majestic four-horse chariot with the Goddess of Peace at the reins. Napoleon took this statue to the Louvre in Paris in 1806. After the Prussians defeated Napoleon and got it back (1813), she was renamed the Goddess of Victory.

The gate sat unused, part of a sad circle dance called the Wall, for more than 25 years. Now postcards all over town show the ecstatic day—November 9, 1989—when the world enjoyed the sight of happy Berliners jamming the gate like flowers on a parade float. Pause a minute and think about struggles for freedom—past and present. (There's actually a special room built into the gate for this purpose.) Around the gate, look at the information boards with pictures of how this area changed throughout the 20th century. There's a TI within the gate (daily 9:30-19:00, S-Bahn: Brandenburger Tor).

The Brandenburg Gate, the center of old Berlin, sits on a major boulevard running east to west through Berlin. The western segment, called Strasse des 17 Juni (named for a workers' uprising against the DDR government on June 17, 1953), stretches for four miles from the Brandenburg Gate and Victory Column to the Olympic Stadium. But we'll follow this city axis in the opposite direction, east, walking along a stretch called Unter den Linden—into the core of old imperial Berlin and past what was once the palace of the Hohenzollern family who ruled Prussia and then Germany. The palace—the reason for just about all you'll see—is a phantom sight, long gone. Alexanderplatz, which marks the end of this walk, is near the base of the giant TV Tower hovering in the distance.

• *Cross through the gate into...*

▲Pariser Platz

"Parisian Square," so named after the Prussians defeated Napoleon in 1813, was once filled with important government buildings—all bombed to smithereens in World War II. For decades, it was an unrecognizable, deserted no-man's-land—cut off from both East and West by the Wall. But now it's rebuilt, and the banks, hotels, and embassies that were here before the bombing have reclaimed their original places—with a few additions: a palace of coffee (Starbucks) and the small Kennedys Museum (described later). The winners of World War II enjoy this prime real estate: The American, French, British, and Soviet (now Russian) embassies are all on or near this square.

Face the gate and look to your left. The **US Embassy** reopened in its historic location in 2008. The building has been controversial: For safety's sake, Uncle Sam wanted more of a security zone around the building, but the Germans wanted to keep Pariser Platz a welcoming people zone. (Throughout the world, American embassies are the most fortified buildings in town.) The compromise: The extra security the US wanted is built into the structure. Easy-on-the-eyes barriers keep potential car bombs at a distance, and its front door is on the side farthest from the Brandenburg Gate.

Just to the left, the **DZ Bank building** is by Frank Gehry, famous for Bilbao's organic Guggenheim Museum, Prague's Dancing House, Seattle's Experience Music Project, Chicago's Millennium Park, and Los Angeles' Walt Disney Concert Hall. Gehry fans might be surprised at the DZ Bank building's low profile. Structures on Pariser Platz are designed to be bland so as not to draw attention away from the Brandenburg Gate. (The glassy facade of the Academy of Arts, next to Gehry's building, is controversial for drawing attention to itself.) For your fix of the good old Gehry, step into the lobby and check out its undulating interior. It's a fish—and you feel like you're both inside and outside of it. The architect's vision is explained on a nearby plaque. The best view of the roof of Gehry's creation is from the Reichstag dome.

• *Enter the Academy of Arts (Akademie der Kunst), next door to Gehry's building. Its doors lead to a lobby (with a small food counter, daily 10:00-20:00), which leads directly to the vast...*

▲▲Memorial to the Murdered Jews of Europe
(Denkmal für die Ermordeten Juden Europas)

This Holocaust memorial, consisting of 2,711 gravestone-like pillars (called "stelae") and completed in 2005, is an essential stop for any visit to Berlin. It was the first formal, German government-sponsored Holocaust memorial. Jewish American architect Peter

Eisenman won the competition for the commission (and built it on time and on budget—€27 million). It's been criticized for focusing on just one of the groups targeted by the Nazis, but the German government has promised to erect memorials to other victims.

Cost and Hours: Free, memorial always open; information center open Tue-Sun 10:00-20:00, Oct-March until 19:00, closed Mon year-round; last entry 45 minutes before closing, S-Bahn: Brandenburger Tor or Potsdamer Platz, tel. 030/2639-4336, www.stiftung-denkmal.de. The €4 audioguide augments the experience.

Visiting the Memorial: The pillars are made of hollow concrete, each chemically coated for easy removal of graffiti. (Notably, the chemical coating was developed by a subsidiary of the former IG Farben group—the company infamous for supplying the Zyklon B gas used in Nazi death camps.) The number of pillars isn't symbolic of anything; it's simply how many fit on the provided land.

Once you enter the memorial, notice that people seem to appear and disappear between the columns, and that no matter where you are, the exit always seems to be up. Is it a labyrinth...a symbolic cemetery...and intentionally disorienting? It's entirely up to the visitor to derive the meaning, while pondering this horrible chapter in human history.

The pondering takes place under the sky. For the learning, go under the field of concrete pillars to the state-of-the-art **information center** (there may be a short line because of the mandatory security check). Inside, a thought-provoking exhibit (well-explained in English) studies the Nazi system of extermination and humanizes the victims, while also providing space for silent reflection. In the Starting Hall, exhibits trace the historical context of the Nazi and WWII era, while six portraits—representing the six million Jewish victims—look out on the visitors. The Room of Dimensions has glowing boxes in the floor containing diaries, letters, and final farewells penned by Holocaust victims. The Room of Families presents case-studies of 15 Jewish families from around Europe, to more fully convey the European Jewish experience. Remember: Behind these 15 stories are millions more tales of despair, tragedy, and survival. In the Room of Names, a continually running soundtrack lists the names and brief biographical sketches of Holocaust victims; reading the names of all those murdered would take more than six and a half years. The Room of Sites documents some 220 different places of genocide. You'll also find exhibits about other Holocaust monuments and memorials, a searchable database of victims, and a video archive of interviews with survivors.

The memorial's location—where the Wall once stood—is coincidental. Nazi propagandist Joseph Goebbels' bunker was discovered during the work and left buried under the northeast corner of the memorial. Hitler's bunker is just 200 yards away, under a nondescript parking lot. Such Nazi sites are intentionally left hidden to discourage neo-Nazi elements from creating shrines.

• *Now backtrack to Pariser Platz (through the yellow building). Across the square (next to Starbucks), consider dropping into...*

The Kennedys Museum

This crisp private enterprise facing the Brandenburg Gate recalls John F. Kennedy's Germany trip in 1963, with great photos and video clips as well as a photographic shrine to the Kennedy clan in America. It's a small, overpriced, yet delightful experience with interesting mementos—such as old campaign buttons and posters, and JFK's notes with the phonetic "Ish bin ein Bearleener." Jacqueline Kennedy commented on how strange it was that this—not even in his native language—was her husband's most quotable quote. Most of the exhibit consists of photographs that, if nothing else, spark a nostalgic longing for the days of Camelot.

Cost and Hours: €7, includes special exhibits, reduced to €3.50 for a broad array of visitors—dream up a discount and ask for it, daily 10:00-18:00, Pariser Platz 4a, tel. 030/2065-3570, www.thekennedys.de.

• *Leave Pariser Platz and begin strolling...*

▲▲Unter den Linden

The street called Unter den Linden is the heart of former East Berlin. In Berlin's good old days, Unter den Linden was one of Europe's grand boulevards. In the 15th century, this carriageway led from the palace to the hunting grounds (today's big Tiergarten). In the 17th century, Hohenzollern princes and princesses moved in and built their palaces here so they could be near the Prussian king.

Named centuries ago for its thousand linden trees, this was the most elegant street of Prussian Berlin before Hitler's time, and the main drag of East Berlin after his reign. Hitler replaced the venerable trees—many 250 years old—with Nazi flags. Popular discontent actually drove him to replant the trees. Today, Unter den Linden is no longer a depressing Cold War cul-de-sac, and its pre-Hitler strolling café ambience has returned. Notice how it is divided, roughly at Friedrichstrasse, into a business section that stretches toward the Brandenburg Gate, and a culture section that spreads out toward Alexanderplatz. Frederick the Great wanted to have culture, mainly the opera and the university, closer to his palace, and to keep business (read: banks) farther away, near the city walls.

↺ Self-Guided Walk: As you walk toward the giant TV Tower, the big building you see jutting out into the street on your right is the **Hotel Adlon.** In its heyday, it hosted such notables as Charlie Chaplin, Albert Einstein, and Greta Garbo. This was the

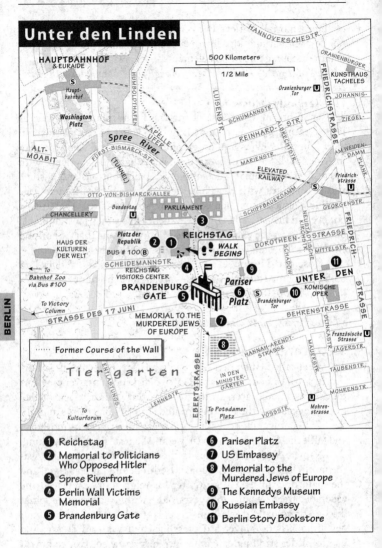

Unter den Linden

500 Kilometers

1/2 Mile

..... Former Course of the Wall

1. Reichstag
2. Memorial to Politicians Who Opposed Hitler
3. Spree Riverfront
4. Berlin Wall Victims Memorial
5. Brandenburg Gate
6. Pariser Platz
7. US Embassy
8. Memorial to the Murdered Jews of Europe
9. The Kennedys Museum
10. Russian Embassy
11. Berlin Story Bookstore

setting for Garbo's most famous line, "I vant to be alone," uttered in the film *Grand Hotel*. Damaged by the Russians just after World War II, the original hotel was closed with the construction of the nearby Wall in 1961 and later demolished. The grand Adlon was rebuilt in 1997. It was here that the late Michael Jackson shocked millions by dangling his baby, Blanket, over the railing (second balcony up, on the side of the hotel next to the Academy of Art). See how far you can get inside.

Descend into the Brandenburger Tor S-Bahn station ahead of you. It's one of Berlin's former **ghost subway stations.** During the

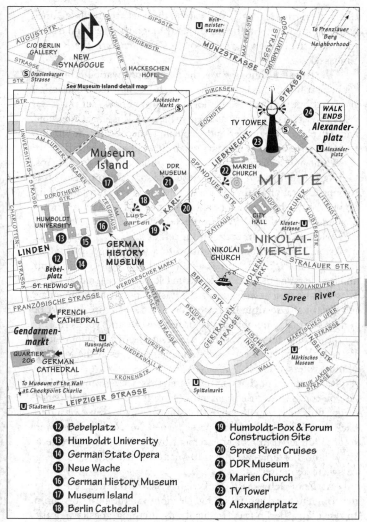

12 Bebelplatz
13 Humboldt University
14 German State Opera
15 Neue Wache
16 German History Museum
17 Museum Island
18 Berlin Cathedral
19 Humboldt-Box & Forum Construction Site
20 Spree River Cruises
21 DDR Museum
22 Marien Church
23 TV Tower
24 Alexanderplatz

BERLIN

Cold War, most underground train tunnels were simply blocked at the border. But a few Western lines looped through the East. To make a little hard Western cash, the Eastern government rented the use of these tracks to the West, but the stations (which happened to be in East Berlin) were strictly off-limits. For 28 years, the stations were unused, as Western trains slowly passed through and passengers saw only eerie DDR (East German) guards and lots of cobwebs. Literally within days of the fall of the Wall, these stations were reopened, and today they are a time warp (looking essentially as they did when built in 1931, with dreary old green tiles and original signage). Walk along the track (the walls are lined with historic photos of the Reichstag through the ages) and exit on the other side, following signs to *Russische Botschaft* (the Russian Embassy).

The **Russian Embassy** was the first big postwar building project in East Berlin. It's built in the powerful, simplified Neoclassical style that Stalin liked. While not as important now as it was a few years ago, it's as immense as ever. It flies the Russian white, blue, and red. Find the hammer-and-sickle motif decorating the window frames—a reminder of the days when Russia was the USSR.

Continuing past the Aeroflot airline offices, look across Glinkastrasse to the right to see the back of the **Komische Oper** (Comic Opera; program and view of ornate interior posted in window). While the exterior is ugly, the fine old theater interior—amazingly missed by WWII bombs—survives.

Back on the main drag, on the left at #40, is an entertaining bookstore, Berlin Story. In addition to a wide range of English-language books, this shop has a modest (but overpriced) museum and a wide range of nostalgic knickknacks from the Cold War. The West lost no time in consuming the East; consequently, some have felt a wave of *Ost*-algia for the old days of East Berlin. At election time, a surprising number of the former East Berlin's voters still opt for the extreme left party, which has ties to the bygone Communist Party, although the East-West divide is no longer at the forefront of most voters' minds.

One symbol of that communist era has been given a reprieve. As you continue to Friedrichstrasse, look at the DDR-style pedestrian lights, and you'll realize that someone had a sense of humor back then. The perky red and green men—*Ampelmännchen*—were recently under threat of replacement by far less jaunty Western-style signs. Fortunately, after a 10-year court battle, the DDR signals were kept after all.

At **Friedrichstrasse,** look right. Before the war, the Unter den Linden/Friedrichstrasse intersection was the heart of Berlin. In the 1920s, Berlin was famous for its anything-goes love of life. This was the cabaret drag, a springboard to stardom for young and vampy entertainers like Marlene Dietrich. (Born in 1901, Dietrich starred in the one of the first German talkies—*The Blue Angel*—and then headed straight to Hollywood.) Over the last few years, this boulevard—lined with super department stores (such as Galeries Lafayette) and big-time hotels (such as the Hilton and Regent)—is attempting to replace Ku'damm as the grand commerce-and-café boulevard of Berlin. More recently, western Berlin is retaliating with some new stores of its own. And so far, Friedrichstrasse gets little more than half the pedestrian traffic that Ku'damm gets in the West. Why? Locals complain that this area has no daily life—

no supermarkets, not much ethnic street food, and so on. Consider detouring to Galeries Lafayette, with its cool marble-and-glass, waste-of-space interior (Mon-Sat 10:00-20:00, closed Sun; check out the vertical garden on its front wall, belly up to its amazing ground-floor viewpoint, or have lunch in its recommended basement cafeteria).

If you continued down Friedrichstrasse, you'd wind up at the sights listed under "South of Unter den Linden," on page 628—including Checkpoint Charlie (a 10-minute walk from here). But for now, continue along Unter den Linden. At the corner, the **VW Automobil Forum** shows off the latest models from the many car companies owned by VW (free, corner of Friedrichstrasse and Unter den Linden, VW art gallery and handy VW WC in the basement).

As you explore Berlin, you may see big, colorful **water pipes** running overground. Wherever there are big construction projects, streets are laced with these drainage pipes. Berlin's high water table means that any new basement comes with lots of pumping out.

Continue down Unter den Linden a few more blocks, past the large equestrian statue of Frederick the Great, and turn right into the square called **Bebelplatz.** Stand on the glass window set into the pavement in the center.

Frederick the Great—who ruled from 1740 to 1786—established Prussia not just as a military power, but as a cultural and intellectual heavyweight as well. This square was the center of the "new Athens" that Frederick envisioned. His grand palace was just down the street (explained later).

Look down through the glass you're standing on: The room of empty bookshelves is a memorial repudiating the notorious Nazi **book burning.** It was on this square in 1933 that staff and students from the university threw 20,000 newly forbidden books (like Einstein's) into a huge bonfire on the orders of the Nazi propaganda minister Joseph Goebbels. A plaque nearby reminds us of the prophetic quote by the German poet Heinrich Heine. In 1820, he wrote, "Where they burn books, at the end they also burn people." The Nazis despised Heine because he was Jewish before converting to Christianity. A century later, his books were among those that went up in flames on this spot.

Great buildings front Bebelplatz. Survey the square counterclockwise:

Humboldt University, across Unter den Linden, is one of Europe's greatest. Marx and Lenin (not the brothers or the sisters) studied here, as did the Grimms (both brothers) and more than two dozen Nobel Prize winners. Einstein, who was Jewish, taught here until taking a spot at Princeton in 1932 (smart guy). Used-book merchants set up their tables in front of the university, selling books by many of the authors whose works were once condemned to Nazi flames just across the street.

The former **state library** (labeled *Juristische Fakultät*, facing Bebelplatz on the right with your back to Humboldt University) is where Vladimir Lenin studied during much of his exile from Russia. If you climb to the second floor of the library and go through the door opposite the stairs, you'll see a 1968 vintage stained-glass window depicting Lenin's life's work with almost biblical reverence. On the ground floor is Tim's Espressobar, a great little café with light food, student prices, and garden seating (€3 plates, Mon-Fri 8:00-20:00, Sat 9:00-17:00, closed Sun, handy WC).

Between the library and the church, the square is closed by one of Berlin's swankiest lodgings—**Hotel de Rome**, housed in a historic bank building with a spa and lap pool fitted into the former vault.

The round, Catholic **St. Hedwig's Church,** nicknamed the "upside-down teacup," was built by the pragmatic Frederick the Great to encourage the integration of Catholic Silesians after his empire annexed their region in 1742. (St. Hedwig is the patron saint of Silesia, a region now shared by Germany, Poland, and the Czech Republic.) When asked what the church should look like, Frederick literally took a Silesian teacup and slammed it upside-down on a table. Like all Catholic churches in Berlin, St. Hedwig's is not on the street, but stuck in a kind of back lot—indicating inferiority to Protestant churches. You can step inside the church to see the cheesy DDR government renovation (generally daily until 17:00).

The **German State Opera** was bombed in 1941, rebuilt to bolster morale and to celebrate its centennial in 1943, and bombed again in 1945; it was renovated in 2013.

Cross Unter den Linden to the university side. The Greek-temple-like building set in the small chestnut-tree-filled park is the **Neue Wache** (the emperor's "New Guardhouse," from 1816). Converted to a memorial to the victims of fascism in 1960, the structure was transformed again, after the Wall fell, into a national memorial. Look inside, where a replica of the Käthe Kollwitz statue, *Mother with Her Dead Son,* is surrounded by thought-provoking silence. This marks the tombs of Germany's unknown soldier and an unknown concentration camp victim. The inscription in front reads, "To the victims of war and tyranny." Read the entire statement in English (on wall, left of entrance). The memorial, open to the sky, incorporates the elements—sunshine, rain, snow—falling on this modern-day *pietà*.

• *After the Neue Wache, the next building you'll see is Berlin's pink-yet-formidable Zeughaus (arsenal). Dating from 1695, it's considered the oldest building on the boulevard, and now houses the...*

▲▲▲German History Museum (Deutsches Historisches Museum)

This fantastic museum is a two-part affair: the pink former Prussian arsenal building and the I. M. Pei-designed annex. The main building (fronting Unter den Linden) houses the permanent collection, offering the best look at German history under one roof, anywhere. The modern annex features good temporary exhibits surrounded by the work of a great contemporary architect. While this city has more than its share of hokey "museums" that slap together WWII and Cold War bric-a-brac, then charge too much for admission, this thoughtfully presented museum—with more than 8,000 artifacts telling not just the story of Berlin, but of all Germany—is clearly the top history museum in town.

Cost and Hours: €8, daily 10:00-18:00, Unter den Linden 2, tel. 030/2030-4751, www.dhm.de.

Audioguide: For the most informative visit, invest in the excellent €3 audioguide, with six hours of info to choose from.

Visiting the Museum: The permanent collection packs two huge rectangular floors of the old arsenal building with historical objects, photographs, and models—all well-described in English and intermingled with multimedia stations to help put everything in context. From the lobby, head upstairs (to the "**first floor**") and work your way chronologically down. This floor traces German history from 1 B.C. to 1918, with exhibits on early cultures, the Middle Ages, Reformation, Thirty Years' War, German Empire, and World War I. You'll see a Roman floor mosaic, lots of models of higgledy-piggledy medieval towns and castles, tapestries, suits of armor, busts of great Germans, a Turkish tent from the Ottoman siege of Vienna (1683), flags from German unification in 1871 (the first time "Germany" existed as a nation), exhibits on everyday life in the tenements of the Industrial Revolution, and much more.

History marches on through the 20th century on the **ground floor,** including the Weimar Republic, Nazism, World War II, Allied occupation, and a divided Germany. Propaganda posters trumpet Germany's would-be post-WWI savior, Adolf Hitler. Look for the model of the impossibly huge, 950-foot-high, 180,000-capacity domed hall Hitler wanted to erect in the heart of Berlin, which he planned to re-envision as Welthauptstadt Germania, the "world capital" of his far-reaching Third Reich. Another model shows the sobering reality of Hitler's grandiosity: a crematorium at Auschwitz-Birkenau concentration camp in occupied Poland. The exhibit wraps up with chunks of the Berlin Wall, reunification, and a quick look at Germany today.

For architecture buffs, the big attraction is the **Pei annex** behind the history museum, which complements the museum with often-fascinating temporary exhibits. From the old building, cross through the courtyard (with the Pei glass canopy overhead) to reach the annex. A striking glassed-in spiral staircase unites four floors with surprising views and lots of light. It's here that you'll experience why Pei—famous for his glass pyramid at Paris' Louvre—is called the "perfector of classical modernism," "master of light," and a magician of uniting historical buildings with new ones. (If the museum is closed, or you don't have a ticket, venture down the street—Hinter dem Giesshaus—to the left of the museum to see the Pei annex from the outside.)

• *Back on Unter den Linden, head toward the Spree River. Just before the bridge, wander left along the canal through a tiny but colorful arts-and-crafts market (weekends only; a larger flea market is just outside the Pergamon Museum). Continue up the riverbank two blocks and cross the footbridge over the Spree. This takes you to...*

Museum Island (Museumsinsel)

This island is filled with some of Berlin's most impressive museums (all part of the Staatliche Museen zu Berlin). The first building—the Altes Museum—went up in the 1820s, and the rest of the complex began development in the 1840s under King Friedrich Wilhelm IV, who envisioned the island as a place of culture and learning. The island's imposing Neoclassical buildings host five grand museums: the **Pergamon Museum** (classical antiquities, including the top-notch Pergamon Altar, with its temple and frieze); the **Neues Museum** ("New Museum," famous for its Egyptian collection with the bust of Queen Nefertiti); the **Old National Gallery** (Alte Nationalgalerie, 19th-century art, mostly German Romantic and Realist paintings); the **Altes Museum** ("Old Museum," more antiquities); and the **Bode Museum** (European statuary and paintings through the ages, coins, and Byzantine art).

• *The museums of Museum Island, worth the better part of a sightseeing day, are described in more detail below. To bypass the museums and other sights on Museum Island for now, skip ahead to the "Museum Island to Alexanderplatz" section on page 626.*

The Museums of Museum Island

A formidable renovation is under way on Museum Island. When complete, a grand entry and unified visitors center will serve the island's five venerable but separate museums; tunnels will lace the complex together; and this will become one of the grandest museum zones in Europe (intended completion date: 2015, www.museumsinsel-berlin.de). In the meantime, pardon their dust.

Cost: The €14 Museum Island Pass combo-ticket—covering all five museums—is a far better value than buying individual entries ranging from €8 to €13 (prices can vary depending on special exhibits). All five museums are also included in the city's €19 Mu-

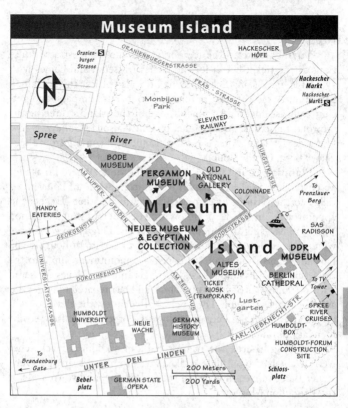

Museum Island

[Map labels: Oranienburger Strasse • ORANIENBURGERSTRASSE • HACKESCHER HÖFE • FRAS-STRASSE • Monbijou Park • Hackescher Markt • ELEVATED RAILWAY • BURGSTRASSE • Spree River • BODE MUSEUM • PERGAMON MUSEUM • OLD NATIONAL GALLERY • AM KUPFER-GRABEN • COLONNADE • To Prenzlauer Berg • HANDY EATERIES • GEORGENSTR. • Museum • BODESTRASSE • SAS RADISSON • UNIVERSITÄTSSTRASSE • NEUES MUSEUM & EGYPTIAN COLLECTION • Island • DDR MUSEUM • DOROTHEENSTR. • ALTES MUSEUM • TICKET KIOSK (TEMPORARY) • AM ZEUGHAUS • BERLIN CATHEDRAL • To TV Tower • HUMBOLDT UNIVERSITY • Lustgarten • SPREE RIVER CRUISES • NEUE WACHE • GERMAN HISTORY MUSEUM • KARL-LIEBKNECHT-STR. • HUMBOLDT-BOX • To Brandenburg Gate • UNTER DEN LINDEN • HUMBOLDT-FORUM CONSTRUCTION SITE • 200 Meters • 200 Yards • Bebelplatz • GERMAN STATE OPERA • Schlossplatz]

seumspass (both passes described on page 585). Special exhibits are extra.

Hours: Pergamon—daily 10:00-18:00, Thu until 21:00. Neues Museum—daily 10:00-18:00, Thu-Sat until 20:00. Old National Gallery and Bode Museum—Tue-Sun 10:00-18:00, Thu until 22:00, closed Mon; same hours for Altes Museum except closes Thu at 20:00. Tel. 030/266-424-242, www.smb.museum.

Required Reservation for Pergamon and Neues Museums: Visiting either the Pergamon Museum or Neues Museum requires a *Zeitfensterticket* ("time-window ticket") that gives you a 30-minute time slot for entering the museum (included with admission; separate appointments required for each museum). Once inside, you can stay as long as you like. Reserve your time online (www. smb.museum) or in person at any Museum Island ticket office. (At less busy times, tickets are sometimes sold without any particular time slot.)

You can usually get a time slot within about an hour, often sooner—except at the busiest times (Sat and Sun mornings), when you may have to wait longer. The least-crowded times are evenings when the museums are open late (Thu for Pergamon, Thu-Sat for Neues).

Buying Tickets: The temporary kiosk on Bodestrasse functions as the ticket booth for the Neues Museum and comes with avoidable lines. Long ticket-buying lines also plague the Pergamon Museum. Avoid them by purchasing your museum pass (and getting your assigned entry time) at one of the island's three never-crowded museums: Altes, Bode, or Old National Gallery. (From Unter den Linden, Altes is most convenient; if coming from Prenzlauer Berg, try the Bode.)

Planning Your Time: I'd start at the Bode, where I'd ask for an entry time to the Pergamon Museum in about an hour, and a ticket to the Neues Museum for 1.5 hours after that. Tickets and appointments in hand, spend any time left before your Pergamon time slot browsing the Bode. Then enjoy the Pergamon collection, where the art is earth-shaking but easy to see in an hour. If you have any extra time before your Neues appointment, nip into the time-tunnel Old National Gallery. Step into the Neues Museum within 30 minutes of your entry time, and be prepared to linger. I'd skip the Altes Museum. For lunch nearby, follow the elevated train tracks away from the Pergamon down Georgenstrasse (see recommendations on page 668).

Getting There: The nearest S-Bahn station is Hackescher Markt, about a 10-minute walk away. From hotels in the Prenzlauer Berg, ride tram #M-1 to the end of line, and you're right at the Pergamon Museum.

▲▲▲Pergamon Museum (Pergamonmuseum)

The star attraction of this world-class museum, part of Berlin's Collection of Classical Antiquities (Antikensammlung), is the fantastic and gigantic Pergamon Altar. The Babylonian Ishtar Gate (slathered with glazed blue tiles from the 6th century B.C.) and the museum's many ancient Greek, Mesopotamian, Roman, and early Islamic treasures are also impressive.

Audioguide: Make ample use of the superb audioguide (included with admission)—it will broaden your experience. Punching #10 on the audioguide gets you the "Pergamon in 30 Minutes" general tour. Or follow my quicker, more succinct self-guided tour.

⊙ Self-Guided Tour: With your timed entry and museum pass, walk boldly by the long line of people who don't have or read guidebooks, and go directly in.

There's a lot to see in this museum (everything is well-described by posted English information and the included audioguide). The best plan for the casual visitor is to focus on a few highlights.

From the entrance, walk straight ahead to find the museum's namesake, the **Pergamon Altar.** Actually a 65-foot-wide temple, this "altar" comes from the second-century B.C. Greek city of Pergamon (near the west coast of today's Turkey). The Pergamon Altar was just one component of a spectacular hilltop ensemble—temples, sanctuaries, palaces, theaters, and other buildings erected to honor the gods—modeled after the Acropolis in Athens. (See a model of the complete Pergamon Acropolis to the right, as you face the stairs.)

Pergamon was excavated from 1878 to 1886 by German archaeologist Carl Humann, who unearthed fragments of the temple's frieze all over the site (many pieces had been "recycled" as building materials in later structures). The bits and pieces were brought here to Berlin, reassembled on this replica of the temple, and put on display in this purpose-built museum in 1930.

The temple replica re-creates the western third of the original building. Stairs lead up to a chamber with a small sacrificial altar, where priests and priestesses sacrificed and burned animals, while toga-clad Greeks assembled in awe at the foot of the stairs below.

Surviving pieces of a 269-foot-long frieze that wrapped around the entire temple dramatically spill onto the stairs and around the room. Called the **Gigantomachy Frieze,** it shows the Greek gods under Zeus and Athena defeating the giants in a dramatic pig pile of mythological mayhem. Imagine how much more evocative these sculptures once were, slathered in colorful paint, gold, and silver trim.

So what's the fight about? Long before the time of man, an epic struggle pitted the titans against the gods. When the gods won, they thrust their foes into a miserable underworld (the mythological equivalent of purgatory) and settled in for a comfy period of rule atop Mount Olympus. But the troublesome race of giants—children of the earth goddess Gaia, mother of the titans—sought revenge. The giants had legs of slithering snakes that kept them in contact with the ground, allowing Gaia to make them immortal. This frieze captures a pivotal event, when the giants Alkyoneus and Porphyrion led a rebellion of their race against the gods. (The people of Pergamon appreciated the parallels between this story and their own noble struggle against unenlightened barbarians.)

With your back to the altar steps, look at the right end of the frieze to find panels with Zeus and Athena, locked in combat with the giants. Faint surviving labels on the cornice above the statues—in Greek, of course—help identify the combatants; the modern English letters below may prove more helpful.

Find the **Athena** panel. Athena (faceless, in the center, with the shield) and Nike (all that's left are her wings, right arm, and left leg) pull the chief giant Alkyoneus (his snake legs curling around his bicep) up by his hair—breaking his connection to the earth, the source of his immortality. Below them, Gaia—the mother of

BERLIN

the giants—rises up from her subterranean realm to lend a hand. (See the fear in Gaia's and Alkyoneus' tortured eyes.) Alkyoneus would survive this brush with Athena, only to be killed soon after by Hercules. (The statue of Hercules is missing—all that survives is one pathetic paw of his lion pelt.)

The **Zeus** panel shows the (headless) king of the gods raining lightning bolts down on his enemies—including the snake-legged Porphyrion, with his back(side) toward us. Notice Zeus' disembodied right hand up above, ready to pitch some serious heat. Fans of Greek mythology can take a slow walk along the entire length of the frieze, identifying their favorite gods and giants...the gang's all here. Before long, the giants will be history, and the gods can go back about their usual business of conspiring against each other and impregnating mortals.

Facing the altar stairs, go through the door to your left. The intricate, ancient Greek **mosaic floor** is finely assembled from miniscule pebbles, with a particularly impressive floral motif decorating the border. In the otherwise undecorated box in the middle, in what looks like an ancient Post-It note, you can see where the artist "signed" his work. The Athena statue standing in the middle of the room is a replica of one that once stood at the center of Athens' Acropolis. Turn around to see the doorway you just came through, surrounded by the original, double-decker ornamental entryway to the Pergamon Acropolis. Ancient pilgrims who had come from far and wide to worship the gods in Pergamon passed through here on their way to the altar.

Return to the altar room, cross straight through it, and go out the door on the far side. From Pergamon, flash-forward 300 years (and travel south 110 miles) to the ancient Roman city of Miletus. Dominating this room (on your right) is the 95-foot-wide, 55-foot-high **Market Gate of Miletus,** destroyed by an earthquake centuries ago and now painstakingly reconstructed here in Berlin. The exquisite mosaic floor from a Roman villa in Miletus has two parts: In the square panel, the musician Orpheus strokes his lyre to charm the animals; in stark contrast, in the nearby rectangular mosaic (from an adjacent room), hunters pursue wild animals.

Step through the market gate and all the way back to 575 B.C., to the Fertile Crescent—Mesopotamia (today's Iraq). The Assyrian ruler Nebuchadnezzar II, who amassed a vast empire and enormous wealth, wanted to build a suitably impressive processional entryway to his capital city, Babylon, to honor the goddess Ishtar. His creation, the **Ishtar Gate,** inspired awe and obedience in anyone who came to his city. This is a reconstruction, using some original components. The gate itself is embellished with two animals: a bull and a mythical dragon-like combination of lion, cobra, eagle, and scorpion. The long hall leading to the main gate—designed for a huge processional of deities to celebrate the new year—is decorated with a chain of blue and yellow glazed tiles with 120 strolling lions (representing the goddess Ishtar). To get the big picture, find the model of the original site in the center of the hall.

These main exhibits are surrounded by smaller galleries. Upstairs is the **Museum of Islamic Art.** It contains fine carpets, tile work, the Aleppo Room (with ornately painted wooden walls from an early 17th-century home in today's Syria; since it was commissioned by a Christian, it incorporates Arabic, Persian, and biblical themes), and the Mshatta Facade (walls and towers from one of the early eighth-century Umayyad "desert castles," from today's Jordan).

▲▲Neues (New) Museum and Egyptian Collection

Oddly, Museum Island's so-called "new" museum features the oldest stuff around. There are three collections here: the Egyptian Collection (with the famous bust of Queen Nefertiti; floor 0 and parts of floors 1-2), the Museum of Prehistory and Early History (floor 3 and parts of floors 1-2), and some items from the Collection of Classical Antiquities (artifacts from ancient Troy—famously excavated by German adventurer Heinrich Schliemann—and Cyprus, just off the entrance).

The top draw here is the Egyptian art—clearly one of the world's best collections. But let's face it: The main reason to visit is to enjoy one of the great thrills in art appreciation—gazing into the still-young-and-beautiful face of Queen Nefertiti. If you're in a pinch for time, make a beeline to her (floor 2, far corner of Egyptian Collection in room 210; for more on the museum, see www.neues-museum.de).

Audioguide: The fine audioguide (included with admission) celebrates new knowledge about ancient Egyptian civilization and offers fascinating insights into workaday Egyptian life as it describes the vivid papyrus collection, slice-of-life artifacts, and dreamy wax portraits decorating mummy cases.

Visiting the Museum: After being damaged in World War II and sitting in ruins for some 40 years, the Neues Museum was recently rebuilt. Everything is well-described by posted English information and the audioguide.

To tour the whole collection, begin by going all the way to the top (floor 3) where you'll find the **prehistory section.** The entire floor is filled with Stone Age, Ice Age, and Bronze Age items. You'll see early human remains, tools, spearheads, and pottery.

The most interesting item on this floor (in corner room 305) is the tall, conehead-like **Golden Hat,** made of paper-thin hammered gold leaf. Created by an early Celtic civilization in Central Europe, it's particularly exquisite for something so old (from the

Bronze Age, around 1000 B.C.). The circles on the hat represent the sun, moon, and other celestial bodies—leading archaeologists to believe that this headwear could double as a calendar, showing how the sun and moon sync up every 19 years.

Down on floor 2, you'll find **early history** exhibits on migrations, barbarians, and ancient Rome (including larger-than-life statues of Helios and an unidentified goddess) as well as a fascinating look at the Dark Ages after the fall of Rome.

Still on floor 2, cross to the other side of the building for the **Egyptian** section. On the way, you'll pass through the impressive Papyrus Collection—a large room of seemingly empty glass cases. Press a button to watch a 3,000-year-old piece of primitive "paper" (made of aquatic reeds) imprinted with primitive text trundle out of its protective home.

Then, finally, in a room all her own, is the 3,000-year-old bust of **Queen Nefertiti** (the wife of King Akhenaton, c. 1340 B.C.)—the most famous piece of Egyptian art in Europe. Called "Berlin's most beautiful woman," Nefertiti has all the right beauty marks: long neck, symmetrical face, and the perfect amount of makeup. And yet, she's not completely idealized. Notice the fine wrinkles that show she's human (though these only enhance her beauty). Like a movie star discreetly sipping a glass of wine at a sidewalk café, Nefertiti seems somehow more dignified in person. The bust never left its studio, but served as a master model for all other portraits of the queen. (That's probably why the left eye was never inlaid.) Stare at her long enough, and you may get the sensation that she's winking at you. Hey, beautiful!

How the queen arrived in Germany is a tale out of *Indiana Jones*. The German archaeologist Ludwig Borchardt uncovered her in the Egyptian desert in 1912. The Egyptian Department of Antiquities had first pick of all the artifacts uncovered on their territory. After the first takings, they divided the rest 50/50 with the excavators. When Borchardt presented Nefertiti to the Egyptians, they passed her over, never bothering to examine her closely. Unsubstantiated rumors persist that Borchardt misled the Egyptians in order to keep the bust for himself—rumors that have prompted some Egyptians to call for the return of Nefertiti (just as the Greeks are lobbying the British to return the Parthenon frieze currently housed in the British Museum). Although this bust is not particularly representative of Egyptian art in general—and despite increasing claims that her long neck suggests she's a Neoclassical fake—Nefertiti has become a symbol of Egyptian art by popular acclaim.

The Egyptian Collection continues with other sculptures, including kneeling figures holding steles (stone tablets inscribed with prayers). On floor 1, a fascinating exhibit examines how depictions of the human image evolved during the 3,000-year span of ancient Egyptian culture. You'll also see entire walls from tombs and (in the basement—floor 0) a sea of large sarcophagi.

▲Old National Gallery (Alte Nationalgalerie)

This gallery, behind the Neues Museum and Altes Museum, is designed to look like a Greek temple. Spanning three floors, it focuses on art (mostly paintings) from the 19th century: Romantic German paintings (which I find most interesting) on the top floor, and French and German Impressionists and German Realists on the first and second floors. You likely won't recognize any specific paintings, but it's still an enjoyable stroll through German culture from the century in which that notion first came to mean something. The included audioguide explains the highlights.

Visiting the Museum: Start on the third floor, with Romantic canvases and art of the Goethe era (roughly 1770-1830), and work your way down. Use the audioguide to really delve into these romanticized, vivid looks at life in Germany in the 19th century and before. As you stroll through the Romantic paintings—the museum's strength—keep in mind that they were created about the time (mid-late 19th century) that Germans were first working toward a single, unified nation. By glorifying pristine German landscapes and a rugged, virtuous people, these painters evoked the region's high-water mark—the Middle Ages, when "Germany" was a patchwork of powerful and wealthy merchant city-states. Linger over dreamy townscapes with Gothic cathedrals and castles that celebrate medieval German might. Still lifes, idealized portraits of tow-headed children, and genre paintings (depicting everyday scenes, often with subtle social commentary) strum the heartstrings of anyone with Teutonic blood. The Düsseldorf School excelled at Romantic landscapes (such as Carl Friedrich Lessing's *Castle on a Rock*). Some of these canvases nearly resemble present-day fantasy paintings. Perhaps the best-known artist in the collection is Caspar David Friedrich, who specialized in dramatic scenes celebrating grandeur and the solitary hero. His *The Monk by the Sea (Der Mönch am Meer)* shows a lone figure standing on a sand dune, pondering a vast, turbulent expanse of sea and sky.

On the second floor, you'll find one big room of minor works by bigger-name French artists, including Renoir, Cézanne, Manet, Monet, and Rodin. Another room is devoted to the Romantic Hans von Marées, the influential early Symbolist Arnold Böcklin, and other artists of the "German Roman" (Deutschrömer) movement—Germans who lived in, and were greatly influenced by, Rome. Artists of the Munich School are represented by naturalistic canvases of landscapes or slice-of-life scenes.

On the first floor, 19th-century Realism reigns. While the Re-

BERLIN

alist Adolph Menzel made his name painting elegant royal gatherings and historical events, his *Iron Rolling Mill (Das Eisenwalzwerk)* captures the gritty side of his moment in history—the emergence of the Industrial Age—with a warts-and-all look at steelworkers toiling in a hellish factory. The first floor also hosts a sculpture collection, with works by great sculptors both foreign (the Italian Canova, the Dane Thorvaldsen) and German (Johann Gottfried Schadow's delightful *Die Prinzessinnen,* showing the dynamic duo of Prussian princesses Louise and Frederike).

Bode Museum

At the "prow" of Museum Island, the Bode Museum (designed to appear as if it's rising up from the river), is worth a quick look. Just inside, a grand statue of Frederick William of Brandenburg on horseback, curly locks blowing in the wind, welcomes you into the lonely halls of the museum. This fine building contains a hodge-podge of collections: Byzantine art, historic coins, ecclesiastical art, sculptures, and medals commemorating the fall of the Berlin Wall and German reunification. For a free, quick look at its lavish interior, climb the grand staircase to the charming café on the first floor.

Altes (Old) Museum

The least interesting of the five museums, this building features the rest of the Collection of Classical Antiquities (the best of which is in the Pergamon Museum)—namely, Etruscan, Roman, and Greek art. I'd pass it up.

Other Sights on and near Museum Island

In addition to the five museums just described, Museum Island is home to the following sights. One more sight (the DDR Museum) sits just across the river.

Lustgarten

For 300 years, the island's big central square has flip-flopped between being a military parade ground and a people-friendly park, depending upon the political tenor of the time. During the revolutions of 1848, the Kaiser's troops dispersed a protesting crowd that had assembled here, sending demonstrators onto footpaths. Karl Marx later commented, "It is impossible to have a revolution in a country where people stay off the grass."

For decades, it was *verboten* to relax or walk on the Lustgarten's grass. But in 1999, the Lustgarten was made into a park (read the history posted in the corner opposite the church). On a sunny day, it's packed with relaxing locals and is one of Berlin's most enjoyable public spaces.

Berlin Cathedral (Berliner Dom)

This century-old church towers over Museum Island. Inside, the great reformers (Luther, Calvin, and company) stand around the brilliantly restored dome like stern saints guarding their theology. Frederick I rests in an ornate tomb (right transept, near entrance to dome). The 270-step climb to the outdoor dome gallery is tough but offers pleasant, breezy views of the city at the finish line. The crypt downstairs is not worth a look.

Cost and Hours: €7 includes access to dome gallery, €10 with audioguide, not covered by Museum Island ticket, Mon-Sat 9:00-20:00, Sun 12:00-20:00, until 19:00 Oct-March, closes early—around 17:30—on some days for concerts, interior closed but dome open during services, tel. 030/2026-9136, www.berliner-dom.de. The cathedral hosts many organ concerts (often on weekends, tickets from about €10 always available at the door).

Humboldt-Forum Construction Site (Former Site of Hohenzollern Palace)

Across Unter den Linden from Berlin Cathedral is a big lawn that for centuries held the Baroque palace of the Hohenzollern dynasty of Brandenburg and Prussia. Much of that palace actually survived World War II but was replaced by the communists with a blocky, Soviet-style "Palace" of the Republic—East Berlin's parliament building/entertainment complex and a showy symbol of the communist days. The landmark building fell into disrepair after reunification and was eventually dismantled in 2007. After much debate about how to use this prime real estate, the German parliament decided to construct the Humboldt-Forum, a huge public venue filled with museums, shops, galleries, and concert halls behind a facade constructed in imitation of the original Hohenzollern palace. With a €1.2 billion price tag, many Berliners consider the reconstruction plan a complete waste of money.

The temporary **Humboldt-Box** has been set up to help the public follow the construction of the new Humboldt-Forum. The multiple floors of the futuristic "box" display building plans and models for the project (€4, daily 10:00-20:00, after that free entry to terrace-café until 23:00, tel. 01805-030-707, www.humboldt-box.com). On the top floor, the terrace-café with unobstructed views over Berlin serves coffee, desserts, and light food until 18:00, and a dinner menu after that (€5-15 lunch dishes, €15-22 dinners).

Spree River Cruises

The recommended Spree River boat tours depart from the riverbank near the bridge by the Berlin Cathedral. For details, see page 597.

• *Directly across the bridge from Museum Island, down along the riverbank, look for the...*

▲DDR Museum

Although this exhibit began as a tourist trap, it has expanded and matured into a genuinely interesting look at life in former East Germany (DDR). It's well-stocked with kitschy everyday items from the communist period, plus photos, video clips, and concise English explanations. The exhibits are interactive—you're encouraged to pick up and handle anything that isn't behind glass. You'll crawl through a Trabant car (designed by East German engineers to compete with the West's popular VW Beetle) and pick up some DDR-era jokes ("East Germany had 39 newspapers, four radio stations, two TV channels...and one opinion."). The reconstructed communist-era home lets you tour the kitchen, living room, bedrooms, and more. You'll learn about the Russian-imported *Dacha*—the simple countryside cottage (owned by one in six East Germans) used for weekend retreats from the grimy city. (Others vacationed on the Baltic Coast, where nudism was all the rage, as a very revealing display explains.) Lounge in DDR movie chairs as you view a subtitled propaganda film or clips from beloved-in-the-East TV shows (including the popular kids' show *Sandmännchen*—"Little Sandman"). Even the meals served in the attached restaurant are based on DDR-era recipes.

Cost and Hours: €6, daily 10:00-20:00, Sat until 22:00, just across the Spree from Museum Island at Karl-Liebknecht-Strasse 1, tel. 030/847-123-731, www.ddr-museum.de.

Museum Island to Alexanderplatz

• *Continue walking down Unter den Linden. Before crossing the bridge (and leaving Museum Island), look across the river. The pointy twin spires of the 13th-century Nikolai Church mark the center of medieval Berlin. This* **Nikolaiviertel** *(Viertel means "quarter") was restored by the DDR and trendy in the last years of communism. Today, it's a lively-at-night riverside restaurant district.*

As you cross the bridge, look left in the distance to see the gilded **New Synagogue** dome, rebuilt after WWII bombing (described later).

Across the river to the left of the bridge, directly below you, is the **DDR Museum** (described earlier). Just beyond that is the giant **SAS Radisson Hotel** and shopping center, with a huge aquarium in the center. The elevator goes right through the middle of a deep-sea world. (You can see it from the unforgettable Radisson hotel lobby—tuck in your shirt and walk past the guards with the confidence of a guest who's sleeping there.) Here in the center of the old communist capital, it seems that capitalism has settled in with a spirited vengeance.

In the park immediately across the street (a big jaywalk from the Radisson) are grandfatherly statues of **Marx and Engels** (nicknamed "the old pensioners"). Surrounding them are stainless-steel monoliths with evocative photos that show the struggles of the workers of the world.

Walk toward **Marien Church** (from 1270), just left of the base of the TV Tower. An artist's rendering helps you follow the interesting but very faded old "Dance of Death" mural that wraps around the narthex inside the door.

The big red-brick building past the trees on the right is the **City Hall,** built after the revolutions of 1848 and arguably the first democratic building in the city.

The 1,200-foot-tall **TV Tower** (Fernsehturm) has a fine view from halfway up (€12, daily March-Oct 9:00-24:00, Nov-Feb 10:00-24:00, www.tv-turm.de). The tower offers a handy city orientation and an interesting view of the flat, red-roofed sprawl of Berlin—including a peek inside the city's many courtyards *(Höfe).* Consider a kitschy trip to the observation deck for the view and lunch in its revolving restaurant (mediocre food, €12 plates, horrible lounge music, reservations smart for dinner, tel. 030/242-3333). The retro tower is quite trendy these days, so it can be crowded (your ticket comes with an assigned entry time). Built (with Swedish know-how) in 1969 for the 20th anniversary of the communist government, the tower was meant to show the power of the atheistic state at a time when DDR leaders were having the crosses removed from church domes and spires. But when the sun shined on their tower—the greatest spire in East Berlin—a huge cross was reflected on the mirrored ball. Cynics called it "The Pope's Revenge." East Berliners dubbed the tower the "Tele-Asparagus." They joked that if it fell over, they'd have an elevator to the West.

Farther east, pass under the train tracks into **Alexanderplatz.** This area—especially the former Kaufhof department store (now Galeria Kaufhof)—was the commercial pride and joy of East Berlin. Today, it's still a landmark, with a major U- and S-Bahn station. The once-futuristic, now-retro "World Time Clock," installed in 1969, is a nostalgic favorite and a popular meeting point. Stop in the square for a coffee and to people-watch. It's a great scene.

• *Our orientation stroll or bus ride (this is the last stop for bus #100) is finished. From here, you can hike back a bit to catch the riverboat tour, take in the sights south of Unter den Linden, venture into the colorful Prenzlauer Berg neighborhood, or consider extending this foray into eastern Berlin.*

Karl-Marx-Allee

The buildings along Karl-Marx-Allee in East Berlin (just beyond Alexanderplatz) were completely leveled by the Red Army in 1945. As an expression of their adoration to the "great Socialist Father" (Stalin), the DDR government decided to rebuild the street better

BERLIN

than ever (the USSR provided generous subsidies). They intentionally made it one meter wider than the Champs-Elysées, named it Stalinallee, and lined it with "workers' palaces" built in the bold "Stalin Gothic" style so common in Moscow in the 1950s. Now renamed after Karl Marx, the street and its restored buildings provide a rare look at Berlin's communist days. Distances are a bit long for convenient walking, but you can cruise Karl-Marx-Allee by taxi, or ride the U-Bahn to Strausberger Platz (which was built to resemble an Italian promenade) and walk to Frankfurter Tor, reading the good information posts along the way. Notice the Social Realist reliefs on the buildings and the lampposts, which incorporate the wings of a phoenix (rising from the ashes) in their design. Once a "workers' paradise," the street now hosts a two-mile-long capitalist beer festival the first weekend in August.

The **Café Sibylle,** just beyond the Strausberger Platz U-Bahn station, is a fun spot for a coffee, traditional DDR ice-cream treats, and a look at its free informal museum that tells the story of the most destroyed street in Berlin. While the humble exhibit is nearly all in German, it's fun to see the ear (or buy a €10 plaster replica) and half a moustache from what was the largest statue of Stalin in Germany (the centerpiece of the street until 1961). It also provides a few intimate insights into apartment life in a DDR flat. The café is known for its good coffee and *Schwedeneisbecher mit Eierlikor*—an ice-cream sundae with a shot of egg liqueur, popular among those nostalgic for communism (Mon-Fri 10:00-20:00, Sat-Sun 12:00-20:00, Karl-Marx-Allee 72, at intersection with Koppenstrasse, a block from U-Bahn: Strausberger Platz, tel. 030/2935-2203).

Heading out to Karl-Marx-Allee (just beyond the TV Tower), you're likely to notice a giant colorful **mural** decorating a blocky communist-era skyscraper. This was the Ministry of Education, and the mural is a tile mosaic trumpeting the accomplishments of the DDR's version of "No Child Left Behind."

South of Unter den Linden

The following sights—heavy on Nazi and Wall history—are listed roughly north to south (as you reach them from Unter den Linden).

▲▲Gendarmenmarkt

This delightful, historic square is bounded by twin churches, a tasty chocolate shop, and the Berlin Symphony's concert hall (designed by Karl Friedrich Schinkel, the man who put the Neoclassical stamp on Berlin and Dresden). In summer, it hosts a few outdoor cafés, *Biergartens*, and sometimes concerts. Wonderfully symmetrical, the square is considered by Berliners to be the finest in town (U6: Französische Strasse; U2 or U6: Stadtmitte).

The name of the square—part French and part German (after

the *Gens d'Armes,* Frederick the Great's royal guard who were head-quartered here)—reminds us that in the 17th century, a fifth of all Berliners were French émigrés—Protestant Huguenots fleeing Catholic France. Back then, Frederick the Great's tolerant Prussia was a magnet for the persecuted (and for their money). These émigrés vitalized Berlin with new ideas and know-how...and their substantial wealth.

Of the two matching churches on Gendarmenmarkt, the one to the south (bottom end of square) is the **German Cathedral** (Deutscher Dom). This cathedral (not to be confused with the Berlin Cathedral on Unter den Linden) was bombed flat in the war and rebuilt only in the 1980s. It houses the thought-provoking Milestones, Setbacks, Sidetracks *(Wege, Irrwege, Umwege)* exhibit, which traces the history of the German parliamentary system—worth ▲. The parliament-funded exhibit—while light on actual historical artifacts—is well done and more interesting than it sounds. It takes you quickly from the revolutionary days of 1848 to the 1920s, and then more deeply through the tumultuous 20th century. As the exhibit is designed for Germans rather than foreign tourists, there are no English descriptions—but you can follow the essential, excellent, and free 1.5-hour English audioguide or buy the wonderfully detailed €10 guidebook. If you think this museum is an attempt by the German government to develop a more sophisticated and educated electorate in the interest of stronger democracy, you're exactly right. Germany knows (from its own troubled history) that a dumbed-down electorate, manipulated by clever spin-meisters and sound-bite media blitzes, is a dangerous thing (free, Tue-Sun May-Sept 10:00-19:00, Oct-April 10:00-18:00, closed Mon year-round, tel. 030/2273-0431).

The **French Cathedral** (Französischer Dom), at the north end of the square, offers a humble museum on the Huguenots (€2, Tue-Sat 12:00-17:00, Sun 11:00-17:00, closed Mon, enter around the right side) and a viewpoint in the dome up top (€3, daily 10:30-19:00, last entry at 18:00, 244 steps, enter through door facing square). Fun fact: Neither of these churches is a true cathedral, as they never contained a bishop's throne; their German title of *Dom* (cathedral) is actually a mistranslation from the French word *dôme* (cupola).

Fassbender & Rausch, on the corner near the German Cathedral, claims to be Europe's biggest chocolate store. After 150 years of chocolate-making, this family-owned business proudly displays its sweet delights—250 different kinds—on a 55-foot-long buffet. Truffles are sold for about €0.60 each; it's fun to compose a fancy little eight-piece box of your own for about €5. Upstairs is an elegant hot chocolate café with fine views. The window displays feature giant chocolate models of Berlin landmarks—Reichstag,

TV Tower, Kaiser Wilhelm Memorial Church, and so on. If all this isn't enough to entice you, I have three words: erupting chocolate volcano (Mon-Sat 10:00-20:00, Sun 11:00-20:00, corner of Mohrenstrasse at Charlottenstrasse 60, tel. 030/2045-8440).

Gendarmenmarkt is buried in what has recently emerged as Berlin's "Fifth Avenue" shopping district. For the ultimate in top-end shops, find the corner of Jägerstrasse and Friedrichstrasse and wander through the **Quartier 206** (Mon-Fri 11:00-20:00, Sat 10:00-18:00, closed Sun, www.quartier206.com). The adjacent, middlebrow **Quartier 205** has more affordable prices.

Nazi and Cold War Sites on Wilhelmstrasse

Fragment of the Wall

Surviving stretches of the Wall are virtually nonexistent in downtown Berlin. One of the most convenient places to see a bit is at the intersection of Wilhelmstrasse and Zimmerstrasse/Niederkirchnerstrasse, a few blocks southwest of Gendarmenmarkt. Many visitors make the short walk over here from the Checkpoint Charlie sights (described later), then drop into the museum listed next.

▲▲Topography of Terror (Topographie des Terrors)

Coincidentally, the patch of land behind the surviving stretch of Wall was closely associated with a different regime: It was once the nerve center for the most despicable elements of the Nazi government, the Gestapo and the SS. This stark-gray, boxy building is one of the few memorial sites that focuses on the perpetrators rather than the victims of the Nazis. It's chilling but thought-provoking to see just how seamlessly and bureaucratically the Nazi institutions and state structures merged to become a well-oiled terror machine. There are few actual artifacts; it's mostly written explanations and photos, like reading a good textbook standing up. And, while you could read this story anywhere, to take this in atop the Gestapo headquarters is a powerful experience. The exhibit's a bit dense, but WWII historians (even armchair ones) will find it fascinating.

Cost and Hours: Free, daily 10:00-20:00, outdoor exhibit closes at sunset in winter, Niederkirchnerstrasse 8, tel. 030/254-5090, www.topographie.de.

Background: This location marks what was once the most feared address in Berlin: the headquarters of the Reich Main Security Office *(Reichssicherheitshauptamt)*. These offices served as the engine room of the Nazi dictatorship, as well as the command center of the SS *(Schutzstaffel*, whose members began as Hitler's personal bodyguards), the Gestapo *(Geheime Staatspolizei*, secret state police), and the SD *(Sicherheitsdienst*, the Nazi intelligence agency). This trio (and others) were ultimately consolidated under Heinrich Himmler to become a state-within-a-state, with talons in every corner of German society. This elite militarized branch of the Nazi machine was also tasked with the "racial purification" of German-held lands, especially Eastern Europe—the Holocaust. It was from these headquarters that the Nazis administered concentration camps, firmed up plans for the "Final Solution to the Jewish Question," and organized the domestic surveillance of anyone opposed to the regime. The building was also equipped with dungeons, where the Gestapo detained and tortured thousands of prisoners.

The Gestapo and SS employed intimidation techniques to coerce cooperation from the German people. The general public knew that the Gestapo was to be feared: It was considered omnipotent, omnipresent, and omniscient. Some political prisoners underwent "enhanced interrogation" right here in this building. The threat of *Schutzhaft* ("protective custody," usually at a concentration camp) was used to terrify any civilians who stepped out of line—or who might make a good example. But Hitler and his cronies also won people's loyalties through propaganda. They hammered home the idealistic notion of the *Volksgemeinschaft* ("people's community") of a purely Germanic culture and race, which empowered Hitler to create a pervasive illusion that "We're all in this together." Anyone who was not an Aryan was *Untermensch*—subhuman—and must be treated as such.

Visiting the Museum: The complex has two parts: indoors, in the modern boxy building; and outdoors, in the trench that runs along the surviving stretch of Wall. Visit the indoor exhibit first.

Inside, you'll find a visitor center with an information desk and an extensive **Topography of Terror** exhibit about the SS and Gestapo, and the atrocities they committed in Berlin and across Europe. A model of the government quarter, circa 1939, sets the stage of Nazi domination in this area. A timeline of events and old photographs, documents, and newspaper clippings illustrate how Hitler and his team expertly manipulated the German people to build a broadly supported "dictatorship of consent."

The exhibit walks you through the evolution of Hitler's regime: the Nazi takeover; institutions of terror (Himmler's "SS State"); terror, persecution, and extermination; atrocities in Nazi-occupied countries; and the war's end and postwar. Some images here are indelible, such as photos of SS soldiers stationed at Auschwitz, gleefully yukking it up on a retreat in the countryside (even as their helpless prisoners were being gassed and burned a few miles away). The exhibit profiles specific members of the various reprehensible SS branches, as well as the groups they targeted: Jews, Roma, and Sinti (Gypsies); the unemployed or homeless; homosexuals; and the physically and mentally ill (considered "useless eaters" who consumed resources without contributing work).

Downstairs is a WC and a library with research books on

BERLIN

these topics. Before heading outside, ask at the information desk to borrow the free audioguide that describes the outdoor exhibits.

Outside, in the trench along the Wall, you'll find the exhibit **Berlin 1933-1945: Between Propaganda and Terror,** which overlaps slightly with the indoor exhibit but focuses on Berlin. The chronological survey begins with the post-WWI Weimar Republic and continues through the ragged days just after World War II. One display explains how Nazis invented holidays (or injected new Aryan meaning into existing ones) as a means of winning over the public. Other exhibits cover the "Aryanization" of Jewish businesses (they were simply taken over by the state and handed over to new Aryan owners); Hitler's plans for converting Berlin into a gigantic "Welthauptstadt (World Capital) Germania"; and the postwar Berlin Airlift, which brought provisions to some 2.2 million West Berliners whose supply lines were cut off by East Berlin.

With more time, explore the grounds around the blocky building on a **"Site Tour."** Posted signs explain 15 different locations, including the scant remains of the prison cellars.

German Finance Ministry
(Bundesministerium der Finanzen)

Across the street (facing the Wall chunk) are the former headquarters of the Nazi Luftwaffe (Air Force), the only major Hitler-era government building that survived the war's bombs. Notice how the whole building gives off a monumental feel, making the average person feel small and powerless. Walk into the stark courtyard. After the war, this was the headquarters for the Soviet occupation. Later the DDR was founded here, and the communists used the building to house their—no joke—Ministry of Ministries. Walk up Wilhelmstrasse (to the north) to see an entry gate (on your left) that looks much like it did when Germany occupied nearly all of Europe. On the north side of the building (farther up Wilhelmstrasse, at corner with Leipziger Strasse) is a wonderful example of communist art. The mural, Max Lingner's *Aufbau der Republik* (*Building the Republic,* 1953), is classic Socialist Realism, showing the entire society—industrial laborers, farm workers, women, and children—all happily singing the same patriotic song. Its subtitle: "The importance of peace for the cultural development of humanity and the necessity of struggle to achieve this goal." This was the communist ideal. For the reality, look at the ground in the courtyard in front of the mural to see an enlarged photograph from a 1953 uprising here against the communists...quite a contrast. Placards explain the events of 1953 in English.

Stasi Museum

This modest exhibit, roughly between the Topography of Terror and Checkpoint Charlie, tells the story of how the communist-era Ministry for State Security (*Staatssicherheit,* a.k.a. Stasi) infiltrated all aspects of German life. Soon after the Wall fell, DDR authorities scrambled to destroy the copious illicit information their agents and informants had collected about the people of East Germany. But the government mandated that these records be preserved as evidence of DDR crimes, and the documents are now managed by the Federal Commissioner for Stasi Records. A timeline traces the history of the archives, and wraparound kiosks profile individual "subversive elements" who were targeted by the Stasi. There are a few actual artifacts, but the exhibit is mostly dryly written texts and reproduced photographs that don't do much to personalize the victims—making this museum worth a visit only for those with a special interest in this period. Temporary exhibits are upstairs.

Cost and Hours: Free, daily 10:00-18:00, Zimmerstrasse 90-91, tel. 030/232-450, www.bstu.bund.de.

Other Stasi Sites: If you're interested in this chapter of East German history, you may find it more satisfying (but time-consuming) to visit two other sites affiliated with the Stasi: a different **Stasi Museum,** in the former State Security headquarters (€5, Mon-Fri 11:00-18:00, Sat-Sun 12:00-18:00, Ruscherstrasse 103, U-5: Magdalenenstrasse, tel. 030/553-6854, www.stasimuseum.de); and the **Stasi Prison,** where "enemies of the state" served time (€4, visits possible only with a tour; English tours daily at 14:30—call to confirm before making the trip; German tours Mon-Fri at 11:00, 13:00, and 15:00, Sat-Sun hourly 10:00-16:00; Genslerstrasse 66, reachable on various trams from downtown—see website for specifics, tel. 030/9860-8230, www.stiftung-hsh.de).

Checkpoint Charlie

This famous Cold War checkpoint was not named for a person, but for its checkpoint number—as in Alpha (#1, at the East-West German border, a hundred miles west of here), Bravo (#2, as you enter Berlin proper), and Charlie (#3, the best known because most foreigners passed through here). While the actual checkpoint has long since been dismantled, its former location is home to a fine museum and a mock-up of the original border crossing. The area has become a Cold War freak show and—as if celebrating the final victory of crass capitalism—is one of Berlin's worst tourist-trap zones. A McDonald's stands defiantly overlooking the former haunt of East German border guards. You can even pay an exorbitant €10 for a full set of Cold War-era stamps in your passport. (For a more sober and intellectually redeeming look at the Wall's history, head for the out-of-the-way Berlin Wall Memorial at Bernauer Strasse, north of here near the Prenzlauer Berg neighborhood and described on page 640. Local officials, likely put off by the touristy crassness of the Checkpoint Charlie scene, have steered local funding to that area.)

▲Checkpoint Charlie Street Scene

Where Checkpoint Charlie once stood, notice the thought-provoking post with larger-than-life **posters** of a young American soldier facing east and a young Soviet soldier facing west. The rebuilt **guard station** now hosts two actors playing American guards who pose for photos. (Across the street is Snack Point Charlie.) A **photo exhibit** stretches down the street, with great English descriptions telling the story of the Wall. While you could get this information from a book, it's poignant to stand here in person and ponder the gripping history of this place.

A few yards away (on Zimmerstrasse), a **glass panel** describes the former checkpoint. From there, a double row of **cobbles** in Zimmerstrasse traces the former path of the Wall. These innocuous cobbles run throughout the city, even through some buildings.

Farther down on Zimmerstrasse, before Charlottenstrasse, find the **Memorial to Peter Fechter** (set just off the sidewalk, barely inside the Wall marker), who was shot and left for dead here in the early days of the Wall.

▲▲Museum of the Wall at Checkpoint Charlie (Mauermuseum Haus am Checkpoint Charlie)

While the famous border checkpoint between the American and Soviet sectors is long gone, its memory is preserved by one of Europe's most cluttered museums. During the Cold War, the House at Checkpoint Charlie stood defiantly—spitting distance from the border guards—showing off all the clever escapes over, under, and through the Wall. Today, while the drama is over and hunks of the Wall stand like trophies at its door, the museum survives as a living artifact of the Cold War days. The yellowed descriptions, which have scarcely changed since that time, tinge the museum with nostalgia. It's dusty, disorganized, and overpriced, with lots of reading involved, but all that just adds to this museum's borderline-kitschy charm. If you're pressed for time, this is a decent after-dinner sight.

Cost and Hours: €12.50, assemble 20 tourists and get in for €8.50 each, €3.50 audioguide, discount with WelcomeCard but not covered by Museumspass, daily 9:00-22:00, U6 to Kochstrasse or—better from Zoo—U2 to Stadtmitte, Friedrichstrasse 43-45, tel. 030/253-7250, www.mauermuseum.de.

Visiting the Museum: Exhibits narrate a gripping history of the Wall, with a focus on the many ingenious **escape attempts** (the early years—with a cruder wall—saw more escapes). You'll see the actual items used to smuggle would-be Wessies—a VW bug whose trunk hid a man, two side-by-side suitcases into which a woman squeezed, a makeshift zip line for crossing over (rather than through) the border, a hot-air balloon in which two families floated to safety (immortalized in the Disney film *Night Crossing*), an inflatable boat that puttered across the dangerous Baltic Sea, primitive homemade aircraft, two surfboards hollowed out to create just enough space for a refugee, and more. One chilling exhibit lists some 43,000 people who died in "Internal Affairs" internment camps during the transition to communism (1945-1950). Profiles personalize various escapees and their helpers, including John P. Ireland, an American who posed as an eccentric antiques collector so he could transport 10 different refugees to safety in his modified Cadillac.

You'll also see **artwork** inspired by the Wall and its fall, and a memorial to Rainer Hildebrandt, who founded this museum shortly after the Wall went up in 1961 (he died in 2004, but the museum lives on as a shrine to his vision). On the **top floor** (easy to miss), that vision broadens to the larger themes of freedom and persecution, including exhibits on Eastern European rebellions (the 1956 uprising in Hungary, 1968's Prague Spring, and the Solidarity movement in 1980s Poland) and Gandhi's protests in India—plus a hodgepodge of displays on world religions and Picasso's *Guernica*. Fans of "the Gipper" appreciate the room honoring President Ronald Reagan, displaying his actual cowboy hat and boots. The small movie theater shows various Wall-related films (a schedule is posted), and the displays include video coverage of those heady days when people power tore down the Wall.

▲▲Jewish Museum Berlin (Jüdisches Museum Berlin)

This museum is one of Europe's best Jewish sights. The highly conceptual building is a sight in itself, and the museum inside—an overview of the rich culture and history of Europe's Jewish community—is excellent, particularly if you take advantage of the informative and engaging audioguide. Rather than just reading dry texts, you'll feel this museum as fresh and alive—an exuberant celebration of the Jewish experience that's accessible to all. Even though the museum is in a nondescript residential neighborhood, it's well worth the trip.

Cost and Hours: €5, sometimes extra for special exhibits, discount with WelcomeCard, daily 10:00-20:00, Mon until 22:00, last entry one hour before closing, closed on Jewish holidays. Tight security includes bag check and metal detectors. The excellent €3 audioguide—with four hours of commentary on 151 different items—is essential to fully appreciate the exhibits. Tel. 030/2599-3300, www.jmberlin.de.

Getting There: Take the U-Bahn to Hallesches Tor, find the exit marked *Jüdisches Museum*, exit straight ahead, then turn right on Franz-Klühs-Strasse. The museum is a five-minute walk ahead on your left, at Lindenstrasse 9.

Eating: The museum's restaurant, Liebermanns, offers good

Jewish-style meals, albeit not kosher (€9 daily specials, lunch served 12:00-16:00, snacks at other times, tel. 030/2593-9760).

Visiting the Museum: Designed by American architect Daniel Libeskind (the master planner for the redeveloped World Trade Center in New York), the zinc-walled building has a zigzag shape pierced by voids symbolic of the irreplaceable cultural loss caused by the Holocaust. Enter the 18th-century Baroque building next door, then go through an underground tunnel to reach the museum interior.

Before you reach the exhibit, your visit starts with three **memorial spaces.** Follow the Axis of Exile to a disorienting slanted garden with 49 pillars (evocative of the Memorial to the Murdered Jews of Europe, across town). Next, the Axis of Holocaust, lined with artifacts from Jews imprisoned and murdered by the Nazis, leads to an eerily empty tower shut off from the outside world. The Axis of Continuity takes you to stairs and the main exhibit. A detour partway up the long stairway leads to the Memory Void, a compelling space of "fallen leaves": heavy metal faces that you walk on, making unhuman noises with each step.

Finish climbing the stairs to the top of the museum, and stroll chronologically through the 2,000-year **story of Judaism** in Germany. The exhibit, on two floors, is engaging, with lots of actual artifacts. Interactive bits (you can, for example, spell your name in Hebrew, or write a prayer and hang it from a tree) make it lively for kids. English explanations interpret both the exhibits and the design of the very symbolic building.

The top floor focuses on everyday life in Ashkenaz (medieval German-Jewish lands). The nine-minute movie "A Thousand Years Ago" sets the stage for your journey through Jewish history. You'll learn what garlic had to do with early Jews in Germany (hint: It's not just about cooking). The Middle Ages were a positive time for Jewish culture, which flourished then in many areas of Europe. But around 1500, many Jews were expelled from the countryside and moved into cities. Viewing stations let you watch nine short, lively videos that pose provocative questions about faith. Moses Mendelssohn's role in the late-18th-century Jewish Enlightenment, which gave rise to Reform Judaism, is highlighted. The Tradition and Change exhibit analyzes how various subgroups of the Jewish faith modified and relaxed their rules to adapt to a changing world.

Downstairs, on the middle floor, exhibits detail the rising tide of anti-Semitism in Germany through the 19th century—ironically, at a time when many Jews were so secularized that they celebrated Christmas right along with Hanukkah. Berlin's glory days (1890-1933) were a boom time for many Jews, though it was at times challenging to reconcile the reformed ways of the more assimilated western (German) Jews with the more traditional Eastern

European Jews. The exhibit segues into the **dark days** of Hitler—the collapse of the relatively tolerant Weimar Republic, the rise of the Nazis, and the horrific night of November 9-10, 1938, when, throughout Germany, hateful mobs destroyed Jewish-owned businesses, homes, synagogues, and even entire villages—called "Crystal Night" (Kristallnacht) for the broken glass that glittered in the streets.

The thought-provoking conclusion brings us to the present day, with the question: How do you keep going after six million of your people have been murdered? You'll see how German society has reacted to the Holocaust blood on its hands (one fascinating exhibit has footage of a 1975 sit-in of German Jews to protest a controversial play with a stereotypical Jewish villain), and listen to headphone commentary of Jewish people describing their experiences growing up in postwar Germany, Austria, and Switzerland.

More Sights South of Unter den Linden

East Side Gallery

The biggest remaining stretch of the Wall is now "the world's longest outdoor art gallery." It stretches for nearly a mile and is covered with murals painted by artists from around the world. The murals (classified as protected monuments) got a facelift in 2009, when the city invited the original artists back to re-create their work for the 20th anniversary of the fall of the Wall. This segment of the Wall makes a poignant walk. For a quick look, take the S-Bahn to the Ostbahnhof station (follow signs to Stralauerplatz exit; once outside, TV Tower will be to your right; go left and at next corner look to your right—the Wall is across the busy street). The gallery is slowly being consumed by developers. If you walk the entire length of the East Side Gallery, you'll find a small Wall souvenir shop at the end and a bridge crossing the river to a subway station at Schlesisches Tor (in Kreuzberg). The bridge, a fine example of Brandenburg Neo-Gothic brickwork, has a fun neon "rock, paper, scissors" installment poking fun at the futility of the Cold War (visible only after dark).

Kreuzberg

This district—once abutting the dreary Wall and inhabited mostly by poor Turkish guest laborers and their families—is still run-down, with graffiti-riddled buildings and plenty of student and Turkish street life. It offers a gritty look at melting-pot Berlin, in a city where original Berliners are as rare as old buildings. Berlin is the largest Turkish city outside of Turkey itself, and Kreuzberg is its "downtown." But to call it a "little Istanbul" insults the big one. You'll see *Döner Kebab* stands, shops decorated with spray paint, and mothers wrapped in colorful scarves. But lately, an influx of immigrants from many other countries has diluted the Turkishness of Kreuzberg. Berliners come here for fun ethnic eateries. For an easy dose of Kreuzberg, joyride on bus #129 (catch it near Jewish Museum). For a colorful stroll, take the U-Bahn to Kottbusser Tor and wander—ideally on Tuesday and Friday between 12:00 and 18:00, when the Turkish Market sprawls along the Maybachufer riverbank.

North of Unter den Linden

There are few major sights to the north of Unter den Linden, but this area has some of Berlin's trendiest, most interesting neighborhoods. I've listed these roughly from south to north, as you'd approach them from the city center and Unter den Linden. On a sunny day, a stroll (or tram ride) through these bursting-with-life areas can be as engaging as any museum in town.

Hackescher Markt

This area, in front of the S-Bahn station of the same name, is a great people scene day and night. The brick trestle supporting the train track is another classic example of the city's Brandenburg Neo-Gothic brickwork. Most of the brick archways are now filled with hip shops, which have official—and newly trendy—addresses such as "S-Bahn Arch #9, Hackescher Markt." Within 100 yards of the S-Bahn station, you'll find Hackeschen Höfe (described next), recommended Turkish and Bavarian restaurants, walking-tour and pub-crawl departure points, and tram #M1 to Prenzlauer Berg.

Hackeschen Höfe (a block in front of the Hackescher Markt S-Bahn station) is a series of eight courtyards bunny-hopping through a wonderfully restored 1907 *Jugendstil* (German Art Nouveau) building. Berlin's apartments are organized like this—courtyard after courtyard leading off the main roads. This complex is full of trendy restaurants (including the recommended Turkish eatery, Hasir), theaters, and cinemas (playing movies in their original languages). This is a wonderful example of how to make huge city blocks livable. Two decades after the Cold War, this area has reached the final evolution of East Berlin's urban restoration. (These courtyards also serve a useful lesson for visitors: Much of Berlin's charm hides off the street front.)

Oranienburger Strasse

Oranienburger Strasse is anchored by an important and somber sight, the New Synagogue. But the rest of this zone (roughly between the synagogue and Torstrasse) is colorful and quirky—especially after dark. The streets behind Grosse Hamburger Strasse flicker with atmospheric cafés, *Kneipen* (pubs), and art galleries. At night (from about 20:00), techno-prostitutes line Oranienburger Strasse. Prostitution is legal throughout Germany. Prostitutes pay taxes and receive health care insurance like anyone else. On this street, they hire security guards (lingering nearby) for safety—and they all seem to buy their Barbarella wardrobes at the same place.

▲New Synagogue (Neue Synagogue)

A shiny gilded dome marks the New Synagogue, now a museum and cultural center. Consecrated in 1866, this was once the biggest and finest synagogue in Germany, with seating for 3,200 worshippers and a sumptuous Moorish-style interior modeled after the Alhambra. It was desecrated by Nazis on Crystal Night (Kristallnacht) in 1938, bombed in 1943, and partially rebuilt in 1990. Only the dome and facade have been restored—a window overlooks the vacant field marking what used to be the synagogue. On its facade, a small plaque—added by East Berlin Jews in 1966—reads "Never forget" *(Vergesst es nie).* At that time East Berlin had only a few hundred Jews, but now that the city is reunited, the Jewish community numbers about 12,000.

Inside, past tight security, the small but moving permanent exhibit called Open Ye the Gates describes the Berlin Jewish community through the centuries (filling three big rooms on the ground floor and first floor, with some good English descriptions). Examine the cutaway model showing the entire synagogue (pre-destruction) and an exhibit of religious items. Stairs lead up (past temporary exhibits, with a separate entry fee) to the dome, where there's not much to see except the unimpressive-from-the-inside dome itself and ho-hum views—not worth the entry price or the climb.

Cost and Hours: Main exhibit-€3.50, dome-€2, temporary exhibits-€3, €7 combo-ticket covers everything, audioguide-€3; March-Oct Sun-Mon 10:00-20:00, Tue-Thu 10:00-18:00, Fri 10:00-17:00—until 14:00 in Oct and March-May, closed Sat; Nov-Feb Sun-Thu 10:00-18:00, Fri 10:00-14:00, closed Sat; Oranienburger Strasse 28/30, enter through the low-profile door in the modern building just right of the domed synagogue facade, S-Bahn: Oranienburger Strasse, tel. 030/8802-8300 and press 1, www.cjudaicum.de.

Nearby: A block from the synagogue (to the right as you face it), walk 50 yards down **Grosse Hamburger Strasse** to a little park. This street was known for 200 years as the "street of tolerance" because the Jewish community donated land to Protestants so they could build a church. Hitler turned it into the "street of death" *(Todesstrasse),* bulldozing 12,000 graves of the city's oldest Jewish cemetery and turning a Jewish nursing home into a deportation center. Because of the small but growing radical Islamic element in Berlin, and a smattering of persistent neo-Nazis, several police officers and an Israeli secret agent keep watch over this park and the Jewish high school nearby.

▲Prenzlauer Berg

Young, in-the-know locals agree that Prenzlauer Berg (PRENTS-low-er behrk) is one of Berlin's most colorful neighborhoods (roughly between Helmholtzplatz and Kollwitzplatz and along Kastanienallee, U2: Senefelderplatz and Eberswalder Strasse; or take the S-Bahn to Hackescher Markt and catch tram #M1 north). Tourists call it "Prenzl'berg" for short, while Berliners just call it "der Berg." This part of the city was largely untouched during World War II, but its buildings slowly rotted away under the communists. After the Wall fell, it was overrun with laid-back hipsters, energetic young families, and clever entrepreneurs who breathed life back into its classic old apartment blocks, deserted factories, and long-forgotten breweries. Ten years of rent control kept things affordable for its bohemian residents. But now landlords are free to charge what the market will bear, and the vibe is changing. This is ground zero for Berlin's baby boom: Tattooed and pierced young moms and dads, who've joined the modern rat-race without giving up their alternative flair, push their youngsters in designer strollers past trendy boutiques and restaurants. You'll count more kids here than just about anywhere else in town. Locals complain that these days the cafés and bars cater to yuppies sipping prosecco, while the working class and artistic types are being pushed out. While it has changed plenty, I still find Prenzlauer Berg a celebration of life and a joy to stroll through. Though it's a few blocks farther out than the neighborhoods described previously, it's a fun area to explore and have a meal (see page 672) or spend the night (see page 658).

▲Berlin Wall Memorial
(Gedenkstätte Berliner Mauer)

While tourists flock to Checkpoint Charlie, local authorities have been investing in this site to develop Berlin's most substantial attraction relating to its gone-but-not-forgotten Wall. Exhibits line up along a two-block stretch of Bernauer Strasse, stretching northeast from the Nordbahnhof S-Bahn station. You can enter two different museums; see several fragments of the Wall, plus various open-air exhibits and memorials; and peer from an observation tower down into a preserved, complete stretch of the Wall system (as it was during the Cold War).

Cost and Hours: Free; Visitor Center and Documentation Center open April-Oct Tue-Sun 9:30-19:00, Nov-March until 18:00, closed Mon year-round; outdoor areas accessible 24 hours daily; last English movie starts at 18:00, memorial chapel closes at 17:00; Bernauer Strasse 111, tel. 030/4679-86666, www.berliner-mauer-gedenkstaette.de.

Getting There: Take the S-Bahn (line S-1, S-2, or S-25—all handy from Potsdamer Platz, Brandenburger Tor, or Friedrichstrasse) to the Nordbahnhof. The Nordbahnhof's underground hallways have history exhibits in English (explained later). Exit by following signs for *Bernauer Strasse,* and you'll pop out across the street from a long chunk of Wall and kitty-corner from the Visitor Center.

Background: The Berlin Wall, which was erected virtually overnight in 1961, ran right along Bernauer Strasse. People were suddenly separated from their neighbors across the street. This stretch was particularly notorious because existing apartment buildings were incorporated into the structure of the Wall itself. Film footage and photographs from the era show Berliners worriedly watching workmen seal off these buildings from the West, brick by brick. Some people attempted to leap to freedom from upper-story windows, with mixed results. One of the unfortunate ones was Ida Siekmann, who fell to her death from her third-floor apartment on August 22, 1961, and is considered the first casualty of the Berlin Wall.

Visiting the Memorial: From the Nordbahnhof station (which has some interesting Wall history in itself), head first to the Visitor Center to get your bearings, then explore the assorted Wall fragments and other sights in the park across the street. Work your way up Bernauer Strasse to the Documentation Center, Wall System, and memorial chapel.

Nordbahnhof

This S-Bahn station was one of the "ghost stations" of Cold War Berlin. As it was a dogleg of the East mostly surrounded by the West, Western subway trains had permission to use the underground tracks to zip through this station (without stopping, of course) en route between stops in the West. Posted information boards show photos comparing 1989 with 2009, and explain that East German border guards, who were stationed here to ensure that nobody got on or off those trains, were literally locked into their surveillance rooms to prevent them from escaping. (But one subway employee and his family used the tunnels to walk to the West and freedom.)

Follow signs down a long yellow hall to Bernauer Strasse. Climbing the stairs up to the Bernauer Strasse exit, ponder that the doorway at the top of these stairs (marked by the *Sperrmauer 1961-1989* plaque) was a bricked-off no-man's-land just 25 years ago. Stepping outside, you'll see the Wall park directly across the street, and the Visitor Center in a low rust-colored building kitty-corner across the street.

Visitor Center (Bezucherzentrum)

This new, small complex has a helpful information desk, a bookstore, and two good movies that provide context for a visit (they run in English at the top of each hour, about 30 minutes for the whole spiel): *History of the Wall* offers a great 12-minute overview of why the Wall was built and how it fell. That's followed by *Walled In!*, an animated 12-minute film illustrating the Wall as it functioned here at Bernauer Strasse (Wall wonks will find it fascinating). Before leaving, pick up the brochure explaining the outdoor exhibits, and ask about any new exhibits.

Wall Fragments and Other Sights

Across the street from the Visitor Center is a long stretch of Wall. The park behind it is scattered with a few more Wall chunks as well as monuments and memorials honoring its victims. To get your bearings, find the small model of the entire area when the Wall still stood (just across the street from the Nordbahnhof). While most items are explained by English plaques, the brochure from the Visitor Center helps you better appreciate what you're seeing. The rusty "Window of Remembrance" monument honors slain would-be escapees with their names, dates of death, and transparent photos viewable from both sides. Before it was the no-man's-land between the walls, this area was the parish graveyard for a nearby church; ironically, DDR officials had to move a thousand graves from here to create a "death strip."

Berlin Wall Documentation Center (Dokumentationszentrum Berliner Mauer)

This "Doku-Center" has two movies, a small exhibit, and a viewpoint tower overlooking the preserved Wall section. The two **films** shown on the ground floor are different from those screened at the Visitor Center: *The View*, dating from 1965, tells the story of an elderly West Berlin woman who lived near the Wall, and could look into the death strip and the East from her window (in German only). *Mauerflug* features aerial photography of Berlin from the spring of 1990—after the Wall had opened, but while most of the 96-mile-long barricade still stood, offering an illuminating look at a divided city (English subtitles).

Upstairs is an **exhibit** with photos and videos detailing the construction of the Wall that began August 13, 1961. At the model of the Wall along Bernauer Strasse, notice how existing buildings were incorporated into the structure. Headphones let you listen to propagandistic, high-spirited oompah music from East Germany that celebrated the construction of the wall: "It was high time!" There's also a list of the 163 people who died attempting to cross the Wall. From the top-floor **viewpoint** look down at the Wall itself (described next).

Wall System

This is the last surviving intact bit of the complete "Wall system" (with both sides of its Wall—capped by the round pipe that made it tougher for escapees to get a grip—and its no-man's-land, or death strip). The guard tower came from a different part of the Wall;

it was actually purchased on that great capitalist invention, eBay (over in Moscow, Stalin spins in his grave). A strip of photos and descriptions explains what you're seeing. Plaques along the sidewalk below you mark the locations of escapes or deaths.

Just beyond the Wall section (to the left), and also viewable from the tower, is a modern, cagelike church (described next).

Chapel of Reconciliation (Kapelle der Versöhnung)
This marks the spot of the late-19th-century Church of Reconciliation, which survived WWII bombs...but did not survive the communists. When the Wall was built, this church wound up, unusable, right in the middle of the death strip. It was torn down in 1985, supposedly because it got in the way of the border guards' sight lines. (This coincided with a period in which anti-DDR opposition movements were percolating in Christian churches, prompting the nonbeliever regime to destroy several houses of worship.) If you're interested, walk around the chapel for a closer look (it closes at 17:00). Notice the larger footprint of the original church in the field around it. The chapel hosts daily prayer services for the victims of the Wall.

More Wall Sights
Over the next few years, the Memorial plans to gradually add more open-air exhibitions about the Berlin Wall farther along Bernauer Strasse. Eventually the chain of sights will stretch all the way to Eberswalder Strasse and Oderberger Strasse, near the heart of Prenzlauer Berg.

Natural History Museum (Museum für Naturkunde)
This museum is worth a visit just to see the largest dinosaur skeleton ever assembled. While you're there, meet "Bobby" the stuffed ape, and tour the new Wet Collections, displaying shelf after shelf of animals preserved in ethanol (about a million all together). The museum is a magnet for the city's children, who love the interactive displays, the "History of the Universe in 120 Seconds" exhibit, and the cool virtual-reality "Jurascope" glasses that put meat and skin on all the dinosaur skeletons.

Cost and Hours: €6, €3.50 for kids, Tue-Fri 9:30-18:00, Sat-Sun 10:00-18:00, closed Mon, last entry 30 minutes before closing, Invalidenstrasse 43, U6: Naturkundemuseum, tel. 030/2093-8591, www.naturkundemuseum-berlin.de.

BERLIN

Sights in Central Berlin

Tiergarten Park and Nearby

Berlin's "Central Park" stretches two miles from Bahnhof Zoo to the Brandenburg Gate.

Victory Column (Siegessäule)

The Tiergarten's newly restored centerpiece, the Victory Column, was built to commemorate the Prussian defeat of Denmark in 1864...then reinterpreted after the defeat of France in 1870. The pointy-helmeted Germans rubbed it in, decorating the tower with French cannons and paying for it all with francs received as war reparations. The three lower rings commemorate Bismarck's victories. I imagine the statues of Moltke and other German military greats—which lurk in the trees nearby—goose-stepping around the floodlit angel at night.

Originally standing at the Reichstag, in 1938 the tower was moved to this position and given a 25-foot lengthening by Hitler's architect Albert Speer, in anticipation of the planned re-envisioning of Berlin as "Germania"—the capital of a worldwide Nazi empire. Streets leading to the circle are flanked by surviving Nazi guardhouses, built in the stern style that fascists loved. At the memorial's first level, notice how WWII bullets chipped the fine marble columns. From 1989 to 2003, the column was the epicenter of the Love Parade (Berlin's city-wide techno-hedonist street party), and it was the backdrop for Barack Obama's summer 2008 visit to Germany as a presidential candidate. (He asked to speak in front of the Brandenburg Gate, but German Chancellor Angela Merkel wanted to save that symbol from "politics.")

Climbing its 270 steps earns you a breathtaking Berlin-wide view and a close-up of the gilded bronze statue of the goddess Victoria (go ahead, call her "the chick on a stick"—everybody here does). You might recognize Victoria from Wim Wenders' 1987 arthouse classic *Wings of Desire*, or the *Stay (Faraway, So Close!)* video he directed for the rock band U2.

Cost and Hours: €2.20; April-Oct Mon-Fri 9:30-18:30, Sat-Sun 9:30-19:00; Nov-March Mon-Fri 10:00-17:00, Sat-Sun 10:00-17:30; closes in the rain, WCs for paying guests only, no elevator, bus #100, tel. 030/8639-8560. From the tower, the grand Strasse des 17 Juni leads east to the Brandenburg Gate.

Flea Market

A colorful flea market thrives weekends on Strasse des 17 Juni, with great antiques, more than 200 stalls, collector-savvy merchants, and fun German fast-food stands (Sat-Sun 6:00-16:00, right next to S-Bahn: Tiergarten).

German Resistance Memorial
(Gedenkstätte Deutscher Widerstand)

This memorial and museum, located in the former Bendlerblock military headquarters just south of the Tiergarten, tells the story of several organized German resistance movements and the more than 42 separate assassination attempts against Hitler. An ill-fated scheme to kill Hitler was plotted in this building (the actual attempt occurred in Rastenburg, eastern Prussia; the event was dramatized in the 2009 Tom Cruise film *Valkyrie*). The conspirators, including Claus Schenk Graf von Stauffenberg, were shot here in the courtyard. While there are no real artifacts, the spirit that haunts the place is multilingual.

Cost and Hours: Free, Mon-Fri 9:00-18:00, Thu until 20:00, Sat-Sun 10:00-18:00, free and good English audioguide—passport required, €3 printed English translation, no crowds, near Kulturforum at Stauffenbergstrasse 13, enter in courtyard, door on left, main exhibit on third floor, bus #M29, tel. 030/2699-5000, www. gdw-berlin.de.

Potsdamer Platz and Nearby

The "Times Square of Berlin," and possibly the busiest square in Europe before World War II, Potsdamer Platz was cut in two by the Wall and left a deserted no-man's-land for 40 years. Today, this immense commercial/residential/entertainment center, sitting on a futuristic transportation hub, is home to the European corporate headquarters of several big-league companies.

▲Potsdamer Platz

The new Potsdamer Platz was a vision begun in 1991, when it was announced that Berlin would resume its position as the capital of Germany. Sony, Daimler, and other major corporations have turned the square once again into a center of Berlin. Like great Christian churches built upon pagan holy grounds, Potsdamer Platz—with its corporate logos flying high and shiny above what was the Wall—trumpets the triumph of capitalism.

While Potsdamer Platz tries to give Berlin a common center, the city has always been—and remains—a collection of towns. Locals recognize 28 distinct neighborhoods that may have grown together but still maintain their historic orientation. While Munich has the single dominant Marienplatz, Berlin will always have Charlottenburg, Savignyplatz, Kreuzberg, Prenzlauer Berg, and so on. In general, Berliners prefer these characteristic neighborhoods to an official city center. They're unimpressed by the grandeur of Potsdamer Platz, simply considering it a good place to go to the movies, with overpriced, touristy restaurants.

While most of the complex just feels big (the arcade is like any huge, modern, American mall), the entrance to the complex and Sony Center are worth a visit, and German-film buffs will enjoy the Deutsche Kinemathek museum (described later).

For an overview of the new construction, and a scenic route to the Sony Center, start at the Bahnhof Potsdamer Platz (east end of Potsdamer Strasse, S- and U-Bahn: Potsdamer Platz, exit following *Leipziger Platz* signs to see the best view of skyscrapers as you emerge). Find the green hexagonal **clock tower** with the traffic lights on top. This is a replica of the first automatic traffic light in Europe, which once stood at the six-street intersection of Potsdamer Platz. On either side of Potsdamer Strasse, you'll see enormous cubical entrances to the underground Potsdamer Platz train station. Near these entrances, notice the slanted **glass cylinders** sticking out of the ground. The mirrors on the tops of the tubes move with the sun to collect light and send it underground (saving piles of euros in energy costs). A line in the pavement indicates where the **Berlin Wall** once stood. On the right side of the street, notice the re-erected slabs of the Wall. Imagine when the first piece was cut out (see photo and history on nearby panel). These hang like scalps at the gate of Fort Capitalism...look up at the towering corporate headquarters: Market forces have won a clear victory. Now descend into one of the train station entrances and follow signs to *Sony Center*. As you walk through the passage, notice the wall panels with historical information.

You'll come up the escalator into the **Sony Center** under a grand canopy (designed to evoke Mount Fuji). At night, multicolored floodlights play on the underside of this tent. Office workers and tourists eat here by the fountain, enjoying the parade of people. The modern Bavarian Lindenbräu beer hall—the Sony boss wanted a *Bräuhaus*—serves traditional food (€11-17, daily 11:00-24:30, big €8 salads, three-foot-long taster boards of eight different beers, tel. 030/2575-1280). Across the plaza, Josty Bar is built around a surviving bit of a venerable hotel that was a meeting place for Berlin's rich and famous before the bombs (€10-17 meals, daily 10:00-24:00, tel. 030/2575-9702). CineStar is a rare cinema that plays mainstream movies in their original language (www.cinestar.de).

Sights near Potsdamer Platz

▲Deutsche Kinemathek Film and TV Museum

This exhibit is the most interesting place to visit in the Sony Center. The early pioneers in filmmaking were German (including Fritz Lang, F. W. Murnau, Ernst Lubitsch, and the Austrian-born Billy Wilder), and many of them also became influential in Hollywood—making this a fun visit for cinephiles. Your admission ticket gets you into several floors of exhibits (including temporary exhibits on floors 1 and 4) made meaningful by the included, essential English audioguide.

Cost and Hours: €6, includes 1.5-hour audioguide, Tue-Sun 10:00-18:00, Thu until 20:00, closed Mon, tel. 030/2474-9888, www.deutsche-kinemathek.de.

Nearby: The Kino Arsenal theater downstairs shows offbeat art-house films in their original language.

Visiting the Museum: From the ticket desk, ride the elevator up to the third floor, where you can turn left (into the film section, floors 3 and 2) or right (into the TV section, floors 3 and 4).

In the **film section,** you'll walk back in time through a fun mirrored entryway. The exhibit starts with the German film industry's beginnings, with an emphasis on the Weimar Republic period in the 1920s, when Berlin rivaled Hollywood. Influential films included the early German Expressionist masterpiece *The Cabinet of Dr. Caligari* (1920) and Fritz Lang's seminal *Metropolis* (1927). Three rooms are dedicated to Marlene Dietrich, who was a huge star both in Germany and, later, in Hollywood. (Dietrich, who performed at USO shows to entertain Allied troops fighting against her former homeland, once said, "I don't hate the Germans, I hate the Nazis.") Another section examines Nazi use of film as propaganda, including Leni Riefenstahl's masterful documentary of the 1936 Berlin Olympics and her earlier, chillingly propagandistic *Triumph of the Will* (1935). The postwar period was defined by two separate East and West German film industries. The exhibit's finale reminds us that German filmmakers are still highly influential and successful—including Wolfgang Petersen *(Das Boot, Air Force One, The Perfect Storm)* and Werner Herzog (the documentary *Grizzly Man* and the drama *Rescue Dawn*). (If this visit gets you curious about German cinema, see the recommendations in the Appendix.)

The **TV section** tells the story of *das Idioten Box* from its in-

BERLIN

fancy (when it was primarily used as a Nazi propaganda tool) to today. The 30-minute kaleidoscopic review—kind of a frantic fast-forward montage of greatest hits in German TV history, both East and West—is great fun even if you don't understand a word of it (it plays all day long, with 10-minute breaks). Otherwise, the TV section is a little more challenging for non-German speakers to appreciate. Upstairs (on the fourth floor) is a TV archive where you can dial through a wide range of new and classic German TV standards.

Panoramapunkt

Across Potsdamer Strasse from the Film and TV Museum, you can ride what's billed as "the fastest elevator in Europe" to skyscraping rooftop views. You'll travel at nearly 30 feet per second to the top of the 300-foot-tall Kollhoff Tower. Its sheltered but open-air view deck provides a fun opportunity to survey Berlin's ongoing construction from above.

Cost and Hours: €5.50, €9.50 VIP ticket lets you skip the line, audioguide-€2.50, daily 10:00-20:00, until 22:00 in summer, last elevator 30 minutes before closing, in red-brick building at Potsdamer Platz 1, tel. 030/2593-07080, www.panoramapunkt.de.

Kulturforum

Just west of Potsdamer Platz, Kulturforum rivals Museum Island as the city's cultural heart, with several top museums and Berlin's concert hall—home of the world-famous Berlin Philharmonic orchestra (admission to all Kulturforum sights covered by a single €8 Bereichskarte Kulturforum combo-ticket—a.k.a. Quartier-Karte—and also by the Museumspass; info for all museums: tel. 030/266-424-242, www.kulturforum-berlin.de). Of its sprawling museums, only the Gemäldegalerie is a must (S- or U-Bahn to Potsdamer Platz, then walk along Potsdamer Platz; or from Bahnhof Zoo, take bus #200 to Philharmonie).

▲▲Gemäldegalerie

Literally the "Painting Gallery," Germany's top collection of 13th-through 18th-century European paintings (more than 1,400 canvases) is beautifully displayed in a building that's a work of art in itself. The North Wing starts with German paintings of the 13th to 16th centuries, including eight by Albrecht Dürer. Then come the Dutch and Flemish—Jan van Eyck, Pieter Brueghel, Peter Paul Rubens, Anthony van Dyck, Frans Hals, and Jan Vermeer. The wing finishes with German, English, and French 18th-century artists, such as Thomas Gainsborough and Antoine Watteau. An octagonal hall at the end features an impressive stash of Rembrandts. The South Wing is saved for the Italians—Giotto, Botticelli, Titian, Raphael, and Caravaggio.

Cost and Hours: Covered by €8 Kulturforum combo-ticket,

Tue-Sun 10:00-18:00, Thu until 22:00, closed Mon, audioguide included with entry, clever little loaner stools, great salad bar in cafeteria upstairs, Matthäikirchplatz 4.

⊃ Self-Guided Tour: I'll point out a few highlights, focusing on Northern European artists (Germans, Dutch, and Flemish), with a few Spaniards and Italians thrown in. To go beyond my selections, make ample use of the excellent audioguide.

The collection spreads out on one vast floor surrounding a central hall. Inner rooms have Roman numerals (I, II, III), while adjacent outer rooms are numbered (1, 2, 3). After showing your ticket, turn right into room I and work your way counterclockwise (and roughly chronologically) through the collection.

Rooms I-III/1-4 kick things off with early German paintings (13th-16th centuries). In room 1, look for the 1532 portrait of wealthy Hanseatic cloth merchant Georg Gisze by **Hans Holbein the Younger** (1497-1543). Gisze's name appears on several of the notes stuck to the wall behind him. And, typical of detail-rich Northern European art, the canvas is bursting with highly symbolic tidbits. Items scattered on the tabletop and on the shelves behind the merchant represent his lofty status and aspects of his life story. In the vase, the carnation represents his recent engagement, and the herbs symbolize his virtue. And yet, the celebratory flowers are already beginning to fade and the scales behind him are unbalanced, reminders of the fleetingness of happiness and wealth.

In room 2 are fine portraits by the remarkably talented **Albrecht Dürer** (1471-1528), who traveled to Italy during the burgeoning days of the early Renaissance and melded the artistic harmony and classical grandeur he discovered there with a Northern European attention to detail. In his *Portrait of Hieronymus Holzschuher* (1526), Dürer skillfully captured the personality of a friend from Nürnberg, right down to the sly twinkle in his sidelong glance. Technically the portrait is perfection: Look closely and see each individual hair of the man's beard and fur coat, and even the reflection of the studio's windows in his eyes. Also notice Dürer's little pyramid-shaped, D-inside-A signature. Signing one's work was a revolutionary assertion of Dürer's renown, at a time when German artists were considered anonymous craftsmen.

Lucas Cranach the Elder (1472-1553), whose works are in room III, was a court painter for the prince electors of Saxony and a close friend of Martin Luther (and his unofficial portraitist). But *The Fountain of Youth* (1546) is a far cry from Cranach's solemn portrayals of the Reformer. Old women helped to the fountain (on the left) emerge as young ladies on the right. Newly nubile, the women go into a tent to dress up, snog with noblemen in the bushes (right foreground), dance merrily beneath the trees, and dine grandly be-

BERLIN

neath a landscape of phallic mountains and towers. This work is flanked by Cranach's Venus nudes. I sense a pattern here.

Netherlandish painters (rooms IV-VI/4-7) were early adopters of oil paint (as opposed to older egg tempera), whose flexibility allowed them to brush the super-fine details for which they are famous. **Rogier van der Weyden** (room IV) was a virtuoso handler of the new medium. In *Portrait of a Young Woman* (c. 1400-1464), the subject wears a typical winged bonnet, addressing the viewer directly with her fetching blue eyes. The subjects (especially women) of most portraits of the time look off to one side; some art historians guess that the confident woman shown here is Van der Weyden's wife. In the same room is a remarkable, rare trio of three-panel altarpieces by Van der Weyden: The *Marienaltar* shows the life of the Virgin Mary; the *Johannesaltar* narrates the life of John the Baptist—his birth, baptizing Christ (with God and the Holy Spirit hovering overhead), and his gruesome death by decapitation; and the *Middelburger Altar* tells the story of the Nativity. Savor the fine details in each panel of these altarpieces.

Flash forward a few hundred years to the 17th century and Flemish (Belgian) painting (rooms VII-VIII/9-10), and it's apparent how much the Protestant Reformation—and resulting Counter-Reformation—changed the tenor of Northern European art. In works by **Peter Paul Rubens** (1577-1640)—including *Jesus Giving Peter the Keys to Heaven*—calm, carefully studied, detail-oriented seriousness gives way to an exuberant Baroque trumpeting of the greatness of the Catholic Church. In the Counter-Reformation world, the Catholic Church had serious competition for the hearts and minds of its congregants. Exciting art like this became a way to keep people in the pews. Notice the quivering brushstrokes and almost too-bright colors. (In the same room are portraits by Rubens' student, Anthony van Dyck, as well as some hunting still lifes from Frans Snyders and others.) In the next rooms (VIII and 9) are more Rubens, including the mythological *Perseus Freeing Andromeda* and *The Martyrdom of St. Sebastian by Arrows* (loosely based on a more famous rendition by Andrea Mantegna).

Dutch painting from the 17th century (rooms IX-XI/10-19) is dominated by the convivial portraits by **Frans Hals** (c. 1582-1666). His 1620 portrait of Catharina Hooft (far corner, room 13) presents a startlingly self-possessed baby (the newest member of a wealthy merchant family) dressed with all the finery of a queen, adorned with lace and jewels, and clutching a golden rattle. The smiling nurse supporting the tyke offers her a piece of fruit, whose blush of red perfectly matches the nanny's apple-fresh cheeks.

But the ultimate Dutch master is **Rembrandt van Rijn** (1606-1669), whose powers of perception and invention propelled him to fame in his lifetime. Displayed here are several storytelling scenes (room 16), mostly from classical mythology or biblical stories, all employing Rembrandt's trademark chiaroscuro technique (with a strong contrast between light and dark). In *The Rape of Persephone*, Pluto grabs Persephone from his chariot and races toward the underworld, while other goddesses cling to her robe, trying to save her. Cast against a nearly black background, the almost overexposed, action-packed scene is shockingly emotional. In the nearby *Samson and Delilah* (1628), Delilah cradles Samson's head in her lap while silently signaling to a goon to shear Samson's hair, the secret to his strength. A self-portrait (room X) of a 28-year-old Rembrandt wearing a beret is paired with the come-hither 1637 *Portrait of Hendrickje Stoffels* (the two were romantically linked). *Samson Threatens His Father-in-Law* (1635) captures the moment just after the mighty Samson (with his flowing hair, elegant robes, and shaking fist) has been told by his wife's father to take a hike. I wouldn't want to cross this guy.

Although **Johannes Vermeer** (1632-1675) is today just as admired as Rembrandt, he was little known in his day, probably because he painted relatively few works for a small circle of Delft collectors. Vermeer was a master at conveying a complicated story through a deceptively simple scene with a few poignant details—whether it's a woman reading a letter at a window, a milkmaid pouring milk from a pitcher into a bowl, or (as in *The Glass of Wine*, room 18) a young man offering a drink to a young lady. The young man had been playing her some music on his lute (which now sits, discarded, on a chair) and is hoping to seal the deal with some alcohol. The woman is finishing one glass of wine, and her would-be suitor stands ready—almost *too* ready—to pour her another. His sly, somewhat smarmy smirk drives home his high hopes for what will come next. Vermeer has perfectly captured the exact moment of "Will she or won't she?" The painter offers some clues—the coat of arms in the window depicts a woman holding onto the reigns of a horse, staying in control—but ultimately, only he (and the couple) know how this scene will end.

Shift south to Italian, French, and Spanish painting of the 17th and 18th centuries (rooms XII-XIV/23-28). Venetian cityscapes by Canaletto (who also painted Dresden) and lots of bombastic Baroque art hang in room XII. Room XIII features big-name Spanish artists Murillo, Zurbarán, and the great **Diego Velázquez** (1599-1660). He gave the best of his talents to his portraits, capturing warts-and-all likenesses that are effortlessly real. His 1630 *Portrait of a Lady* conveys the subject's subtle, sly Mona Lisa smile. Her figure and face (against a dull gray background) are filtered through a pleasant natural light. Notice that if you stand too close, the brushstrokes get muddy—but when you back up, the scene snaps into perfectly sharp relief.

From here, the collection itself takes a step backwards—into Italian paintings of the 13th-16th centuries (rooms XV-XVIII/29-41). This section includes some lesser-known works by great Italian Renaissance painters, including Raphael (rooms XVII and 29, including five different Madonnas, among them the *Terranuova Madonna*, in a round frame) and Sandro Botticelli (room VIII).

New National Gallery (Neue Nationalgalerie)

This gallery features 20th-century art, with ever-changing special exhibits.

Cost and Hours: Covered by €8 Kulturforum combo-ticket, Tue-Fri 10:00-18:00, Thu until 22:00, Sat-Sun 11:00-18:00, closed Mon, café downstairs, Potsdamer Strasse 50.

Museum of Decorative Arts (Kunstgewerbemuseum)

Wander through a mazelike floor plan displaying a thousand years of applied arts—porcelain, fine *Jugendstil* (German Art Nouveau) furniture, Art Deco, and reliquaries. There are no English descriptions and no crowds.

Cost and Hours: Covered by €8 Kulturforum combo-ticket, Tue-Fri 10:00-18:00, Sat-Sun 11:00-18:00, closed Mon, Herbert-von-Karajan-Strasse 10.

▲Musical Instruments Museum (Musikinstrumenten Museum)

This impressive hall is filled with 600 exhibits spanning the 16th century to modern times. Wander among old keyboard instruments and funny-looking tubas. Pick up the included audioguide and free English brochure at the entry. In addition to the English commentary, the audioguide has clips of various instruments being played (just punch in the number next to the instrument you want to hear). This place is fascinating if you're into pianos.

Cost and Hours: €4 but included in €8 Kulturforum ticket, Tue-Fri 9:00-17:00, Thu until 22:00, Sat-Sun 10:00-17:00, closed Mon, low-profile white building east of the big yellow Philharmonic Concert Hall, tel. 030/2548-1178.

Philharmonic Concert Hall

Poke into the lobby of Berlin's yellow Philharmonic building and see if there are tickets available during your stay. The interior is famous for its extraordinary acoustics. Even from the outside, this is a remarkable building, designed by a nautical engineer to look like a ship—notice how different it looks from each angle. Inexpensive and legitimate tickets are often sold on the street before performances. Or you can buy tickets from the box office in person, by phone, or online (ticket office open Mon-Fri 15:00-18:00, Sat-Sun 11:00-14:00, info tel. 030/2548-8132, box office tel. 030/2548-8999—answered daily 9:00-18:00, www.berliner-philharmoniker.

de). For guest performances, you must buy tickets through the organizer (see website for details).

Sights in Western Berlin

Throughout the Cold War, Western travelers—and most West Berliners—got used to thinking of western Berlin's Kurfürstendamm boulevard as the heart of the city. But those days have gone the way of the Wall. With the huge changes the city has undergone since 1989, the real "city center" is now, once again, Berlin's historic center (the Mitte district, around Unter den Linden and Friedrichstrasse). While western Berlin still works well as a home base, it's no longer the obvious place from which to explore Berlin. After the new Hauptbahnhof essentially put Bahnhof Zoo out of business in 2006, the area was left with an identity crisis. Now, more than 20 years after reunification, the west side is back and has fully embraced its historical role as a chic, classy suburb.

In the Heart of Western Berlin

A few interesting sights sit within walking distance of Bahnhof Zoo and the Savignyplatz hotels. For a detailed map of this area, see page 666.

▲Kurfürstendamm

Western Berlin's main drag, Kurfürstendamm boulevard (nicknamed "Ku'damm"), starts at Kaiser Wilhelm Memorial Church and does a commercial cancan for two miles. In the 1850s, when Berlin became a wealthy and important capital, her "new rich" chose Kurfürstendamm as their street. Bismarck made it Berlin's Champs-Elysées. In the 1920s, it became a chic and fashionable drag of cafés and boutiques. During the Third Reich, as home to an international community of diplomats and journalists, it enjoyed more freedom than the rest of Berlin. Throughout the Cold War, economic subsidies from the West made sure that capitalism thrived on Ku'damm. And today, while much of the old charm has been hamburgerized, Ku'damm is still a fine place to enjoy elegant shops (around Fasanenstrasse), department stores, and people-watching.

▲Kaiser Wilhelm Memorial Church (Gedächtniskirche)

This church was originally dedicated to the first emperor of Germany. Reliefs and mosaics show great events in the life of Germany's favorite *Kaiser*, from his coronation in 1871 to his death in 1888. The church's bombed-out ruins have been left standing as a poignant memorial to the destruction of Berlin in World War II.

Cost and Hours: Church—free, daily 9:00-19:00; Memorial Hall—free, Mon-Sat 10:00-18:00, shorter hours on Sun. Located on Breitscheidplatz, U2/U9 and S-Bahn: Zoologischer Garten or U1/U9: Kurfürstendamm, www.gedaechtniskirche.com.

Visiting the Church: The church is actually an ensemble of buildings: a new church, the matching bell tower, a meeting hall, and the bombed-out ruins of the old church, with its Memorial Hall. The church may still be undergoing renovation when you visit (though the interior should still be open to visitors). The renovations were undertaken to strengthen the foundations of all four buildings, which should make it possible for visitors to get to the top of the church for the first time in 60 years.

Under a Neo-Romanesque mosaic ceiling, the **Memorial Hall** features a small exhibit of interesting photos about the bombing and before-and-after models of the church. After the war, some Berliners wanted to tear down the ruins and build it anew. Instead, it was decided to keep what was left of the old church as a memorial and stage a competition to design a modern, add-on section. The winning entry—the short, modern church (1961) next to the Memorial Hall—offers a meditative world of 11,000 little blue windows. The blue glass was given to the church by the French as a reconciliation gift. For more information on both churches, pick up the English flier (€0.50).

As you enter the **church,** a peaceful blue oasis in the middle of the busy city, turn immediately right to find a simple charcoal sketch of the Virgin Mary wrapped in a shawl. During the Battle of Stalingrad, German combat surgeon Kurt Reuber rendered the Virgin on the back of a stolen Soviet map to comfort the men in his care. On the right are the words "Light, Life, Love" from the gospel of John; on the left, "Christmas in the cauldron 1942"; and at the bottom, "Fortress Stalingrad." Though Reuber died in captivity a year later, his sketch had been flown out of Stalingrad on the last medical evacuation flight, and postwar Germany embraced it as a symbol of the wish for peace. Copies of the drawing, now known as the *Stalingrad Madonna,* hang in the Berlin Cathedral, in England's Coventry, and in Russia's Volgograd (formerly Stalingrad) as a sign of peaceful understanding between the nations. As another act of reconciliation, every Friday at 13:00 a "Prayers for Peace" service is held simultaneously with the cathedral in Coventry.

Nearby: The lively square between the churches and the Europa Center (a once-impressive, shiny high-rise shopping center built as a showcase of Western capitalism during the Cold War) usually attracts street musicians and performers—especially in the summer. Berliners call the funky fountain "the wet meatball."

The Story of Berlin
Filling most of what seems like a department store right on Ku'damm (at #207), this sprawling history exhibit tells the stormy 800-year story of Berlin in a creative way. While there are almost

no real historic artifacts, the exhibit does a good job of cobbling together many dimensions of the life and tumultuous times of this great city. It's particularly strong on the story of the city from World War I through the Cold War. However, for similar information, and more artifacts, the German History Museum on Unter den Linden is a far better use of your time and money (see page 615).

Cost and Hours: €10, daily 10:00-20:00, last entry 2 hours before closing, tel. 030/8872-0100, www.story-of-berlin.de. Times for the 30-minute bunker tour are posted at the entry.

▲Käthe Kollwitz Museum

This local artist (1867-1945), who experienced much of Berlin's stormiest century, conveys some powerful and mostly sad feelings about motherhood, war, and suffering through the stark faces of her art. This small yet fine collection (the only one in town of Kollwitz's work) consists of three floors of charcoal drawings, topped by an attic with a handful of sculptures.

Cost and Hours: €6, €1 pamphlet has necessary English explanations of a few major works, daily 11:00-18:00, a block off Ku'damm at Fasanenstrasse 24, U-Bahn: Uhlandstrasse, tel. 030/882-5210, www.kaethe-kollwitz.de.

▲Kaufhaus des Westens (KaDeWe)

The "Department Store of the West" has been a Berlin tradition for more than a century. With a staff of 2,100 to help you sort through its vast selection of 380,000 items, KaDeWe claims to be the biggest department store on the Continent. You can get everything from a haircut and train ticket (third floor) to souvenirs (fourth floor). The theater and concert box office on the sixth floor charges an 18 percent booking fee, but they know all your options (cash only). The sixth floor is a world of gourmet taste treats. The biggest selection of deli and exotic food in Germany offers plenty of classy opportunities to sit down and eat. Ride the glass elevator to the seventh floor's glass-domed Winter Garden, a self-service cafeteria—fun but pricey.

Hours: Mon-Thu 10:00-20:00, Fri 10:00-21:00, Sat 9:30-20:00, closed Sun, S-Bahn: Zoologischer Garten or U-Bahn: Wittenbergplatz, tel. 030/21210, www.kadewe.de.

Nearby: The Wittenbergplatz U-Bahn station (in front of KaDeWe) is a unique opportunity to see an old-time station. Enjoy its interior with classic advertisements still decorating its venerable walls.

Berlin Zoo (Zoologischer Garten Berlin)

More than 1,500 different kinds of animals call Berlin's famous zoo home...or so the zookeepers like to think. The big hit here is the lonely panda bear (straight in from the entrance).

Cost and Hours: €13 for zoo, €13 for world-class aquarium, €20 for both, kids half-price, daily 9:00-18:00, aquarium closes

BERLIN

30 minutes earlier; feeding times—*Fütterungszeiten*—posted just inside entrance, the best feeding show is the sea lions—generally at 15:15; enter near Europa Center in front of Hotel Palace or opposite Bahnhof Zoo on Hardenbergplatz, Budapester Strasse 34, tel. 030/254-010, www.zoo-berlin.de.

Nightlife in Berlin

Berlin is a happening place for nightlife—whether it's clubs, pubs, jazz music, cabaret, hokey-but-fun German variety shows, theater, or concerts.

Sources of Entertainment Info: *Berlin Programm* lists a nonstop parade of concerts, plays, exhibits, and cultural events (€2, in German, www.berlin-programm.de); *Exberliner Magazine* (€3, www.exberliner.com) doesn't have as much hard information, but is colorfully written English (both sold at kiosks and TIs). For the young and determined sophisticate, *Zitty* and *Tip* are the top guides to alternative culture (in German, sold at kiosks). Also pick up the free schedules *Flyer* and *030* in bars and clubs. Visit KaDeWe's ticket office for your music and theater options (sixth floor, 18 percent fee but access to all tickets; see page 655). Ask about "competitive improvisation" and variety shows.

Berlin Jazz
To enjoy live music near my recommended Savignyplatz hotels in western Berlin, consider **A Trane Jazz Club** (all jazz, great stage and intimate seating, €7-18 cover depending on act, opens at 21:00, live music nightly 22:00-2:00 in the morning, Bleibtreustrasse 1—see map on page 666, tel. 030/313-2550, www.a-trane.de). **B-Flat Acoustic Music and Jazz Club,** in the heart of eastern Berlin, also has live music nightly—and shares a courtyard with a tranquil tea house (shows vary from free to €10-12 cover, open Mon-Thu from 20:00 with shows starting at 21:00, Fri-Sat from 21:00 with shows at 22:00, closed Sun, a block from Rosenthaler Platz U-Bahn stop at Rosenthaler Strasse 13—see map on page 670, tel. 030/283-3123, www.b-flat-berlin.de).

Berliner Rock and Roll
Berlin has a vibrant rock and pop scene, with popular venues at the Spandau Citadel and at the outdoor Waldbühne ("Forest Stage"). Check out what's playing on posters in the U-Bahn, in *Zitty*, or at any ticket agency. Great Berlin bands include The Beatsteaks, Jennifer Rostock, and the funky ska band Seeed.

Cabaret
Bar Jeder Vernunft offers modern-day cabaret a short walk from my recommended hotels in western Berlin. This variety show—under a classic old tent perched atop the modern parking lot of the Berliner Festspiele theater—is a hit with German-speakers, but can

BERLIN

still be worthwhile for those who don't speak the language (as some of the music shows are in a sort of "Denglish"). Even some Americans perform here periodically. Tickets are generally about €22-25, and shows change regularly (performances start Mon-Sat at 20:00, Sun at 19:00, seating can be a bit cramped, south of Ku'damm at Schaperstrasse 24—see map on page 666, U-3 or U-9: Spichernstrasse, tel. 030/883-1582, www.bar-jeder-vernunft.de).

German Variety Show

To spend an evening enjoying Europe's largest revue theater, consider "YMA—Too Beautiful to Be True" at the **Friedrichstadt-Palast**. It's a passionate visual spectacle, a weird ballet that pulsates like a visual poem (€17-105, Tue at 18:30, Thu-Sat at 19:30, Sat also at 15:30, Sun at 15:30, no shows Mon or Wed, Friedrichstrasse 107—see map on page 670, U6: Oranienburger Tor, tel. 030/2326-2326, www.show-palace.eu). The Friedrichstrasse area around the Palast and to the south has been synonymous with Berliner entertainment for at least 200 years. The East German government built the current Palast in 1984 on the ruins of an older theater, which itself was a horse barn for the Prussian Army. The current exterior is meant to mimic the interior design of the older theater.

Nightclubs and Pubs

Oranienburger Strasse's trendy scene (page 638) has been eclipsed by the action at Friedrichshain (farther east). To the north, you'll find the hip Prenzlauer Berg neighborhood, packed with everything from smoky pubs to small art bars and dance clubs (best scene is around Helmholtzplatz, U2: Eberswalder Strasse; see page 640).

Dancing

Cut a rug at **Clärchens Ballhaus**, an old ballroom that's been a Berlin institution since 1913. At some point everyone in Berlin comes through here, as the dance hall attracts an eclectic Berlin-in-a-nutshell crowd of grannies, elegant women in evening dresses, yuppies, scenesters, and hippies. The music (swing, waltz, tango, or cha-cha) changes every day, with live music on Friday and Saturday (from 23:15, €4 cover; dance hall open daily from 10:00—12:00 in winter—until the last person goes home, in the heart of the Auguststrasse gallery district at Auguststrasse 24—see map on page 670, S-Bahn: Oranienburger Strasse, tel. 030/282-9295, www.ballhaus.de). Dancing lessons are also available (€8, Mon-Tue at 19:00, Thu at 19:30, 1.5 hours). The "Gypsy" restaurant, which fills a huge courtyard out front, serves decent food and good pizza.

Art Galleries

Berlin, a magnet for new artists, is a great city for gallery visits. Galleries—many of which stay open late—welcome visitors who are "just looking." The most famous gallery district is in eastern Berlin's Mitte neighborhood, along **Auguststrasse** (branches off from Oranienburger Strasse at the ruined Tacheles building).

Check out the Berlin outpost of the edgy-yet-accessible art of the New Leipzig movement at **Galerie Eigen+Art** (Tue-Sat 11:00-18:00, closed Sun-Mon, Auguststrasse 26, tel. 030/280-6605, www.eigen-art.com). The other gallery area is in western Berlin, along **Fasanenstrasse.**

Pub Crawls

Various companies offer pub crawls to some of Berlin's fun watering holes. The (unrelated) binge-drinking death of a 16-year-old in Berlin a few years ago reinforced the tours' strict 18-year-old minimum age limit. Pub crawls depart around 20:15, cost €12, generally visit four bars and two clubs, and provide a great way to drink it up with new friends from around the world while getting a peek at Berlin's bar scene...or at least how its bars look when invaded by 50 loud tourists. You could take a pub crawl offered by **Insider Tour** or **Sandeman's New Europe Berlin** (see contact info on pages 593 and 596), or look around town for fliers from other companies.

Sleeping in Berlin

When in Berlin, I used to sleep in the former West, on or near Savignyplatz—and I still list good options there. But these days, the focus of Berlin is in the East, and I've recommended places in the colorful Prenzlauer Berg district. Berliners say that this sort of homey, homogenous neighborhood is in the heart of the *Kiez* (literally "gravel").

Berlin is packed and hotel prices go up on holidays, including Green Week in mid-January, Easter weekend, the first weekend in May, Ascension weekend in May, German Unity Day (Oct 3), Christmas, and New Year's. Keep in mind that many hotels have limited staff after 20:00, so if you're planning to arrive after that, let the hotel know in advance.

In Eastern Berlin

Prenzlauer Berg

If you want to sleep in the former East Berlin, set your sights on the colorful and fun Prenzlauer Berg district. After decades of neglect, this corner of eastern Berlin has quickly come back to life. Gentrification has brought Prenzlauer Berg great hotels, tasty ethnic and German eateries (see "Eating in Berlin," later), and a happening nightlife scene. Think of all the graffiti as just some people's way of saying they care. The huge and impersonal concrete buildings are enlivened with a street fair of fun little shops and eateries.

This loosely defined area is about 1.5 miles north of Alexanderplatz, roughly between Kollwitzplatz and Helmholtzplatz, and to the west, along Kastanienallee (known affectionately as "Casting Alley" for its generous share of beautiful people). The closest

BERLIN

Sleep Code

(€1 = about $1.30, country code: 49, area code: 030)
S = Single, **D** = Double/Twin, **T** = Triple, **Q** = Quad, **b** = bathroom, **s** = shower only. Unless otherwise noted, credit cards are accepted, English is spoken, and breakfast is included.

To help you sort easily through these listings, I've divided the accommodations into three categories, based on the price for a standard double room with bath:

$$$ **Higher Priced**—Most rooms €125 or more.
$$ **Moderately Priced**—Most rooms between €85-125.
$ **Lower Priced**—Most rooms €85 or less.

Prices can change without notice; verify the hotel's current rates online or by email.

U-Bahn stops are U-2: Senefelderplatz at the south end of the neighborhood, U-8: Rosenthaler Platz in the middle, or U-2: Eberswalder Strasse at the north end. Or, for less walking, take the S-Bahn to Hackescher Markt, then catch tram #M1 north.

$$$ Precise Hotel Myer's Berlin rents 52 simple, small rooms. The gorgeous public spaces include a patio and garden. This peaceful hub—off a quiet garden courtyard and tree-lined street, just a five-minute walk from Kollwitzplatz or the nearest U-Bahn stop (Senefelderplatz)—makes it hard to believe you're in a capital city. Their four classes of rooms range from three to five stars, hence the wide price range (Db-€95-200, price also depends on season—check rates online for your dates, air-con in some rooms, elevator, free Internet access and Wi-Fi, Metzer Strasse 26, tel. 030/440-140, fax 030/4401-4104, www.myershotel.de, myers@precisehotels.com).

$$$ Hotel Jurine (zhoo-REEN—the family name) is a pleasant 53-room business-style hotel whose friendly staff aims to please. In good weather, you can enjoy the breakfast buffet on the lush backyard patio (Sb-€90-110, Db-€130-160, extra bed-€37, rates vary by season, check their website for discounts July-Aug, skip breakfast to save a few euros, elevator, free Wi-Fi, parking garage-€13.50—reserve ahead, Schwedter Strasse 15, 10-minute walk to U2: Senefelderplatz, tel. 030/443-2990, fax 030/4432-9999, www.hotel-jurine.de, mail@hotel-jurine.de).

$$ Hotel Kastanienhof feels less urban-classy and more like a traditional small-town German hotel. It's wonderfully located on the Kastanienallee #M1 tram line, with easy access to the Prenzlauer Berg bustle. Its 38 slightly overpriced rooms come

Eastern Berlin Accommodations

1. Precise Hotel Myer's Berlin
2. Hotel Jurine
3. Hotel Kastanienhof
4. The Circus Hotel
5. Karlito Apartmenthaus
6. easyHotel Berlin Hackescher Markt
7. Hotel Augustinenhof
8. Circus Hostel & Internet Café
9. Meininger Hotels (3)
10. EastSeven Hostel
11. Hotel Transit Loft
12. To Ostel
13. Bike Rentals (2)

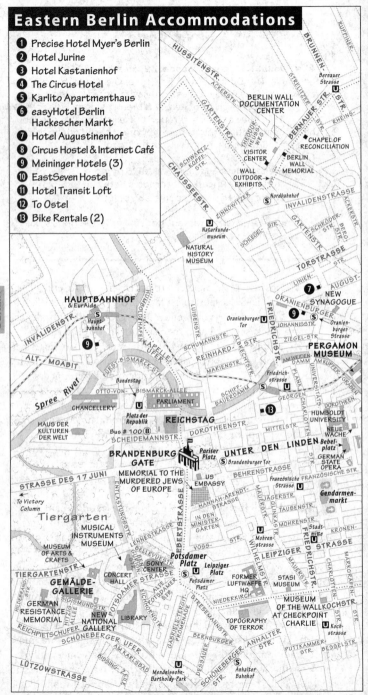

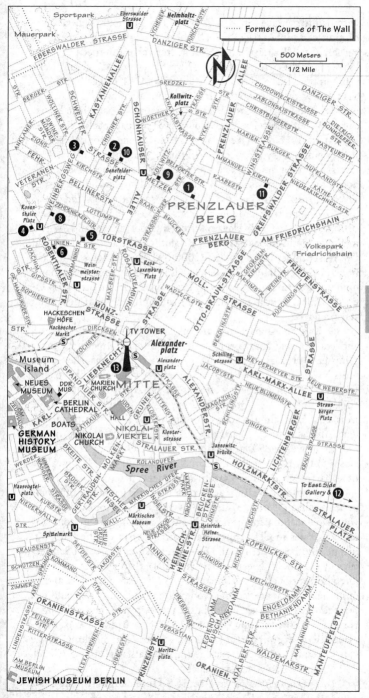

BERLIN

with helpful service (Sb-€79-94, Db-€105-140, extra bed-€29, reception closed 22:00-6:30—call ahead to make arrangements to get key if you'll arrive late, elevator, free cable Internet in rooms, Wi-Fi in lobby, parking-€9/day, 20 yards from #M1 Zionskirche tram stop at Kastanienallee 65, tel. 030/443-050, fax 030/4430-5111, www.kastanienhof.biz, info@kastanienhof.biz).

$$ The **Circus Hotel,** run by the popular hostel listed later, caters to youth hostelers who've outgrown the backpacker lifestyle. Each of its 60 colorful, trendy rooms has a unique bit of decoration. It overlooks a busy intersection, so there's some nighttime noise— try asking for a quieter back room. Owing to its idealistic youth-hostel roots, it's very service-oriented, with lots of included extras, a very "green" attitude, and occasional special events for guests (Sb-€70, small standard Db-€80, larger Db-€90, junior suite Db-€100, breakfast-€4-8, elevator, free Internet access and Wi-Fi, mellow ground-floor restaurant, Rosenthaler Strasse 1, directly at U8: Rosenthaler Platz, tel. 030/2000-3939, www.circus-berlin.de, info@circus-berlin.de). The Circus also offers a range of spacious, modern **apartments** two blocks away on Choriner Strasse (Db-€130-€250 depending on size and furnishings, 3-night minimum stay preferred).

$ **Karlito Apartmenthaus** offers 12 well-located, modern, and comfortable apartments on a tranquil side street and above a hip café near Hackescher Markt. All of the sleek, Ikea-esque units have miniature balconies and are fully equipped (Sb-€62-77, Db-€72-85, price depends on season, extra person-€15, up to 2 children under 8 sleep free with 2 paying adults, breakfast in Café Lois-€5, no minimum stay, elevator, free Wi-Fi, bike rental-€8/day, Linienstrasse 60—check in at Café Lois around the corner on Gormannstrasse, 350 yards from S-Bahn: Hackescher Markt, even closer to U8: Rosenthaler Platz, mobile 0179-704-9041, www.karlito-apartments.de, info@karlito-apartments.de).

$ **easyHotel Berlin Hackescher Markt** is part of an unapologetically cheap Europe-wide chain where you pay for exactly what you use—nothing more, nothing less. Based on parent company easyJet's sales model of nickel-and-dime air travel, the hotel has inexpensive base rates (small Db-€25-65, larger Db-€35-65, prices vary by season, it's cheaper to book earlier), then charges you separately for optional extras (breakfast, Wi-Fi, using the TV, and so on). The 125 orange-and-gray rooms are very small, basic, and feel popped out of a plastic mold, but if you skip the extras, the price is right, and the location—at the Hackescher Markt end of Prenzlauer Berg—is wonderful (air-con, elevator, after booking online call to request a quieter back room, Rosenthaler Strasse 69, tel. 030/4000-6550, www.easyhotel.com).

Near Oranienburger Strasse: **$$$** **Hotel Augustinenhof** is a clean hotel with 66 spacious rooms, nice woody floors, and some of the most comfortable beds in Berlin. While not exactly in Prenzlauer Berg, the hotel is on a side street near all of the Oranienburger Strasse action. Rooms in front overlook the courtyard of the old Imperial Post Office, rooms in back are a bit quieter, and all rooms have old, thin windows (official rates: Sb-€119, Db-€151—but you'll likely pay closer to Db-€99, elevator, free Wi-Fi or cable Internet in rooms, Auguststrasse 82, 50 yards from S-Bahn: Oranienburger Strasse, tel. 030/308-860, fax 030/308-86100, www. hotel-augustinenhof.de, augustinenhof@albrechtshof-hotels.de).

Hostels in Eastern Berlin

Berlin is known among budget travelers for its fun, hip hostels. These range from upscale-feeling hostels with some hotelesque private rooms comfortable enough even for non-hostelers, to more truly backpacker-type places where comfort is secondary to socializing. These are scattered around eastern Berlin, including some (Circus, Meininger, and EastSeven) in the Prenzlauer Berg area just described.

Comfortable Hostels with Hotelesque Rooms

$ Circus is a brightly colored, well-run place with 230 beds, a trendy lounge with upscale ambience, and a bar downstairs. It has typical hostel dorms as well as some very hotel-like private rooms; for a step up in quality, see the listing for the Circus Hotel, earlier (€19/bed in 8- to 10-bed dorms, €23/bed in 4- to 5-bed dorms, S-€43, Sb-€53, D-€56, Db-€70, T-€75, 2-person apartment with kitchen-€85, 4-person apartment-€140, breakfast-€4-8, no curfew, elevator, pay Internet access, free Wi-Fi, bike rental, Weinbergsweg 1A, U8: Rosenthaler Platz, tel. 030/2000-3939, www. circus-berlin.de, info@circus-berlin.de).

$ Meininger is a Europe-wide budget-hotel chain with several locations in Berlin. With sleek, nicely decorated rooms, these are a great-value budget option, even for non-hostelers. They have three particularly appealing branches: in Prenzlauer Berg (Schönhauser Allee 19 on Senefelderplatz), at Oranienburger Strasse 67 (next to the Aufsturz pub), and near the Hauptbahnhof, at Ella-Traebe-Strasse 9 (rates vary by availability, but usually €18-19/bed in 6-bed dorms, Sb-€52, Db-€70, Tb-€86; rates at Hauptbahnhof location about €5-10 more; all locations: breakfast-€5.50, elevator, 24-hour reception, pay Internet access, free Wi-Fi in lobby, tel. 030/666-36100, www.meininger-hostels.de).

Backpacker Havens

$ EastSeven Hostel rents the best cheap beds in Prenzlauer Berg. It's sleek and modern, with all the hostel services and more: 60

beds, inviting lounge, fully equipped guests' kitchen, lockers, garden, and bike rental. Children are welcome. Easygoing people of any age are comfortable here (€18/bed in 8-bed dorms, €22/bed in 4-bed dorms with private bathroom—or €20/bed in dorm with bathroom down the hall, S-€38, D-€52, T-€66, private rooms have bathrooms down the hall, includes sheets, towel-€1, continental breakfast-€2, free Internet access and Wi-Fi, laundry-€5, no curfew, 100 yards from U2: Senefelderplatz at Schwedter Strasse 7, tel. 030/9362-2240, www.eastseven.de, info@eastseven.de).

$ **Hotel Transit Loft,** actually a hostel, is located in a refurbished factory. Its 62 clean, high-ceilinged, modern rooms and wide-open lobby have an industrial touch. The reception—staffed by friendly, hip Berliners—is open 24 hours, with a bar serving drinks all night long (€21/bed in 4- to 6-bed dorms, Sb-€59, Db-€69, Tb-€89, includes sheets and breakfast, elevator, cheap Internet access, free Wi-Fi, fully wheelchair-accessible, down alley facing inner courtyard at Immanuelkirchstrasse 14A; U2/U5/U8 or S-Bahn: Alexanderplatz, then tram #M4 to Hufelandstrasse and walk 50 yards; tel. 030/4849-3773, fax 030/4405-1074, www.transit-loft.de, loft@hotel-transit.de).

$ **Ostel** is a fun retro-1970s-DDR apartment building that re-creates the lifestyle and interior design of a country relegated to the dustbin of history. All the furniture and room decorations have been meticulously collected and restored to their former socialist glory—only the psychedelic wallpaper is a replica. Guests buy ration vouchers (€7.50/person) for breakfast in the attached restaurant. Kitschy, sure—but also clean and memorable (€15/bed in a 4- or 6-bed "Pioneer Camp" room or in 12-bunk dorm—includes lockers, S-€33, Sb-€40, D-€54, Db-€61, 4-person apartments-€120, includes sheets and towels, 24-hour reception, free Wi-Fi in lobby, bike rental, free parking, free collective use of the people's barbeque, right behind Ostbahnhof station on the corner of Strasse der Pariser Kommune at Wriezener Karree 5, tel. 030/2576-8660, www.ostel.eu, contact@ostel.eu).

In Western Berlin: Near Savignyplatz and Bahnhof Zoo

While Bahnhof Zoo and Ku'damm are no longer the center of the action, this western Berlin neighborhood is still a comfortable and handy home base (thanks to its easy transit connections to the rest of the city). The streets around the tree-lined Savignyplatz (a 10-minute walk behind the station) have a neighborhood charm, with an abundance of simple, small, friendly, good-value places to sleep and eat. The area has an artsy aura going back to the cabaret days in the 1920s, when it was the center of Berlin's gay scene. The hotels and pensions I list here—which are all a 5- to 15-minute walk from Bahnhof Zoo and Savignyplatz (with S- and U-Bahn stations)—are generally located a couple of flights up in big, run-down buildings. Inside, they're clean and spacious enough so that their well-worn character is actually charming. Asking for a quieter room in back gets you away from any street noise. Of the accommodations listed here, Pension Peters offers the best value for budget travelers.

$$ Hecker's Hotel is a modern, four-star business hotel with 69 big, fresh rooms and all the Euro-comforts. Their "superior" rooms cost €10 more than their "comfort" rooms, and—while the same size—have more modern furnishings and air-conditioning. Herr Kiesal promises free breakfasts (otherwise €16/person) for those reserving direct with this book (Sb-€85, Db-usually €95-100—though all rooms €180 during conferences, generally €100 July-Aug, look for deals on their website, non-smoking rooms, elevator, free Wi-Fi, parking-€12-18/day, between Savignyplatz and Ku'damm at Grolmanstrasse 35, tel. 030/88900, fax 030/889-0260, www.heckers-hotel.com, info@heckers-hotel.com).

$$ Hotel Askanischerhof, the oldest B&B in Berlin, is posh as can be, with 16 sprawling, antique-furnished living rooms you can call home. Photos on the walls brag of famous movie-star guests. It oozes Old World service and classic Berlin atmosphere (Sb-€110, Db-€120, Tb-€130, elevator, free Wi-Fi, free parking, Ku'damm 53, tel. 030/881-8033, fax 030/881-7206, www.askanischer-hof.de, info@askanischer-hof.de).

$$ Hotel Astoria is a friendly three-star business-class hotel with 32 comfortably furnished rooms and affordable summer and weekend rates (Db-€108-126, often Db-€80 in summer, check their website for deals, non-smoking floors, elevator, free Wi-Fi and Internet access, bike rental, parking-€9/day, around corner from Bahnhof Zoo at Fasanenstrasse 2, tel. 030/312-4067, www.hotelastoria.de, info@hotelastoria.de).

$$ Hotel Carmer 16, with 34 bright and airy (if a bit dated) rooms, is both business-like and homey, and has an inviting lounge and charming balconies (Db-€99, ask for Rick Steves price when reserving direct with this book, extra person-€30, some rooms have balconies, family suites, elevator and a few stairs, free Wi-Fi, parking €9.50/day, Carmerstrasse 16, tel. 030/3110-0500, fax 030/3110-0510, www.hotel-carmer16.de, info@hotel-carmer16.de).

$$ Hotel-Pension Funk, the former home of a 1920s silent-movie star, is a delightfully quirky time warp. Kind manager Herr Michael Pfundt offers 15 elegant old rooms with rich Art Nouveau furnishings (S-€42, Ss-€60, Sb-€72, D-€72, Ds-€85, Db-€99, extra person-€25, cash preferred, free Wi-Fi, a long block south of Ku'damm at Fasanenstrasse 69, tel. 030/882-7193, www.hotel-pensionfunk.de, berlin@hotel-pensionfunk.de).

BERLIN

Western Berlin

1. Hecker's Hotel
2. Hotel Askanischerhof
3. Hotel Astoria
4. Hotel Carmer 16
5. Hotel-Pension Funk
6. Hotel Bogota
7. Pension Peters
8. Restaurant Marjellchen
9. Rest. Leibniz-Klause
10. Dicke Wirtin Pub
11. To Restaurant Weyers
12. Café Literaturhaus
13. Die Zwölf Apostel Rest.
14. Zillemarkt Restaurant
15. Technical University Mensa
16. Ullrich Supermarkt
17. Schleusenkrug Beer Garden
18. Winter Garden Buffet
19. A Trane Jazz Club
20. Bar Jeder Vernunft
21. Internet Café
22. Fat Tire Bikes

$$ Hotel Bogota is a slumbermill just steps off Ku'damm, renting 115 rooms in a sprawling maze of a building that used to house the Nazi Chamber of Culture. A creaky, well-worn place with big, simple rooms and old furniture, it has the feel of a once-grand hotel (S-€49, Ss-€62, Sb-€98, D-€77, Ds-€84, Db-€89-150, extra bed-€21, check their website for deals and great last-minute prices in summer, children under 14 free, elevator, free Wi-Fi and Internet access, little back garden, 10-minute walk from Savigny-platz at Schlüterstrasse 45, tel. 030/881-5001, fax 030/883-5887, www.hotel-bogota.de, info@hotel-bogota.de).

$ Pension Peters, run by a German-Swedish couple, is sunny and central, with a cheery breakfast room and a super-friendly staff who go out of their way to help their guests. With its sleek Scandinavian decor and 34 renovated rooms, it's a good choice. Some of the ground-floor rooms facing the back courtyard are a bit dark—and cheaper for the inconvenience (Sb-€58, Db-€79, big Db-€85, extra bed-€15, family room-€85, ask for Rick Steves price, up to 2

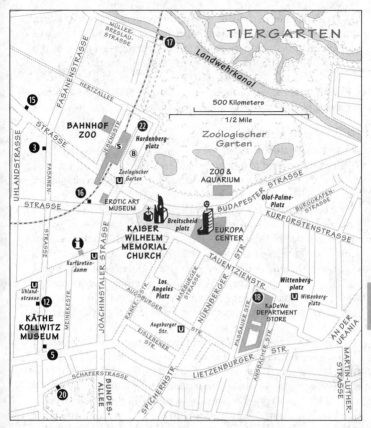

kids under 13 free with 2 paying adults, cash preferred, free Wi-Fi and Internet access, bike rental, 10 yards off Savignyplatz at Kantstrasse 146, tel. 030/312-2278, www.pension-peters-berlin.de, info@pension-peters-berlin.de, Annika and Christoph with help of his sister, Daisy).

Eating in Berlin

There's a world of restaurants to choose from in this ever-changing city. Your best approach may be to select a neighborhood and browse until you find something that strikes your fancy, rather than seeking out a particular restaurant.

Don't be too determined to eat "Berlin-style." The city is known only for its mildly spicy sausage and for its street food (*Currywurst* and *Döner Kebab*). Germans—especially Berliners—consider their food old-school; when they go out to eat, they're not usually looking for the "traditional local fare" many travelers are after. Nouveau

German is California cuisine with scant memories of wurst, kraut, and pumpernickel. If the kraut is getting the wurst of you, take a break with some international or ethnic offerings—try one of the many Turkish, Italian, pan-Asian, and Balkan restaurants.

Colorful pubs—called *Kneipen*—offer light, quick, and easy meals and the fizzy local beer, *Berliner Weiss*. Ask for it *mit Schuss* for a shot of fruity syrup in your suds.

In Eastern Berlin
Near Unter den Linden
While this government/commercial area is hardly a hotspot for eateries, I've listed a few places handy for your sightseeing, all a short walk from Unter den Linden.

Cheap Eats: **Bier's Curry und Spiesse,** under the tracks at the Friedrichstrasse S-Bahn stop, is a great, greasy, cheap, and generous place for an old-fashioned German hot dog. This is the local favorite near Unter den Linden for €2 *Currywurst*. Experiment with variations (the *Flieschspiess* is excellent) and sauces—and don't hold the fried *Zwiebeln* (onions). You'll munch standing at a counter, where the people-watching is great (daily 11:00-5:00 in the morning; from inside the station, take the Friedrichstrasse exit and turn left).

Near the Pergamon Museum: Georgenstrasse, a block behind the Pergamon Museum and under the S-Bahn tracks, is lined with fun eateries filling the arcade of the train trestle—close to the sightseeing action but in business mainly for students from nearby Humboldt University. **Deponie3** is a trendy Berlin *Kneipe* usually filled with students. Garden seating in the back is nice if you don't mind the noise of the S-Bahn passing directly above you. The interior is a cozy, wooden wonderland of a bar with several inviting spaces. They serve basic salads, traditional Berlin dishes, and hearty daily specials (€4-8 breakfasts, good €8 brunch Sun 10:00-15:00, €5-11 lunches and dinners, open daily from 9:00, sometimes live music, Georgenstrasse 5, tel. 030/2016-5740). For Italian food, a branch of **Die Zwölf Apostel** is nearby (daily until 24:00, food served until 22:00; described later, under "Near Savignyplatz").

In the Heart of Old Berlin's Nikolai Quarter: The *Nikolaiviertel* marks the original medieval settlement of Cölln, which would eventually become Berlin. The area was destroyed during the war but was rebuilt for Berlin's 750th birthday in 1987. The whole area has a cute, cobbled, and characteristic old town...Middle Ages meet Socialist Realism. Today, the district is pretty soulless by day but a popular restaurant zone at night. **Bräuhaus Georgbrau** is a thriving beer hall serving homemade suds on a picturesque courtyard overlooking the Spree River. Eat in the lively and woody but mod-feeling interior, or outdoors with fun riverside seating—thriving with German tourists. It's a good place to try one of the few typical Berlin dishes: *Eisbein* (boiled ham hock) with sauerkraut and mashed peas with bacon (€10 with a beer and schnapps). The statue of St. George once stood in the courtyard of Berlin's old castle—until the Nazis deemed it too decadent and not "German" enough, and removed it (€10-13 plates, three-foot-long sampler board with a dozen small glasses of beer, daily 10:00-24:00, 2 blocks south of Berlin Cathedral and across the river at Spreeufer 4, tel. 030/242-4244).

In City Hall: Consider lunching at one of Berlin's many *Kantine*. Located in government offices and larger corporations, *Kantine* offer fast, filling, and cheap lunches, along with a unique opportunity to see Germans at work (though the food can hardly be considered gourmet). There are thousands of *Kantine* in Berlin, but the best is **Die Kantine im Roten Rathaus,** in the basement of City Hall. For less than €4, you can get filling German dishes like *Leberkäse* (German-style baloney) or stuffed cabbage (Mon-Fri 11:00-15:00, closed Sat-Sun, Rathausstrasse 15).

Near Gendarmenmarkt, South of Unter den Linden

BERLIN

The twin churches of Gendarmenmarkt seem to be surrounded by people in love with food. The lunch and dinner scene is thriving with upscale restaurants serving good cuisine at highly competitive prices to local professionals (see map on page 670 for locations). If in need of a quick-yet-classy lunch, stroll around the square and along Charlottenstrasse. For a quick bite, head to the cheap *Currywurst* stand behind the German Cathedral.

Lutter & Wegner Restaurant is well-known for its Austrian cuisine (*Schnitzel* and *Sauerbraten*) and popular with businesspeople. It's dressy, with fun sidewalk seating or a dark and elegant interior (€9-18 starters, €16-22 main dishes, daily 11:00-24:00, Charlottenstrasse 56, tel. 030/202-9540). They have a second location, called **Beisl am Tacheles,** near the New Synagogue (Oranienburger Strasse 52, tel. 030/2478-1078).

Augustiner am Gendarmenmarkt, next door to Lutter & Wegner, lines its sidewalk with trademark Bavarian white-and-blue-checkerboard tablecloths; inside, you'll find a classic Bavarian beer-hall atmosphere. Less pretentious than its neighbor, it offers good beer and affordable Bavarian classics in an equally appealing location (€6-12 light meals, €10-15 bigger meals, daily 9:00-24:00, Charlottenstrasse 55, tel. 030/2045-4020).

Galeries Lafayette Food Circus is a French festival of fun eateries in the basement of the landmark department store. You'll find a good deli and prepared-food stands, dishing up cuisine that's good-quality but not cheap (most options €10-15, cheaper €8-10 sandwiches and savory crepes, Mon-Sat 10:00-20:00, closed

Eastern Berlin Eateries & Nightlife

1. Bier's Curry und Spiesse
2. Deponie3 Pub
3. Die Zwölf Apostel
4. Bräuhaus Georgbrau
5. Die Kantine im Roten Rathaus
6. Lutter & Wegner Restaurant; Augustiner am Gendarmenmarkt
7. Beisl am Tacheles
8. Galeries Lafayette Food Circus
9. Fresco Espresso Bar
10. Hasir Turkish Restaurant
11. Weihenstephaner Bavarian Restaurant
12. Restaurant Simon
13. Aufsturz Pub
14. Prater Biergarten
15. Zum Schusterjungen Speisegaststätte
16. La Bodeguita del Medio Cuban Bar Restaurant
17. Konnopke's Imbiss
18. Restaurant "Die Schule"
19. Kauf Dich Glücklich
20. Fleischmöbel Pub
21. Gugelhof Restaurant
22. Luigi Zuckermann Deli & Transit Restaurant
23. Metzer Eck Pub
24. Lemongrass Scent
25. Humboldt-Box Café
26. To Café Sibylle

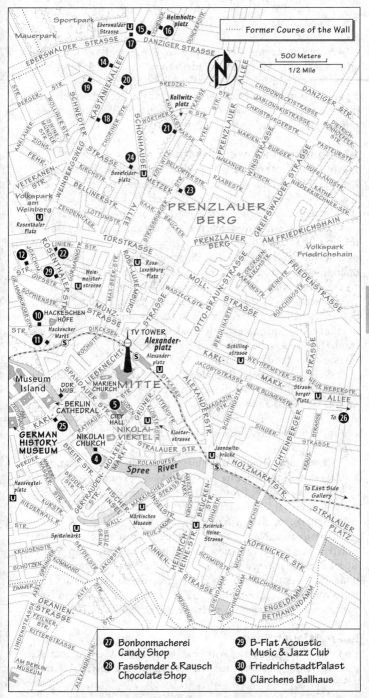

BERLIN

27 Bonbonmacherei Candy Shop

28 Fassbender & Rausch Chocolate Shop

29 B-Flat Acoustic Music & Jazz Club

30 FriedrichstadtPalast

31 Clärchens Ballhaus

Sun, Friedrichstrasse 76-78, U-Bahn: Französische Strasse, tel. 030/209-480).

Near Checkpoint Charlie: **Fresco Espresso Bar** is a touristy joint, handy for made-to-order sandwiches. Israeli-born Sagi makes his own bread daily and piles on the fixin's for €4-6. This is a popular stop for walking-tour groups: If you get here when they do, expect a line (Mon-Sat 7:30-19:00, Sun 8:00-19:00, in summer until 20:30, Friedrichstrasse 200, tel. 030/2061-6693).

At and near Hackescher Markt

Hasir Turkish Restaurant is your chance to dine with candles, hardwood floors, and happy Berliners savoring meaty Anatolian specialties. As Berlin is the world's largest Turkish city outside of Asia Minor, it's no wonder you can find some good Turkish restaurants here. But while most locals think of Turkish food as fast and cheap, this is a dining experience. The restaurant, in a courtyard next to the Hackeschen Höfe shopping complex (see page 638), offers indoor and outdoor tables filled with an enthusiastic local crowd. The service can be a bit questionable, so bring some patience (€6-10 starters, €14-20 main dishes, large and splittable portions, daily 11:30-1:00 in the morning, in late evening the courtyard is dominated by an unpleasantly loud underground disco, a block from the Hackescher Markt S-Bahn station at Oranienburger Strasse 4, tel. 030/2804-1616).

Weihenstephaner Bavarian Restaurant serves upmarket Bavarian traditional food for around €10-15 a plate; offers an atmospheric cellar, an inner courtyard, and a busy people-watching street-side terrace; and, of course, has excellent beer (daily 11:00-23:00, Neue Promenade 5 at Hackescher Markt, tel. 030/8471-0760).

Restaurant Simon dishes up tasty Italian and German specialties—enjoy them either in the restaurant's simple yet atmospheric interior, or opt for streetside seating (€6-12 main dishes, daily 12:00-23:00, Auguststrasse 53, at intersection with Kleine Auguststrasse, tel. 030/2789-0358).

Aufsturz, a lively pub with live music, pours more than 100 different beers and 40 varieties of whiskey, and dishes up "traditional Berliner pub grub"—like nachos—and great potato soup for under €5. The traditional "Berlin board" for €17 can easily feed three voracious carnivores (daily 12:00-24:00, a block beyond New Synagogue at Oranienburger Strasse 67, tel. 030/2804-7407).

In Prenzlauer Berg

Prenzlauer Berg is packed with fine restaurants—German, ethnic, and everything in between. Even if you're not staying in this area, it's worth venturing here for dinner. (For more on Prenzlauer Berg, see page 640; for restaurant locations, see the map on page 670.) Before making a choice, I'd spend at least half an hour strolling and browsing through this bohemian wonderland of creative eateries. Because Prenzlauer Berg sprawls over a wide area, I've organized my listings by neighborhood.

Near Eberswalder Strasse

The area surrounding the elevated Eberswalder Strasse U-Bahn station (on the U2 line, at the confluence of Kastanienallee, Danziger Strasse, Ebwerswalder Strasse, and Schönhauser Allee) is the epicenter of Prenzlauer Berg—a young, hip, and edgy place to eat and drink. While a bit farther north than other areas I recommend (and a 10- to 15-minute walk from most of my recommended hotels), it's worth the trip to immerse yourself in quintessential Prenzlauer Berg.

Prater Biergarten offers two great eating opportunities: a rustic indoor restaurant and a mellow, shaded, super-cheap, and family-friendly outdoor beer garden (with a playground)—each proudly pouring Prater's own microbrew. In the beer garden—Berlin's oldest—you step up to the counter and order (simple €3-5 plates and an intriguing selection of beer munchies, daily in good weather 12:00-24:00). The restaurant serves serious traditional *Biergarten* cuisine and good salads (€7-17 plates, Mon-Sat 18:00-24:00, Sun 12:00-24:00, cash only, Kastanienallee 7, tel. 030/448-5688).

Zum Schusterjungen Speisegaststätte ("The Cobbler's Apprentice") is a classic old-school, German-with-attitude eatery that retains its circa-1986 DDR decor. Famous for its filling €7-10 meals (including various types of schnitzel and Berlin classics such as pork knuckle), it's a no-frills place with quality ingredients and a strong local following. It serves the eating needs of those Berliners lamenting the disappearance of solid traditional German cooking amid the flood of ethnic eateries (small 40-seat dining hall plus outdoor tables, daily 12:00-24:00, corner of Lychener Strasse and Danziger Strasse 9, tel. 030/442-7654).

La Bodeguita del Medio Cuban Bar Restaurant is purely fun-loving Cuba—graffiti-caked walls, Che Guevara posters, animated staff, and an ambience that makes you want to dance. Come early to eat or late to drink. This restaurant has been here since 1994—and in fast-changing Prenzlauer Berg, that's an eternity. The German-Cuban couple who run it take pride in their food, and the main dishes are big enough to split. You can even puff a Cuban cigar at the sidewalk tables (€4-10 tapas, €6 Cuban ribs and salad, Tue-Sun 18:00-24:00, closed Mon, a block from U2: Eberswalder Strasse at Lychener Strasse 6, tel. 030/4050-0601).

BERLIN

Konnopke's Imbiss, a super-cheap German-style sausage stand, has been a Berlin institution for more than 70 years—it was family-owned even during DDR times. Berliners say Konnopke's cooks up some of the city's best *Currywurst* (less than €2). Located beneath the U2 viaduct, the stand was demolished in summer of 2010 during roadwork. Berliners rioted, and Konnopke's was rebuilt in a slick glass-and-steel hut (Mon-Fri 10:00-20:00, Sat 12:00-20:00, closed Sun; Kastanienallee dead-ends at the elevated train tracks, and under them you'll find Konnopke's at Schönhauser Allee 44A). Don't confuse this with the nearby Currystation—look for the real Konnopke's.

Restaurant "Die Schule" is a modern place with a no-frills style where you can sample traditional German dishes tapas-style. Assemble a collection of little €2.50 plates of old-fashioned German food you might not try otherwise (good indoor and outdoor seating, €24 full 3-course dinner, daily 11:00-22:00, Kastanienallee 82, tel. 030/780-089-550).

After-Dinner Dessert and Drinks: There are oodles of characteristic funky pubs and nightspots in the area around Helmholtzplatz (and elsewhere in Prenzlauer Berg). Oderberger Strasse is a fun zone to explore; I've listed two places on this street that I particularly like. **Kauf Dich Glücklich** makes a great capper to a Prenzlauer Berg dinner. It serves an enticing array of sweet Belgian waffles and ice cream in a candy-sprinkled, bohemian lounge on a great Prenzlauer Berg street (daily 11:00-24:00, indoor and outdoor seating—or get your dessert to go, wait possible on busy nights, Oderberger Strasse 44, tel. 030/4435-2182). **Fleischmöbel** ("Meat Furniture") is a fun place to drink with locals, despite the lack of beer on tap. Here you'll find strong cocktails, cool classic rock, and a big blackboard. It's a bit hipster-pretentious, but offers a good glimpse into the Prenzlauer Berg lifestyle. Its two smallish rooms unashamedly offer a bit of 1960s retro in an increasingly trendy part of town; on warm evenings, tables fill the sidewalk out front (daily 12:00 until "whenever," Oderberger Strasse 2).

Near Kollwitzplatz

This square, home of the DDR student resistance in 1980s, is now trendy and upscale, popular with hip parents who take their hip kids to the leafy playground park at its center. It's an especially good area to prowl among upmarket restaurants—walk the square and choose. Just about every option offers sidewalk seats in the summer (great on a balmy evening). It's a long block up Kollwitzstrasse from U2: Senefelderplatz.

Gugelhof, right on Kollwitzplatz, is an institution famous for its Alsatian German cuisine. You'll enjoy French quality with German proportions. It's highly regarded, with a boisterous and enthusiastic local crowd filling its minimalist yet classy interior. In good weather, outdoor seating sprawls along its sidewalk. Their fixed-price meals are fun, and they welcome swapping (€20-30 three-course meal, €5-10 starters, €12-20 main dishes, Mon-Fri 16:00-24:00, Sat-Sun 10:00-24:00, reservations required during peak times, where Knaackstrasse meets Kollwitzplatz, tel. 030/442-9229).

Near Rosenthaler Platz, Closer to Hackescher Markt

Surrounding the U8: Rosenthaler Platz station, a short stroll or tram ride from the Hackescher Markt S-Bahn station, and an easy walk from the Oranienburger Strasse action, this busy neighborhood has a few enticing options.

Luigi Zuckermann is a trendy young deli with Israeli/New York style. It's a great spot to pick up a custom-made deli sandwich (choose your ingredients at the deli counter), hummus plate, salad, fresh-squeezed juice, or other quick, healthy lunch. Linger in the interior, grab one of the few sidewalk tables, or take your food to munch on the go (€5-8 meals, daily 8:00-24:00, Rosenthaler Strasse 67, tel. 030/2804-0644).

Transit is a stylish, innovative, affordable Thai/Indonesian/pan-Asian small-plates restaurant at the bustling Hackescher Markt end of Prenzlauer Berg. Sit at one of the long shared tables and dig into a creative menu of €3 small plates and €7 big plates. Two people can make a filling meal out of three or four dishes (daily 11:00-late, Rosenthaler Strasse 68, tel. 030/2478-1645).

Near Senefelderplatz (near Recommended Hotels on Metzer Strasse and Schwedter Strasse)

While neither of these places—in a sedate corner of Prenzlauer Berg near the Senefelderplatz U-Bahn stop—is worth going out of your way for, they're handy for those staying at one of my recommended accommodations nearby.

Metzer Eck is a time-warp *Kneipe* with a family tradition dating to 1913 and a cozy charm. It serves cheap basic typical Berlin food with five beers on tap, including the Czech Budvar (€5-8 meals, Mon-Fri 16:00-24:00, Sat 18:00-24:00, closed Sun, Metzer Strasse 33, on the corner of Metzer Strasse and Strassburger Strasse, tel. 030/442-7656).

Lemongrass Scent, with a gaggle of inviting sidewalk tables, offers tasty and affordable "Asian street kitchen" food near several recommended hotels (two-course weekday lunch special for less than €5, €3-4 starters, €5-8 main dishes, Mon-Fri 11:30-24:00, Sat-Sun 12:00-24:00, Schwedter Strasse 12, tel. 030/4057-6985).

BERLIN

In Western Berlin
Near Savignyplatz

Many good restaurants are on or within 100 yards of Savignyplatz, near my recommended western Berlin hotels (for locations, see map on page 666). Savignyplatz is lined with attractive, relaxed, mostly Mediterranean-style places. Take a walk and survey these; continue your stroll along Bleibtreustrasse to discover many trendier, more creative little eateries.

Restaurant Marjellchen is a trip to East Prussia. Dine in a soft, jazzy elegance in one of two six-table rooms. While it doesn't have to be expensive (€10-18 main courses, €27 two-course meals), plan to go the whole nine yards here, as this can be a great Prussian experience with caring service. The menu is inviting, and the place family-run—all the recipes were brought to Berlin by the owner's mother after she was expelled from East Prussia. Reservations are smart (daily 17:00-23:30, Mommsenstrasse 9, tel. 030/883-2676).

Restaurant Leibniz-Klause is a good place for a dressy German meal. You'll enjoy upscale presentation on white tablecloths, hunter-sized portions, service that's both friendly and professional, and no pretense. Their *Berliner Riesen-Eisbein* ("super-pork-leg on the bone"), with sauerkraut and horseradish, will stir even the tiniest amount of Teutonic blood in your veins (€15-22 plates, good indoor and outdoor seating, daily 12:00-late, Leibnizstrasse near corner with Mommsenstrasse, tel. 030/323-7068).

Dicke Wirtin is a pub with traditional old-Berlin *Kneipe* atmosphere, six good beers on tap, and solid home cooking at reasonable prices—such as their famously cheap *Gulaschsuppe* (€4). Their interior is fun and pubby, with soccer on the TV; their streetside tables are also inviting. Pickled eggs are on the bar—ask about how these can help you avoid a hangover (€5 daily specials, Bavarian Andechs beer on tap, open daily from 12:00, dinner served from 18:00, just off Savignyplatz at Carmerstrasse 9, tel. 030/312-4952).

Weyers offers modern German cuisine in a simple, elegant setting, with dining tables in the summer spilling out into the idyllic neighborhood park in front (€5-10 starters, €10-16 main plates, daily 8:00-24:00, facing Ludwigkirchplatz at corner of Pariser Strasse and Pfalzburger Strasse, tel. 030/881-9378).

Café Literaturhaus is a neighborhood favorite for a light meal, sandwich, or dessert. It has the ambience of an Old World villa with a big garden perfect for their evening poetry readings (€5-15 meals, daily 9:30-24:00, Fasanenstrasse 23, tel. 030/882-5414).

Die Zwölf Apostel ("The Twelve Apostles") is popular for good Italian food. Choose between indoors with candlelit ambience, outdoors on a sun-dappled patio, or overlooking the people-parade on its pedestrian street. A local crowd packs this restaurant for €12 pizzas and €15-20 meals (long hours daily, cash only, immediately across from Savignyplatz S-Bahn entrance, Bleibtreustrasse 49, tel. 030/312-1433).

Zillemarkt Restaurant, which feels like an old-time Berlin *Biergarten,* serves traditional Berlin specialties in the garden or in the rustic candlelit interior. Their *Berliner Allerlei* is a fun way to sample a bit of nearly everything (cabbage, pork, sausage, potatoes and more for a minimum of two people...but it can feed up to five). They have their own microbrew (€10 meals, daily 10:00-24:00, near the S-Bahn tracks at Bleibtreustrasse 48A, tel. 030/881-7040).

Technical University Mensa puts you in a thriving, modern student scene. It feels like a student union building (because it is), with shops, a travel agency, a lounge, kids making out, and lots of international students to chat with. The main cafeteria *(Mensa)* is upstairs—bustling with students and lots of eating options. Streetside is a cafeteria with a more limited selection. Even with the non-student surcharge, eating here is very cheap (€3-5 meals, Mon-Fri 11:00-14:30, closed Sat-Sun, general public entirely welcome but pays the highest of the three prices, coffee bar downstairs with Internet access, just north of Uhlandstrasse at Hardenbergstrasse 34).

Supermarket: The neighborhood grocery store is **Ullrich** (Mon-Sat 9:00-22:00, Sun 11:00-22:00, Kantstrasse 7, under the tracks near Bahnhof Zoo). There's plenty of fast food near Bahnhof Zoo and on Ku'damm.

Near Bahnhof Zoo

Schleusenkrug beer garden is hidden in the park overlooking a canal between the Bahnhof Zoo and Tiergarten stations. Choose from an ever-changing self-service menu of huge salads, pasta, and some German dishes (€7-12 plates, daily 10:00-24:00, food served until 22:00; standing in front of Bahnhof Zoo, turn left and walk 5 minutes, following the path into the park between the zoo and train tracks; tel. 030/313-9909).

Self-Service Cafeterias: The top floor of the famous department store, **KaDeWe,** holds the Winter Garden Buffet view cafeteria, and its sixth-floor deli/food department is a picnicker's nirvana. Its arterials are clogged with more than 1,000 kinds of sausage and 1,500 types of cheese (Mon-Thu 10:00-20:00, Fri 10:00-21:00, Sat 9:30-20:00, closed Sun, U-Bahn: Wittenbergplatz).

Berlin Connections

By Train

Berlin used to have several major train stations. But now that the Hauptbahnhof has emerged as the single, massive central station, all the others have wilted into glorified subway stations. Virtually all long-distance trains pass through the Hauptbahnhof—ignore the other stations.

EurAide is an agent of Deutsche Bahn (German Railway) that sells reservations for high-speed and overnight trains, with staff that can answer your travel questions in English (located in the Hauptbahnhof; see "Arrival in Berlin" on page 585).

From Berlin by Train to: Frankfurt (hourly, 4 hours), **Bacharach** (hourly, 6.5-7.5 hours, 1-3 changes), **Würzburg** (hourly, 4 hours, change in Göttingen or Fulda), **Rothenburg** (hourly, 5-6 hours, often via Göttingen or Fulda, then Würzburg, then Steinach), **Nürnberg** (hourly, 4.5 hours), **Munich** (1-2/hour, 6-6.75 hours, every 2 hours direct, otherwise change in Göttingen), **Köln** (hourly, 4.25 hours), **Amsterdam** (6/day direct to Amsterdam Zuid, 6.5 hours; plus 1 night train/day to Amsterdam Centraal, 9.5 hours), **London** (8/day, 10-12.75 hours, 2-3 changes—you're better off flying cheap on easyJet or Air Berlin, even if you have a railpass), **Paris** (11/day, 8-9.5 hours, change in Köln—via Belgium—or in Mannheim, 1 direct 13.25-hour night train), **Vienna** (8/day, most with 1-2 changes, 2/day plus 1/night are direct, 9.5-12 hours; some via Czech Republic, but trains with a change in Nürnberg, Munich, or Würzburg avoid that country—useful if it's not covered by your railpass). It's wise but not required to reserve in advance for trains to or from Amsterdam (or Prague). Train info: tel. 0180-599-6633, www.bahn.com. Before buying a ticket for any long train ride from Berlin (over 7 hours), consider taking a cheap flight instead (buy it well in advance to get a super fare).

Night trains run from Berlin to these cities: Munich, Paris, Amsterdam, Vienna, Budapest, Malmö (Sweden, near Copenhagen), Basel, and Zürich. There are no night trains from Berlin to anywhere in Italy or Spain. A *Liegeplatz*, a.k.a. *couchette* berth (€13-36), is a great deal; inquire at EurAide at the Hauptbahnhof for details. Beds generally cost the same whether you have a first- or second-class ticket or railpass. Trains are often full, so reserve your *couchette* a few days in advance from any travel agency or major train station in Europe.

By Plane

Berlin will soon whittle down its three airports to a single main hub, the new **Willy Brandt Berlin-Brandenburg International,** which may open in 2014 (airport code: BER, tel. 01805-000-186), designed to handle all air traffic for the area. (For British Air, tel. 01805-266-522; Delta, tel. 01803-337-880; SAS, tel. 01805-117-002; Lufthansa, tel. 01803-803-803.)

Located about 13 miles from central Berlin, next to the formerly busy Schönefeld Airport, it'll be connected to the city center by fast and frequent Airport Express regional **trains** (ignore the S-Bahn, as there are no direct S-Bahn trains to the city center; likewise, buses to the U-Bahn lines make little sense for anyone heading straight into central Berlin). The airport station (Flughafen Berlin Brandenburg Bahnhof) sits directly under the terminal, a five-minute walk from the airlines' check-in desks. To reach my recommended hotels in eastern Berlin, take the RE7 or RB14 to Alexanderplatz (2/hour, 25 minutes, direction: Dessau or Nauen); for my hotels in western Berlin, take either of those trains to Zoologischer Garten (40 minutes). Two additional trains per hour connect the airport to the main train station, via Potsdamer Platz (RE9, 30 minutes). Any train into the city center costs €3 (railpasses valid—but don't use up a travel day just for this trip). Buy your ticket at a machine and validate it before boarding by stamping it in one of the nearby boxes. A **taxi** to the city center costs about €35 (same rates 24/7).

If you happen to be arriving before the new airport is fully operational, you may find yourself at **Tegel Airport**, four miles from the center (airport code: TXL). Bus #TXL goes between the airport, the Hauptbahnhof (stops by Washingtonplatz entrance), and Alexanderplatz in eastern Berlin. For western Berlin, take bus #X9 to Bahnhof Zoo, or slower bus #109 to Ku'damm and Bahnhof Zoo (€2.30). Bus #128 goes to northern Berlin. A taxi from Tegel Airport costs €15 to Bahnhof Zoo, or €25 to Alexanderplatz (taxis from Tegel levy a €0.50 surcharge).

Berlin is the continental European hub for budget airlines such as easyJet (lots of flights to Spain, Italy, Eastern Europe, the Baltics, and more—book long in advance to get incredible €30-and-less fares, www.easyjet.com). Ryanair (www.ryanair.com), Air Berlin (www.airberlin.com), and German Wings (www.germanwings.com) make the London-Berlin trip (and other routes) dirt-cheap, so consider this option before booking an overnight train. Consequently, British visitors to the city are now outnumbered only by Americans.

BERLIN

GREAT
BRITAIN

LONDON

London is more than 600 square miles of urban jungle—a world in itself and a barrage on all the senses. On my first visit, I felt extremely small.

London is more than its museums and landmarks. It's the L.A., D.C., and N.Y.C. of Britain—a living, breathing, thriving organism...a coral reef of humanity. The city has changed dramatically in recent years, and many visitors are surprised to find how "un-English" it is. ESL (English as a second language) seems like the city's first language, as white people are now a minority in major parts of this city that once symbolized white imperialism. Arabs have nearly bought out the area north of Hyde Park. Chinese takeouts outnumber fish-and-chips shops. Eastern Europeans pull pints in British pubs. Many hotels are run by people with foreign accents (who hire English chambermaids), while outlying suburbs are home to huge communities of Indians and Pakistanis. London is a city of nearly eight million separate dreams, inhabiting a place that tolerates and encourages them. With the English Channel Tunnel and discount airlines making travel between Britain and the Continent easier than ever, London is learning—sometimes fitfully—to live as a microcosm of its formerly vast empire.

The city, which has long attracted tourists, seems perpetually at your service, with an impressive slate of sights, entertainment, and eateries, all linked by a great transit system. You're riding the coattails of a banner year for London—2012—when the city hosted both the Olympics and the Queen's "Diamond Jubilee" celebration for her 60th year on the throne. Consequently, this already spiffy city is even more spruced up than usual.

With just a few days here, you'll get no more than a quick

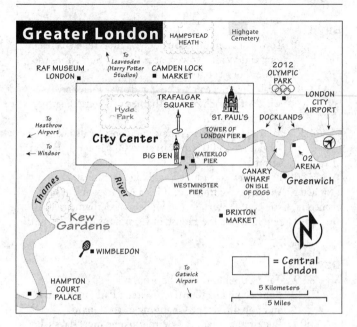

Greater London

HAMPSTEAD HEATH

Highgate Cemetery

To Leavesden (Harry Potter Studios)

RAF MUSEUM LONDON

CAMDEN LOCK MARKET

2012 OLYMPIC PARK

LONDON CITY AIRPORT

Hyde Park

TRAFALGAR SQUARE

ST. PAUL'S

DOCKLANDS

To Heathrow Airport

City Center

TOWER OF LONDON PIER

To Windsor

BIG BEN

WATERLOO PIER

CANARY WHARF ON ISLE OF DOGS

O2 ARENA

Greenwich

Thames River

WESTMINSTER PIER

Kew Gardens

BRIXTON MARKET

WIMBLEDON

To Gatwick Airport

= Central London

HAMPTON COURT PALACE

5 Kilometers

5 Miles

splash in this teeming human tidal pool. But with a good orientation, you'll find London manageable and fun. You'll get a sampling of the city's top sights, history, and cultural entertainment, and a good look at its ever-changing human face.

Blow through the city on a double-decker bus, and take a pinch-me-I'm-in-London walk through the West End. Ogle the crown jewels at the Tower of London, hear the chimes of Big Ben, and see the Houses of Parliament in action. Cruise the Thames River, and take a spin on the London Eye. Hobnob with poets' tombstones in Westminster Abbey, and visit with Leonardo, Botticelli, and Rembrandt in the National Gallery. Enjoy Shakespeare in a replica of the Globe theater and marvel at a glitzy, fun musical at a modern-day theater. Whisper across the dome of St. Paul's Cathedral, then rummage through our civilization's attic at the British Museum. And sip your tea with pinky raised and clotted cream dribbling down your scone.

Planning Your Time

The sights of London alone could easily fill a trip to Great Britain. It's worth at least three busy days. You won't be able to see everything, so don't try. You'll keep coming back to London. After dozens of visits myself, I still enjoy a healthy list of excuses to return. Especially if you hope to enjoy a play or concert, a night or two of jet lag is bad news.

Here's a suggested three-day schedule:

Day 1

9:00	Tower of London (crown jewels first, then Beefeater tour and White Tower; note that on Sun-Mon, the Tower opens at 10:00).
13:00	Grab a picnic, catch a boat at Tower Pier, and relax with lunch on the Thames while cruising to Westminster Pier.
14:30	Tour Westminster Abbey, and consider its evensong service (at 15:00 Sat-Sun, at 17:00 Mon-Fri and Sat in summer).
17:00 (or after evensong)	Follow my self-guided walk of Westminster. When you're finished, if it's a Monday or Tuesday, you could return to the Houses of Parliament and pop in to see the House of Commons in action (until 22:30).

Day 2

8:30	Take a double-decker hop-on, hop-off London sightseeing bus tour (from Green Park or Victoria) and hop off for the Changing of the Guard.
11:00	Buckingham Palace (guards change most days May-July at 11:30, alternate days Aug-April—confirm).
12:00	Walk through St. James's Park to enjoy London's delightful park scene.
13:00	Covent Garden for lunch, shopping, and people-watching.
14:30	Tour the British Museum.
Evening	Have a pub dinner before a play, concert, or evening walking tour.

Day 3

Choose among these remaining London highlights: National Gallery, British Library, Churchill War Rooms, Imperial War Museum, the two Tates (Tate Modern on the South Bank for modern art, Tate Britain on the North Bank for British art), St. Paul's Cathedral, Victoria and Albert Museum, National Portrait Gallery, Natural History Museum, Courtauld Gallery, or the Museum of London; take a spin on the London Eye or a cruise to Kew Gardens; enjoy a play at Shakespeare's Globe; do some serious shopping at one of London's elegant department stores or open-air markets; or take another historic walking tour.

Orientation to London

To grasp London more comfortably, see it as the old town in the city center without the modern, congested sprawl. (Even from that perspective, it's still huge.)

The Thames River (pronounced "tems") runs roughly west to east through the city, with most of the visitor's sights on the North Bank. Mentally, maybe even physically, trim down your map to include only the area between the Tower of London (to the east), Hyde Park (west), Regent's Park (north), and the South Bank (south). This is roughly the area bordered by the Tube's Circle Line. This four-mile stretch between the Tower and Hyde Park (about a 1.5-hour walk) looks like a milk bottle on its side (see map on next page), and holds 80 percent of the sights mentioned in this chapter. With a core focus and a good orientation, you'll get a sampling of London's top sights, history, and cultural entertainment, and a good look at its ever-changing human face.

The sprawling city becomes much more manageable if you think of it as a collection of neighborhoods.

Central London: This area contains Westminster and what Londoners call the West End. The Westminster district includes Big Ben, Parliament, Westminster Abbey, and Buckingham Palace—the grand government buildings from which Britain is ruled. Trafalgar Square, London's gathering place, has many major museums. The West End is the center of London's cultural life, with bustling squares: Piccadilly Circus and Leicester Square host cinemas, tourist traps, and nighttime glitz. Soho and Covent Garden are thriving people-zones with theaters, restaurants, pubs, and boutiques. And Regent and Oxford streets are the city's main shopping zones.

North London: Neighborhoods in this part of town—including Bloomsbury, Fitzrovia, and Marylebone—contain such major sights as the British Museum and the overhyped Madame Tussauds Waxworks. Nearby, along busy Euston Road, is the British Library, plus a trio of train stations (one of them, St. Pancras International, is linked to Paris by the Eurostar "Chunnel" train).

The City: Today's modern financial district, called simply "The City," was a walled town in Roman times. Gleaming skyscrapers are interspersed with historical landmarks such as St. Paul's Cathedral, legal sights (Old Bailey), and the Museum of London. The Tower of London and Tower Bridge lie at The City's eastern border.

East London: Just east of The City is the East End—the increasingly gentrified former stomping ground of Cockney ragamuffins and Jack the Ripper.

The South Bank: The South Bank of the Thames River of-

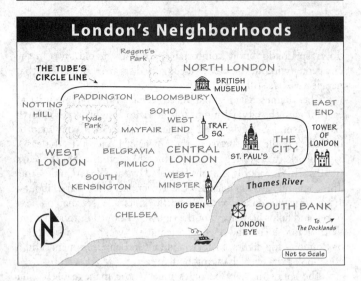

London's Neighborhoods

fers major sights (Tate Modern, Shakespeare's Globe, London Eye) linked by a riverside walkway. Within this area, Southwark (SUTH-uck) stretches from the Tate Modern to London Bridge. Pedestrian bridges connect the South Bank with The City and Trafalgar Square.

West London: This huge area contains neighborhoods such as Mayfair, Belgravia, Pimlico, Chelsea, South Kensington, and Notting Hill. It's home to London's wealthy and has many trendy shops and enticing restaurants. Here you'll find a range of museums (Victoria and Albert Museum, Tate Britain, and more), my top hotel recommendations, lively Victoria Station, and the vast green expanses of Hyde Park and Kensington Gardens.

Outside the Center: The Docklands, London's version of Manhattan, is farther east than the East End; Olympic Park is just north of the Docklands. Kew Gardens is southwest of London.

Tourist Information

For such a big and important city, it's amazing how hard it can be to find unbiased sightseeing information and advice in London. You'll see "Tourist Information" offices advertised everywhere, but most of them are private agencies that make a big profit selling tours and advance sightseeing and/or theater tickets; others are run by Transport for London and are primarily focused on providing public-transit advice.

The only publicly funded (and therefore impartial) "real" TI is the **City of London Information Centre** (Mon-Sat 9:30-17:30, Sun 10:00-16:00; across the busy street from St. Paul's Cathedral—around the right side as you face the main staircase, in the modern, angular building just toward the Millennium Bridge; Tube: St. Paul's, www.visitthecity.co.uk). While officially a service of The City (London's financial district), this office also provides information about the rest of the London. It sells Oyster cards, London Passes, and advance "Fast Track" sightseeing tickets (all described later), and stocks various free publications: *London Planner* (a free monthly that lists all the sights, events, and hours), some walking-tour brochures, the *Official London Theatre Guide*, a *Welcome to London* Tube and bus map, the *Guide to River Thames Boat Services*, and a few brochures describing self-guided walks in The City (various themes, including Dickens, modern architecture, and film locations). They give out a free map of The City, and sell two others (one for £1, or £2 for a mini version of the £2.50 Benson's map sold at newsstands and bookstores); ask if they have yet another free map with a coupon good for 20 percent off admission to St. Paul's. I'd skip their room-booking service and theater box office, both of which charge a commission.

Visit London, which serves the greater London area, doesn't have an office you can visit in person—but does operate a call center and website (tel. 0870-156-6366, www.visitlondon.com).

Fast Track Tickets: To skip the ticket-buying queues at certain London sights, you can buy "Fast Track" tickets in advance—and they're usually cheaper than tickets sold right at the sight. They're particularly smart for the Tower of London, Windsor Castle, and Madame Tussauds Waxworks, all of which get very busy in high season. They're available through various sales outlets around London (including the City of London TI, souvenir stands, and several faux-TIs scattered throughout touristy areas).

London Pass: This pass, which covers many big sights and lets you skip some lines, is expensive but potentially worth the investment for extremely busy sightseers (£46/1 day, £61/2 days, £74/3 days, £99/6 days; days are calendar days rather than 24-hour periods; comes with 160-page guidebook, also sold at TI near St. Paul's, major train stations and airports, tel. 0870-242-9988, www. londonpass.com). Among the many sights it includes are the Tower of London, Westminster Abbey, St. Paul's Cathedral, and Windsor Castle, as well as many temporary exhibits and audioguides at otherwise "free" biggies. Think through your sightseeing plans, study their website to see what's covered, and do the math before you buy.

Arrival in London

For more information on getting to or from London by train, bus, and plane, see "London Connections," near the end of this chapter.

By Train: London has nine major train stations, all connected by the Tube (subway). All have ATMs, and many of the larger stations also have shops, fast food, exchange offices, and luggage storage. From any station, you can ride the Tube or taxi to your hotel. For more info on train travel, see www.nationalrail.co.uk.

By Bus: The main intercity bus station is Victoria Coach Station, one block southwest of Victoria train station (and the Victoria Tube station). For more on bus travel, see www.nationalexpress.com.

By Plane: London has six airports. Most tourists arrive at Heathrow or Gatwick airports, although flights from elsewhere in Europe may land at Stansted, Luton, Southend, or London City airports. For specifics on getting from London's airports to downtown, see "London Connections," near the end of this chapter; for hotels near Heathrow and Gatwick, see page 781.

Helpful Hints

Theft Alert: Wear your money belt. The Artful Dodger is alive and well in London. Be on guard, particularly on public transportation and in places crowded with tourists, who, considered naive and rich, are targeted. The Changing of the Guard scene is a favorite for thieves. And more than 7,500 purses are stolen annually at Covent Garden alone.

Pedestrian Safety: Cars drive on the left side of the road—which can be as confusing for foreign pedestrians as for foreign drivers. Before crossing a street, I always look right, look left, then look right again just to be sure. Most crosswalks are even painted with instructions, reminding foreign guests to "Look right" or "Look left." While locals are champion jaywalkers, you shouldn't try it; jaywalking is treacherous when you're disoriented about which direction traffic is coming from.

Medical Problems: Local hospitals have good-quality 24-hour-a-day emergency care centers, where any tourist who needs help can drop in and, after a wait, be seen by a doctor. Your hotel has details. St. Thomas' Hospital, immediately across the river from Big Ben, has a fine reputation.

Getting Your Bearings: London is well-signed for visitors. Through an initiative called Legible London, the city is erecting thoughtfully designed, pedestrian-focused maps around town. In this sprawling city—where predictable grid-planned streets are relatively rare—it's also smart to buy and use a good map. *Benson's London Street Map* (£2.50), sold at many newsstands and bookstores, is my favorite for efficient sightseeing; the City of London TI sells a mini version of the Benson's map for £2.

Festivals: For one week in February and another in September, fashionistas descend on the city for London Fashion Week (www.londonfashionweek.co.uk). The famous Chelsea Flower

Show blossoms in late May (book ahead for this popular event at www.rhs.org.uk/chelsea). During the annual Trooping the Colour in June, there are military bands and pageantry, and the Queen's birthday parade (www.trooping-the-colour. co.uk). Tennis fans pack the stands at the Wimbledon Tennis Championship in late June to early July (www.wimbledon. org), and partygoers head for the Notting Hill Carnival in late August.

Traveling in Winter: London dazzles year-round, so consider visiting in winter, when airfares and hotel rates are generally cheaper and there are fewer tourists. For ideas on what to do, see the "Winter Activities in London" article at www.rick-steves.com/winteracts.

Internet Access: As nearly all the city's hotels offer Internet access, and cafés all over town have free Wi-Fi, London now has few actual Internet cafés (if you need one, ask your hotelier).

Travel Bookstores: Located between Covent Garden and Leicester Square, the very good **Stanfords Travel Bookstore** stocks current editions of many of my books (Mon-Fri 9:00-20:00, Sat 10:00-20:00, Sun 12:00-18:00, 12-14 Long Acre, second entrance on Floral Street, Tube: Leicester Square, tel. 020/7836-1321, www.stanfords.co.uk).

Two impressive **Waterstones** bookstores have the biggest collection of travel guides in town: on Piccadilly (Mon-Sat 9:00-22:00, Sun 11:30-18:00, Costa Café, great views from top-floor bar, 203 Piccadilly, tel. 0843-290-8549) and on Trafalgar Square (Mon-Sat 9:00-21:00, Sun 12:00-18:00, Costa Café on second floor, tel. 0843-290-8651).

Baggage Storage: Train stations have replaced lockers with more secure baggage-storage counters, known locally as "left luggage." Each bag must go through a scanner (just like at the airport), so lines can be slow. Expect long waits in the morning to check in (up to 45 minutes) and in the afternoon to pick up (each item-£8.50/24 hours, most stations daily 7:00-23:00). You can also store bags at the airports (similar rates and hours, www.excess-baggage.com). If leaving London and returning later, you may be able to store a box or bag at your hotel for free—assuming you'll be staying there again.

"Voluntary Donations": Several sights—the Tower of London, Churchill War Rooms, Kensington Palace, and the Banqueting House—automatically add a "voluntary donation" of about 10 percent to their admission fees. The price posted and quoted includes the donation, though it's perfectly fine to say you want to pay a cheaper price without the donation. If you say nothing, you'll automatically pay the donation price.

Updates to this Book: Check www.ricksteves.com/update for any

Affording London's Sights

London is one of Europe's most expensive cities, with the dubious distinction of having some of the world's steepest admission prices. Fortunately, many sights are free.

Free Museums: Many of the city's biggest and best museums won't charge you a dime, including the British Museum, British Library, National Gallery, National Portrait Gallery, Tate Britain, Tate Modern, Wallace Collection, Imperial War Museum, Victoria and Albert Museum, Natural History Museum, Science Museum, National Army Museum, Sir John Soane's Museum, the Museum of London, and the Geffrye Museum.

Free Churches: Many smaller churches let worshippers (and tourists) in free. The big sightseeing churches—Westminster Abbey and St. Paul's—charge admission fees, but offer free evensong services nearly daily (though you're not allowed to stick around afterward). Westminster Abbey also offers free organ recitals most Sundays at 17:45.

Other Freebies: London has plenty of free performances, such as lunch concerts at St. Martin-in-the-Fields (see page 719) and summertime movies at The Scoop amphitheater near City Hall (Tube: London Bridge, schedule at www.morelondon.com—click on "The Scoop at More London"). For other freebies, check out www.freelondonlistings.co.uk. There's no charge to enjoy the pageantry of the Changing of the Guard, rants at Speaker's Corner in Hyde Park, displays at Harrods, the people-watching scene at Covent Garden, and the colorful streets of the East End. It's free to view the legal action at the Old Bailey and the legislature at work in the Houses of Parliament. And you can get into a bit of the Tower of London and Windsor Castle by attending Sunday services in each place's chapel (chapel access only).

significant changes that have occurred since this book was printed.

Getting Around London

To travel smart in a city this size, you must get comfortable with public transportation. London's excellent taxis, buses, and subway (Tube) system make a car unnecessary.

The helpful *Welcome to London* brochure, produced by the mayor's office and Transport for London (TFL), includes both a Tube map and a handy schematic map of the best bus routes (available free at TFL offices—such as the one in Victoria Station, the TI, and at museums and hotels all over town). For specific directions on how to get from point A to point B on London's transit, call TFL's automated info line at 0843-222-1234.

Sightseeing Deals: If you've bought a paper rail ticket at a National Rail station (such as Paddington or Victoria), you may be eligible for two-for-one discounts at many popular sights, such as the London Eye, Tower of London, and Madame Tussauds Waxworks. This is a great deal if you can get it. To claim the discount, the rail ticket must have been used and validated that day—for instance, if you are arriving by train into London (from elsewhere in England) or taking a short morning side-trip. This even works if you're taking the train in from Gatwick Airport. Get details and print vouchers at www.daysoutguide.co.uk, or look for brochures with coupons at major train stations.

Good-Value Tours: The city walking tours with professional guides (£6-9) are one of the best deals going (see page 700). Hop-on, hop-off big-bus tours, while expensive (£22-27), provide a great overview and include free boat tours as well as city walks. (Or, for the price of a transit ticket, you could get similar views from the top of a double-decker public bus.) A one-hour Thames ride to Greenwich costs £10 one-way, but most boats come with entertaining commentary. A three-hour bicycle tour is about £20.

Theater: Compared with Broadway, London's theater is a bargain. Seek out the freestanding tkts booth at Leicester Square to get 25- to 50-percent discounts on good seats (see page 757). Buying direct at the theater box office can score you a great deal on same-day tickets, and even the most popular shows generally have some seats under £20. A £5 "groundling" ticket for a play at Shakespeare's Globe is the best theater deal in town (see page 760). Tickets to the Open Air Theatre at north London's Regent's Park start at £12 (see page 761).

LONDON

Public-Transit Passes

London has the most expensive public transit system in the world—save money on your Tube and bus rides using a multi-ride pass. You have three options: Pay double by buying individual tickets as you go; buy a £5 Oyster card and top it up as needed to travel like a local for about £1-2 per ride; or get a Travelcard for unlimited travel on either one or seven days.

The transit system has six zones. Since almost all of my recommended accommodations, restaurants, and sights are within Zones 1 and 2, those are the prices I've listed here; you'll pay more to go farther afield. Specific fares and other details change constantly; for a complete and updated list of prices, check www.tfl.gov.uk.

Individual Transit Tickets

These days in London, individual paper tickets are obsolete; there's no point buying one unless you're literally taking just one ride your entire time in the city. Because individual fares (£4.50 per Tube ride, £2.40 per bus ride) are about double the cost of using a pay-as-you-go Oyster card, in just two or three rides you'll recoup the £5 added deposit for the Oyster. If you do buy a single ticket, avoid ticket-window lines in Tube stations by using the coin-op machines; practice on the punchboard to see how the system works (hit "Adult Single" and your destination). These tickets are valid only on the day of purchase.

Oyster Cards

A pay-as-you-go Oyster card (a plastic card embedded with a computer chip) is the standard, smart way to economically ride the Tube, buses, Docklands Light Railway (DLR), and Overground. On each type of transport, you simply lay the card flat against the yellow card reader at the turnstile or entrance, it flashes green, and the fare is automatically deducted. (You'll also tap your card again to "touch out" as you exit the Tube and DLR turnstiles, but not to exit buses.)

With an Oyster card, rides cost about half the price of individual paper tickets (£2.10 or £2.80 per Tube ride—depending on time of day, £1.40 per bus ride). You buy the card itself at any Tube station ticket window for a refundable £5 deposit, then load it up with as much credit as you want. (For extra peace of mind, ask about registering your card against theft or loss.) When your balance gets low, simply add credit—or "top up"—at a ticket window or machine. (American credit cards always work at the ticketing window, but they might not at the automated top-up stations. To avoid wasting time, look for a top-up station that lets you pay either with a credit card or cash—so if your card doesn't work, you can just stick in a bill.) A price cap on the pay-as-you-go Oyster card guarantees you'll never pay more than the One-Day Travelcard price within a 24-hour period.

You can see how much credit remains on your card by touching it to the pad at any automatic ticket machine. Oyster card balances never expire (though they need reactivating at a ticket window every two years), so you can use the card whenever you're in London, or lend it to someone else.

When you're finished with the card (and if you don't mind a short wait), you should be able to reclaim your £5 deposit at any ticket window. However, to make it as easy as possible to recoup your deposit, you should always use the same mode of payment: For example, if you pay the deposit in cash, you need to top up with cash. If you pay the deposit in cash and top up with a credit card, or vice versa, it can be more difficult (or impossible) to get your deposit back.

Transfers: You can change from one Tube line to another on the same Oyster journey (as long as you don't leave the station); however, if you change between buses, or change between bus and Tube, you'll pay a new fare.

Travelcards

Like the Oyster card, Travelcards are valid on the Tube, buses, Docklands Light Railway (DLR), and Overground. The difference is that Travelcards let you ride as many times as you want within a one- or a seven-day period, for one fixed price.

Before you buy a card, estimate where you'll be going; there's a card for Zones 1 and 2, and another for Zones 1-6 (which includes Heathrow Airport). If Heathrow is the only ride you're taking outside Zones 1-2 (which is likely), you can pay a small supplement to make the Zones 1-2 Travelcard stretch to cover that one ride.

The **One-Day Travelcard** gives you unlimited travel for a day (Zones 1-2: £8.80, off-peak version £7.30; Zones 1-6: £16.40, off-peak version £8.90; off-peak cards are good for travel after 9:30 on weekdays and anytime on weekends). This Travelcard works like a traditional paper ticket: Buy it at any Tube station ticket window or machine, then feed it into a turnstile (and retrieve it) to enter and exit the Tube. On a bus, just show it to the driver when you get on.

The **Seven-Day Travelcard** is a great option if you're staying four or more days and plan to use the buses and Tube a lot. It's actually issued on a plastic Oyster card, but gives you unlimited travel anytime, anywhere in Zones 1 and 2 for a week (£30.40 plus the refundable £5 deposit for the Oyster card). As with an Oyster card, you'll touch it to the yellow pad when entering or exiting a Tube turnstile, or when boarding a bus.

The Bottom Line

Struggling to choose which pass works best for your trip? First of all, skip the individual tickets. On a short visit (three days or fewer), if you think you'll be zipping around a lot, consider a One-Day Travelcard for each day you're here (or at least for your busiest days); if you'll be taking fewer, more focused rides, get an Oyster card and pay as you go. If you're in London four days or longer, the Seven-Day Travelcard will likely pay for itself.

By Tube

London's subway system is called the Tube or Underground (but never "subway," which, in Britain, refers to a pedestrian underpass). The Tube is one of this planet's great people-movers and often the fastest long-distance transport in town (runs Mon-Sat about

LONDON

5:00-24:00, Sun about 7:00-23:00). Two other commuter rail lines, while technically not part of the Tube, are tied into the network and use the same tickets: The Docklands Light Railway (called DLR, runs to the Docklands, 2012 Olympics site, and Greenwich) and the Overground.

Get your bearings by studying a map of the system (free at any station).

Each line has a name (such as Circle, Northern, or Bakerloo) and two directions (indicated by the end-of-the-line stops). Find the line that will take you to your destination, and figure out roughly which direction (north, south, east, or west) you'll need to go to get there.

You can use an Oyster card, Travelcard, or individual tickets (all explained earlier) to pay for your journey. At the Tube station, touch your Oyster card flat against the turnstile's yellow card reader, both when you enter and exit the station. If you have a regular paper ticket or a One-Day Travelcard, feed it into the turnstile, reclaim it, and hang on to it—you'll need it later.

Find your train by following signs to your line and the (general) direction it's headed (such as Central Line: east). Since some tracks are shared by several lines, double-check before boarding a train: First, make sure your destination is one of the stops listed on the sign at the platform. Also, check the electronic signboards that announce which train is next, and make sure the destination (the end-of-the-line stop) is the direction you want. Some trains, particularly on the Circle and District lines, split off for other directions, but each train has its final destination marked above its windshield.

Trains run roughly every 3-10 minutes. If one train is absolutely packed and you notice another to the same destination is coming in three minutes, wait to avoid the sardine routine. Rush hours (8:00-10:00 and 16:00-19:00) can be packed and sweaty. Bring something to do to make your waiting time productive. If you get confused, ask for advice from a local, a blue-vested staff person, or at the information window located before the turnstile entry.

At most stations, you can't leave the system without touching your Oyster card to an electronic reader, or feeding your ticket or One-Day Travelcard into the turnstile. (If you have a single-trip paper ticket, the turnstile will eat your now-expired ticket; if it's a One-Day Travelcard, it will spit out your still-valid card.) Some stations, such as Hampton Court, do not have a turnstile, so you'll have to locate a reader to "touch out" your Oyster card. If you skip this step and leave the station, the system assumes you've ridden to the most remote station, and the highest fare will be deducted from your card. When leaving a station, save walking time by choosing the best street exit—check the maps on the walls or ask any station personnel.

The system can be fraught with construction delays and breakdowns (the Circle Line is notorious for problems). Most construction is scheduled for weekends. Closures are known and publicized in advance (online at www.tfl.gov.uk and with posters in the Tube; Google Maps also has real-time service alerts for the Tube). Pay attention to signs and announcements explaining necessary detours. Closed Tube lines are often replaced by temporary bus service, but it can be faster to figure out alternate routes on the Tube; since the lines cross each other constantly, there are several ways to make any journey. For help, check out the "Journey Planner" at www.tfl.gov.uk.

By Bus

If you figure out the bus system, you'll easily conquer sprawling London. Pick up a free bus map; the most user-friendly is in the *Welcome to London* brochure (mentioned earlier). You can also find thicker, more in-depth maps of various sectors of the city (most useful is the Central London Bus Guide). Bus maps are available at Transport for London offices, the City of London TI, and other tourist spots around town. With a mobile phone, you can find out the arrival time of the next bus by texting your bus stop's five-digit code (posted at the stop, above the timetable) to 87287 (if you're using your US phone's SIM card, text the code to 011-44-7797-800-287).

Buses are covered by Travelcards and Oyster cards. You can also buy individual tickets from a machine at bus stops (no change given), but you can't buy tickets on board. Any bus ride in downtown London costs £2.40 for those paying cash, or £1.40 if using an Oyster card (with a cap of £4.40 per day). If you're staying longer, consider the £19.60 Seven-Day bus pass.

The first step in mastering London's bus system is learning how to decipher the bus stop signs. In the first column, find your destination on the list—e.g., Paddington. In the next column, find a bus that goes there—the #23. The final column has a letter within a circle (e.g., "H") that tells you exactly which bus stop you need to stand at to catch your bus. (You'll find the same letter marked on a neighborhood map nearby.) Make your way to that stop—you'll know it's yours because it will have the same letter on its pole—and wait for the bus with your number on it to arrive. Hop on, and you're good to go.

As you board, touch your Oyster card to the electronic card reader, or, if you have a paper ticket or a One-Day Travelcard, show it to the driver. On "Heritage Routes" #9 and #15 (some of which use older double-decker buses), you may still pay a conductor; take

LONDON

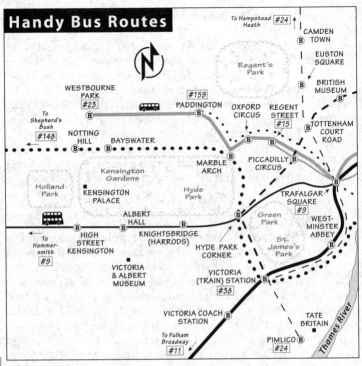

Handy Bus Routes

a seat, and he or she will come around to collect your fare or verify your pass. There's no need to tap your card or show your ticket when you hop off.

If you have an Oyster card or Travelcard, save your feet and get in the habit of hopping buses for quick little straight shots, even just to get to a Tube stop. During bump-and-grind rush hours (8:00-10:00 and 16:00-19:00), you'll usually go faster by Tube.

By Taxi

London is the best taxi town in Europe. Big, black, carefully regulated cabs are everywhere. (While historically known as "black cabs," some of London's official taxis are now covered with wildly colored ads.) Some cabs now run on biofuels—a good way to dispose of all that oil used to fry fish-and-chips.

I've never met a crabby cabbie in London. They love to talk, and they know every nook and cranny in town. I ride in a taxi each day just to get my London questions answered (drivers must pass a rigorous test on "The Knowledge" of London geography to earn their license).

If a cab's top light is on, just wave it down. Drivers flash lights when they see you wave. They have a tight turning radius (on new

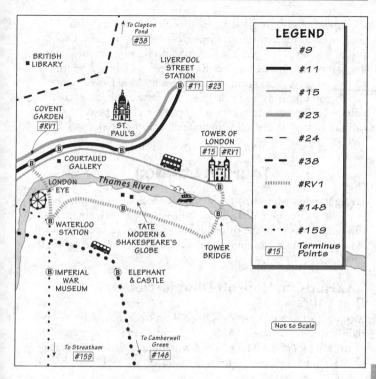

LEGEND

——	#9
▬▬	#11
——	#15
▬▬	#23
– –	#24
– –	#38
⋯⋯	#RV1
•••	#148
• • •	#159
#15	Terminus Points

To Clapton Pond #38

BRITISH LIBRARY

LIVERPOOL STREET STATION

B #11 #23

COVENT GARDEN #RV1

ST. PAUL'S

TOWER OF LONDON #15 #RV1

COURTAULD GALLERY

Thames River

LONDON EYE

WATERLOO STATION

TATE MODERN & SHAKESPEARE'S GLOBE

TOWER BRIDGE

IMPERIAL WAR MUSEUM

ELEPHANT & CASTLE

To Streatham #159

To Camberwell Green #148

Not to Scale

cabs, the back tires actually pivot), so you can hail cabs going in either direction. If waving doesn't work, ask someone where you can find a taxi stand. Telephoning a cab will get you one in a few minutes, but costs a little more (tel. 0871-871-8710; £2 surcharge, plus extra fee to book ahead by credit card).

Rides start at £2.40. The regular tariff #1 covers most of the day (Mon-Fri 6:00-20:00), tariff #2 is during "unsociable hours" (Mon-Fri 20:00-22:00 and Sat-Sun 6:00-22:00), and tariff #3 is for nights (22:00-6:00) and holidays. Rates go up about 15-20 percent with each higher tariff. All extra charges are explained in writing on the cab wall. Tip a cabbie by rounding up (maximum 10 percent).

Connecting downtown sights is quick and easy, and will cost you about £6-8 (for example, St. Paul's to the Tower of London, or between the two Tate museums). For a short ride, three adults in a cab generally travel at close to Tube prices—and groups of four or five adults should taxi everywhere. All cabs can carry five passengers, and some take six, for the same cost as a single traveler.

Don't worry about meter cheating. Licensed British cab meters come with a sealed computer chip and clock that ensures you'll get the correct tariff. The only way a cabbie can cheat you is by taking a needlessly long route. Another pitfall is taking a cab when traffic is bad to a destination efficiently served by the Tube. On one trip to London, I hopped in a taxi at South Kensington for Waterloo Station and hit bad traffic. Rather than spending 20 minutes and £2 on the Tube, I spent 40 minutes and £16 in a taxi.

If you overdrink and ride in a taxi, be warned: Taxis charge £40 for "soiling" (a.k.a., pub puke). If you forget this book in a taxi, call the Lost Property office and hope for the best (tel. 0845-330-9882).

Tours in London

To sightsee on your own, download my series of free audio tours that illuminate some of London's top sights and neighborhoods: the British Museum, the British Library, St. Paul's Cathedral, and my walks around Westminster and The City (see sidebar on page 7 for details).

▲▲▲Hop-on, Hop-off Double-Decker Bus Tours

Two competitive companies (Original and Big Bus) offer essentially the same two tours of the city's sightseeing highlights, with nearly 30 stops on each route. Big Bus tours are a little more expensive (£27), while Original tours are cheaper (£22 with this book) and nearly as good.

These two-to-three hour, once-over-lightly bus tours drive by all the famous sights, providing a stress-free way to get your bearings and see the biggies. They stop at the same core group of sights regardless of which overview tour you're on: Piccadilly Circus, Trafalgar Square, Big Ben, St. Paul's, the Tower of London, Marble Arch, Victoria Station, and elsewhere. With a good guide and nice weather, I'd sit back and enjoy the entire tour. (If you don't like your guide, you can hop off and try your luck with the next departure.)

Each company offers at least one route with live (English-only) guides, and a second (sometimes slightly different route) comes with recorded, dial-a-language narration. In addition to the overview tours, both Original and Big Bus include the Thames River boat trip by City Cruises (between Westminster and the Tower of London) and three 1.5-hour walking tours.

Pick up a map from any flier rack or from one of the countless salespeople, and study the complex system. Sunday morning—when the traffic is light and many museums are closed—is a fine time for a tour. Unless you're using the bus tour mainly for hop-on, hop-off transportation, consider saving time and money by taking a night tour (described on the next page).

Buses run about every 10-15 minutes in summer, every 10-20 minutes in winter, and operate daily. They start at about 8:30 and run until early evening in summer or late afternoon in winter. The last full loop usually leaves Victoria Station at about 19:00 in summer, and at about 17:00 in winter (confirm by checking the schedule or asking the driver).

You can buy tickets from drivers or from staff at street kiosks (credit cards accepted at kiosks at major stops such as Victoria Station, ticket good for 24 hours).

Original London Sightseeing Bus Tour

They offer two versions of their basic highlights loop: **The Original Tour** (live guide, marked with a yellow triangle on the front of the bus) and the **City Sightseeing Tour** (essentially the same route but with recorded narration, a kids' soundtrack option, and a stop at Madame Tussauds; bus marked with a red triangle). Other routes include the blue-triangle **Museum Tour** (connecting far-flung museums and major shopping stops), and green, black, and purple triangle routes (linking major train stations to the central route). All routes are covered by the same ticket. Keep it simple and just take one of the city highlights tours (£26, £22 with this book, limit four discounts per book, they'll rip off the corner of this page—raise bloody hell if the staff or driver won't honor this discount; also online deals, info center at 17 Cockspur Street, tel. 020/8877-1722, www.theoriginaltour.com).

Big Bus London Tours

For £29 (up to 30 percent discount online—requires printer), you get the same basic overview tours: Red buses come with a live guide, while the blue route has a recorded narration and a one-hour longer path that goes around Hyde Park. These pricier Big Bus tours tend to have better, more dynamic guides than the Original tours, and more departures as well—meaning shorter waits for those hopping on and off (daily 8:30-18:00, winter until 16:30, info center at 48 Buckingham Palace Road, tel. 020/7233-9533, www.bigbustours.com).

London by Night Sightseeing Tour

This tour offers a 1.5-hour circuit, but after hours, with no extras (e.g., walks, river cruises), and at a lower price. While the narration can be pretty lame, the views at twilight are grand—though note that it stays light until late on summer nights, and London just doesn't do floodlighting as well as, say, Paris (£19, £15 online). From June through late September, open-top buses depart at 19:00, 20:00, 20:45, 21:30, 22:10, and 22:55 from Victoria Station (Jan-May and late Sept-late Dec departs at 19:00, 20:45, and 22:10 only with closed-top bus, no tours between Christmas and New Year). Buses leave from near Victoria Station (in front of Grosvenor Hotel on Buckingham Palace Road; or you can board at any stop, such as

Marble Arch, Trafalgar Square, London Eye, or Tower of London; tel. 020/8545-6110, www.london-by-night.net). For a memorable and economical evening, munch a scenic picnic dinner on the top deck. (There are plenty of take-away options within the train stations and near the various stops.)

▲▲Walking Tours

Several times a day, top-notch local guides lead (sometimes big) groups through specific slices of London's past. Look for brochures at TIs or ask at hotels, although the latter usually push higher-priced bus tours. *Time Out*, the weekly entertainment guide, lists some, but not all, scheduled walks. Check with the various tour companies by phone or online to get their full picture.

To take a walking tour, simply show up at the announced location and pay the guide. Then enjoy two chatty hours of Dickens, Harry Potter, the Plague, Shakespeare, Legal London, the Beatles, Jack the Ripper, or whatever is on the agenda.

Essential London Walk

Blue Badge Tourist Guides offer their basic two-hour Essential London walk to Rick Steves readers for £6 (otherwise £9, tours depart 365 days a year at 10:00 from the Eros statue on Piccadilly Circus—look for the guide with the Blue Badge umbrella, www.guidelondon.org.uk). Tours go rain or shine, and there's no need to pre-book—just show up. With the discount, this is the best deal going, as you know you'll get a well-trained guide leading you through the historic core of London (from Piccadilly, you walk to Trafalgar Square, Whitehall, Westminster Abbey, the Houses of Parliament, and the Thames, and end at Buckingham Palace—just in time for the last part of the Changing of the Guard).

London Walks

This leading company lists its extensive and creative daily schedule on their website, as well as in a beefy, plain *London Walks* brochure (available at hotels, St. Martin-in-the-Fields' Café in the Crypt on Trafalgar Square, and the City of London TI). Just perusing their fascinating lineup of tours inspires me to stay longer in London. Their two-hour walks, led by top-quality professional guides (ranging from archaeologists to actors), cost £9 (cash only, walks offered year-round, private tours for groups-£130, tel. 020/7624-3978 for a live person, tel. 020/7624-9255 for a recording of today's or tomorrow's walks and the Tube station they depart from, www.walks.com).

London Walks also offers day trips into the countryside, a good option for those with limited time and transportation (£12-16 plus £10-50 for transportation and any admission costs, cash only: Stonehenge/Salisbury, Oxford/Cotswolds, Cambridge, Bath, and so on). These are economical in part because everyone gets group discounts for transportation and admissions.

Sandemans New London "Free Royal London Tour"

This company employs students (rather than licensed guides) who recite three-hour spiels covering the basic London sights. While the fast-moving, youthful tours are light and irreverent, and can be both entertaining and fun, it's misleading to call the tours "free," as tips are expected (the guides actually pay the company for the privilege of asking for tips). With the Essential London Walk (listed earlier) offered daily at a reasonable price by professional Blue Badge guides, taking this "free" tour makes no sense to me (daily at 11:00 and 13:00, meet at Wellington Arch, Tube: Hyde Park Corner, Exit 2). Sandemans also has other guided tours for a charge, including a Pub Crawl (£20, nightly at 19:30, meet at Verve Bar at 1 Upper St. Martin's Lane, Tube: Leicester Square, www. newlondon-tours.com).

Beatles Walks

Fans of the still-Fab Four can take one of three Beatles walks (London Walks has two that run 5 days/week; Big Bus includes a daily walk with their bus tour; both listed earlier).

Jack the Ripper Walks

Each walking tour company seems to make most of its money with "haunted" and Jack the Ripper tours. Many guides are historians and would rather not lead these lightweight tours—but, in tourism as in journalism, "if it bleeds, it leads" (which is why the juvenile London Dungeon is one of the city's busiest sights).

Two reliably good two-hour tours start every night at the Tower Hill Tube station exit. **London Walks'** leave nightly at 19:30 (£9, pay at the start, tel. 020/7624-3978, recorded info tel. 020/7624-9255, www.jacktheripperwalk.com). **Ripping Yarns**, which leaves earlier, is guided by off-duty Yeoman Warders—the Tower of London "Beefeaters" (£7, pay at end, nightly at 18:45, no tours between Christmas and New Year, mobile 07813-559-301, www.jack-the-ripper-tours.com). After taking both, I found the London Walks tour more entertaining, informative, and with a better route (along quieter, once-hooker-friendly lanes, with less traffic), starting at Tower Hill and ending at Liverpool Street Station rather than returning to Tower Hill. Groups can be huge for both, but there's always room—just show up.

Private Walks with Local Guides

Standard rates for London's registered Blue Badge guides are about £140-165 for four hours and £225 or more for nine hours (tel. 020/7611-2545, www.guidelondon.org.uk or www.britainsbest-guides.org). I know and like four fine local guides: **Sean Kelleher** (tel. 020/8673-1624, mobile 07764-612-770, seankelleher@btinternet.com), **Britt Lonsdale** (£190/half-day, £290/day, great with families, tel. 020/7386-9907, mobile 07813-278-077, brittl@btinternet.com), and two others who work in London when they're

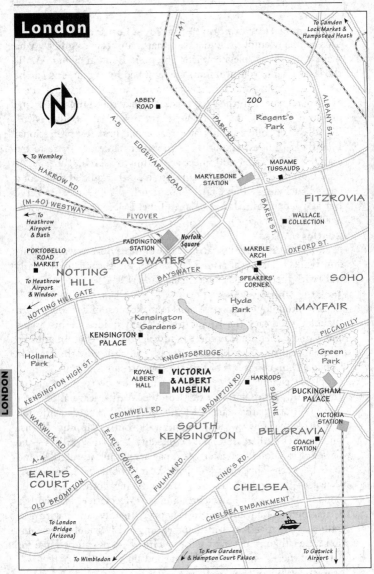

not on the road leading my Britain tours, **Tom Hooper** (mobile 07986-048-047, tomh@ricksteves.net) and **Gillian Chadwick** (mobile 07889-976-598, gillianc@ricksteves.net).

Driver-Guides

These two guides have cars or a minibus (particularly helpful for travelers with limited mobility): **Robina Brown** (£310/half-day, £455/day, tel. 020/7228-2238, www.driverguidetours.com, robina@driverguidetours.com) and **Janine Barton** (£350/half-day,

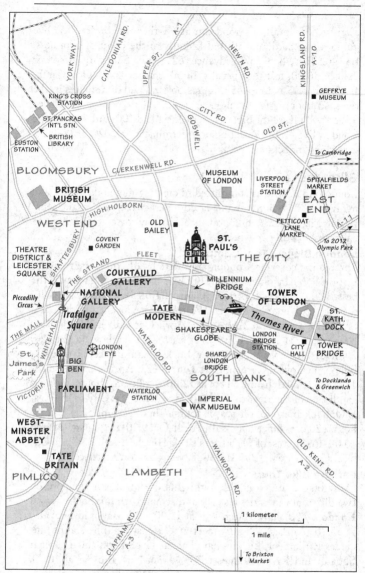

£450/day within London, £550 outside London, tel. 020/7402-4600, http://seeitinstyle.synthasite.com, jbsiis@aol.com).

London Duck Tours

A bright-yellow amphibious WWII-vintage vehicle (the model that landed troops on Normandy's beaches on D-Day) takes a gang of 30 tourists past some famous sights on land—Big Ben, Trafalgar Square, Piccadilly Circus—then splashes into the Thames for a cruise. All in all, it's good fun at a rather steep price. The live guide works hard, and it's kid-friendly to the point of goofiness. Beware: These book up in advance (£21, April-Sept daily, first tour 9:30 or 10:00, last tour usually 18:00, shorter hours Oct-March, 1-4/hour, 1.25 hours—45 minutes on land and 30 minutes in the river, £3 booking fee by phone or online, departs from Chicheley Street—you'll see the big, ugly vehicle parked 100 yards behind the London Eye, Tube: Waterloo or Westminster, tel. 020/7928-3132, www.londonducktours.co.uk).

Bike Tours

London, like Paris, is committed to creating more bike paths, and many of its best sights can be laced together with a pleasant pedal through its parks. A bike tour is a fun way to see the sights and enjoy the city on two wheels.

London Bicycle Tour Company

Three tours covering London are offered daily from their base at Gabriel's Wharf on the South Bank of the Thames. Sunday is the best, as there is less car traffic (**Central Tour**—£19, daily at 10:30, 6 miles, 2.5 hours, includes Westminster, Covent Garden, and St. Paul's; **West End Tour**—£19, April-Oct daily at 14:30, Nov-March daily at 12:00 as long as at least 4 people show up, 7 miles, 2.5 hours, includes Westminster, Buckingham Palace, Hyde Park, Soho, and Covent Garden; **East Tour**—£22, April-Oct Sat-Sun at 14:00, Nov-March only on Sat at 12:00, 9 miles, 3.5 hours, includes south side of the river to Tower Bridge, then The City to the East End; book ahead for off-season tours). They also rent bikes (£3.50/hour, £20/day; office open daily April-Oct 9:30-18:00, Nov-March 10:00-16:00, west of Blackfriars Bridge on the South Bank, 1a Gabriel's Wharf, tel. 020/3318-3088, www.londonbicycle.com).

Fat Tire Bike Tours

Daily bike tours cover the highlights of downtown London, on two different itineraries (ask about discount with this book): **Royal London** (£20, daily March-Nov at 11:00, mid-May-mid-Sept also at 15:30, 7 miles, 4 hours, meet at Queensway Tube station; includes Parliament, Buckingham Palace, Hyde Park, and Trafalgar Square) and **River Thames** (£30, March-Nov Thu-Sat at 10:30, nearly daily in summer, 5 hours, meet at Waterloo Tube station—exit 2; includes London Eye, St. Paul's, Tower of London, Trafalgar Square, Covent Garden, and boat trip on the Thames). The spiel is light and irreverent rather than scholarly, but the price is right. Reservations are easy online, and required for River Thames tours and kids' bikes (off-season tours can be arranged, mobile 078-8233-8779, www.fattirebiketourslondon.com). Confirm the schedule online or by phone.

Weekend Tour Packages for Students in London

Andy Steves (my son) runs **Weekend Student Adventures**, offering active and experiential three-day weekend tours for €199 designed for American students studying abroad (see www.wsaeurope.com for details on tours of London and other great European cities).

▲▲Cruises

Boat tours with entertaining commentaries sail regularly from many points along the Thames. The options are plentiful, with several companies offering essentially the same trip. Your basic options are to use the boats either for a scenic joyride cruise within the city center, or for transportation to an outlying sight (such as Greenwich or Kew Gardens).

Boats come and go from several docks in the city center. The most popular places to embark are Westminster Pier (at the base of Westminster Bridge across the street from Big Ben) and Waterloo Pier (at the London Eye, across the river).

Buy boat tickets at the kiosks on the docks. If you'd like to compare your options in one spot, head to Westminster Pier, where all of the big outfits have ticket kiosks. While individual Tube and bus tickets don't work on the boats, a Travelcard can snare you a 33 percent discount on most cruises (just show the card when you pay for the cruise; no discount with the pay-as-you-go Oyster card except on Thames Clippers). Because different companies vary in the discounts they offer, always ask. Children and seniors generally get discounts. You can purchase drinks and scant, pricey snacks on board. Clever budget travelers pack a picnic and munch while they cruise.

Round-trip fares are only a bit more than one-way. Still, for pleasure and efficiency, consider combining a one-way cruise (to Kew, Greenwich, or wherever) with a Tube or train ride back.

Tourist-Oriented Cruises in the City Center

London offers many made-for-tourist cruises, most on slow-moving, open-top boats accompanied by commentary about passing sights.

City Cruises runs boats from Westminster Pier across the river to Waterloo Pier, then downriver to Tower Pier and on to Greenwich (tel. 020/7740-0400, www.citycruises.com). If you want just a sample, hop on their 30-minute cruise only as far as Tower Pier (£9 one-way, £10.50 round-trip, daily April-Oct roughly 10:00-19:00, until 21:00 in mid-July-mid-Sept, until 18:00 in winter, 2/hour). City Cruises also offers a £15.50 River Red Rover ticket good for all-day hop-on, hop-off travel—though the line's limited stops in the city center make this a lesser deal than it might seem.

Thames River Services runs a similar trip with even fewer stops: Westminster to St. Katharine's Pier to Greenwich (tel. 020/7930-4097, www.thamesriverservices.co.uk). They have classic boats and feel a little friendlier and more old-fashioned.

The **Circular Cruise** offered by Crown River Services is a handy hop-on, hop-off route with stops at the Westminster, Festival, Embankment, Bankside, London Bridge, and St. Katharine's piers (£3 to go one stop, £8.50 one-way for a longer trip, £11 round-trip, daily 11:00-18:30, every 30 minutes late May-early Sept, fewer stops and less frequent off-season, tel. 020/7936-2033, www.crownriver.com).

The **London Eye** operates its own river cruise, offering a 40-minute live-guided circular tour from Waterloo Pier. As it's much pricier than the alternatives for just a short loop, it's a poor value (£12.50, reservations recommended, 10 percent discount if you pre-book online, no Travelcard discounts, departures daily generally at :45 past the hour, April-Oct 10:45-18:45, Nov-March 11:45-16:45, closed mid-Jan-mid-Feb, tel. 0870-500-0600, www.londoneye.com).

Careening at Top Speed Along the Thames: Two competing companies invite you aboard a small, 12-person, high-speed rigid inflatable boat (RIB—similar to a Zodiac) for an adrenaline-fueled tour of the city (London RIB Voyages: stand-up comedian guides, £42/50 minutes, £49/1.25 hours, tel. 020/7928-8933, www.londonribvoyages.com; Thames RIB Experience: £34/50 minutes, £48/1.25 hours, tel. 020/7930-5746, www.thamesribexperience.com).

Away from the Thames, on Regent's Canal: Consider exploring London's canals by taking a cruise on historic Regent's Canal in north London. The good ship *Jenny Wren* offers 1.5-hour guided canal boat cruises from Walker's Quay in Camden Town through scenic Regent's Park to Little Venice (£9.50; Aug daily at 10:30, 12:30, and 16:30, Sat-Sun also at 14:30; April-July and Sept-Oct daily at 12:30 and 14:30, Sat-Sun also at 16:30; Walker's Quay, 250 Camden High Street, 3-minute walk from Tube: Camden Town; tel. 020/7485-4433, www.walkersquay.com). While in Camden Town, stop by the popular, punky Camden Lock Market to browse through trendy arts and crafts (daily 10:00-18:00, busiest on weekends, a block from Walker's Quay, www.camdenlockmarket.com).

Commuting by Clipper

Thames Clippers, which uses fast, sleek, 220-seat catamarans, is designed for commuters rather than sightseers. Think of the boats as express buses on the river—they zip no-nonsense through London every 20-30 minutes, stopping at most of the major docks en route: Embankment, Waterloo/London Eye, Blackfriars or Bankside, London Bridge, Tower, Canary Wharf (Docklands), and Greenwich (roughly 20 minutes from Embankment to Tower, 10 more minutes to Docklands, 10 more minutes to Greenwich). However, the boats are less pleasant for joyriding than the cruises described earlier, with no commentary and no open deck up top (the only outside access is on a crowded deck at the exhaust-choked back of the boat, where you're jostling for space to take photos). Any one-way ride costs £6, and a River Roamer all-day ticket costs £13.60 (33 percent discount with Travelcard, 10 percent off with a pay-as-you-go Oyster card, tel. 020/7001-2222, www.thamesclippers.com).

Thames Clippers also offers two express trips. The **Tate Boat** ferry service, which directly connects the Tate Britain (Millbank Pier) and the Tate Modern (Bankside Pier), is made for art-lovers (£6 one-way, covered by £13.60 River Roamer day ticket; buy ticket at gallery desk or on board; for frequency and times, see the Tate Britain and Tate Modern listings, later, or www.tate.org.uk/visit/tate-boat). The **O2 Express** runs only on nights when there are events going on at the O2 arena; from Waterloo Pier, £7 one-way, £14 round-trip, 30 minutes).

Cruising Upstream, to Kew Gardens

Boats operated by the Westminster Passenger Services Association leave for Kew Gardens from Westminster Pier (£12 one-way, £18 round-trip, cash only; 4/day, April-Oct daily at 10:30, 11:15, 12:00, and 14:00; 1.5 hours, about half the trip is narrated, tel. 020/7930-2062, www.wpsa.co.uk). Romantic as these rides sound, it can be a long trip.

Self-Guided Walk

Westminster Walk

Just about every visitor to London strolls along historic Whitehall from Big Ben to Trafalgar Square. This walk gives meaning to that touristy ramble (most of the sights you'll see are described in more detail later). Under London's modern traffic and big-city bustle lie 2,000 fascinating years of history. You'll get a whirlwind tour as well as a practical orientation to London. (You can download a free, extended Rick Steves audio version of this walk; see page 7.)

Start halfway across ❶ **Westminster Bridge** for that "Wow, I'm really in London!" feeling. Get a close-up view of the **Houses of Parliament** and **Big Ben** (floodlit at night). Downstream you'll

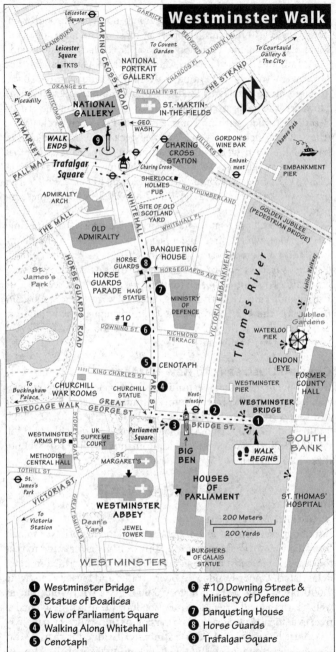

Westminster Walk

1 Westminster Bridge

2 Statue of Boadicea

3 View of Parliament Square

4 Walking Along Whitehall

5 Cenotaph

6 #10 Downing Street & Ministry of Defence

7 Banqueting House

8 Horse Guards

9 Trafalgar Square

see the **London Eye.** Down the stairs to Westminster Pier are boats to the Tower of London and Greenwich (downstream) or Kew Gardens (upstream).

En route to Parliament Square, you'll pass a ❷ **statue of Boadicea,** the Celtic queen defeated by Roman invaders in A.D. 60.

For fun, call home from near Big Ben at about three minutes before the hour to let your loved one hear the bell ring. You'll find four red phone booths lining the north side of ❸ **Parliament Square** along Great George Street—also great for a phone-box-and-Big-Ben photo op.

Wave hello to Winston Churchill and Nelson Mandela in Parliament Square. To Churchill's right is **Westminster Abbey,** with its two stubby, elegant towers. The white building (flying the Union Jack) at the far end of the square houses Britain's new **Supreme Court.**

Head north up Parliament Street, which turns into ❹ **Whitehall,** and walk toward Trafalgar Square. You'll see the thought-provoking ❺ **Cenotaph** in the middle of the boulevard, reminding passersby of the many Brits who died in the last century's world wars. To visit the **Churchill War Rooms,** take a left before the Cenotaph, on King Charles Street.

Continuing on Whitehall, stop at the barricaded and guarded ❻ **#10 Downing Street** to see the British "White House," home of the prime minister. Break the bobby's boredom and ask him a question. The huge building across Whitehall from Downing Street is the **Ministry of Defence** (MOD), the "British Pentagon."

Nearing Trafalgar Square, look for the 17th-century ❼ **Banqueting House** across the street and the ❽ **Horse Guards** behind the gated fence.

The column topped by Lord Nelson marks ❾ **Trafalgar Square**. The stately domed building on the far side of the square is the **National Gallery,** which has a classy café in the Sainsbury wing. To the right of the National Gallery is **St. Martin-in-the-Fields Church** and its Café in the Crypt.

To get to Piccadilly from Trafalgar Square, walk up Cockspur Street to Haymarket, then take a short left on Coventry Street to colorful **Piccadilly Circus** (see map on page 722).

Near Piccadilly, you'll find a number of theaters. **Leicester Square** (with its half-price "tkts" booth for plays—see page 757) thrives just a few blocks away. Walk through seedy **Soho** (north of Shaftesbury Avenue) for its fun pubs. From Piccadilly or Oxford Circus, you can take a taxi, bus, or the Tube home.

Sights in Central London

Westminster

These sights are listed roughly in geographical order from Westminster Abbey to Trafalgar Square, and are linked by my self-guided Westminster Walk, above.

▲▲▲Westminster Abbey

The greatest church in the English-speaking world, Westminster Abbey is the place where England's kings and queens have been crowned and buried since 1066. Like a stony refugee camp huddled outside St. Peter's Pearly Gates, Westminster Abbey has many stories to tell. The steep admission includes an excellent audioguide—worthwhile if you have the time and interest. To experience the church more vividly, take a live tour, or attend evensong or an organ concert (see next page).

Two tiny **museums** ring the cloisters. The Chapter House, where the monks had daily meetings, features fine architecture and stained glass with faded but well-described medieval art. The Abbey Museum has exhibits on royal coronations, funerals, Abbey history, a close-up look at medieval stained glass, and replicas of the crown jewels used for coronation practice. Look into the impressively realistic eyes of Elizabeth I, Charles II, Admiral Nelson, and a dozen others, part of a compelling series of wax-and-wood statues that, for three centuries, graced coffins during funeral processions.

Cost and Hours: £16, £32 family ticket (covers 2 adults and 1 child), cash or credit cards accepted (line up in the correct queue to pay), ticket includes audioguide and entry to cloisters and Abbey Museum; abbey—Mon-Fri 9:30-16:30, Wed until 19:00 (main church only), Sat 9:30-14:30, last entry one hour before closing, closed Sun to sightseers but open for services; museum—daily 10:30-16:00; cloisters—daily 8:00-18:00; no photos, café in solarium, Tube: Westminster or St. James's Park, tel. 020/7654-4834, www.westminster-abbey.org. It's free to enter just the cloisters and Abbey Museum (through Dean's Yard, around the right side as you face the main entrance), but if it's too crowded inside, the marshal at the cloister entrance may not let you in.

When to Go: The place is most crowded every day at mid-morning and on Saturdays and Mondays. Visit early, during lunch, or late to avoid tourist hordes. Weekdays after 14:30 are less congested; come after that time and stay for the 17:00 evensong. The main entrance, on the Parliament Square side, often has a sizable line. Of the two queues (cash or credit) at the admissions desk, the cash line is probably moving faster.

Music and Services: Mon-Fri at 7:30 (prayer), 8:00 (communion), 12:30 (communion), 17:00 evensong (except on Wed, when the evening service is generally spoken—not sung); Sat at 8:00 (communion), 9:00 (prayer), 15:00 (evensong; June-Sept it's at 17:00); Sun services have more music: at 8:00 (communion), 10:00 (sung Matins), 11:15 (sung Eucharist), 15:00 (evensong), 18:30 (evening service). Services are free to anyone, though visitors who haven't paid church admission aren't allowed to linger afterward. Free organ recitals are usually held Sun at 17:45 (30 minutes). For a schedule of services or recitals on a particular day, look for posted signs with schedules or check the Abbey's website.

▲▲Houses of Parliament (Palace of Westminster)

This Neo-Gothic icon of London, the royal residence from 1042 to 1547, is now the meeting place of the legislative branch of government. The Houses of Parliament are located in what was once the Palace of Westminster—long the palace of England's medieval kings—until it was largely destroyed by fire in 1834. The palace was rebuilt in the Victorian Gothic style (a move away from Neo-classicism back to England's Christian and medieval heritage, true to the Romantic Age) and completed in 1860.

Visitors are welcome to view debates in either the bickering House of Commons or the genteel House of Lords. You're only allowed inside when Parliament is in session, indicated by a flag flying atop the Victoria Tower, at the south end of the building (generally Mondays through Thursdays). This isn't really intended as a tourist attraction—it's about letting British citizens observe their leaders at work. Though the actual debates are generally quite dull, it's still a thrill to be inside and see the British government inaction. If you're more interested in the building than the proceedings, join a guided tour (see below).

Cost and Hours: Free, both Houses open to visitors Mon-Tue 14:30-22:30, Wed 11:30-22:00, Thu 10:30-19:00, these are longest possible hours—often closes earlier with no notice, closed Fri-Sun and most of Aug-Sept, less action and no lines after 18:00, Tube: Westminster, tel. 020/7219-4272, see www.parliament.uk for schedule.

Tours: Though Parliament is in recess during much of August and September, you can get a behind-the-scenes peek at the royal chambers of both houses during these months with a tour (£15, 1.25 hours, generally Mon-Sat, times vary, so confirm in advance; book ahead through www.ticketmaster.co.uk). The same tours are offered Saturdays year-round.

Visiting the Houses of Parliament (HOP): Enter the venerable HOP midway along the west side of the building (across the street from Westminster Abbey) through the Visitor Entrance (with the tourist ramp, next to the St. Stephen's Entrance—if lost, ask a guard). As you enter, you'll be asked if you want to visit the House of Commons or the House of Lords. The House of Lords has more pageantry, shorter lines, but less lively debates (tel. 020/7219-3107 for schedule, visit www.parliamentlive.tv for a preview). Inquire about the wait—an hour or two is not unusual. If there's a long line for the House of Commons and you just want a quick look inside the grand halls of this majestic building, start with the House of Lords. Once inside, you can switch if you like. If you have questions, ask one of the attendants (wearing yellow ties).

Just past security (where you'll be photographed and given a badge to wear around your neck), you enter the vast and historic **Westminster Hall,** which survived the 1834 fire. The cavernous hall was built in the 11th century, and its famous self-supporting hammer-beam roof was added in 1397. Racks of brochures here explain how the British government works, and plaques describe the hall. The Jubilee Café, open to the public, has live video feeds showing exactly what's going on in each house. Just seeing the café video is a fun experience (and can help you decide which house—if either—you'd like to see). Walking through the hall and up the stairs, you'll enter the busy world of government with all its high-powered goings-on.

Jewel Tower: Across the street from the Parliament building's St. Stephen's Gate, the Jewel Tower is a rare remnant of the old Palace of Westminster, used by kings until Henry VIII. The crude stone tower (1365-1366) was a guard tower in the palace wall, overlooking a moat. It contains a fine little exhibit on Parliament and the tower (£3, daily March-Oct 10:00-17:00, Nov-Feb 10:00-16:00, tel. 020/7222-2219). Next to the tower (and free) is a quiet courtyard with picnic-friendly benches.

Big Ben: The 315-foot-high clock tower at the north end of the Palace of Westminster is named for its 13-ton bell, Ben. The light above the clock is lit when the House of Commons is sitting. The face of the clock is huge—you can actually see the minute hand moving. For a good view of it, walk halfway over Westminster Bridge.

Other Sights in Westminster
▲▲▲Churchill War Rooms
This excellent sight offers a fascinating walk through the underground headquarters of the British government's fight against the Nazis in the darkest days of the Battle for Britain. It has two parts: the war rooms themselves, and a top-notch museum dedicated to the man who steered the war from here, Winston Churchill. For

details on all the blood, sweat, toil, and tears, pick up the excellent, essential, and included audioguide at the entry, and dive in.

Cost and Hours: £17 (includes 10 percent optional donation), £5 guidebook, daily 9:30-18:00, last entry one hour before closing; on King Charles Street, 200 yards off Whitehall, follow the signs, Tube: Westminster, tel. 020/7930-6961, www.iwm.org.uk/churchill. The museum's gift shop is great for anyone nostalgic for the 1940s.

Cabinet War Rooms: The 27-room, heavily fortified nerve center of the British war effort was used from 1939 to 1945. Churchill's room, the map room, and other rooms are just as they were in 1945. As you follow the one-way route, be sure to take advantage of the audioguide, which explains each room and offers first-person accounts of wartime happenings here (it takes about 45 minutes, not counting the Churchill Museum). Be patient—it's well worth it. While the rooms are spartan, you'll see how British gentility survived even as the city was bombarded—posted signs informed those working underground what the weather was like outside, and a cheery notice reminded them to turn off the light switch to conserve electricity.

Churchill Museum: Don't bypass this museum, which occupies a large hall amid the war rooms. It dissects every aspect of the man behind the famous cigar, bowler hat, and V-for-victory sign. It's extremely well-presented and engaging, using artifacts, quotes, political cartoons, clear explanations, and high-tech interactive exhibits to bring the colorful statesman to life; this museum alone deserves an hour. You'll get a taste of Winston's wit, irascibility, work ethic, passion for painting, American ties, writing talents, and drinking habits. The exhibit shows Winston's warts as well: It questions whether his party-switching was just political opportunism, examines the basis for his opposition to Indian self-rule, and reveals him to be an intense taskmaster who worked 18-hour days and was brutal to his staffers (who deeply respected him nevertheless).

A long touch-the-screen timeline lets you zero in on events in his life from birth (November 30, 1874) to his first appointment as prime minister in 1940. Many of the items on display—such as a European map divvied up in permanent marker, which Churchill brought to England from the postwar Potsdam Conference—drive home the remarkable span of history this man lived through. Imagine: Churchill began his military career riding horses in the cavalry and ended it speaking out against the proliferation of nuclear armaments. It's all the more amazing considering that, in the 1930s, the man who would become my vote for greatest statesman of the 20th century was considered a washed-up loony ranting about the growing threat of fascism.

London at a Glance

▲▲▲Westminster Abbey Britain's finest church and the site of royal coronations and burials since 1066. **Hours:** Mon-Fri 9:30-16:30, Wed until 19:00, Sat 9:30-14:30, closed Sun to sightseers except for worship. See page 710.

▲▲▲Churchill War Rooms Underground WWII headquarters of Churchill's war effort. **Hours:** Daily 9:30-18:00. See page 713.

▲▲▲National Gallery Remarkable collection of European paintings (1250-1900), including Leonardo, Botticelli, Velázquez, Rembrandt, Turner, Van Gogh, and the Impressionists. **Hours:** Daily 10:00-18:00, Fri until 21:00. See page 717.

▲▲▲British Museum The world's greatest collection of artifacts of Western civilization, including the Rosetta Stone and the Parthenon's Elgin Marbles. **Hours:** Daily 10:00-17:30, Fri until 20:30 (selected galleries only). See page 727.

▲▲▲British Library Impressive collection of the most important literary treasures of the Western world. **Hours:** Mon-Fri 9:30-18:00, Tue until 20:00, Sat 9:30-17:00, Sun 11:00-17:00. See page 729.

▲▲▲St. Paul's Cathedral The main cathedral of the Anglican Church, designed by Christopher Wren, with a climbable dome and daily evensong services. **Hours:** Mon-Sat 8:30-16:30, closed Sun except for worship. See page 732.

▲▲▲Tower of London Historic castle, palace, and prison housing the crown jewels and a witty band of Beefeaters. **Hours:** March-Oct Tue-Sat 9:00-17:30, Sun-Mon 10:00-17:30; Nov-Feb Tue-Sat 9:00-16:30, Sun-Mon 10:00-16:30. See page 735.

▲▲▲Victoria and Albert Museum The best collection of decorative arts anywhere. **Hours:** Daily 10:00-17:45, Fri until 22:00 (selected galleries only). See page 749.

▲▲Houses of Parliament London's Neo-Gothic landmark, famous for Big Ben and occupied by the Houses of Lords and Commons. **Hours:** Generally Mon-Tue 14:30-22:30, Wed 11:30-22:00, Thu 10:30-19:00, closed Fri-Sun and most of Aug-Sept. See page 711.

▲▲Trafalgar Square The heart of London, where Westminster, The City, and the West End meet. **Hours:** Always open. See page 717.

▲▲National Portrait Gallery A *Who's Who* of British history, featuring portraits of this nation's most important historical figures.

Hours: Daily 10:00-18:00, Thu-Fri until 21:00, first and second floors open Mon at 11:00. See page 719.

▲▲**Covent Garden** Vibrant people-watching zone with shops, cafés, street musicians, and an iron-and-glass arcade that once hosted a produce market. **Hours:** Always open. See page 720.

▲▲**Changing of the Guard at Buckingham Palace** Hour-long spectacle at Britain's royal residence. **Hours:** Generally May-July daily at 11:30, Aug-April every other day. See page 725.

▲▲**London Eye** Enormous observation wheel, dominating—and offering commanding views over—London's skyline. **Hours:** Daily July-Aug 10:00-21:30, April-June 10:00-21:00, Sept-March 10:00-20:00. See page 738.

▲▲**Imperial War Museum** Exhibits on the military history of the bloody 20th century. **Hours:** Daily 10:00-18:00. See page 740.

▲▲**Tate Modern** Works by Monet, Matisse, Dalí, Picasso, and Warhol displayed in a converted powerhouse. **Hours:** Daily 10:00-18:00, Fri-Sat until 22:00. See page 741.

▲▲**Shakespeare's Globe** Timbered, thatched-roofed reconstruction of the Bard's original wooden "O." **Hours:** Theater complex, museum, and actor-led tours generally daily 9:00-17:00; in summer, morning theater tours only. Plays are also held here. See page 742.

▲▲**Tate Britain** Collection of British painting from the 16th century through modern times, including works by William Blake, the Pre-Raphaelites, and J. M. W. Turner. **Hours:** Daily 10:00-18:00, first Fri of the month until 22:00. See page 746.

▲▲**Kensington Palace** Recently restored former home of British monarchs, with good exhibits on Queen Victoria, as well as William and Mary. **Hours:** Daily 10:00-18:00, until 17:00 Nov-Feb. See page 750.

▲▲**Natural History Museum** Packed with stuffed creatures, engaging exhibits, and enthralled kids. **Hours:** Daily 10:00-17:50. See page 750.

▲**Courtauld Gallery** Fine collection of paintings filling one wing of the Somerset House, a grand 18th-century palace. **Hours:** Daily 10:00-18:00. See page 721.

LONDON

Eating: Get your rations at the Switch Room café (in the museum), or for a nearby pub lunch, try Westminster Arms (food served downstairs, on Storey's Gate, a couple of blocks south of the museum).

Horse Guards

The Horse Guards change daily at 11:00 (10:00 on Sun), and a colorful dismounting ceremony takes place daily at 16:00. The rest of the day, they just stand there—terrible for video cameras (on Whitehall, between Trafalgar Square and #10 Downing Street, Tube: Westminster, www.changing-the-guard.com). Buckingham Palace pageantry is canceled when it rains, but the Horse Guards change regardless of the weather.

▲Banqueting House

England's first Renaissance building (1619-1622) is still standing. Designed by Inigo Jones, built by King James I, and decorated by his son Charles I, the Banqueting House came to symbolize the Stuart kings' "divine right" management style—the belief that God himself had anointed them to rule. The house is one of the few London landmarks spared by the 1698 fire and the only surviving part of the original Palace of Whitehall. Today it opens its doors to visitors, who enjoy a restful 20-minute audiovisual history, a 30-minute audioguide, and a look at the exquisite banqueting hall itself. As a tourist attraction, it's basically one big room, with sumptuous ceiling paintings by Peter Paul Rubens. At Charles I's request, these paintings drove home the doctrine of the legitimacy of the divine right of kings. Ironically, in 1649—divine right ignored—King Charles I was famously executed right here.

Cost and Hours: £5 (includes 10 percent optional donation), includes audioguide, Mon-Sat 10:00-17:00, closed Sun, last entry at 16:30, may close for government functions—though it usually stays open at least until 13:00 (call ahead for recorded information about closures), aristocratic WC, immediately across Whitehall from the Horse Guards, Tube: Westminster, tel. 020/3166-6155, www.hrp.org.uk.

▲▲Trafalgar Square

London's central square—at the intersection of Westminster, The City, and the West End—is the climax of most marches and demonstrations, and a thrilling place to simply hang out. A recent remodeling of the square has rerouted car traffic, helping reclaim the area for London's citizens. At the top of Trafalgar Square (north) sits the domed National Gallery with its grand staircase, and to the right, the steeple of St. Martin-in-the-Fields, built in 1722, inspiring the steeple-over-the-entrance style of many town churches in New England. The pedestal called the Fourth Plinth (see map) is

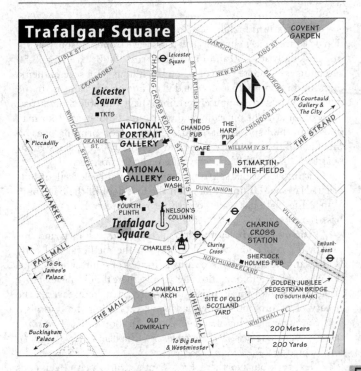

often topped with a temporary work of art. In the center of the square, Lord Horatio Nelson stands atop his 185-foot-tall fluted granite column, gazing out toward Trafalgar, where he lost his life but defeated the French fleet. Part of this 1842 memorial is made from his victims' melted-down cannons. He's surrounded by spraying fountains, giant lions, hordes of people, and—until 2005—even more pigeons. A former London mayor decided that London's "flying rats" were a public nuisance and evicted Trafalgar Square's venerable seed salesmen (Tube: Charing Cross).

▲▲▲National Gallery

Displaying Britain's top collection of European paintings from 1250 to 1900—including works by Leonardo, Botticelli, Velázquez, Rembrandt, Turner, Van Gogh, and the Impressionists—this is one of Europe's great galleries. You'll peruse 700 years of art—from gold-backed Madonnas to Cubist bathers.

Cost and Hours: Free, but suggested donation of £2, temporary (optional) exhibits extra, floor plan-£1; daily 10:00-18:00, Fri until 21:00, last entry to special exhibits 45 minutes before closing; no photos, on Trafalgar Square, Tube: Charing Cross or Leicester Square.

Information: Helpful £1 floor plan available from information desk; free one-hour overview tours leave from Sainsbury Wing info desk daily at 11:30 and 14:30, plus Fri at 19:00; excellent £3.50 audioguides—choose from one-hour highlights tour, several theme tours, or tour option that lets you dial up info on any painting in the museum; ArtStart computer terminals help you study any artist, style, or topic in the museum, and print out a tailor-made tour map (mostly in the Espresso Bar, and a few more non-printing ones on first floor of the Sainsbury Wing); info tel. 020/7747-2885, switchboard tel. 020/7839-3321, www.nationalgallery.org.uk.

Eating: Consider splitting afternoon tea at the excellent-but-pricey National Dining Rooms, on the first floor of the Sainsbury Wing. The National Café, located near the Getty Entrance, also has afternoon tea.

Visiting the Museum: Pick up the handy £1 map and approach the collection chronologically. In the medieval and early Renaissance rooms you'll see shiny paintings of saints, angels, Madonnas, and crucifixions floating in an ethereal gold never-never land. Then comes the Renaissance, where artists rediscovered the beauty of nature and the human body, expressing the optimism and confidence of this new age. Look for Botticelli's *Venus and Mars*, Michelangelo's *The Entombment*, Raphael's *Pope Julius II*, and Leonardo's *The Virgin of the Rocks*.

Next seek out Northern Protestant art, in which Greek gods and Virgin Marys were out, hometown folks and hometown places were in. Highlights include Vermeer's *A Young Woman Standing at a Virginal* and Rembrandt's *Belshazzar's Feast*. The museum's outstanding Baroque collection includes Van Dyck's *Equestrian Portrait of Charles I*, Velázquez's *The Rokeby Venus*, and Caravaggio's *The Supper at Emmaus*. It's no surprise that hometown painters get lots of space here. The reserved British were more comfortable cavorting with nature than with the lofty gods, as seen in Constable's *The Hay Wain* and Turner's *The Fighting Téméraire*.

Then, at the end of the 19th century, a new breed of artists burst out of the stuffy confines of the studio. They donned scarves and berets and set up their canvases in farmers' fields or carried their notebooks into crowded cafés, dashing off quick sketches in order to catch a momentary...impression. Check out Impressionist and Post-Impressionist masterpieces such as Monet's *Gare St. Lazare* and *The Water-Lily Pond*, Renoir's *The Skiff*, Seurat's *Bathers at Asnières*, Van Gogh's *Sunflowers*, and Cézanne's *Bathers*.

Other Sights on Trafalgar Square

▲▲National Portrait Gallery

Put off by halls of 19th-century characters who meant nothing to me, I used to call this "as interesting as someone else's yearbook." But a selective walk through this 500-year-long *Who's Who* of British history is quick and free, and puts faces on the story of England.

Some highlights: Henry VIII and wives; portraits of the "Virgin Queen" Elizabeth I, Sir Francis Drake, and Sir Walter Raleigh; the only real-life portrait of William Shakespeare; Oliver Cromwell and Charles I with his head on; portraits by Gainsborough and Reynolds; the Romantics (William Blake, Lord Byron, William Wordsworth, and company); Queen Victoria and her era; and the present royal family, including the late Princess Diana.

The collection is well-described, not huge, and in historical sequence, from the 16th century on the second floor to today's royal family on the ground floor.

Cost and Hours: Free, but suggested donation of £5, temporary (optional) exhibits extra, audioguide-£3, floor plan-£1; daily 10:00-18:00, Thu-Fri until 21:00, first and second floors open Mon at 11:00, last entry to special exhibits 45 minutes before closing, no photos, basement café and top-floor view restaurant; entry 100 yards off Trafalgar Square (around the corner from National Gallery, opposite Church of St. Martin-in-the-Fields), Tube: Charing Cross or Leicester Square, tel. 020/7306-0055, recorded info tel. 020/7312-2463, www.npg.org.uk.

▲St. Martin-in-the-Fields

The church, built in the 1720s with a Gothic spire atop a Greek-type temple, is an oasis of peace on wild and noisy Trafalgar Square. St. Martin cared for the poor. "In the fields" was where the first church stood on this spot (in the 13th century), between Westminster and The City. Stepping inside, you still feel a compassion for the needs of the people in this neighborhood—the church serves the homeless and houses a Chinese community center. The modern east window—with grillwork bent into the shape of a warped cross—was installed in 2008 to replace one damaged in World War II.

A freestanding glass pavilion to the left of the church serves as the entrance to the church's underground areas. There you'll find the concert ticket office, a gift shop, brass-rubbing center, and the recommended support-the-church Café in the Crypt.

Cost and Hours: Free, but donations welcome, £3.50 audioguide at shop downstairs; hours vary but generally Mon-Fri 8:30-13:00 & 14:00-18:00, Sat 9:30-13:00 & 14:00-18:00, Sun 15:30-17:00; Tube: Charing Cross, tel. 020/7766-1100, www.smitf.org.

Music: The church is famous for its concerts. Consider a free lunchtime concert (suggested £3 donation; Mon, Tue, and Fri at 13:00), an evening concert (£8-28, several nights a week at 19:30), or Wednesday night jazz at the Café in the Crypt (£5.50 or £9, at 20:00). See the church's website for the concert schedule.

The West End and Nearby
Piccadilly and Soho
▲Piccadilly Circus

Although this square is slathered with neon billboards and tacky attractions (think of it as the Times Square of London), the surrounding streets are packed with great shopping opportunities and swimming with youth on the rampage.

Nearby Shaftesbury Avenue and Leicester Square teem with fun-seekers, theaters, Chinese restaurants, and street singers. To the northeast is London's Chinatown and, beyond that, the funky Soho neighborhood (described next). And curling to the northwest from Piccadilly Circus is genteel Regent Street, lined with the city's most exclusive shops.

▲Soho

North of Piccadilly, seedy Soho has become trendy—with many recommended restaurants—and is well worth a gawk. It's the epicenter of London's thriving, colorful youth scene, a fun and funky *Sesame Street* of urban diversity.

Soho is also London's red light district (especially near Brewer and Berwick Streets), where "friendly models" wait in tiny rooms up dreary stairways, voluptuous con artists sell strip shows, and eager male tourists are frequently ripped off. But it's easy to avoid trouble if you're not looking for it. In fact, the sleazy joints share the block with respectable pubs and restaurants, and elderly couples stroll past neon signs that flash *Licensed Sex Shop in Basement.*

Covent Garden and Nearby
▲▲Covent Garden

This large square teems with people and street performers—jugglers, sword swallowers, and guitar players. London's buskers (including those in the Tube) are auditioned, licensed, and assigned times and places where they are allowed to perform.

The square's centerpiece is a covered marketplace. A market has been here since medieval times, when it was the "convent" garden owned by Westminster Abbey. In the 1600s, it became a housing development with this courtyard as its center, done in the Palladian style by Inigo Jones. Today's fine iron-and-glass structure was built in 1830 (when such buildings were all the Industrial Age rage) to house the stalls of what became London's chief produce market. Covent Garden remained a produce market until 1973, when its venerable arcades were converted to boutiques, cafés, and antiques shops. A market still thrives here today.

The "Actors' Church" of St. Paul, the Royal Opera House, and the London Transport Museum (described next) all border the square, and theaters are nearby. The area is a people-watcher's delight, with cigarette eaters, Punch-and-Judy acts, food that's good for you (but not your wallet), trendy crafts, sweet whiffs of marijuana, two-tone hair (neither tone natural), and faces that could set off a metal detector. For better Covent Garden lunch deals, walk a block or two away from the eye of this touristic hurricane (check out the places north of the Tube station, along Endell and Neal Streets).

▲London Transport Museum

This modern, well-presented museum, located right at Covent Garden, is fun for kids and thought-provoking for adults (if a bit overpriced). Whether you're cursing or marveling at the buses and Tube, the growth of Europe's third-biggest city (after Moscow and Istanbul) has been made possible by its public transit system.

After you enter, take the elevator up to the top floor...and the year 1800, when horse-drawn vehicles ruled the road. Next, you descend to the first floor and the world's first underground Metro system, which used steam-powered locomotives (the Circle Line, c. 1865). On the ground floor, horses and trains are replaced by motorized vehicles (cars, taxis, double-decker buses, streetcars), resulting in 20th-century congestion. How to deal with it? In 2003, car drivers in London were slapped with a congestion charge, and today, a half-billion people ride the Tube every year.

Cost and Hours: £13.50, ticket good for one year, Sat-Thu 10:00-18:00, Fri 11:00-18:00, last entry 45 minutes before closing, pleasant upstairs café with Covent Garden view, in southeast corner of Covent Garden courtyard, Tube: Covent Garden, switchboard tel. 020/7379-6344, recorded info tel. 020/7565-7299, www.ltmuseum.co.uk.

▲Courtauld Gallery

While less impressive than the National Gallery, this wonderful and compact collection of paintings is still a joy. The gallery is part of the Courtauld Institute of Art, and the thoughtful descriptions of each piece of art remind visitors that the gallery is still used for teaching. You'll see medieval European paintings and works by Rubens, the Impressionists (Manet, Monet, and Degas), Post-Impressionists (such as Cézanne), and more. Besides the permanent collection, a quality selection of loaners and temporary exhibits are often included in the entry fee. The gallery is located within the grand Somerset House; enjoy the riverside eateries and the courtyard featuring a playful fountain.

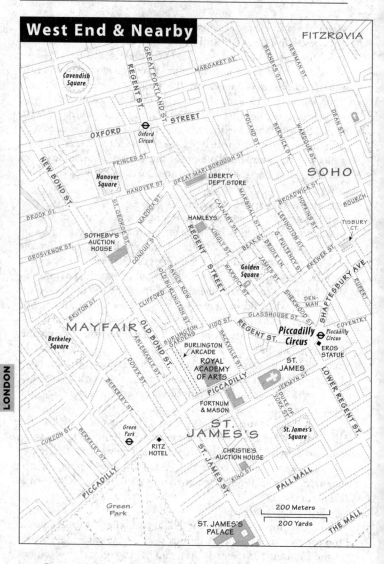

West End & Nearby

FITZROVIA

SOHO

MAYFAIR

ST. JAMES'S

Cavendish Square

Hanover Square

Liberty Dept Store

Hamleys

Sotheby's Auction House

Golden Square

Berkeley Square

Piccadilly Circus

Eros Statue

Burlington Arcade

Royal Academy of Arts

Fortnum & Mason

Green Park

Ritz Hotel

St. James's Square

Christie's Auction House

Green Park

St. James's Palace

The Mall

200 Meters
200 Yards

Cost and Hours: £6, free Mon until 14:00; open daily 10:00–18:00, last entry 30 minutes before closing, occasionally open Thu until 21:00—check website; café; at Somerset House along the Strand, Tube: Temple or Covent Garden, recorded info tel. 020/7848-2526, shop tel. 020/7848-2579, www.courtauld.ac.uk.

Buckingham Palace

Three palace sights require admission: the State Rooms (Aug-Sept only), Queen's Gallery, and Royal Mews. You can pay for

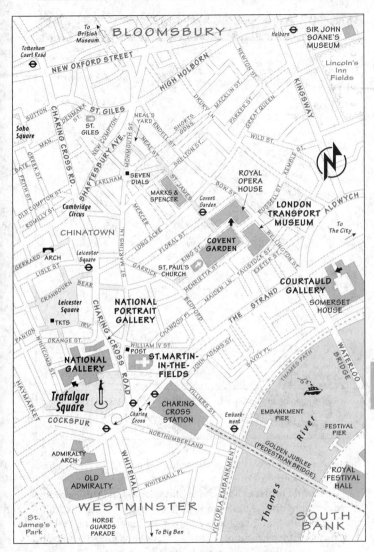

each separately, or buy a combo-ticket. A combo-ticket for £32 admits you to all three sights; a cheaper version for £16 covers the Queen's Gallery and Royal Mews. Many tourists are more interested in the Changing of the Guard, which costs nothing at all to view.

▲State Rooms at Buckingham Palace

This lavish home has been Britain's royal residence since 1837. When the Queen's at home, the royal standard flies (a red, yellow, and blue flag); otherwise, the Union Jack flaps in the wind.

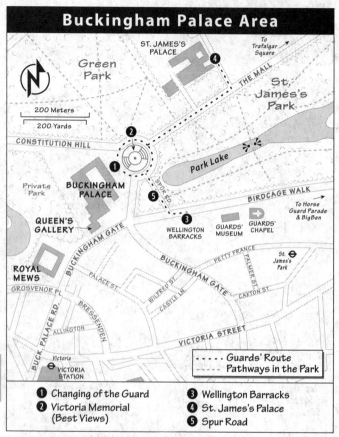

Buckingham Palace Area

Green Park

ST. JAMES'S PALACE

To Trafalgar Square

THE MALL

St. James's Park

200 Meters
200 Yards

CONSTITUTION HILL

Park Lake

BUCKINGHAM PALACE

Private Park

SPUR RD.

QUEEN'S GALLERY

BUCKINGHAM GATE

BIRDCAGE WALK

To Horse Guard Parade & Big Ben

WELLINGTON BARRACKS

GUARDS' MUSEUM

GUARDS' CHAPEL

ROYAL MEWS

PALACE ST.

GROSVENOR PL.

BRESSENDEN

BUCKINGHAM GATE

PETTY FRANCE

PALMER ST.

St. James's Park

BUCK. PALACE RD.

ALLINGTON

WILFRED ST.

CASTLE LN.

CAXTON ST.

VICTORIA STREET

Victoria

VICTORIA STATION

- - - - Guards' Route
- - - - Pathways in the Park

1 Changing of the Guard
2 Victoria Memorial (Best Views)
3 Wellington Barracks
4 St. James's Palace
5 Spur Road

The Queen opens her palace to the public—but only in August and September, when she's out of town.

Cost and Hours: £18 for lavish State Rooms and throne room, includes audioguide; Aug-Sept only, daily 9:30-18:30, last admission 16:15; only 8,000 visitors a day by timed entry; come early to the palace's Visitor Entrance (opens 9:15), or book ahead in person, by phone, or online (£1.25 extra); Tube: Victoria, tel. 020/7766-7300, www.royalcollection.org.uk.

Queen's Gallery at Buckingham Palace

A small sampling of Queen Elizabeth's personal collection of art is on display in five rooms in a wing adjoining the palace. Her 7,000 paintings, one of the largest private art collections in the world, are actually a series of collections, which have been built upon by each successive monarch since the 16th century. The Queen rotates the paintings, enjoying some privately in her many palatial residences while sharing others with her subjects in public galleries in Edinburgh and London.

In addition to the permanent collection, you'll see temporary exhibits and a small room glittering with the Queen's personal jewelry. Compared to the crown jewels at the Tower, it may be Her Majesty's bottom drawer—but it's still a dazzling pile of diamonds. Temporary exhibits change about twice a year and are lovingly described by the included audioguide.

Because the gallery is small and security is tight (involving lines), I'd suggest visiting this gallery only if you're a patient art lover interested in the current exhibit.

While admission tickets come with an entry time, this is only enforced during rare days when crowds are a problem.

Cost and Hours: £7.50-9.25 depending on exhibit, daily 10:00-17:30, last entry one hour before closing, Tube: Victoria, tel. 020/7766-7301—but Her Majesty rarely answers. Men shouldn't miss the mahogany-trimmed urinals.

Royal Mews

Located to the left of Buckingham Palace, the Queen's working stables, or "mews," are open to visitors. The visit is likely to be disappointing unless you follow the included audioguide or the hourly guided tour (April-Oct only, 45 minutes), in which case it's thoroughly entertaining—especially if you're interested in horses and/or royalty. You'll see a few of the Queen's 30 horses, a fancy car, and a bunch of old carriages, finishing with the Gold State Coach (c. 1760, 4 tons, 4 mph). Queen Victoria said absolutely no cars. When she died, in 1901, the mews got its first Daimler. Today, along with the hay-eating transport, the stable is home to five Bentleys and Rolls-Royce Phantoms, with one on display.

Cost and Hours: £8.25, April-Oct daily 10:00-17:00, Nov-March Mon-Sat 10:00-16:00, closed Sun, last entry 45 minutes before closing, guided tours on the hour, Buckingham Palace Road, Tube: Victoria, tel. 020/7766-7302.

▲▲Changing of the Guard at Buckingham Palace

This is the spectacle every visitor to London has to see at least once: stone-faced, red-coated, bearskin-hatted guards changing posts with much fanfare, in an hour-long ceremony accompanied by a brass band.

It's 11:00 at Buckingham Palace, and the on-duty guards (the "Queen's Guard") are ready to finish their shift. Nearby at St. James's Palace (a half-mile northwest), a second set of guards is also ready for a break. Meanwhile, fresh replacement guards (the "New Guard") gather for a review and inspection at Wellington Barracks, 500 yards east of the palace (on Birdcage Walk).

At 11:15, the tired St. James's guards head out to the Mall, and then take a right turn for Buckingham Palace. At 11:30, the replacement troops, led by the band, also head for Buckingham Palace. Meanwhile, a fourth group—the Horse Guard—passes by along the Mall on its way back to Hyde Park Corner from its own changing-of-the-guard ceremony on Whitehall (which just took place at Horse Guards Parade at 11:00, or 10:00 on Sun).

At 11:45, the tired and fresh guards converge on Buckingham Palace in a perfect storm of Red Coat pageantry. Everyone parades around, the guard changes (passing the regimental flag, or "colour") with much shouting, the band plays a happy little concert, and then they march out. At noon, two bands escort two detachments of guards away: the tired guards to Wellington Barracks and the fresh guards to St. James's Palace. As the fresh guards set up at St. James's Palace and the tired ones dress down at the barracks, the tourists disperse.

Cost and Hours: Free, daily May-July at 11:30, every other day Aug-April, no ceremony in very wet weather; exact schedule subject to change—call 020/7766-7300 for the day's plan, or check www.changing-the-guard.com or www.royalcollection.org.uk (click "Visit," then "Changing the Guard"); Buckingham Palace, Tube: Victoria, St. James's Park, or Green Park. Or hop into a big black taxi and say, "Buck House, please."

Sightseeing Strategies: Most tourists just show up and get lost in the crowds, but those who know the drill will enjoy the event more. The action takes place in stages over the course of an hour, at several different locations. The main event is in the forecourt right in front of Buckingham Palace (between Buckingham Palace and the fence) from 11:30 to 12:00. To see it close up, you'll need to get here no later than 10:30 to get a place right next to the fence.

But there's plenty of pageantry elsewhere. Get out your map and strategize. You could see the guards mobilizing at Wellington Barracks or St. James's Palace (11:00-11:15). Or watch them parade with bands down The Mall and Spur Road (11:15-11:30). After the ceremony at Buckingham Palace is over (and many tourists have gotten bored and gone home), the parades march back along those same streets (12:10).

Pick one event and find a good, unobstructed place from which to view it. The key is to get either right up front along the road or fence, or find some raised elevation to stand or sit on—a balustrade or a curb—so you can see over people's heads.

If you get there too late to score a premium spot right along the fence, head for the high ground on the circular Victoria Memorial, which provides the best overall view (come before 11:00 to get a place). From the memorial, you have good (if more distant) views of the palace as well as the arriving and departing parades along The

Mall and Spur Road. The actual Changing of the Guard in front of the palace is a nonevent. It is interesting, however, to see nearly every tourist in London gathered in one place at the same time.

If you arrive too late to get any good spot at all, or you just don't feel like jostling for a view, stroll down to St. James's Palace and wait near the corner for a great photo-op. At about 12:15, the parade marches up The Mall to the palace and performs a smaller changing ceremony—with almost no crowds. Afterward, stroll through nearby St. James's Park.

Sights in North London

▲▲▲British Museum

Simply put, this is the greatest chronicle of civilization...anywhere. A visit here is like taking a long hike through *Encyclopedia Britannica* National Park. While the vast British Museum wraps around its Great Court (the huge entrance hall), the most popular sections of the museum fill the ground floor: Egyptian, Assyrian, and ancient Greek, with the famous frieze sculptures from the Parthenon in Athens. The museum's stately Reading Room—famous as the place where Karl Marx hung out while formulating his ideas on communism and writing *Das Kapital*—sometimes hosts special exhibits.

Cost and Hours: Free, but a £5, US$7, or €6 donation requested; temporary exhibits usually extra (and with timed ticket); daily 10:00-17:30, Fri until 20:30 (selected galleries only), least crowded weekday late afternoons; Great Russell Street, Tube: Tottenham Court Road.

Information: Information desks offer a standard museum map (£1 suggested donation) and a £2 version that highlights important pieces; the *Visitor's Guide* (£3.50) offers 15 different tours and skimpy text.

Tours: Free 30-minute **eyeOpener tours** are led by volunteers, who focus on select rooms (daily 11:00-15:45, generally every 15 minutes). Free 45-minute **gallery talks** on specific subjects are offered Tue-Sat at 13:15. The £5 **multimedia guide** offers dial-up audio commentary and video on 200 objects, as well as several theme tours (must leave photo ID). There's also a fun children's audioguide (£3.50). And finally, you can download a free Rick Steves **audio tour** of the museum (see page 7). General info tel. 020/7323-8299, ticket desk tel. 020/7323-8181, collection questions tel. 020/7323-8838, www.britishmuseum.org.

Visiting the Museum: From the Great Court, doorways lead to all wings. Huge winged lions (which guarded an Assyrian palace 800 years before Christ) guard these great galleries. For a brief tour, connect these ancient dots:

LONDON

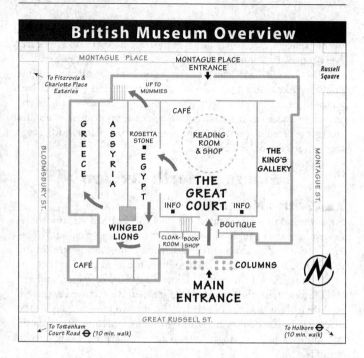

British Museum Overview

MONTAGUE PLACE

MONTAGUE PLACE
ENTRANCE

Russell
Square

To Fitzrovia &
Charlotte Place
Eateries

UP TO
MUMMIES

CAFÉ

GREECE

ASSYRIA

ROSETTA
STONE

EGYPT

READING
ROOM
& SHOP

THE
KING'S
GALLERY

BLOOMSBURY ST.

MONTAGUE ST.

THE
GREAT
COURT

INFO

INFO

WINGED
LIONS

CLOAK-
ROOM

BOOK-
SHOP

BOUTIQUE

CAFÉ

COLUMNS

MAIN
ENTRANCE

GREAT RUSSELL ST.

To Tottenham
Court Road ⊖ (10 min. walk)

To Holborn ⊖
(10 min. walk)

Start with the Egyptian section. Wander from the Rosetta Stone past the many statues. At the end of the hall, climb the stairs to mummy land.

Back at the winged lions, explore the dark, violent, and mysterious **Assyrian** rooms. The Nimrud Gallery is lined with royal propaganda reliefs and wounded lions (from the ninth century B.C.).

The most modern of the ancient art fills the **Greek** section. Find Room 11, behind the winged lions, and start your walk through Greek art history with the simple and primitive Cycladic fertility figures. Later, painted vases show a culture really into partying. The finale is the Parthenon Sculptures (the so-called Elgin Marbles). The much-wrangled-over bits of the Athenian Parthenon (from about 450 B.C.) are even more impressive than they look. To best appreciate these ancient carvings, take the audioguide tour (described earlier).

Be sure to venture upstairs to see artifacts from **Roman Britain** that surpass anything you'll see at Hadrian's Wall or elsewhere in Britain. Nearby, the Dark Age Britain exhibits offer a worthwhile peek at that bleak era; look for the Sutton Hoo Burial Ship artifacts from a seventh-century royal burial on the east coast of England (Room 41). A rare Michelangelo cartoon (preliminary sketch) is in Room 90.

Other Sights in North London

▲▲▲British Library

The British Empire built its greatest monuments out of paper; it's through literature that England has made her lasting contribution to history and the arts. Here, in just two rooms, are the literary treasures of Western civilization, from early Bibles, to the Magna Carta, to Shakespeare's *Hamlet*, to Lewis Carroll's *Alice's Adventures in Wonderland*.

You'll see the Lindisfarne Gospels transcribed on an illuminated manuscript, as well as Beatles lyrics scrawled on the back of a greeting card. Pages from Leonardo da Vinci's notebook show his powerful curiosity, his genius for invention, and his famous backward and inside-out handwriting, which makes sense only if you know Italian and have a mirror. A *Beowulf* manuscript from A.D. 1000, *The Canterbury Tales*, and Shakespeare's First Folio also reside here. (If the First Folio is not out, the library should have other Shakespeare items on display.)

Exhibits change often, and many of the museum's old, fragile manuscripts need to "rest" periodically in order to stay well-preserved. If your heart's set on seeing that one particular rare Dickens book or letter penned by Gandhi, call ahead to make sure it's on display.

Cost and Hours: Free, but £2 suggested donation, admission charged for some (optional) temporary exhibits, Mon-Fri 9:30-18:00, Tue until 20:00, Sat 9:30-17:00, Sun 11:00-17:00, 96 Euston Road, Tube: King's Cross St. Pancras or Euston, tel. 019/3754-6060 or 020/7412-7676, www.bl.uk.

Tours: While the British Library doesn't offer an audioguide or guided tours, you can download a free Rick Steves audio tour that describes its highlights (see page 7).

▲Wallace Collection

Sir Richard Wallace's fine collection of 17th-century Dutch Masters, 18th-century French Rococo, medieval armor, and assorted aristocratic fancies fills the sumptuously furnished Hertford House on Manchester Square. From the rough and intimate Dutch lifescapes of Jan Steen to the pink-cheeked Rococo fantasies of François Boucher, a wander through this little-visited mansion makes you nostalgic for the days of the empire. While this collection would be a big deal in a mid-sized city, it's small potatoes here in London... but enjoyable nevertheless.

Cost and Hours: Free, daily 10:00-17:00, £4 audioguide, free guided tours or lectures almost daily—call to confirm times, just north of Oxford Street on Manchester Square, Tube: Bond Street. Tel. 020/7563-9500, www.wallacecollection.org.

▲Madame Tussauds Waxworks

This waxtravaganza is gimmicky and expensive, but dang good...a hit with the kind of travelers who skip the British Museum. The

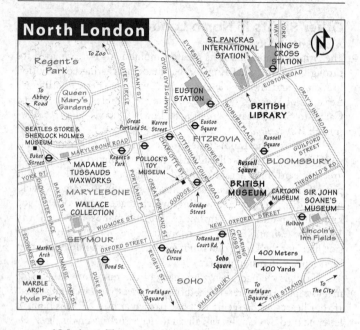

North London

To Zoo

Regent's Park

To Abbey Road

Queen Mary's Gardens

OUTER CIRCLE

ALBANY ST.

HAMPSTEAD ROAD

EVERSHOLT ST.

ST. PANCRAS INTERNATIONAL STATION

KING'S CROSS STATION

YORK WAY

EUSTON ROAD

GRAY'S INN ROAD

EUSTON STATION

BRITISH LIBRARY

WOBURN PLACE

BEATLES STORE & SHERLOCK HOLMES MUSEUM

Great Portland St.

Warren Street

Euston Square

FITZROVIA

GOWER ST.

Russell Square

GUILFORD STREET

Baker Street

Regent's Park

MARYLEBONE ROAD

POLLOCK'S TOY MUSEUM

CHARLOTTE ST.

Russell Square

BLOOMSBURY

THEOBALD'S RD.

MADAME TUSSAUDS WAXWORKS

PORTLAND PL.

GREAT PORTLAND ST.

BRITISH MUSEUM

CARTOON MUSEUM

SIR JOHN SOANE'S MUSEUM

YORK ST.

MARYLEBONE

WALLACE COLLECTION

Goodge Street

NEW OXFORD STREET

Holborn

Lincoln's Inn Fields

WIGMORE ST.

SEYMOUR

GLOUCESTER PLACE

BAKER ST.

Marble Arch

OXFORD STREET

Oxford Circus

Tottenham Court Rd.

CHARING CROSS RD.

400 Meters

400 Yards

EDGWARE RD.

PORTMAN ST.

PARK ST.

DUKE ST.

Bond St.

REGENT ST.

Soho Square

MARBLE ARCH

Hyde Park

To Trafalgar Square

SOHO

SHAFTESBURY

To Trafalgar Square

THE STRAND

To The City

original Madame Tussaud did wax casts of heads lopped off during the French Revolution (such as Marie-Antoinette's). She took her show on the road and ended up in London in 1835. Now it's all about squeezing Tom Cruise's bum, gambling with George Clooney, and partying with Beyoncé, Britney, and Brangelina. In addition to posing with all the eerily realistic wax dummies—from Johnny Depp to Barack Obama to the Beatles—you'll have the chance to tour a hokey haunted-house exhibit; learn how they created this waxy army; hop on a people-mover and cruise through a kid-pleasing "Spirit of London" time trip; and visit with Spider-Man, the Hulk, and other Marvel superheroes. A nine-minute "4-D" show features a 3-D movie heightened by wind, "back ticklers," and other special effects.

Cost: £30, 10 percent discount and no waiting in line if you buy tickets on their website (also consider combo-deal with London Eye, sold cheaper online), £25.50 Fast Track ticket (see page 687), often even bigger discount—up to 50 percent—if you get "Late Saver" ticket online for visits later in the day. Kids also get a discount, and those under 5 are free.

Hours: Mid-July-Aug and school holidays daily 9:00-20:00, Sept-mid-July Mon-Fri 9:30-19:30, Sat-Sun 9:00-20:00, last entry two hours before closing; Marylebone Road, Tube: Baker Street, tel. 0871-894-3000, www.madametussauds.com.

Crowd-Beating Tips: This popular attraction can be

swamped with people. To avoid the line, buy a Fast Track ticket or reserve online. If you wait to buy tickets at the attraction, you'll discover that the ticket-buying line twists endlessly once inside the door (believe the posted signs warning you how long the wait will be—an hour or more is not unusual at busy times). If you buy your tickets at the door, try to arrive after 15:00.

▲Sir John Soane's Museum

Architects love this quirky place, as do fans of interior decor and eclectic knickknacks. Tour this furnished home on a bird-chirping square and see 19th-century chairs, lamps, and carpets, wood-paneled nooks and crannies, and stained-glass skylights. (Note that some sections may be closed for restoration through 2014, but the main part of the house will be open.) The townhouse is cluttered with Soane's (and his wife's) collection of ancient relics, curios, and famous paintings, including Hogarth's series on *The Rake's Progress* (read the fun plot) and several excellent Canalettos. In 1833, just before his death, Soane established his house as a museum, stipulating that it be kept as nearly as possible in the state he left it. If he visited today, he'd be entirely satisfied. You'll leave wishing you'd known the man.

Cost and Hours: Free, but donations much appreciated, Tue-Sat 10:00-17:00, open and candlelit the first Tue of the month 18:00-21:00, closed Sun-Mon, last entry 30 minutes before closing, long entry lines on Sat and first Tue, good £1 brochure, £10 guided tour Sat at 11:00, free downloadable audio tours on their website, 13 Lincoln's Inn Fields, quarter-mile southeast of British Museum, Tube: Holborn, tel. 020/7405-2107, www.soane.org.

Cartoon Museum

This humble but interesting museum is located in the shadow of the British Museum. While its three rooms are filled with British cartoons unknown to most Americans, the satire of famous bigwigs and politicians—including Napoleon, Margaret Thatcher, the Queen, and Tony Blair—shows the power of parody to deliver social commentary. Upstairs, you'll see pages spanning from *Tarzan* to *Tank Girl*, and *Andy Capp* to the British *Dennis the Menace*—interesting only to comic-book diehards.

Cost and Hours: £5.50, Mon-Sat 10:30-17:30, Sun 12:00-17:30, 35 Little Russell Street—go one block south of the British Museum on Museum Street and turn right, Tube: Tottenham Court Road, tel. 020/7580-8155, www.cartoonmuseum.org.

Pollock's Toy Museum

This rickety old house, with glass cases filled with toys and games lining its walls and halls, is a time-warp experience that brings back childhood memories to people who grew up without batteries or computer chips. Though the museum is small, you could spend a lot of time here, squinting at the fascinating toys and dolls that entertained the children of 19th- and early 20th-century England. The included information is great. The story of Theodore Roosevelt refusing to shoot a bear cub while on a hunting trip was celebrated in 1902 cartoons, resulting in a new, huggable toy: the Teddy Bear. It was popular for good reason: It could be manufactured during World War I without rationed products; it coincided with the new belief that soft toys were good for a child's development; it was an acceptable "doll for boys"; and it was *the* toy children kept long after they'd grown up.

Cost and Hours: £6, kids-£3, generally Mon-Sat 10:00-17:00, closed Sun, last entry 30 minutes before closing, 1 Scala Street, Tube: Goodge Street, tel. 020/7636-3452, www.pollock-stoymuseum.com. A fun retro toy shop is attached.

Sights in The City

When Londoners say "The City," they mean the one-square-mile business center in East London that 2,000 years ago was Roman Londinium. The outline of the Roman city walls can still be seen in the arc of roads from Blackfriars Bridge to Tower Bridge. Within The City are 23 churches designed by Sir Christopher Wren, mostly just ornamentation around St. Paul's Cathedral. Today, while home to only 7,000 residents, The City thrives with nearly 300,000 office workers coming and going daily. It's a fascinating district to wander on weekdays, but since almost nobody actually lives there, it's dull in the evenings and on Saturday and Sunday.

You can download a free Rick Steves audio tour of The City, which peels back the many layers of history in this oldest part of London (see page 7).

▲▲▲St. Paul's Cathedral

Sir Christopher Wren's most famous church is the great St. Paul's, its elaborate interior capped by a 365-foot dome. There's been a church on this spot since 604. After the Great Fire of 1666 destroyed the old cathedral, Wren created this Baroque masterpiece. And since World War II, St. Paul's has been Britain's symbol of resilience. Despite 57 nights of bombing, the Nazis failed to destroy the cathedral, thanks to the St. Paul's volunteer fire watchmen, who stayed on the dome.

Cost and Hours: £15, includes church entry, dome climb, crypt, tour, and audioguide; Mon-Sat 8:30-16:30, last entry for sightseeing 16:00 (dome opens at 9:30, last entry at 16:15), closed Sun except for worship, sometimes closed for special events, no photos, café and restaurant in crypt, Tube: St. Paul's.

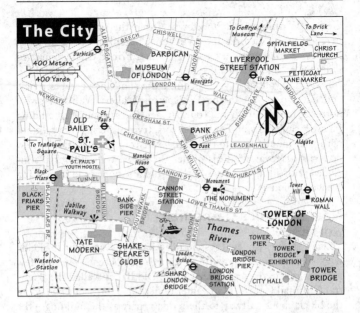

Music and Services: Communion is Mon-Sat at 8:00 and 12:30. Sunday services are held at 8:00, 10:15 (Matins), 11:30 (sung Eucharist), 15:15 (evensong), and 18:00. Additional evensong services are held Tue-Sat at 17:00 (40 minutes, free to anyone—though visitors who haven't paid admission aren't allowed to linger after the service). If you're here for evensong worship and sitting under the dome, at 16:40 you may be able to grab a big wooden stall in the choir, next to the singers.

Information: Admission includes an **audioguide** as well as a 1.5-hour guided tour (Mon-Sat at 10:45, 11:15, 13:30, and 14:00; confirm schedule at church or call 020/7246-8357). Free 15-minute talks are offered throughout the day, and a stand-up, wrap-around **film** program titled *Oculus: An Eye into St. Paul's* gives some historical background and shows the view from atop the dome (find it near Nelson's tomb). You can also download a free Rick Steves **audio tour** of St. Paul's (see page 7). Recorded info tel. 020/7236-4128, reception tel. 020/7246-8350, www.stpauls.co.uk.

Visiting the Cathedral: Inside, this big church feels big. At 515 feet long and 250 feet wide, it's Europe's fourth largest, after Rome (St. Peter's), Sevilla, and Milan. The spaciousness is accentuated by the relative lack of decoration. The simple, cream-colored ceiling and the clear glass in the windows light everything evenly.

There are many legends buried here: Horatio Nelson, who wore down Napoleon; the Duke of Wellington, who finished Napoleon off; and even Charles Cornwallis, who was finished off by

George Washington at Yorktown. Often the site of historic funerals (Queen Victoria and Winston Churchill), St. Paul's most famous ceremony was a wedding—when Prince Charles married Lady Diana Spencer in 1981.

During your visit, you can climb the dome for a great city view and have some fun in the Whispering Gallery. Whisper sweet nothings into the wall, and your partner (and anyone else) standing far away can hear you. For best effects, try whispering (not talking) with your mouth close to the wall, while your partner stands a few dozen yards away with his or her ear to the wall. The crypt (included with admission) is a world of historic bones and interesting cathedral models.

Near St. Paul's Cathedral

▲Old Bailey

To view the British legal system in action—lawyers in little blonde wigs speaking legalese with an upper-crust accent—spend a few minutes in the visitors' gallery at the Old Bailey, called the "Central Criminal Court." Don't enter under the dome; continue down the block about halfway to the modern part of the building—the entry is at Warwick Passage.

Cost and Hours: Free, generally Mon-Fri 9:45-13:00 & 14:00-16:00 depending on caseload, last entry at 15:40, closed Sat-Sun, fewer cases in Aug; no kids under 14; no bags, mobile phones, cameras, iPods, or food, but small purses OK; you can check bags at the Capable Travel agency just down the street at Old Bailey 4—£5/bag, £1 per phone or camera; 2 blocks northwest of St. Paul's on Old Bailey Street, follow signs to public entrance, Tube: St. Paul's, tel. 020/7248-3277.

▲Museum of London

This museum tells the fascinating story of London, taking you on a walk from its pre-Roman beginnings to the present. It features London's distinguished citizens through history—from Neanderthals, to Romans, to Elizabethans, to Victorians, to Mods, to today. The museum's displays are chronological, spacious, and informative without being overwhelming. Scale models and costumes help you visualize everyday life in the city at different periods. In the last room, you'll see the museum's prized possession: the Lord Mayor's Coach, a golden carriage pulled by six white horses, looking as if it had pranced right out of the pages of *Cinderella*. There are enough whiz-bang multimedia displays (including the Plague and the Great Fire) to spice up otherwise humdrum artifacts. This regular stop for the local school kids gives the best overview of London history in town.

Cost and Hours: Free, daily 10:00-18:00, galleries shut down

30 minutes before closing, see the day's events board for special talks and tours, on London Wall at Aldersgate Street, Tube: Barbican or St. Paul's plus a five-minute walk, tel. 020/7001-9844, www. museumoflondon.org.uk.

The Monument

Wren's 202-foot-tall tribute to London's Great Fire was recently restored. Climb the 331 steps inside the column for a view of The City that is still monumental.

Cost and Hours: £3, daily 9:30-17:30, last entry at 17:00, junction of Monument Street and Fish Street Hill, Tube: Monument, tel. 020/7626-2717, www.themonument.info.

▲▲▲Tower of London

The Tower has served as a castle in wartime, a king's residence in peacetime, and, most notoriously, as the prison and execution site of rebels. You can see the crown jewels, take a witty Beefeater tour, and ponder the executioner's block that dispensed with Anne Boleyn, Sir Thomas More, and troublesome heirs to the throne.

Cost and Hours: £21, family-£55 (both prices include a 10 percent optional donation), entry fee includes Beefeater tour (described later), skip the £4 audioguide and the £5 guidebook; March-Oct Tue-Sat 9:00-17:30, Sun-Mon 10:00-17:30; Nov-Feb Tue-Sat 9:00-16:30, Sun-Mon 10:00-16:30; last entry 30 minutes before closing; cafeteria, Tube: Tower Hill, switchboard tel. 0844-482-7777, www.hrp.org.uk.

Advance Tickets: To avoid the long ticket-buying lines at the Tower, buy your ticket at the Trader's Gate gift shop, located down the steps from the Tower Hill Tube stop (tickets here are generally slightly cheaper than at the gate; similar, discounted "Fast Track" tickets are sold at various locations throughout London). You can also buy tickets, with credit card only, at the Tower Welcome Centre to the left of the normal ticket lines—though on busy days, it can be crowded here as well. It's easy to book online (www.hrp.org. uk, £1 discount, no fee) or by phone (tel. 0844-482-7799 within UK or tel. 011-44-20-3166-6000 from the US; £2 fee), then pick up your tickets at the Tower.

More Crowd-Beating Tips: It's most crowded in summer, on weekends (especially Sundays), and during school holidays. Any time of year, the line for the crown jewels—the best on earth—can be just as long as the line for tickets. For fewer crowds, arrive before 10:00 and go straight for the jewels, then tour the rest of the Tower. Crowds die down after 16:30.

Yeoman Warder (Beefeater) Tours: Today, while the Tower's military purpose is history, it's still home to the Beefeaters—the 35 Yeoman Warders and their families. (The original duty of the Yeoman Warders was to guard the Tower, its prisoners, and the jewels.) The free, worthwhile, 1-hour Beefeater tours leave every 30 minutes from inside the gate (first tour at 10:00, last one at 15:30—or 14:30 in Nov-Feb). The boisterous Beefeaters are great entertainers, and their talks include lots of bloody anecdotes about the Tower and its history, and they relish telling corny jokes.

Sunday Worship: For a refreshingly different Tower experience, come on Sunday morning, when visitors are welcome on the grounds—for free—to worship in the Chapel Royal of St. Peter ad Vincula. You get in without the lines, but you can only see the chapel—no sightseeing (9:15 Communion or 11:00 service with fine choral music, meet at west gate 30 minutes early, dress for church, may be closed for ceremonies—call ahead).

Visiting the Tower: William I, still getting used to his new title of "the Conqueror," built the stone "White Tower" (1077-1097) to keep the Londoners in line. The Tower also served as an effective lookout for seeing invaders coming up the Thames. His successors enlarged it to its present 18-acre size. Because of the security it provided, it has served over the centuries as the Royal Mint, the Royal Jewel House, and as a prison and execution site.

The Tower's hard stone and glittering jewels represent the ultimate power of the monarch. The crown jewels include the world's largest cut diamond—the 530-carat Star of Africa—placed in the royal scepter. When Queen Elizabeth II opens Parliament, she checks out the Imperial State Crown with its 3,733 jewels, including Elizabeth I's pearl earrings.

You'll find more bloody history per square inch in this original tower of power than anywhere else in Britain, though the actual execution site (in the courtyard) looks just like a lawn. Not all prisoners died at the block—Richard III supposedly ordered two teenage princes strangled in their prison cells because they were a threat to his throne.

Near the Tower of London

Tower Bridge

The iconic Tower Bridge (often mistakenly called London Bridge) has been recently painted and restored. The hydraulically powered drawbridge was built in 1894 to accommodate the growing East End. While fully modern, its design was a retro Neo-Gothic look.

You can tour the bridge at the **Tower Bridge Exhibition,** with a history display and a peek at the Victorian engine room that lifts the span. It's overpriced at £8, though the city views from the walkways are spectacular (daily 10:00-18:00 in summer, 9:30-17:30 in winter, last entry 30 minutes before closing, enter at the northwest tower, Tube: Tower Hill, tel. 020/7403-3761, www.towerbridge.org.uk).

The bridge is most interesting when the drawbridge lifts to let ships pass, as it does a thousand times a year, but it's best viewed from outside the museum. For the bridge-lifting schedule, check the website or call (see previous page for contact info).

Nearby: The best remaining bit of London's **Roman Wall** is just north of the Tower (at the Tower Hill Tube station). The chic **St. Katharine Dock,** just east of Tower Bridge, has private yachts, mod shops, a recommended medieval banquet, and the classic Dickens Inn, fun for a drink or pub lunch. Across the bridge, on the South Bank, is the upscale Butlers Wharf area, as well as City Hall, museums, the Jubilee Walkway, and, towering overhead, the Shard. Or you can head north to Liverpool Street Station, and stroll London's East End (described next).

Sights in East London

▲East End

This formerly industrial area just beyond Liverpool Street Station has turned into one of London's trendy spots. It boasts a colorful mix of bustling markets, late-night dance clubs, the Bangladeshi ghetto (called "Banglatown"), and tenements of Jack the Ripper's London, all in the shadow of glittering new skyscrapers. Head up Brick Lane for a meal in "the curry capital of Europe," or check out the former Truman Brewery, which now houses a Sunday market, cool shops, and Café 1001 (good coffee). This neighborhood is best on Sunday afternoons, when the Spitalfields, Petticoat Lane, and Backyard markets thrive.

▲Geffrye Museum

This low-key but well-organized museum—housed in an 18th-century almshouse—is located north of Liverpool Street Station in the hip Shoreditch area. Walk past 11 English living rooms, furnished and decorated in styles from 1600 to 2000, then descend the circular stairs to see changing exhibits on home decor. In summer, explore the fragrant herb garden.

Cost and Hours: Free, fees for (optional) special exhibits, Tue-Sat 10:00-17:00, Sun 12:00-17:00, closed Mon, garden open April-Oct, 136 Kingsland Road, tel. 020/7739-9893, www.geffrye-museum.org.uk.

Getting There: Take the Tube to Liverpool Street, then ride the bus 10 minutes north (bus #149 or #242). Or take the East London line on the Overground to the Hoxton stop, which is right next to the museum (Tube tickets and Oyster cards also valid on Overground).

The South Bank

Sights on the South Bank

The South Bank of the Thames is a thriving arts and cultural center, tied together by the riverfront Jubilee Walkway.

▲Jubilee Walkway

This riverside path is a popular, pub-crawling pedestrian promenade that stretches all along the South Bank, offering grand views of the Houses of Parliament and St. Paul's. On a sunny day, this is the place to see Londoners out strolling. The Walkway hugs the river except just east of London Bridge, where it cuts inland for a couple of blocks. It was recently expanded into a 60-mile "Greenway" circling the city, including the 2012 Olympics site.

▲▲London Eye

This giant Ferris wheel, towering above London opposite Big Ben, is the world's highest observational wheel and London's answer to the Eiffel Tower. Riding it is a memorable experience, even though London doesn't have much of a skyline, and the price is borderline outrageous. Whether you ride or not, the wheel is a sight to behold.

The experience starts with a brief (four-minute) and engaging show combining a 3-D movie with wind and water effects. Then it's

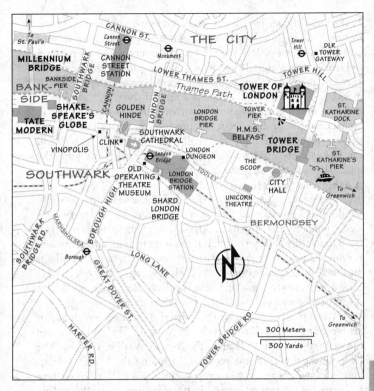

time to spin around the Eye. Designed like a giant bicycle wheel, it's a pan-European undertaking: British steel and Dutch engineering, with Czech, German, French, and Italian mechanical parts. It's also very "green," running extremely efficiently and virtually silently. Twenty-five people ride in each of its 32 air-conditioned capsules for the 30-minute rotation (you go around only once). Each capsule has a bench, but most people stand. From the top of this 443-foot-high wheel even Big Ben looks small.

Cost: £19, or pay roughly twice as much for a combo-ticket with Madame Tussauds Waxworks (sold cheaper online), other packages are available. Buy tickets at the box office (in the corner of the County Hall building nearest the Eye), in advance by calling 0870-500-0600 or save 10 percent by booking online at www. londoneye.com.

Hours: Daily July-Aug 10:00-21:30, April-June 10:00-21:00, Sept-March 10:00-20:00, these are last-ascent times, closed Dec 25 and a few days in Jan for annual maintenance, Tube: Waterloo or Westminster. Thames boats come and go from Waterloo Pier at the foot of the wheel.

Crowd-Beating Tips: The London Eye is busiest between

11:00 and 17:00, especially on weekends year-round and every day in July and August. When it's crowded, you might have to wait up to 30 minutes to buy your ticket, then another 30-45 minutes to board your capsule. If you plan to visit during a busy time, call ahead or go online to pre-book your ticket, then punch your confirmation code into the automated machine in the ticket office (otherwise, you can pick up your ticket in the short "Groups and Ticket Collection" line at desk #5; if you pre-reserve, there's rarely a wait to pick up your ticket, but you'll still wait to board the wheel). You can pay an extra £10 for a Fast Track ticket that lets you jump the queue, but the time you save is probably not worth the expense.

▲▲Imperial War Museum

This impressive museum covers the wars of the last century—from World War I biplanes, to the rise of fascism, to Montgomery's Africa campaign tank, to the Cold War, the Cuban Missile Crisis, the Troubles in Northern Ireland, the wars in Iraq, and terrorism. Rather than glorify war, the museum does its best to shine a light on the 100 million deaths of the 20th century. It shows everyday life for people back home and never neglects the human side of one of civilization's more uncivilized, persistent traits.

Allow plenty of time, as this powerful museum—with lots of artifacts and video clips—can be engrossing. The highlights are the main WWI and WII area, the "Secret War" section, and the Holocaust exhibit. (Some sections, including the WWI exhibit, may be closed for renovation until summer 2014.) War wonks love the place, as do general history buffs who enjoy patiently reading displays. For the rest, there are enough interactive experiences and multimedia exhibits and submarines for the kids to climb in to keep it interesting.

Cost and Hours: Free, daily 10:00-18:00, last entry 17:45, temporary exhibits extra, £3.50 audioguide, guided tours usually Sat-Sun at 11:30 and 13:30—confirm at info desk, Tube: Lambeth North or Elephant and Castle; buses #3, #12, and #159 all come here from Westminster area; tel. 020/7416-5000, www.iwm.org.uk.

Visiting the Museum: Start with the museum's latest pride and joy: the WWI galleries, newly souped up for the centennial anniversary of the start of the "Great War." Exhibits cover the various theaters, then follow the war at sea, the home front, and the Treaty of Versailles and interwar years. The Trench Experience lets you walk through a dark, chaotic, smelly WWI trench. Then head into the WWII section that explains Blitzkrieg and its effects (see an actual Nazi parachute bomb like the ones that devastated London). The Blitz Experience is a walk-through simulator that assaults the senses with the noise and intensity of a WWII air raid on London (begins every 10 minutes). End with a visit to a special exhibit celebrating Field Marshal Bernard Montgomery, and the displays about conflicts since 1945.

The cinema on the ground floor shows a rotating selection of films. Up on the first floor, you'll get the best view of the entry hall's **large exhibits**—including Monty's tank, several field guns, and, dangling overhead, vintage planes. Imagine the awesome power of the 50-foot V-2 rocket (towering up from the ground floor)—the kind the Nazis rained down on London, which could arrive silently and destroy a city block.

Near the first-floor stairwell is the **"Secret War"** exhibit, which peeks into the intrigues of espionage, and poses challenging questions about the role of secrecy in government.

The second floor has temporary exhibits and the **John Singer Sargent room,** an art gallery of military-themed works; hiding behind the entryway is Sargent's *Gassed* (1919) and other giant canvases. Across the hall is a provocative 30-minute **film** about genocide, *Crimes Against Humanity.* The third-floor section on the **Holocaust,** one of the best on the subject anywhere, tells the story with powerful videos, artifacts, and fine explanations.

From Tate Modern to City Hall

These sights are in Southwark (SUTH-uck), the core of the tourist's South Bank. Southwark was for centuries the place Londoners would go to escape the rules and decency of the city and let their hair down. Bearbaiting, brothels, rollicking pubs, and theater—you name the dream, and it could be fulfilled just across the Thames. A run-down warehouse district through the 20th century, it's been gentrified with classy restaurants, office parks, pedestrian promenades, major sights (such as the Tate Modern and Shakespeare's Globe), and a colorful collection of lesser sights. The area is easy on foot and a scenic—though circuitous—way to connect the Tower of London with St. Paul's.

▲▲Tate Modern

Dedicated in the spring of 2000, the striking museum across the river from St. Paul's opened the new century with art from the previous one. Its powerhouse collection of Monet, Matisse, Dalí, Picasso, Warhol, and much more is displayed in a converted powerhouse.

The permanent collection is on the third and fifth floors. Paintings are arranged according to theme, not chronologically or by artist. Paintings by Picasso, for example, are scattered all over the building. Don't just come to see the Old Masters of modernism. Push your mental envelope with more recent works by Pollock, Miró, Bacon, Picabia, Beuys, Twombly, and others.

Of equal interest are the many temporary exhibits featuring cutting-edge art. Each year, the main hall features a different monumental installation by a prominent artist—always one of the highlights of the art world. The Tate is constructing a new wing to the south, which will double its exhibition space. The performance halls should be open in time for your visit; the rest of the complex is set to open later in 2014.

Cost and Hours: Free, but £4 donation appreciated, fee for special exhibitions, audioguide-£4, daily 10:00-18:00, Fri-Sat until 22:00, last entry to temporary exhibits 45 minutes before closing, especially crowded on weekend days (crowds thin out on Fri and Sat evenings), free 45-minute **guided tours** are offered about four times daily (ask for schedule at info desk), no photos beyond entrance hall, several cafés, tel. 020/7887-8888, www.tate.org.uk.

Getting There: Cross the Millennium Bridge from St. Paul's; take the Tube to Southwark, London Bridge, or Mansion House and walk 10-15 minutes; or catch Thames Clippers' Tate Boat ferry service from the Tate Britain (£6 one-way or £13.60 for day ticket, 33 percent discount with Travelcard, buy ticket at gallery desk or on board, departs every 40 minutes from 9:55 to 17:00, 18 minutes, check schedule at www.tate.org.uk/visit/tate-boat).

▲Millennium Bridge

The pedestrian bridge links St. Paul's Cathedral and the Tate Modern across the Thames. This is London's first new bridge in a century. When it opened, the $25 million bridge wiggled when people walked on it, so it promptly closed for repairs; 20 months and $8 million later, it reopened. Nicknamed the "blade of light" for its sleek minimalist design (370 yards long, four yards wide, stainless steel with teak planks), its clever aerodynamic handrails deflect wind over the heads of pedestrians.

▲▲Shakespeare's Globe

This replica of the original Globe Theatre was built, half-timbered and thatched, as it was in Shakespeare's time. (This is the first thatched roof constructed in London since they were outlawed after the Great Fire of 1666.) The Globe originally accommodated 2,200 seated and another 1,000 standing. Today, slightly smaller and leaving space for reasonable aisles, the theater holds 800 seated and 600 groundlings. Its promoters brag that the theater melds "the three A's"—actors, audience, and architecture—with each contributing to the play. The working theater hosts authentic performances of Shakespeare's plays with actors in period costumes, modern interpretations of his works, and some works by other playwrights. For details on attending a play, see page 760.

Visiting the Globe: The complex has four parts: the theater itself, the box office, a museum, and the Jacobean Indoor Theatre. The Globe Exhibition ticket includes both a tour of the Globe theater and the museum.

Museum: First, you browse on your own (with the included audioguide) through displays of Elizabethan-era costumes and makeup, music, script-printing, and special effects. There are early folios and objects that were dug up on site. A video and scale models help put Shakespearean theater within the context of the times. (The Globe opened one year after England mastered the seas by defeating the Spanish Armada. The debut play was Shakespeare's *Julius Caesar.*) You'll also learn how they built the replica in modern times, using Elizabethan materials and techniques. Take advantage of the touchscreens to delve into specific topics.

Theater: You must tour the theater at the time stamped on your ticket, but you can come back to the museum afterward; tickets are good all day. A guide (usually an actor) leads you into the theater to see the stage and the various seating areas for the different classes of people. You take a seat and learn how the new Globe is similar to the old Globe (open-air performances, standing-room by the stage, no curtain) and how it's different (female actors today, lights for night performances, concrete floor). It's not a backstage tour—you don't see dressing rooms or costume shops or sit in on rehearsals, though you may see workers building sets for a new production. You mostly sit and listen. The guides are energetic, theatrical, and knowledgeable, bringing the Elizabethan period to life.

When matinee performances are going on, you can't tour the theater. But you can see the museum, then tour the nearby (and less interesting) Rose Theatre instead.

Cost and Hours: £13.50 includes museum and 40-minute tour, £10 when only the Rose Theatre is available for touring, tickets good all day; complex open daily 9:00-17:00; exhibition and tours: May-Sept—Globe tours offered mornings only with Rose Theatre tours in afternoon; Oct-April—Globe tours run all day, tours start every 15-30 minutes; on the South Bank directly across Thames over Southwark Bridge from St. Paul's, Tube: Mansion House or London Bridge plus a 10-minute walk; tel. 020/7902-1400 or 020/7902-1500, www.shakespearesglobe.com.

Jacobean Indoor Theater: The new Sam Wanamaker Playhouse, attached to the back of the current Globe complex, allows performances to continue through the winter. The intimate, horseshoe-shaped venue seats fewer than 350, and is designed to use authentic candle-lighting for performances focused less on Shakespeare and more on the work of his contemporaries (Jonson, Marlow, Fletcher).

Eating: The Swan at the Globe café offers a sit-down restaurant (for lunch and dinner, reservations recommended, tel. 020/7928-9444), a drinks-and-plates bar, and a sandwich-and-coffee cart (daily 9:00-closing, depending on performance times).

LONDON

Vinopolis: City of Wine

While it seems illogical to have a huge wine museum in beer-loving London, Vinopolis makes a good case. Built over a Roman wine store and filling the massive vaults of an old wine warehouse, the museum offers an excellent audioguide with a light yet earnest history of wine to accompany your sips of various mediocre reds and whites, ports, and champagnes. Allow some time, as the audioguide takes an hour and a half—and the sipping can slow things down pleasantly. This place is popular. Booking ahead for Friday and Saturday nights is a must.

Cost and Hours: Self-guided tour options range from £22.50 to £40—each includes about five wine tastes and an audioguide. Other options are available for guided tours. Some packages also include whiskey (the new wine), other spirits, or a meal. Open Thu-Fri 14:00-22:00, Sat 12:00-22:00, Sun 12:00-18:00, closed Mon-Wed, last entry 2.5 hours before closing, between Shakespeare's Globe and Southwark Cathedral at 1 Bank End, Tube: London Bridge, tel. 020/7940-3000, www.vinopolis.co.uk.

The Clink Prison Museum

Proudly the "original clink," this was, until 1780, where law-abiding citizens threw Southwark troublemakers. Today, it's a low-tech torture museum filling grotty old rooms with papier-mâché gore. Unfortunately, there's little that seriously deals with the fascinating problem of law and order in Southwark, where 18th-century Londoners went for a good time.

Cost and Hours: Overpriced at £7; July-Sept daily 10:00-21:00; Oct-June Mon-Fri 10:00-18:00, Sat-Sun until 19:30; 1 Clink Street, Tube: London Bridge, tel. 020/7403-0900, www.clink.co.uk.

Golden Hinde Replica

This is a full-size replica of the 16th-century warship in which Sir Francis Drake circumnavigated the globe from 1577 to 1580. Commanding this ship, Drake earned his reputation as history's most successful pirate. The original is long gone, but this boat has logged more than 100,000 miles, including a voyage around the world. While the ship is fun to see, its interior is not worth touring.

Cost and Hours: £6, daily 10:00-17:30, sometimes closed for private events, Tube: London Bridge, ticket office just up Pickfords Wharf from the ship, tel. 020/7403-0123, www.goldenhinde.com.

▲Southwark Cathedral

While made a cathedral only in 1905, it's been the neighborhood church since the 13th century, and comes with some interesting history. The enthusiastic docents give impromptu tours if you ask.

Cost and Hours: Free, but donation requested (you'll likely be approached about the donation, so be prepared with at least £1 or a simple "No"), daily 8:00-18:00—though only the back of the nave is open to discreet sightseers during frequent services, last entry 30 minutes before closing, £3.50 guidebook, no photos without permission, Tube: London Bridge. Tel. 020/7367-6700, http://cathedral.southwark.anglican.org.

Music: The cathedral hosts services weekdays at 17:30 and Sat at 16:00—sometimes spoken, sometimes evensong, so call or check the website for details; Sun choral Eucharist at 11:00 and evensong at 15:00. They also host organ recitals Mon at 13:10 and music recitals Tue at 15:15 (call to confirm both).

▲Old Operating Theatre Museum and Herb Garret

Climb a tight and creaky wooden spiral staircase to a church attic where you'll find a garret used to dry medicinal herbs, a fascinating exhibit on Victorian surgery, cases of well-described 19th-century medical paraphernalia, and a special look at "anesthesia, the defeat of pain." Then you stumble upon Britain's oldest operating theater, where limbs were sawed off way back in 1821. The museum occasionally offers "demonstrations." While fun and interesting to some, they can be distressing to those who are squeamish or have a vivid imagination.

Cost and Hours: £6, cash only, borrowable laminated descriptions, ask about planned audioguide, daily 10:30-16:45, closed Dec 15-Jan 5, 9a St. Thomas Street, Tube: London Bridge, tel. 020/7188-2679, www.thegarret.org.uk.

The Shard

Rocketing dramatically 1,020 feet above the south end of the London Bridge, this recent addition to London's skyline is by far the tallest building in Western Europe. Designed by Renzo Piano (best known as the co-architect of Paris' Pompidou Center), the glass-clad building shimmers in the sun and its prickly top glows like the city's nightlight after dark. If you go, you'll take a two-part elevator ride up to the 68th floor, then climb up one story to the main (enclosed) observation platform. Climbing up to the 72nd floor gets you to the open-air deck, where the wind roars over the glass enclosure (£25 if booked a day in advance, £29 for same-day reservations, daily 9:00-22:00, last entry at 20:30, Tube: London Bridge—use London Bridge exit, tel. 0844-499-7111, www.theviewfromtheshard.com).

HMS *Belfast*

"The last big-gun armored warship of World War II" clogs the Thames just upstream from the Tower Bridge. This huge vessel—now manned with wax sailors—thrills kids who always dreamed of sitting in a turret shooting off their imaginary guns. If you're into WWII warships, this is the ultimate. Otherwise, it's just lots of exercise with a nice view of the Tower Bridge.

Cost and Hours: £12.70, or £14 with voluntary donation, includes audioguide, daily March-Oct 10:00-18:00, Nov-Feb 10:00-

17:00, last entry one hour before closing, Tube: London Bridge, tel. 020/7940-6300, www.iwm.org.uk/visits/hms-belfast.

City Hall

The glassy, egg-shaped building near the south end of Tower Bridge is London's City Hall, designed by Sir Norman Foster, the architect who worked on London's Millennium Bridge and Berlin's Reichstag. Nicknamed "the Armadillo," City Hall houses the office of London's mayor—the blonde, flamboyant, conservative former journalist and author Boris Johnson. He consults here with the Assembly representatives of the city's 25 districts. An interior spiral ramp allows visitors to watch and hear the action below in the Assembly Chamber—ride the lift to floor 2 (the highest visitors can go) and spiral down. On the lower ground floor is a large aerial photograph of London and a handy cafeteria. Next to City Hall is the outdoor amphitheater called The Scoop (Tube: London Bridge, schedule at www.morelondon.com—click on "The Scoop at More London").

Cost and Hours: Free, open to visitors Mon-Thu 8:30-18:00, Fri 8:30-17:30, closed Sat-Sun; Tube: London Bridge station plus 10-minute walk, or Tower Hill station plus 15-minute walk; tel. 020/7983-4000, www.london.gov.uk.

Sights in West London

▲▲Tate Britain

One of Europe's great art houses, Tate Britain specializes in British painting from the 16th century through modern times. This is people's art, with realistic paintings rooted in the culture, landscape, and stories of the British Isles.

Look for Hogarth's sketches of gritty London life, Gainsborough's twinkle-toe ladies, Blake's glowing angels, Constable's clouds, the swooning realism of the Pre-Raphaelites, and room after room of J. M. W. Turner's proto-Impressionist tempests. In the modern art wing, there's Francis Bacon's screaming nightmares, Henry Moore statues, and the camera-eye portraits of Hockney and Freud.

If any of these names are new to you, don't worry. You'll likely see a few "famous" works you didn't know were British and exit the Tate Britain with at least one new favorite artist.

Cost and Hours: Free but £4 donation requested, admission fee for (optional) temporary exhibits, map-£1 suggested donation, ask if audioguide is available; daily 10:00-18:00, first Fri of the month until 22:00 (or possibly every Fri—check online or call to confirm), last entry to special exhibitions at 17:15 (or 21:15 when open late), free tours on various topics offered throughout the

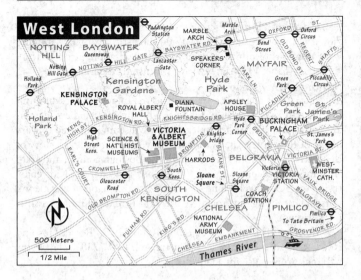

day—ask at the information desk or call ahead; café and restaurant, tel. 020/7887-8888, www.tate.org.uk.

Getting There: It's on the Thames River, south of Big Ben and north of Vauxhall Bridge. Take the Tube to Pimlico, then walk seven minutes. Or hop the Tate Boat museum ferry from the Tate Modern (£6 one-way, £13.60 day ticket, 33 percent discount with Travelcard, buy ticket at gallery desk or on board, departs every 40 minutes from 10:00 to 17:00, 18 minutes, www.tate.org.uk/visit/tate-boat).

Victoria Station

From underneath this station's iron-and-glass canopy, trains depart for the south of England and Gatwick Airport. While Victoria Station is famous and a major Tube stop, few tourists actually take trains from here—most just come to take in the exciting bustle. It's a fun place to just be a "rock in a river" teeming with commuters and services. The station is surrounded by big red buses and taxis, travel agencies, and lousy eateries. It's next to the main intercity bus station (Victoria Coach Station) and the best inexpensive lodgings in town.

Westminster Cathedral

This cathedral, the largest Catholic church in England and just a block from Victoria Station, is strikingly Neo-Byzantine, but not very historic or important to visit. Opened in 1903, the church has an unfinished interior, with a spooky, blackened ceiling waiting for the mosaics that are supposed to be placed there. While it's definitely not Westminster Abbey, half the tourists wandering around inside seem to think it is. Take the lift to the top of the 273-foot bell tower for a view of the glassy office blocks of Victoria Station.

Cost and Hours: Free entry, £5 for the lift; church—daily 7:00-19:00; tower—daily 9:30-17:00, last trip at 16:30; 5-minute walk from bus terminus in front of Victoria Station, just off Victoria Street, Tube: Victoria, www.westminstercathedral.org.uk.

National Army Museum

This museum is not as awe-inspiring as the Imperial War Museum, but it's still fun, especially for kids who are into soldiers, armor, and guns. And while the Imperial War Museum is limited to wars of the 20th century, the National Army Museum tells the story of the British army from 1415 through the Bosnian conflict and Iraq, with lots of Redcoat lore and a good look at Waterloo. Kids enjoy trying on a Cromwellian helmet, seeing the skeleton of Napoleon's horse, and peering out from a World War I trench through a working periscope.

Cost and Hours: Free, daily 10:00-17:30, Royal Hospital Road, Chelsea, Tube: Sloane Square, tel. 020/7730-0717, www. national-army-museum.ac.uk.

Hyde Park and Nearby

A number of worthwhile sights border this grand park, from Apsley House on the east to the newly renovated Kensington Palace on the west.

▲Apsley House (Wellington Museum)

Having beaten Napoleon at Waterloo, Arthur Wellesley, the First Duke of Wellington, was once the most famous man in Europe. He was given a huge fortune, with which he purchased London's ultimate address, #1 London. His refurbished mansion offers a nice interior, a handful of world-class paintings, and a glimpse at the life of the great soldier and two-time prime minister. The highlight is the large ballroom, the Waterloo Gallery, decorated with Anthony van Dyck's *Charles I on Horseback* (over the main fireplace), Diego Velázquez's earthy *The Water-Seller of Seville* (to the left of Van Dyck), Jan Steen's playful *The Dissolute Household* (to the right), and a large portrait of Wellington by Francisco Goya (farther right).

Those who know something about Wellington ahead of time will appreciate the place much more than those who don't, as there's scarce biographical background. The place is well-described by the included audioguide, which has sound bites from the current Duke of Wellington (who still lives at Apsley).

Cost and Hours: £6.50, free on June 18—Waterloo Day, April-Oct Wed-Sun 11:00-17:00, closed Mon-Tue; Nov-March Sat-Sun 10:00-16:00, closed Mon-Fri; 20 yards from Hyde Park Corner Tube station, tel. 020/7499-5676, www.english-heritage. org.uk.

Nearby: Hyde Park's pleasant rose garden is picnic-friendly. **Wellington Arch,** which stands just across the street, is open to the public but not worth the £4 charge (or £8 combo-ticket with Apsley House; elevator up, lousy views and boring exhibits).

▲**Hyde Park and Speakers' Corner**

London's "Central Park," originally Henry VIII's hunting grounds, has more than 600 acres of lush greenery, the huge man-made Serpentine Lake, the royal Kensington Palace and Orangery (described later), and the ornate Neo-Gothic Albert Memorial across from the Royal Albert Hall. The western half of the park is known as Kensington Gardens.

On Sundays, from just after noon until early evening, **Speakers' Corner** offers soapbox oratory at its best (northeast corner of the park, Tube: Marble Arch). Characters climb their stepladders, wave their flags, pound emphatically on their sandwich boards, and share what they are convinced is their wisdom. Regulars have resident hecklers who know their lines and are always ready with a verbal jab or barb. "The grass roots of democracy" is actually a holdover from when the gallows stood here and the criminal was allowed to say just about anything he wanted to before he swung. I dare you to raise your voice and gather a crowd—it's easy to do.

The **Princess Diana Memorial Fountain** honors the "People's Princess," who once lived in nearby Kensington Palace. The low-key circular stream, great for cooling off your feet on a hot day, is in the south-central part of the park, near the Albert Memorial and Serpentine Gallery. A similarly named but different sight, the **Diana, Princess of Wales Memorial Playground,** is in the north-west corner of the park.

▲▲▲**Victoria and Albert Museum**

The world's top collection of decorative arts (vases, stained glass, fine furniture, clothing, jewelry, carpets, and more) is a surprisingly interesting assortment of crafts from the West, as well as Asian and Islamic cultures. The British Galleries are grand, but there's much more to see, including Raphael's tapestry cartoons and a cast of Trajan's Column that depicts the emperor's conquests.

You'll also see one of Leonardo da Vinci's notebooks, underwear through the ages, a Chihuly chandelier, a life-size *David* with detachable fig leaf, Henry VIII's quill pen, and Mick Jagger's sequined jumpsuit. From the worlds of Islam and India, there are stunning carpets, the ring of the man who built the Taj Mahal, and a mechanical tiger that eats Brits.

Best of all, the objects are all quite beautiful. You could spend days in the place. Pick up a museum map and wander at will.

Cost and Hours: Free, but £3 donation requested, sometimes pricey fees for (optional) special exhibits, £1 suggested donation for much-needed museum map, daily 10:00-17:45, some galleries open Fri until 22:00, free one-hour tours daily on the half-hour 10:30-15:30, on Cromwell Road in South Kensington, Tube: South

Kensington, from the Tube station a long tunnel leads directly to museum, tel. 020/7942-2000, www.vam.ac.uk.

▲▲Natural History Museum

Across the street from Victoria and Albert, this mammoth museum is housed in a giant and wonderful Victorian, Neo-Romanesque building. In the main hall, above a big dinosaur skeleton and under a massive slice of sequoia tree, Charles Darwin sits as if upon a throne overseeing it all. Built in the 1870s specifically for the huge collection (50 million specimens), the building has several color-coded "zones" that cover everything from life (creepy-crawlies, human biology, "our place in evolution," and awe-inspiring dinosaurs) to earth science (meteors, volcanoes, earthquakes, and so on). Use the helpful map (£1 suggested donation) to find your way through the collection.

Exhibits are wonderfully explained, with lots of creative, interactive displays. Pop in, if only for the wild collection of dinosaurs and to hear English children exclaim, "Oh my goodness!" Get oriented by talking with one of the many "visit planners" (helpful guides scattered throughout the museum), review the "What's on Today" board for special events and tours, and note which sections are closed (according to the signs, these sections aren't being "renovated," but are "evolving"). While the dinosaur hall often has a long line, everything else is wide open. Don't miss the vault in the mineralogy section (top floor of the green zone), with rare and precious stones, including a meteorite from Mars and the Aurora Pyramid of Hope, displaying 296 diamonds showing their full range of natural colors.

Cost and Hours: Free, fees for (optional) special exhibits, daily 10:00-17:50, until 22:30 last Fri of the month, last entry 20 minutes before closing, long tunnel leads directly from South Kensington Tube station to museum, tel. 020/7942-5000, exhibit info and reservations tel. 020/7942-5011, www.nhm.ac.uk.

▲Science Museum

Next door to the Natural History Museum, this sprawling wonderland for curious minds is kid-perfect, with themes such as measuring time, exploring space, climate change, and the evolution of modern medicine. It offers hands-on fun, from moonwalks to deep-sea exploration, with trendy technology exhibits and a state-of-the-art IMAX theater (shows-£10, £8 for kids).

Cost and Hours: Free, daily 10:00-18:00, until 19:00 during school holidays, Exhibition Road, Tube: South Kensington, tel. 0870-870-4868, www.sciencemuseum.org.uk.

▲▲Kensington Palace

Sitting primly on its pleasant parkside grounds, this newly renovated royal residence provides a glimpse into the courtly lives of several important residents: William and Mary, the Hanovers (the

"Georges"), and Queen Victoria (born and raised in this palace). The spaces are immaculately restored and creatively presented, with engaging, user-friendly exhibits designed to appeal to adults and kids alike—making this a particularly entertaining royal sight. The Victoria exhibit is especially worthwhile.

Kensington was once the residence of King William and Queen Mary, who moved from Whitehall in central London in 1689 to the more pristine and peaceful village of Kensington (since engulfed by London). Sir Christopher Wren converted an existing house into the palace, which became the center of English court life until 1837, when Queen Victoria moved into Buckingham Palace. Since then, lesser royals have bedded down in Kensington Palace. Princess Diana lived here from her 1981 marriage to Prince Charles until her death in 1997. Today it's home to three of Charles' cousins, and the official London home of Will and Kate.

After buying your ticket, you have three different color-coded routes to choose from: the Queen's State Apartments (with highly conceptual exhibits focusing on the later Stuart dynasty—William and Mary, and Mary's sister, Queen Anne); the King's State Apartments (the grandest spaces, from Hanoverian times); and the "Victoria Revealed" exhibit (telling the story, through quotes and artifacts, of Britain's longest-ruling monarch). If you're short on time, choose "Victoria Revealed." A fourth, temporary-exhibit route may also be offered during your visit.

Cost and Hours: £14.50 (includes 10 percent optional donation), save £1 by booking online, daily 10:00-18:00, until 17:00 Nov-Feb, last entry one hour before closing, a 10-minute hike through Kensington Gardens from either Queensway or High Street Kensington Tube station, tel. 0870-751-5170 or 0844-482-7777, www.hrp.org.uk.

Nearby: Garden enthusiasts enjoy popping into the secluded Sunken Garden, 50 yards from the exit. Consider afternoon tea at the nearby Orangery, built as a greenhouse for Queen Anne in 1704 (tea served 14:00-18:00, until 17:00 Nov-Feb, £20 "Orangery tea," à la carte treats, no reservations taken, tel. 020/3166-6113, www.hrp.org.uk).

Sights in Greater London

East of London

Olympic Park

From July 27 to August 12, 2012, London hosted athletes from 205 nations in the 30th Olympiad. Festivities centered around Olympic Park, filling the Lea Valley, about seven miles northeast of downtown London. Lea Valley used to be the site of derelict factories, mountains of discarded tires, and Europe's biggest refrigerator dump. But this area now glistens with gardens, greenery, and state-of-the-art construction.

Olympic Park is huge—bigger than Hyde Park/Kensington Gardens. It's also quite beautiful, laced with canals and tributaries of the Lea River. Now that the games are over, the area is gradually being converted into a public park (and may be open in time for your visit). The best overview of the whole area—with fine views of the stadium, the Orbit (a giant climbable statue), the grounds, the Aquatics Centre, and the other structures—is along a 500-yard-long berm called the **Greenway**, which sits at the park's southern perimeter. The easiest landmark to head for is the View Tube, a covered shelter with a free lookout tower, café, WC, and maps.

Getting There: From downtown London, it's about a 25-minute ride on the Tube and/or DLR to one of the stations that ring Olympic Park.

West of London
▲▲Kew Gardens
For a fine riverside park and a palatial greenhouse jungle to swing through, take the Tube or the boat to every botanist's favorite escape, Kew Gardens. While to most visitors the Royal Botanic Gardens of Kew are simply a delightful opportunity to wander among 33,000 different types of plants, to the hardworking organization that runs the gardens, they are a way to promote the understanding and preservation of the botanical diversity of our planet. The Kew Tube station drops you in a little community of plant-and-herb shops, a two-block walk from Victoria Gate (the main garden entrance). Pick up a map brochure and check at the gate for a monthly listing of best blooms.

Garden-lovers could spend days exploring Kew's 300 acres. For a quick visit, spend a fragrant hour wandering through three buildings: the Palm House, a humid Victorian world of iron, glass, and tropical plants that was built in 1844; a Waterlily House that Monet would swim for; and the Princess of Wales Conservatory, a modern greenhouse with many different climate zones growing countless cacti, bug-munching carnivorous plants, and more. With extra time, check out the Xstrata Treetop Walkway, a 200-yard-long scenic steel walkway that puts you high in the canopy 60 feet above the ground. Young kids will love the Climbers and Creepers indoor/outdoor playground and little zip line, as well as a slow and easy ride on the hop-on, hop-off Kew Explorer tram (£4 for narrated 40-minute ride, departs on the hour from 11:00 from near Victoria Gate).

Cost: £14, discounted to £12 45 minutes before greenhouses close, kids under 17 free, £5.50 for Kew Palace only.

Hours: April-Aug Mon-Fri 9:30-18:30, Sat-Sun 9:30-19:30, closes earlier Sept-March—check schedule online, palace closed Nov-March, last entry to gardens 30 minutes before closing, galleries and conservatories close at 17:30 in high season—earlier off-season, free one-hour walking tours daily at 11:00 and 13:30, Tube: Kew Gardens, boats run April-Oct between Kew Gardens and Westminster Pier—see page 707, switchboard tel. 020/8332-5000, recorded info tel. 020/8332-5655, www.kew.org.

Eating: For a sun-dappled lunch or snack, walk 10 minutes from the Palm House to the Orangery Cafeteria (£4 sandwiches, £8-12 lunches, daily 10:00-17:30, until 15:15 in winter, closes early for events, tel. 0844-482-7777, www.hrp.org.uk).

North of London
Highgate Cemetery
Located in the tea-cozy-cute village of Highgate, north of the city, this Victorian cemetery represents a fascinating, offbeat piece of London history. Built as a private cemetery, this was the fashionable place to bury the wealthy dead in the late 1800s. It has themed mausoleums, professional mourners, and several high-profile residents in its East Cemetery, including Karl Marx, George Eliot, and Douglas Adams. The tomb of "Godfather of Punk" Malcolm McLaren (former manager of the Sex Pistols) is often covered with rotten veggies.

Cost and Hours: East Cemetery—£3, Mon-Fri 10:00-17:00, Sat-Sun 11:00-17:00, closes one hour earlier in winter, last entry 30 minutes before closing; older, creepier West Cemetery—viewable by £7 guided tour only, Mon-Fri at 14:00—arrive by 13:45, Sat-Sun hourly 11:00-15:00, call ahead to reserve; Tube: Archway (Northern Line/High Barnet branch) or—slower—bus #C2 from Victoria Station or Oxford Circus, tel. 020/8340-1834, www.highgate-cemetery.org.

The Making of Harry Potter: Warner Bros. Studio Tour
A nirvana for Potterphiles, this attraction lets fans young and old see the actual sets and props that were used in the films, watch video interviews with the actors and filmmakers, and view exhibits about how the films' special effects were created. Visitors must book a time slot in advance—it's essential to reserve your visit online as far ahead as possible. Since it's located in Leavesden, a 20-minute train ride from London, and takes about three hours to experience, a visit here will eat up the better part of a day.

Cost and Hours: £28, kids ages 5 to 15-£21, family ticket for 2 adults and 2 kids-£83, audio/videoguide-£5, tours depart daily 10:00-18:00, café, still photography allowed, tel. 0845-084-0900, www.wbstudiotour.co.uk.

Getting There: Reaching the studio requires a **train and shuttle bus** connection. First, take the train from London Euston to Watford Junction (about 5/hour, 15-20 minutes). From there, you can take a Mullany's Coaches shuttle bus to the studio tour (2/hour, 15 minutes, arrive at Watford Junction at least 45 minutes before your tour entrance time, £1.50 one-way, £2 round-trip). Golden Tours runs three more direct (and more expensive) **buses** per day between their office near Victoria Station in central London and the studio (price includes round-trip bus and entrance: adults-£55, kids-£50; leaves London at 8:00, 11:00, and 14:00, tour begins 2 hours after bus departs, reserve ahead at www.goldentours.com).

Entertainment in London

For the best list of what's happening and a look at the latest London scene, pick up a current copy of *Time Out* (£3 at newsstands, www.timeout.com). The TI's free monthly *London Planner* covers sights, events, and plays at least as well as *Time Out* does.

Theater (a.k.a. "Theatre")

London's theater rivals Broadway's in quality and usually beats it in price. Choose from 200 offerings—Shakespeare, musicals, comedies, thrillers, sex farces, cutting-edge fringe, revivals starring movie celebs, and more. London does it all well. I prefer big, glitzy—even bombastic—musicals over serious chamber dramas, simply because London can deliver the lights, booming voices, dancers, and multimedia spectacle I rarely get back home. (If you're a regular visitor to Broadway or Las Vegas—where you have access to similar spectacles—you might prefer some of London's more low-key offerings.)

There are also plenty of enticing plays to choose from, ranging from revivals of classics to cutting-edge works by the hottest young playwrights. Many star huge-name celebrities (you'll see the latest offerings advertised all over the Tube and elsewhere). London is a magnet for movie stars who want to stretch their acting chops.

Most theaters, marked on tourist maps, are found in the West End between Piccadilly and Covent Garden. Box offices, hotels, and TIs offer a handy, free, and weekly *Official London Theatre Guide*. From home, you can look online at www.officiallondontheatre.co.uk for the latest on what's currently playing in London.

Most performances are nightly except Sunday, usually with one or two matinees a week. The few shows that run on Sundays are mostly family fare (*Matilda*, *The Lion King*, and so on) and, in summer, Shakespeare at the Globe (late April-early Oct—and possibly year-round once their new indoor Jacobean Theatre opens, possibly in time for your visit). Tickets range from about £15 to £65. Matinees are generally cheaper and rarely sell out.

Theater Lingo: It's helpful to know these terms when booking tickets—stalls (ground floor), dress circle (first balcony), upper circle (second balcony), balcony (sky-high third balcony), slips (cheap seats on the fringes). Many cheap seats have a restricted view (behind a pillar). For floor plans of the various theaters, see www.theatremonkey.com.

Buying Theater Tickets

Choose between waiting to buy your tickets in London (offering you flexibility and the possibility of getting a deal that's available only locally), or prebooking from home (a safer bet if you have your heart set on a particular show that's likely to sell out).

Getting Tickets in London: Many tickets are available on short notice—likely at a discount. While very popular shows sell out early (especially for weekend performances), nearly-as-popular shows may offer discounted tickets to fill seats. Seeing all those glitzy ads in the Tube may make you curious as to what's on: Drop by the discount **tkts** booth on Leicester Square to find out (explained in next section). If you're interested in a particular show, call or check the theater's website carefully to see if they're offering any deals; if not, you might as well book through tkts.

Booking Tickets Before You Go: To book in advance online or by phone, do your homework to figure out what you want; browse your options at www.officiallondontheatre.co.uk. Booking ahead is smart if there's a show you must see, it's very popular, and your time in London is quite limited (e.g., a couple of days—and remember that on weekends, plays are more likely to get booked up). It's also worth checking to see if the tickets for your preferred show are sold at full price even by the discount tkts booth in London (check their website at www.tkts.co.uk to determine this); in this case, it's less likely that you'll score a deal by waiting until you get to London (and more risky that the show will sell out before you arrive).

The easiest way to book seats online is by going through the theater's website; punch in possible dates, check their seating chart for availability, and select your seats. Most theater websites link you to a preferred vendor such as www.ticketmaster.co.uk or www.seetickets.com.

Another option is calling the theater box office (which may ring through to a central ticketing office); ask about seats and available dates. You can call from the US as easily as from England.

Whether you book online or over the phone, you pay with your credit card. A service charge of £3 per ticket is typical if you book direct with the theater. You may be offered the option of having your tickets emailed to you (you print them out); otherwise, you arrive about 30 minutes before the show starts to pick up your tickets at "Will Call."

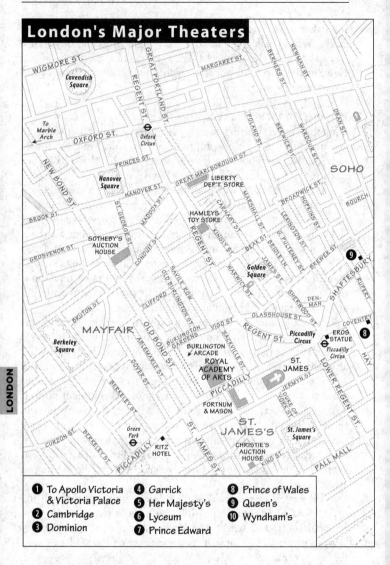

London's Major Theaters

- ❶ To Apollo Victoria & Victoria Palace
- ❷ Cambridge
- ❸ Dominion
- ❹ Garrick
- ❺ Her Majesty's
- ❻ Lyceum
- ❼ Prince Edward
- ❽ Prince of Wales
- ❾ Queen's
- ❿ Wyndham's

Avoid buying tickets through third-party, middleman agencies, which mark up their prices dramatically (explained further in "Booking Through Other Agencies," below).

Ticketing Outlets

You have three basic options for booking tickets: Using the discount tkts booth at Leicester Square (ideal for discounted same-day tickets, and sometimes for tickets up to a week ahead); booking direct at the theater's box office (best if you can get a special deal,

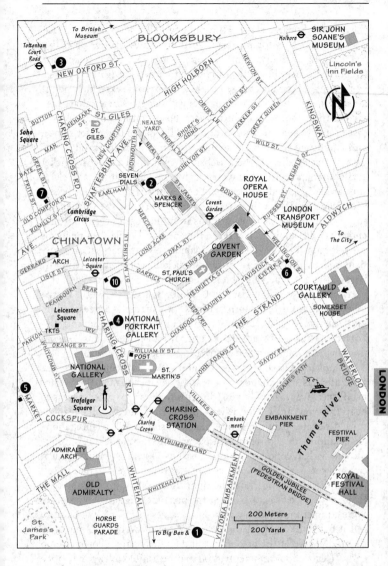

such as a last-minute return or a same-day deal); or buying through an agency (expensive and worthwhile only if you're desperate for a sold-out show). Here are sample prices: A top-notch seat to *Chicago* costs £66 if you buy directly from the theater; the same seat costs £36.75 through tkts at Leicester Square. The cheapest (restricted view) seat is £26 through the theater. If you get tickets from a third-party agency for a popular date that's sold out, you could pay much more than face value.

Discount "tkts" Booth: This famous ticket booth at Leicester

(LESS-ter) Square, run by the Society of London Theatre, sells discounted tickets for top-price seats to shows on the push list. Even big-name shows can turn up on this list. Most tickets are half-price; other shows are discounted 25 percent (in either case, you'll pay a £3 service charge per ticket). For some extremely popular shows, they sell full-price tickets without the service charge (so it costs the same as at the box office). For about half of the shows, discounted tickets are available only on the day of the performance, although more theaters are selling discounted tickets through tkts up to a week ahead. Their website (www.tkts.co.uk) lists ticket availability and prices, but you must buy in person at their kiosk. A similar list is posted next to the kiosk—survey your options before you queue (or if the line is long, while you're in the queue). It's smart to have two or three options in mind, just in case your first choice is sold out when you reach the counter. While the line forms early, it tends to move fast. Unless you have your heart set on a particular show that has only same-day tickets, consider dropping by later in the day, when it's a bit less crowded—many tickets will still be available (open Mon-Sat 10:00-19:00, Sun 11:00-16:00). Warning: Note that the real booth (with its "tkts" name) is a freestanding kiosk at the edge of the garden in Leicester Square. Several dishonest outfits nearby advertise "official half-price tickets"—avoid these, where you'll rarely pay anything close to half-price.

Booking Direct (at the Theater's Box Office): While tkts generally has seats that are as cheap or cheaper than at the theater itself, the advantage of buying direct is that you may have access to deals that you can't get anywhere else. Most theaters offer cheap returned tickets, standing-room, matinee, senior or student standby deals, and more. (Discounted tickets, called "concessions," are indicated with a "conc" or "s" in the listings.) Picking up a late return can get you a great seat at a cheap-seat price. Great seats can sell for low prices—if you know the right time to show up. A good plan for same-day deals is to arrive at the box office right when it opens. For example, the popular show *Wicked* saves its front-row tickets to sell at half-price at 10:00 on the day of the show, but you must buy them in person at the box office...and on busy days, people line up early. (Restrictions may apply: You may be limited to two half-price tickets; if you can buy multiple cheap tickets, the seats may not be together; and with front-row seats, be warned you may not be able to see the stage floor or actors' feet.) To find out about deals, look at the show's website, call the box office, or simply drop in to find out the drill (the theaters are mostly in highly trafficked tourist areas, so you're likely to wander past your chosen theater at some point during your visit). Even if a show is "sold out," there's usually a way to get a seat. Call the theater box office and ask how.

If you don't care where you sit, you can often buy the absolute cheapest seats—those with an obstructed view or in the nosebleed section—at the box office; these tickets often cost less than £20. Some theaters are so small that there's hardly a bad seat. After the lights go down, scooting up is less than a capital offense. Shakespeare did it.

Booking Through Other Agencies: Although booking through a middleman (such as the TI, your hotel, or ticket agency) is quick and easy, prices are inflated by a standard 25 percent fee. Ticket agencies (whether in the US or in London) are just scalpers with an address. If you're buying from an agency, look at the ticket carefully (your price should be no more than 30 percent over the printed face value; the 20 percent VAT is already included in the face value) and understand where you're sitting according to the floor plan (if your view is restricted, it will state this on the ticket).

Agencies are worthwhile only if a show you've just got to see is sold out at the box office. They scarf up hot tickets, planning to make a killing after the show is sold out. US booking agencies get their tickets from another agency, adding to your expense by involving yet another middleman. Many tickets sold on the street are forgeries. Although some theaters use booking agencies to handle their advance sales, you'll likely save money by avoiding the middleman.

Theater Options

West End Theaters: The commercial (nonsubsidized) theaters cluster around Soho (especially along Shaftesbury Avenue) and Covent Garden. With a centuries-old tradition of pleasing the masses, these present London theater at its glitziest.

Plays: If you're interested in straight-up plays rather than bombastic West-End musicals or Shakespeare (explained next), you'll have many choices. A few recent cinematic blockbusters (including *The King's Speech* and *War Horse*) started out as London plays. Straight plays tend to have shorter runs than famous musicals: Check out the latest at www.officiallondontheatre.co.uk, ask at the tkts booth, or just watch for ads on the Tube. One particularly good venue is the **Royal National Theatre,** which has a range of impressive options, often starring recognizable names; while ugly on the outside, the acts that play out upon its stage are beautiful (looming on the South Bank by Waterloo Bridge, www.nationaltheatre.org.uk). Since 2003, Kevin Spacey has been the artistic director of **The Old Vic** theater. He has directed and appeared in several productions, and has enlisted many big-name film directors and actors for others (tucked behind Waterloo Station, www.oldvictheatre.com).

Royal Shakespeare Company: If you'll ever enjoy Shakespeare, it'll be in Britain. The RSC performs at various theaters around London and in Stratford-upon-Avon year-round. To get a schedule, contact the RSC (Royal Shakespeare Theatre, Stratford-upon-Avon, tel. 0844-800-1110, www.rsc.org.uk).

Shakespeare's Globe: To see Shakespeare in a replica of the theater for which he wrote his plays, attend a play at the Globe. In this round, thatch-roofed, open-air theater, the plays are performed much as Shakespeare intended—under the sky, with no amplification.

The play's the thing from late April through early October (usually Mon 19:30, Tue-Sat 14:00 and 19:30, Sun either 13:00 and/or 18:30, tickets can be sold out months in advance). You'll pay £5 to stand and £15-39 to sit, usually on a backless bench. Because only a few rows and the pricier Gentlemen's Rooms have seats with backs, £1 cushions and £3 add-on back rests are considered a good investment by many. Dress for the weather.

The £5 "groundling" tickets—which are open to rain—are most fun. Scurry in early to stake out a spot on the stage's edge, where the most interaction with the actors occurs. You're a crude peasant. You can lean your elbows on the stage, munch a picnic dinner (yes, you can bring in food), or walk around. I've never enjoyed Shakespeare as much as here, performed as it was meant to be in the "wooden O." If you can't get a ticket, consider waiting around. Plays can be long, and many groundlings leave before the end. Hang around outside and beg or buy a ticket from someone leaving early (groundlings are allowed to come and go). A few non-Shakespeare plays are also presented each year. If you can't attend a show, you can take a guided tour of the theater and museum by day (see page 742).

The Globe is opening a new, indoor Jacobean Theatre within the Globe complex (hopefully in time for your visit) that will allow top-quality Shakespearean and other plays to be performed through the winter. Check online or call the Globe box office for details.

To reserve tickets for plays at the Globe, call or drop by the box office (Mon-Sat 10:00-18:00, Sun 10:00-17:00, open one hour later on performance days, New Globe Walk entrance, no extra charge to book by phone, tel. 020/7401-9919). You can also reserve online (www.shakespearesglobe.com, £2.50 booking fee). If the tickets are sold out, don't despair; a few often free up at the last minute. Try calling around noon the day of the performance to see if the box office expects any returned tickets. If so, they'll advise you to show up a little more than an hour before the show, when these tickets are sold (first-come, first-served).

The theater is on the South Bank, directly across the Thames over the Millennium Bridge from St. Paul's Cathedral (Tube: Mansion House or London Bridge). The Globe is inconvenient for public transport, but the courtesy phone in the lobby lets you get a minicab in minutes. (These minicabs have set fees—e.g., £8 to South Kensington—but generally cost less than a metered cab and provide fine and honest service.) During theater season, there's a regular supply of black cabs outside the main foyer on New Globe Walk.

Outdoor Theater in Summer: Enjoy Shakespearean drama and other plays under the stars at the Open Air Theatre, in leafy Regent's Park in north London. Food is allowed: You can bring your own picnic; order à la carte from the theater menu; or pre-order a £25 picnic supper from the theater at least 48 hours in advance (tickets £12-50; season runs late May-mid-Sept, order tickets online after mid-Jan or by phone Mon-Sun 9:00-21:00—£1 booking fee by phone, no fee if ordering online or in person; tel. 0844-826-4242, www.openairtheatre.org; grounds open 1.5 hours prior to evening performances, one hour prior to matinees; 10-minute walk north of Baker Street Tube, near Queen Mary's Gardens within Regent's Park; detailed directions and more info at www.openairtheatre.org).

Fringe Theater: London's rougher evening-entertainment scene is thriving, filling pages in *Time Out*. Choose from a wide range of fringe theater and comedy acts (generally £5).

Classical Music
Concerts at Churches
For easy, cheap, or free concerts in historic churches, ask the TI (or check *Time Out*) about **lunch concerts,** especially:
- St. Bride's Church, with free lunch concerts twice a week at 13:15 (generally Tue and Fri—confirm by phone or online, church tel. 020/7427-0133, www.stbrides.com).
- St. James's at Piccadilly, with 50-minute concerts on Mon, Wed, and Fri at 13:10 (suggested £3.50 donation, info tel. 020/7381-0441, www.st-james-piccadilly.org).
- St. Martin-in-the-Fields, offering concerts on Mon, Tue, and Fri at 13:00 (suggested £3.50 donation, church tel. 020/7766-1100, www.smitf.org).

St. Martin-in-the-Fields also hosts fine **evening concerts** by candlelight (£8-28, several nights a week at 19:30) and live jazz in its underground Café in the Crypt (£5.50 or £9, Wed at 20:00).

Evensong and Organ Recitals at Churches
Evensong services are held at several churches, including:
- St. Paul's Cathedral (Tue-Sat at 17:00, Sun at 15:15, tel. 020/7246-8350, www.stpauls.co.uk).
- Westminster Abbey (Mon-Tue and Thu-Fri at 17:00, Sat-Sun at 15:00 except Sat at 17:00 in summer; there's a service Wed

but it's spoken, not sung; tel. 020/7654-4834, www.westminster-abbey.org).

- Southwark Cathedral (Sun at 15:00; also Mon-Fri at 17:30 and Sat at 16:00 but sometimes spoken, not sung—call to confirm; tel. 020/7367-6700, www.southwark.anglican.org/cathedral).
- St. Bride's Church (Sun at 17:30, tel. 020/7427-0133, www.stbrides.com).

Free **organ recitals** are usually held on Sunday at 17:45 in Westminster Abbey (30 minutes, tel. 020/7222-5152). Many other churches have free concerts; ask for the *London Organ Concerts Guide* at the TI.

Performances

Prom Concerts: For a fun classical event (mid-July-mid-Sept), attend a Prom Concert (shortened from "Promenade Concert") during the annual festival at the Royal Albert Hall. Nightly concerts are offered at give-a-peasant-some-culture prices (£5 "Promming"—standing-room spots—sold at the door, £7 restricted-view seats, most £20-54 but depends on performance, Tube: South Kensington, tel. 0845-401-5045, www.bbc.co.uk/proms).

Opera: Some of the world's best opera is belted out at the prestigious Royal Opera House, near Covent Garden (box office tel. 020/7304-4000, www.roh.org.uk), and at the London Coliseum (English National Opera, St. Martin's Lane, Tube: Leicester Square, box office tel. 0871-911-0200, www.eno.org). Or consider taking in an unusual opera at the King's Head pub in Islington, home of London's Little Opera House (11 Upper Street, Tube: Angel, tel. 020/7478-0160, www.kingsheadtheatre.com).

Dance: Sadler's Wells Theatre features both international and UK-based dance troupes (Rosebery Avenue, Islington, Tube: Angel, info tel. 020/7863-8198, box office tel. 0844-412-4300, www.sadlerswells.com).

Sightseeing

Tours: Guided **walks** are offered several times a day and vary by theme: ancient London, museums, legal London, Dickens, Beatles, Jewish quarter, Christopher Wren, and so on. In the evening, expect a more limited choice: ghosts, Jack the Ripper, pubs, or literature. See a list of walking-tour companies on page 700.

To see the city illuminated at night, consider a **bus tour.** A two-hour London by Night Sightseeing Tour leaves several times an evening from Victoria Station and other points (see page 699).

Cruises: In summer, boats sail as late as 19:00 between Westminster Pier (near Big Ben) and the Tower of London. (For details, see page 705.)

A handful of outfits run Thames River evening cruises with

four-course meals and dancing. **London Showboat** offers the best value (£75, May-Sept Wed-Sun, April and Oct Thu-Sun, March and Nov Thu-Sat, Jan-Feb Fri-Sat, 3.5 hours, departs at 19:30 from Westminster Pier and returns by 23:00, reservations necessary, tel. 020/7740-0400, www.citycruises.com). Dinner cruises are also offered by **Bateaux London** (£76-143, tel. 020/7695-1800, www. bateauxlondon.com). For more on cruising, get the *River Thames Boat Services* brochure from a London TI.

Sleeping in London

London is an expensive city for lodging. Cheaper rooms are relatively dumpy. Don't expect £130 cheeriness in an £80 room. For £70, you'll get a double with breakfast in a safe, cramped, and dreary place with minimal service and the bathroom down the hall. For £90, you'll get a basic, clean, reasonably cheery double with a private bath in a usually cramped, cracked-plaster building, or a soulless but comfortable room without breakfast in a huge Motel 6-type place. My London splurges, at £160-290, are spacious, thoughtfully appointed places good for entertaining or romancing.

Looking for Hotel Deals Online: Given London's high hotel prices, using the Internet can help you score a deal. Various websites list rooms in high-rise, three- and four-star business hotels. You'll give up the charm and warmth of a family-run establishment, and breakfast probably won't be included, but you might find that the price is right.

Start by browsing the websites of several chains to get a sense of typical rates and online deals. For listings of no-frills, Motel 6-type places, see "Big, Good-Value, Modern Hotels," later.

Pricier London hotel chains include Millennium/Copthorne (www.millenniumhotels.com), Thistle (www.thistle.com), Intercontinental/Holiday Inn (www.ichotelsgroup.com), Radisson (www.radisson.com), Hilton (www.hilton.com), and Red Carnation (www.redcarnationhotels.com).

Auction-type sites (such as www.priceline.com or www.hotwire.com) match flexible travelers with empty hotel rooms, often at prices well below the hotel's normal rates.

My readers report good experiences with these accommodation discount sites: www.londontown.com (an informative site with a discount booking service), http://athomeinlondon.co.uk and www.londonbb.com (both list central B&Bs), www.lastminute.com, www.visitlondon.com, http://roomsnet.com, and www.eurocheapo.com.

Using a Booking Agency: Cross-Pollinate is an online agency representing B&Bs and apartments in a handful of European cities, including London. They handpick their listings, presenting

Sleep Code

(£1 = about $1.60, country code: 44, area code: 020)
S = Single, **D** = Double/Twin, **T** = Triple, **Q** = Quad, **b** = bathroom, **s** = shower only. Unless otherwise noted, credit cards are accepted and breakfast is included.

To help you sort through these listings easily, I've divided the accommodations into three categories based on the price for a standard double room with bath:

  $$$ **Higher Priced**—Most rooms £125 or more.
    $$ **Moderately Priced**—Most rooms between £75-125.
      $ **Lower Priced**—Most rooms £75 or less.

Prices can change without notice; verify the hotel's current rates online or by email.

each one as if recommending it to a friend. Search their website for a listing you like, then submit your reservation online. If the place is available, you'll be charged a small deposit and emailed the location and check-in details. Policies vary from owner to owner, but in most cases you'll pay the balance on arrival in cash. Minimum stays vary from one to five nights (US tel. 800-270-1190, UK tel. 020/3514-0083, www.cross-pollinate.com, info@cross-pollinate.com).

Victoria Station Neighborhood

The streets behind Victoria Station teem with little, moderately priced-for-London B&Bs. It's a safe, surprisingly tidy, and decent area without a hint of the trashy, touristy glitz of the streets in front of the station. I've divided these accommodations into two broad categories: Belgravia, west of the station, feels particularly posh, while Pimlico, to the east, is still upscale and dotted with colorful eateries. While I wouldn't go out of my way just to dine here, each area has plenty of good restaurants (see page 795). All of the recommended hotels are within a five-minute walk of the Victoria Tube, bus, and train stations. On hot summer nights, request a quiet back room; most of these B&Bs lack air-conditioning and may front busy streets.

The best laundry options are on the east side (Pimlico): **Pimlico Launderette** is a bit farther out—about five blocks southwest of Warwick Square—but the low prices and friendly George make it worth the effort (£7.20 same-day full service, £5-6 self-service, daily 8:00-19:00; 3 Westmoreland Terrace—go down Clarendon

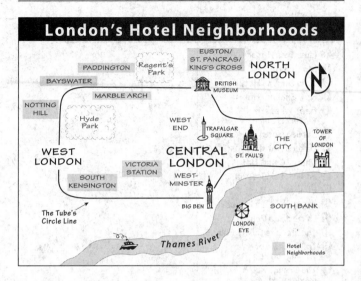

London's Hotel Neighborhoods

Map showing: EUSTON/ST. PANCRAS/KING'S CROSS, NORTH LONDON, PADDINGTON, Regent's Park, BAYSWATER, BRITISH MUSEUM, MARBLE ARCH, NOTTING HILL, Hyde Park, WEST END, TRAFALGAR SQUARE, THE CITY, TOWER OF LONDON, WEST LONDON, CENTRAL LONDON, ST. PAUL'S, VICTORIA STATION, WEST-MINSTER, SOUTH KENSINGTON, The Tube's Circle Line, BIG BEN, LONDON EYE, SOUTH BANK, Thames River, Hotel Neighborhoods

LONDON

Street, turn right on Sutherland, and look for the launderette on the left at the end of the street; tel. 020/7821-8692).

Drivers like the 400-space Semley Place NCP **parking garage**, near the hotels on the west—Belgravia—side (£40/day, possible discounts with hotel voucher, just west of the Victoria Coach Station at Buckingham Palace Road and Semley Place, tel. 0845-050-7080, www.ncp.co.uk).

West of Victoria Station (Belgravia)

Here in Belgravia, the prices are a bit higher and your neighbors include Andrew Lloyd Webber and Margaret Thatcher (her policeman stands outside 73 Chester Square). All of these places line up along tranquil Ebury Street, two blocks over from Victoria Station.

$$$ Lime Tree Hotel, enthusiastically run by Charlotte and Matt, comes with 25 spacious, stylish, comfortable, thoughtfully decorated rooms and a fun-loving breakfast room (Sb-£99, Db-£150, larger superior Db-£175, Tb-£195, family room-£210, usually cheaper Jan-Feb, free Internet access and Wi-Fi, small lounge opens onto quiet garden, 135 Ebury Street, tel. 020/7730-8191, www.limetreehotel.co.uk, info@limetreehotel.co.uk, Ariane manages the office, trusty Alan covers the night shift).

$$ Morgan House, a great budget choice in this neighborhood, has 11 rooms and is entertainingly run, with lots of travel tips and friendly chat from owner Rachel Joplin and her staff (S-£58, D-£84, Db-£108, T-£108, family suites: Tb-£148, Qb-£158, free Wi-Fi, 120 Ebury Street, tel. 020/7730-2384, www.morganhouse.co.uk, morganhouse@btclick.com).

Victoria Station Neighborhood

1. Lime Tree Hotel
2. Morgan House
3. Luna Simone Hotel
4. New England Hotel
5. Best Western Victoria Palace
6. Jubilee Hotel
7. Bakers Hotel
8. Cherry Court Hotel
9. easyHotel Victoria
10. Ebury Wine Bar
11. Jenny Lo's Tea House
12. La Bottega Deli
13. The Thomas Cubitt Pub
14. To The Duke of Wellington Pub
15. The Orange Pub & Daylesford Deli
16. Grumbles Restaurant
17. Seafresh Fish Restaurant
18. The Jugged Hare Pub
19. St. George's Tavern
20. Grocery Stores (4)
21. To Launderette
22. Bus Tours – Day (2)
23. Bus Tours – Night
24. Tube, Taxis, City Buses
25. Green Line Coach Terminal
26. Buses to Luton & Stansted Airports
27. Apollo Victoria Theatre
28. Victoria Palace Theatre

LONDON

East of Victoria Station (Pimlico)

This area is a bit less genteel-feeling than Belgravia, but still plenty inviting, with eateries and grocery stores. Most of these hotels are on or near Warwick Way, the main drag through this area. Generally the best Tube stop for this neighborhood is Victoria (though the Pimlico stop works equally well for the Luna Simone Hotel). Bus #24 runs right through the middle of Pimlico, connecting Tate Britain to the south with Victoria Station,

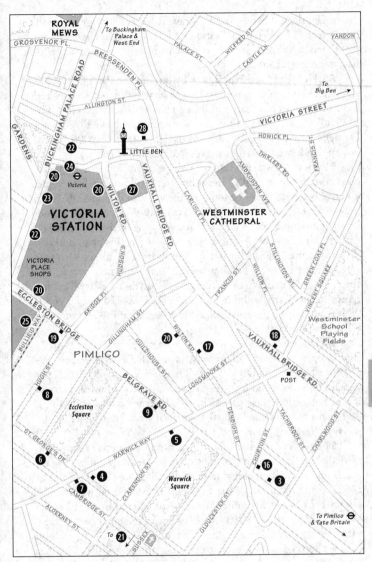

the Houses of Parliament, Trafalgar Square, and much more to the north.

$$ Luna Simone Hotel rents 36 fresh, spacious, nicely remodeled rooms with modern bathrooms. It's a smartly managed place, run for more than 40 years by twins Peter and Bernard—and Bernard's son Mark—and they still seem to enjoy their work (Sb-£75, Db-£110, Tb-£135, Qb-£165, ask about discount with cash and this book, free Internet access and Wi-Fi, near the corner of Charlwood Street and Belgrave Road at 47 Belgrave Road, handy bus #24 to Victoria Station and Trafalgar Square stops out front, tel. 020/7834-5897, www.lunasimonehotel.com, stay@lunasimonehotel.com).

$$ New England Hotel, run by Jay and the Patel family, has slightly worn public spaces and somewhat faded but well-priced rooms in a tight old corner building (small Sb-£59, Db-£89, Tb-£119, Qb-£129, prices soft during slow times, pay Wi-Fi, 20 Saint George's Drive, tel. 020/7834-8351, fax 020/7834-9000, www.newenglandhotel.com, mystay@newenglandhotel.com).

$$ Best Western Victoria Palace offers modern business-class comfort compared to the other creaky old hotels listed here. Choose between the 43 rooms in the main building (Db-£120, includes breakfast, elevator, 60-64 Warwick Way), or pay a quarter less by booking a nearly identical room in one of the two annexes, each a half-block away—an excellent value for this neighborhood if you skip breakfast. All three buildings have been recently renovated (annex Db-£89, breakfast-£12.50, air-con, no elevator, free Internet access and Wi-Fi, 17 Belgrave Road and 1 Warwick Way, reception at main building, tel. 020/7821-7113, fax 020/7630-0806, www.bestwesternvictoriapalace.co.uk, info@bestwestern-victoriapalace.co.uk).

$$ Jubilee Hotel is a well-run, colorful slumbermill with 24 tiny, simple rooms and many tiny, neat beds (S-£39-45, Sb-£59-65, tiny D-£55-65, Db-£79-89, Tb-£89-95, Qb-£99-109, rates depend on season and length of stay, ask for Rick Steves discount if you book direct and pay cash, free Internet access and Wi-Fi, 31 Eccleston Square, tel. 020/7834-0845, www.jubileehotel.co.uk, stay@jubileehotel.co.uk, Bob Patel).

$$ Bakers Hotel shoehorns 11 brightly painted rooms into a small building, but it's conveniently located and offers modest prices and a small breakfast (S-£50, D-£65, Db-£85, T-£85, Tb-£105, family room-£120, less for longer stays and on weeknights, ask for Rick Steves discount when booking direct, free Wi-Fi, 126 Warwick Way, tel. 020/7834-0729, www.bakershotel.co.uk, reservations@bakershotel.co.uk, Amin Jamani).

$ Cherry Court Hotel, run by the friendly and industrious Patel family, rents 12 very small but bright and well-designed rooms in a central location. Considering London's sky-high prices, this is a fine budget choice (Sb-£55, Db-£65, Tb-£105, Qb-£120, Quint/b-£130, ask for best Rick Steves price with this book, 5 percent fee to pay with credit card, fruit-basket breakfast in room, air-con, free Internet access and Wi-Fi, laundry, peaceful garden patio, 23 Hugh Street, tel. 020/7828-2840, fax 020/7828-0393, www.cherrycourthotel.co.uk, info@cherrycourthotel.co.uk).

$ easyHotel Victoria, at 36 Belgrave Road, is part of the budget chain described on page 779.

"South Kensington," She Said, Loosening His Cummerbund

To stay on a quiet street so classy it doesn't allow hotel signs, surrounded by trendy shops and colorful restaurants, call "South Ken" your London home. Shoppers like being a short walk from Harrods and the designer shops of King's Road and Chelsea. When I splurge, I splurge here. Sumner Place is just off Old Brompton Road, 200 yards from the handy South Kensington Tube station (on Circle Line, two stops from Victoria Station; and on Piccadilly Line, direct from Heathrow).

$$$ Aster House, well-run by friendly and accommodating Simon and Leonie Tan, has a cheerful lobby, lounge, and breakfast room. Its 13 rooms are comfy and quiet, with TV, phone, and air-conditioning. Enjoy breakfast or just lounging in the whisper-elegant Orangery, a glassy greenhouse. Simon and Leonie offer free loaner mobile phones to their guests (Sb-£125, Db-£190, bigger Db-£235 or £270, does not include 20 percent VAT; ask about discount with this book—up to 20 percent discount if you book three or more nights, up to 25 percent discount for five or more nights; additional discount with cash, check website for specials, pay Internet access, free Wi-Fi, 3 Sumner Place, tel. 020/7581-5888, fax 020/7584-4925, www.asterhouse.com, asterhouse@gmail.com).

$$$ Number Sixteen, for well-heeled travelers, packs over-the-top formality and class into its 41 rooms, plush lounges, and tranquil garden. It's in a labyrinthine building, with boldly modern decor—perfect for an urban honeymoon (Sb-from £140, Db-from £225—but soft, ask for discounted "seasonal rates," especially on weekends and in Aug—subject to availability, does not include 20 percent VAT, breakfast buffet in the garden-£18 continental or £19 full English, elevator, free Internet access, pay Wi-Fi, 16 Sumner Place, tel. 020/7589-5232, fax 020/7584-8615, US tel. 800-553-6674, www.firmdalehotels.com, sixteen@firmdale.com).

$$$ The Pelham Hotel, a 52-room business-class hotel with crisp service and a pricey mix of pretense and style, is not quite sure which investment company owns it. It's genteel, with low lighting and a pleasant drawing room among the many perks (Db-£190-290, rate depends on room size and season, breakfast-£15 continental or £18 full English, does not include 20 percent VAT, lower prices on weekends and in Aug, Web specials can include free breakfast, air-con, elevator, free Internet access, pay Wi-Fi, fitness room, 15 Cromwell Place, tel. 020/7589-8288, fax 020/7584-8444, US tel. 1-888-757-5587, www.pelhamhotel.co.uk, reservations@pelhamhotel.co.uk).

LONDON

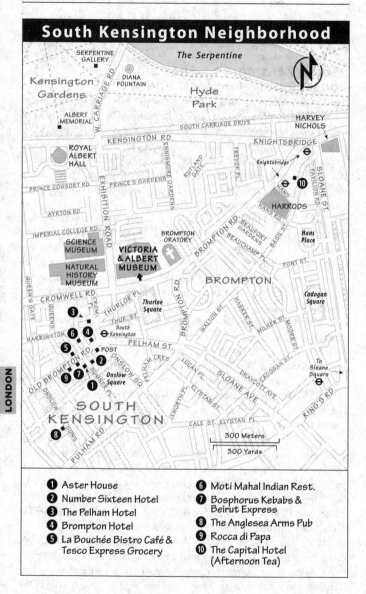

South Kensington Neighborhood

1. Aster House
2. Number Sixteen Hotel
3. The Pelham Hotel
4. Brompton Hotel
5. La Bouchée Bistro Café & Tesco Express Grocery
6. Moti Mahal Indian Rest.
7. Bosphorus Kebabs & Beirut Express
8. The Anglesea Arms Pub
9. Rocca di Papa
10. The Capital Hotel (Afternoon Tea)

$$ Brompton Hotel is a humble, borderline-dreary, last-resort place with 24 rooms above a jumble of cafés and clubs. There's a noisy bar and some street noise, so ask for a room in the back if you want quiet. It has old carpet and no public spaces, and they serve breakfast in your room. In spite of all this, its rates are reasonable for this upscale neighborhood (Sb-£100, Db-£110, Tb-£160, "deluxe" rooms are just like the others but with a tub, save a little by booking via their website, includes continental breakfast, free Wi-Fi, across from the South Kensington Tube station at 30 Old Brompton Road, tel. 020/7584-4517, fax 020/7823-9936, www. bromhotel.com, book@bromhotel.com).

Notting Hill and Bayswater Neighborhoods

Residential Notting Hill has quick bus and Tube access to downtown, and, for London, is very "homely" (Brit-speak for cozy). It's also peppered with trendy bars and restaurants, and is home to the famous Portobello Road Market (offbeat antiques shops open daily are enlivened on Saturdays with 2,000 additional stalls until 19:00, most shops closed Sun, Tube: Notting Hill Gate, tel. tel. 020/7727-76847229-8354), www.portobelloroad.co.uk).

Popular with young international travelers, the Bayswater street called Queensway is a multicultural festival of commerce and eateries. The neighborhood does its dirty clothes at **Galaxy Launderette** (£6-8 self-service, £10-12 full-service, Mon-Sat 8:00-20:00, Sun 9:00-20:00, staff on hand with soap and coins, 65 Moscow Road, at corner of St. Petersburgh Place and Moscow Road, tel. 020/7229-7771). For **Internet access,** you'll find several stops along busy Queensway, and a self-serve bank of computer terminals on the food-circus level—third floor—of Whiteleys Shopping Centre (daily 8:30-24:00, corner of Queensway and Porchester Gardens—see page 799).

Near Kensington Gardens Square

Several big, old hotels line quiet Kensington Gardens Square (not to be confused with the much bigger Kensington Gardens adjacent to Hyde Park), a block west of bustling Queensway, north of Bayswater Tube station. These hotels are quiet for central London, but the area feels a bit sterile, and the hotels here tend to be impersonal.

$$$ Vancouver Studios offers 45 modern, tastefully furnished rooms with fully equipped kitchenettes (utensils, stove, microwave, and fridge) rather than breakfast. It faces Kensington Gardens Square in front and its own tranquil garden patio out back (Sb-£92, Db-£135, Tb-£175, extra bed-£20, discount for seven or more nights, pay Internet access, free Wi-Fi, welcoming lounge, 30 Prince's Square, tel. 020/7243-1270, fax 020/7221-8678, www. vancouverstudios.co.uk, info@vancouverstudios.co.uk).

$$$ Garden Court Hotel is understated, with 37 simple rooms (Sb-£50-75, D-£80, Db-£130, Tb-£160, Qb-£180, ask for Rick Steves price if booking direct, elevator, pay Internet access, free Wi-Fi, 30-31 Kensington Gardens Square, tel. 020/7229-2553, fax 020/7727-2749, www.gardencourthotel.co.uk, info@gardencourthotel.co.uk).

Notting Hill & Bayswater Neighborhoods

LONDON

1. Vancouver Studios
2. Garden Court Hotel
3. London House Hotel
4. Phoenix Hotel
5. Kensington Gardens Hotel
6. Princes Square Guest Accommodation
7. Westland Hotel
8. London Vicarage Hotel
9. The Gate Hotel
10. To Norwegian YWCA
11. To Caring Hotel
12. Maggie Jones Restaurant
13. The Churchill Arms Pub & Thai Kitchen
14. Hereford Road Restaurant
15. The Prince Edward Pub
16. Café Diana
17. Royal China Restaurant
18. Whiteleys Shopping Centre (Food Court, Grocery, Internet)
19. Tesco Grocery
20. Spar Market
21. The Orangery (Afternoon Tea)
22. Launderette

$$$ London House Hotel has 103 cookie-cutter rooms right on Kensington Gardens Square. While the place lacks personality, the rates are decent considering the fine location (rates fluctuate, but generally Db-£105 weekdays and £130 on weekends, smaller rooms not facing the square are about £10 cheaper, basement family rooms-£140, check online for specific rates and last-minute deals, continental breakfast-£6, free Wi-Fi in lobby, pay Wi-Fi in rooms, 81 Kensington Gardens Square, tel. 020/7243-1810, www. londonhousehotels.com, reservations@londonhousehotels.com).

$$ Phoenix Hotel, a Best Western modernization of a 125-room hotel, offers American business-class comforts; spacious, plush public spaces; and big, modern-feeling rooms. Its prices—which range from fine value to rip-off—are determined by a greedy computer program, with huge variations according to expected demand. Book online to save money (flexible prices, but usually Sb-£65, Db-£100, elevator, free Internet access and Wi-Fi, 1-8 Kensington Gardens Square, tel. 020/7229-2494, fax 020/7727-1419, US tel. 800-528-1234, www.phoenixhotel.co.uk, info@phoenix-hotel.co.uk).

$$ Kensington Gardens Hotel, which has the same owners as the Phoenix Hotel down the street (see above), laces 17 pleasant, slightly scuffed rooms together in a tall, skinny building with lots of stairs and no elevator (Ss-£59, Sb-£66, Db-£89, Tb-£112; book by phone or email and ask for best Rick Steves price—if booking on their website, look for the Rick Steves discount under "Additional Information"; continental breakfast served at Phoenix Hotel, free Wi-Fi, 9 Kensington Gardens Square, tel. 020/7243-7600, fax 020/7792-8612, www.kensingtongardenshotel.co.uk, info@kensingtongardenshotel.co.uk, Rowshanak).

$$ Princes Square Guest Accommodation is a big, soulless place renting 50 businesslike rooms with modern decor. It's well-located, practical, and a good value, especially if you can score a good rate (prices fluctuate with demand, but generally Sb-£65-70, Db-£80-90, Tb-£100-120, email to ask for best price, elevator, pay Wi-Fi, 23-25 Princes Square, tel. 020/7229-9876, www.princessquarehotel.co.uk, info@princessquarehotel.co.uk).

Near Kensington Gardens

$$$ Westland Hotel, conveniently located on a busy street a five-minute walk from the Notting Hill neighborhood, feels like a wood-paneled hunting lodge with a fine lounge. The 32 spacious rooms are comfortable, with old-fashioned charm. Their £173 doubles are the best value, but check their website for specials. It's been run by the Isseyegh family for three generations (Sb-£112, deluxe Sb-£124, Db-£133, deluxe Db-£155, cavernous premier Db-£176, sprawling Tb-£220, gargantuan Qb-£247, 15 percent discount if you book at least three weeks in advance, elevator, free Wi-Fi, garage-£20/day, between Notting Hill Gate and Queensway Tube stations at 154 Bayswater Road, tel. 020/7229-9191, fax 020/7727-1054, www.westlandhotel.co.uk, reservations@westlandhotel.co.uk, Shirley and Bertie).

$$$ London Vicarage Hotel is family-run, understandably popular, and elegantly British in a quiet, classy neighborhood. It has 17 rooms furnished with taste and quality, a TV lounge, a grand staircase, and facilities on each floor. Mandy and Monika maintain a homey atmosphere (S-£63, Sb-£107, D-£107, Db-£136, T-£136, Tb-£178, Q-£152, Qb-£200, 20 percent less in winter—check website, free Wi-Fi; 8-minute walk from Notting Hill Gate and High Street Kensington Tube stations, near Kensington Palace at 10 Vicarage Gate; tel. 020/7229-4030, fax 020/7792-5989, www.londonvicaragehotel.com, vicaragehotel@btconnect.com).

$$ The Gate Hotel has seven cramped but decent rooms on a delightful curved street near the start of the Portobello Road Market, in the heart of the characteristic Notting Hill neighborhood. While the lodgings are basic and could be cleaner, the prices are low for this area and the romantic setting might be worth it for some (Sb-£60, Db-£85, bigger "luxury" Db-£95, Tb-£115; higher prices Fri-Sat; 5 percent fee to pay with credit card, continental breakfast in room, no elevator, pay Wi-Fi, 6 Portobello Road, Tube: Notting Hill Gate, tel. 020/7221-0707, fax 020/7221-9128, www.gatehotel.co.uk, bookings@gatehotel.co.uk, Jasmine).

Near Holland Park

$ Norwegian YWCA (Norsk K.F.U.K.)—where English is definitely a second language—is open to any Norwegian woman, and to non-Norwegian women under 30. (Men must be under 30 with a Norwegian passport.) Located on a quiet, stately street, it offers a study, TV room, piano lounge, and an open-face Norwegian ambience (goat cheese on Sundays!). They have mostly quads, so those willing to share a room with strangers are most likely to get a bed (July-Aug: Ss-£46, shared double-£44/bed, shared triple-£40/bed, shared quad-£37/bed, includes sheets and towels, includes breakfast year-round plus sack lunch and dinner Sept-June, £20 key deposit and £3 membership fee required, pay Wi-Fi, 52 Holland Park, Tube: Holland Park, tel. 020/7727-9346 or 020/7727-9897, www.kfukhjemmet.org.uk, kontor@kfukhjemmet.org.uk). With each visit, I wonder which is easier to get—a sex change or a Norwegian passport?

Paddington Station Neighborhood

At the far-east end of Bayswater, the neighborhood around Paddington Station—while much less charming than the other areas

I've recommended—is pleasant enough, and very convenient to the Heathrow Express airport train. The area is flanked by the Paddington and Lancaster Gate Tube stops. Most of my recommendations circle Norfolk Square, just two blocks in front of Paddington Station, yet are still quiet and comfortable. The main drag, London Street, is lined with handy eateries—pubs, Indian, Italian, Greek, Lebanese, and more—plus convenience stores and an Internet café. (Better restaurants are a short stroll to the west, near Queensway and Notting Hill—see page 797.) To reach this area, exit the station toward Praed Street (with your back to the tracks, it's to the left). Once outside, continue straight across Praed Street and down London Street; Norfolk Square is a block ahead on the left.

On Norfolk Square

These places (and many more on the same street) are similar; all offer small rooms at a reasonable price, in tall buildings with lots of stairs and no elevator. I've chosen the ones that offer the most reasonable prices and the warmest welcome.

$$ St. David's Hotels, run by the Neokleous family, has 60 rooms in several adjacent buildings. The rooms are small—as is typical for less expensive hotels in London—and basic, with minimal amenities, but the staff is friendly (S-£50-60, Sb-£70-85, D-£70-85, Db-£90-120, Tb-£100-130, free Wi-Fi, 14-20 Norfolk Square, tel. 020/7723-3856, fax 020/7402-9061, www.stdavidshotels.com, info@stdavidshotels.com).

$$ Tudor Court Hotel has 38 colorful rooms conscientiously run by Connan and the Gupta family. While the tiny rooms are tight (with prefab plastic bathrooms) and the rates are a bit high, this place distinguishes itself with its warm welcome and attention to detail. If you smell them cooking up a big batch of curry rice, the Guptas are getting ready to take it to the homeless shelter, where they volunteer each week (S-£54-63, Sb-£95-108, "compact" Db-£99-120, larger "standard" Db-£135-165, "compact" Tb-£144-180, larger "standard" Tb-£162-198, family room-£180-225, higher rates are for Fri-Sat and other busy times, free Wi-Fi, 10-12 Norfolk Square, tel. 020/7723-5157, fax 020/7723-0727, www.tudorcourtpaddington.co.uk, reservations@tudorcourtpaddington.co.uk).

$$ Falcon Hotel, a lesser value, has less personality and 19 simple, old-school, slightly musty rooms (S-£59, Sb-£69, D-£85, Db-£95, twin Db-£99, Tb-£139, Qb-£149, rates flex with demand, free Internet access, pay Wi-Fi, 11 Norfolk Square, tel. 020/7723-8603, www.falcon-hotel.com, info@falcon-hotel.com).

$ easyHotel, the budget chain described on page 779, has a branch at 10 Norfolk Place.

LONDON

Elsewhere near Paddington Station

To reach these hotels, follow the directions on the previous page, but continue past Norfolk Square to the big intersection with Sussex Gardens; the Royal Park is a couple of blocks to the right, and the others are immediately to the left.

$$$ The Royal Park is the neighborhood's classy splurge, with 48 plush rooms, polished service, a genteel lounge (free champagne for guests nightly 19:00-20:00), and all the little extras ("classic" Db-official rates-£189-279, but prepaid/nonrefundable offers are as low as £139-189, bigger "executive" Db for £20 more, prices vary with demand, does not include 20 percent VAT, breakfast-£10-18, elevator, free Internet access and Wi-Fi, 3 Westbourne Terrace, tel. 020/7479-6600, fax 020/7479-6601, www.theroyalpark.com, info@theroyalpark.com).

$$ Stylotel feels like the stylish, super-modern, aluminum-clad big sister of the easyHotel chain (described on page 779). Instead of peeling wallpaper and ancient carpets held together with duct tape, they've opted for sleek styling in their 39 rooms, all with clean, hard surfaces—hardwood floors, prefab plastic bathrooms, and metallic walls. You may feel like an astronaut in a science-fiction film, but if you don't need ye olde doilies, this place offers a good value (Sb-£69, Db-£99, Tb-£119, Qb-£139, can vary with demand—book early and direct for best rates, elevator, pay Wi-Fi, 160-162 Sussex Gardens, tel. 020/7723-1026, www.stylotel.com, info@stylotel.com, well-run by Andreas). They also have eight fancier, pricier, air-conditioned suites across the street.

$$ Olympic House Hotel has stark public spaces and a stern welcome, but its 39 business-class rooms offer predictable comfort and fewer old-timey quirks than many hotels in this price range (Sb-£75, Db-£105, rates vary with demand, air-con in most rooms costs extra, elevator, pay Wi-Fi, 138-140 Sussex Gardens, tel. 020/7723-5935, www.olympichousehotel.co.uk, olympichouse-hotel@btinternet.com).

Between Paddington and Bayswater: About halfway between these two hotel neighborhoods, **$$ Caring Hotel,** plain but affordable, has 25 tidy, nondescript rooms in a nice, quiet location just off of Hyde Park (basic D-£70, Ds-80, small Db-£90, standard Db-£100, superior Db-£120, free Wi-Fi, cheaper rooms are higher up—more stairs, 24 Craven Hill Gardens—it's the second road with this name as you come from the park, Tube: Queensway, tel. 020/7262-8708, www.caringhotel.com, caring-hotel@tiscali.co.uk).

Marble Arch Neighborhood

This neighborhood is located north of Hyde Park and near Oxford Street, a busy shopping destination. There's a convenient Marks & Spencer department store within walking distance.

$$$ The 22 York Street B&B offers a casual alternative in the city center, renting 10 traditional, hardwood, comfortable rooms, each named for a notable London landmark (Sb-£95, Db-£129, free Internet access and Wi-Fi, inviting lounge; from Baker Street Tube station, walk 2 blocks down Baker Street and take a right to 22 York Street—since there's no sign, just look for #22; tel. 020/7224-2990, www.22yorkstreet.co.uk, mc@22yorkstreet.co.uk, energetically run by Liz and Michael Callis).

$$$ The Sumner Hotel rents 19 rooms in a 19th-century Georgian townhouse. Decorated with fancy modern Italian furniture, this swanky place packs in all the extras (Db-£170-220 depending on size, ask about discount with this book, cheaper off-season, extra bed-£60, air-con, elevator, free Wi-Fi, 54 Upper Berkeley Street, a block and a half off Edgware Road, Tube: Marble Arch, tel. 020/7723-2244, fax 0870-705-8767, www.thesumner.com, hotel@thesumner.com).

Big, Good-Value, Modern Hotels

London has an abundance of modern, impersonal, American-style chain hotels. While they lack the friendliness and funkiness of a memorable B&B, the value they provide is undeniable; doubles generally go for around £90-100 (or less—often possible with promotional rates). As these hotels are often located on busy streets in dreary train-station neighborhoods, use common sense after dark and wear your money belt.

Premier Inn

For any of these, your best option is to book online at www.premierinn.com. You can also call their reservations line at 0871-527-9222 (UK toll call) or, from North America, 011-44-1582-567-890.

$$ Premier Inn London County Hall, literally down the hall from a $400-a-night Marriott Hotel, fills one end of London's massive former County Hall building. This family-friendly place is wonderfully located near the base of the London Eye and across the Thames from Big Ben. Its 313 efficient rooms come with all the necessary comforts, though it's quite impersonal—rather than a real reception desk, you'll find self-service check-in kiosks with a couple of clerks standing by to help (Db-£99-199 for 2 adults and up to 2 kids under age 16, elevator, pay Wi-Fi, some accessible rooms, 500 yards from Westminster Tube stop and Waterloo Station, Belvedere Road, tel. 0871-527-8648, easiest to book online at www.premierinn.com).

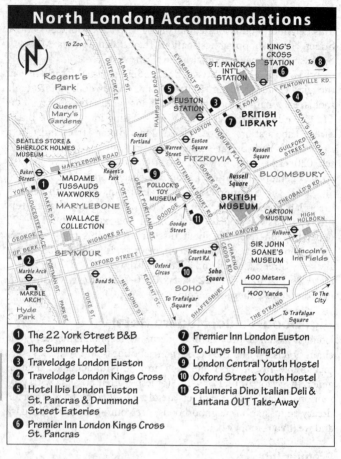

North London Accommodations

1. The 22 York Street B&B
2. The Sumner Hotel
3. Travelodge London Euston
4. Travelodge London Kings Cross
5. Hotel Ibis London Euston St. Pancras & Drummond Street Eateries
6. Premier Inn London Kings Cross St. Pancras
7. Premier Inn London Euston
8. To Jurys Inn Islington
9. London Central Youth Hostel
10. Oxford Street Youth Hostel
11. Salumeria Dino Italian Deli & Lantana OUT Take-Away

$$ Premier Inn London Southwark/Borough Market, with 59 rooms, is near Shakespeare's Globe on the South Bank (Db for up to 2 adults and 2 kids-£99-189, elevator, pay Wi-Fi, Bankside, 34 Park Street, Tube: London Bridge, tel. 0871-527-8676, www. premierinn.com). Another location is nearby, on Great Suffolk Street, called **Premier Inn London Southwark/Tate Modern.**

$$ Premier Inn London Kings Cross St. Pancras, with 276 rooms, is across the street from the east end of King's Cross Station and near the Eurostar terminus at St. Pancras Station (Db-£89-189, air-con, elevator, pay Wi-Fi, 26-30 York Way, Tube: King's Cross St. Pancras, tel. 0871-527-8672, www.premierinn.com).

Other **$$ Premier Inns** charging £89-189 per room include **London Euston** (big, blue Lego-type building packed with vacationing families, on handy but noisy street at corner of Euston Road and Dukes Road, Tube: Euston, tel. 0871-527-8656), **Lon-**

don **Kensington Earl's Court** (11 Knaresborough Place, Tube: Earl's Court or Gloucester Road, tel. 0871-527-8666), **London Victoria** (82-83 Eccleston Square, Tube: Victoria, tel. 0871-527-8680), and **London Putney Bridge** (farther out, 3 Putney Bridge Approach, Tube: Putney Bridge, tel. 0871-527-8674). Avoid the **Tower Bridge** location, which is an inconvenient 15-minute walk from the nearest Tube stop.

Other Chains

Travelodge: **$$ Travelodge London Kings Cross** is another typical chain hotel with 140 cookie-cutter rooms, just 200 yards south (in front) of King's Cross Station (Db-usually £60-90, family rooms, can be noisy, elevator, pay Wi-Fi, Grays Inn Road, Tube: King's Cross St. Pancras, tel. 0871-984-6256). Other convenient Travelodge London locations are nearby **Kings Cross Royal Scot, Euston, Marylebone, Covent Garden, Liverpool Street,** and **Farringdon.** For details on all Travelodge hotels, see www.travelodge.co.uk.

Ibis: **$$$ Hotel Ibis London Euston St. Pancras** rents 380 rooms on a quiet street a block west of Euston Station (Db-£117-149, usually £139, no family rooms, elevator, pay Internet access and Wi-Fi, 3 Cardington Street, Tube: Euston, tel. 020/7388-7777, fax 020/7388-0001, www.ibishotel.com, h0921@accor.com). There's also an **Ibis London City** (5 Commercial Street, Tube: Aldgate East, tel. 020/7422-8400), but the other Ibis locations are far from the center.

Jurys Inn: **$$$ Jurys Inn Islington** rents 200-plus compact, comfy rooms near King's Cross Station (Db/Tb-£209-230, some discounted rooms available online, 2 adults and 2 kids under age 12 can share one room, 60 Pentonville Road, Tube: Angel, tel. 020/7282-5500, fax 020/7282-5511, www.jurysinns.com). You'll also find Jurys Inns at **Chelsea** (Imperial Road, Tube: Imperial Wharf, tel. 020/7411-2200) and near **Heathrow Airport** (see "Heathrow and Gatwick Airports," later).

easyHotel

With several hotels in good neighborhoods around London, easyHotel is a radical concept—offering what you need to sleep well and safely, and nothing more. Most of them are fitted into old buildings, so the rooms are all odd shapes, from tiny windowless closets to others that are quite spacious. All rooms are well-ventilated and come with an efficient "bathroom pod" that looks like it was popped out of a plastic mold—just big enough to take care of business. While they do have a 24-hour reception, everything else is spartan: You get two towels, liquid soap, and a clean bed—no breakfast, no fresh towels, and no daily cleaning. The base rate ranges from £30 to 85, depending on the room size and when you book—"The earlier you book, the less you pay." Prices are the same for one person or two, but then you're nickel-and-dimed with optional charges for the TV, Wi-Fi, luggage storage, and so on.

If you go with the basic package, it's like hosteling with privacy—a hard-to-beat value. But you get what you pay for; in my experience, easyHotels are cheap in every sense of the word (no elevator, thin walls, noisy halls filled with loud travelers seeking bargain beds, flimsy construction that often results in broken things in the room). And they're only a good deal if you book far enough ahead to get a good price, and skip the many extras...which can add up fast.

Regardless of the location, you must reserve through their website (www.easyhotel.com).

$ easyHotel Victoria is well-located in an old building near Victoria Station (77 rooms, 34-40 Belgrave Road—for location, see map on page 766, Tube: Victoria, enquiries@victoria.easyhotel. com). They also have branches at **South Kensington** (34 rooms, 14 Lexham Gardens, Tube: Earl's Court or Gloucester Road, tel. 020/7136-2870, enquiries@southken.easyhotel.com), **Earl's Court** (80 rooms, 44-48 West Cromwell Road, Tube: Earl's Court, enquiries@earlscourt.easyhotel.com), **Paddington** (47 rooms, 10 Norfolk Place, Tube: Paddington, enquiries@paddington.easyhotel.com), and **Heathrow** and **Luton** airports (Heathrow location described on page 782).

Hostels

For more London hostel listings, try www.hostellondon.com.

$ London Central Youth Hostel is the flagship of London's hostels, with 300 beds and all the latest in security and comfortable efficiency. Families and travelers of any age will feel welcome in this wonderful facility. You'll pay the same price for any bed in a 4- to 8-bed single-sex dorm—with or without private bathroom—so try to grab one with a bathroom (£16-30/bunk depending on demand, twin D-£40-60, £3/night less for members, breakfast-£4, includes sheets, rental towels, lockers—BYO lock, families welcome to book an entire room, pay Internet access and Wi-Fi, members' kitchen, laundry, open 24 hours, book long in advance, between Oxford Circus and Great Portland Street Tube stations at 104 Bolsover Street—see map on page 778, tel. 0845-371-9154, www.yha.org.uk, londoncentral@yha.org.uk).

$ Oxford Street Youth Hostel is right in the shopping and clubbing zone in Soho, with 90 beds (£20-30/bunk, twin D-£50-60, members pay £3 less, includes sheets, rental towels, pay Internet access and Wi-Fi, lockers—BYO lock, members' kitchen, laundry, open 24 hours, 14 Noel Street, Tube: Oxford Street, tel. 0845-371-9133, www.yha.org.uk, oxfordst@yha.org.uk).

$ St. Paul's Youth Hostel, near St. Paul's Cathedral, is modern, friendly, well-run, and a bit scruffy. Most of the 210 beds are in shared, single-sex 3- to 11-bunk rooms (£20-30/bunk depending on demand, twin D-£50-60, includes locker and sheets but not breakfast, members pay £3 less, laundry, pay Internet access and Wi-Fi, cheap meals, open 24 hours, 36 Carter Lane, Tube: St. Paul's, tel. 020/7236-4965 or 0845-371-9012, www.yha.org.uk, stpauls@yha.org.uk).

$ A cluster of three **St. Christopher's Inn** hostels, south of the Thames near London Bridge, have cheap dorm beds; one branch (the Oasis) is for women only. All have loud and friendly bars attached (£22-32, includes sheets, lockers, small breakfast, must be over 18 years old, free Wi-Fi, open 24 hours, 161-165 Borough High Street, Tube: Borough or London Bridge, reservations tel. 020/8600-7500, www.st-christophers.co.uk).

Dorms

$$ The **University of Westminster** opens its dorm rooms to travelers during summer break, from June through mid-September. Located in several high-rise buildings scattered around central London, the rooms—some with private bathrooms, others with shared bathrooms nearby—come with access to well-equipped kitchens and big lounges (S-£32-41, Sb-£61, D-£108, Db-£182, tel. 020/7911-5181, www.westminster.ac.uk/business/summer-accommodation, summeraccommodation@westminster.ac.uk).

$$ The **London School of Economics** has openings in its dorms from July through September (S-£28-34, Sb-£56-65, D-£52-60, Db-£76-95, tel. 020/7955-7676, www.lsevacations.co.uk, vacations@lse.ac.uk).

$ **University College London** also has rooms for travelers, from late June until mid-September (S-£33-37, Sb-£49, 2-night minimum, cable Internet access in rooms, Wi-Fi in some common areas, tel. 020/7278-3895, www.ucl.ac.uk/residences, accommodation@ucl.ac.uk).

Heathrow and Gatwick Airports

At or near Heathrow Airport

It's so easy to get to Heathrow from central London, I see no reason to sleep there. But if you do, here are some options. The Yotel is actually inside the airport, while the rest are a short bus or taxi ride away. In addition to public buses, the cleverly named £4 "Hotel Hoppa" shuttle buses connect the airport to many nearby hotels (different routes serve the various hotels and terminals—may take a while to spot your particular bus at the airport).

$$ Yotel, at the airport inside Terminal 4, has small sleep dens that offer a popular place to catch a quick nap (four hours-

LONDON

£37-64), or to stay overnight (tiny "standard cabin"—£65/8 hours, "premium cabin"—£87/8 hours; cabins sleep 1-2 people; price is per cabin—not person, reserve online for free or by phone for small fee). Prices vary by day, week, and time of year, so check their website. All rooms are only slightly larger than a double bed, and have private bathrooms and free Internet access and Wi-Fi. These windowless rooms have oddly purplish lighting (tel. 020/7100-1100, www.yotel.com, customer@yotel.com).

$$ Jurys Inn, another hotel chain, tempts tired travelers with 300-plus cookie-cutter rooms (Db-£89-106, check website for deals, breakfast extra; on Eastern Perimeter Road, Tube: Hatton Cross plus 5-minute walk; take the Tube one stop from Terminals 1 or 3; or two stops from Terminals 4 or 5; or the "Hotel Hoppa" #H9 from Terminals 1 or 3, or #H53 or #H56 from Terminals 4 or 5; or buses #285, #482, #490, or #555; tel. 020/8266-4664, fax 020/8266-4665, www.jurysinns.com).

$ easyHotel, your cheapest bet, is in a low-rent residential neighborhood a £5 taxi ride from the airport. Its 53 no-frills, pod-like rooms are on two floors. Before booking at this very basic place, read the explanation on page 779 (Db-£35-53, no breakfast, no elevator, pay Internet access and Wi-Fi, Brick Field Lane; take local bus #140 from airport's Central Bus Station or the "Hotel Hoppa" #H8 from Terminals 1 or 3, or the hotel can arrange a taxi to the airport; tel. 020/8897-9237, www.easyhotel.com, enquiries@heathrow.easyhotel.com).

$ Hotel Ibis London Heathrow is a chain hotel offering predictable value (Db-£40-55, check website for specials as low as £35, breakfast-£7, pay Internet access and Wi-Fi; 112-114 Bath Road, take local bus #105, #111, #140, #285, #423, or #555 from airport's Central Bus Station or Terminal 4, or the "Hotel Hoppa" #H6 from Terminals 1 or 3, or #H56 from Terminals 4 or 5; tel. 020/8759-4888, fax 020/8564-7894, www.ibishotel.com, h0794@accor.com).

At or near Gatwick Airport

$$ Yotel, with small rooms, has a branch right at the airport (Gatwick South Terminal; see prices and contact info in Heathrow listing, previous page).

$ Gatwick Airport Central Premier Inn rents cheap rooms 350 yards from the airport (Db-£45-90, breakfast-£5-8, £2.50 shuttle bus from airport—must reserve in advance, Longbridge Way, North Terminal, tel. 0871-527-8406, frustrating phone tree, www.premierinn.com). Five more Premier Inns are within a five-mile radius of the airport.

$ Gatwick Airport Travelodge has budget rooms about two miles from the airport (Db-£30-60, breakfast extra, pay Wi-Fi,

Church Road, Lowfield Heath, Crawley, £3.20 shuttle bus to/from airport, tel. 0871-984-6031, www.travelodge.co.uk).

Eating in London

With "modern English" cuisine on the rise, you could try a different cuisine for each meal in London and never eat "local" English food, even during a lengthy stay. The sheer variety of foods—from every corner of its former empire and beyond—is astonishing. You'll be amazed at the number of hopping, happening new restaurants of all kinds.

If you want to dine (as opposed to eat), drop by a London newsstand to get a weekly entertainment guide or an annual restaurant guide (both have extensive restaurant listings). Visit www.london-eating.co.uk or www.squaremeal.co.uk for more options.

The thought of a £50 meal in Britain generally ruins my appetite, so my London dining is limited mostly to easygoing, fun, moderately priced alternatives. I've listed places by neighborhood—handy to your sightseeing or hotel. Considering how expensive London can be, if there's any good place to cut corners to stretch your budget, it's by eating cheaply. Pub grub (at one of London's 7,000 pubs) and ethnic restaurants (especially Indian and Chinese) are good low-cost options. Of course, picnicking is the fastest and cheapest way to go. Good grocery stores and sandwich shops, fine park benches, and polite pigeons abound in Britain's most expensive city.

London (and all of Britain) is smoke-free. Expect restaurants and pubs that sell food to be non-smoking indoors, with smokers occupying patios and doorways outside. When ready to pay, Brits generally ask for the "bill" rather than the "check."

Central London

I've arranged these options by neighborhood, but they're all within about a 15-minute walk of each other. Survey your options before settling on a place.

Near Soho and Chinatown

London has a trendy scene that most Beefeater-seekers miss entirely. Foodies who want to eat well skip the more staid and touristy zones near Piccadilly and Trafalgar Square, and head to Soho instead. Make it a point to dine in Soho at least once, to feel the pulse of London's eclectic urban melting pot of international flavors. These restaurants are scattered throughout a chic, creative, and borderline-seedy zone that teems with hipsters, theatergoers, and London's gay community. Even if you plan to have dinner elsewhere, it's a treat just to wander around Soho.

Note: While gentrification has mostly stripped this area (no pun intended) of its former "red light district" vibe, a few pockets of sex for sale survive. Beware of the extremely welcoming women standing outside the strip clubs (especially on Great Windmill Street). Enjoy the sales pitch—but know that only fools fall for the "£5 drink and show" lure.

On and near Wardour Street, in the Heart of Soho

Running through the middle of Soho, rumbling past what's left of the strip-club zone, Wardour Street is ground zero for creative restaurateurs hoping to break into the big leagues. Strolling up this street—particularly from Brewer Street northward—you can take your pick from a world of options: Thai, Indonesian, Vietnamese, Italian, French and even...English. Not yet tarnished by the corporatization creeping in from areas to the south, this drag still seems to hit the right balance between trendy and accessible. While I've listed several choices below (including some that are a block or two off of Wardour Street), simply strolling the length of the street and following your appetite to the place that looks best is a great plan.

The **Busaba Eathai** is a hit with locals for its snappy (sometimes rushed) service, casual-yet-high-energy ambience, and good, inexpensive Thai cuisine. Be prepared to be wedged communally around big, square 16-person hardwood tables or in two-person tables by the window—with everyone in the queue staring at your noodles. On a busy night, the place really gets rollicking—not ideal for quiet conversation. They don't take reservations, so arrive by 19:00 or line up (£7-12 meals, Mon-Thu 12:00-23:00, Fri-Sat 12:00-23:30, Sun 12:00-22:00, 106 Wardour Street, tel. 020/7255-8686). They're adding new locations all the time; convenient outlets include nearby Panton Street (at #35), just below Piccadilly Circus; at 44 Floral Street, near Covent Garden; at 22 Store Street, near the British Museum and Goodge Street Tube; and at 8-13 Bird Street, just off Oxford Street and across from the Bond Street Tube.

Princi is a vast, bright, efficient, wildly popular Italian deli/bakery with Milanese flair. Along one wall is a long counter with display cases offering a tempting array of pizza rustica, panini sandwiches, focaccia, a few pasta dishes, and desserts (look in the window from the street to see their wood-fired oven in action). Order your food at the counter, then find a space at a long shared table; or get it "to go" for an affordable and fast meal (£7-13 meals, Mon-Sat 8:00-24:00, Sun 8:30-22:00, 135 Wardour Street, tel. 020/7478-8888).

Bi Bim Bap is named for what it sells: *bibimbap* (literally "mixed rice"), a scalding stone bowl filled with rice, thinly sliced veggies, and topped with a fried egg. Mix it all up with your spoon, flavor it to taste with the two sauces, then dig in with your chopsticks. While purists go with the straightforward rice bowl, you can pay a few pounds extra to add other toppings—including chicken, *bulgogi* (marinated beef strips), and mushrooms. Though the food is traditional Korean, the stylish, colorful interior lets you know you're in Soho (£7-10 meals, Mon-Fri 12:00-15:00 & 18:00-23:00, Sat 12:00-23:00, closed Sun, 11 Greek Street, tel. 020/7287-3434).

Mooli's is made-to-order for a quick, affordable, flavorful jolt of Indian street food. Their £5-6 *mooli* wraps, sort of like an Indian burrito, are filled with pork, chicken, beef, *paneer* (cheese), chickpea, or spicy goat. Top it with your choice of chutneys and Indian salsas. Eat in or grab one to go; their "mini" version makes a good £3.50 snack (Mon-Sat 8:30-23:30, closed Sun, 50 Frith Street, tel. 020/7494-9075).

Bocca di Lupo, a pricey and popular splurge, serves small portions of classic regional Italian food. Dressy and a bit snooty, it's a place where you're glad you made a reservation. The counter seating, on cushy stools with a view into the open kitchen, is particularly memorable. Most diners assemble a sampler meal with a series of £7-10 small plates—but be careful, because at these prices, your bill can add up. A short selection of more affordable £10-15 "one-dish meals" is available for lunch and until 19:00 (Mon-Sat 12:00-15:00 & 17:30-23:00, Sun 12:30-15:15 & 17:00-21:00, 12 Archer Street, tel. 020/7734-2223).

Gelupo, Bocca di Lupo's sister gelateria across the street, has a wide array of ever-changing but always creative and delicious dessert favorites—ranging from popular standbys like the incredibly rich chocolate sorbet to fresh-mint *stracciatella* to hay (yes, hay). A £3 sampler cup or cone gets you two flavors (and little taster spoons are generously offered to help you choose). Everything is homemade, and the white subway-tile interior feels clean and bright. They also have espresso drinks and—at lunchtime—£4-5 deli sandwiches (Mon-Thu 12:00-23:00, Fri-Sat 12:00-1:00 in the morning, Sun 12:00-22:00, 7 Archer Street, tel. 020/7287-5555).

Yalla Yalla is a hole-in-the-wall serving up high-quality Beirut street food—hummus, baba ghanoush, tabbouleh, and *shawarmas*. Stylish as you'd expect for Soho, it's tucked down a seedy alley between a sex shop and a tattoo parlor. Eat in the cramped and cozy interior or one of the few outdoor tables, or get your food to go (£3-4 sandwiches, £4-6 *mezes*, £7 *mezes* platter available until 17:00, £10-12 bigger dishes, Mon-Sat 10:00-23:00, Sun 10:00-22:00, 1 Green's Court—just north of Brewer Street, tel. 020/7287-7663).

Byron, an upscale-hamburger chain, has a particularly appeal-

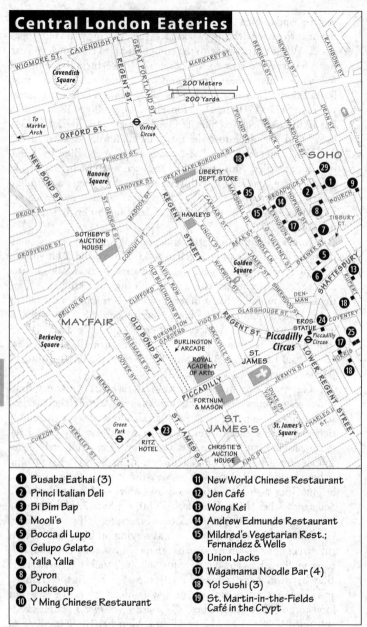

Central London Eateries

1. Busaba Eathai (3)
2. Princi Italian Deli
3. Bi Bim Bap
4. Mooli's
5. Bocca di Lupo
6. Gelupo Gelato
7. Yalla Yalla
8. Byron
9. Ducksoup
10. Y Ming Chinese Restaurant
11. New World Chinese Restaurant
12. Jen Café
13. Wong Kei
14. Andrew Edmunds Restaurant
15. Mildred's Vegetarian Rest.; Fernandez & Wells
16. Union Jacks
17. Wagamama Noodle Bar (4)
18. Yo! Sushi (3)
19. St. Martin-in-the-Fields Café in the Crypt

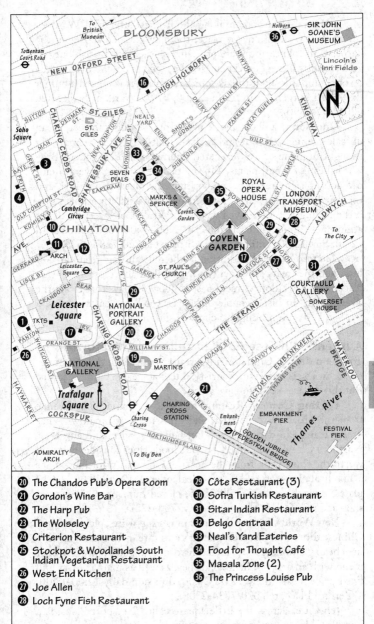

20 The Chandos Pub's Opera Room
21 Gordon's Wine Bar
22 The Harp Pub
23 The Wolseley
24 Criterion Restaurant
25 Stockpot & Woodlands South Indian Vegetarian Restaurant
26 West End Kitchen
27 Joe Allen
28 Loch Fyne Fish Restaurant
29 Côte Restaurant (3)
30 Sofra Turkish Restaurant
31 Sitar Indian Restaurant
32 Belgo Centraal
33 Neal's Yard Eateries
34 Food for Thought Café
35 Masala Zone (2)
36 The Princess Louise Pub

LONDON

ing industrial-mod branch along the liveliest stretch of Wardour Street. In this high-energy place, the open kitchen sizzles in the corner while old cartoons are projected on the wall. British burgers aren't exactly like American ones—they tend to be a bit overcooked by our standards—but this is your best option if you need a burger fix (£7-10 burgers, daily 12:00-23:00, 97-99 Wardour Street, tel. 020/7297-9390).

Ducksoup, a short block over from Wardour Street, is an upscale-feeling yet cool and relaxed little bar, with a small but thoughtful menu of well-executed international and modern British dishes (£7 small plates, £14 big plates—sharing several items can add up). The menu is handwritten, the music is on vinyl, and the rough woodwork and cramped-but-convivial atmosphere give it the feeling of a well-loved wine bar. While a bit overpriced, the atmosphere is memorable (Mon-Sat 12:00-24:00, food served until 22:30, Sun 13:00-16:00, 41 Dean Street, tel. 020/7287-4599).

And for Dessert: In addition to the outstanding gelato at **Gelupo** and the treats at **Princi** (both described above), several other places along Wardour Street boast window displays that tickle the sweet tooth. In just a couple of blocks, you'll see pastry shops, a *crêperie*, and a Hummingbird cupcake shop.

Authentic Chinese Food in and near Chinatown

The main drag of Chinatown (Gerrard Street, with the ornamental archways) is lined with touristy, interchangeable Chinese joints. But these places seem to have an edge.

Y Ming Chinese Restaurant—across Shaftesbury Avenue from the ornate gates, clatter, and dim sum of Chinatown—has dressy European decor, serious but helpful service, and authentic Northern Chinese cooking. London's food critics consider this well worth the short walk from the heart of Chinatown for food that's a notch above (good £12 meal deal offered 12:00-18:00, £8-12 plates, open Mon-Sat 12:00-23:45, closed Sun, turquoise corner shop at 35-36 Greek Street, tel. 020/7734-2721).

New World Chinese Restaurant is a sprawling, old-fashioned Chinese diner that just feels real. It's a fixture in Chinatown, serving cheap Cantonese food, including dim sum and a similar dinner menu with an array of little £3 dishes, as well as main courses and fixed-price meals (daily 12:00-24:00, dim sum daily 12:00-18:00, 1 Gerrard Place, tel. 020/7734-2508).

Jen Café, across the little square called Newport Place, is a humble Chinese corner eatery much loved for its homemade dumplings. It's just stools and simple seating, with fast service, a fun, inexpensive menu, and a devoted following (£3-6 plates, Mon-Wed 10:30-20:30, Thu-Sun 10:30-21:30, cash only, 4 Newport Place, tel. 020/7287-9708).

Wong Kei Chinese restaurant, at the Wardour Street (west) end of the Chinatown drag, offers a bewildering variety of dishes served by notoriously brusque waiters in a setting that feels like a hospital cafeteria. Londoners put up with the abuse to enjoy one of the satisfying BBQ rice dishes or hot pots. Individuals and couples are usually seated at communal tables, while larger parties are briskly shuffled up or down stairs (£7-12 main dishes, cash only, Mon-Sat 12:00-23:30, Sun 12:00-22:30, 41-43 Wardour Street, tel. 020/7437-8408).

More Sedate and Upscale Options, on Lexington Street, in the Heart of Soho

Andrew Edmunds Restaurant is a tiny, candlelit place where you'll want to hide your camera and guidebook and not act like a tourist. This little place—with a jealous and loyal clientele—is the closest I've found to Parisian quality in a cozy restaurant in London. The modern European cooking and creative seasonal menu are worth the splurge (£5-7 starters, £12-20 main dishes, Mon-Sat 12:30-15:00 & 18:00-22:45, Sun 13:00-15:30 & 18:00-22:30, come early or call ahead, request ground floor rather than basement, 46 Lexington Street, tel. 020/7437-5708).

Mildred's Vegetarian Restaurant, across from Andrew Edmunds, has cheap prices, an enjoyable menu, and a pleasant interior filled with happy eaters (£8-11 meals, Mon-Sat 12:00-23:00, closed Sun, vegan options, 45 Lexington Street, tel. 020/7494-1634).

Fernandez & Wells is a cozy, convivial, delightfully simple little wine, cheese, and ham bar. Drop in and grab a stool as you belly up to the big wooden bar. Share a plate of top-quality cheeses and/or Spanish, Italian, or French hams with fine bread and oil, while sipping a nice glass of wine (Mon-Fri 11:00-22:00, Sat-Sun 12:00-22:00, quality sandwiches at lunch, wine/cheese/ham bar after 16:00, 43 Lexington Street, tel. 020/7734-1546).

Just East of Soho

Union Jacks, the latest venture of British celebrity chef Jamie Oliver, takes a classic dish—pizza—and turns it on its ear by fusing it with British ingredients. Jamie's wood-fired "flats" (flatbreads) are topped not with cheese and tomatoes, but roast pig shoulder or oxtail and brisket. While this sounds risky, he pulls it off with great flavors, plus tasty salads and fun "fizzy drinks." It's improbably located in a sterile-feeling glass office park just a couple of blocks east of central Soho (across from St. Giles Church), but—predictably—plans to expand all over London are underway (£5-7 small plates and salads, £10-13 pizzas, £9-15 classic British dishes, daily 12:00-23:00, Sun until 22:00, 4 Central St. Giles Piazza, tel. 020/3597-7888).

Soho Chain Restaurants

Some of Britain's most popular chain restaurants for ethnic eats started out here in Soho. In this fast-evolving neighborhood, the restaurants listed below are a little like stale sushi. While I wouldn't waste a Soho meal on one of these places (since you can find an identical menu at branches all over town—and all over the UK), they're a convenient fallback if some of the other places I recommend are full. Two places I recommend above, Busaba Eathai and Byron, have quickly expanded and may soon join the global-domination ranks of Wagamama and Yo! Sushi. Princi, Bi Bim Bap, Mooli's, and Union Jacks seem poised to explode next.

Wagamama Noodle Bar is a noisy, pan-Asian, organic slurp-athon. As you enter, check out the kitchen and listen to the roar of the basement, where benches rock with happy eaters. Everybody sucks. Portions are huge and splitting is allowed. While the quality has gone downhill a bit as they've expanded, this remains a re-liable choice for variety at reasonable prices (£8-12 meals, Mon-Sat 11:30-23:00, Sun 12:00-22:00, 10A Lexington Street, tel. 020/7292-0990 but no reservations taken). Other handy branches are all over town, including near the British Museum (4 Streatham Street), Kensington (26 High Street), in the Harvey Nichols de-partment store (109 Knightsbridge), Covent Garden (1 Tavistock Street), Leicester Square (14 Irving Street), Piccadilly Circus (8 Norris Street), Fleet Street (#109), and next to the Tower of Lon-don (2B Tower Place).

Yo! Sushi is a Japanese-food-extravaganza experience, com-plete with thumping rock, Japanese cable TV, and a 195-foot-long conveyor belt. For £1.50, you get unlimited green tea (water for £1.05). Snag a bar stool and grab dishes as they rattle by (priced by color of dish; check the chart: £1.80-5 per dish, Mon-Fri 12:00-22:30, Sat-Sun 12:00-23:00, until 24:00 in summer, 2 blocks south of Oxford Street, where Lexington Street becomes Poland Street, 52 Poland Street, tel. 020/7287-0443). If you like Yo!, you're in the right city: There are about 40 other locations around town, in-cluding a handy branch a block from the London Eye on Belve-dere Road, as well as outlets on Haymarket a block from Piccadilly Circus, within Selfridges and Harvey Nichols department stores, in the Whiteleys Shopping Centre on Queensway, and in several major train stations.

Traditional Choices near Trafalgar Square

These places, all of which provide a more "jolly olde" experience than high cuisine, are within about 100 yards of Trafalgar Square.

St. Martin-in-the-Fields Café in the Crypt is just right for a tasty meal on a monk's budget—maybe even on a monk's tomb.

You'll dine sitting on somebody's gravestone in an ancient crypt. Their enticing buffet line is kept stocked all day, serving breakfast, lunch, and dinner (£6-10 cafeteria plates, hearty traditional desserts, free jugs of water). They also serve a restful cream tea (£6, daily 14:00-18:00). You'll find the café directly under the St. Martin-in-the-Fields Church, facing Trafalgar Square—enter through the glass pavilion next to the church (Mon-Tue 8:00-20:00, Wed 8:00-22:30, Thu-Sat 8:00-21:00, Sun 11:00-18:00, profits go to the church, Tube: Charing Cross, tel. 020/7766-1158 or 020/7766-1100). Wednesday evenings at 20:00 come with a live jazz band (£6-9 tickets). While here, check out the concert schedule for the busy church upstairs (or visit www.smitf.org).

The Chandos Pub's Opera Room floats amazingly apart from the tacky crush of tourism around Trafalgar Square. Look for it opposite the National Portrait Gallery (corner of William IV Street and St. Martin's Lane) and climb the stairs (to the right of the pub entrance) to the Opera Room. This is a fine Trafalgar rendezvous point and wonderfully local pub. They serve traditional, plain-tasting £5-8 pub meals—meat pies and fish-and-chips are their specialty. The ground-floor pub is stuffed with regulars and offers snugs (private booths), the same menu, and more serious beer drinking. Chandos proudly serves the local Samuel Smith beer at £4 a pint (kitchen open daily 11:00-19:00, Fri and Sun until 18:00, order and pay at the bar, 29 St. Martin's Lane, Tube: Leicester Square, tel. 020/7836-1401).

Gordon's Wine Bar, with a simple, steep staircase leading into a candlelit 15th-century wine cellar, is filled with dusty old bottles, faded British memorabilia, and nine-to-fivers. At the "English rustic" buffet, choose a hot meal or cold meat dish with a salad (figure around £7-8/dish); the £8.20 cheese plate comes with two cheeses, bread, and a pickle. Then step up to the wine bar and consider the many varieties of wine and port available by the glass (this place is passionate about port). The low, carbon-crusted vaulting deeper in the back seems to intensify the Hogarth-painting atmosphere. Although it's crowded, you can normally corral two chairs and grab the corner of a table. On hot days, the crowd spills out onto a leafy back patio, where a barbecue cooks for a long line of tables (arrive before 17:00 to get a seat, Mon-Sat 11:00-23:00, Sun 12:00-22:00, 2 blocks from Trafalgar Square, bottom of Villiers Street at #47, Tube: Embankment, tel. 020/7930-1408, manager Gerard Menan).

Ales: **The Harp,** clearly a local favorite, is a crowded and cluttered little pub just a block above Trafalgar Square. While they serve no food, this is a good, central spot to nurse a fine ale and make a new friend with one of the Londoners crowded around the coaster-coated bar. This is a top choice for an après-work pint among nine-to-fivers, who stand in the dozens out front after the workday, sipping their beers (Mon-Sat 10:30-23:30, Sun 12:00-22:30, 47 Chandos Place, tel. 020/7836-0291).

Near Piccadilly

The first two places are upscale and snooty—but if you want something cheaper in this same area, you'll find plenty of other options.

Swanky Splurges

The Wolseley is the grand 1920s showroom of a long-defunct British car. The last Wolseley drove out with the Great Depression, but today this old-time bistro bustles with formal waiters serving traditional Austrian and French dishes in an elegant black-marble-and-chandeliers setting fit for its location next to the Ritz. Although the food can be unexceptional, prices are reasonable, and the presentation and setting are grand. Reservations are a must (£13-30 main courses; cheaper soup, salad, and sandwich "café menu" available; both menus available in all areas of restaurant, Mon-Fri 7:00-24:00, Sat 8:00-24:00, Sun 8:00-23:00, 160 Piccadilly, tel. 020/7499-6996). They're popular for their fancy cream or afternoon tea.

The palatial **Criterion** offers grand-piano ambience beneath gilded tiles and chandeliers in a dreamy Byzantine church setting from 1880. It's right on Piccadilly Circus but a world away from the punk junk. It's a deal for the visual experience during lunch and if you order the £19-23 fixed-price meal (except on Sun, when you must order from the expensive à la carte menu)...and, at any hour, the service couldn't care less. Anyone can drop in for coffee or a drink (Mon-Sat 12:00-14:30 & 17:30-23:30, Sun 12:00-15:30 & 17:30-22:30, 224 Piccadilly, tel. 020/7930-0488).

Cheaper Options near Piccadilly

Hungry and broke in the theater district? Head for Panton Street (off Haymarket, two blocks southeast of Piccadilly Circus), where several hardworking little places compete, all seeming to offer a three-course meal for about £9. Peruse the entire block (vegetarian, Pizza Express, Moroccan, Thai, Chinese, and two famous diners) before making your choice.

Stockpot is a meat, potatoes, gravy, and mushy-peas kind of place, famous and rightly popular for its edible, cheap English meals (£6-12, daily 7:00-23:00, 38 Panton Street, tel. 020/7839-5142). The **West End Kitchen** (across the street at #5, same hours and menu) is a direct competitor that's also well-known and just as good (£5-11 meals). Vegetarians may prefer the **Woodlands South**

Indian Vegetarian Restaurant, which serves an impressive £19 *thali* (otherwise £7 main courses, 37 Panton Street).

Near Covent Garden

Covent Garden bustles with people and touristy eateries. The area feels overrun, but if you must eat around here, you have some good choices.

Joe Allen, tucked in a brick cellar a block away from the market, serves modern international and American cuisine with both style and hubbub. Downstairs off a quiet street with candles and white tablecloths, it's comfortably spacious and popular with the theater crowd. It feels a bit old-fashioned and cluttered, but in a welcoming way (£7 starters, £10-22 main courses, £16 two-course specials and £19.50 three-course specials available at lunch and from 17:00-18:45, open Mon-Fri 12:00-24:00, Sat-Sun 10:00-24:00, piano music after 21:00, 13 Exeter Street, tel. 020/7836-0651).

Loch Fyne Fish Restaurant is part of a Scottish chain that grows its own oysters and mussels. It offers an inviting atmosphere with a fine fishy energy and no pretense (£10-17 main dishes, £10 two-course special and £12 three-course special served 12:00-19:00, open Mon-Sat 8:00-22:30, Sun 9:00-22:00, a couple of blocks behind Covent Garden at 2 Catherine Street, tel. 020/7240-4999).

Côte Restaurant is a contemporary French bistro chain serving good-value French cuisine at the right prices (£9-14 mains, £14 three-course early dinner specials if you order by 19:00, open Mon-Tue 8:00-23:00, Wed-Fri 8:00-24:00, Sat 9:00-24:00, Sun 9:00-22:30, 17-21 Tavistock Street, tel. 020/7379-9991). Côte also has locations in Soho (124-126 Wardour Street) and near St. Martin-in-the-Fields (50-51 St. Martin's Lane).

Sofra Turkish Restaurant is good for quality Turkish with a touch of class. They have several menus: *meze* (Turkish tapas, £4-7), vegetarian, and £10 fixed-price meals (also £10-15 main dishes, daily 9:00-24:00, 36 Tavistock Street, tel. 020/7240-3773).

Sitar Indian Restaurant is a well-respected Indian/Bangladeshi place serving dishes from many regions, fine fish, and a tasty £15 vegetarian *thali*. It's small and dressy, with snappy service (£10-17 main dishes, Mon-Fri 12:00-24:00, Sat-Sun 15:00-23:00, next to Somerset House at 149 Strand, tel. 020/7836-3730).

Belgo Centraal serves hearty Belgian specialties in a vast 400-seat underground lair. It's a mussels, chips, and beer emporium dressed up as a mod-monastic refectory—with noisy acoustics and waiters garbed as Trappist monks. The classy restaurant section is more comfortable and less rowdy, but usually requires reserva-

LONDON

tions. It's often more fun just to grab a spot in the boisterous beer hall, with its tight, communal benches (no reservations accepted). Both sides have the same menu and specials. Belgians claim they eat as well as the French and as heartily as the Germans. This place, which offers a stunning array of dark, blonde, and fruity Belgian beers, actually makes Belgian things trendy—a formidable feat (£10-14 main dishes, open daily 12:00-23:00; Mon-Fri £5-6.30 "beat the clock" meal specials 17:00-18:30—the time you order is the price you pay—including main dishes and fries; no meal-splitting after 18:30, and you must buy food with beer; daily £8 lunch special 12:00-17:00; 1 kid eats free for each parent ordering a regular entrée; 1 block north of Covent Garden Tube station at 50 Earlham Street, tel. 020/7813-2233).

Neal's Yard is a surprisingly colorful courtyard full of cheap, hip, and healthy eateries near Covent Garden. The neighborhood is a tabouli of fun, hippie-type cafés. One of the best—nearby—is the venerable and ferociously vegetarian **Food for Thought,** packed with local health nuts (good £5 vegetarian meals, £8 dinner plates, Mon-Sat 12:00-20:30, Sun 12:00-17:30, 2 blocks north of Covent Garden Tube station at 31 Neal Street, tel. 020/7836-0239).

Masala Zone is a colorful London chain serving up accessible and reliably good Indian food. You can order a curry-and-rice dish, a *thali* (metal platter with several small dishes), or their street food specials. Each branch has its own personality; the one at Covent Garden has giant, colorful marionettes suspended from the ceiling (£8-12 meals, daily 12:00-23:00, just off the top end of Covent Garden at 48 Floral Street, tel. 020/7379-0101). Other locations include Soho (9 Marshall Street) and Bayswater (75 Bishops Bridge Road).

Near the British Museum, in Fitzrovia

To avoid the touristy crush right around the museum (and just southwest, in Soho), Londoners head a few blocks west, to the Fitzrovia area. Here, tiny Charlotte Place is lined with small eateries (including the two listed below); nearby, the much bigger Charlotte Street has several more good options. The higher street signs you'll notice on Charlotte Street are a holdover from a time when they needed to be visible to carriage drivers. This area is a short walk from the Goodge Street Tube station—convenient to the British Museum, and right next to Pollock's Toy Museum (see map on page 778).

Salumeria Dino serves up hearty sandwiches, pasta, and Italian coffee. Dino, a native of Naples, has run his little shop for more than 30 years and has managed to create a classic Italian deli that's so authentic, you'll walk out singing "O Sole Mio" (£3-5 sandwiches, £1 take-away cappuccinos, Mon-Fri 9:00-17:00, closed Sat-Sun, 15 Charlotte Place, tel. 020/7580-3938).

Lantana OUT, next door to Salumeria Dino, is an Australian coffee shop that sells modern soups, sandwiches, and salads at their take-away window. Their changing menu features a soup-salad-sweet combo deal for £5.50 (£3-7 meals, pricier sit-down café next door, Mon-Fri 7:30-15:00, café open Sat-Sun 9:00-17:00, 13 Charlotte Place, tel. 020/7637-3347).

Note that Jamie Oliver's **Union Jacks** is also handy to the British Museum (see page 789).

West London
Near Victoria Station Accommodations
These restaurants are within a few blocks of Victoria Station—and all are places where I've enjoyed eating. As with the accommodations in this area, I've grouped them by location: east or west of the station (see the map on page 766).

Cheap Eats: For groceries, a handy **M&S Simply Food** is inside Victoria Station (Mon-Sat 7:00-24:00, Sun 8:00-23:00, near the front, by the bus terminus), along with a **Sainsbury's Local** (daily 6:00-23:00, at rear entrance, on Eccleston Street). A larger Sainsbury's is on Wilton Road near Warwick Way, a couple of blocks southeast of the station (Mon-Fri 7:00-23:00, Sat 7:00-22:00, Sun 11:00-17:00). A string of good ethnic restaurants lines Wilton Road (near the recommended Seafresh Fish Restaurant). For affordable if forgettable meals, try the row of cheap little eateries on Elizabeth Street.

West of Victoria Station (Belgravia)
Ebury Wine Bar, filled with young professionals, provides a cut-above atmosphere. In the delightful back room, the fancy menu features modern European cuisine with a French accent, including delicious £15-20 main dishes and a £19 two-course and £25 three-course special (available Mon-Fri at lunch and daily 18:00-20:00; three-course meal includes a glass of champagne that you're welcome to swap for house wine). At the wine bar, find a cheaper bar menu that's better than your average pub grub (£8-15 meals). This is emphatically a "traditional wine bar," with no beers on tap (restaurant open daily 12:00-15:00 & 18:00-22:30, wine bar open all day long, reservations smart, at intersection of Ebury and Elizabeth Streets, 139 Ebury Street, tel. 020/7730-5447).

Jenny Lo's Tea House is a simple budget place serving up a short menu of £8-9 eclectic Chinese-style meals to locals in the know. Jenny clearly learned from her father, Ken Lo, one of the most famous Cantonese chefs in Britain, whose fancy place is just around the corner (also £5.50 take-out lunches, Mon-Fri 12:00-14:45 & 18:00-22:00, closed Sat-Sun, cash only, 14 Eccleston Street, tel. 020/7259-0399).

La Bottega is an Italian delicatessen that fits its upscale Belgravia neighborhood. It offers tasty, freshly cooked pastas (£6), lasagnas, and salads (£8 lasagna and salad meal), along with great sandwiches (£3) and a good coffee bar with pastries. While not cheap, it's fast (order at the counter), and the ingredients would please an Italian chef. Grab your meal to go, or enjoy the Belgravia good life with locals, either sitting inside or on the sidewalk (Mon-Fri 8:00-19:00, Sat 9:00-18:00, Sun 9:00-17:00, on corner of Ebury and Eccleston Streets, tel. 020/7730-2730).

The Thomas Cubitt pub, named for the urban planner who designed much of Belgravia, is a trendy neighborhood gastropub packed with young professionals. It's pricey and a pinch pretentious, and prides itself on using sustainable ingredients in its modern English cooking. With a bright but slightly cramped interior and fine sidewalk seating, it's great for a drink or meal (£6 small plates, £14-17 main dishes, 44 Elizabeth Street, tel. 020/7730-6060). Upstairs is a more refined restaurant with the same kitchen, but an emphasis on finer technique and presentation (£8-11 starters, £17-20 main courses, reservations recommended, Mon-Sat 12:00-15:00 & 18:00-22:00, Sun 12:00-15:00 only).

The Duke of Wellington pub is a classic neighborhood place with forgettable grub, sidewalk seating, and an inviting interior. A bit more lowbrow than my other Belgravia listings, this may be your best shot at meeting a local (£5 sandwiches, £7-10 meals, food served Mon-Sat 12:00-15:00 & 18:00-21:00, Sun lunch only, 63 Eaton Terrace, tel. 020/7730-1782).

South End of Ebury Street: A five-minute walk down Ebury Street, where it intersects with Pimlico Road, you'll find a pretty square with a few more eateries to consider—including **The Orange,** a high-priced gastropub with the same owners and a similar menu to the Thomas Cubitt (described earlier); and **Daylesford,** the deli and café of an organic farm (£3-5 light meals to go—a good picnic option).

East of Victoria Station (Pimlico)

Grumbles brags it's been serving "good food and wine at nonscary prices since 1964." Offering a delicious mix of "modern eclectic French and traditional English," this unpretentious little place with cozy booths inside (on two levels, including a cellar) and four nice sidewalk tables is *the* spot to eat well in this otherwise workaday neighborhood. Their traditional dishes are their forte (£10-16 plates, £11 early-bird specials 18:00-19:00, open Mon-Sat 12:00-

LONDON

14:30 & 18:00-23:00, Sun 12:00-22:30, reservations wise, half a block north of Belgrave Road at 35 Churton Street, tel. 020/7834-0149, Alex).

Seafresh Fish Restaurant is the neighborhood place for plaice—and classic and creative fish-and-chips cuisine. You can either take out on the cheap or eat in, enjoying a white fish ambience. Though Mario's father started this place in 1965, it feels like the chippie of the 21st century (meals-£5-7 to go, £12-17 to sit, Mon-Sat 12:00-15:00 & 17:00-22:30, closed Sun, 80-81 Wilton Road, tel. 020/7828-0747).

The Jugged Hare pub, a 10-minute walk from Victoria Station, sits in a lavish old bank building, with vaults replaced by tankards of beer and a fine kitchen. They have a fun, traditional menu with more fresh veggies than fries, and a plush, vivid pub scene good for a meal or just a drink (£6.25 sandwiches, £10 meals, Mon-Sat 11:00-23:00, Sun 12:00-23:30, food served daily 12:00-22:00, Sun until 21:30, quiz night Wed at 19:00, 172 Vauxhall Bridge Road, tel. 020/7828-1543).

St. George's Tavern is *the* pub for a meal in this neighborhood. They serve dinner from the same fun menu in three zones: on the sidewalk to catch the sun and enjoy some people-watching, in the sloppy pub, and in a classier back dining room. They're proud of their sausages and "toad in the hole." The scene is inviting for just a beer, too (£8-14 meals, Mon-Sat 10:00-22:00, Sun until 21:30, corner of Hugh Street and Belgrave Road, tel. 020/7630-1116).

Near Notting Hill and Bayswater Accommodations

For locations, see the map on page 772.

Maggie Jones's, a Charles Dickens-meets-Ella Fitzgerald splurge, is exuberantly rustic and very English, with a 1940s-jazz soundtrack. It's a longer walk than most of my recommendations, but worth the hike. You'll get solid English cuisine, including huge plates of crunchy vegetables, served by a young and casual staff. It's pricey, but the portions are huge (especially the meat-and-fish pies, their specialty). You're welcome to save lots by splitting your main course. The candlelit upstairs is the most romantic, while the basement is kept lively with the kitchen, tight seating, and lots of action. If you eat well once in London, eat here—and do it quick, before it burns down (lunch—£5 starters, £7 main dishes; dinner—£6-9 starters, £15-24 main dishes; Mon-Sat 12:00-15:00 & 18:00-23:00, Sun 12:00-15:00 & 18:00-22:30, reservations recommended, 6 Old Court Place, just east of Kensington Church Street, near High Street Kensington Tube stop, tel. 020/7937-6462).

LONDON

The Churchill Arms pub and **Thai Kitchen** (same location) are local hangouts, with good beer and a thriving old-English ambience in front, and hearty £8 Thai plates in an enclosed patio in the back. You can eat the Thai food in the tropical hideaway (table service) or in the atmospheric pub section (order at the counter and they'll bring it to you). They also serve basic English pub food at lunch (£3 sandwiches, £5-7 meals). The place is festooned with Churchill memorabilia and chamber pots (including one with Hitler's mug on it—hanging from the ceiling farthest from Thai Kitchen—sure to cure the constipation of any Brit during World War II). Arrive by 18:00 or after 21:00 to avoid a line. During busy times, diners are limited to an hour at the table (food served daily 12:00-22:00, 119 Kensington Church Street, tel. 020/7727-4242).

Hereford Road is a cozy, mod eatery tucked at the far end of Prince's Square. It's stylish but not pretentious, serving heavy, meaty English cuisine executed with modern panache. Cozy two-person booths face the open kitchen up top; the main dining room is down below. There are also a few sidewalk tables (£6-8 starters, £14-16 main courses, reservations smart, Mon-Sat 12:00-15:00 & 18:00-22:00, Sun 12:00-16:00 & 18:00-22:00, 3 Hereford Road, tel. 020/7727-1144).

The Prince Edward serves good grub in a quintessential pub setting (£7-12 meals, Mon-Wed 10:00-23:00, Thu-Sat 10:00-23:30, Sun 10:00-22:30, plush-pubby indoor seating or sidewalk tables, family-friendly, pay Wi-Fi, 2 blocks north of Bayswater Road at the corner of Dawson Place and Hereford Road, 73 Prince's Square, tel. 020/7727-2221).

Café Diana is a healthy little eatery serving sandwiches, salads, and Middle Eastern food. It's decorated—almost shrine-like—with photos of Princess Diana, who used to drop by for pita sandwiches. You can dine in the simple interior, or order some food from the counter to go (£3-5 sandwiches, £6-8 meat dishes, daily 8:00-23:00, 5 Wellington Terrace, on Bayswater Road, opposite Kensington Palace Garden Gates, where Di once lived, tel. 020/7792-9606, Abdul).

On Queensway: The road called Queensway is a multiethnic food circus, lined with lively and inexpensive eateries—browse the options along here and choose your favorite. For a cut above, head for **Royal China Restaurant**—filled with London's Chinese, who consider this one of the city's best eateries. It's dressed up in black, white, and gold, with candles and brisk waiters. While it's pricier than most neighborhood Chinese restaurants, the food is noticeably better (£9-13 dishes, Mon-Thu 12:00-23:00, Fri-Sat 12:00-23:30, Sun 11:00-22:00, dim sum until 17:00, 13 Queensway, tel. 020/7221-2535). For a lowbrow alternative, **Whiteleys Shopping**

Centre Food Court—at the top end of Queensway—offers a fun selection of ethnic and fast-food chain eateries among Corinthian columns, and a multiscreen theater in a delightful mall (most restaurants daily 12:00-23:00, some eateries open shorter hours; options include Yo! Sushi, good salads at Café Rouge, pizza, Starbucks, and a coin-op Internet place; third floor, corner of Porchester Gardens and Queensway).

Supermarkets: **Tesco** is a half-block from the Notting Hill Gate Tube stop (Mon-Sat 7:00-24:00, Sat until 23:00, Sun 12:00-18:00, near intersection with Pembridge Road, 114-120 Notting Hill Gate). Queensway is home to several supermarkets, including the smaller **Spar Market** at #18 (Mon-Sat 7:00-24:00, Sun 8:00-24:00). Nearby, **Marks & Spencer** can be found in Whiteleys Shopping Centre (Mon-Sat 8:30-22:00, Sun 12:00-18:00).

South Kensington

Popular eateries line Old Brompton Road and Thurloe Street (Tube: South Kensington), and a good selection of cheap eateries are clumped around the Tube station. For locations, see the map on page 770.

La Bouchée Bistro Café is a classy hole-in-the-wall touch of France. This candlelit and woody bistro, with very tight seating, serves a special fixed-price meal (£14.50/2 courses, £16.50/3 courses) on weekdays during lunch and from 17:00-19:00, and £15 *plats du jour* all *jour* (also £15-20 à la carte main courses). Reservations are smart in the evening (daily 12:00-15:00 & 17:00-23:00, 56 Old Brompton Road, tel. 020/7589-1929).

Moti Mahal Indian Restaurant, with minimalist-yet-classy mod ambience and attentive service, serves mostly Bangladeshi cuisine that's delicious. Consider chicken *jalfrezi* if you like spicy food, and buttery chicken if you don't (£8-21 main courses, daily 12:00-15:00 & 17:30-23:00, 3 Glendower Place, tel. 020/7240-9329).

Bosphorus Kebabs is the student favorite for a quick, fast, and hearty Turkish dinner. While mostly for take-away, they have a few tight tables indoors and on the sidewalk (£5-6 meals, Turkish kebabs, daily 10:30-24:00, 59 Old Brompton Road, tel. 020/7584-4048).

Beirut Express has fresh, well-prepared Lebanese cuisine. In the front, you'll find take-away service as well as barstools for quick service (£5 sandwiches). In the back is a sit-down restaurant with £14-16 plates and £5-8 *mezes* (daily 11:00-24:30, 65 Old Brompton Road, tel. 020/7591-0123).

The Anglesea Arms, with a great terrace surrounded by classy South Kensington buildings, is a destination pub that feels like the classic neighborhood favorite. It's a thriving and happy place, with a woody ambience and a mellow step-down back dining room a world away from any tourism. Chef Julian Legge freshens up traditional English cuisine and prints up a daily menu listing his creative meals. While it'd be a shame to miss his cooking, this is also a fine place to just have a beer (£6-8 starters, £12-17 main dishes, meals served daily 12:00-15:00 & 18:00-22:00; from Old Brompton Road, turn left at Onslow Gardens and go down a few blocks to 15 Selwood Terrace; tel. 020/7373-7960).

Rocca di Papa is a bright and dressy Italian place with a heated terrace (£6-8 pizza, pasta, and salads; daily 11:30-23:30, 73 Old Brompton Road, tel. 020/7225-3413).

Supermarket: **Tesco Express** is handy for picnics (daily 7:00-24:00, 50-52 Old Brompton Road).

Elsewhere in London

Between St. Paul's and the Tower: **The Counting House,** formerly an elegant old bank, offers great £7-11 meals, nice homemade £10-11 meat pies, fish, and fresh vegetables. The fun "nibbles menu," with £3-6 snacks, is available starting in the early evening until 22:00 (or until 21:00 on Mon; open Mon-Fri 11:00-23:00, gets really busy with the buttoned-down 9-to-5 crowd after 12:15 especially Thu-Fri, closed Sat-Sun, near Mansion House in The City, 50 Cornhill, tel. 020/7283-7123).

Near St. Paul's: **De Gustibus Sandwiches** is where an artisan bakery meets the public, offering fresh, you-design-it sandwiches, salads, and soups. Communication can be difficult, but it's worth the effort. Just one block below St. Paul's, it has simple seating or take-out picnic sacks for lugging to one of the great nearby parks (£4-8 sandwiches, £6 hot dishes, Mon-Fri 7:00-17:00, closed Sat-Sun, from church steps follow signs to youth hostel a block downhill, 53-55 Carter Lane, tel. 020/7236-0056; another outlet is inside the Borough Market in Southwark).

Near the British Library: Drummond Street (running just west of Euston Station—see map on page 778) is famous for cheap and good Indian vegetarian food (£5-10 dishes, £7 lunch buffets). Consider **Chutneys** (124 Drummond, tel. 020/7388-0604) and **Ravi Shankar** (133-135 Drummond, tel. 020/7388-6458) for a good *thali* (both open long hours daily).

Near the Tower of London: In **The Medieval Banquet**'s underground, brick-arched room, costumed wenches bring you a tasty four-course medieval-themed meal (includes ale and red wine) while minstrels, knights, jesters, and contortionists perform. If you enjoy one of the acts, pound on the table. Reserve in advance online or by phone (adult-£50, child-£30, family deal for 2 adults and 2 kids-£110—Sun-Thu only, ask about discount for Rick Steves readers, Mon-Sat around 20:00, Sun around 18:00, veggie option possible, rentable medieval garb, The Medieval Banquet Ivory House, St. Katharine Docks, enter docks off East Smithfield Street, Tube: Tower Hill, tel. 020/7480-5353, www.medievalbanquet.com).

London Connections

By Plane

A number of discount airlines fly into and out of London's smaller airports, making London a great jumping-off point for other destinations.

Heathrow Airport

Heathrow Airport is one of the world's busiest airports. Think about it: 68 million passengers a year on 470,000 flights from 180 destinations riding 90 airlines, like some kind of global maypole dance. For Heathrow's airport, flight, and transfer information, call the switchboard at 0844-335-1801, or visit the helpful website at www.heathrowairport.com (airport code: LHR).

Heathrow has five terminals, numbered T-1 through T-5 (though T-2 is closed for renovation through 2014). Each terminal is served by different airlines and alliances; for example, T-5 is exclusively for British Airways and Iberia Air flights, while T-1 serves mostly Star Alliance flights—such as United, USAir, and Lufthansa—plus plenty more British Airways flights. Screens posted throughout the airport identify which terminal each airline uses; this information should also be printed on your ticket or boarding pass.

To navigate, read signs and ask questions. You can walk between T-1, T-2 (when it's open), and T-3. From this central hub, T-4 and T-5 split off in opposite directions (and are not walkable). To travel between T-1/T-2/T-3 and either T-4 or T-5, you can take a shuttle bus (free, serves all terminals), or the Tube (requires a ticket, serves all terminals). You can also connect T-1/T-2/T-3 and T-5 by Heathrow Express train (free, every 15-20 minutes, does not serve T-4).

If you're flying out of Heathrow, it's critical to confirm which terminal your flight will use (look carefully at your ticket/boarding pass, check online, or call your airline in advance)—because if it's T-4 or T-5, you'll need to allow extra time. Taxi drivers generally know which terminal you'll need based on the airline, but bus drivers may not.

Services: Each terminal has an airport information desk (generally daily 5:00-22:00), car-rental agencies, exchange bureaus,

London's Airports

50 Kilometers
50 Miles

ENGLAND

LUTON

Cambridge

STANSTED

North Sea

LONDON CITY

SOUTHEND

Reading

Bath

HEATHROW

LONDON

CHANNEL TUNNEL

GATWICK

English Channel

To Paris & Brussels

---- Rail
---- Bus

ATMs, a pharmacy, a VAT refund desk (tel. 020/8910-3682; you must present the VAT claim form from the retailer here to get your tax rebate on items purchased in Britain), room-booking services, and baggage storage (£5/item for up to 4 hours, £8.50/item for 24 hours, hours vary by terminal but generally daily 5:30-23:00, www. excess-baggage.co.uk). Get online 24 hours a day at Heathrow's Internet access points (at each terminal—T-4's is up on the mezzanine level). Pay Wi-Fi is available throughout the airport (provided by Boingo, www.boingo.com). A post office is on the first floor of T-3 (departures area). Each terminal has cheap eateries.

Heathrow's small **"TI"** (tourist info shop), even though it's a for-profit business, is worth a visit, if you're nearby, to pick up free information: a simple map, the *London Planner*, and brochures (daily 6:30-22:00, 5-minute walk from T-3 in Tube station, follow signs to Underground; bypass queue for transit info to reach window for London questions).

Getting to London from Heathrow Airport

You have five basic options for traveling the 14 miles between Heathrow Airport and downtown London: Tube (£5.30/person), bus (£5/person), direct shuttle bus (£22.50/person), express train with connecting Tube or taxi (about £20/person), or taxi (about £55/group).

By Tube (Subway): The Tube takes you from any Heathrow terminal to downtown London in 50-60 minutes on the Piccadilly Line (6/hour, buy ticket at Tube station ticket window or self-service machine). Depending on your destination in London, you may need to transfer (for example, if headed to the Victoria Station neighborhood, transfer at South Kensington to the Circle or District lines and ride two more stops). If you plan to use the Tube for transport in London, it may make sense to buy a Travelcard or pay-as-you-go Oyster card at the airport's Tube station ticket window. (For details on these passes, see page 691.) If your Travelcard covers only Zones 1-2, it does not include Heathrow (Zone 6); however, you can pay a small supplement for the initial trip from Heathrow to downtown.

If you're taking the Tube from downtown London *to* the airport, note that Piccadilly Line trains don't stop at every terminal. Trains either stop at T-4, then T-1/T-2/T-3 (also called Heathrow Central), in that order; or T-1/T-2/T-3, then T-5. When leaving central London on the Tube, allow extra time if going to T-4 or T-5; to ensure you get on a train going to your terminal, carefully check the destination before you board.

By Bus: Most buses depart from the outdoor common area in the heart of the Heathrow complex called the Central Bus Station. It serves T-1/T-2/T-3, and is a five-minute walk from these terminals. To connect between T-4 or T-5 and the Central Bus Station, use Heathrow's free shuttle buses; to reach T-5 only, you could instead ride the free Heathrow Express train.

National Express links Heathrow's Central Bus Station with London's Victoria Coach Station, near several of my recommended hotels. While slow, the bus is cheap and handy for those staying near Victoria Station (£5, 1-2/hour, less frequent from Victoria Station to Heathrow, 45-60 minutes, tel. 0871-781-8178, www.nationalexpress.com). A less-frequent National Express bus goes from T-5 directly to Victoria Coach Station (3/day).

Heathrow Shuttle is an economical shuttle-bus service that goes to/from your hotel and your terminal at Heathrow. You'll share a minivan with other travelers who are also being picked up or dropped off (£15/person, progressive discounts for groups of two or more operates daily 4:00-18:00, book at least 24 hours in advance, office open daily 6:00-22:00, tel. 0845-257-8068, www.heathrowshuttle.com, info@heathrowshuttle.com). The rival **Hotel by Bus** service is pricey in comparison (£22.50/person).

By Train: Two different trains run between Heathrow Airport and London's Paddington Station. At Paddington Station, you're in the thick of the Tube system, with easy access to any of my recommended neighborhoods—my Paddington hotels are just outside the front door, and Notting Hill Gate is just two Tube stops away. The **Heathrow Connect** train is the slightly slower, much cheaper option, serving T-1/T-2/T-3 at one station called Heathrow Central; use free transfers if you're coming from either

T-4 or T-5 (£9.10 one-way, £17.80 round-trip, 2/hour Mon-Sat, 1-2/hour Sun, 30 minutes, tel. 0845-678-6975, www.heathrow-connect.com). The **Heathrow Express** train is fast and runs more frequently, but it's pricey (£19 "express class" one-way, £34 round-trip, 4/hour; 15 minutes to downtown from T-1/T-2/T-3, 21 minutes from T-5; transfer by shuttle bus required from T-4; ask about discount promos at ticket desk, buy ticket before you board, covered by BritRail pass, daily 5:10-23:25, tel. 0845-600-1515, www.heathrowexpress.co.uk). At the airport, you can use the Heathrow Express as a free transfer between T-1/T-2/T-3 and T-5 (but not T-4).

By Taxi: Taxis from the airport cost about £45-70 to west and central London (one hour). For groups of four, this can be a deal. Hotels can often line up a cab back to the airport for about £30-40. For the cheapest taxi to the airport, don't order one from your hotel. Simply flag down a few and ask for their best "off-meter" rate. Locals refer to hired cars that do the trip off-meter as "mini-cabs." These are reliable and generally cost what you'd pay for a taxi in good traffic, but—with a fixed price—they can save you money when taxis are snarled in congestion with the meter running.

Gatwick Airport

More and more flights land at Gatwick Airport, which is half-way between London and the South Coast (airport code: LGW, tel. 0844-892-0322, www.gatwickairport.com). Gatwick has two terminals, North and South, which are easily connected by a free monorail (two-minute trip, runs 24 hours daily). Note that boarding passes say "Gatwick N" or "Gatwick S" to indicate your terminal. British Airways flights generally use Gatwick North. The Gatwick Express trains (described next) stop only at Gatwick South. Schedules in each terminal show only arrivals and departures from that terminal.

Getting to London: Gatwick Express trains are clearly the best way into London from this airport. They shuttle conveniently between Gatwick South and London's Victoria Station, with many of my recommended hotels close by (£19 one-way, £33 round-trip, 10 percent discount if purchased online, 4/hour, 30 minutes, runs 5:00-24:00 daily, a few trains as early as 3:30, tel. 0845-850-1530, www.gatwickexpress.com). If you buy your tickets at the station before boarding, ask about their deal where three or four adults travel for the price of two. (If you see others in the ticket line, suggest buying your tickets together—you'll save up to 50 percent.) When going *to* the airport, at Victoria Station note that Gatwick Express has its own ticket windows right by the platform (tracks 13 and 14).

You can save a few pounds by taking Southern Railway's

slower and less frequent **shuttle train** between Gatwick South and Victoria Station (£13.30, up to 4/hour, 45 minutes, tel. 0845-127-2920, www.southernrailway.com).

A train also runs between Gatwick South and **St. Pancras International Station** (£9, 8/hour, 1 hour, www.firstcapitalconnect.co.uk)—useful for travelers taking the Eurostar train (to Paris or Brussels) or staying in the St. Pancras/King's Cross neighborhood.

Even slower, but cheap and handy to the Victoria Station neighborhood, you can take the **bus** (1.25 hours). National Express runs a bus from Gatwick direct to Victoria Station (£8, hourly, tel. 0871-781-8181, www.nationalexpress.com); easyBus has one going to near the Earls Court Tube stop (£2-9 depending on how far ahead you book, 2-3/hour, www.easybus.co.uk).

London's Other Airports

Stansted Airport: If you're using Stansted (airport code: STN, tel. 0844-335-1803, www.stanstedairport.com), you have several options for getting into or out of London. Two different **buses** connect the airport and London's Victoria Station neighborhood: National Express (£10.50, every 20 minutes, 1.75 hours, runs 24 hours a day, picks up and stops throughout London, ends at Victoria Coach Station, tel. 0871-781-8181, www.nationalexpress.com) and Terravision (£9, 2-3/hour, 1.25 hours, ends at Green Line Coach Station just south of Victoria Station). Or you can take the faster, pricier Stansted Express **train** (£21, connects to London's Tube system at Tottenham Hale and Liverpool Street, 4/hour, 45 minutes, 5:30-23:00, tel. 0845-850-0150, www.stanstedexpress.com). Stansted is expensive by **cab**; figure £100-120 one-way from central London.

Luton Airport: For Luton (airport code: LTN, airport tel. 01582/405-100, www.london-luton.co.uk), there are two choices into or out of London. The fastest way to go is by **train** to London's St. Pancras International Station (£14.50 one-way, 1-5/hour, 25-45 minutes—check schedule to avoid slower trains, tel. 0845-712-5678, www.eastmidlandstrains.co.uk); catch the 10-minute shuttle bus (£1.50) from outside the terminal to the Luton Airport Parkway Station. The Green Line express **bus** #757 runs to Buckingham Palace Road, just south of London's Victoria Station (£16-17, small discount for easyJet passengers who buy online, 2-4/hour, 1.25-1.5 hours, 24 hours a day, tel. 0844-801-7261, www.greenline.co.uk). If you're sleeping at Luton, consider easyHotel (see listing on page 779).

Other Airports: There's a slim chance you might use **London City Airport** (airport code: LCY, tel. 020/7646-0088, www.londoncityairport.com). To get into London, take the Docklands Light Railway (DLR) to the Bank Tube station, which is one stop east of

St. Paul's on the Central Line (£4.30 one-way, covered by Travelcard, £2.60-3.10 on Oyster card, 22 minutes, www.tfl.gov.uk/dlr). Some Easyjet flights land even farther out, at **Southend Airport** (airport code: SEN, tel. 01702/608-100, www.southendairport. com). Trains connect the airport to London's Liverpool Street Station (£15 one-way, 8/hour, 50 minutes, www.greateranglia.co.uk).

Connecting London's Airports by Bus
A handy **National Express bus** runs between Heathrow, Gatwick, Stansted, and Luton airports—easier than having to cut through the center of London—although traffic can be bad and can increase travel times (tel. 0871-781-8181, www.nationalexpress.com).

From Heathrow Airport to: **Gatwick Airport** (1-6/hour, about 1.25 hours—but allow at least three hours between flights, £20-25), **Stansted Airport** (1-2/hour, about 1.5 hours, £22.50), **Luton Airport** (hourly, 1-1.5 hours, £21).

By Train
Britain is covered by a myriad of rail systems (owned by different companies), which together are called National Rail. London, the country's major transportation hub, has a different train station for each region. There are nine main stations:

Euston—Serves northwest England, North Wales, and Scotland.

King's Cross—Serves northeast England and Scotland, including York and Edinburgh.

Liverpool Street—Serves east England, including Essex and Harwich.

London Bridge—Serves south England, including Brighton.

Marylebone—Serves southwest and central England, including Stratford-upon-Avon.

Paddington—Serves south and southwest England, including Heathrow Airport, Windsor, Bath, South Wales, and the Cotswolds.

St. Pancras International—Serves north and south England, plus the Eurostar to Paris or Brussels.

Victoria—Serves Gatwick Airport, Canterbury, Dover, and Brighton.

Waterloo—Serves southeast England, including Salisbury.

In addition, there are other, smaller train stations in London that you are not likely to use, such as **Charing Cross** or **Blackfriars.**

Any train station has schedule information, can make reservations, and can sell tickets for any destination. Most stations offer a baggage-storage service (£8.50/bag for 24 hours, look for *left luggage* signs); because of long security lines, it can take a while to

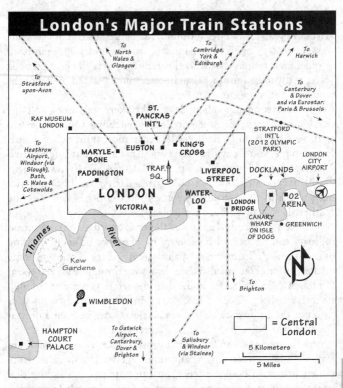

London's Major Train Stations

To North Wales & Glasgow

To Cambridge, York & Edinburgh

To Harwich

To Stratford-upon-Avon

To Heathrow Airport, Windsor (via Slough), Bath, S. Wales & Cotswolds

RAF MUSEUM LONDON

ST. PANCRAS INT'L

To Canterbury & Dover and via Eurostar: Paris & Brussels

STRATFORD INT'L (2012 OLYMPIC PARK)

MARYLE-BONE

EUSTON

KING'S CROSS

LONDON CITY AIRPORT

PADDINGTON

TRAF. SQ.

LIVERPOOL STREET

DOCKLANDS

LONDON

WATER-LOO

O2 ARENA

VICTORIA

LONDON BRIDGE

CANARY WHARF ON ISLE OF DOGS

GREENWICH

Thames River

Kew Gardens

To Brighton

WIMBLEDON

HAMPTON COURT PALACE

To Gatwick Airport, Canterbury, Dover & Brighton

To Salisbury & Windsor (via Staines)

= Central London

5 Kilometers

5 Miles

check or pick up your bag (www.excess-baggage.com). For more details on the services available at each station, see www.national-rail.co.uk/stations.

Train Connections from London
To Paris or Brussels via Eurostar Train
From St. Pancras International Station to: Paris (12-15/day, 2.5-3 hours), **Bruges** (via Brussels: 10/day, 2.5 hours to Brussels Midi; then transfer, backtracking to Bruges: 2/hour, 1 hour, entire trip just a few dollars more with Eurostar ticket). Arrive at least 30 minutes early; security procedures for the Eurostar are similar to airport check-in.

Eurostar Fares: Unlike most trains in Western Europe, Eurostar is not covered by railpasses and always requires a separate, reserved train ticket. Eurostar fares (essentially the same between London and Paris or Brussels) vary depending on how far ahead you reserve, whether you can live with restrictions, and whether you're eligible for any discounts (such as those for early purchase or round-trip travel).

A **one-way, full-fare ticket** (with no restrictions on refundability) runs about $400 for first-class and $300 for second-class. **Discounts** can lower fares substantially (figure $60-160 for second-class, one-way) for children under 12, youths under 26, seniors 60 or older, and railpass holders. The early bird gets the best price. If you're ready to commit, you can book tickets as early as 6-9 months in advance at www.eurostar.com.

A tour company called BritainShrinkers sells one- or two-day tours to Paris, Brussels, or Bruges, enabling you to side-trip to these cities from London for less than most train tickets alone. For example, you'll pay £129 for a one-day Paris "tour" (unescorted Mon-Sat day trip with Métro pass; tel. 020/7404-5100, www.britainshrinkers.com). This can be a particularly good option if you need to get to Paris from London on short notice, when only the costliest Eurostar fares are available.

Once you're confident about the time and date of your crossing, you can check and book fares by phone or online. Ordering online through Eurostar or major agents offers a print-at-home eticket option. You can also order by phone through Rail Europe at US tel. 800-387-6782 for home delivery before you go, or through Eurostar (tel. 0870-518-6186, priced in euros) and pick up your ticket at the train station. In Britain, tickets can be issued only at the Eurostar office in St. Pancras International Station. In continental Europe, you can buy your Eurostar ticket at any major train station in any country or at any travel agency that handles train tickets (expect a booking fee). You can purchase passholder discount tickets at Eurostar departure stations, through US agents, or by phone with Eurostar, but they may be harder to get at other train stations and travel agencies, and are a discount category that can sell out.

To Points West in Britain

From Paddington Station to: Bath (2/hour, 1.5 hours), **Oxford** (2/hour direct, 1 hour, more possible with transfer in Reading), **Penzance** (every 1-2 hours, 5-5.5 hours, possible change in Plymouth), and **Cardiff** (2/hour, 2 hours).

To Points North in Britain

From King's Cross Station to: Trains run at least hourly, stopping in **York** (2 hours), **Durham** (3 hours), and **Edinburgh** (4.5 hours). Trains to **Cambridge** also leave from here (3/hour, 45-60 minutes).

From Euston Station to: Conwy (nearly hourly, 3.25 hours, transfer in Chester or Crewe), **Liverpool** (hourly, 2 hours, more with transfer), **Blackpool** (hourly, 3 hours, transfer at Preston), **Keswick** (hourly, 4.5 hours, transfer to bus at Penrith), and **Glasgow** (1-2/hour, 4.5-5 hours).

Public Transportation near London

To North England & Scotland
To York & Scotland
King's Lynn
Norwich
Coventry
ENGLAND
Stratford-upon-Avon
Warwick
Long Buckby
Leam. Spa
Bedford
Hunt.
Ely
Cambridge
Worcester
Moreton
Banbury
Luton
Stansted
To Hoek van Holland
Chelten-ham
Stow
Oxford
Harwich
COTSWOLDS
Blenheim
Swindon
Didcot
London City
Southend
To Cardiff
Avebury
Reading
Slough
London
Greenwich
To Ostende
Bristol
Windsor
Heathrow
EUROSTAR
Ramsgate
Canterbury
Bath
Bedwyn
Stonehenge
Dover
Wells
Gatwick
Ashford
(CHUNNEL)
Calais
Glaston-bury
Salisbury
South-ampton
Brighton
Rye
East-bourne
Hastings
Calais-Fréthun
To Paris
To Cornwall
Poole
Portsmouth
English Channel
FRANCE
Weymouth
Bourne-mouth
Isle of Wight

----- Rail
- - - Bus
········ Boat

Area covered by London Plus Pass

30 Kilometers
30 Miles (approx. scale)

Note: Bus Lines Follow Most Rail Lines

From London's Other Stations

Trains run between London and **Canterbury,** leaving from St. Pancras International Station and arriving in Canterbury West (1-2/hour, 1 hour), as well as from London's Victoria Station and arriving in Canterbury East (2/hour, 1.5 hours).

Direct trains leave for **Stratford-upon-Avon** from Marylebone Station, located near the southwest corner of Regent's Park (5/day direct, more with transfers, 2.25 hours).

To Other Destinations: Windsor (2/hour, 1 hour, direct from Waterloo Station; also 2-3/hour, 35 minutes, from Paddington Station with change in Slough), **Greenwich** (from Bank or Monument Tube stop take the DLR—Docklands Light Railway—to Cutty Sark Station), **Dover** (hourly, 1.25 hours, from St. Pancras International Station; also hourly, 2 hours, direct from Victoria Station or Charing Cross Station), **Brighton** (4-5/hour, 1 hour, from Victoria Station and London Bridge Station), **Portsmouth** (3/hour, 1.5-2 hours, most from Waterloo Station, a few from Victoria Station), and **Salisbury** (1-2/hour, 1.5 hours, from Waterloo Station).

By Bus

Buses are slower but considerably cheaper than trains for reaching destinations around Britain, and beyond. Most depart from

Victoria Coach Station, which is one long block south of Victoria Station (near many recommended accommodations and Tube: Victoria). Inside the station, you'll find basic eateries, kiosks, and a helpful information desk stocked with schedules and ready to point you to your bus or answer any questions. Watch your bags carefully—luggage thieves thrive at the station.

Most domestic buses are operated by **National Express** (tel. 0871-781-8181, www.nationalexpress.com); their international departures are called **Eurolines** (tel. 0871-781-8177, www.eurolines.co.uk).

A newer, smaller company called **Megabus** undersells National Express with deeply discounted promotional fares—the further ahead you buy, the less you pay (some trips for just £1.50, toll tel. 0900-160-0900, www.megabus.com). While Megabus can be much cheaper than National Express—even half the price—they tend to be slower than their competitor and their routes mainly connect cities (rather than include smaller towns). They also sell discounted train tickets on selected routes.

Try to avoid bus travel on Friday and Sunday evenings, when weekend travelers are more likely to make buses sell out.

To ensure getting a ticket—and to save money with special promotions—you can book your ticket in advance online (see websites above). The cheapest pre-purchased tickets can be changed (for a £5 fee), but they're usually nonrefundable within 72 hours of travel. If you have a British mobile phone, you can order online and have a "text ticket" sent right to your phone.

Ideally you'll buy your tickets online. But if you must buy one at the station, try to arrive an hour before the bus departs—or drop by the day before. (For buses to Stansted Airport and Oxford, you can buy the ticket on board; otherwise you'll buy it at a ticket window.) Automated ticketing machines are scattered around the station (separate machines for National Express/Eurolines and Megabus; you can buy either for today or for tomorrow); there's also a ticket counter near gate 21.

To Other Destinations in Britain: National Express buses go to **Bath** (nearly hourly, 3.5 hours), **Oxford** (2/hour, about 2 hours, **Cambridge** (hourly, 2-2.5 hours), **Canterbury** (about hourly, 2-2.5 hours), **Dover** (about hourly, 2.5-3.25 hours), **Brighton** (hourly, 2 hours), **Penzance** (5/day, 8.5-10 hours, overnight available), **Cardiff** (hourly, 3.25 hours), **Stratford-upon-Avon** (3/day, 3.5 hours), **Liverpool** (8/day direct, 5.25-6 hours, overnight available), **Blackpool** (4/day direct, 6.25-7 hours, overnight available), **York** (4/day direct, 5.25 hours), **Durham** (4/day direct, 6.5-7.5 hours), **Glasgow** (4/day direct, 8-9 hours, train is a much better option), **Edinburgh** (2/day direct, 8.75-9.75 hours, go by train instead).

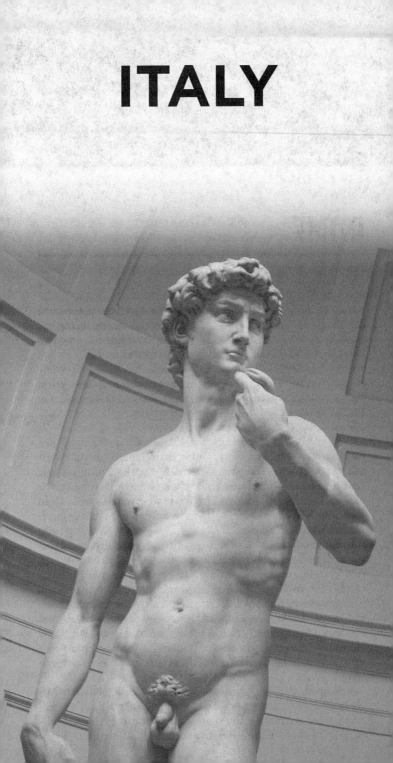

ITALY

ROME

Roma

Rome is magnificent and brutal at the same time. It's a showcase of Western civilization, with astonishingly ancient sights and a modern vibrancy. But if you're careless, you'll be run down or pickpocketed. And with the wrong attitude, you'll be frustrated by the kind of chaos that only an Italian can understand. On my last visit, a cabbie struggling with the traffic said, *"Roma chaos."* I responded, *"Bella chaos."* He agreed.

While Paris is an urban garden, Rome is a magnificent tangled forest. If your hotel provides a comfortable refuge; if you pace yourself; if you accept—and even partake in—the siesta plan; if you're well-organized for sightseeing; and if you protect yourself and your valuables with extra caution and discretion, you'll love it. (And Rome is much easier to live with if you can avoid the mid-summer heat.)

For me, Rome is in a three-way tie with Paris and London as Europe's greatest city. Two thousand years ago, the word "Rome" meant civilization itself. Everything was either civilized (part of the Roman Empire, Latin- or Greek-speaking) or barbarian. Today, Rome is Italy's political capital, the capital of Catholicism, and the center of the ancient world, littered with evocative remains. As you peel through its fascinating and jumbled layers, you'll find Rome's buildings, cats, laundry, traffic, and 2.7 million people endlessly entertaining. And then, of course, there are its stupendous sights.

Visit St. Peter's, the greatest church on earth, and scale Michelangelo's 448-foot-tall dome, the world's tallest. Learn something about eternity by touring the huge Vatican Museum. You'll find the story of creation—bright as the day it was painted—in the

Rome's Neighborhoods

VATICAN MUSEUM

NORTH ROME

VILLA BORGHESE

PIAZZA DEL POPOLO

BORGHESE GALLERY

VATICAN CITY

ST. PETER'S

"SHOPPING TRIANGLE"

SPANISH STEPS

TERMINI

TRAIN STATION

NATIONAL MUSEUM

PANTHEON NEIGHBORHOOD

PIAZZA VENEZIA

CAPITOLINE HILL

EAST ROME

Tiber River

ANCIENT ROME

FORUM

PILGRIM'S ROME

SAN GIOVANNI IN LATERANO

SANTA MARIA

COLOSSEUM

TRASTEVERE

TESTACCIO

SOUTH ROME

SOUTH OF TESTACCIO

E.U.R.

APPIAN WAY

Not to Scale

restored Sistine Chapel. Do the "Caesar Shuffle" through ancient Rome's Forum and Colosseum. Savor Europe's most sumptuous building, the Borghese Gallery, and take an early evening "Dolce Vita Stroll" down Via del Corso with Rome's beautiful people. Enjoy an after-dark walk from Campo de' Fiori to the Spanish Steps, lacing together Rome's Baroque and bubbly nightspots. Dine well at least once.

ROME

Planning Your Time

Rome is wonderful, but it's huge and exhausting. On a first-time visit, many travelers find that Rome is best done quickly—Italy is more charming elsewhere. But whether you're here for a day or a week, you won't be able to see all of these sights, so don't try— you'll keep coming back to Rome. After several dozen visits, I still have a healthy list of excuses to return.

Rome in a Day: Some people actually try to "do" Rome in a day. Crazy as that sounds, if all you have is a day, it's one of the most exciting days Europe has to offer. Start at 8:30 at the Colosseum. Then explore the Forum, hike over Capitoline Hill, and cap your "Caesar Shuffle" with a visit to the Pantheon. After a quick lunch, taxi to the Vatican Museum (the lines usually die down mid-afternoon, or you can reserve a visit online in advance). See the Vatican Museum, then St. Peter's Basilica (open until 19:00 April-Sept). Taxi back to Campo de' Fiori to find dinner. Finish your day lacing together all the famous floodlit spots (follow my self-guided Heart of Rome Walk). If you only want a day in Rome, consider side-tripping from Florence, or fit it in before taking the night train to Venice (via Milan).

Rome in Two to Three Days: On the first day, do the "Caesar Shuffle" from the Colosseum to the Forum, then over Capitoline Hill to the Pantheon. After a siesta, join the locals strolling from Piazza del Popolo to the Spanish Steps (follow my self-guided "Dolce Vita Stroll"). On the second day, see Vatican City (St. Peter's, climb the dome, tour the Vatican Museum). Have dinner on the atmospheric Campo de' Fiori, and then walk to the Trevi Fountain and Spanish Steps (following my Heart of Rome Walk). With a third day, add the Borghese Gallery (reservations required) and the National Museum of Rome.

Orientation to Rome

Sprawling Rome actually feels manageable once you get to know it. The old core, with most of the tourist sights, sits in a diamond formed by Termini train station (in the east), the Vatican (west), Villa Borghese Gardens (north), and the Colosseum (south). The Tiber River runs through the diamond from north to south. In the center of the diamond sits Piazza Venezia, a busy square and traffic hub. It takes about an hour to walk from Termini Station to the Vatican.

Think of Rome as a series of neighborhoods, huddling around major landmarks.

Ancient Rome: In ancient times, this was home for the grandest buildings of a city of a million people. Today, the best of the classical sights stand in a line from the Colosseum to the Forum to the Pantheon.

Pantheon Neighborhood: The Pantheon anchors the neighborhood I like to call the heart of Rome. It stretches eastward from the Tiber River through Campo de' Fiori and Piazza Navona, past the Pantheon to the Trevi Fountain.

Vatican City: Located west of the Tiber, it's a compact world of its own, with two great, huge sights: St. Peter's Basilica and the Vatican Museum.

North Rome: With the Spanish Steps, Villa Borghese Gardens, and trendy shopping streets (Via Veneto and the "shopping triangle"), this is a more modern, classy area.

East Rome: This includes the area around Termini Station, with its many recommended hotels and public-transportation connections. Nearby is the neighborhood I call "Pilgrim's Rome," with several prominent churches dotting the area south of the station.

South Rome: South of Vatican City is Trastevere, the seedy, colorful wrong-side-of-the-river neighborhood that provides a look at village Rome. It's the city at its crustiest—and perhaps most "Roman." Across the Tiber River, directly south of the city center, is the Appian Way, home of the catacombs.

Within each of these neighborhoods, you'll find elements from the many layers of Rome's 2,000-year history: the marble ruins of ancient times; tangled streets of the medieval world; early Christian churches; grand Renaissance buildings and statues; Baroque fountains and church facades; 19th-century apartments; and 20th-century boulevards choked with traffic.

Since no one is allowed to build taller than St. Peter's dome, and virtually no buildings have been constructed in the city center since Mussolini got distracted in 1938, Rome has no modern skyline. The Tiber River is basically ignored—after the last floods (1870), the banks were built up very high, and Rome turned its back on its naughty river.

Tourist Information

Rome has two tourist information offices and several TI kiosks. The TI offices are at the airport (Terminal 3, daily 9:00-18:30) and Termini train station (daily 8:00-21:00, 100 yards down track 24, look for signs). Little kiosks (generally open daily 9:30-19:00) are near the Forum (on Piazza del Tempio della Pace), on Via Nazionale (at Palazzo delle Esposizioni), near Castel Sant'Angelo (at Piazza Pia), near Piazza Navona (at Piazza delle Cinque Lune), and near the Trevi Fountain (at Via del Corso and Via Minghetti). The TI's website is http://en.turismoroma.it. The TIs don't offer room-booking services. If a commercial info-center offers to book you a room, just say no—you'll save money by booking direct.

At any TI, ask for a city map and a listing of sights and hours (in the free *Evento* booklet with English-language pages listing the month's cultural events). Your hotel will have a freebie map and may also have the free *Evento* booklet, saving you a trip to the TI if that's all you need. The best map I found is published by Rough Guide (€9 in bookstores).

Rome's single best source of up-to-date tourist information is its **call center,** with English-speakers on staff. Dial 06-0608 (answered daily 9:00-21:00, press 2 for English, www.060608.it).

ROME

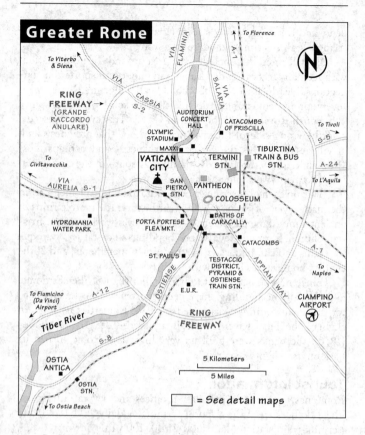

Several English-oriented **websites** provide insight into events and daily life in the city: www.inromenow.com (light tourist info on lots of topics), www.wantedinrome.com (events and accommodations), and http://rome.angloinfo.com (on living in and moving to Rome).

Arrival in Rome
By Train at Termini Station

Termini, Rome's main train station, is a buffet of tourist services. While information desks are jammed with travelers, very handy red info kiosks at the head of the tracks can answer your simple questions. The Customer Care window near the main entrance and ticket booths can also be helpful for schedule questions.

Along track 24, about 100 yards down, you'll find the **TI** (daily 8:00-21:00), a **post office** (Mon-Fri 8:30-14:00, Sat 8:30-13:00, closed Sun), a **hotel booking** office, and **car rental** desks. The **baggage storage** (deposito bagagli) is downstairs (€5/5 hours, then cheaper, daily 6:00-24:00).

The **"Leonardo Express" train** to Fiumicino Airport runs from track 24 (see page 940). A good self-service **cafeteria,** Ciao, is near the head of track 24, upstairs, with fine views (daily 11:00-22:30). For **sandwiches** to go, try VyTA in the atrium across from track 1.

Near track 1, you'll find a **pharmacy** (daily 7:30-22:00); along the same track is a **waiting room** and **Despar Express,** selling everything from groceries to electronics (daily 7:00-21:30). If you can't find what you're looking for there, try downstairs at **Conad** (daily 6:00-24:00) or one of the many other specialty shops.

Elsewhere in the station are **ATMs,** late-hours banks, and 24-hour thievery. In the station's main entrance lobby, **Borri Books** sells books in English, including popular fiction, Italian history and culture, and kids' books, plus maps upstairs (daily 7:00-23:00).

Termini is also a local transportation hub. The city's two Metro lines (A and B) intersect downstairs at Termini Metro station. Buses (including Rome's hop-on, hop-off bus tours—see "Tours in Rome," later) leave across the square directly in front of the main station hall. The Metro and bus areas have been under construction but should be open in time for your visit—look for signs directing you to the Metro platform or bus stop. Taxis queue in front; avoid con men hawking "express taxi" services in unmarked cars (only use cars marked with the word *taxi* and a phone number). To avoid the long taxi line, simply hike out past the buses to the main street and hail one.

From Termini, most of my recommended hotels are easily accessible by foot (for those near this train station) or by Metro (for those in the Colosseum and Vatican neighborhoods).

The station has some sleazy sharks with official-looking business cards; avoid anybody selling anything unless they're in a legitimate shop at the station.

ROME

By Train or Bus at Tiburtina Station

Tiburtina, Rome's second-largest train station, is located in the city's northeast corner. In general, slower trains (from Milan, Bolzano, Bologna, Udine, and Reggio di Calabria) and some night trains (from Munich, Milan, Venice, Innsbruck, and Udine) use Tiburtina, as does the night bus to Fiumicino Airport. Direct night trains from Paris and Vienna use Termini train station instead.

Tiburtina has been newly redeveloped for high-speed rail, including some Eurostar Italia trains and the new Italo service (run by a private operator). Some Italo trains may also stop at Ostiense Station. A separate "Casa Italo" area in each station has dedicated service counters, red ticket machines, and waiting areas. You can also book Italo tickets by phone (tel. 06-0708) or online (www.italotreno.it). Because this is a new company, it's hard to predict the level of service or even its long-term survival.

Tiburtina is also known as a hub for bus service to destinations all across Italy. Buses depart from the piazza in front of the station. Ticket offices are located in the piazza and around the corner on Circonvallazione Nomentana (just beyond the elevated freeway).

The Tiburtina Station is on Metro line B, with easy connections to Termini (a straight shot, four stops away) and the entire Metro system. Or take bus #492 from Tiburtina to various city-center stops (such as Piazza Barberini, Piazza Venezia, and Piazza Cavour) and the Vatican neighborhood.

By Car

The Grande Raccordo Anulare circles greater Rome. This ring road has spokes that lead you into the center. Entering from the north, leave the autostrada at the Settebagni exit. Following the ancient Via Salaria (and the black-and-white *Centro* signs), work your way doggedly into the Roman thick of things. This will take you along the Villa Borghese Gardens and dump you right on Via Veneto in downtown Rome. Avoid rush hour and drive defensively: Roman cars stay in their lanes like rocks in an avalanche.

Parking in Rome is dangerous. Park near a police station or get advice at your hotel. The Villa Borghese underground garage is handy (Metro: Spagna). Garages charge about €24 per day.

Consider this: Your car is a worthless headache in Rome. Avoid a pile of stress and save money by parking at the huge, easy, and relatively safe lot behind the train station in the hill town of Orvieto (follow *P* signs from autostrada) and catching the train to Rome (hourly, 1-1.5 hours).

If you absolutely must drive and park a car in Rome, try to avoid commuter traffic by arriving Friday evening, or anytime during the weekend, and by leaving town during the weekend. Park your car at Tiburtina Station (€1/hour, www.atac.roma.it) and take a 10-minute ride on the Metro line B into the center.

By Plane

For information on Rome's airports, see the end of this chapter.

Helpful Hints

Sightseeing Tips: Avid sightseers can save money by buying the Roma Pass (see "Tips on Sightseeing in Rome" sidebar, later), available at TIs and participating sights—buy one before visiting the Colosseum or Forum, and you can skip the long lines there. If you want to see the Borghese Gallery, remember to reserve ahead (see page 887). To bypass the long Vatican Museum line, reserve an entry time online (see page 879 for details).

Internet Access: If your hotel doesn't offer free or cheap Internet access, your hotelier can point you to the nearest Internet café.

Bookstores: These stores (all open daily except Anglo American and Open Door) sell travel guidebooks, including mine. The first two are chains, while the others have a more personal touch. **Borri Books** is at Termini Station, and **Feltrinelli International** has two branches (at Largo Argentina, and just off Piazza della Repubblica at Via Vittorio Emanuele Orlando 84, tel. 06-482-7878). **Anglo American Bookshop** has great art and history sections (closed all day Sun and Mon morning, a few blocks south of Spanish Steps at Via della Vite 102, tel. 06-679-5222). **Libreria Fanucci** has a small selection but is centrally located (a block toward the Pantheon from Piazza Navona at Piazza Madama 8, tel. 06-686-1141). In Trastevere, Irishman Dermot at the **Almost Corner Bookshop** stocks an Italian-interest section (Via del Moro 45, tel. 06-583-6942), and the **Open Door Bookshop** carries the only used books in English in town (closed Sun, Via della Lungaretta 23, tel. 06-589-6478).

Laundry: Your hotelier can direct you to the nearest launderette. The **ondablu** chain usually comes with Internet access; one of their more central locations is near Termini Station (€2/hour, about €8 to wash and dry a 15-pound load, usually open daily 8:00-22:00, Via Principe Amedeo 70b, tel. 06-474-4647).

Travel Agencies: You can get train tickets and railpass-related reservations and supplements at travel agencies (at little or no additional cost), avoiding a trip to a train station. Your hotelier will know of a convenient agency nearby.

Updates to this Book: Check www.ricksteves.com/update for any significant changes that have occurred since this book was printed.

Dealing with (and Avoiding) Problems

Theft Alert: While violent crime is rare in the city center, petty theft is rampant. With sweet-talking con artists meeting you at the station, well-dressed pickpockets on buses, and thieving gangs of children at the ancient sites, Rome is a gauntlet of rip-offs. Although it's not as bad as it was a few years ago, and pickpockets don't want to hurt you—they usually just want your money—green or sloppy tourists will be scammed. Thieves strike when you're distracted. Don't trust kind strangers. Keep nothing important in your pockets. Be most on guard while boarding and leaving buses and subways. Thieves crowd the door, then stop and turn while others crowd and push from behind. You'll find less crowding and commotion—and less

ROME

Tips on Sightseeing in Rome

These tips can help you use your time and money efficiently, making the Eternal City seem less eternal and more entertaining.

Passes

Roma Pass: Rome offers several sightseeing passes to help you save money. For most visitors, the Roma Pass (www.romapass. it) is the clear winner. The Roma Pass costs €30 and is valid for three days, covering public transportation and free or discounted entry to Roman sights. You get free admission to your first two sights (where you also get to skip the ticket line) and then a discount on the rest within the three-day window. Sights covered (or discounted) by the pass include the following: Colosseum/Palatine Hill/Roman Forum, Borghese Gallery (though you still must make a reservation), Capitoline Museums, Castel Sant'Angelo, Montemartini Museum, Ara Pacis, Museum of Roman Civilization, Etruscan Museum, Baths of Caracalla, Trajan's Market, and some of the Appian Way sights. The pass also covers four branches of the National Museum of Rome, considered as a single "sight": Palazzo Massimo (the most important of the lot), Crypta Balbi (medieval art), Palazzo Altemps (sculpture collection), and Museum of the Bath (ancient inscriptions).

If you'll be visiting any two of the major sights in a three-day period, get the pass. It's sold at participating sights, TIs, and many tobacco shops or newsstands (look for a *Roma Pass* sign; all should offer the same price). Try to buy it at a less crowded TI or sight (you can buy it at a sight even if you don't intend to use it there). Don't bother to order it online—you have to physically pick up the pass in Rome, which negates any time-saving advantage.

Validate your Roma Pass by writing your name and validation date on the card. Then insert it directly into the turnstile at your first two (free) sights. At other sights, show it at the ticket office to get your reduced (*ridotto*) price—about 30 percent off.

To get the most of your pass, visit the two most expensive sights first—for example, the Colosseum (€12) and the National Museum (€10). Definitely use it to bypass the long ticket-buying line at the Colosseum. For sights that normally sell a combined ticket (such as the Colosseum/Palatine Hill/Roman Forum or the National Museum branches), visiting the combined sight counts as a single entry.

The Roma Pass comes with a three-day transit pass. Write your name and birth date on the transit pass, validate it on your first bus or Metro ride by passing it over a sensor at a turnstile or validation machine (look for a yellow circle), and you can take unlimited rides within Rome's city limits until midnight of the third day.

The TI's other passes—Roma & Più Pass ("Rome & More") and the Archeologia Card—are generally not worth the trouble for most tourists.

Combo-Ticket for Colosseum, Forum, and Palatine Hill: A €12 combo-ticket covers these three adjacent sights (no individual tickets are sold per sight). The combo-ticket allows one entry per sight and is valid for two days. Note that these sights are also covered by the Roma Pass. To avoid ticket-buying lines at the Colosseum and Forum, purchase your combo-ticket or Roma Pass at the lesser-visited Palatine Hill. Between the combo-ticket or Roma Pass, the pass is the better deal, unless you're planning on seeing only the sights covered by the combo-ticket.

Top Tips

Museum Reservations: The marvelous Borghese Gallery requires reservations in advance (for specifics, see page 887). You can reserve online to avoid long lines at the Vatican Museum (see page 879).

Opening Hours: Rome's sights have notoriously variable hours from season to season. Get a current listing of opening times—ask for the free booklet *Evento* at a TI or your hotel. Or check online at www.060608.it/en (find "Cultural Heritage" in the menu under "Culture and Leisure"; search by using the Italian names of sights). On holidays, expect shorter hours or closures.

Churches: Many churches, which have divine art and free entry, open early (around 7:00-7:30), close for lunch (roughly 12:00-15:00), and close late (about 19:00). Kamikaze tourists maximize their sightseeing hours by visiting churches before 9:00 or late in the day and, during the siesta, seeing major sights that stay open all day (St. Peter's, Colosseum, Forum, Capitoline Museums, Pantheon, and National Museum of Rome). Dress modestly for church visits.

Picnic Discreetly: Public drinking and eating is not allowed at major sights, though the ban has proven difficult to enforce. To avoid the risk of being fined, choose an empty piazza for your picnic, or keep a low profile.

Miscellaneous Tips: I carry a plastic water bottle and refill it at Rome's many public drinking spouts. Because public restrooms are scarce, use toilets at museums, restaurants, and bars.

ROME

risk—waiting for the end cars of a subway rather than the middle cars. The sneakiest thieves pretend to be well-dressed businessmen (generally with something in their hands), or tourists wearing fanny packs and toting cameras and even Rick Steves guidebooks.

Scams abound: Don't give your wallet to self-proclaimed "police" who stop you on the street, warn you about counterfeit (or drug) money, and ask to see your cash. If a bank machine eats your ATM card, see if there's a thin plastic insert with a tongue hanging out that thieves use to extract it.

If you know what to look out for, fast-fingered moms with babies and gangs of children picking the pockets and handbags of naive tourists are not a threat, but an interesting, albeit sad, spectacle. Pickpockets troll through the tourist crowds around the Colosseum, Forum, Vatican, and train and Metro stations. Watch them target tourists who are overloaded with bags or distracted with a camera. The kids look like beggars and hold up newspapers or cardboard signs to confuse their victims. They scram like stray cats if you're on to them.

Reporting Losses: To report lost or stolen items, file a police report (at Termini Station, with *polizia* at track 11 or with Carabinieri at track 20; offices are also at Piazza Venezia). You'll need the report to file an insurance claim for lost gear, and it can help with replacing your passport—first file the police report, then call your embassy to make an appointment (US embassy: tel. 06-46741, Via Vittorio Veneto 121, www.usembassy.it). For information on how to report lost or stolen credit cards, see page 12.

Emergency Numbers: Police—tel. 113. Ambulance—tel. 118.

Pedestrian Safety: Your main safety concern in Rome is crossing streets safely. Use extreme caution. Scooters don't need to stop at red lights, and even cars exercise what drivers call the "logical option" of not stopping if they see no oncoming traffic. Each year, as noisy gasoline-powered scooters are replaced by electric ones, the streets get quieter (hooray), but more dangerous for pedestrians. Follow locals like a shadow when you cross a street (or spend a good part of your visit stranded on curbs). When you do cross alone, don't be a deer in the headlights. Find a gap in the traffic and walk with confidence while making eye contact with approaching drivers—they won't hit you if they can tell where you intend to go.

Staying/Getting Healthy: The siesta is a key to survival in summertime Rome. Lie down and contemplate the extraordinary power of gravity in the Eternal City. I drink lots of cold, refreshing water from Rome's many drinking fountains (the Forum has three).

There's a pharmacy (marked by a green cross) in every neighborhood. Pharmacies stay open late in Termini Station (daily 7:30-22:00) and at Piazza dei Cinquecento 51 (open 24 hours daily, next to Termini Station on the corner of Via Cavour, tel. 06-488-0019).

Embassies can recommend English-speaking doctors. Consider MEDline, a 24-hour home-medical service; doctors speak English and make calls at hotels for €150 (tel. 06-808-0995). Anyone is entitled to free emergency treatment at public hospitals. The hospital closest to Termini Station is Policlinico Umberto 1 (entrance for emergency treatment on Via Lancisi, translators available, Metro: Policlinico). Readers report that the staff at Santa Susanna Church, home of the American Catholic Church in Rome, offers useful advice and medical referrals (see page 897).

Getting Around Rome

Sightsee on foot, by city bus, by Metro, or by taxi. I've grouped your sightseeing into walkable neighborhoods. Make it a point to visit sights in a logical order. Needless backtracking wastes precious time.

The public transportation system, which is cheap and efficient, consists primarily of buses, a few trams, and the two underground subway (Metro) lines. Consider it part of your Roman experience.

The walking-tour company, Rome Walks, has produced an orientation video to Rome's transportation system; find it on You-Tube by searching for "Understanding Rome's Public Transport."

For information, visit www.atac.roma.it, which has a useful route planner in English, or call 06-57003.

Buying Tickets

All public transportation uses the same ticket. It costs €1.50 and is valid for one Metro ride—including transfers underground—plus unlimited city buses and *elettrico* buses during a 100-minute period. Passes good on buses and the Metro are sold in increments of one day (€6, good until midnight), three days (€16.50), one week (€24, about the cost of three taxi rides), and one month (€35, valid for a calendar month).

You can purchase tickets and passes at some newsstands, tobacco shops (*tabacchi*, marked by a black-and-white *T* sign), and major Metro stations and bus stops, but not on board. It's smart to stock up on tickets early, or to buy a pass or a Roma Pass (which includes a three-day transit pass—see page 820). That way, you don't have to run around searching for an open tobacco shop when you spot your bus approaching. Metro stations rarely have human

ROME

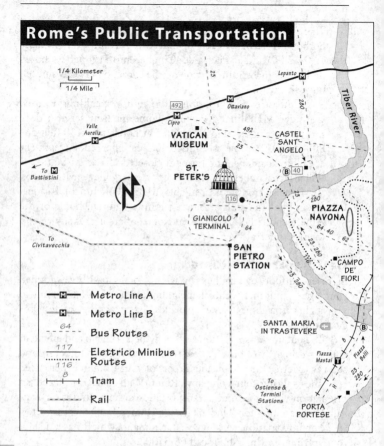

Rome's Public Transportation

1/4 Kilometer

1/4 Mile

Lepanto

Tiber River

Ottaviano

Valle
Aurelia

Cipro

VATICAN
MUSEUM

CASTEL
SANT'
ANGELO

To
Battistini

ST.
PETER'S

PIAZZA
NAVONA

GIANICOLO
TERMINAL

CAMPO
DE'
FIORI

To
Civitavecchia

SAN
PIETRO
STATION

SANTA MARIA
IN TRASTEVERE

Piazza
Mastai

Piazza
Belli

To
Ostiense &
Termini
Stations

PORTA
PORTESE

---M--- Metro Line A
---M--- Metro Line B
- 64 - Bus Routes
- 117 - Elettrico Minibus
- 116 - Routes
|—|—| Tram
~~~~ Rail

ticket-sellers, and the machines are often either broken or require exact change (it helps to insert your smallest coin first).

Validate your ticket by sticking it in the Metro turnstile (magnetic-strip-side up, arrow-side first) or in the machine when you board the bus (magnetic-strip-side down, arrow-side first)—watch others and imitate. It'll return your ticket with your expiration time printed. To get through a Metro turnstile with a transit pass or Roma Pass, use it just like a ticket (on buses, however, you need to validate your pass only if that's your first time using it).

By Metro

The Roman subway system (Metropolitana, or "Metro") is simple, with two clean, cheap, fast lines—A and B—that intersect at Termini Station. The Metro runs from 5:30 to 23:30 (Fri-Sat until 1:30 in the morning). The subway's first and last compartments are generally the least crowded (and the least likely to harbor pickpockets).

You'll notice lots of big holes in the city as a new line is built.

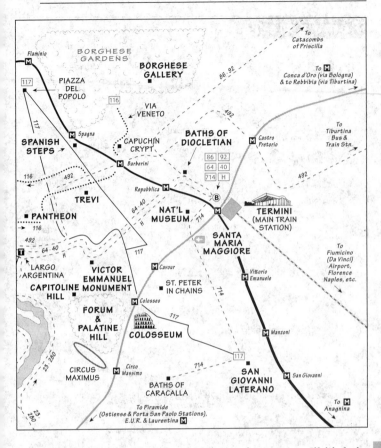

Line C, from the Colosseum to Largo Argentina, will likely be done in 2020. Because of this construction, you may find the system closed at 21:00 on some nights.

While much of Rome is not served by its skimpy subway, the following stops are helpful:

Termini (intersection of lines A and B): Termini Station, shuttle train to airport, National Museum of Rome, and recommended hotels

Repubblica (line A): Baths of Diocletian, Via Nazionale, and recommended hotels

Barberini (line A): Capuchin Crypt, Trevi Fountain, and Villa Borghese

Spagna (line A): Spanish Steps and classy shopping area

Flaminio (line A): Piazza del Popolo, start of recommended "Dolce Vita Stroll" down Via del Corso

Ottaviano (line A): St. Peter's Basilica, Vatican Museum, and recommended hotels

Rome's Metro

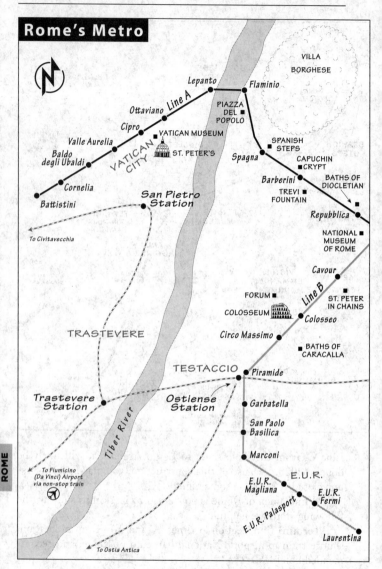

Tiburtina (line B): Tiburtina train and bus station

Colosseo (line B): Colosseum, Roman Forum, bike rental, and recommended hotels

By Bus

The Metro is handy, but it won't get you everywhere—take the bus. Bus routes are clearly listed at the stops. TIs usually don't have bus maps, but with some knowledge of major stops, you won't necessar-

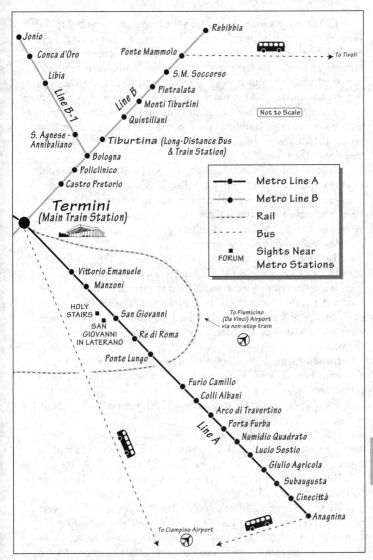

ily need one (though if you do want a route map, find one printed inside the free-at-hotels *Evento* magazine, or buy it from tobacco shops).

Buses—especially the touristy #40 and #64—are havens for thieves and pickpockets. Assume any commotion is a thief-created distraction. If one bus is packed, there's likely a second one on its tail with far fewer crowds and thieves. Once you know the bus system, you'll find it's easier than searching for a cab.

Tickets have a barcode and must be stamped on the bus in the yellow box with the digital readout (be sure to retrieve your ticket). Validate your ticket as you board (magnetic-strip-side down, arrow-side first), otherwise you're cheating. While relatively safe, riding without a stamped ticket on the bus is stressful. Inspectors fine even innocent-looking tourists €50. There's no need to validate a transit pass or Roma Pass on the bus, unless your pass is new and hasn't yet been stamped elsewhere in the transit system. Bus etiquette (not always followed) is to board at the front or rear doors and exit at the middle.

Regular bus lines start running at about 5:30, and during the day they run every 5-10 minutes. After 23:30, and sometimes earlier (such as on Sundays), buses are less frequent but still dependable. Night buses are also reliable, and are marked with an *N* and an owl symbol on the bus-stop signs.

These are the major bus routes:

Bus #64: This bus cuts across the city, linking Termini Station with the Vatican, stopping at Piazza della Repubblica (sights), Via Nazionale (recommended hotels), Piazza Venezia (near Forum), Largo Argentina (near Pantheon), St. Peter's Basilica (get off just past the tunnel), and San Pietro Station. Ride it for a city overview and to watch pickpockets in action. The #64 can get horribly crowded.

Bus #40: This express bus, which mostly follows the #64 route (but branches off on the Vatican side of the river), is especially helpful—fewer stops and crowds.

The following three routes conveniently connect Trastevere with other parts of Rome:

Bus #H: This express bus, linking Termini Station and Trastevere, makes a few stops on Via Nazionale (for Trastevere, get off at Piazza Belli, just after crossing the Tiber River).

Bus #8: This tram connects Largo Argentina with Trastevere (get off at Piazza Belli).

Buses #23 and #280: These link the Vatican with Trastevere and Testaccio, stopping at the Vatican Museum (nearest stop is Via Leone IV), Castel Sant'Angelo, Trastevere (Piazza Belli), Porta Portese (Sunday flea market), and Piramide (Metro and gateway to Testaccio).

Other useful routes include:

Bus #62: Largo Argentina to St. Peter's Square.

Bus #81: San Giovanni in Laterano, Largo Argentina, and Piazza Risorgimento (Vatican).

Buses #85 and #87: Piazza Venezia, Colosseum, San Clemente, and San Giovanni in Laterano.

Bus #492: Travels east-west across the city, connecting Tiburtina (train and bus stations), Largo Santa Susanna (near Piazza della Repubblica), Piazza Barberini, Piazza Venezia, Largo Argentina, Piazza Cavour (Castel Sant'Angelo), and Piazza Risorgimento (St. Peter's Basilica and Vatican).

Bus #714: Termini Station, Santa Maria Maggiore, San Giovanni in Laterano, and Terme di Caracalla (Baths of Caracalla).

Elettrico **Minibuses:** Two cute *elettrico* minibuses that wind through the narrow streets of old and interesting neighborhoods are great for transport or simple joyriding.

Elettrico **#116** runs through the medieval core of Rome: Ponte Vittorio Emanuele II (near Castel Sant'Angelo) to Campo de' Fiori, Pantheon, Piazza Barberini, and the southern edge of the scenic Villa Borghese Gardens.

Elettrico **#117** connects San Giovanni in Laterano, Colosseo, Via dei Serpenti, Trevi Fountain, Piazza di Spagna, and Piazza del Popolo—and vice versa. Where Via del Corso hits Piazza del Popolo, a #117 is usually parked and ready to go. Riding it from here to the end of the line, San Giovanni in Laterano, makes for a fine joyride that leaves you, conveniently, at a great sight.

By Taxi

I use taxis in Rome more often than in other cities. They're reasonable and useful for efficient sightseeing in this big, hot metropolis. Taxis start at €3, then charge about €1.50 per kilometer (surcharges: €1.50 on Sun, €3.50 for nighttime hours of 22:00-7:00, one regular suitcase or bag rides free, tip by rounding up to the nearest euro). Sample fares: Termini Station to Vatican-€10; Termini Station to Colosseum-€6; Colosseum to Trastevere-€7 (or look up your route at www.worldtaximeter.com). Three or four companions with more money than time should taxi almost everywhere.

It's tough to wave down a taxi in Rome, especially at night. Find the nearest taxi stand by asking a passerby or a clerk in a shop, *"Dov'è una fermata dei taxi?"* (doh-VEH OO-nah fehr-MAH-tah DEHee TAHK-see). Some taxi stands are listed on my maps. To save time and energy, have your hotel or restaurant call a taxi for you; the meter starts when the call is received (generally adding a euro or two to the bill). To call a cab on your own, dial 06-4994 or 06-6645. It's routine for Romans to ask the waiter in a restaurant to call a taxi when they ask for the bill. The waiter will tell you how many minutes you have to enjoy your coffee.

Beware of corrupt taxis. A common cabbie scam is to take your €20 note, drop it, and pick up a €5 note (similar color), claiming that's what you gave him. To avoid this scam, pay in small bills; if you only have a large bill, show it to the cabbie as you state its face value. Keep an eye on the meter, if the cabbie turns it off abruptly when he stops and announces a too-high fare, you'll know what you owe.

If hailing a cab on the street, be sure the meter is restarted when you get in (should be around €3, or around €5 if you or your hotelier phoned for the taxi). Many meters show both the fare and the time elapsed during the ride—and some tourists pay €10 for an eight-minute trip (more than the fair meter rate).

When you arrive at the train station or airport, beware of hustlers conning naive visitors into unmarked, rip-off "express taxis." Only use official taxis, with a *taxi* sign and phone number marked on the door. By law, they must display a multilingual official price chart. If you have any problems with a taxi, point to the chart and ask the cabbie to explain it to you. Making a show of writing down the taxi number (to file a complaint) can motivate a driver to quickly settle the matter.

If you take a Rome city cab from Fiumicino Airport to anywhere in central Rome within the old city walls, the cost should be €48 (covering up to four people and their bags); however, every year some readers report being ripped off. The catch is that cabbies *not* based in Rome or Fiumicino can charge €70. At the airport, look specifically for a Rome city cab, with the "SPQR" shield on the door. By law, they can charge only €48 for the ride (still, be sure to establish the price before you get in).

Tired travelers arriving at the airport will likely find it less stressful to take an airport shuttle van to their hotel, or catch the train to Termini Station and take the Metro or a cheaper taxi from there (for details on getting from the airport to downtown Rome via taxi, shuttle, or train, see "Rome Connections," near the end of this chapter).

By Bike

Biking in the big city of Rome can speed up sightseeing or simply be an enjoyable way to explore. Though Roman traffic can be stressful, Roman drivers are respectful of cyclists. Still, use caution and never assume the right of way. The best rides are on small streets in the city center. A bike path along the banks of the Tiber River makes a good 20-minute ride (easily accessed from the ramps at Porta Portese and Ponte Regina Margherita near Piazza del Popolo). Get a bike with a well-padded seat—the little stones that pave Roman streets are unforgiving.

Top Bike Rental and Tours is professionally run by Roman bike enthusiasts who want to show off their city. Your rental comes with a handy map that suggests a route and indicates less-trafficked streets. Owner Ciro also offers four-hour-long English-only guided tours around the city and the Ancient Appian Way; check his website for days and times (rental: €15/day, discount with this book, best to reserve in advance via email; bike tours: start at €35, reservations required; daily 10:00-19:00, leave ID for deposit, from

Santa Maria Maggiore go up Via dell'Olmata and turn left at the end of the block, Via dei Quattro Cantoni 40, tel. 06-488-2893, www.topbikerental.com, info@topbikerental.com).

Cool Rent, near the Colosseo Metro stop, is cheaper but less helpful (€3/hour, €10/day, 3-person bike cart €10/hour, daily 9:30-20:00, driver's license or other ID for deposit, 10 yards to the right as you exit the Metro). A second outlet is just off Via del Corso (on Largo di Lombardi, near corner of Via del Corso and Via della Croce, mobile 388-695-9303, Sasin).

Tours in Rome

To sightsee on your own, download my series of **free audio tours** that illuminate some of Rome's top sights and neighborhoods: the Colosseum, Roman Forum, St. Peter's Basilica, Sistine Chapel, Trastevere, Jewish Ghetto, and Ostia Antica (see sidebar on page 7 for details).

Walking Tours

Finding the best guided tours in Rome is challenging. Local guides are good but pricey. Tour companies are cheaper, but quality and organization are unreliable.

If you do hire a private Italian guide, consider organizing a group of four to six people from your hotel to split the cost (€180 for a half-day tour); this ends up costing about the same per person as going on a scheduled tour from one of the walking-tour companies listed below (about €25, generally expat guides).

Local Guides

I've worked with each of these licensed independent local guides. They're worth every euro. They speak excellent English and enjoy tailoring tours to your interests. Their prices (roughly €50/hour) flex with the day, season, and demand. Arrange your date and price by email.

Francesca Caruso loves to teach and share her appreciation of her city, and has contributed generously to this chapter (francescainroma@gmail.com). Popular with my readers, Francesca understandably books up quickly; if she's busy, she'll recommend one of her colleagues. **Carla Zaia** is an engaging expert on all things Roman (mobile 349-759-0723, carlaromeguide@gmail.com). **Cristina Giannicchi** has an archaeology background (mobile 338-111-4573, www.crisacross.com, crisgiannicchi@gmail.com). **Sara Magister** is a Roman with a doctorate in art history and author of a book on Renaissance Rome (mobile 339-379-3813, a.magister@iol.it). **Giovanna Terzulli** is a personable, knowledgeable art historian (terzulli@tiscali.it). **Alessandra Mazzoccoli** is experienced, easygoing, and good with all ages (alemazzoccoli@gmail.com). Italian-

American **Sean Finelli,** known as "The Roman Guy," offers several walking tours and a trip-planning service (www.theromanguy. com).

Walking-Tour Companies

Rome has many highly competitive tour companies, each offering a series of themed walks through various slices of Rome. Three-hour guided walks generally cost €25-30 per person. Guides are usually native English speakers, often American expats. Tours are limited to small groups, geared to American tourists, and given in English only. I've listed some here, but without a lot of details on their offerings. Before your trip, spend some time on these companies' websites to get to know your options, as each company has a particular teaching and guiding personality. Some are highbrow, and others are less scholarly. It's sometimes required, and always smart, to book a spot in advance (easy online). I must add that we get a lot of negative feedback on some of these tour companies. Readers report that their advertising can be misleading, and scheduling mishaps are common.

Context Rome's walking tours are more intellectual than most, designed for travelers with longer-than-average attention spans. They are more expensive than others and are led by "docents" rather than guides (tel. 06-9672-7371, US tel. 800-691-6036, www.contextrome.com). **Enjoy Rome** offers a number of different walks and a website filled with helpful information (Via Marghera 8a, tel. 06-445-1843, www.enjoyrome.com, info@enjoyrome.com). **Rome Walks** has put together several particularly creative itineraries (mobile 347-795-5175, www.romewalks.com, info@romewalks. com, Annie). **Roman Odyssey** gives readers of this book a discount on their walks (tel. 06-580-9902, mobile 328-912-3720, www.romanodyssey.com, Rahul). **Through Eternity** offers travelers with this book a discount on most tours; book through their website and enter the promotional code "RICKSTEVES" for the best discount (tel. 06-700-9336, mobile 347-336-5298, www.througheternity.com, office@througheternity.com, Rob). **Walks of Italy** has fun guides who lead a variety of good walks for groups no bigger than 12 people at a time (discount for readers of this book, US tel. 202/684-6916, Italian mobile 334-974-4274, www.walksofitaly. com, Jason Spiehler).

Hop-on, Hop-off Bus Tours

Several different agencies, including the ATAC public bus company, run hop-on, hop-off tours around Rome. These tours are constantly evolving and offer varying combinations of sights. You can grab one (and pay as you board) at any stop; Termini Station and Piazza Venezia are handy hubs. Although the city is perfectly walkable and traffic jams can make the bus dreadfully slow, these open-top bus tours remain popular.

Trambus 110 seems to be the best. Operated by the ATAC city-bus lines, it offers an orientation tour on big red double-decker buses with an open-air upper deck. In less than two hours, you'll have 80 sights pointed out to you (with a next-to-worthless record-ed narration). While you can hop on and off, the service can be er-ratic (mobbed midday, not ideal in bad weather), and it can be very slow in heavy traffic. It's best to think of this as a two-hour quickie orientation with scant information and lots of images. Stops in-clude Ara Pacis, Piazza Cavour, St. Peter's Square, Corso Vittorio Emanuele (for Piazza Navona), Piazza Venezia, Colosseum, and Via Nazionale. Bus #110 departs every 20 minutes. You can catch it at any stop, including Termini Station. Buy the ticket as you board (runs daily April-Oct 8:30-20:30, shorter hours off-season, single tour-€12, 48-hour ticket-€18, tel. 800-281-281, www.trambuso-pen.com).

Archeobus is an open-top bus, also operated by ATAC, that runs twice hourly from Termini Station out to the ancient Appian Way (with stops at the Colosseum, Baths of Caracalla, San Cal-listo, San Sebastiano, and the Tomb of Cecilia Metella). This is a handy way to see the sights down this ancient Roman road, but it can be frustrating for various reasons—sparse narration, sporadic service, and not ideal for hopping on and off (€15, €25 combo-ticket with Trambus 110, ticket valid 48 hours, 1.5-hour loop, daily 9:00-16:30, less frequent off-season, from Termini Station and Pi-azza Venezia, tel. 800-281-281, www.trambusopen.com). A simi-lar bus laces together all the Christian sights.

Car and Minibus Tours

Autoservizi Monti Concezio, run by gentle, capable, and Eng-lish-speaking Ezio, offers private cars or minibuses with driver/ guides (car-€40/hour, minibus-€45/hour, 3-hour minimum for city sightseeing, long rides outside Rome are more expensive, mo-bile 335-636-5907 or 349-674-5643, www.tourservicemonti.it, info@tourservicemonti.it).

Miles & Miles Private Tours is a family-run company of-fering a number of tours (all explained on their website) in Mer-cedes minibuses and cars, all with good English-speaking driver/ guides (€60/hour for up to 8 people, 5-hour minimum, Rick Steves readers booking direct get a discount off any web prices they offer, mobile 331-466-4900, www.milesandmiles.net, info@milesand-miles.net, Francesco answers the mobile phone, while Kimberly—an American—runs their office). They can also provide unguided long-distance transportation; if traveling with a small group or a

ROME

family from Rome to Florence or the Amalfi Coast, consider paying extra to turn the trip into a memorable day tour with door-to-door service.

Self-Guided Walks

Here are three walks that give you a moving picture of Rome, an ancient yet modern city. You'll walk through history (Roman Forum Tour), take a refreshing early-evening walk (Dolce Vita Stroll), and enjoy the thriving local scene, best at night (Heart of Rome Walk).

Roman Forum Tour

The Forum was the political, religious, and commercial center of the city. Rome's most important temples and halls of justice were here. This was the place for religious processions, political demonstrations, elections, important speeches, and parades by conquering generals. As Rome's empire expanded, these few acres of land became the center of the civilized world.

Cost: €12 combo-ticket covers both the Roman Forum/Palatine Hill (grouped as one sight for the purposes of the ticket) and the Colosseum; also covered by the Roma Pass. The combo-ticket is valid two consecutive days, but once your ticket is scanned for either the Forum/Palatine Hill or the Colosseum, you can't re-enter that sight (even the next day).

Hours: The Roman Forum, Colosseum, and Palatine Hill are all open daily 8:30 until one hour before sunset: April-Sept until 19:15, Oct until 18:30, Nov-mid-Feb until 16:30, mid-Feb-mid-March until 17:00, mid-March-late March until 17:30; last entry one hour before closing.

Avoiding Lines: See "Avoiding Lines" on page 854.

Getting There: The closest Metro stop is Colosseo. The Forum has two entrances. The main entrance is on Via dei Fori Imperiali ("Road of the Imperial Forums"). From the Colosseo Metro stop, walk away from the Colosseum on Via dei Fori Imperiali to find the low-profile Forum ticket office (look closely), located where Via Cavour spills into Via dei Fori Imperiali.

The other entrance is at the Palatine Hill ticket office on Via di San Gregorio—after buying your ticket, take the path to the right (not up the hill), and wind around to enter the Forum at the Arch of Titus.

Information: A free visitors center (called I Fori di Roma), located across Via dei Fori Imperiali from the Forum's main entrance, has a TI (which sells the Roma Pass), bookshop, small café, WCs, and a film (daily 9:30-18:30). A bookstore is at the Forum entrance. Vendors at outside sell *Rome: Past and Present* books with

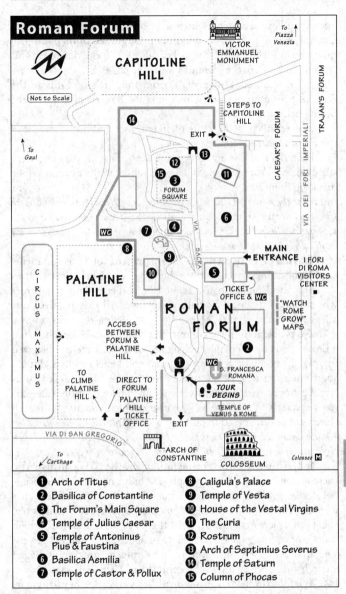

Roman Forum

Not to Scale

CAPITOLINE HILL

VICTOR EMMANUEL MONUMENT

To Piazza Venezia

TRAJAN'S FORUM

STEPS TO CAPITOLINE HILL

EXIT

CAESAR'S FORUM

VIA DEI FORI IMPERIALI

To Gaul

⑭

⑬

⑫

⑮ ③

FORUM SQUARE

⑪

⑥

WC

⑦ ④

VIA SACRA

MAIN ENTRANCE

I FORI DI ROMA VISITORS CENTER

⑧

⑨

⑤

TICKET OFFICE & WC

"WATCH ROME GROW" MAPS

⑩

CIRCUS MAXIMUS

PALATINE HILL

R O M A N F O R U M

②

ACCESS BETWEEN FORUM & PALATINE HILL

① WC

S. FRANCESCA ROMANA

TOUR BEGINS

TO CLIMB PALATINE HILL

DIRECT TO FORUM

PALATINE HILL TICKET OFFICE

EXIT

TEMPLE OF VENUS & ROME

VIA DI SAN GREGORIO

To Carthage

ARCH OF CONSTANTINE

COLOSSEUM

Colosseo Ⓜ

ROME

① Arch of Titus
② Basilica of Constantine
③ The Forum's Main Square
④ Temple of Julius Caesar
⑤ Temple of Antoninus Pius & Faustina
⑥ Basilica Aemilia
⑦ Temple of Castor & Pollux

⑧ Caligula's Palace
⑨ Temple of Vesta
⑩ House of the Vestal Virgins
⑪ The Curia
⑫ Rostrum
⑬ Arch of Septimius Severus
⑭ Temple of Saturn
⑮ Column of Phocas

plastic overlays that restore the ruins (includes DVD, smaller book marked €15, prices soft, so offer €10). Info office tel. 06-3996-7700, http://archeoroma.beniculturali.it/en.

Tours: An unexciting yet informative **audioguide** helps decipher the rubble (€5/2 hours, €7 version includes Palatine Hill and lasts 3 hours, must leave ID), but you'll have to return it to one of the Forum entrances instead of being able to exit directly to Capitoline Hill or the Colosseum. Official **guided tours** in English might be available (inquire at ticket office). You can download this walk as a free Rick Steves **audio tour** (see page 7).

With Limited Time: Walk from the Arch of Titus to the Arch of Septimius Severus. Don't miss the Basilica of Constantine hiding behind the trees.

Services: WCs are at the main entrance and in the middle of the Forum, near #8 on the map.

Plan Ahead: The ancient paving at the Forum is uneven; wear sturdy shoes. I carry a water bottle and refill it at the Forum's public drinking fountains.

• *Start at the Arch of Titus (Arco di Tito). It's the white triumphal arch that rises above the rubble on the east end of the Forum (closest to the Colosseum). Stand at the viewpoint alongside the arch and gaze over the valley known as the Forum.*

❶ **Arch of Titus (Arco di Tito):** The Arch of Titus commemorated the Roman victory over the province of Judaea (Israel) in A.D. 70. The Romans had a reputation as benevolent conquerors who tolerated the local customs and rulers. All they required was allegiance to the empire, shown by worshipping the emperor as a god. No problem for most conquered people, who already had half a dozen gods on their prayer lists anyway. But Israelites believed in only one god, and it wasn't the emperor. Israel revolted. After a short but bitter war, the Romans defeated the rebels, took Jerusalem, destroyed their temple (leaving only the foundation wall—today's revered "Wailing Wall"), and brought home 50,000 Jewish slaves...who were forced to build this arch (and the Colosseum).

• *Walk down the Via Sacra into the Forum. After about 50 yards, turn right and follow a path uphill to the three huge arches of the...*

❷ **Basilica of Constantine (a.k.a. Basilica Maxentius):** Yes, these are big arches. But they represent only one-third of the original Basilica of Constantine, a mammoth hall of justice. The arches were matched by a similar set along the Via Sacra side (only a few squat brick piers remain). Between them ran the central hall, which was spanned by a roof 130 feet high—about 55 feet higher than the side arches you see. (The stub of brick you see sticking up began an arch that once spanned the central hall.) The hall itself was as long as a football field, lavishly furnished with colorful inlaid marble, a gilded bronze ceiling, and statues, and filled with strolling Romans. At the far (west) end was an enormous marble statue of Emperor Constantine on a throne. (Pieces of this statue, including a hand the size of a man, are on display in Rome's Capitoline Museums.)

The basilica was begun by the emperor Maxentius, but after he was trounced in battle, the victor Constantine completed the massive building. No doubt about it, the Romans built monuments on a more epic scale than any previous Europeans, wowing their "barbarian" neighbors.

• *Now stroll deeper into the Forum, downhill along the Via Sacra, through the trees. Many of the large basalt stones under your feet were walked on by Caesar Augustus 2,000 years ago. Pass by the only original bronze door still swinging on its ancient hinges (the green door at the Tempio di Romolo, on the right—if it happens to be open, peek in), and continue between ruined buildings until the Via Sacra opens up to a flat, grassy area.*

❸ **The Forum's Main Square**: The original Forum, or main square, was this flat patch about the size of a football field, stretching to the foot of Capitoline Hill. Surrounding it were temples, law courts, government buildings, and triumphal arches.

Rome was born right here. According to legend, twin brothers Romulus (Rome) and Remus were orphaned in infancy and raised by a she-wolf on top of Palatine Hill. Growing up, they found it hard to get dates. So they and their cohorts attacked the nearby Sabine tribe and kidnapped their women. After they made peace, this marshy valley became the meeting place and then the trading center for the scattered tribes on the surrounding hillsides.

The square was the busiest and most crowded—and often the seediest—section of town. Besides the senators, politicians, and currency exchangers, there were even sleazier types—souvenir hawkers, pickpockets, fortune-tellers, gamblers, slave marketers, drunks, hookers, lawyers, and tour guides.

The Forum is now rubble, but imagine it in its prime: blindingly brilliant marble buildings with 40-foot-high columns and shining metal roofs; rows of statues painted in realistic colors; processional chariots rattling down the Via Sacra. Mentally replace tourists in T-shirts with tribunes in togas. Imagine the buildings towering and the people buzzing around you while an orator gives a rabble-rousing speech from the Rostrum. If things still look like just a pile of rocks, at least tell yourself, "But Julius Caesar once leaned against these rocks."

• *At the near (east) end of the main square (the Colosseum is to the east) are the foundations of a temple now capped with a peaked wood-and-metal roof.*

❹ **Temple of Julius Caesar (Tempio del Divo Giulio, or Ara di Cesare):** Julius Caesar's body was burned on this spot (under the metal roof) after his assassination. Peek behind the wall into the small apse area, where a mound of dirt usually has fresh flowers—given to remember the man who, more than any other, personified the greatness of Rome.

Caesar (100-44 B.C.) changed Rome—and the Forum—dramatically. He cleared out many of the wooden market stalls and

ROME

began to ring the square with even grander buildings. Caesar's house was located behind the temple, near that clump of trees. He walked right by here on the day he was assassinated ("Beware the Ides of March!" warned a street-corner Etruscan preacher).

Though he was popular with the masses, not everyone liked Caesar's urban design or his politics. When he assumed dictatorial powers, he was ambushed and stabbed to death by a conspiracy of senators, including his adopted son, Brutus *("Et tu, Brute?")*.

The funeral was held here, facing the main square. The citizens gathered, and speeches were made. Mark Antony stood up to say (in Shakespeare's words), "Friends, Romans, countrymen, lend me your ears. I come to bury Caesar, not to praise him." When Caesar's body was burned, the citizens who still loved him threw anything at hand on the fire, requiring the fire department to come put it out. Later, Emperor Augustus dedicated this temple in his name, making Caesar the first Roman to become a god.

• *Behind and to the left of the Temple of Julius Caesar are 10 tall columns. These belong to the...*

❺ **Temple of Antoninus Pius and Faustina:** The Senate built this temple to honor Emperor Antoninus Pius (A.D. 138-161) and his deified wife, Faustina. The 50-foot-tall Corinthian (leafy) columns must have been awe-inspiring to out-of-towners who grew up in thatched huts. Although the temple has been inhabited by a church, you can still see the basic layout—a staircase led to a shaded porch (the columns), which admitted you to the main building (now a church), where the statue of the god sat. Originally, these columns supported a triangular pediment decorated with sculptures.

Picture these columns, with gilded capitals, supporting brightly painted statues in the pediment, and the whole building capped with a gleaming bronze roof. The stately gray rubble of today's Forum is a faded black-and-white photograph of a 3-D Technicolor era.

The building is a microcosm of many changes that occurred after Rome fell. In medieval times, the temple was pillaged. Note the diagonal cuts high on the marble columns—a failed attempt by scavengers to cut through the pillars to pull them down for their precious stone. (They used vinegar and rope to cut the marble... but because vinegar also eats through rope, they abandoned the attempt.) In 1550, a church was housed inside the ancient temple. The green door shows the street level at the time of Michelangelo. The long staircase was underground until excavated in the 1800s.

• *There's a ramp next to the Temple of A. and F. Walk halfway up it and look to the left to view the...*

❻ **Basilica Aemilia:** A basilica was a covered public forum, often serving as a Roman hall of justice. In a society that was as legal-minded as America is today, you needed a lot of lawyers—and a big place to put them. Citizens came here to work out matters such as inheritances and building permits, or to sue somebody.

Notice the layout. It was a long, rectangular building. The stubby columns all in a row form one long, central hall flanked by two side aisles. Medieval Christians required a larger meeting hall for their worship services than Roman temples provided, so they used the spacious Roman basilica as the model for their churches. Cathedrals from France to Spain to England, from Romanesque to Gothic to Renaissance, all have the same basic floor plan as a Roman basilica.

• *Return again to the Temple of Julius Caesar. To the right of the temple are the three tall Corinthian columns of the Temple of Castor and Pollux. Beyond that is Palatine Hill—the corner of which may have been...*

❼ **Caligula's Palace (a.k.a. the Palace of Tiberius):** Emperor Caligula (ruled A.D. 37-41) had a huge palace on Palatine Hill overlooking the Forum. It actually sprawled down the hill into the Forum (some supporting arches remain in the hillside).

Caligula was not a nice person. He tortured enemies, stole senators' wives, and parked his chariot in handicap spaces. But Rome's luxury-loving emperors only added to the glory of the Forum, with each one trying to make his mark on history.

• *To the left of the Temple of Castor and Pollux, find the remains of a small white circular temple.*

❽ **Temple of Vesta:** This is perhaps Rome's most sacred spot. Rome considered itself one big family, and this temple represented a circular hut, like the kind that Rome's first families lived in. Inside, a fire burned, just as in a Roman home. And back in the days before lighters and butane, you never wanted your fire to go out. As long as the sacred flame burned, Rome would stand. The flame was tended by priestesses known as Vestal Virgins.

• *Around the back of the Temple of Vesta, you'll find two rectangular brick pools. These stood in the courtyard of the...*

❾ **House of the Vestal Virgins:** The Vestal Virgins lived in a two-story building surrounding a long central courtyard with these two pools at one end. Rows of statues depicting leading Vestal Virgins flanked the courtyard. This place was the model—both architecturally and sexually—for medieval convents and monasteries.

Chosen from noble families before they reached the age of 10, the six Vestal Virgins served a 30-year term. Honored and revered by the Romans, the Vestals even had their own box opposite the emperor in the Colosseum. The statues that line the courtyard honor dutiful Vestals.

As the name implies, a Vestal took a vow of chastity. If she served her term faithfully—abstaining for 30 years—she was given a huge dowry and allowed to marry. But if they found any Virgin who wasn't, she was strapped to a funeral car, paraded through the streets of the Forum, taken to a crypt, given a loaf of bread and a lamp...and buried alive. Many women suffered the latter fate.

• *Return to the Temple of Julius Caesar and head to the Forum's west end (opposite the Colosseum). As you pass alongside the big open space of the Forum's main square, consider how the piazza is still a standard part of any Italian town. It has reflected and accommodated the gregarious and outgoing nature of the Italian people since Roman times.*

Stop at the big, well-preserved brick building (on right) with the triangular roof. Look in at...

⑩ The Curia (Senate House): The Curia was the most important political building in the Forum. While the present building dates from A.D. 283, this was the site of Rome's official center of government since the birth of the republic. (Ongoing archaeological work may restrict access to the Curia, as well as the Arch of Septimius Severus—described later—and the exit to Capitoline Hill.) Three hundred senators, elected by the citizens of Rome, met here to debate and create the laws of the land. Their wooden seats once circled the building in three tiers; the Senate president's podium sat at the far end. The marble floor is from ancient times. Listen to the echoes in this vast room—the acoustics are great.

Rome prided itself on being a republic. Early in the city's history, its people threw out the king and established rule by elected representatives. Each Roman citizen was free to speak his mind and have a say in public policy. Even when emperors became the supreme authority, the Senate was a power to be reckoned with. The Curia building is well-preserved, having been used as a church since early Christian times. In the 1930s, it was restored and opened to the public as a historic site. (Note: Although Julius Caesar was assassinated in "the Senate," it wasn't here—the Senate was temporarily meeting across town.)

A statue and two reliefs inside the Curia help build our mental image of the Forum. The statue, made of porphyry marble in about A.D. 100 (with its head, arms, and feet now missing), was a tribute to an emperor, probably Hadrian or Trajan. The two relief panels may have decorated the Rostrum. Those on the left show people (with big stone tablets) standing in line to burn their debt records following a government amnesty. The other shows the distribution of grain (Rome's welfare system), some buildings in the background, and the latest fashion in togas.

• *Go back down the Senate steps and find the 10-foot-high wall just to the left of the big arch, marked...*

⑪ Rostrum (Rostri): Nowhere was Roman freedom more apparent than at this "Speaker's Corner." The Rostrum was a raised platform, 10 feet high and 80 feet long, decorated with statues, columns, and the prows of ships (rostra).

On a stage like this, Rome's orators, great and small, tried to draw a crowd and sway public opinion. Mark Antony rose to offer Caesar the laurel-leaf crown of kingship, which Caesar publicly (and hypocritically) refused while privately becoming a dictator. Men such as Cicero railed against the corruption and decadence that came with the city's newfound wealth. In later years, daring citizens even spoke out against the emperors, reminding them that Rome was once free. Picture the backdrop these speakers would have had—a mountain of marble buildings piling up on Capitoline Hill.

In front of the Rostrum are trees bearing fruits that were sacred to the ancient Romans: olives (provided food, light, and preservatives), figs (tasty), and wine grapes (made a popular export product).

• *The big arch to the right of the Rostrum is the...*

⑫ Arch of Septimius Severus: In imperial times, the Rostrum's voices of democracy would have been dwarfed by images of the empire, such as the huge six-story-high Arch of Septimius Severus (A.D. 203). The reliefs commemorate the African-born emperor's battles in Mesopotamia. Near ground level, see soldiers marching captured barbarians back to Rome for the victory parade. Despite Severus' efficient rule, Rome's empire was crumbling under the weight of its own corruption, disease, decaying infrastructure, and the constant attacks by foreign "barbarians."

• *Pass underneath the Arch of Septimius Severus and turn left. If the path is blocked, backtrack toward the Temple of Julius Caesar and around the square. On the slope of Capitoline Hill are the eight remaining columns of the...*

⑬ Temple of Saturn: These columns framed the entrance to the Forum's oldest temple (497 B.C.). Inside was a humble, very old wooden statue of the god Saturn. But the statue's pedestal held the gold bars, coins, and jewels of Rome's state treasury, the booty collected by conquering generals.

• *Standing here, at one of the Forum's first buildings, look east at the lone, tall...*

⑭ Column of Phocas—Rome's Fall: This is the Forum's last monument (A.D. 608), a gift from the powerful Byzantine Empire to a fallen empire—Rome. Given to commemorate the pagan Pantheon's becoming a Christian church, it's like a symbolic last nail in ancient Rome's coffin. After Rome's 1,000-year reign, the city was looted by Vandals, the population of a million-plus shrank to about 10,000, and the once-grand city center—the Forum—was abandoned, slowly covered up by centuries of silt and dirt. In the 1700s, an English historian named Edward Gibbon overlooked this spot from Capitoline Hill. Hearing Christian monks singing at these pagan ruins, he looked out at the few columns poking up from the ground, pondered the decline and fall of the Roman Empire, and thought, "Hmm, that's a catchy title...."

• *From here, you have several options:*

    1. Exiting past the Arch of Titus lands you at the Colosseum (page 851).

    2. Exiting past the Arch of Septimius Severus leads you to the stairs up to Capitoline Hill (page 863).

    3. The Forum's main entrance spills you back out onto Via dei Fori Imperiali (for Trajan's Column, Market, and Museum of the Imperial Forums, page 862).

    4. From the Arch of Titus, you can climb Palatine Hill (page 860).

▲▲Dolce Vita Stroll

This is the city's chic stroll, from Piazza del Popolo (Metro: Flaminio) down a wonderfully traffic-free section of Via del Corso, and up Via Condotti to the Spanish Steps. It takes place from around 17:00 to 19:00 each evening (Fri and Sat are best), except on Sunday, when it occurs earlier in the afternoon. Leave before 18:00 if you plan to visit the Ara Pacis (Altar of Peace), which closes at 19:00 and is closed Monday.

As you stroll, you'll see shoppers, people-watchers, and flirts on the prowl filling this neighborhood of some of Rome's most fashionable stores (some open after siesta 16:30-19:30). While both the crowds and the shops along Via del Corso have gone downhill recently, elegance survives in the grid of streets between here and the Spanish Steps. If you get hungry during your stroll, see page 933 for descriptions of neighborhood wine bars and restaurants.

To reach **Piazza del Popolo,** where the stroll starts, take Metro line A to Flaminio and walk south to the square. Delightfully car-free, Piazza del Popolo is marked by an obelisk that was brought to Rome by Augustus after he conquered Egypt. (It used to stand in the Circus Maximus.) In medieval times, this area was just inside Rome's main entry (for more background on the square, see page 891).

If starting your stroll early enough, the Baroque church of **Santa Maria del Popolo** is worth popping into (Mon-Sat until 18:30, Sun until 19:30, next to gate in old wall on north side of square). Inside, look for Raphael's Chigi Chapel (KEE-gee, second chapel on left) and two paintings by Caravaggio (in the Cerasi Chapel, left of altar; see listing on page 892).

From Piazza del Popolo, shop your way down **Via del Corso.** With the proliferation of shopping malls, many chain stores lining Via del Corso are losing customers and facing hard times. Still, this remains a fine place to feel the pulse of Rome at twilight.

Historians side-trip right down Via Pontefici past the fascist architecture to see the massive, rotting, round-brick **Mausoleum**

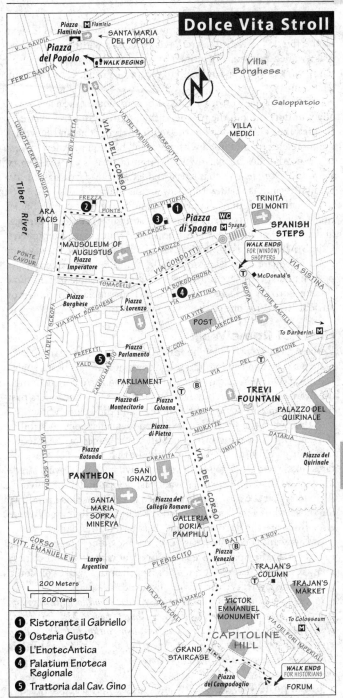

Dolce Vita Stroll

Piazza Flaminio · Ⓜ Flaminio

SANTA MARIA DEL POPOLO

V. L. SAVOIA

Piazza del Popolo

FERD. SAVOIA

● **WALK BEGINS**

Villa Borghese

Galoppatoio

VIA DEL CORSO

VIA DI RIPETTA

VIA DEL BABUINO

MARGUTTA

VILLA MEDICI

LUNGOTEVERE IN AUGUSTA

Tiber River

FREZZA

❷ PONTE

VIA VITTORIA

VIA DEL CORSO

❶

❸ VIA CROCE

Piazza di Spagna

WC

Ⓜ Spagna

TRINITÀ DEI MONTI

SPANISH STEPS

ARA PACIS

MAUSOLEUM OF AUGUSTUS
Piazza Imperatore

VIA CAROZZE

VIA CONDOTTI

WALK ENDS
FOR (WINDOW) SHOPPERS

VIA SISTINA

PONTE CAVOUR

Ⓣ ◆ McDonald's

VIA PUE MACELLI

TOMACELLI

VIA BORGOGNONA

❹ VIA FRATTINA

PKOPA

Piazza Borghese

Piazza S. Lorenzo

VIA VITE

POST

V. MERCEDE

To Barberini Ⓜ

VIA DELLA SCROFA

VIA FONT. BORGHESE

PREFETTI

❺ VALD.

CAMPO MARZO

Piazza Parlamento

V. CON.

TRITONE

Ⓣ

VIA DEL

PARLIAMENT

Ⓣ

Ⓑ

SABINA

TREVI FOUNTAIN

Piazza di Montecitorio

Piazza Colonna

MURATTE

PALAZZO DEL QUIRINALE

Piazza di Pietra

DATARIA

Piazza del Quirinale

Piazza Rotonda

CARAVITA

VIA DEL CORSO

VIA DELLA SCROFA

PANTHEON

SAN IGNAZIO

SANTA MARIA SOPRA MINERVA

Piazza del Collegio Romano

GALLERIA DORIA PAMPHLIJ

BATT. V. A NOV.

CORSO VITT. EMANUELE II

Largo Argentina

PLEBISCITO

Ⓑ

Piazza Venezia

TRAJAN'S COLUMN

Ⓣ

TRAJAN'S MARKET

Ⓜ To Colosseum

200 Meters

200 Yards

VIA D'ARA COELI

SAN MARCO

VICTOR EMMANUEL MONUMENT

VIA DEI FORI IMPERIALI

❶ Ristorante il Gabriello
❷ Osteria Gusto
❸ L'EnotecAntica
❹ Palatium Enoteca Regionale
❺ Trattoria dal Cav. Gino

CAPITOLINE HILL

GRAND STAIRCASE

Piazza del Campodoglio

WALK ENDS
FOR HISTORIANS

FORUM

ROME

of Augustus, topped with overgrown cypress trees. Beyond it, next to the river, is Augustus' **Ara Pacis,** enclosed within a protective glass-walled museum (described on page 893). From the mausoleum, walk down Via Tomacelli to return to Via del Corso and the 21st century.

From Via del Corso, window-shoppers should take a left down **Via Condotti** to join the parade to the **Spanish Steps.** The streets that parallel Via Condotti to the south (Borgognona and Frattina) are more elegant and filled with high-end boutiques. A few streets to the north hides the narrow Via Margutta. This is where Gregory Peck's *Roman Holiday* character lived (at #51); today it has a leafy tranquility and is filled with pricey artisan shops.

Historians: Ignore Via Condotti and forget the Spanish Steps. Stay on Via del Corso, which has been straight since Roman times, and walk a half-mile down to the Victor Emmanuel Monument. Climb Michelangelo's stairway to his glorious (especially when floodlit) square atop Capitoline Hill. Stand on the balcony (just past the mayor's palace on the right), which overlooks the Forum. As the horizon reddens and cats prowl the unclaimed rubble of ancient Rome, it's one of the finest views in the city.

Heart of Rome Walk

Rome's most colorful neighborhood features narrow lanes, intimate piazzas, fanciful fountains, and some of Europe's best people-watching. During the day, this walk shows off the colorful Campo de' Fiori market and trendy fashion boutiques as it meanders past major monuments such as the Pantheon and the Spanish Steps.

But, when the sun sets, unexpected magic happens. A stroll in the cool of the evening brings out all the romance of the Eternal City. Sit so close to a bubbling fountain that traffic noise evaporates. Jostle with kids to see the gelato flavors. Watch lovers straddling more than the bench. Jaywalk past *polizia* in flak-proof vests. And marvel at the ramshackle elegance that softens this brutal city for those who were born here and can't imagine living anywhere else. These are the flavors of Rome, best tasted after dark.

This walk is equally pleasant in reverse order. You could ride the Metro to the Spanish Steps and finish at Campo de' Fiori, near many recommended restaurants. To lengthen this walk, you could start in Trastevere; see directions on page 899.

• *Start this walk at Campo de' Fiori, my favorite outdoor dining room (especially after dark—see "Eating in Rome," page 923). It's a few blocks east of Largo Argentina, a major transportation hub. Buses #40, #64, and #492 stop at both Largo Argentina and along Corso Vittorio Emanuele II, a long block north of Campo de' Fiori. A taxi from Termini Station costs about €8.*

Campo de' Fiori: One of Rome's most colorful spots, this bohemian piazza hosts a fruit and vegetable **market** in the morning, cafés in the evening, and pub-crawlers at night. In ancient times, the "Field of Flowers" was an open meadow. Later, Christian pilgrims passed through on their way to the Vatican, and a thriving market developed.

Lording over the center of the square is a statue of **Giordano Bruno,** an intellectual heretic who was burned on this spot in 1600. When the statue of Bruno was erected in 1889, riots overcame Vatican protests against honoring a heretic. Bruno faces his nemesis, the Vatican Chancellory (the big white building just outside the far-right corner of the square), while his pedestal reads, "And the flames rose up." Check out the reliefs on the pedestal for scenes from Bruno's trial and execution. Even today, this neighborhood is known for its free spirit and occasional demonstrations.

Campo de' Fiori is the product of centuries of unplanned urban development. At the east end of the square (behind Bruno), the ramshackle apartments are built right into the old outer wall of ancient Rome's mammoth Theater of Pompey. This entertainment complex covered several city blocks, stretching from here to Largo Argentina. Julius Caesar was assassinated in the Theater of Pompey, where the Senate was renting space.

The square is lined with and surrounded by fun eateries. Bruno faces the **Forno** (in the left corner of the square). Step in, at least to observe the frenzy as pizza is sold hot out of the oven. You can order *un etto* (100 grams, an average serving) by pointing, then take your snack to the counter to pay. The many bars lining the square are fine for drinks and watching the scene. On weekend nights, when the Campo is packed with beer-drinking kids, this medieval square is transformed into one vast Roman street party.

• *If Bruno did a hop, step, and jump forward, then turned right on Via dei Baullari and marched 200 yards, he'd cross the busy Corso Vittorio Emanuele; then, continuing another 150 yards on Via Cuccagna, he'd find...*

Piazza Navona: This oblong square retains the shape of the original racetrack that was built around A.D. 80 by the emperor Domitian. (To see the ruins of the original entrance, exit the square at the far—or north—end, then take an immediate left, and look down to the left 25 feet below the current street level.) Since ancient times, the square has been a center of Roman life. In the 1800s, the city would flood the square to cool off the neighborhood.

The **Four Rivers Fountain** in the center is the most famous fountain by the man who remade Rome in Baroque style, Gian Lorenzo Bernini. Four burly river gods (representing the four continents that were known in 1650) support an Egyptian obelisk. The water of the world gushes everywhere. The Nile has his head cov-

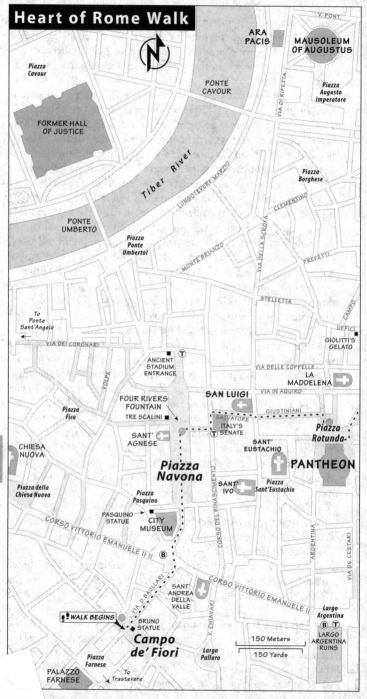

Heart of Rome Walk

N

ARA PACIS

MAUSOLEUM OF AUGUSTUS

V. PONT

Piazza Cavour

PONTE CAVOUR

VIA DI RIPETTA

Piazza Augusto Imperatore

FORMER HALL OF JUSTICE

Tiber River

LUNGOTEVERE MARZIO

Piazza Borghese

CLEMENTINO

PONTE UMBERTO

Piazza Ponte Umberto I

MONTE BRIANZO

VIA DELLA SCROFA

PREFETTI

STELLETTA

CAMPO

UFFICI

To Ponte Sant'Angelo

VIA DEI CORONARI

GIOLITTI'S GELATO

VIA DELLE COPPELLE

VOLPE

ANCIENT STADIUM ENTRANCE T

SAN LUIGI

VIA IN AQUIRO

LA MADDELENA

Piazza Fico

FOUR RIVERS FOUNTAIN
TRE SCALINI

GIUSTINIANI

SALVATORE
ITALY'S SENATE T

Piazza Rotunda

CHIESA NUOVA

SANT' AGNESE

SANT' EUSTACHIO

PANTHEON

Piazza Navona

SANT' IVO

Piazza Sant'Eustachio

Piazza della Chiesa Nuova

Piazza Pasquino

CORSO DEL RINASCIMENTO

ARGENTINA

CORSO VITTORIO EMANUELE II II

PASQUINO STATUE
CITY MUSEUM

B

VIA DE CESTARI

SANT' ANDREA DELLA VALLE

CORSO VITTORIO EMANUELE II

Largo Argentina

WALK BEGINS

VIA D. BAULLARI

B T

BRUNO STATUE

V. CHIAVARI

LARGO ARGENTINA RUINS

PALAZZO FARNESE

Piazza Farnese

Campo de' Fiori

To Trastevere

Largo Pallaro

150 Meters

150 Yards

ROME

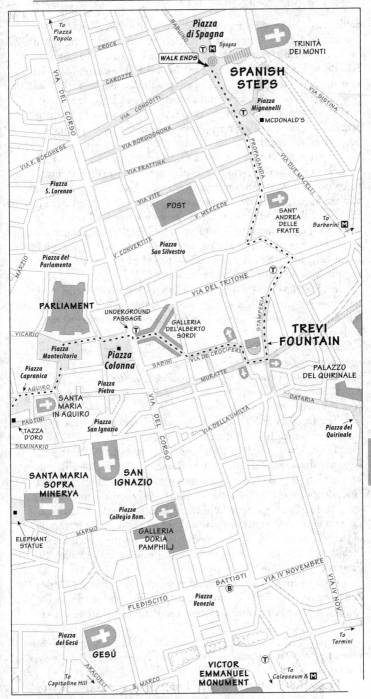

To Piazza Popolo

BABUINO

CROCE

CAROZZE

VIA DEL CORSO

Piazza di Spagna

WALK ENDS

Spagna

TRINITÀ DEI MONTI

SPANISH STEPS

VIA SISTINA

VIA CONDOTTI

Piazza Mignanelli

■ MCDONALD'S

VIA BORGOGNONA

PROPAGANDA

VIA DUE MACELLI

VIA FRATTINA

VIA F. BORGHESE

Piazza S. Lorenzo

VIA VITE

POST

V. MERCEDE

SANT' ANDREA DELLE FRATTE

To Barberini Ⓜ

V. CONVERTITE

Piazza San Silvestro

MARZIO

Piazza del Parlamento

VIA DEL TRITONE

STAMPERIA

PARLIAMENT

UNDERGROUND PASSAGE

GALLERIA DEL'ALBERTO SORDI

TREVI FOUNTAIN

VICARIO

Piazza Montecitorio

Piazza Colonna

SABINI

VIA DE CROCIFERI

MURATTE

PALAZZO DEL QUIRINALE

Piazza Capranica

AQUIRO

Piazza Pietra

VIA DEL CORSO

DATARIA

PASTINI

SANTA MARIA IN AQUIRO

VIA DELLA UMILTÀ

Piazza del Quirinale

TAZZA D'ORO

SEMINARIO

Piazza San Ignazio

SANTA MARIA SOPRA MINERVA

SAN IGNAZIO

ROME

ELEPHANT STATUE

Piazza Collegio Rom.

MARMO

GALLERIA DORIA PAMPHILJ

BATTISTI

VIA IV NOVEMBRE

VIA IV NOV.

PLEBISCITO

Piazza Venezia

Ⓑ

To Termini

Piazza del Gesù

GESÙ

ARACOELI

S. MARCO

VICTOR EMMANUEL MONUMENT

To Capitoline Hill

To Colosseum & Ⓜ

ered, since the headwaters were unknown then. The Ganges holds an oar. The Danube turns to admire the obelisk, which Bernini had moved here from a stadium on the Appian Way. And Uruguay's Río de la Plata tumbles backward in shock, wondering how he ever made the top four. Bernini enlivens the fountain with horses plunging through the rocks and exotic flora and fauna from these newly discovered lands. Homesick Texans may want to find the armadillo. (It's the big, weird, armor-plated creature behind the Plata river statue.)

The Plata river god is gazing upward at the **Church of St. Agnes,** worked on by Bernini's former student-turned-rival, Francesco Borromini. Borromini's concave facade helps reveal the dome and epitomizes the curved symmetry of Baroque. Tour guides say that Bernini designed his river god to look horrified at Borromini's work. Or maybe he's shielding his eyes from St. Agnes' nakedness, as she was stripped before being martyred. But either explanation is unlikely, since the fountain was completed two years before Borromini even started work on the church.

Piazza Navona is Rome's most interesting night scene, with street music, artists, fire-eaters, local Casanovas, ice cream, and outdoor cafés that are worthy of a splurge if you've got time to sit and enjoy Italy's human river.

• *Leave Piazza Navona directly across from Tre Scalini (famous for its rich chocolate ice cream), and go east down Corsia Agonale, past rose peddlers and palm readers. Jog left around the guarded building (where Italy's senate meets), and follow the brown sign to the Pantheon, which is straight down Via del Salvatore.*

The Pantheon: Sit for a while under the portico of the Pantheon (romantically floodlit and moonlit at night).

The 40-foot, single-piece granite columns of the Pantheon's entrance show the scale the ancient Romans built on. The columns support a triangular Greek-style roof with an inscription that says "M. Agrippa" built it. In fact, it was built *(fecit)* by Emperor Hadrian (A.D. 120), who gave credit to the builder of an earlier structure. This impressive entranceway gives no clue that the greatest wonder of the building is inside—a domed room that inspired later domes, including Michelangelo's St. Peter's and Brunelleschi's Duomo (in Florence).

If it's open, pop into the Pantheon for a look around (interior described on page 869). If you have extra time, consider detouring to several interesting churches near the Pantheon (listed on page 870).

• *With your back to the Pantheon, veer to the right, uphill toward the* ... *sign that reads* Casa del Caffè *at the Tazza d'Oro coffee shop on* ... *fani.*

...om the Pantheon to the Trevi Fountain: Tazza d'Oro

Casa del Caffè, one of Rome's top coffee shops, dates back to the days when this area was licensed to roast coffee beans. Locals come here for a shot of espresso or, when it's hot, a refreshing *granita di caffè con panna* (coffee slush with cream).

• *Continue up Via Orfani to...*

Piazza Capranica is home to the big, plain Florentine Renaissance-style Palazzo Capranica (directly opposite as you enter the square). Big shots, like the Capranica family, built towers on their palaces—not for any military use, but just to show off.

• *Leave the piazza to the right of the palace, heading down Via in Aquiro.*

The street Via in Aquiro leads to a sixth-century B.C. **Egyptian obelisk** taken as a trophy by Augustus after his victory in Egypt over Mark Antony and Cleopatra. The obelisk was set up as a sundial. Follow the zodiac markings to the well-guarded front door. This is Italy's **parliament building,** where the lower house meets; you may see politicians, political demonstrations, and TV cameras.

• *To your right is Piazza Colonna, where we're heading next—unless you like gelato...*

A one-block detour to the left (past Albergo Nazionale) brings you to Rome's most famous *gelateria.* **Giolitti's** is cheap for takeout or elegant and splurge-worthy for a sit among classy locals (open daily until past midnight, Via Uffici del Vicario 40); get your gelato in a cone *(cono)* or cup *(coppetta)*.

Piazza Colonna features a huge second-century column. Its reliefs depict the victories of Emperor Marcus Aurelius over the barbarians. When Marcus died in A.D. 180, the barbarians began to get the upper hand, beginning Rome's long three-century fall. The big, important-looking palace houses the headquarters for the prime minister's cabinet.

Noisy **Via del Corso** is Rome's main north-south boulevard. It's named for the Berber horse races—without riders—that took place here during Carnevale. This wild tradition continued until the late 1800s, when a series of fatal accidents (including, reportedly, one in front of Queen Margherita) led to its cancellation. Historically the street was filled with meat shops. When it became one of Rome's first gas-lit streets in 1854, these butcher shops were banned and replaced by classier boutiques, jewelers, and antiques dealers. Nowadays the northern part of Via del Corso is closed to traffic, and for a few hours every evening it becomes a wonderful parade of Romans out for a stroll (see the "Dolce Vita Stroll," earlier).

• *Cross Via del Corso to enter a big palatial building with columns, which houses the Galleria Alberto Sordi shopping mall (with conv? WCs). Inside, take the fork to the right and exit at the back. (If after 22:00, when the mall is closed, circle around the right side of the Galleria on Via dei Sabini.) Once out the back, head up Via de Crociferi, to the roar of the water, lights, and people at the...*

Trevi Fountain: The Trevi Fountain shows how Rome took full advantage of the abundance of water brought into the city by its great aqueducts. This watery Baroque avalanche by Nicola Salvi was completed in 1762. Salvi used the palace behind the fountain as a theatrical backdrop for the figure of "Ocean," who represents water in every form. The statue surfs through his wet kingdom—with water gushing from 24 spouts and tumbling over 30 different kinds of plants—while Triton blows his conch shell.

The magic of the square is enhanced by the fact that no streets directly approach it. You can hear the excitement as you draw near, and then—*bam!*—you're there. The scene is always lively, with lucky Romeos clutching dates while unlucky ones clutch beers. Romantics toss a coin over their shoulder, thinking it will give them a wish and assure their return to Rome. That may sound silly, but every year I go through this tourist ritual...and it actually seems to work.

Take some time to people-watch (whisper a few breathy *bellos* or *bellas*) before leaving. There's a peaceful zone at water level on the far right.

• *From the Trevi Fountain, we're 10 minutes from our next stop, the Spanish Steps. Just use a map to get there, or follow these directions: Facing the Trevi Fountain, go forward, walking along the right side of the fountain on Via della Stamperia. Cross busy Via del Tritone. Continue 100 yards and veer right at Via delle Fratte, a street that changes its name to Via Propaganda before ending at the...*

Spanish Steps: Piazza di Spagna, with the very popular Spanish Steps, is named for the Spanish Embassy to the Vatican, which has been here for 300 years. It's been the hangout of many Romantics over the years (Keats, Wagner, Openshaw, Goethe, and others). In the 1700s, British aristocrats on the "Grand Tour" of Europe came here to ponder Rome's decay. The British poet John Keats pondered his mortality, then died of tuberculosis at age 25 in the pink building on the right side of the steps. Fellow Romantic Lord Byron lived across the square at #66.

The **Sinking Boat Fountain** at the foot of the steps, built by Bernini or his father, Pietro, is powered by an aqueduct. Actually, all of Rome's fountains are aqueduct-powered; their spurts are determined by the water pressure provided by the various aqueducts. This one, for instance, is much weaker than Trevi's gush.

The piazza is a thriving scene at night. Window-shop along which stretches away from the steps. This is where big names cater to the trendsetting jet set. It's clear that the main sight around here is not the famous steps, but the people who sit on them.

• *Our walk is finished. If you'd like to reach the top of the steps sweat-free, take the free elevator just outside the Spagna Metro stop (to the left, as you face the steps; elevator closes at 21:00). A free WC is underground in the piazza near the Metro entrance, by the middle palm tree (10:00-19:30). The nearby McDonald's (as you face the Spanish Steps, go right one block) is big and lavish, with a salad bar and WC. When you're ready to leave, you can zip home on the Metro (usually open until 23:30, Fri-Sat until 1:30 in the morning) or grab a taxi at either the north or south side of the piazza.*

Sights in Rome

I've clustered Rome's sights into walkable neighborhoods, some quite close together (see the "Rome's Neighborhoods" map on page 813). Save transit time by grouping your sightseeing according to location. For example, the Colosseum and the Forum are a few minutes' walk from Capitoline Hill; a 15-minute walk beyond that is the Pantheon. I like to tour these sights in one great day, starting at the Colosseum and ending at the Pantheon.

Ancient Rome

The core of ancient Rome, where the grandest monuments were built, is between the Colosseum and Capitoline Hill. Among the ancient forums, a few modern sights have popped up.

The Colosseum and Nearby

▲▲▲Colosseum (Colosseo)

Built when the Roman Empire was at its peak in A.D. 80, the Colosseum represents Rome at its grandest. The Flavian Amphitheater (the Colosseum's real name) was an arena for gladiator contests and public spectacles. When killing became a spectator sport, the Romans wanted to share the fun with as many people as possible, so they stuck two semicircular theaters together to create a freestanding amphitheater. The outside (where slender cypress trees stand today) was decorated with a 100-foot-tall bronze statue of Nero that gleamed in the sunlight. In a later age, the colossal structure was nicknamed a "coloss-eum," the wonder of its age. It could accommodate 50,000 roaring fans (100,000 thumbs).

This 2,000-year-old building is the classic example of Roman engineering. The Romans pioneered the use of concrete and the rounded arch, which enabled them to build on this tremendous scale. The exterior is a skeleton of 3.5 million cubic feet of travertine stone. (Each of the pillars flanking the ground-level arches

ROME

Rome at a Glance

▲▲▲**Colosseum** Huge stadium where gladiators fought. **Hours:** Daily 8:30 until one hour before sunset: April-Sept until 19:15, Oct until 18:30, off-season closes as early as 16:30. See page 851.

▲▲▲**Roman Forum** Ancient Rome's main square, with ruins and grand arches. **Hours:** Same hours as Colosseum. See page 860.

▲▲▲**Pantheon** The defining domed temple. **Hours:** Mon-Sat 8:30-19:30, Sun 9:00-18:00, holidays 9:00-13:00, closed for Mass Sat at 17:00 and Sun at 10:30. See page 869.

▲▲▲**St**. **Peter's Basilica** Most impressive church on earth, with Michelangelo's *Pietà* and dome. **Hours:** Church—daily April-Sept 7:00-19:00, Oct-March 7:00-18:00, often closed Wed mornings; dome—daily April-Sept 8:00-18:00, Oct-March 8:00-16:45. See page 872.

▲▲▲**Vatican Museum** Four miles of the finest art of Western civilization, culminating in Michelangelo's glorious Sistine Chapel. **Hours:** Mon-Sat 9:00-18:00. Closed on religious holidays and Sun, except last Sun of the month (open 9:00-14:00). May be open some Fri nights by online reservation only. Hours are subject to change. See page 877.

▲▲▲**Borghese Gallery** Bernini sculptures and paintings by Caravaggio, Raphael, and Titian in a Baroque palazzo. Reservations mandatory. **Hours:** Tue-Sun 9:00-19:00, closed Mon. See page 887.

▲▲▲**National Museum of Rome** Greatest collection of Roman sculpture anywhere. **Hours:** Tue-Sun 9:00-19:45, closed Mon. See page 895.

▲▲**Palatine Hill** Ruins of emperors' palaces, Circus Maximus view, and museum. **Hours:** Same as Colosseum. See page 860,

▲▲**Capitoline Museums** Ancient statues, mosaics, and expansive view of Forum. **Hours:** Tue-Sun 9:00-20:00, closed Mon. See page 865.

▲▲**Ara Pacis** Shrine marking the beginning of Rome's Golden Age. **Hours:** Tue-Sun 9:00-19:00, closed Mon. See page 893.

▲▲**Dolce Vita Stroll** Evening *passeggiata*, where Romans strut their stuff. **Hours:** Roughly Mon-Sat 17:00-19:00 and Sun afternoons. See page 842.

▲▲**Catacombs** Underground tombs, mainly Christian, some outside the city. **Hours:** Generally open 10:00-12:00 & 14:00-17:00. See pages 892 and 907.

▲**Arch of Constantine** Honors the emperor who legalized Christianity. **Hours:** Always viewable. See page 858.

▲**St. Peter-in-Chains Church** with Michelangelo's *Moses*. **Hours:** Daily 8:00-12:30 & 15:00-19:00, until 18:00 in winter. See page 859.

▲**Trajan's Column, Market, and Museum of the Imperial Forums** Tall column with narrative relief, and museum with entry to Trajan's Market. **Hours:** Column always viewable; museum open Tue-Sun 9:00-19:00, closed Mon. See page 862.

▲ **Piazza del Campidoglio** Square atop Capitoline Hill, designed by Michelangelo, with a museum, grand stairway, and Forum overlooks. **Hours:** Always open. See page 863.

▲**Victor Emmanuel Monument** Gigantic edifice celebrating Italian unity, with Rome from the Sky elevator ride up to 360-degree city view. **Hours:** Monument open daily 9:30-18:30; elevator open Mon-Thu 9:30-18:30, Fri-Sun 9:30-19:30. See page 867.

▲**Trevi Fountain** Baroque hot spot into which tourists throw coins to ensure a return trip to Rome. **Hours:** Always flowing. See page 871.

▲**Castel Sant'Angelo** Hadrian's Tomb turned castle, prison, papal refuge, now museum. **Hours:** Tue-Sun 9:00-19:30, closed Mon. See page 885.

▲**Capuchin Crypt** Decorated with the bones of 4,000 Franciscan friars. **Hours:** Daily 9:00-19:00. See page 890.

▲**Baths of Diocletian** Once ancient Rome's immense public baths, now a Michelangelo church. **Hours:** Mon-Sat 7:00-18:30, Sun 7:00-19:30, closed to sightseers during Mass. See page 896.

▲**Santa Maria della Vittoria** Church with Bernini's swooning *St. Teresa in Ecstasy*. **Hours:** Mon-Sat 8:30-12:00 & 15:30-18:00, Sun 15:30-18:00. See page 897.

ROME

weighs five tons.) It took 200 ox-drawn wagons shuttling back and forth every day for four years just to bring the stone here from Tivoli. The Romans stacked stone blocks (without mortar) into the shape of an arch, supported temporarily by wooden scaffolding. Finally, they wedged a keystone into the top of the arch—it not only kept the arch from falling, it could bear even more weight above. Iron pegs held the larger stones together—notice the small holes that pockmark the sides.

While the essential structure of the Colosseum is Roman, the four-story facade is decorated with mostly Greek columns—Doric-like Tuscan columns on the ground level, Ionic on the second story, Corinthian on the next level, and at the top, half-columns with a mix of all three. Originally, copies of Greek statues stood in the arches of the middle two stories, giving a veneer of sophistication to this arena of death.

This was where ancient Romans—whose taste for violence was the equal of modern America's—enjoyed their *Dirty Harry*s and *Terminator*s. Gladiators, criminals, and wild animals fought to the death in every conceivable scenario. The bit of reconstructed Colosseum floor gives you an accurate sense of the original floor and the subterranean warren where animals were held, then lifted up in elevators. Released at floor level, animals would pop out from behind blinds into the arena—the gladiator didn't know where, when, or by what he'd be attacked.

Only a third of the original Colosseum remains. Earthquakes destroyed some of it, but most was carted off as easy pre-cut stones for other buildings during the Middle Ages and Renaissance.

Cost and Hours: €12 combo-ticket includes Roman Forum and Palatine Hill, open daily 8:30 until one hour before sunset, last entry one hour before closing—for specifics, see "Hours" on page 834, audioguide-€5.50, Metro: Colosseo, tel. 06-3996-7700, http://archeoroma.beniculturali.it/en.

Avoiding Lines: Crowds tend to be thinner (and lines shorter) in the afternoon (especially after 15:00 in summer); this is also true at the Forum.

You can save lots of time by buying your combo-ticket in advance, having the Roma Pass, booking a guided tour, or renting an audioguide or videoguide. Here are the options:

1. Buy your combo-ticket (or Roma Pass) at the less-crowded Palatine Hill entrance, 150 yards away on Via di San Gregorio (facing the Forum, with Colosseum at your back, go left down the street). You can also buy a Roma Pass at the tobacco shop in the Colosseo Metro station, the I Fori di Roma visitors center on Via dei Fori Imperiali (see page 834), or other sights around town. It should cost the same no matter where you buy it. (Avoid buying your ticket or Roma Pass at the Forum, which also tends to have lines.)

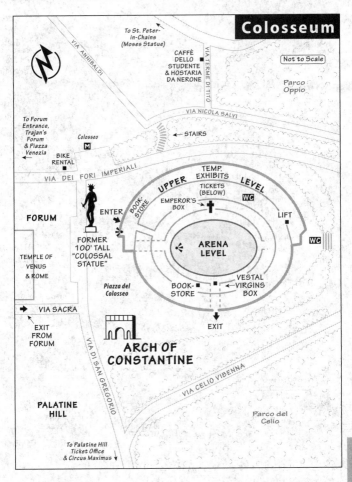

Colosseum

Not to Scale

To St. Peter-
in-Chains
(Moses Statue)

CAFFÈ
DELLO
STUDENTE
& HOSTARIA
DA NERONE

Parco
Oppio

VIA ANNIBALDI

VIA TERME DI TITO

VIA NICOLA SALVI

To Forum
Entrance,
Trajan's
Forum
& Piazza
Venezia

Colosseo
M

← STAIRS

BIKE
RENTAL

VIA DEI FORI IMPERIALI

TEMP.
EXHIBITS

UPPER LEVEL

TICKETS
(BELOW)

WC

EMPEROR'S
BOX

BOOK-
STORE

ENTER

FORUM

FORMER
100' TALL
"COLOSSAL
STATUE"

LIFT

ARENA
LEVEL

WC

TEMPLE OF
VENUS
& ROME

Piazza del
Colosseo

BOOK-
STORE

VESTAL
VIRGINS
BOX

VIA SACRA

EXIT
FROM
FORUM

EXIT

VIA DI SAN GREGORIO

ARCH OF
CONSTANTINE

VIA CELIO VIBENNA

PALATINE
HILL

Parco del
Celio

To Palatine Hill
Ticket Office
& Circus Maximus ↓

2. Buy a combo-ticket online at www.ticketclic.it (€1.50 booking fee, not changeable). The "free tickets" you'll see listed are valid only for EU citizens with ID.

3. Pay to join an official guided tour, or rent an audioguide or videoguide (see "Tours," page 858). This lets you march right up to the Colosseum's guided visits *(Visite Guidate)* desk, thus bypassing the ticket lines. Even if you don't use the device or accompany the guided tour, the extra cost might be worth it just to skip the ticket line.

4. Hire a private walking-tour guide. Guides of varying quality linger outside the Colosseum, offering tours that allow you to skip the line. Be aware that these private guides may try to mislead you into thinking the Colosseum lines are longer than they really are. For more on this option, see "Tours" on page 858.

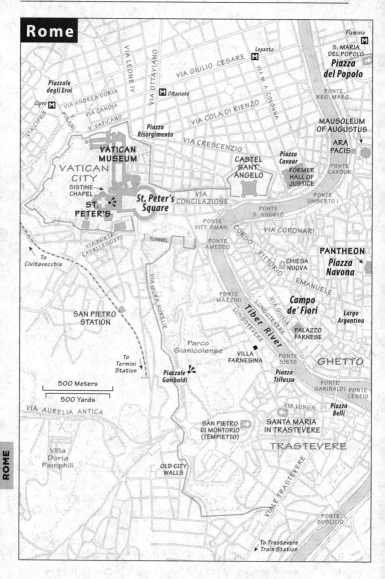

Rome

Flaminio
S. MARIA DEL POPOLO
Piazza del Popolo
Lepanto
VIA GIULIO CESARE
PONTE REG. MARG.
Piazzale degli Eroi
VIA LEONE IV
VIA OTTAVIANO
VIA A. M. A. COLONNA
Cipro
VIA ANDREA DORIA
Ottaviano
VIA COLA DI RIENZO
MAUSOLEUM OF AUGUSTUS
VIA CIPRO
VIA GANDIA
V. VATICANO
Piazza Risorgimento
VIA CRESCENZIO
Piazza Cavour
ARA PACIS
VIA PISANI
VATICAN MUSEUM
CASTEL SANT' ANGELO
FORMER HALL OF JUSTICE
PONTE CAVOUR
VATICAN CITY
SISTINE CHAPEL
ST. PETER'S
St. Peter's Square
VIA CONCILAZIONE
PONTE UMBERTO I
PONTE S. ANGELO
VIA CORONARI
PANTHEON
PONTE VITT. EMAN.
CORSO VITTORIO
Piazza Navona
To Civitavecchia
VIA PORTA CAVALLEGGERI
TUNNEL
PONTE AMEDEO
CHIESA NUOVA
EMANUELE
Campo de' Fiori
SAN PIETRO STATION
VIA MURA AURELIE
PONTE MAZZINI
VIA GIULIA
LUNGOTEVERE
Largo Argentina
PALAZZO FARNESE
Parco Gianicolense
VILLA FARNESINA
PONTE SISTO
GHETTO
To Termini Station
Piazzale Garibaldi
Piazza Trilussa
PONTE GARIBALDI
PONTE CESTIO
500 Meters
500 Yards
Piazza Belli
VIA AURELIA ANTICA
VIA LUNGA
SAN PIETRO DI MONTORIO (TEMPIETTO)
SANTA MARIA IN TRASTEVERE
Villa Doria Pamphili
OLD CITY WALLS
TRASTEVERE
VIALE TRASTEVERE
PONTE SUBLICIO
To Trastevere Train Station

ROME

Restoration: The arena is being cleaned from top to bottom, given permanent lighting, and outfitted with new shops and services. Long-range plans include building a free-standing ticket booth outside the Colosseum. These ongoing renovations, scheduled to last several years, may affect your visit.

Warning: Beware of the **greedy gladiators.** For a fee, the incredibly crude, modern-day gladiators snuff out their cigarettes and pose for photos. They're officially banned from panhandling in

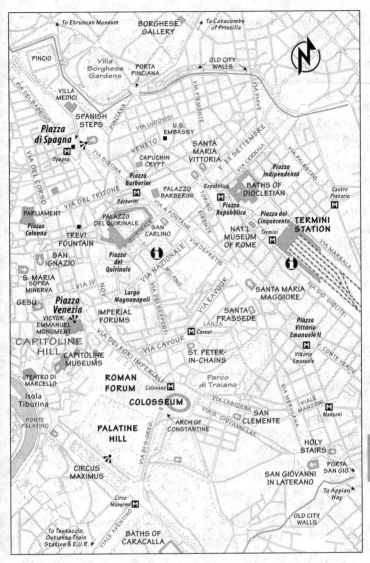

this area, but you may still see them, hoping to intimidate easy-to-swindle tourists into paying too much money for a photo op. (If you go for it, €4-5 for one photo usually keeps them appeased.) Also, look out for **pickpockets** and con artists in this prime tourist spot.

Getting There: The Colosseo Metro stop on line B is just across the street from the monument. Bus #60 is handy for hotels near Via Firenze and Via Nazionale. Bus #87 links Largo Argentina with the Colosseum.

Getting In: If you need to buy a ticket or sign up for a guided tour, follow the signs for the appropriate line. With a combo-ticket or Roma Pass in hand, look for signs for *ticket holders* or *Roma Pass*, allowing you to bypass the long lines.

Tours: A dry but fact-filled **audioguide** is available just past the turnstiles (€5.50/2 hours). A handheld **videoguide** senses where you are in the site and plays related video clips (€6).

Official **guided tours** in English depart nearly hourly between 10:00 and 17:00, and last 45-60 minutes (€5 plus Colosseum ticket, purchase inside the Colosseum near the ticket booth marked *Visite Guidate;* if you're lost, ask a guard to direct you to the desk).

Private guides stand outside the Colosseum, looking for business (€25-30/2-hour tour of the Colosseum, Palatine Hill, and Forum). If booking a private guide, make sure that your tour will start right away and that the ticket you receive covers all three sights: the Colosseum, Forum, and Palatine Hill.

You can also download a free Rick Steves **audio tour** of the Colosseum; see page 7.

A 1.5-hour **behind-the-scenes tour** takes you through restricted areas, including underground passageways and the third floor, which are off-limits to regular Colosseum visitors. It's generally offered April-Nov only, and closes during and after bad weather, as the underground passageways flood easily. While interesting, this tour certainly isn't essential to appreciating the Colosseum. It's operated by Pierreci, a private company; to book, contact them at least a day in advance (€8 plus Colosseum ticket, www.pierreci.it, call 06-3996-7700 during business hours: Mon-Fri 9:00-18:00, Sat 9:00-14:00, closed Sun, no same-day reservations). After dialing, wait for English instructions on how to reach a live operator, then reserve a time and pre-pay with a credit card. Without a reservation, you can try to join the next available tour (may be in Italian): Once you have your Colosseum entrance ticket and are at the turnstiles, look for the tour meeting point just past the ticket desk; pay the guide directly.

With Limited Time: With a single glance, you can basically see the entire interior. It's not necessary to go upstairs or circle the place.

▲Arch of Constantine

If you are a Christian, were raised a Christian, or simply belong to a so-called "Christian nation," ponder this arch. It marks one of the great turning points in history: the military coup that made Christianity mainstream. In A.D. 312, Emperor Constantine defeated his rival Maxentius in the crucial Battle of the Milvian Bridge. The night before, he had seen a vision of a cross in the sky. Constantine—whose mother and sister had already become Christians—became sole emperor and legalized Christianity. With this one battle, a once-obscure Jewish sect with a handful of followers became the state religion of the entire Western world. In A.D. 300, you could be killed for being a Christian; a century later, you could be killed for not being one. Church enrollment boomed.

The restored arch is like an ancient museum. It's decorated entirely with recycled carvings originally made for other buildings. By covering it with exquisite carvings of high Roman art—works that glorified previous emperors—Constantine put himself in their league. Hadrian is featured in the round reliefs, with Marcus Aurelius in the square reliefs higher up. The big statues on top are of Trajan and Augustus. Originally, Augustus drove a chariot similar to the one topping the modern Victor Emmanuel II Monument. Fourth-century Rome may have been in decline, but Constantine clung to its glorious past.

▲St. Peter-in-Chains Church (San Pietro in Vincoli)

Built in the fifth century to house the chains that held St. Peter, this church is most famous for its Michelangelo statue. Check out the much-venerated chains under the high altar, then focus on mighty Moses. (Note that this isn't the famous St. Peter's Basilica, which is at Vatican City.)

Pope Julius II commissioned Michelangelo to build a massive tomb, with 48 huge statues, topped with a grand statue of this egomaniacal pope. The pope had planned to have his tomb placed in the center of St. Peter's Basilica. When Julius died, the work had barely been started, and no one had the money or necessary commitment to Julius to finish the project.

In 1542, some of the remnants of the tomb project were brought to St. Peter-in-Chains and pieced together by Michelangelo's assistants. Some of the best statues ended up elsewhere, such as the *Prisoners* in Florence and the *Slaves* in the Louvre. *Moses* and the Louvre's *Slaves* are the only statues Michelangelo personally completed for the project. Flanking *Moses* are the Old Testament sister-wives of Jacob, Leah (to our right) and Rachel, both begun by Michelangelo but probably finished by pupils.

This powerful statue of Moses—mature Michelangelo—is worth studying. The artist worked on it in fits and starts for 30 years. Moses has received the Ten Commandments. As he holds the stone tablets, his eyes show a man determined to stop his tribe from worshipping the golden calf and idols...a man determined to win salvation for the people of Israel. Why the horns? Centuries ago, the Hebrew word for "rays" was mistranslated as "horns."

Cost and Hours: Free, daily April-Sept 8:00-12:30 & 15:00-19:00, Oct-March 8:00-12:30 & 15:00-18:00, modest dress required; the church is a 10-minute uphill walk from the Colosseum, or a shorter, simpler walk from the Cavour Metro stop.

ROME

The Roman Forum and Nearby

▲▲▲Roman Forum (Foro Romano)

This is ancient Rome's birthplace and civic center, and the common ground between Rome's famous seven hills. As just about anything important that happened in ancient Rome happened here, it's arguably the most important piece of real estate in Western civilization. While only a few fragments of that glorious past remain, history-seekers find plenty to ignite their imaginations amid the half-broken columns and arches.

Cost and Hours: €12 combo-ticket includes Colosseum and Palatine Hill—see page 821, open daily 8:30 until one hour before sunset, last entry one hour before closing, audioguide-€5, Metro: Colosseo, tel. 06-3996-7700, http://archeoroma.beniculturali.it/en.

See my Roman Forum Tour, on page 834.

▲▲Palatine Hill (Monte Palatino)

The hill overlooking the Forum is jam-packed with history—"the huts of Romulus," the huge Imperial Palace, a view of the Circus Maximus—but there's only the barest skeleton of rubble left to tell the story.

We get our word "palace" from this hill, where the emperors chose to live. The Palatine Hill was once so filled with palaces that later emperors had to build out. (Looking up at it from the Forum, you see the substructure that supported these long-gone palaces.)

The Palatine museum contains statues and frescoes that help you imagine the luxury of the imperial Palatine. From the pleasant garden, you'll get an overview of the Forum. On the far side, look down into an emperor's private stadium and then beyond at the grassy Circus Maximus, once a chariot course. Imagine the cheers, jeers, and furious betting.

While many tourists consider the Palatine Hill just extra credit after the Forum, it offers an insight into the greatness of Rome. (And, if you're visiting the Colosseum or Forum, you've got a ticket whether you like it or not.)

Cost and Hours: €12 combo-ticket covers both the Roman Forum/Palatine Hill (grouped as one sight for the purposes of the ticket) and the Colosseum. The combo-ticket is valid two consecutive days, but once your ticket is scanned for either the Forum/Palatine Hill or the Colosseum, you can't re-enter that sight (even the next day)—see page 821; open same hours as Forum and Colosseum.

The closest Metro stop is Colosseo. The entrance is on Via di San Gregorio (facing the Forum with the Colosseum at your back, it's down the street to your left). You can also enter the Palatine from within the Roman Forum—just climb the hill from the Arch of Titus.

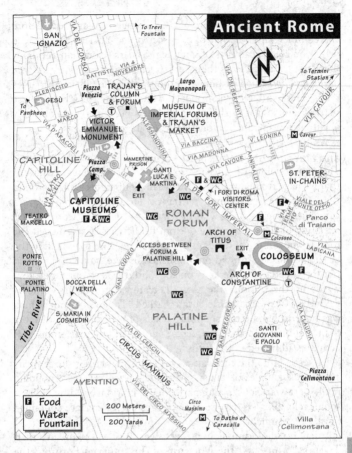

Ancient Rome

San Ignazio • To Trevi Fountain • To Termini Station • To Pantheon • Piazza Venezia • Trajan's Column & Forum • Largo Magnanapoli • Museum of Imperial Forums & Trajan's Market • Victor Emmanuel Monument • Capitoline Hill • Piazza Camp. • Mamertine Prison • Santi Luca e Martina • I Fori di Roma Visitors Center • St. Peter-in-Chains • Capitoline Museums • Roman Forum • Teatro Marcello • Ponte Rotto • Bocca della Verità • Access Between Forum & Palatine Hill • Arch of Titus • Colosseum • Ponte Palatino • S. Maria in Cosmedin • Arch of Constantine • Tiber River • Palatine Hill • Santi Giovanni e Paolo • Piazza Celimontana • Aventino • Circus Maximus • Circo Massimo • To Baths of Caracalla • Villa Celimontana • Parco di Traiano

🅵 Food
⦿ Water Fountain

200 Meters
200 Yards

Audioguides cost €5/2 hours (€7 version includes Roman Forum and lasts 3 hours, must leave ID). Guided tours in English might be available (inquire at the ticket booth). WCs are at the ticket office when you enter, up the hill near the stadium, at the museum in the center of the site, and hiding among the orange trees in the Farnese Gardens.

Mamertine Prison

This 2,500-year-old cistern-like prison is where, according to Christian tradition, the Romans imprisoned Saints Peter and Paul. Though it was long a charming and historic sight, its artifacts have been removed, and today it's run by a commercial tour-bus company charging €10 for a cheesy "multimedia" walk-through. Don't go in. Instead, stand outside and imagine how this dank cistern once housed prisoners of the emperor. Amid fat rats and rotting corpses, unfortunate humans awaited slow deaths. It's said that a miraculous fountain sprang up inside so Peter could convert and baptize his jailers, who were also subsequently martyred. Before the commercial ruination of this sacred and ancient site, on the walls you could read lists of notable prisoners (Christian and non-Christian) and the ways they were executed: *strangolati, decapitato, morto per fame* (died of hunger). The sign by the Christian names read, "Here suffered, victorious for the triumph of Christ, these martyr saints." Today this sight itself has been martyred by a city apparently desperate to monetize its heritage.

▲Trajan's Column, Market, and Museum of the Imperial Forums

This grand column is the best example of "continuous narration" that we have from antiquity. More than 2,500 figures spiral around the 140-foot-high column, telling of Trajan's victorious Dacian campaign (circa A.D. 103, in present-day Romania), from the assembling of the army at the bottom to the victory sacrifice at the top. At one point, the ashes of Trajan and his wife were held in the base, and the sun glinted off a polished bronze statue of Trajan at the top. (Today, St. Peter is on top.) Study the propaganda that winds up the column like a scroll, trumpeting Trajan's wonderful military exploits. This column marked "Trajan's Forum," which was built to handle the shopping needs of a wealthy city of more than a million people. Commercial, political, religious, and social activities all mixed in the forum.

Nestled into the cutaway curve of Quirinal Hill is the semicircular brick complex of Trajan's Market. It was likely part shopping mall, part warehouse, and part administration building. Or, as some archaeologists have recently suggested, it may have contained mostly government offices.

Paying the admission fee gets you inside Trajan's Market, Trajan's Forum, and the **Museum of the Imperial Forums**. The museum features discoveries from the forums of emperors Julius Caesar, Augustus, Nerva, and Trajan, with fragments of statues and a slideshow that reconstructs how the forum looked in each emperor's time.

Cost and Hours: Museum—€11, includes entry to the market ruins—also viewable for free from Via dei Fori Imperiali, Tue-Sun 9:00-19:00, closed Mon, last entry one hour before closing, audioguide-€3.50, entrance is uphill from the column on Via IV Novembre 94, tel. 06-0608, www.mercatiditraiano.it.

Getting There: Trajan's Column is just a few steps off Piazza Venezia (a hub for major bus routes #40, #64, #85, and #87) on Via dei Fori Imperiali, across the street from the Victor Emmanuel Monument. Trajan's Market can be entered only through the Museum of the Imperial Forums at Via IV Novembre 94 (up the staircase from Trajan's Column). Trajan's Forum stretches southeast of the column toward the Colosseo Metro stop and the Colosseum itself.

Bocca della Verità

The legendary "Mouth of Truth" at the Church of Santa Maria in Cosmedin draws a playful crowd. Stick your hand in the mouth of the gaping stone face in the porch wall. As the legend goes (and was popularized by the 1953 film *Roman Holiday*, starring Gregory Peck and Audrey Hepburn), if you're a liar, your hand will be gobbled up. The mouth is only accessible when the church gate is open, but it's always (partially) visible through the gate, even when closed. If the church itself is open, step inside to see one of the few unaltered medieval church interiors in Rome. Notice the mismatched ancient columns and beautiful *cosmatesque* floor—a centuries-old example of recycling.

Cost and Hours: €0.50, daily 9:30-17:50, closes earlier off-season, Piazza Bocca della Verità, near the north end of Circus Maximus.

Capitoline Hill

Of Rome's famous seven hills, this is the smallest, tallest, and most famous—home of the ancient Temple of Jupiter and the center of city government for 2,500 years. There are several ways to get to the top of Capitoline Hill. If you're coming from the north (from Piazza Venezia), take Michelangelo's impressive stairway to the right of the big, white Victor Emmanuel Monument. Coming from the southeast (the Forum), take the steep staircase near the Arch of Septimius Severus. From near Trajan's Forum along Via dei Fori Imperiali, take the winding road. All three converge at the top, in the square called Campidoglio (kahm-pee-DOHL-yoh).

▲Piazza del Campidoglio (Capitoline Hill Square)

This square atop the hill, once the religious and political center of ancient Rome, is still the home of the city's government. In the 1530s, the pope called on Michelangelo to re-establish this square as a grand center. Michelangelo placed the ancient equestrian statue of Marcus Aurelius as the square's focal point. Effective. (The original statue is now in the adjacent museum.) The twin buildings on either side are the Capitoline Museums. Behind the replica of the statue is the mayoral palace (Palazzo Senatorio).

Michelangelo intended that people approach the square from his grand stairway off Piazza Venezia. From the top of the stairway, you see the new Renaissance face of Rome, with its back to the Forum. Michelangelo gave the buildings the "giant order"—huge pilasters make the existing two-story buildings feel one-storied and more harmonious with the new square. Notice how the statues atop these buildings welcome you and then draw you in.

The terraces just downhill (past either side of the mayor's palace) offer grand views of the Forum. To the left of the mayor's palace is a copy of the famous She-Wolf statue on a column. Farther

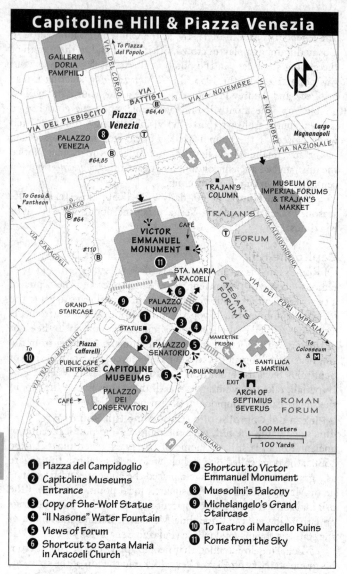

Capitoline Hill & Piazza Venezia

1. Piazza del Campidoglio
2. Capitoline Museums Entrance
3. Copy of She-Wolf Statue
4. "Il Nasone" Water Fountain
5. Views of Forum
6. Shortcut to Santa Maria in Aracoeli Church
7. Shortcut to Victor Emmanuel Monument
8. Mussolini's Balcony
9. Michelangelo's Grand Staircase
10. To Teatro di Marcello Ruins
11. Rome from the Sky

down is *il nasone* ("the big nose"), a refreshing water fountain. Block the spout with your fingers, and water spurts up for drinking. Romans joke that a cheap Roman boy takes his date out for a drink at *il nasone*. Near the She-Wolf statue is the staircase leading to a shortcut to the Victor Emmanuel Monument (see sidebar).

Shortcut to the Victor Emmanuel Monument and Aracoeli Church

A clever shortcut lets you go directly from Piazza del Campidoglio, the square atop Capitoline Hill, to Santa Maria in Aracoeli Church and an upper level of the Victor Emmanuel Monument, avoiding long flights of stairs. Facing the square's equestrian statue, head to the left, climbing the wide set of stairs near the She-Wolf statue. Midway up the stairs (at the column), turn left to reach the back entrance to the Aracoeli Church. To reach the Victor Emmanuel Monument, pass the column and continue to the top of the steps, pass through the iron gate, and enter the small unmarked door at #13 on the right. You'll soon emerge on a café terrace that leads to the monument and the Rome from the Sky elevator.

▲▲Capitoline Museums (Musei Capitolini)

Some of ancient Rome's most famous statues and art are housed in the two palaces (Palazzo dei Conservatori and Palazzo Nuovo) that flank the equestrian statue in Piazza del Campidoglio. They're connected by an underground passage that leads to the vacant Tabularium and panoramic views of the Roman Forum.

Cost and Hours: €12, €14 combo-ticket includes Montemartini Museum, Tue-Sun 9:00-20:00, closed Mon, last entry one hour before closing, audioguide-€5, tel. 06-8205-9127 or 06-0608, www.museicapitolini.org.

Visiting the Museums: The museum's layout—with two different buildings connected by an underground passage—can be confusing, but you're likely to happen upon all of the highlights. You'll enter at the Palazzo dei Conservatori (on your right as you face the equestrian statue), cross underneath the square (beneath the Palazzo Senatorio, the mayoral palace, not open to public), and exit from the Palazzo Nuovo (on your left).

The **Palazzo dei Conservatori** claims to be one of the world's oldest museums, founded in 1471 when a pope gave ancient statues to the citizens of Rome. In the courtyard, enjoy the massive chunks of Constantine: his head, hand, and foot. When intact, this giant held the place of honor in the Basilica of Constantine in the Forum.

The museum is worthwhile, with lavish rooms and several great statues, including the *Boy Extracting a Thorn*. In one grand room, you'll see the 13th-century *Capitoline She-Wolf* (the little statues of Romulus and Remus were added in the Renaissance), the enchanting *Commodus as Hercules,* and a marvelous statue of Marcus Aurelius (the father of Commodus) on a horse. The great-

ROME

est surviving equestrian statue of antiquity, this was the original centerpiece of the square (where a copy stands today).

Christians in the Dark Ages thought that the statue's hand was raised in blessing, which probably led to their misidentifying him as Constantine, the first Christian emperor. While most pagan statues were destroyed by Christians, "Constantine" was spared.

The second-floor café, **Caffè Capitolino,** has a splendid patio offering city views. It's lovely at sunset (public entrance for non-museum-goers off Piazza Caffarelli and through door #4).

Go downstairs to the **Tabularium.** Built in the first century B.C., these sturdy vacant rooms once held the archives of ancient Rome. The word Tabularium comes from "tablet," on which Romans wrote their laws. You won't see any tablets, but you will see a stunning head-on view of the Forum from the windows.

Leave the Tabularium and enter the **Palazzo Nuovo,** which houses mostly portrait busts of forgotten emperors. But it also has two must-see statues: the *Dying Gaul* and the *Capitoline Venus* (both on the first floor up).

Santa Maria in Aracoeli Church

The church atop Capitoline Hill is old and dear to the hearts of Romans. It stands on the site where Emperor Augustus (supposedly) had a premonition of the coming of Mary and Christ standing on an "altar in the sky" *(ara coeli).* The church is Rome in a nutshell, where you can time-travel across 2,000 years by standing in one spot.

Cost and Hours: Free, daily April-Oct 9:00-12:30 & 15:00-18:30, Nov-March 9:00-12:30 & 14:30-17:30. While dedicated pilgrims climb up the long, steep staircase from street level (the right side of Victor Emmanuel Monument, as you face it), savvy sightseers prefer to enter through the shortcut atop Capitoline Hill (see sidebar).

Piazza Venezia

This vast square, dominated by the big, white Victor Emmanuel Monument, is a major transportation hub and the focal point of modern Rome. (The square has been dug up for years—Metro line C is under construction, and when anything of archaeological importance is uncovered, progress is interrupted, hence the canopied site on the square today.) With your back to the monument (you'll get the best views from the terrace by the guards and eternal flame), look down Via del Corso, the city's axis, surrounded by Rome's classiest shopping district. In the 1930s, Benito Mussolini whipped up Italy's nationalistic fervor from a balcony above the square (it's the less-grand balcony on the left). Fascist masses filled the square screaming, "Four more years!"—or something like that. Mussolini created the boulevard Via dei Fori Imperiali (to your right) to open up views of the Colosseum in the distance to impress his visiting friend Adolf

Hitler. Mussolini lied to his people, mixing fear and patriotism to push his country to the right and embroil the Italians in expensive and regrettable wars. In 1945, they shot Mussolini and hung him from a meat hook in Milan. (Former Prime Minister Silvio Berlusconi's headquarters are still located—thought-provokingly—just behind Mussolini's. That explains all the security on Via del Plebiscito.)

With your back still to the monument, circle around the left side, and look down into the ditch on your left to see the ruins of an ancient apartment building from the first century A.D.; part of it was transformed into a tiny church (faded frescoes and bell tower). Rome was built in layers—almost everywhere you go, there's an earlier version beneath your feet. (The hop-on, hop-off Trambus 110 stops just across the busy intersection from here.)

Continuing on, you reach two staircases leading up Capitoline Hill. One is Michelangelo's grand staircase up to the Campidoglio. The longer of the two leads to the Santa Maria in Aracoeli Church, a good example of the earliest style of Christian churches (described earlier). The contrast between this climb-on-your-knees ramp to God's house and Michelangelo's elegant stairs illustrates the changes Renaissance humanism brought civilization.

From the bottom of Michelangelo's stairs, look right several blocks down the street to see a condominium actually built upon the surviving ancient pillars and arches of Teatro di Marcello.

▲Victor Emmanuel Monument

This oversize monument to Italy's first king, built to celebrate the 50th anniversary of the country's unification in 1861, was part of Italy's push to overcome the new country's strong regionalism and create a national identity. At the base of this statue, Italy's Tomb of the Unknown Soldier—flanked by Italian flags and armed guards—is watched over by the goddess Roma (with the gold mosaic background).

The scale of the monument is over-the-top: 200 feet high, 500 feet wide. The 43-foot-long statue of the king on the horse is one of the biggest equestrian statues in the world. The king's moustache forms an arc five feet long, and a person could sit within the horse's hoof. With its gleaming white sheen (from a recent scrubbing) and enormous scale, the monument provides a vivid sense of what Ancient Rome looked like at its peak—imagine the Forum filled with shiny, grandiose buildings like this one.

The "Vittoriano" (as locals call it) is open and free to the public. You can simply climb the front stairs, or go inside from one of several entrances: midway up the monument through doorways flanking the central statue, on either side at street level, and at the base of the colonnade (two-thirds of the way up, near the shortcut from Capitoline Hill). The little-visited **Museum of the Risorgimento** fills several floors with displays (free, well-described in English) on

ROME

the movement and war that led to the unification of Italy in 1870. A section on the lower east side hosts temporary exhibits of minor works by major artists (free to enter museum, exhibits around €10, tel. 06-322-5380, www.comunicareorganizzando.it/home.asp). A café is at the base of the top colonnade, on the monument's east side.

You can climb the stairs to the midway point for a decent view, keep climbing to the base of the colonnade for a better view, or, for the best view, ride the **Rome from the Sky** elevator, which zips you from the top of the stair climb (at the back of the monument) to the rooftop for the grandest, 360-degree view of the center of Rome—even better than from the top of St. Peter's dome. Helpful panoramic diagrams describe the skyline, with powerful binoculars available for zooming in on particular sights. It's best in late afternoon, when it's beginning to cool off and Rome glows.

Cost and Hours: Monument—Free, daily 9:30-18:30, a few WCs scattered throughout, tel. 06-679-3598. Elevator—€7, Mon-Thu 9:30-18:30, Fri-Sun 9:30-19:30, ticket office closes 45 minutes earlier, WC at entrance, tel. 06-6920-2049; follow *ascensori panoramici* signs inside the Victor Emmanuel Monument or take the shortcut from Capitoline Hill (no elevator access from street level).

Pantheon Neighborhood

Besides being home to ancient sights and historic churches, this neighborhood gives Rome its urban-village feel. Wander narrow streets, sample the many shops and eateries, and gather with the locals in squares marked by bubbling fountains. Exploring is especially good in the evening, when the restaurants bustle and streets are jammed with foot traffic. For a self-guided walk of this neighborhood, from Campo de' Fiori to the Trevi Fountain, see my "Heart of Rome Walk" on page 844.

Getting There: To reach the Pantheon neighborhood, you can walk (it's a 15-minute walk from Capitoline Hill), take a taxi, or catch a bus. Buses stop at a chaotic square called Largo Argentina, a few blocks south of the Pantheon—from here you can walk north on either Via dei Cestari or Via di Torre Argentina to the Pantheon. Buses #40 and #64 carry tourists and pickpockets frequently between the Termini train station and Vatican City (#492 serves the same areas via a different route). Bus #87 connects to the Colosseum. The *elettrico* minibus #116 runs between Campo de' Fiori and Piazza Barberini via the Pantheon. The most dramatic approach is on foot coming from Piazza Navona along Via Giustiniani, which spills directly into Piazza della Rotonda, offering the classic Pantheon view.

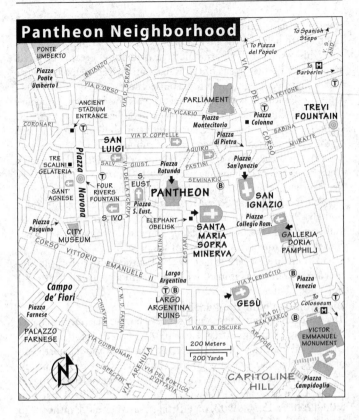

Pantheon Neighborhood

To Spanish Steps

PONTE UMBERTO

Piazza Ponte Umberto I

BRIANZO

VIA D. SCROFA

VIA D'ORSO

To Piazza del Popolo

To Barberini

ANCIENT STADIUM ENTRANCE

PARLIAMENT

CORONARI

UFF. VICARIO

Piazza Montecitorio

Piazza Colonna

TREVI FOUNTAIN

VIA D. COPPELLE

AQUIRO

Piazza di Pietra

SAN LUIGI

SALV.

GIUST.

Piazza Rotunda

PASTINI

Piazza San Ignazio

TRE SCALINI GELATERIA

Piazza Navona

VIA DELLA SCROFA

S. EUST.

SEMINARIO

SANT' AGNESE

FOUR RIVERS FOUNTAIN

PANTHEON

SAN IGNAZIO

Piazza S. Eust.

Piazza Pasquino

S. IVO

ELEPHANT OBELISK

Piazza Collegio Rom.

GALLERIA DORIA PAMPHILJ

CITY MUSEUM

CORSO

VITTORIO

ARGENTINA

CESTARI

SANTA MARIA SOPRA MINERVA

EMANUELE II

V. M. D. FARINA

Largo Argentina

VIA PLEBISCITO

Piazza Venezia

To Colosseum & M

Campo de' Fiori

Piazza Farnese

CHIAVARI

LARGO ARGENTINA RUINS

GESÙ

VIA DI SAN MARCO

PALAZZO FARNESE

VIA GIUBBONARI

VIA D. B. OSCURE

ARACOELI

200 Meters

200 Yards

VICTOR EMMANUEL MONUMENT

SPECCHI

VIA ARENULA

VIA DEL PORTICO D'OTTAVIA

N

CAPITOLINE HILL

Piazza Campidoglio

▲▲▲Pantheon

For the greatest look at the splendor of Rome, antiquity's best-preserved interior is a must. Built two millennia ago, this influential domed temple served as the model for Michelangelo's dome of St. Peter's and many others.

Because the Pantheon became a church dedicated to the martyrs just after the fall of Rome, the barbarians left it alone, and the locals didn't use it as a quarry. The portico is called "Rome's umbrella"—a fun local gathering in a rainstorm. Walk past its one-piece granite columns (biggest in Italy, shipped from Egypt) and through the original bronze doors. Sit inside under the glorious skylight and enjoy classical architecture at its best.

The dome, 142 feet high and wide, was Europe's biggest until the Renaissance. Michelangelo's dome at St. Peter's, while much higher, is about three feet narrower. The brilliance of this dome's construction astounded architects through the ages. During the Renaissance, Brunelleschi was given permission to cut into the dome (see the little square hole above and to the right of the en-

ROME

trance) to analyze the material. The concrete dome gets thinner and lighter with height—the highest part is volcanic pumice.

This wonderfully harmonious architecture greatly inspired Raphael and other artists of the Renaissance. Raphael, along with Italy's first two kings, chose to be buried here.

The Pantheon is the only ancient building in Rome continuously used since its construction. When you leave, notice that the building is sunken below current street level, showing how the rest of the city has risen on 20 centuries of rubble.

The nearest WCs are at bars and cafés on the Pantheon's square. Several reasonable eateries are a block or two north up Via del Pantheon. Some of Rome's best gelato is nearby.

Cost and Hours: Free, Mon-Sat 8:30-19:30, Sun 9:00-18:00, holidays 9:00-13:00, closed for Mass Sat at 17:00 and Sun at 10:30, audioguide-€5, tel. 06-6830-0230. You can download a free Rick Steves **audio tour** of the Pantheon; see page 7.

When to Go: Try to get to the Pantheon first thing in the morning: While it's jammed with people midday, you'll have it all to yourself before 9:00.

▲▲Churches near the Pantheon

The **Church of San Luigi dei Francesi** has a magnificent chapel painted by Caravaggio (free, daily 10:00-12:30 & 15:00-19:00 except closed Thu afternoon, between the Pantheon and the north end of Piazza Navona). The only Gothic church in Rome is the **Church of Santa Maria sopra Minerva,** with a little-known Michelangelo statue, *Christ Bearing the Cross* (free, Mon-Fri 7:00-19:00, Sat-Sun 8:00-12:30 & 15:30-19:00, on a little square behind Pantheon, to the east). The **Church of San Ignazio,** several blocks east of the Pantheon, is a riot of Baroque illusions with a false dome (free, Mon-Sat 7:30-19:00, Sun 9:00-19:00). A few blocks away, across Corso Vittorio Emanuele, is the rich and Baroque **Gesù Church,** headquarters of the Jesuits in Rome (free, daily 7:00-12:30 & 16:00-19:45, interesting daily service at 17:30).

▲Galleria Doria Pamphilj

This underappreciated gallery, in the heart of the old city, offers a rare chance to wander through a noble family's lavish rooms with the prince who calls this downtown mansion home. Well, almost. Through an audioguide, the prince lovingly narrates his family's story as you tour the palace and its world-class art. Don't miss Velázquez's intense, majestic, ultra-realistic portrait of Pope Innocent X (1574-1655), patriarch of the Pamphilj (pahm-FEEL-yee) family. It stands alongside an equally impressive bust of the pope by Bernini. Stroll through a mini-Versailles-like hall of mirrors to more paintings, including works by Titian and Raphael. Finally, relax along with Mary, Joseph, and Jesus, and let the angel serenade you in Caravaggio's *Rest on the Flight to Egypt.*

Cost and Hours: €10.50, includes worthwhile 1.5-hour audioguide, daily 10:00-17:00, last entry 45 minutes before closing, elegant café, from Piazza Venezia walk 2 blocks up Via del Corso to #305, tel. 06-679-7323, www.dopart.it/roma.

Piazza di Pietra (Piazza of Stone)

The square was actually a quarry set up to chew away at the abandoned Temple of Hadrian, dedicated to the emperor responsible for building the Pantheon (look for his bust and a model of the temple in a window on the square). You can still see the holes that hungry medieval scavengers chipped into the columns to steal the metal pins that held the slabs together. Look over the railing to see ground level 1,900 years ago (two blocks toward Via del Corso from Pantheon).

▲Trevi Fountain

The bubbly Baroque fountain, worth ▲▲ by night, is a minor sight to art scholars...but a major nighttime gathering spot for teens on the make and tourists tossing coins. The coins tourists deposit daily are collected to feed Rome's poor (for more on the fountain, see page 850).

Palazzo del Quirinale

This presidential palace, the former home of several popes and the Italian royal family, feels like a combination of the White House and the Palace of Versailles. Guided tours—on Sundays only—take you through its opulent public rooms. Named after the highest of Rome's seven hills, the square in front offers fine views of St. Peter's Basilica.

Cost and Hours: €5, Sun 8:30-12:00 only—closed rest of the week, expect a line, square always open, 200 yards east and up the hill from Trevi Fountain on Piazza del Quirinale, tel. 06-46991, www.quirinale.it.

ROME

Vatican City

Vatican City, the world's smallest country, contains St. Peter's Basilica (with Michelangelo's exquisite *Pietà*) and the Vatican Museum (with Michelangelo's Sistine Chapel). A helpful **TI** is just to the left of St. Peter's Basilica as you're facing it (Mon-Sat 8:30-18:15, closed Sun, tel. 06-6988-1662, Vatican switchboard tel. 06-6982, www.vatican.va). The entrances to St. Peter's and to the Vatican Museum are a 15-minute walk apart (follow the outside of the Vatican wall, which links the two sights). The nearest Metro stop, Ottaviano, is about 10 minutes from either sight.

Modest dress is required of men, women, and children throughout Vatican City, even outdoors. Otherwise the Swiss Guard can turn you away. Cover your shoulders; bring a light jacket or cover-up if you're wearing a tank top. Wear long pants instead of shorts. Skirts or dresses should extend below your knee.

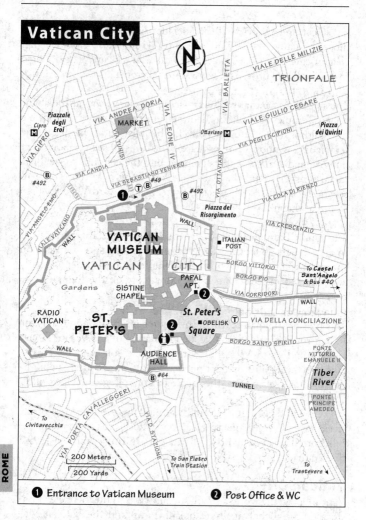

1 Entrance to Vatican Museum **2** Post Office & WC

▲▲▲St. Peter's Basilica (Basilica San Pietro)

There is no doubt: This is the richest and grandest church on earth. To call it vast is like calling Einstein smart. Plaques on the floor show where other, smaller churches would end if they were placed inside. The ornamental cherubs would dwarf a large man. Birds roost inside, and thousands of people wander about, heads craned heavenward, hardly noticing each other. Don't miss Michelangelo's *Pietà* (behind bulletproof glass) to the right of the entrance. Bernini's altar work and twisting, towering canopy are brilliant.

Cost: Free entry to basilica and crypt. Dome climb-€6 if you take the stairs all the way up, or €7 to ride an elevator partway (to the roof), then climb to the top of the dome (for details, see "Dome Climb," later). Museum-Treasury–€6.

Hours: The **church** is open daily April-Sept 7:00-19:00, Oct-March 7:00-18:00. It closes on Wednesday mornings during papal audiences. **Mass** is held daily, generally in Italian and in the south (left) transept, though other possible locations are the apse and the Blessed Sacrament Chapel (on right side of nave). Mass is typically scheduled on Mon-Sat at 8:30, 9:00, 10:00, 11:00, 12:00, and 17:00 (in Latin, in the apse); and on Sun and holidays at 9:00, 10:30 (in Latin), 11:30, 12:15, 13:00, 16:00, and 17:45. Confirm the schedule and location on site, or go to www.vatican.va (click on "Basilicas and Papal Chapels" link).

The **Museum-Treasury** is open daily April-Sept 9:00-18:15, Oct-March 9:00-17:15. The **crypt** is open daily 9:00-16:00. The **dome** is open to climbers daily April-Sept 8:00-18:00, Oct-March 8:00-16:45, last entry 30 minutes before closing.

When to Go: The best time to visit the church is early (before 10:00) or late; at 17:00, when the church is fairly empty, sunbeams can work their magic, and the late-afternoon Mass fills the place with spiritual music. The downside to visiting late is that the area around the altar and beyond is often roped off from around 16:00 to prepare for Mass. Still, the shorter line, smaller crowds, and ambience might make it worthwhile.

Avoiding Lines: The security-checkpoint lines can get quite long and there's no reliable way to avoid them (thankfully, they move relatively quickly). Occasionally, St. Peter's is accessible from the Vatican Museum (though the museum comes with its own long lines, which can be avoided if you reserve your entry time). If you visit the Vatican Museum first, pray that the shortcut from the Sistine Chapel directly to St. Peter's is open (depends on crowd levels—see page 880 for specifics.)

Dress Code: No shorts, above-the-knee skirts, or bare shoulders (this applies to men, women, and children). Attendants strictly enforce this dress code, even in hot weather.

Getting There: Take the Metro to Ottaviano, then walk 10 minutes south on Via Ottaviano. There are several good bus options: The #40 express bus drops off at Piazza Pio, next to Castel Sant'Angelo—a 10-minute walk to St. Peter's. The more crowded bus #64 is convenient for pickpockets and stops just outside St. Peter's Square to the south (get off the bus after it crosses the Tiber, at the first stop past the tunnel; backtrack toward the tunnel and turn left when you see the rows of columns). Bus #492 heads through the center of town, stopping at Largo Argentina, and gets you near Piazza Risorgimento (get off when you see the Vatican walls). A taxi from Termini train station to St. Peter's costs about €11.

ROME

Tours: The Vatican TI conducts free 1.5-hour tours of St. Peter's (depart from TI Mon-Fri 14:15, plus Tue and Thu 9:45, confirm schedule at TI, tel. 06-6988-1662). Audioguides can be rented near the checkroom (€5 plus ID, for church only, daily 9:00-17:00). You can download a free Rick Steves **audio tour** of St. Peter's; see page 7.

To see St. Peter's original grave, you can take a **Scavi "Excavations"** tour into the Necropolis (€12, 1.5 hours, ages 15 and older only, no photos). Book at least two months in advance by phone (tel. 06-6988-5318), email (scavi@fsp.va), or fax (06-6987-3017), following the detailed instructions at www.vatican.va (search on "Excavations Office"); no response means they're booked up.

Dome Climb (Cupola): To get to the roof (which is about the halfway point to the dome), you can either take the elevator (€7) or stairs (€6, 231 steps); from the roof, you'll have to climb 323 steps to the top of the dome. Allow an hour to go up and down. The entry to the elevator is just outside the basilica on the north side of St. Peter's (near the secret exit from the Sistine Chapel). Look for signs to the cupola.

Vatican Gardens: If you want to walk through the Vatican Gardens, you must book a tour online at least two days in advance at http://biglietteriamusei.vatican.va. No response means they're booked up (€31, 2 hours, usually daily except Wed and Sun, includes entry to Vatican Museum; tours start at 9:30 or 10:00 at Vatican Museum tour desk). Roma Cristiana's open-bus tours of the gardens can usually be booked on short notice (€15, 1 hour, 2/hour Mon-Tue and Thu-Sat 8:00-13:00, best to reserve a couple days in advance but same-day availability possible, Opera Romana Pellegrinaggi office in front of St. Peter's Square, Piazza Pio XII 9, tel. 06-6989-6380 or 06-698-961).

With Limited Time: Stroll the nave, glance up at the dome and down at the marker of St. Peter's tomb. Don't miss the Pietà. Skip the crypt and the dome climb.

Baggage Check: The free bag check (mandatory for bags larger than a purse or daypack) is outside the basilica (to the right as you face the entrance) and just inside the security checkpoint.

Services: WCs are to the right and left on St. Peter's Square (just outside the security checkpoint and exit), near baggage storage down the steps on the right side of the entrance, and on the roof.

❷ **Self-Guided Tour:** For a quick walk through the basilica, follow these points:

❶ The atrium is itself bigger than most churches. The huge white columns on the portico date from the first church (fourth century). Notice the historic doors (the Holy Door, on the right, won't be opened until the next Jubilee Year, in 2025).

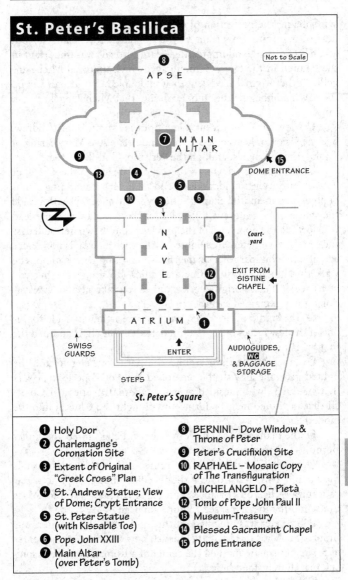

St. Peter's Basilica

Not to Scale

APSE

MAIN ALTAR

DOME ENTRANCE

NAVE

Court-yard

EXIT FROM SISTINE CHAPEL

ATRIUM

SWISS GUARDS

ENTER

AUDIOGUIDES, **WC** & BAGGAGE STORAGE

STEPS

St. Peter's Square

❶ Holy Door
❷ Charlemagne's Coronation Site
❸ Extent of Original "Greek Cross" Plan
❹ St. Andrew Statue; View of Dome; Crypt Entrance
❺ St. Peter Statue (with Kissable Toe)
❻ Pope John XXIII
❼ Main Altar (over Peter's Tomb)

❽ BERNINI – Dove Window & Throne of Peter
❾ Peter's Crucifixion Site
❿ RAPHAEL – Mosaic Copy of The Transfiguration
⓫ MICHELANGELO – Pietà
⓬ Tomb of Pope John Paul II
⓭ Museum-Treasury
⓮ Blessed Sacrament Chapel
⓯ Dome Entrance

❷ The purple, circular porphyry stone marks the site of Charlemagne's coronation in A.D. 800 (in the first St. Peter's church that stood on this site). From here, get a sense of the immensity of the church, which can accommodate 60,000 worshippers standing on its six acres.

❸ Michelangelo planned a Greek-cross floor plan, rather than the Latin-cross standard in medieval churches. A Greek cross, symbolizing the perfection of God, and by association the goodness of man, was important to the humanist Michelangelo. But accommodating—and impressing—large crowds was important to the Church in the fancy Baroque age, which followed Michelangelo, so the original nave length was doubled. Stand halfway up the nave and imagine the stubbier design that Michelangelo had in mind.

❹ View the magnificent dome from the statue of St. Andrew. See the vision of heaven above the windows: Jesus, Mary, a ring of saints, rings of angels, and, on the very top, God the Father.

Visitors can go down to the crypt (labeled as the *Grotte* or *Tombe*) within the foundations of Old St. Peter's, containing tombs of popes and memorial chapels. The crypt entrance is usually beside the statue of St. Andrew, to the left of the main altar. Stairs lead you down to the floor level of the previous church, where you'll pass the sepulcher of Peter. This lighted niche with an icon is not Peter's actual tomb, but part of a shrine that stands atop Peter's tomb. The walk through the crypt is free and quick (15 minutes)—but you won't see St. Peter's original grave unless you take a Scavi "Excavations" tour (explained earlier).

❺ The statue of St. Peter, with an irresistibly kissable toe, is one of the few pieces of art that predate this church. It adorned the first St. Peter's church.

❻ Circle to the right around the statue of Peter to find the lighted glass niche with the red-robed body of Pope John XXIII (r. 1958-1963), who presided over the landmark Vatican II Council that instituted major reforms and brought the Church into the modern age.

❼ The main altar sits directly over St. Peter's tomb and under Bernini's seven-story bronze canopy.

❽ St. Peter's throne and Bernini's starburst dove window is the site of a daily Mass (check the schedule on site, or go to www.vatican.va—click on "Basilicas and Papal Chapels" link; for Mass times in other locations, see "Hours" on page 873).

❾ St. Peter was crucified on this spot when this location was simply "the Vatican Hill." The obelisk now standing in the center of St. Peter's square marked the center of a Roman racecourse long before a church stood here.

❿ The church is filled with mosaics, not paintings. Notice the mosaic copy of Raphael's *Transfiguration*.

⓫ Michelangelo sculpted his *Pietà* when he was 24 years old. (A *pietà* is a work that represents Mary with the body of Christ taken down from the cross.) Michelangelo's mastery of the body is obvious in this powerfully beautiful masterpiece. Jesus is believably dead, and Mary, the eternally youthful "handmaiden" of the Lord, accepts God's will...even if it means giving up her son.

⓬ The tomb of Pope John Paul II was moved to the chapel of San Sebastian in 2011, after he was beatified by Pope Benedict XVI (a step on the road to sainthood). He lies beneath a painting of the steadfast St. Sebastian, his favorite saint.

⓭ Outside on the north side of St. Peter's, an elevator leads to the roof and the stairway up the dome. The dome, Michelangelo's last work, is (you guessed it) the biggest anywhere. Taller than a football field is long, it's well worth the sweaty climb for a great view of Rome, the Vatican grounds, and the inside of the basilica—particularly heavenly while there is singing. Look around—Rome has no modern skyline. No building in Rome is allowed to exceed the height of St. Peter's. The elevator takes you to the rooftop of the nave. From there, a few steps take you to a balcony at the base of the dome looking down into the church interior. After that, the one-way, 323-step climb (for some people, it's claustrophobic) to the cupola begins. The rooftop level (below the dome) has a gift shop, WC, drinking fountain, and a commanding view.

⓮ For most, the museum-treasury (on the left side of the nave, near the altar) is not worth the admission.

⓯ You're welcome to step through the metalwork gates into the Blessed Sacrament Chapel, an oasis of peace reserved for prayer and meditation (on the right-hand side of the church, about midway to the altar).

▲▲▲Vatican Museum (Musei Vaticani)

The four miles of displays in this immense museum—from ancient statues to Christian frescoes to modern paintings—culminate in the Raphael Rooms and Michelangelo's glorious Sistine Chapel. This is one of Europe's top three or four houses of art. It can be exhausting, so plan your visit carefully, focusing on a few themes. Allow two hours for a quick visit, three or four hours for enough time to enjoy it.

Cost and Hours: €15 plus optional €4 reservation fee, Mon-Sat 9:00-18:00, last entry at 16:00 (though the official closing time is 18:00, the staff starts ushering you out at 17:30), closed on religious holidays and Sun except last Sun of the month (when it's free, more crowded, and open 9:00-14:00, last entry at 12:30); may be open Fri nights May-July and Sept-Oct 19:00-23:00 (last entry at 21:30) by online reservation only. Hours are subject to constant change and frequent holidays; check http://mv.vatican.va for current times. Lines are extremely long in the morning—go in the afternoon, or skip the ticket-buying line altogether by reserving an entry time on their website. A €7 audioguide is available (ID required).

The museum is closed on many holidays (mainly religious ones), including, for 2014: Jan 1 (New Year's), Jan 6 (Epiphany),

ROME

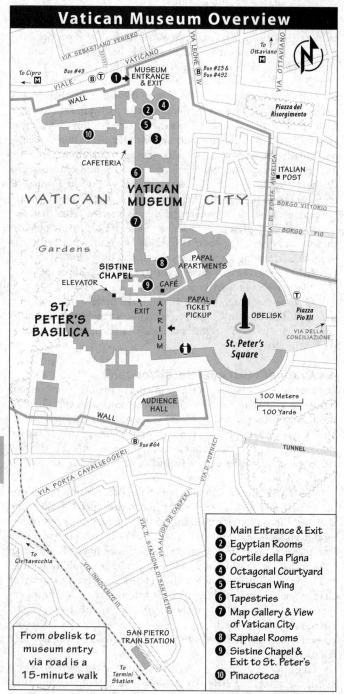

Vatican Museum Overview

1 Main Entrance & Exit

2 Egyptian Rooms

3 Cortile della Pigna

4 Octagonal Courtyard

5 Etruscan Wing

6 Tapestries

7 Map Gallery & View of Vatican City

8 Raphael Rooms

9 Sistine Chapel & Exit to St. Peter's

10 Pinacoteca

From obelisk to museum entry via road is a 15-minute walk

ROME

Feb 11 (Vatican City established), March 19 (St. Joseph), April 1 (Easter Monday), May 1 (Labor Day), June 29 (Saints Peter and Paul), Aug 15 plus either Aug 14 or 16—it varies year to year (Assumption of the Virgin), Nov 1 (All Saints' Day), Dec 8 (Immaculate Conception), and Dec 25 and 26 (Christmas).

Individual rooms may close at odd hours, especially in the afternoon. The rooms described here are usually open.

Reservations: Bypass the long ticket lines by reserving an entry time online at http://mv.vatican.va. It costs €19 (€15 ticket plus €4 booking fee, pay with credit card). It's easy. You choose your day and time, they email you a confirmation immediately, and you print out the voucher with its reservation bar code. At the Vatican Museum, bypass the ticket-buying line and queue up at the "Entrance with Reservations" line (to the right). Show your voucher to the guard, who will scan it and let you in. Once inside the museum, go to a ticket window *(a cassa)*, either in the lobby or upstairs, present your voucher and ID, and they'll issue your ticket.

When to Go: The museum is generally hot and crowded, with waits of up to two hours to buy tickets (figure about a 10-minute wait for every 100 yards in line). The worst days are Saturdays, the last Sunday of the month (when it's free), Mondays, rainy days, and any day before or after a holiday closure. Mornings are most crowded. To see the Sistine Chapel with fewer crowds, visit at the end of the day.

Avoiding Lines: The best way to skip the long lines is to **reserve tickets** in advance (described above). If you book a **guided tour** (see "Tours," next page), you can approach the guard with your voucher and go right in. If you book with a private tour company, you may still have a short wait at crowded times.

You can often buy **same-day, skip-the-line tickets** through the TI in St. Peter's Square (to the left, as you face the basilica). You pay the same price (€15 ticket plus €4 reservation fee) that you would online. If the TI doesn't have tickets, you could try the tour company called Roma Cristiana, which sells higher-priced, same-day tickets from their kiosk at St. Peter's Square (€15 ticket plus €11 booking fee, entrances almost hourly, tel. 06-6980-6380, www.operaromanapellegrinaggi.org).

If you don't have a reservation, **try arriving after 14:00,** when crowds subside somewhat. Another good time is during the papal audience, on Wednesday at 10:30, when many tourists are at St. Peter's Basilica.

Make sure you get in the right line. Generally, individuals without tickets line up against the Vatican City wall (to the left of the entrance as you face it), and reservation holders (both individuals and groups) enter on the right.

ROME

Dress Code: Remember, modest dress is required (no shorts, above-knee skirts, or bare shoulders).

Getting There: Metro stop Ottaviano is a 10-minute walk away. (The Cipro Metro stop also works for the museum, but involves a big stair climb, and is farther from the end of the ticket-buying line.) Bus #49 from Piazza Cavour stops right at the entrance. Bus #23 from Trastevere hugs the west bank of the Tiber and stops on Via Leone IV, just downhill from the entrance. Bus #492 heads from the city center past Piazza Risorgimento and the Vatican walls, and also stops on Via Leone IV. Bus #64 stops on the other side of St. Peter's Square, a 15- to 20-minute walk (facing the church from the obelisk, take a right through the colonnade and follow the Vatican Wall). Taxis are reasonable (hop in and say, "moo-ZAY-ee vah-tee-KAH-nee").

Tours: A €7 **audioguide** is available at the top of the spiral ramp/escalator (ID required). If you rent an audioguide, you lose the option of taking the shortcut from the Sistine Chapel to St. Peter's (described later, under "Museum Strategies"), since audioguides must be returned to the museum entrance/exit.

You can download a free Rick Steves **audio tour** of the Sistine Chapel; see page 7.

The Vatican offers **English tours** that are easy to book online (€31, includes admission, http://mv.vatican.va). As with individual ticket reservations, present your confirmation voucher to a guard to the right of the entrance; then, once inside, go to the Guided Tours desk (in the lobby, up a few stairs).

Both **private tour** companies and private guides offer English tours of the museum, usually allowing you to skip the long ticket-buying line. For a listing of several companies, see page 831.

With Limited Time: See the octagonal courtyard (Laocoön), then follow the crowd flow directly to the Sistine Chapel, sightseeing along the way. Skip the Etruscan Wing and the Pinacoteca. From the Sistine Chapel, head straight to St. Peter's via the shortcut, if open (see "Museum Strategies," below).

Security and Baggage Check: To enter the museum, you pass through a metal detector (no pocket knives allowed). The baggage check (to the right after security) takes only bigger bags; you'll need to carry your day bag with you.

Museum Strategies: The museum has two exits, and you'll want to decide which you'll take before you enter. The **main exit** is right near the entrance. Use this one if you want to rent an audioguide (which you must return at the entrance) or if you plan on following this self-guided tour exactly as laid out, visiting the Pinacoteca (painting gallery) at the end.

The other exit is a handy but sometimes closed) **shortcut** that leads from the Sistine Chapel directly to St. Peter's Basilica (spilling out alongside the church; see map on page 878). This route saves you a 30-minute walk (15 minutes back to the Vatican Museum entry/exit, then 15 minutes to St. Peter's) and lets you avoid the often-long security line at the basilica's main entrance. If you take this route, you'll have to forgo an audioguide and skip the Pinacoteca (or tour it earlier). Officially, this exit is for Vatican guides and their groups only. However, it's often open to anyone (depending on how crowded the chapel is and how the guards feel). It's worth a shot (try blending in with a group that's leaving), but be prepared for the possibility that you won't get through.

Photography: No photos are allowed in the Sistine Chapel. Elsewhere in the museum, photos without a flash are permitted.

◐ Self-Guided Tour: Start, as Western civilization did, in **Egypt and Mesopotamia.** Decorating the museum's courtyard are some of the best **Greek and Roman statues** in captivity, including the *Laocoön* group (first century B.C., Hellenistic) and the *Apollo Belvedere* (a second-century Roman copy of a Greek original). The centerpiece of the next hall is the *Belvedere Torso* (just a 2,000-year-old torso, but one that had a great impact on the art of Michelangelo). Finishing off the classical statuary are two fine fourth-century porphyry sarcophagi. These royal purple tombs were made (though not used) for the Roman emperor Constantine's mother and daughter. They were Christians—and therefore outlaws—until Constantine made Christianity legal in A.D. 312, and they became saints. Both sarcophagi were quarried and worked in Egypt. The technique for working this extremely hard stone (a special tempering of metal was required) was lost after this, and porphyry marble was not chiseled again until Renaissance times in Florence.

After long halls of tapestries, old maps, broken penises, and fig leaves, you'll come to what most people are looking for: the Raphael Rooms and Michelangelo's Sistine Chapel.

After fancy rooms illustrating the "Immaculate Conception of Mary" (in the 19th century, the Vatican codified this hard-to-sell doctrine, making it a formal part of the Catholic faith) and the triumph of Constantine (with divine guidance, which led to his conversion to Christianity), you enter rooms frescoed by **Raphael** and his assistants. The highlight is the restored *School of Athens.* This is remarkable for its blatant pre-Christian classical orientation, especially since it originally wallpapered the apartments of Pope Julius II. Raphael honors the great pre-Christian thinkers—Aristotle, Plato, and company—who are portrayed as the leading artists of Raphael's day. There's Leonardo da Vinci, whom Raphael worshipped, in the role of Plato. Michelangelo broods in the foreground, added later. When Raphael snuck a peek at the Sistine Chapel, he decided that his arch-competitor was so good that he had to put their personal differences aside and include him in this

ROME

Vatican City

This tiny independent country of little more than 100 acres, contained entirely within Rome, has its own postal system, armed guards, helipad, mini-train station, and radio station (KPOP). It also has two huge sights: St. Peter's Basilica (with Michelangelo's *Pietà*) and the Vatican Museum (with the Sistine Chapel). Politically powerful, the Vatican is the religious capital of 1.1 billion Roman Catholics. If you're not a Catholic, become one for your visit.

The pope is both the religious and secular leader of Vatican City. For centuries, locals referred to him as "King Pope." Italy and the Vatican didn't always have good relations. In fact, after unification (in 1870), when Rome's modern grid plan was built around the miniscule Vatican, it seemed as if the new buildings were designed to be just high enough so no one could see the dome of St. Peter's from street level. Modern Italy was created in 1870, but the Holy See didn't recognize it as a country until 1929, when the pope and Mussolini signed the Lateran Pact, giving sovereignty and a few nearby churches to the Vatican.

Like every European country, Vatican City has its own versions of the euro coin (with a portrait of Pope Benedict XVI and, before him, of Pope John Paul II). You're unlikely to find one in your pocket, though, as they are snatched up by collectors before falling into circulation.

Post Offices: The Vatican postal service is famous for its stamps, which you can get from offices on St. Peter's Square (next to TI or between the columns just before the security checkpoint) or in the Vatican Museum (Mon-Sat 8:30-18:30, closed Sun). Vatican stamps are good throughout Rome, but to use the Vatican's mail service, you need to mail your cards from the Vatican; write your postcards ahead of time. (Note that the Vatican won't mail cards with Italian stamps.)

Seeing the Pope: Your best chances for a sighting are on Sunday or Wednesday. The pope usually gives a blessing at noon on Sunday from his apartment on St. Peter's Square (except in July and August, when he speaks at his summer residence at Cas-

tribute to the artists of his generation. Today's St. Peter's was under construction as Raphael was working. In the *School of Athens*, he gives us a sneak preview of the unfinished church.

Next is the brilliantly restored **Sistine Chapel.** This is the pope's personal chapel and also the place where, upon the death (or resignation) of the ruling pope, a new pope is elected.

The Sistine Chapel is famous for Michelangelo's pictorial culmination of the Renaissance, showing the story of creation, with a powerful God weaving in and out of each scene through that busy first week. This is an optimistic and positive expression of the High tel Gandolfo, 25 miles from Rome, reachable by train from Rome's Termini train station). St. Peter's is easiest (just show up) and, for most, enough of a "visit." Those interested in a more formal appearance (though not more intimate) can get a ticket for the Wednesday general audience (at 10:30) when the pope, arriving in his Popemobile, greets and blesses the crowds at St. Peter's from a canopied platform on the square (except in winter, when he speaks at 10:30 in the 7,000-seat Paolo VI Auditorium, next to St. Peter's Basilica). If you only want to see St. Peter's—but not the pope—avoid these times (the basilica closes during papal audiences and crowds are substantial).

For the Wednesday audience, while anyone can observe from a distance, you need a (free) ticket to get close to the papal action (and get a seat). To find out the pope's schedule and request a ticket, see www.vatican.va (click on the "Prefecture of the Papal Household" link) or call 06-6988-3114.

The American Catholic Church in Rome, Santa Susanna, lets you order tickets online (free, no booking fee but donations appreciated) for the Wednesday general audience. Pick up your reserved tickets, or check for last-minute availability, at the church the Tuesday before the audience between 17:00 and 18:45 (consider staying for the 18:00 Mass in English, near Via Firenze hotels, at Via XX Settembre 15, Metro: Repubblica, tel. 06-4201-4554—charming Rosanna speaks English, details at www.santa-susanna.org).

Probably less convenient—unless you're already at the basilica—is getting a ticket at St. Peter's Square from the Vatican guard at their station at the bronze doors (open Tue 12:00-19:30; last-minute tickets may be available Wed morning—just join the line). It's under the "elbow" of Bernini's colonnade, on the right side of the square as you face the basilica (see map on page 878).

While many visitors come hoping for a more intimate audience, private audiences ended with the death of Pope John Paul II. Pope Benedict doesn't do them.

Renaissance and a stirring example of the artistic and theological maturity of the 33-year-old Michelangelo, who spent four years on this work.

The ceiling shows the history of the world before the birth of Jesus. We see God creating the world, creating man and woman, destroying the earth by flood, and so on. God himself, in his purple robe, actually appears in the first five scenes. Along the sides (where the ceiling starts to curve), we see the Old Testament prophets and pagan Greek prophetesses who foretold the coming of Christ. Dividing these scenes and figures are fake niches (a painted

3-D illusion) decorated with nude statue-like figures with symbolic meaning.

When the ceiling was finished and revealed to the public, it simply blew 'em away—it was unlike anything seen before. It both caps the Renaissance and turns it in a new direction. In perfect Renaissance spirit, it mixes Old Testament prophets with classical figures. But the style is more dramatic, shocking, and emotional than the balanced Renaissance works before it. This is a very personal work—the Gospel according to Michelangelo—but its themes and subject matter are universal. Many art scholars contend that the Sistine ceiling is the single greatest work of art by any one human being.

Later, after the Reformation wars had begun and after the Catholic army of Spain had sacked the Vatican, the reeling Church began to fight back. As part of its Counter-Reformation, a much older Michelangelo was commissioned to paint the *Last Judgment* (behind the altar).

It's Judgment Day, and Christ—the powerful figure in the center, raising his arm to spank the wicked—has come to find out who's naughty and who's nice. Beneath him, a band of angels blows its trumpets Dizzy Gillespie-style, giving a wake-up call to the sleeping dead. The dead at lower left leave their graves and prepare to be judged. The righteous, on Christ's right hand (the left side of the picture), are carried up to the glories of heaven. The wicked on the other side are hurled down to hell, where demons wait to torture them. Charon, from the underworld of Greek mythology, waits below to ferry the souls of the damned to hell.

When *The Last Judgment* was unveiled to the public in 1541, it caused a sensation. The pope is said to have dropped to his knees and cried, "Lord, charge me not with my sins when thou shalt come on the Day of Judgment."

And it changed the course of art. The complex composition, with more than 300 figures swirling around the figure of Christ, went far beyond traditional Renaissance balance. The twisted figures shown from every imaginable angle challenged other painters to try and top this master of 3-D illusion. And the sheer terror and drama of the scene was a striking contrast to the placid optimism of, say, Raphael's *School of Athens*. Michelangelo had Baroque-en all the rules of the Renaissance, signaling a new era of art.

For a **shortcut directly to St. Peter's Basilica** (see "Museum Strategies," earlier), you'll exit at the far-right corner of the Sistine Chapel (with your back to the altar). This route saves you a 30-minute walk and the wait in the St. Peter's security line, but if you exit here, you're done with the museum—you can't get back to the main entrance/exit (where audioguides need to be returned) or the **Pinacoteca** (the Vatican's small but fine collection of paintings, with Raphael's *Transfiguration*, Leonardo's unfinished *St. Jerome*, and Caravaggio's *Deposition*).

If you skip the shortcut and take the long march back, you'll find, along with the Pinacoteca, a cafeteria (long lines, uninspired food), the underrated early-Christian art section, and the exit via the souvenir shop.

Near Vatican City
▲Castel Sant'Angelo

Built as a tomb for the emperor, used through the Middle Ages as a castle, prison, and place of last refuge for popes under attack, and today a museum, this giant pile of ancient bricks is packed with history.

Cost and Hours: €8.50, Tue-Sun 9:00-19:30, closed Mon, last entry one hour before closing, near Vatican City, Metro: Lepanto or bus #40 or #64, tel. 06-681-9111, www.castelsantangelo. beniculturali.it.

Background: Ancient Rome allowed no tombs—not even the emperor's—within its walls. So Emperor Hadrian grabbed the most commanding position just outside the walls and across the river and built a towering tomb (c. A.D. 139) well within view of the city. His mausoleum was a huge cylinder (210 by 70 feet) topped by a cypress grove and crowned by a huge statue of Hadrian himself riding a chariot. For nearly a hundred years, Roman emperors (from Hadrian to Caracalla, in A.D. 217) were buried here.

In the year 590, the archangel Michael appeared above the mausoleum to Pope Gregory the Great. Sheathing his sword, the angel signaled the end of a plague. The fortress that was Hadrian's mausoleum eventually became a fortified palace, renamed for the "holy angel."

Castel Sant'Angelo spent centuries of the Dark Ages as a fortress and prison, but was eventually connected to the Vatican via an elevated corridor at the pope's request (1277). Since Rome was repeatedly plundered by invaders, Castel Sant'Angelo was a handy place of last refuge for threatened popes. In anticipation of long sieges, rooms were decorated with papal splendor (you'll see paintings by Carlo Crivelli, Luca Signorelli, and Andrea Mantegna). In 1527, during a sack of Rome by troops of Charles V of Spain, the pope lived inside the castle for months with his entourage of hundreds (an unimaginable ordeal, considering the food service at the top-floor bar).

Visiting the Castle: Touring the place is a stair-stepping workout. After you walk around the entire base of the castle, take the small staircase down to the original Roman floor (following the route of Hadrian's funeral procession). In the atrium, study the model of the mausoleum as it was in Roman times. Imagine

ROME

being surrounded by a veneer of marble, and the niche in the wall filled with a towering "welcome to my tomb" statue of Hadrian. From here, a ramp leads to the right, spiraling 400 feet. While some of the fine original brickwork and bits of mosaic survive, the marble veneer is long gone (notice the holes in the wall that held it in place).

At the end of the ramp, a bridge crosses over the room where the ashes of the emperors were kept. From here, the stairs continue out of the ancient section and into the medieval structure (built atop the mausoleum) that housed the papal apartments. Don't miss the Sala del Tesoro (Treasury), where the wealth of the Vatican was locked up in a huge chest. (*Do* miss the 58 rooms of the military museum.) From the pope's piggy bank, a narrow flight of stairs leads to the rooftop and perhaps the finest view of Rome anywhere (pick out landmarks as you stroll around). From the safety of this dramatic vantage point, the pope surveyed the city in times of siege. Look down at the bend of the Tiber, which for 2,700 years has cradled the Eternal City.

Ponte Sant'Angelo
The bridge leading to Castel Sant'Angelo was built by Hadrian for quick and regal access from downtown to his tomb. The three middle arches are actually Roman originals and a fine example of the empire's engineering expertise. The statues of angels (each bearing a symbol of the passion of Christ—nail, sponge, shroud, and so on) are Bernini-designed and textbook Baroque. In the Middle Ages, this was the only bridge in the area that connected St. Peter's and the Vatican with downtown Rome. Nearly all pilgrims passed this bridge to and from the church. Its shoulder-high banisters recall a tragedy: During a Jubilee Year festival in 1450, the crowd got so huge that the mob pushed out the original banisters, causing nearly 200 to fall to their deaths.

North Rome
Borghese Gardens and Via Veneto
▲Villa Borghese Gardens
Rome's semi-scruffy three-square-mile "Central Park" is great for its shade and for people-watching plenty of modern-day Romeos and Juliets. The best entrance is at the head of Via Veneto (Metro: Barberini, then 10-minute walk up Via Veneto and through the old Roman wall at Porta Pinciana, or catch a cab to Via Veneto—Porta Pinciana). There you'll find a cluster of buildings with a café, a kiddie arcade, and bike rental (€4/hour). Rent a bike or, for romantics, a pedaled rickshaw (*riscio*). Bikes come with locks to allow you to make sightseeing stops. Follow signs to discover the park's cafés, fountains, statues, lake, great viewpoint over Piazza del Popolo, and prime picnic spots. Some sights require paid admis-

sion, including Rome's zoo, the National Gallery of Modern Art (which holds 19th-century art; not to be confused with MAXXI, described later), and the Etruscan Museum (also described later).

▲▲▲Borghese Gallery (Galleria Borghese)

This plush museum, filling a cardinal's mansion in the park, offers one of Europe's most sumptuous art experiences. You'll enjoy a collection of world-class Baroque sculpture, including Bernini's *David* and his excited statue of Apollo chasing Daphne, as well as paintings by Caravaggio, Raphael, Titian, and Rubens. The museum's slick, mandatory reservation system keeps crowds to a manageable size.

The essence of the collection is the connection of the Renaissance with the classical world. As you enter, notice the second-century Roman reliefs with Michelangelo-designed panels above either end of the portico. The villa was built in the early 17th century by the great art collector Cardinal Scipione Borghese, who wanted to prove that the glories of ancient Rome were matched by the Renaissance.

In the main entry hall, high up on the wall, is a thrilling first-century Greek sculpture of a horse falling. The Renaissance-era rider was added by Pietro Bernini, father of the famous Gian Lorenzo Bernini.

Each room seems to feature a Baroque masterpiece. The best of all is in Room III: Bernini's *Apollo and Daphne.* It's the perfect Baroque subject—capturing a thrilling, action-filled moment. In the mythological story, Apollo—made stupid by Cupid's arrow of love—chases after Daphne, who has been turned off by the "arrow of disgust." Just as he's about to catch her, she calls to her father to save her. Magically, her fingers begin to sprout leaves, her toes become roots, her skin turns to bark, and she transforms into a tree. Frustrated Apollo will end up with a handful of leaves. Walk slowly around the statue. It's more air than stone.

Cost and Hours: €12.50; drops to €8.50 when there's no temporary exhibit, both prices include basic €2 reservation fee, credit cards accepted, Tue-Sun 9:00-19:00, closed Mon, ticket office closes one hour before museum, no photos, all bags and cameras must be checked (free).

Reservations: Reservations are mandatory and simple to get. It's easiest by booking online (www.ticketeria.it, €1 extra booking fee, user-friendly website). You can also reserve by telephone (tel. 06-32810, press 2 for English, pay for tickets on arrival). Call during Italian office hours: Mon-Fri 9:00-18:00, Sat 9:00-13:00, office closed Sat in Aug and Sun year-round.

Every two hours, 360 people are allowed to enter the museum Entry times are 9:00, 11:00, 13:00, 15:00, and 17:00. Reser~ *minimum* of several days in advance for a weekday visit, and

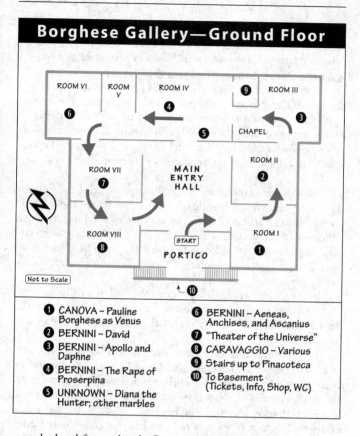

Borghese Gallery—Ground Floor

ROOM VI · ROOM V · ROOM IV · ❾ · ROOM III

❻ · ❹ · ❸

❺ · CHAPEL

ROOM VII · MAIN ENTRY HALL · ROOM II

❼ · ❷

ROOM VIII · START · ROOM I

❽ · PORTICO · ❶

Not to Scale

❿

❶ CANOVA – Pauline Borghese as Venus

❷ BERNINI – David

❸ BERNINI – Apollo and Daphne

❹ BERNINI – The Rape of Proserpina

❺ UNKNOWN – Diana the Hunter; other marbles

❻ BERNINI – Aeneas, Anchises, and Ascanius

❼ "Theater of the Universe"

❽ CARAVAGGIO – Various

❾ Stairs up to Pinacoteca

❿ To Basement (Tickets, Info, Shop, WC)

a week ahead for weekends. Reservations are tightest at 11:00 and 15:00, on Tuesdays, and on weekends. For off-season weekdays (but not weekends), your chances of getting a same-day reservation are fairly high if you're flexible about the entry time (but you must go in person—you can't call to reserve same-day tickets).

After you reserve a day and time, you'll get a claim number. Be at the Borghese Gallery 30 minutes before your appointed time to pick up your ticket in the lobby on the lower level. Punctuality is critical (arriving late can mean forfeiting your reservation). You can try skipping the ticket pickup line by paying with a credit card at one of the computer kiosks (but they don't always work).

You can use a Roma Pass for entry, but you still need to make a reservation (by phone only—not online; specify that you have the Roma Pass). If you don't have a reservation, try arriving near the top of the hour, when the museum sells unclaimed tickets to those standing by. Generally, out of 360 reservations, a few will fail to show (but more than a few may be waiting to grab them). You're most likely to land a stand-by ticket at 9:00.

Getting There: The museum is set idyllically but inconveniently in the vast Villa Borghese Gardens. To avoid missing your appointment, allow yourself plenty of time to find the place. A taxi drops you 100 yards from the museum. Your destination is the Galleria Borghese (gah-leh-REE-ah bor-GAY-zay). Be sure *not* to tell the cabbie "Villa Borghese"—which is the park, not the museum.

Bus #910 goes from Termini train station to the Via Pinciana stop (a few steps from the villa). Coming from Campo de' Fiori or Via del Corso (at Via Minghetti), bus #116 drops you off at the southern edge of the park. From Largo Argentina, bus #63 takes you to the US Embassy on Via Veneto; walk uphill on Via Veneto to the southern edge of the park.

By Metro, from the Barberini Metro stop, walk 10 minutes up Via Veneto, enter the park, and turn right, following signs another 10 minutes to the Borghese Gallery.

Tours: Guided English tours are offered at 9:10 and 11:10 (€6.50; may also be offered on busy weekends at 13:10 and 15:10). You can't book a tour when you make your museum reservation—sign up as soon as you arrive. Or consider the excellent 1.5-hour audioguide tour (€5).

With Limited Time: Focus on the ground-floor sculptures, especially Bernini.

Museum Strategy: Visits are strictly limited to two hours. Budget most of your time for the more interesting ground floor, but set aside 30 minutes for the paintings of the Pinacoteca upstairs (highlights are marked by the audioguide icons). Avoid the crowds by seeing the Pinacoteca first. The fine bookshop and cafeteria are best visited outside your two-hour entry window (the bookshop closes 30 minutes before the gallery).

Etruscan Museum (Villa Giulia Museo Nazionale Etrusco)
The fascinating Etruscan civilization thrived in Italy around 600 B.C., when Rome was an Etruscan town. The Villa Giulia (a fine Renaissance palace in the Villa Borghese Gardens) hosts a museum that tells the story. The displays are clean and bright, with good English information.

The star of the museum is the famous "husband and wife sarcophagus"—a dead couple seeming to enjoy an everlasting banquet from atop their tomb (sixth century B.C. from Cerveteri). Historians also dig the gold sheets from Pyrgi, with inscriptions in two languages—the "Etruscan Rosetta Stone" that has helped scholars decipher their odd language, and the Apollo of Veio, which stood atop Apollo's temple. The smiling god welcomes Hercules, while his mother Latona stands nearby cradling baby Apollo.

Cost and Hours: €8, Tue-Sun 8:30-19:30, closed Mon, last entry one hour before closing, good English information, 20-min-

ROME

ute walk from Borghese Gallery, Piazzale di Villa Giulia 9, tel. 06-322-6571.

Via Veneto

In the 1960s, movie stars from around the world paraded down curvy Via Veneto, one of Rome's glitziest nightspots. Today it's still lined with the city's poshest hotels and the US Embassy, but any hint of local color has faded to bland.

▲Capuchin Crypt

If you want to see artistically arranged bones, this is the place. The crypt is below the Church of Santa Maria della Immacolata Concezione at Via Veneto 27, just up from Piazza Barberini. In 2012, church officials added a new six-room museum, which shows the clothing, footwear, books, and other religious artifacts used by members of the order. For most travelers, however, the morbid attraction remains the crypt.

The bones of more than 4,000 friars who died between 1528 and 1870 are in the basement, all lined up in a series of six crypts for the delight—or disgust—of the always-wide-eyed visitor. The monastic message on the wall explains that this is more than just a macabre exercise: "We were what you are...you will become what we are now."

As you leave (humming "the foot bone's connected to the..."), pick up a few of Rome's most interesting postcards—the proceeds support Capuchin mission work. Head back outside, where it's not just the bright light that provides contrast with the crypt. Within a few steps are: the US Embassy, Hard Rock Cafe, and fancy Via Veneto cafés, filled with the poor and envious keeping an eye out for the rich and famous.

Cost and Hours: €6, daily 9:00-19:00, last entry 30 minutes before closing, modest dress required, no photos, turn off mobile phones, Metro: Barberini, tel. 06-487-1185.

Piazza del Popolo

This vast oval square marks the traditional north entrance to Rome. From ancient times until the advent of trains and airplanes, this was just about any visitor's first look at Rome. Today the square, known for its symmetrical design and its art-filled churches, is the starting point for the city's evening *passeggiata* (see my "Dolce Vita Stroll" on page 842).

From the Flaminio Metro stop, pass through the third-century Aurelian Wall via the Porta del Popolo, and look south. The 10-story obelisk in the center of the square once graced the temple of Ramses II in Egypt and the Roman Circus Maximus racetrack. The obelisk was brought here in 1589 as one of the square's beautification projects. (The piazza's oval shape dates from the early 19th century.) At the south side of the square, twin domed churches mark the spot where three main boulevards exit the square and form a trident. The central boulevard (running between the churches) is Via del Corso, which since ancient times has been the main north-south drag through town, running to Capitoline Hill (the governing center) and the Forum.

Along the north side of the square (flanking the Porta del Popolo) are two 19th-century buildings that give the square its pleasant symmetry: the Carabinieri station and the Church of Santa Maria del Popolo.

Two large fountains grace the sides of the square—Neptune to the west and Roma to the east (marking the base of Pincio Hill). Though the name Piazza del Popolo means "Square of the People" (and it is a popular hangout), the word was probably derived from the Latin *populus,* after the poplar trees which once stood here.

ROME

Church of Santa Maria del Popolo

One of Rome's most overlooked churches, this features two chapels with top-notch art and a facade built of travertine scavenged from the Colosseum. The church is brought to you by the Rovere family, which produced two popes, and you'll see their symbol—the oak tree and acorns—throughout.

Go inside. The Chigi Chapel (second on the left) was designed by Raphael and inspired (as Raphael was) by the Pantheon. Notice the Pantheon-like dome, pilasters, and capitals. Above in the oculus, God looks in, aided by angels who power the eight known planets. Raphael built the chapel for his wealthy banker friend Agostino Chigi, buried in the pyramid-shaped tomb in the wall to the right of the altar. Later, Chigi's great-grandson hired Bernini to make two of the four statues, and Bernini delivered a theatrical episode. In one corner, Daniel straddles a lion and raises his praying hands to God for help. Kitty-corner across the chapel, an angel grabs Habbakuk's hair and tells him to go take some food to poor Daniel.

In the Cerasi Chapel (left of altar), Caravaggio's *The Conversion on the Way to Damascus* shows Paul sprawled on his back beside his horse while his servant looks on. The startled future saint is blinded by the harsh light as Jesus' voice asks him, "Why do you persecute me?" In the style of the Counter-Reformation, Paul receives his new faith with open arms.

In the same chapel, Caravaggio's *Crucifixion of St. Peter* is shown as a banal chore; the workers toil like faceless animals. The light and dark are in high contrast. Caravaggio liked to say, "Where light falls, I will paint it."

Cost and Hours: Free, Mon-Sat 7:00-12:00 & 16:00-18:30, Sun 8:00-13:30 & 16:30-19:30, often partially closed to accommodate its busy schedule of Masses, on north side of Piazza del Popolo—as you face the gate in the old wall from the square, the church entrance is to your right.

▲▲Catacombs of Priscilla (Catacombe di Priscilla)

While most tourists and nearly all tour groups go out to the ancient Appian Way to see the famous catacombs of San Sebastiano and San Callisto, the Catacombs of Priscilla (on the other side of town) are less commercialized and crowded, and just feel more intimate, as catacombs should.

You enter from a convent and explore the result of 250 years of tunneling that occurred from the second to the fifth centuries. Visits are by 30-minute guided tour only (English-language tours go whenever a small group gathers—generally every 20 minutes or so). You'll see a few thousand of the 40,000 niches carved here, along with some beautiful frescoes, including what is considered the first depiction of Mary nursing the Baby Jesus.

Cost and Hours: €8, Tue-Sun 8:30-12:00 & 14:30-17:00, closed Mon, last entry 30 minutes before closing, closed one random month a year—check website or call first, tel. 06-8620-6272, www.catacombepriscilla.com.

Getting There: The catacombs are northeast of Termini train station (at Via Salaria 430), far from the center (a €15 taxi ride) but well-served by buses (20-30 minutes). From Termini, take bus #92 or #86 from Piazza Cinquecento. From Piazza Venezia and along Via del Corso, take bus #63 or #630. Tell the driver "Piazza Crati" and "kah-tah-KOHM-bay" and he'll let you off near Piazza Crati (at the Nemorense/Crati stop). From there, walk through the little market in Piazza Crati, then down Via di Priscilla (about 5 minutes). The entrance is in the orange building on the left at the top of the hill.

MAXXI

Rome's "National Museum of Art of the 21st Century" is the big news on the museum scene here—as you can imagine it would be, after the 10 years and €150 million it took to make it happen. Like many contemporary art museums, it's notable more for the building than the art inside. To me, it comes off as a second-rate Pompidou Center. While not to my taste, it's one of the few places in the city where fans of contemporary architecture can see the latest trends.

Cost and Hours: €11, Tue-Sun 11:00-19:00, Thu and Sat until 22:00, closed Mon, last entry one hour before closing; no permanent collection, several rotating exhibits throughout the year—preview on their site; tram #2 from Piazza del Popolo to Piazza Apollo Doro, Via Guido Reni 4a, tel. 06-322-5178, www.fondazionemaxxi.it.

From the Spanish Steps to the Ara Pacis

▲Spanish Steps

The wide, curving staircase, culminating with an obelisk between two Baroque church towers, makes for one of Rome's iconic sights. Beyond that, it's a people-gathering place. By day, the area hosts shoppers looking for high-end fashions; on warm evenings, it attracts young people in love with the city. For more, see the "Heart of Rome Walk" on page 844.

"Shopping Triangle"

The triangular-shaped area between the Spanish Steps, Piazza Venezia, and Piazza del Popolo (along Via del Corso, see map on page 890) contains Rome's highest concentration of upscale boutiques and fashion stores.

▲▲Ara Pacis (Altar of Peace)

On January 30, 9 B.C., soon-to-be-emperor Augustus led a procession of priests up the steps and into this newly built "Altar of

Peace." They sacrificed an animal on the altar and poured an offering of wine, thanking the gods for helping Augustus pacify barbarians abroad and rivals at home. This marked the dawn of the Pax Romana (c. A.D. 1-200), a Golden Age of good living, stability, dominance, and peace *(pax)*. The Ara Pacis (AH-rah PAH-chees) hosted annual sacrifices by the emperor until the area was flooded by the Tiber River. Buried under silt, it was abandoned and forgotten until the 16th century, when various parts were discovered and excavated. Mussolini gathered the altar's scattered parts and reconstructed them here in 1938. In 2006, the Altar of Peace reopened to the public in a striking modern building. As the first new building allowed to be built in the old center since 1938, it's been controversial, but its quiet, air-conditioned interior may have signaled the dawn of another new age in Rome.

The Altar of Peace was originally located east of here, along today's Via del Corso. The model shows where it stood in relation to the Mausoleum of Augustus (now next door) and the Pantheon. Approach the Ara Pacis and look through the doorway to see the raised altar. This simple structure has just the basics of a Roman temple: an altar for sacrifices surrounded by cubicle-like walls that enclose a consecrated space.

The reliefs on the north and south sides probably depict the parade of dignitaries who consecrated the altar, while the reliefs on the west side (near the altar's back door) celebrate the two things Augustus brought to Rome: peace (goddess Roma as a conquering Amazon, right side) and prosperity (fertility goddess surrounded by children, plants, and animals).

Cost and Hours: €7.50, tightwads can look in through huge windows for free; Tue-Sun 9:00-19:00, closed Mon, last entry one hour before closing; €3.50 audioguide available as free download at www.arapacis.it, good WC downstairs. The Ara Pacis is a long block west of Via del Corso on Via di Ara Pacis, on the east bank of the Tiber near Ponte Cavour, Metro: Spagna; a 10-minute walk down Via dei Condotti, tel. 06-0608.

▲Fausto delle Chiaie (Fausto of the Beach)

This eccentric fellow (who's likely more sane than the rest of us) is a self-appointed part of the Ara Pacis. Fausto's installation art, usually strewn along the curb that runs between the Ara Pacis and Mausoleum of Augustus, aims to take you to a different dimension. Though he sits next to the local art academy, he stresses that the proximity is merely a coincidence. Charming Fausto speaks English and reminds you that his "plastic secretary" (a tip box) is at the end of the curb. He may be mini compared to the nearby museum, but for me he's more entertaining than the MAXXI.

East Rome

Near Termini Train Station

These sights are within a 10-minute walk of the train station. By Metro, use the Termini stop for the National Museum and the Repubblica stop for the rest.

▲▲▲National Museum of Rome
(Museo Nazionale Romano Palazzo Massimo alle Terme)

The National Museum's main branch, at Palazzo Massimo, houses the greatest collection of ancient Roman art anywhere. It's a historic yearbook of Roman marble statues with some rare Greek originals. On the ground floor alone, you can look eye-to-eye with Julius and Augustus Caesar, Alexander the Great, and Socrates.

On the first floor, along with statues and busts showing such emperors as Trajan and Hadrian, you'll see the best-preserved Roman copy of the Greek *Discus Thrower*. Statues of athletes like this commonly stood in the baths, where Romans cultivated healthy bodies, minds, and social skills, hoping to lead well-rounded lives. Other statues on this floor originally stood in the pleasure gardens of the Roman rich—surrounded by greenery with the splashing sound of fountains, all painted in bright, lifelike colors. Though executed by Romans, the themes are mostly Greek, with godlike humans and human-looking gods.

The second floor contains frescoes and mosaics that once decorated the walls and floors of Roman villas. They're remarkably realistic and unstuffy, featuring everyday people, animals, flowery patterns, and geometrical designs. The Villa Farnesina frescoes—in black, red, yellow, and blue—are mostly architectural designs, with fake columns, friezes, and garlands. The Villa di Livia frescoes, owned by the wily wife of Augustus, immerse you in a leafy green garden full of birds and fruit trees, symbolizing the gods.

Finally, descend into the basement to see fine gold jewelry, dice, an abacus, and vault doors leading into the best coin collection in Europe, with fancy magnifying glasses maneuvering you through cases of coins from ancient Rome to modern times.

Cost and Hours: €10 combo-ticket covers three other branches—all skippable, Tue-Sun 9:00-19:45, closed Mon, last entry 45 minutes before closing, audioguide-€5, about 100 yards from train station, Metro: Repubblica or Termini, tel. 06-3996-7700, http://archeoroma.beniculturali.it/en. The museum is about 100 yards from Termini train station—as you leave the station, it's the sandstone-brick building on your left. Enter at the far end, at Largo di Villa Peretti.

ROME

Near Termini Station

(Map locations include: Piazza Della Croce Rossa, To Villa Borghese Gardens, US Embassy, To Spanish Steps, CAPUCHIN CRYPT, SANTA MARIA DELLA VITTORIA, Piazza Barberini, SANTA SUSANNA, Piazza di San Bernardo, BATHS OF DIOCLETIAN, Piazza Indipendenza, Repubblica, STA. MARIA DEGLI ANGELI, Piazza Repubblica, Piazza dei Cinquecento, Castro Pretorio, PALAZZO DEL QUIRINALE, SAN CARLINO, To Trevi & Pantheon, Piazza del Quirinale, NAT'L MUSEUM OF ROME, TERMINI STATION, SANTA MARIA MAGGIORE, Largo Magnanapoli, SANTA PRASSEDE, Cavour, To Colosseum & Forum, MUSEUM OF ASIAN ART, Piazza Vittorio Emanuele II, Vittorio Emanuele; scale: 250 Meters / 250 Yards)

▲Baths of Diocletian (Terme di Diocleziano)

Around A.D. 300, Emperor Diocletian built the largest baths in Rome. This sprawling meeting place—with baths and schmoozing spaces to accommodate 3,000 bathers at a time—was a big deal in ancient times.

While much of it is still closed, the best part is open: the Church of Santa Maria degli Angeli. From noisy Piazza della Repubblica, step into the vast and cool church built upon the remains of a vast and steamy Roman bath complex. The church we see today was (at least partly) designed by Michelangelo (1561), who used the baths' main hall as the nave. Later, when Piazza della Repubblica became an important Roman intersection, another architect renovated the church. To allow people to enter from the grand new piazza, he spun it 90 degrees, turning Michelangelo's nave into a long transept. The eight red granite columns are original, from ancient Rome—stand next to one and feel its five-foot girth. (Only the eight in the transept proper are original. The others are made of plastered-over brick.) In Roman times, this hall was covered with mosaics, marble, and gold, and lined with statues.

Cost and Hours: Free, Mon-Sat 7:00-18:30, Sun 7:00-19:30, closed to sightseers during Mass, faces Piazza della Repubblica.

ROME

▲Church of Santa Maria della Vittoria

This church houses Bernini's statue, the swooning *St. Teresa in Ecstasy*. Inside the church, you'll find St. Teresa to the left of the altar. Teresa has just been stabbed with God's arrow of fire. Now, the angel pulls it out and watches her reaction. Teresa swoons, her eyes roll up, her hand goes limp, she parts her lips...and moans. The smiling, cherubic angel understands just how she feels. Teresa, a 16th-century Spanish nun, later talked of the "sweetness" of "this intense pain," describing her oneness with God in ecstatic, even erotic, terms.

Bernini, the master of multimedia, pulls out all the stops to make this mystical vision real. Actual sunlight pours through the alabaster windows, bronze sunbeams shine on a marble angel holding a golden arrow. Teresa leans back on a cloud and her robe ripples from within, charged with her spiritual arousal. Bernini has created a little stage-setting of heaven. And watching from the "theater boxes" on either side are members of the family who commissioned the work.

Cost and Hours: Free, pay €0.50 for light, Mon-Sat 8:30-12:00 & 15:30-18:00, Sun 15:30-18:00, about 5 blocks northwest of Termini train station on Largo Susanna, Metro: Repubblica.

Santa Susanna Church

The home of the American Catholic Church in Rome, Santa Susanna holds Mass in English daily at 18:00 and on Sunday at 9:00 and 10:30. They arrange papal audience tickets (see page 882), and their excellent website contains tips for travelers and a list of convents that rent out rooms.

Cost and Hours: Free, daily 9:00-12:00 & 16:00-18:00, Via XX Settembre 15, near recommended Via Firenze hotels, Metro: Repubblica, tel. 06-4201-4554, www.santasusanna.org.

Pilgrim's Rome

East of the Colosseum (and south of Termini train station) are several venerable churches that Catholic pilgrims make a point of visiting. Near one of the churches is a small WWII museum.

Church of San Giovanni in Laterano

Built by Constantine, the first Christian emperor, this was Rome's most important church through medieval times. A building alongside the church houses the Holy Stairs (Scala Santa) said to have been walked up by Jesus, which today are ascended by pilgrims on their knees.

Cost and Hours: Free, church—daily 7:00-18:30; Holy Stairs—daily April-Sept 6:15-12:00 & 15:30-18:45, Oct-March 6:15-12:00 & 15:00-18:15; audioguide—€5; Piazza di San Giovanni in Laterano, Metro: San Giovanni, or bus #85 or #87; tel. 06-6988-6409.

ROME

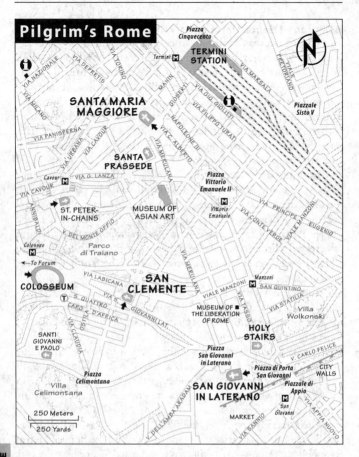

Pilgrim's Rome

Museum of the Liberation of Rome
(Museo Storico della Liberazione di Roma)

This small memorial museum, near the Church of San Giovanni in Laterano, is housed in the prison wing of the former Nazi police headquarters of occupied Rome. Other than a single printed sheet to help, there's little in English. Still, for those interested in resistance movements and the Nazi occupation, it's a stirring visit. You'll see a few artifacts, many photos of heroes, and a couple of cells preserved as they were found on June 4, 1944, when the city was liberated.

Cost and Hours: Free, Tue-Sun 9:30-12:30, Tue and Thu-Fri also 15:30-19:30, closed Mon and Aug, just behind the Holy Stairs at Via Tasso 145; tel. 06-700-3866.

Church of Santa Maria Maggiore

Some of Rome's best-surviving mosaics line the nave of this church built as Rome was falling. The nearby Church of Santa Prassede has still more early mosaics.

Cost and Hours: Free, daily 7:00-19:00, audioguide-€5, Piazza Santa Maria Maggiore, Metro: Termini or Vittorio Emanuele, tel. 06-6988-6802.

▲Church of San Clemente

Besides visiting the church itself, with frescoes by Masolino, you can also descend into the ruins of an earlier church. Descend yet one more level and enter the eerie remains of a pagan temple to Mithras.

Cost and Hours: Upper church—free, lower church—€5, both open Mon-Sat 9:00-12:30 & 15:00-18:00, Sun 12:00-18:00, last entry to lower church 20 minutes before closing; Via di San Giovanni in Laterano, Metro: Colosseo, or bus #85 or #87; tel. 06-774-0021, www.basilicasanclemente.com.

South Rome

The area south of the center contains some interesting but widely scattered areas, from Trastevere to the Jewish Quarter to the Ancient Appian Way.

Trastevere and Nearby

Trastevere is the colorful neighborhood across *(tras)* the Tiber *(Tevere)* River. Trastevere (trahs-TAY-veh-ray) offers the best look at medieval-village Rome. The action unwinds to the chime of the church bells. Go there and wander. Wonder. Be a poet. This is Rome's Left Bank. (You can download a free Rick Steves **audio tour** of this neighborhood; see page 7.)

This proud neighborhood was long a working-class area. Now that it's becoming trendy, high rents are driving out the source of so much color. Still, it's a great people scene, especially at night. Stroll the back streets (for restaurant recommendations, see page 924).

To reach Trastevere by foot from Capitoline Hill, cross the Tiber on Ponte Fabricio to Isola Tiberina; from there, Ponte Cestio takes you to Trastevere. You can also take tram #8 from Largo Argentina, or bus #H from Termini and Via Nazionale (get off at Piazza Belli). From the Vatican (Piazza Risorgimento), it's bus #23 or #271.

Linking Trastevere with the Heart of Rome Walk: You can walk from Trastevere to Campo de' Fiori to link up with the beginning of my Heart of Rome Walk (see page 844): From Trastevere's church square (Piazza di Santa Maria), take Via del Moro to the river and cross at Ponte Sisto, a pedestrian bridge that has a good view of St. Peter's dome. Continue straight ahead for one block.

ROME

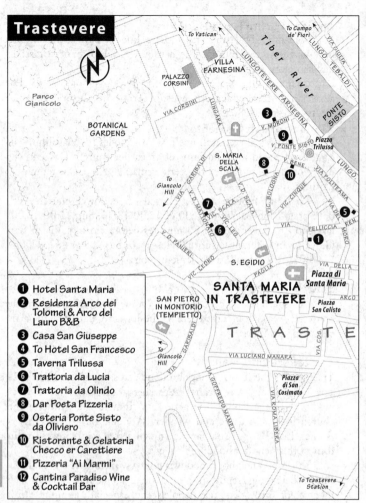

Trastevere

- **1** Hotel Santa Maria
- **2** Residenza Arco dei Tolomei & Arco del Lauro B&B
- **3** Casa San Giuseppe
- **4** To Hotel San Francesco
- **5** Taverna Trilussa
- **6** Trattoria da Lucia
- **7** Trattoria da Olindo
- **8** Dar Poeta Pizzeria
- **9** Osteria Ponte Sisto da Oliviero
- **10** Ristorante & Gelateria Checco er Carettiere
- **11** Pizzeria "Ai Marmi"
- **12** Cantina Paradiso Wine & Cocktail Bar

Take the first left, which leads down Via di Capo di Ferro through the scary and narrow darkness to Piazza Farnese, with the imposing Palazzo Farnese. Michelangelo contributed to the facade of this palace, now the French Embassy. The fountains on the square feature huge one-piece granite hot tubs from the ancient Roman Baths of Caracalla. One block from there (opposite the palace) is the atmospheric square, Campo de' Fiori.

▲Church of Santa Maria in Trastevere

One of Rome's oldest church sites, a basilica was erected here in the fourth century, when Christianity was legalized. It is said to have been the first church in Rome dedicated to the Virgin Mary. The structure you see today dates mainly from the 12th century. Its por-

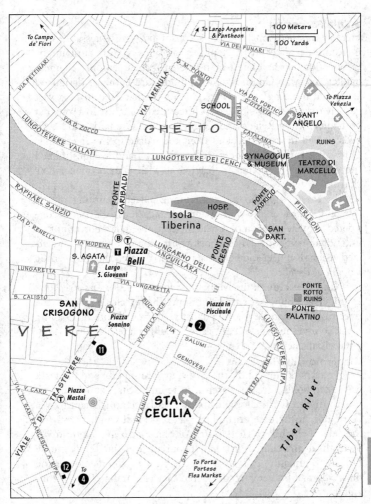

tico (covered area just outside the door) is decorated with fascinating fragments of stone—many of them lids from catacomb burial niches—and filled with early Christian symbolism. The church is on Piazza di Santa Maria, the Trastevere neighborhood's most important meeting place. With its broad and inviting steps, the 17th-century fountain was actually designed to be the "sofa" of the neighborhood. During major soccer games, a large screen is set up here so that everybody can share in the tension and excitement. At other times, children gather here with a ball and improvise matches of their own.

Cost and Hours: Free, daily 7:30-21:00.

▲Villa Farnesina

Here's a unique opportunity to see a sumptuous Renaissance villa in Rome decorated with Raphael paintings. It was built in the early 1500s for the richest man in Renaissance Europe, Siennese banker Agostino Chigi. Architect Baldassare Peruzzi's design—a U-shaped building with wings enfolding what used to be a vast garden—successfully blended architecture and nature in a way that both ancient and Renaissance Romans loved. Orchards and flower beds flowed down in terraces from the palace to the riverbanks. Later construction of modern embankments and avenues robbed the garden of its grandeur, leaving it with a more melancholy charm.

In the Loggia of Galatea, find Raphael's painting of the nymph Galatea (on the wall by the entrance door). Galatea is considered Raphael's vision of female perfection—not a portrait of an individual woman, but a composite of his many lovers in an idealized vision. Raphael and his assistants also painted the subtly erotic Loggia of Psyche.

Cost and Hours: €5; Mon and Sat 9:00-17:00, Tue-Fri 9:00-14:00, closed Sun, last entry 20 minutes before closing; across the river from Campo de' Fiori, a short walk from Ponte Sisto and a block behind the river at 230 Via della Lungara; tel. 06-6802-7268, www.villafarnesina.it.

Gianicolo Hill Viewpoint

From this park atop a hill, the city views are superb, and the walk to the top holds a treat for architecture buffs. Start at Trastevere's Piazza di San Cosimato, and follow Via Luciano Manara to Via Garibaldi, at the base of the hill. Via Garibaldi winds its way up the side of the hill to the Church of San Pietro in Montorio. To the right of the church, in a small courtyard, is the Tempietto by Donato Bramante. This tiny church, built to commemorate the martyrdom of St. Peter, is considered a jewel of Italian Renaissance architecture.

Continuing up the hill, Via Garibaldi connects to Passeggiata del Gianicolo. From here, you'll find a pleasant park with panoramic city views. Ponder the many Victorian-era statues, including that of baby-carrying, gun-wielding, horse-riding Anita Garibaldi. She was the Brazilian wife of the revolutionary General Giuseppe Garibaldi, who helped forge a united Italy in the late 19th century.

Near Trastevere: Jewish Quarter

From the 16th through the 19th centuries, Rome's Jewish population was forced to live in a cramped ghetto at an often-flooded bend of the Tiber River. While the medieval Jewish ghetto is long gone, this area—just across the river and toward Capitoline Hill from

Trastevere—is still home to Rome's synagogue and fragments of its Jewish heritage.

You can download a free Rick Steves **audio tour** of this neighborhood; see page 7.

Synagogue (Sinagoga) and Jewish Museum (Museo Ebraico)

Rome's modern synagogue stands proudly on the spot where the medieval Jewish community was sequestered for more than 300 years. The site of a historic visit by Pope John Paul II, this synagogue features a fine interior and a museum filled with artifacts of Rome's Jewish community. Modest dress is required. The only way to visit the synagogue—unless you're here for daily prayer service—is with a tour.

Cost and Hours: €10 ticket includes museum and guided hourly tour of synagogue; mid-June-mid-Sept Sun-Thu 10:00-19:00, Fri 10:00-16:00, closed Sat; mid-Sept-mid-June Sun-Thu 10:00-17:00, Fri 9:00-14:00, closed Sat; last entry 45 minutes before closing, English tours usually at :15 past the hour, 30 minutes, check schedule at ticket counter; on Lungotevere dei Cenci, tel. 06-6840-0661, www.museoebraico.roma.it. Walking tours of the Jewish Ghetto are conducted at least once a day except Saturday.

Ancient Appian Way

Southeast of the city center lie several ancient sights that make the trek here worthwhile.

Baths of Caracalla (Terme di Caracalla)

Inaugurated by Emperor Caracalla in A.D. 216, this massive bath complex could accommodate 1,600 visitors at a time. Today it's just a shell—a huge shell—with all of its sculptures and most of its mosaics moved to museums. You'll see a two-story roofless brick building surrounded by a garden, bordered by ruined walls. The two large rooms at either end of the building were used for exercise. In between the exercise rooms was a pool flanked by two small mosaic-floored dressing rooms. Niches in the walls once held statues. The baths' statues are displayed elsewhere: For example, the immense *Toro Farnese* (a marble sculpture of a bull surrounded by people) snorts in Naples' Archaeological Museum.

In its day, this was a remarkable place to hang out. For ancient Romans, bathing was a social experience. The Baths of Caracalla functioned until Goths severed the aqueducts in the sixth century. In modern times, grand operas are performed here.

Cost and Hours: €6, includes the Tomb of Cecilia Metella and the Villa dei Quintili on the Appian Way, Mon 9:00-14:00, Tue-Sun 9:00 until one hour before sunset (19:00 in summer, 16:30 in winter), last entry one hour before closing, audioguide-€5, good €8 guidebook; Metro: Circus Maximus, plus a 5-minute walk south

ROME

along Via delle Terme di Caracalla; bus #714 from Termini train station or bus #118 from the Appian Way—see "Getting There" on page 905; tel. 06-3996-7700.

▲Appian Way

For a taste of the countryside around Rome and more wonders of Roman engineering, take the four-mile trip from the Colosseum out past the wall to a stretch of the ancient Appian Way, where the original pavement stones are lined by several interesting sights. Ancient Rome's first and greatest highway, the Appian Way once ran from Rome to the Adriatic port of Brindisi, the gateway to Greece. Today you can walk (or bike) some stretches of the road, rattling over original paving stones, past crumbling monuments that once lined the sides.

The wonder of its day, the Appian Way was the largest, widest, fastest road ever, called the "Queen of Roads." Built in 312 B.C. and named after Appius Claudius Caecus (a Roman official), it connected Rome with Capua (near Naples), running in a straight line for much of the way, ignoring the natural contour of the land. Eventually, this most important of Roman roads stretched 430 miles to the port of Brindisi—the gateway to the East—where boats sailed for Greece and Egypt. Twenty-nine such roads fanned out from Rome. Just as Hitler built the Autobahn system in anticipation of empire maintenance, the expansion-minded Roman government realized the military and political value of a good road system. Today the road and the landscape around it are preserved as a cultural park.

For the tourist, the ancient Appian Way offers three attractions: the road itself, with its ruined monuments; the two major Christian catacombs open to visitors; and the peaceful atmosphere, which provides a respite from the city. Be aware, however, that the road today is busy with traffic—and actually quite treacherous in spots.

The road starts at the massive **San Sebastiano Gate and Museum of the Walls,** about two miles south of the Colosseum. The stretch that's of most interest to tourists starts another two miles south of the gate. I like to begin near the Tomb of Cecilia Metella, at the far (southern) end of the key sights, and work northward (mostly downhill) toward central Rome.

Cost and Hours: San Sebastiano Gate and Museum of the Walls—€4, Tue-Sun 9:00-14:00, closed Mon, last entry 30 minutes before closing, tel. 06-7047-5284.

When to Go: Visit in the morning or late afternoon, since many of the sights—including the Catacombs of San Callisto—shut down from 12:00 to 14:00. All the recommended sights are open on Tuesday, Thursday, Friday, and Saturday. On Monday, several sights are closed, including the Tomb of Cecilia Metella,

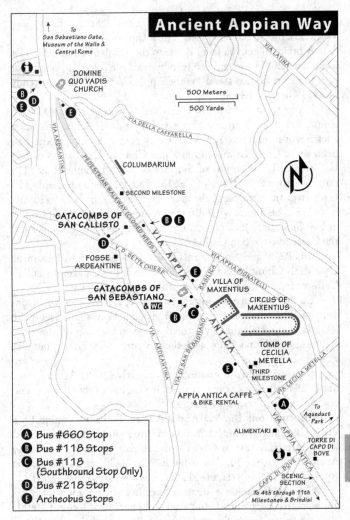

Ancient Appian Way

To
San Sebastiano Gate,
Museum of the Walls &
Central Rome

DOMINE
QUO VADIS
CHURCH

500 Meters

500 Yards

VIA LATINA

VIA DELLA CAFFARELLA

VIA ARDEATINA

PEDESTRIAN WALKWAY (CLOSED WEDS.)

COLUMBARIUM

SECOND MILESTONE

CATACOMBS OF
SAN CALLISTO

V. D. SETTE CHIESE

FOSSE
ARDEANTINE

CATACOMBS OF
SAN SEBASTIANO
& WC

VIA APPIA

VIA APPIA PIGNATELLI

BASILICA

VILLA OF
MAXENTIUS

CIRCUS OF
MAXENTIUS

VIA ARDEATINA

VIA DI SAN SEBASTIANO

VIA APPIA ANTICA

TOMB OF
CECILIA
METELLA

THIRD
MILESTONE

VIA CECILIA METELLA

APPIA ANTICA CAFFÈ
& BIKE RENTAL

ALIMENTARI

VIA APPIA ANTICA

To
Aqueduct
Park

TORRE DI
CAPO DI BOVE

CAPO DI BOVE

SCENIC
SECTION

To 4th through 11th
Milestones & Brindisi

- **A** Bus #660 Stop
- **B** Bus #118 Stops
- **C** Bus #118
  (Southbound Stop Only)
- **D** Bus #218 Stop
- **E** Archeobus Stops

ROME

the Circus and Villa of Maxentius, and the San Sebastiano Gate and Museum of the Walls. On Wednesday, the Catacombs of San Callisto and the pedestrian path through the park are closed. On Sunday, the Catacombs of San Sebastiano are closed; however, the Appian Way is closed to car traffic, making it a great day for walking or biking (although the old stones are bumpy).

Getting There: Bus #660 drops you off at the Tomb of Cecilia Metella. In Rome, take Metro line A to the Colli Albani stop, where you catch bus #660 (2/hour, along Via Appia Nuova) and ride 10 minutes to the last stop—Cecilia Metella/Via Appia Antica (at the intersection of Via Cecilia Metella and Via Appia

Antica). As it can be frustrating to buy a bus ticket on the Appian Way, have one in hand for your return trip.

A **taxi** will get you from Rome to the Tomb of Cecilia Metella for about €20. However, to return by taxi, you'll have to phone for one; there are no taxi stands on the Appian Way (or just take handy bus #118 back to Rome).

If you want to visit just a few sights, consider **bus #118.** In Rome, catch #118 from either the Piramide or Circo Massimo Metro stops; going away from the city center, it stops at the San Sebastiano Gate, Domine Quo Vadis Church, Catacombs of San Callisto, and Catacombs of San Sebastiano. Although bus #118 does not stop at the Tomb of Cecilia Metella, the tomb is only 500 yards away from the San Sebastiano bus stop. Going back to Rome, bus #118 takes a somewhat different route (skipping the Catacombs of San Sebastiano); catch this northbound bus just up the road at the Catacombs of San Callisto.

Bus #218 goes from San Giovanni in Laterano to Domine Quo Vadis Church and the west entrance of the Catacombs of San Callisto, but isn't that useful for other Appian Way sights.

The handy, but much more expensive, **Archeobus** runs from Termini train station to the major Appian Way sights (see page 833). It stops at all the key attractions—you can hop off, tour the sights, and pick up a later bus (officially runs twice hourly, but service can be spotty).

Getting Back: No matter how you arrive at the Appian Way, **bus #118** is an easy, cheap way to return to Rome (get off at the end of the line, the Piramide Metro stop).

Information: The **Via Appia Antica TI** near Domine Quo Vadis Church gives out maps and information on the entire park, which stretches east and south of the visit outlined here (daily April-Oct 9:30-17:30, Nov-March 9:30-16:30, rents bikes, Via Appia Antica 58/60, tel. 06-513-5316, www.parcoappiaantica).

Capo di Bove has a small info center with a good €4 map/guide, active excavations, and a relaxing garden (Mon-Sat 10:00-16:00, Sun 10:00-18:00, great place for discreet picnic, clean WCs, Via Appia Antica 222, tel. 06-3996-7700); it's 100 yards uphill from **Appia Antica Caffè,** which also has maps and rents bikes (mobile 340-319-8060).

Services: Free WCs are at the San Sebastiano and San Callisto catacombs and at Capo di Bove, and WCs for paying customers are at the Tomb of Cecilia Metella and the Appia Antica Caffè. There are several water fountains along the way to refill water bottles.

▲▲Catacombs of San Sebastiano

A guide leads you underground through the tunnels where early Christians were buried. You'll see faded frescoes and graffiti by ear-

ROME

ly-Christian tag artists. Besides the catacombs themselves, there's a historic fourth-century basilica with holy relics.

Cost and Hours: €8, includes 35-minute tour, 2/hour, Mon-Sat 10:00-17:00, closed Sun and mid-Nov-mid-Dec, last entry 30 minutes before closing, Via Appia Antica 136, tel. 06-785-0350, www.catacombe.org.

▲▲Catacombs of San Callisto

The larger of the two sets of catacombs, San Callisto also is the more prestigious, having been the burial site for several early popes.

Cost and Hours: €8, includes 30-minute tour, at least 2/hour, Thu-Tue 9:00-12:00 & 14:00-17:00, closed Wed and Feb, Via Appia Antica 110, tel. 06-5130-1580 or 06-513-0151, www.catacombe.roma.it.

Near Rome

▲▲Ostia Antica

For an exciting day trip, pop down to the Roman port of Ostia, which is similar to Pompeii but a lot closer and, in some ways, more interesting. Because Ostia was a working port town, it shows a more complete and gritty look at Roman life than wealthier Pompeii. Wandering around today, you'll see warehouses, apartment flats, mansions, shopping arcades, and baths that served a once-thriving port of 60,000 people. Later, Ostia became a ghost town, and it's now excavated. Buy a map, then explore the town, including the 2,000-year-old theater. Finish with its fine little museum.

Cost and Hours: €8.50 for the site and museum, April-Oct Tue-Sun 8:30-19:00, Nov-Feb Tue-Sun 8:30-17:00, March Tue-Sun 8:30-18:00, closed Mon year-round, last entry one hour before closing. The museum closes from 13:30 to 14:30 for lunch. Tel. 06-5635-0215. Helpful websites include www.ostia-antica.org and http://archeoroma.beniculturali.it/en. A map of the site with suggested itineraries is available for €2 from the ticket office.

Audioguides: Although you'll see little audioguide markers throughout the site, there are no audioguides for rent. But you can download a free Rick Steves **audio tour** of Ostia Antica; see page 7.

Getting There: Getting to Ostia Antica from downtown Rome is a snap—it's a 45-minute combination Metro/train ride. (Since the train is part of the Metro system, it only costs one Metro ticket each way—€3 total round-trip.)

From Rome, take Metro line B to the Piramide stop, which is also the Roma Porta San Paolo train station. The train tracks are just a few steps from the Metro tracks: Follow signs to *Lido*—go up the escalator, turn left, and go down the steps into the Roma-Lido station. All trains depart in the direction of Lido, leave every 15 minutes, and stop at Ostia Antica along the way. The lighted schedule reads something like, "*Prossima partenza alle ore 13.25, bin*

3," meaning, "Next departure at 13:25 from track 3." Look for the next train, hop on, ride for about 30 minutes (no need to stamp your Metro ticket again, but keep it handy in case they decide to check), and get off at the Ostia Antica stop.

Leaving the train station in Ostia Antica, cross the road via the blue skybridge and walk straight down Via della Stazione di Ostia Antica, continuing straight until you reach the parking lot. The entrance is to your left. (If you don't have a ticket to get back, purchase one at the ticket window at the station, or from the nearby snack bar.)

Sleeping in Rome

Double rooms listed in this chapter range from about €65 (very simple, toilet and shower down the hall) to €400 (maximum plumbing and more), with most clustering around €150 (with private bathrooms). I've favored these pricier options, because intense Rome is easier to enjoy with a welcoming oasis to call home.

Some places give you a small discount (about 5 percent) if you pay cash. Haggle if you arrive late in the day during off-season (roughly mid-July through August and November through mid-March). It's common for hotels in Rome to lower their prices 10-50 percent in the off-season, although prices at hostels and the cheaper hotels won't fluctuate much. Room rates are lowest in sweltering August.

Traffic in Rome roars. Thanks to double-paned windows and air-conditioning, night noise is not the problem it once was. Even so, light sleepers who ask for a *tranquillo* room will likely get a room in the back...and sleep better. Once you actually see your room, consider the potential problem of night noise. If necessary, don't hesitate to ask for a quieter room.

Almost no hotels have parking, but nearly all have a line on spots in a nearby garage (about €24/day).

Convents: Although I list just a few, Rome has many convents that rent out rooms. See the Church of Santa Susanna's website for a list (www.santasusanna.org, select "Coming to Rome"). At convents, the beds are twins and English is often in short supply, but the price is right. Consider these nun-run places, all listed in this chapter: the expensive but divine **Casa di Santa Brigida** (near Campo de' Fiori), **Suore di Santa Elisabetta** (near Santa Maria Maggiore), **Casa Sant'Sofia** (near the Colosseum), **Casa Il Rosario** (near Piazza Venezia), and **Casa per Ferie Santa Maria alle Fornaci** (near the Vatican).

Hostels: If going the hostel route, consider the ones I list in this chapter (within a 10-minute walk of Termini train station), or check www.backpackers.it for more listings.

Sleep Code

(€1 = about $1.30)
S = Single, **D** = Double/Twin, **T** = Triple, **Q** = Quad, **b** = bathroom, **s** = shower only. Unless otherwise noted, breakfast is included, hotel staff speak basic English, and credit cards are accepted.

To help you easily sort through these listings, I've divided the accommodations into three categories based on the price for a double room with bath during high season:

$$$ **Higher Priced**—Most rooms €180 or more.
  $$ **Moderately Priced**—Most rooms between €130-180.
    $ **Lower Priced**—Most rooms €130 or less.

Rome charges a hotel tax of €2-3 per person, per night that must be paid in cash at checkout. This tax is typically not included in the prices I've listed here.

Prices can change without notice; verify the hotel's current rates online or by email.

Near Termini Train Station

While not as atmospheric as other areas of Rome, the hotels near Termini train station are less expensive, and public-transportation options link these places easily with the entire city. The city's two Metro lines intersect at the station, and most buses leave from here. Piazza Venezia is a 20-minute walk down Via Nazionale.

West of the Station

Most of these hotels are on or near Via Firenze, a safe, handy, central, and relatively quiet street that's a 10-minute walk from Termini train station and the airport train, and two blocks beyond Piazza della Repubblica. The Defense Ministry is nearby, so you've got heavily armed guards watching over you all night.

The neighborhood is well-connected by public transportation (with the Repubblica Metro stop nearby). Virtually all the city buses that rumble down Via Nazionale (#64, #70, #115, #640, #492, and the #40 express) take you to Piazza Venezia (Forum) and Largo Argentina (Pantheon). From Largo Argentina, bus #64 (jammed with people and thieves), the #40 express bus, and bus #492 continue to the Vatican. Or, at Largo Argentina, you can transfer to electric trolley #8 to Trastevere (get off at first stop after crossing the river).

To stock your closet pantry, pop over to **Despar Supermarket** (daily 8:00-21:00, Via Nazionale 213, at the corner of Via Venezia).

ROME

A 24-hour **pharmacy** near the recommended hotels is Farmacia Piram (Via Nazionale 228, tel. 06-488-4437).

$$$ Residenza Cellini feels like the guest wing of a gorgeous Neoclassical palace. It offers 11 rooms, "ortho/anti-allergy beds," four-star comforts and service, and a breezy breakfast terrace (Db-€190, larger Db-€210, extra bed-€25, show this book and ask for best Rick Steves price if paying with cash, air-con, elevator, Internet access and Wi-Fi, Via Modena 5, tel. 06-4782-5204, fax 06-4788-1806, www.residenzacellini.it, residenzacellini@tin.it, Barbara, Gaetano, and Donato).

$$$ Hotel Modigliani, a delightful 23-room place, is energetically run in a clean, bright, minimalist yet in-love-with-life style that its artist namesake would appreciate. It has a vast and plush lounge, a garden, and a newsletter introducing you to each of the staff (Db-€195, but check website for deals and ask about additional Rick Steves discount; air-con, Wi-Fi; northwest of Via Firenze—from Tritone Fountain on Piazza Barberini, go 2 blocks up Via della Purificazione to #42; tel. 06-4281-5226, www.hotel-modigliani.com, info@hotelmodigliani.com, Giulia and Marco).

$$$ IQ Hotel, facing the Opera House, is a beautifully designed place. It feels almost Scandinavian in its efficiency, without a hint of the Old World. Its 88 rooms are fresh and spacious, the roof garden comes with a swing set, and vending machines dispense bottles of wine (Db-€100-220 depending on room size and season—likely €200 in peak season, €40 extra for 3rd and 4th person, discount off best Web price for Rick Steves readers—must book direct and request at time of booking, breakfast-€10, air-con, elevator, Internet access and Wi-Fi, cheap self-service laundry, gym, Via Firenze 8, tel. 06-488-0465, fax 06-4893-0442, www. iqhotelroma.it, info@iqhotelroma.it, manager Diego).

$$ Hotel Oceania is a peaceful slice of air-conditioned heaven. This 24-room manor house-type hotel is spacious and quiet, with tastefully decorated rooms. Stefano runs a fine staff, serves wonderful coffee, provides lots of thoughtful extra touches, and works hard to maintain a caring family atmosphere (Sb-€135, Db-€168, Tb-€198, Qb-€220, show this book and ask for best Rick Steves price if paying with cash, deep discounts summer and winter, roof terrace, family suite, Internet access and Wi-Fi, videos in the TV lounge, Via Firenze 38, third floor, tel. 06-482-4696, fax 06-488-5586, www.hoteloceania.it, info@hoteloceania.it; Anna and Radu round out the staff).

$$ Hotel Aberdeen, which perfectly combines high quality and friendliness, is warmly run by Annamaria, with support from sister Laura and cousin Cinzia, and staff members Mariano and Costel. The 37 comfy, modern rooms are a good value (Sb-€102,

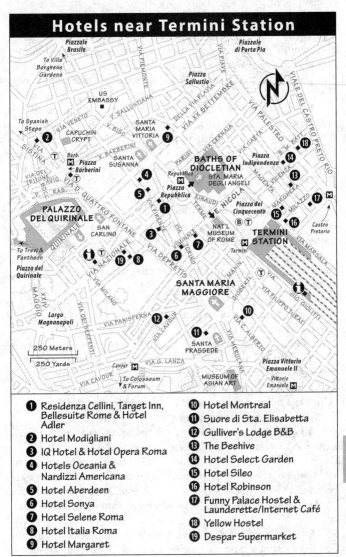

Hotels near Termini Station

1. Residenza Cellini, Target Inn, Bellesuite Rome & Hotel Adler
2. Hotel Modigliani
3. IQ Hotel & Hotel Opera Roma
4. Hotels Oceania & Nardizzi Americana
5. Hotel Aberdeen
6. Hotel Sonya
7. Hotel Selene Roma
8. Hotel Italia Roma
9. Hotel Margaret
10. Hotel Montreal
11. Suore di Sta. Elisabetta
12. Gulliver's Lodge B&B
13. The Beehive
14. Hotel Select Garden
15. Hotel Sileo
16. Hotel Robinson
17. Funny Palace Hostel & Launderette/Internet Café
18. Yellow Hostel
19. Despar Supermarket

ROME

Db-€170, Tb-€180, Qb-€200, for these rates—or better—book direct via email or use the "Rick Steves reader reservations" link on their website, much cheaper rates off-season, air-con, Internet access and Wi-Fi, Via Firenze 48, tel. 06-482-3920, fax 06-482-1092, www.hotelaberdeen.it, info@hotelaberdeen.it).

\$\$ Hotel Opera Roma, with contemporary furnishings and marble accents, boasts 15 spacious, modern, and thoughtfully appointed rooms. It's quiet and just a stone's throw from the Opera House (Db-€165, Tb-€190, show this book and ask for best Rick Steves price, additional cash discount, air-con, elevator, Internet access and loaner laptop on request, Via Firenze 11, tel. 06-487-1787, www.hoteloperaroma.com, info@hoteloperaroma.com, Rezza, Litu, and Federica).

$$ Hotel Sonya offers 34 well-equipped rooms, a hearty breakfast, a central location, and decent prices (Sb-€90, Db-€150, Tb-€165, Qb-€185, Quint/b-€200, show this book and ask for best Rick Steves price if paying cash, air-con, elevator, loaner laptops in room and Wi-Fi, faces the Opera House at Via Viminale 58, Metro: Repubblica or Termini, tel. 06-481-9911, fax 06-488-5678, www.hotelsonya.it, info@hotelsonya.it, Francesca and Ivan).

$$ Hotel Selene Roma spreads its 40 rooms out on a few floors of a big palazzo. With elegant furnishings and room to breathe, it's a fine value (Db-€150, Tb-€165, email direct for discount, additional cash discount, air-con, elevator, Wi-Fi, Via del Viminale 8, tel. 06-474-4781, www.hotelseleneroma.it, reception@hotelseleneroma.it).

$$ Bellesuite Rome offers six bright, modern rooms with all the comforts in a quiet building (Db-€150, Tb-€190, Qb-€215, air-con, elevator, Wi-Fi, Via Modena 5, tel. 06-9521-3049, www.bellesuiterome.com, mail@bellesuiterome.com).

$$ Target Inn is a sleek, practical-but-forgettable six-room place next to Residenza Cellini (listed earlier). It's owned by the same people who run the recommended Target Restaurant nearby (Db-€150, air-con, elevator, Wi-Fi, Via Modena 5, tel. 06-474-5399, www.targetinn.com, info@targetinn.com).

$ Hotel Adler evokes a more genteel age of travel, with a small garden patio and eight basic rooms on a wide and elegant hall (Db-€125, Tb-€165, Qb-€190, Quint/b-€210, discount with this book, additional discount if you pay cash, air-con, elevator, Internet access and Wi-Fi, Via Modena 5, second floor, tel. 06-484-466, fax 06-488-0940, www.hoteladler-roma.com, info@hoteladler-roma.com).

$ Hotel Nardizzi Americana, with 33 decent rooms and a delightful rooftop terrace, is another solid value (Sb-€95, Db-€125, Tb-€155, Qb-€175; to get the best rates, check their "Rick Steves readers reservations" link along with the rest of their website; additional cash discount, air-con, elevator, Internet access and Wi-Fi, Via Firenze 38, fourth floor, tel. 06-488-0035, fax 06-488-0368, www.hotelnardizzi.it, info@hotelnardizzi.it; friendly Stefano, Fabrizio, Mario, and Giancarlo).

$ Hotel Italia Roma, in a busy and handy locale, is located safely on a quiet street next to the Ministry of the Interior. Thoughtfully run by Andrea, Sabrina, Abdul, and Gabriel, it has

35 modest but comfortable rooms (Sb-€90, Db-€130, Tb-€180, Qb-€200, 30 percent cheaper July-Aug, air-con-€10 extra per day, elevator, Internet access and Wi-Fi, Via Venezia 18, just off Via Nazionale, Metro: Repubblica, tel. 06-482-8355, fax 06-474-5550, www.hotelitaliaroma.it, info@hotelitaliaroma.it). The four "residenza" rooms upstairs on the third floor are newer and a bit more expensive. They also have eight similar annex rooms across the street.

$ **Hotel Margaret** fills its walls with Impressionist prints and offers 12 decent rooms at a fair price (Db-€110, Tb-€150, Qb-€170, mention this book for best rates, air-con, elevator, Wi-Fi, north of Piazza Repubblica at Via Antonio Salandra 6, fourth floor, tel. 06-482-4285, fax 06-482-4277, www.hotelmargaret.net, info@hotelmargaret.net, Emanuela).

Southwest of the Station

These good-value places cluster around the basilica of Santa Maria Maggiore, on the edge of Rome's international district.

$ **Hotel Montreal** is a basic three-star place with 27 small rooms on a big street a block southeast of Santa Maria Maggiore (Sb-€90, Db-€110, Tb-€135, may be less if you email direct and ask for a Rick Steves discount, air-con, elevator, Internet access and Wi-Fi, small garden terrace, good security, Via Carlo Alberto 4, 1 block from Metro: Vittorio Emanuele, 3 blocks from Termini train station, tel. 06-445-7797, fax 06-446-5522, www.hotelmontreal-roma.com, info@hotelmontrealroma.com, Pasquale).

$ **Suore di Santa Elisabetta** is a heavenly Polish-run convent with a serene garden and 70 beds in tidy twin-bedded (only) rooms. Often booked long in advance, with such tranquility it's a super value (S-€40, Sb-€48, D-€66, Db-€85, Tb-€106, Qb-€128, Quint/b-€142, no air-con, elevator serves top floors only, fine view roof terrace and breakfast hall, 23:00 curfew, a block southwest of Santa Maria Maggiore at Via dell'Olmata 9, Metro: Termini or Vittorio Emanuele, tel. 06-488-8271, fax 06-488-4066, www.csse-roma.eu, ist.it.s.elisabetta@libero.it).

$ **Gulliver's Lodge B&B** has four fun, colorful rooms on the ground floor of a large, secure building. While on a busy street, the rooms are quiet. Although the public spaces are few, in-room extras like DVD players (and DVDs, including my Italy shows) make it a fine home base (Db-€120, Tb-€135, mention the book for these prices, cash only, air-con, Internet access and Wi-Fi, a 15-minute walk southwest of Termini train station at Via Cavour 101, Metro: Cavour, tel. 06-9727-3787, www.gulliverslodge.com, info@gulliverslodge.com, Sara and Mary).

ROME

Sleeping Cheaply, Northeast of Termini Train Station

The cheapest places in town are northeast of Termini train station (Metro: Termini). Some travelers feel this area is weird and spooky after dark, but these hotels feel plenty safe. With your back to the train tracks, turn right and walk two blocks out of the station. **Splashnet** launderette/Internet café is handy (€8 full-serve wash and dry, Internet access-€1.50/hour, €2 luggage storage per day—or free if you wash and go online, daily 8:30-23:00, just off Via Milazzo at Via Varese 33, tel. 06-4470-3523).

$ The Beehive gives vagabonds—old and young—a cheap, clean, and comfy home in Rome, thoughtfully and creatively run by Steve and Linda, a friendly American couple, and their hard-working staff. They offer six great-value artsy-mod double rooms (D-€80, T-€105), and an eight-bed dorm (€30 bunks). Their nearby annex, The Sweets, has similar style and several rooms with private baths (Sb-€60, Db-€100, air-con-€10, Internet access and Wi-Fi, private garden terrace, 2 blocks from Termini train station at Via Marghera 8, tel. 06-4470-4553, www.the-beehive.com, info@the-beehive.com).

$ Hotel Select Garden, a modern and comfortable 21-room hotel run by the cheery Picca family, boasts lively modern art adorning the walls and a beautiful lemon-tree garden. It's a safe, tranquil, and welcoming refuge just a couple of blocks from the train station (Sb-€95, Db-€120, Tb-€140, show this book and ask for best Rick Steves price, air-con, Wi-Fi, Via V. Bachelet 6, tel. 06-445-6383, fax 06-444-1086, www.hotelselectgarden.com, info@hotelselectgarden.com, Armando).

$ Hotel Sileo, with shiny chandeliers in dim rooms, is a homely little place renting 10 basic rooms (Db-€75, Tb-€90, air-con, elevator, Wi-Fi, Via Magenta 39, fourth floor, tel. & fax 06-445-0246, www.hotelsileo.com, info@hotelsileo.com). Friendly Alessandro and Maria Savioli don't speak English, but daughter Anna does.

$ Hotel Robinson is just a few steps from the station, but tucked away from the commotion. Set on an interior courtyard, it has 20 simple rooms that are a fine value (Sb-€65, Db-€85, Tb-€120, mention this book for these rates and a small breakfast, air-con-€10, Wi-Fi, Via Milazzo 3, tel. 06-491-423, fax 06-8968-5644, www.hotelrobinsonrome.com, info@hotelrobinsonrome.com).

$ Funny Palace Hostel, adjacent to Splashnet and run by its entrepreneurial owner Mabri, rents dorm beds in quiet four-person rooms and 18 stark-but-clean private rooms (dorm beds-€25, Db-€100, cash only, reception in the launderette—described earlier, Via Varese 33/31, tel. 06-4470-3523, www.hostelfunny.com).

$ Yellow Hostel rents 130 beds in 4-, 6-, and 12-bed coed dorms to 18- through 39-year-olds only (they also have 11 private rooms). Hip yet sane, it's well-run with fine facilities, including lockers. There's no curfew, and its café/late-night bar is next door (€18-35/bed depending on plumbing, size, and season; reserve via email—no telephone reservations accepted, Wi-Fi and iPad rental available, 6 blocks from station, just past Via Vicenza at Via Palestro 40/44, tel. 06-493-82682, www.yellowhostel.com).

Near Ancient Rome

Stretching from the Colosseum to Piazza Venezia, this area is central. Sightseers are a short walk from the Colosseum, Roman Forum, and Trajan's Column.

Near the Colosseum

$$$ Hotel Lancelot is a comfortable yet elegant refuge—a 60-room hotel with the ambience of a B&B. It's quiet and safe, with a shady courtyard, restaurant, bar, and tiny communal sixth-floor terrace. It's well-run by Faris and Lubna Khan, who serve a good €25 dinner—a chance to connect with your hotel neighbors and the staff. No wonder it's popular with returning guests (Sb-€126, Db-€194, Tb-€224, Qb-€264, €20 extra for sixth-floor terrace room with a Colosseum view, discount with this book, air-con, elevator, wheelchair-accessible, Wi-Fi, parking-€10/day, 10-minute walk behind Colosseum near San Clemente Church at Via Capo d'Africa 47, tel. 06-7045-0615, fax 06-7045-0640, www.lancelothotel.com, info@lancelothotel.com). Faris and Lubna speak the Queen's English.

$$ Hotel Paba has seven fresh rooms, chocolate-box-tidy and lovingly cared for by Alberta Castelli. Though it overlooks busy Via Cavour just two blocks from the Colosseum, it's quiet enough (Db-€135, extra bed-€40, ask about cash discount, big beds, breakfast served in room, air-con, elevator, Wi-Fi, Via Cavour 266, Metro: Cavour, tel. 06-4782-4902, fax 06-4788-1225, www.hotelpaba.com, info@hotelpaba.com).

$$ Nicolas Inn Bed & Breakfast, a delightful little four-room place with thoughtful touches, is spacious and bright. It's run by François and American expat Melissa, who make you feel like you have caring friends in Rome (Db-€150-170, ask about discount with this book, cash only, included breakfast served at neighboring bar, air-con, Wi-Fi, Via Cavour 295, tel. 06-9761-8483, www.nicolasinn.com, info@nicolasinn.com).

$ Hotel Pensione Rosetta, homey and family-run, rents 18 rooms. It's pretty minimal, with no lounge and no breakfast, but has a good location and reasonable prices (Sb-€70, Db-€95, Tb-€110, air-con, Wi-Fi, Via Cavour 295, tel. 06-478-23069, www.

ROME

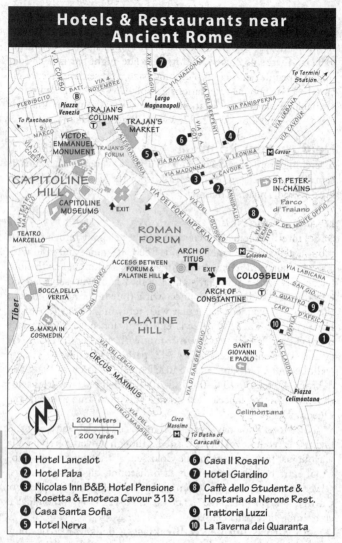

Hotels & Restaurants near Ancient Rome

1. Hotel Lancelot
2. Hotel Paba
3. Nicolas Inn B&B, Hotel Pensione Rosetta & Enoteca Cavour 313
4. Casa Santa Sofia
5. Hotel Nerva
6. Casa Il Rosario
7. Hotel Giardino
8. Caffè dello Studente & Hostaria da Nerone Rest.
9. Trattoria Luzzi
10. La Taverna dei Quaranta

rosettahotel.com, info@rosettahotel.com, Antonietta and Francesca).

$ Casa Santa Sofia, while stern and sterile, is still a welcoming and cozy convent that rents 60 rooms to travelers. Built for Russian and Brazilian pilgrims, it's well-run and situated on a characteristic square near a Metro stop and the Roman Forum (Sb-€50, Db-€80, dinner-€20, Piazza della Madonna dei Monti 3, Metro: Cavour, tel. 06-485-778, www.casasantasofia.it).

Near Piazza Venezia

$$$ Hotel Nerva is a three-star slice of tranquility with 19 small, overpriced (but often discounted) rooms on a surprisingly quiet back street just steps away from the Roman Forum (Sb-€130, Db-€190, extra bed-€40, ask for Rick Steves discount, rates very soft—especially off-season, air-con, elevator, Wi-Fi, Via Tor de' Conti 3, tel. 06-678-1835, fax 06-6992-2204, www.hotelnerva.com, info@hotelnerva.com, Antonio, Paolo, Anna).

$ Casa Il Rosario is a peaceful, well-run Dominican convent renting 40 rooms with monastic simplicity to both pilgrims and tourists in a good neighborhood (reserve several months in advance, S-€42, Sb-€56, Db-€94, Tb-€120, single beds only, fans, free Internet access, roof-terrace picnics welcome, 23:00 curfew, midway between Quirinale and Colosseum near bottom of Via Nazionale at Via Sant'Agata dei Goti 10, bus #40 or #170 from Termini, tel. 06-679-2346, fax 06-6994-1106, irodopre@tin.it).

$ Hotel Giardino offers 11 basic rooms in a central location three blocks northeast of Piazza Venezia (but may close in 2014). With a tiny central lobby and a small breakfast room, it suits travelers who prize location over big-hotel amenities (Sb-€85, Db-€130, one smaller Db for 15 percent less, these prices with cash and this book, air-con, Wi-Fi, effective double-paned windows, on a busy street off Piazza di Quirinale at Via XXIV Maggio 51, tel. 06-679-4584, fax 06-8928-1175, www.hotel-giardino-roma.com, info@hotel-giardino-roma.com, helpful Gianluca).

In the Pantheon Neighborhood

Winding, narrow lanes filled with foot traffic and lined with boutique shops and tiny trattorias...this is village Rome at its best. The atmosphere isn't cheap, but this is where you want to be—especially at night, when Romans and tourists gather in the floodlit piazzas for the evening stroll, the *passeggiata*.

ROME

Near Campo de' Fiori

You'll pay a premium (and endure a little extra night noise) to stay in the old center. But each of these places is romantically set deep in the tangled back streets near the idyllic Campo de' Fiori and, for many, worth the extra money.

$$$ Casa di Santa Brigida overlooks the elegant Piazza Farnese. With soft-spoken sisters gliding down polished hallways and pearly gates instead of doors, this lavish 20-room convent makes exhaust-stained Roman tourists feel like they've died and gone to heaven. If you don't need a double bed or a TV in your room, it's worth the splurge—especially if you luxuriate in its ample public spaces or on its lovely roof terrace (Sb-€120, twin Db-€200, book well in advance, air-con, elevator, Internet access and Wi-Fi,

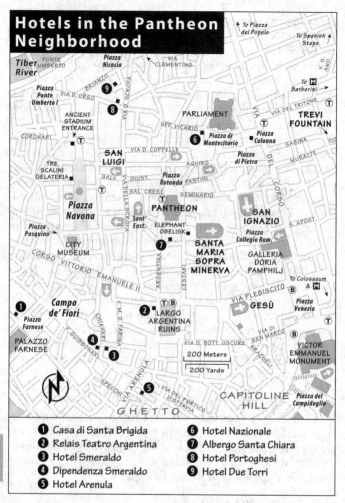

Hotels in the Pantheon Neighborhood

To Piazza del Popolo

To Spanish Steps

Tiber River

PONTE UMBERTO

Piazza Nicosia

VIA CLEMENTINO

Piazza Ponte Umberto I

VIA D'ORSO

VIA D. SCROFA

VIA DEL TRITONE

To M Barberini

TREVI FOUNTAIN

ANCIENT STADIUM ENTRANCE

CORONARI

PARLIAMENT

UFF. VICARIO

Piazza di Montecitorio

Piazza Colonna

SABINA

MURATTE

SAN LUIGI

VIA D. COPPELLE

AQUIRO

Piazza di Pietra

TRE SCALINI GELATERIA

SALV. GIUST.

VIA DELLA SCROFA

Piazza Rotonda

PASTINI

SAL. CRESC.

SEMINARIO

Piazza Navona

Sant' Eust.

PANTHEON

SAN IGNAZIO

S. APOST.

Piazza Pasquino

ELEPHANT OBELISK

Piazza Collegio Rom.

CITY MUSEUM

SANTA MARIA SOPRA MINERVA

GALLERIA DORIA PAMPHILJ

CORSO VITTORIO EMANUELE II

ARGENTINA

CESTARI

To Colosseum & M

VIA PLEBISCITO

Piazza Venezia

Campo de' Fiori

GESÙ

Piazza Farnese

CHIAVARI

V. M. D. FARINA

LARGO ARGENTINA RUINS

VIA DI SAN MARCO

VICTOR EMMANUEL MONUMENT

PALAZZO FARNESE

V. GIUBBONARI

VIA D. BOTT. OSCURE

ARACOELI

200 Meters

200 Yards

VIA ARENULA

SPECCHI

VIA DEL PORTICO D'OTTAVIA

CAPITOLINE HILL

Piazza del Campidoglio

GHETTO

❶ Casa di Santa Brigida
❷ Relais Teatro Argentina
❸ Hotel Smeraldo
❹ Dipendenza Smeraldo
❺ Hotel Arenula

❻ Hotel Nazionale
❼ Albergo Santa Chiara
❽ Hotel Portoghesi
❾ Hotel Due Torri

ROME

tasty €25 dinners, roof garden, plush library, Monserrato 54, tel. 06-6889-2596, fax 06-6889-1573, piazzafarnese@brigidine.org, many of the sisters are from India and speak English—pray you get to work with wonderful sister Gertrude).

$$$ **Relais Teatro Argentina,** a six-room gem, is steeped in tasteful old-Rome elegance, but has all the modern comforts. It's cozy and quiet like a B&B and couldn't be more centrally located (Db-€210, Tb-€240, discounts for cash and for stays of 3 days or more, air-con, no elevator, 3 flights of stairs, Internet access and Wi-Fi, Via del Sudario 35, tel. 06-9893-1617, www.relaisteatroargentina.com, info@relaisteatroargentina.com, Carlotta).

$$ Hotel Smeraldo, with 50 rooms, is strictly run by an impersonal staff, but it's clean and a reasonable deal (Sb-€110, Db-€150, Tb-€170, show this book for best rates, air-con, elevator, Internet access and Wi-Fi, flowery roof terrace, midway between Campo de' Fiori and Largo Argentina at Vicolo dei Chiodaroli 9, tel. 06-687-5929, fax 06-6880-5495, www.smeraldoroma.com, info@smeraldo-roma.com, Massimo and Walter). Their **Dipendenza Smeraldo,** 10 yards around the corner at Via dei Chiavari 32, has 16 similar rooms (same price and free breakfast, same reception and contact info).

In the Jewish Ghetto

$$ Hotel Arenula, with 50 decent rooms, is the only hotel in Rome's old Jewish ghetto. Though it has the ambience of a gym and attracts lots of students, it is in the thick of old Rome (Sb-€75-98, Db-€133, ask about high-season discount with this book, extra bed-€21, air-con, no elevator, Wi-Fi, opposite the fountain in the park on Via Arenula at Via Santa Maria de' Calderari 47, tel. 06-687-9454, fax 06-689-6188, www.hotelarenula.com, info@hotelarenula.com).

Close to the Pantheon

These places are buried in the pedestrian-friendly heart of ancient Rome, each within about a five-minute walk of the Pantheon. You'll pay more here—but you'll save time and money by being exactly where you want to be for your early and late wandering.

$$$ Hotel Nazionale, a four-star landmark, is a 16th-century palace that shares a well-policed square with the Parliament building. Its 100 rooms are accentuated by lush public spaces, fancy bars, a uniformed staff, and a marble-floored restaurant. It's a big, stuffy hotel with a revolving front door, but it's a worthy splurge if you want security, comfort, and the heart of Rome at your doorstep (Sb-€220, Db-€350, giant deluxe Db-€480, extra person-€70, check online for summer and weekend discounts—you'll typically save 30 percent off their sky-high rack rates, air-con, elevator, Wi-Fi, Piazza Montecitorio 131, tel. 06-695-001, fax 06-678-6677, www.hotelnazionale.it, info@hotelnazionale.it).

$$$ Albergo Santa Chiara, in the old center, is big, solid, and hotelesque. Flavia, Silvio, and their fine staff offer marbled elegance (but basic furniture) and all the hotel services. Its ample public lounges are dressy and professional, and its 99 rooms are quiet and spacious (Sb-€138, Db-€190, Db-€215 April-June and Oct, Tb-€260, check website for discounts, book online direct and request special Rick Steves rates, elevator, air-con, Wi-Fi, behind Pantheon at Via di Santa Chiara 21, tel. 06-687-2979, fax 06-687-3144, www.albergosantachiara.com, info@albergosantachiara.com).

ROME

$$$ Hotel Portoghesi is a classic hotel with 28 rooms in the medieval heart of Rome. It's peaceful, quiet, and calmly run, and comes with a delightful roof terrace—though you pay for the location (Sb-€130-160, Db-€160-200, price range reflects low and high season, breakfast on roof, air-con, elevator, Wi-Fi, Via dei Portoghesi 1, tel. 06-686-4231, fax 06-687-6976, www.hotelportoghesiroma.it, info@hotelportoghesiroma.it).

$$$ Hotel Due Torri, hiding out on a tiny quiet street, is beautifully located. It feels professional yet homey, with an accommodating staff, generous public spaces, and 26 small rooms. While the location and lounge are great, the rooms are overpriced (Sb-€125, Db-€195, family apartment-€240 for 3 and €260 for 4, check website for frequent discounts, air-con, elevator, Wi-Fi, a block off Via della Scrofa at Vicolo del Leonetto 23, tel. 06-6880-6956, fax 06-686-5442, www.hotelduetorriroma.com, info@hotelduetorriroma.com, Cinzia).

In Trastevere

Colorful and genuine in a gritty sort of way, Trastevere is a treat for travelers looking for a less touristy and more bohemian atmosphere. Choices are few here, but by trekking across the Tiber, you can have the experience of being comfortably immersed in old Rome. To locate the following places, see the map on page 900.

$$$ Hotel Santa Maria sits like a lazy hacienda in the midst of Trastevere. Surrounded by a medieval skyline, you'll feel as if you're on some romantic stage set. Its 20 small but well-equipped, air-conditioned rooms—former cells in a cloister—are all on the ground floor, as are a few suites for up to six people. The rooms circle a gravelly courtyard of orange trees and stay-awhile patio furniture (Db-€180, Tb-€220; show this book and ask for best Rick Steves price, higher rates for stays shorter than three nights; family rooms, free loaner bikes, Internet access and Wi-Fi, face church on Piazza Maria Trastevere and go right down Via della Fonte d'Olio 50 yards to Vicolo del Piede 2, tel. 06-589-4626, fax 06-589-4815, www.hotelsantamaria.info, info@hotelsantamaria.info). Some rooms come with family-friendly fold-down bunks for €30 extra per person. Their freshly renovated six-room **Residenza Santa Maria** is a couple of blocks away (same prices and contact info).

$$$ Residenza Arco dei Tolomei is your most poetic Trastevere experience imaginable, with six small, unique, antique-filled rooms boasting fragrant balconies. With its quiet and elegant setting, you can pretend you're visiting aristocratic relatives (Db-€200, discounts for cash and for stays of three days or more, reserve well in advance, Internet access and Wi-Fi, from Piazza Piscinula a block up Via dell'Arco de' Tolomei at #27, tel. 06-5832-0819, fax

06-6456-1375, www.bbarcodeitolomei.com, info@bbarcodeitolomei.com; Marco, Gianna Paola, and dog Pixel).

$$ Casa San Giuseppe is down a characteristic laundry-strewn lane with a sunny roof terrace and views of Aurelian Walls. While convent-owned, it's a secular place renting 29 plain but peaceful, spacious, and spotless rooms (Sb-€115, Db-€155, Tb-€185, Qb-€215, garden-facing rooms are quiet, air-con, elevator, Internet access, parking-€15, just north of Piazza Trilussa at Vicolo Moroni 22, tel. 06-5833-3490, fax 06-5833-5754, www.casasangiuseppe.it, info@casasangiuseppe.it, Andrea).

$$ Arco del Lauro B&B rents six white, minimalist rooms in a good location. Facing a courtyard (no views but little noise), the friendly welcome and good value make up for the lack of public spaces (Db-€135, Qb-€185, prices good if booked direct, cash only, includes breakfast served in a café, air-con, Internet access and Wi-Fi, from Piazza Piscinula a block up Via dell'Arco de' Tolomei at #29, tel. 06-9784-0350, mobile 346-244-3212, fax 06-9725-6541, www.arcodellauro.it, info@arcodellauro.it, Lorenza and Daniela).

$$ Hotel San Francesco, big and blocky yet welcoming, stands like a practical and efficient oasis at the edge of all the Trastevere action. Renting 24 trim rooms in this authentic district, it comes with an inviting roof terrace and a helpful staff. Handy trams to Largo Argentina are just a block away (Db-€90-180, prices vary wildly, email direct and mention this book for best rates, air-con, elevator, Wi-Fi, Via Jacopa de' Settesoli 7, tel. 06-5830-0051, www.hotelsanfrancesco.net, info@hotelsanfrancesco.net).

Near Vatican City

Sleeping near the Vatican is expensive, but some enjoy calling this more relaxed, residential neighborhood home. Even though it's handy to the Vatican (when the rapture hits, you're right there), everything else is a long way away. Fortunately, it's well-served by public transit—use the Metro (line A) and bus (ask your hotel for the most convenient routes) to easily connect with the center.

$$$ Hotel Alimandi Vaticano, facing the Vatican Museum, is beautifully designed. Run by the Alimandi family (Enrico, Irene, and Germano), it features four stars, 24 spacious rooms, and all the modern comforts you can imagine (Sb-€170, standard Db-€170-200, big Db with 2 double beds-€240-260, Tb-€230-260, cash discount, air-con, elevator, Internet access and Wi-Fi, Viale Vaticano 99, Metro: Ottaviano, tel. 06-397-45562, fax 06-397-30132, www.alimandivaticanohotel.com, alimandivaticano@alimandi.com).

$$ Hotel Alimandi Tunisi is a good value, run by other members of the friendly and entrepreneurial Alimandi family—Paolo, Luigi, Marta, and Barbara. They have 27 modest but comfortable

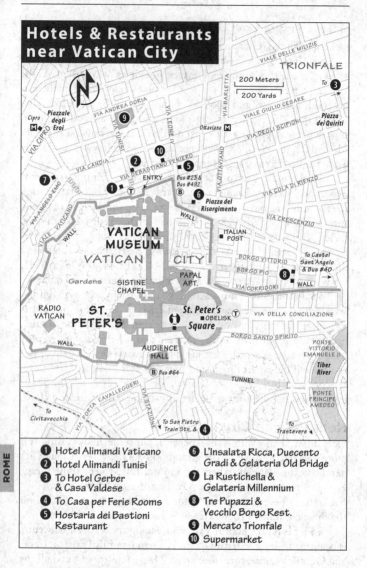

Hotels & Restaurants near Vatican City

1 Hotel Alimandi Vaticano
2 Hotel Alimandi Tunisi
3 To Hotel Gerber & Casa Valdese
4 To Casa per Ferie Rooms
5 Hostaria dei Bastioni Restaurant

6 L'Insalata Ricca, Duecento Gradi & Gelateria Old Bridge
7 La Rustichella & Gelateria Millennium
8 Tre Pupazzi & Vecchio Borgo Rest.
9 Mercato Trionfale
10 Supermarket

ROME

rooms and vast public spaces, including a piano lounge, pool table, and rooftop terrace where the grand buffet breakfast is served (Sb-€90, Db-€130-175, cash discount, elevator, air-con, Internet access and Wi-Fi, down the stairs directly in front of Vatican Museum, Via Tunisi 8, Metro: Ottaviano, tel. 06-3972-3941, fax 06-3972-3943, www.alimanditunisi.com, alimandi@tin.it).

$$ Hotel Gerber, set in a quiet residential area, is family-run with 27 well-polished, businesslike rooms (Sb-€140, Db-€180, Tb-€200, Qb-€220, ask about discount with this book when you book direct, air-con, elevator, Wi-Fi, leafy terrace; from Lepanto Metro station, go one block down Via M. Colonna and turn right to Via degli Scipioni 241; tel. 06-321-6485, fax 06-321-7048, www. hotelgerber.it, info@hotelgerber.it; Peter, Simonetta, and friendly dog Kira).

$ Casa Valdese is an efficient, well-managed, church-run hotel that's popular with Germans. Its 33 big, quiet rooms are located just over the Tiber River and near the Vatican. It feels safe if a bit institutional, with the bonus of two breezy, communal roof terraces with incredible views (two external Sb-€58, Db-€130, Tb-€180, Qb-€210, discounts for 3-night stays, air-con, Internet access and Wi-Fi; from Lepanto Metro station, go one block down Via M. Colonna, turn left on Via degli Scipioni, then continue for a block to the intersection with Via Alessandro Farnese 18; tel. 06-321-5362, fax 06-321-1843, www.casavaldeseroma.it, reception@ casavaldeseroma.it, Matteo).

$ Casa per Ferie Santa Maria alle Fornaci is simple and efficient, housing pilgrims and secular tourists just a short walk south of the Vatican in 54 identical, stark, utilitarian, mostly twin-bedded rooms. Reserve at least three months in advance (Sb-€70, Db-€100, Tb-€135, air-con, elevator; take bus #64 from Termini train station to San Pietro train station, then walk 100 yards north along Via della Stazione di San Pietro to Piazza Santa Maria alle Fornaci 27; tel. 06-393-67632, fax 06-393-66795, www.trinitaridematha. it, cffornaci@tin.it, Carmine).

Eating in Rome

I've listed a number of restaurants I enjoy. While most are in quaint and therefore pricey and touristy areas (Piazza Navona, the Pantheon neighborhood, Campo de' Fiori, and Trastevere), many are tucked away just off the tourist crush.

I'm impressed by how small the price difference can be between a mediocre Roman restaurant and a fine one. You can pay about 20 percent more for double the quality. If I had $90 for three meals in Rome, I'd spend $50 for one and $20 each for the other two, rather than $30 on all three. For splurge meals, I'd consider Gabriello, Fortunato, and Taverna Trilussa (in that order).

Rome's fabled nightspots (most notably Piazza Navona, near the Pantheon, and Campo de' Fiori) are lined with the outdoor tables of touristy restaurants with enticing menus and formal-vested waiters. The atmosphere is super-romantic: I, too, like the idea of dining under floodlit monuments, amid a constantly flowing parade of people. But you'll likely be surrounded by tourists, and noisy English-speakers can kill the ambience of the spot...leaving you with just a forgettable and overpriced meal. Restaurants in these areas are notorious for surprise charges, forgettable food, microwaved ravioli, and bad service.

I enjoy the view by savoring just a drink or dessert on a famous square, but I dine with locals on nearby low-rent streets, where the proprietor needs to serve a good-value meal and nurture a local following to stay in business. If you're set on eating—or just drinking and snacking—on a famous piazza, you don't need a guidebook listing to choose a spot; enjoy the ritual of slowly circling the square, observing both the food and the people eating it, and sit where the view and menu appeal to you.

In Trastevere

Colorful Trastevere is now pretty touristy. Still, Romans join the tourists to eat on the rustic side of the Tiber River. Start at the central square, Piazza di Santa Maria. This is where the tourists dine, while others wander the back streets in search of mom-and-pop places with barely a menu. My recommendations are within a few minutes' walk of each other (between Piazza di Santa Maria in Trastevere and Ponte Sisto; see map on page 900).

Taverna Trilussa is your best bet for dining well in Trastevere. Brothers Massimo and Maurizio offer quality and value without pretense. With a proud 100-year-old tradition, this place has the right mix of style and informality. The service is fun-loving (they're happy to let you split plates into smaller portions to enjoy a family-style meal), yet professional. The menu celebrates local classics and seasonal specials, and comes with a big wine selection. The spacious dining hall is strewn with eclectic Roman souvenirs. For those who'd rather eat outdoors, Trilussa has an actual terrace rather than just tables jumbled together on the sidewalk (€15 pastas, €20 *secondi*, Mon-Sat from 19:30 for dinner, closed Sun, reservations very smart, Via del Politeama 23, tel. 06-581-8918).

Trattoria da Lucia lets you enjoy simple, traditional food at a good price. It's your basic old-school, Trastevere dining experience, and has been family-run since World War II. You'll meet four generations of the family, including Giuliano and Renato, their uncle Ennio, and Ennio's mom—pictured on the menu in the 1950s. The family specialty is *spaghetti alla Gricia,* with pancetta (€9 pastas, €11 *secondi,* Tue-Sun 12:30-15:00 & 19:30-23:00, closed Mon, cash only, evocative outdoor or comfy indoor seating—but avoid back room, just off Via del Mattonato at Vicolo del Mattonato 2, tel. 06-580-3601).

Trattoria da Olindo takes homey to extremes. You really feel like you dropped in on a family that cooks for the neighborhood to supplement their income. Don't expect any smiles here (€8 pastas, €10 *secondi,* Mon-Sat dinner served 20:00-22:30, closed Sun, cash

ROME

only, indoor and funky outdoor seating, on the corner of Vicolo della Scala and Via del Mattonato at #8, tel. 06-581-8835).

Dar Poeta Pizzeria, tucked in a back alley and a hit with local students, cranks out some of the best wood-fired pizza I've had in Rome. It's run by three friends—Marco, Paolo, and another Marco—who welcome you into the informal restaurant beneath exposed brick arches. If you're in a spicy mood, order *lingua di fuoco* (tongue of fire). If you're extra hungry, pay an extra euro for *pizza alto* (thicker crust). Choose between their classic, cramped interior and lively tables outside on the cobblestones. Their chocolate dessert calzone is a favorite (€6-9 pizzas, daily 12:00-24:00, Vicolo del Bologna 45, tel. 06-588-0516).

Osteria Ponte Sisto da Oliviero, small and Mediterranean, specializes in traditional Roman cuisine, but has frequent Neapolitan specials as well. Just outside the tourist zone, it caters mostly to Romans and offers beautiful desserts and a fine value (€9 pastas, €12 *secondi*, Thu-Tue 12:30-15:30 & 19:30-24:00, closed Wed, Via Ponte Sisto 80, tel. 06-588-3411, reservations smart, Oliviero). If you're coming from the city center, cross Ponte Sisto (pedestrian bridge), continue across the little square (Piazza Trilussa), and you'll see it on the right.

Ristorante Checco er Carettiere is a big, family-run place that's been a Trastevere fixture for four generations—as the photos on the wall attest. With white tablecloths, well-presented food, and dressy local diners, this is a popular place for a special meal in Trastevere. While it's overpriced, you'll eat well amid lots of fun commotion (€18 pastas, €22 *secondi*, daily 12:30-15:00 & 19:30-23:15, Via Benedetta 10, tel. 06-580-0985). Their *osteria* next door (at #13) shares the same kitchen and offers less ambience, lower prices, and a more basic menu (€11 pastas, €15 *secondi*). Many Romans consider their *gelateria* (next door at #7) to be among the best on this side of the river.

Pizzeria "Ai Marmi" is a bright and noisy festival of pizza, where the oven and pizza-assembly line are surrounded by marble-slab tables (hence the nickname "the Morgue"). It's a classic Roman scene, whether you enjoy the chaos inside or sit at a sidewalk table, with famously good €8 pizzas and very tight seating. Expect a long line between 20:00 and 22:00 (Thu-Tue 19:00-24:00, closed Wed, cash only, tram #8 from Largo Argentina to first stop over bridge, just beyond Piazza Sonnino at Viale di Trastevere 53, tel. 06-580-0919).

Cantina Paradiso Wine and Cocktail Bar, a block over Viale di Trastevere from the touristy action, has a funky romantic charm. During happy hour (18:00-21:00), the €8 drinks come with a well-made little buffet that can turn into a cheap, light dinner (€8 pastas, daily 12:00-24:00, Via San Francesco a Ripa 73, tel. 06-589-9799, Weronika).

And for Dessert: **Gelateria alla Checco er Carettiere,** run by and next door to the famous, recommended restaurant of the same name, is many locals' favorite spot for gelato in Trastevere (daily 12:00-24:00, Via Benedetta 7).

In the Jewish Ghetto

The Jewish Ghetto sits just across the river from Trastevere (see map on page 900).

Sora Margherita, hiding without a sign on a cluttered square, has been a rustic neighborhood favorite since 1927. Amid a picturesque commotion, families chow down on old-time Roman and Jewish dishes for a decent price. It's technically not a real restaurant (it avoids red tape by officially registering itself an *associazione culturale*)—you can even sign a card to join the "cultural association" (don't worry; membership has no obligations except that you enjoy your meal). The menu's crude term for the fettuccini gives you some idea of the mood of this place: *nazzica culo* ("shaky ass"—what happens while it's made). Reservations are almost always necessary (€10 pastas, €12 *secondi*; Sept-May Mon-Sat 12:30-15:00, dinner seatings on Mon, Wed, Fri, and Sat at 20:00 and 21:30, closed Sun; June-July same hours except closed Sat, closed in Aug, just south of Via del Portico d'Ottavia at Piazza delle Cinque Scole 30—look for the red curtain, tel. 06-687-4216).

In the Pantheon Neighborhood

For the restaurants in this central area, I've listed them based on which landmark they're closest to: Campo de' Fiori, Piazza Navona, the Trevi Fountain, or the Pantheon itself.

On and near Campo de' Fiori

While it is touristy, Campo de' Fiori offers a sublimely romantic setting. And, since it's so close to the heart of the Roman people, it remains popular with locals, even though its restaurants offer greater atmosphere than food value. The square is lined with popular and interesting bars, pizzerias, and small restaurants—all great for people-watching over a glass of wine. Later at night it's taken over by a younger clubbing crowd.

Osteria da Giovanni ar Galletto is nearby, on the more elegant and peaceful Piazza Farnese. Angelo entertains an upscale Roman clientele and has magical outdoor seating. Regrettably, service can be horrible, you need to double-check the bill, and single diners aren't treated very well. Still, if you're in no hurry and ready to savor my favorite al fresco setting in Rome (while humoring the waiters), this can be a good bet (€12 pastas, €15-20 *secondi*, Mon-Sat 12:15-15:00 & 19:30-23:00, closed Sun, reservations smart for outdoor seating, tucked in corner of Piazza Farnese at #104, tel. 06-686-1714).

Osteria Enoteca al Bric is a mod bistro run by helpful Roberto and Barbara, who love to cook, serve fine wine, and listen to jazz. Wine-case lids decorate the wall like happy memories. They offer a fun, €22 happy-hour deal for two from 19:30 to 20:30 that includes a plate of cheeses and meats, two glasses of good wine, water, and bread (Tue-Sun from 19:30 for dinner, closed Mon, reserve if dining after 20:30, can be pricey, 100 yards off Campo de' Fiori at Via del Pellegrino 51, tel. 06-687-9533).

Vineria Salumeria Roscioli is an elegant *enoteca* that's a hit with local foodies, so reservations are a must. While it's just a salami toss away from touristy Campo de' Fiori, you'll dine with classy locals, and feel like you're sitting in a romantic (and expensive) deli after hours. They have a good selection of fine cheeses, meats, local dishes, and top-end wines by the glass (€15-25 plates, Mon-Sat 12:30-16:00 & 19:00-24:00, closed Sun, 3 blocks east of Campo de' Fiori at Via dei Giubbonari 21, tel. 06-687-5287).

Filetti di Baccalà is a cheap and basic Roman classic, where nostalgic regulars cram into wooden tables and savor their old-school favorites—fried cod finger-food fillets (€5 each) and raw *puntarelle* greens (slathered with anchovy sauce in spring and winter). Study what others are eating, and order from your grease-stained server by pointing at what you want. Sit in the fluorescently lit interior or try to grab a seat out on the little square, a quiet haven a block east of Campo de' Fiori (Mon-Sat 17:30-23:00, closed Sun, cash only, Largo dei Librari 88, tel. 06-686-4018). If you're not into greasy spoons, avoid this place.

Trattoria der Pallaro, an eccentric and well-worn eatery that has no menu, has a slogan: "Here, you'll eat what we want to feed you." Paola Fazi—with a towel wrapped around her head turban-style—and her gang dish up a five-course meal of homey Roman food. You have three menu choices: €25 for the works; €20 for appetizers, *secondi*, and dessert; or €15 for appetizers and pasta. Any option is filling, includes wine and coffee, and is capped with a thimble of mandarin juice. While the service can be odd and the food is rustic, the experience is fun (daily 12:00-16:00 & 19:00-24:00, reserve if dining after 20:00, cash only, indoor/outdoor seating on quiet square, a block south of Corso Vittorio Emanuele, down Largo del Chiavari to Largo del Pallaro 15, tel. 06-6880-1488).

Pizzeria da Baffetto 2 makes pizza Roman-style: thin crust, crispy, and wood-fired. Eat in the cramped informal interior, or outside on the busy square (€7-9 pizzas, daily 18:30-24:00, Sat-Sun

ROME

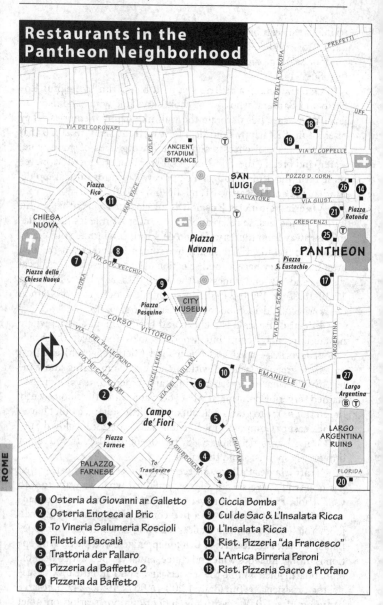

Restaurants in the Pantheon Neighborhood

1. Osteria da Giovanni ar Galletto
2. Osteria Enoteca al Bric
3. To Vineria Salumeria Roscioli
4. Filetti di Baccalà
5. Trattoria der Pallaro
6. Pizzeria da Baffetto 2
7. Pizzeria da Baffetto
8. Ciccia Bomba
9. Cul de Sac & L'Insalata Ricca
10. L'Insalata Ricca
11. Rist. Pizzeria "da Francesco"
12. L'Antica Birreria Peroni
13. Rist. Pizzeria Sacro e Profano

ROME

also open for lunch 12:30-15:30, a block north of Campo de' Fiori at Piazza del Teatro di Pompeo 18, tel. 06-6821-0807).

Near Piazza Navona

Piazza Navona is the quintessential setting for dining on a Roman square. Whether you eat here or not, you'll want to stroll the piazza

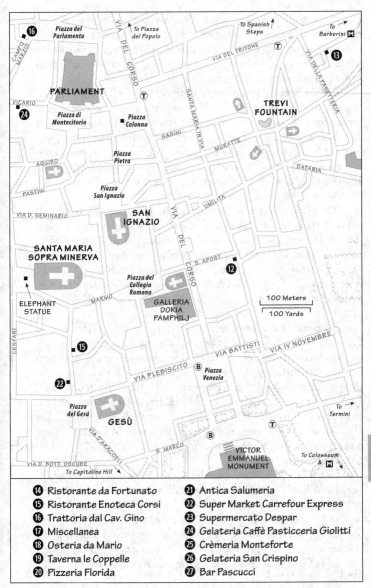

⑭ Ristorante da Fortunato
⑮ Ristorante Enoteca Corsi
⑯ Trattoria dal Cav. Gino
⑰ Miscellanea
⑱ Osteria da Mario
⑲ Taverna le Coppelle
⑳ Pizzeria Florida
㉑ Antica Salumeria
㉒ Super Market Carrefour Express
㉓ Supermercato Despar
㉔ Gelateria Caffè Pasticceria Giolitti
㉕ Crèmeria Monteforte
㉖ Gelateria San Crispino
㉗ Bar Pascucci

ROME

before or after your evening meal. This is where many people fall in love with Rome. The tangled streets just to the west are lined with popular eateries of many stripes.

Ciccia Bomba is a traditional trattoria where Gianpaolo, Gianluca, and their crew serve up tasty homemade pasta, wood-fired pizza, and other Roman specialties (consider their daily-special sheet)—all at a good price. While you can sit at a table on ancient pavement next to your own column, I like the ambience upstairs (€7 pastas, €9 *secondi*, Thu-Tue 12:30-15:00 & 19:00-24:00, closed Wed, Via del Governo Vecchio 76, a block west of Piazza Navona, just north from Piazza Pasquino, tel. 06-6880-2108).

Cul de Sac, a corridor-wide trattoria lined with wine bottles, is packed with an enthusiastic crowd enjoying a wide-ranging menu, from pasta to homemade pâté. They have fun tasting-plates of *salumi* and cheese, more than a thousand different wines, and fine outdoor seating. It's small, and they don't take reservations— come early to avoid a wait (€7-15 plates, daily 12:00-16:00 & 18:00-24:00, a block off Piazza Navona on Piazza Pasquino, tel. 06-6880-1094).

Ristorante Pizzeria "da Francesco," bustling and authentic, has a 50-year-old tradition, a hardworking young waitstaff, great indoor seating, and classic outdoor seating on a cluttered little square that makes you want to break out a sketchpad. Their blackboard explains the daily specials (€9 pizzas and pastas, €15 *secondi,* open daily 12:00-15:00 & 19:00-24:00 except closed Tue at lunch, 3 blocks west of Piazza Navona at Piazza del Fico 29, tel. 06-686-4009).

Pizzeria da Baffetto, buried deep in the old quarter behind Piazza Navona, is a Roman favorite, offering tasty pizza but rude service. Its tables are tightly arranged amid the mishmash of photos and sketches littering the walls. The pizza-assembly kitchen keeps things energetic, and the pizza oven keeps the main room warm (you can opt for a table on the cobbled street). Come early or late, or be prepared to wait (€7 pizzas, daily from 18:30, cash only; order "P," "M," or "D"—small, medium, or large; west of Piazza Navona on the corner of Via Sora at Via del Governo Vecchio 114, tel. 06-686-1617).

L'Insalata Ricca is a popular local chain that specializes in healthy, filling €8 salads and less-healthy pastas and main courses (daily 12:00-15:45 & 18:45-24:00). They have a handy branch on Piazza Pasquino (next to the recommended Cul de Sac, tel. 06-6830-7881) and a more spacious and enjoyable location a few blocks away, on a bigger square next to busy Corso Vittorio Emanuele (near Campo de' Fiori at Largo dei Chiavari 85, tel. 06-6880-3656).

Near the Trevi Fountain

L'Antica Birreria Peroni is Rome's answer to a German beer hall. Serving hearty mugs of the local Peroni beer and lots of just plain fun beer-hall food and Italian classics, the place is a hit with Romans for a cheap night out (Mon-Sat 12:00-24:00, closed Sun, midway between Trevi Fountain and Capitoline Hill, a block off Via del Corso at Via di San Marcello 19, tel. 06-679-5310).

Ristorante Pizzeria Sacro e Profano fills an old church with spicy southern Italian (Calabrian) cuisine and satisfied tourists. Run with enthusiasm by Emiliano and friends, this is just far enough away from the Trevi mobs. Their pizza oven is wood-fired, and their hearty €15 *antipasti* plate is a filling montage of Calabrian taste treats (Mon-Sat 12:00-15:00 & 18:00-23:00, closed Sun, a block off Via del Tritone at Via dei Maroniti 29, tel. 06-679-1836).

Close to the Pantheon

Eating on the square facing the Pantheon is a temptation, and I'd consider it just to relax and enjoy the Roman scene. But if you walk a block or two away, you'll get less view and better value. Here are some suggestions.

Ristorante da Fortunato is an Italian classic, with fresh flowers on the tables and white-coated, black-tie career waiters politely serving good meat and fish to politicians, foreign dignitaries, and tourists with good taste. Don't leave without perusing the photos of their famous visitors—everyone from former Iraqi Foreign Minister Tariq Aziz to Bill Clinton seems to have eaten here. All are pictured with the boss, Fortunato, who, since 1975, has been a master of simple edible elegance. (His son Jason is now on the team.) The outdoor seating is fine for watching the river of Roman street life flow by, but the real atmosphere is inside. For a dressy night out, this is a reliable and surprisingly reasonable choice—but be sure to reserve ahead (plan to spend €45 per person, daily 12:30-15:30 & 19:30-23:30, a block in front of the Pantheon at Via del Pantheon 55, tel. 06-679-2788).

Ristorante Enoteca Corsi is a wine shop that grew into a thriving lunch-only restaurant. The Paiella family serves straightforward, traditional cuisine at great prices to an appreciative crowd of office workers. Check the blackboard for daily specials (gnocchi on Thursday, fish on Friday, and so on). Friendly Giuliana, Claudia, Sara, and Manuela welcome eaters to step into their wine shop and pick out a bottle. For the cheap take-away price, plus €2-4 (depending on the wine), they'll uncork it at your table. With €9 pastas, €13 main dishes, and fine wine at a third of the price you'd pay in normal restaurants, this can be a good value. And guests with this book finish their meal with a free glass of homemade *limoncello* (Mon-Sat 12:00-15:30, closed Sun, no reservations possible, a block toward the Pantheon from the Gesù Church at Via del Gesù 87, tel. 06-679-0821).

Trattoria dal Cav. Gino, tucked away on a tiny street behind the Parliament, has been a favorite since 1963. Photos on the

ROME

wall recall the days when it was the haunt of big-time politicians. Grandpa Gino shuffles around grating the parmesan cheese while his English-speaking children Carla and Fabrizio serve up traditional Roman favorites and make sure things run smoothly. Reserve ahead, even for lunch, as you'll be packed in with savvy locals (€8 pastas, €11 *secondi*, cash only, Mon-Sat 13:00-14:45 & 20:00-22:30, closed Sun, fish on Friday, behind Piazza del Parlamento and just off Via di Campo Marzio at Vicolo Rosini 4, tel. 06-687-3434).

Miscellanea is run by much-loved Mikki, who's on a mission to keep foreign students well-fed. Welcoming travelers as well as locals, he offers hearty €4 sandwiches and a long list of €7 salads, along with pasta and other staples. Mikki (and his son Romeo) often tosses in a fun little extra, including—if you have this book on the table—a free glass of Mikki's "sexy wine" (from *fragoline*, strawberry-flavored grapes). While basic, it's convenient and inexpensive (daily 8:00-24:00, indoor/outdoor seating, facing the rear of the Pantheon at Via della Palombella 34, tel. 06-6813-5318).

Osteria da Mario, a homey little mom-and-pop joint with a no-stress menu, serves traditional favorites in a fun dining room or on tables spilling out onto a picturesque old Roman square (€8 pastas, €10 *secondi*, Mon-Sat 13:00-15:30 & 19:00-23:00, closed Sun; from the Pantheon walk 2 blocks up Via del Pantheon, go left on Via delle Coppelle, and take first right to Piazza delle Coppelle 51; tel. 06-6880-6349, Marco).

Taverna le Coppelle is simple, basic, family-friendly, and inexpensive—especially for pizza—with a checkered-tablecloth ambience (€9 pizzas, daily 12:30-15:00 & 19:30-23:30, Via delle Coppelle 39, tel. 06-6880-6557, Alfonso).

Pizzeria Florida, about four blocks south of the Pantheon, offers cheap pizza slices and sandwiches to go (daily 10:00-22:00, Via Florida 25, across from cat sanctuary, tel. 06-6880-3236).

Picnicking Close to the Pantheon
It's fun to munch a picnic with a view of the Pantheon. (Remember to be discreet.) Here are some options.

Antica Salumeria is an old-time *alimentari* (grocery store) on the Pantheon square. While they hustle most tourists into premade €5 sandwiches, you can make your own picnic. Find your way to the back to buy artichokes, mixed olives, bread, cheese, and meat (daily 8:00-21:00, mobile 334-340-9014).

Supermarkets near the Pantheon: Food is relatively cheap at Italian supermarkets. **Super Market Carrefour Express** is a convenient place for groceries a block from the Gesù Church (Mon-Sat 8:00-21:00, Sun 9:00-19:30, 50 yards off Via del Plebiscito at

Via del Gesù 59). Another place, **Supermercato Despar,** is half a block from the Pantheon toward Piazza Navona (daily 8:30-22:00, Via Giustiniani 18).

Gelato Close to the Pantheon

Three fine *gelaterie* and bars specializing in fresh-fruit smoothies are within a five-minute walk of the Pantheon.

Gelateria Caffè Pasticceria Giolitti, Rome's most famous and venerable ice-cream joint, has reasonable take-away prices and elegant Old World seating (daily 7:00-24:00, just off Piazza Colonna and Piazza Monte Citorio at Via Uffici del Vicario 40, tel. 06-699-1243).

Crèmeria Monteforte is known for its traditional, quality gelato and super-creamy sorbets *(cremolati)*. The fruit flavors are especially refreshing—think gourmet slushies (Tue-Sun 10:00-24:00, off-season closes earlier, closed Mon and Dec-Jan, faces the west side of the Pantheon at Via della Rotonda 22, tel. 06-686-7720).

Gelateria San Crispino serves small portions of particularly tasty gourmet gelato using creative ingredients. Because of their commitment to natural ingredients, the colors are muted; gelato purists consider bright colors a sign of unnatural chemicals, used to attract children. They serve cups, but no cones (daily 12:00-24:00, a block in front of the Pantheon on Piazza della Maddalena, tel. 06-6889-1310).

Bar Pascucci is a hole in the wall that's been making refreshing fruit *frullati* and frappés (like smoothies and shakes) for more than 75 years. Add a sandwich or fruit salad to make a healthy light meal (Mon-Sat 6:00-23:00, closed Sun, near Largo Argentina at Via di Torre Argentina 20, tel. 06-686-4816).

In North Rome: Near the Ara Pacis and Spanish Steps

To locate these restaurants, see the map on page 843.

Ristorante il Gabriello is inviting and small—modern under medieval arches—and provides a peaceful and local-feeling respite from all the top-end fashion shops in the area. Claudio serves with charisma, while his brother Gabriello cooks creative Roman cuisine using fresh, organic products from his wife's farm. Italians normally just trust their waiter and say, "Bring it on." Tourists are understandably more cautious, but you can be trusting here. Simply close your eyes and point to anything on the menu. Or invest €45 in "Claudio's Extravaganza" (not including wine), and he'll shower you with edible kindness. Specify whether you'd prefer fish, meat, or both. (Romans think raw shellfish is the ultimate in fine dining. If you differ, make that clear.) When finished, I stand up, hold my

ROME

belly, and say, *"Ahhh, la vita è bella"* (€10 pastas, €15 *secondi*, dinner only, Mon-Sat 19:00-23:00, closed Sun, reservations smart, air-con, dress respectfully—no shorts please, 3 blocks from Spanish Steps at Via Vittoria 51, tel. 06-6994-0810).

Osteria Gusto is thriving with trendy locals. While pricey, it's untouristy, gives a glimpse of today's Roman scene, and is fine for a glass of good wine over an artisanal cheese plate or a complete dinner (€13 pastas, €18 *secondi*, daily 12:30-15:30 & 19:00-24:00, opens at 18:30 for drinks and appetizers only, reservations recommended after 20:00 and on weekends, on the corner of Via Soderini at Via della Frezza 16, tel. 06-3211-1482). Their more expensive *ristorante* and more casual wine bar (which offers lighter bites) are directly adjacent.

L'EnotecAntica, an upbeat, atmospheric 200-plus-year-old *enoteca,* has around 60 Italian-only wines by the glass (€4-10, listed on a big blackboard) and a fresh €14 *antipasti* plate of veggies, *salumi,* and cheese. Very crowded on summer evenings, it comes with wonderful ambience both inside and out; its outside tables are set on a quiet cobbled street (daily 12:00-24:00, Via della Croce 76b, tel. 06-679-0896).

Palatium Enoteca Regionale is a crisp, modern restaurant funded by the region of Lazio (home to Rome) to show off its finest agricultural fare. Surrounded by locals, you'll enjoy generous, shareable plates of cheeses and *salumi,* a limited menu of pasta and meat, and a huge selection of local wine (€12-16 dishes, Mon-Sat 12:30-15:30 & 19:30-23:00, closed Sun, 5 blocks in front of the Spanish Steps at Via Frattina 94, tel. 06-6920-2132).

In Ancient Rome: Near the Colosseum and Forum

You'll find good views but poor value at the restaurants directly behind the Colosseum. To get your money's worth, eat at least a block away. Here are several handy eateries, all shown on the map on page 916: one at the foot of Via Cavour, two at the top of Terme di Tito (a long block uphill from the Colosseum, near St. Peter-in-Chains church—of Michelangelo's *Moses* fame; for directions, see page 859), and two a couple of blocks to the east.

Enoteca Cavour 313 is a wine bar with a mission: to offer good wine and quality food with an old-fashioned commitment to value and friendly service. It's also a convenient place for a good lunch near the Forum and Colosseum. Angelo and his three partners enjoy creating a mellow ambience under lofts of wine bottles (limited menu of daily specials and fine wines by the glass, daily 12:30-14:45 & 19:00-24:00, 100 yards off Via dei Fori Imperiali at Via Cavour 313, tel. 06-678-5496).

Hostaria da Nerone is a traditional place serving hearty classics, including tasty homemade pasta dishes. Their *antipasti* plate—with a variety of veggies, fish, and meat—is a good value for a quick lunch. While the *antipasti* menu indicates specifics, you can have a plate of whatever's out—just direct the waiter to assemble the €9 *antipasti* plate of your lunchtime dreams (€10 pastas, €12 *secondi*, Mon-Sat 12:00-15:00 & 19:00-23:00, closed Sun, indoor/outdoor seating, Via delle Terme di Tito 96, tel. 06-481-7952, run by Teo and Eugenio).

Caffè dello Studente, next door to Hostaria da Nerone, is popular with engineering students attending the nearby University of Rome. Pina, Mauro, and their perky daughter Simona (who speaks English) give my readers a royal welcome and serve average, microwaved *bar gastronomia* fare—toasted sandwiches, salads, and mixed bruschetta. If it's not busy, show this book when you order at the bar and sit without paying extra at a table (Mon-Sat 7:30-22:30, April-Oct Sun 9:00-22:30, Nov-March closed Sun, Via delle Terme di Tito, tel. 06-488-3240).

Trattoria Luzzi is a well-worn, no-frills eatery serving simple food in a high-energy environment (as they've done since 1945). With good prices, big portions, and proximity to the Colosseum, it draws a crowd—reserve or expect a short wait at lunch and after 19:30 (€6 pastas, €7 pizzas, €9 *secondi*, Thu-Tue 12:00-24:00, closed Wed, Via San Giovanni in Laterano 88, tel. 06-709-6332).

La Taverna dei Quaranta, a casual neighborhood favorite, is a bit more refined than nearby Luzzi, but still far from pretentious. In the evening, they fire up the wood oven for pizza, to go along with a basic menu of Roman classics and seasonal specialties. As the place caters mostly to locals, service can be a bit slow and straightforward—but it's a good bet in this touristy area (€8 pastas, €13 *secondi*, daily 12:00-15:30 & 19:00-24:00, Via Claudia 24, tel. 06-700-0550).

Near Termini Station

These restaurants are near my recommended hotels on Via Firenze. Several are clustered on Via Flavia, others are nearby (Target, etc.), and a few, such as Bar Tavola Calda, are good options for quick meals.

On (or near) Via Flavia

To easily check out a fun and varied selection of eateries within a block of each other, walk to Via Flavia (a block behind the Church of Santa Maria della Vittoria of *St. Teresa in Ecstasy* fame) and survey these choices—an old-time restaurant, a good pizzeria, a small romantic place, and a friendly wine bar.

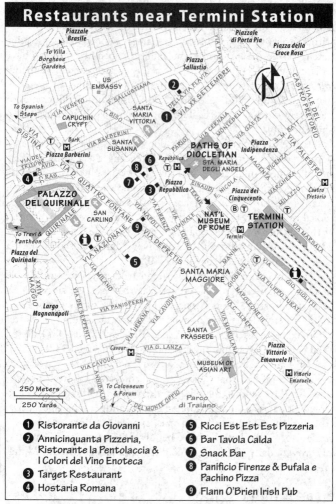

Restaurants near Termini Station

1. Ristorante da Giovanni
2. Annicinquanta Pizzeria, Ristorante la Pentolaccia & I Colori del Vino Enoteca
3. Target Restaurant
4. Hostaria Romana
5. Ricci Est Est Est Pizzeria
6. Bar Tavola Calda
7. Snack Bar
8. Panificio Firenze & Bufala e Pachino Pizza
9. Flann O'Brien Irish Pub

Ristorante da Giovanni, well-worn and old-fashioned, makes no concessions to tourism or the modern world—just hardworking cooks and waiters serving standard dishes at great prices to a committed clientele. It's simply fun to eat in the middle of this high-energy, Roman time warp (€6-10 pastas and *secondi,* daily specials, Mon-Sat 12:00-15:00 & 19:00-22:00, closed Sun and Aug, corner of Via XX Settembre at Via Antonio Salandra 1, tel. 06-485-950).

Annicinquanta Pizzeria, big and classic, serves the neighborhood's favorite pizzas in a calm ambience with outdoor seating (€8 Neapolitan-style pizzas, daily 12:15-15:30 & 19:30-24:00 except no lunch on Sat, Via Flavia 3, tel. 06-4201-0460).

Ristorante la Pentolaccia, pricier and more romantic than the nearby Da Giovanni, is a dressy, tourist-friendly place with tight seating and traditional Roman cooking—consider their daily specials. This is a local hangout, and reservations are smart (daily 12:00-15:00 & 17:30-23:00, a block off Via XX Settembre at Via Flavia 38, tel. 06-483-477). To start things off with a free bruschetta, leave this book on the table.

I Colori del Vino Enoteca is a modern wine bar that feels like a laboratory of wine appreciation. It has woody walls of bottles, a creative menu of meats and cheeses with different regional themes, and a great list of fine wines by the glass. Helpful, English-speaking Marco carries on a long family tradition of celebrating the fundamentals of good nutrition: fine wine, cheese, meat, and bread (Mon-Fri 12:00-15:00 & 17:30-23:00, closed Sat-Sun because Marco doesn't cater to noisy weekend drinkers, corner of Via Flavia and Via Aureliana, tel. 06-474-1745). Remember Shakespeare's sage warning about drinking: "It provokes the desire, but it takes away the performance."

More Eateries near the Station

Target Restaurant seems to be the favorite recommendation of every hotel receptionist and tour guide for this neighborhood. It has reliably good food, a sleek look, capable service, and practical prices (€8-12 salads, pastas, and pizzas; €20 *secondi,* daily 12:00-15:00 & 19:00-24:00 except no lunch on Sun, reserve to specify seating outside or inside—avoid getting seated in basement, Via Torino 33, tel. 06-474-0066).

Hostaria Romana is a busy bistro with a hustling and fun-loving gang of waiters, and noisy walls graffitied by happy eaters. As its menu specializes in traditional Roman dishes, it's a good place to try *saltimbocca alla romana* or *bucatini all'amatriciana.* Their €10 *antipasti* plate, with a variety of vegetables and cheeses, makes a hearty start to your meal (€9 pastas, €14 *secondi,* Mon-Sat 12:15-15:00 & 19:15-23:00, closed Sun, reservations smart, a block up the lane just past the entrance to the big tunnel near the Trevi Fountain at Via del Boccaccio 1, tel. 06-474-5284).

Ricci Est Est Est Pizzeria, a venerable family-run pizzeria, has plenty of historical ambience, good €8 pizzas, and dangerously tasty *fritti,* such as fried *baccalà* (cod) and zucchini flowers (Tue-Sun 19:00-24:00, closed Mon and Aug, Via Genova 32, tel. 06-488-1107).

Fast, Simple Meals near the Station

Bar Tavola Calda is a workers' favorite for a quick, cheap lunch. They have good, fresh, hot dishes ready to go for a fine price. Head back past the bar to peruse their enticing display, point at what you want, then grab a seat and the young waitstaff will serve you (Mon-Sat 6:00-18:00, closed Sun, Via Torino 40).

Snack Bar puts out a lunchtime display of inexpensive pastas, colorful sandwiches, fresh fruit, and salad. Their loyal customers appreciate the fruit salad with yogurt (daily 6:00-24:00, Via Firenze 33, mobile 339-393-1356, Enrica).

Panificio Firenze makes hearty sandwiches, has a selection of well-priced wine, and stocks other goodies for a picnic to go (sandwiches priced by weight, Mon-Fri 7:00-19:00, Sat 7:00-14:00, closed Sun, Via Firenze 51-52, tel. 06-488-5035, Giovanni).

Bufala e Pachino Pizza is a convenient place for pizza by the slice *(al taglio)* and priced by weight—just point and tell them how much you'd like. Their *supplì* (fried rice balls filled with mozzarella), at just €1 each, make for cheap, filling snacks (daily 10:00-23:00, Via Firenze 54).

Flann O'Brien Irish Pub is an entertaining place for a light meal of pasta...or something *other* than pasta, such as grilled meats and giant salads, served early and late, when other places are closed. They have Irish beer, live sporting events on TV, and perhaps the most Italian crowd of all. Walk way back before choosing a table. Live bands often play on Friday evenings (daily 7:00-24:00, Via Nazionale 17, at intersection with Via Napoli, tel. 06-488-0418).

Near Vatican City

Avoid the restaurant-pushers handing out fliers near the Vatican: They're hawking places with bad food and expensive menu tricks. Try any of these instead (see map on page 922).

Handy Lunch Places near Piazza Risorgimento

These are a stone's throw from the Vatican wall, located halfway between St. Peter's Basilica and the Vatican Museum. They're all fast and cheap, with a good *gelateria* next door.

Hostaria dei Bastioni, run by Antonio while Emilio cooks, has noisy street-side seating and a quiet interior (€8 pastas, €12 *secondi*, Mon-Sat 12:00-15:30 & 18:30-23:00, closed Sun, at corner of Vatican wall at Via Leone IV 29, tel. 06-3972-3034).

L'Insalata Ricca is another branch of the popular chain that serves salads and pastas (daily 12:30-15:30 & 18:30-23:45, across from Vatican walls at Piazza Risorgimento 5, tel. 06-3973-0387).

Duecento Gradi is a good bet for fresh and creative €5 sandwiches. Munch your lunch on a stool or take it away (daily 11:00-24:00, Piazza Risorgimento 3, tel. 06-3975-4239).

Gelato: **Gelateria Old Bridge** scoops up hearty portions of fresh gelato for tourists and nuns alike—join the line (daily 10:00-23:00, just off Piazza Risorgimento across from Vatican walls at Via Bastioni 3).

Other Good Options in the Vatican Area

The first three listings—the restaurant, the streets with pizza shops, and the covered market—are near the Vatican Museum. The Borgo Pio eateries are near St. Peter's Basilica.

La Rustichella serves tasty wood-fired pizza and the usual pasta in addition to their sprawling *antipasti* buffet (€8 for a single plate). Arrive when it opens at 19:00 to avoid a line and have the pristine buffet to yourself. Do like the Romans do—take a moderate amount and make one trip only (Tue-Sun 12:30-15:00 & 19:00-24:00, closed Mon, near Metro: Cipro, opposite church at end of Via Candia, Via Angelo Emo 1, tel. 06-3972-0649). Consider the fun and fruity **Gelateria Millennium** next door.

Viale Giulio Cesare and *Via Candia:* These streets are lined with cheap *pizza rustica* shops, self-serve places, and basic eateries.

Covered Market: As you collect picnic supplies, turn your nose loose in the wonderful **Mercato Trionfale** covered market. It's one of the best in the city, located three blocks north of the Vatican Museum (Mon-Sat roughly 7:00-14:00, Tue and Fri some stalls stay open until 19:00, closed Sun, corner of Via Tunisi and Via Andrea Doria). If the market is closed, try several nearby supermarkets; the most convenient is **Carrefour Express** (Mon-Sat 8:00-20:00, Sun 9:00-20:00, Via Sebastiano Veniero 16).

Along Borgo Pio: The pedestrians-only Borgo Pio—a block from Piazza San Pietro—has restaurants worth a look, such as **Tre Pupazzi** (Mon-Sat 12:00-15:00 & 19:00-23:00, closed Sun, at corner of Via Tre Pupazzi and Borgo Pio, tel. 06-686-8371). At **Vecchio Borgo,** across the street, you can get pasta, pizza slices, and veggies to go (Mon-Sat 9:00-21:00, closed Sun, Borgo Pio 27a, tel. 06-8117-3585).

Rome Connections

Rome is well-connected with the rest of the planet: by train, bus, plane, car, and cruise ship. This section addresses your arrival and departure from the city. It explains the various options and gives a rundown on their points of departure.

By Train

Rome's main train station is the centrally located **Termini** train station, which has connections to the airport. Rome's other major station is the **Tiburtina** bus/train station, which is starting to get some high-speed rail connections. For in-depth descriptions of both Termini and Tiburtina stations, see page 816. Smaller stations include **Ostiense** (useful for going to South Rome and Testaccio, also may have some high-speed rail) and its neighbor, **Porta San**

Paolo (with connections to Ostia Antica). If you're staying near the Vatican and taking a regional train, it saves time to get off at the **San Pietro** train station rather than at Termini.

Nearly all of the most convenient connections for travelers depart from Termini, but as a precaution, it's always smart to confirm whether your train departs from Termini or Tiburtina.

From Rome's Termini Station by Train to: Venice (roughly hourly, 3.75 hours, overnight possible with transfer in Milan), **Florence** (at least hourly, 1.5 hours), **Siena** (1-2/hour, 1 change, 3-4 hours), **La Spezia Centrale** (8/day direct, more with transfers in Pisa, 3-4.5 hours), **Milan** (hourly, 3-8 hours, overnight possible), **Milan's Malpensa Airport** (1 direct express/day, 4.5 hours), **Amsterdam** (6/day, 20 hours), **Interlaken** (5/day, 6.5-8 hours), **Frankfurt** (6/day, 11-12 hours), **Munich** (5/day, 10-11.5 hours, 1 direct night train, 11.5 hours), **Nice** (7/day, 8.75-10.5 hours,), **Paris** (4/day, 10.75-12.75 hours; 1 night train, 14 hours, transfer in Milan, important to reserve ahead at www.thello.com), **Vienna** (2/day, 11.75 hours, 1 direct night train, 12 hours).

From Rome's Tiburtina Station by Train to: Florence (8/day, 1.5 hours), **Milan** (8/day, 3.5 hours), **Naples** (5/day, 1.25 hours).

By Plane

Rome's two airports—**Fiumicino** (a.k.a. Leonardo da Vinci, airport code: FCO) and the small **Ciampino** (airport code: CIA)—share the same website (www.adr.it).

Fiumicino Airport

Rome's major airport has a TI (in Terminal 3, daily 9:00-18:30), ATMs, banks, luggage storage, shops, and bars. The Rome Walks website (www.romewalks.com) has a useful video on options for getting into the city from the airport.

The slick, direct **"Leonardo Express" train** connects the airport and Rome's central Termini train station in 30 minutes for €14. Trains run twice hourly in both directions from roughly 6:00 to 23:00 (leaving the airport at :07 and :37). From the airport's arrival gate, follow signs to the train car icon or *Stazione/Railway Station*. Buy your ticket from a machine, the Biglietteria office, or a newsstand at the platform; then validate it in a yellow machine near the track. Make sure the train you board is going to the central "Roma Termini" station, not "Roma Orte" or others.

Going from Termini train station to the airport, trains depart at about :22 and :52 past the hour, from track 24. Check the departure boards for "Fiumicino Aeroporto"—the local name for the airport—and confirm with an official or a local on the platform that the train is indeed going to the airport (€14, buy ticket from any tobacco shop or a newsstand in the station, or at the self-service machines, Termini-Fiumicino trains run 5:52-22:52). Read your ticket: If it requires validation, stamp it in the yellow machine near the platform before boarding. From the train station at the airport, you can access most of the terminals. American airlines flying direct to the US depart from Terminal 5, which is a separate building not connected to the rest of the terminals. If you arrive by train, catch the T5 shuttle bus *(navetta)* on the sidewalk in front of Terminal 3—it's too far to walk with luggage.

Allow lots of time going in either direction; there's a fair amount of transportation involved, including moving walkways, escalators, and walking (e.g., getting from your hotel to Termini, from Termini to the train platform, the ride to the airport, getting from the airport train station to check-in, etc.). Flying to the US involves an extra level of security—plan on getting to the airport even earlier than normal (I like to arrive 2.5 hours ahead of my flight).

The **Terravision Express bus** connects Fiumicino and Termini train station, departing every 40 minutes (€6 one-way, €11 round-trip; leaves the airport from Terminal 3, leaves Termini Station from Via Marsala—just outside the exit closest to track 1; one hour, www.terravision.eu). The **SIT Bus Shuttle** also connects Fiumicino and Termini (€8 one-way, €15 round-trip, similar schedule and info to Terravision, tel. 06-592-3507, www.sitbusshuttle.com). While cheaper than the train, the buses take twice as long and can potentially fill up (allow plenty of extra time).

Shuttle van services run to and from the airport and can be economical for one or two people. It's cheaper from the airport to downtown, as several companies compete for this route; by surveying the latest deals, you should be able to snare a ride into town for around €10. To get from your hotel to the airport, consider Rome Airport Shuttle (€25/1 person, extra people-€6 each, by reservation only, tel. 06-4201-4507 or 06-4201-3469, www.airportshuttle.it).

A **taxi** between Fiumicino and downtown Rome takes 45 minutes in normal traffic (for tips on taxis, see page 829). If you're catching a taxi at the airport, be sure to wait at the taxi stand. Avoid unmarked, unmetered taxis; these guys will try to tempt you away from the taxi-stand lineup by offering an immediate (rip-off) ride. Rome's and Fiumicino's official taxis have a fixed rate to and from the airport (€48 for up to four people with bags).

Cabbies not based in Rome or Fiumicino are allowed to charge €70 for the ride. That sign is posted next to the €48-fare sign—confusing many tourists and allowing dishonest cabbies to overcharge. It's best to use a Rome city cab, with the "SPQR" shield on the

ROME

door. They can only charge €48 for the ride to anywhere in the historic center (within the old city walls, where most of my recommended hotels are located).

If your cab driver tries to charge you more than €48 from the airport into town, say, *"Quarant'otto euro—è la legge"* (kwah-rahnt-OH-toh AY-oo-roh—ay lah LEJ-jay; which means, "Forty-eight euros—it's the law"), and they should back off.

To get from the airport into town cheaply by taxi, try teaming up with any tourist also just arriving (most are heading for hotels near yours in the center). When you're departing Rome, your hotel can arrange a taxi to the airport at any hour.

For **airport information,** call 06-65951. To inquire about flights, call 06-6595-3640.

Ciampino Airport

Rome's smaller airport (tel. 06-6595-9515) handles charter flights and some budget airlines (including all Ryanair and some easyJet flights).

To get to downtown Rome from the airport, you can take the Cotral bus, which leaves every 40 minutes (€5, 20-minute ride, toll-free tel. 800-174-471, www.cotralspa.it), to the Anagnina Metro stop, where you can connect by Metro to the stop nearest your hotel. Rome Airport Shuttle also offers service to and from Ciampino (€25/1 person, listed earlier). The Terravision Express Shuttle connects Ciampino and Termini train station, leaving every 20 minutes (€4 one-way, €8 round-trip, www.terravision.eu). The SIT Bus Shuttle also connects Termini to Ciampino (€4, about 2/hour, 45 minutes, runs 7:45-23:15 Ciampino to Termini, 4:30-21:30 Termini to Ciampino, pickup on Via Marsala just outside the train exit closest to track 1, tel. 06-592-3507, www.sitbusshuttle.it). A taxi should cost €30 to downtown (within the old city walls, including most of my recommended hotels).

ROME

VENICE

Venezia

Soak all day in this puddle of elegant decay. Venice is Europe's best-preserved big city. This car-free urban wonderland of a hundred islands—laced together by 400 bridges and 2,000 alleys—survives on the artificial respirator of tourism.

Born in a lagoon 1,500 years ago as a refuge from barbarians, Venice is overloaded with tourists and is slowly sinking (not because of the tourists). In the Middle Ages, the Venetians became Europe's clever middlemen for East-West trade and created a great trading empire. By smuggling in the bones of St. Mark (San Marco) in A.D. 828, Venice gained religious importance as well. With the discovery of America and new trading routes to the Orient, Venetian power ebbed. But as Venice fell, her appetite for decadence grew. Through the 17th and 18th centuries, Venice partied on the wealth accumulated through earlier centuries as a trading power.

Today, Venice is home to 58,000 people in its old city, down from about twice that number just three decades ago. While there are about 270,000 people in greater Venice (counting the mainland, not counting tourists), the old town has a small-town feel. Locals seem to know everyone. To see small-town Venice away from the touristic flak, escape the Rialto-San Marco tourist zone and savor the town early and late, without the hordes of vacationers day-tripping in from cruise ships and nearby beach resorts. A 10-minute walk from the madness puts you in an idyllic Venice that few tourists see.

Planning Your Time

Venice is worth at least a day on even the speediest tour. Hyper-efficient train travelers take the night train in and/or out. Sleep in the old center to experience Venice at its best: early and late. For a one-day visit, cruise the Grand Canal, do the major sights on St. Mark's Square (the square itself, Doge's Palace, Correr Museum, and St. Mark's Basilica), see the Frari Church for art, and wander the back streets on a pub crawl. Enjoy an evening gondola ride. Venice's greatest sight is the city itself. While doable in a day, Venice is worth two. It's a medieval cookie jar, and nobody's looking. Make time to simply wander.

Orientation to Venice

The island city of Venice is shaped like a fish. Its major thorough-fares are canals. The Grand Canal winds through the middle of the fish, starting at the mouth where all the people and food enter, passing under the Rialto Bridge, and ending at St. Mark's Square (Piazza San Marco). Park your 21st-century perspective at the mouth and let Venice swallow you whole.

Venice is a car-less kaleidoscope of people, bridges, and odor-less canals. There are six districts (*sestieri*, shown on map on page 945):

San Marco (from St. Mark's Square to the Accademia Bridge), Castello (the area east of St. Mark's Square), Dorsoduro (the belly of the fish, on the far side the Accademia Bridge), Cannaregio (between the train station and the Rialto Bridge), San Polo (west of the Rialto Bridge), and Santa Croce (the "eye" of the fish, across the canal from the train station).

To find your way, navigate by landmarks, not streets. Many street corners have a sign pointing you to *(per)* the nearest major landmark, such as San Marco, Accademia, Rialto, and Ferrovia (train station). Obedient visitors stick to the main thoroughfares as directed by these signs...and miss the charm of back-street Venice.

Beyond the city's core lie several other islands, including San Giorgio (with great views of Venice), Giudecca (more views), San Michele (old cemetery), Murano (famous for glass), Burano (lace-making), Torcello (old church), and the skinny Lido beach.

Tourist Information

With this book, a free city map from your hotel, and the events schedule on the TI's website, there's little need to make an in-person visit to a TI in Venice. That's fortunate, because the city's TIs are crowded and clunky. If you need to check or confirm something, try phoning the TI at 041-529-8711 or visit www.turismovenezia.it

Venice Overview

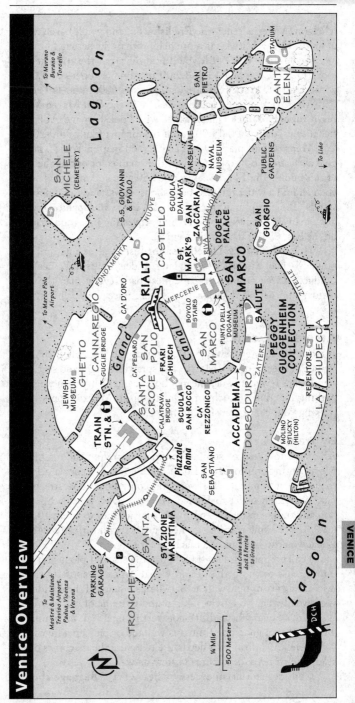

VENICE

(click on "Venezia," then the English icon, and you'll have a world of help). This website is far more helpful than the actual TI office.

If you must visit a TI, you'll find offices at the **train station** (next to track 1, daily 13:00-19:00 in summer, opens at 9:00 in winter), on **St. Mark's Square** (daily 9:00-19:00, in far-left corner with your back to the basilica), nearby at the **San Marco-Vallaresso vaporetto dock** (shares office with bookshop and Alilaguna ticket sales, daily 9:00-19:00), or at the **airport** (daily 9:00-20:00).

Maps: Of all places, you need a good map in Venice. Hotels give away freebies (no better than the small color one at the front of this book). The TI sells a decent €2.50 map and miniguide—but you can find a wider range at bookshops, newsstands, and postcard stands. The cheap maps are pretty bad, but if you spend €5, you'll get a map that shows you everything. Investing in a good map can be the best €5 you'll spend in Venice.

Helpful History Timelines: For historical orientation, local guide Michael Broderick (listed later, under "Tours in Venice") has produced three poster-size timelines that cleverly map the city's history and art (sold at local bookstores; see www.venicescapes. org).

Arrival in Venice

A two-mile-long causeway (with highway and train lines) connects Venice to the mainland. Mestre, the sprawling mainland section of Venice, has fewer crowds, cheaper hotels, and plenty of inexpensive parking lots, but zero charm. Don't stop in Mestre unless you're parking your car or transferring trains.

By Train

All trains to "Venice" stop at Venezia Mestre (on the mainland). Most continue on to Santa Lucia Station (a.k.a. Venezia S.L.) on the island of Venice itself. If your train only stops at Mestre, worry not. Your train ticket to Venice will get you to Venezia S.L. Just hop any train coming by and finish your journey (6/hour, 10 minutes). If, for some reason, you need a ticket from Mestre to Santa Lucia, you can buy one at a machine for €1.

Venice's Santa Lucia train station (Ferrovia) plops you right into the old town on the Grand Canal, an easy vaporetto ride or fascinating 40-minute walk to St. Mark's Square. If the station's TI is crowded when you arrive, skip it and visit one of the two TIs at St. Mark's Square instead. It's not worth a long wait for a minimal TI map (buy a good one from a newsstand or pick up a free one at your hotel). Confirm your departure plan (use the machines or just study the *partenze*/departures posters on walls).

Consider storing unnecessary heavy bags. **Baggage check** is

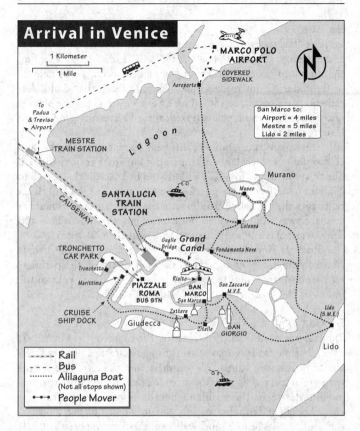

Arrival in Venice

1 Kilometer

1 Mile

To Padua & Treviso Airport

MARCO POLO AIRPORT

COVERED SIDEWALK

Aeroporto

San Marco to:
Airport = 4 miles
Mestre = 5 miles
Lido = 2 miles

MESTRE TRAIN STATION

Lagoon

Murano

Museo

SANTA LUCIA TRAIN STATION

Colonna

CAUSEWAY

TRONCHETTO CAR PARK

Guglie Bridge

Grand Canal

Fondamenta Nove

Tronchetto

Marittima

Rialto

San Zaccaria M.V.E.

PIAZZALE ROMA BUS STN

SAN MARCO

San Marco

CRUISE SHIP DOCK

Zattere

Giudecca

Zitelle

SAN GIORGIO

Lido (S.M.E.)

Lido

- - - - Rail
- - - - Bus
· · · · · Alilaguna Boat
(Not all stops shown)
•—•—• People Mover

at track 1 (€5/5 hours, €11/24 hours, daily 6:00-23:50, no lockers). **WCs** (€0.80) are at track 1 and in the back of the big bar/cafeteria area inside the station.

Minimize your time in the station—the banks of user-friendly automated ticket machines are handy but cover Italian destinations only. They take euros and credit cards, display schedules, and issue tickets. If you need international tickets or live help, the ticket windows are open from 6:00 to 20:30. Or you could take care of these tasks online or for a fee at downtown travel agencies (see page 952).

To get from the train station to downtown Venice, walk straight out of the station to the canal. You'll see vaporetto docks and ticket booths on both sides. For vaporetto #2 (fast boat down Grand Canal), go left. For vaporetto #1 (slow boat down Grand Canal), go right. See page 953 for details on vaporetto tickets and passes. A water taxi from the train station to a hotel in central Venice will cost about €60.

By Bus

Venice's "bus station" is actually an open-air parking lot called Piazzale Roma. If you arrive at the Piazzale Roma bus station, find the vaporetto docks (just left of the modern bridge) and take #1 or the faster #2 down the Grand Canal to reach the Rialto, Accademia, or San Marco (St. Mark's Square) stops. If your hotel is near the train station, you can walk there by crossing the modern Calatrava Bridge.

The square is a jumble of different operators, platforms, and crosswalks over busy lanes of traffic. But bus stops are well-signed. The ticket windows for ACTV (local public buses, including #5 to Marco Polo Airport) are by the vaporetto stop. The ATVO ticket office is in the big, white building, on the right side of the square as you face away from the canal (for express buses to Marco Polo and Treviso airports and to Padua; office open daily 6:40-19:35).

Piazzale Roma has two big parking garages and the People Mover monorail (going to the cruise port and then the parking-lot island of Tronchetto). A baggage-storage office is next to the monorail at #497m (€5/24 hours, daily 6:00-21:00).

By Car

The freeway dead-ends after crossing the causeway to Venice. At the end of the road you have two parking choices: garages at Tronchetto or Piazzale Roma. As you drive into the city, sign boards with green and red lights indicate which lots are full. (You can also park in Mestre, on the mainland, but this is less convenient.)

Parking at Tronchetto: This garage is much bigger, a bit farther out, a bit cheaper, and well-connected by vaporetto (€3-4/hour, €21/24 hours, discounts for longer stays, tel. 041-520-7555, www.veniceparking.it).

After parking in the big Tronchetto garage, cross the street. While you can head left for a long walk to the ill-conceived People Mover (which takes you to Piazzale Roma for €1), it's easiest to go right to the vaporetto dock (not well-signed, look for *ACTV*). At the dock, catch vaporetto #2 in one of two directions: via the Grand Canal (more scenic, stops at Rialto, 40 minutes to San Marco), or via Giudecca (around the city, faster, no Rialto stop, 30 minutes to San Marco).

Don't be waylaid by aggressive water taxi boatmen. They charge €100 to take you where the vaporetto will take you for €7. Also avoid the travel agencies masquerading as TIs; deal only with the ticket booth at the vaporetto dock or the HelloVenezia public transport office. If you're going to buy a local transport pass, do it now.

If you're staying near the train station and don't mind a walk, you can take the €1 People Mover monorail instead of paying €7 for

VENICE

the two-stop vaporetto ride. The monorail brings you from Tronchetto to the bus station at Piazzale Roma, then it's a five-minute walk across the Calatrava Bridge to the train station (buy monorail tickets with coins from machine, 3-minute trip, runs Mon-Sat 7:00-23:00, Sun 8:30-21:00).

Parking at Piazzale Roma: The two garages here are closer in and more convenient—but a bit more expensive and likelier to be full. Both garages face the busy square (Piazzale Roma) where the road ends. The big white building on your right is a 2,200-space public parking garage, the Autorimessa Communale (€25/24 hours, tel. 041-272-7211, www.asmvenezia.it). In a back corner of the square is the private Garage San Marco (€30/24 hours, tel. 041-523-2213, www.garagesanmarco.it). At either of these, you'll have to give up your keys.

Parking in Mestre: Parking in the garage across from the train station in Mestre (on the mainland) only makes sense if you have light bags and are staying within walking distance of the Santa Lucia train station (€8/day Mon-Fri, €12-16/day Sat-Sun; www.sabait.it).

By Plane

For information on Venice's airport, see the end of this chapter.

Helpful Hints

Theft Alert: The dark, late-night streets of Venice are generally safe. Even so, pickpockets (often elegantly dressed) work the crowded main streets, docks, and *vaporetti*. Your biggest risk of pickpockets is inside St. Mark's Basilica or on a tightly packed vaporetto.

A handy *polizia* station is on the right side of St. Mark's Square (near Caffè Florian). To call the police, dial 113. The Venice TI handles complaints—which must be submitted in writing—about local crooks, including gondolier, restaurant, or hotel rip-offs (fax 041-523-0399, complaint.apt@turismovenezia.it).

It's illegal for street vendors to sell knock-off handbags and it's also illegal for you to buy them; both you and the vendor can get big fines.

Medical Help: Venice's Santi Giovanni e Paolo hospital (tel. 118) is a 10-minute walk from both the Rialto and San Marco neighborhoods, located on Fondamenta dei Mendicanti toward Fondamente Nove. You can take vaporetto #4.1 from San Zaccaria-Jolanda, or #5.2 from the train station or Piazzale Roma, to the Ospedale stop.

Be Prepared to Splurge: Venice is expensive for residents as well as tourists, as everything must be shipped in and hand-trucked to its destination. I find that the best way to enjoy Venice is just to succumb to its charms and blow a little money.

Crowd Control: The city is inundated with cruise-ship crowds and tours from mainland hotels daily from 10:00 to about 17:00. Crowds can be a serious problem at **St. Mark's Basilica.** Try going early or late, or even better, you can bypass the line if you have a bag to check (see page 975). At the **Doge's Palace,** avoid the long line by purchasing your ticket at the less-crowded Correr Museum. You can also visit late in the day, buy your ticket online, or book a tour. For the **Campanile,** ascend late (it's open until 21:00 July-Sept), or skip it entirely if you're going to the similar San Giorgio Maggiore bell tower. For the **Accademia,** go early or late—or you can reserve a ticket at least a day in advance by phone or online.

Sights that have crowd problems get even more crowded when it rains.

Take Breaks: Venice's endless pavement, crowds, and tight spaces are hard on tourists, especially in hot weather. Schedule breaks in your sightseeing. Grab a cool place to sit down, relax, and recoup—meditate on a pew in an uncrowded church, or stop in a café.

Etiquette: On St. Mark's Square, a "decorum patrol" admonishes snackers and sunbathers. Picnicking is forbidden (keep a low profile). The only place for a legal picnic is in Giardinetti Reali, the small park along the waterfront west of the Piazzetta near St. Mark's Square.

Dress Modestly: When visiting St. Mark's Basilica or other major churches, men, women, and even children must cover their shoulders and knees (or risk being turned away). Remove hats when entering a church.

Public Toilets: Handy public WCs (€1.50) are near major landmarks, including: St. Mark's Square (behind the Correr Museum and at the waterfront park, Giardinetti Reali), Rialto, and the Accademia Bridge. Use free toilets whenever you can—in a museum you're visiting or a café you're eating in. You could also get a drink at a bar (cheaper) and use their WC for free.

Best Views: On St. Mark's Square, enjoy views from the soaring Campanile or the balcony of St. Mark's Basilica (both require admission). The Rialto and Accademia bridges provide free, expansive views of the Grand Canal, along with a cooling breeze. Or get off the main island for a view of the Venetian skyline: Ascend the Church of San Giorgio Maggiore's bell tower, or venture to Giudecca Island to visit the swanky bar of the Molino Stucky Hilton Hotel (free shuttle boat leaves from near the San Zaccaria-M.V.E. vaporetto dock).

Pigeon Poop: If your head is bombed by a pigeon, resist the initial response to wipe it off immediately—it'll just smear into your hair. Wait until it dries, and it should flake off cleanly. But if the poop splatters on your clothes, wipe it off immediately to avoid a stain.

Water: I carry a water bottle to refill at public fountains. Venetians pride themselves on having pure, safe, and tasty tap water piped in from the foothills of the Alps. You can actually see the mountains from Venice's bell towers on crisp, clear winter days.

Updates to this Book: For news about changes to this book's coverage since it was published, see www.ricksteves.com/update.

Services

Internet Access: Almost all hotels have Wi-Fi, many have a computer that guests can use, and most provide these services for free. Otherwise, handy if pricey little Internet places are scattered around town (usually on back streets, marked with an @ sign, and charging €5/hour).

Post Office: The main post office is on Marzaria San Salvador, a few blocks toward St. Mark's Square from the Rialto, just beyond the Bata shoe store (Mon-Fri 8:30-19:10, Sat 8:30-12:30, closed Sun). You'll find branch offices around town. Use post offices only as a last resort, as simple transactions can take 45 minutes if you get in the wrong line. You can buy stamps from tobacco shops and mail postcards at any of the red postboxes in town.

Bookstores: In keeping with its literary heritage, Venice has classy and inviting bookstores. The small **Libreria Studium,** a block behind St. Mark's Basilica, has a carefully chosen selection of new English books, including my guidebooks (daily 9:00-19:30, on Calle de la Canonica at #337—see map on page 973, tel. 041-522-2382). Used-bookstore lovers shouldn't miss the funky **Acqua Alta** ("high water") bookstore, whose quirky owner Luigi has prepared for the next flood by displaying his wares in a selection of vessels, including bathtubs and a gondola (daily 9:00-21:00, large and classically disorganized selection includes prints of Venice, just beyond Campo Santa Maria Formosa on Calle Lunga Santa Maria Formosa at #5176, tel. 041-296-0841). For a solid selection of used books in English, visit **Marco Polo,** on Calle del Teatro Malibran, close to the St. Mark's side of the Rialto Bridge on the way to Corte del Milion (Mon-Sat 9:30-13:00 & 15:30-19:30, closed Sun, tel. 041-522-6343).

Laundry: You'll find coin-operated launderettes near the train station and off Campo Santa Maria Formosa. I've listed details

VENICE

for a self-service *lavanderia* and a competitively priced full-service laundry near St. Mark's Square (see page 993), and for a self-serve laundry near the train station (page 1006). Or ask your hotelier for the nearest launderette.

Travel Agencies: If you need to get train tickets, make seat reservations, or arrange a *cuccetta* (koo-CHET-tah—a berth on a night train), save a time-consuming trip to Venice's crowded train station by using a downtown travel agency. Most trains between Venice, Florence, and Rome require reservations, even for railpass holders. A travel agency can also give advice on cheap flights (book at least a week in advance for the best fares).

Near St. Mark's Square, **Oltrex Change and Travel** sells train tickets and books reservations for a €4 fee (tickets sold daily 9:00-18:00; on Riva degli Schiavoni, one bridge past the Bridge of Sighs—see map on page 973; tel. 041-524-2828, Luca and Beatrice).

Near Rialto, **Kele & Teo Travel** sells train tickets for a €4 per-person service charge (Mon-Fri 9:00-18:00, Sat 9:00-12:00, closed Sun; leaving the Rialto Bridge heading for St. Mark's, it's half a block away, tucked down a side street on the right; tel. 041-520-8722).

English Church Services: San Zulian Church offers a Mass in English (generally May-Sept Mon-Fri at 9:30 and Sun at 11:30, Sun only Oct-April, 2 blocks toward Rialto off St. Mark's Square, tel. 041-523-5383). **St. George's Anglican Church** welcomes all to its English-language Eucharist (Sun at 10:30, located on Campo San Zio in Dorsoduro, midway between Accademia and Peggy Guggenheim Collection, www.stgeorgesvenice.com).

Getting Around Venice
On Foot

The city's "streets" are narrow pedestrian walkways connecting its docks, squares, bridges, and courtyards. To navigate, look for yellow signs on street corners pointing you to *(per)* the nearest major landmark. The first landmarks you'll get to know are San Marco (St. Mark's Square), Rialto (the bridge), Accademia (another bridge), Ferrovia (the train station), and Piazzale Roma (the bus station). Determine whether your destination is in the direction of a major signposted landmark, then follow the signs through the maze.

Dare to turn off the posted routes and make your own discoveries. While 80 percent of Venice is, in fact, not touristy, 80 percent of the tourists never notice. Escape the crowds and explore on foot. Walk and walk to the far reaches of the town. Don't worry about getting lost—in fact, get as lost as possible. Keep reminding yourself, "I'm on an island, and I can't get off." When it comes time to find your way, just follow the arrows on building corners or simply ask a local, *"Dov'è San Marco?"* ("Where is St. Mark's?") People in the tourist business (that's most Venetians) speak some English. If they don't, listen politely, watch where their hands point, say *"Grazie,"* and head off in that direction. If you're lost, refer to your map, or pop into a hotel and ask for their business card—it probably comes with a map and a prominent "You are here."

If you need to find a specific address, it helps to know its district, street, house number, and nearby landmarks. Every building in Venice has a house number. The numbers relate to the district (each with about 6,000 address numbers), not the street.

Some helpful street lingo: *Campo* means square, *campiello* is a small square, *calle* is a street, *fondamenta* is the embankment along a canal or the lagoon, *rio* is a small canal, *rio terà* is a street that was once a canal and has been filled in, *sotoportego* is a covered passageway, and *ponte* is a bridge. Don't get hung up on the exact spelling of street and square names, which may sometimes appear in the Venetian dialect and other times in standard Italian.

By Vaporetto

Venice's public transit system, run by a company called ACTV, is a fleet of motorized bus-boats called *vaporetti*. They work like city buses except that they never get a flat, the stops are docks, and if you get off between stops, you might drown.

For most travelers, only two vaporetto lines matter: line #1 and line #2. These lines leave every 10 minutes or so and go up and down the Grand Canal, between the "mouth of the fish" at one end and San Marco at the other. Line #1 is the slow boat, taking 45 minutes and making every stop along the way. Line #2 is the fast boat that zips down the Grand Canal in 25 minutes, stopping only at Tronchetto (parking lot), Piazzale Roma (bus station), Ferrovia (train station), Rialto Bridge, San Tomà (Frari Church), San Samuele, Accademia Bridge, San Marco (west end of St. Mark's Square), and San Zaccaria (east end of St. Mark's Square).

Catching a vaporetto is very much like catching a city bus. You can buy either single-ride tickets (valid for 1 hour) or passes (valid for a variety of durations, from 12 hours to 7 days) from any ticket window or HelloVenezia office. HelloVenezia, run by ACTV, is a string of shops selling tickets and passes at the same prices as ticket windows (www.hellovenezia.com).

Before you board, validate your ticket by holding it up to the small white machine on the dock until you hear a pinging sound. The machine readout shows how long your ticket is valid—and inspectors do come by now and then to check tickets. If you board

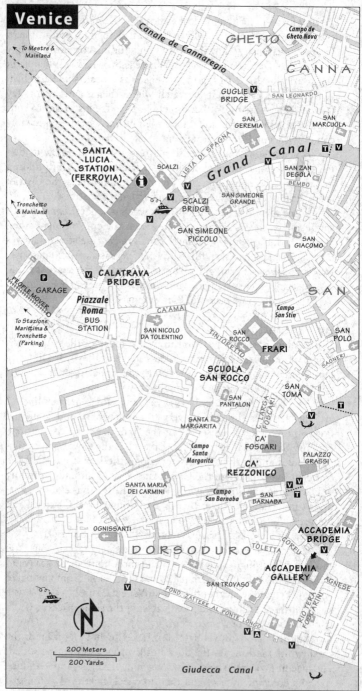

Venice

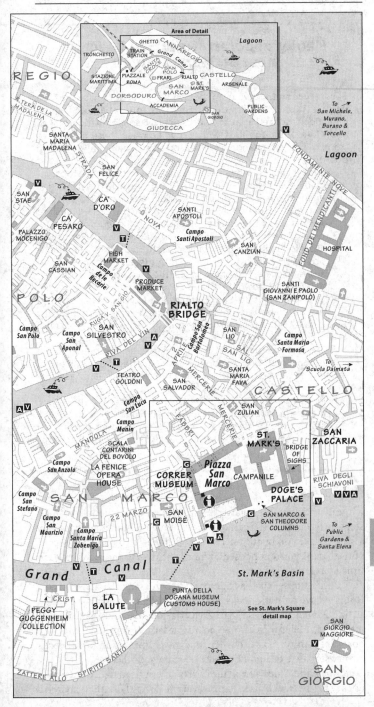

Area of Detail

TRONCHETTO

GHETTO CANNAREGIO

Lagoon

TRAIN STATION

Grand Canal

STAZIONE MARITTIMA

PIAZZALE ROMA

SANTA CROCE

SAN POLO

FRARI

RIALTO

CASTELLO

DORSODURO

SAN MARCO

ST. MARK'S

ARSENALE

ACCADEMIA

SAN GIORGIO

PUBLIC GARDENS

GIUDECCA

To
San Michele,
Murano,
Burano &
Torcello

REGIO

R. TERA DE LA MADALENA

Lagoon

FONDAMENTE NOVE

SANTA MARIA MADALENA

STRADA

SAN FELICE

SAN STAE

CA' D'ORO

NOVA

SANTI APOSTOLI

Campo Santi Apostoli

CA' PESARO

PALAZZO MOCENIGO

FISH MARKET

Campo de le Becarie

SAN CANZIAN

SANTI GIOVANNI E PAOLO (SAN ZANIPOLO)

HOSPITAL

FOND. DEI MENDICANTI

SAN CASSIAN

PRODUCE MARKET

POLO

RUGA V. SAN GIO

RIALTO BRIDGE

Campo San Polo

Campo San Aponal

SAN SILVESTRO

RIVA DEL VIN

Campo San Bartolomeo

SAN LIO

SAL SAN LIO

Campo Santa Maria Formosa

To Scuola Dalmata

APRILE

TEATRO GOLDONI

MERCERIE

SANTA MARIA FAVA

SAN SALVADOR

SAN MARCO

MANDOLA

Campa San Luca

Campo Manin

SCALA CONTARINI DEL BOVOLO

LA FENICE OPERA HOUSE

Campo San Anzolo

Campo San Stefano

22 MARZO

Campo San Maurizio

Campo Santa Maria Zobenigo

Grand Canal

PEGGY GUGGENHEIM COLLECTION

LA SALUTE

CRIST

ZATTERE ALLO

SPIRITO SANTO

CASTELLO

FABBRI

MERCERIE

SAN ZULIAN

ST. MARK'S

BRIDGE OF SIGHS

SAN ZACCARIA

CORRER MUSEUM

Piazza San Marco

CAMPANILE

DOGE'S PALACE

RIVA DEGLI SCHIAVONI

SAN MOISÈ

SAN MARCO & SAN THEODORE COLUMNS

To Public Gardens & Santa Elena

St. Mark's Basin

PUNTA DELLA DOGANA MUSEUM (CUSTOMS HOUSE)

See St. Mark's Square detail map

SAN GIORGIO MAGGIORE

SAN GIORGIO

VENICE

Handy *Vaporetti* from San Zaccaria, near St. Mark's Square

Several *vaporetti* leave from the San Zaccaria docks, located 150 yards east of St. Mark's Square. There are four separate San Zaccaria docks spaced about 70 yards apart: Danieli, Jolanda, M.V.E., and Pietà. Although I list which specific dock these lines leave from, they often change from season to season—confirm before boarding.

- Line #1 goes up the Grand Canal, making all the stops, including San Marco-Vallaresso, Rialto, Ferrovia (train station), and Piazzale Roma (but it does not go as far as Tronchetto). In the other direction, it goes from San Zaccaria-Danieli to Arsenale and Giardini before ending on the Lido.
- Line #2 begins at San Zaccaria-M.V.E. and zips over to San Giorgio Maggiore, the island church across from St. Mark's Square (5 minutes, €4 ride). From there, it continues on to stops on the island of Giudecca, the parking lot at Tronchetto, and then down the Grand Canal.
- Line #4.1 goes to San Michele and Murano in 45 minutes (usually departs from the San Zaccaria-Jolanda dock).
- Line #7 is the summertime express boat to Murano (25 minutes, most likely from the San Zaccaria-Jolanda dock).
- The Molino Stucky shuttle boat takes even non-guests to the Hilton Hotel, with its popular view bar (free, 20-minute ride, leaves at 0:20 past the hour from near the San Zaccaria-M.V.E. dock).
- Lines #5.1 and #5.2 are the *circulare* (cheer-koo-LAH-ray), making a loop around the perimeter of the island, with a stop at the Lido—perfect if you just like riding boats. Line #5.1 goes counterclockwise (usually from the San Zaccaria-

without a ticket (because ticket windows at odd hours or small stops may be closed), seek out the conductor immediately to buy a single ticket on board (or risk a €50 fine). If you purchase a vaporetto pass, you're supposed to touch the pass to the machine each time you board the boat.

Large stops—such as San Marco, San Zaccaria, and Piazzale Roma—have multiple docks, and each dock has its own name, such as San Marco-Vallaresso, San Zaccaria-Jolanda, and Piazzale Roma-Parisi. Helpful electronic boards at larger stops display which boats are coming next and when, and give information for all docks at that stop. Make a point to take advantage of these.

At smaller stops, check the charts and signs to figure out which dock your boat will use. Signs on each dock show the vaporetto

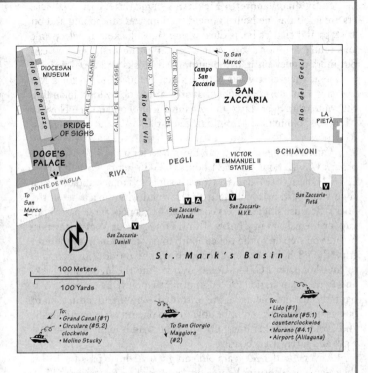

Danieli dock), and #5.2 goes clockwise (usually from the San Zaccaria-Jolanda dock).
- The Alilaguna airport shuttle to and from the airport stops here as well (generally at the San Zaccaria-Jolanda dock).

lines that stop there and the direction they are headed: Along the Grand Canal, a #1 or #2 boat might be headed toward St. Mark's Square (signposted *San Marco*), or back toward the mainland (signposted *Ferrovia*, *Piazzale Roma*, or *Tronchetto*). Sorting out the different directions of travel can be confusing, especially as boats on some circular routes travel in one direction only (true for lines #5.1 and #5.2, plus the non-Murano sections of lines #4.1 and #4.2).

To clear up any confusion, ask a ticket-seller or conductor for help (sometimes they're stationed on the dock to help confused tourists), or look at the most current ACTV timetable (in English and Italian, free at ticket booths but often unavailable—can be downloaded from the ACTV website, www.actv.it).

These are your ticket and pass options:

Individual Vaporetto Tickets: A single ticket costs €7. Tickets are good for one hour in one direction; you can hop on and off at stops and change boats during that time. Tickets are electronic and refillable—don't toss your ticket after the first use. You can put more money on it at the automated kiosks and avoid waiting in line at the ticket window. The fare is reduced to €4 for a few one-stop runs *(corsa semplice)* that are hard to do by foot, including the route from San Marco to La Salute, from Fondamente Nove to Murano-Colonna, and from San Zaccaria-M.V.E. to San Giorgio Maggiore.

Vaporetto Passes: You can buy a pass for unlimited use of *vaporetti*: €18/12 hours, €20/24 hours, €25/36 hours, €30/48 hours, €35/72 hours, €50/7-day pass (pass is supposed to be validated each time you board by touching it to the small white machine on the dock). Because single tickets cost a hefty €7 a pop, these passes can pay for themselves in a hurry. Think through your Venice itinerary before you step up to the ticket booth to pay for your first vaporetto trip. The 48-hour pass pays for itself with five rides (for example: to your hotel, on a Grand Canal joyride, into the lagoon and back, and to the train station). Keep in mind that outlying stops, such as Santa Elena and Biennale, are unstaffed—another good reason to buy a pass. And it's fun to be able to hop on and off spontaneously, and avoid long ticket lines. On the other hand, many tourists just walk and rarely use a boat.

Anyone under 30 years old can get a 72-hour pass for €18 if they also buy a **Rolling Venice** discount card for €4 (see page 972). Those settling in for a longer stay can ride like a local by buying the **CartaVenezia** ID card (€40/5 years, which lets you ride for €1.10 per trip). See www.actv.it for details.

Passes are also valid on ACTV's mainland buses, including bus #5 to the airport (but not the airport buses run by ATVO, a separate company).

Vaporetto Tips: For fun, take my Grand Canal Cruise. Boats can be literally packed during the tourist rush hour (during mornings heading in from Piazzale Roma, and in evenings heading out to Piazzale Roma). Riding at night, with nearly empty boats and chandelier-lit palace interiors viewable from the Grand Canal, is an entirely different experience.

By *Traghetto*

Only four bridges cross the Grand Canal, but *traghetti* (shuttle gondolas) ferry locals and in-the-know tourists across the Grand Canal at seven handy locations. Just step in, hand the gondolier €2, and enjoy the ride—standing or sitting. Note that some *traghetti* are seasonal, some stop running as early as 12:30, and all stop by 18:00.

VENICE

By Water Taxi

Venetian taxis, like speedboat limos, hang out at busy points along the Grand Canal. Prices are regulated and listed on the TI's website: €15 for pick-up, then €2 per minute; €5 per person for more than four passengers; and €10 between 22:00 and 6:00. Extra bags cost €3 apiece. (For information on taking the water taxi to/from the airport, see "Venice Connections," at the end of this chapter.) Despite regulation, prices can be soft; negotiate and settle on the price or rate before stepping in. For travelers with lots of luggage or small groups who can split the cost, taxi boat rides can be a worthwhile and time-saving convenience—and skipping across the lagoon in a classic wooden motorboat is a cool indulgence. For a little more than €100 an hour, you can have a private, unguided taxi-boat tour.

By Gondola

If you're interested in hiring a gondolier for your own private cruise, see page 989.

Tours in Venice

Tours of Venice on foot and afloat abound. To sightsee on your own, download my series of free audio tours that illuminate some of Venice's top sights and experiences: St. Mark's Square, St. Mark's Basilica, the Frari Church, and a cruise along the Grand Canal (see sidebar on page 7 for details).

Avventure Bellissime Venice Tours

This company offers several English-only two-hour walks, including a basic St. Mark's Square introduction called the "Original Venice Walking Tour" (€22, includes church entry, most days at 11:00, Sun at 14:00; 45 minutes on the square, 15 minutes in the church, one hour along back streets), a 70-minute private boat tour of the Grand Canal (€43, daily at 16:30, eight people maximum), and excursions on the mainland (discount for Rick Steves readers, see descriptions at www.tours-italy.com, tel. 041-970-499, info@tours-italy.com, Monica or Jonathan).

Classic Venice Bars Tour

Debonair guide Alessandro Schezzini is a connoisseur of Venetian *bacari*—classic old bars serving wine and traditional *cicchetti* snacks. He organizes two-hour Venetian pub tours (€30, any night on request at 18:00, depart from top of Rialto Bridge, better to book by email—alessandro@schezzini.it—than by phone, mobile 335-530-9024, www.schezzini.it). Alessandro's tours include sampling *cicchetti* with wines at three different *bacari*. (If you think of this tour as a light dinner with a local friend, it's a particularly good value.)

VENICE

Artviva.

This company offers a busy program of tours, including Venice in a day, four themed tours (Grand Canal, Venice Walk, Doge's Palace, Gondola Tour), and a "Learn to Be a Gondolier" tour (for details, see www.italy.artviva.com).

Venicescapes

Michael Broderick's private theme tours of Venice are intellectually demanding and beyond the attention span of most mortal tourists. But travelers with a keen interest and desire to learn find him passionate and engaging. Your time with Michael is like a rolling, graduate-level lecture (see his website for various 4-6-hour itineraries, 2 people-$250-290 or the euro equivalent, $60/person after that, admissions and transport not included, book in advance, tel. 041-850-5742, mobile 349-479-7406, www.venicescapes.org, info@venicescapes.org).

Local Guides

Plenty of licensed, trained guides are available. If you organize a small group from your hotel at breakfast to split the cost (figure on €70/hour with a 2-hour minimum), the fee becomes more reasonable. The following guides work with individuals, families, and small groups:

Walks Inside Venice is a dynamic duo of women enthusiastic about teaching (€70/hour per group with this book, 3-hour minimum; Roberta: mobile 347-253-0560; Sara: mobile 335-522-9714; www.walksinsidevenice.com, info@walksinsidevenice.com). Roberta has been a big help in the making of this book. They also do regularly scheduled small-group, English-only walking tours (€60, departs daily at 14:30, 2.5 hours).

Elisabetta Morelli is a fine licensed guide (€70/hour, 2-hour minimum, tel. 041-526-7816, mobile 328-753-5220, www.elisabettamorelli.it, bettamorelli@inwind.it).

Venice with a Guide is a co-op of 10 good guides (www.venicewithaguide.com).

Alessandro Schezzini, mentioned earlier for his Classic Venice Bars Tour, isn't a licensed guide, so he can't take you into sights. But his relaxed, 1.5-hour back-streets tour gets you beyond the clichés and into off-beat Venice (€15/person, departs daily at 16:00, mobile 335-530-9024, www.schezzini.it, alessandro@schezzini.it). He also does lagoon tours.

Weekend Tour Packages for Students in Venice

Andy Steves (my son) runs Weekend Student Adventures, offering experiential three-day weekend tours for €199, designed for American students studying abroad (www.wsaeurope.com for details on tours of Venice and other great cities).

Self-Guided Cruise in Venice

▲▲▲Grand Canal Cruise

Take a joyride and introduce yourself to Venice by boat. Cruise the Canal Grande all the way to San Marco, starting at the train station (Ferrovia) or the bus station (Piazzale Roma).

If it's your first trip down the Grand Canal, you might want to stow this book and just take it all in—Venice is a barrage on the senses that hardly needs narration. But these notes give the cruise a little meaning and help orient you to this great city.

This tour is designed to be done on the slow boat #1 (which takes about 45 minutes). The express boat #2 travels the same route, but it skips many stops and takes only 25 minutes, making it hard to sightsee. Also, some #2 boats terminate at Rialto; confirm that you're on a boat that goes all the way to San Marco.

To help you enjoy the visual parade of canal wonders, I've organized this tour by boat stop. I'll point out both what you can see from the current stop, and what to look forward to as you cruise to the next stop. You can download this self-guided cruise as a free Rick Steves audio tour (see page 7).

A Few Tips: You're more likely to find an empty seat if you catch the vaporetto at Piazzale Roma. You can break up the tour by hopping on and off at various sights described in greater depth elsewhere in this chapter (but remember, a single-fare vaporetto ticket is good for just one hour; passes let you hop on and off all day). The trip is best in a boat with seats in the bow, but many boats no longer offer these great front-row view seats. If they do, make a beeline for these seats as soon as you board. From the front, you can easily look left, right, and forward. If you find yourself stuck on the side or in the cabin, do your best. Avoid sitting in the back, only because you'll miss the wonderful forward views.

Overview

The Grand Canal is Venice's "Main Street." At more than two miles long, nearly 150 feet wide, and nearly 15 feet deep, it's the city's largest canal, lined with its most impressive palaces. It's the remnant of a river that once spilled from the mainland into the Adriatic. The sediment it carried formed barrier islands that cut Venice off from the sea, forming a lagoon.

VENICE

Venice was built on the marshy islands of the former delta, sitting on wood pilings driven nearly 15 feet into the clay (alder was the preferred wood). About 25 miles of canals drain the city, dumping like streams into the Grand Canal. Technically, Venice has only three canals: Grand, Giudecca, and Cannaregio. The 45 small waterways that dump into the Grand Canal are referred to as rivers (e.g., Rio Novo).

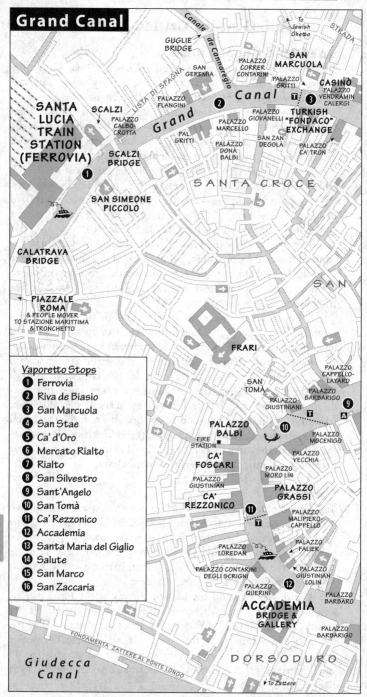

Grand Canal

To Jewish Ghetto

STRADA

GUGLIE BRIDGE

Canale de Cannaregio

SAN MARCUOLA

PALAZZO CORRER CONTARINI

SAN GEREMIA

PALAZZO GRITTI

CASINÒ

PALAZZO VENDRAMIN CALERGI

LISTA DI SPAGNA

PALAZZO FLANGINI

Grand Canal

❷

❸

TURKISH "FONDACO" EXCHANGE

SANTA LUCIA TRAIN STATION (FERROVIA)

SCALZI

PALAZZO CALBO-CROTTA

PALAZZO GIOVANELLI

PALAZZO MARCELLO

PAL GRITTI

PALAZZO DONA BALBI

SAN ZAN DEGOLA

PALAZZO CA' TRON

❶

SCALZI BRIDGE

SAN SIMEONE PICCOLO

SANTA CROCE

SAN

CALATRAVA BRIDGE

PIAZZALE ROMA
& PEOPLE MOVER TO STAZIONE MARITTIMA & TRONCHETTO

FRARI

PALAZZO CAPPELLO-LAYARD

SAN TOMÀ

PALAZZO BARBARIGO

Vaporetto Stops

❶ Ferrovia
❷ Riva de Biasio
❸ San Marcuola
❹ San Stae
❺ Ca' d'Oro
❻ Mercato Rialto
❼ Rialto
❽ San Silvestro
❾ Sant'Angelo
❿ San Tomà
⓫ Ca' Rezzonico
⓬ Accademia
⓭ Santa Maria del Giglio
⓮ Salute
⓯ San Marco
⓰ San Zaccaria

PALAZZO GIUSTINIANI

❾

A

❿

PALAZZO MOCENIGO

PALAZZO BALBI

FIRE STATION

CA' FOSCARI

PALAZZO VECCHIA

PALAZZO MORO LIN

PALAZZO GIUSTINIAN

CA' REZZONICO

PALAZZO GRASSI

⓫

PALAZZO MALIPIERO-CAPPELLO

PALAZZO LOREDAN

PALAZZO FALIER

PALAZZO CONTARINI DEGLI SCRIGNI

PALAZZO GIUSTINIAN LOLIN

PALAZZO QUERINI

⓬

PALAZZO BARBARO

ACCADEMIA BRIDGE & GALLERY

PALAZZO BARBARIGO

VENICE

FONDAMENTA ZATTERE AL PONTE LONGO

Giudecca Canal

DORSODURO

To Zattere

NOVA

Lagoon

FONDAMENTE NOVE

PALAZZO
MARCELLO

PALAZZO
MOLIN

PALAZZO
ZULLAN

(4)

**SAN
STAE**

PALAZZO
BARBARIGO

PALAZZO
FONTANA

PALAZZO
GIUSTI

CANNAREGIO

PALAZZO
SAGREDO

**CA'
PESARO**

PALAZZO
DONÀ

PALAZZO
FAVRETTO

**CA'
D'ORO**

STRADA NOVA

PALAZZO
MICHIEL
COLONNE

PALAZZO
CORNER
DELLA REGINA

PALAZZO
BRANDOLIN

(5)

PALAZZO
VALMARANA

PALAZZO
CA' DA MOSTO

**FISH
MARKET**

(6)

**PRODUCE
MARKET**

PALAZZO
CIVRAN

P O L O

**GERMAN
EXCHANGE**
(FORMER POST)

S. MARIA
FORMOSA

**RIALTO
BRIDGE**

SAL. S. LIO

(7)

PALAZZO
PAPADOPOLI

PALAZZO
BARZIZZA

PALAZZO
DOLFIN-
MANIN

PALAZZO
DONÀ

PALAZZO
CORNER-
CONTARINI

(8)

PALAZZO
BEMBO

MERCERIE

PALAZZO
BERNARDO

PALAZZO
FARSETTI-
DANDOLO

C A S T E L L O

PALAZZO
BENZON

PALAZZO
MARTINENGO

PALAZZO
GRIMANI

PALAZZO
CORNER-
SPINELLI

FABBRI

MERCERIE

**ST.
MARK'S
BASILICA**

CAMPANILE

**BRIDGE
OF SIGHS**

S A N   M A R C O

**DOGE'S
PALACE**

**SAN
MARCO**

CALLE LARGA
XXII MARZO

(16)

SAN MARCO &
SAN THEODORE
COLUMNS

**HARRY'S
AMERICAN
BAR**

(15)

To
Lido

**CA'
GRANDE**

**GRITTI
PALACE
HOTEL**

PALAZZO
FLANGINI

**St. Mark's
Basin**

Grand

(13)

Canal

(14)

PALAZZO
DARIO

PALAZZO
GENOVESE

**LA
SALUTE
CHURCH**

**PEGGY
GUGGENHEIM
COLLECTION**

**PUNTA DELLA
DOGANA MUSEUM**
(CUSTOMS HOUSE)

To
San Giorgio
Maggiore &
Giudecca

200 Meters

200 Yards

VENICE

Venice is a city of palaces, dating from the days when the city was the world's richest. The most lavish palaces formed a grand architectural cancan along the Grand Canal. Once frescoed in reds and blues, with black-and-white borders and gold-leaf trim, they made Venice a city of dazzling color. This cruise is the only way to truly appreciate the palaces, approaching them at water level, where their main entrances were located. Today, strict laws prohibit any changes in these buildings, so while landowners gnash their teeth, we can enjoy Europe's best-preserved medieval city—slowly rotting. Many of the grand buildings are now vacant. Others harbor chandeliered elegance above mossy, empty (often flooded) ground floors.

The Grand Canal Cruise Begins

This tour starts at the Ferrovia vaporetto stop (at Santa Lucia train station). It also works if you board upstream from Ferrovia at Piazzale Roma, a short walk from Ferrovia over the Calatrava Bridge. Just start the tour when your vaporetto reaches Ferrovia.

Ferrovia: The **Santa Lucia train station,** one of the few modern buildings in town, was built in 1954. It's been the gateway into Venice since 1860, when the first station was built. "F.S." stands for "Ferrovie dello Stato," the Italian state railway system.

More than 20,000 people a day commute in from the mainland, making this the busiest part of Venice during rush hour. The **Calatrava Bridge,** spanning the Grand Canal between the train station and Piazzale Roma upstream, was built in 2008 to alleviate some of the congestion and make the commute easier (see page 987).

Opposite the train station, atop the green dome of **San Simeon Piccolo** church, St. Simeon waves *ciao* to whoever enters or leaves the "old" city. The pink church with the white Carrara-marble facade, just beyond the train station, is the **Church of the Scalzi** (Church of the Barefoot, named after the shoeless Carmelite monks), where the last doge (Venetian ruler) rests. It looks relatively new because it was partially rebuilt after being bombed in 1915 by Austrians aiming (poorly) at the train station.

Riva de Biasio: Venice's main thoroughfare is busy with all kinds of boats: taxis, police boats, garbage boats, ambulances, construction cranes, and even brown-and-white UPS boats. Somehow they all manage to share the canal in relative peace.

About 25 yards past the Riva de Biasio stop, you'll look left down the broad **Cannaregio Canal** to see what was the **Jewish Ghetto** (described on page 986). The twin, pale-pink, eight-story "skyscrapers"—the tallest buildings you'll see at this end of the canal—are reminders of how densely populated the world's original ghetto was. Set aside as the local Jewish quarter in 1516, this area became extremely crowded. This urban island developed into one of the most closely knit business and cultural quarters of all the Jewish communities in Italy, and gave us our word "ghetto" (from *geto*, the copper foundry located here).

San Marcuola: At this stop, facing a tiny square just ahead, stands the unfinished church of San Marcuola, one of only five churches fronting the Grand Canal. Centuries ago, this canal was a commercial drag of expensive real estate in high demand by wealthy merchants. About 20 yards ahead on the right stands the stately gray **Turkish "Fondaco" Exchange,** one of the oldest houses in Venice. Its horseshoe arches and roofline of triangles and dingleballs are reminders of its Byzantine heritage. Turkish traders in turbans docked here, unloaded their goods into the warehouse on the bottom story, then went upstairs for a home-style meal and a place to sleep. Venice in the 1500s was very cosmopolitan, welcoming every religion and ethnicity, so long as they carried cash. (Today the building contains the city's Museum of Natural History—and Venice's only dinosaur skeleton.)

Just 100 yards ahead on the left, Venice's **Casinò** is housed in the palace where German composer Richard *(The Ring)* Wagner died in 1883. See his distinct, strong-jawed profile in the white plaque on the brick wall. In the 1700s, Venice was Europe's Vegas, with casinos and prostitutes everywhere. *Casinòs* ("little houses" in Venetian dialect) have long provided Italians with a handy escape from daily life. Today they're run by the state to keep Mafia influence at bay. Notice the fancy front porch, rolling out the red carpet for high rollers arriving by taxi or hotel boat.

San Stae: The San Stae Church sports a delightful Baroque facade. Opposite the San Stae stop is a little canal opening—on the second building to the right of that opening, look for the peeling plaster that once made up **frescoes** (you can barely distinguish the scant remains of little angels on the lower floors). Imagine the facades of the Grand Canal at their finest. Most of them would have been covered in frescoes by the best artists of the day. As colorful as the city is today, it's still only a faded, sepia-toned remnant of a long-gone era, a time of lavishly decorated, brilliantly colored palaces.

Just ahead, jutting out a bit on the right, is the ornate white facade of **Ca' Pesaro** (which houses the International Gallery of Modern Art—see page 984). *"Ca'"* is short for *casa* (house). Because only the house of the doge (Venetian ruler) could be called a palace *(palazzo),* all other Venetian palaces are technically *"Ca'."*

In this city of masks, notice how the rich marble facades along the Grand Canal mask what are generally just simple, no-nonsense brick buildings. Most merchants enjoyed showing off. However, being smart businessmen, they only decorated the side of the build-

VENICE

ings that would be seen and appreciated. But look back as you pass Ca' Pesaro. It's the only building you'll see with a fine side facade. Ahead, on the left, with its glorious triple-decker medieval arcade (just before the next stop) is Ca' d'Oro.

Ca' d'Oro: The lacy **Ca' d'Oro** (House of Gold) is the best example of Venetian Gothic architecture on the canal. Its three stories offer different variations on balcony design, topped with a spiny white roofline. Venetian Gothic mixes traditional Gothic (pointed arches and round medallions stamped with a four-leaf clover) with Byzantine styles (tall, narrow arches atop thin columns), filled in with Islamic frills. Like all the palaces, this was originally painted and gilded to make it even more glorious than it is now. Today the Ca' d'Oro is an art gallery (described on page 988).

Look at the Venetian chorus line of palaces in front of the boat. On the right is the arcade of the covered **fish market,** with the open-air **produce market** just beyond. It bustles in the morning but is quiet the rest of the day. This is a great scene to wander through—even though European Union hygiene standards have made it cleaner but less colorful than it once was.

Find the *traghetto* gondola ferrying shoppers—standing like Washington crossing the Delaware—back and forth. There are seven *traghetto* crossings along the Grand Canal, each one marked by a classy low-key green-and-black sign. As a public service, all gondoliers are obliged to row the *traghetto* a few days a month. Make a point to use them. At €2 a ride, *traghetti* offer the cheapest gondola ride in Venice (but at this price don't expect them to sing to you).

Mercato Rialto: This stop was opened in 2007 to serve the busy market (boats only stop here between 8:00 and 20:00). The long and officious-looking building at this stop is the Venice courthouse. Straight ahead in the distance, rising above the huge post office, is the tip of the Campanile (bell tower), crowned by its golden angel at St. Mark's Square, where this tour will end. The **German Exchange** (100 yards directly ahead, on left side) was the trading center for German metal merchants in the early 1500s (once a post office, it will soon be a shopping center).

You'll cruise by some trendy and beautifully situated wine bars on the right, but look ahead as you round the corner and see the impressive Rialto Bridge come into view.

A major landmark of Venice, the **Rialto Bridge** is lined with shops and tourists. Constructed in 1588, it's the third bridge built on this spot. Until the 1850s, this was the only bridge crossing the Grand Canal. With a span of 160 feet and foundations stretching 650 feet on either side, the Rialto was an impressive engineering feat in its day. Earlier Rialto Bridges could open to let big ships in, but not this one. When this new bridge was completed, much

VENICE

of the Grand Canal was closed to shipping and became a canal of palaces.

When gondoliers pass under the fat arch of the Rialto Bridge, they take full advantage of its acoustics: *"Volare, oh, oh..."*

Rialto: Rialto, a separate town in the early days of Venice, has always been the commercial district, while San Marco was the religious and governmental center. Today, a winding street called the Mercerie connects the two, providing travelers with human traffic jams and a mesmerizing gauntlet of shopping temptations. This is the only stretch of the historic Grand Canal with landings upon which you can walk. They unloaded the city's basic necessities here: oil, wine, charcoal, iron. Today, the quay is lined with tourist-trap restaurants.

Venice's sleek, black, graceful **gondolas** are a symbol of the city (for more on gondolas, see page 989). With about 500 gondoliers joyriding amid the churning *vaporetti*, there's a lot of congestion on the Grand Canal. Pay attention—this is where most of the gondola and vaporetto accidents take place. While the Rialto is the highlight of many gondola rides, gondoliers understandably prefer the quieter small canals. Watch your vaporetto driver curse the better-paid gondoliers.

Ahead 100 yards on the left, two gray-colored **palaces** stand side by side (the City Hall and the mayor's office). Their horseshoe-shaped, arched windows are similar and their stories are the same height, lining up to create the effect of one long balcony.

San Silvestro: We now enter a long stretch of important **merchants' palaces,** each with proud and different facades. Because ships couldn't navigate beyond the Rialto Bridge, the biggest palaces—with the major shipping needs—line this last stretch of the navigable Grand Canal.

Palaces like these were multi-functional: ground floor for the warehouse, offices and showrooms upstairs, and the living quarters above the offices on the "noble floors" (with big windows designed to allow in maximum light). Servants lived and worked on the top floors (with the smallest windows). For fire-safety reasons, the kitchens were also located on the top floors. Peek into the noble floors to catch a glimpse of their still-glorious chandeliers of Murano glass.

Sant'Angelo: Notice how many buildings have a foundation of waterproof white stone *(pietra d'Istria)* upon which the bricks sit high and dry. Many canal-level floors are abandoned as the rising water level takes its toll. The **posts**—historically painted gaily with the equivalent of family coats of arms—don't rot underwater. But the wood at the waterline, where it's exposed to oxygen, does. On the smallest canals, little blue gondola signs indicate that these docks are for gondolas only (no taxis or motorboats).

VENICE

Venice at a Glance

▲▲▲**St. Mark's Square** Venice's grand main square. **Hours:** Always open. See page 973.

▲▲▲**St. Mark's Basilica** Cathedral with mosaics, saint's bones, treasury, museum, and viewpoint of square. **Hours:** Mon-Sat 9:45-17:00, Sun 14:00-17:00 (until 16:00 Nov-March). See page 974.

▲▲▲**Doge's Palace** Art-splashed palace of former rulers, with prison accessible through Bridge of Sighs. **Hours:** Daily April-Oct 8:30-18:30, Nov-March 8:00-17:30. See page 978.

▲▲▲**Rialto Bridge** Distinctive bridge spanning the Grand Canal, with a market nearby. **Hours:** Bridge—always open; market—souvenir stalls open daily, produce market closed Sun, fish market closed Sun-Mon. See page 985.

▲▲**Correr Museum** Venetian history and art. **Hours:** Daily April-Oct 10:00-19:00, Nov-March 10:00-17:00. See page 979.

▲▲**Accademia** Venice's top art museum. **Hours:** Mon 8:15-14:00, Tue-Sun 8:15-19:15. See page 981.

▲▲**Peggy Guggenheim Collection** Popular display of 20th-century art. **Hours:** Wed-Mon 10:00-18:00, closed Tue. See page 983.

▲▲**Frari Church** Franciscan church featuring Renaissance masters. **Hours:** Mon-Sat 9:00-18:00, Sun 13:00-18:00. See page 985.

▲▲**Scuola San Rocco** "Tintoretto's Sistine Chapel." **Hours:** Daily 9:30-17:30. See page 986.

▲**Campanile** Dramatic bell tower on St. Mark's Square with elevator to the top. **Hours:** Daily Easter-June and Oct 9:00-19:00, July-Sept 9:00-21:00; Nov-Easter 9:30-16:45. See page 980.

VENICE

San Tomà: Fifty yards ahead, on the right side (with twin obelisks on the rooftop) stands Palazzo Balbi, the palace of an early-17th-century captain general of the sea. These Venetian equivalents of five-star admirals were honored with twin obelisks decorating their palaces. This palace, like so many in the city, flies three flags: Italy (green-white-red), the European Union (blue with ring of stars), and Venice (a lion on a field of red and gold). Today it houses the administrative headquarters of the regional government.

Just past the admiral's palace, look immediately to the right,

▲**Bridge of Sighs** Famous enclosed bridge, part of Doge's Palace, near St. Mark's Square. **Hours:** Always viewable. See page 981.

▲**La Salute Church** Striking church dedicated to the Virgin Mary. **Hours:** Daily 9:00-12:00 & 15:00-17:30. See page 983.

▲**Ca' Rezzonico** Posh Grand Canal palazzo with 18th-century Venetian art. **Hours:** April-Oct Wed-Mon 10:00-18:00, Nov-March Wed-Mon 10:00-17:00, closed Tue year-round. See page 984.

▲**Punta della Dogana** Museum of contemporary art. **Hours:** Wed-Mon 10:00-19:00, closed Tue. See page 984.

▲**Ca' Pesaro International Gallery of Modern Art** in a canalside palazzo. **Hours:** Tue-Sun 10:00-18:00, until 17:00 in winter, closed Mon. See page 984.

▲**Scuola Dalmata di San Giorgio** Exquisite Renaissance meeting house. **Hours:** Mon 14:45-18:00, Tue-Sat 9:15-13:00 & 14:45-18:00, Sun 9:15-13:00. See page 988.

Church of San Zaccaria Final resting place of St. Zechariah, plus a Bellini altarpiece and an eerie crypt. **Hours:** Mon-Sat 10:00-12:00 & 16:00-18:00, Sun 16:00-18:00. See page 981.

Church of San Polo Ninth-century church with works by Tintoretto, Veronese, and Tiepolo. **Hours:** Mon-Sat 10:00-17:00, closed Sun. See page 986.

▲**San Giorgio Maggiore** Island across the lagoon featuring church with Palladio architecture, Tintoretto paintings, and fine views back on Venice. **Hours:** April-Oct Mon-Sat 9:00-19:00, Sun 9:00-11:00 & 12:00-19:00; Nov-March daily 9:00-17:30. See page 981.

VENICE

down a side canal. On the right side of that canal, before the bridge, see the traffic light and the **fire station** (the 1930s Mussolini-era building with four arches hiding fireboats parked and ready to go).

The impressive **Ca' Foscari,** with a classic Venetian facade (on the corner, across from the fire station), dominates the bend in the canal. This is the main building of the University of Venice, which has about 25,000 students. Notice the elegant lamp on the corner—needed in the old days to light this intersection.

The grand, heavy, white **Ca' Rezzonico,** just before the stop of the same name, houses the Museum of 18th-Century Venice (see page 984). Across the canal is the cleaner and leaner **Palazzo Grassi,** the last major palace built on the canal, erected in the late 1700s. It was purchased by a French tycoon and now displays a contemporary art collection.

Ca' Rezzonico: Up ahead, the Accademia Bridge leads over the Grand Canal to the **Accademia Gallery** (right side), filled with the best Venetian paintings (see page 981). The bridge was put up in 1934 as a temporary structure. Locals liked it, so it stayed. It was rebuilt in 1984 in the original style.

Accademia: From here, look through the graceful bridge and way ahead to enjoy a classic view of **La Salute Church,** topped by a crown-shaped dome supported by scrolls (see page 983). This Church of Saint Mary of Good Health was built to thank God for delivering Venetians from the devastating plague of 1630 (which had killed about a third of the city's population).

The low, white building among greenery (100 yards ahead, on the right, between the Accademia Bridge and the church) is the **Peggy Guggenheim Collection.** The American heiress "retired" here, sprucing up a palace that had been abandoned in mid-construction. Peggy willed the city her fine collection of modern art (see page 983).

As you approach the next stop, notice on the right how the fine line of higgledy-piggledy palaces evokes old-time Venice. Two doors past the Guggenheim, Palazzo Dario has a great set of characteristic **funnel-shaped chimneys.** These forced embers through a loop-the-loop channel until they were dead—required in the days when stone palaces were surrounded by humble, wooden buildings, and a live spark could make a merchant's workforce homeless. Notice this early Renaissance building's flat-feeling facade with "pasted-on" Renaissance motifs. Three doors later is the **Salviati building,** which once served as a glassworks. Its fine mosaic, done by Art Nouveau in the early 20th century, features Venice as a queen being appreciated by the big shots of society.

Santa Maria del Giglio: Back on the left stands the fancy Gritti Palace hotel. Hemingway and Woody Allen both stayed here (but not together).

Take a deep whiff of Venice. What's all this nonsense about stinky canals? All I smell is my shirt. By the way, how's your captain? Smooth dockings? To get to know him, stand up in the bow and block his view.

Salute: The huge La Salute Church towers overhead as if squirted from a can of Catholic Reddi-wip. Like Venice itself, the church rests upon pilings. To build the foundation for the city, more than a million trees were piled together, reaching beneath the mud to the solid clay. Much of the surrounding countryside was deforested by Venice. Trees were imported and consumed locally—to fuel the furnaces of Venice's booming glass industry, to build Europe's biggest merchant marine, to form light and flexible beams for nearly all of the buildings in town, and to prop up this city in the mud.

As the Grand Canal opens up into the lagoon, the last building on the right with the golden ball is the 17th-century **Customs House,** which now houses the Punta della Dogana Museum of Contemporary Art (listed on page 984). Its two bronze Atlases hold a statue of Fortune riding the ball. Arriving ships stopped here to pay their tolls.

San Marco: Up ahead on the left, the green pointed tip of the Campanile marks **St. Mark's Square,** the political and religious center of Venice...and the final destination of this tour. You could get off at the San Marco stop and go straight to St. Mark's Square. But I'm staying on the boat for one more stop, just past St. Mark's Square (it's a quick walk back).

Survey the lagoon. Opposite St. Mark's Square, across the water, the ghostly white church with the pointy bell tower is **San Giorgio Maggiore,** with great views of Venice (see page 981). Next to it is the residential island Giudecca, stretching from close to San Giorgio Maggiore past the Venice youth hostel (with a nice view, directly across) to the Hilton Hotel (good nighttime view, far right end of island).

Still on board? If you are, as we leave the San Marco stop, prepare for a drive-by view of St. Mark's Square. First comes the bold white facade of the old mint (marked by a tiny cupola, where Venice's golden ducat, the "dollar" of the Venetian Republic, was made) and the library facade. Then come the twin columns, topped by St. Theodore and St. Mark, who've welcomed visitors since the 15th century. Between the columns, catch a glimpse of two giant figures atop the **Clock Tower**—they've been whacking their clappers every hour since 1499. The domes of **St. Mark's Basilica** are soon eclipsed by the lacy facade of the **Doge's Palace.** Next you'll see the **Bridge of Sighs** (leading from the palace to the prison—check out the maximum security bars), many gondolas with their green breakwater buoys, and then the grand harborside promenade—the **Riva.**

Follow the Riva with your eye, past elegant hotels to the green area in the distance. This is the largest of Venice's few **parks,** which hosts the annual Biennale festival (see page 989). Much farther in the distance is the **Lido,** the island with Venice's beach. Its sand and casinos are tempting, but its car traffic disrupts the medieval charm of Venice.

San Zaccaria: OK, you're at your last stop (likely San Zacca-

VENICE

ria-Danieli or San Zaccaria-M.V.E.). Quick—muscle your way off this boat! (If you don't, you'll eventually end up at the Lido.)

At San Zaccaria, you're right in the thick of the action. A number of other *vaporetti* depart from here (see page 956). Otherwise, it's a short walk back along the Riva to St. Mark's Square. Ahoy!

Sights in Venice

For information on sightseeing passes, see below. Venice's city museums offer youth and senior discounts to Americans and other non-EU citizens.

Sightseeing Passes for Venice

Venice offers a combo-ticket and an array of passes. For most people, the best choice is the Museum Pass, which covers entry into the Doge's Palace, Correr Museum, and more. Note that some major sights (Accademia, Peggy Guggenheim Collection, Scuola San Rocco, Campanile, and the three sights within St. Mark's Basilica that charge admission) are not covered on any pass.

Combo-Ticket: To visit either the Doge's Palace or the Correr Museum, you must buy a €16 combo-ticket that includes both. To bypass the long line at the Doge's Palace, buy your combo-ticket at the never-crowded Correr Museum.

Museum Pass: Busy sightseers may prefer this more expensive pass, which covers these museums: the Doge's Palace; Correr Museum; Ca' Rezzonico (Museum of 18th-Century Venice); Palazzo Mocenigo Costume Museum; Casa Goldoni (home of the Italian playwright); Ca' Pesaro (modern art); Museum of Natural History in the Santa Croce district; the Glass Museum on the island of Murano; and the Lace Museum on the island of Burano. At €20, this pass is the best value if you plan to see the Doge's Palace and even just one of the other covered museums. You can buy it at any of the participating museums.

Chorus Pass: This pass gives church lovers admission to 16 of Venice's churches and their art (generally €3 each)—including the Frari Church—for €10, although the typical tourist is unlikely to see more than two of them.

Venice Card: This pass combines the 11 city-run museums and the 16 churches covered by the Chorus Pass, plus a few minor discounts, for €40, but it's hard to make it pay off.

Rolling Venice: This youth pass offers discounts at dozens of sights and shops, but its best deal is for transit. If you're under 30 and want to buy a three-day transit pass, it'll cost you just €18—rather than €35—with the Rolling Venice pass (€4 for ages 14-29, sold at TIs and HelloVenezia shops).

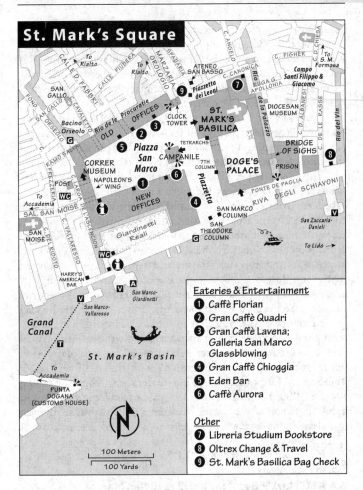

St. Mark's Square

Eateries & Entertainment
1. Caffè Florian
2. Gran Caffè Quadri
3. Gran Caffè Lavena; Galleria San Marco Glassblowing
4. Gran Caffè Chioggia
5. Eden Bar
6. Caffè Aurora

Other
7. Libreria Studium Bookstore
8. Oltrex Change & Travel
9. St. Mark's Basilica Bag Check

100 Meters
100 Yards

Transportation Passes: Venice sells transit-only passes that cover *vaporetti* and mainland buses. For a rundown on these, see "Getting Around Venice," earlier.

San Marco District

▲▲▲St. Mark's Square (Piazza San Marco)

This grand square is surrounded by splashy, historic buildings and sights: St. Mark's Basilica, the Doge's Palace, the Campanile bell tower, and the Correr Museum. The square is filled with music, lovers, pigeons, and tourists by day, and is your private rendezvous with the Venetian past late at night, when Europe's most magnificent dance floor is *the* romantic place to be.

With your back to the church, survey one of Europe's great urban spaces, and the only square in Venice to merit the title "Piazza." Nearly two football fields long, it's surrounded by the offices of the republic. On the right are the "old offices" (16th-century Renaissance). At left are the "new offices" (17th-century High Renaissance). Napoleon called the piazza "the most beautiful drawing room in Europe," and added to the intimacy by building the final wing, opposite the basilica, that encloses the square.

For a slow and pricey evening thrill, invest €12-20 (including the cover charge for the music) for a drink at one of the elegant cafés with the dueling orchestras. For an unmatched experience that offers the best people-watching, it's worth the small splurge.

The **Clock Tower** (Torre dell'Orologio), built during the Renaissance in 1496, marks the entry to the main shopping drag, called the Mercerie (or "Marzarie," in Venetian dialect), which connects St. Mark's Square with the Rialto Bridge. From the piazza, you can see the bronze men (Moors) swing their huge clappers at the top of each hour. In the 17th century, one of them knocked an unsuspecting worker off the top and to his death—probably the first-ever killing by a robot. Notice one of the world's first "digital" clocks on the tower facing the square (with dramatic flips every five minutes). You can go inside the Clock Tower with a pre-booked guided tour that takes you close to the clock's innards and out to a terrace with good views over the square and city rooftops (€12.50 combo-ticket includes Correr Museum—where tour starts—but not Doge's Palace; tours in English Mon-Wed at 10:00 and 11:00, Thu-Sun at 14:00 and 15:00; no kids under age 6; reserve by calling 848-082-000, booking online at http://torreorologio.visitmuve.it, going in person at the Correr Museum a day in advance, or even just showing up at the Correr prior to a scheduled tour to see if space is available).

You can download a free Rick Steves audio tour of St. Mark's Square (see page 7).

▲▲▲St. Mark's Basilica (Basilica di San Marco)

Built in the 11th century to replace an earlier church, this basilica's distinctly Eastern-style architecture underlines Venice's connection with Byzantium (which protected it from the ambition of Charlemagne and his Holy Roman Empire). It's decorated with booty from returning sea captains—a kind of architectural Venetian trophy chest. The interior glows mysteriously with gold mosaics and colored marble. Since about A.D. 830, the saint's bones have been housed on this site.

Cost and Hours: Basilica entry is free, three interior sights charge admission (see below), open Mon-Sat 9:45-17:00, Sun 14:00-17:00 (Sun until 16:00 Nov-March), interior brilliantly lit daily 11:30-12:30, St. Mark's Square, vaporetto: San Marco or San Zaccaria. No photos are allowed inside. Tel. 041-270-8311, www.basilicasanmarco.it.

Three separate exhibits within the church charge admission: the **Treasury** (€3, includes free audioguide), **Golden Altarpiece** (€2), and **San Marco Museum** (€5). The San Marco Museum has the original bronze horses (copies of these overlook the square), a balcony offering a remarkable view over St. Mark's Square, and various works related to the church.

Dress Code: Modest dress (no bare knees or bare shoulders) is strictly enforced, even for kids. Shorts are OK if they cover the knees.

Bag Check (and Skipping the Line): Small purses and shoulder-slung bags are allowed inside, but larger bags and backpacks are not. Check them for free for up to one hour at the nearby church called Ateneo San Basso, 30 yards to the left of the basilica, down narrow Calle San Basso (see map page 976; daily 9:30-17:00). Note that Ateneo San Basso will not let you check small bags that would be allowed inside.

Those with a bag to check actually get to skip the line, as do their companions (up to three or so). Leave your bag at Ateneo San Basso and pick up your claim tag. Take your tag to the basilica's tourist entrance. Keep to the left of the railing where the line forms and show your tag to the gatekeeper. He'll let you in, ahead of the line. After touring the church, come back and pick up your bag.

Theft Alert: St. Mark's Basilica is the most dangerous place in Venice for pickpocketing—inside, it's always a crowded jostle.

Tours: Free, hour-long English **tours** (heavy on the mosaics' religious symbolism) are offered many days at 11:00 (meet in atrium, schedule varies, see schedule board). You can download a free Rick Steves audio tour of St. Mark's Basilica (see page 7).

Visiting the Basilica: St. Mark's Basilica has 4,750 square yards of Byzantine mosaics, though many were designed by artists from the Italian Renaissance and later. Start outside in the square, far enough back to take in the whole facade. Then zero in on the details. The mosaic over the far left door shows the theft of ❶ **St. Mark's relics** that put Venice on the pilgrimage map.

The best and oldest mosaics are in the atrium (turn right as you enter and stop under the last dome). Facing the piazza, look domeward for the story of ❷ **Noah, the ark, and the flood** (two by two, the wicked being drowned, Noah sending out the dove, a happy rainbow, and a sacrifice of thanks).

Step inside the church and follow the one-way tourist route. Notice how the marble floor is richly decorated in mosaics. As in many Venetian buildings, because the best foundation pilings were made around the perimeter, the floor rolls. The church is laid out with four equal arms, topped with domes, radiating out from the center to form a ❸ **Greek cross** (+). Those familiar with Eastern Orthodox churches will find common elements in St. Mark's: a

VENICE

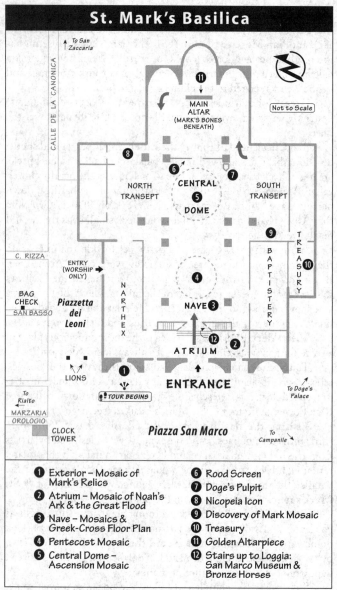

St. Mark's Basilica

Not to Scale

To San Zaccaria

CALLE DE LA CANONICA

MAIN ALTAR (MARK'S BONES BENEATH) — ⑪

NORTH TRANSEPT — ⑧

CENTRAL DOME — ⑤ ⑥ ⑦

SOUTH TRANSEPT

C. RIZZA

ENTRY (WORSHIP ONLY)

BAG CHECK
SAN BASSO

Piazzetta dei Leoni

NARTHEX

NAVE — ③ ④

BAPTISTERY — ⑨

TREASURY — ⑩

ATRIUM — ⑫ ②

LIONS

To Rialto
MARZARIA OROLOGIO

CLOCK TOWER

ENTRANCE — ①

✎ TOUR BEGINS

Piazza San Marco

To Doge's Palace

To Campanile

❶ Exterior – Mosaic of Mark's Relics
❷ Atrium – Mosaic of Noah's Ark & the Great Flood
❸ Nave – Mosaics & Greek-Cross Floor Plan
❹ Pentecost Mosaic
❺ Central Dome – Ascension Mosaic
❻ Rood Screen
❼ Doge's Pulpit
❽ Nicopeia Icon
❾ Discovery of Mark Mosaic
❿ Treasury
⓫ Golden Altarpiece
⓬ Stairs up to Loggia: San Marco Museum & Bronze Horses

VENICE

central floor plan, domes, mosaics, and iconic images of Mary and Christ as Pantocrator—ruler of all things.

Find the chandelier near the entrance doorway, and run your eyes up to the ❹ **Pentecost** mosaic in the dome above. In a golden heaven, the dove of the Holy Spirit shoots out a pinwheel of spiritual lasers, igniting tongues of fire on the heads of the 12 apostles below.

Shuffle under the central dome, and look up for the ❺ **Ascension** mosaic. Christ—having lived his miraculous life and having been crucified for man's sins—ascends into the starry sky on a rainbow.

Look around at the church's furniture: the ❻ **rood screen,** topped with 14 saints, separates the congregation from the high altar. The ❼ **pulpit** on the right was reserved for the doge, who led prayers and made important announcements.

In the north transept, today's Venetians pray to a painted wooden icon of Mary and baby Jesus known as ❽ **Nicopeia,** or "Our Lady of Victory." This Madonna has helped Venice persevere through plagues, wars, and crucial soccer games.

In the south transept (to right of main altar), find the dim ❾ **Discovery of Mark** mosaic high up on the west wall. This mosaic re-creates the happy scene in 1094 when Mark's misplaced relics were found within a hollow column.

Additional Sights: The ❿ **Treasury** (ask for the included and informative audioguide when you buy your ticket) and ⓫ **Golden Altarpiece** give you the easiest way outside of Istanbul or Ravenna to see the glories of the Byzantine Empire. Venetian crusaders looted the Christian city of Constantinople and brought home piles of lavish loot (perhaps the lowest point in Christian history until the advent of TV evangelism). Much of this plunder is stored in the Treasury (Tesoro) of San Marco. As you view these treasures, remember that most were made in about A.D. 500, while Western Europe was stuck in the Dark Ages. Beneath the high altar lies the body of St. Mark ("Marce") and the Golden Altarpiece (Pala d'Oro), made of 250 blue-backed enamels with religious scenes, all set in a gold frame and studded with 15 hefty rubies, 300 emeralds, 1,500 pearls, and assorted sapphires, amethysts, and topaz (c. 1100).

In the ⓬ **San Marco Museum** (Museo di San Marco) upstairs you can see an up-close mosaic exhibition, a fine view of the church interior, a view of the square from the balcony with bronze horses, and (inside, in their own room) the original horses. Art historians don't know how old the horses are—they could be from ancient Greece (fourth century B.C.) or from ancient Rome, during its Fall (fourth century A.D.). Legend says these well-traveled horses were taken to Rome by Nero. We know they were taken to Constanti-

VENICE

nople/Istanbul by Constantine, to Venice by crusaders, to Paris by Napoleon, back "home" to Venice when Napoleon fell, and finally indoors and out of the acidic air. The staircase up to the museum is in the atrium, near the basilica's main entrance, marked by a sign that says *Loggia dei Cavalli, Museo.*

▲▲▲Doge's Palace (Palazzo Ducale)

The seat of the Venetian government and home of its ruling duke, or doge, this was the most powerful half-acre in Europe for 400 years. The Doge's Palace was built to show off the power and wealth of the Republic. The doge lived with his family on the first floor, near the halls of power. From his once-lavish (now sparse) quarters, you'll follow the one-way tour through the public rooms of the top floor, finishing with the Bridge of Sighs and the prison. The place is wallpapered with masterpieces by Veronese and Tintoretto. Don't worry much about the great art. Enjoy the building.

Cost and Hours: €16 combo-ticket also includes Correr Museum, daily April-Oct 8:30-18:30, Nov-March 8:00-17:30, last entry one hour before closing, café, next to St. Mark's Basilica, just off St. Mark's Square, vaporetto stops: San Marco or San Zaccaria, tel. 041-271-5911, http://palazzoducale.visitmuve.it.

Avoiding Lines: If the line is long at the Doge's Palace, buy your combo-ticket at the Correr Museum across the square; then you can go straight to the Doge's Palace turnstile, skirting along to the right of the long ticket-buying line and entering at the "prepaid tickets" entrance. It's also possible to buy your ticket online—at least 48 hours in advance—on the museum website.

Tours: The audioguide tour is dry but informative (€5, 1.5 hours, need ID or credit card for deposit). For a 1.25-hour live guided tour, consider the Secret Itineraries Tour, which takes you into palace rooms otherwise not open to the public (€20, includes Doge's Palace admission but not Correr Museum admission; €14 with combo-ticket; three English-language tours each morning). Though the tour skips the palace's main hall, you're welcome to visit the hall afterward on your own. Reserve ahead for this tour in peak season—it can fill up as much as a month in advance. Book online at http://palazzoducale.visitmuve.it or reserve by phone (tel. 848-082-000, from the US dial 011-39-041-4273-0892), or you can try just showing up at the info desk.

Visiting the Doge's Palace: You'll see the restored facades from the **courtyard.** Notice a grand staircase (with nearly naked Moses and Paul Newman at the top). Even the most powerful visitors climbed this to meet the doge. This was the beginning of an architectural power trip.

In the **Senate Hall,** the 120 senators met, debated, and passed laws. Tintoretto's large *Triumph of Venice* on the ceiling (central painting, best viewed from the top) shows the city in all its glory.

Lady Venice is up in heaven with the Greek gods, while barbaric lesser nations swirl up to give her gifts and tribute.

The **Armory**—a dazzling display originally assembled to intimidate potential adversaries—shows remnants of the military might that the empire employed to keep the East-West trade lines open (and the local economy booming).

The giant **Hall of the Grand Council** (175 feet by 80 feet, capacity 2,600) is where the entire nobility met to elect the senate and doge. It took a room this size to contain the grandeur of the Most Serene Republic. Ringing the room are portraits of the first 76 doges (in chronological order). The one at the far end that's blacked out is the notorious Doge Marin Falier, who opposed the will of the Grand Council in 1355. He was tried for treason, beheaded, and airbrushed from history.

On the wall over the doge's throne is Tintoretto's monster-piece, *Paradise,* the largest oil painting in the world. Christ and Mary are surrounded by a heavenly host of 500 saints. The painting leaves you feeling that you get to heaven not by being a good Christian, but by being a good Venetian.

Cross the covered **Bridge of Sighs** over the canal to the **prisons.** Circle the cells. Notice the carvings made by prisoners—from olden days up until 1930—on some of the stone windowsills of the cells, especially in the far corner of the building.

Cross back over the Bridge of Sighs, pausing to look through the marble-trellised windows at all of the tourists.

▲▲Correr Museum (Museo Correr)

This uncrowded museum gives you a good, easy-to-manage overview of Venetian history and art. The doge memorabilia, armor, banners, statues (by Canova), and paintings (by the Bellini family and others) re-create the festive days of the Venetian Republic. There are English descriptions and breathtaking views of St. Mark's Square throughout the museum. But the Correr Museum has one more thing to offer, and that's a quiet refuge—a place to rise above St. Mark's Square when the piazza is too hot, too rainy, or too overrun with tourists.

Cost and Hours: €16 combo-ticket also includes the Doge's Palace and two lesser museums inside the Correr (National Archaeological Museum and the Monumental Rooms of the Marciana National Library); daily April-Oct 10:00-19:00, Nov-March 10:00-17:00, last entry one hour before closing; bag check free and mandatory for bags bigger than a large purse, no photos, elegant café, enter at far end of square directly opposite basilica, tel. 041-240-5211, http://correr.visitmuve.it.

Avoid long lines at the crowded Doge's Palace by buying your combo-ticket at the Correr Museum. For €12.50 you can see the Correr Museum and tour the Clock Tower on St. Mark's Square,

VENICE

but this ticket doesn't include the Doge's Palace (and the €16 combo-ticket mentioned above doesn't include the Clock Tower). For more on reserving a Clock Tower tour, see page 974.

▲Campanile (Campanile di San Marco)

This dramatic bell tower replaced a shorter tower, part of the original fortress that guarded the entry of the Grand Canal. That tower crumbled into a pile of bricks in 1902, a thousand years after it was built. Today you'll see construction work being done to strengthen the base of the rebuilt tower. Ride the elevator 325 feet to the top of the bell tower for the best view in Venice (especially at sunset). For an ear-shattering experience, be on top when the bells ring. The golden archangel Gabriel at the top always faces into the wind. Beat the crowds and enjoy the crisp morning air at 9:00 or the cool evening breeze at 18:00.

Cost and Hours: €8, daily Easter-June and Oct 9:00-19:00, July-Sept 9:00-21:00, Nov-Easter 9:30-16:45, tel. 041-522-4064, www.basilicasanmarco.it.

La Fenice Opera House (Gran Teatro alla Fenice)

During Venice's glorious decline in the 18th century, this was one of seven opera houses in the city, and one of the most famous in Europe. For 200 years, great operas and famous divas debuted here, applauded by ladies and gentlemen in their finery. Then in 1996, an arson fire completely gutted the theater. But La Fenice ("The Phoenix") has risen from the ashes, thanks to an eight-year effort to rebuild the historic landmark according to photographic archives of the interior. To see the results at their most glorious, attend an evening **performance** (theater box office open daily 9:30-18:00, tel. 041-2424, www.teatrolafenice.it).

You can also **tour the opera house** during the day. All you really see is the theater itself; there's no "backstage" tour of dressing rooms, or an opera museum. The auditorium, ringed with box seats, is impressive: pastel blue with sparkling gold filigree, muses depicted on the ceiling, and a starburst chandelier. It's also a bit saccharine and brings sadness to Venetians who remember the place before the fire. Other than a minor exhibit of opera scores and Maria Callas memorabilia, there's little to see from the world of opera. A dry 45-minute audioguide recounts two centuries of construction.

Cost and Hours: €8 tours, generally open daily 9:30-13:30, but can vary wildly, depending on the performance schedule—to confirm, call box office number (listed above) or check www.festfenice.com. La Fenice is on Campo San Fantin, between St. Mark's Square and the Accademia Bridge.

VENICE

Behind St. Mark's Basilica

▲Bridge of Sighs

This much-photographed bridge connects the Doge's Palace with the prison. Travelers popularized this bridge in the Romantic 19th century. Supposedly, a condemned man would be led over this bridge on his way to the prison, take one last look at the glory of Venice, and sigh. Though overhyped, the Bridge of Sighs is undeniably tingle-worthy—especially after dark, when the crowds have dispersed and it's just you and floodlit Venice.

Getting There: The Bridge of Sighs is around the corner from the Doge's Palace. Walk toward the waterfront, turn left along the water, and look up the first canal on your left. You can walk across the bridge (from the inside) by visiting the Doge's Palace.

Church of San Zaccaria

This historic church is home to a sometimes-waterlogged crypt, a Bellini altarpiece, a Tintoretto painting, and the final resting place of St. Zechariah, the father of John the Baptist.

Cost and Hours: Free, €1 to enter crypt, €0.50 coin to light up Bellini's altarpiece, Mon-Sat 10:00-12:00 & 16:00-18:00, Sun 16:00-18:00 only, 2 canals behind St. Mark's Basilica.

Across the Lagoon from St. Mark's Square

▲San Giorgio Maggiore

This is the dreamy church-topped island you can see from the waterfront by St. Mark's Square. The striking church, designed by Palladio, features art by Tintoretto, a bell tower, and good views of Venice.

Cost and Hours: Free entry to church; April-Oct Mon-Sat 9:00-19:00, Sun 9:00-11:00 & 12:00-19:00; Nov-March daily 9:00-17:30. The bell tower costs €3 and is accessible by elevator (runs from 30 minutes after the church opens until 30 minutes before the church closes).

Getting There: To reach the island from St. Mark's Square, take the five-minute ride on vaporetto #2 (€4, 6/hour, ticket valid for one hour; leaves from San Zaccaria-M.V.E. dock located east of Bridge of Sighs by equestrian statue, direction: Tronchetto).

Dorsoduro District

▲▲Accademia (Galleria dell'Accademia)

Venice's top art museum, packed with highlights of the Venetian Renaissance, features paintings by the Bellini family, Titian, Tintoretto, Veronese, Tiepolo, Giorgione, Canaletto, and Testosterone. It's just over the wooden Accademia Bridge from the San Marco action.

The Accademia is the greatest museum anywhere for Venetian Renaissance art and a good overview of painters whose works you'll

VENICE

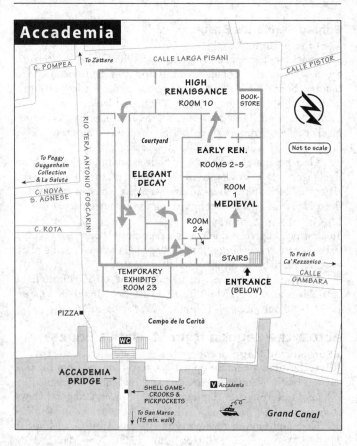

Accademia

see all over town. Venetian art is underrated and, I think, misunderstood. It's nowhere near as famous today as the work of the florescent Florentines, but—with historical slices of Venice, ravishing nudes, and very human Madonnas—it's livelier, more colorful, and simply more fun. The Venetian love of luxury shines through in this collection, which starts in the Middle Ages and runs to the 1700s. Look for grand canvases of colorful, spacious settings, peopled with happy locals in extravagant clothes having a great time.

Medieval highlights include elaborate altarpieces and golden-haloed Madonnas, all painted at a time when realism, depth of field, and emotion were considered beside the point. Medieval Venetians, with their close ties to the East, borrowed techniques such as gold-leafing, frontal poses, and "iconic" faces from the religious icons of Byzantium (modern-day Istanbul).

Among early masterpieces of the Renaissance are Mantegna's studly *St. George* and Giorgione's mysterious *The Tempest*. As the Renaissance reaches its heights, so do the paintings, such as Titian's magnificent *Presentation of the Virgin*. It's a religious scene, yes, but it's really just an excuse to display secular splendor (Titian was the most famous painter of his day—perhaps even more famous than Michelangelo). Veronese's sumptuous *Feast in the House of Levi* also has an ostensibly religious theme (in the middle, find Jesus eating his final meal)—but it's outdone by the luxury and optimism of Renaissance Venice. Life was a good thing and beauty was to be enjoyed. (Veronese was hauled before the Inquisition for painting such a bawdy Last Supper...so he fine-tuned the title). End your tour with Guardi's and Canaletto's painted "postcards" of the city—landscapes for visitors who lost their hearts to the romance of Venice.

Cost and Hours: €11, dull audioguide-€5, Mon 8:15-14:00, Tue-Sun 8:15-19:15, last entry 45 minutes before closing, no photos allowed. At Accademia Bridge, vaporetto: Accademia, tel. 041-522-2247, www.gallerieaccademia.org.

Avoiding Lines: In peak season, visit early or late to miss the crowds (300 people are allowed in at any one time).

Renovation: This museum seems to be in a constant state of disarray. A major expansion and renovation has been dragging on for years, and the halls feel like a gallery from the 1960s. Paintings come and go, but still, the museum contains sumptuous art—the best in Venice. Be flexible: You'll probably just end up wandering around and matching descriptions to blockbuster paintings when you find them.

▲▲Peggy Guggenheim Collection

The popular museum of far-out art, housed in the American heiress' former retirement palazzo, offers one of Europe's best reviews of the art of the first half of the 20th century. Stroll through styles represented by artists whom Peggy knew personally—Cubism (Picasso, Braque), Surrealism (Dalí, Ernst), Futurism (Boccioni), American Abstract Expressionism (Pollock), and a sprinkling of Klee, Calder, and Chagall.

Cost and Hours: €12, usually includes temporary exhibits, audioguide-€7, Wed-Mon 10:00-18:00, closed Tue, no photos inside, pricey café, 5-minute walk from the Accademia Bridge, vaporetto: Accademia or Salute, tel. 041-240-5411, www.guggenheim-venice.it.

▲La Salute Church (Santa Maria della Salute)

This impressive church with a crown-shaped dome was built and dedicated to the Virgin Mary by grateful survivors of the 1630 plague.

Cost and Hours: Free entry to church, €3 to enter the Sacristy; daily 9:00-12:00 & 15:00-17:30. It's a 10-minute walk from the Accademia Bridge; the Salute vaporetto stop is at its doorstep, tel. 041-241-1018, www.seminariovenezia.it.

VENICE

▲Ca' Rezzonico (Museum of 18th-Century Venice)

This grand Grand Canal palazzo offers the best look in town at the life of Venice's rich and famous in the 1700s. Wander under ceilings by Tiepolo, among furnishings from that most decadent century, enjoying views of the canal and paintings by Guardi, Canaletto, and Longhi.

Cost and Hours: €8, audioguide-€4; April-Oct Wed-Mon 10:00-18:00, Nov-March Wed-Mon 10:00-17:00, closed Tue year-round; ticket office closes one hour before museum does, café, at Ca' Rezzonico vaporetto stop, tel. 041-241-0100, http://carezzonico.visitmuve.it.

▲Punta della Dogana

This museum of contemporary art, opened in 2009, makes the Dorsoduro a major destination for art lovers. Housed in the former Customs House at the end of the Grand Canal, it features cutting-edge 21st-century art in spacious rooms. This isn't Picasso and Matisse, or even Pollock and Warhol—those guys are ancient history. But if you're into the likes of Jeff Koons, Cy Twombly, Rachel Whiteread, and a host of newer artists, the museum is world-class. The displays change completely about every year, drawn from the museum's large collection. In fact, the art spreads over two locations—the triangular Customs House and Palazzo Grassi.

Cost and Hours: €15 for one locale, €20 for both; Wed-Mon 10:00-19:00, closed Tue, last entry one hour before closing; audioguide-€5 or €8 for both museums, small café, tel. 199-139-139, www.palazzograssi.it.

Getting There: Punta della Dogana is near La Salute Church (Dogana *traghetto* or vaporetto: Salute). Palazzo Grassi is a bit upstream, on the east side of the Grand Canal (vaporetto: San Samuele).

Santa Croce District

▲Ca' Pesaro International Gallery of Modern Art

This museum features 19th- and early 20th-century art in a 17th-century canalside palazzo. The collection is strongest on Italian (especially Venetian) artists, but also presents a broad array of other well-known artists. The highlights are in one large room: Klimt's beautiful/creepy *Judith II,* with eagle-talon fingers; Kandinsky's *White Zig Zags* (plus other recognizable shapes); the colorful *Nude in the Mirror* by Bonnard that flattens the 3-D scene into a 2-D pattern of rectangles; and Chagall's surprisingly realistic portrait of his hometown rabbi, *The Rabbi of Vitebsk.* The adjoining room VII features small-scale works by Matisse, Max Ernst, Mark Tobey, and a Calder mobile.

Cost and Hours: €8, Tue-Sun 10:00-18:00, until 17:00 in winter, closed Mon, last entry one hour before closing, 2-minute walk from San Stae vaporetto stop, tel. 041-524-0662, http://cape-saro.visitmuve.it.

Palazzo Mocenigo Costume Museum

The Museo di Palazzo Mocenigo offers a walk through six rooms of a fine 17th-century mansion with period furnishings, family portraits, ceilings painted (c. 1790) with family triumphs (the Mocenigos produced seven doges), Murano glass chandeliers in situ, and a paltry collection of costumes with sparse descriptions.

Cost and Hours: €5, Tue-Sun 10:00-17:00, closed Mon, last entry one hour before closing, a block in from San Stae vaporetto stop, tel. 041-721-798, http://mocenigo.visitmuve.it.

San Polo District

▲▲▲Rialto Bridge

One of the world's most famous bridges, this distinctive and dramatic stone structure crosses the Grand Canal with a single confident span. The arcades along the top of the bridge help reinforce the structure...and offer some enjoyable shopping diversions, as does the **market** surrounding the bridge (produce market closed Sun, fish market closed Sun-Mon).

▲▲Frari Church
(Basilica di Santa Maria Gloriosa dei Frari)

My favorite art experience in Venice is seeing art in the setting for which it was designed—as it is at the Frari Church. The Franciscan "Church of the Brothers" and the art that decorates it are warmed by the spirit of St. Francis. It features the work of three great Renaissance masters: Donatello, Giovanni Bellini, and Titian—each showing worshippers the glory of God in human terms.

Cost and Hours: €3, Mon-Sat 9:00-18:00, Sun 13:00-18:00, last entry 30 minutes before closing, modest dress recommended, on Campo dei Frari, near San Tomà vaporetto and *traghetto* stops, tel. 041-272-8618, www.basilicadeifrari.it.

Audioguides: You can rent an audioguide for €2, or you can download a free Rick Steves audio tour of the Frari (see page 7).

Concerts: The church occasionally hosts evening concerts and small theatrical performances (€8-20, buy tickets at church, for details see the church website on previous page).

Visiting the Frari Church: In **Donatello's wood statue of St. John the Baptist** (just to the right of the high altar), the prophet of the desert—dressed in animal skins and nearly starving from his diet of bugs 'n' honey—announces the coming of the Messiah. Donatello was a Florentine working at the dawn of the Renaissance.

Bellini's *Madonna and Child with Saints and Angels* painting (in the sacristy farther to the right) came later, done by a Venetian in a more Venetian style—soft focus without Donatello's harsh realism. While Renaissance humanism demanded Madonnas and

VENICE

saints that were accessible and human, Bellini places them in a physical setting so beautiful that it creates its own mood of serene holiness. The genius of Bellini, perhaps the greatest Venetian painter, is obvious in the pristine clarity, rich colors (notice Mary's clothing), believable depth, and reassuring calm of this three-paneled altarpiece.

Finally, glowing red and gold like a stained-glass window over the high altar, **Titian's** *The Assumption of the Virgin* sets the tone of exuberant beauty found in the otherwise sparse church. Titian the Venetian—a student of Bellini—painted steadily for 60 years... you'll see a lot of his art. As stunned apostles look up past the swirl of arms and legs, the complex composition of this painting draws you right to the radiant face of the once-dying, now-triumphant Mary as she joins God in heaven.

Feel comfortable to discreetly freeload off passing tours. For many, these three pieces of art make a visit to the Accademia Gallery unnecessary (or they may whet your appetite for more). Before leaving, check out the Neoclassical pyramid-shaped Canova monument and (opposite that) the grandiose tomb of Titian. Compare the carved marble *Assumption* behind Titian's tombstone portrait with the painted original above the high altar.

▲▲Scuola San Rocco

Sometimes called "Tintoretto's Sistine Chapel," this lavish meeting hall (next to the Frari Church) has some 50 large, colorful Tintoretto paintings plastered to the walls and ceilings. The best paintings are upstairs, especially the *Crucifixion* in the smaller room. View the neck-breaking splendor with the mirrors available in the Grand Hall.

Cost and Hours: €8, audioguide-€1, daily 9:30-17:30, last entry 30 minutes before closing, tel. 041-523-4864, www.scuola-grandesanrocco.it.

Church of San Polo

This nearby church, which pales in comparison to the two sights just listed, is only worth a visit for art lovers. One of Venice's oldest churches (from the ninth century), San Polo features works by Tintoretto, Veronese, and Tiepolo and son.

Cost and Hours: €3, Mon-Sat 10:00-17:00, closed Sun.

Cannaregio District

Jewish Ghetto

Tucked away in the Cannaregio District is the ghetto where Venice's Jewish population once lived, segregated from their non-Jewish neighbors. While today's Jewish population is dwindling, the neighborhood still has centuries of history, not to mention Jewish-themed sights and eateries.

In medieval times, Jews were grudgingly allowed to do business in Venice, but they weren't permitted to live here until 1385 (subject to strict laws and special taxes). Anti-Semitic forces tried to oust them from the city, but in 1516, the doge compromised by restricting Jews to a special (undesirable) neighborhood. It was located on an easy-to-isolate island near the former foundry *(geto)*—in time the word "ghetto" caught on across Europe as a term for any segregated neighborhood.

The population swelled with immigrants from elsewhere in Europe, reaching 5,000 in the 1600s, the Golden Age of Venice's Jews. Restricted within their tiny neighborhood (the Gheto Novo, or "New Ghetto"), they expanded upward, building six-story "skyscrapers" that still stand today. The community's five synagogues were built atop the high-rise tenements. (As space was very tight and you couldn't live above a house of worship, this was the most practical use of precious land.) Only two synagogues are still active. You can spot them (with their five windows) from the square, but to visit them you have to book a tour through the Jewish Museum.

This original ghetto becomes most interesting after touring the **Jewish Museum** (Museo Ebraico) at #2902b, a worthwhile stop with just three rooms. Exhibits include silver menorahs, cloth covers for Torah scrolls, and a concise bilingual exhibit on the Venetian Jewish community up through 1797 (€3, June-Sept Sun-Fri 10:00-19:00, Oct-May Sun-Fri 10:00-17:30, closed Jewish holidays and Sat year-round, bookstore, small café, Campo de Gheto Novo, tel. 041-715-359, www.museoebraico.it). You can see three of the ghetto's five **synagogues** with the 45-minute English tour (€8.50, tours run hourly on the half-hour June-Sept Sun-Fri 10:30-17:30, Oct-May Sun-Fri 10:30-16:30, no tours Sat and Jewish holidays). Group sizes are limited (the 11:30 and 12:30 tours are the most popular), so show up 20 minutes early to be sure you get in.

Getting There: From either the San Marcuola vaporetto stop or the train station, walk five minutes to the Ponte de Guglie bridge that crosses the Cannaregio Canal. Cross the bridge and turn left. About 50 yards north of the bridge, a small covered alleyway (Calle del Gheto Vechio) leads between the *farmacia* and the Gam-Gam Kosher Restaurant, through a newer Jewish section, across a bridge, and into the historic core of the ghetto at Campo de Gheto Novo.

Calatrava Bridge (a.k.a. Ponte della Costituzione)

This controversial bridge, designed by Spanish architect Santiago Calatrava, is just upstream from the train station. Only the fourth bridge to cross the Grand Canal, it carries foot traffic between the train station and bus terminal at Piazzale Roma. After delays, cost overruns, and questions about its stability, the bridge finally opened in 2008.

The bridge draws snorts from Venetians. Its modern design is a sore point for a city with such rich medieval and Renaissance architecture. With an original price tag of €4 million, the cost rose to around €11 million. Then someone noticed that people in wheelchairs couldn't cross, so the bridge was retrofitted with a special carriage on a track. And, to add practical insult to aesthetic injury, critics say the heavy bridge is crushing the centuries-old foundations at either end, threatening nearby buildings.

Ca' d'Oro
This "House of Gold" palace, fronting the Grand Canal, is quintessential Venetian Gothic (Gothic seasoned with Byzantine and Islamic accents—see "Ca' d'Oro" on page 966). Inside, the permanent collection includes a few big names in Renaissance painting (Ghirlandaio, Signorelli, and Mantegna), a glimpse at a lush courtyard, and a grand view of the Grand Canal.

Cost and Hours: €6, dry audioguide-€4, Mon 8:15-14:00, Tue-Sun 8:15-19:15, free peek through hole in door of courtyard, at vaporetto: Ca' d'Oro, www.cadoro.org.

Castello District
▲Scuola Dalmata di San Giorgio
This little-visited "school" (which means "meeting place") features an exquisite wood-paneled chapel decorated with the world's best collection of paintings by Vittorio Carpaccio (1465-1526).

The Scuola, a reminder that cosmopolitan Venice was once Europe's trade hub, was one of a hundred such community centers for various ethnic, religious, and economic groups, supported by the government partly to keep an eye on foreigners. It was here that the Dalmatians (from present-day Croatia) worshipped in their own way, held neighborhood meetings, and preserved their culture.

Cost and Hours: €4, Mon 14:45-18:00, Tue-Sat 9:15-13:00 & 14:45-18:00, Sun 9:15-13:00, midway between St. Mark's Square and the Arsenale, on Calle dei Furlani at #3259a, tel. 041-522-8828.

Naval Museum and Arsenale
The mighty Republic of Venice was home to the first great military industrial complex: a state-of-the-art shipyard that could build a powerful warship of standardized parts in an assembly line (and did so to intimidate visiting heads of state). While the Arsenale is still a military base and is therefore closed to the public, its massive and evocative gate, the Porta Magna, is worth a look (to see the gate, turn left at the Naval Museum—described next—and follow the canal). At the waterfront end of the canal, in front of the Arsenale, stands the Naval Museum (Museo Storico Navale). It's very old-school and military-run, but anyone into maritime history or sailing will find its several floors of exhibits interesting. You'll

see the evolution of warships, displays on old fishing boats, and gondolas (all described in English).

Cost and Hours: Museum—€2, Mon-Sat 8:45-13:30, closed Sun, tel. 041-244-1399.

Santa Elena

For a pleasant peek into a completely non-touristy, residential side of Venice, walk or catch vaporetto #1 from St. Mark's Square to the neighborhood of Santa Elena (at the fish's tail). This 100-year-old suburb lives as if there were no tourism. You'll find a kid-friendly park, a few lazy restaurants, and beautiful sunsets over San Marco.

La Biennale

From roughly June through November, Venice hosts an annual world's fair—contemporary art in odd years, modern architecture in even years—in buildings and pavilions scattered throughout Giardini park and the Arsenale. The festival is an excuse for temporary art exhibitions, concerts, and other cultural events around the city (for more information, see www.labiennale.org).

Experiences in Venice

Gondola Rides

Riding a gondola is simple, expensive, and one of the great experiences in Europe. Gondoliers hanging out all over town are eager to have you hop in for a ride. A rip-off for some, this is a traditional must for romantics.

The price for a gondola starts at €80 for a 40-minute ride during the day. Prices jump about 30 percent after 19:00—when it's most romantic and relaxing. Prices are standard and listed on the gondoliers' association website (go to www.gondolavenezia.it, click on "Using the Gondola," and look under "*charterage*"). You can divide the cost—and the romance—among up to six people per boat, but only two get the love seat. Adding a singer and an accordionist will cost an additional €120.

Because you might get a narration plus conversation with your gondolier, talk with several and choose one you like. You're welcome to review the map and discuss the route. Doing so is also a good way to see if you enjoy the gondolier's personality and language skills. Establish the price, route, and duration of the trip before boarding, enjoy your ride, and pay only when you're finished. While prices are pretty firm, you might find them softer during the day. Most gondoliers honor the official prices, but a few might try to scam you out of some extra euros, particularly by insisting on a tip.

If you've hired musicians and want to hear a Venetian song *(un canto Veneziano)*, try requesting "*Venezia La Luna e Tu.*" Asking to

VENICE

hear *"O Sole Mio"* (which comes from Naples) is like asking a lounge singer in Cleveland to sing "The Eyes of Texas."

Glide through nighttime Venice with your head on someone's shoulder. Follow the moon as it sails past otherwise unseen buildings. Silhouettes gaze down from bridges while window glitter spills onto the black water. You're anonymous in the city of masks, as the rhythmic thrust of your striped-shirted gondolier turns old crows into songbirds. This is extremely relaxing (and, I think, worth the extra cost to experience at night). Suggestion: Put the camera down and make a point for you and your partner to enjoy a threesome with Venice. Warning: Women, beware...while gondoliers can be extremely charming, local women say that anyone who falls for one of these Venetian Romeos "has slices of ham over her eyes."

For cheap gondola thrills during the day, stick to the €2 one-minute ferry ride on a Grand Canal *traghetto*. At night, *vaporetti* are nearly empty, and it's a great time to cruise the Grand Canal on the slow boat #1. Or hang out on a bridge along the gondola route and wave at romantics.

Nightlife in Venice

You must experience Venice after dark. The city is quiet at night, as tour groups stay in the cheaper hotels of Mestre on the mainland, and the masses of day-trippers return to their beach resorts and cruise ships. Gondolas cost more, but are worth the extra expense (described earlier). At night, *vaporetti* are nearly empty, and it's a great time to cruise the Grand Canal on the slow boat #1.

Venice has a busy schedule of events, church concerts, festivals, and entertainment. Check at the TI or the TI's website (www.turismovenezia.it) for listings. The free monthly *Un Ospite di Venezia* lists all the latest happenings in English (free at fancy hotels, or check www.aguestinvenice.com).

Baroque Concerts

Venice is a city of the powdered-wig Baroque era. For about €25, you can take your pick of traditional Vivaldi concerts in churches throughout town. Homegrown Vivaldi is as ubiquitous here as Strauss is in Vienna and Mozart is in Salzburg. In fact, you'll find frilly young Vivaldis hawking concert tickets on many corners. Most shows start at 20:30 and generally last 1.5 hours. You'll see posters in hotels all over town (hotels sell tickets at face-value). A one-stop shop for concerts is the Vivaldi Store (east end of Rialto Bridge, at Fontego dei Tedeschi #5537, tel. 041-522-1343). Tickets for Baroque concerts in Venice can usually be bought the same day as the concert, so don't bother with websites that sell tickets with a surcharge. The general rule of thumb: Musicians in wigs and tights offer better spectacle; musicians in black-and-white suits are better performers.

The **Interpreti Veneziani orchestra**, considered the best group in town, generally performs 1.5-hour concerts nightly at 21:00 at the San Vidal Church (€25, church ticket booth open daily 9:30-21:00, north end of Accademia Bridge, tel. 041-277-0561, www.interpretiveneziani.com). If you're attending a concert at **Scuola San Rocco** (tickets €15-30), arrive 30 minutes early to enjoy the art (which you'd have to pay €8 to see during the day).

Other Performances

Venice's most famous theaters are **La Fenice** (grand old opera house, box office tel. 041-2424, see page 980), **Teatro Goldoni** (mostly Italian live theater), and **Teatro della Fondamenta Nuove** (theater, music, and dance).

Musica a Palazzo is a unique evening of opera at a Venetian palace on the Grand Canal. You'll spend about 45 delightful minutes in each of three sumptuous rooms as eight musicians (generally four instruments and four singers) perform. They generally present three different operas on successive nights—enthusiasts can experience more than one. With these kinds of surroundings, under Tiepolo frescoes, you'll be glad you dressed up. As there are only 70 seats, you must book by phone or online in advance (€60, nightly shows at 20:30, Palazzo Barbarigo-Minotto, Fondamenta Duodo o Barbarigo, vaporetto: Giglio, mobile 340-971-7272, www.musicapalazzo.com).

Venezia is advertised as "the show that tells the great story of Venice" and "simply the best show in town." I found the performance to be slow-moving and a bit cheesy, and the venue was disappointing (€39, nightly May-Oct at 20:00, Nov-April at 19:00; 80 minutes, just off St. Mark's Square on Campo San Gallo, tel. 041-241-2002, www.teatrosangallo.net).

St. Mark's Square

For tourists, St. Mark's Square is the highlight, with lantern light and live music echoing from the cafés. Just being here after dark is a thrill, as **dueling café orchestras** entertain. Every night, enthusiastic musicians play the same songs, creating the same irresistible magic. Hang out for free behind the tables (allowing you to move easily on to the next orchestra when the musicians take a break), or spring for a seat and enjoy a fun and gorgeously set concert. If you sit a while, it can be €12-20 well spent (for a drink and the cover charge for music). Dancing on the square is free—and encouraged.

Several venerable cafés and bars on the square serve expensive drinks outside but cheap drinks inside at the bar. The scene in a bar like **Gran Caffè Lavena** (in spite of its politically incorrect chandelier) can be great. The touristy **Bar Americano** is lively until late (under the Clock Tower). You'll hear people talking about the famous **Harry's American Bar,** which sells overpriced food and American cocktails to dressy tourists near the San Marco-Vallaresso vaporetto stop. But it's a rip-off...and the last place Hemingway would drink today. It's far cheaper to get a drink at any of the bars just off St. Mark's Square; you can even get prosecco to go in a plastic cup.

Wherever you end up, streetlamp halos, live music, floodlit history, and a ceiling of stars make St. Mark's magic at midnight. You're not a tourist, you're a living part of a soft Venetian night...an alley cat with money. In the misty light, the moon has a golden hue. Shine with the old lanterns on the gondola piers, where the sloppy lagoon splashes at the Doge's Palace...reminiscing.

Sleeping in Venice

For hassle-free efficiency and the sheer magic of being close to the action, I favor hotels that are handy to sightseeing activities. I've listed rooms in four neighborhoods: St. Mark's bustle, the Rialto action, the quiet Dorsoduro area behind the Accademia art museum, and near the train station (handy for train travelers, but far from the action). I also mention several apartment rentals, big fancy hotels, cheap dorms, and places on the mainland. For additional listings of B&Bs and apartments, try **Cross-Pollinate,** a reputable online booking agency (www.cross-pollinate.com).

Book your accommodations well in advance if you'll be traveling during busy times. Contact the hotel directly, not through any room-finding service (they can't give opinions on quality).

Note that hotel websites are particularly valuable for Venice, because they often include detailed directions that can help you get to your rooms with a minimum of wrong turns in this navigationally challenging city.

Over the past decade, Venice has seen the opening of several big new hotels, countless little boutique hotels, and the conversion of many private homes to short-term rental apartments, nearly doubling Venice's hotel capacity. Now the city is overbuilt for hotels. Demand is soft and, therefore, so are prices. Most hotels change prices from day to day, according to demand.

The prices I've listed are for one-night stays in peak season (April, May, June, Sept, and Oct) and assume you're booking directly (not through a TI or online hotel-booking engine). Prices can spike up during festivals. Almost all places drop prices from November through March (except during Carnevale— Feb 22-March 4 in 2014 —and Christmas) and in July and August. A €180 double can cost €80-90 in winter. Off-season, don't pay the rates I list.

To save money during a relatively slow time, consider arriv-

Sleep Code

(€1 = about $1.30, country code: 39)
S = Single, **D** = Double/Twin, **T** = Triple, **Q** = Quad, **b** = bathroom, **s** = shower only. Unless otherwise noted, credit cards are accepted, breakfast is included, and English is generally spoken. There's almost always Wi-Fi and/or Internet access available, either free or for a fee. Venice charges a hotel tax of €1-4 per person, per night. This tax is typically not included in the prices I've listed here.

To help you easily sort through these listings, I've divided the accommodations into three categories based on the price for a standard double room with bath:

$$$ Higher Priced—Most rooms €180 or more.
  $$ Moderately Priced—Most rooms between €130-180.
    $ Lower Priced—Most rooms €130 or less.

Prices can change without notice; verify the hotel's current rates online or by email.

---

ing without a reservation and dropping in at the last minute. Big, fancy hotels put empty rooms on an aggressive push list, offering great prices. Many hotels in Venice list rooms on www.venere.com, especially for last-minute vacancies (two to three weeks before the date).

Near St. Mark's Square

To get here from the train station or Piazzale Roma bus station, ride the vaporetto to San Zaccaria—either the slow #1 or the fast #2 (from the Tronchetto parking lot, it's #2 only). Consider using your ride to follow my tour of the Grand Canal (see page 961); to make sure you arrive via the Grand Canal, confirm that your boat goes "*via Rialto.*"

To locate the following hotels, see the map on page 996.

Nearby Laundries: Lavanderia Gabriella offers full service a few streets north of St. Mark's Square (€15/load includes wash, dry, and fold; drop off Mon-Fri 8:00-12:30, closed Sat-Sun; pick up 2 hours later or next working day; with your back to the door of San Zulian Church, go over Ponte dei Ferali, take first right down Calle dei Armeni, then first left on Rio Terà de le Colonne to #985; tel. 041-522-1758, Elisabetta).

Effe Erre, a modern self-service *lavanderia,* is near the recommended Hotel al Piave on Ruga Giuffa at #4826 (€12/load, daily 6:30-24:00, mobile 349-058-3881, Massimo).

East of St. Mark's Square

Located near the Bridge of Sighs, just off the Riva degli Schiavoni waterfront promenade, these places rub drainpipes with Venice's most palatial five-star hotels.

$$$ Hotel Campiello, lacy and bright, was once part of a 19th-century convent. Ideally located 50 yards off the waterfront, on a tiny square, its 16 rooms offer a tranquil, friendly refuge for travelers who appreciate comfort and professional service (Sb-€130, Db-€180, cash discount with this book if you reserve direct, air-con, elevator; just steps from the San Zaccaria vaporetto stop, Castello 4647; tel. 041-520-5764, fax 041-520-5798, www.hcampiello.it, campiello@hcampiello.it; family-run for four generations, currently by Thomas, Nicoletta, and Marco). They also rent three modern family apartments, under rustic timbers just steps away (up to €380/night).

$$$ Hotel Fontana is a nice, old-time, family-run place with 15 rooms near a school, two bridges behind St. Mark's Square (Sb-€120, Db-€180, family rooms, cash discount, quieter rooms on garden side, 2 rooms have terraces for €20 extra, air-con, elevator, free Internet access, on Campo San Provolo at Castello 4701, tel. 041-522-0579, fax 041-523-1040, www.hotelfontana.it, info@hotelfontana.it, cousins Diego and Gabriele).

$$$ Hotel la Residenza is a grand old palace facing a peaceful square. It has 15 small rooms on three levels and a huge, luxurious lounge that comes with a piano and a stingy breakfast. This is a good value for romantics—you'll feel like you're in the Doge's Palace after hours (Sb-€105, Db-€175-220, air-con, on Campo Bandiera e Moro at Castello 3608, tel. 041-528-5315, fax 041-523-8859, www.venicelaresidenza.com, info@venicelaresidenza.com, Giovanni).

$$ Locanda al Leon, which feels a little like a medieval tower house, rents 13 reasonably priced rooms just off Campo Santi Filippo e Giacomo (Db-€150-160, Tb-€190, Qb-€230, ask for Rick Steves price and show this book if paying cash, air-con, Campo Santi Filippo e Giacomo, Castello 4270, tel. 041-277-0393, fax 041-521-0348, www.hotelalleon.com, leon@hotelalleon.com, Giuliano and Marcella).

$ Albergo Doni is dark and quiet—a bit of a time-warp—with 13 well-worn, once-classy rooms up a creaky stairway. It's run by friendly Tessa and her brother, an Italian stallion named Nikos (S-€75, D-€105, Db-€130, T-€135, Tb-€170, ask about discount with this book, ceiling fans, 3 Db rooms have air-con, 3 nice overflow apartments are same price but no breakfast, on Fondamenta del Vin at Castello 4656, tel. & fax 041-522-4267, www.albergodoni.it, albergodoni@hotmail.it).

$ Casa per Ferie Santa Maria della Pietà is a wonderful

church-run facility renting 55 beds in 16 rooms just a block off the Riva, with a fabulous lagoon-view roof terrace that could rival the most luxurious hotels in town. Institutional with generous public spaces and dorm-style comfort, there are no sinks, toilets, or showers in any of its rooms, but there's plenty of plumbing down the hall (€40 beds in 4-8-bed dorms, S-€55, D-€100, straight price all year, only twin beds, reserve with credit card but pay cash, partial air-con, profits go to church care for poor, 100 yards from San Zaccaria-Pietà vaporetto dock, down Calle de la Pietà from La Pietà Church, tel. 041-522-2171, www.pietavenezia.org, info.admin@pietavenezia.org).

North of St. Mark's Square

$$ Hotel al Piave, with 28 fine, air-con rooms above a bright and classy lobby, is fresh, modern, and comfortable. You'll enjoy the neighborhood and always get a cheery welcome (Db-€150, Tb-€200; family suites-€280 for 4, €300 for 5, or €310 for 6; Rick Steves discount when booked directly and paid in cash, on Ruga Giuffa at Castello 4838, tel. 041-528-5174, fax 041-523-8512, www.hotelalpiave.com, info@hotelalpiave.com, Mirella, Paolo, Ilaria, and Federico speak English).

$$ Locanda Silva is a big, basic, beautifully located hotel with a functional 1960s feel, renting 23 decent old-school rooms (S-€70, Sb-€85, D-€90, Db-€140, Tb-€160, Qb-€180, book direct and ask about Rick Steves discount, additional discount if you stay at least 2 nights, discounts valid only with cash, closed Dec-Jan, air-con, on Fondamenta del Remedio at Castello 4423, tel. 041-522-7643, fax 041-528-6817, www.locandasilva.it, info@locandasilva.it, Sandra, Katia and Massimo).

$$ Locanda Casa Querini rents six bright, high-ceilinged rooms on a quiet square tucked away behind St. Mark's. You can enjoy your breakfast or a sunny happy-hour picnic sitting at their tables right on the sleepy little square (Db-€150, third person-€20-25, one cheaper small double, ask for Rick Steves rate with this book and cash, air-con, halfway between San Zaccaria vaporetto stop and Campo Santa Maria Formosa at Castello 4388 on Campo San Zaninovo/Giovanni Novo, tel. 041-241-1294, fax 041-523-6188, www.locandaquerini.com, info@locandaquerini.com; Silvia, Patrizia, and Caterina).

$ Hotel Riva, with gleaming marble hallways, big exposed beams, fine antique furnishings, and lots of stairs, is romantically situated on a canal along the gondola serenade route. This has long been a standby in this book, but how it'll stack up when it reopens after a major renovation remains to be seen (see website for latest prices, on Ponte de l'Anzolo at Castello 5310, tel. 041-522-7034, www.hotelriva.it, info@hotelriva.it, Daniella).

VENICE

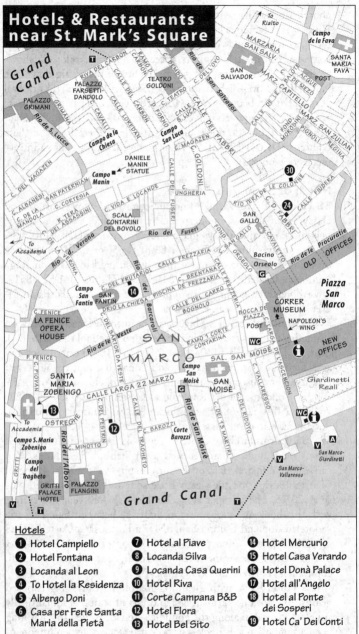

Hotels & Restaurants near St. Mark's Square

VENICE

Hotels

1. Hotel Campiello
2. Hotel Fontana
3. Locanda al Leon
4. To Hotel la Residenza
5. Albergo Doni
6. Casa per Ferie Santa Maria della Pietà
7. Hotel al Piave
8. Locanda Silva
9. Locanda Casa Querini
10. Hotel Riva
11. Corte Campana B&B
12. Hotel Flora
13. Hotel Bel Sito
14. Hotel Mercurio
15. Hotel Casa Verardo
16. Hotel Donà Palace
17. Hotel all'Angelo
18. Hotel al Ponte dei Sosperi
19. Hotel Ca' Dei Conti

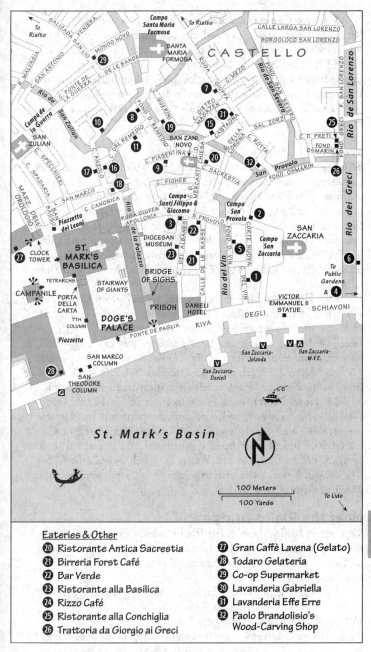

Eateries & Other

20 Ristorante Antica Sacrestia
21 Birreria Forst Café
22 Bar Verde
23 Ristorante alla Basilica
24 Rizzo Café
25 Ristorante alla Conchiglia
26 Trattoria da Giorgio ai Greci

27 Gran Caffè Lavena (Gelato)
28 Todaro Gelateria
29 Co-op Supermarket
30 Lavanderia Gabriella
31 Lavanderia Effe Erre
32 Paolo Brandolisio's
   Wood-Carving Shop

$ Corte Campana B&B, run by enthusiastic and helpful Riccardo, rents three quiet and characteristic rooms just behind St. Mark's Square. One room has a private bath down the hall (Db-€125, Tb-€165, Qb-€190, prices are soft, cash only, 2-night minimum, at least €10/night less for stays of 4 nights, air-con, free Internet access, on Calle del Remedio at Castello 4410, tel. & fax 041-523-3603, mobile 389-272-6500, www.cortecampana.com, info@cortecampana.com).

West of St. Mark's Square

$$$ Hotel Flora sits buried in a sea of fancy designer boutiques and elegant hotels almost on the Grand Canal. It's formal, with uniformed staff and grand public spaces, yet the 40 rooms have a homey warmth and the garden oasis is a sanctuary for well-heeled, foot-weary guests (generally Db-€260, check website for special discounts or email Sr. Romanelli for Rick Steves discount off standard prices, air-con, elevator, family apartment, San Marco 2283a, tel. 041-520-5844, fax 041-522-8217, www.hotelflora.it, info@hotelflora.it).

$$$ Hotel Bel Sito offers pleasing yet well-worn Old World character, 34 rooms, generous public spaces, a peaceful courtyard, and a picturesque location—facing a church on a small square between St. Mark's Square and the Accademia (Sb-€110, Db-€185, air-con, elevator; near Santa Maria del Giglio vaporetto stop—line #1, San Marco 2517; tel. 041-522-3365, fax 041-520-4083, www.hotelbelsitovenezia.it, info@hotelbelsito.info, manager Rossella).

$$ Hotel Mercurio, a block in front of La Fenice Opera House, offers a warm welcome and 29 peaceful, comfortable rooms, some with canal views (Sb-€130, Db-€170, Tb-€200, Qb-€230-250, €10 less when booked direct and paid in cash, air-con, on Calle del Fruttariol at San Marco 1848, tel. 041-522-0947, fax 041-241-1079, www.hotelmercurio.com, info@hotelmercurio.com, Monica, Vittorio, and Natale).

Near the Rialto Bridge

Vaporetto #2 brings you to the Rialto quickly from the train station, the Piazzale Roma bus station, and the parking-lot island of Tronchetto. You can also take the slower vaporetto #1 (but not from Tronchetto).

To locate the following hotels, see the map on page 1001.

West of the Rialto Bridge

$$ Pensione Guerrato, above the colorful Rialto produce market and just two minutes from the Rialto Bridge, is run by friendly, creative, and hardworking Roberto and Piero. Their 800-year-old building—with 24 spacious, air-conditioned, and charming rooms—is simple, airy, and wonderfully characteristic (D-€90, Db-€140, Tb-€160, Qb-€175, Quint/b-€185, check website for special discounts, ask about Rick Steves discount with this book and cash, on Calle drio la Scimia at San Polo 240a, tel. & fax 041-528-5927, www.pensioneguerrato.it, info@pensioneguerrato. it, Monica and Rosanna). My tour groups book this place for 60 nights each year. Sorry. The Guerrato also rents family apartments in the old center (great for groups of 4-8) for around €55 per person.

East of the Rialto Bridge

$$$ Hotel al Ponte Antico is exquisite, professional, and small. With nine plush rooms, a velvety royal living/breakfast room, and its own dock for water taxi arrivals, it's perfect for a romantic anniversary. Because its wonderful terrace overlooks the Grand Canal, Rialto Bridge, and market action, its non-canal-view rooms may be a better value (Db-€320, superior Db-€400, deluxe canal-front Db-€490, air-con, 100 yards from Rialto Bridge at Cannaregio 5768, tel. 041-241-1944, fax 041-241-1828, www.alponteantico. com, info@alponteantico.com, Matteo makes you feel like royalty).

$$ Locanda la Corte is perfumed with elegance without being snooty. Its 17 attractive, high-ceilinged, wood-beamed rooms—Venetian-style, done in earthy pastels—circle a small, quiet courtyard (standard Db-€150, deluxe Db-€170, cash discount, ask about discount with this book, suites and family rooms available, air-con, on Calle Bressana at Castello 6317, tel. 041-241-1300, fax 041-241-5982, www.locandalacorte.it, info@locandalacorte.it, Marco, Abel, and Tommy the cat).

$ Alloggi Barbaria rents eight backpacker-type rooms on one floor around a bright but institutional-feeling common area. Beyond Campo Santi Giovanni e Paolo, it's a long walk from the action, in a residential neighborhood, and only a step above a youth hostel (Db-€90-100, third or fourth person-€25 each, pay cash for best price, family deals, limited breakfast, air-con, on Calle de le Capucine at Castello 6573, tel. 041-522-2750, fax 041-277-5540, www.alloggibarbaria.it, info@alloggibarbaria.it, Giorgio and Fausto).

Near the Accademia Bridge

As you step over the Accademia Bridge, the commotion of touristy Venice is replaced by a sleepy village laced with canals. This quiet area, next to the best painting gallery in town, is a 15-minute walk from the Rialto or St. Mark's Square.

The fast vaporetto #2 connects the Accademia Bridge with the train station (15 minutes), Piazzale Roma bus station (20 minutes), Tronchetto parking lot (25 minutes), and St. Mark's Square (5 minutes). For hotels south of the Accademia Bridge, vaporetto #5.1

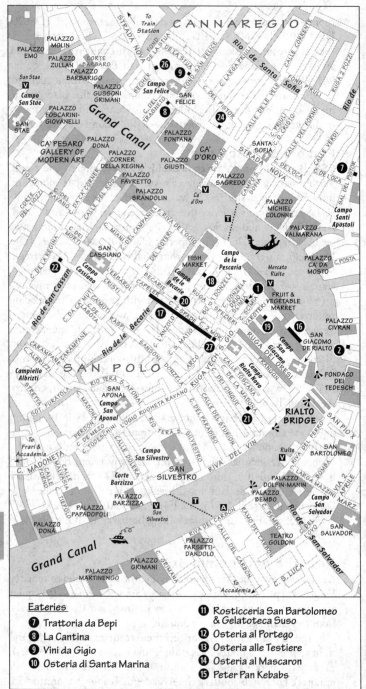

Eateries

7 Trattoria da Bepi

8 La Cantina

9 Vini da Gigio

10 Osteria di Santa Marina

11 Rosticceria San Bartolomeo & Gelatoteca Suso

12 Osteria al Portego

13 Osteria alle Testiere

14 Osteria al Mascaron

15 Peter Pan Kebabs

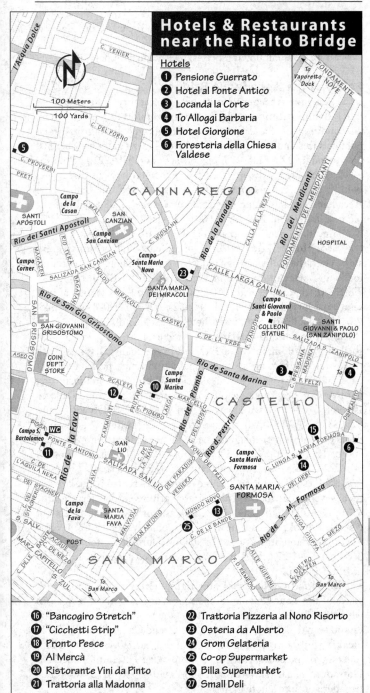

Hotels & Restaurants near the Rialto Bridge

Hotels

1. Pensione Guerrato
2. Hotel al Ponte Antico
3. Locanda la Corte
4. To Alloggi Barbaria
5. Hotel Giorgione
6. Foresteria della Chiesa Valdese

16. "Bancogiro Stretch"
17. "Cicchetti Strip"
18. Pronto Pesce
19. Al Mercà
20. Ristorante Vini da Pinto
21. Trattoria alla Madonna

22. Trattoria Pizzeria al Nono Risorto
23. Osteria da Alberto
24. Grom Gelateria
25. Co-op Supermarket
26. Billa Supermarket
27. Small Deli

VENICE

to Zattere (or the Alilaguna speedboat from the airport to Zattere) is a good option.

To locate the following hotels, see the map on page 1005.

South of the Accademia Bridge

$$$ **Pensione Accademia** fills the 17th-century Villa Maravege like a Bellini painting. Its 27 rooms are comfortable, elegant, and air-conditioned. You'll feel aristocratic gliding through its grand public spaces and lounging in its wistful, breezy gardens (Sb-€80-160, standard Db-€145-295, bigger "superior" Db-€210-390, Qb-€360, Rick Steves discount on balance when booked direct and paid in cash; on Fondamenta Bollani at Dorsoduro 1058; facing Accademia art museum, go right to where the small canal hits the big one; tel. 041-521-0188, fax 041-523-9152, www.pensioneaccademia.it, info@pensioneaccademia.it).

$$$ **Hotel Belle Arti** has a grand entry and a formal, stern staff. With the ambience of a modern American hotel, its 64 rooms feel out of place in musty Old World Venice (Sb-€150, Db-€240, Tb-€270, air-con, elevator; 100 yards behind Accademia art museum at Dorsoduro 912a; tel. 041-522-6230, fax 041-528-0043, www.hotelbellearti.com, info@hotelbellearti.com).

$$ **Pensione la Calcina,** the home of English writer John Ruskin in 1876, maintains a 19th-century formality. It comes with three-star comforts in a professional yet intimate package. Its 27 nautical-feeling rooms are squeaky clean, with nice wood furniture, hardwood floors, and a peaceful canalside setting facing Giudecca Island (Sb-€140, Sb with view-€170, Db-€150-250, Db with view-€290-350, Qb-€320, air-con, rooftop terrace, buffet breakfast outdoors on platform over lagoon, near Zattere vaporetto stop at south end of Rio de San Vio at Dorsoduro 780, tel. 041-520-6466, fax 041-522-7045, www.lacalcina.com, info@lacalcina.com).

$$ **Casa Rezzonico,** a tranquil getaway far from the crowds, rents seven quiet rooms with a grassy private garden terrace (Sb-€130, Db-€170, Tb-€200, Qb-€230, ask for Rick Steves discount when you book, air-con, near Ca' Rezzonico vaporetto stop—line #1, on Fondamenta Gherardini at Dorsoduro 2813, tel. 041-277-0653, fax 041-277-5435, www.casarezzonico.it, info@casarezzonico.it, Matteo).

$$ **Hotel Galleria** has nine tight, velvety rooms, most with views of the Grand Canal. Some rooms are quite narrow. It's run with a family feel by Luciano and Stefano (S-€85, D-€130, skinny Grand Canal view Db-€160, palatial Grand Canal view Db-€185, breakfast in room, ceiling fans, free mini-bar, 30 yards from Accademia art museum, next to recommended Foscarini pizzeria at Dorsoduro 878a, tel. 041-523-2489, fax 041-520-4172, www.hotelgalleria.it, info@hotelgalleria.it).

$$ Don Orione Religious Guest House is a big cultural center dedicated to the work of a local man who became a saint in modern times. Filling an old monastery, it feels institutional, like a modern retreat center—clean, peaceful, and strictly run, with 74 rooms. It's beautifully located, comfortable, and a fine value (Sb-€88, Db-€146, Tb-€188, Qb-€226, profits go to mission work in the developing world, groups welcome, air-con, elevator, on Rio Terà A. Foscarini, Dorsoduro 909a, tel. 041-522-4077, fax 041-528-6214, www.donorione-venezia.it, info@donorione-venezia.it). From the Zattere vaporetto stop, turn right, then turn left. It's just after the church at #909a.

$ Ca' San Trovaso rents seven simple rooms split between the main building and a nearby annex. The location is peaceful, on a small desolate-feeling canal (Sb-€90, Db-€115, Db with bigger canal view and air-con-€130, Tb-€145, pay cash for best prices, breakfast in your room, air-con in most rooms, no common space except small roof terrace, near Zattere vaporetto stop, off Fondamenta de le Romite at Dorsoduro 1350/51, tel. 041-277-1146, mobile 339-445-8821, fax 041-277-7190, www.casantrovaso.com, info@casantrovaso.com, Mark and his son Alessandro).

$ Casa di Sara, a colorfully decorated B&B, is hidden in a leafy courtyard in a humble back-street area. Their four quiet rooms and tiny roof terrace offer the maximum in privacy (Sb-€85, Db-€110, Tb-€130, mobile 342-596-3563, fax 041-241-2296, www.casadisara.com, info@casadisara.com, Aniello).

North of the Accademia Bridge

$$$ Novecento Hotel rents nine plush rooms on three floors. This boutique hotel is decorated circa-1920s throughout, with a big, welcoming lounge and an elegant living room (Db-€240-260, air-con, lots of stairs; on Calle del Dose, off Campo San Maurizio at San Marco 2683; tel. 041-241-3765, fax 041-521-2145, www.novecento.biz, info@novecento.biz).

$$ Istituto Ciliota is a big, efficient, and sparkling-clean place—well-run, well-located, and church-owned—with an Ikea-style charm, 30 dorm-like rooms, and a peaceful garden. If you want industrial-strength comfort at a good price with no stress and little character, this is a fine value. Rooms come with twin beds and a fridge. During the school year, half the rooms are used by students (Sb-€80, twin Db-€80-160 but generally €140, air-con, cheaper with longer stays, on Calle delle Muneghe just off Campo San Stefano near the Accademia Bridge and vaporetto stop, tel. 041-520-4888, www.ciliota.it, info@ciliota.it).

$$ Foresteria Levi, run by a foundation that promotes research on Venetian music, offers 20 quiet, institutional yet comfortable and spacious rooms (some are lofts). Prices vary wildly—

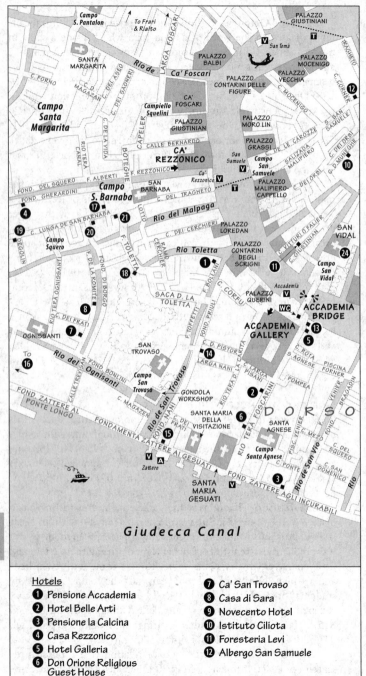

Hotels

1. Pensione Accademia
2. Hotel Belle Arti
3. Pensione la Calcina
4. Casa Rezzonico
5. Hotel Galleria
6. Don Orione Religious Guest House
7. Ca' San Trovaso
8. Casa di Sara
9. Novecento Hotel
10. Istituto Ciliota
11. Foresteria Levi
12. Albergo San Samuele

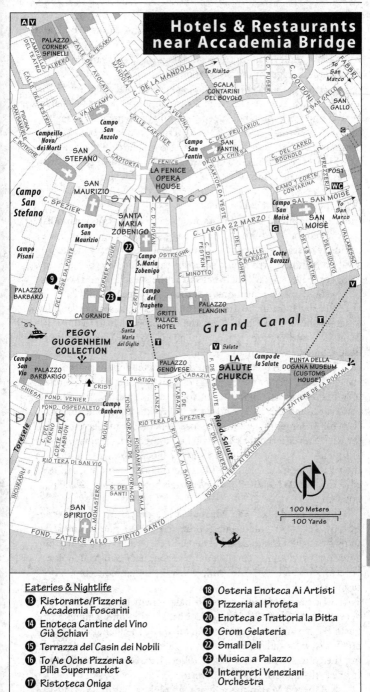

Hotels & Restaurants near Accademia Bridge

A **V**

PALAZZO CORNER-SPINELLI

PALAZZO DEL TEATRO

CALLE DEL PESTRIN

PISCINA SAN SAMUELE

C. BOTEGHE

Campeillo Novo/ dei Morti

RIO TERA DE LA MANDOLA

C. DE LA MANDOLA

C. DE LA VERONA

CALLE DEL AVOCATI

VA IN CAMPO

CALLE CAFETIER

Campo San Anzolo

SAN STEFANO

C. CAOTORTA

C. FENICE

Campo San Fantin

SAN FANTIN

C. DEL FRUTARIOL

RIO SAN FANTIN

D.O SAOR DA VESTE

LA FENICE OPERA HOUSE

To Rialto

SCALA CONTARINI DEL BOVOLO

C. D. FUSERI

C. GOLDONI

To San Marco

C. SAN GALLO

SAN GALLO

G

FREZZERIA

POST

WC

CAMO 1 CORTE CONTARINA

SAL SAN MOISÈ

To San Marco

SAN MOISÈ

G

Campo San Moisè

C. DEL CARRO BOGNOLO

C. DEL RIDOTTO

DEI 13 MARTIRI

C. VALLARESSO

SAN MAURIZIO

Campo San Stefano

C. SPEZIER

SAN MAURIZIO

Campo San Maurizio

Campo Pisani

C. D. PIOVAN

SANTA MARIA ZOBENIGO

SAN MARCO

C. DEL PIOVAN

C. LARGA 22 MARZO

C. DEL PESTRIN

CALLE BAROZZI

Corte Barozzi

OSTREGHE

Campo S. Maria Zobenigo

C. MINOTTO

C. DEL TRAGHETO

22

CORNER ZAGUR

C. DELLE DOSE DA PONTE

9

PALAZZO BARBARO

CA' GRANDE

23

C. GRITTI

Campo del Tragheto

GRITTI PALACE HOTEL

PALAZZO FLANGINI

V

Santa Maria del Giglio

T

T

Grand Canal

V Salute

Campo de la Salute

T

PUNTA DELLA DOGANA MUSEUM (CUSTOMS HOUSE)

PEGGY GUGGENHEIM COLLECTION

Campo San Vio

PALAZZO BARBARIGO

CRIST.

PALAZZO GENOVESE

C. BASTION

C. DE L'ABAZIA

LA SALUTE CHURCH

F. DE LA SALUTE

F. ZATTERE DE LA DOGANA

C. CHIESA

FOND. VENIER

FOND. OSPEDALETO

Campo Barbaro

C. LANZA

C. DE L'ABAZIA

RIO TERA DEL SPEZIER

RIO TERA AI SALONI

C. DEL SQUERO

FOND. ZATTERE AI SALONI

DURO

Torèsete

C. DEL FORNO

CORTE DEL SABBION

C. MOLIN

FONDAMENTA CA' BALA

FONDAMENTA SORANZO DE LA FORNACE

Rio d Salute

INCURABILI

RIO TERA DI SAN VIO

S. DEI SANTI

SAN SPIRITO

FOND. ZATTERE ALLO SPIRITO SANTO

100 Meters
100 Yards

N

VENICE

Eateries & Nightlife

13 Ristorante/Pizzeria Accademia Foscarini

14 Enoteca Cantine del Vino Già Schiavi

15 Terrazza del Casin dei Nobili

16 To Ae Oche Pizzeria & Billa Supermarket

17 Ristoteca Oniga

18 Osteria Enoteca Ai Artisti

19 Pizzeria al Profeta

20 Enoteca e Trattoria la Bitta

21 Grom Gelateria

22 Small Deli

23 Musica a Palazzo

24 Interpreti Veneziani Orchestra

ask for the Rick Steves deal (Db-€100-190, fans, elevator, on Calle Giustinian at San Marco 2893, tel. 041-786-711, fax 041-786-766, www.foresterialevi.it, info@foresterialevi.it). It's 80 yards from the Accademia Bridge on the St. Mark's side.

$ Albergo San Samuele is a backpacker place: dumpy but in a great locale. It rents 12 basic rooms in a crumbling old palace near Campo San Stefano. Sleep here only if their price is far less than other listings (S-€70, D-€90, Db-€110, extra bed-€15, no breakfast, on Salizada San Samuele at San Marco 3358, tel. 041-520-5165, fax 041-522-8045, www.hotelsansamuele.com, info@hotelsansamuele.com).

Near the Train Station

I don't recommend the train station area. It's crawling with noisy, disoriented tourists with too much baggage and people whose life's calling is to scam visitors out of their money. It's so easy just to hop a vaporetto upon arrival and sleep in the Venice of your dreams. Still, some like to park their bags near the station, and if so, these places stand out (for locations, see the map on page 1008).

Nearby Laundry: Orange, the nearest self-service laundry, is across the Grand Canal from the station (€14/load, daily 7:30-22:30, follow directions to recommended Albergo Marin, on Ramo de le Chioverete at Santa Croce 665b).

$$$ Hotel Abbazia, in the dreary hotel zone near the train station, fills a former abbey with both history and class. The refectory makes a grand living room for guests, a garden fills the old courtyard, and the halls leading to 50 rooms are monkishly wide (Db-€200, larger Db-€230—choose Venetian or modern style, ask for Rick Steves discount when you book direct, air-con, no elevator but plenty of stairs, fun-loving staff, 2 blocks from the station on the very quiet Calle Priuli dei Cavaletti, Cannaregio 68, tel. 041-717-333, fax 041-717-949, www.abbaziahotel.com, info@abbazia-hotel.com).

$$ Locanda Ca' San Marcuola is a peaceful and characteristic, if well-worn, oldie-but-goodie renting 14 fine rooms a few steps from the Grand Canal (Db-€140, €10 more for slightly bigger room overlooking small canal, air-con, near San Marcuola vaporetto stop, tel. 041-716-048, www.casanmarcuola.com, info@casanmarcuola).

$ Locanda Herion rents 16 beige-tiled, homey rooms for a decent price (Db-€120, cash discount, air-con, on Campiello Augusto Picutti at Cannaregio 1697a, tel. 041-275-9426, fax 041-275-6647, www.locandaherion.com, info@locandaherion.com). Exiting the train station, turn left to follow Rio Terà Lista de Spagna. It's near the San Marcuola vaporetto stop.

$ Albergo Marin has a depressing lobby, but its 19 good-value, quiet rooms are handy to the train station (Sb-€110, D-€100, Db-€120, Tb-€150, cash discount, fans on request, on Ramo de le Chioverete at Santa Croce 670b, tel. 041-718-022, fax 041-721-485, www.albergomarin.it, info@albergomarin.it, Giacomo). From the station, cross the stone bridge over the Grand Canal and go right along the embankment. Take the first left, then the first right, then right again to #670b.

$ Hotel S. Lucia, 150 yards from the train station, is oddly modern and sterile, with bright and spacious rooms and tight showers. Its 15 rooms are simple and clean. Guests enjoy their sunny garden area out front (S-€60, D-€90, Db-€110, Tb-€130, cash discount, breakfast-€5, air-con, closed Nov-Feb, on Calle de la Misericordia at Cannaregio 358, tel. 041-715-180, fax 041-710-610, www.hotelslucia.com, info@hotelslucia.com, Gianni and Alessandra). Exit the station, head left, then take the second left onto Calle de la Misericordia.

$ Hotel Henry, a tiny family-owned hotel, rents 15 simple and flowery rooms without any public spaces. It's in a quiet residential neighborhood near the Jewish Ghetto, a 10-minute walk from the train station (D-€80, Db-€100, Tb-€130, Qb-€160, show this book and ask for Rick Steves price if paying cash, ask about discount with 3-night stay, no breakfast, air-con, on Calle Ormesini at Campiello Briani, Cannaregio 1506e, tel. 041-523-6675, fax 041-715-680, www.alloggihenry.com, info@alloggihenry.com, Manola and Henry).

$ Hotel Rossi sits quietly at the end of a dead-end street. It's tired and quiet, renting 17 inexpensive, well-worn rooms (S-€56, D-€80, Db-€95, Tb-€115, air-con, a short walk from the station and a block away from the main street at Lista di Spagna 262, tel. 041-715-164, www.hotelrossi.ve.it, into@hotelrossi.ve.it).

Big, Fancy Hotels that Discount Shamelessly

Here are several big, plush, four-star places with greedy, sky-high rack rates (around Db-€300) that often have great discounts (as low as Db-€120) for online booking through their websites. All are on the map on page 996, except for Hotel Giorgione. If you want sliding-glass-door, uniformed-receptionist kind of comfort and formality in the old center, these are worth considering: **$$$ Hotel Giorgione** (big, garish, shiny, near Rialto Bridge, www.hotelgiorgione.com, see map on page 1001); **$$$ Hotel Casa Verardo** (elegant and quietly parked on a canal behind St. Mark's, more stately, www.casaverardo.it); **$$$ Hotel Donà Palace** (sitting like Las Vegas in the touristy zone a few blocks behind St. Mark's Basilica, works with neighbors **$$$ Hotel all'Angelo** and **$$$ Hotel al Ponte dei Sosperi** to rent 100 overpriced but often discounted rooms, all on Calle Larga San Marco, www.donapal-

VENICE

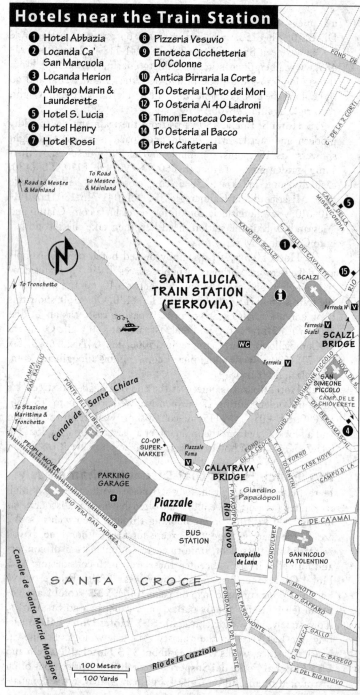

Hotels near the Train Station

1. Hotel Abbazia
2. Locanda Ca' San Marcuola
3. Locanda Herion
4. Albergo Marin & Launderette
5. Hotel S. Lucia
6. Hotel Henry
7. Hotel Rossi
8. Pizzeria Vesuvio
9. Enoteca Cicchetteria Do Colonne
10. Antica Birraria la Corte
11. To Osteria L'Orto dei Mori
12. To Osteria Ai 40 Ladroni
13. Timon Enoteca Osteria
14. To Osteria al Bacco
15. Brek Cafeteria

VENICE

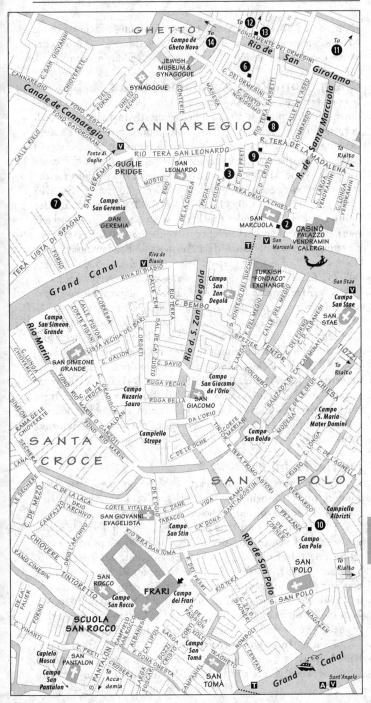

VENICE

ace.it); and **$$$ Hotel Ca' Dei Conti** (5 minutes northeast of St. Mark's Square, palatial and perfectly located but €500 rooms are worth it only when deeply discounted, www.cadeiconti.com).

Cheap Dormitory Accommodations

$ Foresteria della Chiesa Valdese is ramshackle, chilly, and run-down yet charming. It rents 70 beds—mostly in tight (6-10-bed) dorms, but with nine fine doubles and some larger private rooms sleeping up to six. It comes with generous public spaces and classic paintings on the walls and ceilings. Its profits support the charity work of the Methodist Church. They take reservations for the rooms, but only accept walk-ins for the dorms (dorm bed-€34, Db-€100-135, Tb-€115-130, Qb-€175, 5b-€190, €5/person less for multi-night stays; includes breakfast, sheets, towels, and lockers; must check in and out when office is open—8:30-20:00, no air-con, elevator, near Campo Santa Maria Formosa on Fondamenta Cavagnis at Castello 5170, see map on page 1001, tel. 041-528-6797, fax 041-241-6238, www.foresteriavenezia.it, info@foresteriavenezia.it).

$ Venice's youth hostel, on Giudecca Island with 260 beds and grand views across the Bay of San Marco, is a godsend for backpackers shell-shocked by Venetian prices. It's an old-school hostel—big rooms stacked with bunk beds (€26 beds with sheets and breakfast in 8-20-bed dorms, cheaper for hostel members, lockers, towels-€5, room lock-out 10:00-13:30, office open 24 hours, Fondamenta Zitelle 86, tel. 041-523-8211, fax 041-523-5689, www.ostellovenezia.it, info@ostellovenezia.it). Take vaporetto #4.1 from the bus or train stations (from the Tronchetto parking lot, take vaporetto #2) to the Zitelle stop, then walk right along the embankment to #86.

On the Mainland

While I prefer to stay in the heart of the action, these two places combine fine prices with easy bus links into Venice and are particularly good options for those who need to park a car.

$ Villa Dolcetti is a 1635 building with six comfortable rooms in a suburb of Venice. Art lovers Diego and Tatiana provide a buffet breakfast, free parking, and lots of sightseeing advice (Db-€75, superior Db-€85, Tb-€90-110, these prices for Rick Steves readers booking direct, air-con, tel. 041-563-1077, www.villadolcetti.com, info@villadolcetti.com). It's in the town of Oriago di Mira, at Via Venezia 85. Steps away is a bus stop on the Venice-Padua line that connects you to Venice's Piazzale Roma (2/hour, 25 minutes).

$ Villa Mocenigo Agriturismo, about 10 miles from Marco Polo Airport, is a working, family-run farm in a peaceful rural location between Venice and Padua. Its 10 rooms are furnished with antiques, and regional specialties are served for dinner (Sb-€40-55, Db-€60-74, extra bed-€20-25, dinner about €20/person, air-con, free parking, Via Viasana 59 in Mirano-Venezia, tel. 041-433-246, mobile 335-547-4728, www.villamocenigo.com, info@villamo-cenigo.com). Email for directions. Buses to Venice leave directly from the villa (3/hour, 45 minutes).

Eating in Venice

While touristy restaurants are the scourge of Venice, the following places are popular with actual Venetians and respect the tourists who happen in. First trick: Walk away from triple-language menus. Second trick: For freshness, eat fish. Most seafood dishes are the catch-of-the-day. (But remember that seafood can be sold by weight—per 100 grams or *etto*—rather than a set price.) Third trick: Eat later. A place may feel really touristy at 19:00, but if you come back at 21:00 it can be filled with locals. Tourists eat barbarically early, which is fine with the restaurants because they fill tables that would otherwise be used only once in an evening.

If you want a meal with a canal view, it generally comes with lower quality or a higher price. But if you're aiming for a canal-side memory, these two next-door neighbors offer good value: **Ristorante alla Conchiglia** and **Trattoria da Giorgio ai Greci,** several blocks behind St. Mark's, both have a few tables next to one of the smaller canals frequented by gondoliers. While tourist traps, they are lit up like Venetian Christmas trees after dark, and you can't argue with their setting (on Fondamenta San Lorenzo near the Ponte dei Greci bridge).

Unique to Venice, *cicchetti* **bars** specialize in finger foods and appetizers that can combine to make a quick and tasty meal. The selection and ambience are best on workdays (Mon-Sat lunch and early dinner).

Near the Rialto Bridge
North of the Bridge
These restaurants are located beyond Campo Santi Apostoli, along the Strada Nova, the main drag going from Rialto toward the train station. Unless otherwise noted, for locations see the map on page 1001.

Trattoria da Bepi, bright and alpine-paneled, feels like a classic, where Loris carries on his mother's passion for good, traditional Venetian cuisine. Ask for the seasonal specialties: The seafood appetizer plate and crab dishes are excellent. There's good seating inside and out. If you trust Loris, you'll walk away with a wonderful dining memory (€8-10 pastas, €14-18 *secondi*, €2 cover, Fri-Wed

VENICE

12:00-14:30 & 19:00-22:00, closed Thu, half a block off Campo Santi Apostoli on Salizada Pistor at #4550, tel. 041-528-5031).

La Cantina is an elegant *enoteca*—both rustic and sophisticated. There's no menu. Rather than cook (there's no kitchen here), Francesco and Andrea prepare wonderful gourmet plates of meat, cheese, and fish. Though it's not cheap (meat-and-cheese plates-€15/person, seafood plates-€30/person), you'll enjoy the very best ingredients paired with fine wines. You can sit inside and watch the preparation scene, or enjoy the parade of passersby from great seats right on the Strada Nova. For a budget alternative, have a *cicchetti* (€1.50) at the bar with a glass of fine wine (closed Sun, facing Campo San Felice on Strada Nova near Ca' d'Oro, tel. 041-522-8258).

Vini da Gigio has an enthusiasm for good food and a traditional Venetian menu (€12-16 pastas, €18-22 *secondi,* no cover, Wed-Sun 12:00-14:30 & 19:00-22:30, closed Mon-Tue, 4 blocks from Ca' d'Oro vaporetto stop on Fondamenta San Felice at #3628a—behind the church on Campo San Felice, tel. 041-528-5140).

Pizzeria Vesuvio serves some of the best and most popular pizza in town. A neighborhood favorite, it has classy indoor seating and pleasant tables outside (long hours, closed Tue, on Rio Terà Farsetti up from San Marcuola vaporetto stop, tel. 041-795-688).

Enoteca Cicchetteria Do Colonne is a local dive with a loyal following and a good spread of *cicchetti* and sandwiches. It's handy for a drink and a snack. While the food is mediocre, the scene (both at the bar and at the tables outside) feels real and is fun (daily, up from San Marcuola vaporetto stop just before Strada Nova on Rio Terà del Cristo, a block from Pizzeria Vesuvio—listed above, see map on page 1008, tel. 041-524-0453).

East of the Bridge

Osteria di Santa Marina, serving pricey, near-gourmet cuisine in a dressy dining room, is highly regarded by Venetians. The presentation is impressive, but you feel there's more pretense than love of food. Cheap-eating tricks are frowned on in this elegant, borderline stuffy restaurant (€15 pastas, €25 *secondi*, €3 cover, €75-80 fixed-price meals, Mon-Sat 12:30-14:30 & 19:30-22:00, closed Sun, reserve for dinner, eat indoors or outdoors on pleasant Campo Marina at #5911, between Rialto Bridge and Campo Santa Maria Formosa, tel. 041-528-5239).

Rosticceria San Bartolomeo is a cheap—if confusing—self-service diner. This throwback budget eatery has a surly staff: Don't take it personally. Take out, grab one of the few tiny tables, or munch at the bar—I'd skip their upper-floor restaurant option (€6-7 pastas, great fried *mozzarella al prosciutto* for €1.50, fruit salad, €1 glasses of wine, prices listed on wall behind counter, no cover and no service charge, daily 9:00-21:30, tel. 041-522-3569). To find it, imagine the statue on Campo San Bartolomeo walking backward 20 yards, turning left, and going under a passageway—now, follow him.

Osteria al Portego is a friendly neighborhood eatery. Carlo serves good meals and excellent *cicchetti*—best enjoyed early, around 18:00 (from 19:00 to 21:00, their six tables are reserved for those ordering from the menu; the *cicchetti* are picked over by 21:00). The *cicchetti* here can make a great meal, but consider sitting down for a dinner from their fine menu. Reserve ahead if you want a table (€13 pastas, €1 glasses of house wine, daily 10:30-15:00 & 18:00-22:00, near Campo Marina at #6015 on Calle Malvasia, tel. 041-522-9038). From Rosticceria San Bartolomeo (listed above), continue over a bridge to Campo San Lio, turn left, and follow Calle Carminati straight 50 yards over another bridge.

Near Campo Santa Maria Formosa: **Osteria alle Testiere** is my top dining splurge in Venice. Hugely respected, Luca and his staff are dedicated to quality, serving up creative, artfully presented market-fresh seafood (there's no meat on the menu), homemade pastas, and fine wine in what the chef calls a "Venetian Nouvelle" style. With only 22 seats, it's tight and homey, with the focus on food and service. They have daily specials, 10 wines by the glass, and one agenda: a great dining experience. This is a good spot to let loose and trust your host. Reservations are a must for their three seatings: 12:30, 19:00, and 21:30 (€20 pastas, €26 *secondi*, plan on spending €50 for dinner, closed Sun-Mon; on Calle del Mondo Novo, just off Campo Santa Maria Formosa, at #5801; tel. 041-522-7220).

Osteria al Mascaron is where I've gone for years to watch Gigi, Momi, and their food-loving band of ruffians dish up rustic-yet-sumptuous pastas with steamy seafood to salivating foodies. The seafood pastas seem pricey at €24-32, but they're meant for two (it's OK to ask for single portions). The €16 *antipasto misto* plate—have fun pointing—and two glasses of wine make a terrific light meal (€2.50 cover, Mon-Sat 12:00-15:00 & 19:00-23:00, closed Sun, reservations smart Fri-Sat; on Calle Lunga Santa Maria Formosa, a block past Campo Santa Maria Formosa, at #5225; tel. 041-522-5995).

Fast and Cheap Eats: The veggie stand on Campo Santa Maria Formosa is a fixture. For *döner kebabs* (€3.50) and pizza to go (€2/slice), head down Calle Lunga Santa Maria Formosa to **Peter Pan** at #6249 (daily 11:00-24:00).

Rialto Market Area

As with market neighborhoods anywhere, you'll find lots of hard-

VENICE

working hole-in-the walls with a line on the freshest of ingredients and catering to local shoppers needing a quick, affordable, and tasty bite. This area is very crowded by day, nearly empty early in the evening, and packed with young Venetian clubbers later.

Most of these places are informal, serving *cicchetti* and/or light meals. At each place, look for the list of snacks and wine by the glass at the bar or on the wall. When you're ready for dessert, try dipping a Burano biscuit in a glass of strawberry-flavored *fragolino* or another sweet dessert wine. Most bars are closed 15:00-18:00, and offer glasses of house wine for under €1, better wine for around €2.50, and *cicchetti* for €1-2.

My listings below include a strip of trendy places fronting the Grand Canal, a stretch of dark and rustic pubs serving regional tapas, three little places on the market (one for sandwiches, one for seafood, and a cheap and cheery low-end restaurant), a venerable old Venetian diner, and a couple of solid places for pasta and pizza (see map on page 1001). Most of these eateries are within 200 yards of the market and each other.

The Bancogiro Stretch: Five Places Overlooking the Grand Canal

Just past the Rialto Bridge, between Campo San Giacomo and the Grand Canal, this strip of five popular places has some of the best canalside seating in Venice. I call this the "Bancogiro Stretch" (Bancogiro is the strip of old banking buildings they front). Each place has a unique character and formula. During meals, they charge more and limit table seating to those ordering full lunches or dinners; but between meal times you can enjoy a drink or a snack at fine prices. After dinner hours, the Bancogiro Stretch becomes a youthful and trendy night spot. Before or after dinner, this strip is one of the best places in town for a *spritz*.

Here's the rundown (in the order you'd reach them from the Rialto Bridge): **Bar Naranzaria** serves Japanese and Italian dishes (€15-20 plates); **Caffè Vergnano**, your cheapest option—especially during meal times—is just a café with no cover (€9-12 salads, pizzas, and pastas, and a busy microwave oven); **Osteria al Pescador** is a more serious restaurant; **Bar Ristorante Bancogiro** is really good, with the only full kitchen on the strip, romantic dining upstairs (no canal views), a passion for the best cheese, and good *cicchetti* options at the bar (€16 pastas, €22 *secondi*, nice €15 cheese plate, €3.50 cover, closed Mon, tel. 041-523-2061); and the more modern **Bar Ancora**, which seems to be most popular with the local bar crowd (€13 pastas, €17 *secondi*, *cicchetti* at the bar).

The *Cicchetti* Strip: Four Venetian Tapas Bars

The 100-yard-long stretch starting two blocks inland from the Rialto Market (along Sotoportego dei Do Mori and Calle de le Do Spade) is beloved among Venetian *cicchetti* enthusiasts for its delightful bar munchies, good wine by the glass, and fun stand-up conviviality. These four places serve food all day, but the spread is best at around noon (generally open daily 12:00-15:00 & 18:00-20:00 or 21:00; two of the places I list are closed Sun). While each place offers a fine bar-and-stools scene, you might instead choose to treat one like a restaurant, order from their rustic menu, and grab a table. Scout these four places in advance to help decide which ambience is right for the experience you have in mind. Then pick one, dig in, and drink up.

Bar all'Arco, a bustling one-room joint, is particularly enjoyable for its tiny open-face sandwiches (closed Sun; Francisco, Anne, Matteo).

Osteria ai Storti, with a cool photo of the market in 1909, is run by Alessandro, who speaks English and enjoys helping educate travelers (€8 pastas, €12 *secondi*, 20 yards from Cantina Do Mori—listed below, around the corner on Calle San Matio).

Cantina Do Mori has been famous with locals (since 1462) and savvy travelers (since 1982) as a convivial place for fine wine. They serve a forest of little edibles on toothpicks and *francobolli* (a spicy selection of 20 tiny, mayo-soaked sandwiches nicknamed "stamps"). Go here to be abused in a fine atmosphere—the frowns are part of the shtick (closed Sun).

Cantina Do Spade is expertly run by Francesco, who clearly lists the *cicchetti* and wines of the day (also good for sit-down meals, 30 yards down Calle de le Do Spade from Osteria ai Storti at #860).

Other Good Eateries near the Rialto Market

Pronto Pesce is the perfect place to sample fish while watching the market action. Bruno and Umberto speak English and like to explain what's good. They serve a €10 mixed fish plate with bread (daily from 13:00 until it's sold out) that locals plan their day around. Consider their "express plates" of pasta (€10-12, served daily 12:45-14:15), fish risotto specials, artful fish hors d'oeuvres, and many other fresh fish tidbits. This fancy hole-in-the-wall is fun for a quick bite—eat standing up or take it to go (Tue-Sat 10:00-15:00 & 17:30-19:30, closed Sun-Mon, facing the fish market on Calle de le Becarie o Panataria at #319, tel. 041-822-0298).

Al Mercà ("At the Market"), a few steps away and off the canal, is a lively little nook with a happy crowd, where law-office workers have lunch and young locals gather in the evening for drinks and little snacks. The price list is clear, and I've found the crowd to be welcoming to tourists interested in connecting (stand at the bar or in the square—there are no tables and no interior, Mon-Sat 9:30-14:30 & 18:00-21:00, closed Sun, on Campo Cesare Battisti at #213).

Ristorante Vini da Pinto is a cheap, tourist-friendly eatery with a basic menu and forgettable food at decent prices. It has good service and relaxing outdoor seating (daily, long hours, facing the fish market, tel. 041-522-4599).

Trattoria alla Madonna is a big, bustling, classic Italian eatery with old-school formal waiters, a huge menu, and about a hundred tables. Tour groups find it efficient, and local families have come here for lunch after church for generations. There's no romance—just solid, reliable, traditional food from a menu that hasn't changed since World War II (€10 pastas, €13 *secondi*, €2 cover, closed Wed, tel. 041-522-3824, tucked away on Calle della Madonna, 2 minutes west of Rialto Bridge).

Antica Birraria la Corte is an everyday eatery on the delightful Campo San Polo, between the Rialto Bridge and the Frari Church. Popular for its €8-11 pizza, calzones, and wonderful selection of hearty €10 salads, it fills the far side of this cozy, family-filled square. While the interior is a sprawling beer hall, it's a joy to eat on the square, where metal tables teeter on the cobbles, the wind plays with the paper mats, and children run free (€11-12 pastas, €14-19 *secondi,* €2 cover, daily 12:00-15:30 & 18:00-22:30, Campo San Polo 2168, tel. 041-275-0570, see the map on page 1008).

Trattoria Pizzeria al Nono Risorto is unpretentious, inexpensive, youthful, and famous for serving good pizza in a nice setting. You'll sit in a gravelly garden under a leafy canopy, surrounded by Italians enjoying huge €8 salads, pastas, and pizzas, and €12-17 grilled meat or fish dishes (Thu 19:00-22:30, Fri-Tue 12:00-14:30 & 19:00-22:30, closed Wed, reservations smart on weekends; from Rialto fish market, get out your map and walk 3 minutes away from the Rialto to Campo San Cassiano—it's just over the bridge on Sotoportego de Siora Bettina at #2338; tel. 041-524-1169).

Near St. Mark's Square: Dining Fine and Cheap 'n' Cheery

For locations, see the map on page 996.

Ristorante Antica Sacrestia is a classic restaurant where the owner, Pino, takes a hands-on approach to greeting guests. His staff serves creative €33-50 fixed-price meals and a humdrum €20 *turistico* one. You can also order à la carte; try the delightful €21 antipasto spread. This is a good place if you're looking for quality pizza in a lovely setting near St. Mark's for lunch, or a romantic splurge for dinner. My readers are welcome to a free *sgroppino* (lemon vodka after-dinner drink) upon request (€12-16 pastas and pizzas, €17-30 *secondi*, Tue-Sun 11:30-15:00 & 18:00-23:00, closed Mon, immediately behind San Zaninovo/Giovanni Novo Church on Calle de la Sacrestia at #4442, may move in 2014 to nearby spot on Calle Corona at Castello 4463, tel. 041-523-0749).

"Sandwich Row": On Calle de le Rasse, just steps away from the tourist intensity at St. Mark's Square, is a handy strip I call "Sandwich Row." Lined with sandwich bars, it's the closest place to St. Mark's to get a decent sandwich at an affordable price with a place to sit down (most places open daily 7:00-24:00, €1 extra to sit; from the Bridge of Sighs, head down the Riva and take the second lane on the left). I particularly like **Birreria Forst,** a café that serves a selection of meaty €3 sandwiches with tasty sauce on wheat bread, or made-to-order sandwiches for €4 (daily 10:00-21:00, air-con, rustic wood tables, Calle de le Rasse at #4540, tel. 041-523-0557), and **Bar Verde,** a more modern sandwich bar with fun people-watching views from its corner tables (big €5 sandwiches, splittable €9 salads, fresh pastries, at the end of Calle de le Rasse at #4526, facing Campo Santi Filippo e Giacomo).

Ristorante alla Basilica, just one street behind St. Mark's Basilica, is a church-run, indoor, institutional-feeling place that serves a solid €14 fixed-price lunch (including water) daily from 11:45 to 15:00. It's not self-serve—you'll be seated and can choose a pasta, a *secondi,* and a vegetable side dish off the menu (air-con, on Calle dei Albanesi at #4255, tel. 041-522-0524).

Rizzo, like most Venetian "bars," is an eat-at-the-counter café with sandwiches, pizza, pastries, and other reasonably priced snacks. It stands out for its handy location, north of St. Mark's Square on the main drag of Calle dei Fabbri, and its tiny grocery shelf with yogurt and other quick bites (Mon-Sat 8:00-20:00, closed Sun, on Calle dei Fabbri at #933a, tel. 041-522-3388).

Picnicking: Though you can't picnic on St. Mark's Square, you can legally take your snacks to the nearby Giardinetti Reali, the small park along the waterfront west of the Piazzetta.

In Dorsoduro

All of these recommendations are within a 10-minute walk of the Accademia Bridge (for locations, see the map on page 1005). Dorsoduro is great for restaurants and well-worth the walk from the more touristy Rialto and San Marco areas. The first two listings are near the Accademia (and best for lunch). The next two are in Zattere, overlooking the Giudecca Canal. And the last four (best for dinner) are near Campo San Barnaba.

VENICE

Near the Accademia Bridge

Ristorante/Pizzeria Accademia Foscarini, next to the Accademia Bridge and Galleria, offers decent €10-11 pizzas in a great canalside setting. Their toasted *farciti* stuffed sandwich is a local favorite (€6.50 at the table). Though the pizzas may be forgettable, this place is both scenic and practical—on each visit to Venice, I grab a pizza lunch here while I ponder the Grand Canal bustle. They also serve a €10 breakfast (no cover or service charge, May-Oct Wed-Mon 7:00-22:30, Nov-April Wed-Mon 7:00-21:00, closed Tue year-round, on Rio Terà A. Foscarini at #878c, tel. 041-522-7281, Paolo).

Enoteca Cantine del Vino Già Schiavi is much-loved for its €1 *cicchetti* and €3.50 sandwiches (order from list on board). It's also a good place for a €1-2 glass of wine and appetizers. You're welcome to enjoy your wine and finger food at the bar or out on the sidewalk. This is primarily a wine shop with great prices for bottles to go—and plastic glasses for picnickers (Mon-Sat 8:00-20:30, closed Sun, 100 yards from Accademia art museum on San Trovaso canal; facing Accademia, take a right and then a forced left at the canal to the second bridge—it's at #992, tel. 041-523-0034).

In Zattere

Terrazza del Casin dei Nobili takes full advantage of the warm, romantic evening sun. They serve finely crafted, regional specialties with creativity at tolerable prices. The canalside seating is breezy and beautiful, but comes with the rumble of *vaporetti* from the nearby stop. The interior is bright and hip (good €9-10 pizzas, €10-13 pastas, €15-25 *secondi*, €2 cover, Fri-Wed 12:00-23:00, closed Thu; from Zattere vaporetto stop, turn left to #924; tel. 041-520-6895, Ruggiero and Eleonora). On Wednesday and Sunday evenings in summer, there's live music nearby on the Zattere promenade.

Ae Oche Pizzeria is playful, with casual tables on the canal and a sprawling pizza parlor interior. It's a hit with young Venetians for its fun atmosphere and good prices (daily 12:00-15:00 & 19:00-23:00, a couple of hundred yards from the Zattere vaporetto stop, tel. 041-520-6601).

On or near Campo San Barnaba

This small square is a delight—especially in the evening. As these places are within a few steps of each other—and the energy and atmosphere can vary—I like to survey the options before choosing (although reservations may be necessary to dine later in the evening).

Ristoteca Oniga is all about fresh fish, with a chic-and-ship-shape interior, great tables on the square, and the enthusiastic direction of Raffaele. The menu is accessible and always includes a good vegetarian dish (€12 pastas, €20 *secondi*, €2 cover, closed Tue, reservations smart, Campo San Barnaba, tel. 041-522-4410).

Osteria Enoteca Ai Artisti serves well-presented quality dishes either in its tight little wine-snob interior or at six petite, romantic canalside tables. They serve good wines by the glass from their prize-winning list (€15 pastas, €20 *secondi*, closed Sun, Fondamenta della Toletta, tel. 041-523-8944).

Pizzeria al Profeta is a casual place popular for great pizza and steak. It's big, woody interior seems to stoke conviviality, as does its leafy garden out back (€8-10 pizzas, closed Tue; from Campo San Barnaba, walk to the end of Calle Lunga San Barnaba; tel. 041-523-7466).

Enoteca e Trattoria la Bitta is dark and woody, with a soft-jazz bistro feel, tight seating, and a small, forgettable back patio. They serve beautifully presented, traditional Venetian food with—proudly—no fish. Their helpful waitstaff and small, handwritten daily menu are clearly focused on quality, with local ingredients and a "slow food" ethic. As it has an avid following, there are two seatings (19:00 and 21:00), reservations are required, and service can be intense (€10 pastas, €16-25 *secondi*, €2 cover, dinner only, Mon-Sat 18:30-23:00, closed Sun, cash only, just off Campo San Barnaba on Calle Lunga San Barnaba, tel. 041-523-0531, Debora and Marcellino).

In Cannaregio

Cannaregio offers the classic chance in Venice to "get off the beaten path." Beyond the Jewish Ghetto, this neighborhood—more residential than touristic—features a grid layout with straight and spacious canalside walks (part of an expansion from the 1400s). Although it lacks the higgledy-piggledy feel of the older part of town, it's worth the long walk for a look. Rather than come here just for a meal, I'd make time to explore and then grab a bite while in the neighborhood. Cannaregio is most peaceful at sunset. For locations, see the map on page 1008.

Osteria L'Orto dei Mori is a chic place serving nicely presented, creative Venetian cuisine. You can eat in the elegant, modern interior or on a great neighborhood square with 10 tables surrounded by a classic scene of wellhead, bridges, and canal (€13 pastas, €25 *secondi*, €3 cover, closed Tue, on Rio della Sensa at Calle Larga, on Campo dei Mori, tel. 041-524-3677).

Osteria Ai 40 Ladroni ("The Forty Thieves") is a characteristic old standby with a few tables on the canal, a rustic interior, and a convivial garden out back. The action is near the bar (€10 pastas, €15 *secondi*, they're proud of their mixed seafood *antipasti*, closed Mon, Fondamenta della Sensa at Calle del Capitello, reserve for dinner, tel. 041-715-736).

Timon Enoteca Osteria, while nothing earthshaking, has a relaxing canalside setting with nice wines and *cicchetti* (a block past the Jewish Ghetto on Fondamenta Ormesini at Calle Malvasia, tel. 041-524-6066).

Osteria al Bacco is simple and rustic, with a typical Venetian menu and a couple of canalside tables (€10 pastas, €16 *secondi*, €2 cover, closed Mon, on Fondamenta Capuzine at Calle Girolamo, tel. 041-721-415).

Elsewhere in Venice

On Giudecca Island: **I Figli delle Stelle Ristorante** offers a delightful dining experience with an excuse to ride the boat from St. Mark's Square across to the island of Giudecca. Simone and his staff artfully serve Venetian classics with a dash of Rome and Puglia and a passion for fish and lamb. While they have inside seating, the reason to venture here is to sit canalside with fine views of Venice across the broad Giudecca Canal and all the water traffic. Reserve ahead to specify "first line" seating along the water, "second line" seating a few steps away, or a table inside (€15 pastas, €22 *secondi*, €3.50 cover, daily 12:30-14:30 & 19:00-22:30, 50 yards from Zitelle vaporetto dock—from San Marco ride line #4.2 or #2, tel. 041-523-0004).

On Fondamente Nove: **Ristorante Algiubagio,** though not cheap, is a good place to eat well overlooking the northern lagoon. The name is a combination of the owners' four names—Alberto, Giulio, Barbara, and Giovanna—who strive to impress visitors with quality, creative Venetian cuisine made using the best ingredients. Reserve a table on the lagoon facing the island of San Michele or in their classy cantina dining room (€16-18 pastas, €24-25 *secondi*, €3.50 cover, €30-42 fixed-price meals, Wed-Mon 12:00-15:00 & 19:00-22:30, closed Tue; on Fondamente Nove, to the left of the vaporetto dock as you face the water, at #5039; tel. 041-523-6084).

Near Campo Santa Maria Nova: **Osteria da Alberto,** with excellent daily specials, €13 seafood dishes, €11 pastas, a good house wine, and a woody and characteristic interior, is one of my standbys. It's smart to reserve at night—I'd request a table in the front (€2 cover, Mon-Sat 12:00-15:00 & 18:30-22:30, closed Sun; on Calle Larga Giacinto Gallina, midway between Campo Santi Apostoli and Campo Santi Giovanni e Paolo, next to Ponte de la Panada bridge at #5401—see map on page 1001; tel. 041-523-8153, run by Graziano and Giovanni).

Near the Train Station: There are piles of eateries near the station. The buffet in the station itself is quite good, with peaceful garden seating out back in summer, big €3-4 sandwiches, and slices of pizza for €3. A block away is a small branch of the efficient and economic **Brek,** a popular self-service cafeteria chain (€5 pastas, €7-9 *secondi,* daily 11:30-22:00, head left as you leave the station and walk about 50 yards past the bridge along Rio Terà Lista di Spagna to #124—see map on page 1008).

Cheap Meals

The keys to eating affordably in Venice are pizza, *döner kebabs,* bars/cafés, cafeterias, and picnics. *Panini* and *tramezzini* (sandwiches) are sold fast and cheap at bars everywhere and can stave off mid-morning hunger. There's a great "sandwich row" of cheap cafés near St. Mark's Square (see page 1016). For speed, value, and ambience, you can get a filling plate of typically Venetian appetizers at nearly any bar. For quick, fun eating, I like small, stand-up mini-meals at *cicchetti* **bars** best (several are recommended in this chapter). Those on a hard-core budget equip their room with a pantry stocked at the market (fruits and veggies are remarkably cheap) or pick up a kebab (or the equivalent), then dine in at picnic prices.

Pizza

While not the home of pizza, Venice is enthusiastic about it. For tourists, a great way to enjoy a delightful Venetian setting at a pain-less price is to have a pizza with a beer or carafe of house wine at a canalside restaurant. Pizza ranges from €4 for takeout to €6 in a cheap restaurant to €12 in a finest restaurant. Personally, I like to go top-end on pizza: Invest the extra euros, and enjoy a great set-ting, classy service, and the best quality.

If you're in the mood for pizza, here are my recommendations (all of these places are described in more detail earlier):

For fun-loving, youthful places featuring inexpensive and good pizzas, big pizza parlor-type interiors, and relaxing outdoor seating, try **Pizzeria al Profeta** (with a leafy garden, near Campo San Barnaba), **Ae Oche Pizzeria** (with casual tables overlooking the Giudecca Canal), **Antica Birraria la Corte** (on a big, breezy neighborhood square), or **Trattoria Pizzeria al Nono Risorto** (near the Rialto Bridge with a garden full of tables).

For simple pizza from little more than a bar—with great tables on the Grand Canal under the Accademia Bridge—check out **Ristorante/Pizzeria Accademia Foscarini.**

For top-shelf pizza served in a more formal restaurant setting, consider **Terrazza del Casin dei Nobili** (with elegant seating over-looking the Giudecca Canal), **Ristorante Antica Sacrestia** (in a classy restaurant near St. Mark's Square), and **Pizzeria Vesuvio** (with fine outdoor seating too, near the Jewish Ghetto).

VENICE

Picnics

The **fruit and vegetable market** that sprawls for a few blocks just past the Rialto Bridge is a fun place to assemble a picnic (best Mon-Sat 8:00-13:00, closed Sun). The adjacent **fish market** is wonderfully slimy (closed Sun-Mon). Side lanes in this area are speckled with fine little hole-in-the-wall munchie bars, bakeries, and cheese shops.

A handy (but often mobbed) **Co-op** supermarket is between St. Mark's and Campo Santa Maria Formosa, on the corner of Salizada San Lio and Calle del Mondo Novo at #5817. It has a great selection of picnic supplies, including packaged salads for €2 (daily 8:30-20:00). The largest supermarket in town is the **Co-op** at Piazzale Roma, next to the vaporetto stop at #504-507 (daily 8:30-20:00). It's an easy walk from the train station, as is the **Billa** supermarket on Campo San Felice (at #3660, along the Strada Nova between the train station and Rialto area, Mon-Sat 8:30-20:00, Sun 9:00-20:00). Another **Billa** supermarket is convenient for those staying in Dorsoduro: It's at #1492, as far west as possible on the Zattere embankment, by the San Basilio vaporetto stop and the cruise-ship docks (Mon-Sat 8:00-20:00, Sun 9:00-19:00).

The only legal place to picnic in public in Venice is Giardinetti Reali, the waterfront park near St. Mark's Square. Eating anywhere outdoors, you may be besieged by pigeons. A picnic in your room can be a better bet.

Gelato

You'll find good *gelaterie* in every Venetian neighborhood, offering one-scoop cones for about €1.50. Look for the words *artigianale* or *produzione propria*, which indicates that a shop makes its own gelato.

The popular, inventive, upscale **Grom** ice-cream chain has two branches in Venice, one on Campo San Barnaba at #2761 (beyond the Accademia Bridge), and another one on the Strada Nova at #3844, not far from the Rialto (cheapest cone-€2.50, both open long hours daily). A competing gourmet gelato shop, **Gelatoteca Suso,** serves up delectable flavors such as fig and nut (daily 12:00-23:00, next to recommended Rosticceria San Bartolomeo on Calle de la Bissa).

On St. Mark's Square, two venerable cafés have gelato counters: **Gran Caffè Lavena** (April-Oct daily until 24:00, no gelato Nov-March, first café to left of the Clock Tower, behind the first orchestra, at #134) and **Todaro** (on the corner of the Piazzetta at #5, near the water and just under the column topped by St. Theodore slaying a crocodile).

Venice Connections

By Train

From Venice by Train to: Florence (hourly, 2-3 hours, often crowded so make reservations), **Milan** (hourly, 2.5-3.5 hours), **Cinque Terre/Monterosso** (5/day, 6 hours, change in Milan), **Rome** (roughly hourly, 3.75 hours, also 1 direct night train, 7 hours),

International Destinations: Interlaken (5/day, 6-8.5 hours, 2-5 changes, no pleasant overnight option), **Luzern** (7/day, 6.5-7 hours, 1 direct, others change in Milan and Arth-Goldau), **Bern** (3/day, 6 hours, change in Milan or Brig), **Munich** (4-6/day, 7 hours, change in Verona; 1 direct night train, 9 hours; most trains reservable only via www.bahn.de), **Salzburg** (4/day, 6-7 hours, 1-2 changes, 1 direct night train, 7 hours), **Paris** (2/day, 10-12 hours with change in Milan; 1 direct night train, 13.5 hours, important to reserve ahead, no railpasses accepted, www.thello.com), **Ljubljana** (3/day, 7.5 hours—buy ticket at train station, take bus from Piazzale Roma to Villach in Austria, then transfer to train; 1 direct night train, 4 hours, but arrives at 2:00 in the morning), and **Vienna** (3/day, 8 hours—same system as Ljubljana; 1 direct night train, 11 hours).

By Plane

Marco Polo is Venice's main airport. Some budget flights, including Ryanair, use the smaller airport in the nearby city of Treviso.

Marco Polo Airport

Venice's small, modern airport is on the mainland shore of the lagoon, six miles north of the city (airport code: VCE). There's one sleek terminal, with a TI (daily 9:00-20:00), car-rental agencies, ATMs, a bank, and a few shops and eateries. For flight information, call 041-260-9260, visit www.veniceairport.com, or ask your hotel.

Getting Between the Airport and Venice

Here are four ways to transfer between the airport and downtown Venice:

- Alilaguna boats—Slowest trip, medium cost
- Water taxis—Fastest trip, most expensive
- Airport shuttle buses to Piazzale Roma (Venice's bus station)—Faster than Alilaguna, slower than water taxi, least expensive
- Private shuttle bus to Piazzale Roma—Medium speed, medium cost

Each of these options is explained in detail (next). An advantage of the Alilaguna boats is that you can reach most of this chapter's recommended hotels very simply, with no changes—except hotels near the train station, which are better served by the bus to Piazzale Roma.

Both Alilaguna boats and water taxis leave from the airport's boat dock, an eight-minute walk from the terminal. Exit the arrivals hall and turn left, following signs along a paved, level, covered sidewalk (easy for wheeled bags).

When flying out of Venice, allow yourself plenty of time to get to the airport. Water transport can be slow. Plan to arrive at the airport two hours before your flight, and remember that getting there can easily take another two hours. Alilaguna boats are small and can fill up. In an emergency, you can always hop in a water taxi and get to the airport in 30 minutes.

Alilaguna Airport Boats

These boats make the scenic (if slow) journey across the lagoon, each shuttling passengers between the airport and a number of different stops on the island of Venice (€15, €25 round-trip, €1 surcharge if bought on boat, roughly 2/hour, 1-1.5-hour trip depending on destination). Alilaguna boats are not part of the ACTV vaporetto system, so they aren't covered by city transit passes. But they do use the same docks and ticket windows as the regular *vaporetti*.

There are three Alilaguna lines—blue, red, and orange. Stops near recommended hotels include: San Marco, San Zaccaria, Zattere, Guglie, Rialto, and Fondamente Nove. For a full schedule, visit the TI, see the website (www.alilaguna.it), call 041-240-1701, ask your hotelier, or scan the schedules posted at the docks.

From the Airport to Venice: You can buy Alilaguna tickets at the airport's TI, the ticket desk in the terminal, and at the ticket booth at the dock. Any ticket-seller can tell you which line to catch to get to your destination. Boats from the airport run roughly twice an hour from 7:00 to midnight.

From Venice to the Airport: Ask your hotelier what dock and what line is best. Boats start leaving Venice as early as 3:40 in the morning so that passengers can catch early flights. Scope out the dock and buy your ticket in advance to avoid last-minute stress.

Water Taxis

Luxury taxi speedboats zip directly between the airport and the closest dock to your hotel, getting you within steps of your final destination in about 30 minutes. The official price is €110 for up to four people; add €10 for every extra person (10-passenger limit). You may get a higher quote—politely talk it down. A taxi can be a smart investment for small groups and those with an early departure.

From the airport, arrange your ride at the water-taxi desk or with the boat captains lounging at the dock. From Venice, book your taxi trip the day before you leave. Your hotel will help (since they get a commission), or you can book directly with the Consorzio Motoscafi water taxi association (tel. 041-522-2303, www.motoscafivenezia.it).

Airport Shuttle Buses

Buses between the airport and Venice are fast, frequent, and cheap. They take you across the bridge from the mainland to the island, dropping you at Venice's bus station, at the "mouth of the fish" on a square called Piazzale Roma. From there, you can catch a vaporetto down the Grand Canal—convenient for hotels near the Rialto Bridge and St. Mark's Square. If you're staying near the train station, you can walk from Piazzale Roma to your hotel.

Two bus companies run between Piazzale Roma and the airport: ACTV and ATVO. ATVO buses take 20 minutes and go nonstop. ACTV buses make a few stops en route and take slightly longer (30 minutes). They are equally good; just jump on whichever one's leaving next (either bus: €5, runs about 5:00-24:00, 2/hour, just 1/hour early and late, check schedules at www.atvo.it or www.actv.it).

From the Airport to Venice: Both buses leave from just outside the arrivals terminal. Buy tickets from the TI, the ticket desk in the terminal, ticket machines, or the driver. ATVO tickets are not valid on ACTV buses and vice versa. Double-check the destination; you want Piazzale Roma. If taking ACTV, you want bus #5.

From Venice to the Airport: At Piazzale Roma, buy your ticket from the ACTV windows or ATVO office before heading out to the platforms. The newsstand in the center of the lot also sells tickets. ACTV buses leave from platform A1; ATVO buses leave from platforms near the center of the lot and are well-signed.

Private Shuttle Bus

Treviso Car Service offers a private minivan service between Marco Polo Airport and Piazzale Roma or the cruise port (minivan-€55, seats up to 8; car-€50, seats up to 3; mobile 348-900-0700 or 333-411-2840, www.tourleadervenice.com, info@tourleadervenice.com).

Treviso Airport

Several budget airlines, such as Ryanair, Wizz Air, and Germanwings, use Treviso Airport, 12 miles northwest of Venice (airport code: TSF, tel. 042-231-5111, www.trevisoairport.it).

VENICE

Regular ATVO buses take you from the airport to Piazzale Roma (€7, about 2/hour, 1.25 hours, www.atvo.it). Buy your tickets at the ATVO desk in the airport and stamp them on the bus. Treviso Car Service offers minivan service to Piazzale Roma (minivan-€75, seats up to 8; car-€65, seats up to 3; for contact info, see private shuttle bus listing above).

FLORENCE

Firenze

Florence, the home of the Renaissance and birthplace of our modern world, has the best Renaissance art in Europe. In a single day, you could look Michelangelo's *David* in the eyes, fall under the seductive sway of Botticelli's *Birth of Venus,* and climb the modern world's first dome, which still dominates the skyline.

Get your bearings with a Renaissance walk. Florentine art goes beyond paintings and statues—enjoy the food, fashion, and street markets. You can lick Italy's best gelato while enjoying some of Europe's best people-watching.

Planning Your Time

If you're in Italy for three weeks, Florence deserves at least one well-organized day: see the Accademia *(David),* tour the Uffizi Gallery (Renaissance art), visit the underrated Bargello (best statues), and do the Renaissance Walk (explained on page 1043; to avoid heat and crowds, do this walk in the morning or late afternoon). Art lovers will want to chisel out another day of their itinerary for the many other Florentine cultural treasures. Shoppers and ice-cream lovers may need to do the same.

Plan your sightseeing carefully; follow the tips and tricks in this chapter to save time and avoid lines. This is particularly important if you'll be in town for only a day or two during the crowded summer months.

The Uffizi Gallery and Accademia nearly always have long ticket-buying lines, especially in peak season (April-Oct) and on holiday weekends. Crowds thin out weekdays in the off-season. You can easily avoid the wait by making reservations (see page 1045) or buying a Firenze Card (see page 1044).

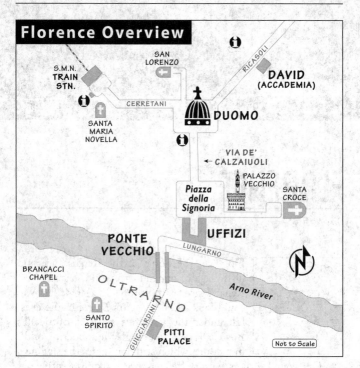

Florence Overview

S.M.N. TRAIN STN.

SAN LORENZO

RICASOLI

DAVID (ACCADEMIA)

CERRETANI

SANTA MARIA NOVELLA

DUOMO

VIA DE' CALZAIUOLI

PALAZZO VECCHIO

SANTA CROCE

Piazza della Signoria

UFFIZI

PONTE VECCHIO

LUNGARNO

BRANCACCI CHAPEL

OLTRARNO

Arno River

SANTO SPIRITO

GUICCIARDINI

PITTI PALACE

Not to Scale

Note that both the Uffizi and Accademia are closed on Monday. Some sights close early—even before 14:00; other museums close early only on certain days (e.g., the first Sunday of the month, second and fourth Monday, etc.). In general, Sundays and Mondays are bad, with many museums either closed or with shorter hours.

Connoisseurs of smaller towns should consider taking the bus to Siena for a day or evening trip (1.25 hours one-way, confirm when last bus returns).

Orientation to Florence

The best of Florence lies on the north bank of the Arno River. The main historical sights cluster around the red-brick dome of the cathedral (Duomo). Everything is within a 20-minute walk of the train station, cathedral, or Ponte Vecchio (Old Bridge). The less famous but more characteristic Oltrarno area (south bank) is just over the bridge. Though small, Florence is intense. Prepare for scorching summer heat, slick pickpockets, few WCs, steep prices, and long lines. Easy tourist money has corrupted some locals, making them greedy and dishonest (check your bill carefully). The big news for visitors to Florence is the energetic young mayor's passion

FLORENCE

for traffic-free zones. Once brutal for pedestrians, the city is now a delight on foot.

Tourist Information

Florence has two separate TI organizations, which are equally helpful.

One TI has two different branches, both with a focus on the city. The main branch is across the square from the **train station** and very crowded (Mon-Sat 8:30-19:00, Sun 8:30-14:00; with your back to tracks, exit the station—it's 100 yards away, across the square in wall near corner of church at Piazza Stazione 4; if you see a "tourist information" desk inside the train station, it's a hotel-booking service in disguise; tel. 055-212-245, www.firenze-turismo.it). The other branch is very centrally located at **Piazza del Duomo**, at the west corner of Via Calzaiuoli (it's inside the Bigallo Museum/Loggia; Mon-Sat 9:00-19:00, Sun 9:00-14:00).

The other TI organization covers both the city and the greater province of Florence. Its main branch is a couple of blocks **north of the Duomo** (Mon-Sat 8:30-18:30, closed Sun, just past Medici-Riccardi Palace at Via Cavour 1 red, tel. 055-290-832, international bookstore across street); a second branch is at the **airport** (daily 8:30-20:30).

At any TI, peruse these free, handy resources in English (though, since they overlap quite a bit, you probably don't need them all):

- city map (also ask for the transit map, which has bus routes of interest to tourists on the back; your hotel likely has freebie maps, too)
- current museum-hours listing (very important, since no guide-book—including this one—has ever been able to accurately predict the hours of Florence's sights for the coming year; you can also download this list at www.firenzeturismo.it)
- a list of current exhibitions
- a printout of what's happening that day
- the compact *Firenze Info* booklet, loaded with useful practical details
- the *Firenze: The Places of Interest* fold-out, with brief descriptions of sightseeing options
- information on entertainment, including the TI's monthly *Florence & Tuscany News* (good for events and entertainment listings)
- the glossy monthly *Florence Concierge Information* magazine (stuffed with ads for shopping and restaurants, but also includes some practical information)
- *The Florentine* newspaper (published every other Thu in Eng-

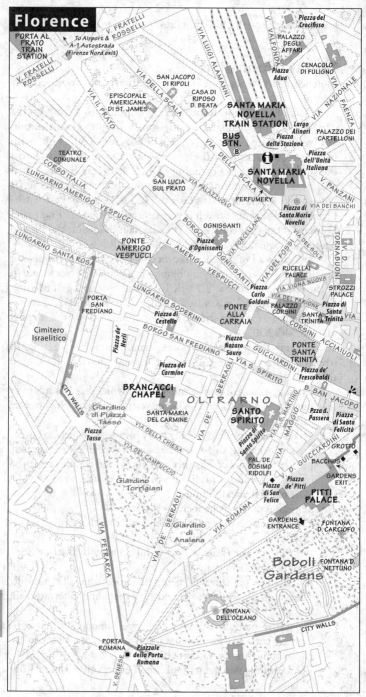

Florence

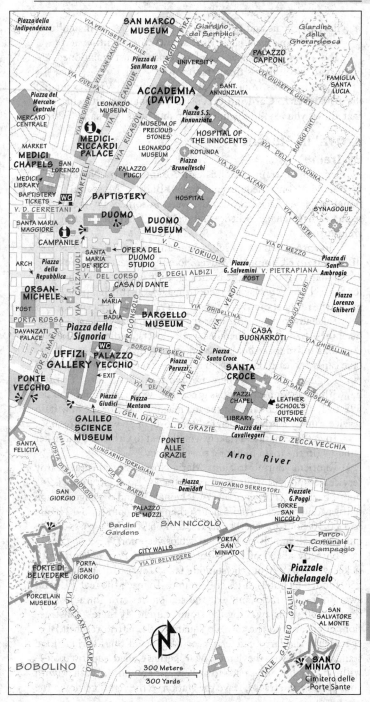

FLORENCE

lish, for expats and tourists, with great articles giving cultural insights; download latest issue at www.theflorentine.net)

The Florence magazine and newspaper just mentioned are often available at hotels throughout town.

The TIs across from the train station and on Via Cavour sell the €50 **Firenze Card,** an expensive but handy sightseeing pass that allows you to skip the lines at top museums (see page 1044).

Arrival in Florence
By Train

Florence's main train station is called **Santa Maria Novella** (*Firenze S.M.N.* on schedules and signs). Built in Mussolini's "Rationalism" style back between the wars, in some ways the station seems to have changed little—notice the 1930s-era lettering and architecture.

Florence also has two suburban train stations: **Firenze Rifredi** and **Firenze Campo di Marte.** Note that some trains don't stop at the main station—before boarding, confirm that you're heading for S.M.N., or you may overshoot the city. (If this happens, don't panic; the other stations are a short taxi ride from the center.)

Take advantage of the user-friendly, automated "Fast Ticket" machines that display schedules, issue tickets, and even make reservations for railpass-holders. Some take only credit cards; others take cards and cash. Using them is easy—it actually can be fun; just tap "English." Be aware there are two train companies: TrenItalia, with most connections, has green-and-white machines (toll tel. 892-021, www.trenitalia.it); the red machines are for the new Italo service, run by a private operator (tel. 06-0708, www.italotreno.it).

To get international tickets, you'll need to either go to a ticket window (in the main hall) or a travel agency.

To orient yourself to Santa Maria Novella Station and nearby services, stand with your back to the tracks. Look left to see a 24-hour pharmacy (*Farmacia,* near McDonald's) and baggage storage halfway down track 16 (€5/5 hours, then €0.70/hour for 6-12 hours and €0.30/hour for over 12 hours, daily 6:00-23:50, passport required, maximum 40 pounds, no explosives—sorry).

Directly ahead of you is the main hall (*salone biglietti,* with ticket windows). Avoid the station's fake "Tourist Information" office, funded by hotels, if it's still around. To reach the real TI, walk away from the tracks and exit the station; it's straight across the square, 100 yards away, by the stone church. (If there's construction, circle around the torn-up square to the left to reach it.) For cheap eats, the large cafeteria near McDonald's has various food stands. Better yet, the handy Margherita/Conad supermarket—with sandwiches and salads to go—is just around the corner (with your back to the tracks, leave the station to the right, go down the steps, and it's immediately on your right on Via Luigi Alamanni; Mon-Sat 8:00-20:00, closed Sun).

Getting to the Duomo and City Center: The Duomo and town center are to your left (with your back to the tracks). Out the doorway to the left, you'll find city buses and the taxi stand. Taxis cost about €8 to the Duomo, and the line moves fast, except on holidays. To walk into town (10-15 minutes), exit the station to the left and find the stairs/escalators down to the underground passageway/mall called Galleria S.M. Novella. Head toward the Church of Santa Maria Novella. (Warning: Pickpockets—often dressed as tourists—frequent this tunnel, especially the surface point near the church.) You come out on the other side of the square; head down Via dei Panzani, which leads directly to the Duomo.

By Bus

The bus station is next to the train station, with the TI across the square. Exit the station through the main door, and turn left along the busy street toward the brick dome. The train station is on your left, while downtown Florence is straight ahead and a bit to the right. For more information on buses, see page 1037.

By Car

The autostrada has several exits for Florence. Get off at the *Nord*, *Sud*, or *Certosa* exits and follow signs toward—but not into—the *Centro*.

Don't even attempt driving into the city center. Florence has a traffic-reduction system that's complicated and confusing even to locals. Every car passing into the *Zona Traffico Limitato (ZTL)* is photographed; those who haven't jumped through bureaucratic hoops to get a permit can expect to receive a €100 ticket in the mail. If you get lost and cross the line several times...you get several fines. The no-go zone (defined basically by the old medieval wall, now a boulevard circling the historic center of town—watch for *Zona Traffico Limitato* signs) is roughly the area between the river, main train station, Piazza della Libertà, Piazza Donatello, and Piazza Beccaria.

Parking: The city center is ringed with big, efficient parking lots (signposted with the standard big *P*), each with taxi and bus service into the center. Check www.firenzeparcheggi.it for details on parking lots, availability, and prices. From the freeway, follow the signs to *Centro*, then *Stadio*, then *P*. I usually head for "Parcheggio del Parterre," just beyond Piazza della Libertà (€2/hour, €20/day, €65/week, open 24 hours daily, tel. 055-500-1994, 600 spots, automated, pay with cash or credit card, never fills up completely). To get into town, find the taxi stand at the elevator exit, or ride one of the minibuses that connect all of the major parking lots with the city center (see www.ataf.net for routes).

FLORENCE

You can park for free along any suburban curb near a bus stop that feels safe and take the bus into the city center from there. Check for signs that indicate parking restrictions—for example, a circle with a slash through it and "*dispari giovedi, 0,00-06,00*" means "don't park on Thursdays between midnight and six in the morning."

Free parking is easy up at Piazzale Michelangelo (see page 1070), but don't park where the buses drop off passengers; park on the side of the piazza farthest from the view. To get from Piazzale Michelangelo to the center of town, take bus #12 or #13.

Car Rental: If you're picking up a rental car upon departure, don't struggle with driving into the center. Taxi with your luggage to the car-rental office, and head out from there.

By Plane

For information on Florence's **Amerigo Vespucci Airport,** see "Florence Connections," near the end of this chapter.

Helpful Hints

Theft Alert: Florence has particularly hardworking thief gangs who hang out where you do: near the train station, the station's underpass (especially where the tunnel surfaces), and at major sights. American tourists—especially older ones—are considered easy targets. Some thieves even dress like tourists to fool you. Be on guard at two squares frequented by drug pushers (Santa Maria Novella and Santo Spirito). Bus #7 (to the nearby town of Fiesole, with great Florence views) is a favorite with tourists and, therefore, with thieves.

Medical Help: There's no shortage of English-speaking medical help in Florence. To reach a doctor who speaks English, call **Medical Service Firenze** at 055-475-411; the phone is answered 24/7. Rates are reasonable. For a doctor to come to your hotel within an hour of your call, you'd pay €100-200 (higher rates apply on Sun, holidays, or for late visits). You pay only €50 if you go to the clinic when the doctor's in (Mon-Fri 11:00-12:00 & 17:00-18:00, Sat 11:00-12:00, closed Sun, no appointment necessary, between the Duomo and Piazza della Repubblica at Via Roma 4).

  Dr. Stephen Kerr is an English doctor specializing in helping sick tourists (drop-in clinic open Mon-Fri 15:00-17:00, other times by appointment, €50/visit, Piazza Mercato Nuovo 1, between Piazza della Repubblica and Ponte Vecchio, tel. 055-288-055, mobile 335-836-1682, www.dr-kerr.com). The TI has a list of other English-speaking doctors.

  There are 24-hour **pharmacies** at the train station and on Borgo San Lorenzo (near the Baptistery).

Museum Strategies: If you want to see a lot of museums, the pricey Firenze Card—which saves you from having to wait in line or make reservations for the Uffizi and Accademia—can be a good value (see page 1044).

Churches: Some churches operate like museums, charging an admission fee to see their art treasures. Modest dress for men, women, and even children is required in some churches (including the Duomo, Santa Maria Novella, Santa Croce, Santa Maria del Carmine—with the Brancacci Chapel, and the Medici Chapels), and recommended for all of them—no bare shoulders, short shorts, or short skirts. At many churches, you can borrow or buy a cheap, disposable poncho for instant respectability. Be respectful of worshippers and the paintings; don't use a flash. Churches usually close from 12:00 or 12:30 to 15:00 or 16:00.

Addresses: For reasons beyond human understanding, Florence has a ridiculously confusing system for street addresses, with separate numbering for businesses (red) and residences (black). In print, this designation is sometimes indicated by a letter following the number: "r" = red; no indication or "n" = black, for *nero*. While usually black, B&B addresses can be either. The red and black numbers each appear in roughly consecutive order on streets but bear no apparent connection with each other. While the numbers are sometimes color-coded on street signs, in many cases they appear in neither red nor black, but in blue! I'm lazy and don't concern myself with the distinction (if one number's wrong, I look nearby for the other) and can easily find my way around.

Chill Out: Schedule several cool breaks into your sightseeing where you can sit, pause, and refresh yourself with a sandwich, gelato, or coffee. Carry a water bottle to refill at Florence's twist-the-handle public fountains. Try the *fontanello* (dispenser of free cold water) on Piazza della Signoria, behind the statue of Neptune (to the left of the Palazzo Vecchio).

Internet Access: Bustling, tourist-filled Florence has many small Internet cafés. **VIP Internet** has cheap rates, numerous terminals, and long hours (€1.50/hour, daily 9:00-24:00, near recommended hotel Katti House at Via Faenza 49 red, tel. 055-264-5552). **Internet Train,** the dominant chain, is pricier, with bright and cheery rooms, speedy computers, and decent hours (€4.30/hour, cheaper for students, reusable card good for any other Internet Train location, open daily roughly 9:00-20:00, www.internettrain.it). Find branches near Piazza della Repubblica (Via Porta Rossa 38 red), behind the Duomo (Via dell'Oriolo 40), and on Piazza Santa Croce (Via de'Benci 36 red). Internet Train also offers Wi-Fi, phone cards, and other services.

FLORENCE

Most hotels have Wi-Fi. If you have a smartphone with an Italian mobile number, you can access free Wi-Fi for an hour at various hotspots around town (the TI can give you a list of hotspots and instructions).

Bookstores: Local guidebooks (sold at kiosks) are cheap, and give you a map and a decent commentary on the sights. For brand-name guidebooks in English (including mine), try **Feltrinelli International** (Mon-Sat 9:00-19:30, closed Sun, a few blocks north of the Duomo and across the street from TI and Medici-Riccardi Palace at Via Cavour 12 red, tel. 055-219-524); **Edison Bookstore** (also has CDs, plus novels on the Renaissance and much more on its four floors; Mon-Sat 9:00-24:00, Sun 10:00-24:00, facing Piazza della Repubblica, tel. 055-213-110); **Paperback Exchange** (cheaper, all books in English, bring in your used book for a discount on a new one, Mon-Fri 9:00-19:30, Sat 10:30-19:30, closed Sun, just south of the Duomo on Via delle Oche 4 red, tel. 055-293-460); or **BM Bookshop** (with perhaps the city's largest collection of English books and guidebooks—including mine; Mon-Sat 9:30-19:30, closed Sun, near Ponte alla Carraia at Borgognissanti 4 red, tel. 055-294-575).

Services: WCs are scarce. Use them when you can, in any café or museum you patronize.

Laundry: The **Wash & Dry Lavarapido** chain offers long hours and efficient, self-service launderettes at several locations (about €7 for wash and dry, bring plenty of coins, daily 8:00-22:00, tel. 055-580-480). These are close to recommended hotels: Via dei Servi 102 red (near *David*), Via del Sole 29 red and Via della Scala 52 red (between train station and river), Via Ghibellina 143 red (Palazzo Vecchio), and Via dei Serragli 87 red (across the river in Oltrarno neighborhood). For more options, the TI has a complete list of launderettes.

Bike Rental: The **city of Florence** rents bikes cheaply at several locations: the train station, Piazza Santa Croce, and Piazza Ghiberti (€2/1 hour, €5/5 hours, €10/day, tel. 055-650-5295; information at any TI). **Florence by Bike** rents two-wheelers of all sizes (€3.50/hour, €9/5 hours, includes bike lock and helmet, child seat-€3 extra; April-Oct daily 9:00-19:30; Nov-March Mon-Sat 9:00-13:00 & 15:30-19:30, closed Sun; Via San Zanobi 120 red, tel. 055-488-992, www.florencebybike.it, info@florencebybike.it).

Travel Agency: While it's easy to buy train tickets to destinations within Italy at handy machines at the station, travel agencies can be more convenient and helpful for getting international tickets, reservations, and supplements. The cost may be the same, or there may be a minimal charge. Ask your hotelier for the nearest travel agency.

FLORENCE

Updates to this Book: For updates to this book, check www.ricksteves.com/update.

Getting Around Florence

I organize my sightseeing geographically and do it all on foot. I think of Florence as a Renaissance treadmill—it requires a lot of walking. You likely won't need public transit, except maybe to head up to Piazzale Michelangelo and San Miniato Church for the view, or to Fiesole.

Buses: The city's full-size buses don't cover the old center well (the whole area around the Duomo is off-limits to motorized traffic). The TI hands out a map of transit routes. Of the many bus lines, I find these to be of most value for seeing outlying sights:

Buses **#12** and **#13** go from the train station to Porta Romana, up to San Miniato Church and Piazzale Michelangelo, and on to Santa Croce.

Bus **#7** goes from Piazza San Marco (near the Accademia and Museum of San Marco) to Fiesole, a small town with big views of Florence.

The train station and Piazza San Marco are two major hubs near the city center; to get between these two, either walk (about 15 minutes) or take bus #1, #6, #14, or #23.

Fun little **minibuses** (many of them electric, *elettrico*) wind through the tangled old center of town and up and down the river—just €1.20 gets you a 90-minute joyride. These buses, which run every 10 minutes, are popular with sore-footed sightseers and eccentric local seniors.

Bus **#C1** stops behind the Palazzo Vecchio and Piazza Santa Croce, then heads north up to Piazza Libertà.

Bus **#C2** twists through the congested old center from the train station to Piazza Beccaria.

Bus **#C3** goes up and down the Arno River, with stops near Ponte Vecchio, the Carraia bridge to Oltrarno, and beyond.

Bus **#D** goes from the train station to Ponte Vecchio, cruises through Oltrarno, and finishes at Ponte San Niccolò.

The minibuses connect many major parking lots with the historical center (tickets sold at machines at lots).

Buy bus tickets at tobacco shops *(tabacchi)*, newsstands, or the ATAF bus office just east of the train station, on Piazza della Stazione (€1.20/90 minutes, €4.70/4 tickets, €5/24 hours, €12/3 days, 1-day and 3-day passes aren't always available in tobacco shops, validate in machine on the bus, tel. 800-424-500, www.ataf.net). You can buy tickets on board, but you'll pay more (€2) and you'll need exact change. City buses are free with the Firenze Card (see page 1044). Follow general bus etiquette: Board at front or rear doors, exit out the center.

Taxi: The minimum cost for a taxi ride is €5, or €6 after 22:00 and on Sundays (rides in the center of town should be charged as tariff #1). A taxi ride from the train station to the Duomo costs about €8. Taxi fares and supplements (e.g., €2 extra if you call a cab rather than hail one) are clearly explained on signs in each taxi. It can be hard to find a cab on the street; to call one, dial 055-4390 or 055-4242.

Tours in Florence

To sightsee on your own, download my series of free audio tours that illuminate some of Florence's top sights and neighborhoods: my Renaissance Walk, the Accademia, and the Uffizi Gallery (see page 7 for details).

Tour companies big and small offer plenty of tours that go out to smaller towns in the Tuscan countryside (the most popular day trips: Siena, San Gimignano, Pisa, and into Chianti country for wine-tasting). They also do Florence city tours, but for most people, the city is really best on foot.

For insight with a personal touch, consider the tour companies and individual Florentine guides listed here. Hardworking and creative, they offer a worthwhile array of organized sightseeing activities. Study their websites for details. If you're taking a city tour, remember that individuals save money with a scheduled public tour (such as those offered daily by Florencetown or ArtViva). If you're traveling as a family or small group, however, you're likely to save money by booking a private guide (since rates are based on roughly €55/hour for any size of group).

Walking (and Biking) Tours
ArtViva Walking Tours
This company offers a variety of tours (up to 12/day year-round) featuring downtown Florence, museum highlights, and Tuscany and Cinque Terre day trips. Their guides are native English-speakers. The three-hour "Original Florence" walk hits the main sights but gets offbeat to weave a picture of Florentine life in medieval and Renaissance times. Tours go rain or shine with as few as four participants (€25, daily at 9:15). Museum tours include the Uffizi Gallery (€39, includes admission, 2 hours), Accademia (called "Original *David*" tour, €35, includes admission, 1 hour), and "Original Florence in One Day" (€94, includes admission to Uffizi and Accademia plus 3-hour town walk, 6 hours). Their brochure and website list more activities, including biking and hiking tours, wine tours, and cooking classes (Mon-Sat 8:00-18:00, Sun 8:30-13:30, near Piazza della Repubblica at Via de' Sassetti 1, second floor, above Odeon Cinema, tel. 055-264-5033 during day or mobile 329-613-2730 from 18:00-20:00, www.artviva.com).

FLORENCE

Florencetown Tours on Foot or by Bike

This well-organized company runs a variety of English-language tours. The boss, Luca Perfetto, offers student rates to anyone with this book, with an additional discount for second tours (if booking on their website, enter the code "RICK2013" when prompted). Three tours—their basic town walk, bike tour, and cooking class—are worth considering: The "Walk and Talk Florence" tour, which takes 2.5 hours, hits all the basic spots, including the Oltrarno neighborhood (€19, daily at 10:00). The "I Bike Florence" tour gives you 2.5 hours on a vintage one-speed bike following a fast-talking guide on a blitz of the town's top sights (€25, daily at 10:00 and 15:00, helmets optional, 15 stops on both sides of the river; in bad weather, the bike tours go as a €19 walking tour). The cooking class costs €79 and includes a market tour; see the listing later. Their office is two blocks from the Palazzo Vecchio at Via de' Lamberti 1 (find steps off Via de' Calzaiuoli on the river side of Orsanmichele Church); they also have an "info point" kiosk on Piazza della Repubblica, at the corner with Via Pellicceria (tel. 055-012-3994, www.florencetown.com).

Walks Inside Florence

Three art historians—Paola Barubiani and her partners Emma Molignoni and Marzia Valbonesi—provide quality guiding. Their company offers a daily 2.5-hour introductory tour (€50/person, 6 people maximum; outside except for a visit inside to see *David*, Accademia entry fee not included) and three-hour private tours (€180, €60/hour for more time, price is for groups of up to 4 people). They also offer an artisans-and-shopping tour, a guided evening walk, cooking classes with a market visit, private cruise excursions from the port of Livorno, and more—see their website for details (ask about Rick Steves discount for any tour, Paola's mobile 335-526-6496, www.walksinsideflorence.com, paola@walksinsideflorence.it).

Florentia

Top-notch private walking tours—geared for thoughtful, well-heeled travelers with longer-than-average attention spans—are led by Florentine scholars. The tours range from introductory city walks and museum visits to in-depth thematic walks, such as the Oltrarno neighborhood, Jewish Florence, and family-oriented tours (tours start at €250, includes personal assistance by email as you plan your trip, reserve in advance, www.florentia.org, info@florentia.org).

Context Florence

This scholarly group of graduate students and professors leads "walking seminars," such as a 3.5-hour study of Michelangelo's work and influence (€75/person, plus museum admission) and a two-hour evening orientation stroll (€40/person). I enjoyed the

Florence at a Glance

▲▲▲**Accademia** Michelangelo's *David* and powerful (unfinished) *Prisoners*. Reserve ahead or get a Firenze Card. **Hours:** Tue-Sun 8:15-18:50, closed Mon. See page 1046.

▲▲▲**Duomo Museum** Underrated cathedral museum with sculptures. **Hours:** Mon-Sat 9:00-19:30, Sun 9:00-13:40. See page 1056.

▲▲▲**Bargello** Underappreciated sculpture museum (Michelangelo, Donatello, Medici treasures). **Hours:** Tue-Sat 8:15-13:50, until 16:50 during special exhibits (typically April-Oct); also open first, third, and fifth Mon and second and fourth Sun of each month. See page 1057.

▲▲▲**Uffizi Gallery** Greatest collection of Italian paintings anywhere. Reserve well in advance or get a Firenze Card. **Hours:** Tue-Sun 8:15-18:35, closed Mon. See page 1060.

▲▲**Museum of San Marco** Best collection anywhere of artwork by the early Renaissance master Fra Angelico. **Hours:** Tue-Fri 8:15-13:50, Sat 8:15-16:50; also open 8:15-13:50 on first, third, and fifth Mon and 8:15-16:50 on second and fourth Sun of each month. See page 1048.

▲▲**Medici Chapels** Tombs of Florence's great ruling family, designed and carved by Michelangelo. **Hours:** Tue-Sat April-Oct 8:15-16:50, Nov-March 8:15-13:50; also open second and fourth Mon and first, third, and fifth Sun of each month. See page 1050.

▲▲**Duomo** Gothic cathedral with colorful facade and the first dome built since ancient Roman times. **Hours:** Mon-Fri 10:00-17:00, Thu until 16:00 Oct-May, Sat 10:00-16:45, Sun 13:30-16:45. See page 1052.

▲▲**Palazzo Vecchio** Fortified palace, once home to the Medici, wallpapered with history. **Hours:** Fri-Wed 9:00-19:00, until 24:00 April-Sept; Thu 9:00-14:00 year-round. See page 1063.

▲▲**Galileo Science Museum** Fascinating old clocks, telescopes, maps, and Galileo's finger in a bottle. **Hours:** Wed-Mon 9:30-18:00, Tue 9:30-13:00. See page 1064.

▲▲**Santa Croce Church** Precious art, tombs of famous Florentines, and Brunelleschi's Pazzi Chapel in 14th-century church. **Hours:** Mon-Sat 9:30-17:30, Sun 14:00-17:30. See page 1065.

▲▲**Church of Santa Maria Novella** Thirteenth-century Dominican church with Masaccio's famous 3-D painting. **Hours:** Church—Mon-

FLORENCE

Thu 9:00-17:30, Fri 11:00-17:30, Sat 9:00-17:00, Sun 13:00-17:00; museum—Fri-Mon 9:00-16:00, closed Tue-Thu. See page 1066.

▲▲**Pitti Palace** Several museums in lavish palace plus sprawling Boboli and Bardini gardens. **Hours:** Palatine Gallery, Royal Apartments, and Gallery of Modern Art: Tue-Sun 8:15-18:50, closed Mon; Boboli and Bardini gardens, Costume Gallery, Argenti/Silverworks Museum, and Porcelain Museum: Daily 8:15-18:30, until 19:30 June-Aug, gardens close as early as 16:30 in winter, closed first and last Mon of each month. See page 1066.

▲▲**Brancacci Chapel** Works of Masaccio, early Renaissance master who reinvented perspective. **Hours:** Mon and Wed-Sat 10:00-17:00, Sun 13:00-17:00, closed Tue. Reservations required, though often available on the spot. See page 1068.

▲▲**San Miniato Church** Sumptuous Renaissance chapel and sacristy showing scenes of St. Benedict. **Hours:** Daily Easter-mid-Oct 8:00-20:00 or possibly later, in winter 8:30-13:00 & 15:30-19:00. See page 1071.

▲**Medici-Riccardi Palace** Lorenzo the Magnificent's home, with fine art, frescoed ceilings, and Gozzoli's lovely Chapel of the Magi. **Hours:** Thu-Tue 9:00-18:00, closed Wed. See page 1051.

▲**Climbing the Duomo's Dome** Grand view into the cathedral, close-up of dome architecture, and, after 463 steps, a glorious Florence vista. **Hours:** Mon-Fri 8:30-19:00, Sat 8:30-17:40, closed Sun. Long and slow lines—go early, or try reserving online (if that's offered). See page 1053.

▲**Campanile** Bell tower with views similar to Duomo's, 50 fewer steps, and fewer lines. **Hours:** Daily 8:30-19:30. See page 1053.

▲**Baptistery** Bronze doors fit to be the gates of paradise. **Hours:** Doors always viewable; interior open Mon-Sat 12:15-19:00 except first Sat of each month 8:30-14:00, Sun 8:30-14:00. See page 1056.

▲**Ponte Vecchio** Famous bridge lined with gold and silver shops. **Hours:** Bridge always open (shops closed at night). See page 1063.

▲**Casa Buonarroti** Early, lesser-known works by Michelangelo. **Hours:** Wed-Mon 10:00-17:00, closed Tue. See page 1065.

▲**Piazzale Michelangelo** Hilltop square with stunning view of Duomo and Florence, with San Miniato Church just uphill. **Hours:** Always open. See page 1070.

FLORENCE

fascinating three-hour fresco workshop (€75/person plus materials, you take home a fresco you make yourself). See their website for other innovative offerings: Medici walk, lecture series, food walks, kids' tours, and programs in Venice, Rome, Naples, London, and Paris (tel. 06-967-27371, US tel. 215/609-4888 or 800-691-6036, www.contexttravel.com, info@contexttravel.com).

Cooking Classes and Market Tour

For something special, consider this five-hour experience offered by **Florencetown.** You'll start with a trip to the Mercato Centrale for shopping and tasting, then settle into their kitchen for a cooking lesson that finishes with a big feast of everything you've cooked. You'll meet butchers and bakers, and make bruschetta, pasta, a main course, and dessert (likely tiramisu). Groups are intimate and small (from 1-25 people, €79/person, ask for Rick Steves discount, Mon-Sat 10:00-15:00, runs rain or shine, chef Giovanni, Via de Lamberti 1, tel. 055-012-3994, www.florencetown.com).

Local Guides for Private Tours

Alessandra Marchetti, a Florentine who has lived in the US, gives private walking tours of Florence and driving tours of Tuscany (€60-75/hour, mobile 347-386-9839, aleoberm@tin.it).

Paola Migliorini and her partners offer museum tours, city walking tours, private cooking classes, wine tours, and Tuscan excursions by van—you can tailor tours as you like (€60/hour without car, €70/hour in an 8-seat van, tel. 055-472-448, mobile 347-657-2611, www.florencetour.com, info@florencetour.com); they also do private tours from the cruise-ship port of Livorno.

Karin Kibby, an Oregonian living in Livorno who leads Rick Steves tours, also offers day trips throughout Tuscany, including private excursions for cruise-ship passengers docking at Livorno. She'll work with you to find the best solution for your budget and interests (2-10 people, mobile 333-108-6348, karinkintuscany@yahoo.it).

Roberto Bechi, a great guide based in Siena, can come pick you up in Florence for off-the-beaten-path tours of the Tuscan countryside (mobile 328-425-5648, www.toursbyroberto.com, toursbyroberto@gmail.com). If you book any tour with Roberto, he can advise you on other aspects of your trip.

Hop-on, Hop-off Bus Tours

Around town, you'll see big double-decker sightseeing buses double-parking near major sights. Tourists on the top deck can listen to brief recorded descriptions of the sights, snap photos, and enjoy a drive-by look at major landmarks (€16/1 calendar day, €22/48 hours, pay as you board, www.firenze.city-sightseeing.it). As the name implies, you can hop off when you want and catch the next bus (usually every 30 minutes). But since the most important sights are buried in the old center where big buses can't go, Florence doesn't really lend itself to this kind of tour bus. Look at the route map before committing.

Driving Tours

500 Touring Club offers a unique look at Florence: from behind the wheel of one of the most iconic Italian cars, a vintage, restored Fiat 500. After a lesson *in la doppietta* (double-clutching), you'll head off in a guided convoy, following a lead car with live commentary via the radio and photo stops at the best viewpoints. Tours depart from a 15th-century villa on the edge of town; the Fiats are restored models from the 1960s and 1970s. Itineraries vary from basic sightseeing to countryside excursions with wine-making and lunch; see their website for options (2-hour tour–€60/person, US tel. 347/535-0030, Italian mobile 346-826-2324, Via Gherardo Silvani 149a, www.500touringclub.com, info@500touringclub.com, Andrea).

Weekend Tour Packages for Students

Andy Steves (my son) runs **Weekend Student Adventures,** offering active and experiential three-day weekend tours from €199, designed for American students studying abroad (www.wsaeurope.com for details on tours of Florence and other great cities).

Self-Guided Walk

A Renaissance Walk Through Florence

During the Dark Ages, it was especially obvious to the people of Italy—sitting on the rubble of Rome—that there had to be a brighter age on the horizon. The long-awaited rebirth, or Renaissance, began in Florence for good reason. Wealthy because of its cloth industry, trade, and banking; powered by a fierce city-state pride (locals would pee into the Arno with gusto, knowing rival city-state Pisa was downstream); and fertile with more than its share of artistic genius (imagine guys like Michelangelo and Leonardo attending the same high school)—Florence was a natural home for this cultural explosion.

Take a two-hour walk through the core of Renaissance Florence from the Duomo (cathedral) to Ponte Vecchio on the Arno River. You can download a free Rick Steves audio tour of this walk (see page 7).

Begin at the Duomo to marvel at the dome that kicked off the architectural Renaissance. Step inside the Baptistery to view a ceiling covered with preachy, flat, 2-D, medieval mosaic art. Then, to learn what happened when art met math, check out the realistic 3-D reliefs on the doors; the man who painted them, Giotto, also designed the bell tower—an early example of a Renaissance genius who excelled in many areas.

Continue toward the river on Florence's great pedestrian mall, Via de' Calzaiuoli—part of the original grid plan given to the city by the ancient Romans. Stop by any gelato shop for some cool refreshment. Down a few blocks, compare medieval and Renaissance statues on the exterior of the Orsanmichele Church. Via de' Calzaiuoli connects the cathedral with the central square (Piazza della Signoria), the city palace (Palazzo Vecchio), and the Uffizi Gallery, which contains the greatest collection of Italian Renaissance paintings in captivity. Finally, walk through the Uffizi courtyard—a statuary thinktank of Renaissance greats—to the Arno River and Ponte Vecchio.

Sights in Florence

Avoid long ticket-buying lines at many sights and museums (especially the Uffizi and Accademia) by buying a Firenze Card or making advance reservations. Unfortunately, no single option works for every sight, so it's well worth your time to study the following options and plan ahead.

Firenze Card

The Firenze Card (€50) is pricey but convenient. This three-day sightseeing pass gives you admission to many of Florence's sights, including the Uffizi Gallery and Accademia. Just as important, it lets you skip the ticket-buying lines without making reservations. For busy sightseers, the card can save some money. And for anyone, it can certainly save time. For people seeing five or six major sights in a short time, the card is well worth it. (But if you only want to see the Uffizi and Accademia, you'll save at least €20 by making individual reservations instead; see "Advance Reservations," later.)

With the card, you simply go to the entrance at a covered sight (if there's a "with reservations" door, use it), show the card, and they let you in (though there may be delays on especially crowded days).

The Firenze Card is valid for 72 hours from when you validate it at your first museum (e.g., Tue at 15:00 until Fri at 15:00). It includes regular admission price as well as any temporary exhibits (which are commonly tacked on at major sights such as the Uffizi). The card is good for one visit per sight. It also gives you free use of Florence city buses. The card is not shareable, and there are no family or senior discounts for Americans or Canadians.

To figure out if the Firenze Card is a good deal for you, tally up the entry fees of what you want to see. For example, here's a list of popular sights and their admission fees:

- Uffizi Gallery (€6.50 base price, usually €11 with temporary exhibits, as much as €15 with €4 reservation fee)
- Accademia (same fees as Uffizi)
- Palazzo Vecchio (€6.50)
- Bargello (€4 base, €7 with exhibits)
- Medici Chapels (€6 base, €9 with exhibits)
- Museum of San Marco (€4)
- Medici-Riccardi Palace (€7)

If you saw these sights without the card you'd pay about €60, including the exhibit and reservation fees. Other covered sights featured in this chapter include the various Duomo-related sights (dome climb, Campanile, Duomo Museum, and Baptistery), Pitti Palace (both Palatine Gallery and Boboli Gardens), Brancacci Chapel, Church of Santa Maria Novella, Museum of Santa Maria Novella, Santa Croce Church, Casa Buonarroti, Casa di Dante, Museum of Precious Stones, Palazzo Davanzati, and Galileo Science Museum. The card is great for popping into lesser sights you otherwise wouldn't pay for. For a complete list of included sights, see www.firenzecard.it.

The two Leonardo museums are not covered by the Firenze Card. The Baptistery, Campanile, dome climb, and Duomo Museum are also covered by a combo-ticket.

Getting the card makes the most sense from April through October, when crowds are worst. Off-season travelers could do without it.

You can buy the card at TIs and many participating sights. The handiest places are the TI at Via Cavour 1 red (a couple of blocks north of the Duomo), the Museum of Santa Maria Novella (next to the church of that name), and the Uffizi's door #2. See the full list of outlets at www.firenzecard.it.

Validate your card only when you're ready to tackle the covered sights on three consecutive days. Make sure the sights you want to visit will be open (many sights are closed Sun or Mon).

Advance Reservations

Florence has an optional reservation system (€4 booking fee) for its state-run sights—including the Accademia, Uffizi Gallery, Bargello, Medici Chapels, and the Pitti Palace. (The Brancacci Chapel technically *requires* an advance reservation, but you can work around that—see page 1069.) I'd recommend reservations only for the Uffizi and Accademia. For the Uffizi, book a month in advance for April-Oct travel (less off-season). For the Accademia, book a few days ahead for April-Oct (less off-season. From November to March, you can probably get in without a reservation after 16:00,

FLORENCE

but why risk it? After seeing hundreds of bored tourists waiting in lines, it's hard not to be amazed at their cluelessness.

Here are your reservation options:

• **Through Your Hotel:** When you make your hotel reservation, ask if they can book your museum reservations for you. Some hoteliers may charge a €3-5 fee above the €4 booking fee. They'll reserve by phone and give you a confirmation number that you'll take to the museum, where you'll pay cash for your ticket. This is your easiest reservation option.

• **By Phone:** From the US, dial 011-39-055-294-883, or within Italy call 055-294-883. The lines are open (Italian time) Mon-Fri 8:30-18:30, Sat 8:30-12:30, closed Sun. The reservation line is often busy. Be persistent. When you get through, an English-speaking operator walks you through the process—a few minutes later you say *grazie*, having secured an entry time and a confirmation number. You'll need to present your confirmation number at the museum and pay cash for your ticket plus the €4 reservation fee.

• **Online:** Sites such as www.uffizi.com and www.tickitaly.com are easy and reliable, but they require paying in advance with a credit card and charge a hefty €10-per-ticket reservation fee. The city's official site (www.firenzemusei.it) is only €4, but it's troublesome and not user-friendly.

• **Reserve in Florence:** Try to score a same-day reservation (€4) at the booking window at Orsanmichele Church (daily 10:00-17:00, along Via de' Calzaiuoli—see location on map on page 1048); the My Accademia Libreria bookstore across from the Accademia (Tue-Sun 8:15-17:30, closed Mon, Via Ricasoli 105 red—see map on page 1054); or the Uffizi's door #2—skirt to the left of the long ticket-buying line (Tue-Sun 8:15-18:35).

• **Private Tour:** Take a tour that includes your museum admission (see listings of tour companies on page 1038).

Sights North of the Arno River
North of the Duomo (Cathedral)
▲▲▲Accademia (Galleria dell'Accademia)

When you look into the eyes of Michelangelo's magnificent sculpture of *David*, you're looking into the eyes of Renaissance Man.

In 1501, Michelangelo Buonarroti, a 26-year-old Florentine, was commissioned to carve a large-scale work. The figure comes from a Bible story. The Israelites are surrounded by barbarian warriors, who are led by a brutish giant named Goliath. When the giant challenges the Israelites to send out someone to fight him, a young shepherd boy steps forward. Armed only with a sling, David defeats the giant. This 17-foot-tall symbol of divine victory over evil represents a new century and a whole new Renaissance outlook.

Originally, *David* was meant to stand on the roofline of the Duomo, but was placed more prominently at the entrance of the Palazzo Vecchio (where a copy stands today). In the 19th century, *David* was moved indoors for his own protection, and stands under a wonderful Renaissance-style dome designed just for him.

Nearby are some of the master's other works, including his powerful (unfinished) *Prisoners*, *St. Matthew*, and a *Pietà* (possibly by one of his disciples). Florentine Michelangelo Buonarroti, who would work tirelessly through the night, believed that the sculptor was a tool of God, responsible only for chipping away at the stone until the intended sculpture emerged. Beyond the magic marble are some mildly interesting pre-Renaissance and Renaissance paintings, including a couple of lighter-than-air Botticellis, the plaster model of Giambologna's *Rape of the Sabine Women*, and a musical instrument collection with an early piano.

Cost and Hours: €6.50, up to €11 with mandatory exhibits, plus €4 reservation fee; Tue-Sun 8:15-18:50, closed Mon, last entry 30 minutes before closing; no photos, Via Ricasoli 60, reservation tel. 055-294-883, www.polomuseale.firenze.it. To avoid long lines in peak season, get the Firenze Card (described earlier) or make reservations (see page 1045).

Avoiding Lines: In peak season (April-Oct), the museum is most crowded on Sunday, Tuesday, and between about 11:00 and 13:00. It's smart to buy a Firenze Card or reserve ahead (see pages 1044 and 1045 for info on both options). Those with reservations or the Firenze Card line up at the entrance labeled *With Reservations*. If you show up without a reservation or Firenze Card, and there's a long line, try dropping by the My Accademia Libreria reservation office, just across the street from the exit, to see if they have any reservations available later that day (€4 reservation charge). On off-season weekdays (Nov-March) before 8:30 or after 16:00, you can sometimes get in with no reservation and no lines.

Audioguides: The museum rents a €6 audioguide (€10/2 people; rent from souvenir counter in ticket lobby). You can download a free Rick Steves audio tour of the Accademia; see page 7.

Nearby: Piazza S.S. Annunziata, behind the Accademia, displays lovely Renaissance harmony. Facing the square are two fine buildings: the 15th-century Santissima Annunziata church (worth a peek) and Filippo Brunelleschi's Hospital of the Innocents (Spedale degli Innocenti, not worth going inside), with terra-cotta medallions by Luca della Robbia. Built in the 1420s, the hospital is considered the first Renaissance building. I love sleeping on this square (at the recommended Hotel Loggiato dei Serviti) and picnicking here during the day (with the riffraff, who remind me of the persistent gap—today as in Renaissance times—between those who appreciate fine art and those just looking for some cheap wine).

FLORENCE

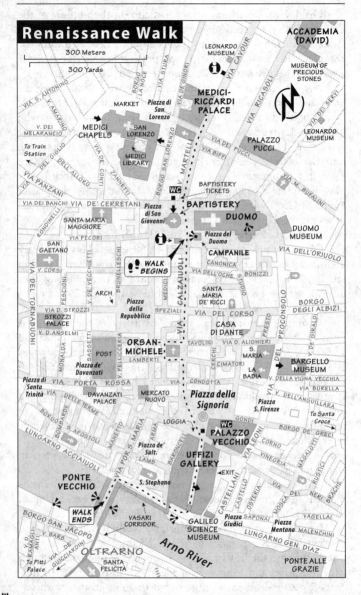

Renaissance Walk

300 Meters

300 Yards

ACCADEMIA (DAVID)

LEONARDO MUSEUM

MUSEUM OF PRECIOUS STONES

MEDICI-RICCARDI PALACE

LEONARDO MUSEUM

MARKET

Piazza di San Lorenzo

PALAZZO PUCCI

MEDICI CHAPELS

SAN LORENZO

To Train Station

MEDICI LIBRARY

BAPTISTERY TICKETS

WC

Piazza di San Giovanni

BAPTISTERY

DUOMO

DUOMO MUSEUM

SANTA MARIA MAGGIORE

Piazza del Duomo

CAMPANILE

CANONICA

SAN GAETANO

WALK BEGINS

ARCH

Piazza della Repubblica

SANTA MARIA DE' RICCI

CASA DI DANTE

STROZZI PALACE

ORSAN-MICHELE

VIA DEL CORSO

S. MARIA LA BADIA

BARGELLO MUSEUM

Piazza di Santa Trinita

Piazza de' Davanzati

POST

DAVANZATI PALACE

MERCATO NUOVO

Piazza della Signoria

Piazza S. Firenze

To Santa Croce

LOGGIA

WC

PALAZZO VECCHIO

Piazza de' Salt.

UFFIZI GALLERY

S. Stephano

PONTE VECCHIO

WALK ENDS

VASARI CORRIDOR

GALILEO SCIENCE MUSEUM

Piazza Giudici

Piazza Mentana

To Pitti Palace

SANTA FELICITA

OLTRARNO

Arno River

PONTE ALLE GRAZIE

FLORENCE

▲▲Museum of San Marco (Museo di San Marco)

Located one block north of the Accademia, this 15th-century monastery houses the greatest collection anywhere of frescoes and paintings by the early Renaissance master Fra Angelico. The ground floor features the monk's paintings, along with some works by Fra Bartolomeo. Upstairs are 43 cells decorated by Fra Angelico and his assistants. While the monk/painter was trained in the medieval religious style, he also learned and adopted Renaissance techniques and sensibilities, producing works that blended Christian symbols and Renaissance realism. Don't miss the cell of Savonarola, the charismatic monk who rode in from the Christian right, threw out the ruling Medici family, turned Florence into a theocracy, sponsored "bonfires of the vanities" (burning books, paintings, and so on), and was finally burned himself when Florence decided to change channels.

Cost and Hours: €4, covered by Firenze Card, Tue-Fri 8:15-13:50, Sat 8:15-16:50; also open 8:15-13:50 on first, third, and fifth Mon and 8:15-16:50 on second and fourth Sun of each month; last entry 30 minutes before closing, reservations possible but unnecessary, no photos, on Piazza San Marco, tel. 055-238-8608, www.polomuseale.firenze.it.

Museum of Precious Stones
(Museo dell'Opificio delle Pietre Dure)

This unusual gem of a museum features room after room of exquisite mosaics of inlaid marble and other stones. The Medici loved colorful stone tabletops and floors; you'll even find landscapes and portraits (find Cosimo I in Room I). Upstairs, you'll see wooden work benches from a workshop funded by the art-patron Medici family (1588), complete with foot-powered power tools. Rockhounds can browse 500 different stones (lapis lazuli, quartz, agate, marble, and so on) and the tools used to cut and inlay them. Borrow the English descriptions in each room.

Cost and Hours: €4, covered by Firenze Card, Mon-Sat 8:15-14:00, closed Sun, last entry 30 minutes before closing, around corner from Accademia at Via degli Alfani 78, tel. 055-265-1357.

Church of San Lorenzo

This red-brick dome—which looks like the Duomo's little sister—marks the burial place of Giovanni di Bicci de' Medici (1360-1429), founder of the influential Medici family. Part *Sopranos*, part Kennedys, part John-D-and-Catherine-T art patrons, the Medici dominated Florentine politics for 300 years (c. 1434-1737). Immeasurably wealthy from their cloth, silk, and banking businesses, the family rose to the ranks of Europe's nobility, producing popes and queens.

Cost and Hours: €3.50, buy ticket just inside cloister next door, €6 combo-ticket covers Laurentian Library; March-Oct Mon-Sat 10:00-17:30, Sun 13:30-17:30; Nov-Jan Mon-Sat 10:00-17:30, closed Sun; last entry 30 minutes before closing.

Visiting the Church: The facade is big, ugly, and unfinished, because Pope Leo X (also a Medici) pulled the plug on the project due to dwindling funds—after Michelangelo had labored on it for four years (1516-1520). Inside, though, is the spirit of Florence in the 1420s, with gray-and-white columns and arches in perfect

Renaissance symmetry and simplicity. The Brunelleschi-designed church is lit by an even, diffused light. The Medici coat of arms (with the round pills of these "medics") decorates the ceiling, and everywhere are images of St. Lawrence, the Medici patron saint who was martyred on a grill.

Highlights of the church include two finely sculpted Donatello pulpits (in the nave). In the Martelli Chapel (left wall of the left transept), Filippo Lippi's *Annunciation* features a smiling angel greeting Mary in a sharply 3-D courtyard. Light shines through the vase in the foreground, like the Holy Spirit entering Mary's womb. The Old Sacristy (far left corner), designed by Brunelleschi, was the burial chapel for the Medici. Bronze doors by Donatello flank the sacristy's small altar. Overhead, the dome above the altar shows the exact arrangement of the heavens on July 4, 1442, leaving scholars to hypothesize about why that particular date was used. Back in the nave, the round inlaid marble in the floor before the main altar marks where Cosimo the Elder is buried. Assistants in the church provide information on request, and the information brochure is free and in English.

Nearby: Outside the church, just to the left of the main door, is a **cloister** with peek-a-boo Duomo views and the **San Lorenzo Museum.** This collection of fancy reliquaries is included in your church admission, but is hardly worth the walk, except to see Donatello's grave. Also in the cloister is the **Laurentian Library** (€3, €6 combo-ticket with church, includes special exhibits, generally Mon and Fri-Sat 9:30-13:30, Tue-Thu 9:30-17:15, closed Sun). The library, largely designed by Michelangelo, stars his impressive staircase, which widens imperceptibly as it descends. Michelangelo also did the walls in the vestibule (entrance) that feature empty niches, scrolls, and oddly tapering pilasters. Climb the stairs and enter the Reading Room—a long, rectangular hall with a coffered-wood ceiling—designed by Michelangelo to host scholars enjoying the Medici's collection of manuscripts.

A **street market** bustles outside the church (listed after the Medici Chapels, next). Around the back end of the church is the entrance to the Medici Chapels and the New Sacristy, designed by Michelangelo for a later generation of dead Medici.

▲▲Medici Chapels (Cappelle Medicee)

The burial site of the ruling Medici family in the Church of San Lorenzo includes the dusky Crypt; the big, domed Chapel of Princes; and the magnificent New Sacristy, featuring architecture, tombs, and statues almost entirely by Michelangelo. The Medici made their money in textiles and banking, and patronized a dream team of Renaissance artists that put Florence on the cultural map. Michelangelo, who spent his teen years living with the Medici, was commissioned for the family's final tribute.

Cost and Hours: €6, €9 with mandatory exhibits, covered by Firenze Card; Tue-Sat April-Oct 8:15-16:50, Nov-March 8:15-13:50; also open second and fourth Mon and first, third, and fifth Sun of each month; last entry 30 minutes before closing; reservations possible but unnecessary, audioguide-€6 (€10/2 people), modest dress required, no photos, tel. 055-238-8602, www.polo-museale.firenze.it.

▲San Lorenzo Market

Florence's vast open-air market sprawls around the Church of San Lorenzo. Most of the leather stalls are run by Iranians selling South American leather that was tailored in Italy. Prices are soft (daily 9:00-19:00, closed Mon in winter, between the Duomo and train station).

▲Mercato Centrale (Central Market)

Florence's giant iron-and-glass-covered central market, a wonderland of picturesque produce, is fun to explore. While the nearby San Lorenzo Market—with its garment stalls in the streets—feels like a step up from a haphazard flea market, the Mercato Centrale retains a Florentine elegance. Wander around. You'll see parts of the cow you'd never dream of eating (no, that's not a turkey neck), enjoy generous free samples, watch pasta-making, and have your pick of plenty of fun eateries sloshing out cheap and tasty pasta to locals (Mon-Sat 7:00-14:00, in winter open Sat until 17:00, closed Sun year-round). For eating ideas in and around the market, see "Eating in Florence," later.

▲Medici-Riccardi Palace (Palazzo Medici-Riccardi)

Lorenzo the Magnificent's home is worth a look for its art. The tiny Chapel of the Magi contains colorful Renaissance gems such as the *Procession of the Magi* frescoes by Benozzo Gozzoli. The former library has a Baroque ceiling fresco by Luca Giordano, a prolific artist from Naples known as "Fast Luke" *(Luca fa presto)* for his speedy workmanship. While the Medici originally occupied this 1444 house, in the 1700s it became home to the Riccardi family, who added the Baroque flourishes. While the palace is rarely mobbed, you may encounter a slight bottleneck at the Chapel of the Magi (Cappella di Gozzoli). Only 10 people are allowed in at a time, but the line moves quickly.

Cost and Hours: €7, covered by Firenze Card, Thu-Tue 9:00-18:00, closed Wed, last entry 30 minutes before closing, ticket entrance is north of the main gated entrance, audio/videoguide-€4, no photos in Chapel of the Magi, Via Cavour 3, tel. 055-276-0340, www.palazzo-medici.it.

Leonardo Museums

Two different-but-similar entrepreneurial establishments several blocks apart show off reproductions of Leonardo's ingenious inventions. Either one is fun for anyone who wants to crank the shaft

FLORENCE

and spin the ball bearings of Leonardo's fertile imagination. While there are no actual historic artifacts, each museum shows several dozen of Leonardo's inventions and experiments made into working models. You might see a full-size armored tank, walk into a chamber of mirrors, operate a rotating crane, or watch experiments in flying. The exhibits are described in English, and what makes these places special is that you're encouraged to touch and play with the models—it's great for kids. The museum on Via dei Servi is a bit larger.

Cost and Hours: Admission to each museum is €7. Museo Leonardo da Vinci—daily 10:00-19:00, Nov-March until 18:00, Via dei Servi 66 red, tel. 055-282-966, www.mostredileonardo. com. Le Macchine di Leonardo da Vinci—April-Oct daily 9:30-19:30; Nov-March Mon-Fri 11:00-17:00, Sat-Sun 9:30-19:30; for €1 extra they'll throw in a slice of pizza and a Coke, in Galleria Michelangelo at Via Cavour 21, tel. 055-295-264, www.macchin-edileonardo.com.

Duomo and Nearby

The following Duomo-related sights are all covered with a single combo-ticket. This €10 ticket admits you to the Baptistery, dome, Campanile, Duomo Museum, and church crypt (the church itself is free). Two good places to buy your ticket are at the rarely crowded Duomo Museum and the Centro Arte e Cultura (a few steps north of the Baptistery at Piazza di San Giovanni 7).

The Firenze Card (see page 1044) also covers all of these sights (except the uninteresting crypt).

▲▲Duomo (Cattedrale di Santa Maria del Fiore)

Florence's Gothic cathedral has the third-longest nave in Christendom. The church's noisy facade looks old, but it's actually Neo-Gothic, from the 1870s. Covered with pink, green, and white Tuscan marble, the facade was rushed to completion (about 600 years after the building began) to celebrate Italian unity, here in the city that briefly served as the young country's capital. Its "retro" look is meant to capture the feel of the original medieval facade.

In the interior, you'll see a huge *Last Judgment* by Giorgio Vasari and Federico Zuccari (inside the dome). Much of the church's great art is stored behind the church in the Duomo Museum (which is partially closed for renovation until 2015).

The cathedral's claim to artistic fame is Brunelleschi's magnificent dome—the first Renaissance dome and the model for domes to follow. Think of the confidence of the age: The Duomo was built with a big hole in its roof, awaiting a dome...but it was built before the technology to span the hole with a dome even existed. No *problema*. They knew that someone soon could rise to the challenge... and the local architect Filippo Brunelleschi did. First, he built the

FLORENCE

grand white skeletal ribs, which you can see, then filled them in with interlocking bricks in a herringbone pattern. The dome grew upward like an igloo, supporting itself as it proceeded from the base. When the ribs reached the top, Brunelleschi arched them in and fixed them in place with the cupola at the top. His dome, built in only 14 years, was the largest since Rome's Pantheon.

Visible from all over the city, the dome of Florence's cathedral has inspired Florentines to do great things. Most recently, it inspired the city to make the area around the cathedral delightfully traffic-free.

Cost and Hours: Cathedral interior—free; Mon-Fri 10:00-17:00, Thu until 16:00 May and Oct, until 16:30 Nov-April; Sat 10:00-16:45, Sun 13:30-16:45, audioguide-€5, free English tours offered but fill up fast, modest dress code enforced, tel. 055-230-2885, www.operaduomo.firenze.it.

Crowd-Beating Tips: Massive crowds line up to see the huge church: Although it's a major sight, it's not worth a long wait. To avoid the lines, go late, as crowds tend to subside by late afternoon.

▲Climbing the Duomo's Dome

Brunelleschi's dome was the wonder of the age, the model for many domes to follow, from St. Peter's to the US Capitol. People gave it the ultimate compliment, saying, "Not even the ancients could have done it."

For a grand view into the cathedral from the base of the dome, a peek at some of the tools used in the dome's construction, a chance to see Brunelleschi's "dome-within-a-dome" construction, a glorious Florence view from the top, and the equivalent of 463 plunges on a Renaissance StairMaster, climb the dome. Michelangelo, setting out to construct the dome of St. Peter's in Rome, drew inspiration from the dome of Florence. He said, "I'll make its sister...bigger, but not more beautiful."

Cost and Hours: €10 ticket covers all Duomo sights, also covered by Firenze Card, Mon-Fri 8:30-19:00, Sat 8:30-17:40, closed Sun, last entry 40 minutes before closing, arrive by 8:30 or drop by very late for the fewest crowds, enter from outside church on north side, tel. 055-230-2885.

▲Campanile (Giotto's Tower)

The 270-foot bell tower has 50 fewer steps than the Duomo's dome (but that's still 413 steps—no elevator); offers a faster, relatively less-crowded climb; and has a view of that magnificent dome to boot. On the way up, there are several intermediate levels where you can catch your breath and enjoy ever-higher views. The stairs narrow as you go up, creating a mosh-pit bottleneck near the very top—but the views are worth the hassle. While the various viewpoints are enclosed by cage-like bars, the gaps are big enough to let you snap great photos.

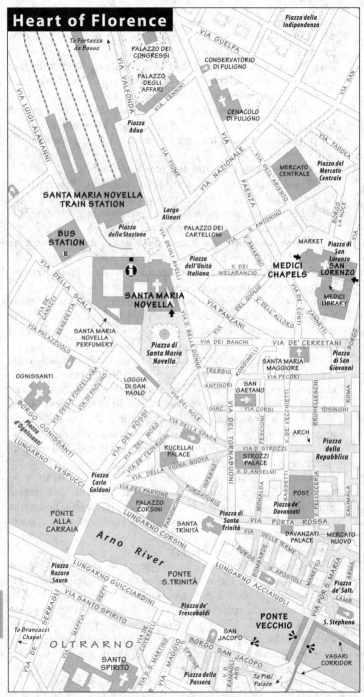

Heart of Florence

FLORENCE

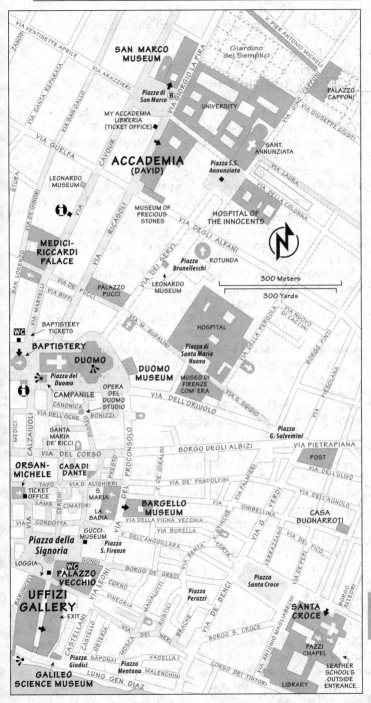

Cost and Hours: €10 ticket covers all Duomo sights, also covered by Firenze Card, daily 8:30-19:30, last entry 40 minutes before closing.

▲Baptistery

Michelangelo said its bronze doors were fit to be the gates of paradise. Check out the gleaming copies of Lorenzo Ghiberti's bronze doors facing the Duomo (the original panels are in the Duomo Museum). Making a breakthrough in perspective, Ghiberti used mathematical laws to create the illusion of receding distance on a basically flat surface.

The doors on the north side of the building were designed by Ghiberti when he was young; he'd won the honor and opportunity by beating Brunelleschi in a competition (the rivals' original entries are in the Bargello).

Inside, sit and savor the medieval mosaic ceiling, where it's always Judgment Day and Jesus is giving the ultimate thumbs-up and thumbs-down.

Cost and Hours: €10 ticket covers all Duomo sights, also covered by Firenze Card, interior open Mon-Sat 12:15-19:00 except first Sat of month 8:30-14:00, Sun 8:30-14:00, last entry 30 minutes before closing, audioguide-€2, tel. 055-230-2885. The bronze doors are on the outside, so they are always "open" and viewable.

▲▲▲Duomo Museum (Museo dell'Opera del Duomo)

The underrated cathedral museum, behind the church (at Via del Proconsolo 9), is great if you like sculpture (parts may be closed for renovation during your visit). It holds many of the original creations that defined the 1400s (the Quattrocento) in Florence, when the city blossomed and classical arts were reborn. On the ground floor, look for a late Michelangelo *Pietà* that was intended as his sculptural epitaph, and statues from the original Baptistery facade. The museum also features Ghiberti's original bronze "Gates of Paradise" panels (the ones on the Baptistery's doors today are replicas). While copies now decorate the exteriors of the Duomo (cathedral) and Campanile (bell tower, called Giotto's Tower), the original sculptured masterpieces from both are now restored and displayed safely indoors at the Duomo Museum. Upstairs, you'll find Brunelleschi's models for his dome, as well as Donatello's anorexic *Mary Magdalene* and playful choir loft. Though overlooked by most visitors to Florence, this refurbished museum is a delight.

Cost and Hours: €10 ticket covers all Duomo sights, also covered by Firenze Card; Mon-Sat 9:00-19:30, Sun 9:00-13:40, last entry 40 minutes before closing, one of the few museums in Florence always open on Mon, audioguide-€5, Via del Proconsolo 9, tel. 055-282-226, www.operaduomo.firenze.it.

Tours: The audioguide costs €5. Guided English tours are generally offered daily in summer for €3 (as they use volunteer guides, schedules vary—stop by or call to ask).

Nearby: If you find this church art intriguing, head to the left around the back of the Duomo to find Via dello Studio (near the south transept), then walk a block toward the river to #23a (freestanding yellow house on the right). You can look through the open doorway of the **Opera del Duomo art studio** and see workers sculpting new statues, restoring old ones, or making exact copies. They're carrying on an artistic tradition that dates back to the days of Brunelleschi. The "opera" continues.

Between the Duomo and Piazza della Signoria

▲▲▲Bargello (Museo Nazionale)

This underappreciated sculpture museum is in a former police station-turned-prison that looks like a mini-Palazzo Vecchio. The Renaissance began with sculpture—the great Florentine painters were "sculptors with brushes." You can see the birth of this revolution of 3-D in the Bargello (bar-JEL-oh), which boasts the best collection of Florentine sculpture. It's a small, uncrowded museum and a pleasant break from the intensity of the rest of Florence.

The Bargello has Donatello's very influential, painfully beautiful *David* (the first male nude to be sculpted in a thousand years), works by Michelangelo, and rooms of Medici treasures. Moody Donatello, who embraced realism with his lifelike statues, set the personal and artistic style for many Renaissance artists to follow. The best pieces are in the ground-floor room at the foot of the outdoor staircase (with fine works by Michelangelo, Cellini, and Giambologna) and in the "Donatello room" directly above (with plenty by Donatello, including two different *David*s, plus Ghiberti and Brunelleschi's revolutionary dueling door panels and yet another *David* by Verrocchio).

Cost and Hours: €4, €7 with mandatory exhibits, covered by Firenze Card, Tue-Sat 8:15-13:50, until 16:50 during special exhibits (generally April-Oct); also open first, third, and fifth Mon and the second and fourth Sun of each month; last entry 30 minutes before closing, reservations possible but unnecessary, audioguide-€6 (€10/2 people), photos in courtyard only, Via del Proconsolo 4, reservation tel. 055-238-8606, www.polomuseale.firenze.it.

Casa di Dante (Dante's House)

Dante Alighieri (1265-1321), the poet who gave us *The Divine Comedy,* is the Shakespeare of Italy, the father of the modern Italian language, and the face on the country's €2 coin. However, most Americans know little of him, and this museum is not the ideal place to start. Even though it has English information, this small museum (in a building near where he likely lived) assumes visitors have prior knowledge of the poet. It's not a medieval-flavored house with period furniture—it's just a small, low-tech museum about Dante. Still, Dante lovers can trace his interesting life and works through pictures, models, and artifacts. And because the exhibits are as much about medieval Florence as they are about the man, novices can learn a little about Dante and the city he lived in.

Cost and Hours: €4, covered by Firenze Card; April-Sept daily 10:00-18:00; Oct-March Tue-Sun 10:00-17:00, closed Mon; last entry 30 minutes before closing, near the Bargello at Via Santa Margherita 1, tel. 055-219-416, www.museocasadidante.it.

▲Orsanmichele Church

In the ninth century, this loggia (covered courtyard) was a market used for selling grain (stored upstairs). Later, it was enclosed to make a church.

Outside are dynamic, statue-filled niches, some with accompanying symbols from the guilds that sponsored the art. Donatello's *St. Mark* and *St. George* (on the northeast and northwest corners) step out boldly in the new Renaissance style.

The interior has a glorious Gothic tabernacle (1359) housing the painted wooden panel that depicts *Madonna delle Grazie* (1346). The iron bars spanning the vaults were the Italian Gothic answer to the French Gothic external buttresses. Look for the rectangular holes in the piers—these were once wheat chutes that connected to the upper floors. The museum upstairs (limited hours) displays most of the originals from the niches outside the building, by Ghiberti, Donatello, Brunelleschi, and others.

Cost and Hours: Free, daily 10:00-17:00, museum also free but open only Mon, niche sculptures always viewable from the outside. You can give the *Madonna della Grazie* a special thanks if you're in town when an evening concert is held inside the Orsanmichele (tickets sold on day of concert from door facing Via de' Calzaiuoli; also books Uffizi and Accademia tickets, ticket window open daily 10:00-17:00).

▲Mercato Nuovo (a.k.a. the Straw Market)

This market loggia is how Orsanmichele looked before it became a church. Originally a silk and straw market, Mercato Nuovo still functions as a rustic yet touristy market (at the intersection of Via Calimala and Via Porta Rossa). Prices are soft, but the San Lorenzo Market (listed earlier) is much better for haggling. Notice the circled X in the center, marking the spot where people hit after being hoisted up to the top and dropped as punishment for bankruptcy. You'll also find *Porcellino* (a statue of a wild boar nicknamed "little pig"), which people rub and give coins to in order to ensure their return to Florence. This new copy, while only a few years old, already has a polished snout. At the back corner, a wagon sells tripe (cow innards) sandwiches—a local favorite (daily 9:00-20:00).

▲Piazza della Repubblica and Nearby

This large square sits on the site of the original Roman Forum. Florence was a riverside garrison town set below the older town of Fiesole—essentially a rectangular fort with the square marking the intersection of the two main roads (Via Corso and Via Roma). The square's lone column—nicknamed "the belly button of Florence"—once marked the intersection (the Roman streets were about nine feet below the present street level). All that survives of Roman Florence is this column and the city's street plan. Look at any map of Florence today, and you'll see the ghost of Rome in its streets: a grid-plan city center surrounded by what was the Roman wall. The Braille model of the city makes the design clear.

Venerable cafés and stores line the square. During the 19th century, intellectuals met in cafés here. The La Rinascente department store, facing Piazza della Repubblica, is one of the city's mainstays (WC on fourth floor, continue up the stairs from there to the bar with a rooftop terrace with great Duomo and city views).

▲Palazzo Davanzati

This five-story, late-medieval tower house offers a rare look at a noble dwelling built in the 14th century. Currently only the ground, first, and second floors are open to visitors, though the remaining floors can be visited with an escort (usually at 10:00, 11:00, and 12:00; ask when you arrive or call ahead to be sure there's space). Like other buildings of the age, the exterior is festooned with 14th-century horse-tethering rings made out of iron, torch holders, and poles upon which to hang laundry and fly flags. Inside, though the furnishings are pretty sparse, you'll see richly painted walls, a long chute that functioned as a well, plenty of fireplaces, a lace display, and even an indoor "outhouse." While there's little posted information, you can borrow English descriptions in each room.

Cost and Hours: €2, covered by Firenze Card, Tue-Sat 8:15-13:50; also open first, third, and fifth Sun and second and fourth Mon of each month; Via Porta Rossa 13, tel. 055-238-8610.

On and near Piazza della Signoria

The main civic center of Florence is dominated by the Palazzo Vecchio, Uffizi Gallery, and marble greatness of old Florence littering the cobbles. Piazza della Signoria still vibrates with the echoes of Florence's past—executions, riots, and great celebrations. Today, it's a tourist's world with pigeons, postcards, horse buggies, and tired hubbies. If it would make your weary companion happy, stop in at the recommended but expensive **Rivoire** café to enjoy its fine desserts, pudding-thick hot chocolate, and the best view seats in town. It's expensive—but if you linger, it can be a great value.

FLORENCE

▲▲▲Uffizi Gallery

This greatest collection of Italian paintings anywhere features works by Giotto, Leonardo, Raphael, Caravaggio, Titian, and Michelangelo, and a roomful of Botticellis, including the *Birth of Venus*. Northern Renaissance masters (Dürer, Rembrandt, and Rubens) are also well represented.

Cost and Hours: €6.50, €11 with mandatory exhibits, extra €4 for recommended reservation, cash required to pick up tickets reserved by phone; Tue-Sun 8:15-18:35, closed Mon, last entry 30 minutes before closing, no photos, museum info tel. 055-238-8651, reservation tel. 055-294-883, www.uffizi.firenze.it.

Avoiding Lines: To avoid the notoriously long ticket-buying lines, either get a Firenze Card or book ahead (for details on both, see page 1044). During summer and on weekends, the Uffizi can be booked up a month or more in advance. Sometimes, by the end of the day (an hour before closing), you can just walk right in, but generally you'll encounter lines even off-season (and waits up to three hours in peak season, April-Oct). The busiest days are Tuesday, Saturday, and Sunday.

Getting In: There are several entrances (see map). Which one you use depends on whether you have a Firenze Card, a reservation, or neither. Firenze Card-holders enter at door #1 (labeled *Reservation Entrance*), close to the Palazzo Vecchio. Read the signs carefully, as there are two lines at this entrance; get in the line for individuals, not groups. People buying a ticket on the spot line up with everyone else at door #2. (The wait can be up to two hours.)

To buy a Firenze Card, or to see if there are any same-day reservations available (€4 extra, but could save you time in the ticket line), enter door #2 to the left of the ticket-buying line (marked *Booking Service and Today*).

If you've already made a reservation and need to pick up your ticket, go to door #3 (labeled *Reservation Ticket Office,* across the courtyard from doors #1 and #2). Tickets are available for pick-up 10 minutes before your appointed time. If you booked online, you've already prepaid with your credit card and just need to exchange your voucher for a ticket. If you (or your hotelier) booked by phone, you need to give them your confirmation number and pay for the ticket (cash only). Once you have your ticket, walk briskly past the 200-yard-long ticket-buying line—pondering the IQ of this gang—to door #1. Show your ticket and walk in.

Audioguides: A 1.5-hour audioguide costs €6 (€10/2 people; must leave ID). You can also download a free Rick Steves audio tour of the Uffizi (see page 7).

Visiting the Museum: The museum is not nearly as big as it is great. Few tourists spend more than two hours inside. Most of the paintings are displayed on one comfortable, U-shaped floor in

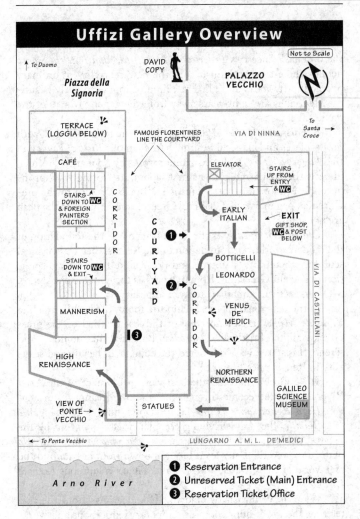

Uffizi Gallery Overview

Not to Scale

↑ To Duomo

DAVID COPY

PALAZZO VECCHIO

Piazza della Signoria

TERRACE (LOGGIA BELOW)

FAMOUS FLORENTINES LINE THE COURTYARD

VIA DI NINNA

To Santa Croce →

CAFÉ

ELEVATOR

STAIRS UP FROM ENTRY & **WC**

STAIRS DOWN TO **WC** & FOREIGN PAINTERS SECTION

CORRIDOR

COURTYARD

EARLY ITALIAN

EXIT
GIFT SHOP, **WC** & POST BELOW

STAIRS DOWN TO **WC** & EXIT

BOTTICELLI

LEONARDO

CORRIDOR

MANNERISM

VENUS DE' MEDICI

❸

VIA DI CASTELLANI

HIGH RENAISSANCE

NORTHERN RENAISSANCE

VIEW OF PONTE VECCHIO →

STATUES

GALILEO SCIENCE MUSEUM

← To Ponte Vecchio

LUNGARNO A. M. L. DE'MEDICI

Arno River

❶ Reservation Entrance
❷ Unreserved Ticket (Main) Entrance
❸ Reservation Ticket Office

chronological order from the 13th through 17th centuries. The left wing, starring the Florentine Middle Ages to the Renaissance, is the best. The connecting corridor contains sculpture, and the right wing focuses on the High Renaissance and Baroque.

Medieval (1200-1400): Paintings by **Duccio, Cimabue,** and **Giotto** show the baby steps being made from the flat Byzantine style toward realism. In his *Madonna and Child with Angels,* Giotto created a "stage" and peopled it with real beings. The triumph here is Mary herself—big and monumental, like a Roman statue. Beneath her robe, she has knees and breasts that stick out at us. This three-dimensionality was revolutionary, a taste of the Renaissance a century before it began.

Early Renaissance (mid-1400s): Paolo Uccello's *Battle of San Romano* is an early study in perspective with a few obvious flubs. Piero della Frencesca's *Federico da Montefeltro and Battista Sforza* heralds the era of humanism and the new centrality of ordinary people in art, warts and all. Fra Filippo Lippi's radiantly beautiful Madonnas are light years away from the generic Marys of the medieval era.

Renaissance (1450-1500): The Botticelli room is filled with masterpieces and classical fleshiness (the famous *Birth of Venus* and the *Allegory of Spring*), plus two minor works by Leonardo da Vinci. Here is the Renaissance in its first bloom, its "springtime" of innocence. Madonna is out, Venus is in. This is a return to the pre-Christian pagan world of classical Greece, where things of the flesh are not sinful.

Classical Sculpture: If the Renaissance was the foundation of the modern world, the foundation of the Renaissance was classical sculpture. Sculptors, painters, and poets alike turned for inspiration to ancient Greek and Roman works as the epitome of balance, 3-D perspective, human anatomy, and beauty.

In the octagonal classical sculpture room, the highlight is the *Venus de' Medici*, a Roman copy of the lost original of the great Greek sculptor Praxiteles' *Aphrodite*. Balanced, harmonious, and serene, this statue was considered the epitome of beauty and sexuality in Renaissance Florence.

The sculpture hall has the best view in Florence of the Arno River and Ponte Vecchio through the window, dreamy at sunset.

High Renaissance (1500-1550): Don't miss Michelangelo's *Holy Family*, the only surviving completed easel painting by the greatest sculptor in history; Raphael's *Madonna of the Goldfinch*, with Mary and the Baby Jesus brought down from heaven into the real world of trees, water, and sky; and Titan's voluptuous *Venus of Urbino*.

Wrap up your visit by enjoying Duomo views from the café terrace. The lower floor contains temporary exhibitions and works by Caravaggio and foreign painters.

In the Uffizi's Courtyard: Enjoy the courtyard (free), full of artists and souvenir stalls. (Swing by after dinner when it's completely empty.) The surrounding statues honor earthshaking Florentines: artists (Michelangelo), philosophers (Niccolò Machiavelli), scientists (Galileo), writers (Dante), cartographers (Amerigo Vespucci), and the great patron of so much Renaissance thinking, Lorenzo "the Magnificent" de' Medici.

Nearby: The Loggia dei Lanzi, across from the Palazzo Vecchio and facing the square, is where Renaissance Florentines once debated the issues of the day; a collection of Medici-approved sculptures now stand (or writhe) under its canopy, including Cellini's bronze *Perseus.* The plaque on the pavement in front of the fountain marks the spot where the monk Savonarola was burned in MCDXCVIII, or 1498.

▲▲Palazzo Vecchio

This castle-like fortress with the 300-foot spire dominates Florence's main square. In Renaissance times, it was the Town Hall, where citizens pioneered the once-radical notion of self-rule. Its official name—the Palazzo della Signoria—refers to the elected members of the city council. In 1540, the tyrant Cosimo I de' Medici made the building his personal palace, redecorating the interior in lavish style. Today the building functions once again as the Town Hall, home to the mayor's office and the city council.

Entry to the ground-floor courtyard is free, so even if you don't go upstairs to the museum, you can step inside and feel the essence of the Medici. Paying customers can see Cosimo's (fairly) lavish royal apartments, decorated with (fairly) top-notch paintings and statues by Michelangelo and Donatello. The highlight is the Grand Hall (Salone dei Cinquecento), a 13,000-square-foot hall lined with huge frescoes and interesting statues. People who pay to climb the tower are rewarded with a magnificent city view.

Cost and Hours: Courtyard—free to enter; museum—€6.50, €8 combo-ticket with Brancacci Chapel, covered by Firenze Card; tower only-€6.50 (418 steps), museum plus tower-€10; Fri-Wed 9:00-19:00, until 24:00 April-Sept; Thu 9:00-14:00 year-round; ticket office closes one hour earlier, Piazza della Signoria, tel. 055-276-8224, www.museicivicifiorentini.it.

Nighttime Terrace Visits: In summer, you can join an escort for an unnarrated walk along the "patrol path"—the balcony that runs just below the crenellated top of the building (€2 plus regular admission ticket, every 30 minutes between 20:00 and 23:00, no tours Oct-March). Note that this tour doesn't go to the top of the tower, but just to the top of the main building.

▲Ponte Vecchio

Florence's most famous bridge has long been lined with shops. Originally these were butcher shops that used the river as a handy disposal system. Then, when the powerful and princely Medici built the Vasari Corridor (described next) over the bridge, the stinky meat market was replaced by the more elegant gold and silver shops that remain there to this day. A statue of Benvenuto Cellini, the master goldsmith of the Renaissance, stands in the center, ignored by the flood of tacky tourism. This is a very romantic spot late at night (when lovers gather, and a top-notch street musician performs).

Vasari Corridor

This elevated and enclosed passageway, constructed in 1565, gave the Medici a safe, private commute over Ponte Vecchio from their

FLORENCE

Pitti Palace home to their Palazzo Vecchio offices. It's open only by special appointment, and while enticing to lovers of Florence, the actual tour experience isn't much. Entering from inside the Uffizi Gallery, you walk along a modern-feeling hall (wide enough to carry a Medici on a sedan chair) across Ponte Vecchio, and end in the Pitti Palace. Half the corridor is lined with Europe's best collection of self-portraits, along with other paintings (mostly 17th- and 18th-century) that seem like they didn't make the cut to be hung on the walls of the Uffizi. The best way to get inside the corridor is to go with a tour company such as Florencetown (€89, daily at 15:30, tel. 055-012-3994, www.florencetown.com) or Art-Viva (€84, Tue and Sat at 13:30, tel. 055-264-5033, www.artviva.com). The three-hour tours, which include a tour of the Uffizi, are expensive because of steep city entrance fees and the requirement that groups be accompanied by attendants and a guide.

▲▲Galileo Science Museum
(Museo Galilei e Istituto di Storia della Scienza)

When we think of the Florentine Renaissance, we think of visual arts: painting, mosaics, architecture, and sculpture. But when the visual arts declined in the 1600s (abused and co-opted by political powers), music and science flourished in Florence. The first opera was written here. And Florence hosted many scientific breakthroughs, as you'll see in this fascinating collection of Renaissance and later clocks, telescopes, maps, and ingenious gadgets. Trace the technical innovations as modern science emerges from 1000 to 1900. One of the most talked-about bottles in Florence is the one here that contains Galileo's finger. Exhibits include various tools for gauging the world, from a compass and thermometer to Galileo's telescopes. Other displays delve into clocks, pumps, medicine, and chemistry. It's friendly, comfortably cool, never crowded, and just a block east of the Uffizi on the Arno River.

Cost and Hours: €9, €22 family ticket, cash only, covered by Firenze Card, Wed-Mon 9:30-18:00, Tue 9:30-13:00, last entry 30 minutes before closing, Piazza dei Giudici 1, tel. 055-265-311, www.museogalileo.it.

Tours: The €5 audioguide is well-produced, and offers both a highlights tour as well as dial-up info (with video) on each exhibit. The 1.5-hour English-language guided tour covers the collection plus behind-the-scenes areas, and includes hands-on demonstrations of some of the devices (€50 flat fee for 2-14 people, cash only, doesn't include museum entry, book at least a week in advance, great for kids, tel. 055-234-3723, groups@museogalileo.it).

East of Piazza della Signoria

▲▲Santa Croce Church

This 14th-century Franciscan church, decorated with centuries of precious art, holds the tombs of great Florentines. The loud 19th-century Victorian Gothic facade faces a huge square ringed with tempting shops and littered with tired tourists. Escape into the church and admire its sheer height and spaciousness.

On the left wall (as you face the altar) is the **tomb of Galileo Galilei** (1564-1642), the Pisan who lived his last years under house arrest near Florence for having defied the Church by saying that the earth revolved around the sun. His heretical remains were only allowed in the church long after his death. Directly opposite (on the right wall) is the **tomb of Michelangelo Buonarroti** (1475-1564).

The first chapel to the right of the main altar features the famous fresco by Giotto of the *Death of St. Francis*. With simple but eloquent gestures, Francis' brothers bid him a sad farewell.

In the hallway near the bookstore, notice the photos of the devastating flood of 1966. Beyond that is the leather school (free entry).

Exit between the Rossini and Machiavelli tombs into the delightful cloister (open-air courtyard). On the left, enter Brunelleschi's Pazzi Chapel, which captures the Renaissance in miniature.

Cost and Hours: €6, €8.50 combo-ticket with nearby Casa Buonarroti, covered by Firenze Card, Mon-Sat 9:30-17:30, Sun 14:00-17:30, last entry 30 minutes before closing, audioguide-€5 (€8/2 people), modest dress required, 10-minute walk east of the Palazzo Vecchio along Borgo de' Greci, tel. 055-246-6105, www.santacroceopera.it. The **leather school** is free and sells tickets to the church. If the church has a long line, come here to avoid it (daily 10:00-18:00, has own entry behind church plus an entry within the church, www.leatherschool.com).

▲Casa Buonarroti (Michelangelo's House)

Fans enjoy a house standing on property once owned by Michelangelo. The house was built after Michelangelo's death by the artist's grand-nephew, who turned it into a little museum honoring his famous relative. You'll see some of Michelangelo's early, less-than-monumental statues and a few sketches. Be warned: Michelangelo's descendants attributed everything they could to their famous relative, but very little here (beyond two marble relief panels and a couple of sketches) is actually by Michelangelo.

Cost and Hours: €6.50, €8.50 combo-ticket with Santa Croce Church, covered by Firenze Card, Wed-Mon 10:00-17:00, closed Tue, English descriptions, Via Ghibellina 70, tel. 055-241-752.

FLORENCE

Santa Maria Novella Sights near the Train Station

▲▲Church of Santa Maria Novella

This 13th-century Dominican church is rich in art. Along with crucifixes by Giotto and Brunelleschi, it contains every textbook's example of the early Renaissance mastery of perspective: *The Holy Trinity* by Masaccio. The exquisite chapels trace art in Florence from medieval times to early Baroque. The outside of the church features a dash of Romanesque (horizontal stripes), Gothic (pointed arches), Renaissance (geometric shapes), and Baroque (scrolls). Step in and look down the 330-foot nave for a 14th-century optical illusion. Next to the church are the cloisters and the museum, located in the old Dominican convent of Santa Maria Novella. The museum's highlight is the breathtaking Spanish Chapel, with walls covered by a series of frescos by Andrea di Bonaiuto.

Cost and Hours: €5 for church and museum, covered by Firenze Card; church open Mon-Thu 9:00-17:30, Fri 11:00-17:30, Sat 9:00-17:00, Sun 13:00-17:00, last entry 30 minutes before closing, audioguide-€5 (€8/2 people), modest dress required, no photos, tel. 055-219-257, www.museicivicifiorentini.it; museum open Fri-Mon 9:00-16:00, closed Tue-Thu, tel. 055-282-187.

Farmacia di Santa Maria Novella

This palatial perfumery has long been run by the Dominicans of Santa Maria Novella. Thick with the lingering aroma of centuries of spritzes, it started as the herb garden of the Santa Maria Novella monks. Well-known even today for its top-quality products, it is extremely Florentine. Pick up the history sheet at the desk, and wander deep into the shop. The first room features perfumes, the middle (green) room offers items for the home, and the third room, which sells herbal products and dates from 1612, is the most historic. From here, you can peek at one of Santa Maria Novella's cloisters with its dreamy frescoes and imagine a time before Vespas and tourists.

Cost and Hours: Free but shopping encouraged, inconsistent hours but likely daily 9:30-19:30, a block from Piazza Santa Maria Novella, 100 yards down Via della Scala at #16—located on map on page 1030, tel. 055-216-276, www.smnovella.com.

Sights South of the Arno River

To locate these sights, see the map on page 1068.

▲▲Pitti Palace

The imposing Pitti Palace, several blocks southwest of Ponte Vecchio, is not only home to the second-best collection of paintings in town, the **Palatine Gallery,** but also happens to be the most sumptuous palace you can tour in Florence. The building itself is mammoth, holding several different museums and anchoring two gardens. Stick primarily to the gallery, forget about everything else, and the palace becomes a little less exhausting.

You'll walk through one palatial room after another, walls sagging with masterpieces by 16th- and 17th-century masters, including Rubens, Titian, and Rembrandt. Its Raphael collection is the second-biggest anywhere—the Vatican beats it by one. Each room has some descriptions in English, though the paintings themselves have limited English labels.

The collection is all on one floor. To see the highlights, walk straight down the spine through a dozen or so rooms. Before you exit, consider a visit to the Royal Apartments. These 14 rooms (of which only a few are open at any one time) are where Florence's aristocrats lived in the 18th and 19th centuries. Each room features a different color and time period. Here, you get a real feel for the splendor of the dukes' world.

The rest of the Pitti Palace is skippable, unless the various sights match your interests: the **Gallery of Modern Art** (second floor, features Romantic, Neoclassical, and Impressionist works by 19th- and 20th-century Tuscan painters), **Argenti/Silverworks Museum** (on the ground and mezzanine floors; displays Medici treasures from jeweled crucifixes to gilded ostrich eggs), **Costume Gallery**, **Porcelain Museum**, and **Boboli and Bardini gardens** (behind the palace; enter from Pitti Palace courtyard).

The main reason to visit the Pitti Palace is to see the Palatine Gallery, but you can't buy a ticket for the gallery alone; to see it you'll need to buy ticket #1, which includes the Palatine Gallery, Royal Apartments, and Gallery of Modern Art. Ticket #2 covers the Boboli and Bardini gardens, Costume Gallery, Argenti/Silverworks Museum, and Porcelain Museum. Behind door #3 is a combo-ticket covering the whole shebang.

Cost and Hours: Ticket #1—€8.50, Tue-Sun 8:15-18:50, closed Mon. Ticket #2—€7, daily 8:15-18:30, except closed first and last Mon of each month, until 19:30 June-Aug, gardens close as early as 16:30 in winter, last entry 30-60 minutes before closing. An €11.50 combo-ticket (valid 3 days) covers the entire palace complex. All tickets are cash only and increase in price with mandatory special exhibits. Reservations are possible but unnecessary, and everything is covered by the Firenze Card. The €6 audioguide (€10/2 people) explains the sprawling palace. No photos are allowed in the Palatine Gallery. Tel. 055-238-8614, www.polomuseale.firenze.it.

Getting In: If there's a long line, you can bypass it by making a €3 "reservation" on the spot for immediate entry. The ticket office is at the far right of the massive facade; just march up to the head of the line and go to the window on the right, marked *reservation desk*. You can also skip lines if you have a Firenze Card. Once you have your ticket, enter through the main doorway in the center of the fa-

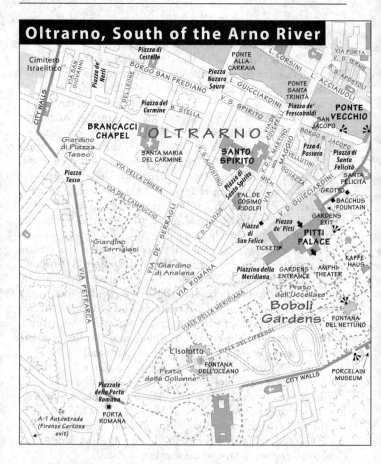

Oltrarno, South of the Arno River

cade. Firenze Card-holders should go directly to the main entrance (where you may be ushered to the head of the security checkpoint); then go to the bookstore on the left side of the courtyard to have your card swiped and get your tickets.

▲▲Brancacci Chapel

For the best look at works by Masaccio (one of the early Renaissance pioneers of perspective in painting), see his restored frescoes here. Instead of medieval religious symbols, Masaccio's paintings feature simple, strong human figures with facial expressions that reflect their emotions. The accompanying works of Masolino and Filippino Lippi provide illuminating contrasts.

Your ticket includes a 40-minute film in English on the church, the frescoes, and Renaissance Florence (reserve a viewing time when you book your entry). The film starts promptly at the top of the hour (first shown at 10:00, last shown at 15:00). Computer animation brings the paintings to life—making them appear

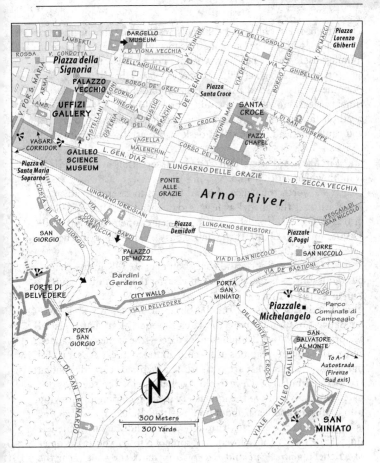

to move and giving them 3-D depth—while narration describes the events depicted in the panels. Yes, it's a long time commitment, and the film takes liberties with the art. But it's visually interesting and your best way to see the frescoes close up. The film works great either before or after you visit the frescoes.

Cost and Hours: €4, covered by Firenze Card, free and easy reservations required—although on weekdays and any day off-season, it's usually possible to walk right in if you arrive before 15:30, €8 combo-ticket with Palazzo Vecchio, includes worthwhile 40-minute film in English—reserve viewing time when you book entry, Mon and Wed-Sat 10:00-17:00, Sun 13:00-17:00, closed Tue, last entry 30 minutes before closing, in Church of Santa Maria del Carmine, reservations tel. 055-276-8224 or 055-276-8558, ticket desk tel. 055-284-361, www.museicivicifiorentini.it.

Reservations: Reserving an entry time is required (and free), but if you come before 15:30, you can usually just show up and be assigned a time more or less right away. Officially, reservation times begin every 15 minutes, with a maximum of 30 visitors per time slot (you have 15 minutes inside the chapel). But when it's not too busy, they generally let people come and go at will, and stay as long as they like.

The most crowded time is around 16:00, just before closing time; the least crowded time tends to be 12:00-14:00. If, before you head out for the sight, you want to find out if there's a long line, you can call ahead to the ticket desk just to ask how busy it is (tel. 055-284-361).

Firenze Card users don't need a reservation at all, and can walk in whenever they like.

If it's worth the peace of mind for you to reserve in advance, you must call the chapel at least a day ahead (tel. 055-276-8224 or 055-276-8558, English spoken, call center open Mon-Sat 9:30-17:00, Sun 9:30-12:30). If the line is busy, keep trying—it's best to call around 13:00-15:00.

Dress Code: Shorts and bare shoulders are OK in the chapel, but modest dress is requested when visiting the rest of the church.

Santo Spirito Church

This church has a classic Brunelleschi interior—enjoy its pure Renaissance lines (and ignore the later Baroque altar that replaced the original). Notice Brunelleschi's "dice"—the stone cubes added above the column capitals that contribute to the nave's playful lightness. The church's art treasure is a painted, carved wooden crucifix attributed to 17-year-old Michelangelo. The sculptor donated this early work to the monastery in appreciation for allowing him to dissect and learn about bodies. The Michelangelo *Crocifisso* is displayed in the sacristy, through a door midway down the left side of the nave (if it's closed, ask someone to let you in). Copies of Michelangelo's *Pietà* and *Risen Christ* flank the nave (near the main door). Beer-drinking, guitar-playing rowdies decorate the church steps.

Cost and Hours: Free, Mon-Tue and Thu-Sat 9:30-12:30 & 16:00-17:30, Sun 16:00-17:30 only, closed Wed, Piazza di Santo Spirito, tel. 055-210-030.

▲Piazzale Michelangelo

Overlooking the city from across the river (look for the huge statue of *David*), this square has a superb view of Florence and the stunning dome of the Duomo.

It's worth the 30-minute hike, drive (free parking), or bus ride (either #12 or #13 from the train station—takes 20-30 minutes, or even more in bad traffic). It makes sense to take a taxi or ride the bus up, and then enjoy the easy downhill walk back into town. An inviting café with great views is just below the overlook. The best photos are taken from the street immediately below the overlook (go around to the right and down a few steps). Off the west side of the piazza is a somewhat hidden terrace, an excellent place to retreat from the mobs. After dark, the square is packed with schoolkids licking ice cream and each other. About 200 yards beyond all the tour groups and teenagers is the stark, beautiful, crowd-free, Romanesque San Miniato Church (next listing).

The hike down is quick and enjoyable. Take the steps between the two bars on the San Miniato Church side of the parking lot (Via San Salvatore al Monte), and in a couple of minutes you walk through the old wall (Porta San Miniato) and emerge in the delightful little Oltrarno neighborhood of San Niccolò.

▲▲San Miniato Church

According to legend, the martyred St. Minias—this church's namesake—was beheaded on the banks of the Arno in A.D. 250. He picked up his head and walked here (this was before the #12 bus), where he died and was buried in what became the first Christian cemetery in Florence. In the 11th century, this church was built to house Minias' remains. The church's green-and-white marble facade (12th century) is classic Florentine Romanesque, one of the oldest in town. The church has wonderful 3-D paintings, a plush ceiling of glazed terra-cotta panels by Luca della Robbia, and an exquisite Renaissance chapel (on the left side of the nave). The highlight for me is the brilliantly preserved art in the sacristy (upstairs to right of altar, in the room on right) showing scenes from the life of St. Benedict (circa 1350, by a follower of Giotto). Drop €2 into the electronic panel in the corner to light the room for five minutes. The evening Mass with the monks chanting in Latin offers a meditative worship experience—a peaceful way to end your visit.

Cost and Hours: Free, daily Easter-mid-Oct 8:00-20:00 or possibly later, in winter 8:30-13:00 & 15:30-19:00, tel. 055-234-2731, www.sanminiatoalmonte.it.

Getting There: It's about 200 yards above Piazzale Michelangelo. From the station, bus #12 takes you right to the San Miniato al Monte stop (hop off and hike up the grand staircase); bus #13 from the station takes you to Piazzale Michelangelo, from which you'll hike up the rest of the way up.

Gregorian Chants: To experience this mystical medieval space at its full potential, time your visit to coincide with a Mass of Gregorian chants. In general, these are held each evening in summer (Easter-mid-Oct) at 18:30, and in winter at 17:00 or 17:30—but as the schedule is subject to change, double-check with any TI, check the church's website, or call ahead.

Sleeping in Florence

Competition among hotels is stiff. When things slow down, fancy hotels drop their prices and become a much better value for travelers than the cheap, low-end places.

Nearly all of my recommended accommodations are located in the center of Florence, within minutes of the great sights. If arriving by train, you can either walk (usually around 10 minutes) or take a taxi (roughly €8-10) to reach most of my recommended accommodations, as buses don't cover the center very well. For additional listings of B&Bs and apartments, try Cross-Pollinate, a trustworthy online booking agency (www.cross-pollinate.com).

Florence is notorious for its mosquitoes. If your hotel lacks air-conditioning, request a fan and don't open your windows, especially at night. Many hotels furnish a small plug-in bulb *(zanzariere)*—usually set in the ashtray—that helps keep the blood-suckers at bay. If not, you can purchase one cheaply at any pharmacy *(farmacia)*.

Museumgoers take note: If you don't plan to get a Firenze Card (see page 1044), ask if your hotelier will reserve entry times for you to visit the popular Uffizi Gallery and the Accademia (Michelangelo's *David*). Request this service when you book your room; it's fast, easy, and offered free or for a small fee by most hotels—the only requirement is advance notice. Ask them to reserve your visits for any time the day after your arrival. If you'd rather make the reservations yourself, see page 1045 for details.

North of the Arno River
Between the Duomo and the Train Station

$$$ Hotel Centrale is indeed central, just a short walk from the Duomo. The 31 spacious but slightly overpriced rooms—with a tasteful mix of old and new decor—are over a businesslike conference center (Db-€170, bigger superior Db-€212, Tb-€210, suites available, discount with this book, ask for Rick Steves rate when you reserve, additional discount if booked 3 months in advance, air-con, elevator, free Internet access and Wi-Fi, Via dei Conti 3, check in at big front desk on ground floor, tel. 055-215-761, fax 055-215-216, www.hotelcentralefirenze.it, info@hotelcentralefirenze.it, Margherita and Roberto).

$$ Hotel Accademia, which comes with marble stairs, parquet floors, and attractive public areas, has 21 pleasant rooms and a floor plan that defies logic (Db-€145, Tb-€170, discount with this book if you book direct and pay cash, air-con, free Internet access and Wi-Fi, Via Faenza 7, tel. 055-293-451, fax 055-219-771, www.hotelaccademiafirenze.com, info@hotelaccademiafirenze.com, Tea and Paolo).

$ Hotel Lorena, just across from the Medici Chapels, has 19 rooms (six of which have shared bathrooms) and a tiny lobby.

Sleep Code

(€1 = about $1.30, country code: 39)
S = Single, **D** = Double/Twin, **T** = Triple, **Q** = Quad, **b** = bathroom, **s** = shower only. You can assume a hotel takes credit cards unless you see "cash only" in the listing. Unless otherwise noted, hotel staff speak basic English and breakfast is included.

Florence charges a hotel tax of €1 per star (according to the hotel's official star rating), per person, per night. So a couple staying at a three-star hotel would pay €3 each, or €6 total, per night. This tax is generally not included in the prices I've listed here.

To help you easily sort through these listings, I've divided the accommodations into three categories based on the price for a standard double room with bath during high season:

$$$ **Higher Priced**—Most rooms €160 or more.
$$ **Moderately Priced**—Most rooms between €100-160.
$ **Lower Priced**—Most rooms €100 or less.

Prices can change without notice; verify the hotel's current rates online or by email.

Though it's a bit like a youth hostel, it's cheap and conveniently located. Chatty Roberto speaks little English, but is eager to please (S-€35, Sb-€50, D-€60, Db-€75, Tb-€95, very flexible rates, breakfast-€5, air-con, free Wi-Fi, Via Faenza 1, tel. 055-282-785, fax 055-288-300, www.hotellorena.com, info@hotellorena.com).

$ Katti House and the nearby **Soggiorno Annamaria** are run by house-proud mama-and-daughter team Maria and Katti, who rent a total of 15 rooms on a bustling pedestrian street. While both offer comparable comfort, Soggiorno Annamaria has a more historic setting, with frescoed ceilings, unique tiles, timbered beams, and quieter rooms. Katti House serves as reception for both places, but mostly you interact with Maria; while she's a fine hostess, she speaks virtually no English so communication can be challenging (Sb-€85, D-€85, Db-€100, skimpy breakfast served in your room, air-con, free Internet access and Wi-Fi—only in Katti, Via Faenza 21, if no answer check in at Trattoria Katti next door, tel. & fax 055-213-410, www.kattihouse.com, info@kattihouse.com).

North of the Duomo
North of the Mercato Centrale

After dark, this neighborhood can feel a little deserted, but I've never heard of anyone running into harm here. It's a short walk from the train station and an easy stroll to all the sightseeing action. While workaday, it's practical, with plenty of good budget restaurants and markets nearby.

$$ Grand Tour Firenze has six charming rooms on a nondescript street between the train station and the Accademia. This cozy B&B will make you feel right at home; it's thoughtfully appointed and the owners, Cristina and Giuseppe, live there. The delightful and spacious suites come with a garden ambience on the ground floor (Db-€110, suite-€130, ask for discount when you book direct and pay cash, includes breakfast voucher for the corner bar—or skip it to save €10/person, air-con, free Wi-Fi, Via Santa Reparata 21, tel. 055-283-955, www.florencegrandtour.com, info@florencegrandtour.com). They run another more romantic, pricier place a couple of blocks away.

$$ Galileo Hotel, a classy business hotel with 31 rooms on a chaotic and congested street, is run with familial warmth (Sb-€100, Db-€130, Tb-€150, ask for Rick Steves discount when you book direct and pay cash, quadruple-pane windows effectively shut out street noise, air-con, elevator, free Internet access and Wi-Fi, Via Nazionale 22a, tel. 055-496-645, fax 055-496-447, www.galileohotel.it, info@galileohotel.it).

$ Hotel Il Bargellino, run by Bostonian Carmel and her Italian husband Pino, feels like it's in a residential neighborhood. They rent 10 summery rooms decorated with funky antique furniture and Pino's modern paintings. Guests enjoy relaxing with Carmel and Leopoldo the parrot on the big, breezy, momentum-slowing terrace adorned with lemon shrubs (S-€45, D-€80, Db-€90, ask for Rick Steves discount if you book direct and pay cash, extra bed-€25, no breakfast, free Wi-Fi, north of the train station at Via Guelfa 87, tel. 055-238-2658, www.ilbargellino.com, carmel@ilbargellino.com).

$ Casa Rabatti is the ultimate if you always wanted to have a Florentine mama. Its four simple, clean rooms are run with warmth by Marcella. This is a great place to practice your Italian, since Marcella loves to chat and speaks minimal English. Seeing nearly two decades of my family Christmas cards on their walls, I'm reminded of how long she has been keeping budget travelers happy (D-€50, Db-€60, €25 extra per bed in shared quad or quint, show this book and ask for best Rick Steves price, cash only but secure reservation with credit card, no breakfast, fans available, free Wi-Fi, 5 blocks from station at Via San Zanobi 48 black, tel. 055-212-393, casarabatti@inwind.it). If Marcella's booked, she'll put you up in her daughter's place nearby, at Via Nazionale 20 (five big, airy, family-friendly rooms; €25/person, fans, no breakfast, closer to the station). While daughter Patrizia works, her mom runs the place. Getting bumped to Patrizia's gives you slightly more comfort and slightly less personality...certainly not a net negative.

$ Soggiorno Magliani, which may close in 2014, has six bright, no-frills rooms (sharing two baths) that feel and smell like a great-grandmother's home. It's run by the friendly duo Vincenza and her English-speaking daughter Cristina, and the price is right (S-€36, D-€46, T-€65, cash only but secure reservation with credit card, no breakfast, near Via Guelfa at Via Santa Reparata 1, tel. 055-287-378, hotel-magliani@libero.it).

$ Hotel Enza rents 19 dark, musty, straightforward rooms. The prices are reasonable for predictable hotel comfort (S-€45, Sb-€55, Db-€80, show this book and ask for best Rick Steves price, extra bed-€20, optional breakfast-€8, air-con, free Internet access and Wi-Fi, Via San Zanobi 45 black, tel. 055-490-990, fax 055-473-672, www.hotelenza.it, info@hotelenza.it, Diana).

Near the Accademia

$$$ Hotel Loggiato dei Serviti, at the most prestigious address in Florence on the most Renaissance square in town, gives you Old World romance with hair dryers. Stone stairways lead you under open-beam ceilings through this 16th-century monastery's monumental public rooms—it's so artful, you'll be snapping photos everywhere. The 38 cells—with air-conditioning, TVs, mini-bars, free Wi-Fi, and telephones—would be unrecognizable to their original inhabitants. The hotel staff is both professional and warm (Sb-€140, Db-€160, superior Db-€180, family suites from €263, ask for Rick Steves rate when you book, elevator, valet parking-€21/day, Piazza S.S. Annunziata 3, tel. 055-289-592, fax 055-289-595, www.loggiatodeiservitihotel.it, info@loggiatodeiservitihotel.it; Simonetta, Gianni, and two Chiaras). When full, they rent five spacious and sophisticated rooms in a 17th-century annex a block away. While it lacks the monastic mystique, the annex rooms are bigger, gorgeous, and cost the same.

$$$ Hotel dei Macchiaioli offers 15 fresh and spacious rooms on one high-ceilinged, noble floor in a restored *palazzo* owned for generations by a well-to-do Florentine family. You'll eat breakfast under original frescoed ceilings while enjoying modern comforts (Sb-€100, Db-€180, Tb-€220, Rick Steves discount if you book direct and pay cash, air-con, free Wi-Fi, Via Cavour 21, tel. 055-213-154, www.hoteldeimacchiaioli.com, info@hoteldeimacchiaioli.com, helpful Francesca and Paolo).

$$ Hotel Morandi alla Crocetta, a former convent, envelops you in a 16th-century cocoon. Located on a quiet street with 12 rooms, period furnishings, parquet floors, and wood-beamed or painted ceilings, it takes you back a few centuries and up a few social classes (Sb-€105, Db-€155, Tb-€185, low-season discounts online, air-con, free Wi-Fi, a block off Piazza S.S. Annunziata at Via Laura 50, tel. 055-234-4747, fax 055-248-0954, www.hotel-

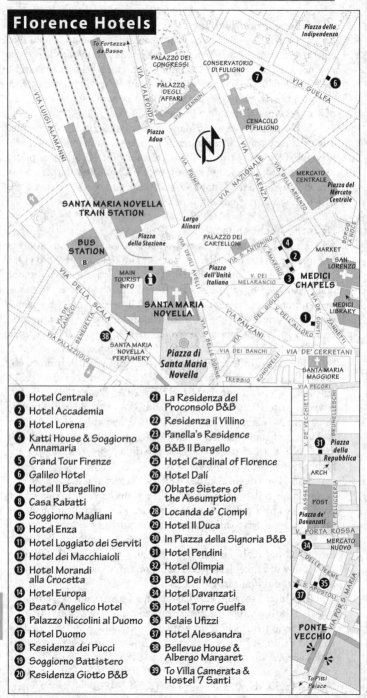

Florence Hotels

1. Hotel Centrale
2. Hotel Accademia
3. Hotel Lorena
4. Katti House & Soggiorno Annamaria
5. Grand Tour Firenze
6. Galileo Hotel
7. Hotel Il Bargellino
8. Casa Rabatti
9. Soggiorno Magliani
10. Hotel Enza
11. Hotel Loggiato dei Serviti
12. Hotel dei Macchiaioli
13. Hotel Morandi alla Crocetta
14. Hotel Europa
15. Beato Angelico Hotel
16. Palazzo Niccolini al Duomo
17. Hotel Duomo
18. Residenza dei Pucci
19. Soggiorno Battistero
20. Residenza Giotto B&B
21. La Residenza del Proconsolo B&B
22. Residenza il Villino
23. Panella's Residence
24. B&B Il Bargello
25. Hotel Cardinal of Florence
26. Hotel Dalí
27. Oblate Sisters of the Assumption
28. Locanda de' Ciompi
29. Hotel Il Duca
30. In Piazza della Signoria B&B
31. Hotel Pendini
32. Hotel Olimpia
33. B&B Dei Mori
34. Hotel Davanzati
35. Hotel Torre Guelfa
36. Relais Ufizzi
37. Hotel Alessandra
38. Bellevue House & Albergo Margaret
39. To Villa Camerata & Hostel 7 Santi

FLORENCE

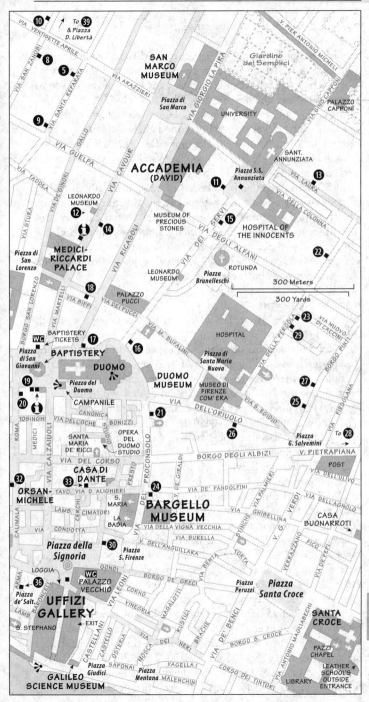

morandi.it, welcome@hotelmorandi.it, well-run by Maurizio, Rolando, and Ertol).

$$ Hotel Europa, run by cheery Miriam, Roberto, and daughters Priscilla and Isabel since 1970, has a welcoming atmosphere. The breakfast room is spacious, and some of the 20 rooms have views of the Duomo (Sb-€89, Db-€150, Tb-€180, Qb-€250, a little extra for a private balcony, €10-15 more for bigger "deluxe" room, discount if you pay cash, mention Rick Steves to get their best available room, air-con, old-timey elevator, free Wi-Fi, Via Cavour 14, tel. 055-239-6715, fax 055-268-984, www.webhoteleuropa.com, firenze@webhoteleuropa.com).

$$ Beato Angelico Hotel rents 11 large, tastefully furnished rooms well-located on a quiet street just far enough away from the tourist scene. Unfortunately, this pleasant place may close in 2014 (Db-€135, ask for Rick Steves price if you book direct and pay cash, third bed-€30, breakfast-€10, air-con, elevator, free Wi-Fi, Via dei Servi 38, tel. 055-272-9924, www.beatoangelicohotel.com, info@beatoangelicohotel.com, Cesare).

Near the Duomo

All of these places are within a block of Florence's biggest church and main landmark.

$$$ Palazzo Niccolini al Duomo, one of five elite Historic Residence Hotels in Florence, is run by Niccolini da Camugliano. The lounge (where free chamomile tea is served in the evenings) is palatial, but the 12 rooms, while splendid, vary wildly in size. If you have the money and want a Florentine palace to call home, this can be a good bet (Db-€180-€450 depending on type of room, ask for Rick Steves discount when you book, check online to choose a room and consider last-minute deals, elevator, free Internet access and Wi-Fi, Via dei Servi 2, tel. 055-282-412, fax 055-290-979, www.niccolinidomepalace.com, info@niccolinidomepalace.com).

$$$ Hotel Duomo, big and venerable, rents 24 rooms four floors up. The Duomo looms like a monster outside the hotel's windows; most (but not all) rooms come with views. The rooms are modern and comfortable enough, and the location can't be beat (Sb-€90, Db-€160, Tb-€180, discount with this book if you pay cash, air-con, elevator, free Wi-Fi, Piazza del Duomo 1, tel. 055-219-922, www.hotelduomofirenze.it, info@hotelduomofirenze.it; Alberto, Sonia, and Karen).

$$ Residenza dei Pucci rents 12 pleasant rooms (each one different) spread over three floors. The decor, a mix of soothing earth tones and aristocratic furniture, makes this place feel upscale for this price range (Sb-€135, Db-€150, Tb-€170, Qb-€238, rates can vary, discount with cash and this book, air-con, no elevator, free slow Wi-Fi or pay for fast Wi-Fi, reception open 9:00-20:00—

let them know if you'll arrive late, Via dei Pucci 9, tel. 055-281-886, fax 055-264-314, www.residenzadeipucci.com, residenzadei-pucci@residenzadeipucci.com, Mirella and Marina).

$$ Soggiorno Battistero rents seven simple, airy rooms, most with great views, overlooking the Baptistery and the Duomo square. Choose a view or a quieter room in the back when you book by email. It's a pristine, fresh, and minimalist place run by Italian Luca and his American wife Kelly, who makes the hotel particularly welcoming (Sb-€83, Db-€110, Tb-€145, Qb-€155, show this book and ask for Rick Steves price, discount if you book direct and pay cash, breakfast served in room, air-con available June-Aug, free Wi-Fi, Piazza San Giovanni 1, third floor—new elevator may be ready in time for your visit, tel. 055-295-143, fax 055-268-189, www.soggiornobattistero.it, info@soggiornobattistero.it).

$$ Residenza Giotto B&B offers you the chance to stay on Florence's upscale shopping drag, Via Roma. Occupying the top floor of a 19th-century building, this place has six bright, smallish rooms and a terrace with knockout views of the Duomo's tower. Reception is generally open 9:00-17:00; let them know your arrival time in advance (Sb-€90, Db-€130, view rooms-€10 extra, extra bed-€25, discount if you book direct and pay cash, air-con, elevator, free Wi-Fi, Via Roma 6, tel. 055-214-593, fax 055-264-8568, www.residenzagiotto.it, info@residenzagiotto.it, Giorgio).

$$ La Residenza del Proconsolo B&B, run by helpful Mariano, has five older-feeling rooms a minute from the Duomo (three rooms have Duomo views). The place lacks public spaces, but the rooms are quite large and nice—perfect for eating breakfast, which is served in your room (Sb-€90, Db-€120, Tb-€140, air-con, free Wi-Fi, Via del Proconsolo 18 black, tel. 055-264-5657, mobile 335-657-4840, www.proconsolo.com, info@proconsolo.com).

East of the Duomo

$$ Residenza il Villino, popular and friendly, aspires to offer a Florentine home away from home. It has 10 charmingly rustic rooms and a picturesque, peaceful little courtyard. As it's in a "little villa" (as the name implies) set back from the street, this is a quiet refuge from the bustle of Florence (small Db-€110, Db-€130, family suite that sleeps up to six—price upon request, discount with cash and this book, air-con, free Internet access and Wi-Fi, just north of Via degli Alfani at Via della Pergola 53, tel. 055-200-1116, fax 055-200-1101, www.ilvillino.it, info@ilvillino.it; Sergio—who looks a bit like Henry Winkler, Elisabetta, and son Lorenzo).

$$ Panella's Residence, once a convent and today part of owner Graziella's extensive home, is a classy B&B, with six chic, romantic, and ample rooms, antique furnishings, and historic architectural touches (Db-€140, bigger superior Db-€165, even big-

FLORENCE

ger deluxe Db-€180, more if paying by credit card, discounts for 3 or more nights, air-con, free Wi-Fi, Via della Pergola 42, tel. & fax 055-234-7202, mobile 345-972-1541, www.panellaresidence.com, panella_residence@yahoo.it).

$ B&B Il Bargello is a home away from home, run by friendly and helpful Canadian expat Gabriella. Hike up three long flights (no elevator) to reach six smart, relaxing rooms. Gabriella offers a cozy communal living room, kitchen access, and an inviting roof-top terrace with close-up views of Florence's towers (Db-€100, ask for Rick Steves rate when you book direct and pay cash, air-con, free Internet access and Wi-Fi, 20 yards off Via Proconsolo at Via de' Pandolfini 33 black, tel. 055-215-330, mobile 339-175-3110, www.firenze-bedandbreakfast.it, info@firenze-bedandbreakfast. it).

$ Hotel Cardinal of Florence is a third-floor walk-up with 17 spartan, tidy, and sun-splashed rooms overlooking either a silent courtyard (many with views of Brunelleschi's dome) or quiet street. Relax and enjoy Florence's rooftops from the sun terrace (Sb-€60, Db-€95, ask for Rick Steves rate, additional discount if you pay cash, air-con, free Wi-Fi, Borgo Pinti 5, tel. 055-234-0780, fax 055-234-3389, www.hotelcardinalofflorence.com, info@hotelcar-dinalofflorence.com, Mauro and Ida).

$ Hotel Dalí has 10 cheap and cheery rooms with new baths and floors in a nice location for a great price. Samanta and Marco, who run this guesthouse with a charming passion and idealism, are a delight to know (S-€40, D-€70, Db-€85, extra bed-€25, no breakfast, fans but no air-con, request quiet room when you book, no elevator, free Wi-Fi, free parking, 2 blocks behind the Duomo at Via dell'Oriuolo 17 on the second floor, tel. & fax 055-234-0706, www.hoteldali.com, hoteldali@tin.it).

$ Oblate Sisters of the Assumption run an institutional 30-room hotel in a Renaissance building with a dreamy garden, great public spaces, appropriately simple rooms, and a quiet, prayerful ambience (€45/person in single, double, triple, or quad rooms with bathrooms, €38/person with shared bathrooms, cash only, single beds only, air-con, elevator, Wi-Fi with suggested donation, €10/day limited parking—request when you book, Borgo Pinti 15, tel. 055-248-0582, fax 055-234-6291, sroblateborgopinti@virgilio.it, sisters are likely to speak French but not English, Sister Theresa is very helpful).

$ Locanda de' Ciompi, overlooking the inviting Piazza dei Ciompi antiques market in a young and lively neighborhood, is just right for travelers who want to feel like a part of the town. Alessio and Lisa run a minimalist place—just five quiet, clean, taste-ful rooms along a thin hallway (Db-€100, Tb-€115, discount with this book if you book direct and pay cash, includes breakfast at nearby bar, air-con, free Wi-Fi, 8 blocks behind the Duomo at Via Pietrapiana 28, tel. 055-263-8034, www.locandadeciompi.it, locandadeciompi@yahoo.it).

$ Hotel Il Duca—a big, bright place on a quiet street a few blocks behind the Duomo—seems like a basic building wearing a fancy coat. Its 13 pleasant rooms are a great value, but don't expect a warm welcome or personal service (Sb-€85, Db-€90, third bed-€25, air-con, free Wi-Fi, Via della Pergola 34, tel. 055-906-2167, www.hotelilduca.it, info@hotelilduca.it, Angela).

South of the Duomo
Between the Duomo and Piazza della Signoria

These are the most central of my accommodations recommendations (and therefore a little overpriced). While worth the extra cost for many, given Florence's walkable, essentially traffic-free core, nearly every hotel I recommend can be considered central.

$$$ In Piazza della Signoria B&B, overlooking Piazza della Signoria, is peaceful, refined, and homey at the same time. Fit for a honeymoon, the 10 rooms come with all the special touches and little extras you'd expect in a top-end American B&B. However, the rates are high, and the "partial view" rooms require craning your neck to see anything—not worth the extra euros (viewless Db-€250, partial-view Db-€280, full-view "deluxe" Db-€300, Tb-€280, partial-view Tb-€300, ask for discount when you book direct with this book, family apartments, lavish bathrooms, air-con, tiny elevator, free Internet access and Wi-Fi, Via dei Magazzini 2, tel. 055-239-9546, mobile 348-321-0565, fax 055-267-6616, www.inpiazzadellasignoria.com, info@inpiazzadellasignoria.com, Sonia and Alessandro).

$$$ Hotel Pendini, with 42 rooms and three slightly tarnished stars, fills the top floor of a grand building constructed to celebrate Italian unification in the late 19th century. It overlooks Piazza della Repubblica, and as you walk into the lobby, you feel as if you are walking back in time (Sb-€139, Db-€189, deluxe Db with square view and noise-€239, air-con, elevator, free Internet access and Wi-Fi, Via degli Strozzi 2, tel. 055-211-170, www.hotelpendini.it, info@hotelpendini.it).

$$$ Hotel Olimpia is a friendly, well-worn, established place renting 24 quite dated rooms on the fourth floor overlooking Piazza della Repubblica (some rooms have views and noise). You pay for the location (Db-€160, air-con, elevator, pay Wi-Fi, Piazza della Repubblica 2, tel. 055-219-781, fax 055-267-0383, www.hotelolimpia.it, hotelolimpia@tin.it, Marziano).

$$ B&B Dei Mori, a peaceful haven with a convivial and welcoming living room, rents five tastefully appointed rooms ideally located on a quiet pedestrian street near Casa di Dante—

within a five-minute walk of the Duomo, the Bargello, or Piazza della Signoria. Accommodating Suzanne, Daniele, and Peter pride themselves on offering personal service, including lots of tips on dining and sightseeing in Florence. But if they're full, I'd skip their offer of an apartment nearby (D-€100, Db-€120, discount for my readers—ask when you book, air-con-€5, free Wi-Fi, reception open 8:00-19:00, Via Dante Alighieri 12, tel. 055-211-438, www. deimori.com, deimori@bnb.it).

Near Ponte Vecchio

$$$ Hotel Davanzati, bright and shiny with artistic touches, has 22 cheerful rooms with all the comforts. The place is a family affair, thoughtfully run by friendly Tommaso and father Fabrizio, who offer drinks and snacks each evening at their candlelit happy hour, plus lots of other extras (Sb-€132, Db-€199, Tb-€259, show this book and ask for Rick Steves rate, prices soft off-season, discount if you pay cash, free loaner laptop in every room, free on-demand movies—including my Italy TV shows—on your room TV, air-con, free Wi-Fi, next to Piazza Davanzati at Via Porta Rossa 5—easy to miss so watch for low-profile sign above the door, tel. 055-286-666, fax 055-265-8252, www.hoteldavanzati.it, info@hoteldavanzati.it).

$$$ Hotel Torre Guelfa has grand (almost royal) public spaces and is topped by a fun medieval tower with a panoramic rooftop terrace. Its 31 pricey rooms vary wildly in size and layout. Room 315, with a private terrace (€245), is worth reserving several months in advance (Db-€170-190, Db junior suite-€230, ask for Rick Steves discount, family deals, check their website for promotions, air-con, elevator, free Internet access and Wi-Fi in lobby, a couple blocks northwest of Ponte Vecchio, Borgo S.S. Apostoli 8, tel. 055-239-6338, fax 055-239-8577, www.hoteltorreguelfa.com, info@hoteltorreguelfa.com, Sandro and Barbara).

$$$ Relais Uffizi is a peaceful little gem, with 15 classy rooms tucked away down a tiny alleyway off Piazza della Signoria. The lounge has a huge window overlooking the action in the square below (Sb-€120, Db-€180, Tb-€220, more for deluxe rooms, buffet breakfast, air-con, elevator, free Wi-Fi, Chiasso de Baroncelli/Chiasso del Buco 16, tel. 055-267-6239, fax 055-265-7909, www. relaisuffizi.it, info@relaisuffizi.it, charming Alessandro and Elizabetta).

$$ Hotel Alessandra is 16th-century, tranquil, and sprawling, with 27 big, tasteful rooms and an old-school, peeling-wallpaper vibe (S-€67-€88, Sb-€110, D-€110, Db-€150, Tb-€195, Qb-€215, cash discount, air-con, free Internet access and Wi-Fi, Borgo S.S. Apostoli 17, tel. 055-283-438, fax 055-210-619, www.hotelalessandra.com, info@hotelalessandra.com, Anna and son Andrea).

Near the Train Station

$ Bellevue House is a third-floor (no elevator) oasis of tranquility, with six spacious, old-fashioned rooms flanking a long, mellow-yellow lobby. It's a peaceful time warp thoughtfully run by Rosanna and Antonio di Grazia (Db-€70-95, family deals; discount if you stay two nights, pay cash, and book direct; optional €3 breakfast in street-level bar, air-con, free Wi-Fi, Via della Scala 21, tel. 055-260-8932, mobile 333-612-5973, fax 055-265-5315, www.bellev-uehouse.it, info@bellevuehouse.it).

$ Albergo Margaret, homey yet minimalist, doesn't have a public lounge or offer breakfast. Run by the Cristantielli family, it has seven peaceful and simple rooms (D-€40, Ds-€60, Db-€75, ask for discount if you book direct and pay cash, extra bed-€10, air-con, free Wi-Fi, near Santa Maria Novella at Via della Scala 25, tel. & fax 055-210-138, www.hotel-margaret.it, info@hotel-margaret.it; Francesco, Anna, and Graziano).

Hostels away from the Center

These two hostels, northeast of downtown, are a bus ride from the action. A far more central hostel is in the Oltrarno (listed at the end of the next section).

$ Villa Camerata, classy for an IYHF hostel, is in a pretty villa three miles northeast of the train station, on the outskirts of Florence (€18/bed with breakfast, 4- to 6-bed rooms, nonmembers pay €3/night more, free Wi-Fi, self-serve laundry, Via Righi 2—take bus #11 from the train station to Salviatino or bus #17 to Via Cento Stelle, tel. 055-601-451, fax 055-610-300, www.aighostels.com, firenze@aighostels.com).

$ Hostel 7 Santi calls itself a "travelers' haven." It fills a former convent, but you'll feel like you're in an old school. Still, it offers some of the best cheap beds in town, is friendly to older travelers, and comes with the services you'd expect in a big, modern hostel, including free Wi-Fi and self-serve laundry. It's in a more residential neighborhood near the Campo di Marte stadium, about a 10-minute bus ride from the center (200 beds in 60 rooms, mostly 4- or 6-bed dorms with a floor of doubles and triples, €16-18/dorm bed, Sb-€45, Db-€60, Tb-€75, Qb-€85, includes sheets and towels, breakfast and dinner available but cost extra, no curfew, free Internet access and Wi-Fi; Viale dei Mille 11—from train station, take bus #10, #17, or #20, direction: Campo di Marte, to bus stop Chiesa dei Sette Santi; tel. 055-504-8452, www.7santi.com, info@7santi.com).

South of the Arno River, in the Oltrarno

Across the river in the Oltrarno area, between the Pitti Palace and Ponte Vecchio, you'll find small, traditional crafts shops, neigh-

FLORENCE

Oltrarno Hotels & Restaurants

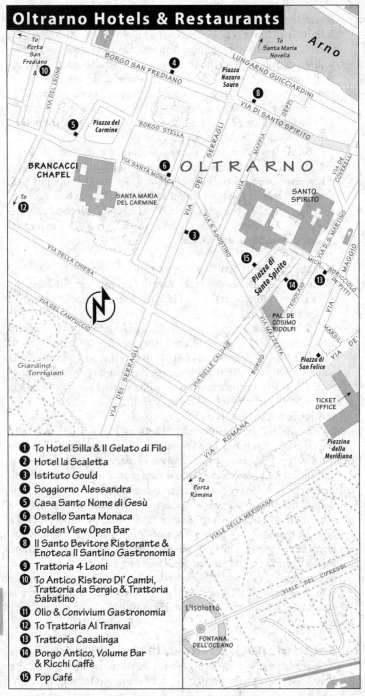

1. To Hotel Silla & Il Gelato di Filo
2. Hotel la Scaletta
3. Istituto Gould
4. Soggiorno Alessandra
5. Casa Santo Nome di Gesù
6. Ostello Santa Monaca
7. Golden View Open Bar
8. Il Santo Bevitore Ristorante & Enoteca Il Santino Gastronomia
9. Trattoria 4 Leoni
10. To Antico Ristoro Di' Cambi, Trattoria da Sergio & Trattoria Sabatino
11. Olio & Convivium Gastronomia
12. To Trattoria Al Tranvai
13. Trattoria Casalinga
14. Borgo Antico, Volume Bar & Ricchi Caffè
15. Pop Café

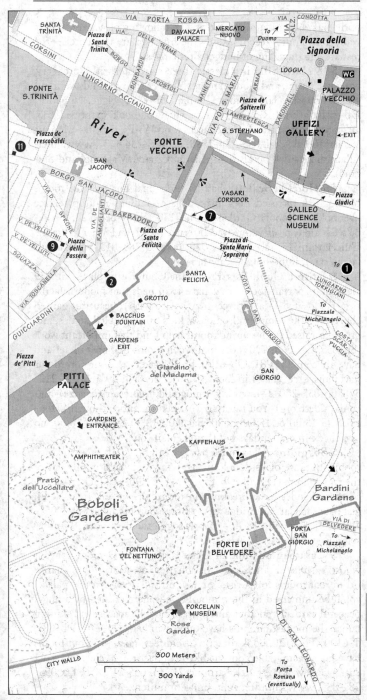

borly piazzas, and family eateries. The following places are an easy walk from Ponte Vecchio. Only the first two are real hotels—the rest are a ragtag gang of budget alternatives.

$$$ Hotel Silla is a classic three-star hotel with 36 cheery, spacious, pastel, and modern rooms. It faces the river and overlooks a park opposite Santa Croce Church (Db-€180, bigger "superior" Db-€210, ask for Rick Steves rate when you book, extra bed-€35, air-con, elevator, free Internet access and Wi-Fi, parking-€19/day, Via dei Renai 5, tel. 055-234-2888, fax 055-234-1437, www.hotel-silla.it, hotelsilla@hotelsilla.it; Laura, Chiara, Massimo, and Stefano).

$$ Hotel la Scaletta has 17 functional but colorful rooms hiding in a tortured floor plan, plus a fabulous rooftop terrace overlooking Boboli Gardens (Db-€130, third bed-€20, breakfast-€7, air-con, elevator, free Internet access and Wi-Fi, Via de' Guicciardini 13, tel. 055-283-028, fax 055-283-013, www.hotel-lascaletta.it, info@hotellascaletta.it).

$ Istituto Gould is a Protestant Church-run place with 39 clean and spartan rooms that have twin beds and modern facilities. It's located in a 17th-century palace with a beautiful garden courtyard. The complex also houses kids from troubled homes, and proceeds raised from renting rooms help fund that important work (Sb-€55, Db-€60, €20 more for garden rooms that are quieter and have air-con, Tb-€81, Qb-€100, breakfast-€6, non-air-con rooms have fans, free Wi-Fi in lobby, Via dei Serragli 49, tel. 055-212-576, fax 055-280-274, www.istitutogould.it, foresteriafirenze@diaconiavaldese.org). You must arrive when the office is open (Mon-Fri 8:45-13:00 & 15:00-19:30, Sat 9:00-13:30 & 14:30-18:00, no live check-in on Sundays but they'll email you a code).

$ Soggiorno Alessandra has five bright, comfy, and smallish rooms. Because of its double-paned windows, you'll hardly notice the traffic noise (D-€73, Db-€78, Tb-€98, Qb-€128, cheaper off-season, includes basic breakfast in room, air-con-€8, free Wi-Fi, just past the Carraia Bridge at Via Borgo San Frediano 6, tel. 055-290-424, fax 055-218-464, www.soggiornoalessandra.it, info@soggiornoalessandra.it, Alessandra).

$ Casa Santo Nome di Gesù is a grand, 29-room convent whose sisters—Franciscan Missionaries of Mary—are thankful to rent rooms to tourists. Staying in this 15th-century palace, you'll be immersed in the tranquil atmosphere created by a huge, peaceful garden, generous and prayerful public spaces, and smiling nuns. The monastic rooms have only twin beds (D-€70, Db-€85, T-€100, Tb-€120, book direct to avoid fees, no air-con but rooms have fans, memorable convent-like breakfast room, elevator, strict 23:29 curfew, Piazza del Carmine 21, tel. 055-213-856, fax 055-281-835, www.fmmfirenze.it, info@fmmfirenze.it).

Hostel: **$ Ostello Santa Monaca,** a well-run, institutional-feeling hostel a long block south of the Brancacci Chapel. As clean as its guests, its 112 beds in 15 rooms (2- to 20-bed dorms) attract a young backpacking crowd (€18-26/bed with sheets and towel, 10:00-14:00 lock-out, 2:00 in the morning curfew, free Internet access and Wi-Fi, self-serve laundry, kitchen, bike rental, Via Santa Monaca 6, tel. 055-268-338, fax 055-280-185, www.ostellosantamonaca.com, info@ostellosantamonaca.com).

Rural *Agriturismo* South of Florence

The countryside south of Florence is loaded with enticing rural farms offering accommodations, called *agriturismi.* This option is about 45 minutes south of Florence, in the Chianti region.

$$$ I Greppi di Silli is a lovely, family-run *agriturismo* set among rolling hills south of Florence. Owners Anna and Giuliano Alfani cultivate Chianti grapes and olive trees, and offer six carefully remodeled apartments with beds for 2-6 people, some with panoramic views and/or terraces; a seventh apartment (sleeps 8) is a mile away in an old country house (Db-€115-250 or €735-1,900/week, price depends on apartment, less off-season; one-week minimum—Sat-to-Sat—in July-Aug, fewer nights possible in shoulder and low season—but generally still a 3-night minimum; breakfast-€9, pool, kids' play area, table tennis, bocce ball court, loaner bikes, weekly farm dinners-€28/person—less for kids, Via Vallacchio 19, near San Casciano and just outside the village of Mercatale Val di Pesa, about 45 minutes' drive to Florence or San Gimignano and one hour from Siena, tel. 055-821-7959, www.igreppidisilli.it, info@igreppidisilli.it).

Eating in Florence

Remember, restaurants like to serve what's fresh. If you're into flavor, go for the seasonal best bets—featured in the *piatti del giorno* ("special of the day") section on menus. For dessert, it's gelato (see sidebar later in this section).

To save money and time for sights, keep lunches fast and simple, eating in one of the countless pizzerias and self-service cafeterias. Picnicking is easy—there's no shortage of corner *supermercatos,* or you can picnic your way through the Mercato Centrale.

North of the Arno River
Near the Church of Santa Maria Novella
Trattoria al Trebbio serves traditional food, especially rabbit and steak, with simple Florentine elegance in its candlelit interior. Inside, it feels like a throwback; the room is decorated with

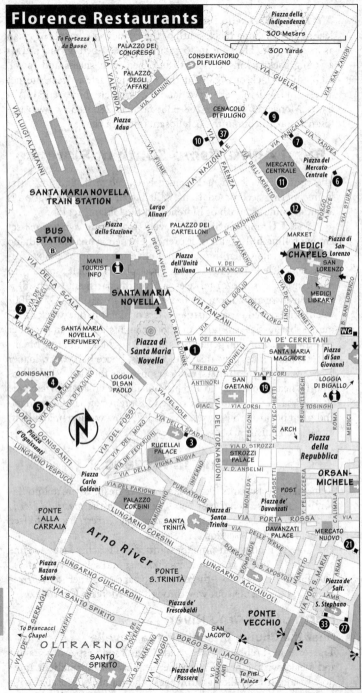

Florence Restaurants

Piazza della Indipendenza

300 Meters

300 Yards

To Fortezza da Basso

PALAZZO DEI CONGRESSI

PALAZZO DEGLI AFFARI

CONSERVATORIO DI FULIGNO

CENACOLO DI FULIGNO

Piazza Adua

9

10 **37**

7

11

MERCATO CENTRALE

Piazza del Mercato Centrale

6

SANTA MARIA NOVELLA TRAIN STATION

Largo Alinari

PALAZZO DEI CARTELLONI

12

BUS STATION

Piazza della Stazione

MARKET

MEDICI CHAPELS

Piazza di San Lorenzo

SAN LORENZO

MAIN TOURIST INFO

Piazza dell'Unità Italiana

V. DEI MELARANCIO

8

MEDICI LIBRARY

SANTA MARIA NOVELLA

WC

2

SANTA MARIA NOVELLA PERFUMERY

Piazza di Santa Maria Novella

1

SANTA MARIA MAGGIORE

Piazza di San Giovanni

LOGGIA DI BIGALLO

OGNISSANTI

LOGGIA DI SAN PAOLO

4

SAN GAETANO

19

Piazza della Repubblica

5

RUCELLAI PALACE

3

STROZZI PALACE

ORSAN-MICHELE

Piazza Carlo Goldoni

PALAZZO CORSINI

SANTA TRINITÀ

Piazza di Santa Trinita

POST

Piazza de' Davanzati

DAVANZATI PALACE

MERCATO NUOVO

21

PONTE ALLA CARRAIA

Arno River

PONTE S. TRINITÀ

Piazza Nazaro Sauro

Piazza de' Frescobaldi

Piazza de' Salt.

S. Stephano

33 **27**

OLTRARNO

SANTO SPIRITO

SAN JACOPO

PONTE VECCHIO

To Brancacci Chapel

Piazza della Passera

To Pitti Palace

1 Trattoria al Trebbio
2 Trattoria "da Giorgio"
3 Trattoria Marione
4 Trattoria Sostanza-Troia
5 Trattoria 13 Gobbi
6 Trattoria Zà-Zà & Trattoria Mario's
7 Trattoria la Burrasca
8 Trattoria Lo Stracotto
9 Osteria Vineria i'Brincello
10 Trattoria Nerone Pizzeria
11 Mercato Centrale & Nerbone in the Market
12 Casa del Vino
13 Pugi Pizza
14 Barbecue Döner Kebab
15 Pasticceria Robiglio
16 La Mescita Fiaschetteria
17 Il Centro Supermercati
18 To Antica Trattoria da Tito
19 Self-Service Rist. Leonardo
20 Turkuaz Döner Kebab
21 Rivoire Café
22 Frescobaldi Rist. & Wine Bar
23 Ristorante Paoli, Cantinetta dei Verrazzano & Perchè No! Gelateria
24 Osteria Vini e Vecchi Sapori
25 I Fratellini
26 L'Antico Trippaio, Pizzeria Totò & Supermarket
27 'Ino Bottega di Alimentari e Vini
28 Ristorante del Fagioli
29 Boccadama Enoteca Rist.
30 Trattoria Anita
31 Trattoria l'cche C'è C'è
32 Gelateria Grom
33 Gelateria Carrozze
34 Gelateria Carabè
35 Vivoli's Gelateria
36 Gelateria de' Neri
37 The Bermuda Triangle

FLORENCE

old movie posters. Outside, tables spill out onto a romantic little square—an oasis of Roman Trastevere-like charm (€7-10 pastas, €10-14 *secondi*, daily 12:00-15:00 & 19:15-23:00, closed for lunch Tue off-season, reserve for outdoor seating, half a block off of Piazza Santa Maria Novella at Via delle Belle Donne 47, tel. 055-287-089, Antonio).

Trattoria "da Giorgio" is a family-style diner on a sketchy street serving up piping-hot, delicious home cooking to happy locals and tourists alike. Their three-course, fixed-price meal, including water and a drink, is a great value (€12 at lunch, €13 at dinner). Choose from among the daily specials or the regular menu (Mon-Sat 12:00-14:30 & 18:30-22:00, closed Sun, Via Palazzuolo 100 red, tel. 055-284-302, Silvano).

Trattoria Marione serves sincerely home cooked-style meals to a mixed group of tourists and Florentines beneath hanging ham hocks. The ambience is happy, crowded, food-loving, and steamy (€8-11 pastas, €10-12 *secondi*, daily 12:00-17:30 & 19:00-23:00, Via della Spada 27 red, tel. 055-214-756, Fabio).

Trattoria Sostanza-Troia, characteristic and well established, is famous for its beef. Hearty steaks and pastas are splittable. Whirling ceiling fans and walls strewn with old photos evoke earlier times, while the artichoke pies remind locals of Grandma's cooking. Crowded, shared tables with paper tablecloths give this place a bistro feel. They offer two dinner seatings, at 19:30 and 21:00, which require reservations (dinners for about €30 plus wine, cash only, lunch Mon-Sat 12:30-14:00, closed Sun, closed Sat off-season, Via del Porcellana 25 red, tel. 055-212-691).

Trattoria 13 Gobbi ("13 Hunchbacks") is a trendy and slightly self-important eatery, atmospherically cluttered and glowing with candles around a tiny garden. Romantic in front and more kid-friendly in back, it serves beautifully presented Tuscan food (they're enthusiastic about their steak) on big, fancy plates to a mostly tourist crowd (€10-12 pastas, €14-19 *secondi*, daily 12:30-15:00 & 19:30-23:00, Via del Porcellana 9 red, tel. 055-284-015, Enrico).

Near the Mercato Centrale

The following market-neighborhood eateries all have a distinct vibe. They're within a few blocks of each other: Scout around and choose your favorite.

Trattoria Zà-Zà is a fun, characteristic, high-energy place facing the Mercato Centrale. It offers a family-friendly festival of standard Tuscan dishes such as *ribollita* and *bistecca alla fiorentina*, plus a variety of big, splittable €8 salads. Though it's more touristy than ever, the food is still great, and everyone's happy. Arrive early or make a reservation. Choose between the folkloric interior or the fine outdoor piazza. Understand your itemized bill, and don't mistake their outside seating with the neighboring restaurant's (€8-10 pastas, €10-16 *secondi*, daily 11:00-23:00, Piazza del Mercato Centrale 26 red, tel. 055-215-411). Their **bar/osteria,** nearby, has a similar menu (with a few differences, including more of an emphasis on seafood and *taglieri*—cheese-and-meat plates), a trendier-feeling interior, and a smaller, more open outdoor-dining zone.

Trattoria la Burrasca is Flintstone-chic. Friendly duo Elio and Simone offer a limited menu with good-value seasonal specials of Tuscan home cooking. It's small—10 tables—and often filled with my readers. If Archie Bunker were Italian, he'd eat at this trattoria for special nights out (€6 pastas, €7-15 *secondi,* no cover or service charge, Tue-Sun 12:00-15:00 & 19:00-22:30, closed Mon, Via Panicale 6, north corner of Mercato Centrale, tel. 055-215-827).

Trattoria Lo Stracotto is a truffle-colored eatery with sophisticated ambience just steps away from the Medici Chapels. It's run by cousins Francesco and Tommaso, who serve up tasty, traditional dishes such as *bistecca alla fiorentina* and *ribollita* (based on grandfather's recipe), and good chocolate soufflé. Enjoy the candlelit ambience and soft music as you sit either in the dining room or out on the terrace (€8-10 pastas, €9-15 *secondi,* daily 12:00-15:00 & 18:00-22:30, Piazza Madonna degli Aldobrandi 16/17, tel. 055-230-2062).

Osteria Vineria i'Brincello is a bright, happy, no-frills diner with tasty food, lots of spirit, friendly service, and no hint of snobbishness. It features a list of Tuscan daily specials hanging from the ceiling and great prices on good bottled wine (€7-8 pastas, €8-15 *secondi*, €5 takeout homemade pasta, daily 12:00-15:00 & 19:00-23:00, near corner of Via Nazionale and Via Chiara at Via Nazionale 110 red, tel. 055-282-645, Fredi cooks while Claudia serves).

Trattoria Nerone Pizzeria, serving up cheap, hearty Tuscan dishes and decent pizzas, is a tourist-friendly, practical standby in the hotel district. The lively, flamboyantly outfitted space (once the garden courtyard of a convent) feels like a good but kitschy Italian-American chain restaurant (€5-8 pizzas, €6-8 pastas, €8-12 *secondi,* daily 12:00-15:00 & 18:30-23:00, just north of Via Nazionale at Via Faenza 95-97 red, tel. 055-291-217, Tulio).

Eating Cheaply in or near the Mercato Centrale

Note that none of these eateries is open for dinner.

The **Mercato Centrale (Central Market)** is great for an ad-lib lunch. It offers colorful piles of picnic produce, people-watching, and rustic sandwiches (Mon-Sat 7:00-14:00, Sat in winter until 17:00, closed Sun, a block north of San Lorenzo street market). Meat, fish, and cheese are sold on the ground level, with fruit and veggies mostly upstairs. The thriving ground-level eateries within the market (such as Nerbone, described next) serve some of the cheapest hot meals in town. The fancy deli, Perini, is famous for its quality products and generous free samples. Buy a picnic of fresh mozzarella cheese, olives, fruit, and crunchy bread to munch on the steps of the nearby Church of San Lorenzo, overlooking the bustling street market.

Nerbone in the Market is a venerable café and the best place for a sit-down meal within the Mercato Centrale. Join the shoppers and workers who crowd up to the bar to grab their €4-6 plates. Of the several cheap market diners, this feels the most authentic. As intestines are close to Florentines' hearts, tripe is very big here (lunch menu served Mon-Sat 12:00-14:00, sandwiches available 8:00-12:00, closed Sun, cash only, inside the Mercato Centrale on the side closest to the Church of San Lorenzo, mobile 339-648-0251).

Trattoria Mario's, around the corner from Trattoria Zà-Zà (listed earlier), has been serving hearty lunches to market-goers since 1953 (Fabio and Romeo are the latest generation). Their simple formula: bustling service, old-fashioned good value, a lunch-only fixed-price meal, and shared tables. It's *cucina casalinga*— home cooking *con brio*. This place is high-energy and jam-packed. Their best dishes often sell out first, so go early. If there's a line, put your name on the list (€5-6 pastas, €8 *secondi*, cash only, Mon-Sat 12:00-15:30, closed Sun and Aug, no reservations, Via Rosina 2, tel. 055-218-550).

Casa del Vino, Florence's oldest operating wine shop, offers glasses of wine from among 25 open bottles (see the list tacked to the bar). Owner Gianni, whose family has owned the Casa for more than 70 years, is a class act. Gianni's *carta dei panini* lists delightful €3.50 sandwiches and €1 crostini; the *I Nostri Panini* (classic sandwiches) richly reward adventurous eaters. During busy times, it's a mob scene. You'll eat standing outside alongside workers on a quick lunch break (Mon-Fri 9:30-20:00 year-round, Sat 9:30-17:00 June-Sept only, closed Sun year-round and Sat off-season, hidden behind stalls of San Lorenzo Market at Via dell'Ariento 16 red, tel. 055-215-609).

Near the Accademia
Budget-Lunch Places Surrounding the Accademia

For pizza by the slice, try **Pugi**, at Piazza San Marco 10. For a break from pasta and pizza, grab a quick kebab lunch from **Barbecue: The Taste of Istanbul** (Via Cavour 41).

Pasticceria Robiglio, a smart little café, opens up its stately dining area and sets out a few tables on the sidewalk for lunch. They have a small menu of daily pasta and *secondi* specials, and seem determined to do things like they did in the elegant, pre-tourism days (generous €9-10 plates, a great €8 niçoise-like "fantasy salad," pretty pastries, smiling service, daily 12:00-15:00, longer hours as a café, a block toward the Duomo off Piazza S.S. Annunziata at Via dei Servi 112 red, tel. 055-212-784). Before you leave, be tempted by their pastries—famous among Florentines.

La Mescita Fiaschetteria is a characteristic hole-in-the-wall just around the corner from *David*—but a world away from all the tourism. It's where locals and students enjoy daily pasta specials and hearty sandwiches with good €1.50 house wine. You can trust Mirco and Alessio (as far as you can throw them)—just point to what looks good (such as their €5-6 pasta plate or €6-7 *secondi*), and you'll soon be eating well and inexpensively. The place can either be mobbed by students or in a peaceful time warp, depending on when you stop by (Mon-Sat 10:45-16:00, closed Sun, Via degli Alfani 70 red, mobile 347-795-1604 or 338-992-2640).

Picnic on the Ultimate Renaissance Square: **Il Centro Supermercati,** a handy supermarket a half-block north of the Accademia, has a curbside sandwich bar (Panineria) with an easy English menu that includes salads to go (Mon-Sat 9:00-19:30, Sun 10:00-19:00, sandwich bar may close earlier, Via Ricasoli 109). With your picnic in hand, hike around the block and join the bums on Piazza S.S. Annunziata, the first Renaissance square in Florence (don't confuse this with the less-interesting Piazza San Marco, closer to the supermarket). There's a fountain for washing fruit on the square. Grab a stony seat anywhere you like, and savor one of my favorite cheap Florence eating experiences. Or, drop by any of the places listed earlier for an easy lunch (pizza, kebab, or sandwich plus juice) to go.

Dining with Bobo away from the Center

Antica Trattoria da Tito, a 10-minute hike from the Accademia along Via San Gallo, is a long, drawn-out event of a meal. The boss, Bobo, is a fire hose of restaurateur energy who has clearly found his niche—making people happy with quality traditional food and lots of wine. His staff is as loyal as his clientele. While the food is great, there's no pretense. It's just a playground of Tuscan cuisine with "no romance allowed." As for the music he plays, Bobo says, "We are slaves of '80s." I'd come late and plan to party. To gorge on a feast of *antipasti* (meats, cheeses, fava beans, and bruschetta), consider ordering *fermami* (literally "stop me")—for €14, Bobo brings you food until you say, *"Fermami!"* A couple can get *fermami*, desserts, and a nice bottle of wine for €60 total. Ask for *vino* recommendations to experience that perfect pairing of food and wine. If you go with the flow here, you'll walk back to your hotel fat and filled with memories (€10 pastas, €12 *secondi*, €14 *gran tagliere*—big plate of cheese and meat, travelers with this book get a free after-dinner drink, Mon-Sat 12:30-15:00 & 19:00-23:00, closed Sun, reservations generally necessary, Via San Gallo 112 red, tel. 055-472-475).

Fast and Cheap near the Duomo

Self-Service Ristorante Leonardo is inexpensive, air-conditioned, quick, and handy. Eating here, you'll get the sense that they're passionate about the quality of their food. Stefano and Luciano (like Pavarotti) run the place with enthusiasm and put out free pitchers of tap water. It's just a block from the Duomo, southwest of the Baptistery (tasty €5 pastas, €6 main courses, Sun-Fri 11:45-14:45 & 18:45-21:45, closed Sat, upstairs at Via Pecori 11, tel. 055-284-446).

Döner Kebab: A good place to try this cheap Middle Eastern specialty is **Turkuaz**, a couple of blocks northeast of the Duomo (Via dei Servi 65).

Near Piazza della Signoria

Piazza della Signoria, the scenic square facing the Palazzo Vecchio, is ringed by beautifully situated yet touristy eateries serving over-priced, bad-value, and probably microwaved food. If you're determined to eat on the square, have pizza at Ristorante il Cavallino or bar food from the Irish pub next door. Piazza della Signoria's saving grace is **Rivoire** café, famous for its fancy desserts and thick hot chocolate. While obscenely expensive, it has the best view tables on the square (Tue-Sun 7:30-24:00, closed Mon, tel. 055-214-412).

Fine Dining

Frescobaldi Ristorante and Wine Bar, the showcase of Italy's aristocratic wine family, is a good choice for a formal dinner in Florence. Candlelight reflects off glasses of wine, and high-vaulted ceilings complement the sophisticated dishes. They offer the same menu in three different dining areas: cozy interior, woody wine bar, and breezy terrace. If coming for dinner, make a reservation, dress up, and hit an ATM (€11-14 appetizers and pastas, €18-24 *secondi,* lighter wine-bar menu at lunch, Tue-Sat 12:00-14:30 & 19:00-22:30, Mon 19:00-22:30, closed Sun and much of Aug, air-con, half a block north of the Palazzo Vecchio at Via dei Magazzini 2-4 red, tel. 055-284-724, Francesco is the lead waiter).

Ristorante Paoli dishes up wonderful, traditional cuisine to loads of cheerful eaters being served by jolly little old men under a richly frescoed Gothic vault. It feels old-school and Old World...it's all about the setting. Because of its fame and central location, it's filled mostly with tourists, but for a sophisticated, traditional Tuscan splurge meal, this is a fine choice. Salads are dramatically cut and mixed from a trolley right at your table. The walls are sweaty with memories that go back to 1824, and the service is flamboyant and fun-loving (but don't get taken—confirm prices). Woodrow Wilson slurped spaghetti here—his bust looks down on you as you eat (€10-15 pastas, €12-20 *secondi*, daily 12:00-15:00 & 19:00-23:00, reserve for dinner, between Piazza della Signoria and the Duomo at Via dei Tavolini 12 red, tel. 055-216-215).

Eating Cheaply and Simply near Piazza della Signoria

Cantinetta dei Verrazzano, a long-established bakery/café/wine bar, serves delightful sandwich plates in an old-time setting. Their *selection Verrazzano* is a fine plate of four little crostini (like mini-bruschetta) proudly featuring different breads, cheeses, and meats from the Chianti region (€7.50). The *tagliere di focacce*, a sampler plate of mini-focaccia sandwiches, is also fun (€14 for big plate for two). Add a €5 glass of Chianti to either of these dishes to make a fine, light meal. Office workers pop in for a quick lunch, and it's traditional to share tables. Be warned: Prices can add up here in a hurry (Mon-Sat 8:00-21:00, Sun 10:00-17:00, no reservations taken, just off Via de' Calzaiuoli, across from Orsanmichele Church at Via dei Tavolini 18, tel. 055-268-590). They also have benches and tiny tables for eating at takeout prices. Simply step to the back and point to a hot *focacce* sandwich (€3), order a drink at the bar, and take away your food or sit with Florentines and watch the action while you munch.

Osteria Vini e Vecchi Sapori, half a block north of the Palazzo Vecchio, is a colorful 16-seat hole-in-the-wall restaurant serving Tuscan food with a fun, accessible menu of delicious €7-9 pastas and €9-10 *secondi* (Tue-Sat 12:30-15:00 & 19:30-22:00, Sun 12:30-15:00, closed Mon, reserve for dinner; facing the bronze equestrian statue in Piazza della Signoria, go behind its tail into the corner and to your left; Via dei Magazzini 3 red, tel. 055-293-045, run by Mario while wife Rosanna cooks and son Thomas serves).

I Fratellini is an informal eatery where the "little brothers" have served peasants 29 different kinds of sandwiches and cheap glasses of Chianti wine (see list on wall) since 1875. Join the local crowd to order, then sit on a nearby curb or windowsill to eat, placing your glass on the wall rack before you leave (€2.50 sandwiches, daily 9:00-20:00 or until the bread runs out, closed Sun in winter, 20 yards in front of Orsanmichele Church on Via dei Cimatori, tel. 055-239-6096). Be adventurous with the menu (easy-order by number). Consider *finocchiona* (#15, a special Tuscan salami), *lardo di Colonnata* (#22, lard aged in Carrara marble), and *cinghiale* (#19, spicy wild boar) sandwiches. Order the most expensive wine they're selling by the glass (Brunello for €5; bottles are labeled).

Cheap Takeout on Via Dante Alighieri: Three handy places line up on this street, just a couple of blocks from the Duomo. **L'Antico**

Trippaio, an antique tripe stand, is a fixture in the town center. Cheap and authentic as can be, this is where locals come daily for €4-6 sandwiches *(panini),* featuring specialties like *trippa alla fio-rentina* (tripe), *lampredotto* (cow's stomach), and a list of more appetizing options. Roberto and Maurizio offer a free plastic glass of rotgut Chianti with each sandwich for travelers with this book (daily 9:00-20:00, on Via Dante Alighieri, mobile 339-742-5692). If tripe isn't your cup of offal, **Pizzeria Totò,** just next to the tripe stand, has very good €2.50-3 slices (Via Dante Alighieri 28 red, tel. 055-290-406). And a few steps in the opposite direction is a **Metà supermarket**, with cheap drinks and snacks and a fine *antipasti* case inside (daily 8:30-21:30, Sun from 9:00, Via Dante Alighieri 20-24). If you pick up lunch at any of these, the best people-watching place to enjoy your sandwich is three blocks away, on Piazza della Signoria.

Wine Bar near Ponte Vecchio

'Ino Bottega di Alimentari e Vini is a mod little shop filled with gifty edibles. Alessandro and his staff serve sandwiches and wine—you'll get your €5-8 sandwich on a napkin with an included glass of their wine of the day as you perch on a tiny stool. They can also make a fine €12 *piatto misto* of cheeses and meats with bread (daily 11:00-16:30, immediately behind Uffizi Gallery on Ponte Vecchio side, Via dei Georgofili 3 red, tel. 055-219-208).

Between the Palazzo Vecchio and Santa Croce Church

Ristorante del Fagioli is an enthusiastically run eatery where you feel the heritage. The dad, Gigi, commands the kitchen while family members Antonio, Maurizio, and Simone keep the throngs of loyal customers returning. The cuisine: home-style bread-soups, hearty steaks, and Florentine classics. Don't worry—while *fagioli* means "beans," that's the family name, not the extent of the menu (€9 pastas, €9 *secondi,* cash only, Mon-Fri 12:30-14:30 & 19:30-24:00, closed Sat-Sun, reserve for dinner, between Santa Croce Church and the Alle Grazie bridge at Corso dei Tintori 47, tel. 055-244-285).

Boccadama Enoteca Ristorante is a stylish, shabby-chic wine bistro serving an easy-to-navigate menu of capably executed traditional Tuscan fare based on seasonal produce. Eat in the intimate dining room with candles reflecting off bottle-lined walls or at one of the few tables on the dramatic Piazza Santa Croce. As this place is popular with groups, reservations are smart (€8-9 *primi,* €12-16 *secondi,* daily 11:00-16:00 & 18:30-24:00, on south side of Piazza Santa Croce at 25-26 red, tel. 055-243-640, Marco).

Trattoria Anita, midway between the Uffizi and Santa Croce, feels old-school, with wood paneling and rows of wine bottles. Brothers Nicola, Gianni, and Maurizio offer a good lunch special: three hearty Tuscan courses for €9 on weekdays (€7-8 pastas, €7-12 *secondi*, Mon-Sat 12:00-14:30 & 19:00-22:15, closed Sun, on the corner of Via Vinegia and Via del Parlagio at #2 red, tel. 055-218-698).

Trattoria I'cche C'è C'è (EE-kay chay chay; dialect for "whatever there is, there is") is a small, family-style restaurant where fun-loving Gino and his wife Mara serve functional local food, including a €13 three-course, fixed-price meal. While filled with tourists, the place has a charming mom-and-pop warmth (€7-12 pastas, €12-18 *secondi*, Tue-Sun 12:30-14:30 & 19:30-22:30, closed Mon and two weeks in Aug, midway between Bargello and river at Via Magalotti 11 red, tel. 055-216-589).

South of the River, in the Oltrarno

In general, dining in the Oltrarno offers a more authentic experience; although it's quite close to the old center, tourists imagine that it's another world and tend to stay away. At many of these places, Florentines may even outnumber my readers. For locations, see the map on page 1088.

Dining with a Ponte Vecchio View

Golden View Open Bar is a lively, trendy bistro, good for a romantic meal or just a salad, pizza, or pasta with fine wine and a fine view of Ponte Vecchio and the Arno River. Its white, minimalist interior is a stark contrast to atmospheric old Florence. Reservations for window tables are essential unless you drop in early for dinner (€10 pizzas, €11-15 pastas, big €11-14 salads, €20-30 *secondi*, daily 11:30-24:00, impressive wine bar, 50 yards east of Ponte Vecchio at Via dei Bardi 58, tel. 055-214-502, run by Antonio, Marco, and Tomaso). They have four seating areas (with the same menu and prices) for whatever mood you're in: a riverside pizza place, a classier restaurant, a jazzy lounge, and a wine bar (they also serve a buffet of appetizers free with your drink from 19:00 to 21:00). Mixing their fine wine, river views, and live jazz makes for a wonderful evening (jazz nightly at 21:00 except Tue and Thu off-season).

Dining Well in the Oltrarno

Of the many good and colorful restaurants in the Oltrarno, these are my favorites. Reservations are a good idea in the evening.

Il Santo Bevitore Ristorante, lit like a Rembrandt painting and filled with dressy tables, serves creative Tuscan cuisine. They're enthusiastic about matching quality produce from the area with the right wine. This is a good break from the big, sloppy plates of pasta you'll get at many Florence eateries (€9-12 pastas,

FLORENCE

Gelato

Gelato is an edible art form. Italy's best ice cream is in Florence—one souvenir that can't break and won't clutter your luggage. But beware of scams at touristy joints on busy streets that turn a simple request for a cone into a €10 "tourist special" rip-off. To avoid this, survey the size options and be very clear in your order (for example, "a €3 cone").

A key to gelato appreciation is sampling liberally and choosing flavors that go well together. Ask, as Italians do, for *"Un assaggio, per favore?"* (A taste, please?; oon ah-SAH-joh pehr fah-VOH-ray) and *"Che si sposano bene?"* (What marries well?; kay see spoh-ZAH-noh BEN-ay).

Artiginale, nostra produzione, and *produzione propia* mean gelato is made on the premises; also, gelato displayed in covered metal tins (rather than white plastic) is more likely to be home-made. Gelato aficionados avoid colors that don't appear in nature—for fewer chemicals and real flavor, go for mellow hues (bright colors attract children). If you see giant mounds of bright colors, skip it.

All of these places, which are a cut above, are open daily for long hours.

Near the Duomo: The recent favorite in town, **Grom** uses organic ingredients and seasonal fresh fruit, along with biodegradable spoons and tubs. This clever Italy-wide chain markets its traditional approach with a staff quick to tell customers, "This gelato reminds me of my childhood." A few purists grumble that a chain *gelateria* can't possibly compare with a local one-off, but so far Grom has maintained an impressively high quality—likely because the menu follows what's in season, changing every month (Via delle Oche 24 red).

€8-12 meat-and-cheese *taglieri*, €10-17 *secondi*, good wine list by the glass or bottle, daily 12:30-14:30 & 19:30-22:30, closed Sun for lunch, come early or make reservations, no outside seating, Via di Santo Spirito 64, tel. 055-211-264). Their smaller wine bar next door, **Enoteca Il Santino Gastronomia,** feels like the perfect after-work hangout for foodies who'd like a glass of wine and some light food. Tight, cozy, and atmospheric, one wall is occupied by the bar, where you can assemble an €8-12 *tagliere* of local cheeses and *salumi* (also available to take away). They also have a few €6-8 hot dishes. Both the food and the wine is locally sourced from small producers (daily 12:30-23:00, Via di Santo Spirito 60 red, tel. 055-230-2820).

Trattoria 4 Leoni creates the quintessential Oltrarno dinner scene. The Tuscan-style food is made with an innovative twist and an appreciation for vegetables. You'll enjoy the fun energy and

Near Ponte Vecchio: **Gelateria Carrozze** is a longtime favorite (on riverfront 30 yards from Ponte Vecchio toward the Uffizi at Piazza del Pesce 3).

Near the Accademia: A Sicilian choice on a tourist thoroughfare, **Gelateria Carabè** is particularly famous for its luscious granite—Italian ices made with fresh fruit. A cremolata is a granita with a dollop of gelato—a delicious combination (from the Accademia, it's a block toward the Duomo at Via Ricasoli 60 red).

Near Orsanmichele Church: **Perchè No!** is located just off the busy main pedestrian drag, Via de' Calzaiuoli, and serves a wide array of flavors (Via dei Tavolini 19).

Near the Church of Santa Croce: The venerable favorite, **Vivoli's** still has great gelato—but it's more expensive and stingy in its servings. Before ordering, try a free sample of their rice flavor—*riso* (closed Mon, Aug, and Jan; opposite the Church of Santa Croce, go down Via Torta a block and turn right on Via Stinche). Locals flock to **Gelateria de' Neri** (Via de' Neri 26 red), also owned by Vivoli's.

Near the Mercato Centrale: The **Bermuda Triangle** (a.k.a., I Gelati Del Bondi) is a hit both for its fresh ingredients and for the big-hearted energy of its owner, Vetulio (Via Nazionale 61 red, where it crosses Via Faenza, tel. 055-287-490).

Across the River: If you want an excuse to check out the little village-like neighborhood across the river from Santa Croce, enjoy a gelato at the tiny **Il Gelato di Filo** (named for Filippo and Lorenzo) at Via San Miniato 5 red, a few steps toward the river from Porta San Miniato. Gelato chef Edmir is proud of his fruity sorbet as well.

characteristic seating, both outside on the colorful square, Canto ai Quattro Pagoni, and inside, where you'll dine in exposed-stone sophistication. While the wines by the glass are pricey, the house wine is very good (€10 pastas, €10-15 *secondi*, daily 12:00-24:00, dinner reservations smart; from Ponte Vecchio walk four blocks up Via de' Guicciardini, turn right on Via dello Sprone, then slightly left to Via de' Vellutini 1; tel. 055-218-562).

Antico Ristoro Di' Cambi is a meat-lover's dream—thick with Tuscan traditions, rustic touches, and T-bone steaks. The bustling scene has a memorable, beer-hall energy. As you walk in, you'll pass a glass case filled with red chunks of Chianina beef that's priced by weight (for the famous *bistecca alla fiorentina*, €40/kilo, standard serving is half a kilo per person). Before you OK your investment, they'll show you the cut and tell you the weight. While the steak comes nearly uncooked, it's air dried for 21 days so it's not really raw, just very tasty and tender—making you so happy you're sitting at the top of the food chain. Sit inside the convivial woody interior or outside on a square (€8-10 pastas, €10-18 *secondi*, Mon-Sat 12:00-14:30 & 18:30-22:30, closed Sun, reserve on weekends and to sit outside, Via Sant'Onofrio 1 red, one block south of Ponte Amerigo Vespucci, tel. 055-217-134, run by Stefano and Fabio, the Cambi cousins).

Olio & Convivium Gastronomia is primarily a catering company for top-end events, and this is where they showcase their cooking. It started as an elegant deli whose refined olive-oil-tasting room morphed into a romantic, aristocratic restaurant. Their three intimate rooms are surrounded by fine *prosciutti*, cheeses, and wine shelves. It can seem intimidating and a little pretentious, but well-dressed foodies will appreciate this place for its quiet atmosphere. Their list of €14-25 *gastronomia* plates offers an array of taste treats and fine wines by the glass (€14-16 pastas, €20-22 *secondi*, stylish €18 lunches with wine, Tue-Sat 12:00-14:30 & 19:00-22:30, Mon 12:00-14:30 only, closed Sun, strong air-con, Via di Santo Spirito 4, tel. 055-265-8198, Monica).

Trattoria da Sergio is a tiny eatery about a block before Porta San Frediano, one of Florence's medieval gates. It has charm and a strong following, so reservations are a must. The food is on the gourmet side of home cooking—mama's favorites with a modern twist—and therefore a bit more expensive (€9-10 pastas, €12-20 *secondi*, Tue-Sun 12:00-14:00 & 19:30-22:45, closed Mon, Borgo San Frediano 145 red, tel. 055-223-449, Sergio and Marco).

Trattoria Al Tranvai, with tight seating and small dark-wood tables, looks like an old-time tram filled with the neighborhood gang. A 10-minute walk from the river at the edge of the Oltrarno, it feels like a small town's favorite eatery (€9 pastas, €10-13 *secondi*, Mon 19:00-24:00, Tue-Sat 11:00-15:00 & 19:00-24:00, closed Sun, Piazza T. Tasso 14 red, tel. 055-225-197).

Eating Cheaply in the Oltrarno

Trattoria Sabatino, farthest away and least touristy of my Oltrarno listings, is a spacious, brightly lit mess hall—disturbingly cheap—with family character and a simple menu. It's a super place to watch locals munch. You'll find it just outside Porta San Frediano, a 15-minute walk from Ponte Vecchio (€4 pastas, €5 *secondi*, Mon-Fri 12:00-15:00 & 19:15-22:00, closed Sat-Sun, Via Pisana 2 red, tel. 055-225-955, little English spoken).

Trattoria Casalinga, an inexpensive standby, comes with aproned women bustling around the kitchen. Florentines and tourists alike pack the place and leave full and happy, with euros to spare for gelato (€7 pastas, €8-10 *secondi*, Mon-Sat 12:00-14:30 & 19:00-21:45, after 20:00 reserve or wait, closed Sun and Aug, just off Piazza di Santo Spirito, near the church at Via de' Michelozzi 9 red, tel. 055-218-624, Andrea and Paolo).

Borgo Antico is the hit of Piazza di Santo Spirito, with enticing pizzas, big deluxe plates of pasta, a delightful setting, and a trendy and boisterous young crowd (€8-10 pizza and pasta, €14-18 *secondi*, daily 12:00-23:00, best to reserve for a seat on the square, Piazza di Santo Spirito 6 red, tel. 055-210-437, Andrea and Michele—feel his forearm). **Volume,** the bar next door, is run by the same gang.

Ricchi Caffè, next to Borgo Antico, has fine gelato, home-made desserts, shaded outdoor tables, and €9 pasta dishes at lunch (daily 7:00-24:00, tel. 055-215-864). After noting the plain facade of the Brunelleschi church facing the square, step inside the café and pick your favorite picture of the many ways it might be finished.

Florence Connections

Florence is Tuscany's transportation hub, with fine train, bus, and plane connections to virtually anywhere in Italy. The city has several train stations, a bus station (next to the main train station), and an airport (plus Pisa's airport is nearby). Livorno, on the coast west of Florence, is a major cruise-ship port for passengers visiting Florence, Pisa, and other nearby destinations.

By Train
From Florence by Train to: La Spezia (for the Cinque Terre, 5/day direct, 2.5 hours, otherwise nearly hourly with change in Pisa, €11.30), **Milan** (hourly, 1.75 hours, €53), **Milan's Malpensa Airport** (2/day direct, 2.75 hours, €58), **Venice** (hourly, 2-3 hours, may transfer in Bologna; often crowded—reserve ahead, €43), **Rome** (at least hourly, 1.5 hours, most connections require seat reservations, €45), **Interlaken** (5/day, 5.5-6 hours, 2-3 changes), **Frankfurt** (1/day, 12 hours, 1-3 changes), **Paris** (3/day, 10-15 hours, 1-2 changes, important to reserve overnight train ahead), **Vienna** (1 direct overnight train, or 5/day with 1-3 changes, 10-16 hours). Note that these are all TrenItalia connections; the new Italo company may offer additional options (check www.italotreno.it).

By Bus
The SITA bus station (100 yards west of the Florence train station on Via Santa Caterina da Siena) is traveler-friendly—a big, old-school lot with numbered stalls and all the services you'd expect. Schedules for regional trips are posted everywhere, and TV monitors show imminent departures. Bus service drops dramatically on Sunday.

From Florence by Bus to: Florence's **Amerigo Vespucci Airport** (2/hour, 30 minutes, €5, pay driver and immediately validate

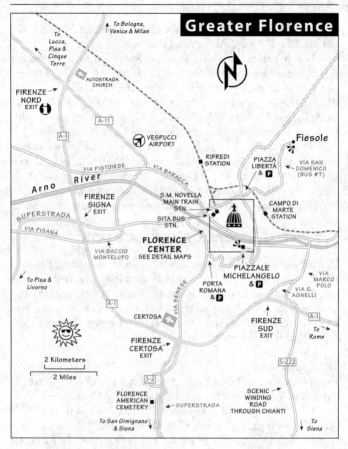

ticket, always from platform 1). Generally, buy bus tickets in the station, as you'll pay 30 percent more if you buy tickets on the bus. Bus info: www.sitabus.it or tel. 800-373-760 (Mon-Fri 8:30-12:30 & 15:00-18:00, closed Sat-Sun).

By Taxi

For small groups with more money than time, zipping to nearby towns by taxi can be a good value (e.g., €120 from your Florence hotel to your Siena hotel).

A more comfortable alternative is to hire a private car service. Florence-based **Transfer Chauffeur Service** has a fleet of modern vehicles with drivers who can whisk you between cities, to and from the cruise ship port at Livorno, and through the Tuscan countryside for around the same price as a cab (tel. 055-614-2182, mobile 338-862-3129, www.transfercs.com, marco.masala@transfercs.com, Marco).

By Plane

Florence's **Amerigo Vespucci Airport,** also called Peretola Airport, is about five miles northwest of the city (open 5:10-24:00, no overnighting allowed, TI, cash machines, car-rental agencies, airport code: FLR, airport info tel. 055-306-1630, flight info tel. 055-306-1700—domestic only, www.aeroporto.firenze.it). Shuttle buses (far right of airport as you exit arrivals hall) connect the airport with Florence's SITA bus station, 100 yards west of the train station on Via Santa Caterina da Siena (2/hour, 30 minutes, €5, buy ticket on board and validate immediately, daily 6:00-23:30, first bus leaves for airport from Florence at 5:30). If you're changing to a different intercity bus in Florence (for instance, one bound for Siena), stay on the bus through the first stop (at the train station); it will continue on to the bus station nearby. Allow about €25 and 30 minutes for a taxi.

Pisa's **Galileo Galilei Airport** also handles international and domestic flights (TI open daily 8:30-23:30, cash machine, car-rental agencies, baggage storage from 8:00-20:00 only, €7/bag; self-service cafeteria, airport code: PSA, tel. 050-849-300, www.pisa-airport.com).

You can connect to **Florence** easily by train (2-3/hour, 1.25 hours, €5.80, most transfer at Pisa Centrale) or by Terravision bus (about hourly, 1.25 hours, €10 one-way, ticket kiosk is at the right end of the arrivals hall as you're facing the exits, catch bus outside and to the far right of the bus parking lot, www.terravision.eu).

THE CINQUE TERRE

The Cinque Terre (CHINK-weh TAY-reh), a remote chunk of the Italian Riviera, is the traffic-free, lowbrow, underappreciated alternative to the French Riviera. There's not a museum in sight—just sun, sea, sand (well, pebbles), wine, and pure, unadulterated Italy. Enjoy the villages, swimming, hiking, and evening romance of one of God's great gifts to tourism. For a home base, choose among five *(cinque)* villages, each of which fills a ravine with a lazy hive of human activity—calloused locals, sunburned travelers, and no Vespas. While the Cinque Terre is now discovered (and can be quite crowded midday, when tourist boats and cruise-ship excursions drop by), I've never seen happier, more relaxed tourists.

The chunk of coast was first described in medieval times as "the five lands." In the feudal era, this land was watched over by castles. Tiny communities grew up in their protective shadows, ready to run inside at the first hint of a Turkish Saracen pirate raid. Marauding pirates from North Africa were a persistent problem until about 1400. Many locals were kidnapped and ransomed or sold into slavery, and those who remained built fires on flat-roofed watchtowers to relay warnings—alerting the entire coast to imminent attacks. The last major raid was in 1545.

As the threat of pirates faded, the villages prospered, catching fish and cultivating grapes. Churches were enlarged with a growing population. But until the advent of tourism in this generation, the towns remained isolated. Even today, traditions survive, and each of the five villages comes with a distinct dialect and its own proud heritage.

Sadly, a few ugly, noisy Americans give tourism a bad name here. Even hip, young residents are put off by loud, drunken tour-

ists. They say—and I agree—that the Cinque Terre is an exceptional place. It deserves a special dignity. Party in Viareggio or Portofino, but be mellow in the Cinque Terre. Talk softly. Help keep it clean. In spite of the tourist crowds, it's still a real community, and we are its guests.

In this chapter, I cover the five towns in order from south to north—from Riomaggiore to Monterosso. Since I still get the names of the towns mixed up, I think of them by number: #1 Riomaggiore (a workaday town), #2 Manarola (picturesque), #3 Corniglia (on a hilltop), #4 Vernazza (the region's cover girl, the most touristy and dramatic), and #5 Monterosso al Mare (the closest thing to a beach resort of the five towns).

Flooding Damage and Closures: On October 25, 2011, the Cinque Terre region was hit hard by a devastating flood. Two towns in particular—Monterosso and Vernazza—were seriously damaged. After a winter of hard work, both Monterosso and Vernazza reopened for tourism in 2012; nearly all of the trails, beaches, hotels, and restaurants of the entire Cinque Terre are wide-open for visitors, though a few businesses may lag behind. After this exhausting period of rebuilding, locals are offering visitors, who provide their livelihood, a warm and hearty welcome. For all the latest on the recovery in **Vernazza,** see www.savevernazza.com; for **Monterosso,** see www.rebuildmonterosso.com.

Arrival in the Cinque Terre

By Train: Big, fast trains from elsewhere in Italy speed right past the Cinque Terre (though some stop in Monterosso and Riomaggiore). Unless you're coming from a nearby town, you'll have to change trains at least once to reach Manarola, Corniglia, or Vernazza.

Generally, if you're coming from the north, you'll change trains in Sestri Levante or Genoa (specifically, Genoa's Piazza Principe station). If you're coming from the south or east, you'll most likely have to switch trains in La Spezia (change at La Spezia Centrale station—don't make the mistake of getting off at La Spezia Migliarina). No matter where you're coming from, it's best to check in the station before you leave to see your full schedule and route options (use the computerized kiosks or ask at a ticket window). Don't forget to validate your ticket by stamping it—ka-CHUNK!—in the machines located on train platforms and elsewhere in the station. Conductors here are notorious for levying stiff fines on forgetful tourists. For more information on riding the train between Cinque Terre towns, see "Getting Around the Cinque Terre," later.

Planning Your Time

The ideal stay is two or three full days; my recommended minimum stay is two nights and a completely uninterrupted day. The Cinque Terre is served by the local train from Genoa and La Spezia. Speed demons arrive in the morning, check their bags in La Spezia, take the five-hour hike through all five towns, laze away the afternoon on the beach or rock of their choice, and zoom away on the overnight train to somewhere back in the real world. But be warned: The Cinque Terre has a strange way of messing up your momentum. (The evidence is the number of Americans who have fallen in love with the region and/or one of its residents...and are still here.) Frankly, staying fewer than two nights is a mistake that you'll likely regret.

The towns are just a few minutes apart by hourly train or boat. There's no checklist of sights or experiences—just a hike, the towns themselves, and your fondest vacation desires. Study this chapter in advance and piece together your best day, mixing hiking, swimming, trains, and a boat ride. For the best light and coolest temperatures, start your hike early.

Market days perk up the towns from 8:00 to 13:00 on Tuesday in Vernazza, Wednesday in Levanto, Thursday in Monterosso and Sestri Levante, and Friday in La Spezia.

The winter is really dead—most hotels and some restaurants close in December and January. The long Easter weekend and June and July are the peak of peak periods, the toughest times to find rooms. In spring, the towns can feel inundated with Italian school groups day-tripping on spring excursions (they can't afford to sleep in this expensive region).

For more information on the region, see www.cinqueterre.it.

Cinque Terre Park Cards

Visitors hiking between the towns on coastal trails need to pay a park entrance fee. This fee keeps the trails safe and open, and pays for viewpoints, picnic spots, WCs, and more. The popular coastal trail generates enough revenue to subsidize the development of trails and outdoor activities higher in the hills.

You have two options for covering the park fee: the Cinque Terre Park Card or the Cinque Terre Treno Park Card. Both are valid until midnight on the expiration date. Write your name on your card or risk a big fine. The configuration and pricing of these cards seem to always be in flux—be aware that the following details may change before your visit, and cuts to park funding may cause the park to stop offering these cards.

The **Cinque Terre Park Card** costs €5 for one day of hiking or €9 for two (covers trails and shuttle buses but not trains, buy at trailheads and at most train stations, no validation required).

The **Cinque Terre Treno Park Card** covers what the Cinque Terre Park Card does, plus the use of the local trains (from Levanto to La Spezia, including all Cinque Terre towns). It's sold at TIs inside train stations, but not at trailheads (€10/1 day, €19/2 days, validate card at train station by punching it in the yellow machine). With this card, you have to hike and take three train trips every day just to break even.

Cards cost a bit more on weekends and in August. Those under 18 or over 70 get a discount, as do families of four or more (see www.parconazionale5terre.it).

Getting Around the Cinque Terre

Within the Cinque Terre, you can connect towns in three ways: by train, boat, or foot. Trains are cheaper, boats are more scenic, and hiking lets you enjoy more pasta. From a practical point of view, you should consider supplementing the often frustrating train with the sometimes more convenient boat. The trail between Riomaggiore and Manarola is a delight and takes just a few minutes, making the train not worth waiting for. The trail from Manarola to Corniglia is likely closed (after a huge 2011 landslide).

By Train

Along the coast here, trains go in only two directions: *"per* [to] *Genova"* (the Italian spelling of Genoa), northbound; or *"per La Spezia,"* southbound. Assuming you're on vacation, accept the unpredictability of Cinque Terre trains (they're often late...unless you are, too—in which case they're on time). Relax while you wait—buy a cup of coffee at a station bar. When the train comes (know which direction to look for: La Spezia or Genova), casually walk over and hop on. This is especially easy in Monterosso, with its fine café-with-a-view on track #1 (direction: Milano/Genova), and in Vernazza, where you can hang out at the Blue Marlin Bar with a prepaid drink and dash when the train pulls in.

Use the handy TV monitors in the station, which display upcoming departures for the next hour or so (as well as notes about which track they're on and whether they're late—*in ritardo*). Most of the northbound trains that stop at all Cinque Terre towns and are headed toward Genova will list Sestri Levante as the *destinazione*.

By train, the five towns are just a few minutes apart. Know your stop. Once the train leaves the town just before your destination, go to the door and get ready to slip out before the mobs flood in, making it impossible to get off. Words to the wise for novice tourists, who often miss their stop: The stations are small and the trains are long, so (especially in Vernazza) you might have to get off deep in a tunnel. Also, the doors don't open automatically—you may have to open the handle of the door yourself (twist the black handle, or lift up the red one). If a door isn't working, go quickly to the next car to leave. (When leaving a town by train, if you find the platform jammed with people, walk down the platform into the tunnel, where things quiet down.)

It costs about €1.80 per ride within the region. Tickets are good for 75 minutes in one direction, so you could conceivably use one for a brief stopover. To make the ticket good for six hours (in one direction only), you need to buy a ticket good for 40 kilometers (€3.50). Stamp the ticket at the station machine before you board. Machines are often broken or out of ink (good luck explaining that to conductors), but riding without a validated ticket can be expensive (usually €50). You can buy several tickets at once and use them as you like, validating as you go. If you have a Eurail Pass, don't spend one of your valuable travel days on the cheap Cinque Terre.

Cinque Terre Train Schedule: Since the train is the Cinque Terre's lifeline, many shops and restaurants post the current schedule, and most hotels offer copies of it (one also comes with the Cinque Terre Park Card). But beware: The printed schedules can be misleading (half the listed departures don't go every day); the monitors in the stations are your best source of actual, current departure information. Note that fast trains leaving La Spezia zip right through the Cinque Terre; some stop only in Monterosso (town #5) and Riomaggiore (town #1). But any train that stops in Manarola, Corniglia, and Vernazza (towns #2, #3, and #4)—

including the trains on the schedule below—will stop in all five towns.

The times below are accurate as of this printing, but confirm schedules locally. These are the daily train times (a few do not run on Sunday; more trains are added in the busiest season, June-Sept):

Trains leave La Spezia Centrale for all or most of the Cinque Terre villages at 7:12, 10:06, 11:10, 12:00, 13:15, 14:09, 15:10, 15:58, 17:10, 17:20, 18:06, 19:10, 20:18, 21:25, 23:10, and 00:50.

Going back to La Spezia, trains leave Monterosso at 6:20, 8:15, 9:29, 11:00, 11:55, 12:19, 13:28, 14:20, 15:22, 16:17, 17:30, 18:18, 19:22, 20:07 or 20:20, 21:32, 22:22, and 23:45 (these same trains depart Vernazza about four minutes later).

Again, convenient TV monitors posted at several places in each station clearly show exactly what times the next trains are leaving in each direction (and, if they're late, how late they are expected to be). I trust these monitors much more than my ability to read any printed schedule.

By Boat

From Easter through October, a daily boat service connects Monterosso, Vernazza, Manarola, Riomaggiore, and Portovenere. Boats provide a scenic way to get from town to town and survey what you just hiked. And boats offer the only efficient way to visit the nearby resort of Portovenere (the alternative is a tedious train-bus connection via La Spezia). In peaceful weather, the boats can be more reliable than the trains, but if seas are rough, they don't run at all. Because the boats nose in and tourists have to gingerly disembark onto little more than a plank, even a small chop can cancel some or all of the stops.

I see the tour boats as a syringe, injecting each town with a boost of euros. The towns are addicted, and they shoot up hourly through the summer. (Between 10:00 and 15:00—especially on weekends—masses of gawkers unload from boats, tour buses, and cruise ships, inundating the villages and changing the feel of the region.)

Boats depart Monterosso about hourly (10:30-17:00), stopping at the Cinque Terre towns (except at Corniglia) and ending up an hour later in Portovenere. (Portovenere-Monterosso boats run 8:50-17:00.) The ticket price depends on the length of the boat ride (short hops-€4, longer hops-€8, one-way with stops-€10, five-town all-day pass-€15). Round-trip tickets are slightly cheaper than two one-way trips. You can buy tickets at little stands at each town's harbor (tel. 0187-732-987 and 0187-818-440). Another all-day boat pass for €25 extends to Portovenere and includes a 40-minute scenic ride around three small islands (2/day). Boats are not covered by the Cinque Terre Park Card. Boat schedules are posted at docks, harbor bars, Cinque Terre park offices, and hotels (www.navigazionegolfodeipoeti.it).

By Shuttle Bus

Green shuttle buses connect each Cinque Terre town with its distant parking lot and various points in the hills (for example, a shuttle runs from Corniglia's train station to its hilltop town center). Note that these shuttle buses do not connect the towns with each other. Most rides cost €1.50 (and are covered by the Cinque Terre Park Card)—pick up bus schedules from TIs or note the times posted on bus doors and at bus stops. Departures often coordinate with train arrival times. Some (but not all) departures from Vernazza, Manarola, and Riomaggiore go beyond the parking lots and high into the hills. To soak in the scenery, you can pay for a round-trip ride and just cruise both ways (30-45 minutes round-trip). Be aware that cuts to park funding may eliminate or reduce the frequency of these buses.

Hiking the Cinque Terre

All five towns are connected by good trails, marked with red-and-white paint, white arrows, and some signs. You'll experience the area's best by hiking all the way from one end to the other (although, unfortunately, the Manarola-Corniglia stretch is likely closed). While you can detour to dramatic hilltop sanctuaries, I'd keep it simple by following trail #2—the low route between the villages. The entire seven-mile hike can be done in about four hours, but allow five for dawdling. Germans (with their task-oriented *Alpenstock* walking sticks) are notorious for marching too fast through the region. Take it slow...smell the cactus flowers and herbs, notice the lizards, listen to birds singing in the olive groves, and enjoy vistas on all sides.

Trails can be closed in bad weather or because of landslides. Remember that hikers need to pay a fee to enter the trails (see "Cinque Terre Park Cards," earlier). If you're hiking the entire five-town route, consider that the trail between Riomaggiore (#1) and Manarola (#2) is easiest. The hike between Manarola and Corniglia (#3) has minor hills (but may be closed during your visit). The trail from Corniglia to Vernazza (#4) is demanding, and the path from Vernazza to Monterosso (#5) is the most challenging. For that hike, you might want to start in Monterosso in order to tackle the toughest section while you're fresh—and to enjoy the region's most dramatic scenery as you approach Vernazza. If you plan to hike all five towns, it's best to start early in the day, beginning at Monterosso (#5) and ending with Riomaggiore (#1).

Other than the wide, easy Riomaggiore-Manarola segment, the trail is generally narrow, steep, rocky, and comes with lots of steps. Be warned that I get many emails from readers who say the trail was tougher than they expected. The rocks and metal grates can be slippery in the rain. While the trail is a bit of a challenge, it's perfectly doable for any fit hiker...and worth the sweat.

Maps aren't necessary for the basic coastal hikes described here. But for the expanded version of this hike (12 hours, from Portovenere to Levanto) and more serious hikes in the high country, pick up a good hiking map (about €5, sold everywhere). The *Cinque Terre Walking Guide* (by a German publisher, but sold locally in an English-language edition) is worth seeking out for anyone planning a serious hike.

To leave the park cleaner than you found it, bring a plastic bag *(sacchetto di plastica)* and pick up a little trail trash along the way. It would be great if American visitors—who get so much joy out of this region—were known for this good deed.

Riomaggiore-Manarola (20 minutes): Facing the front of the train station in Riomaggiore (#1), go up the stairs to the right, following signs for *Via dell'Amore*. The photo-worthy promenade—wide enough for baby strollers—winds along the coast to Manarola (#2), but may be closed in 2014. While there's no beach along the trail, stairs lead down to sunbathing rocks. A long tunnel and mega-nets protect hikers from mean-spirited falling rocks. A wine bar—Bar & Vini A Piè de Mà—is located at the Riomaggiore trailhead and offers light meals, awesome town views, and clever boat storage under the train tracks (for more info, see page 1123). There's a picnic zone with a water fountain, shade, and a seagull that must have been human in a previous life hanging out just above the Manarola station (WC at Manarola station).

Manarola-Corniglia (45 minutes, likely closed during your visit): The walk from Manarola (#2) to Corniglia (#3) is a little longer, more rugged, and steeper than the Via dell'Amore. It's also less romantic. To avoid the last stretch (switchback stairs leading up to the hill-capping town of Corniglia), end your hike at Corniglia's train station and catch the shuttle bus to the town center (2/hour, €1.50, free with Cinque Terre Park Card, usually timed to meet the trains).

Corniglia-Vernazza (1.5 hours): The hike from Corniglia (#3) to Vernazza (#4)—the wildest and greenest section of the coast— is very rewarding but very hilly (going the other direction, from Vernazza to Corniglia, is steeper). From the Corniglia station and beach, zigzag up to the town (via the steep stairs, the longer road, or the shuttle bus). Ten minutes past Corniglia, toward Vernazza, you'll see Guvano beach far beneath you (once the region's nude beach). The scenic trail leads past a bar and picnic tables, through lots of fragrant and flowery vegetation, into Vernazza. If you need a break before reaching Vernazza, stop by Franco's Ristorante and Bar la Torre; it has a small menu but big views.

Vernazza-Monterosso (1.5 hours): The trail from Vernazza (#4) to Monterosso (#5) is a scenic up-and-down-a-lot trek and the most challenging of the bunch. Trails are narrow, steep, and crumbly, with a lot of steps (some readers report "very dangerous"), but easy to follow. Locals frown on camping at the picnic tables located midway. The views just out of Vernazza, looking back at the town, are spectacular.

Longer Hikes: Above the trails that run between the towns, higher-elevation hikes crisscross the region. Shuttle buses make the going easier, connecting coastal villages and trailheads in the hills. Ask locally about the more difficult six-mile inland hike to Volastra. This tiny village, perched between Manarola and Corniglia, hosts lots of Germans and Italians in the summertime. Just below its town center, in the hamlet of Groppo, is the Cinque Terre Cooperative Winery (open daily). For the whole trip on the high road between Manarola and Corniglia, allow two hours one-way. In return, you'll get sweeping views and a closer look at the vineyards. Shuttle buses run from Manarola to Volastra (€2.50 or free with Cinque Terre Park Card, pick up schedule from park office, 8/day, more departures in summer, 15 minutes); consider taking the bus up and hiking down.

Swimming, Kayaking, and Biking

Every town in the Cinque Terre has a beach or a rocky place to swim. Monterosso has the biggest and sandiest beach, with umbrellas and beach-use fees (but it's free where there are no umbrellas). Vernazza's is tiny—better for sunning than swimming. Manarola and Riomaggiore have the worst beaches (no sand), but Manarola offers the best deep-water swimming.

Wear your walking shoes and pack your swim gear. Several of the beaches have showers (no shampoo, please). Underwater sightseeing is full of fish—goggles are sold in local shops. Sea urchins can be a problem if you walk on the rocks, and sometimes jellyfish wash up on the pebbles.

You can rent kayaks or boats in Riomaggiore, Vernazza, and Monterosso. (For details, see individual town listings in this chapter.) Some readers say kayaking can be dangerous—the kayaks tip easily, training is not provided, and lifejackets are not required.

Sleeping in the Cinque Terre

If you think too many people have my book, avoid Vernazza. You get fewer crowds and better value for your money in other towns. Monterosso is a good choice for sun-worshipping softies, those who prefer the ease of a real hotel, and the younger crowd (more nightlife). Hermits, anarchists, wine lovers, and mountain goats like Corniglia. Sophisticated Italians and Germans choose Manarola. Riomaggiore—bigger than Vernazza and less resorty than Monterosso—has the cheapest beds.

While the Cinque Terre is too rugged for the mobs that ravage the Spanish and French coasts, it's popular with Italians, Germans, and in-the-know Americans. Hotels charge more and are packed on holidays (including Easter); in June, July, and September; and on Fridays and Saturdays all summer. (With global warming, sweltering August is no longer considered peak season on this stretch of the Riviera.) While you can find doubles for €65 or €70 most of the season, you'll pay extra (around €80) in June and July. The prices I've listed are the maximum for April through October. For a terrace or view, you might pay an extra €20 or more. Apartments for four can be economical for families—figure around €120.

It's smart to reserve your room in advance in May, June, July, and September, and on weekends and holidays. At other times, you can land a double room on any day by just arriving in town (ideally by noon) and asking around at bars and restaurants, or simply by approaching locals on the street. Many travelers enjoy the opportunity to shop around a bit and get the best price by bargaining. Private rooms—called *affitta camere*—are no longer an intimate stay with a family. They are generally comfortable apartments (often with small kitchens) where you get the key and come and go as you like, rarely seeing your landlord. Many landowners rent the buildings by the year to local managers, who then attempt to make a profit by filling them night after night with tourists. While air-conditioning is essential in the summer elsewhere in Italy, in the breezy Cinque Terre you can generally manage fine without it.

For the best value, visit several private rooms and snare the best. Going direct cuts out the middleman and softens prices. Staying more than one night gives you bargaining leverage. Plan on paying cash. Private rooms are generally bigger and more comfortable than those offered by pensions and have the same privacy as a hotel room.

If you want the security of a reservation, make it at a hotel long in advance (smaller places generally don't take reservations very far ahead). Query by email, not fax. If you do reserve, honor your reservation (or, if you must cancel, do it as early as possible). Since people renting rooms usually don't take deposits, they lose money if you don't show up.

Eating in the Cinque Terre

Hanging out at a sea-view restaurant while sampling local specialties could become one of your favorite memories.

Tegame alla Vernazza is the most typical main course in Vernazza: anchovies, potatoes, tomatoes, white wine, oil, and herbs. Anchovies (*acciughe*; ah-CHOO-gay) are ideally served the day they're caught. There's nothing cool about being an anchovy virgin. If you've always hated anchovies (the harsh, cured-in-salt American kind), try them fresh here. *Pansotti* are ravioli with ricotta and a mixture of greens, often served with a walnut sauce...delightful and filling.

While antipasto means cheese and salami in Tuscany, here you'll get *antipasti frutti di mare* (or *antipasti misti*), a plate of mixed "fruits of the sea" and a fine way to start a meal. Many restaurants are particularly proud of their *antipasti frutti di mare*—it's how they show off. For two diners, splitting one of these and a pasta dish can be plenty.

This region is the birthplace of pesto. Basil, which loves the temperate Ligurian climate, is ground with cheese (half parmigiano cow cheese and half pecorino sheep cheese), garlic, olive oil, and pine nuts, and then poured over pasta. Try it on spaghetti, *trenette* (the long, flat Ligurian noodle), or *trofie* (made of flour with a bit of potato, designed specifically for pesto to cling to). Many also like pesto lasagna, always made with white sauce, never red. If you become addicted, small jars of pesto are sold in the local grocery stores and gift shops. If it's refrigerated, it's fresh; this is what you want if you're eating it today. For taking home, get the jar-on-a-shelf pesto.

Focaccia, the tasty pillowy bread, also originates here in Liguria. Locals say the best focaccia is made between the Cinque Terre and Genoa. It's simply flatbread with olive oil and salt. The baker roughs up the dough with finger holes, then bakes it. Focaccia comes plain or with onions, sage, or olive bits, and is a local favorite for a snack on the beach. Bakeries sell it in rounds or slices by the weight (a portion is about 100 grams, or *un etto*).

Farinata, a humble fried-bread snack, is made from chickpea meal, water, oil, and pepper, and baked on a copper tray in a wood-burning stove. *Farinata* is sold at pizza and focaccia places.

The *vino delle Cinque Terre*, while not one of Italy's top wines, flows cheap and easy throughout the region. It's white—great with seafood. For a sweet dessert wine, the *sciacchetrà* wine is worth the splurge (€4 per small glass, often served with a cookie). You could order the fun dessert *torta della nonna* ("grandmother's cake") and dunk chunks of it into your glass. Aged *sciacchetrà* is dry and costly (up to €12/glass). While 10 kilos of grapes yield seven liters of local wine, *sciacchetrà* is made from near-raisins, and 10 kilos of grapes make only 1.5 liters of *sciacchetrà*. The word means "push and pull"—push in lots of grapes, pull out the best wine. If your room is up a lot of steps, be warned: *Sciacchetrà* is 18 percent alcohol, while regular wine is only 11 percent.

In the cool, calm evening, sit on Vernazza's breakwater with a glass of wine and watch the phosphorescence in the waves.

Nightlife in the Cinque Terre

While the Cinque Terre is certainly not noted for bumping beach-town nightlife like nearby Viareggio, you'll find some sort of travel-tale-telling hub in Monterosso, Vernazza, and Riomaggiore (Manarola and Corniglia are sleepy). Monterosso (where bars can stay open until 2:00 in the morning) has a lively scene, especially in the summertime—but no *discoteca* yet. In Vernazza, the nightlife centers in the bars on the waterfront piazza, which is the small-town-style place to "see and be seen." A town law requires all bars to shut by midnight. Bar Centrale in Riomaggiore is, well, the central place for cocktails and meeting fellow travelers. (For details, see the "Nightlife" sections for these three villages.) Wherever your night adventures take you, have fun, but please remember that residents live upstairs.

Helpful Hints for the Cinque Terre

Tourist and Park Information: Each town (except Corniglia) has a well-staffed TI and park office (listed throughout this chapter). Be aware that budget cuts may cause TIs and park offices to reduce their hours or close.

Money: Banks and ATMs are plentiful throughout the region.

Baggage Storage: You can store bags at La Spezia's train station (€3/12 hours, 8:00-22:00, along track 1, next to WC, allow plenty of time to pick up your baggage before departing) and at Lucia's Lavarapido in Monterosso (€5/day).

Services: Every train station has a handy public WC. Otherwise, pop into a bar or restaurant.

Taxi: Cinqueterre Taxi covers all five towns (mobile 328-583-4969, www.cinqueterretaxi.com, info@cinqueterretaxi.com).

Local Guides: Andrea Bordigoni is both knowledgeable and a delight (€110/half-day, €175/day, mobile 347-972-3317, bordigo@inwind.it). Other local guides are **Marco Brizzi** (mobile 328-694-2847, marco_brizzi@yahoo.it) and **Paola Tommarchi** (paolatomma@alice.it).

Booking Agency: Miriana and Filippo at **Cinque Terre Riviera** book rooms in the Cinque Terre towns, Portovenere, and La Spezia for a 10 percent markup over the list price (can also arrange transportation, cooking classes, and weddings; Via Picedi 18 in La Spezia; tel. 0187-520-702, Miriana—mobile 340-794-7358, Filippo—mobile 393-939-1901, www.cinqueterreriviera.com, info@cinqueterreriviera.com, English spoken).

Riomaggiore (Town #1)

The most substantial non-resort town of the group, Riomaggiore is a disappointment from the train station. But once you leave that neighborhood, you'll stumble upon a fascinating tangle of pastel homes leaning on each other like drunken sailors. Just walk through the tunnel next to the train tracks, and you'll discover a more real, laid-back, and workaday town than its touristy neighbors.

Orientation to Riomaggiore

Tourist Information

The TI is in the train station at the ticket desk (daily 8:00-18:00, tel. 0187-920-633). If the TI in the station is crowded, buy your hiking pass at the Cinque Terre park shop/information office next door by the mural (daily 8:00-19:30, tel. 0187-760-515, netpointriomaggiore@parconazionale5terre.it). For an informal information source, try Ivo and Alberto, who run Bar Centrale (see "Nightlife in Riomaggiore," later).

Arrival in Riomaggiore

The bus shuttles locals and tourists up and down Riomaggiore's steep main street and continues to the parking lot outside town (€1.50 one-way, €2.50 round-trip, free with Cinque Terre Park Card, 2/hour but almost comically erratic, main stop at the fork of Via Colombo and Via Malborghetto, or flag it down as it passes).

Helpful Hints

Internet Access: The **park shop/information office** has four Internet terminals upstairs, plus Wi-Fi (€1.50/20 minutes, daily May-Sept 8:00-22:00, Oct-April 8:00-19:30). **La Zorza Café** and **Bar Centrale** both offer free Wi-Fi with the purchase of a drink (see "Nightlife in Riomaggiore," later).

Laundry: A self-service launderette is on the main street (€3.50/wash, €3.50/dry, daily 9:00-19:30, run by Edi's Rooms next door, Via Colombo 111).

Self-Guided Walk

Welcome to Riomaggiore

Here's an easy loop trip that maximizes views and minimizes uphill walking.

• *Start at the train station. (If you arrive by boat, cross beneath the tracks and take a left, then hike through the tunnel along the tracks to reach the station.) You'll come to some...*

Colorful Murals: These murals, with subjects modeled after real-life Riomaggiorians, glorify the nameless workers who constructed the nearly 300 million cubic feet of dry-stone walls (without cement) that run throughout the Cinque Terre. These walls give the region its characteristic *muri a secco* terracing for vineyards and olive groves. The murals, done by Argentinean artist Silvio Benedetto, are well-explained in English.

• *Head to the railway tunnel entrance, and ride the elevator to the top of town (€0.50 or €1 family ticket, free with Cinque Terre Park Card, daily 8:00–19:45). If the elevator is closed (likely), hike around to the left, following the road up and then right to the...*

Top o' the Town: Here you're treated to spectacular sea views. To continue the viewfest, go right and follow the walkway (ignore the steps marked *Marina Seacoast* that lead to the harbor). It's a five-minute level stroll to the church. You'll pass under the offices of the disgraced national park president and the city hall (flying two flags), with murals celebrating the heroic grape-pickers and fishermen of the region (also by Silvio Benedetto).

• *Before reaching the church, pause to enjoy the...*

Town View: The major river of this region once ran through this valley, as implied by the name Riomaggiore (local dialect for "river" and "major"). As in the other Cinque Terre towns, the river ravine is now paved over, and the romantic arched bridges that once connected the two sides have been replaced by a practical modern road.

Notice the lack of ugly aerial antennae. In the 1980s, every residence got cable. Now, the TV tower on the hilltop behind the church steeple brings the modern world into each home. The church was rebuilt in 1870, but was first established in 1340. It's dedicated to St. John the Baptist, the patron saint of Genoa, the maritime republic that once dominated the region.

• *Continue past the church down to Riomaggiore's main street, named...*

Via Colombo: Walk about 30 feet beyond the WC, go down the stairs, and—if it's open—pop into the tiny Cinque Terre Antiche museum (€0.50, free with Cinque Terre Park Card, generally closed). Inside, sit down for a few minutes to watch a circa-1950 video of the Cinque Terre.

Continuing down Via Colombo, you'll pass a bakery, a couple of grocery shops, and the self-service laundry. There's homemade gelato next to the Bar Centrale. Above where Via Colombo dead-ends, a park-like square built over the train tracks gives the children of the town a level bit of land upon which to kick their soccer balls. The murals above celebrate the great-grandparents of these very children—the salt-of-the-earth locals who earned a humble living before the age of tourism. To the left, stairs lead down to the Marina neighborhood, with the harbor, the boat dock, a 200-yard

THE CINQUE TERRE

1 Locanda del Sole
2 Locanda Ca' dei Duxi
3 Hotel & Café la Zorza
4 Locanda dalla Compagnia
5 Riomaggiore Reservations
6 La Dolce Vita Rooms
7 Edi's Rooms & Launderette
8 Camere Patrizia
9 Trattoria la Grotta
10 La Lanterna Ristorante
11 Te la Do lo la Merenda Snack Bar
12 Enoteca & Ristorante Dau Cila
13 Bar & Vini A Piè de Mà
14 Bar Centrale & Gelateria
15 Madonna di Montenero Trail
16 Park Office Kiosk

trail to the beach *(spiaggia)*, and an inviting little art gallery. To the right of the stairs is the pedestrian tunnel, running alongside the tracks, which takes you directly back to the station and the trail to the other towns. From here, you can take a train, hop a boat, or hike to your next destination.

Sights in Riomaggiore

Beach
Riomaggiore's rugged and tiny "beach" is rocky, but it's clean and peaceful. Take a two-minute walk from the harbor: Face the harbor, then follow the path to your left. Passing the rugged boat landing, stay on the path to the pebbly beach. There's a shower there in the summer, and another closer to town by the boat landing—where many enjoy sunning on and jumping from the rocks.

Kayaks and Water Sports
The town has a diving center (scuba, snorkeling, kayaks; office down the stairs and under the tracks on Via San Giacomo, daily May-Sept 9:00-18:00, tel. 0187-920-011, www.5terrediving.it).

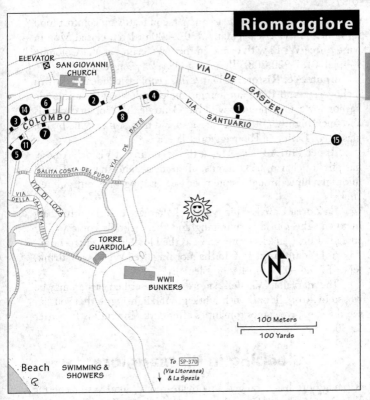

Hikes

The cliff-hanging Torre Guardiola trail, a steep 20-minute climb from the beach up to old WWII bunkers and a hilltop botanical pathway, has been closed because of a rock slide. Another trail rises from Riomaggiore scenically to the 14th-century Madonna di Montenero sanctuary, high above the town (45 minutes, take the main road inland until you see signs, or ride the green shuttle bus 12 minutes from the town center to the sanctuary trail, then walk uphill 10 minutes).

Nightlife in Riomaggiore

Bar Centrale, run by sociable Ivo, Alberto, and the gang, offers "nightlife" any time of day—making it a good stop for Italian breakfast and music. Ivo, who lived in San Francisco, fills his bar with San Franciscan rock and a fun-loving vibe. During the day, this is a shaded place to relax with other travelers; it feels a little like the village's living room. At night, it offers the younger set the liveliest action (and best mojitos) in town. They also serve €5 fast-food pastas and microwaved pizzas, and a menu featuring comfort food for homesick Americans (daily 7:30-24:00 or later, closed Mon in winter, free Wi-Fi with drink, in the town center at Via Colombo 144, tel. 0187-920-208). There's a good *gelateria* next door.

Enoteca & Ristorante Dau Cila, a cool little hideaway with a mellow jazz-and-Brazilian-lounge ambience down at the miniscule harbor, is a counterpoint to wild Bar Centrale. It's cool for cocktails and open nightly until 24:00 (snacks and meals, fine wine by the glass; see "Eating in Riomaggiore," later).

Bar & Vini A Piè de Mà, at the beginning of Via dell'Amore, has piles of charm, €6 cocktails, often music, and stays open until midnight June through September (see "Eating in Riomaggiore," later).

La Zorza Café is a hip, youthful alternative to the other bars in town. The music is thumping and the cocktails come with a spread of little snacks (same space as the Hotel la Zorza reception, €6 drinks, daily until 1:00 in the morning, free Wi-Fi with drink, tel. 0187-920-036, fun-loving Elenia).

The marvelous **Via dell'Amore** trail (described earlier, may be closed in 2014), lit only with subtle ground lighting so that you can see the stars, welcomes romantics after dark. The trail is free after 19:30.

Sleeping in Riomaggiore

Riomaggiore has arranged its private-room rental system better than its neighbors. Several agencies—with regular office hours, English-speaking staff, and email addresses—line up within a few yards of each other on the main drag. Each manages a corral of local rooms for rent. These offices keep erratic hours, so it's smart to settle up the day before you leave in case they're closed when you need to depart. Expect lots of stairs. If you don't mind the hike, the street above town has safe overnight parking (free 20:00-8:00).

Hotels

$$$ Locanda del Sole has seven modern, basic, and overpriced rooms with a shared and peaceful terrace. Located at the utilitarian top end of town, it's a five-minute walk downhill to the center. Easy (and free with this book) parking makes it especially appealing to drivers (Db-€110-120, air-con, Wi-Fi, Via Santuario 114, tel. 0187-920-773, mobile 340-983-0090, www.locandadelsole. net, info@locandadelsole.net, Enrico).

$$$ Locanda Ca' dei Duxi rents 10 good rooms from an efficient little office on the main drag (Db-€100-130 depending on view and season, extra person-€20, air-con, Wi-Fi, open

---

Sleep Code

(€1 = about $1.30, country code: 39)
S = Single, **D** = Double/Twin, **T** = Triple, **Q** = Quad, **b** = bathroom, **s** = shower only. Unless otherwise noted, credit cards are accepted, English is spoken, and breakfast is included (except in Vernazza). Many towns in Italy levy a hotel tax of €2 per person, per night, which must be paid in cash (not included in the rates I've quoted).

To help you sort easily through these listings, I've divided the accommodations into three categories based on the price for a standard double room with bath:

$$$ Higher Priced—Most rooms €100 or more.
$$ Moderately Priced—Most rooms between €50-100.
$ Lower Priced—Most rooms €50 or less.

Prices can change without notice; verify the hotel's current rates online or by email.

---

year-round, Via Colombo 36, mobile 329-825-7836, www.duxi.it, info@duxi.it, Samuele and Anna). They also manage **Ca' dei Lisci**, with simpler and cheaper rooms (D-€60, Db-€70-80, www.cade-ilisci.com).

$$$ Hotel la Zorza rents 11 decent, cave-like, and overpriced rooms in the tangled lanes in the center of town (Db-€110-140, Qb apartment-€150, air-con, Wi-Fi, Via Colombo 231, tel. 0187-920-036, mobile 329-825-7836, www.hotelzorza.com, info@duxi.it).

$$ Locanda dalla Compagnia rents five modern rooms at the top of town, just 300 yards below the parking lot and the little church. All rooms—nice but rather dim—are on the same tranquil ground floor, and share an inviting lounge. Franca runs it with the help of son Allessandro (Db-€80, air-con, mini-fridge, no view, Via del Santuario 232, tel. 0187-760-050, www.dallacompagnia.it, lacomp@libero.it).

Room-Booking Services

$$ Riomaggiore Reservations offers 12 rooms and 15 apartments, with American expats Amy and Maddy smoothing communications (Db-€60-90 depending on view, Db suite with top view-€120, cash only, reception open 9:00-17:00 in season, Via Colombo 181, tel. 0187-760-575, www.riomaggiorereservations.com, info@riomaggiorereservations.com).

$$ La Dolce Vita offers three fine, good-value rooms on the main drag and two apartments around town (Db-€60-80, open daily 9:30-19:30; if they're closed, they're full; Via Colombo 167, tel. 0187-762-283, mobile 329-099-2741, agonatal@libero.it, helpful Giacomo and Simone).

$$ Edi's Rooms rents 20 rooms and apartments. You pay extra for views (Db-€70-90 depending on room, apartment Qb-€100-180, reserve with credit card, office open daily in summer 8:30-20:00, in winter 10:30-12:30 & 14:30-19:00, some rooms involve climbing a lot of steps—ask before viewing or reserving, reception at Via Colombo 111, tel. 0187-760-842, tel. 0187-920-325, www.appartamenticinqueterre.net, edi-vesigna@iol.it).

Backpacker Dorms

$ Riomaggiore Reservations (also listed above) runs a mini-hostel in a fine communal apartment with nine beds in three rooms, a cool living room, terrace, and kitchen in a good, quiet location. Take care of this little treasure so it survives (€25/bed, reception open 9:00-17:00 in season, Via Colombo 181, tel. 0187-760-575, www.riomaggiorereservations.com, info@riomaggiorereservations.com).

$ Camere Patrizia rents cheap doubles and dorm bunk beds at €25 per person from its reception at Via Colombo 25, but books only through www.hostelworld.com or to drop-ins (mobile 333-165-6362).

Eating in Riomaggiore

Trattoria la Grotta, right in the town center (with no view), serves reliably good food with a passion for anchovies and mussels. You'll enjoy friendly service surrounded by historic photos and wonderful stonework in a dramatic, dressy, cave-like setting. Venessa is warm and helpful, while her mother, Isa, is busy cooking (€12 pastas, €15 *secondi*, cash discount, Thu-Tue 12:00-14:30 & 17:30-22:30, closed Wed, Via Colombo 247, tel. 0187-920-187).

La Lanterna, with a gray-and-white interior and a few appealing harborside tables outside, is wedged into a niche in the Marina, overlooking the harbor under the tracks. Chef Massimo serves traditional plates, loves anchovies, and bakes fresh bread daily (€10 pastas, €18 *secondi*, no cover, daily 12:00-22:00, Via San Giacomo 10, tel. 0187-920-589).

Te La Do Io La Merenda ("I'll Give You a Snack") is good for a snack, pizza, or takeout. Their counter is piled with an assortment of munchies, and they have pastas, roasted chicken, and focaccia sandwiches to go (daily 9:00-21:00, Via Colombo 161, mobile 340-400-3256).

Enoteca & Ristorante Dau Cila is decked out like a black-and-white movie set in a centuries-old boat shed with extra tables outside on a rustic deck over dinghies. Try their antipasto specialty of several seafood appetizers, and listen to jazz with the waves lap-ping at the harbor below (€12 pastas, €18 *secondi*, March-Jan daily until 24:00, Via San Giacomo 65, tel. 0187-760-032, Luca).

Bar & Vini A Piè de Mà, at the trailhead on the Manarola end of town, is good for a scenic light bite or quiet drink at night. Enjoying a meal at a table on its dramatically situated terrace provides an indelible Cinque Terre memory (daily 10:00-20:00, June-Sept until 24:00, tel. 0187-921-037).

Picnics: Groceries and delis lining Via Colombo sell food to go, including pizza slices, for a picnic at the harbor or beach. Look for *Co-Op* grocery store signs for the best prices.

Manarola (Town #2)

Like Riomaggiore, Manarola is attached to its station by a 200-yard-long tunnel (lined with interesting photos). During WWII air raids, these tunnels provided refuge and a safe place for rattled villagers to sleep. The town itself fills a ravine, bookended by its wild little harbor to the west and a diminutive church square inland to the east. A delightful and gentle stroll from the church down to the harborside park provides the region's easiest vineyard walk (described in my "Self-Guided Walk," below).

Orientation to Manarola

The **TI** at the train station is open daily 7:00-20:00.

A **shuttle bus** runs between the low end of Manarola's main street (at the tobacco shop and newsstand) and the parking lot (€1.50 one-way, €2.50 round-trip, free with Cinque Terre Park Card, 2/hour, just flag it down). Shuttle buses also run about hourly from Manarola to Volastra, near the Cinque Terre Cooperative Winery.

To get to the **dock** and the boats that connect Manarola with the other Cinque Terre towns, find the steps to the left of the harbor view—they lead down to the ticket kiosk. Continue around the left side of the cliff (as you're facing the water) to catch the boats.

Self-Guided Walk

Welcome to Manarola

From the harbor, this 30-minute circular walk shows you the town and surrounding vineyards, and ends at a fantastic viewpoint, perfect for a picnic.

• *Start down at the waterfront.*

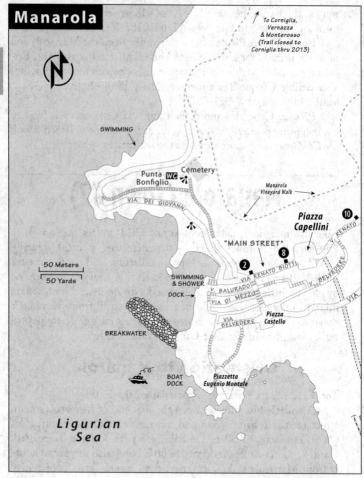

The Harbor: Manarola is tiny and picturesque, a tumble of buildings bunny-hopping down its ravine to the fun-loving waterfront. Notice how the I-beam crane launches the boats. Facing the water, look to the right, at the hillside Punta Bonfiglio cemetery and park (where this walk ends).

The town's swimming hole is just below. Manarola has no sand, but offers the best deep-water swimming in the area. The first "beach" has a shower, ladder, and wonderful rocks. The second has tougher access and no shower, but feels more remote and pristine (follow the paved path toward Corniglia, just around the point). For many, the tricky access makes this beach dangerous.

• Hiking inland up the town's main drag, you'll come to the train tracks covered by Manarola's new square, called...

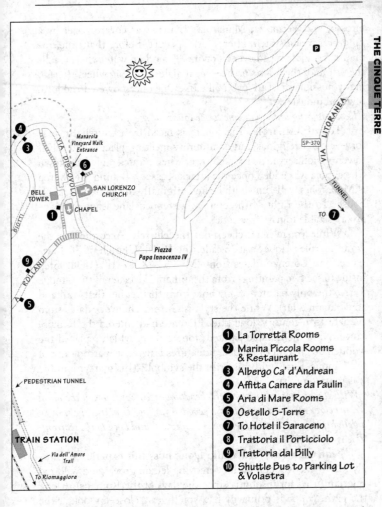

1 La Torretta Rooms

2 Marina Piccola Rooms & Restaurant

3 Albergo Ca' d'Andrean

4 Affitta Camere da Paulin

5 Aria di Mare Rooms

6 Ostello 5-Terre

7 To Hotel il Saraceno

8 Trattoria il Porticciolo

9 Trattoria dal Billy

10 Shuttle Bus to Parking Lot & Volastra

Piazza Capellini: Built in 2004, this square is an all-around great idea, giving the town a safe, fun zone for kids. Locals living near the tracks also enjoy a little less noise. Check out the mosaic that displays the varieties of local fish in colorful enamel.

• *Fifty yards uphill, you'll find the...*

Sciacchetrà Museum: Run by the national park, it's hardly a museum. But if it's open, pop in to its inviting room to see a tiny exhibit on the local wine industry (€0.50, free with Cinque Terre Park Card, generally closed, 15-minute video in English by request, 100 yards uphill from train tracks, across from the post office).

• *Hiking farther uphill, you can still hear...*

Manarola's Stream: Like the streams in Riomaggiore, Monterosso, and Vernazza, Manarola's rivulet was covered over by a modern sewage system after World War II. Before that time, romantic bridges arched over its ravine. A modern waterwheel recalls the origin of the town's name—local dialect for "big wheel" (one of many possible derivations). Mills like this once powered the local olive oil industry.

• *Keep climbing until you come to the square at the...*

Top of Manarola: The square is faced by a church, an oratory—now a religious and community meeting place—and a bell tower, which served as a watchtower when pirates raided the town (the cupola was added once the attacks ceased). Behind the church is Manarola's well-run youth hostel, originally the church's schoolhouse. To the right of the oratory, a stepped lane leads to Manarola's sizable tourist-free zone.

While you're here, check out the **church**. According to the white marble plaque in its facade, the Parish Church of St. Lawrence (San Lorenzo) dates from "MCCCXXXVIII" (1338). Step inside to see two paintings from the unnamed Master of the Cinque Terre, the only painter of any note from this region (left wall and above main altar). While the style is Gothic, the work dates from the late 15th century, long after Florence had entered the Renaissance. Note the humble painted stone ceiling, which replaced the wooden original in the 1800s. It features Lawrence, patron saint of the Cinque Terre, with his grill, the symbol of his martyrdom (he was roasted on it).

• *With the bell tower on your left, head about 20 yards down the main street below the church and find a wooden railing. It marks the start of a delightful stroll around the high side of town, and back to the seafront. This is the beginning of the...*

Manarola Vineyard Walk: Don't miss this experience. Simply follow the wooden railing, enjoying lemon groves and wild red valerian (used for insomnia since the days of the Romans). Along the path, which is primarily flat, you'll get a close-up look at the region's famous dry-stone walls and finely crafted vineyards (with dried-heather thatches to protect the grapes from the southwest winds). Smell the rosemary. Study the structure of the town, and pick out the scant remains of an old fort. Notice the S-shape of the main road—once a riverbed—that flows through town. The town's roofs are traditionally made of locally quarried slate, rather than tile, and are held down by rocks during windstorms. As the harbor comes into view, you'll see the breakwater, added just a decade ago.

Above you on the right are simple wooden religious scenes, the work of local resident Mario Andreoli. Before his father died, Mario promised him he'd replace the old cross on the family's vineyard. Mario has been adding figures ever since. After recovering from a rare illness, he redoubled his efforts. On religious holidays, everything's lit up: the Nativity, the Last Supper, the Crucifixion, the Resurrection, and more. Some of the scenes are left up year-round.

High above, a recent fire burned off the tree cover, revealing ancient terraces that line the terrain like a topographic map.

• *Follow this trail all the way to a T-intersection, where it hits the main coastal trail. Turn left. (A right takes you to the trail to Corniglia, likely closed during your visit.) Before descending back into town, take a right, detouring into...*

The Cemetery: Ever since Napoleon—who was king of Italy in the early 1800s—decreed that cemeteries were health risks, Cinque Terre's burial spots have been located outside the towns. The result: The dearly departed generally get first-class sea views. Each cemetery—with its evocative yellowed photos and finely carved Carrara marble memorial reliefs—is worth a visit. (The basic structure for all of them is the same, but Manarola's is the most easily accessible.)

In cemeteries like these, there's a hierarchy of four places to park your mortal remains: a graveyard, a spacious death condo *(loculo)*, a mini bone-niche *(ossario)*, or the communal ossuary. Because of the tight space, a time limit is assigned to the first three options (although many older tombs are grandfathered in). Bones go into the ossuary in the middle of the chapel floor after about a generation. Traditionally, locals make weekly visits to loved ones here, often bringing flowers. The rolling stepladder makes access to top-floor *loculi* easy.

• *The Manarola cemetery is on Punta Bonfiglio. Take the stairs just below it, then walk farther out through a park (playground, drinking water, WC, and picnic benches). Your Manarola finale: the bench at the tip of the point, offering one of the most commanding views of the entire region. The easiest way back to town is to take the stairs at the end of the point, which join the main walking path.*

Sleeping in Manarola

(€1 = about $1.30, country code: 39)

Manarola has plenty of private rooms. Ask in bars and restaurants. There's a modern three-star place halfway up the main drag, a sea-view hotel on the harbor, a big modern hostel, and a cluster of options around the church at the peaceful top of the town (a 5-minute hike from the train tracks).

$$$ La Torretta is a trendy, upscale 13-room place that caters to a demanding clientele. Probably the most elegant retreat in the region, it's a peaceful refuge with all the comforts for those happy to pay, including a communal hot tub with a view. Enjoy a complimentary snack and glass of prosecco on arrival, free wine-tastings during your stay, breakfast in your room, and a free minibar. Each chic room is distinct and described on their website (smaller Db-€145, regular Db-€190, Db suite-€250-400, cash discount, book several months in advance as it's justifiably popular, closed mid-Nov-mid-March, free Wi-Fi, on Piazza della Chiesa beside the bell tower at Vico Volto 20, tel. 0187-920-327, www.torrettas.com, torretta@cdh.it).

$$$ Marina Piccola offers 13 bright, slick rooms on the water—so they figure a warm welcome is unnecessary (Db-€120, air-con, free Wi-Fi, Via Birolli 120, tel. 0187-762-065, www.hotelmarinapiccola.com, info@hotelmarinapiccola.com).

$$$ Albergo Ca' d'Andrean, run by Simone, is quiet, comfortable, and modern—except for its antiquated reservation system. While the welcome is formal at best, it has 10 big, sunny, air-conditioned rooms and a cool garden oasis complete with lemon trees (Sb-€75, Db-€105, breakfast-€6, free Wi-Fi, cash only, send personal check to reserve from US—or call if you're reserving from the road, closed Nov-Christmas, up the hill at Via A. Discovolo 101, tel. 0187-920-040, www.cadandrean.it, cadandrean@libero.it).

$$ At Affitta Camere da Paulin, charming Donatella and Eraldo (the town's retired policeman) rent very nice, well-equipped rooms with a large and inviting common living room. It's in a modern setting a few minutes' walk uphill from the train tracks (Db-€70-80, view apartment Db-€105-130, 3-night minimum stay, free Wi-Fi, Via Discovolo 126, tel. 0187-920-706, mobile 334-389-4764, www.dapaulin.it, prenotazioni@dapaulin.it).

$$ Aria di Mare Rooms rents four sunny rooms and an apartment 20 yards beyond Trattoria dal Billy at the very top of town. Three rooms have spacious terraces with knockout views and lounge chairs. Maurizio speaks a little English, while Mamma Franca communicates with lots of Italian and toothy smiles (Db-€65, 2 adults and 1 child-€80, Db apartment-€90, ask for Rick Steves price, basic breakfast, free Wi-Fi, up stairs on the left at Via Aldo Rollandi 137, tel. 0187-920-367, mobile 349-058-4155, www.ariadimare.info, info@ariadimare.info, ask at Billy's if no one's home).

$ Ostello 5-Terre, Manarola's modern and pleasant hostel, occupies the former parochial school above the church square and offers 48 beds in four- to six-bed rooms. Nicola and Riccardo run a calm and peaceful place—it's not a party hostel—and quiet is greatly appreciated. They rent dorm rooms as doubles. Reserve well in advance. Full means full—they don't accommodate the desperate on the floor (Easter-mid-Oct: dorm beds-€23, Db-€65, Qb-€100; less off-season, normally closed Dec-Feb but can open on demand, not co-ed except for couples and families, no membership necessary, open to all ages, optional €5 breakfast and bargain dinners, office closed 13:00-16:00, rooms closed 10:00-13:00, check-in until 22:00, elevator, free Internet access and Wi-Fi, safe, laundry, book exchange, Via B. Riccobaldi 21, tel. 0187-920-039, www.hostel5terre.com, info@hostel5terre.com).

For Drivers: **$$$ Hotel il Saraceno,** with seven spacious, modern rooms, is a deal for drivers. Located above Manarola in the tiny town of Volastra (chock-full of vacationing Germans and Italians in summer), it's serene, clean, and right by the shuttle bus to Manarola (Db-€100, buffet breakfast, Wi-Fi, free parking, Via Volastra 8, tel. 0187-760-081, www.thesaraceno.com, hotel@the-saraceno.com, friendly Antonella).

Eating in Manarola

Many hardworking places line the main drag. The Scorza family works hard at **Trattoria il Porticciolo** (free glass of *sciacchetrà* dessert wine with this book, closed Wed, below train tracks at Via R. Birolli 92, tel. 0187-920-083). The harborside **Marina Piccola** is famous for great views, lousy service, and gouging naive tourists.

Trattoria dal Billy, hiding out high on the hill, is a hit, with good food and impressive views over the valley. With Edoardo and Enrico's black pasta with seafood and squid ink, green pasta with artichokes, mixed seafood starters, and homemade desserts, many find it worth the climb. Dinner reservations are a must (€11 pastas, €14 *secondi,* generally daily 8:00-15:00 & 19:00-23:30, closed Thu, Via Aldo Rollandi 122, tel. 0187-920-628).

Corniglia (Town #3)

This is the quiet town—the only one of the five not on the water—with a mellow main square. According to a (likely fanciful) local legend, the town was originally settled by a Roman farmer who named it for his mother, Cornelia (how Corniglia is pronounced). The town and its ancient residents produced a wine so famous that—some say—vases found at Pompeii touted its virtues. Regardless of the veracity of the legends, wine remains Corniglia's lifeblood today. Follow the pungent smell of ripe grapes into an alley cellar and get a local to let you dip a straw into a keg.

Remote and less visited than the other Cinque Terre towns, Corniglia has fewer tourists, cooler temperatures, a few restaurants, a windy overlook on its promontory, and plenty of private rooms for rent (ask at any bar or shop, no cheaper than other towns). If you think of the Cinque Terre as the Beatles, Corniglia is Ringo.

Corniglia

1. Pan e Vin Bar (Ricci Rooms Check-In)
2. Il Carugio Rooms & Butiega Shop
3. Villa Cecio Rooms
4. Corniglia Hostel
5. La Lanterna Restaurant
6. Osteria Mananan
7. Enoteca il Pirun
8. La Posada Ristorante
9. Gelateria

Orientation to Corniglia

Arrival in Corniglia

From the station, a footpath zigzags up about 380 steps to the town. Or take the green shuttle bus, generally timed to meet arriving trains (€1.50 one-way, €2.50 round-trip; free with Cinque Terre Park Card—to catch the waiting bus, ideally buy the card before you arrive in Corniglia; 2/hour). If you're driving, be aware that only residents can park on the main road between the recommended Villa Cecio and the point where the steep switchback staircase meets the road. Beyond that area, parking is €1.50 per hour.

Self-Guided Walk

Welcome to Corniglia

We'll explore this tiny town—population 240—and end at a scenic viewpoint.

• *Begin near the bus stop, located at a...*

Town Square: The gateway to this community is "Ciappà" square, with an ATM, phone booth, old wine press, and bus stop. The Cinque Terre's designation as a national park sparked a revitalization of the town. Corniglia's young generation is more likely now to stay put, rather than migrate into big cities the way locals did in the past.

• *Look for the arrow pointing to the center* (centro). *Stroll the spine of Corniglia, Via Fieschi. In the fall, the smell of grapes (on their way to becoming wine) wafts from busy cellars. Along this main street, you'll see...*

Corniglia's Enticing Shops: Alberto's Gelateria dishes up the best homemade gelato in town. Before ordering, get a free taste of Alberto's *miele di Corniglia*, made from local honey. His local lemon slush takes pucker to new heights. **Enoteca il Pirun**— named for a type of oddly shaped old-fashioned wine pitcher designed to aerate the wine and give the alcohol more kick—is located in a cool cantina at Via Fieschi 115. Sample some local wines (generally free for small tastes). If you buy a bottle, they may gift you with a souvenir bib. In the **Butiega** shop at Via Fieschi 142, Vincenzo sells organic local specialties (daily 8:00-19:30). For picnickers, they offer €4 made-to-order ham-and-cheese sandwiches and a fun €5 *antipasti misti* to go. (There are good places to picnic farther along on this walk.)

• *Following Via Fieschi, you'll end up at the...*

Main Square: On Largo Taragio, tables from two bars and a trattoria spill around a WWI memorial and the town's old well. It once piped in natural spring water from the hillside to locals living without plumbing. What looks like a church is the Oratory of Santa Caterina. (An oratory is a kind of a spiritual clubhouse for a service group doing social work in the name of the Catholic Church. For more information, see "Oratory of the Dead" on page 1158.) Behind the oratory, you'll find a clearing that local children have made into a soccer field. The stone benches and viewpoint make this a peaceful place for a picnic (less crowded than the end-of-town viewpoint, described below).

• *Opposite the oratory, notice how steps lead steeply down on Via alla Marina to Corniglia's non-beach. It's a five-minute paved climb to sunning rocks, a shower, and a small deck (with a treacherous entry into the water). From the square, continue up Via Fieschi to the...*

End-of-Town Viewpoint: The Santa Maria Belvedere, named for a church that once stood here, marks the scenic end of Corniglia. This is a super picnic spot. From here, look high to the west, where the village and sanctuary of San Bernardino straddle a ridge (a good starting point for a hike; accessible by shuttle bus from Monterosso or a long uphill hike from Vernazza). Below is the tortuous harbor, where locals hoist their boats onto the cruel rocks.

Sights in Corniglia

Beaches

This hilltop town has rocky sea access below its train station (toward Manarola). Once a beach, it's all been washed away and offers no services. Look for signs that say *al mare* or *Marina*. A trail leads from the town center steeply down to sunning rocks on the closest thing Corniglia has to a beach (with a shower).

The infamous **Guvano beach** (a bit along the coast toward Vernazza) is now essentially closed down. Guvano was created by an 1893 landslide that cost the village a third of its farmland. Notorious throughout Italy as a nude beach, Guvano was accessed via an unused train tunnel and attracted visitors with an appetite for drug use. Now the tunnel is closed, and the national park wants people to keep their clothes on and forget about Guvano.

Sleeping in Corniglia

(€1 = about $1.30, country code: 39)
Perched high above the sea on a hilltop, Corniglia has plenty of private rooms. To get to the town from the station, catch the shuttle bus or make the 15-minute uphill hike. The town is riddled with humble places that charge too much (generally Db-€65) and have meager business skills and a limited ability to converse with tourists—so it's almost never full.

$$ Cristiana Ricci is an exception to the rule. She communicates well and is reliable, renting four small, clean, and peaceful rooms—two with kitchens and one with a terrace and sweeping view—just inland from the bus stop (Db-€60-70, Qb-€90, €10/day less when you stay 2 or more nights, free Internet access, check in at the Pan e Vin bar at Via Fieschi 123, mobile 338-937-6547, cri_affittacamere@virgilio.it). Her mom rents a big, modern apartment (€90 for 2-4 people).

$$ Il Carugio has nine modern, sunny rooms right in the center of the village, most with sea views. The communal rooftop terrace offers a commanding view of the coast (Db-€70-80, no breakfast, tel. 0187-812-293, mobile 335-175-7946, www.ilcarugiodicorniglia.com, info@ilcarugiodicorniglia.com, Lidia).

$$ Villa Cecio (pronounced "chay-choe") feels like an abandoned hotel. They offer eight well-worn rooms on the outskirts of town, with saggy beds and little character or warmth (Db-€65, ask about Rick Steves rate, breakfast-€5, cash preferred, great views, on main road 200 yards toward Vernazza at Via Serra 58, tel. 0187-812-043, mobile 334-350-6637, www.cecio5terre.com, info@cecio5terre.com, Giacinto). They also rent eight similar rooms (Db-€60) in an annex on the square where the bus stops.

$ Corniglia Hostel was formerly the town's schoolhouse. It rents 24 beds in a pastel-yellow building up some steps from the main square, where the bus stops. The playground in front is often busy with happy kids. Despite its strict and institutional atmosphere, the hostel's prices, central location, and bright and clean rooms ensure its popularity. Its hotelesque double rooms are open to anyone (€24/bed in two 8-bed dorms, €27 with minimal breakfast; four Db-€55, €60 with breakfast; office open 7:00-13:00 & 15:00-24:00, rooms closed 13:00-15:00, 1:30 curfew, air-con, lockers, Internet access and Wi-Fi, self-serve laundry, no public spaces except lobby, Via alla Stazione 3, tel. 0187-812-559, www.ostellocorniglia.com but reserve at www.hostelworld.com, ostellocorniglia@gmail.com).

Eating in Corniglia

Corniglia has few restaurants.

The trattoria **La Lanterna,** on the main square, is the most atmospheric (but without particularly charming service).

Osteria Mananan—between the Ciappà bus stop and the main square at Via Fieschi 117—serves what many consider the best food in town in its small, stony, elegant interior (Wed-Mon 12:15-14:30 & 19:45-22:00, closed Tue, no outdoor seating, tel. 0187-821-166).

Enoteca il Pirun, also on Via Fieschi, has a small restaurant above the wine bar, where Mario serves typical local dishes (€28 fixed-price meal includes homemade wine, daily 12:00-16:00 & 19:30-23:30, tel. 0187-812-315).

La Posada Ristorante offers dinner in a garden under trees, overlooking the Ligurian Sea. To get here, stroll out of town to the top of the stairs from the station (€10 pastas, €10 *secondi*, €15 tourist *menu*, nightly from 19:00, tel. 0187-821-174)

Vernazza (Town #4)

With the closest thing to a natural harbor—overseen by a ruined castle and a stout stone church—Vernazza is the jewel of the Cinque Terre. Only the occasional noisy slurping up of the train by the mountain reminds you of the modern world.

The action is at the harbor, where you'll find outdoor restaurants, a bar hanging on the edge of the castle, and a breakwater with a promenade, corralled by a natural amphitheater of terraced hills. In the summer, the beach becomes a soccer field, where teams fielded by local bars and restaurants provide late-night entertainment. In the dark, locals fish off the promontory, using glowing bobbers that shine in the waves.

Proud of their Vernazzan heritage, the town's 500 residents like to brag: "Vernazza is locally owned. Portofino has sold out." Fearing the change it would bring, keep-Vernazza-small proponents stopped the construction of a major road into the town and

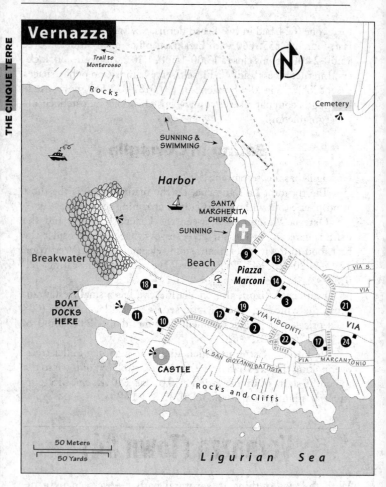

region. Families are tight and go back centuries; several generations stay together. In the winter, the population shrinks, as many people return to their more comfortable big-city apartments to spend the money they reaped during the tourist season.

Sadly, Vernazza was hit harder than any other Cinque Terre town by the flood on October 25, 2011. Essentially every business in town was destroyed as the flood raged through the town, burying it in mud. Every shop, restaurant, and hotel on the main drag had to be re-wired, re-plumbed, and re-equipped. Around town, you'll see photos and hear stories of what was, perhaps, the most tumultuous day ever in the town's thousand-year history.

The flood's impact for visitors today? Almost nothing. Just enjoy. Now that things are mostly back to normal, leisure time is devoted to taking part in the *passeggiata*—strolling lazily together

To Parking & Coastal Road

Piazza Fontana Vecchia

B BUS STOP

4

VIA BRIGATE PARTIGIANE

POST

23

BANK & ATM

5

Little "River"

1

FRAN.

TUNNEL

DEL SANTO

7

I TRAIN STATION

6

16

8

ROMA

CHAPEL

15

CARATTINO

20

Trail to Corniglia, Manarola & Riomaggiore

1. Pensione Sorriso
2. Trattoria Gianni Rooms/Ristorante
3. Albergo Barbara
4. La Marina Rooms, Tonino Basso Rooms & Il Pirata della Cinque Terre
5. Camere Fontana Vecchia
6. Giuliano Basso Rooms
7. Vernazza Rooms
8. Blue Marlin Bar & Café
9. Ananasso Bar
10. Ristorante al Castello
11. Ristorante Belforte
12. Gambero Rosso Ristorante
13. Trattoria del Capitano
14. Ristorante Pizzeria Vulnetia
15. Trattoria da Sandro
16. Antica Osteria il Baretto
17. Ristorante Incadase da Piva
18. Bar Baia Saracena
19. Burgus Wine Bar
20. Franco's Ristorante & Bar la Torre
21. Forno (Bakery)
22. Gelateria
23. Launderette
24. Internet Point

up and down the main street. Sit on a bench and study the passers-by doing their *vasche* (laps). Explore the characteristic alleys, called *carugi*. Learn—and live—the phrase *"la vita pigra di Vernazza"* (the lazy life of Vernazza).

Orientation to Vernazza

Tourist Information

The TI/park information/train ticket office is one desk buried in a gift shop between the two tracks at the train station (daily 8:00-19:30, tel. 0187-812-524). Public WCs are nearby in the station.

Save Vernazza: Led by a group of American women who married into the community, Save Vernazza brought relief to the town in the immediate aftermath of the 2011 flood, and has since morphed into an organization to help preserve and foster healthy tourism. For the latest on the town, its recovery, and their activities—including leads on locals with rooms and apartments for rent—visit www.savevernazza.com.

Arrival in Vernazza

By Train: Vernazza's train station is only about three cars long, but the trains are much longer—so most of the cars come to a stop in a long, dark tunnel. Get out anyway, and walk through the tunnel to the station.

By Car: Because many roads and parking lots were washed out in the 2011 flood, road access and parking above Vernazza may be in flux. There are plans to create a nonresident pay parking lot 500 yards above the town (but don't count on it). In the past, visitors could connect between the parking lot and downtown on a hard-working shuttle service. This may or may not be back up and running for your visit. Yellow lines mark parking spots for residents only.

Helpful Hints

Internet Access: The slick, expensive, six-terminal **Internet Point,** run by Alberto and Isabella, is in the village center (daily June-Oct 9:30-23:00, until 20:00 Nov-May, Wi-Fi, will burn your digital photos to a CD or DVD for €5). The **Il Pirata delle Cinque Terre** bar (at the top of the town) and **Burgus Wine Bar** (on the harbor) both offer free Wi-Fi with a purchase.

Laundry: Domenico's Lavanderia, at the top of town next to the post office, is completely self-serve (coin-op, €6/wash, €5/dry, daily 8:00-22:00, operated by Domenico and Barbara at the fish shop).

Massage: Kate Allen offers a super-relaxing fusion of aromatic/Swedish/holistic massage for €50 per hour in her little studio adjacent to the clinic at the top of Vernazza (mobile 333-568-4653, www.vernazzamassage5terre.com).

Best Views: A steep 10-minute hike in either direction from Vernazza gives you a classic village photo op (for the best light, head toward Corniglia in the morning, and toward Monterosso in the evening).

Self-Guided Walks

Welcome to Vernazza

This tour includes Vernazza's characteristic town squares and ends on its scenic breakwater.

• *From the train station, walk uphill until you hit what was the pre-flood parking lot, with a post office and a barrier that keeps out all but service vehicles. As you survey the post-flood reconstruction work, it is easy to imagine how this ravine could be susceptible to flash flooding. The stream in this ravine once powered Vernazza's water mill. Vernazza's shuttle buses run from here to hamlets and sanctuaries in the hills above.*

Walk to the tidy, modern square called...

Fontana Vecchia: Named after a long-gone fountain, this is where older locals remember the river filled with townswomen doing their washing. A lane leads from here up to the cemetery. Imagine the entire village sadly trudging up here during funerals. (The cemetery is peaceful and evocative at sunset, when the fading light touches each crypt.)

• *Glad to be here in happier times, begin your saunter downhill to the harbor. Just before the* Pensione Sorriso *sign, on your right (big brown wood doors), you'll see the...*

Ambulance Barn: A group of volunteers is always on call for a dash to the hospital, 40 minutes away in La Spezia. Opposite the barn is a big empty lot. Like many landowners, the owner of Pensione Sorriso had plans to expand, but since the 1980s, the government has said "No." While some landowners are frustrated, the old character of these towns survives. A few steps farther down is the town clinic. The *guarda medica* (emergency doctor—see buzzer) sleeps upstairs.

• *At the corner across from the playground, on a marble plaque in the wall on the left, you'll see a...*

World Wars Monument: This is dedicated to those killed in the World Wars. Not a family in Vernazza was spared. Listed on the left are soldiers *morti in combattimento,* who died in World War I; on the right is the World War II section. Some were deported to *Germania;* others—labeled *Part* (stands for *partigiani,* or partisans, generally communists)—were killed while fighting against Mussolini. Cynics considered partisans less than heroes. After 1943, Hitler called up Italian boys over 15. Rather than die on the front for Hitler, they escaped to the hills. They became "resistance fighters" in order to remain free.

The path to Corniglia leaves from here (behind and above the plaque). Behind you is a small square and playground, decorated with three millstones, once used to grind local olives into oil. There's a good chance you'll see an expat mom here at the village playground with her kids. I've met many American women who fell in love with a local guy, stayed, and are now happily raising families here. (But I've rarely met an American guy who moved in with a local girl.)

From here, Vernazza's tiny river goes underground. Until the 1950s, the river ran openly through the center of town. Old-timers recall the days before the breakwater, when the river cascaded down and the surf sent waves rolling up Vernazza's main drag. Back then, this place was nicknamed "Little Venice" for the series of romantic bridges that arched over the stream, connecting the two sides of the town before the main road was built.

Corralling this stream under the modern street, and forcing it to take a hard right turn here, contributed to the damage caused by the 2011 flood. Following the flood, alpine engineers were imported from Switzerland to redesign this drainage system, so any future floods will be less destructive. They also put nets above the town to protect it from more landslides.

Before the flood, the walls under the tracks served as a community information center, with historic photos of the old town, maps showing trails in the hills, a list of local volunteers and when they are on call to drive the ambulance, and an events board. Look around here for photos of the flood and the shops that it devastated. "The 25th of October" is a day that will live forever in this town's lore. The second set of tracks (nearer the harbor) was recently renovated to lessen the disruptive noise, but locals say it made no difference.

• Follow the road downhill to...

Vernazza's "Business Center": Here, you'll pass many locals doing their *vasche* (laps). Next, you'll pass souvenir shops, wine shops, the Blue Marlin Bar (Vernazza's top nightspot), and the tiny Chapel of Santa Marta (the small stone chapel with iron grillwork over the window), where Mass is celebrated only on special Sundays. Farther down, you'll walk by a *gelateria*, bakery, pharmacy, a grocery, and another *gelateria*. There are plenty of fun and cheap food-to-go options here.

• On the left, in front of the second gelateria, a stone arch was blasted away by the flood. The hole in the rock leads to a beach created by the flood. This is where the town's stream used to hit the sea back in the 1970s.

Continue downhill. Just before the harbor, the main street becomes very narrow. This was the bottleneck that caused water to back up into the town during the flood. And these buildings are about the only ones in town to suffer structural damage from the force of the water.

A few steps farther take you to the...

Harbor Square and Breakwater: Vernazza, with the only natural harbor of the Cinque Terre, was established as the sole place boats could pick up the fine local wine. The two-foot-high square stone at the foot of the stairs by the Burgus Wine Bar is marked *Sasso del Sego* (stone of tallow). Workers crushed animal flesh and fat in its basin to make tallow, which drained out of the tiny hole below. The tallow was then used to waterproof boats or wine barrels. For more town history, step into the Burgus to see fascinating old photos of Vernazza on the wall. Stonework is the soul of the region. Take some time to appreciate the impressive stonework of the restaurant interiors facing the harbor.

On the far side (behind Ristorante Pizzeria Vulnetia), peek into the tiny street with its commotion of arches. Vernazza's most characteristic side streets, called *carugi*, lead up from here. The trail (above the church, toward Monterosso) leads to the quintessential view of Vernazza.

Located in front of the harborside church, the tiny piazza—decorated with a river-rock mosaic—is a popular hangout spot. It's where Vernazza's old ladies soak up the last bit of sun, and kids enjoy a patch of level ball field.

Vernazza's harborfront **church** is unusual for its strange entryway, which faces east (altar side). With relative peace and prosperity in the 16th century, the townspeople doubled the church in size, causing it to overtake a little piazza that once faced the west facade. From the square, use the "new" entry and climb the steps, keeping an eye out for the level necessary to keep the church high and dry. Inside, the lighter pillars in the back mark the 16th-century extension. Three historic portable crosses hanging on the walls are carried through town during Easter processions. They are replicas of crosses that (locals like to believe) Vernazza ships once carried on crusades to the Holy Land. In 1998, Vernazza's priest was gruesomely and mysteriously murdered. While circumstantial evidence points to fascinating conspiracy theories, no one knows whodunit (or, at least, no one's telling). Today's priest, Don Giovanni, is popular—he stopped the church bells from ringing through the night (light sleepers rejoiced). In the wake of the 2011 flood, he opened up the church as a staging ground for recovery services.

• *Finish your town tour seated out on the breakwater (perhaps with a glass of local white wine or something more interesting from a nearby bar—borrow the glass, they don't mind). Face the town, and see...*

The Harbor: In a moderate storm, you'd be soaked, as waves routinely crash over the *molo* (breakwater, built in 1972). Waves can rearrange the huge rocks—depositing them from the breakwater onto the piazza and its benches. Freak waves have even washed away tourists squinting excitedly into their cameras. (I've seen it happen.) In 2007, an American woman was swept away and killed by a rogue wave. Enjoy the waterfront piazza—carefully.

The train line (to your left) was constructed in 1874 to tie together a newly united Italy, and linked Turin and Genoa with Rome. A second line (hidden in a tunnel at this point) was built in the 1920s. The yellow building alongside the tracks was Vernazza's first train station. You can see the four bricked-up alcoves where people once waited for trains. Notice the wonderful concrete sunbathing strip (and place for late-night privacy) laid below the tracks along the rocks.

Vernazza's fishing fleet is down to just a couple of boats (with the net spools). While the 2011 flood washed away many of the town's boats and cars (one boat was actually recovered in Spain), Vernazzans are still more likely to own a boat than a car, and it's said that you stand a better chance of surviving if you mess with a local man's wife than with his boat. On a recent visit just after the flood, I ran into Tonino, who showed me photo of his boat, *Gustina*, with this caption: "Tonino loved me and the flood kidnapped me." Tonino said he was lucky to have been stranded across the street when *Gustina* was swept away, or he likely would have been swept out to sea with her.

Boats are on buoys, except in winter or when the red storm flag (see the pole at the start of the breakwater) indicates bad seas. At these times, the boats are pulled up onto the square—which is usually reserved for restaurant tables. In the 1970s, tiny Vernazza had one of Italy's top water polo teams, and the harbor was their "pool." Later, when the league required a real pool, Vernazza dropped out.

The Castle: On the far right, the castle, which is now a grassy park with great views (and nothing but stones), still guards the town (€1.50 donation, daily 10:00-19:00; from harbor, take stairs by Trattoria Gianni and follow *Ristorante al Castello* signs, tower is a few steps beyond). This was the town's watchtower back in pirate days, and a Nazi lookout in World War II. The castle tower looks new because it was rebuilt after the British bombed it, chasing out the Germans. The highest umbrellas mark the recommended Ristorante Al Castello. The squat tower on the water is great for a glass of wine or a meal. From the breakwater, you could follow the rope to the Ristorante Belforte and pop inside, past the actual submarine door. A photo of a major storm showing the entire tower under a wave (not uncommon in the winter) hangs near the bar.

The Town: Before the 12th century, pirates made the coast uninhabitable, so the first Vernazzans lived in the hills above (near the Reggio Sanctuary). The town itself—and its towers, fortified walls, and hillside terracing—are mostly from the 12th through the 15th centuries, when Vernazza was allied with the Republic of Genoa.

Vernazza has two halves. *Sciuiu* (Vernazzan dialect for "flowery") is the sunny side on the left, and *luvegu* (dank) is the shady side on the right. Houses below the castle were connected by an interior arcade—ideal for fleeing attacks. The "Ligurian pastel" colors are regulated by a commissioner of good taste in the regional government. The square before you is locally famous for some of the area's finest restaurants. The big red central house—on the site where Genoan warships were built in the 12th century—used to be a guardhouse.

In the Middle Ages, there was no beach or square. The water went right up to the buildings, where boats would tie up, Venetian-style. Imagine what Vernazza looked like in those days, when it was the biggest and richest of the Cinque Terre towns. Buildings had a water gate (facing today's square) and a front door on the higher inland side. There was no pastel plaster—just fine stonework (traces of which survive above the Trattoria del Capitano). Apart from the added plaster, the general shape and size of the town has changed little in five centuries. Survey the windows and notice inhabitants quietly gazing back.

While the town has 1,500 residents in summer, only 500 stay here through the winter. Vernazza has accommodations for about 500 tourists.

Above the Town: The small, round tower above the red guardhouse—another part of the city fortifications—reminds us of the town's importance in the Middle Ages. Back then, its key ally Genoa's enemies (i.e., the other maritime republics, especially Pisa) were Vernazza's enemies. Franco's Ristorante and Bar la Torre, just behind the tower, welcomes hikers who are finishing, starting, or simply contemplating the Corniglia-Vernazza hike, with great town views. That tower recalls a time when the entire town was fortified by a stone wall.

Vineyards fill the mountainside beyond the town. Notice the many terraces. Someone—probably after too much of that local wine—calculated that the roughly 3,000 miles of dry-stone walls built to terrace the region's vineyards have the same amount of stonework as the Great Wall of China.

For six centuries, the economy was based on wine and olive oil. Then came the 1980s—and the tourists. Locals turned to tourism to make a living, and stopped tending the land. Many vineyards were abandoned, and the terraces fell into disrepair. But it's the stonework of the terracing in the surrounding hills that helps prevent flooding—a lesson learned in the worst possible way on October 25, 2011.

Although many locals still maintain their tiny plots and proudly serve their family wines, the patchwork of local vineyards is atomized and complex because of inheritance traditions. Historically, families divided their land between their children. Parents wanted each child to get some good land. Because some lots were "kissed by the sun" while others were shady, the lots were split into increasingly tiny and eventually unviable pieces—another reason why many have been abandoned.

A single steel train line winds up the gully behind the tower. It is for the vintner's *trenino,* the tiny service train. Play "Where's *trenino?*" and see if you can find two trains. The vineyards once stretched as high as you can see, but since fewer people sweat in the fields these days, the most distant terraces have gone wild again.

The Church, School, and City Hall: Vernazza's Ligurian Gothic church, built with black stones quarried from Punta

Mesco (the distant point behind you), dates from 1318. Note the gray stone that marks the church's 16th-century expansion. The gray-and-red house above the spire is the local elementary school (about 25 children attend; education through age 14 is obligatory). High-schoolers go to the "big city," La Spezia. The red building to the right of the schoolhouse, a former monastery, is the City Hall. Vernazza and Corniglia function as one community. Through most of the 1990s, the local government was Communist. In 1999, residents elected a coalition of many parties working to rise above ideologies and simply make Vernazza a better place. That practical notion of government continues here today. The city was led through the trauma and challenges of the flood by Mayor Vincenzo Resasco. He worked so tirelessly and heroically that, suffering from complete exhaustion after the initial recovery period, he had to be helicoptered to the hospital.

Finally, on the top of the hill, with the best view of all, is the town cemetery.

Activities in Vernazza

Tuesday-Morning Market
Vernazza's skimpy business community is augmented Tuesday mornings (8:00-13:00) when a meager gang of cars and trucks pulls into town for a tailgate market.

Beach
The harbor's sandy cove has sunning rocks and showers by the breakwater. There's also a ladder on the breakwater for deep-water access. The sunbathing lane directly under the church also has a shower.

Boat Rental
Before the flood, Vincenzo of Nord Est rented canoes and small motorboats from his stand on the harbor, and also took people out for mini-cruises. He lost his little fleet; how he'll put it back together remains to be seen (contact him for the latest: mobile 338-700-0436, info@manuela-vernazza.com). With a rental boat, you can reach a tiny *acqua pendente* (waterfall) cove between Vernazza and Monterosso; locals call it their *laguna blu*.

Shuttle Bus Joyride
For a cheap and scenic joyride, with a chance to chat about the region with friendly, English-speaking Beppe, Simone, or Pietro, ride the shuttle bus from the top of town to the sanctuaries and hamlets San Bernadino and Reggio—the ancient birthplace of Vernazza—and back again (entire route for the cost of a round-trip ticket, 5/day—usually at 7:00, 9:45, 12:00, 15:00, and 17:30; schedule posted at park office, train station, and bus stop in front

of post office; €2.50 one-way, free with Cinque Terre Park Card, churches at sanctuaries are usually closed).

Nightlife in Vernazza

Vernazza's younger generation of restaurant workers lets loose after-hours. They work hard through the tourist season, travel in the winter, speak English, and enjoy connecting with international visitors. After the restaurants close down, the town is quiet except for a couple of nightspots. For more information on the Blue Marlin, Ananasso, Il Pirata, and Ristorante Incadase, see their listings under "Eating in Vernazza," later. All Vernazza bars must close by 24:00.

Blue Marlin Bar dominates the late-night scene with a mix of locals and tourists, home-cooked food until 22:00, good drinks, and piano jam sessions. If you're young and hip, this is *the* place to hang out. There's a new piano, and if you play, you're welcome to contribute to the scene. They also host a free book-swap shelf.

Ananasso Bar offers early-evening happy-hour fun and cocktails *(aperitivi)* that both locals and visitors enjoy. Its harborfront tables get the last sunshine of the day.

Burgus Wine Bar, chic and cool with a jazzy ambience, is a popular early-evening and after-dinner harborside hangout. Sip local wine or a cocktail. Valerio and Lorenza specialize in Ligurian wines and can explain the historic town photos and museum cases of artifacts (closed Tue, free Wi-Fi with a drink, Piazza Marconi 4).

Il Pirata delle Cinque Terre, at the top of the town, was completely destroyed by the flood—but is back in business. This place features the entertaining Cannoli brothers, who fill a happy crowd of tourists with wonderful Sicilian pastries and drinks each evening. Many come for dinner and end up staying because of these two wild and crazy guys and the camaraderie they create among their diners (erratic hours driven by demand, free Wi-Fi).

Ristorante Incadase da Piva (tucked up the lane behind the pharmacy) is the haunt of Piva, Vernazza's troubadour. Piva often gets out his guitar and sings traditional local songs as well as his own compositions. If you're looking for a local Hemingway, check here.

Really Late: There's a little cave on the beach just under the church that lends itself to fun in the wee hours, when everything else is closed.

Sleeping in Vernazza

(€1 = about $1.30, country code: 39)

Vernazza, the spindly and salty essence of the Cinque Terre, is my top choice for a home base. Off-season (Oct-March), you can generally arrive without a reservation and find a place, but at other times, it's smart to book ahead (especially June-July and weekends).

People recommended here are listed for their communication skills (they speak English, have email, and are reliable with bookings) and because they rent several rooms. Consequently, my recommendations cost more than comparable rooms you'll find if you shop around. Comparison-shopping will likely save you €10-20 per double per night—and often get you a better place and view to boot. The real Vernazza gems are stray single rooms with owners who have no interest in booking in advance or messing with email. Arrive by early afternoon and drop by any shop or bar and ask; most locals know someone who rents rooms.

Anywhere you stay here requires some climbing, but keep in mind that more climbing means better views. Most do not include breakfast (for suggestions, see "Eating in Vernazza," later). Cash is preferred or required almost everywhere. Night noise can be a problem if you're near the station. Rooms on the harbor come with church bells (but only between 7:00 and 22:00).

Expect Changes: Following the 2011 flooding, most accommodations in town had to rebuild from scratch. While many are likely open for your visit, specifics have likely changed. When inquiring about rooms, carefully confirm the prices, amenities, and other information noted below.

Pensions

These pensions are located on the Vernazza map.

$$$ Pensione Sorriso, the oldest pension in town (where I stayed on my first visit in 1975), rents 19 overpriced rooms above the train station. While the main building has the charm, it comes with train noise and saggy beds; the annex, up the street, is in a quieter apartment that feels forgotten (S-€65, Sb-€80, D-€100, Db-€140-150, Tb-€130, includes breakfast, some with air-con, Wi-Fi, Via Gavino 4, tel. 0187-812-224, www.pensionesorriso. com, info@pensionesorriso.com, Francesca and Aldo).

$$$ Trattoria Gianni rents 27 small rooms and three apartments just under the castle. The rooms are in three buildings—one funky, two modern—up a hundred tight, winding spiral stairs. The funky ones, which may or may not have private baths, are artfully decorated à la shipwreck, with tiny balconies and grand sea views *(con vista sul mare)*. The comfy new *(nuovo)* rooms lack views. Both have modern bathrooms and access to a super-scenic cliff-hanging guests' garden. Steely Marisa requires check-in before 16:00 or a phone call to explain when you're coming. Emanuele (Gianni's son, who now runs the restaurant), Simona, and the staff speak a little English (S-€45, D-€80, Db-€100-120, Tb-€120-140, for best prices pay cash and mention this book when you reserve, cancellations less than a week in advance are charged one night's deposit, closed Jan-Feb, Piazza Marconi 5, tel. 0187-812-228, tel. 0187-821-003, on Wed call mobile 393-9008-155 instead, www. giannifranzi.it, info@giannifranzi.it). Pick up your keys at Trattoria Gianni's restaurant on the harbor square.

$$ Albergo Barbara rents nine simple, clean, and modern rooms overlooking the harbor square—most with small windows and small views. It's run by English-speaking Giuseppe and his no-nonsense Swiss wife, Patricia (D-€55, Db-€65-70, big Db with nice harbor view-€110, extra bed-€10, 2-night stay preferred, closed Dec-Feb, reserve online with credit card but pay cash, free Wi-Fi, Piazza Marconi 30, tel. 0187-812-398, mobile 338-793-3261, www.albergobarbara.it, info@albergobarbara.it).

Private Rooms *(Affitta Camere)*

Vernazza is honeycombed with private rooms year-round, offering the best values in town. Owners may be reluctant to reserve rooms far in advance. Doubles cost €55-100, depending on the view, season, and plumbing—you get what you pay for. Most places accept only cash. Some have killer views, come with lots of stairs, and cost the same as a small, dark place on a back lane over the train tracks. Little English is spoken at many of these places. If you call ahead to let them know your arrival time (or call when you arrive, using your mobile phone), they'll meet you at the train station.

Note: Many of the places listed next were not yet open during my last visit to Vernazza—but they'll likely be ready in time for your visit. Contact those that interest you to see if they're taking guests. A helpful source of information is **Save Vernazza,** which began as a post-flood relief organization but has now evolved into an all-purpose Vernazza advocacy group, with info on local rooms and apartments for rent (check their website for details: www. savevernazza.com).

Well-Run Rooms in the Inland Part of Town

Some of my favorite places in town, located in the ravine above the train station, were hardest hit by the flood. Exactly how and when they will reopen is hard to say, but if they're open, they're well worth considering. For the latest, visit their websites or inquire via Save Vernazza. These rooms are located on the Vernazza map, earlier in this chapter.

$$$ Tonino Basso's four rooms, which come with tranquility but no views, will likely be run by Alessandra (www.toninobasso. com).

$$ La Marina Rooms—is run by hardworking Christian, who speaks English and happily meets his guests at the station to carry their bags. There are five beautiful, top-end, pricey units: Three €90 doubles share a fine ocean-view terrace, and two €120 apartments are more spacious, with fine terraces and views (mobile 338-476-7472, www.lamarinarooms.com, mapcri@yahoo.it).

$$ Camere Fontana Vecchia has four spacious, quiet, non-view rooms near the post office, run by Anne (Via Gavino 15, tel. 0187-821-130, mobile 333-454-9371, www.cinqueterrecamere. com, m.annamaria@libero.it).

$$ Giuliano Basso's four carefully crafted rooms are just above town, straddling a ravine among orange trees. It's proudly built out of stone by Giuliano himself—the town's last stone-layer (more train noise than others, above train station, take the ramp just before Pensione Sorriso, mobile 333-341-4792, www.cdh.it/giuliano, giuliano@cdh.it).

Other Reliable Places Scattered Through Town and the Harborside

These places are not located on this book's map; ask for directions when you reserve.

$$$ La Malà is Vernazza's jetsetter pad. Four pristine white rooms boast four-star-hotel-type extras and a common terrace looking out over the rocky shore. It's a climb—way, way up to the top of town—but they'll gladly carry your bags to and from the station (Db-€155, Db suite-€220, includes breakfast at a bar, air-con, Wi-Fi, mobile 334-287-5718, www.lamala.it, info@lamala. it, Giamba and Armanda). They also rent the simpler "Armanda's Room" nearby (no view, Db-€75, ring bell at Piazza Marconi 15).

$$$ Martina Callo's four air-conditioned rooms overlook the square; they're up plenty of steps near the silent-at-night church tower (room #1: Tb-€110 or Qb-€120 with harbor view; room #2: huge Qb family room with no view-€110; room #3: Db with grand view terrace-€100; room #4: roomy Db with no view-€60; free Wi-Fi, ring bell at Piazza Marconi 26, tel. 0187-812-365, mobile 329-435-5344, www.roomartina.com, roomartina@roomartina.com).

$$ Monica Lercari rents several classy rooms with modern comforts, perched at the top of town. Guests are welcome to borrow the family rowboat or mountain bike (Db-€80, sea-view D-€100, grand sea-view terrace D-€120, "honeymoon suite" Db-€180, includes breakfast, air-con, Wi-Fi, next to recommended Ristorante al Castello, tel. 0187-812-296, alcastellovernazza@yahoo.it).

$$ Memo Rooms has three clean and spacious rooms that offer good value. They overlook the main street, in what feels like a miniature hotel. Enrica will meet you if you call upon arrival (Db-€70, Via Roma 15, tel. 0187-812-360, mobile 338-285-2385, www.memorooms.com, info@memorooms.com).

$$ Nicolina rents five recently renovated units with double-paned windows. Two rooms are in the center over the pharmacy, up a few steep steps—one has only sleeper sofas (Db-€80); two others are in a different building beyond the church with great views (Db-€100, Tb-€120, Qb-€150); and the last unit is a two-bedroom quadruple with even better views (€200). Inquire at Pizzeria Vulnetia on the harbor square (Piazza Marconi 29, tel. 0187-821-193, www.camerenicolina.it, camerenicolina.info@cdh.it).

$$ Rosa Vitali rents two four-person apartments across from the pharmacy overlooking the main street (and beyond the train noise). One has a terrace and fridge (top floor); the other has windows and a full kitchen (Db-€95, Tb-€115, Qb-€125, reception at Via Visconti 10 between the grotto and Piazza Marconi, tel. 0187-821-181, mobile 340-267-5009, www.rosacamere.it, rosa.vitali@libero.it).

$$ Francamaria and her kind husband Andrea rent eight sharp, comfortable, and creatively renovated but expensive rooms—all described in detail on her website. While their reception desk is on the harbor square (on the ground floor facing the harbor at Piazza Marconi 30—don't confuse it with Albergo Barbara at same address), the rooms they manage are all over town (Db-€80-120 depending on size and view, Qb-€125-160, extra person-€20, tel. 0187-812-002, mobile 328-711-9728, www.francamaria.com, info@francamaria.com).

More Private Rooms in Vernazza

$$ Maria Capellini rents a couple of simple, clean rooms, including one on the ground floor right on the harbor (Db with kitchen-€85, Tb-€110, cash only, fans, mobile 338-436-3411, www.mariacapellini.com, mariacapellini@hotmail.it, Maria and Giacomo).

$$ Ivo's Camere rents two simple no-terrace rooms high above the main street, as well as a studio apartment (Db-€75, studio-€100, free Wi-Fi, Via Roma 6, reception at Pizzeria Fratelli Basso—Via Roma 1, tel. 0187-812-103, mobile 333-477-5521, www.ivocamere.com, post@ivocamere.com).

$$ Vernazza Rooms, run by Daria Bianchi, Chiara, and Davide, rents 12 decent rooms from their office near the station. Four rooms are above the Blue Marlin Bar looking down on the main street, and eight are below the City Hall (Db-€60-95, Qb-€100-120, fans, reception next to Blue Marlin Bar at Via del Santo 9, tel. 0187-812-151, mobile 338-581-4688 or 338-418-8696, www.vernazzarooms.com, info@vernazzarooms.com).

$$ Emanuela Colombo has two rooms—one spacious and

basic on the harbor square, the other *molto* chic and located on a quiet side street (Db-€90, Tb-€110, tel. 339-834-2486, www.vacanzemanuela.it, manucap64@libero.it).

More Options: **$$ Affitta Camere Alberto Basso** (a clean, modern room with a noisy harbor/piazza view, Db-€75, check in at Internet Point, albertobasso@hotmail.com); **$$ Capitano Rooms** (3 recently remodeled rooms above the main drag, Db-€90, ask for Paolo or Barbara at the Trattoria del Capitano restaurant, tel. 0187-812-201); **$$ Eva's Rooms** (3 rooms overlooking main street with train noise, Db-€60-80, ring at Via Roma 56, tel. 0187-821-134, www.evasrooms.it, evasrooms@yahoo.it); **$$ Manuela Moggia** (3 rooms, Db-€80, Tb-€95, Qb with kitchen-€125, top of the town at Via Gavino 22, tel. 0187-812-397, mobile 333-413-6374, www.manuela-vernazza.com, info@manuela-vernazza.com); and **$$ Elisabetta Rooms** (3 tired rooms at the tip-top of town with Vernazza's ultimate 360-degree roof terrace, Db-€65, Tb-€90, Qb-€100, fans, Via Carattino 62, mobile 347-451-1834, www.elisabettacarro.it, carroelisabetta@hotmail.com, Elisabetta and Pino).

Eating in Vernazza

As many Vernazza restaurants were wiped out by the 2011 flood, it's possible that a few of the places listed here may still be under construction or have different hours for your visit.

Breakfast

Locals take breakfast about as seriously as flossing. A cappuccino and a pastry or a piece of focaccia from a bar or bakery does it. Most of my recommended accommodations don't come with breakfast (when they do, I've noted so in my listings). Assuming you're on your own, you have four basic options: Blue Marlin Bar for its extensive menu, including bacon and eggs; Il Pirata delle Cinque Terre for sugary stuff and a lively welcome; Ananasso Bar for coffee and a sweet roll on the harborfront; or any bakery for picnic goodies.

Blue Marlin Bar (mid-town, just below the train station) serves a good array of clearly priced à la carte items including eggs and bacon (only after 8:45), adding up to the priciest breakfast in town (likely to total €10). It's run by Massimo and Carmen with the capable assistance of Jeff, an American who now lives in Vernazza. If you're awaiting a train any time of day, the Blue Marlin's outdoor seating beats the platform (Thu-Tue 7:00-24:00, closed Wed, tel. 0187-821-149).

Il Pirata delle Cinque Terre is located at the top of the town, where the dynamic Sicilian duo Gianluca and Massimo (hardworking twins, a.k.a. the Cannoli brothers) enthusiastically offer a great assortment of handcrafted authentic Sicilian pastries. Their fun and playful service makes up for the lack of a view. Gianluca is a pastry artist, hand-painting fanciful sculptured marzipan. Their sweet pastry breakfasts are a hit, with a stunning array of hot-out-of-the-oven treats like *panzerotto* (made of ricotta, cinnamon, and vanilla, €2.50) and hot cheese and pesto bruschetta (€3). They proudly serve no bacon and eggs (since "this is Italy"). While the atmosphere of the place seems like suburban Milan, it has a curious charisma among its customers—bringing Vernazza a welcome bit of Sicily (daily 6:30-24:00, Via Gavino 36, tel. 0187-812-047).

Ananasso Bar feels Old World, with youthful energy and a great location with little tables right on the harbor. They offer toasted *panini,* pastries, and designer cappuccino. You can eat a bit cheaper at the bar (you're welcome to picnic on the nearby bench or seawall rocks with a Mediterranean view) or enjoy the best-situated tables in town (Fri-Wed 8:00-late, closed Thu).

Picnic Breakfast: Drop by one of Vernazza's several little bakeries, focaccia shops, or grocery stores to assemble a breakfast to eat on the breakwater. Top it off with a coffee in a nearby bar.

Lunch and Dinner

If you enjoy Italian cuisine and seafood, Vernazza's restaurants are worth the splurge. All take pride in their cooking. Wander around at about 20:00 and compare the ambience, but don't wait too late to eat—many kitchens close at 22:00. (Immigrants, who are doing more and more of the hard work of cooking and cleaning, need to wrap things up in time to catch the last train back to La Spezia, where many of them live.) To get an outdoor table on summer weekends, reserve ahead. Expect to spend €10 for pastas, €12-16 for *secondi,* and €2-3 for a cover charge. Harborside restaurants and bars are easygoing. You're welcome to grab a cup of coffee or glass of wine and disappear somewhere on the breakwater, returning your glass when you're done. If you dine in Vernazza but are staying in another town, be sure to check train schedules before sitting down to eat, as trains run less frequently in the evening. Anchovies are the specialty, and any restaurant loves to show off with dazzling *antipasti misti* plates of seafood and anchovies.

Above the Harbor, by the Castle

Ristorante al Castello is run by gracious and English-speaking Monica, her husband Massimo, kind Mario, and the rest of her family. Hike high above town to just below the castle for commanding views. Their *lasagne al pesto,* "spaghetti on the rocks" (noodles with shellfish), and scampi crêpes are time-honored family specialties. For simple fare and a special evening, reserve one of the dozen romantic cliffside sea-view tables for two. Some of these tables snake around the castle, where you'll feel like you're eating all alone with the Mediterranean. Monica offers a free *sciacchetrà* or *limoncello* with biscotti if you have this book (€10 pastas, €12 *secondi*, Thu-Tue 12:00-15:00 for lunch, 19:00-22:00 for dinner, closed Wed and Nov-April, tel. 0187-812-296).

Ristorante Belforte's experimental, beautifully presented, creative cuisine includes a hearty *zuppa Michela* (€23 for a boatload of seafood), fishy *spaghetti Bruno* (€13), and *trofie al pesto* (hand-rolled noodles with pesto). Their classic *antipasto del nostro chef* (€36 for six plates) is plenty for two people. From the breakwater, follow either the stairs or the rope that leads up and around to the restaurant. You'll find a tangle of tables embedded in four levels of the lower part of the old castle. For the ultimate seaside perch, call and reserve one of four tables on the *terrazza con vista* (view terrace). Most of Belforte's seating is outdoors—if the weather's bad, the interior can get crowded (€15 pastas, €23 *secondi*, €3 cover, Wed-Mon 12:00-15:00 & 19:00-22:00, closed Tue and Nov-March, tel. 0187-812-222, Michela).

Harborside

Gambero Rosso ("Red Prawn," the same name as Italy's top restaurant guide) is considered Vernazza's most venerable restaurant. It feels dressy and costs more than the others. Try Chef Claudio's namesake risotto (€15 pastas, €20 *secondi*, €3 cover, Tue-Sun 12:00-15:00 & 19:00-22:00, closed Mon and Dec-Feb, Piazza Marconi 7, tel. 0187-812-265).

Trattoria del Capitano serves *spaghetti con frutti di mare* (pasta entangled with various types of seafood) and *grigliata mista* (a mix of seasonal Mediterranean fish) among their offerings (€10 pastas, €16 *secondi*, €2 cover, Wed-Mon 12:00-15:00 & 19:00-22:00, closed Tue except in Aug, closed Nov-Dec, tel. 0187-812-201, while Paolo and Eduardo speak English, grandpa Giacomo doesn't need to).

Trattoria Gianni is an old standby for locals and tourists who appreciate the best prices on the harbor. You'll enjoy well-prepared seafood and receive steady, reliable, and friendly service from Emanuele and Alessandro. Ask about "off-menu specials." While the outdoor seating is basic, the indoor setting is classy (€15 pastas, €15 *secondi*, €3 cover, check their *menù cucina tipica Vernazza*, Thu-Tue 12:00-15:00 & 19:00-22:00, closed Wed except July-Aug, tel. 0187-812-228).

Ristorante Pizzeria Vulnetia is simpler, serving regional specialties such as prizewinning *tegame alla Vernazza*—anchovies, tomatoes, and potatoes baked in the oven (€8 pizzas, €12 pastas, €16 *secondi*, €2 cover, Tue-Sun 12:00-15:30 & 18:30-22:00, closed Thu, Piazza Marconi 29, tel. 0187-821-193, Giuliano).

Inland, on or near the Main Street

Several of Vernazza's inland eateries manage to compete without the harbor ambience, but with slightly cheaper prices.

Trattoria da Sandro, on the main drag, mixes Genovese and Ligurian cuisine with friendly service. It can be a peaceful alternative to the harborside scene, plus they dish up award-winning stuffed mussels (€13 pastas, €15 *secondi*, Wed-Mon 12:00-15:00 & 18:30-22:00, closed Tue, Via Roma 62, tel. 0187-812-223, Gabriella and Alessandro).

Antica Osteria il Baretto is another solid bet for homey, reasonably priced traditional cuisine, run by Simone and Jenny. As it's off the harbor and a little less glitzy than the others, it's favored by locals who prefer less noisy English while they eat great homemade fish ravioli. Sitting deep in their interior can be a peaceful escape (€12 pasta, €14 *secondi*, Tue-Sat 12:00-15:00 & 19:00-22:00, closed Mon, indoor and outdoor seating, Via Roma 31).

Ristorante Incadase da Piva is a rare bit of old Vernazza. For 25 years, charismatic Piva has been known for his *tegame alla Vernazza*, his *riso Piva* (seafood risotto), and his love of music. The town troubadour, he often serenades his guests when the cooking's done. Piva is now joined by his son, Raphael, who speaks English (€10 pastas, €14 *secondi*, Fri-Wed 12:00-15:00 & 19:00-22:30, closed Thu, tucked away 20 yards off the main drag, up a lane behind the pharmacy).

Other Eating Options

Il Pirata delle Cinque Terre, popular for breakfast, is also a favorite for lunch and dinner (€9 pastas, great salads, Sicilian specialties), and its homemade desserts and drinks. The Cannoli twins entertain while they serve, as diners enjoy delicious meals while laughing out loud in this simple café/pastry shop. The menu offers a break from the predictable Ligurian fare, and the bread is literally hot out of the oven (at the top of town; for complete description, see listing under "Breakfast," earlier).

Bar Baia Saracena ("Saracen Bay") serves decent pizza and pastas out on the breakwater. Eat here for the economy and the view (€5-7 salads, €9 pizza, tel. 0187-812-113, Luca).

Pizzerias, Sandwiches, and Groceries: Vernazza's main-street eateries were among the last businesses to reopen after the flood. Two **pizzerias** stay busy, and while they mostly do takeout, each will let you sit and eat for the same cheap price. One has tables on the street, and the other, called Ercole, hides a tiny terrace and a few tables out back. **Forno Bakery** has good focaccia and veggie tarts, and several bars sell sandwiches and pizza by the slice. **Pino's grocery store** also makes inexpensive sandwiches to order (generally Mon-Sat 8:00-13:00 & 17:00-19:30, closed Sun). Tiny jars of pesto spread give elegance to picnics.

Gelato: The town's three *gelaterias* are good. What looks like **Gelateria Amore Mio** (near the grotto, mid-town) is actually Gelateria Stalin—founded in 1968 by a pastry chef with that unfortunate name. His niece Sonia, who "speaks ice cream," and nephew Francesco now run the place, and are generous with free tastes. They also have good coffee (daily 8:00-24:00, closes at 19:00 off-season, 24 flavors, sit there or take it to go).

Monterosso al Mare (Town #5)

This is a resort with a few cars and lots of hotels, rentable beach umbrellas, crowds, and a little more late-night action than the neighboring towns. Monterosso al Mare—the only Cinque Terre town built on flat land—has two parts: A new town (called Fegina) with a parking lot, train station, and TI; and an old town (Centro Storico), which cradles Old World charm in its small, crooked lanes. In the old town, you'll find hole-in-the-wall shops, pastel townscapes, and a new generation of creative small-businesspeople eager to keep their visitors happy.

A pedestrian tunnel connects the old with the new—but take a small detour around the point for a nicer walk. It offers a close-up view of two sights: a 16th-century lookout tower, built after the last serious pirate raid in 1545; and a Nazi "pillbox," a small, low concrete bunker where gunners hid. (During World War II, nearby La Spezia was an important Axis naval base, and Monterosso was bombed while the Germans were here.)

Strolling the waterfront promenade, you can pick out each of the Cinque Terre towns decorating the coast. After dark, they sparkle. Monterosso is the most enjoyable of the five for young travelers wanting to connect with others looking for a little evening action. Even so, Monterosso is not a full-blown Portofino-style resort—and locals appreciate quiet, sensitive guests.

Monterosso sustained serious damage in the 2011 flood, but within just a few months, it was back up and running at nearly 100 percent. Walking through the town today, you'll have to know where to look to find evidence of the devastation. Big grates on the six roads cover the historic canals (which drain runoff from the surrounding hills into the sea), and the sound of rushing water reassures townsfolk that the streams are flowing unimpeded below. The old town is filled with newly furnished and equipped shops and restaurants, and photos on walls commemorate the historic deluge.

But for the most part, the town is moving on—and eager to welcome visitors.

Orientation to Monterosso

Tourist Information

The TI Proloco is next to the train station (April-Oct daily 9:00-19:00, closed Nov-March, exit station and go left a few doors, tel. 0187-817-506, www.prolocomonterosso.it). If you arrive late on a summer day, the old town's Internet café is helpful with tourist information (see later).

Rebuild Monterosso: Led by a group of American women who married into the community, Rebuild Monterosso brought relief to the town in the immediate aftermath of the flood, and has since morphed into an organization to help preserve and foster healthy tourism. For the latest on the town, its recovery, and their activities, visit www.rebuildmonterosso.com.

Arrival in Monterosso

By Train: Train travelers arrive in the new town, from which it's a scenic, flat 10-minute stroll to all the old-town action (leave station to the left; to reach hotels in the new town, turn right out of the station). The bar at track 1, which overlooks both the tracks and the beach, is a handy place to hang out while waiting for your train to pull in (salads, sandwiches, drinks). As many trains run late, this can turn a frustration into a blessing.

Shuttle buses run roughly hourly along the waterfront between the old town (Piazza Garibaldi, just beyond the tunnel), the train station, and the parking lot at the end of Via Fegina (*Campo Sportivo* stop). While the buses can be convenient—saving you a 10-minute schlep with your bags—they only go once an hour, and are likely not worth the trouble (€1.50, free with Cinque Terre Park Card).

The other alternative is to take a **taxi** (certain vehicles have permission to drive in the old city center). They usually wait outside the train station, but you may have to call (€7 from station to the old town, mobile 335-616-5842 or 335-628-0933).

By Car: Monterosso is 30 minutes off the freeway (exit: Levanto-Carrodano). Note that about three miles above Monterosso, a fork directs you to either *Centro Storico* (old part of town—Via Roma parking lot with a few spots, and possibly the new Loreto garage) or *Fegina* (the new town and beachfront parking, most likely where you want to go). At this point you must choose which area, because you can't drive directly from the new town to the old center (which is closed to cars without special permits).

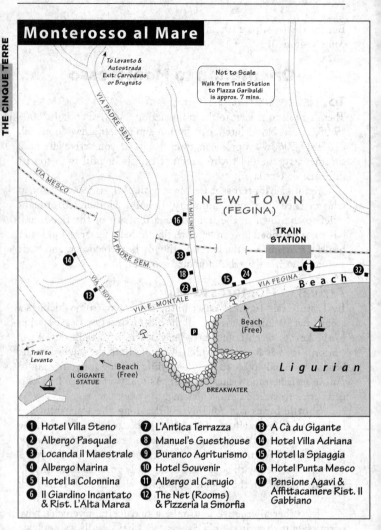

Monterosso al Mare

To Levanto &
Autostrada
Exit: Carrodano
or Brugnato

VIA PADRE SEM.

VIA MESCO

VIA PADRE SEM.

VIA 4 NOV.

Not to Scale

Walk from Train Station
to Piazza Garibaldi
is approx. 7 mins.

NEW TOWN
(FEGINA)

TRAIN
STATION

VIA MOLINELLI

16

33

18

23

15 24

VIA E. MONTALE

14

13

VIA FEGINA

Beach

32

Beach
(Free)

Trail to
Levanto

P

Beach
(Free)

IL GIGANTE
STATUE

BREAKWATER

Ligurian

❶ Hotel Villa Steno	❼ L'Antica Terrazza	⓭ A Cà du Gigante
❷ Albergo Pasquale	❽ Manuel's Guesthouse	⓮ Hotel Villa Adriana
❸ Locanda il Maestrale	❾ Buranco Agriturismo	⓯ Hotel la Spiaggia
❹ Albergo Marina	❿ Hotel Souvenir	⓰ Hotel Punta Mesco
❺ Hotel la Colonnina	⓫ Albergo al Carugio	⓱ Pensione Agavi &
❻ Il Giardino Incanto	⓬ The Net (Rooms)	Affittacamere Rist. Il
& Rist. L'Alta Marea	& Pizzeria la Smorfia	Gabbiano

Parking is easy (except July-Aug and summer weekends) in the huge beachfront guarded lot in the new town (€14/24 hours). If you're heading to the old town, you'll find the big Loreto parking garage on Via Roma, a 10-minute downhill walk to the main square (€1.70/hour, €18/24 hours). For the cheapest Monterosso rates, park along the blue lines (a few minutes farther uphill from the Loreto garage) for €8 per day.

Helpful Hints

Thursday Morning Market: Each Thursday morning, trucks pull into the old town and fill the public area by the beach with

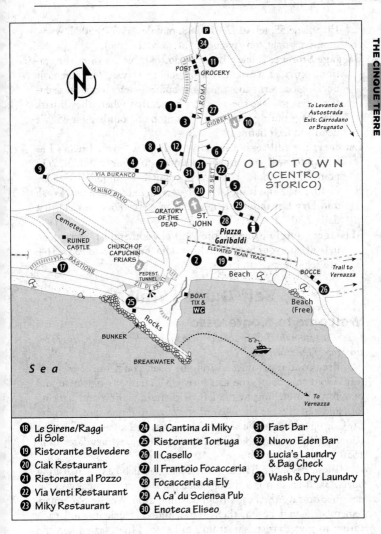

18 Le Sirene/Raggi di Sole
19 Ristorante Belvedere
20 Ciak Restaurant
21 Ristorante al Pozzo
22 Via Venti Restaurant
23 Miky Restaurant

24 La Cantina di Miky
25 Ristorante Tortuga
26 Il Casello
27 Il Frantoio Focacceria
28 Focacceria da Ely
29 A Ca' du Sciensa Pub
30 Enoteca Eliseo

31 Fast Bar
32 Nuovo Eden Bar
33 Lucia's Laundry & Bag Check
34 Wash & Dry Laundry

temporary stalls where locals get the items not otherwise available in this small town.

Medical Help: The town's bike-riding, leather bag-toting, English-speaking physician is **Dr. Vitone,** who charges €50-80 for a simple visit (less for poor students, mobile 338-853-0949).

Internet Access: The Net, a few steps off the old town's main drag (Via Roma), has eight high-speed computers (€1/10 minutes) and Wi-Fi. Enzo happily provides information on the Cinque Terre, rents rooms (see "Sleeping in Monterosso," later), and can burn your photos onto a DVD for €6 (daily 9:30-23:00, off-season closes for lunch and dinner breaks, Via Vittorio

Emanuele 55, tel. 0187-817-288, mobile 335-778-5085, www.monterossonet.com, enzo@monterossonet.com).

Baggage Storage: Lucia's Lavarapido, two blocks from the station, provides a wonderful bag-check service (courageously bucking concerns about terrorist bombs—which can cause entire cities to leave their visitors wondering where they'll park their bags during their visit). Just drop off your bag for €5 (see details in next listing).

Laundry: For full-service laundry in the new town, **Lucia's Lavarapido** will return your laundry to your hotel (€12/13 pounds, daily 8:30-22:00, Via Molinelli 17, mobile 339-484-0940, Lucia and Ivano). For self-service in the old town, **Wash and Dry Lavanderia** is new and modern (€6/wash and dry, daily 7:30-23:30, Via Roma 43).

Massage: Giorgio Moggia, the local physiotherapist, gives good massages at your hotel or in his studio (€60/hour, tel. 339-314-6127, giomogg@tin.it).

Self-Guided Walk

Welcome to Monterosso

· *Hike out from the dock in the old town and climb five rough steps to the very top of the concrete...*

Breakwater: If you're visiting by boat, you'll start here anyway. From this point, you can survey Monterosso's old town and new town (stretching to the left, with train station and parking lot), and actually see all *cinque* of the *terre* from one spot: Vernazza, Corniglia (above the shore), Manarola, and a few buildings of Riomaggiore beyond that. The little fort above, which dates from 1550, is now a private home.

These days, the harbor hosts more paddleboats than fishing boats. Sand erosion is a major problem. The partial breakwater is designed to save the beach from washing away. While old-timers remember a vast beach, their grandchildren truck in sand each spring to give tourists something to lie on. (The Nazis liked the Cinque Terre, too—find two of their bomb-hardened bunkers, near left and far right.)

The fancy €300-a-night, four-star Hotel Porto Roca (on the far right) marks the trail to Vernazza. High above, you see an example of the costly roads built in the 1980s to connect the Cinque Terre towns with the freeway over the hills. The two capes (Punta di Montenero and Punta Mesco) define the Cinque Terre region. The closer cape, Punta Mesco, marks an important sea-life sanctuary, home to a rare sea grass that provides an ideal home for fish eggs. Buoys keep fishing boats away. The cape was once a quarry, providing employment to locals who chipped out the stones used to build the local towns (the green stones making up part of the breakwater below you are from there).

On the far end of the new town, marking the best free beach around, you can just see the statue named *Il Gigante*. It's 45 feet tall and once held a trident. While it looks as if it were hewn from the rocky cliff, it's actually made of reinforced concrete and dates from the beginning of the 20th century, when it supported a dancing terrace for a *fin de siècle* villa. A violent storm left the giant holding nothing but memories of Monterosso's glamorous age.

• *From the breakwater, walk into the old town. At the top of the beach, notice the openings of two big drains, ready to let flash floods rip through town without destroying things. Walking under the train tracks, venture right into the square and find the statue of a dandy holding what looks like a box cutter.*

Piazza Garibaldi: The statue honors Giuseppe Garibaldi, the dashing firebrand revolutionary who, in the 1860s, helped unite the people of Italy into a modern nation. Facing Garibaldi, with your back to the sea, you'll see (from right to left) the City Hall (with the now-required European Union flag beside the Italian one) and a big home and recreation center for poor and homeless elderly. You'll also see A Ca' du Sciensa pub (with historic town photos inside and upstairs; you're welcome to pop in for a look—see "Nightlife in Monterosso," later).

After the 2011 flood, it was on this square that the National Guard set up an emergency tent, used for staging emergency deliveries, community meals, Christmas Eve Mass, and the New Year's Eve disco. In the aftermath of the flood, many moving stories emerged. Old ladies who couldn't help dig, helped cook. People worried that Laura, whose bakery—loved for her secret recipes—was destroyed, wouldn't be able to reopen. But she rebuilt, and that beautiful aroma of her sweet cakes again helps locals greet each new day. The motorbike of Diego's dreams, which he had bought just 10 days before the flood, was buried by the mud. He excavated it, cleaned it up, and—to the cheers of his friends—it started. The local civil protection unit is now named for 40-year-old volunteer Sandro Usai, Monterosso's one death from the flood. Sandro was last seen heroically trying to open up a grate to increase canal drainage when he was swept out to sea. When his body washed ashore a week later, his funeral was the first time the community stopped working and was silent together. Sandro posthumously received the highest civilian award the Italian government gives.

Just under the bell tower (with your back to the sea, it's on your left), a set of covered arcades facing the sea is where the old-timers hang out (they see all and know all). The crenellated bell tower marks the church.

• *Go to church (the entrance is on the inland side).*

Church of St. John the Baptist (Chiesa di San Giovanni Battista): This black-and-white church, with white marble from Carrara and green marble from Punte Mesco, is typical of this region's Romanesque style. Note the lacy, stone rose window above the entrance. It's as delicate as crochet work, with 18 slender mullions (the petals of the rose). The marble stripes get narrower the higher they go, creating the illusion of a church that's taller than it really is.

Step inside for more Ligurian Gothic: original marble columns and capitals with pointed arches to match. The octagonal baptismal font (in the back of the church) was carved from Carrara marble in 1359. Imagine the job getting that from the quarries to here. Nearby is a wooden statue of St. Anthony, carved about 1400, which once graced a church that stood atop Punta Mesco. The church itself dates from 1307—see the proud inscription on the middle column inside: "MilleCCCVII." Outside the church, on the side facing the main street, find the high-water mark from a November 1966 flood (the same month as the flood that devastated Florence). Nearly half a century later, the crippling October 2011 flood hit Monterosso. But the church's statues survived, thanks to townspeople who came to their rescue, carrying them through raging waters to safety. Later, when there was enough help in the streets, excess volunteers came into the church and lovingly polished the candlesticks, just to keep caring for their town.

• *Leaving the church, immediately turn left and go to church again.*

Oratory of the Dead (Oratorio dei Neri): During the Counter-Reformation, the Catholic Church offset the rising influence of the Lutherans by creating brotherhoods of good works. These religious Rotary clubs were called "confraternities." Monterosso had two, nicknamed White and Black. This building is the oratory of the Black group, whose mission—as the macabre decor filling the interior indicates—was to arrange for funerals and take care of widows, orphans, the shipwrecked, and the souls of those who ignore the request for a €1 donation. It dates from the 16th century, and membership has passed from father to son for generations. Notice the fine carved choir stalls (c. 1700) just inside the door, and the haunted-house chandeliers. Look up at the ceiling to find the symbol of the confraternity: a skull-and-crossbones and an hourglass...death awaits us all.

• *Return to the beach and find the brick steps that lead up to the hill-capping convent (starting between the train tracks and the pedestrian tunnel). Stop above the castle at a statue of St. Francis and a wolf taking in a grand view. Enjoy another opportunity to see all five of the Cinque Terre towns. From here, backtrack 20 yards and continue uphill.*

The Switchbacks of the Friars: Follow the yellow brick road (OK, it's orange...but I couldn't help singing as I skipped skyward).

Climb uphill until you reach a convent church, then a cemetery, in a ruined castle at the summit. The lane *(Salita dei Cappuccini)* is nicknamed *Zii di Frati* ("switchbacks of the friars").

• *When you reach a gate marked* Convento e Chiesa Cappuccini, *you have arrived.*

Church of the Capuchin Friars: The former convent is now manned by a single caretaker friar. Before stepping inside, notice the church's striped Romanesque facade. It's all fake. Tap it—no marble, just cheap 18th-century stucco. Sit in the rear pew. The high altarpiece painting of St. Francis can be rolled up on special days to reveal a statue of Mary standing behind it. Look at the statue of St. Anthony to the right and smile (you're on convent camera). Wave at the security camera—they're nervous about the precious painting to your left.

This fine painting of the Crucifixion is attributed to Anthony van Dyck, the 17th-century Flemish master who lived and worked for years in nearby Genoa (though art historians suspect that, at best, it was painted by someone in the artist's workshop). When Jesus died, the earth went dark. Notice the eclipsed sun in the painting, just to the right of the cross. Do the electric candles work? Pick one up, pray for peace, and plug it in. (Leave €0.50, or unplug it and put it back.)

• *Leave and turn left to hike 100 yards uphill to the cemetery that fills the remains of the castle, capping the hill. Look out from the gate and enjoy the view.*

Cemetery in the Ruined Castle: In the Dark Ages, the village huddled within this castle. Slowly it expanded. Notice the town view from here—no sea. You're looking at the oldest part of Monterosso, huddled behind the hill, out of view of 13th-century pirates. Explore the cemetery, but remember that cemeteries are sacred and treasured places (as is clear by the abundance of fresh flowers). Ponder the black-and-white photos of grandparents past. *Q.R.P.* is *Qui Riposa in Pace* (a.k.a. R.I.P.). Rich families had their own little tomb buildings. Climb to the very summit—the castle's keep, or place of last refuge. Priests are buried in a line of graves closest to the sea, but facing inland, toward the town's holy sanctuary high on the hillside (above the road, with its triangular steeple peeking above the trees). Each Cinque Terre town has a lofty sanctuary, dedicated to Mary and dear to the village hearts.

• *From here, your tour is over—any trail leads you back into town.*

Sights in Monterosso

Beaches

Monterosso's beaches, immediately in front of the train station, are easily the Cinque Terre's best and most crowded. This town is a sandy resort with rentable beach extras: Figure €20 to rent two chairs and an umbrella for the day. Light lunches are served by beach cafés to sunbathers at their lounge chairs. It's often worth the euros to enjoy a private beach. If you see umbrellas on a beach, it means you'll have to pay a rental fee; otherwise the sand is free (all the beaches are marked on this book's Monterosso al Mare map). Prices get very soft in the afternoon. Don't use your white hotel towels; most hotels will give you beach towels—sometimes for a fee. The local hidden beach, which is free, gravelly, and generally less crowded, is tucked away under Il Casello restaurant at the east end of town, near the trailhead to Vernazza. There's another free beach at the far-west end, near the Gigante statue. The bocce ball court (next to Il Casello) is busy with the old boys enjoying their favorite pastime.

Kayaks

Samba rents kayaks on the beach (€7/hour for 1-person kayak, €12/hour for 2-person kayak, to the right of train station as you exit, mobile 339-681-2265, Domenico). The paddle to Vernazza is a favorite.

Shuttle Buses for High-Country Hikes

Monterosso's bus service (described earlier, under "Arrival in Monterosso") continues beyond the town limits, but check the schedules—only one or two departures a day head into the high country. Some buses go to the Sanctuary of Our Lady of Soviore, from where you can hike back down to Monterosso (1.5 hours, moderately steep). Rides cost €1.50 (free with Cinque Terre Park Card, pick up schedule from park office). Or you can hike to Levanto (no Cinque Terre Park card necessary, not as stunning as the rest of the coastal trail, 2.5 hours, straight uphill and then easy decline, follow signs at west end of the new town). For hiking details, ask at the train station TI.

Wine-Tasting

Buranco Agriturismo offers visits to their vineyard and cantina daily (just about anytime). You'll taste two of their wines plus a grappa and a *limoncino*, along with home-cooked food (up to €25/person with snacks, English may be limited, follow Via Buranco uphill to path, 10 minutes above town, tel. 0187-817-677, www.burancocinqueterre.it). They also rent apartments; see "Sleeping in Monterosso," later.

Boat Rides

From the old-town harbor, boats run nearly hourly (10:30-17:00) to Vernazza, Manarola, Riomaggiore, and Portovenere. Schedules are posted in Cinque Terre park offices (for details, see "Getting Around the Cinque Terre—By Boat" on page 1109).

Nightlife in Monterosso

A Ca' du Sciensa has nothing to do with science—it's the nickname of the town moneybags, who had a couple of years of higher education and owned this old mansion. The antique dumbwaiter is still in use—a remnant from the days when servants toiled downstairs while the big shots wined and dined up top. This classy yet laid-back pub offers breezy square seating, bar action on the ground level, an intimate lounge upstairs, and discreet balconies overlooking the square to share with your best travel buddy. It's a good place for light meals from a fun and accessible menu: €5-6 sandwiches, salads, and microwaved pastas. They offer €6 cocktails and mojitos with free *aperitivo* snacks from 17:30 to 20:30. Luca welcomes you to wander around the place and view the old Cinque Terre photo collection (daily 10:00-24:00, Piazza Garibaldi 17, tel. 0187-818-233).

Enoteca Eliseo, the first (and I'd say best) wine bar in town, comes with operatic ambience. Eliseo and his wife, Mary, love music and wine. You can select a fine bottle from their shop shelf, and for €7 extra, enjoy it and the village action from their cozy tables. If you've ever wanted an education in grappa, talk to Eliseo—he stocks 96 varieties. Wines sold by the glass *(bicchiere)* are posted (Wed-Mon 9:00-24:00, closed Tue, Piazza Matteotti 3, a block inland behind church, tel. 0187-817-308).

Fast Bar, the best bar in town for young travelers and night owls, is located on Via Roma in the old town. Customers mix travel tales with big, cold beers, and the crowd (and the rock 'n' roll) gets noisier as the night rolls on. Come here to watch Italian or American sporting events on TV any time of day (sandwiches and snacks usually served until midnight, open nightly until 2:00, closed Nov-March, Alex, Francisco, and Stefano).

La Cantina di Miky, in the new town just beyond the train station, is a trendy bar-restaurant with an extensive cocktail and grappa menu. The seating is in three zones: overlooking the beach, in the garden, or in the cellar. Run by Manuel, son of well-known local restaurateur Miky, it sometimes hosts live music. Manuel offers a fun "five villages" wine-tasting with local meats and cheeses. Microbrews are becoming popular in Italy, and this is the best place in town for top-end Italian beers (daily until well after 24:00, Via Fegina 90, tel. 0187-802-525).

Nuovo Eden Bar, overlooking the beach by the big rock just east of the train station, is a fine place to enjoy a cocktail or fancy ice cream with a sea view. Their happy hour (daily 16:30-21:00) means €6 cocktails come with a snack. Locals consider their ice cream (either to go from the streetside stand, or fancy and sit-down) the best in town. Consider this place for a pre-dinner drink or dessert with a view.

Sleeping in Monterosso

(€1 = about $1.30, country code: 39)

Monterosso, the most beach-resorty of the five Cinque Terre towns, offers maximum comfort and ease. The TI Proloco just outside the train station can give you a list of €70-80 double rooms. Rooms in Monterosso are a better value for your money than similar rooms in crowded Vernazza, and the proprietors seem more genuine and welcoming. To locate the hotels, see the Monterosso al Mare map.

In the Old Town

$$$ Hotel Villa Steno is lovingly managed and features great view balconies, panoramic gardens and a roof terrace with sun beds, air-conditioning, and the friendly help of English-speaking Matteo and his wife, Carla. Of their 16 rooms, 12 have view balconies (Sb-€110, Db-€170, Tb-€195, Qb-€225, includes hearty buffet breakfast, ask about discount with cash and this book, Internet access and Wi-Fi, laundry, parking-€8—reserve in advance, Via Roma 109, tel. 0187-817-028 or 0187-818-336, www.villasteno.com, steno@pasini.com). It's a 15-minute hike (or €8 taxi ride) from the train station to the top of the old town. Readers get a free Cinque Terre info packet and a glass of the local sweet wine, *sciacchetrà*, when they check in—ask for it.

$$$ Albergo Pasquale is a modern, comfortable place with 15 rooms, run by the same family as the Hotel Villa Steno (above). It's conveniently located just a few steps from the beach, boat dock, tunnel entrance to the new town, and train tracks. While there is some train noise, it's mostly a lullaby of waves. Located right on the harbor, it has an elevator and offers easier access than most (same prices and welcome drink as Villa Steno; air-con, all rooms with sea view, Via Fegina 8, tel. 0187-817-550 or 0187-817-477, www.hotelpasquale.com, pasquale@pasini.com, Felicita and Marco).

$$$ Locanda il Maestrale rents six small, stylish rooms in a sophisticated and peaceful little inn. Although renovated with all the modern comforts, it retains centuries-old character under frescoed ceilings. Its peaceful sun terrace overlooking the old town and Via Roma action is a delight (small Db-€115, Db-€145, suite-€170, less off-season, discount with cash and this book, air-con, Wi-Fi, Via Roma 37, tel. 0187-817-013, mobile 338-4530-531, www.locandamaestrale.net, maestrale@monterossonet.com, Stefania).

$$$ Albergo Marina, creatively run by enthusiastic husband-and-wife team Marina and Eraldo, has 23 decent rooms and a garden with lemon trees. With a free and filling buffet featuring local specialties from 14:00 to 17:00 daily, they offer a fine value (standard Db-€135, ask about discount with cash and this book, elevator, air-con, Wi-Fi, free use of kayak and snorkel equipment, Via Buranco 40, tel. 0187-817-613, www.hotelmarina5terre.com, marina@hotelmarina5terre.com).

$$$ **Hotel la Colonnina,** a comfy, modern place with 21 big and pretty rooms, generous public spaces, and several leafy, peaceful sun terraces, is buried in the town's fragrant and sleepy back streets (Db-€140-150, Tb-€200, Qb-€230, €15 more for rooms with viewless terrace, cash only, air-con, Internet access and Wi-Fi, fridges, elevator, inviting rooftop terrace with sun beds, garden, in the old town a block inland from the main square at Via Zuecca 6, tel. 0187-817-439, www.lacolonninacinqueterre.it, info@lacolonninacinqueterre.it, Christina).

$$$ **Il Giardino Incantato** ("The Enchanted Garden") is a charming four-room B&B in a tastefully renovated 16th-century Ligurian home in the heart of the old town. Breakfast is served in a hidden garden, which is illuminated with candles in the evening (Db-€150-170, Db suite-€200, ask for Rick Steves discount, air-con, Wi-Fi, free minibar and tea and coffee service, Via Mazzini 18, tel. 0187-818-315, mobile 333-264-9252, www.ilgiardinoincantato.net, giardino_incantato@libero.it, kind and eager-to-please Fausto and Mariapia).

$$$ **L'Antica Terrazza** rents four classy rooms right in town. With a pretty terrace overlooking the pedestrian street and minimal stairs, Raffaella and John offer a good deal (Db-€115, cash discount, air-con, Internet access and Wi-Fi, Vicolo San Martino 1, tel. 380-138-0082, mobile 347-132-6213, www.anticaterrazza.com, post@anticaterrazza.com).

$$$ **Manuel's Guesthouse,** perched high above the town among terraces, is a garden getaway ruled by disheveled artist Manuel and run by his nephew Lorenzo (who is happy to carry your bags up the hill). They have six big, bright rooms and a grand view. After climbing the killer stairs from the town center, their killer terrace is hard to leave—especially after a few drinks (Db-€100, big Db with grand-view balcony-€120, cash only, air-con, Internet access and Wi-Fi, in old town, up about 100 steps behind church, Via San Martino 39, mobile 333-439-0809 or 329-547-3775, www.manuelsguesthouse.com, manuelsguesthouse@libero.it).

$$$ **Buranco Agriturismo,** a 10-minute hike above the old town, has wonderful gardens and views over the vine-covered valley. Its primary business is wine and olive-oil production, but they offer three apartments at a good price. It's a rare opportunity to stay in a farmhouse but still be able to get to town on foot (2-6

people-€60/person including breakfast, €30/child under 12, dinner on request, air-con, free shuttle from station, tel. 0187-817-677, mobile 349-434-8046, www.burancocinqueterre.it, info@buranco.it, informally run by Loredana, Mary, and Giulietta).

$$ Hotel Souvenir is Monterosso's cash-only backpacker hotel. It has 30 rooms in two buildings, each utilitarian but comfortable. Both share a lounge and pleasant leafy courtyard. The basic one is popular with students (S-€30, Sb-€35, D-€55, Db-€70, T-€105, breakfast-€5); the other is less stark and pricier (Sb-€45, Db-€80, Tb-€120, includes breakfast; walk three blocks inland to Via Gioberti 24, tel. 0187-817-822, tel. 0187-817-595, hotel_souvenir@yahoo.com, Beppe).

$$ Albergo al Carugio is a simple, practical nine-room place in a big apartment-style building at the top of the old town. It's quiet, comfy, and functional (Db-€80, book direct and mention this book for best price, no breakfast, air-con, Wi-Fi, Via Roma 100, tel. 0187-817-453, www.alcarugio.it, info@alcarugio.it, Andrea and Simona).

$ The Net Room Service is run by Enzo, who owns the Internet point in town (and speaks perfect English). He manages several apartments, offering Monterosso's least expensive accommodations. Enzo's office functions as your reception (Db-€60-70 any time of year, 2- or 3-night minimum stay, Via Vittorio Emanuele 55, tel. 0187-817-288, www.monterossonet.com, info@monterossonet.com).

In the New Town

$$$ A Cà du Gigante, despite its name, is a tiny yet stylish refuge with nine rooms. About 100 yards from the beach (and surrounded by blocky apartments on a modern street), the interior is tastefully done with modern comfort in mind (Db-€160, Db sea-view suite-€180, ask about discount with 3-night stay and this book, occasional last-minute deals, air-con, free parking, Via IV Novembre 11, tel. 0187-817-401, www.ilgigantecinqueterre.it, gigante@ilgigantecinqueterre.it, Claudia).

$$$ Hotel Villa Adriana is a big, modern, bright hotel on a church-owned estate set in a peaceful garden with a pool, free parking, and a no-stress style. They rent 54 rooms at the same price as much simpler places on the water (Sb-€110, Db-€140-160, all with showers, includes big breakfast, air-con, Wi-Fi, Via IV Novembre 23, tel. 0187-818-109, www.villaadriana.info, info@villaadriana.info).

$$$ Hotel la Spiaggia is a venerable old 19-room place facing the beach and run with attitude by Andrea Poggi and his gentle daughter Maria. Half of the rooms come with air-con and half with sea views, but all are the same price—request what you like when you reserve (Db-€160, extra bed-€30, discount for 2-night stays, includes breakfast and parking, elevator, Via Lungomare 98, tel. 0187-817-567, www.laspiaggiahotel.com, hotellaspiaggia@libero. it, friendly Ele at the desk).

$$$ Hotel Punta Mesco is a tidy, well-run little haven renting 17 quiet, modern rooms. While none have views, 10 rooms have small terraces. For the price, it may offer the best comfort in town (Db-€132, Tb-€178, cash discount, air-con, Wi-Fi, free loaner bikes, free parking, Via Molinelli 35, tel. 0187-817-495, www.hotelpuntamesco.it, info@hotelpuntamesco.it, Diego and Anna).

$$$ Pensione Agavi has 10 spartan, bright, hostel-like, over-priced rooms, about half overlooking the beach near the big rock. This is not a place to party—it feels like an old hospital with narrow hallways (D-€80, Db-€110, Tb-€145, same price with or without view, discount for 2 nights or more, no breakfast, cash only, re-frigerators, turn left out of station to Fegina 30, tel. 0187-817-171, mobile 333-697-4071, hotel.agavi@libero.it, Hillary).

$$ Affittacamere Ristorante il Gabbiano is a charming, family-run restaurant right on the beach, renting five quiet, air-conditioned rooms upstairs. Three rooms face the sea, with small balconies (Db-€100, the largest can be Tb-€130, Qb-€160), while two are at the back (Db-€90). The Gabbiano family restaurant serves as your reception (cash only, refrigerators in rooms, Via Fegina 84, tel. 0187-817-578, lella-v71@hotmail.it).

$ Le Sirene/Raggi di Sole, with nine simple rooms in two humble buildings, is about the cheapest place in town. It's run from a hole-in-the-wall reception desk a block from the station, just off the water. I'd request the Le Sirene building, which doesn't have train noise and is a bit more spacious and airy than Raggi di Sole (Db-€90, third person-€45, fans, Via Molinelli 10, mobile 393-935-7683, www.sirenerooms.com, sirenerooms@gmail.com, Ermanna).

Eating in Monterosso

Restaurants

Ristorante Belvedere, big and sprawling, is *the* place for a good-value meal indoors or outdoors on the harborfront. Their *amfora belvedere*—mixed seafood stew—is huge, and can easily be split among up to four diners (€48). Share with your group and add pasta for a fine meal. Mussel fans will enjoy the *tagliolini della casa* (€8). Their *antipasti misti* (2-person minimum, €15/person), a fishy treat, can nearly make an entire meal. It's energetically run by Federico and Roberto (€9 pastas, €12 *secondi*, Wed-Mon 12:00-14:30 & 19:00-22:00, usually closed Tue, on the harbor in the old town, tel. 0187-817-033).

L'Alta Marea offers special fish ravioli, the catch of the day, and huge crocks of fresh, steamed mussels. Young chef Marco cooks with charisma, while his wife, Anna, takes good care of the guests. This place is quieter, buried in the old town two blocks off the beach, and has covered tables out front for people-watching (€9 pastas and pizza, €12-15 *secondi,* ask for discount with cash and this book, Thu-Tue 12:00-15:00 & 18:00-22:00, closed Wed, Via Roma 54, tel. 0187-817-170).

Ciak, high-energy and tightly packed, is a local institution with reliably good food and higher prices. It's known for its huge, sizzling terra-cotta crock for two crammed with the day's catch and accompanied by risotto or spaghetti, or served swimming in a soup *(zuppa).* Other popular choices are fish ravioli with shrimp sauce and the seafood *antipasto Lampara.* Stroll a couple of paces past the outdoor tables up Via Roma to see what Signore Ciak (who wears his Popeye cap in the kitchen) has on the stove. His son, Lorenzo, made the new tables himself after the 2011 flood (Thu-Tue 12:00-15:00 & 19:00-22:30, closed Wed, tel. 0187-817-014).

Ristorante al Pozzo is a favorite among locals. It's family-run, with good old-fashioned quality, as Gino (with his long white beard) cooks, and his engaging English-speaking son, Manuel, serves. They have one of the best wine lists in town, serve only homemade pasta, and are known for their raw fish and wonderful seafood *antipasti misti* (€10-15 pastas, €15-20 *secondi,* closed Thu, Via Roma 24, tel. 0187-817-575).

Via Venti is a quiet little trattoria, hidden in an alley deep in the heart of the old town, where Papa Ettore creates imaginative seafood dishes using the day's catch and freshly made pasta. Ilaria and her partner Michele serve up delicate and savory gnocchi (tiny potato dumplings) with crab sauce, tender ravioli stuffed with fresh fish, and pear-and-cheese pasta. There's nothing pretentious here... just good cooking, service, and prices (€11 pastas, €16 *secondi,* Fri-Wed 12:00-15:00 & 18:30-22:30, closed Thu, tel. 0187-818-347). From the bottom of Via Roma, with your back to the sea and the church to your left, head to the right down Via XX Settembre and follow it to the end, to #32.

Miky is packed with well-dressed locals who know their seafood and want to eat it in a classy environment. For elegantly presented, top-quality food, this is my Cinque Terre favorite. It's clearly a proud family operation: Miky (dad), Simonetta (mom), and charming Sara (daughter, who greets guests) all work hard. All their pasta is "pizza pasta"—cooked normally but finished in a bowl that's encased in a thin pizza crust. They cook the concoction in a wood-fired oven to keep in the aroma. Miky's has a fine wine list with many available by the glass if you ask. If I were ever to require a dessert, it would be their mixed sampler plate, *dolce mista*—€10 and plenty for two (€15 pastas, €22 *secondi*, €8 sweets, Wed-Mon 12:00-15:00 & 19:00-23:00, closed Tue, reservations wise in summer, diners tend to dress up a bit, in the new town 100 yards north of train station at Via Fegina 104, tel. 0187-817-608).

La Cantina di Miky, a few doors down (toward the station), serves Ligurian specialties that follow in Miky's family tradition of quality. Run by son Manuel—and Christine from New Jersey— it's more trendy, youthful, and informal than Miky's. You can sit downstairs, in the garden, or overlooking the sea (€16 anchovy tasting plate, €13 pastas, €15 *secondi*, creative desserts, large selection of Italian microbrews, daily 12:00-24:00 or later, Via Fegina 90, tel. 0187-802-525). This place doubles as a cocktail bar in the evenings—see "Nightlife in Monterosso," earlier.

Ristorante Tortuga is the top option in Monterosso for sea-view elegance, with gorgeous outdoor seating on a bluff and an elegant white-tablecloth-and-candles interior. If you're looking for a place to propose, this offers the prettiest and most romantic dining in town. When you're out and about, drop by to consider which table you'd like to reserve for later. House specialties include *cannelloni tortuga* and *filetto sciacchetrà* (€15 pastas, €20 *secondi*, Tue-Sun 12:00-14:30 & 18:00-22:00, closed Mon, just outside the tunnel that connects the old and new town, tel. 0187-800-065, mobile 333-240-7956, Silvia and Giamba).

Il Casello is the only place for a fun meal on a terrace overlooking the old-town beach. With outdoor tables on a rocky outcrop, it's a pleasant spot for a salad, pasta, or *secondi* (€10 pastas, €15 *secondi*, daily April-Oct, closed Nov-March, mobile 333-492-7629, Bacco).

Light Meals, Take-Out Food, and Breakfast

Lots of shops and bakeries sell pizza and focaccia for an easy picnic at the beach or on the trail. **Pizzeria la Smorfia**—the local favorite for pizza—cooks up good pizza to eat in or take out. Pizzas come in two sizes; the large can feed three (closed Thu, Via Vittorio Emanuele 73).

At **Il Frantoio,** Simone makes tasty pizza to go or to munch perched on a stool (closed Thu, just off Via Roma at Via Gioberti 1).

Focacceria da Ely makes airy focaccia and thick-crust pizzas for casual seating or takeout (daily 10:30-20:00, until 24:00 in summer, Emigliano).

For a quick bite right at the train station (or on the beach), consider **Il Massimo della Focaccia**. Massimo and Daniella serve local quiche-like tortes, sandwiches, focaccia pizzas, and desserts. With benches just in front, this is a good bet for a €4 light meal with a sea view (daily, Via Fegina 50 at the entry to the station).

Breakfast: Most hotels include breakfast in the room rate. But if you're out looking for breakfast, consider **Bar Gio,** near the train station on the waterfront (continental breakfasts), or **Bar Davi,** under the arch on Via Roma in the old town (with an American-style option, daily from 7:00).

Cinque Terre Connections

By Train

The five towns of the Cinque Terre are on a pokey milk-run train line (described in "Getting Around the Cinque Terre—By Train" on page 1107). Erratically timed but roughly hourly trains connect each town with the others, plus La Spezia, Genoa, and Riviera towns to the north. While a few of these local trains go to more distant points (Milan or Pisa), it's much faster to change in La Spezia, Monterosso, or Sestri Levante to a bigger train (local train info tel. 0187-817-458, www.trenitalia.com).

From La Spezia Centrale by Train to: Rome (7/day, 3-4.5 hours, more with changes, €45; an evening train—departing around 20:00—gives you a complete day in the region while still getting you to Rome that night), **Pisa** (about hourly, 1-1.5 hours, €5), **Florence** (5/day direct, otherwise nearly hourly, 2.5 hours, €11.30), **Milan** (about hourly, 3 hours direct or with change in Genoa, €22), **Venice** (about hourly, 5-6 hours, 1-3 changes, €50).

From Monterosso by Train to: Venice (about hourly, 6-7 hours, 1-3 changes, €52), **Milan** (8/day direct, otherwise hourly with change in Genoa, 3-4 hours, €22), **Genoa** (hourly, 1.2-2 hours, €8), **La Spezia** (2-3/hour, 15-30 minutes), **Rome** (hourly, 4.5 hours, change in La Spezia, €50). For destinations in **France,** change trains in Genoa.

THE
NETHERLANDS

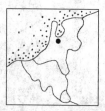

AMSTERDAM

Amsterdam still looks much like it did in the 1600s—the Dutch Golden Age—when it was the world's richest city, an international sea-trading port, and the cradle of capitalism. Wealthy, democratic burghers built a city upon millions of pilings, creating a wonderland of canals lined with trees and townhouses topped with fancy gables. Immigrants, Jews, outcasts, and political rebels were drawn here by its tolerant atmosphere, while painters such as young Rembrandt captured that atmosphere on canvas.

Today's Amsterdam is a progressive place of 820,000 people and almost as many bikes. It's a city of good living, cozy cafés, great art, street-corner jazz, stately history, and a spirit of live and let live. In 2013, Amsterdam celebrated the 400th birthday of its canal system with a series of art festivals, concerts, and special exhibits.

Amsterdam also offers the Netherlands' best people-watching. The Dutch are unique, and observing them is a sightseeing experience all in itself. They're a handsome and healthy people, and among the world's tallest. They're also open and honest—I think of them as refreshingly blunt—and they like to laugh. As connoisseurs of world culture, they appreciate Rembrandt paintings, Indonesian food, and the latest French film—but with an un-snooty, blue-jeans attitude.

Be warned: Amsterdam, a bold experiment in freedom, may box your Puritan ears. For centuries, the city has taken a tolerant approach to things other places try to forbid. Traditionally, the city attracted sailors and businessmen away from home, so it was profitable to allow them to have a little fun. In the 1960s, Amsterdam became a magnet for Europe's hippies. Since then, it's become a world capital of alternative lifestyles. Stroll through any neighbor-

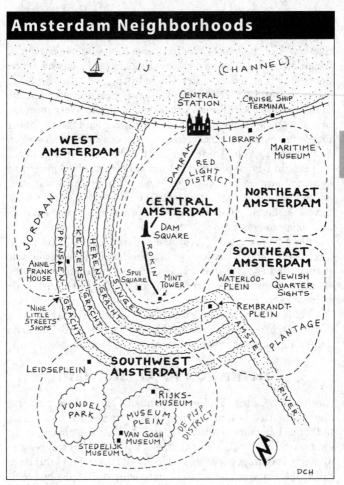

Amsterdam Neighborhoods

hood and see things that are commonplace here but rarely found elsewhere. Prostitution is allowed in the Red Light District, while "smartshops" sell psychedelic drugs and marijuana is openly sold and smoked. (The Dutch aren't necessarily more tolerant or decadent than the rest of us—just pragmatic and looking for smart solutions.)

Approach Amsterdam as an ethnologist observing a strange culture. It's a place where carillons chime quaintly from spires towering above coffeeshops where yuppies go to smoke pot. Take it all in, then pause to watch the clouds blow past stately old gables—and see the Golden Age reflected in a quiet canal.

Planning Your Time

Amsterdam is worth a full day of sightseeing on even the busiest itinerary. And though the city has a couple of must-see museums, its best attraction is its own carefree ambience. The city's a joy on foot—and a breezier and faster delight by bike.

In the morning, see Amsterdam's two great art museums: the Van Gogh and the Rijksmuseum (cafeteria lunch). Walk from the museums to the Singel canal flower market, then take a relaxing hour-long, round-trip canal cruise from the dock at Spui (described later, under "Tours in Amsterdam"). After the cruise, stroll through the peaceful Begijnhof courtyard and tour the nearby Amsterdam Museum. Visiting the Anne Frank House after 18:00 may save you an hour in line in summer (see page 1193 for last-entry times). Have a memorable dinner: Try Dutch pancakes or a *rijsttafel*—an Indonesian smorgasbord.

On a balmy evening, Amsterdam has a Greek-island ambience. Stroll through the Jordaan neighborhood for the idyllic side of town and wander down Leidsestraat to Leidseplein for the roaring café-and-people scene. Tour the Red Light District while you're at it.

With More Time: With two days in the Netherlands, I'd side-trip by bike, bus, or train to Haarlem. With a third day, I'd do the other great Amsterdam museums.

Orientation to Amsterdam

Amsterdam's Central Station (Amsterdam Centraal), on the north edge of the city, is your starting point, with the TI, bike rental, and trams branching out to all points. Damrak is the main north-south axis, connecting Central Station with Dam Square (people-watching and hangout center) and its Royal Palace. From this main street, the city spreads out like a fan, with 90 islands, hundreds of bridges, and a series of concentric canals—named Herengracht (Gentleman's Canal), Keizersgracht (Emperor's Canal), and Prinsengracht (Prince's Canal)—that were laid out in the 17th century, Holland's Golden Age. Amsterdam's major sights are all within walking distance of Dam Square.

To the east of Damrak is the oldest part of the city (today's Red Light District), and to the west is the newer part, where you'll find the Anne Frank House and the peaceful Jordaan neighborhood. Museums and Leidseplein nightlife cluster at the southern edge of the city center.

Tourist Information

"VVV" (pronounced "fay fay fay") is Dutch for "TI," a tourist information office. Amsterdam's tourist offices are crowded and inefficient—avoid them if you can. You can save yourself a trip by calling the TI at 020/201-8800 (Mon-Fri 8:00-18:00) or trying 0900-400-4040 (Mon-Fri 9:00-17:00). From the US dial 011-31-20-551-2525.

The main TI at Central Station is busy, but is convenient for anyone arriving by train (July-Aug Mon-Sat 9:00-19:00, Sun 10:00-17:00; Sept-June Mon-Sat 9:00-18:00, Sun 10:00-17:00). An affiliated office is in the AUB/Last Minute Ticket Shop on Leidseplein, tucked into the side of the giant Stadsschouwburg Theater (Mon-Fri 10:00-19:00, Sat 10:00-18:00, Sun 12:00-18:00; doesn't book hotel rooms). These TIs outside of Amsterdam are helpful and less crowded: at Schiphol Airport (daily 7:00-22:00) and in the town of Haarlem (see next chapter).

Tickets: Although Amsterdam's main TI sells tickets to the Anne Frank House (€1 extra per ticket, same-day tickets available) and the Van Gogh and Stedelijk museums (no fee), it's quicker to get tickets in advance online (see below).

Maps and Brochures: Given the city's maze of streets and canals, I'd definitely get a good city map (€2.50 at Central Station TI, same map given away free at the TI in the AUB/Last Minute Ticket Shop—go figure). Also consider picking up any of the walking-tour brochures (€3 each, including tours covering city center, former Jewish Quarter, Jordaan, and funky De Pijp neighborhood). For entertainment, get a copy of *Time Out Amsterdam* (€3, €1.50 if bought with city map); for additional entertainment ideas, see "Entertainment in Amsterdam," later.

Currency Exchange: At Central Station, **GWK Currency Exchange** offices have hotel reservation windows where clerks sell international phone cards and mobile-phone SIM cards, and answer basic tourist questions, with shorter lines than the TI (Mon-Sat 8:00-22:00, Sun 9:00-22:00, near front of station in both the east and west corridors, tel. 020/627-2731).

Resources for Gay Travelers: A short walk from Central Station down Damrak is **GAYtic,** a TI specifically oriented to the needs of gay travelers. The office stocks maps, magazines, and brochures, and dispenses advice on nightlife and general sightseeing (daily 11:00-20:00, Spuistraat 44, tel. 020/330-1461, www.gaytic.nl). **Pink Point,** in a kiosk outside Westerkerk, next to the Homomonument, is less of a resource, but has advice about nightlife (usually daily 10:00-18:00).

Advance Tickets and Sightseeing Cards

During high season (late March-Oct), you can avoid long ticket lines at the **Rijksmuseum, Van Gogh Museum,** and **Stedelijk** modern-art museum by booking tickets online, getting a Museumkaart sightseeing pass (described later), or buying tickets in advance. At the **Anne Frank House**, the only line-skipping option is booking tickets ahead (or, if you'll be buying a Museumkaart, reserving an entry time). The I amsterdam Card, also described later, only lets you skip the line at the Van Gogh Museum.

Advance Tickets for Major Sights: It's easy to buy tickets online through each museum's website: www.annefrank.org (€0.50 surcharge per ticket, but worth it), www.rijksmuseum.nl, www. vangoghmuseum.com, and www.stedelijk.nl (no extra fee for Rijks, Van Gogh, or Stedelijk). Print out your ticket and bring it to the ticket-holder's line for a quick entry. Before you get your tickets online, however, consider whether you'll save money by buying a sightseeing card.

You can also buy tickets for these sights in advance at the TIs (main TI only for Anne Frank House), but TI lines seem almost as long as the ones you're trying to avoid at the sights.

If You Don't Have Advance Tickets: If you end up visiting the Anne Frank House without a reservation, trim your wait in line by showing up the minute it opens, or late in the day; this works better in early spring and fall than in summer, when even after-dinner lines can be long. Visit the Van Gogh Museum on a Friday evening, when it's open until 22:00, with no lines and few crowds, even in peak season.

Sightseeing Cards: Two cards merit consideration for heavy-duty sightseers: The Museumkaart and the I amsterdam Card. If your trip includes any other Dutch city, you'll save more money by purchasing the Museumkaart, which covers many sights throughout the Netherlands, than the overpriced I amsterdam Card, which is valid only in Amsterdam. (There's no reason to buy both.) However, if Amsterdam's your only stop in the Netherlands, and if you plan to get around on transit (rather than by bike), the I amsterdam Card makes sense, as it includes a transit pass. Both cards allow you free entry to most sights in Amsterdam (including the Van Gogh Museum), but neither card covers the Heineken Brewery, Westerkerk tower, or any sights dealing with sex or marijuana. The Anne Frank House and Rijksmuseum are covered by the Museumkaart but not by the I amsterdam Card. The Museumkaart is a better option for avoiding crowds (it lets you skip ticket-buying lines everywhere except the Anne Frank House; the I amsterdam Card lets you skip only at the Van Gogh). Note: Even if you skip the ticket line, you have to go through security (like everyone else). You'll also see ads for the Holland Pass, but it's not worth it.

The **Museumkaart,** which costs €50 and is valid for a year throughout the Netherlands, is a no-brainer for anyone visiting at least six museums (for example, an itinerary that includes these museums, for a total of €65: Rijksmuseum-€15, Van Gogh Museum-€15, Anne Frank House-€9, Amsterdam Museum-€10, Amstelkring Museum-€8, and the Dutch Resistance Museum-€8). The Museumkaart is sold at all participating museums (buy it at a less-crowded one to avoid lines).

The **I amsterdam Card,** which focuses on Amsterdam and includes most transportation, is not worth the cost unless you're planning on a day or two of nonstop sightseeing, and connecting it all by public transit (it doesn't cover bike rental). This pass doesn't cover the Rijksmuseum or the Anne Frank House. It does, however, include most other Amsterdam sights (including the Van Gogh Museum), one free canal boat tour (otherwise about €13), and unlimited use of trams, buses, and metro (except for the canal tour, all of these public-transit options are also covered by a normal transit pass—see "Getting Around Amsterdam," later). Remember, this card's line-skipping perks are limited to the Van Gogh Museum. You have a set number of consecutive hours to use it (for example: Visit your first museum at 14:00 Monday with a 24-hour pass, and it's good until 13:59 on Tuesday). It's sold at major museums, TIs, and with shorter lines at the GVB public-transit office across from Central Station, next to the TI (€40/24 hours, €50/48 hours, or €60/72 hours; www.iamsterdamcard.com).

Arrival in Amsterdam

By Train

The portal connecting Amsterdam to the world is its aptly named Central Station (Amsterdam Centraal). Through at least 2014, expect the station and the plaza in front of it to be a construction zone and therefore in a state of some flux.

Trains arrive on a level above the station. Go down the stairs or the escalator (at the "A" end of the platform). As you descend from the platforms, you'll find yourself in one of the corridors leading to the street exit for the city center *(Centrum)*. Those wanting buses and river ferries should head in the opposite direction—to the north *(Noord)* exit.

The station is fully equipped for the traveler. You'll find GWK Travelex counters in both the east and west corridors, and international train-ticket offices near the exit of both corridors. Luggage lockers are in the east corridor, under the "B" end of the platforms (€5-7/24 hours, depending on size of bag, always open, can fill up on busy summer weekends). The station has plenty of shops and places to grab a bite to eat. On the train level, platform 2 is lined with eateries, including the tall, venerable, 1920s-style **First Class Grand Café.** Handy **Albert Heijn** "to go" supermarkets are easy to find at the end of the east corridor and in the main north-south underground passage.

Exiting the station, you're in the heart of the city. Straight ahead, just past the canal, is Damrak street, leading to Dam

Square. To your left are the TI and GVB public-transit office. Farther to your left is a fascinating exhibit about the big construction project going on all around you (specifically, the digging of a new subway line). Past the exhibit are two bike rental places: **MacBike** (in the station building), and **Star Bikes** (a five-minute walk past the station), both listed on page 1180. To the right of the station are the postcard-perfect neighborhoods of West Amsterdam; some of my recommended hotels are within walking distance.

Just beyond the taxis are the platforms for the city's blue trams, which come along frequently, ready to take you anywhere your feet won't (buy ticket or pass from conductor). Trams #1, #2, and #5 (which run to nearly all my recommended hotels) leave from in front of the station's west (main) entrance. All trams leaving Central Station stop at Dam Square along their route. For more on the transit system, see page 1178.

By Plane

For details on getting from Schiphol Airport into downtown Amsterdam, see page 1236.

Helpful Hints

Theft Alert: Tourists are considered green and rich, and the city has more than its share of hungry thieves—especially in the train station, on trams, in and near crowded museums, at places of drunkenness, and at the many hostels. Wear your money belt.

Emergency Telephone Number: Throughout the Netherlands, dial 112.

Street Smarts: Beware of silent transportation—trams, electric mopeds, and bicycles—when walking around town. Don't walk on tram tracks or pink/maroon bicycle paths. Before you step off any sidewalk, do a double- or triple-check in both directions to make sure all's clear.

Sightseeing Strategies: To beat the lines at Amsterdam's most popular sights, plan ahead—either buy a sightseeing pass or advance online tickets (see details in the previous section). Friday night is a great time to visit the Van Gogh Museum, when it's open until 22:00 (with far smaller crowds). On Saturday nights in summer, the Anne Frank House stays open until 22:00.

Shop Hours: Most shops are open Tuesday through Saturday 10:00-18:00, and Sunday and Monday 12:00-18:00. Some shops stay open later (21:00) on Thursdays. Supermarkets are generally open Monday through Saturday 8:00-20:00 and have shorter hours or are closed on Sundays.

Busy Weekends: Every year, **King's Day** (Koningsdag, April 27 most years, but April 26 in 2014) and **Gay Pride** (Aug 1-3 in 2014) bring big crowds, fuller hotels, and inflated room prices.

Cash Only: Thrifty Dutch merchants, who hate paying the unusually high fees charged by credit-card companies here, rarely take US credit cards; expect to pay cash in unexpected places, including grocery stores, cafés, budget hotels, train-station machines and windows, and at some museums.

Internet Access: It's easy at cafés all over town, but the best place for serious surfing and email is the towering **Central Library,** which has hundreds of fast terminals and Wi-Fi (€1/30 minutes, Openbare Bibliotheek Amsterdam, daily 10:00-22:00, a 10-minute walk from train station, described on page 1201). The café across the street from Central Station (next to the TI) also has pay Internet access and Wi-Fi. "Coffeeshops," which sell marijuana, usually also offer Internet access—letting you surf with a special bravado.

English Bookstores: For fiction and guidebooks, try the **American Book Center** at Spui 12, right on the square (generally daily 10:00-20:00, tel. 020/535-2575). The huge and helpful **Selexyz Scheltema** is at Koningsplein 20 near the Leidsestraat (generally daily 9:30-18:00; lots of English novels, guidebooks, and maps; tel. 020/523-1411). **Waterstone's Booksellers,** a UK chain, also sells British newspapers (near Spui at 152 Kalverstraat, generally daily 10:00-18:30, tel. 020/638-3821). Expect shorter hours on Monday and Sunday.

Language Barrier: This is one of the easiest places in the non-English-speaking world for an English speaker. Nearly all signs and services are offered in two languages: Dutch and "non-Dutch" (i.e., English).

Maps: The free tourist maps can be confusing, except for *Amsterdam Museums: Guide to 37 Museums* (includes tram info and stops, ask for it at the big museums, such as the Van Gogh). If you want a top-notch map, buy one (about €2.50). I like the *Carto Studio Centrumkaart Amsterdam.* Amsterdam Anything's virtual "Go Where the Locals Go" city map is worth checking out, especially if you have mobile Internet access (www.amsterdamanything.nl).

Pharmacy: The shop named **DA** (Dienstdoende Apotheek) has all the basics—shampoo and toothpaste—as well as a pharmacy counter hidden in the back (Mon-Sat 9:00-22:00, Sun 11:00-22:00, Leidsestraat 74-76 near where it meets Keizersgracht, tel. 020/627-5351). Near Dam Square, there's **BENU Apotheek** (Mon-Fri 8:30-17:30, Sat 10:00-17:00, Sun 12:00-17:00, Damstraat 2, tel. 020/624-4331).

Laundry: Try **Clean Brothers Wasserij** in the Jordaan (daily 8:00-20:00 for €7 self-service, €9 drop-off—ready in an hour—

Mon-Fri 9:00-17:00, Sat 9:00-18:00, no drop-off Sun, West-erstraat 26, one block from Prinsengracht, tel. 020/627-9888) or **Powders,** near Leidseplein (daily 8:00-22:00, €6.50 self-service, €12 drop-off available Mon-Wed and Fri 8:00-17:00, Sat-Sun 9:00-15:00, no drop-off Thu, Kerkstraat 56, one block south of Leidsestraat, mobile 06-2630-6057).

Best Views: Although sea-level Amsterdam is notoriously hori-zontal, there are a few high points where you can get the big picture. The best city views are from the **Central Library** (Openbare Bibliotheek Amsterdam; see page 1201). The **Westerkerk**—described on page 1193 and convenient for any-one visiting the Anne Frank House—has a climbable tower with fine views. The tower of the **Old Church** (Oude Kerk), the top floor of the **Kalvertoren** shopping complex, and the rooftop terrace at the **NEMO science museum** also provide good views.

Updates to this Book: Check www.ricksteves.com/update for any significant changes that have occurred since this book was printed.

Getting Around Amsterdam

Amsterdam is big, and you'll find the trams handy. The longest walk a tourist would make is an hour from Central Station to the Rijksmuseum. When you're on foot, be extremely vigilant for silent but potentially painful bikes, trams, and crotch-high bollards.

By Tram, Bus, and Metro

Amsterdam's public transit system includes trams, buses, and an underground metro; of these, trams are most useful for most tour-ists.

The helpful **GVB public-transit information office** in front of Central Station can answer questions (next to TI, Mon-Fri 7:00-21:00, Sat-Sun 10:00-18:00). Its free, multilingual *Public Transport Amsterdam Tourist Guide* includes a transit map and explains ticket options and tram connections to all the sights. For more public transit information, visit www.gvb.nl.

Tickets: The entire country's public transit network operates on a single ticket system called the OV-Chipkaart (for "Openbaar Vervoer"—public transit). For locals, it couldn't be easier. With a single pre-paid card, they can hop on any form of public transit in the country, scan their card, and the (discounted) fare is immedi-ately deducted. Cards can be reloaded automatically, straight from residents' bank accounts. While it's possible for tourists to purchase an OV-Chipkaart, they cost a non-refundable €7.50 and can only be reloaded at train stations—unless you're staying in the Nether-lands for more than a week, don't bother.

Most travelers instead rely on either single tickets or multi-day passes. (While officially classified as "OV-Chipkaarten," these tickets and passes with electronic chips are nothing like the reloadable, valid-nationwide, plastic cards locals use.)

Within Amsterdam, a single transit ticket costs €2.80 and is good for one hour on the tram, bus, and metro, including transfers. Passes good for unlimited transportation are available for 24 hours (€7.50), 48 hours (€12), 72 hours (€16.50), and 96 hours (€21). (The I amsterdam sightseeing card, described on page 1175, includes a transit pass.) Given how expensive single tickets are, consider buying a pass before you buy that first ticket. (A rental bike—described later—costs about the same as a transit pass...but is way more fun.)

The easiest way to buy a ticket or transit pass is to simply board a tram or bus and pay the conductor (no extra fee). Tickets and passes are also available at metro-station vending machines (which take cash but not US credit cards), at GVB public-transit offices, and at TIs.

Trams: Board the tram at any entrance not marked with a red/white "do not enter" sticker. If you need a ticket or pass, pay the conductor (in a booth at the back); if there's no conductor, pay the driver in front. You must always "check in" as you board by scanning your ticket or pass at the pink-and-gray scanner, and "check out" by scanning it again when you get off. The scanner will beep and flash a green light after a successful scan. Be careful not to accidentally scan your ticket or pass twice while boarding, or it becomes invalid. Checking in and out is very important, as controllers do pass through and fine violators. To open the door when you reach your stop, press a green button on one of the poles near an exit.

Trams #2 *(Nieuw Sloten)* and #5 *(A'veen Binnenhof)* travel the north-south axis, from Central Station to Dam Square to Leidseplein to Museumplein (Van Gogh and Rijks museums). Tram #1 (marked *Osdorp*) also runs to Leidseplein. At Central Station, these three trams depart from the west side of Stationsplein (with the station behind you, they're to your right).

Tram #14, which doesn't connect to Central Station, goes east-west (Westerkerk-Dam Square-Muntplein-Waterlooplein-Plantage). If you get lost in Amsterdam, don't sweat it—10 of the city's 17 trams take you back to Central Station.

Buses and Metro: Tickets and passes work on buses and the metro just as they do on the trams—scan your ticket or pass to "check in" as you enter and again to "check out" when you leave. The metro system is scant—used mostly for commuting to the suburbs—but it does connect Central Station with some sights east of Damrak (Nieuwmarkt-Waterlooplein-Weesperplein). The glacial speed of the metro-expansion project is a running joke among cynical Amsterdammers.

AMSTERDAM

By Bike

Everyone—bank managers, students, pizza delivery boys, and police—uses this mode of transport. It's by far the smartest way to travel in a city where 40 percent of all traffic rolls on two wheels. You'll get around town by bike faster than you can by taxi. On my last visit, I rented a bike for five days, chained it to the rack outside my hotel at night, and enjoyed wonderful mobility. I highly encourage this for anyone who wants to get maximum fun per hour in Amsterdam. One-speed bikes, with *"brrringing"* bells, rent for about €10 per day (cheaper for longer periods) at any number of places—hotels can send you to the nearest spot.

Rental Shops: Star Bikes Rental has cheap rates, long hours, and inconspicuous black bikes. They're happy to arrange an after-hours drop-off if you give them your credit-card number and pre-pay (€5/3 hours, €7/day, €9/24 hours, €12/2 days, €17/3 days, daily 9:00-19:00, requires ID but no monetary deposit, 5-minute walk from east end of Central Station—walk underneath tracks near Doubletree Hotel and then turn right, De Ruyterkade 127, tel. 020/620-3215, www.starbikesrental.com).

MacBike, with thousands of bikes, is the city's bike-rental powerhouse—you'll see their bright-red bikes all over town (they do stick out a bit). It has a huge and efficient outlet at Central Station (€7/3 hours, €9.50/24 hours, €14/48 hours, €19/72 hours, more for 3 gears, 25 percent discount with I amsterdam Card; either leave €50 deposit plus a copy of your passport, or leave a credit-card imprint; free helmets, daily 9:00-17:45; at east end of station—on the left as you're leaving; tel. 020/620-0985, www.macbike.nl). They have two smaller satellite stations at Leidseplein (Weteringschans 2) and Waterlooplein (Nieuwe Uilenburgerstraat 116). Return your bike to the station where you rented it. MacBike sells several pamphlets outlining bike tours with a variety of themes in and around Amsterdam for €1-2.

Frederic Rent-a-Bike, a 10-minute walk from Central Station, has quality bikes and a helpful staff (€8/3 hours, €15/24 hours—€10 if returned by 17:30, €25/48 hours, €50/week, 10 percent discount with this book, daily 9:00-17:30, no after-hours drop-off, Brouwersgracht 78, tel. 020/624-5509, www.frederic.nl, Frederic and son Marne).

Lock Your Bike: Bike thieves are bold and brazen in Amsterdam. Bikes come with two locks and stern instructions to use both. The wimpy ones go through the spokes, whereas the industrial-strength chains are meant to be wrapped around the actual body of the bike and through the front wheel, and connected to something stronger than any human. (Note the steel bike-hitching racks sticking up all around town, called "staples.") Follow your rental agency's locking directions diligently. Once, I used both locks, but my chain wasn't around the main bar of my bike's body. In the morning, I found only my front tire (still safely chained to the metal fence). If you're sloppy, it's an expensive mistake and one that any "included" theft insurance won't cover.

More Tips: As the Dutch believe in fashion over safety, no one here wears a helmet. They do, however, ride cautiously, and so should you: Use arm signals, follow the bike-only traffic signals, stay in the obvious and omnipresent bike lanes, and yield to traffic on the right. Fear oncoming trams and tram tracks. Carefully cross tram tracks at a perpendicular angle to avoid catching your tire in the rut. Warning: Police ticket cyclists just as they do drivers. Obey all traffic signals, and walk your bike through pedestrian zones. Fines for biking through pedestrian zones are reportedly €30-50. A handy bicycle route-planner can be found at www.routecraft. com (select "bikeplanner," then click British flag for English). For a "Do-It-Yourself Bike Tour of Amsterdam" and for bike tours, see page 1184.

By Boat

While the city is great on foot, bike, or tram, you can also get around Amsterdam by boat. **Rederij Lovers** boats shuttle tourists on a variety of routes covering different combinations of the city's top sights. Their Museum Line, for example, costs €16 and stops near the Hermitage, Rijksmuseum/Van Gogh Museum, and Central Station (at least every 45 minutes, 4 stops, 1.5 hours). Sales booths in front of Central Station (and the boats) offer free brochures listing museum hours and admission prices. Most routes come with recorded narration and run daily 10:00-17:30 (tel. 020/530-1090, www.lovers.nl).

The similar **Canal Bus** is actually a boat, offering 17 stops on three different boat routes (€24/24-hour pass, departures daily 9:30-18:30, until 19:00 April-Oct, leaves near Central Station and Rederij Lovers dock, tel. 020/623-9886, www.canal.nl).

If you're simply looking for a floating, nonstop tour, the regular canal tour boats (without the stops) give more information, cover more ground, and cost less (see "Tours in Amsterdam," next page).

For do-it-yourself canal tours and lots of exercise, Canal Bus also rents "canal bikes" (a.k.a. paddleboats) at several locations: near the Anne Frank House, near the Rijksmuseum, near Leidseplein, and where Leidsestraat meets Keizersgracht (€8/hour per person, daily July-Aug 10:00-22:00, Sept-June 10:00-18:00).

By Taxi

For short rides, Amsterdam is a bad town for taxis. Given the good tram system and ease of biking, I use taxis less in Amsterdam than in just about any other city in Europe. The city's taxis have a high drop charge (€7.50) for the first two kilometers (e.g., from Central Station to the Mint Tower), after which it's €2.30 per kilometer (no extra fee for luggage; it's worth trying to bargain a lower rate, as competition among cabbies is fierce). You can wave them down, find a rare taxi stand, or call one (tel. 020/677-7777). You'll also see **bike taxis,** particularly near Dam Square and Leidseplein. Negotiate a rate for the trip before you board (no meter), and they'll wheel you wherever you want to go (€1/3 minutes, no surcharge for baggage or extra weight, sample fare from Leidseplein to Anne Frank House: about €6).

By Car
If you've got a car, park it—all you'll find are frustrating one-way streets, terrible parking, and meter maids with a passion for booting cars parked incorrectly. You'll pay €60 a day to park safely in a central garage. If you must bring a car to Amsterdam, it's best to leave it at one of the city's supervised park-and-ride lots (follow *P&R* signs from freeway, €8/24 hours, includes round-trip transit into city center for up to five people, 4-day maximum).

Tours in Amsterdam

To sightsee on your own, download my series of **free audio tours** that illuminate some of Amsterdam's top neighborhoods: my Amsterdam City Walk, Red Light District Walk, and Jordaan Walk (see sidebar on page 7 for details).

By Boat
▲▲Canal Boat Tours
These long, low, tourist-laden boats leave continually from several docks around town for a relaxing, if uninspiring, one-hour introduction to the city (with recorded headphone commentary). Select a boat tour based on convenience of its starting point, or whether it's included with your I amsterdam Card (which covers Blue Boat Company and Holland International boats). Tip: Boats leave only when full, so jump on a full boat to avoid waiting at the dock. No fishing allowed—but bring your camera. Some prefer to cruise at night, when the bridges are illuminated.

Choose from one of these three companies:

Rederij P. Kooij is cheapest (€9, 3/hour in summer 10:00-22:00, 2/hour in winter 10:00-17:00, at corner of Spui and Rokin streets, about 10 minutes from Dam Square, tel. 020/623-3810, www.rederijkooij.nl).

Blue Boat Company's boats depart from near Leidseplein (€14; every half-hour April-Sept 10:00-18:00, also at 19:00; hourly Oct-March 10:00-17:00; 1.25 hours, Stadhouderskade 30, tel. 020/679-1370, www.blueboat.nl). Their 1.5-hour evening cruise has a live English-speaking guide (€17.50, nightly at 20:00, April-Sept also at 21:00 and 22:00, reservations required).

Holland International offers a standard one-hour trip and a variety of longer tours from the docks opposite Central Station (€14, 1-hour "100 Highlights" tour with recorded commentary, 4/hour daily 9:00-18:00, 2/hour 18:00-22:00; Prins Hendrikkade 33a, tel. 020/625-3035, www.hir.nl).

Hop-On, Hop-Off Canal Boats
Small, 12-person electric Canal Hopper boats leave every 20-30 minutes with live commentary on two different hop-on, hop-off routes (€24 day pass, €17 round-trip ticket, July-Aug daily 10:00-17:00, Sept-June Fri-Sun only, "yellow" west route runs 2/hour and stops near Anne Frank House and Rijksmuseum, "orange" east route runs 3/hour and stops near Red Light District and Damrak, tel. 020/626-5574, www.canal.nl).

Wetlands Safari, Nature Canoe Tours near Amsterdam
If you want some exercise and a dose of village life, consider this five-hour tour. Majel Tromp, a friendly villager who speaks great English, takes groups limited to 15 people. The program: Meet at the bus stops behind Central Station (leave the station from the west corridor and take the escalator up to the buses) at 9:30, catch a public bus, stop for coffee, take a 3.5-hour canoe trip (2-3 people per canoe) with several stops, tour a village by canoe, munch a rural canalside picnic lunch (included), then canoe and bus back into Amsterdam by 15:00 (€43, €27 for kids ages 7-16, €3 discount with this book, May-mid-Sept Sun-Fri, reservations required, tel. 020/686-3445, mobile 06-5355-2669, www.wetlandssafari.nl, info@wetlandssafari.nl).

On Foot
Red Light District Tours
Randy Roy's Red Light Tours consists of one expat American woman, Kimberley. She lived in the Red Light District for years and gives fun, casual, yet informative 1.5-hour walks through this fascinating and eye-popping neighborhood. Though the actual information is light, you'll walk through various porn and drug shops and have an expert to answer your questions. Call or email to reserve (€15 includes a drink in a colorful bar at the end, nightly at 20:00, Fri and Sat also at 22:00, no tours Dec-Feb, tours meet in front of Victoria Hotel—in front of Central Station, mobile 06-4185-3288, www.randyroysredlighttours.com, kimberley@randy-roysredlighttours.com).

Free City Walk

New Europe Tours "employs" native, English-speaking students to give irreverent and entertaining three-hour walks (using the same "free tour, ask for tips, sell their other tours" formula popular in so many great European cities). While most guides lack a local's deep understanding of Dutch culture, not to mention professional training, they're certainly high-energy. This long walk covers a lot of the city with an enthusiasm for the contemporary pot-and-prostitution scene (free but tips expected, daily at 11:15 and 13:15, www.neweuropetours.eu). They also offer paid tours (Red Light District—€12, daily at 19:00; coffeeshop scene—€12, daily at 16:00; city by bike—€19, includes bike, daily at 14:00). Their walking tours leave from the National Monument on Dam Square; the bike tour leaves from Central Station.

Adam's Apple Tours

Frank Sanders' walking tour offers a two-hour, English-only look at the historic roots and development of Amsterdam. You'll have a small group of generally 5-6 people and a caring guide, starting off at Central Station and ending up at Dam Square (€25; May-Sept daily at 10:00, 12:30, and 15:00 based on demand; call 020/616-7867 to confirm times and book).

Private Guide

Albert Walet is a likeable, hardworking, and knowledgeable local guide who enjoys personalizing tours for Americans interested in knowing his city. Al specializes in history, architecture, and water management, and exudes a passion for Amsterdam (€70/2 hours, €120/4 hours, up to 4 people, on foot or by bike, mobile 06-2069-7882, abwalet@yahoo.com). Ab also takes travelers to nearby towns, including Haarlem, Leiden, and Delft.

By Bike

Yellow Bike Guided Tours offers city bike tours of either two hours (€19.50, daily at 10:30) or three hours (€23.50, daily at 13:30), which both include a 20-minute break. They also offer a four-hour, 15-mile tour of the dikes and green pastures of the countryside (€29.50, lunch extra, includes 45-minute break, April-Oct daily at 10:30). All tours leave from Nieuwezijds Kolk 29, three blocks from Central Station (reservations smart, tel. 020/620-6940, www.yellowbike.nl). If you'd prefer a private guide, see Albert Walet, above.

Joy Ride Bike Tours is a creative little company run by English-speaking Sean and Allison Cody. Their most popular tours start just behind the Rijksmuseum (city by bike—€26, 2.5-3 hours, May-Sept departs Fri-Mon at 16:00, none Tue-Thu, no kids under 13; countryside by bike—€30, 4-4.5 hours, May-Sept departs Thu-Mon at 10:30, none Tue-Wed, no kids under 10; no tours off-season). Both tours are limited to 10-15 people, so it's smart to book ahead (save €3 by booking online, €7 cheaper with your own bike—must email or call ahead, tours meet 15 minutes before departure time, helmets and rain gear available, mobile 06-4361-1798, www.joyridetours.nl). Their four-hour "bespoke" tours, offered year-round, are tailored to match your interests (Jewish history, Amsterdam for kids, WWII history, or cannabis; €125/3 people).

Do-It-Yourself Bike Tour of Amsterdam

A day enjoying the bridges, bike lanes, and sleepy, off-the-beaten-path canals on your own one-speed is an essential Amsterdam experience. The real joys of Europe's best-preserved 17th-century city are the countless intimate glimpses it offers: the laid-back locals sunning on their porches under elegant gables, rusted bikes that look as if they've been lashed to the same lamppost since the 1960s, wasted hedonists planted on canalside benches, and happy sailors permanently moored, but still manning the deck.

For a good day trip, rent a bike at or near Central Station (see "By Bike" on page 1180). Head west down Haarlemmerstraat, working your wide-eyed way down Prinsengracht (drop into Café 't Papeneiland at Prinsengracht 2) and detouring through the small, gentrified streets of the Jordaan neighborhood before popping out at the Westerkerk under the tallest spire in the city.

Pedal south to the lush and peaceful Vondelpark, then cut back through the center of town (Leidseplein to the Mint Tower, along Rokin street to Dam Square). From there, cruise the Red Light District, following Oudezijds Voorburgwal past the Old Church (Oude Kerk) to Zeedijk street, and return to the train station.

Weekend Tour Packages for Students

Andy Steves (my son) runs **Weekend Student Adventures,** offering experiential three-day weekend tours for €199, designed for American students studying abroad (www.wsaeurope.com for details on tours of Amsterdam and other great cities).

Sights in Amsterdam

One of Amsterdam's delights is that it has perhaps more small specialty museums than any other city its size. From houseboats to sex, from marijuana to Old Masters, you can find a museum to suit your interests.

For tips on how to save time otherwise spent in the long ticket-buying lines of the big three museums—the Anne Frank House, Van Gogh Museum, and Rijksmuseum—see "Advance Tickets and Sightseeing Cards" on page 1173. Admission prices are high: A sightseeing card such as the Museumkaart (or I amsterdam Card)

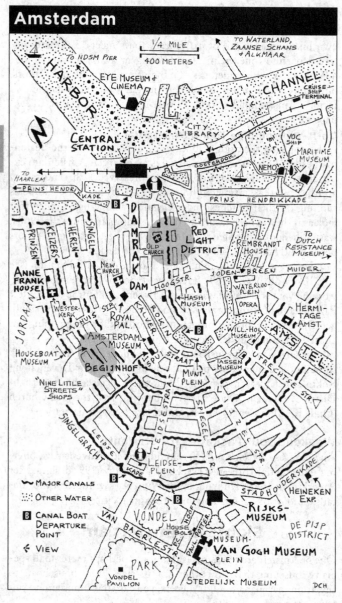

Amsterdam

can pay for itself quickly. Entry to most sights is free with a card (I've noted those that aren't covered).

Most museums require baggage check (usually free, often in coin-op lockers where you get your coin back).

The following sights are arranged by neighborhood for handy sightseeing.

Southwest Amsterdam

▲▲▲Rijksmuseum

At the Rijksmuseum ("Rijks" rhymes with "bikes"), Holland's Golden Age shines with the best collection anywhere of the Dutch Masters—from Vermeer's quiet domestic scenes, to Steen's raucous family meals, to Hals' snapshot portraits, to Rembrandt's moody brilliance. Recently much improved after a long renovation, this delightful museum offers one of the most exciting and enjoyable art experiences in Europe.

The 17th century saw the Netherlands at the pinnacle of its power. The Dutch had won their independence from Spain, trade and shipping boomed, wealth poured in, the people were understandably proud, and the arts flourished. This era was later dubbed the Dutch Golden Age. With no church bigwigs or royalty around to commission big canvases in the Protestant Dutch republic, artists had to find different patrons—and they discovered the upper-middle-class businessmen who fueled Holland's capitalist economy. Artists painted their portraits and decorated their homes with pretty still lifes and nonpreachy, slice-of-life art.

Dutch art is meant to be enjoyed, not studied. It's straightforward, meat-and-potatoes art for the common man. The Dutch love the beauty of everyday things painted realistically and with exquisite detail. Set your cerebral cortex on "low" and let this art pass straight from the eyes to the heart, with minimal detours.

Cost and Hours: €15, not covered by I amsterdam Card, audioguide-€5, videoguide also available, daily 9:00-17:00, last entry 30 minutes before closing, tram #2 or #5 from Central Station to Hobbemastraat, info tel. 020/674-7047 or switchboard tel. 020/674-7000, www.rijksmuseum.nl. The entrance is off the passageway that tunnels right through the center of the building.

Avoiding Crowds: The museum is most crowded from April to September (especially April-June), on weekends, and during morning hours. You can avoid crowds by coming later in the day (it's least crowded after 16:00—but most visitors will want more than an hour here). Avoid waits in the ticket-buying line by buying your ticket or pass in advance. No one can completely avoid the security line.

You can buy and print your ticket in advance online at www.

rijksmuseum.nl. The ticket is good any time (no entry time specified). Buying online has the added advantage of letting you enter through the "direct entry" doorway, scooting you to the front of the security line. You can also buy tickets at many hotels.

▲▲▲Van Gogh Museum

Near the Rijksmuseum, the Van Gogh Museum (we say "van GO," the Dutch say "van HHHOCK") is a cultural high even for those not into art. This remarkable museum features works by the troubled Dutch artist whose art seemed to mirror his life. Vincent, who killed himself in 1890 at age 37, is best known for sunny, Impressionist canvases that vibrate and pulse with vitality. The museum's 200 paintings—which offer a virtual stroll through the artist's work and life—were owned by Theo, Vincent's younger, art-dealer brother. If you like brightly colored landscapes in the Impressionist style, you'll like this museum. If you enjoy finding deeper meaning in works of art, you'll really love it. The mix of Van Gogh's creative genius, his tumultuous life, and the traveler's determination to connect to it makes this museum as much a walk with Vincent as with his art.

The main collection of Van Gogh paintings on the first floor is arranged chronologically, taking you through the changes in Vincent van Gogh's life and styles. The paintings are divided into five periods of Vincent's life—the Netherlands, Paris, Arles, St. Rémy, and Auvers-sur-Oise—proceeding clockwise around the floor. Highlights include *Sunflowers, The Bedroom, The Potato Eaters*, and many brooding self-portraits.

The third floor shows works that influenced Vincent, from Monet and Pissarro to Gauguin, Cézanne, and Toulouse-Lautrec. The worthwhile audioguide includes insightful commentaries and quotes from Vincent himself. Temporary exhibits fill the new wing, down the escalator from the ground-floor lobby.

Cost and Hours: €15, more for special exhibits, audioguide-€5, kids' audioguide-€2.50, daily 9:00-17:00, Fri until 22:00—with no crowds in evening, Paulus Potterstraat 7, tram #2 or #5 from Central Station to Van Baerlestraat stop, tel. 020/570-5200, www.vangoghmuseum.com.

Avoiding Lines: Skip the 15-30-minute wait in the ticket-buying line by getting your ticket in advance, or by getting a Museumkaart or I amsterdam Card. You can buy and print tickets online (at www.vangoghmuseum.com) or at the TI.

▲▲Stedelijk Museum

The Netherlands' top modern-art museum is filled with a fun, far-out, and refreshing collection that includes post-1945 experimental and conceptual art as well as works by Picasso, Chagall, Cézanne, Kandinsky, and Mondrian. The Stedelijk (STAYD-eh-lik), like the

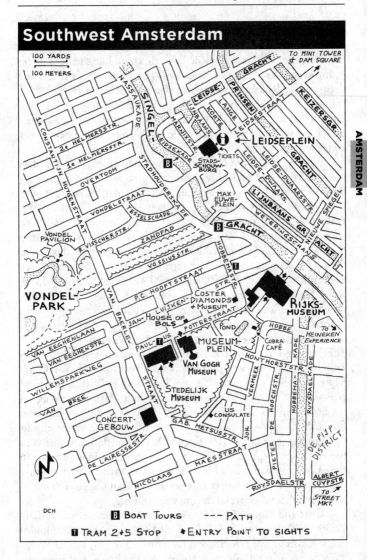

Southwest Amsterdam

AMSTERDAM

B BOAT TOURS --- PATH
T TRAM 2+5 STOP ↟ ENTRY POINT TO SIGHTS

Rijksmuseum, also boasts a newly spiffed-up building, which now flaunts an architecturally daring entry facing Museumplein (near the Van Gogh Museum).

Cost and Hours: €15, Tue-Wed 11:00-17:00, Thu 11:00-22:00, Fri-Sun 10:00-18:00, closed Mon, café with outdoor seating, top-notch shop, Paulus Potterstraat 13/Museumplein 10, tel. 020/573-2911, www.stedelijk.nl.

▲Museumplein

Bordered by the Rijks, Van Gogh, and Stedelijk museums, and the Concertgebouw (classical music hall), this park-like square is interesting even to art-haters. Amsterdam's best acoustics are found underneath the Rijksmuseum, where street musicians perform everything from chamber music to Mongolian throat singing. Mimes, human statues, and crafts booths dot the square. Skateboarders careen across a concrete tube, while locals enjoy a park bench or a coffee at the Cobra Café.

Nearby is **Coster Diamonds,** a handy place to see a diamond-cutting and polishing demo (free, frequent, and interesting 30-minute tours followed by sales pitch, popular for decades with tour groups, prices marked up to include tour guide kickbacks, daily 9:00-17:00, Paulus Potterstraat 2, tel. 020/305-5555, www. costerdiamonds.com). The end of the tour leads you straight into their Diamond Museum, which is worthwhile only for those who have a Museumkaart (which covers entry) or feel the need to see even more diamonds (€7.50, daily 9:00-17:00, tel. 020/305-5300, www.diamantmuseumamsterdam.nl). The tour at **Gassan Diamonds** is free and better (see page 1206), but Coster is convenient to the Museumplein scene.

House of Bols: Cocktail & Genever Experience

This leading Dutch distillery runs a pricey and polished little museum/marketing opportunity across the street from the Van Gogh Museum. The "experience" is a self-guided walk through what is essentially an ad for Bols—"four hundred years of working on the art of mixing and blending...a celebration of gin"—with some fun sniffing opportunities and a drink at a modern, mirrored-out cocktail bar for a finale. (It's essentially the gin-flavored version of the Heineken Experience, listed next.) The highlight is a chance to taste up to five different local gins with a talkative expert guiding you. Then have your barista mix up the cocktail of your dreams—based on what you learned during your sniffing.

Cost and Hours: €12.50, not covered by Museumkaart, daily 12:00-17:30, Fri until 21:00, Sat until 19:00, last entry 45 minutes before closing, must be 18, Paulus Potterstraat 14, tel. 020/570-8575, www.houseofbols.com. If you like the booze and hang out and talk, this can be a good deal (but do it after the Van Gogh Museum).

Heineken Experience

This famous brewery, having moved its operations to the suburbs, has converted its original headquarters into a slick, Disneyesque beerfest—complete with a beer-making simulation ride. The "experience" also includes do-it-yourself music videos, photo ops that put you inside Heineken logos and labels, and no small amount of hype about the Heineken family and the quality of their beer. It's a fun trip, if you can ignore the fact that you're essentially paying for an hour of advertising (overpriced at €17, includes two drinks, daily 11:00-19:00, last entry at 17:30; tram #16, #24, or #25 to Heinekenplein; an easy walk from Rijksmuseum, tel. 020/523-9222, www. heinekenexperience.com).

De Pijp District

This former working-class industrial and residential zone (behind the Heineken Experience, near the Rijksmuseum) is emerging as a colorful, vibrant district. Its spine is Albert Cuypstraat, a street taken over by a long, sprawling produce market packed with interesting people. The centerpiece is **Restaurant Bazar** (marked by a roof-capping golden angel), a church turned into a Middle Eastern food circus (see listing on page 1229).

▲Leidseplein

Brimming with cafés, this people-watching mecca is an impromptu stage for street artists, accordionists, jugglers, and unicyclists. It's particularly bustling on sunny afternoons. The Boom Chicago theater fronts this square (see "Entertainment in Amsterdam," later). Stroll nearby Lange Leidsedwarsstraat (one block north) for a taste-bud tour of ethnic eateries, from Greek to Indonesian.

▲▲Vondelpark

This huge, lively city park is popular with the Dutch—families with little kids, romantic couples, strolling seniors, and hippies sharing blankets and beers. It's a favored venue for free summer concerts. On a sunny afternoon, it's a hedonistic scene that seems to say, "Parents...relax."

Rembrandtplein and Tuschinski Theater

One of the city's premier nightlife spots is the leafy Rembrandtplein (the artist's statue stands here, along with a jaunty group of statues giving us *The Night Watch* in 3-D) and the adjoining Thorbeckeplein. Several late-night dance clubs keep the area lively into the wee hours. Utrechtsestraat is lined with upscale shops and restaurants. Nearby Reguliersdwarsstraat (a street one block south of Rembrandtplein) is a center for gay and lesbian nightclubs.

The **Tuschinski Theater,** a movie palace from the 1920s (a half-block from Rembrandtplein down Reguliersbreestraat), glitters inside and out. Still a working theater, it's a delightful old place to see first-run movies (always in their original language—usually English—with Dutch subtitles). The exterior is an interesting hybrid of styles, forcing the round peg of Art Nouveau into the square hole of Art Deco. The stone-and-tile facade features stripped-down, functional Art Deco squares and rectangles, but is ornamented with Art Nouveau elements—Tiffany-style windows, garlands, curvy iron lamps, Egyptian pharaohs, and exotic gold lettering over the door. Inside (lobby is free), the sumptuous decor features fancy carpets, slinky fixtures, and semi-abstract designs.

Grab a seat in the lobby and watch the ceiling morph (Reguliers-breestraat 26-28).

Pipe Museum (Pijpenkabinet)

This small and quirky-yet-classy museum holds 300 years of pipes in a 17th-century canal house. (It's almost worth the admission price just to see the inside of one of these elegant homes.) You enter through the street-level shop, Smokiana, which is almost interesting enough to be a museum itself. It sells new and antique pipes, various smoking curiosities, and scholarly books written by the shop's owner. If you want more, pay to enter the museum, and a volunteer docent will accompany you upstairs through a tour of smoking history. You begin with some pre-Columbian terra-cotta pipes (from the discoverers of tobacco, dating from around 500 B.C.), followed by plenty of intricate, finely decorated Baroque and Victorian smoking paraphernalia. Ask questions—your guide is happy to explain why the opium pipes have their bowls in the center of the stem, or why some white clay pipes are a foot long.

Cost and Hours: €8, Wed-Sat 12:00-18:00, usually closed Sun-Tue, tel. 020/421-1779, just off Leidsestraat at Prinsengracht 488, www.pijpenkabinet.nl.

Houseboat Museum (Woonbootmuseum)

In the 1930s, modern cargo ships came into widespread use—making small, sail-powered cargo boats obsolete. In danger of extinction, these little vessels found new life as houseboats lining the canals of Amsterdam. Today, 2,500 such boats—their cargo holds turned into classy, comfortable living rooms—are called home. For a peek into this *gezellig* (cozy) world, visit this tiny museum. Captain Vincent enjoys showing visitors around the houseboat, which feels lived-in because, until 1997, it was.

Cost and Hours: €3.75, not covered by Museumkaart; March-Oct Tue-Sun 11:00-17:00, closed Mon; Nov-Dec and Feb Fri-Sun 11:00-17:00, closed Mon-Thu; closed most of Jan; on Prinsengracht, opposite #296 facing Elandsgracht, tel. 020/427-0750, www.houseboatmuseum.nl.

West Amsterdam

▲▲▲Anne Frank House

A pilgrimage for many, this house offers a fascinating look at the hideaway of young Anne during the Nazi occupation of the Netherlands. Anne, her parents, an older sister, and four others spent a little more than two years in a "Secret Annex" behind her father's business. While in hiding, 13-year-old Anne kept a diary chronicling her extraordinary experience. Acting on a tip, the Nazis arrested the group in August of 1944 and sent them to concentration camps in Poland and Germany. Anne and her sister died of typhus in March of 1945, only weeks before their camp was liberated. Of the eight inhabitants of the Secret Annex, only Anne's father, Otto Frank, survived. He returned to Amsterdam and arranged for his daughter's diary to be published in 1947. It was followed by many translations, a play, and a movie.

The thoughtfully designed exhibit offers thorough coverage of the Frank family, the diary, the stories of others who hid, and the Holocaust. The Franks' story was that of Holland's Jews. The seven who died were among the more than 100,000 Dutch Jews killed during the war years. (Before the war, 135,000 Jews lived in the Netherlands.) Of Anne's school class of 87 Jews, only 20 survived. When her father returned to Amsterdam, he fought to preserve this house, wanting it to become, in his words, "more than a museum." It was his dream that visitors come away from the Anne Frank House with an indelible impression—and a better ability to apply the lessons of the Holocaust to our contemporary challenges.

Cost and Hours: €9, not covered by I amsterdam Card; March 15-Sept 14 daily 9:00-21:00, Sat and July-Aug until 22:00; Sept 15-March 14 daily 9:00-19:00, Sat until 21:00; last entry 30 minutes before closing, often less crowded right when it opens or after 18:00, no baggage check, no large bags allowed inside, tel. 020/556-7100, www.annefrank.org.

Getting There: It's at Prinsengracht 267, near Westerkerk and about a 20-minute walk from Central Station. You can also take tram #13, #14, or #17—or bus #170 or #172—to the Westermarkt stop, about a block south of the museum's entrance.

Avoiding Lines: Skip the long ticket-buying line (which is especially bad in the daytime during summer) by purchasing your ticket and reserving an entry time online at www.annefrank.org (€0.50/person fee). Museumkaart holders can purchase an online reservation without buying a separate Anne Frank House ticket. Book as soon as you're sure of your itinerary.

You must present a print-out of your ticket and/or reservation; if you don't have access to a printer, try emailing your confirmation to your hotel and asking them to print it—or bring your confirmation number to the museum and explain the situation. With your ticket (or Museumkaart plus reservation) in hand, you can skip the line and ring the buzzer at the low-profile door marked *Entrance: Reservations Only*. Without a reservation, try arriving when the museum opens (at 9:00) or after 18:00.

Westerkerk

Located near the Anne Frank House, this landmark church has a barren interior, Rembrandt's body buried somewhere under the pews, and Amsterdam's tallest steeple.

The tower is open only for tours and offers a grand city view. The tour guide, who speaks English and Dutch, tells of the church

AMSTERDAM

Amsterdam at a Glance

▲▲▲**Rijksmuseum** Best collection anywhere of the Dutch Masters—Rembrandt, Hals, Vermeer, and Steen—in a spectacular setting. **Hours:** Daily 9:00-17:00. See page 1187.

▲▲▲**Van Gogh Museum** 200 paintings by the angst-ridden artist. **Hours:** Daily 9:00-17:00, Fri until 22:00. See page 1188.

▲▲▲**Anne Frank House** Young Anne's hideaway during the Nazi occupation. **Hours:** March 15-Sept 14 daily 9:00-21:00, Sat and July-Aug until 22:00; Sept 15-March 14 daily 9:00-19:00, Sat until 21:00. See page 1192.

▲▲**Stedelijk Museum** The Netherlands' top modern-art museum, recently and extensively renovated. **Hours:** Tue-Wed 11:00-17:00, Thu 11:00- 22:00, Fri-Sun 10:00-18:00, closed Mon. See page 1188.

▲▲**Vondelpark** City park and concert venue. **Hours:** Always open. See page 1191.

▲▲**Amsterdam Museum** City's growth from fishing village to trading capital to today, including some Rembrandts and a playable carillon. **Hours:** Mon-Fri 10:00-17:00, Sat-Sun 11:00-17:00. See page 1198.

▲▲**Amstelkring Museum** Catholic church hidden in the attic of a 17th-century merchant's house. **Hours:** Mon-Sat 10:00-17:00, Sun and holidays 13:00-17:00. See page 1199.

▲▲**Red Light District Walk** Women of the world's oldest profession on the job. **Hours:** Best from noon into the evening; avoid late at night. See page 1199.

▲▲**Netherlands Maritime Museum** Rich seafaring story of the Netherlands, told with vivid artifacts. **Hours:** Daily 9:00-17:00. See page 1202.

▲▲**Hermitage Amsterdam** Russia's Tsarist treasures, on loan from St. Petersburg. **Hours:** Daily 10:00-17:00. See page 1205.

▲▲**Dutch Resistance Museum** History of the Dutch struggle against the Nazis. **Hours:** Tue-Fri 10:00-17:00, Sat-Mon 11:00-17:00. See page 1206.

▲**Museumplein** Square with art museums, street musicians, crafts, and nearby diamond demos. **Hours:** Always open. See page 1190.

▲**Leidseplein** Lively square with cafés and street musicians. **Hours:** Always open, best on sunny afternoons. See page 1191.

▲**Royal Palace** Lavish City Hall that takes you back to the Golden Age of the 17th century. **Hours:** Daily 11:00-17:00 when not closed for official ceremonies. See page 1196.

▲**Begijnhof** Quiet courtyard lined with picturesque houses. **Hours:** Always open. See page 1198.

▲**Hash, Marijuana, and Hemp Museum** All the dope, from history and science to memorabilia. **Hours:** Daily 10:00-23:00. See page 1200.

▲**EYE Film Institute Netherlands** Film museum and cinema complex housed in a futuristic new building. **Hours:** Exhibits open daily 11:00-18:00, cinemas open roughly 10:00-24:00. See page 1202.

▲**Rembrandt's House** The master's reconstructed house, displaying his etchings. **Hours:** Daily 10:00-17:00. See page 1203.

▲**Diamond Tours** Offered at shops throughout the city. **Hours:** Generally daily 9:00-17:00. See page 2306.

▲**Willet-Holthuysen Museum** Elegant 17th-century house. **Hours:** Mon-Fri 10:00-17:00, Sat-Sun 11:00-17:00. See page 1204.

▲**Jewish Historical Museum** The Great Synagogue and exhibits on Judaism and culture, with Portuguese Synagogue across the street. **Hours:** Daily 11:00-17:00. See page 1206.

▲**Dutch Theater** Moving memorial in former Jewish detention center. **Hours:** Daily 11:00-16:00. See page 1206.

▲**Tropical Museum** Re-creations of tropical-life scenes. **Hours**: Tue-Sun 10:00-17:00, closed Mon. See page 1207.

Houseboat Museum Your chance to see one of these floating homes from the inside. **Hours:** March-Oct Tue-Sun 11:00-17:00, closed Mon; Nov-Dec and Feb Fri-Sun 11:00-17:00, closed Mon-Thu; closed most of Jan. See page 1192.

Central Library Architecturally fun spot—with great view terrace—to take a breather among Amsterdam's bookworms. **Hours:** Daily 10:00-22:00. See page 1201.

and its carillon. Only six people are allowed at a time (it's first-come, first-served), so lines can be long.

Cost and Hours: Church—free, generally April-Sept Mon-Sat 11:00-15:00, closed Sun and Oct-March. Tower—€7 for 30-minute tour—departures on the half hour April-Sept Mon-Sat 10:00-18:00, July-Aug until 20:00; Oct Mon-Sat 11:00-16:00; closed Sun year-round, last tour departs 30 minutes before closing, Nov-March tourable only by appointment—call 020/689-2565 or email anna@westertorenamsterdam.nl.

Reypenaer Tasting Rooms

While essentially just a fancy cheese emporium, this place does a great job of showcasing Dutch cheese. You can pop into the delightful shop any time for a few samples, or experience an hour-long cheese tasting in the basement (which has just 20 seats—it's smart to reserve ahead). The tasting session starts with a video that's somewhere between an ad for cheese and dairy soft porn. Then, with an English-speaking guide, you guillotine six different cheeses and taste them with a nice wine accompaniment.

Cost and Hours: €15 for tasting; Mon-Tue at 13:00 and 15:00, Wed-Sun at 12:00, 13:30, 15:00, and 16:30; book by phone or online, Singel 182, tel. 020/320-6333, www.wijngaardkaas.nl/en/proeflokaal.

The Canal House (Het Grachtenhuis)

This recently opened and aggressively promoted museum sounds exciting and tells an interesting story—but, for most visitors, it's not worth the time or money. There aren't any artifacts on display, and as you shuffle through a series of rooms showing video presentations, you get no sense of the great canalside mansion you came to experience.

Cost and Hours: €12, Tue-Sun 10:00-18:00, closed Mon, Herrengracht 386, www.hetgrachtenhuis.nl.

Nearby: Next door is the **Biblical Museum,** which, like its neighbor, has the potential to be fascinating. Instead, it's an old-school jumble of all things Biblical, with temporary exhibits that'll disappoint most visitors (€8, Mon-Sat 10:00-17:00, Sun 11:00-17:00, Herrengracht 366-368, tel. 020/624-2436, www.bijbels-museum.nl).

Central Amsterdam, near Dam Square

▲Royal Palace (Koninklijk Huis)

This palace was built as a lavish City Hall (1648-1655), when Holland was a proud new republic and Amsterdam was the richest city on the planet—awash in profit from trade. The building became a "Royal Palace" when Napoleon installed his brother Louis as king (1806). After Napoleon's fall, it continued as a royal residence for the Dutch royal family, the House of Orange. Today, it's one of

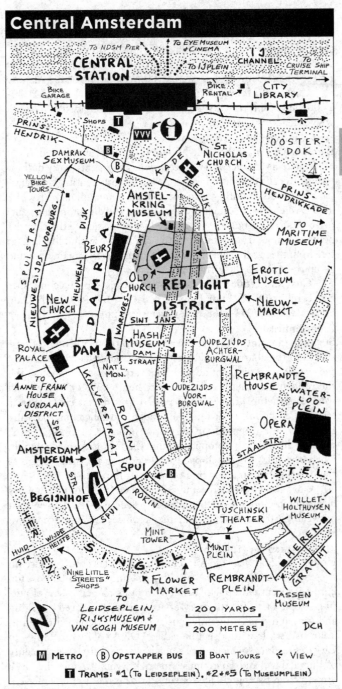

Central Amsterdam

To NDSM Pier   To EYE Museum + Cinema   IJ CHANNEL   To Cruise Ship Terminal

To IJPlein

CENTRAL STATION

BIKE GARAGE   BIKE RENTAL   CITY LIBRARY

SHOPS

PRINS HENDRIK-KADE

VVV

DAMRAK SEX MUSEUM

ST. NICHOLAS CHURCH

OOSTER-DOK

ZEEDIJK

PRINS-HENDRIKKADE

YELLOW BIKE TOURS

AMSTEL-KRING MUSEUM

TO MARITIME MUSEUM

SPUISTRAAT   VOORBURG.   DIJK   NIEUWE-   WARMOES-STRAAT

BEURS

Old Church   **RED LIGHT**

EROTIC MUSEUM

NEW CHURCH   DAMRAK

DISTRICT

NIEUW-MARKT

SINT JANS

HASH MUSEUM

OudeZijds Achter-Burgwal

ROYAL PALACE   **DAM**   DAM-STRAAT

NAT'L. MON.

OudeZijds Voor-Burgwal

REMBRANDT'S HOUSE

WATER-LOO-PLEIN

To ANNE FRANK HOUSE + JORDAAN DISTRICT

KALVERSTRAAT   ROKIN

OPERA

STAALSTR.

AMSTERDAM MUSEUM

SPUI

REMBRANDT'S HOUSE

SPUI-STR.   ROKIN

AMSTEL

BEGIJNHOF

HER-   SPUI

TUSCHINSKI THEATER

WILLET-HOLTHUYSEN MUSEUM

HUID-STR.   WIJDE HEISTE

SINGEL

MINT TOWER

MUNT-PLEIN

REMBRANDT-PLEIN

HEREN-GRACHT

TASSEN MUSEUM

"NINE LITTLE STREETS" SHOPS

FLOWER MARKET

N

TO LEIDSEPLEIN, RIJKSMUSEUM + VAN GOGH MUSEUM

200 YARDS
200 METERS

DCH

Ⓜ METRO   Ⓑ OPSTAPPER BUS   🅱 BOAT TOURS   ⤶ VIEW

🅣 TRAMS: #1 (To LEIDSEPLEIN), #2 + #5 (To MUSEUMPLEIN)

AMSTERDAM

King Willem-Alexander's official residences, with a single impressive floor open to the public. Visitors can gawk at a grand hall and stroll about 20 rooms branching off from it, all of them lavishly decorated with chandeliers, paintings, statues, and furniture that reflect Amsterdam's former status as the center of global trade.

Cost and Hours: €7.50, includes audioguide, daily 11:00-17:00 but often closed for official business, tel. 020/620-4060, www.paleisamsterdam.nl.

New Church (Nieuwe Kerk)

Barely newer than the "Old" Church (located in the Red Light District), this 15th-century sanctuary has an intentionally dull interior, after the decoration was removed by 16th-century iconoclastic Protestants seeking to unclutter their communion with God. This is where many Dutch royal weddings and all coronations take place. A steep entrance fee is charged for admission to the church's popular temporary exhibits, but you can view the church itself for free from the landing above the shop (enter to left of main door and go up the stairs in the gift shop).

Cost and Hours: Free to view from gift-shop balcony, special exhibits-€8-15, audioguide-€3, daily 10:00-17:00, on Dam Square, tel. 020/353-8168, www.nieuwekerk.nl.

▲Begijnhof

Stepping into this tiny, idyllic courtyard in the city center, you escape into the charm of old Amsterdam. (Please be considerate of the people who live around the courtyard, and don't photograph the residents or their homes.) Notice house #34, a 500-year-old wooden structure (rare, since repeated fires taught city fathers a trick called brick). Peek into the hidden Catholic church, dating from the time when post-Reformation Dutch Catholics couldn't worship in public. It's opposite the English Reformed church, where the Pilgrims worshipped while waiting for their voyage to the New World—marked by a plaque near the door.

Cost and Hours: Free and always open (though the churches have sporadic hours), on Begijnensteeg lane, just off Kalverstraat between #130 and #132, pick up flier at office near entrance, www.ercadam.nl.

▲▲Amsterdam Museum

Housed in a 500-year-old former orphanage, this creative museum tries hard to make the city's history engaging and fun (almost too hard—it recently dropped "history" from its name for fear of putting people off). But the story of Amsterdam is indeed engaging and fun, and this is the only museum in town designed to tell it. Your visit starts with a section called "DNA—City on Pilings to City of Freedom," which gives a quick overview. Then, with plenty of interactivity and fancy museum tricks, you'll follow the city's growth from fishing village to world trade center to hippie haven.

On the way you'll enjoy Rembrandt paintings, good English descriptions, and a particularly interesting section on challenges of the 20th and 21st centuries (life during World War I, the gay scene in the 1920s, squatter riots, drug policy, immigration issues, prostitution, and so on). The museum's free pedestrian corridor—lined with old-time group portraits—is a powerful teaser.

Cost and Hours: €10, good audioguide-€4.50, Mon-Fri 10:00-17:00, Sat-Sun 11:00-17:00, pleasant restaurant, next to Begijnhof at Kalverstraat 92, tel. 020/523-1822, www.ahm.nl. This museum is a fine place to buy the Museumkaart, which you can then use to skip long lines at various museums (for details, see page 1174).

Red Light District
▲▲Amstelkring Museum
(Our Lord in the Attic/Museum Ons' Lieve Heer op Solder)

Although Amsterdam has long been known for its tolerant attitudes, 16th-century politics forced Dutch Catholics to worship discreetly. At this museum near Central Station, you'll find a fascinating, hidden Catholic church filling the attic of three 17th-century merchants' houses.

For two centuries (1578-1795), Catholicism in Amsterdam was illegal but tolerated (like pot in the 1970s). When hardline Protestants took power in 1578, Catholic churches were vandalized and shut down, priests and monks rounded up and kicked out of town, and Catholic kids razzed on their way to school. The city's Catholics were forbidden to worship openly, so they gathered secretly to say Mass in homes and offices. In 1663, a wealthy merchant built Our Lord in the Attic (Museum Ons' Lieve Heer op Solder), one of a handful of places in Amsterdam that served as a secret parish church until Catholics were once again allowed to worship in public.

This unique church—embedded within a townhouse in the middle of the Red Light District—comes with a little bonus: a rare glimpse inside a historic Amsterdam home straight out of a Vermeer painting. Don't miss the silver collection and other exhibits of daily life from 300 years ago.

Cost and Hours: €8, includes audioguide, Mon-Sat 10:00-17:00, Sun and holidays 13:00-17:00, no photos, Oudezijds Voorburgwal 40, tel. 020/624-6604, www.opsolder.nl.

▲▲Red Light District Walk

Europe's most popular ladies of the night tease and tempt here, as they have for centuries, in several hundred display-case windows around Oudezijds Achterburgwal and Oudezijds Voorburgwal, surrounding the Old Church (Oude Kerk, described later). Drunks and druggies make the streets uncomfortable late at night after the

AMSTERDAM

gawking tour groups leave (about 22:30), but it's a fascinating walk earlier in the evening.

The neighborhood, one of Amsterdam's oldest, has hosted prostitutes since 1200. Prostitution is entirely legal here, and the prostitutes are generally entrepreneurs, renting space and running their own businesses, as well as filling out tax returns and even paying union dues. Popular prostitutes net about €500 a day (for what's called "S&F" in its abbreviated, printable form, charging €30-50 per customer).

Sex Museums

Amsterdam has two sex museums: one in the Red Light District and another one a block in front of Central Station on Damrak street. While visiting one can be called sightseeing, visiting both is harder to explain. The one on Damrak is cheaper and more interesting. Here's a comparison:

The **Erotic Museum** in the Red Light District is five floors of uninspired paintings, videos, old photos, and sculpture (€7, not covered by Museumkaart, daily 11:00-1:00 in the morning, along the canal at Oudezijds Achterburgwal 54, tel. 020/624-7303).

The **Damrak Sex Museum** tells the story of pornography from Roman times through 1960. Every sexual deviation is revealed in various displays. The museum includes early French pornographic photos; memorabilia from Europe, India, and Asia; a Marilyn Monroe tribute; and some S&M displays (€4, not covered by Museumkaart, daily 9:30-23:00, Damrak 18, a block in front of Central Station, tel. 020/622-8376).

Old Church (Oude Kerk)

This 14th-century landmark—the needle around which the Red Light District spins—has served as a reassuring welcome-home symbol to sailors, a refuge to the downtrodden, an ideological battlefield of the Counter-Reformation, and, today, a tourist sight with a dull interior.

Cost and Hours: €5, more for temporary exhibits, Mon-Sat 11:00-17:00, Sun 13:00-17:00, tel. 020/625-8284, www.oudekerk. nl. It's 167 steps to the top of the church tower (€7, April-Sept Thu-Sat 13:00-17:00, closed Sun-Wed and Oct-March).

Marijuana Sights in the Red Light District

Three related establishments cluster together along a canal in the Red Light District. The **Hash, Marijuana, and Hemp Museum,** worth ▲, is the most worthwhile of the three; it shares a ticket with the less substantial **Hemp Gallery.** Right nearby is **Cannabis College,** a free nonprofit center that's "dedicated to ending the global war against the cannabis plant through public education." For more information, see "Smoking in Amsterdam" on page 1230.

Cost and Hours: Museum and gallery—€9, daily 10:00-23:00, Oudezijds Achterburgwal 148, tel. 020/624-8926, www.

hashmuseum.com. College—free, daily 11:00-19:00, Oudezijds Achterburgwal 124, tel. 020/423-4420, www.cannabiscollege. com.

Northeast Amsterdam

Central Library (Openbare Bibliotheek Amsterdam)

This huge, striking, multistory building holds almost 1,400 seats—many with wraparound views of the city—and lots of Internet terminals, not to mention Wi-Fi (€1/30 minutes, sign up at the desk). It's a classy place to check email. The library, which opened in 2007, demonstrates the Dutch people's dedication to a freely educated populace (the right to information, they point out, is enshrined in the UN's Universal Declaration of Human Rights). Everything's relaxed and inviting, from the fun kids' zone and international magazine and newspaper section on the ground floor to the cafeteria, with its dramatic view-terrace dining on the top (La Place, €10 meals, salad bar, daily 10:00-21:00). The library is a 10-minute walk from the east end of Central Station.

Cost and Hours: Free, daily 10:00-22:00, tel. 020/523-0900, www.oba.nl.

NEMO (National Center for Science and Technology)

This kid-friendly science museum is a city landmark. Its distinctive copper-green building, jutting up from the water like a sinking ship, has prompted critics to nickname it the *Titanic*. Designed by Italian architect Renzo Piano (known for Paris' Pompidou Center and Berlin's Sony Center complex on Potsdamer Platz), the building's shape reflects its nautical surroundings as well as the curve of the underwater tunnel it straddles.

Several floors feature permanent and rotating exhibits that allow kids (and adults) to explore topics such as light, sound, and gravity, and play with bubbles, topple giant dominoes, and draw with lasers. The museum's motto: "It's forbidden NOT to touch!" Whirring, room-size pinball machines reputedly teach kids about physics. English explanations are available. Up top is a restaurant with a great city view, as well as a sloping terrace that becomes a popular "beach" in summer, complete with lounge chairs, a sandbox, and a lively bar. On the bottom floor is a cafeteria offering €5 sandwiches.

Cost and Hours: €13.50, June-Aug daily 10:00-17:00, Sept-May generally closed Mon, tel. 020/531-3233, www.e-nemo.nl. The roof terrace—open until 19:00 in the summer—is generally free.

Getting There: It's above the entrance to the IJ tunnel at Oosterdok 2. From Central Station, you can walk there in 15 minutes, or take bus #22, #42, or #43 to the Kadijksplein stop.

▲▲Netherlands Maritime Museum (Nederlands Scheepvaartmuseum)

This huge, kid-friendly collection of model ships, maps, and sea-battle paintings fills the 300-year-old Dutch Navy Arsenal (cleverly located a little ways from the city center, as this was where they stored the gunpowder). The museum's core collection, on the east side of the courtyard, includes globes, an exhibit on the city's busy shipping port, original navigational tools, displays of ship ornamentation, and a beautifully lit gallery of maritime paintings, depicting dramatic 17th-century naval battles against the British and Romantic seascapes from the 19th century. On the west side of the courtyard are exhibits on whaling, and seafaring in the Dutch Golden Age. Just outside the museum is a replica of the *Amsterdam*, an 18th-century cargo ship. Given the Dutch seafaring heritage, this is an appropriately important and impressive place.

Cost and Hours: €15 covers both museum and ship, both open daily 9:00-17:00, bus #22 or #48 from Central Station to Kattenburgerplein 1, tel. 020/523-2222, www.scheepvaartmuseum.nl.

▲EYE Film Institute Netherlands

The newest and most striking feature of the Amsterdam skyline is EYE, a film museum and cinema housed in an übersleek modern building immediately across the water from Central Station. Heralding the coming gentrification of the north side of the IJ, EYE (a play on "IJ") is a complex of museum spaces and four theaters playing mostly art films (shown in their original language, with selections organized around various themes). Its many other offerings include a monthly program of silent films with live musical accompaniment, special exhibits on film-related themes, a free permanent exhibit in the basement, a shop, and a trendy terrace café with great waterside seating. Helpful attendants at the reception desk can get you oriented.

Cost and Hours: General entry is free, films cost €10, and exhibits cost around €10 (no cash accepted, but standard US credit cards OK), exhibits open 11:00-18:00, cinemas open daily at 10:00 until last screening (ticket office usually closes at 22:00 or 23:00), tel. 020/589-1400, eyefilm.nl.

Getting There: From the docks behind Central Station, catch the free ferry (labeled *Buiksloterweg*) across the river and walk left to IJpromenade 1.

Southeast Amsterdam

To reach the following sights from the train station, take tram #9 or #14. All of these sights (except the Tropical Museum) are close to one another and can easily be connected into an interesting walk—or, better yet, a bike ride. Several of the sights in southeast

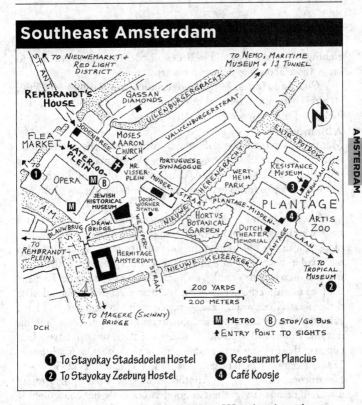

Southeast Amsterdam

Amsterdam cluster near the large square, Waterlooplein, dominated by the modern opera house.

Waterlooplein Flea Market

For more than a hundred years, the Jewish Quarter flea market has raged daily except Sunday (at the Waterlooplein metro station, behind Rembrandt's House). The long, narrow park is filled with stalls selling cheap clothes, hippie stuff, old records, tourist knick-knacks, and garage-sale junk.

▲Rembrandt's House (Museum Het Rembrandthuis)

A middle-aged Rembrandt lived here from 1639 to 1658 after his wife's death, as his popularity and wealth dwindled down to obscurity and bankruptcy. As you enter, ask when the next etching demonstration is scheduled and pick up the excellent audioguide.

Tour the place this way: Explore Rembrandt's reconstructed house (filled with exactly what his bankruptcy inventory of 1656 said he owned); imagine him at work in his reconstructed studio; marvel at his personal collection of exotic objects, many of which he included in paintings; attend the etching demonstration and ask the printer to explain the etching process (drawing in soft wax on a metal plate that's then dipped in acid, inked up, and printed);

and then, for the finale, enjoy several rooms of original Rembrandt etchings. You're not likely to see a single painting, but the master's etchings are marvelous and well-described. I came away wanting to know more about the man and his art.

Cost and Hours: €10, includes audioguide, daily 10:00-17:00, etching demonstrations almost hourly, Jodenbreestraat 4, tel. 020/520-0400, www.rembrandthuis.nl.

▲Diamonds

Many shops in this "city of diamonds" offer tours. These tours come with two parts: a chance to see experts behind magnifying glasses polishing the facets of precious diamonds, followed by a visit to an intimate sales room to see (and perhaps buy) a mighty shiny yet very tiny souvenir.

The handy and professional **Gassan Diamonds** facility fills a huge warehouse one block from Rembrandt's House. A visit here plops you in the big-tour-group fray (notice how each tour group has a color-coded sticker so they know which guide gets the commission on what they buy). You'll get a sticker, join a free 15-minute tour to see a polisher at work, and hear a general explanation of the process. Then you'll have an opportunity to sit down and have color and clarity described and illustrated with diamonds ranging in value from $100 to $30,000. Before or after, you can have a free cup of coffee in the waiting room across the parking lot (daily 9:00-17:00, Nieuwe Uilenburgerstraat 173, tel. 020/622-5333, www.gassan.com, handy WC). Another company, **Coster,** also offers diamond demos. They're not as good as Gassan's, but convenient if you're near the Rijksmuseum (described on page 1190).

▲Willet-Holthuysen Museum
(a.k.a. Herengracht Canal Mansion)

This 1687 townhouse is a must for devotees of Hummel-topped sugar bowls and Louis XVI-style wainscoting. For others, it's a pleasant look inside a typical (rich) home with much of the original furniture and decor. Forget the history and just browse through a dozen rooms of beautiful saccharine objects from the 19th century.

Cost and Hours: €8, audioguide-€3, Mon-Fri 10:00-17:00, Sat-Sun 11:00-17:00; take tram #4, #9, or #14 to Rembrandt-plein—it's a 2-minute walk southeast to Herengracht 605, tel. 020/523-1822, www.willetholthuysen.nl. The museum also hands out a free brochure that covers the house's history.

Tassen Museum (Hendrikje Museum of Bags and Purses)

This hardworking little museum fills an elegant 1664 canal house with 500 years of bag and purse history—from before the invention of pockets through the 20th century. The collection, with lots of artifacts, is well-described in English and gives a fascinating insight into fashion through the ages that fans of handbags will love, and their partners might even enjoy. The creative and surreal bag styles of the 1920s and 1930s are particularly interesting.

Cost and Hours: €8.50, daily 10:00-17:00, three floors—one houses temporary exhibits and two hold the permanent collection, start on top floor, behind Rembrandtplein at Herengracht 573, tel. 020/524-6452, www.tassenmuseum.nl.

▲▲Hermitage Amsterdam

The famous Hermitage Museum in St. Petersburg, Russia, loans art to Amsterdam for a series of rotating, and often exquisitely beautiful, special exhibits in the Amstelhof, a 17th-century former nursing home that takes up a whole city block along the Amstel River.

Why is there Russian-owned art in Amsterdam? The Hermitage collection in St. Petersburg is so vast that they can only show about 5 percent of it at any one time. Therefore, the Hermitage is establishing satellite collections around the world. The one here in Amsterdam is the biggest, filling the large Amstelhof. By law, the great Russian collection can only be out of the country for six months at a time, so the collection is always changing (check the museum's website to see what's on during your visit). Curators in Amsterdam make a point to display art that complements—rather than just repeats—what the city's other museums show so well. The one small permanent "History Hermitage" exhibit explains the historic connection between the Dutch (Orange) and Russian (Romanov) royal families.

Cost and Hours: Generally €15, but price varies with exhibit; audioguide-€4, daily 10:00-17:00; come later in the day to avoid crowds, mandatory free bag check, café, Nieuwe Herengracht 14, tram #9 from the train station, recorded info tel. 020/530-7488, www.hermitage.nl.

De Hortus Botanical Garden

This is a unique oasis of tranquility within the city (no mobile phones are allowed, because "our collection of plants is a precious community—treat it with respect"). One of the oldest botanical gardens in the world, it dates from 1638, when medicinal herbs were grown here. Today, among its 6,000 different kinds of plants—most of which were collected by the Dutch East India Company in the 17th and 18th centuries—you'll find medicinal herbs, cacti, several greenhouses (one with a fluttery butterfly house—a hit with kids), and a tropical palm house. Much of it is described in English: "A Dutch merchant snuck a coffee plant out of Ethiopia, which ended up in this garden in 1706. This first coffee plant in Europe was the literal granddaddy of the coffee cultures of Brazil—long the world's biggest coffee producer."

Cost and Hours: €7.50, not covered by Museumkaart, daily

10:00-17:00, Plantage Middenlaan 2A, tel. 020/625-9021, www. dehortus.nl. The inviting Orangery Café serves tapas.

▲Jewish Historical Museum (Joods Historisch Museum)

This interesting museum tells the story of the Netherlands' Jews through three centuries, serving as a good introduction to Judaism and Jewish customs and religious traditions.   Originally opened in 1932, the museum was forced to close during the Nazi years. Recent renovations have brought it into the 21st century. Its current location comprises four historic former synagogues that have been joined by steel and glass to make one modern complex.

The centerpiece of the museum is the Great Synagogue. First see its ground floor (for an overview of Jewish culture), then go upstairs to the women's gallery (for history from 1600 to 1900). From there, follow the sky bridge to the New Synagogue (for the 20th century story), and poke into the Aanbouw Annex (contemporary exhibits). Then, with the same ticket, finish your visit by crossing the street to the Portuguese Synagogue, with its treasury.

Cost and Hours: €12, includes Portuguese Synagogue, more for special exhibits, ticket also covers Dutch Theater—see next listing; museum daily 11:00-17:00, Portuguese Synagogue daily 10:00-16:00, last entry 30 minutes before closing; free audioguide, displays all have English explanations, children's museum, Jonas Daniel Meijerplein 2, tel. 020/531-0310, www.jhm.nl. The museum has a modern, minimalist, kosher café.

▲Dutch Theater (Hollandsche Schouwburg)

Once a lively theater in the Jewish neighborhood, and today a moving memorial, this building was used as an assembly hall for local Jews destined for Nazi concentration camps. On the wall, 6,700 family names pay tribute to the 104,000 Jews deported and killed by the Nazis. Some 70,000 victims spent time here, awaiting transfer to concentration camps. Upstairs is a small history exhibit with a model of the ghetto, plus photos and memorabilia (such as shoes and letters) of some victims, putting a human face on the staggering numbers. Television monitors show actual footage of the Nazis rounding up Amsterdam's Jews. You can also see a few costumes from the days when the building was a theater. While the exhibit is small, it offers plenty to think about. Back in the ground-floor courtyard, notice the hopeful messages that visiting school groups attach to the wooden tulips.

Cost and Hours: Covered by €12 Jewish Historical Museum ticket, daily 11:00-16:00, Plantage Middenlaan 24, tel. 020/531-0340, www.hollandscheschouwburg.nl.

▲▲Dutch Resistance Museum (Verzetsmuseum)

This is an impressive look at how the Dutch resisted (or collaborated with) their Nazi occupiers from 1940 to 1945. You'll see propaganda movie clips, study forged ID cards under a magnifying glass, and read about ingenious and courageous efforts—big and small—to hide local Jews from the Germans and undermine the Nazi regime.

The museum does a good job of presenting the Dutch people's struggle with a timeless moral dilemma: Is it better to collaborate with a wicked system to effect small-scale change—or to resist outright, even if your efforts are doomed to fail? You'll learn why some parts of Dutch society opted for the former, and others for the latter. While proudly describing acts of extraordinary courage, it doesn't shy away from the less heroic side of the story (for example, the fact that most of the population, though troubled by the persecution of their Jewish countrymen, only became actively anti-Nazi after gentile Dutch men were deported to forced-labor camps). The exhibit is interspersed with riveting first-person accounts of what it was like to go underground, strike, starve, or return from the camps—with every tragic detail translated into English.

Cost and Hours: €8 includes audioguide; Tue-Fri 10:00-17:00, Sat-Mon 11:00-17:00, English descriptions, no flash photos, mandatory and free bag check, tram #9 from station or #14 from Dam Square, Plantage Kerklaan 61. Tel. 020/620-2535, www.verzetsmuseum.org.

Nearby: Two recommended eateries—Restaurant Plancius and Café Koosje—are on the same block as the museum (see listings on page 1229), and Amsterdam's famous zoo is just across the street.

▲Tropical Museum (Tropenmuseum)

As close to the Third World as you'll get without lots of vaccinations, this imaginative museum offers wonderful re-creations of tropical life and explanations of Third World problems (largely created by Dutch colonialism and the slave trade). Ride the elevator to the top floor, and circle your way down through this immense collection, opened in 1926 to give the Dutch people a peek at their vast colonial holdings. Don't miss the display case where you can see and hear the world's most exotic musical instruments. The Ekeko cafeteria serves tropical food.

Cost and Hours: €10, Tue-Sun 10:00-17:00, closed Mon, tram #9 to Linnaeusstraat 2, tel. 020/568-8200, www.tropenmuseum.nl.

Entertainment in Amsterdam

Many Amsterdam hotels serve breakfast until 11:00 because so many people—visitors and locals—live for nighttime in this city.

On summer evenings, people flock to the main squares for drinks at outdoor tables. Leidseplein is the liveliest square, surrounded by theaters, restaurants, and nightclubs. The slightly qui-

AMSTERDAM

eter Rembrandtplein (with adjoining Thorbeckeplein and nearby Reguliersdwarsstraat) is the center of gay clubs and nightlife. Spui features a full city block of bars. And Nieuwmarkt, on the east edge of the Red Light District, is a bit rough, but is probably the least touristy.

The Red Light District (particularly Oudezijds Achterburgwal) is less sleazy in the early evening, and almost carnival-like as the neon lights come on and the streets fill with tour groups. But it starts to feel scuzzy after about 22:30.

Information

Newsstands sell *Time Out Amsterdam* and Dutch newspapers (Thu editions generally list events). The free, irreverent *Boom!* has the basics on the youth and nightlife scene, and is packed with practical tips and countercultural insights (includes €5 discount on Boom Chicago comedy theater act described on next page; available at TIs and many bars). *Uitkrant* is in Dutch, but it's just a calendar of events, and anyone can figure out the name of the event and its date, time, and location (available at TIs, bars, and bookstores).

Box Office: The **AUB/Last Minute Ticket Shop** at Stadsschouwburg Theater is the best one-stop-shopping box office for theater, classical music, and major rock shows. The Last Minute window sells half-price, same-day tickets to certain shows; half-price sales start at noon (Mon-Fri 10:00-19:00, Sat 10:00-18:00, Sun 12:00-18:00, Leidseplein 26, tel. 0900-0191—€0.40/minute, www.lastminuteticketshop.nl).

Music

You'll find classical music at the **Concertgebouw** (free 12:30 lunch concerts on Wed; arrive at 12:00 for best first-come, first-serve seating; at far south end of Museumplein, tel. 0900-671-8345, www.concertgebouw.nl). For chamber music and contemporary works, visit the **Muziekgebouw aan 't IJ,** a mod concert hall on the waterfront, near the train station (Piet Heinkade 1, tel. 020/788-2000, www.muziekgebouw.nl). For opera and dance, try the **opera house** in the Stopera building (Waterlooplein 22, tel. 020/625-5455). In the summer, Vondelpark hosts open-air concerts.

Three of Amsterdam's historic churches have extensive music programs. In summer, the **Westerkerk** has free lunchtime concerts on Fridays at 13:00 (April-Oct) plus an annual Bach organ concert cycle in August (Prinsengracht 281, tel. 020/624-7766, www.westerkerk.nl). The **New Church** offers periodic organ concerts and a religious music festival in June (included in €8 church entry, covered by Museumkaart, Dam Square, tel. 020/638-6909, www.nieuwekerk.nl). The Red Light District's **Old Church** (Oude Kerk) has carillon concerts Tuesday at 14:00 and Saturday at 16:00, and holds an organ music competition in early September (Oudekerk-splein, tel. 020/625-8284, www.oudekerk.nl).

Two rock music (and hip-hop) clubs near Leidseplein are **Melkweg** (Lijnbaansgracht 234a, tel. 020/531-8181, www.melk-weg.nl) and **Paradiso** (Weteringschans 6, tel. 020/626-4521, www.paradiso.nl). They present big-name acts that you might recognize…if you're younger than I am.

Jazz has a long tradition at the **Bimhuis** nightclub, now housed in a black box jutting out from the Muziekgebouw performance hall, right on the waterfront. Its great bar has citywide views, and is open to the public after concerts (Piet Heinkade 3, tel. 020/788-2188, www.bimhuis.nl).

The nearby town of Haarlem offers free pipe-organ concerts on Tuesday evenings in summer at its 15th-century church, the **Grote Kerk** (at 20:15 mid-May-mid-Oct, additional concerts Thu at 16:00 July-Aug; see next chapter).

Comedy

Boom Chicago, an R-rated comedy improv act, was started 15 years ago by a group of Americans on a graduation tour. They have been entertaining tourists and locals ever since. The two-hour English-only show is a series of rude, clever, and high-energy improvisational skits offering a raucous look at Dutch culture and local tourism (€22 weekdays, generally €26 Fri-Sat; Sun-Fri shows at 20:15, Sat at 22:00; confirm times when you buy your ticket, ticket office open daily from 13:00 until 15 minutes after curtain time, no Mon shows Jan-March, tel. 020/423-0101, www.boomchicago.nl). It all happens at the 300-seat Leidseplein Theater at Leidseplein 12; enter through the skinny Boom Bar (optional meal and drink service).

They do *Can't Dutch This* (a collection of their greatest hits over the years) as well as new shows for locals and return customers. When sales are slow, ticket-sellers on the street out front offer steeply discounted tickets, with a drink included. Drop by that afternoon and see what's up.

Theater

Amsterdam is one of the world centers for experimental live theater (much of it in English). Many theaters cluster around the street called the Nes, which stretches south from Dam Square.

Movies

In the Netherlands, most movies are subtitled, rather than dubbed, so English-only speakers have plenty of cinematic options. It's not unusual for movies at many cinemas to be sold out—consider buying tickets during the day. Catch modern movies in the 1920s setting of the classic **Tuschinski Theater** (between Muntplein and Rembrandtplein, described on page 1191).

The new and splashy **EYE Film Institute Netherlands,** across the water from Central Station, is a very memorable place to see a movie (described on page 1202).

Museums

Several museums stay open late. The **Anne Frank House** always stays open until at least 19:00 year-round; it's open daily until 22:00 in July and August and closes late on Saturday year-round (22:00 peak-season, 21:00 off-season). The **Hermitage Amsterdam** stays open until 20:00 on Wednesday, and the **Stedelijk Museum's** collection of modern art is on view until 22:00 on Thursday. The **Van Gogh Museum** is open on Friday until 22:00 and sometimes has music and a wine bar in the lobby.

The **Hash, Marijuana, and Hemp Museum** is open daily until 23:00. And the **sex museums** always stay open late (Damrak Sex Museum until 23:00, Erotic Museum until 1:00 in the morning).

Skating After Dark

Amsterdammers get their skating fix every Friday night in summer and early fall in Vondelpark. Huge groups don inline skates and meet at the round bench near the Vondel Pavilion (around 20:15, www.fridaynightskate.com). Anyone can join in. You can rent skates at the shop at the far end of the park (Vondeltuin Rental, daily 11:00-20:00 in good weather; first hour-€5, then €2.50/hour, €20 deposit and ID required; price includes helmet, wrist guards, and knee guards; at southeastern edge of park, mobile 0627-565-576, www.vondeltuin.nl).

Sleeping in Amsterdam

Greeting a new day by descending steep stairs and stepping into a leafy canalside scene—graceful bridges, historic gables, and bikes clattering on cobbles—is a fun part of experiencing Amsterdam. But Amsterdam is a tough city for budget accommodations, and any hotel room under €140 (or B&B room under €100) will have rough edges. Still, you can sleep well and safely in a great location for €100 per double.

I've grouped my hotel listings into three neighborhoods, each of which has its own character.

West Amsterdam (which includes the Jordaan) has Old World ambience, with quiet canals, old gabled buildings, and candle-lit restaurants. It's also just minutes on foot to Dam Square. Many of

Sleep Code

(€1 = about $1.30, country code: 31, area code: 020)
S = Single, **D** = Double/Twin, **T** = Triple, **Q** = Quad, **b** = bathroom, **s** = shower only. Nearly everyone speaks English. Credit cards are accepted, and prices include breakfast and tax unless otherwise noted.

To help you easily sort through these listings, I've divided the accommodations into three categories, based on the price for a standard double room with bath:

$$$ **Higher Priced**—Most rooms €140 or more.
$$ **Moderately Priced**—Most rooms between €80-140.
$ **Lower Priced**—Most rooms €80 or less.

Prices can change without notice and most do not include the city's 6 percent room tax; verify the hotel's current rates online or by email.

my hotels are charming, friendly gabled mansions. The downside here is that you'll pay more and likely have lots of stairs to climb.

Southwest Amsterdam has two main areas for accommodations: near Leidseplein (more central) and near Vondelpark (farther away). The streets near the bustling Leidseplein have restaurants, tourist buzz, nightlife, canalside charm, B&B coziness, and walkable (or easy tram) access to the center of town. Farther afield is the quieter semi-suburban neighborhood around Vondelpark and Museumplein, close to the Rijks and Van Gogh museums. You'll find good hotel values and ready access to Vondelpark and the art museums, but it's a half-hour walk (or 10-minute tram ride) to Dam Square.

Staying in **Central Amsterdam** is ideal for people who like shopping, tourist sights, and easy access to public transportation (including Central Station). On the downside, the area has traffic noise, concrete, and urban grittiness, and the hotels can lack character.

Some national holidays merit your making reservations far in advance. Amsterdam is jammed during tulip season (late March-mid-May), conventions, festivals, and on summer weekends. During peak season, some hoteliers won't take weekend bookings for those staying fewer than two or three nights.

Around just about every corner in downtown Amsterdam, you'll see construction: cranes for big transportation projects and small crews of bricklayers repairing the wobbly, cobbled streets that line the canals. Canalside rooms can come with great views—and early-morning construction-crew noise. If you're a light sleeper, ask the hotelier for a quiet room in the back. Smoking is illegal in hotel rooms throughout the Netherlands. Parking in Amsterdam is even worse than driving—if you must park a car, ask your hotelier for advice.

Canal houses were built tight. They have steep stairs with narrow treads; almost none have elevators. If steep stairs are potentially problematic, book a hotel with an elevator.

If you'd rather trade big-city action for small-town coziness, consider sleeping in Haarlem, 20 minutes away by train (see next chapter).

West Amsterdam
Stately Canalside Hotels
These hotels, a half-mile apart, both face historic canals. They come with lovely lobbies (some more ornate than others) and rooms that can feel like they're from another century. This area oozes elegance and class, and it is fairly quiet at night.

$$$ **The Toren** is a chandeliered, historic mansion with a pleasant, canalside setting and a peaceful garden out back for guests. Run by Eric and Petra Toren, this smartly renovated, super-romantic hotel is classy yet friendly, with 38 rooms in a great location on a quiet street two blocks northeast of the Anne Frank House. The capable staff is a great source of local advice. The gilt-frame, velvet-curtained rooms are an opulent splurge (tiny Sb-€115, Db-€200, deluxe Db-€250, third person-€40, prices bump way up during conferences and decrease in winter, rates do not include 6 percent tax, breakfast buffet-€14, air-con, elevator, Internet access and Wi-Fi, Keizersgracht 164, tel. 020/622-6033, fax 020/626-9705, www.thetoren.nl, info@thetoren.nl). To get the best prices, check their website for their "daily rate," book direct, and in the "remarks" field, ask for the 10 percent Rick Steves cash discount.

$$$ **Hotel Ambassade,** lacing together 59 rooms in a maze of connected houses, is elegant and fresh, sitting aristocratically on Herengracht. The staff is top-notch, and the public areas (including a library and a breakfast room) are palatial, with antique furnishings and modern art (Sb-€210, Db-€265, more expensive deluxe canal-view doubles and suites, Tb-€245-295, extra bed-€40, ask for Rick Steves discount when booking, see website for specials, rates do not include 6 percent tax, breakfast-€18, air-con, elevator, free Internet access and Wi-Fi, Herengracht 341, for location see map on page 1214, tel. 020/555-0222, www.ambassade-hotel.nl, info@ambassade-hotel.nl, Roos—pronounced "Rose").

Simpler Canalside Hotels
These places have basic rooms—some downright spare, none

plush—and most do without an elevator or other extras. Each of them, however, offers a decent night's sleep in a lovely area of town.

$$$ Wiechmann Hotel's 37 pricey rooms are sparsely furnished with just the dark-wood essentials, but they're spacious, and the *gezellig* public areas are chock-full of Old World charm (Sb-€70-110, Db-€150-170, Tb-€210, Qb-€225, Db suite-€265, check online for best price, 15 percent cheaper for 3 or more nights if booking through their website, some canal views, back rooms are quiet, free Internet access and Wi-Fi, nicely located at Prinsengracht 328-332, tel. 020/626-3321, www.hotelwiechmann.nl, info@hotelwiechmann.nl, John and Taz the welcome dog).

$$ Hotel Brouwer is a woody and homey old-time place. It's situated in a tranquil yet central location on the Singel canal and rents eight rooms with canal views, old furniture, and soulful throw rugs. It's so popular that it's often booked four or five months in advance—reserve as soon as possible (Sb-€60, Db-€95, Tb-€120, rates don't include 6 percent tax, cash only, breakfast-€7, small elevator, free Internet access and Wi-Fi, located between Central Station and Dam Square, near Lijnbaanssteeg at Singel 83, tel. 020/624-6358, www.hotelbrouwer.nl, akita@hotelbrouwer.nl).

$$ Hotel Hoksbergen is a welcoming, well-run canalside place in a peaceful location where helpful, hands-on owners Tony and Bert rent 14 rooms with newly remodeled bathrooms (Db-€98, Tb-€143, five Qb apartments-€165-198, fans, free Wi-Fi, Singel 301, tel. 020/626-6043, www.hotelhoksbergen.com, info@hotelhoksbergen.nl).

$$ Hotel Hegra is cozy, with nine rooms filling a 17th-century merchant's house overlooking the canal (Db-€80-€160, Tb-€119-149, breakfast-€6.50, some rooms with canal view, pay Internet access, free Wi-Fi, bike and boat rentals, just north of Wolvenstraat at Herengracht 269, tel. 020/623-7877, www.hotelhegra.nl, info@hotelhegra.nl, Robert).

$$ Hotel Chic & Basic Amsterdam has a boutique-hotel feel, even though it's part of a Spanish chain. With its mod utilitarian design and younger clientele, it provides a break from all the lace curtains. Located in a quiet neighborhood near Central Station, it offers 25 minimalist rooms and public areas that are bathed in space-age white. Rooms with canal views are pricier and breezier (Sb-€95-130, Db-€120-155, €20 more on holiday weekends, less in winter, cheaper prices are for less sleek "vintage" rooms without canal views, free coffee, continental breakfast, fans on request, tangled floor plan connecting three canalside buildings, free Internet access and Wi-Fi, Herengracht 13, tel. 020/522-2345, www.chicandbasic.com, amsterdam@chicandbasic.com, manager Bernardo Campo).

Hotels & Restaurants in West Amsterdam

AMSTERDAM

Anne Frank House
Homomon.
Nine Little Streets Shops
Westerkerk
To

T TRAM #13, 14 & 17 STOP

DCH

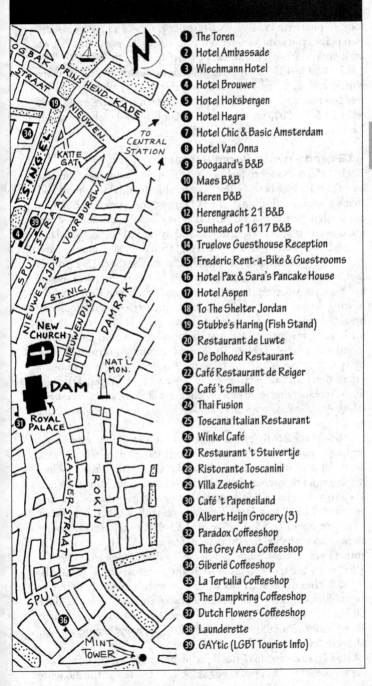

1. The Toren
2. Hotel Ambassade
3. Wiechmann Hotel
4. Hotel Brouwer
5. Hotel Hoksbergen
6. Hotel Hegra
7. Hotel Chic & Basic Amsterdam
8. Hotel Van Onna
9. Boogaard's B&B
10. Maes B&B
11. Heren B&B
12. Herengracht 21 B&B
13. Sunhead of 1617 B&B
14. Truelove Guesthouse Reception
15. Frederic Rent-a-Bike & Guestrooms
16. Hotel Pax & Sara's Pancake House
17. Hotel Aspen
18. To The Shelter Jordan
19. Stubbe's Haring (Fish Stand)
20. Restaurant de Luwte
21. De Bolhoed Restaurant
22. Café Restaurant de Reiger
23. Café 't Smalle
24. Thai Fusion
25. Toscana Italian Restaurant
26. Winkel Café
27. Restaurant 't Stuivertje
28. Ristorante Toscanini
29. Villa Zeesicht
30. Café 't Papeneiland
31. Albert Heijn Grocery (3)
32. Paradox Coffeeshop
33. The Grey Area Coffeeshop
34. Siberië Coffeeshop
35. La Tertulia Coffeeshop
36. The Dampkring Coffeeshop
37. Dutch Flowers Coffeeshop
38. Launderette
39. GAYtic (LGBT Tourist Info)

$$ Hotel Van Onna has 41 simple, industrial-strength rooms, some with canal views. The price is right, and the leafy location makes you want to crack out your easel. The popular top-floor attic rooms are cozy hideaways (Sb-€45-65, Db-€80-110, Tb-€125-145, Qb-€170-200, price depends on season, 5 percent more with credit card, cot-like beds are sufficient, no phones or TVs, free Internet access and Wi-Fi, in the Jordaan at Bloemgracht 104, tel. 020/626-5801, www.hotelvanonna.nl, info@hotelvanonna.nl, Leon and Tsibo).

B&Bs and Private-Room Rentals

B&Bs offer a chance to feel like a local during your visit. The first and third listings here are in a peaceful residential neighborhood that's a short walk from Central Station; the second and fourth are in slightly busier areas. The last two listings are services that manage and rent many apartments and rooms in West Amsterdam.

$$ Boogaard's B&B is a delightful pad on a narrow lane right out of Mister Rogers' neighborhood. The B&B, which has four comfortable rooms and an inviting public living room, is run by Peter, an American expat opera singer. Peter, who clearly enjoys hosting Americans in his home, serves his fresh-baked goodies at breakfast and treats you royally. As his place is popular with my readers, it's smart to book as soon as possible—even as much as six months in advance (Db-€130, 2-night minimum; furnished family apartment with kitchen-€250 for 4 people, 3-night minimum; prices don't include 6 percent tax, air-con, free Wi-Fi, DVD library, free laundry, loaner cell phones and laptops, Langestraat 34, tel. 064/358-6835, www.boogaardsbnb.com, info@boogaardsbnb.com).

$$ Maes B&B (pronounced "mahss") is a dynamite value, renting tastefully cozy rooms for much less than you'd pay at a hotel. Instead of a reception desk, you get antique-filled rooms, the use of a full kitchen, and a warm welcome from Ken and Vlad. They also run **Heren B&B**, a crisply modern space around the corner from Maes, with large rooms—one with a canal view (both locations: Sb-€105, Db-€125, extra bed-€30, suites and full apartments also available, free Internet access and Wi-Fi, if street noise bothers you ask for room in back, Herenstraat 26, tel. 020/427-5165, www.bedandbreakfastamsterdam.com, maesinfo@xs4all.nl).

$$ Herengracht 21 B&B has two stylish, intimate rooms in a canal house filled with art and run by lovely Loes Olden (2-floor Db-€125, canal-view Db-€135, air-con, free Wi-Fi, Herengracht 21, tel. 020/625-6305, mobile 06-2812-0962, www.herengracht21.nl, loes@herengracht21.nl).

$$ Sunhead of 1617 B&B justifiably calls itself a "bed and delicious breakfast," but you're just as likely to remember the thoughtfully decorated, flower-filled rooms and the personality of owner Carlos (Db-€90-150, Db apartment-€130-150, more on holidays, free Wi-Fi, mobile 06-2865-3572, Herengracht 152, www.sunhead.com, carlos@sunhead.com).

$$ With **Truelove Guesthouse,** a room-rental service, you'll feel like you're staying at your Dutch friends' house while they're out of town. Sean and Paul—whose tiny antique store on Prinsenstraat doubles as the reception desk for their rental service—have 15 rooms and apartments in houses sprinkled throughout the northern end of the Jordaan neighborhood. The apartments are stylish and come with kitchens and pull-out beds (Db-€90-140, Db apartment-€130-150, prices soft in off-season and midweek, 10 percent more with credit card, 2-night minimum on weekends, no breakfast, pick up keys in store at Prinsenstraat 4, store tel. 020/320-2500, mobile 06-2480-5672, fax 084-711-4950, www.cosyandwarm-amsterdam.com, trueloveantiek@zonnet.nl).

$ Frederic Rent-a-Bike & Guestrooms, with a bike-rental shop as the reception, is a collection of private rooms on a gorgeous canal just outside the Jordaan, a five-minute walk from Central Station. Frederic has amassed about 100 beds, ranging from dumpy €75 doubles behind the bike-rental shop, to spacious and elegant apartments (from €46/person; these places require a 2-night minimum, occasionally more). Some places are ideal for families and groups of up to eight. He also rents houseboat apartments. All are displayed on his website (phone bookings preferred, book with credit card but pay with cash, no breakfast, Brouwersgracht 78, tel. 020/624-5509, www.frederic.nl, info@frederic.nl, Frederic and Marjolijn). His excellent bike shop, which serves as the reception, is open daily 9:00-17:30 (€15/24 hours). My readers who rent a houseboat or apartment get a 50 percent discount on Frederic's bikes.

Southwest Amsterdam
Charming B&Bs near Leidseplein

The area around Amsterdam's rip-roaring nightlife center (Leidseplein) is colorful, comfortable, and convenient. These canalside mom-and-pop places are within a five-minute walk of rowdy Leidseplein, but generally are in quiet and typically Dutch settings. Within walking distance of the major museums, and steps off the tram line, this neighborhood offers a perfect mix of charm and location.

$$ Hotel de Leydsche Hof, a hidden gem located on a canal, doesn't charge extra for its views. Its four large rooms are a symphony in white, some overlooking a tree-filled backyard, others a canal. Frits and Loes give their big, elegant, old building a stylish air, but be prepared for lots of stairs. Breakfast is served in the grand canal-front room (Db-€120, cash only, 2-night minimum, free Internet access and Wi-Fi, Leidsegracht 14, tel. 020/638-2327, mobile 06-5125-8588, www.freewebs.com/leydschehof, loespiller@planet.nl).

$$ Wildervanck B&B, run by Helene and Sjoerd Wildervanck, offers two tasteful rooms in an elegant 17th-century canal house (big Db on first floor-€135, Db with twin beds on ground floor-€130, extra bed-€35, 2-night minimum, breakfast in their pleasant dining room, free Wi-Fi, family has three girls, just west of Leidsestraat at Keizersgracht 498, tel. 020/623-3846, www.wildervanck.com, info@wildervanck.com).

$$ Hotel Keizershof is wonderfully Dutch, with six bright, airy rooms—some with canal views—in a 17th-century canal house with a lush garden and a fine living room. A very steep spiral staircase leads to rooms named after old-time Hollywood stars. The enthusiastic hospitality of Mrs. de Vries and her daughter, Hanneke, give this place a friendly, almost small-town charm (S-€70, D-€95, Ds-€110, Db-€115, 2-night minimum, reserve with credit card but pay with cash, free Internet access and Wi-Fi; tram #16, #24, or #25 from Central Station; Keizersgracht 618, where Keizersgracht crosses Nieuwe Spiegelstraat; tel. 020/622-2855, www.hotelkeizershof.nl, info@hotelkeizershof.nl).

Near Vondelpark and Museumplein

These options cluster around Vondelpark in a safe neighborhood. Though they don't have a hint of Old Dutch or romantic canalside flavor, they're reasonable values and only a short walk from the action. Unless noted, the places below have elevators. Many are in a pleasant nook between rollicking Leidseplein and the park, and most are a 5- to 15-minute walk to the Rijks and Van Gogh museums. They are easily connected with Central Station by trams #1, #2, and/or #5.

$$$ Hotel Piet Hein offers 81 stylishly sleek yet comfortable rooms as well as a swanky lounge, good breakfast, and a pleasant garden, all on a quiet street (Sb-€100, Db-€165, extra-posh Db-€200-250, Tb-€205, extra bed-€30, specials on website, breakfast-€15, air-con in some rooms, free Internet access and Wi-Fi, Vossiusstraat 51-53, tel. 020/662-7205, www.hotelpiethein.nl, info@hotelpiethein.nl).

$$$ Hotel Fita has 15 bright rooms in a great location—100 yards from the Van Gogh Museum, an even shorter hop from the tram stop, and on a corner with no car traffic. The decor may not be the latest, but all the amenities are there—including espresso machines in every room—and the welcome is very warm (Sb-€109, two small ground-floor Db-€139, Db-€139-169 depending on size, Tb-€205, free Internet access and Wi-Fi in lobby, free laundry ser-

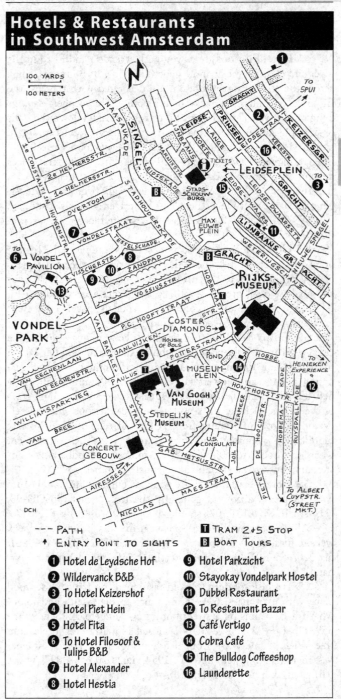

Hotels & Restaurants in Southwest Amsterdam

--- PATH
♦ ENTRY POINT TO SIGHTS

🔳 TRAM 2+5 STOP
🔳 BOAT TOURS

1 Hotel de Leydsche Hof
2 Wildervanck B&B
3 To Hotel Keizershof
4 Hotel Piet Hein
5 Hotel Fita
6 To Hotel Filosoof & Tulips B&B
7 Hotel Alexander
8 Hotel Hestia

9 Hotel Parkzicht
10 Stayokay Vondelpark Hostel
11 Dubbel Restaurant
12 To Restaurant Bazar
13 Café Vertigo
14 Cobra Café
15 The Bulldog Coffeeshop
16 Launderette

vice, Jan Luijkenstraat 37, tel. 020/679-0976, fax 020/664-3969, www.fita.nl, info@fita.nl, owner Roel de Haas).

$$ Hotel Filosoof greets you with Aristotle and Plato in the foyer and classical music in its generous lobby. Its 38 rooms, some across the street from reception, are decorated with themes; the Egyptian room has a frieze of hieroglyphics. Philosophers' sayings hang on the walls, and thoughtful travelers wander down the halls or sit in the garden, rooted in deep discussion. The rooms are small, but the hotel is endearing (Db-€110-130 weeknights, €130-150 Fri-Sat, bigger "deluxe" rooms-€20 extra, suites-€60 extra, prices depend on season and don't include 6 percent tax; breakfast-€15, free Internet access and Wi-Fi, 3-minute walk from tram line #1, get off at Jan Pieter Heijestraat, Anna van Den Vondelstraat 6, tel. 020/683-3013, fax 020/685-3750, www.hotelfilosoof.nl, reservations@hotelfilosoof.nl).

$$ Hotel Alexander is a modern, newly renovated 32-room hotel on a quiet street. Some of the rooms overlook the garden patio out back (Db-€135, prices soft in winter—call or check their website for best deal, breakfast-€10, free Internet access and Wi-Fi, tel. 020/589-4020, fax 020/589-4025, Vondelstraat 44-46, www.hotelalexander.nl, info@hotelalexander.nl).

$$ Tulips B&B, with a bunch of cozy rooms—some on a canal—is run by a friendly Englishwoman, Karen, and her Dutch husband, Paul. Rooms are clean, white, and bright, with red carpeting, plants, and flowers (D-€85, Db-€120, suite-€150, extra bed-€30, discounts for longer stays, cash only, prefer 3-night stays on weekends, includes milk-and-cereal breakfast, no shoes, no elevator but not a lot of stairs, free Wi-Fi, south end of Vondelpark at Sloterkade 65, 7-minute walk from trams #1 and #2, directions sent when you book, tel. 020/679-2753, rooms@bedandbreakfastamsterdam.net, www.bedandbreakfastamsterdam.net).

$$ Hotel Hestia, on a safe street, is efficient and family-run, with 18 clean, airy, and generally spacious rooms (Sb-€83-93, very small Db-€101-107, standard Db-€128-148, Tb-€158-176, Qb-€188-206, Quint/b-€218-236, can be less in winter—check website for best price, Roemer Visscherstraat 7, tel. 020/618-0801, fax 020/685-1382, www.hotel-hestia.nl, info@hotel-hestia.nl, Arnaud).

$$ Hotel Parkzicht, an old-fashioned, no-frills, dark-wood place with extremely steep stairs, rents 13 big, plain, and somewhat frayed rooms on a street bordering Vondelpark (S-€49, Sb-€59, Db-€79-92, Tb-€120-140, closed Nov-March, no elevator, free Wi-Fi, some noise from neighboring youth hostel, Roemer Visscherstraat 33, tel. 020/618-1954, fax 020/618-0897, www.parkzicht.nl, hotel@parkzicht.nl).

Central Amsterdam
Basic Hotels in the City Center

You won't get a warm welcome at either of the two following hotels. But if you're looking for a no-nonsense room that's convenient to plenty of tram lines, these hotels fit the bill.

$$$ Hotel Résidence Le Coin offers 42 larger-than-average rooms complete with small kitchenettes. Located near the Mint Tower, this hotel is a two-minute walk to the Flower Market and a five-minute walk to Rembrandtplein (Sb-€125, small Db-€145, bigger Db-€160, Qb-€240, extra bed-€37, breakfast-€12, pay Wi-Fi, by the University at Nieuwe Doelenstraat 5, tel. 020/524-6800, fax 020/524-6801, www.lecoin.nl, hotel@lecoin.nl).

$$$ Hotel Ibis Amsterdam Centre, located next door to the Central Station, is a modern, efficient, 363-room place. It offers a central location, comfort, and good value, without a hint of charm (Db-€140-160 Nov-Aug, Db-€200 Sept-Oct, breakfast-€16, check website for deals, book long in advance—especially for Sept-Oct, air-con, elevators, free Wi-Fi, pay Internet access; facing Central Station, go left toward the multistory bicycle garage to Stationsplein 49; tel. 020/522-2899, fax 020/522-2889, www.ibishotel.com, h1556@accor.com). When business is slow, usually in mid-summer, they occasionally rent rooms to same-day drop-ins for around €110.

Budget Hotels Between Dam Square and the Anne Frank House

Inexpensive, well-worn hotels line the convenient but noisy and unromantic main drag, Raadhuisstraat. Expect a long, steep, and depressing stairway, with noisy rooms in the front and quieter rooms in the back. Though neither of the places below serves breakfast, they're both steps from a recommended pancake house. For locations, see the map on page 1214.

$ Hotel Pax has 11 large, plain, but airy rooms with Ikea furniture—a lot like a European dorm room (S-€35-45, D-€65, Db-€85, T-€100, Tb-€120, prices drop dramatically in winter, no breakfast, five rooms share two showers and two toilets, Raadhuisstraat 37, tel. 020/624-9735, hotelpax@tiscali.nl, run by go-getters Philip and Pieter).

$ Hotel Aspen, a few doors away and a great value for a budget hotel, has eight tidy, stark, and well-maintained rooms (S-€40, tiny D-€55-65, Db-€75-80, Tb-€95, Qb-€110, prices same 365 days a year, no breakfast, free Internet access and Wi-Fi, Raadhuisstraat 31, tel. 020/626-6714, fax 020/620-0866, www.hotelaspen.nl, info@hotelaspen.nl, run by kindhearted Rudy and Esam).

Hotels & Restaurants in Central Amsterdam

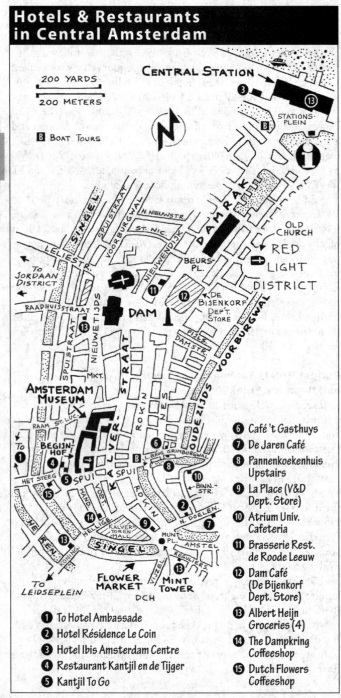

200 YARDS
200 METERS

B BOAT TOURS

CENTRAL STATION

STATIONS-PLEIN

OLD CHURCH
RED LIGHT DISTRICT

TO JORDAAN DISTRICT

SINGEL
SPUISTRAAT
VOORBURGWAL
N. NIEUWSTR.
ST. NIC.
LELIESTR.
NIEUWENDIJK
DAMRAK
RAADHUISSTRAAT
BEURS-PL.
DE BIJENKORF DEPT. STORE
DAM
VOORBURGWAL
NIEUWE ZIJDS
PIJLS.
DAM.STR.
OUDE ZIJDS
SPUI STRAAT
VER-
STRAAT
ROKIN
NES
AMSTERDAM MUSEUM
RAAM
ST. LUC.
BEGIJN-HOF
SPUI J VER-
HET STEEG
SPUI
L. BRG. GRIMBURGWAL
BINN.-STR.
N. DOELEN.
HAND.
 VOET.
HELLIGE
KALVER-TOREN MALL
N. DOELEN.
MUNT PL.
AMSTEL
SINGEL
REGULIERS
TO LEIDSEPLEIN
FLOWER MARKET
MINT TOWER
HE REN
KONING
DCH

TO LEIDSEPLEIN

AMSTERDAM

Legend

1. To Hotel Ambassade
2. Hotel Résidence Le Coin
3. Hotel Ibis Amsterdam Centre
4. Restaurant Kantjil en de Tijger
5. Kantjil To Go
6. Café 't Gasthuys
7. De Jaren Café
8. Pannenkoekenhuis Upstairs
9. La Place (V&D Dept. Store)
10. Atrium Univ. Cafeteria
11. Brasserie Rest. de Roode Leeuw
12. Dam Café (De Bijenkorf Dept. Store)
13. Albert Heijn Groceries (4)
14. The Dampkring Coffeeshop
15. Dutch Flowers Coffeeshop

Hostels

Amsterdam has a world of good, cheap hostels located throughout the city. Most are designed for the party crowd, but here are a few quieter options. They all offer dorm beds; Stayokay Vondelpark also has some basic doubles.

In the Jordaan: **$ The Shelter Jordan** is a scruffy, friendly, Christian-run, 90-bed place in a great neighborhood. Although most of Amsterdam's hostels are pretty wild, this place is drug- and alcohol-free, with boys on one floor and girls on another. These are Amsterdam's best budget beds (bunks dorms-€26-31; higher prices for 4-5-bed rooms; includes sheets and breakfast, Internet access in lobby, free Wi-Fi, near Anne Frank House at Bloemstraat 179, tel. 020/624-4717, www.shelter.nl, jordan@shelter.nl). The Shelter serves hot meals; runs a snack bar in its big, relaxing lounge; offers lockers; and leads nightly Bible studies.

In the Red Light District: **$ The Shelter City** is Shelter Jordan's sister—similar, but definitely not preaching to the local choir. And though its 180 beds are buried in the heart of the red lights, it feels very well-run and perfectly safe (same prices as Shelter Jordan, bunks in Qb-€6 extra, D-€49 for spouses or single-sex; same amenities, rules, and Bible study; Barndesteeg 21, tel. 020/625-3230, fax 020/623-2282, www.shelter.nl, city@shelter.nl).

In Vondelpark: **$ Stayokay Vondelpark (IYHF),** with 536 beds in 130 rooms, is one of Amsterdam's top hostels for the under-25 set—but over-25s will feel comfortable here too (€21-42/bed in 4- to 20-bed dorms, D-€60-105—most with bunk beds, higher prices are for March-Oct, members save €2.50, price depends on demand—cheapest when booked in advance, family rooms, lots of school groups, lockers, laundry, pay Internet access, free Wi-Fi, bike rental, right on Vondelpark at Zandpad 5, tel. 020/589-8996, fax 020/589-8955, www.stayokay.com, vondelpark@stayokay.com). Though Stayokay Vondelpark and Stayokay Stadsdoelen (listed next) are generally booked long in advance, occasionally a few beds open up each day at 11:00.

Near Waterlooplein: **$ Stayokay Stadsdoelen (IYHF),** smaller and simpler than its Vondelpark sister (listed above), has only large dorms and no private bathrooms, but is free of large school groups. Because of the lower prices, this one caters mostly to twentysomethings (€18-35/bed with sheets and breakfast in 10-bed dorms, members save €2.50, price depends on demand—cheapest when booked in advance, lockers, pay Internet access, free Wi-Fi, bike rental, Kloveniersburgwal 97, see map on page 1203, tel. 020/624-6832, fax 020/639-1035, www.stayokay.com, stadsdoelen@stayokay.com).

Farthest East: **$ Stayokay Zeeburg (IYHF)** is a 500-bed hostel with all the modern services. While it's pretty far from the center, by tram or bike you're just 15 minutes from Damrak street. Oldsters fit in here with the youngsters (€24-42/bed in 4- to 9-bed dorms, price depends on demand—cheapest when booked in advance, pay Internet access, free Wi-Fi, lockers, games, restaurant, bike rental, tram #14 to Timorplein 21, tel. 020/551-3190, fax 020/623-4986, www.stayokay.com, zeeburg@stayokay.com).

Eating in Amsterdam

Of Amsterdam's thousand-plus restaurants, no one knows which are best. I'd pick an area and wander. The rowdy food ghetto thrives around Leidseplein; if you don't mind eating in a touristy area, wander along "Restaurant Row" (on Leidsedwarsstraat). The area around Spui Square and that end of Spuistraat is also trendy, and not as noisy. For fewer crowds and more charm, find something in the Jordaan district. Most hoteliers keep a reliable eating list for their neighborhood and know which places keep their travelers happy. I've listed some handy places to consider.

To dine cheaply yet memorably alongside the big spenders, grab a meal to go, then find a bench on a lively neighborhood square or along a canal. Sandwiches *(broodjes)* of delicious cheese on fresh bread are cheap at snack bars, delis, and *broodjes* restaurants. Ethnic restaurants serve cheap, splittable carryout meals. Ethnic fast-food stands abound, offering a variety of meats wrapped in pita bread. Easy to buy at grocery stores, yogurt in the Netherlands (and throughout northern Europe) is delicious and often drinkable right out of its plastic container.

Central Amsterdam

For the locations of these eateries, see the "Hotels and Restaurants in Central Amsterdam" map on page 1222.

On and near Spui

Restaurant Kantjil en de Tijger is a thriving place with a plain and noisy ambience, full of happy eaters who know a good value. The food is purely Indonesian; the waiters are happy to explain your many enticing options. Their three *rijsttafels* (traditional "rice tables" with about a dozen small courses) range from €24 to €30 per person. Though they are designed for two people, three people can make a meal by getting a *rijsttafel* for two plus a soup or light dish (daily 12:00-23:00, reservations smart, mostly indoor with a little outdoor seating, Spuistraat 291, tel. 020/620-0994).

Kantjil to Go, run by Restaurant Kantjil, is a tiny take-out bar serving up inexpensive but delicious Indonesian fare. Their printed menu explains the mix-and-match plan (€5 for 300 grams, €6.50 for 600 grams, vegetarian specials, daily 12:00-21:00, storefront at Nieuwezijds Voorburgwal 342, around the back of the sit-down restaurant listed above, tel. 020/620-3074). Split a large box, grab a bench on the charming Spui Square around the corner, and you've got perhaps the best cheap, hot meal in town.

Near the Mint Tower

Café 't Gasthuys, one of Amsterdam's many brown cafés (so called for their smoke-stained walls), has a busy dumbwaiter cranking out light lunches, sandwiches, and reasonably priced, if uncreative, dinners. It offers a long bar, a lovely secluded back room, peaceful canalside seating, and sometimes slow service (€6-10 lunch plates, €10 three-course dinner, €11-15 main courses, daily 11:00-16:30 & 17:30-22:00, Grimburgwal 7—from the Rondvaart Kooij boat dock, head down Langebrugsteeg, and it's one block down on the left; tel. 020/624-8230).

De Jaren Café ("The Years") is a chic yet inviting place— clearly a favorite with locals. Upstairs is a minimalist restaurant with a top-notch salad bar and canal-view deck (serving €16-20 dinners after 17:30, prices include salad bar plus fish, meat, and veggie dishes; €14 for salad bar only). Downstairs is a modern café, great for light lunches (soups, salads, and sandwiches served all day and evening) or just coffee over a newspaper. On a sunny day, the café's canalside patio is a fine spot to nurse a drink; this is also a nice place to go just for a drink in the evening and to enjoy the spacious Art Deco setting (daily 9:30-23:00, a long block up from Muntplein at Nieuwe Doelenstraat 20-22, tel. 020/625-5771).

Pannenkoekenhuis Upstairs is a tiny, characteristic perch up some extremely steep stairs, where Arno and Ali cook and serve delicious €6-12 pancakes to four tables throughout the afternoon. They'll tell you that I discovered this place long before Anthony Bourdain did (Mon-Fri 12:00-19:00, Sat 12:00-18:00, Sun 12:00-17:00, Grimburgwal 2, tel. 020/626-5603).

La Place, on the ground floor of the V&D department store, has an abundant, colorful array of fresh, appealing food served cafeteria-style. A multistory eatery that seats 300, it has a small outdoor terrace upstairs. Explore before you make your choice. This bustling spot has a lively market feel, with everything from made-on-the-spot beef stir-fry, to fresh juice, to veggie soups (€4 pizza and €5 sandwiches, Sun-Mon 11:00-19:00, Tue-Wed 10:00-19:30, Thu-Sat 10:00-21:00, at the end of Kalverstraat near Mint Tower, tel. 020/622-0171). For fast and healthy take-out food (sandwiches, yogurt, fruit cups, and more), try the bakery on the department store's ground floor. (They run another branch, which has the city's ultimate view terrace, on the top floor of the **Central Library**— Openbare Bibliotheek Amsterdam—near Central Station.)

Atrium University Cafeteria, a three-minute walk from Mint

Tower, feeds travelers and students from Amsterdam University for great prices, but only on weekdays (€7 meals, Mon-Fri 11:00-15:00 & 17:00-19:30; from Spui, walk west down Landebrug Steeg past canalside Café 't Gasthuys three blocks to Oudezijds Achterburgwal 237, then go through arched doorway on the right; tel. 020/525-3999).

Between Central Station and Dam Square

Brasserie Restaurant de Roode Leeuw ("Red Lion") offers a peaceful respite from the crush of Damrak. While this old standby is somewhat overpriced these days, you can still get a menu filled with traditional Dutch food, good service, and the company of plenty of tourists. The *stamppot* (pickled pork loin with bacon and mashed potatoes) is an adventure in Dutch comfort food. Call ahead to reserve a window seat (€17-25 entrées, €33 three-course fixed-price meal with traditional Dutch choices; daily 12:00-22:00, Damrak 93-94, tel. 020/555-0666).

Dam Café, on the first floor of the De Bijenkorf department store on Dam Square, has a small lineup of tasty salads, sandwiches, and desserts. Enjoying views of busy Damrak, comfortable (but limited) seating, and an upscale café vibe, you'll feel miles above the chaotic streets below (€8-11 salads; Sun-Mon 11:00-20:00; Tue-Sat 10:00-20:00, Thu-Fri until 21:00; Dam 1, tel. 088-245-9080). For a much wider range of dishes and lots of seating—but no Dam views—head up to **Kitchen,** the store's swanky fifth-floor self-service restaurant (similar prices and hours as café).

Munching Cheap

Traditional fish stands sell €4 herring sandwiches and other salty treats, usually from easy photo menus. **Stubbe's Haring,** where the Stubbe family has been selling herring for 100 years, is handy and well-established, a few blocks from Central Station (Tue-Fri 10:00-18:00, Sat 10:00-17:00, closed Sun-Mon, at the locks on Singel canal, near the train station, see map on page 1214). Grab a sandwich and have a canalside picnic.

Supermarkets: You'll see **Albert Heijn** grocery stores (daily 8:00-22:00) all over town. They have great deli sections with picnic-perfect take-away salads and sandwiches. Helpful, central locations include behind the Royal Palace on Dam Square (Nieuwezijds Voorburgwal 226), near the Mint Tower (Koningsplein 4), on Leidsestraat (at Konigsplein, on the corner of Leidsestraat and Singel), and inside Central Station (far end of passage under the tracks). Be aware that none of their stores accept US credit cards: Bring cash, and don't get in the checkout lines marked *PIN alleen*.

West Amsterdam
Near the Anne Frank House and in the Jordaan District

Nearly all of these places are within a few scenic blocks of the Anne Frank House, providing handy lunches and atmospheric dinners in Amsterdam's most charming neighborhood. For locations, see the map on page 1214.

Restaurant de Luwte is romantic, located on a picturesque street overlooking a canal. It has lots of candles, a muted but fresh modern interior, spacious seating, a few cool outdoor canalside tables, and French Mediterranean cuisine (€20 main dishes, €30 three-course fixed-price dinners, big salads for €18, daily 18:00-22:00, Leliegracht 26-28, tel. 020/625-8548, manager Maarten).

De Bolhoed has serious vegetarian and vegan food in a colorful setting that Buddha would dig, with a clientele that appears to dig Buddha (big splittable portions, €15 dinners, light lunches, daily 12:00-22:00, dinner starts at 17:00, Prinsengracht 60, tel. 020/626-1803).

Café Restaurant de Reiger must offer the best cooking of any *eetcafé* in the Jordaan. Famous for its fresh ingredients and delightful bistro ambience, it's part of the classic Jordaan scene. In addition to an English menu, ask for a translation of the daily specials (€18-20) on the chalkboard. They're proud of their fresh fish and French-Dutch cuisine. The café, which is crowded late and on weekends, takes no reservations, but you're welcome to have a drink (€3 house wine and fun little bar munchies menu) at the bar while you wait (Tue-Sun 17:00-24:00, closed Mon, veggie options, Nieuwe Leliestraat 34, tel. 020/624-7426).

Café 't Smalle is extremely charming, with three zones where you can enjoy a light lunch or a drink: canalside, inside around the bar, and up some steep stairs in a quaint little back room. The café is open late, and simple meals (salads, soup, and fresh sandwiches) are served 11:00-17:30 (plenty of fine €3-4 Belgian beers on tap, interesting wines by the glass, at Egelantiersgracht 12—where it hits Prinsengracht, tel. 020/623-9617).

Thai Fusion, despite the name, serves straight-up top-quality Thai food in a sleekly modern, black-and-white room wedged neatly in the middle of the Nine Little Streets action (€15-20 main courses, €25-30 two-course meals, daily 16:30-22:30, good veggie options, Berenstraat 8, tel. 020/320-8332).

Toscana Italian Restaurant is the Jordaan's favorite place for good, inexpensive Italian cuisine, served in a woody, Dutch-beer-hall setting (€6-9 pizza and pastas, €16 main courses, Sun-Wed 16:00-23:30, Thu-Sat 12:00-23:30, fast service, Haarlemmerstraat 130, tel. 020/622-0353).

Winkel, the North Jordaan's cornerside hangout, serves appetizing Euro-Dutch meals at its plentiful outside tables and easygoing interior. It really gets hopping on Monday mornings, when the Noordermarkt flea market is underway, but Amsterdammers come from across town all week for the *appeltaart* (€11-14 dinner plates, €5 snacks served after 16:00, daily 8:00-late, Noordermarkt 43, tel. 020/623-0223).

Sara's Pancake House is a basic pancake diner where extremely hardworking Sara cranks out sweet and savory €8-12 flapjacks made from fresh, organic ingredients (daily until 22:30, later on weekends, breakfast served until noon, Raadhuisstraat 45, tel. 020/320-0662).

Restaurant 't Stuivertje is a small, family-run neighborhood eatery tucked away in the Jordaan, serving French-inspired Dutch cuisine in an elegantly cozy but unpretentious atmosphere (€15-25 main courses, dinner salads, Wed-Sun 17:30-22:00, closed Mon-Tue, near Elandsgracht at Hazenstraat 58, tel. 020/623-1349).

Ristorante Toscanini is an up-market Italian place that's always packed. It's so popular that the staff can be a bit arrogant, but the lively, spacious ambience and great Italian cuisine more than make up for that—if you can get a seat. Reservations are essentially required (the staff recommends two weeks' notice for Fri and Sat). Otherwise your best bet is to arrive when they open at 18:00 (€10-14 first courses, €16-25 main courses, Mon-Sat 18:00-22:30, closed Sun, deep in the Jordaan at Lindengracht 75, tel. 020/623-2813).

Villa Zeesicht has all the romantic feel of a classic European café. The cozy interior is crammed with tiny tables topped by tall candlesticks, and wicker chairs outside gather under a wisteria-covered awning. The menu is uninventive—come here instead for the famous *appeltaart* and for the great people-watching on Torensluis bridge (€11-16 plates, daily 9:00-21:30, Torensteeg 7, tel. 020/626-7433).

Drinks Only: **Café 't Papeneiland** is a classic brown café with Delft tiles, an evocative old stove, and a stay-awhile perch overlooking a canal with welcoming benches. It's been the neighborhood hangout since the 17th century (drinks but no food, overlooking northwest end of Prinsengracht at #2, tel. 020/624-1989). It feels a little exclusive; patrons who come here to drink and chat aren't eager to see it overrun by tourists. The café's name means "Papists' Island," since this was once a refuge for Catholics; there used to be an escape tunnel here for priests on the run.

Southwest Amsterdam
Near Leidseplein
Stroll through the colorful cancan of eateries on Lange Leidsedwarsstraat, the "Restaurant Row" just off Leidseplein, and choose

your favorite (but don't expect intimacy or good value). Nearby, busy Leidsestraat offers plenty of starving-student options (between Prinsengracht and Herengracht) offering fast and fun food for around €5 a meal.

To escape the crowds without too long a walk from Leidseplein, wander a few blocks away from the hubbub to Lijnbaansgracht (via Kleine Gartmanplantsoen, the street to the right of The Bulldog Café). At **Restaurant Dubbel,** for example, the steak, fish, and veggie dishes are reasonably priced (€12-15), the bartenders are extra friendly, and you'll actually hear customers speaking Dutch (daily 17:00-24:00, Lijnbaansgracht 256, tel. 020/620-0909).

Beyond the Rijksmuseum

Restaurant Bazar offers one of the most memorable and fun budget eating experiences in town. Converted from a church, it has spacious seating and mod belly-dance music, and is filled with young locals enjoying good, cheap Middle Eastern and North African cuisine. Reservations are a good idea if you plan to eat after 20:00 (fill up with the €8.50 daily plate, delicious €13 couscous, or €16 main dishes; Mon-Fri 11:00-late, Sat-Sun 9:00-late, Albert Cuypstraat 182, tel. 020/675-0544). Restaurant Bazar marks the center of the thriving Albert Cuyp market, which is wrapped up by about 17:00, though the restaurant stays busy late into the evening.

In Vondelpark

Café Vertigo offers a fun selection of excellent soups, salads, and sandwiches, plus main courses such as steak, fish, and *satays*. It's a surprisingly large complex of outdoor tables, an indoor pub, and an elegant, candlelit back-room restaurant beneath the grand, Italian Renaissance Vondel Pavilion. Inside, try to guess the names of the Hollywood icons on the walls. The service can be slow, but if you grab an outdoor table, you can watch the world spin by (daily 10:00-24:00 except opens at 11:00 on off-season weekdays, Vondelpark 3, tel. 020/612-3021).

Southeast Amsterdam

Near the Dutch Resistance Museum

For locations of the following eateries, see the map on page 1203.

Restaurant Plancius, adjacent to the Dutch Resistance Museum, is a handy, modern spot for lunch. Its good indoor and outdoor seating make it popular with the museum staff and broadcasters from the nearby local TV studios (creative breakfasts, hearty fresh sandwiches, light €6-9 lunches and €16-19 dinners, daily 10:00-22:00, Plantage Kerklaan 61a, tel. 020/330-9469).

Café Koosje, located halfway between the Dutch Resistance

Museum and the Dutch Theater, is a corner lunchtime pub/bar ringed with outdoor seating. Inside, casual wooden tables and benches huddle under chandeliers, and the hip, young waitstaff serve beer and salads big enough for two (€5 sandwiches, €11 salads, €14-17 dinners, food served daily 9:00-22:00, on the corner of Plantage Kerklaan at Plantage Middenlaan 37, tel. 020/320-0817).

Smoking in Amsterdam

Tobacco

A quarter of Dutch people smoke tobacco. Holland has a long tradition as a smoking culture, being among the first to import the tobacco plant from the New World. (For a history of smoking, visit the fascinating Pipe Museum, described on page 1192.)

Since 2008, a Dutch law has outlawed smoking tobacco almost everywhere indoors: trains, hotel rooms, restaurants, bars... and even marijuana-dealing coffeeshops.

Marijuana (a.k.a. Cannabis)

For tourists from lands where you can do hard time for lighting up, the open use of marijuana here can feel either somewhat disturbing, or exhilaratingly liberating...or maybe just refreshingly sane. Several decades after being legalized in the Netherlands, marijuana causes about as much excitement here as a bottle of beer. When tourists call an ambulance after smoking too much pot, medics just say, "Drink something sweet and walk it off."

Marijuana Laws and "Coffeeshops"

Throughout the Netherlands, you'll see "coffeeshops"—cafés selling marijuana, with display cases showing various joints or baggies for sale.

Rules and Regulations: The retail sale of marijuana is strictly regulated, and proceeds are taxed. The minimum age for purchase is 18, and coffeeshops can sell up to five grams of marijuana per person per day. It's also illegal for these shops (or anyone) to advertise marijuana. In fact, in many places, the prospective customer has to take the initiative, and ask to see the menu. In some coffeeshops, you actually have to push and hold down a button to see an illuminated menu—the contents of which look like the inventory of a drug bust.

Shops sell marijuana and hashish both in pre-rolled joints and in little baggies. Joints are generally sold individually (€3-5, depending on the strain you choose), though some places sell only small packs of three or four joints. Baggies usually cost €10-15. Some shops charge per gram. The better pot, though costlier, is actually a better value, as it takes less to get high—and it's a better high.

Each coffeeshop is allowed to keep an inventory of about a pound of pot in stock: The tax authorities don't want to see more than this on the books at the end of each accounting cycle, and a shop can lose its license if it exceeds this amount. A popular shop—whose supply must be replenished five or six times a day—simply has to put up with the hassle of constantly taking small deliveries. A shop can sell a ton of pot with no legal problems, as long as it maintains that tiny stock and just refills it as needed. The reason? Authorities want shops to stay small and not become export bases.

In recent years, various Dutch politicians have proposed new laws that would forbid sales of marijuana to nonresidents. Their big worry is European drug dealers who drive over the Dutch border, buy up large quantities of pot, and return home to sell it illegally. This law would be devastating for these Dutch businesses, who depend on out-of-towners to stay in business. The current mayor of Amsterdam is adamant that the city's coffeeshops will remain open—for the sake of the businesses, and because the city believes that the law would just drive business back into a black market, and cause an increase in street crime.

Smoking Tips: The Dutch (like most Europeans) are accustomed to mixing tobacco with marijuana—but any place that caters to Americans will have joints without tobacco; you just have to ask specifically for a "pure" joint. Shops have loaner bongs and inhalers, and dispense rolling papers like toothpicks. As long as you're a paying customer (e.g., you buy a cup of coffee), you can pop into any coffeeshop and light up, even if you didn't buy your pot there.

Tourists who haven't smoked pot since their college days are famous for overindulging in Amsterdam. Coffeeshop baristas nickname tourists about to pass out "Whitey"—the color their faces turn just before they hit the floor. They warn Americans (who aren't used to the strength of the local stuff) to try a lighter leaf. If you do overdo it, the key is to eat or drink something sweet to avoid getting sick. Cola is a good fast fix, and coffeeshops keep sugar tablets handy.

Don't ever buy pot on the street in Amsterdam. Well-established coffeeshops are considered much safer, and coffeeshop owners have an interest in keeping their trade safe and healthy. They're also generally very patient in explaining the varieties available.

Coffeeshops

Most of downtown Amsterdam's coffeeshops feel grungy and foreboding to American travelers who aren't part of the youth-hostel crowd. The neighborhood places (and those in small towns around the countryside) are much more inviting to people without piercings, tattoos, and favorite techno artists. I've listed a few places with a more pub-like ambience for Americans wanting to go local, but within reason. For locations, see the maps in the "Sleeping in Amsterdam" section, earlier.

Paradox is the most *gezellig* (cozy) coffeeshop I found—a mellow, graceful place. The managers, Ludo and Wiljan, and their staff are patient with descriptions and happy to walk you through all your options. This is a rare coffeeshop that serves light meals. The juice is fresh, the music is easy, and the neighborhood is charming (single tobacco-free joints—€3, loaner bongs, games, free Wi-Fi, daily 10:00–20:00, two blocks from Anne Frank House at Eerste Bloemdwarsstraat 2, tel. 020/623-5639, www.paradoxcoffeeshop.com).

The Grey Area—a hole-in-the-wall spot with three tiny tables—is a cool, welcoming, and smoky place appreciated among local aficionados as a perennial winner of Amsterdam's Cannabis Cup awards. Judging by the autographed photos on the wall, many famous Americans have dropped in (say hi to Willie Nelson). You're welcome to just nurse a bottomless cup of coffee. It's run by friendly American Jon, with helpful Adam and Stevan. They even have a vaporizer if you want to try "smoking" without smoking (daily 12:00–20:00, they close relatively early out of consideration for their neighbors, between Dam Square and Anne Frank House at Oude Leliestraat 2, tel. 020/420-4301, www.greyarea.nl).

Siberië Coffeeshop is a short walk from Central Station, but feels cozy, with a friendly canalside ambience. Clean, big, and bright, this place has the vibe of a mellow Starbucks (daily 11:00–23:00, Fri-Sat until 24:00, free Wi-Fi for customers, helpful staff, English menu, Brouwersgracht 11, tel. 020/623-5909, www.coffeeshopsiberie.nl).

La Tertulia is a sweet little mother-and-daughter-run place with pastel decor and a cheery terrarium atmosphere (Tue-Sat 11:00–19:00, closed Sun-Mon, sandwiches, brownies, games, Prinsengracht 312).

The Bulldog Café is the high-profile, leading touristy chain of coffeeshops. These establishments are young but welcoming, with reliable selections. They're pretty comfortable for green tourists wanting to just hang out for a while. The flagship branch, in a former police station right on Leidseplein, is very handy, offering alcohol upstairs, pot downstairs, and fun outdoor seating. It's the rare place where you can have a beer while you smoke and watch the world skateboard by (daily 10:00–1:00 in the morning, Fri-Sat until 3:00, Leidseplein 17, tel. 020/625-6278, www.thebulldog.com). Their original café still sits on the canal near the Old Church in the Red Light District.

The Dampkring is a rough-and-ready constant party. It's

a high-profile, busy place, filled with a young clientele and loud music, but the owners still take the time to explain what they offer. Scenes from the movie *Ocean's Twelve* were filmed here (daily 10:00-1:00 in the morning, close to Spui at Handboogstraat 29, tel. 020/638-0705, www.dampkring.nl).

Dutch Flowers, conveniently located near Spui square on Singel canal, has a very casual "brown café" ambience, with a mature set of regulars. A couple of tables overlooking the canal are perfect for enjoying the late-afternoon sunshine (daily 10:00-23:00, until later Fri-Sat, on the corner of Heisteeg and Singel at Singel 387, tel. 020/624-7624).

Smartshops

Sprinkled across the city are plenty of "smartshops," little grocery stores selling mind-bending natural ingredients. They're clean, well-lit, fully professional retail outlets that sell powerful drugs, many of which are illegal in America. Prices are clearly marked, with brief descriptions of the drugs, their ingredients, and effects. The knowledgeable salespeople can give you more information on their "100 percent natural products that play with the human senses."

Their "natural" drugs include harmless nutrition boosters (such as royal jelly), harmful but familiar tobacco, and herbal versions of popular dance-club drugs (such as herbal Ecstasy). Marijuana seeds, however, are the big sellers. You'll also see mind-bending truffles, a recent trend that caught on after the EU forbade the retailing of hallucinogenic mushrooms. (Truffles grow underground—so they're technically not mushrooms.)

Still, my fellow travelers, *caveat emptor!* We've grown used to thinking, "If it's legal, it must be safe. If it's not, I'll sue." Though perfectly legal and aboveboard in the Netherlands, some of these substances can cause powerful, often unpleasant reactions.

Amsterdam Connections

The Netherlands is so small, level, and well-covered by trains and buses that transportation is a snap. The easy-to-navigate airport is well-connected to Amsterdam and other destinations by bus and train. Use the comprehensive transit website www.9292.nl to plan connections inside the Netherlands by train, bus, or both.

By Train

Amsterdam is the country's hub, but all major cities are linked by speedy trains that come and go every 15 minutes or so. Dutch rail schedules are online at www.ns.nl (domestic) and www.nshispeed.nl (international).

Amsterdam Central Station

Amsterdam's Central Station is being renovated—a messy construction project that's expected to last through 2014 (see "Arrival in Amsterdam" on page 1175 for more details on the station). The station's train-information center can require a long wait. Save lots of time by getting train tickets and information at a small-town station (such as Haarlem), at the airport upon arrival (wonderful service), or at a travel agency. You can buy tickets ahead of time for travel the next day.

If you have a railpass, it's quicker to validate it when you arrive at Schiphol Airport than in Amsterdam's Central Station, where ticket-counter lines are long; you can stretch your railpass by buying an inexpensive ticket from the airport into Amsterdam and using your first "flexi" day for a longer trip.

From Amsterdam Central Station by Train to: Schiphol Airport (4-6/hour, 15 minutes, €4.30, have coins handy to buy from a machine to avoid lines), **Haarlem** (6/hour, 20 minutes, €3.80 one-way, €7.60 same-day round-trip), **Delft** (3/hour direct, 1 hour, more with transfer in Leiden or The Hague), **Bruges** (hourly, 3 hours, transfer at Antwerp Central or Brussels Midi; transfer can be tight—be alert and check with conductor), **Brussels** (hourly, 2 hours), **Ostend** (for ferries to UK; hourly, 4 hours, 3 changes), **London** (6/day, 4.75-5.5 hours, with transfer to Eurostar Chunnel train in Brussels; Eurostar discounted with railpass, www.eurostar. com), **Copenhagen** (3/day, 11.25 hours, multiple transfers; one direct night train), **Bacharach/St. Goar** (roughly every 2 hours, 4.5-6 hours), **Frankfurt** (every 2 hours, 4 hours direct), **Berlin** (5/day, 6.5 hours; 1 direct night train, 9.5 hours), **Munich** (roughly hourly, 7.5-8.75 hours, 1-2 transfers; one direct night train, 10.5 hours), **Bern** (5/day, 8-9 hours, fastest trains change once in Frankfurt), **Paris** (nearly hourly, 3.25 hours direct on fast Thalys train or 4 hours with change to Thalys train in Brussels, www.thalys. com). When booking Thalys trains, even railpass-holders need to buy a seat reservation (generally €26-33 in second class or €41-54 in first class—the first-class reservation generally gets you a meal). If your railpass covers France but not Benelux, the reservation will cost more. (Railpasses that don't include France are not accepted on Thalys trains.) Save money by taking a bus to Paris—described next.

By Bus

To Paris by Bus: If you don't have a railpass, the cheapest way to get to Paris is by Eurolines bus (about 6/day, 8 hours, €46 one-way, €70-86 round-trip; price depends on demand—nonrefundable, advance-purchase one-way tickets as cheap as €17 and round-trip as cheap as €28, check online for deals, Julianaplein 5, Amstel Station, five stops by metro from Central Station, tel. 020/560-8788, www.eurolines.com).

By Plane
Amsterdam's Schiphol Airport

Schiphol (SKIP-pol) Airport is located about 10 miles southwest of Amsterdam's city center.

Information: Schiphol flight information can give you flight times and your airline's contact info (airport code: AMS, toll tel. 0900-0141, from other countries dial +31-20-794-0800, www.schiphol.nl).

Orientation: Schiphol has four terminals. Terminal 1 is for flights to the Schengen European countries (not including the UK); Terminals 2 and 3 are for flights to the UK, US, and other non-European countries; and the new, smaller Terminal 4 (attached to Terminal 3) is for low-cost carriers. Inside the airport, the terminal waiting areas are called lounges; an inviting shopping and eating zone called Holland Boulevard runs between Lounges 2 and 3.

Arrival at Schiphol: Baggage-claim areas for all terminals empty into the same arrival zone, called Schiphol Plaza—with ATMs, shops, eateries, a busy **TI** (near Terminal 2, daily 7:00-22:00), a train station, and bus stops for getting into the city. You can validate your railpass and hit the rails immediately, or, to stretch your railpass, buy an inexpensive ticket into Amsterdam today and start the pass later.

Airport Services: The ABN/AMRO **banks** offer fair exchange rates (in both arrivals and lounge areas). **Service Point,** in Schiphol Plaza at the end of the shopping mall near Terminal 4, is a useful all-purpose service counter that sells SIM cards, has an ATM, and ships packages. The **GWK Travelex** currency-exchange office is located in Arrivals 3 and sells SIM cards for mobile phones. Avoid the Orbitel mobile shop just outside Terminal 2; it sells only one brand of SIM cards, and for an exorbitant rate.

You can surf the **Internet** (for a price) and make phone calls at the Communication Centres (one on the top level of Lounge 2, another on the ground floor of Lounge 1; both are behind customs and not available once you've left the security checkpoint). Convenient luggage **lockers** are at various points around the airport—allowing you to leave your bag here on a lengthy layover (both short- and long-term lockers, credit card only; biggest bank of lockers near the train station at Schiphol Plaza).

Airport Train Ticket Counter: To get train information, buy a ticket, or validate your railpass, take advantage of the fantastic "Train Tickets and Services" counter (Schiphol Plaza ground level, just past Burger King). They have an easy info desk and almost no lines (much quicker than the ticket desk at Amsterdam's Central Station), take US credit cards (unlike most Dutch train stations), and issue tickets for a fee (€0.50 for domestic tickets, €3.50 for tickets to Belgium, Luxembourg, and nearby German cities; up to €10 for other international tickets).

Time-Killing Tips: If you have extra time at Schiphol, check out the Rijksmuseum Amsterdam Schiphol, a little art gallery and museum store on Holland Boulevard, the lively shopping/eating zone between Lounges 2 and 3. The Rijksmuseum loans a dozen or so of its minor masterpieces from the Dutch Golden Age to this unique airport museum, including actual Dutch Masters by Rembrandt, Vermeer, and others (free, daily 6:00-20:00).

To escape the airport crowds, follow signs for the Panorama Terrace to the third floor of Terminal 2, where you'll find a quieter, full-of-locals cafeteria, a kids' play area, and a view terrace where you can watch planes come and go while you nurse a coffee. If you plan to visit the terrace on arrival, stop there before you pass through customs.

From Schiphol Airport to Amsterdam: Direct **trains** to Amsterdam's Central Station run frequently (4-6/hour, 15 minutes, €4.30). The Connexxion **shuttle bus** takes you to your hotel neighborhood; there are three different routes, so ask the attendant which one works best for your hotel (2/hour, 20 minutes, €16 one-way, €26 round-trip, one route stops at Westerkerk near Anne Frank House and many recommended hotels, other routes may cost a couple euros more, departs from lane A7 in front of airport, reserve at least 2 hours ahead for shuttles to airport, tel. 088-339-4741, www.airporthotelshuttle.nl). Allow about €60-70 for a **taxi** to downtown Amsterdam. **Bus** #197 is handiest for those staying in the Leidseplein district (€4, buy ticket from driver, departs from lane B9 in front of airport).

From Schiphol Airport to Haarlem: The big red #300 **bus** departs from lane B6 in front of airport; for details, see "Haarlem Connections" at the end of the next chapter.

HAARLEM

Cute and cozy, yet authentic and handy to the airport, Haarlem is a good home base, giving you small-town warmth overnight, with easy access (20 minutes by train) to wild-and-crazy Amsterdam during the day.

Bustling Haarlem gave America's Harlem its name back when New York was New Amsterdam, a Dutch colony. For centuries Haarlem has been a market town, buzzing with shoppers heading home with fresh bouquets, nowadays by bike.

Enjoy the market on Monday (clothing) or Saturday (general), when the town's atmospheric main square bustles like a Brueghel painting, with cheese, fish, flowers, and families. Make yourself at home; buy some flowers to brighten your hotel room.

Orientation to Haarlem

Tourist Information

Haarlem's TI (VVV), in the town center, is friendlier, more helpful, and less crowded than Amsterdam's, so ask your Amsterdam questions here (April-Sept Mon-Fri 9:30-18:00, Sat 9:30-17:00, Sun 12:00-16:00; Oct-March Mon 13:00-17:30, Tue-Fri 9:30-17:30, Sat 10:00-17:00, closed Sun; across from V&D department store at Verwulft 11, toll tel. 0900-616-1600—€0.50/minute, www.haarlem.nl, info@vvvhaarlem.nl).

The TI offers a good selection of maps and sightseeing- and walking-tour brochures, and sells discounted tickets (€1-2 off) for the Frans Hals Museum and the Teylers Museum.

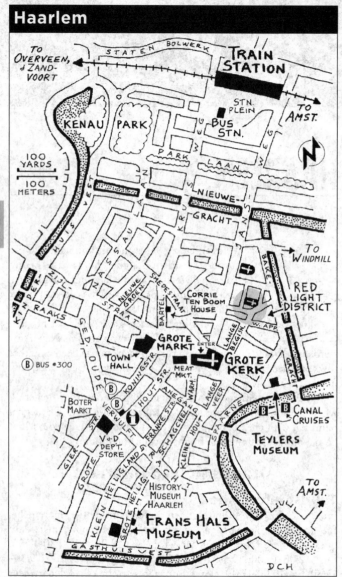

Haarlem

Arrival in Haarlem

By Train: Lockers are available at the station at the very end of platform 3a (€3.70/day, no coins—use a credit card or buy a "Chipknip" prepaid debit card at a ticket window). Two parallel streets flank the train station (Kruisweg and Jansweg). Head up either street, and you'll reach the town square and church within 10 minutes. If you need help, ask a local person to point you toward Grote Markt (Market Square).

By Bus: Buses from Schiphol Airport stop both in the center (Centrum/Verwulft stop, a short walk from Grote Markt) and at the train station.

By Car: Parking is expensive on the streets (€2.70/hour). It's cheaper (€1/30 minutes; €2.50 overnight—19:00-8:00) in these central garages: at the train station, at the southern end of Gedempte Oude Gracht (the main thoroughfare), near the recommended Die Raeckse Hotel, and near the Frans Hals Museum. The most central garage, near the Teylers Museum, is pricier (€1.50 every 40 minutes—essentially, €2.75/hour).

By Plane: For details on getting from Schiphol Airport to Haarlem, see page 1236.

Helpful Hints

Blue Monday and Early Closures: Most sights are closed on Monday, except the church, De Adriaan Windmill (closed Tue), and History Museum Haarlem. The **Corrie Ten Boom House** is closed Sunday-Monday, and closes early the rest of the week (15:00).

Internet Access: Try **Suny Teletechniques** (€2/hour, daily 10:00-24:00, near train station at Lange Herenstraat 4, tel. 023/551-0037) or **High Times Coffeeshop** (free if you buy some pot, Lange Veerstraat 47).

Post Office: There isn't one. To buy stamps, head to a newsstand with the orange *TNT* logo; if you need to send a package, ask your hotelier for help.

Laundry: My Beautiful Launderette is handy and fairly central (€6 self-service wash and dry, daily 8:30-20:30, €9 full service available Mon-Fri 9:00-17:00, near V&D department store at Boter Markt 20).

Bike Rental: You can rent bikes from **Pieters Fietsverhuur** inside the train station (fixed-gear bike only-€6.50/day, €50 deposit and passport number required, Mon-Sat 6:00-24:00, Sun 7:30-24:00, Stationsplein 7, tel. 023/531-7066). They have only 50 bikes to rent and often run out by midmorning—especially when the weather's good. **Rent a Bike Haarlem** charges more, but is friendly and efficient, and carries plenty of new, good-quality bikes. If you're renting for less than a full day, negotiate a cheaper price (fixed-gear bike-€10/day, 3-speed bike-€13.50/day, mountain bikes available, after-hours drop-off possible, ID required for deposit—if you don't want to leave ID, there's a €150 cash deposit; April-Sept daily 9:00-18:00; Oct-March Tue-Fri 10:00-17:30, Thu until 18:00, Sat 10:00-

17:00, closed Sun-Mon; near station at Lange Herenstraat 36, tel. 023/542-1195, www.rentabikehaarlem.nl).

Taxi: The drop charge of €7.50 gets you a little over a mile.

Local Guide: Consider hiring **Walter Schelfhout,** a bearded repository of Haarlem's historical fun facts. If you're into beer lore, Walter's your guy (€85/2 hours, also leads a beer walk sponsored by the Jopenkerk brewpub, tel. 023/535-5715, mobile 06-1258-9299, schelfhout@dutch.nl).

Best View: At **La Place** (top-floor cafeteria of the V&D department store—see page 1249), you get wraparound views of the city as you sip your €2 self-serve tea.

Best Ice Cream: Gelateria Bartoli (on the south side of the Grote Kerk) is the local favorite (daily April-Sept 10:00-22:00, March and Oct-Dec 12:00-17:30 in good weather, closed Jan-Feb).

Sights in Haarlem

▲▲Grote Markt (Market Square)

Haarlem's Grote Markt, where 10 streets converge, is the town's delightful centerpiece...as it has been for 700 years. To enjoy a coffee or beer here, simmering in Dutch good living, is a quintessential European experience. Observe. Sit and gaze at the church, appreciating essentially the same scene that Dutch artists captured centuries ago in oil paintings that now hang in museums.

Just a few years ago, trolleys ran through the square, and cars were parked everywhere. But today it's a pedestrian zone, with market stalls filling the square on Mondays and Saturdays, and café tables dominating on other days.

This is a fun place to build a picnic with Haarlem finger foods and enjoy great seating on the square. Look for pickled herring (take-away stand on the square), local cheese (Gouda and Edam—tasty shop a block away on Barteljorisstraat), french fries with mayonnaise (recommended old-time fries place behind the church on Warmoesstraat), and, in the summer, *stroopwafels* (waffles with built-in syrup) and *poffertjes* (little sugar doughnuts, cooked on the spot).

▲Church (Grote Kerk)

This 15th-century Gothic church (now Protestant) is worth a look, if only to see Holland's greatest pipe organ (from 1738, 100 feet high). Its more than 5,000 pipes impressed both Handel and Mozart. Note how the organ, which fills the west end, seems to steal the show from the altar. Quirky highlights of the church include a replica of Foucault's pendulum, the "Dog-Whipper's Chapel," and a 400-year-old cannonball.

To enter, find the small *Entrée* sign behind the Coster statue on Grote Markt.

Cost and Hours: €2.50, Mon-Sat 10:00-17:00, closed Sun to tourists, tel. 023/553-2040, www.bavo.nl.

Concerts: Consider attending (even part of) a **concert** to hear the Oz-like pipe organ (regular free concerts Tue at 20:15 mid-May-mid-Oct, additional concerts Thu at 16:00 July-Aug; bring a sweater—the church isn't heated).

▲▲Frans Hals Museum

Haarlem is the hometown of Frans Hals, the foremost Dutch portrait painter of the 17th-century Golden Age. This refreshing museum, once an almshouse for old men back in 1610, displays many of Hals' greatest paintings, crafted in his nearly Impressionistic style. You'll see group portraits and paintings of old-time Haarlem. Stand eye-to-eye with life-size, lifelike portraits of Haarlem's citizens—brewers, preachers, workers, bureaucrats, and housewives. Take a close look at the people who built the Dutch Golden Age, and then watched it start to fade.

Along with Frans Hals' work, the museum features a copy of Pieter Brueghel the Younger's *Flemish Proverbs*, a fun painting that shows 72 charming Flemish scenes representing different folk sayings. Pick up the chart to identify these clever bits of everyday wisdom. It's near the 250-year-old dollhouse on display in a former chapel.

Cost and Hours: €10, often €13 with special exhibits, Tue-Sat 11:00-17:00, Sun 12:00-17:00, closed Mon, Groot Heiligland 62, tel. 023/511-5775, www.franshalsmuseum.nl.

History Museum Haarlem

This small museum, across the street from the Frans Hals Museum, offers a glimpse of old Haarlem. Request the English version of the 10-minute video, low-key Haarlem's version of a sound-and-light show. Study the large-scale model of Haarlem in 1822 (when its fortifications were still intact), and wander the three rooms without English descriptions.

Cost and Hours: Overpriced at €5, Mon-Sat 12:00-17:00, Sun 13:00-17:00, Groot Heiligland 47, tel. 023/542-2427, www. historischmuseumhaarlem.nl. The adjacent architecture center (free) may be of interest to architects.

▲Corrie ten Boom House

Haarlem was home to Corrie ten Boom, popularized by her inspirational 1971 book (and the 1975 movie that followed), *The Hiding Place*. Both tell about the Ten Boom family's experience protecting Jews from the Nazis. Corrie ten Boom gives the other half of the Anne Frank story—the point of view of those who risked their lives to hide Dutch Jews during the Nazi occupation (1940-1945).

The Ten Boom House is open only for English tours—check

the sign on the door for the next start time. The gentle and loving one-hour tours come with a little evangelizing that some may find objectionable.

Cost and Hours: Free, but donations accepted; April-Oct Tue-Sat first tour at 10:00, last tour at 15:30; Nov-March Tue-Sat first tour at 11:00, last tour around 15:00; closed Sun-Mon year-round; 50 yards north of Grote Markt at Barteljorisstraat 19; the clock-shop people get all wound up if you go inside—wait in the little side street at the door, where tour times are posted; tel. 023/531-0823, www.corrietenboom.com.

Background: The clock shop was the Ten Boom family business. The elderly father and his two daughters—Corrie and Betsy, both in their 50s—lived above the store and in the brick building attached in back (along Schoutensteeg alley). Corrie's bedroom was on the top floor at the back. This room was tiny to start with, but then the family built a second, secret room (less than a yard deep) at the very back—"the hiding place," where they could hide six Jews at a time. Devoutly religious, the family had a long tradition of tolerance, having hosted prayer meetings here in their home for both Jews and Christians for generations.

The Gestapo, tipped off that the family was harboring Jews, burst into the Ten Boom house. Finding a suspicious number of ration coupons, the Nazis arrested the family, but failed to find the six Jews (who later escaped) in the hiding place. Corrie's father and sister died while in prison, but Corrie survived the Ravensbrück concentration camp to tell her story in her memoir.

▲Teylers Museum

Famous as the oldest museum in Holland, Teylers is a time-warp experience, filled with all sorts of fun curios for science buffs: fossils, minerals, primitive electronic gadgetry, and examples of 18th- and 19th-century technology (it also has two lovely painting galleries and hosts good temporary exhibits).

Cost and Hours: Overpriced at €10, includes excellent (and I'd say, essential) audioguide, Tue-Sat 10:00-17:00, Sun 12:00-17:00, closed Mon, Spaarne 16, tel. 023/516-0960, www.teylersmuseum.nl. The museum's modern café has good prices and faces a delightful garden.

Visiting the Museum: The science-oriented sections of this place feel like a museum of a museum. They're serious about authenticity here: The presentation is perfectly preserved, right down to the original labels. Since there was no electricity in the olden days, you'll find little electric lighting...if it's dark outside, it's dark inside. The museum's benefactor, Pieter Teyler van der Hulst, was a very wealthy merchant who willed his estate, worth the equivalent of €80 million today, to a foundation whose mission was to "create and maintain a museum to stimulate art and science." The museum opened in 1784, six years after Teyler's death (his last euro was spent in 1983—now it's a national museum). Add your name to the guest book, which goes back to before Napoleon's visit here. The freshly renovated oval room—a temple of science and learning—is the core of the museum; in the art salons paintings are hung in the old style.

▲De Adriaan Windmill

Haarlem's old-time windmill, located just a 10-minute walk from the station and Teylers Museum, welcomes visitors with a short video, a little museum, and fine town views.

Cost and Hours: €3; April-Oct Mon and Wed-Fri 13:00-17:00, Sat-Sun 10:30-17:00, closed Tue; same hours in winter except only open Fri-Sun, Papentorenvest 1, tel. 023/545-0259, www.molenadriaan.nl.

Canal Cruise

Making a scenic 50-minute loop through and around Haarlem with a live guide who speaks Dutch and sometimes English, **Post Verkade Cruise**'s little trips are more relaxing than informative (€11; April-Oct daily departures at the top of the hour 12:00-16:00; Nov-March same hours Wed-Sun, reservations required; also evening cruises, across canal from Teylers Museum at Spaarne 11a, tel. 023/535-7723, www.postverkadecruises.nl). For a similar experience in an open boat, find **Haarlem Canal Tours,** farther down Spaarne, across from #17 (€13.50, reservations smart, 70-75 minutes, leaves every 1.5 hours daily 10:00-19:00, may not run in bad weather and off-season, www.haarlemcanaltours.com).

▲Red Light District

Wander through a little Red Light District that's as precious as a Barbie doll—and legal since the 1980s (2 blocks northeast of Grote Markt, off Lange Begijnestraat, no senior or student discounts). Don't miss the mall on Begijnesteeg marked by the red neon sign reading *'t Steegje* ("free"). Just beyond that, the nearby 't Poortje ("office park") costs €6 to enter. Jog to the right to pop into the much more inviting "Red Lantern" (window-shopping welcome, at Korte Begijnestraat 27). As you wander through this area, remember that the people here don't condone prostitution any more than your own community back home probably does; they just find it practical not to criminalize it and drive it underground, but instead to regulate it and keep the practice as safe as possible.

Nightlife in Haarlem

Haarlem's evening scene is great. Consider four basic zones: Grote Markt in the shadow of the Grote Kerk; Lange Veerstraat; Boter Grote Markt; and Vijfhoek (Five Corners).

Grote Markt is lined with trendy bars that seem made for

nursing a drink—**Café Studio** is generally the hot spot for a drink here (at Grote Markt 25); I'd also duck into the dark interior of **In Den Uiver** (near the Grote Kerk entry at Riviervischmarkt 13, live jazz Thu and Sun). Lange Veerstraat (behind the Grote Kerk) is colorful and bordered with lively spots. Boter Grote Markt is more convivial and local, as it's less central and away from the tourists—try the nearby **Jopenkerk** brewpub (described later). Vijfhoek, named for the five lanes that converge here, is incredibly charming, although it has only one pub (with plenty of drinks, bar snacks, a relaxed crowd, and good indoor or outdoor seating). Also worth exploring is the area from this cutest corner in town to the New Church (Nieuwe Kerk), a couple blocks away. If you want a more high-powered scene, Amsterdam is just 20 minutes away by train.

Sleeping in Haarlem

The helpful Haarlem TI can nearly always find you a €29 bed in a private home (€5.50/person fee, plus a cut of your host's money; two-night minimum). Avoid this if you can; it's cheaper to reserve by calling direct. Nearly every Dutch person you'll encounter speaks English.

Haarlem is most crowded in April, particularly on Easter weekend (April 18-21 in 2014, April 3-6 in 2015), during the flower parade (April 26 in 2014), on King's Day (also on April 26 in 2014, but usually on April 27), and in May, July, and August (especially during Haarlem's jazz festival on the third weekend of August). Also see the list of holidays in the appendix.

The prices listed here include breakfast (unless otherwise noted) but don't include the €2.20-per-person-per-day tourist tax. To avoid excessive street noises, forgo views for a room in the back. Hotels and the TI have a useful parking brochure.

In the Center
Hotels and B&Bs

$$$ Hotel Lion D'Or is a classy 34-room business hotel with all the professional comforts, pleasingly posh decor, and a handy but less-than-quaint location (Db-€150, Fri-Sat Db-€125, extra bed-€15, check website for special deals, ask for Rick Steves discount with 2-night stay if you book direct, air-con, elevator, free Internet access and Wi-Fi, across the street from train station at Kruisweg 34, tel. 023/532-1750, fax 023/532-9543, www.hotelliondor.nl, reservations@hotelliondor.nl, friendly Dirk Pauw).

$$$ Stempels Hotel, modern yet elegant, is located in a renovated 300-year-old building. With bare floors, comfy high-quality beds, and minimalist touches in its 17 rooms, what it lacks in warmth it makes up for in style and value. Double-paned windows

Sleep Code

(€1 = about $1.30, country code: 31, area code: 023)
S = Single, **D** = Double/Twin, **T** = Triple, **Q** = Quad, **b** = bathroom, **s** = shower only. Nearly everyone speaks English. Credit cards are accepted and breakfast is included unless otherwise noted.

To help you easily sort through these listings, I've divided the accommodations into three categories, based on the price for a standard double room with bath:

$$$ Higher Priced—Most rooms €85 or more.
$$ Moderately Priced—Most rooms between €60-85.
$ Lower Priced—Most rooms €60 or less.

Prices can change without notice; verify the hotel's current rates online or by email.

help keep down the noise—it's just a block east of Grote Markt—with a bustling brasserie and bar downstairs (standard Sb-€95, standard Db-€112-150, pricier rooms and suites available, breakfast-€12.50, in-room computers with free Internet access and Wi-Fi, elevator, Klokhuisplein 9, tel. 023/512-3910, www.stempelsinhaarlem.nl, info@stempelsinhaarlem.nl).

$$$ Hotel Amadeus, on Grote Markt, has 15 small, bright, and basic rooms, some with views of the square. This charming hotel, ideally located above an early 20th-century dinner café, is relatively quiet, especially if you take a room in the back. Its lush old lounge/breakfast room on the second floor overlooks the square, and Mike and Inez take good care of their guests (Sb-€60, Db-€85, check website for special deals, ask for Rick Steves discount with 2-night stay and cash, free Wi-Fi, Grote Markt 10—from square it's a steep climb to lounge, elevator inside ground-floor café if you need it, tel. 023/532-4530, fax 023/532-2328, www.amadeus-hotel.com, info@amadeus-hotel.com). Hotel Amadeus' breakfast room overlooking the main square is a great place to watch the town greet a new day—and one of my favorite Haarlem moments.

$$$ Ambassador City Centre Hotel, with 46 comfortable rooms in a big, plain hotel, is located just behind the Grote Kerk. If you're willing to trade some street noise for amazing church views, ask for a room in the front (Db-€100, often less off-season, breakfast buffet-€13.50, free Internet access and Wi-Fi, Oude Groenmarkt 20, tel. 023/512-5300, www.acc-hotel.nl, info@acc-hotel.nl). They also run **Hotel Joops,** with 32 rooms, a block away (rooms are €10 cheaper; studios and apartments with kitchenettes for 2-4 people—€110-140 depending on season and number of people).

$$ Central **Hotel Malts** rents 12 bright, simple, and fresh rooms for a good price. The rooms in front are big, but not recommended for light sleepers (small D-€75, small Db-€79, standard Db-€89, big Db-€95, check website for best prices, no elevator, free Wi-Fi, Zijlstraat 56, tel. 023/551-2385, www.maltshotel.nl, info@maltshotel.nl, Marco and Andrea). They also offer €65 studio apartments with kitchenettes near the Red Light District.

Rooms in Restaurants

These places are all run as sidelines by restaurants, and you'll know it by the style of service and rooms. Lobbies are in the restaurant, and there are no public spaces. Still, they are handy and—for Haarlem—inexpensive.

$$ **Hotel Carillon** overlooks the town square and comes with bell-tower chimes and a little traffic. With run-down public spaces and st-e-e-e-p stairs, it's an old-school, over-the-restaurant place. The rooms themselves, however, are freshly updated and pleasant. The front rooms come with more street noise and great town-square views (tiny loft S-€45, Db-€80-90, Tb-€110, Qb-€150, ask for Rick Steves discount when you reserve—must show book on arrival, no elevator, free Wi-Fi, Grote Markt 27, tel. 023/531-0591, fax 023/531-4909, www.hotelcarillon.com, info@hotelcarillon. com, owners Kelly Kuo, Andres Haas, and June).

$$ **Die Raeckse Hotel,** family-run and friendly, is not as central as the others and has less character and more traffic noise—but its 21 rooms are decent and comfortable. Quiet rooms in back cost more than the noisy rooms on the street—but they're worth it (Sb-€55, smaller Db-€80-85, big Db-€85-90, Tb-€120, Qb-€130-145, €5/night discount for 2-night stay, ask for Rick Steves discount if you book direct and show this book on arrival—good only Nov-March, free but time-limited Internet access, free Wi-Fi, Raaks Straat 1, tel. 023/532-6629, fax 023/531-7937, www.die-raeckse. nl, dieraeckse@zonnet.nl).

Near Haarlem

$$$ **Hotel Haarlem Zuid,** with 300 modern rooms, is sterile but a good value for drivers. It sits in an industrial zone a 20-minute walk from the center, on the road to the airport. They are renovating about two-thirds of the rooms; rates may rise as a result (Db-€89-140, breakfast-€13, elevator, free Wi-Fi, free parking, laundry service, free fitness center, reasonable hotel restaurant, Toekanweg 2, tel. 023/536-7500, fax 023/536-7980, www.hotelhaarlemzuid. nl, haarlemzuid@valk.com). Bus #300 conveniently connects the

Haarlem Hotels & Restaurants

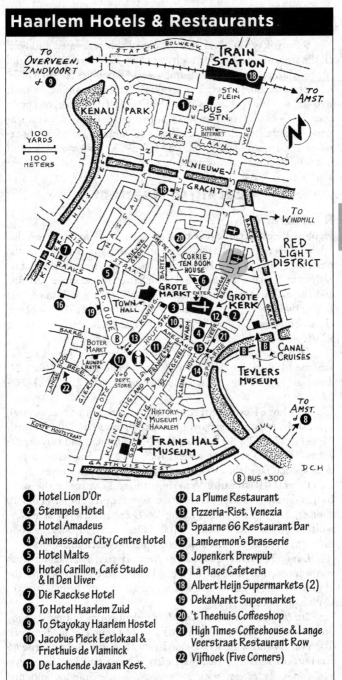

1. Hotel Lion D'Or
2. Stempels Hotel
3. Hotel Amadeus
4. Ambassador City Centre Hotel
5. Hotel Malts
6. Hotel Carillon, Café Studio & In Den Uiver
7. Die Raeckse Hotel
8. To Hotel Haarlem Zuid
9. To Stayokay Haarlem Hostel
10. Jacobus Pieck Eetlokaal & Friethuis de Vlaminck
11. De Lachende Javaan Rest.
12. La Plume Restaurant
13. Pizzeria-Rist. Venezia
14. Spaarne 66 Restaurant Bar
15. Lambermon's Brasserie
16. Jopenkerk Brewpub
17. La Place Cafeteria
18. Albert Heijn Supermarkets (2)
19. DekaMarkt Supermarket
20. 't Theehuis Coffeeshop
21. High Times Coffeehouse & Lange Veerstraat Restaurant Row
22. Vijfhoek (Five Corners)

hotel with the train station, Grote Markt, and the airport (every 10 minutes, stop: Europaweg).

$ Stayokay Haarlem Hostel, completely renovated and with all the youth-hostel comforts, charges €25-30 for beds in four- and six-bed dorms. They also rent simple €60-80 doubles (€2.50 less for members, includes sheets and breakfast, save by booking on their website, pay Internet access, free Wi-Fi, laundry service, reception open 8:00-23:00, Jan Gijzenpad 3, two miles from Haarlem station—take bus #2 from station, or a 10-minute walk from Santpoort Zuid train station, tel. 023/537-3793, www.stayokay.com/haarlem, haarlem@stayokay.com).

Eating in Haarlem

Restaurants

Jacobus Pieck Eetlokaal is popular with locals for its fine-value "global cuisine," good salads, and unpretentious flair. Sit in the peaceful garden courtyard, at a sidewalk table, or in the romantically cozy interior. The Oriental Peak Salad is a perennial favorite, and the dish of the day (*dagschotel*, €12.50) always sells out (great €7 sandwiches at lunch, Tue-Sat 11:00-16:00 & 17:30-22:00, closed Sun-Mon, cash only, Warmoesstraat 18, behind church, tel. 023/532-6144).

De Lachende Javaan ("The Laughing Javanese") is a long-established Indonesian place serving a memorable *rijsttafel* (€20-24, Tue-Sun 17:00-22:00, closed Mon, Frankestraat 27, tel. 023/532-8792).

La Plume Restaurant steakhouse is noisy, with a happy, local, and carnivorous crowd enjoying the candlelit scene (€20-25 meals, Mon-Fri 17:30-23:00, Sat-Sun 17:00-23:00, *satay* and ribs are favorites, Lange Veerstraat 1, tel. 023/531-3202). The relaxing outdoor seating faces the church and a lively pedestrian street.

Pizzeria-Ristorante Venezia, run for 25 years by the same Italian family from Bari, is *the* place to go for pizza or pasta (€8-10 choices, daily 13:00-23:00, facing V&D department store at Verwulft 7, tel. 023/531-7753). You'll feel like you're in Rome at a good indoor table, or sit outdoors for good people-watching.

Lange Veerstraat Restaurant Row: If you don't know what you want to eat, stroll the delightful Lange Veerstraat behind the church and survey a fun range of restaurants (from cheap falafels to Cuban, and much more).

On the Spaarne River Canal: Haarlem seems to turn its back on its river with most of the eating energy a couple of blocks away. To enjoy a meal with a nice canal view, consider the **Spaarne 66 Restaurant Bar.** The Lemmers girls (a mom and her daughters) run this cozy eatery, with a woody, old-time interior and fine

outdoor canalside seating (light €7 lunches, €20 Mediterranean/
Dutch dinner plates, €31.50 three-course fixed-price meal, daily in
summer 10:00-24:00, closed Mon-Tue in winter, Spaarne 66, tel.
023/551-3800).

Dressy Splurge: At **Lambermon's,** expert chef Michèl Lambermon serves chichi pan-European cuisine in a suave, modern,
corner restaurant. The Michelin-rated brasserie offers €29 two-
course fixed-price lunches and €45 three-course dinners (€29-32
main courses, daily 12:00-15:00 & 18:00-22:00; Korte Veerstraat
1, tel. 023/542-7804).

Trendy Brewpub: While beer-drinking is a religion in Belgium, it's also getting that way in Haarlem, where the Jopen brewery has converted a church into a flashy gastropub called **Jopenkerk**. With 18 brews on tap, including a *Hoppenbier* from a 1501
recipe, this is a beer lover's mecca. Budget pub grub is served on
the ground floor, or try the upstairs restaurant for more elegant fare
(€8-10 burgers, salads, and quiche in the pub, €15-23 main dishes in the restaurant, daily 10:00-1:00 in the morning, Gedempte
Voldersgracht 2, tel. 023/533-4114).

Budget Options

La Place is a snazzy chain cafeteria that dishes up fresh, healthy
budget food. Sit on the top floor or the roof garden of the V&D
department store with Haarlem's best view. If you're too hungry to
ride six floors of escalators, they offer the same food on the ground
floor (Mon 11:00-18:00, Tue-Sat 9:30-18:00, Thu until 21:00, Sun
12:00-17:00, Grote Houtstraat 70, on corner of Gedempte Oude
Gracht, tel. 023/515-8700).

Friethuis de Vlaminck is your best bet for a cone of old-fashioned, fresh Flemish-style fries (€2, Tue-Sun 12:00-17:00, closed
Mon, Warmoesstraat 3, behind church, tel. 023/532-1084). Ali offers a dazzling array of sauces. With his help, you can be adventurous.

Supermarkets: **Albert Heijn** has two convenient locations.
One is in the train station (Mon-Fri 6:30-21:00, Sat 10:00-21:00,
Sun 9:00-21:00, cash only), the other is at Kruisstraat 10 (Mon-Sat
8:00-22:00, closed Sun, cash only). The **DekaMarkt** is a few blocks
west of Grote Markt (Mon-Sat 8:00-20:00, Thu-Fri until 21:00,
Sun 16:00-21:00, Gedempte Oude Gracht 54, near the V&D department store).

Haarlem Connections

From Haarlem by Train to: Zandvoort (2/hour, 11 minutes),
Amsterdam (6/hour, 20 minutes, €3.70 one-way, €7.10 same-day
round-trip), **Delft** (2/hour, 40 minutes), **Brussels** (hourly, 2.75

hours, transfer in Rotterdam), **Bruges/Brugge** (hourly, 3.5 hours, 2-3 changes—avoid Thalys connections if traveling with a railpass).

To Schiphol Airport: Your best option is the **bus** (4-10/hour, 40 minutes, €4—buy ticket from driver, bus #300). For most of the trip, this bus travels on its own limited-access roadway—what transit wonks call a "busway." To catch the bus from the middle of Haarlem, head to the Centrum/Verwulft stop, near the V&D department store. To catch it from the train station, look for the "A" bus stop marked *R Net*. You can also get there by **train** (6/hour, 30-40 minutes, transfer at Amsterdam-Sloterdijk station, €5.40 one-way) or **taxi** (about €30-40).

SPAIN

BARCELONA

Barcelona may be Spain's second city, but it's undoubtedly the first city of the proud and distinct region of Catalunya. Catalan flags wave side by side with the Spanish flag, and locals, while fluent in both languages, stubbornly insist on speaking Catalan first. This lively culture is on an unstoppable roll in Spain's most cosmopolitan and European corner.

Barcelona bubbles with life in its narrow Barri Gòtic alleys, along the pedestrian boulevard called the Ramblas, in the funky bohemian quarter of El Born, and throughout the chic, grid-planned new part of town called the Eixample. Its Old City is made for seeing on foot, full of winding lanes that emerge into secluded squares dotted with palm trees and ringed with cafés and boutiques. The waterfront bristles with life, overlooked by the park-like setting of Montjuïc. Everywhere you go, you'll find the city's architecture to be colorful, playful, and unique. Rows of symmetrical ironwork balconies are punctuated with fanciful details: bay windows, turrets, painted tiles, hanging lanterns, flower boxes, and carved reliefs.

Barcelona is full of history. You'll see Roman ruins, a medieval cathedral, twisty Gothic lanes, and traces of Columbus and the sea trade. As the Age of Exploration steered trade from the Mediterranean to the Atlantic, things got pretty quiet here (kept carefully under the thumb of Spanish rulers). But by the late 19th century, the city had boomed into an industrial powerhouse and a cradle of Modernism. A teenage Picasso lived in Barcelona right when he was on the verge of reinventing painting; his legacy is today's Picasso Museum. Catalan architects including Antoni Gaudí, Lluís Domènech i Montaner, and Josep Puig i Cadafalch forged the

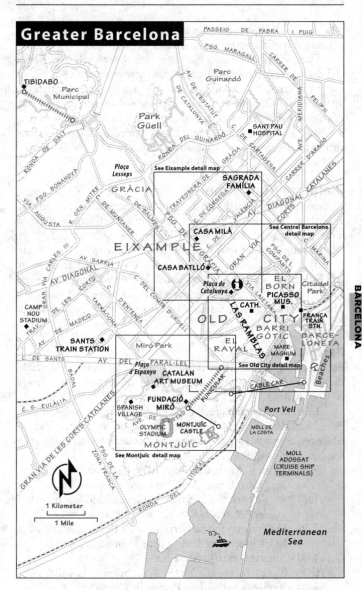

Modernista style and remade the city's skyline with curvy fantasy buildings—culminating in Gaudí's over-the-top Sagrada Família, a church still under construction. Salvador Dalí and Joan Miró join the long list of world-changing 20th-century artists with ties to this city. Meanwhile, World's Fairs in 1888 and 1929 helped spruce up the city, and in 1992, Barcelona hosted the Summer Olympics—an event that once again re-energized this dynamic city and left a wealth of attractive public areas and great sights.

Today's Barcelona is as vibrant as ever. Locals still join hands and dance the everyone's-welcome *sardana* in front of the cathedral every weekend. Neighborhood festivals jam the events calendar. The cafés are filled by day, and people crowd the streets at night, pausing to fortify themselves with a perfectly composed bite of seafood and a drink at a tapas bar. Every hidden back lane provides shelter for an array of inviting shops. If you're in the mood to surrender to a city's charms, let it be in Barcelona.

Planning Your Time

Barcelona is easily worth two days, and no one would regret having a third day (or more). If you can spare only one full day for the city, it can be a scramble but a day you'll never forget.

When planning your time, be aware that many top sights are closed on Monday—making them especially crowded on Tuesday and Sunday (for a rundown of hours, see "At a Glance" on page 1290). Some of Barcelona's major sights can have long lines; it's smart to make advance reservations. If you're here on a weekend, dance the *sardana*.

Barcelona in 1 Day

For a relaxing day, stroll the Ramblas, see the Sagrada Família, add the Picasso Museum if you're a fan, and have dinner in the trendy El Born district.

To cram in much more, try the following ambitious but doable plan. You'll have to rush through the big sights (cathedral, Picasso Museum, Sagrada Família), having just enough time to visit each one but not to linger.

9:00 From Plaça de Catalunya (with its handy TI), follow my "Barri Gòtic Walk" and tour the cathedral.

11:00 Circle back to Plaça de Catalunya and follow my self-guided "Ramblas Ramble" to the harborfront.

12:30 Walk along the harborfront to El Born, grabbing a quick lunch and doing a little shopping.

14:00 Tour the Picasso Museum.

16:00 Take a taxi or the Metro to the Sagrada Família.

18:00 Taxi, bus, or walk to Passeig de Gràcia in the Eixample to see the exteriors of Gaudí's Casa Milà and the Block of Discord. Stroll back down toward Plaça de Catalunya.

19:00 If your energy is holding out, wander down the Ramblas again, at prime paseo time. Enjoy an early tapas dinner in the Eixample or a restaurant dinner later in the Old City.

Barcelona in 2 or 3 Days

To better sample the city's ample charm, spread your visit over several days. With at least two days, divide and conquer the town geographically: Spend one day in the Old City (Ramblas, Barri Gòtic/cathedral area, Picasso Museum/El Born) and another on the Eixample and Gaudí sights (Casa Milà, Sagrada Família, Park Güell). Do Montjuïc on whichever day you're not exhausted (if any)—or, better yet, on a third day.

With extra time on any day, consider taking a hop-on, hop-off bus tour for a sightseeing overview (for instance, the Tourist Bus' blue route links most Gaudí sights, and could work well on Day 2).

Day 1 (Old City)

9:00	Follow my "Barri Gòtic Walk" and tour the cathedral.
11:00	Head back to the Ramblas, then follow my "Ramblas Ramble" (touring Palau Güell if you're a Gaudí fan) down to the harborfront.
13:00	Grab lunch in El Born or the Barri Gòtic.
14:00	Tour the Palace of Catalan Music in El Born (advance reservation required).
15:00	Explore El Born, and tour the Picasso Museum.
Evening	Take your pick of activities: Assemble a tapas dinner by hopping from bar to bar in El Born, and take "A Short, Sweet Walk" (page 1352) for dessert. (Other good neighborhoods for tapas are the ritzy Eixample or touristy Barri Gòtic.) Or wait to dine at a restaurant when locals do, around 21:00. Take in a performance of Spanish guitar, flamenco, or jazz, or a concert in a fancy setting (Casa Milà, Palace of Catalan Music, and more). Zip up to Montjuïc for the sunset and a drink (on the Catalan Art Museum's terrace), then head down to the illuminated Magic Fountains (Fri-Sun, plus Thu in summer).

Day 2 (Modernisme)

9:00	Spend the morning in the Eixample, and tour Casa Milà and/or Casa Batlló.
12:00	Grab an early lunch in the Eixample, then take a taxi or bus to the Sagrada Família.
14:00	Taxi or bus to Park Güell (for more Gaudí), or take a bus to Montjuïc and the 1929 World Expo Fairgrounds (if you're not going to Montjuïc on Day 3).
Evening	See options for Day 1, above.

Barcelona Neighborhood Overview

GRÀCIA

Park Güell

EIXAMPLE

SAGRADA
■ FAMÍLIA

CASA
MILÀ ■

PASSEIG DE GRÀCIA

CASA
BATLLÓ ■

Citadel
Park

EL
BORN

Plaça de
Catalunya ●

CITY

VIA LAIETANA

■ PICASSO
MUSEUM

CATHEDRAL ■

LAS RAMBLAS

BARRI
GÒTIC

OLD

SANTS
STATION ■

EL
RAVAL

BARCELONETA

Plaça
d'Espanya ●

■ FUNDACIÓ
JOAN MIRÓ

MONTJUÏC

Port
Vell

Not to Scale

CRUISE
PORT

Mediterranean Sea

← To Airport

BARCELONA

Day 3 (Montjuïc)

Tour Montjuïc from top to bottom, stopping at sights of interest. The top priorities for most visitors are the Catalan Art Museum, CaixaForum, and Fundació Joan Miró. If the weather is good, see Montjuïc in the morning and spend the afternoon on the beach in Barceloneta. Find your favorite *chiringuito* beach bar for dinner.

Orientation to Barcelona

Like Los Angeles, Barcelona is a basically flat city that sprawls out under the sun between the sea and the mountains. It's huge (1.6 million people, with about 5 million people in greater Barcelona), but travelers need only focus on four areas: the Old City, the harbor/Barceloneta, the Eixample, and Montjuïc.

A large square, **Plaça de Catalunya,** sits at the center of Barcelona, dividing the older and newer parts of town. Sloping downhill from the Plaça de Catalunya is the Old City, with the boulevard called the Ramblas running down to the harbor. Above Plaça de Catalunya is the modern residential area called the Eixample. The Montjuïc hill overlooks the harbor. Outside the Old City, Barcelona's sights are widely scattered, but with a map and a willingness to figure out the sleek Metro system (or a few euros for taxis), all is manageable.

Here are more details per neighborhood:

Old City (Ciutat Vella): This is the compact core of Barcelona—ideal for strolling, shopping, and people-watching—where you'll probably spend most of your time. It's a labyrinth of narrow streets that once were confined by the medieval walls. The lively pedestrian drag called the **Ramblas**—one of Europe's most entertaining streets—runs through the heart of the Old City from Plaça de Catalunya down to the harbor. The Old City is divided into thirds by the Ramblas and another major thoroughfare, Via Laietana. Between the Ramblas and Via Laietana is the characteristic **Barri Gòtic** (BAH-ree GOH-teek, Gothic Quarter), with the cathedral as its navel. Locals call it simply "El Gòtic" for short. To the east of Via Laietana is the trendy **El Born** district (a.k.a. "La Ribera"), a shopping, dining, and nightlife mecca centered on the Picasso Museum and the Church of Santa Maria del Mar. To the west of the Ramblas is the **Raval** (rah-VAHL), enlivened by its university and modern-art museum. The Raval is of least interest to tourists (and, in fact, some parts of it are quite seedy and should be avoided).

Harborfront: This area has been energized since the 1992 Olympics. A pedestrian bridge links the Ramblas with the modern Maremagnum shopping/aquarium/entertainment complex. On the peninsula across the quaint sailboat harbor is **Barceloneta,** a traditional fishing neighborhood with gritty charm and some good seafood restaurants. Beyond Barceloneta, a gorgeous man-made **beach** several miles long leads east to the commercial and convention district called the **Fòrum.**

Eixample: North of the Old City, beyond the bustling hub of Plaça de Catalunya, is the elegant Eixample (eye-SHAM-plah) district, its grid plan softened by cut-off corners. Much of Barcelona's Modernista architecture is found here—especially along the swanky artery Passeig de Gràcia, an area called the **Quadrat d'Or** ("Golden Quarter"). To the north is the **Gràcia** district and beyond that, Antoni Gaudí's **Park Güell.**

Montjuïc: The large hill overlooking the city to the southwest is Montjuïc (mohn-jew-EEK), home to a variety of attractions, including some excellent museums (Catalan Art, Joan Miró) and the Olympic Stadium. At the base of Montjuïc, stretching toward Plaça d'Espanya, are the former **1929 World Expo Fairgrounds**, with additional fine attractions (including the CaixaForum art gallery and the bullring-turned-mall, Las Arenas).

Apart from your geographical orientation, you'll need to orient yourself linguistically to a language distinct from Spanish. Although Spanish ("Castilian"/*castellano*) is widely spoken, the native tongue in this region is Catalan—nearly as different from Spanish as Italian.

Tourist Information

Barcelona's TI has several branches (central tel. 932-853-834, www.barcelonaturisme.cat). The primary one is beneath the main square, **Plaça de Catalunya** (daily 8:30-20:30, entrance along southeast side of square, across from Hard Rock Café—look for red sign, tel. 932-853-832).

Several other convenient branches include a kiosk near the top of the **Ramblas** (daily 8:30-20:30, at #115, mobile 618-783-479); on **Plaça de Sant Jaume,** just south of the cathedral (Mon-Fri 8:30-20:30, Sat 9:00-19:00, Sun 9:00-14:00, in the Barcelona City Hall at Ciutat 2); inside the base of the **Columbus Monument** at the harbor (daily 8:30-19:30); at the **airport**, in both terminals 1 and 2B (both open daily 9:00-21:00); and at **Sants train station** (daily 8:00-20:00).

You'll also find smaller info kiosks in other touristy locales: on **Plaça d'Espanya,** in the park across from the **Sagrada Família** entrance, near the **Columbus Monument** (where the shuttle bus from the cruise port arrives), at the **Nord bus station,** at the various **cruise terminals** along the port, and two on **Plaça de Catalunya.** In addition, throughout the summer, young red-jacketed tourist-info helpers appear in the most touristy parts of town; although they work for the hop-on, hop-off Tourist Bus, they are happy to answer questions.

At any TI, pick up the free city map (although the free El Corte Inglés map provided by most hotels is better), the small Metro map, the monthly *Barcelona Planning.com* guidebook (with basic tips on sightseeing, shopping, events, and restaurants), and the quarterly *See Barcelona* guide (with more in-depth practical information on museums and a neighborhood-by-neighborhood sightseeing rundown). The monthly *In BCN Culture & Leisure* agenda offers a thorough but concise day-by-day list of events. And the monthly *Barcelona Metropolitan* magazine has timely and substantial coverage of local topics and events. All of these are free.

The TI is a handy place to buy tickets for the Tourist Bus (described later, under "Getting Around Barcelona") or for the TI-run walking tours (described later, under "Tours in Barcelona"). All of the TIs (except the kiosks) provide a room-booking service.

Catalunya TI: The all-Catalunya TI works fine for the entire region, and even Madrid (Mon-Sat 10:00-19:00, Sun 10:00-14:00, on Plaça de Joan Carlos I, at the intersection of Passeig de Gràcia and Diagonal at Passeig de Gràcia 107, tel. 932-388-091, www.catalunya.com).

Modernisme Route: Inside the Plaça de Catalunya TI is the privately run **Ruta del Modernisme** desk, which gives out a handy route map showing all 116 Modernista buildings and offers a sightseeing discount package (€12 for a great guidebook and 20-50-percent discounts to many Modernista sights—worthwhile if going beyond the biggies I cover in depth; for €18 you'll also get a guidebook to Modernista bars and restaurants; www.rutadelmodernisme.com).

Sightseeing Passes: The **Articket BCN** ticket covers admission to seven art museums and their temporary exhibits, letting you skip the ticket-buying lines. Sights include the recommended Picasso Museum, Casa Milà, Catalan Art Museum, and Fundació Joan Miró (€30, valid for three months, sold at Plaça de Catalunya and Sants train station TIs and at participating museums, www.articketbcn.org). If you're planning to go to three or more of the museums, this ticket will save you money and time, especially at sights prone to long lines, such as the Picasso Museum and Casa Milà. To skip the ticket-buying line at a museum, show your Articket BCN (to the ticket-taker, at the info desk, or at the group entrance), and you'll get your entrance ticket pronto.

On the other hand, I'd skip the **Barcelona Card,** which covers public transportation (buses, Metro, Montjuïc funicular, and *golondrinas* harbor tour) and includes free admission to a few minor sights and small discounts on many major sights (€29/2 days, €35/3 days, €40/4 days, €47/5 days, sold at TIs and El Corte Inglés department stores).

Arrival in Barcelona

For more information on getting to or from Barcelona by train, plane, bus, or cruise ship, see "Barcelona Connections," at the end of this chapter.

By Train: Virtually all trains end up at Barcelona's **Sants train station,** west of the Old City (for details on getting downtown from Sants Station, see page 1353). AVE trains from Madrid go only to Sants Station and the new **Sagrera Station,** far to the northeast. But many other trains also pass through other stations en route, such as **França Station** (between the El Born and Barceloneta neighborhoods), or the downtown **Passeig de Gràcia** or **Plaça de Catalunya** stations (which are also Metro stops—and very close to most of my recommended hotels). Figure out which stations your train stops at (ask the conductor), and get off at the one most convenient to your hotel.

By Plane: Most international flights arrive at **El Prat de Llobregat Airport,** eight miles southwest of town. Some budget airlines, including Ryanair, fly into **Girona–Costa Brava Airport,** located 60 miles north of Barcelona near Girona. See page 1355 for details on connecting either of these airports to central Barcelona.

By Car: Barcelona's parking fees are outrageously expensive (the lot behind La Boqueria market charges upward of €25/day). You won't need a car in Barcelona, because the taxis and public transportation are so good.

Central Barcelona

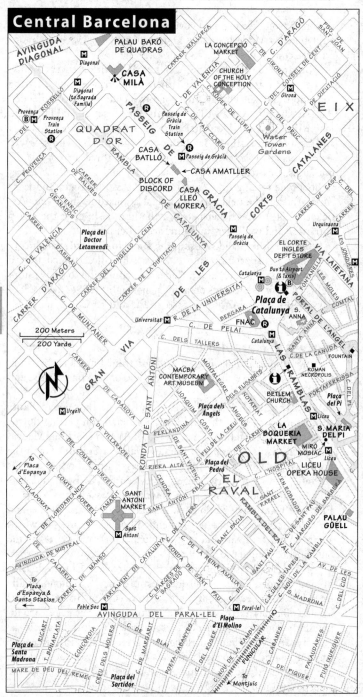

BARCELONA

AVINGUDA DIAGONAL

Diagonal

PALAU BARÓ DE QUADRAS

CARRER MALLORCA

LA CONCEPCIÓ MARKET

C. DE C. D'ARAGÓ

PSG SANT JOAN

CASA MILÀ

Diagonal (to Sagrada Familia)

C. DE VALÈNCIA

CHURCH OF THE HOLY CONCEPTION

C. DEL CONSELL DE CENT

C. DE GIRONA

Girona

C. DE DIPUTACIÓ

EIX

Provença

Provença Train Station

QUADRAT D'OR

C. PROVENÇA

C. DE ROGER DE LLÚRIA

C. DEL BRUC

CATALANES

Passeig de Gràcia Train Station

Passeig de Gràcia

Water Tower Gardens

CARRER DE ROSSELLÓ

C. D'ENRIC GRANADOS

CASA BATLLÓ

CASA AMATLLER

BLOCK OF DISCORD

CASA LLEÓ DE MORERA

CORTS

CARRER DE CASP C. DE

C. DE BALMES

Plaça del Doctor Letamendi

CARRER DEL CONSELLO DE CENT

CARRER DE LA DIPUTACIÓ

Passeig de Gràcia

Urquinaona

LES JONQUERES

CARRER DE VALÈNCIA

CARRER D'ARAGÓ

EL CORTE INGLÉS DEPT STORE

VIA LAIETANA

FONTANELLA MOLES

PORTAL DE L'ANGEL

COMTAL

C. DE MUNTANER

200 Meters

200 Yards

Catalunya

Bus to Airport (& Taxis)

Plaça de Catalunya

S. ANNA

SANTA ANNA

N

GRAN DE CASANOVA

RONDA DE SANT ANTONI

R. DE LA UNIVERSITAT

Universitat

Bergara

C. DE PELAI

Catalunya

FNAC

C. DE LA CANUDA

FOUNTAIN

ROMAN NECROPOLIS

Urgell

C. DE VILLARROEL

C. DELS TALLERS

MACBA CONTEMPORARY ART MUSEUM

MONTALEGRE

JOAQUIM COSTA

DELS ÀNGELS

DELS ELISABETS

NOTARIAT

LAS RAMBLAS

BETLEM CHURCH

PORTAFERRISSA

Plaça del Pi

C. DEL

To Plaça d'Espanya

C. DEL COMTE D'URGELL

PERLANDINA

DE SANT VICENÇ

PEU DE LA CREU

DEL CARME

LA BOQUERIA MARKET

Plaça dels Àngels

S. MARIA DEL PI

Liceu

C. DE FLORIDABLANCA

C. DEL COMTE BORRELL

RIERA ALTA

Plaça del Pedró

OLD EL RAVAL

L'HOSPITAL

MIRÓ MOSAIC

Liceu

LICEU OPERA HOUSE

CENDRA

SANT ANTONI MARKET

SANT ANTONI ABAT

SANT ANTONI DE LA CERA

EN ROBADOR

SANT RAFAEL

RAMBLA DEL RAVAL

C. DE SANT PAU

C. MARQUÈS DE BARBERÀ

PALAU GÜELL

Sant Antoni

DE CALÀBRIA

DE MISTRAL

CARRER DE MANSO

RONDA DE SANT ANTONI

RONDA DE LA REINA AMÀLIA

C. MARGES DE SANT PAU

SANT PACIÀ

SANT PAU

C. DE LES TÀPIES

C. NOU DE LA RAMBLA

AV. DE LES

AVINGUDA DE MISTRAL

To Plaça d'Espanya & Sants Station

CARRER DE

C. MARGES DE C. SAGRADÓ

Poble Sec

Paral-lel

C. DE S. MADRONA

C. DEL CID

AVINGUDA DEL PARAL-LEL

Plaça d'El Molino

Plaça de Santa Madrona

RICART

T. BONAPLATA

CONCORDIA

CREU DELS MOLERS

C. DE MARGARIT

BLAI

POETA CABANYES

C. DEL ROSER

C. NOU DE LA RAMBLA

FUNICULAR

CABANES

PALAUDÀRIES

PUIG XURIGUER

MARE DE DÉU DEL REMEI

Plaça del Sortidor

DE PIQUER

To Montjuïc

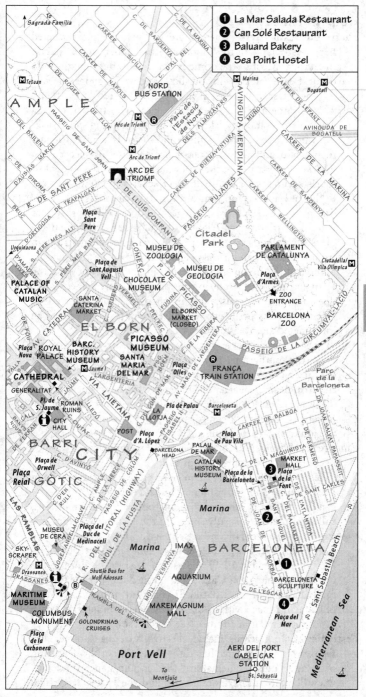

BARCELONA

Helpful Hints

Theft and Scam Alert: You're more likely to be pickpocketed here—especially on the Ramblas—than about anywhere else in Europe. Most of the crime is nonviolent, but muggings do occur. Leave valuables in your hotel and wear a money belt.

Street scams are easy to avoid if you recognize them. Most common is the too-friendly local who tries to engage you in conversation by asking for the time, talking sports, asking whether you speak English, and so on. If a super-friendly man acts drunk and wants to dance because his soccer team just won, he's a pickpocket. Beware of thieves posing as lost tourists who ask for your help. A typical street gambling scam is the pea-and-carrot game, a variation on the shell game. The people winning are all ringers, and you can be sure that you'll lose if you play. Also beware of groups of women aggressively selling carnations, people offering to clean off a stain from your shirt, and people picking things up in front of you on escalators. If you stop for any commotion or show on the Ramblas, put your hands in your pockets before someone else does. Assume any scuffle is simply a distraction by a team of thieves. Crooks are inventive, so keep your guard up. Don't be intimidated...just be smart.

Some areas feel seedy and can be unsafe after dark; I'd avoid the southern part of the Barri Gòtic (basically the two or three blocks directly south and east of Plaça Reial—though the strip near the Carrer de la Mercè tapas bars is better), and I wouldn't venture too deep into the Raval (just west of the Ramblas). One block can separate a comfy tourist zone from the junkies and prostitutes.

Emergency Phone Numbers: General emergencies—112, police—092, ambulance—061 or 112.

Sight Reservations: Several of Barcelona's top sights can have long lines of up to an hour or more. To avoid needless waiting, you can buy tickets in advance by going online (or in some cases, calling). This is especially smart for the Picasso Museum (see page 1294), Sagrada Família (see page 1308), Casa Batlló (see page 1303), and Casa Milà (see page 1307). An Articket BCN (described on page 1259) allows you to skip the lines at the Picasso Museum and Casa Milà, but it doesn't cover the Sagrada Família or Casa Batlló. If you want to tour the Palace of Catalan Music, with its oh-wow Modernista interior, you'll need to reserve it in advance (see page 1296).

Festivals: Major festivals include Festival Grèc, a summer arts festival (June-July, grec.bcn.cat); Montjuïc de Nit, featuring one day of music, cinema, art, theater, and dance (mid-July, www.bcn.cat/cultura/montjuicnit); and the Festes de Gràcia, an eight-day street party (mid-Aug, www.festamajordegracia.cat).

Language Barrier: In posted information throughout the city (such as museum descriptions), English plays third fiddle. You'll see Catalan first, Spanish *(castellano)* second, and English a distant third...or often not at all. Fortunately, many locals speak English.

Web Addresses: If a website doesn't work, try replacing the ".com" or ".es" with ".cat"—the web suffix for Catalunya. Many businesses are switching to this.

Internet Access: Navega Web has hundreds of computers for accessing the Internet and burning pictures onto a disc. It's cheap (€2/hour) and conveniently located across from La Boqueria market, downstairs in the bright Centre Comercial New Park (daily 10:00-23:00, Ramblas 88-94, tel. 933-179-193).

Pharmacy: A 24-hour pharmacy is across from La Boqueria market at #98 on the Ramblas. Another is on the corner of Passeig de Gràcia and Provença, just opposite the entrance to Casa Milà.

Laundry: Several self-service launderettes are located around the Old City. **Wash 'n Dry** is centrally located just off the Ramblas, near a seedy neighborhood just down the street past Palau Güell (self-service-€6.50/load, full service-€14.50/load, daily 9:00-23:00, Carrer Nou de la Rambla 19—see map on page 1330, tel. 934-121-953).

Updates to this Book: For any changes to this book's coverage since it was published, see www.ricksteves.com/update.

Getting Around Barcelona

By Metro

Barcelona's Metro, among Europe's best, connects just about every place you'll visit. Rides cost €2. The T10 Card is a great deal— €9.25 gives you 10 rides (cutting the per-ride cost more than in half). The card is shareable, even by companions traveling with you (insert the card in the machine per passenger). The back of your T10 card will show how many trips were taken, with the time and date of each ride. One "ride" covers you for 1.25 hours of unlimited use on all Metro and local bus lines, as well as local rides on the RENFE and Rodalies de Catalunya train lines (including rides to the airport and train station) and the suburban FGC lines (with service to Montserrat).

Full- and multi-day passes are also available (€7/1 day, €13/2 days, €19/3 days, €24/4 days, €27/5 days, www.tmb.cat). Automated machines at the Metro entrance have English instructions and sell all types of tickets (these can be temperamental about accepting bills, so try to have change on hand).

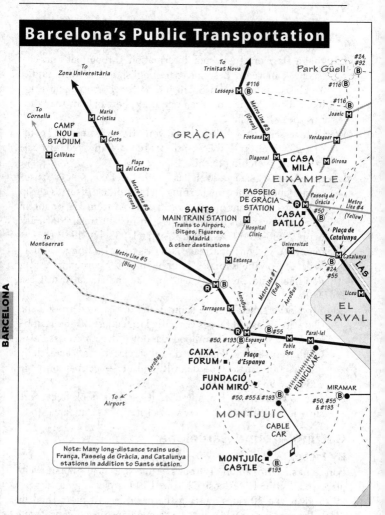

Barcelona's Public Transportation

To Zona Universitària

To Trinitat Nova

To Cornella

Park Güell

#24, #92

Lesseps

#116

#116

#116

Joanic

CAMP NOU STADIUM

Collblanc

Maria Cristina

Les Corts

GRÀCIA

Metro Line #5 (Green)

Fontana

Verdaguer

Plaça del Centre

Diagonal

CASA MILÀ

Girona

EIXAMPLE

Metro line #3 (Green)

SANTS MAIN TRAIN STATION
Trains to Airport, Sitges, Figueres, Madrid & other destinations

PASSEIG DE GRÀCIA STATION

Passeig de Gràcia

#50

Metro Line #4 (Yellow)

To Montserrat

Metro Line #5 (Blue)

Hospital Clinic

CASA BATLLÓ

Plaça de Catalunya

Universitat

Catalunya

#24, #55

Entença

AeroBus

Metro Line #1 (Red)

AeroBus

Liceu

LAS

Tarragona

#50, #193

Espanya

#55

EL RAVAL

CAIXA-FORUM

AeroBus

To Airport

Plaça d'Espanya

Poble Sec

Paral-lel

FUNDACIÓ JOAN MIRÓ

#50, #55 & #193

FUNICULAR

MIRAMAR

#50, #55 & #193

MONTJUÏC

CABLE CAR

Note: Many long-distance trains use França, Passeig de Gràcia, and Catalunya stations in addition to Sants station.

MONTJUÏC CASTLE

#193

Pick up the free Metro map (at any TI) and study it to get familiar with the system. Barcelona has several color-coded lines, but most useful for tourists is the **L3 (green)** line. Handy city-center stops on this line include (in order):

Sants Estació—Main train station

Espanya—Plaça d'Espanya, with access to the lower part of Montjuïc and trains to Montserrat

Paral-lel—Funicular to the top of Montjuïc

Drassanes—Bottom of the Ramblas, near Maritime Museum and Maremagnum mall

Liceu—Middle of the Ramblas, near the heart of the Barri Gòtic and cathedral

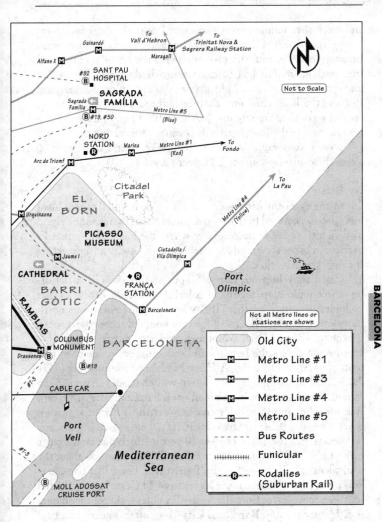

Plaça de Catalunya—Top of the Ramblas and main square with TI, airport bus, and lots of transportation connections

Passeig de Gràcia—Classy Eixample street at the Block of Discord; also connection to L2 (purple) line to Sagrada Família and L4 (yellow) line (described below)

Diagonal—Gaudí's Casa Milà

The **L4 (yellow)** line, which crosses the L3 (green) line at Passeig de Gràcia, is also useful. Helpful stops include **Joanic** (bus #116 to Park Güell), **Jaume I** (between the Barri Gòtic/cathedral and El Born/Picasso Museum), and **Barceloneta** (at the south end of El Born, near the harbor action).

When you enter the Metro, first look for your line number

and color, then follow signs to take that line in the direction you're going. The names of the end stops are used to indicate directions. Insert your ticket into the turnstile (with the arrow pointing in), then reclaim it. On board, most trains have handy Metro-line diagrams with dots that light up next to upcoming destinations. Because the lines cross one another multiple times, there can be several ways to make any one journey. (It's a good idea to keep a general map with you—especially if you're transferring.)

Watch your valuables. If I were a pickpocket, I'd set up shop along the made-for-tourists L3 (green) line.

By Bus

Given the excellent Metro service, it's unlikely you'll take a **local bus** (also €2, covered by T10 Card, insert ticket in machine behind driver), although I've noted places where the bus makes sense. In particular, buses are useful for reaching Park Güell and connecting the sights on Montjuïc.

The handy **hop-on, hop-off Tourist Bus** (Bus Turístic) offers three multi-stop circuits in colorful double-decker buses that go topless in sunny weather. The two-hour blue route covers north Barcelona (most Gaudí sights); the two-hour red route covers south Barcelona (Barri Gòtic, Montjuïc); and the shorter, 40-minute green route covers the beaches and modern Fòrum complex (this route runs April-Oct only). All have headphone commentary (daily 9:00-20:00 in summer, 9:00-19:00 in winter, buses run every 5-25 minutes, most frequent in summer, www.barcelonabusturistic.cat). Ask for a brochure (includes city map) at the TI or at a pick-up point. One-day (€24) and two-day (€31) tickets, which you can buy on the bus or at the TI, offer 10 to 20 percent discounts on the city's major sights and walking tours, which will likely save you about the equivalent of half the cost of the Tourist Bus. From Plaça de Catalunya, the blue northern route leaves from El Corte Inglés; the red southern route leaves from the west—Ramblas—side of the square. A different company, **Barcelona City Tour,** offers a nearly identical service (same price and discounts, two loops instead of three, www.barcelonacitytour.cat).

By Taxi

Barcelona is one of Europe's best taxi towns. Taxis are plentiful (there are more than 10,000) and honest, whether they like it or not. The light on top shows which tariff they're charging; a green light on the roof indicates that a taxi is available. Cab rates are reasonable (€2.50 drop charge, €1/kilometer, these *"Tarif 2"* rates are in effect 7:00-21:00, pay higher *"Tarif 1"* rates off-hours, luggage-€1/piece, €2.10 surcharge to/from train station or cruise port, €3.10 surcharge for airport, other fees posted in window).

Save time by hopping a cab (figure €10 from Ramblas to Sants Station).

Tours in Barcelona

On Foot

Walking Tours

The TI at Plaça de Sant Jaume offers great guided walks through the **Barri Gòtic** in English. You'll learn the medieval story of the city as you walk from Plaça de Sant Jaume through the cathedral neighborhood (€14, daily at 9:30, 2 hours, groups limited to 35, buy your ticket 15 minutes early at the TI desk—not from the guide, in summer stop by the office a day ahead to reserve, tel. 932-853-832, www.barcelonaturisme.cat).

The TI at Plaça de Catalunya offers a **Picasso** walk, taking you through the streets of his youth and early career and finishing in the Picasso Museum (€20, includes museum admission; Tue, Thu, and Sat at 15:00; 2 hours plus museum visit). There are also **gourmet** walks (€20, Fri and Sat at 10:00, 2 hours), **Modernisme** walks (€14, Fri and Sat June-Sept at 18:00, Oct-May at 16:00, 2 hours), and a **Maritime** tour that includes a *golondrinas* boat trip on the harbor (€18, Fri and Sat at 10:00, 2 hours). Other themes include Bohemian Barcelona, the Civil War, movie locations, and a literary tour (drop by the office for a full list). These tours depart from the TI at Plaça de Catalunya (except the Maritime tour, which begins at the Columbus Monument); it's always smart to reserve in advance.

The Ruta del Modernisme desk inside the Plaça de Catalunya TI also does tours of specific **Modernista buildings** that are otherwise not open to the public (see www.rutadelmodernisme.com).

"Free" Walking Tours

Several companies offer "free" walks that rely on—and expect—tips to stay in business. Though led by young people who've basically memorized a clever script (rather than trained historians), these walks can be a fun, casual way to get your bearings.

I like **Runner Bean Tours,** run by Gorka, Ann-Marie, and a handful of local guides. They offer 2.5-hour, English-only walks covering the Old City and Gaudí (both tours depart from Plaça Reial at 11:00 daily year-round, plus daily at 16:30 in April-Oct, www.runnerbeantours.com, mobile 636-108-776). They also do night tours, family walks, and more. Groups can range from just a couple of people up to 30.

Discover Walks does similar tours, with three different two-hour itineraries: Gaudí (daily at 10:00, meet in front of Casa Batlló); Ramblas and Barri Gòtic (daily at 15:00, meet in front of Liceu Opera House on the Ramblas); and Trendy Barcelona, covering the

El Born neighborhood (daily at 17:00, meet at Plaça de l'Angel next to Jaume I Metro stop). This company distinguishes itself by using exclusively native-born guides—no expats (suggested tips: €5/person for a bad guide, €10 for a good one, €15 for a great one, www.discoverwalks.com, tel. 931-816-810).

Local Guides

The **Barcelona Guide Bureau** is a co-op with about 20 local guides who give personalized four-hour tours (weekdays-€216, per-person price drops as group gets bigger; weekends and holidays-€256, no price break with size of group); **Joana Wilhelm** and **Carles Picazo** are excellent (Via Laietana 54, tel. 932-682-422 or 933-107-778, www.bgb.es).

José Soler is a great and fun-to-be-with local guide who enjoys tailoring a walk through his hometown to your interests (€195/half-day per group, mobile 615-059-326, www.pepitotours.com, info@pepitotours.com).

Cristina Sanjuán of Live Barcelona is another good, professional guide who leads walking tours and can also arrange cruise excursions. It's best to reserve by email (€155/2 hours, €20/each additional hour; €195 extra for a car for up to 2 people, €220 extra for up to 6, can combine with airport transfer; tel. 936-327-259, mobile 609-205-844, www.livebarcelona.com, info@livebarcelona.com).

On Wheels

Guided Bus Tours

The **Barcelona Guide Bureau** offers several sightseeing tours leaving from Plaça de Catalunya. Departure times can change. Tours are designed to end at a major sight in case you'd like to spend more time there. The Gaudí tour visits the facades of Casa Batlló and Casa Milà, as well as Park Güell and the Sagrada Família (€50, includes Sagrada Família admission, daily at 9:00, also mid-April-Oct Mon-Sat at 15:15, 3.5 hours). Other tours offered year-round include the Montjuïc tour (€30, includes Spanish Village admission, daily at 12:30, 3 hours) and the All Barcelona Highlights tour (€66, includes Sagrada Família and Spanish Village admissions, daily at 9:00, 6 hours). During the high season, there's also the Gaudí Plus tour, which combines the Gaudí tour with some "off-the-beaten-path masterpieces" (€55, mid-April-Oct Mon-Sat at 9:00, 4 hours). You can get detailed information and book tickets at a TI, on their website, or simply by showing up at their departure point on Plaça de Catalunya in front of the Hard Rock Café—look for the guides holding orange umbrellas. Buying tickets online can save you about 10 percent. You can buy tickets at many hotels for no extra charge (tel. 933-152-261, www.barcelonaguidebureau.com).

Catalunya Tourist Bus also runs excursions to nearby destinations, including some that are difficult to reach by public transportation. Trips include **Montserrat** (€59, 8 hours, includes Gaudí's unfinished Colònia Güell development) and **Salvador Dalí sights** in Figueres and Girona (€71, 11 hours). Both itineraries depart Tuesday through Sunday at 8:30 from Plaça de Catalunya (€8 discount for groups of 4 or more—team up with other travelers to save; live trilingual commentary in Catalan, Spanish, and English; €5 extra for a more in-depth English audioguide; book at TIs, by phone, or online; tel. 932-853-832, www.catalunyabusturistic.com).

For information on **hop-on, hop-off bus tours,** see "Getting Around Barcelona," earlier.

Bike Tours

Several companies run bike tours around Barcelona.

Un Cotxe Menys ("One Car Less") organizes three-hour English-only bike tours daily at 11:00 year-round (April-midSept also Fri-Mon at 16:30). Your guide leads you from sight to sight, mostly on bike paths and through parks, with a stop-and-go commentary (€22 includes bike rental and drink, no reservations needed, tours meet just outside TI on Plaça Sant Jaume in Barri Gòtic—or, 10 minutes later, at their bike shop in El Born near the Church of Santa Maria del Mar; Carrer de l'Esparteria 3—see map on page 1330, tel. 932-682-105, www.bicicletabarcelona.com). The bike shop also rents bikes (€5/hour, €10/4 hours, €18/24 hours, daily 10:00-19:00, leave €150 or photo ID for deposit).

Barcelona CicloTour runs a similar itinerary (€22, departs from Hard Rock Café on Plaça de Catalunya daily at 11:00, midApril-Oct also at 16:30; night tour departs June-Sept Thu-Sun at 19:30, Oct Fri-Sat at 19:30; tel. 933-171-970, www.barcelonaciclotour.com).

Self-Guided Walks

These walks through the atmospheric Old City introduce you to places you may want to explore further. They're easy to follow, pass by some major sights, and provide background to this complex metropolis. The first begins at Barcelona's main square and leads you down the city's main drag: the Ramblas. The second walk guides you into the heart of the Barri Gòtic, the neighborhood around Barcelona's cathedral.

▲▲▲The Ramblas Ramble: From Plaça de Catalunya to the Waterfront

For more than a century, this walk down Barcelona's main boulevard has drawn locals and visitors alike. While its former elegance has been tackified somewhat by tourist shops and fast-food joints, this still has the best people-watching in town. Walk the Ramblas at least once to get the lay of the land, then venture farther afield. It's a one-hour, downhill stroll, with an easy way to get back by Metro. The Ramblas is two different streets by day and by night; stroll it from top to bottom in the evening and again the next morning, grabbing breakfast on a stool in a market café.

The word "Ramblas" is plural; the street is actually a succession of five separately named segments. But street signs and addresses treat it as a single long street—"La Rambla," singular. This pedestrian-only Champs-Elysées takes you from rich (at the top) to rough (at the port). You'll raft the river of Barcelonese life past a grand opera house, elegant cafés, flower stands, retread prostitutes, brazen pickpockets, power-dressing con men, artists, street mimes, an outdoor bird market, great shopping, and people looking to charge more for a shoeshine than what you paid for the shoes.

• *Start your ramble at the top of the Ramblas, where it connects with Plaça de Catalunya.*

❶ **Plaça de Catalunya:** Dotted with fountains, statues, and pigeons, and ringed by grand Art Deco buildings, this plaza is Barcelona's center. The square's stern, straight lines are a reaction to the curves of Modernisme (which predominates in the Eixample district, just to the north). Plaça de Catalunya is the hub for the Metro, bus, airport shuttle, and Tourist Bus. It's where Barcelona congregates to watch soccer matches on the big screen, to demonstrate, to celebrate, and to enjoy outdoor concerts and festivals. It's the center of the world for the Catalan people.

Geographically, the 12-acre square links old Barcelona (the narrow streets to the south) with the new (the broad boulevards to the north). Four great thoroughfares radiate from here. The Ramblas is the popular pedestrian promenade. Passeig de Gràcia has fashionable shops and cafés (and noisy traffic). Rambla de Catalunya is equally fashionable but cozier and more pedestrian-friendly. Avinguda Portal de l'Angel (shopper-friendly and traffic-free) leads to the Barri Gòtic (note that my self-guided "Barri Gòtic Walk" begins from right here).

Historically, Plaça de Catalunya links the modern city with its past. In the 1850s, when Barcelona tore down its medieval walls to expand the city, this square on the edge of the walls was one of the first places to be developed.

The odd, inverted-staircase **monument** at the Ramblas end of the square, representing the shape of Catalunya, honors a former president of Catalunya, Francesc Macià i Llussà, who declared independence for the breakaway region in 1931. (It didn't quite stick.) It was designed by the sculptor Josep Maria Subirachs, whose work you'll see at the Sagrada Família (see page 1308).

The venerable Café Zürich, just across the street from the monument, is a popular downtown rendezvous spot for locals. Homesick Americans might prefer the nearby Hard Rock Café.

• *Cross the street and start heading down the Ramblas. To get oriented, pause 20 yards down, at the ornate lamppost with a fountain as its base (on the right, near #129).*

❶ **Top of the Ramblas (Fountain of Canaletes):** The black-and-gold fountain has been a local favorite for more than a century. When Barcelona tore down its medieval wall and transformed the Ramblas from a drainage ditch into an elegant promenade, this fountain was one of its early attractions. Legend says that a drink from the fountain ensures that you'll come back to Barcelona one day. Watch the tourists—eager to guarantee a return trip—struggle with the awkwardly high water pressure. It's still a popular let's-meet-at-the-fountain rendezvous spot and a gathering place for celebrations and demonstrations. Fans of the Barcelona soccer team rally here before a big match—some touch their hand to their lips, then "kiss" the fountain with their hand for good luck. It's also a good spot to fill up your water bottle.

• *Continue strolling downhill.*

All along the Ramblas are **newsstands** (open 24 hours). Among their souvenirs, you'll see soccer paraphernalia, especially the scarlet-and-blue of FC Barcelona (known as "Barça"). The team is owned by its more than 170,000 "members"—fans who buy season tickets, which come with a share of ownership (the team's healthy payroll guarantees that they're always in contention). Their motto, "More than a club" *(Mes que un club)*, suggests that Barça represents not only athletic prowess but Catalan cultural identity. This comes to a head during a match nicknamed "El Clásico," in which they face their bitter rivals, Real Madrid (whom many Barça fans view as stand-ins for Castilian cultural chauvinism).

Walk 100 yards downhill to #115, where the **Royal Academy of Science's** clock marks official Barcelona time—synchronize. Notice the **TI** kiosk right on the Ramblas—a handy stop for any questions. The **Carrefour** supermarket just behind it has cheap groceries (at #113, Mon-Sat 10:00-22:00, closed Sun).

• *You're now standing at the...*

❸ **Rambla of the Little Birds:** Traditionally, kids brought their parents here to buy pets, especially on Sundays. Today, only a couple of these traditional pet stalls survive. For Barcelona's apartment-dwellers, birds, turtles, fish, hamsters, and rabbits are easier to handle than dogs and cats. But animal-rights groups started lobbying to cut back on these stalls because so many families were making impulse buys with no serious interest in taking care of these cute little critters—and many ended up being flushed. Still,

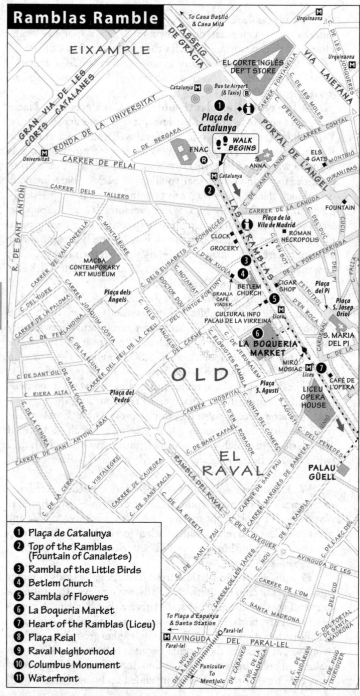

Ramblas Ramble

① Plaça de Catalunya
② Top of the Ramblas (Fountain of Canaletes)
③ Rambla of the Little Birds
④ Betlem Church
⑤ Rambla of Flowers
⑥ La Boqueria Market
⑦ Heart of the Ramblas (Liceu)
⑧ Plaça Reial
⑨ Raval Neighborhood
⑩ Columbus Monument
⑪ Waterfront

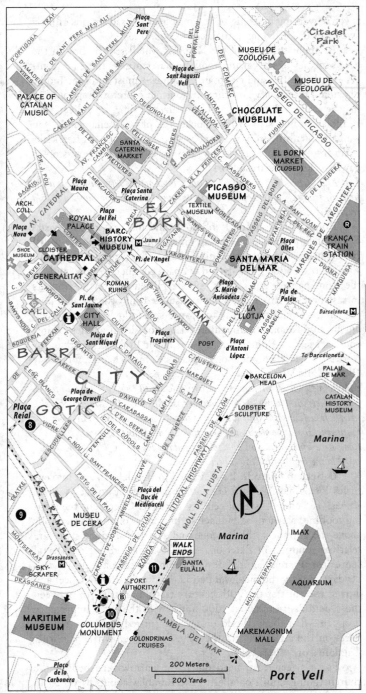

if you're walking by at night, you may hear the sad sounds of little tweety birds locked up in their collapsed kiosks.

At about this part of the Ramblas, you'll see the first of the drag's medley of surreal and goofy **human statues.** These performers—with creative and elaborate costumes—must audition and be registered by the city government; to avoid overcrowding, only 15 may be at work along the Ramblas at any one time. To enliven your Ramblas ramble, stroll with a pocket full of small change. As you wander downhill, drop coins into their cans (the money often kicks them into entertaining gear). Warning: Wherever people stop to gawk, pickpockets are at work.

• *At #122 (the big, modern Citadines Hotel on the left, just behind the first bird kiosk), a 100-yard detour through the passageway leads to a recently discovered...*

Roman Necropolis: Look down and imagine a 2,000-year-old tomb-lined road. In Roman cities, tombs (outside the walls) typically lined the roads leading into town. Emperor Augustus spent a lot of time in modern-day Spain conquering new land, so the Romans were sure to incorporate Hispania into the empire's infrastructure. This road, Via Augusta, led into the Roman port of Barcino (today's highway to France still follows the route laid out by this Roman thoroughfare). Looking down at these ruins, you can see how Roman Barcino was about 10 feet lower than today's street level. For more on this city's Roman chapter, follow my "Barri Gòtic Walk," later.

• *Return to the Ramblas and continue downhill 100 yards or so to the next street. At Carrer de la Portaferrissa (across from the big church), turn left a few steps and look right to see the **decorative tile** over the fountain. The scene shows the original city wall with the gate that once stood here and the action on what is today's Ramblas. Cross the boulevard to the front of the big church.*

❹ **Betlem Church:** It's dedicated to Bethlehem, and for centuries locals have flocked here at Christmastime to see Nativity scenes. The church is 17th-century Baroque: Check out the sloping roofline, ball-topped pinnacles, corkscrew columns, and scrolls above the entrance. The Baroque and also Renaissance styles are relatively unusual in Barcelona because it missed out on several centuries of architectural development. Barcelona enjoyed two heydays: during the medieval period (before the Renaissance) and during the turn of the 20th century (after Baroque). In between those periods, from about 1500 until 1850, the city's importance dropped—first, New World discoveries shifted lucrative trade to ports on the Atlantic, and then the Spanish crown kept unruly Catalunya on a short leash.

For a sweet treat, head down the narrow lane behind the church (going uphill parallel to the Ramblas about 30 yards) to the recommended **Café Granja Viader,** which has specialized in baked and dairy delights since 1870. Step inside to see Viader family photos and early posters advertising Cacaolat—the local chocolate milk Barcelonans love. (For more sugary treats nearby, follow "A Short, Sweet Walk" on page 1352.)

• *Continue down the boulevard, through the stretch called the...*

❺ **Rambla of Flowers:** This colorful block, lined with flower stands, is the Rambla of Flowers. On the left, at #100, **Gimeno** sells cigars. Step inside and appreciate the dying art of cigar boxes. Go ahead, do something forbidden in America but perfectly legal here...buy a Cuban (little singles for €1). Tobacco shops sell stamps and phone cards, plus bongs and marijuana gear—the Spanish approach to pot is very casual. While people can't legally sell marijuana, they're allowed to grow it for personal use and consume it. (You'll smell its sweet smoke all over the city.)

• *Continue to the Metro stop marked by the red M. At #91 (on the right) is the arcaded entrance to Barcelona's great covered market, La Boqueria. If this main entry is choked with visitors (as it often is), you can skirt around the sides by entering one block in either direction (look for the round arches that mark passages into the market colonnade).*

❻ **La Boqueria:** This lively market hall is an explosion of chicken legs, bags of live snails, stiff fish, delicious oranges, odd odors, and sleeping dogs. The best day for a visit is Saturday, when the market is thriving. It's closed on Sundays, and locals avoid it on Mondays, when it's open but (they believe) vendors are selling items that aren't necessarily fresh—especially seafood, since fishermen stay home on Sundays.

Since as far back as 1200, Barcelonans have bought their animal parts here. The market was originally located by the walled city's entrance, as many medieval markets were (since it was more expensive to trade within the walls). It later expanded into the colonnaded courtyard of a now-gone monastery before being topped with a colorful arcade in 1850.

While tourists are drawn like moths to a flame to the area around the main entry (below the colorful stained-glass sign), locals know that the stalls up front pay the highest rent—and therefore have to inflate their prices and cater to out-of-towners. For example, the juices along the main drag just inside the entrance are tempting, but if you venture to the right a couple of alleys, the clientele gets more local and the prices drop dramatically.

Stop by the recommended **Pinotxo Bar**—it's just inside the market, under the sign—and snap a photo of Juan. Animated Juan and his family are always busy feeding shoppers. Getting Juan to crack a huge smile and a thumbs-up for your camera makes a great shot...and he loves it. The stools nearby are a fine perch for enjoying both your coffee and the people-watching.

The market and lanes nearby are busy with tempting little eateries (several are listed on page 1340). Drop by a café for an *espresso con leche* or breakfast *tortilla española* (potato omelet). Once you get past the initial gauntlet, do some exploring. The small square on the north side of the market hosts a farmers market in the mornings. Wander around—as local architect Antoni Gaudí used to—and gain inspiration.

• *Head back out to the street and continue down the Ramblas.*

It's clear that, as you walk the Ramblas, you're skirting along the west boundary of the old Barri Gòtic neighborhood. As you walk, glance to the left through a modern archway for a glimpse of the medieval church tower of **Santa Maria del Pi,** a popular venue for concerts (see page 1328). This also marks Plaça del Pi and a great shopping street, Carrer Petritxol, which runs parallel to the Ramblas.

At the corner directly opposite the modern archway, find the highly regarded **Escribà** bakery (look for the *Antigua Casa Figueras* sign arching over the doorway), with its fine Modernista facade and interior. Notice the beautiful mosaics, stained glass, and woodwork. In the sidewalk in front of the door is a plaque explaining that the building dates from 1902 (plaques like these identify historic shops all over town).

• *After another block, you reach the Liceu Metro station, marking the...*

❼ **Heart of the Ramblas (Liceu):** At the Liceu Metro station's elevators, the Ramblas widens a bit into a small, lively square (Plaça de la Boqueria). Liceu marks the midpoint of the Ramblas, halfway between Plaça de Catalunya and the waterfront.

Underfoot in the center of the Ramblas, find the much-trodupon red-white-yellow-and-blue **mosaic** by homegrown abstract artist Joan Miró. The mosaic's black arrow represents an anchor, a reminder of the city's attachment to the sea. Miró's childlike designs are found all over the city, from murals to mobiles to the La Caixa bank logo. The best place in Barcelona to see his work is in the Fundació Joan Miró at Montjuïc (see page 1322).

The surrounding buildings have playful ornamentation typical of the city. The **Chinese dragon** holding a lantern (at #82) decorates a former umbrella shop (notice the fun umbrella mosaics high up). While the dragon may seem purely decorative, it's actually an important symbol of Catalan pride for its connection to the local patron saint, St. Jordi (George).

Hungry? The recommended **Taverna Basca Irati** tapas bar is a block up Carrer del Cardenal Casanyes. This is one of many userfriendly, Basque-style tapas bars in town; instead of ordering, you can just grab or point to what looks good on the display platters, then pay per piece.

Back on the Ramblas, a few steps down (on the right) is the **Liceu Opera House** (Gran Teatre del Liceu), which hosts world-class opera, dance, and theater (box office around the right side, open Mon-Fri 13:30-20:00). Opposite the opera house is Café de l'Opera (#74), an elegant stop for an expensive beverage. This bustling café, with Modernista decor and a historic atmosphere, boasts that it's been open since 1929, even during the Spanish Civil War.

• *We've seen the best stretch of the Ramblas; from here, it's all downhill (in every sense) to the port. To cut this walk short, you could catch the Metro back to Plaça de Catalunya. Otherwise, continue down the Ramblas another 30 yards. The wide, straight street that crosses the Ramblas at this point (Carrer de Ferran) leads left to Plaça de Sant Jaume, the government center.*

Continue down the Ramblas another 50 yards (to #46), and turn left down an arcaded lane (Correr de Colom) to the square called...

❽ **Plaça Reial:** Dotted with palm trees, surrounded by an arcade, and ringed by yellow buildings with white Neoclassical trim, this elegant square has a colonial ambience. It comes complete with old-fashioned taverns, modern bars with patio seating, and a Sunday coin-and-stamp market (10:00-14:00). Completing the picture are Gaudí's first public works (the two colorful helmeted lampposts). While this used to be a seedy and dangerous part of town, recent gentrification efforts have given it new life, making it inviting and accessible. (The small streets stretching toward the water from the square remain a bit sketchier.) It's a lively hangout by day or by night. Big spaces like this (as well as the site of La Boqueria market) often originated as monasteries. When these were dissolved in the 19th century, their fine colonnaded squares were incorporated into what were considered generally more useful public spaces.

Head back out to the Ramblas. Across the boulevard, a half-block detour down Carrer Nou de la Rambla brings you to **Palau Güell,** designed by Antoni Gaudí (on the left, at #3-5). Even from the outside, you get a sense of this innovative apartment, the first of Gaudí's Modernista buildings. As this is early Gaudí (built 1886-1890), it's darker and more Neo-Gothic than his more famous later work. The two parabolic-arch doorways and elaborate wrought-iron work signal his emerging nonrectangular style. Recently renovated, Palau Güell offers an informative look at a Gaudí interior (see listing on page 1302). Pablo Picasso had a studio at #10 (though there's nothing to see there today).

• *Continue downhill on the Ramblas.*

❾ **Raval Neighborhood (Barri Xines):** The neighborhood on the right-hand side of this stretch of the Ramblas is El Raval. Its nickname was Barri Xines—the world's only Chinatown with nothing even remotely Chinese in or near it. Named for the prejudiced notion that Chinese immigrants went hand-in-hand with poverty, prostitution, and drug dealing, the neighborhood's actual inhabitants were poor Spanish, North African, and Roma (Gypsy) people. At night, the Barri Xines was frequented by prostitutes, many of them transvestites, who catered to sailors wandering up from the port. Today, it's becoming gentrified, but it's still a pretty rough neighborhood.

The seedy zone attracts plenty of characters who don't need the palm trees to be shady. You're likely to see some good old-fashioned **shell games.** Stand back and observe these nervous no-necks at work. They swish around their little boxes, making sure to show you the pea. Their shills play and win. Then, in hopes of making easy money, fools lose big time.

Near the bottom of the Ramblas, take note of the Drassanes Metro stop (close to the Museo de Cera, or wax museum), which can take you back to Plaça de Catalunya when this walk is over. The skyscraper to the right of the Ramblas is the Edificio Colón. When it was built in 1970, the 28-story structure was Barcelona's first high-rise. Near the skyscraper is the Maritime Museum, housed in what were the city's giant medieval shipyards (permanent collection likely closed through 2014; see listing on page 1299).

• *Up ahead is the...*

❿ **Columbus Monument and Waterfront:** The 200-foot column commemorates Christopher Columbus' stop in Barcelona after his first trip to America (see listing on page 1299).

Continue ahead to the waterfront. Barcelona is one of Europe's top 10 ports, though this stretch of the harbor is a pleasant marina with sailboats.

Stand here and survey some of your sightseeing options: At your feet are the *golondrinas* harbor cruise boats (page 1299). Across the harbor (though not really visible from here) is the spit of land called Barceloneta, home to some nice restaurants and sandy beaches (see page 1351). To the right of the harbor rises the majestic, 570-foot bluff of Montjuïc, a park-like setting dotted with a number of sights and museums (see page 1317).

The pedestrian bridge jutting into the harbor is a modern extension of the Ramblas called La Rambla del Mar ("Rambla of the Sea"). This popular wooden bridge—with waves like the sea—leads to Maremagnum, a shopping mall with a cinema, a huge aquarium, restaurants, and piles of people. Late at night, it's a rollicking youth hangout.

• *Your ramble is over. If it's a nice day, consider strolling the promenade and looping back around on La Rambla del Mar. Or maybe explore El Born. Or, if you're truly on vacation, walk through Barceloneta to the beach.*

If you'd like to get to other points in town, your best bet is to back-track to the Drassanes Metro stop. Alternatively, you can catch buses #14 or #59 from along the top of the promenade to Plaça de Catalunya.

▲▲The Barri Gòtic: From Plaça de Catalunya to the Cathedral

Barcelona's Barri Gòtic, or Gothic Quarter, is a bustling world of shops, bars, and nightlife packed into narrow, winding lanes and undiscovered courtyards. This is Barcelona's birthplace—where the ancient Romans built a city, where medieval Christians built their cathedral, and where Barcelonans lived within a ring of protective walls until the 1850s, when the city expanded.

Today, this area—nicknamed simply "El Gòtic"—is Barcelona's most historic neighborhood. Concentrate on the area around the cathedral (since the section near the port is somewhat dull and seedy). The Barri Gòtic is a tangled-yet-inviting grab bag of grand squares, schoolyards, Art Nouveau storefronts, musty junk shops, classy antiques shops (on Carrer de la Palla), street musicians strumming Catalan folk songs, and balconies with domestic jungles behind wrought-iron bars. Go on a cultural scavenger hunt. Write a poem. Take artsy pictures. This self-guided walk gives you a structure, covering the major sights and offering a historical overview before you get lost.

• *Start on Barcelona's grand, main square, Plaça de Catalunya (described on page 1270). From the southeast corner (near El Corte Inglés), head downhill along the broad pedestrian boulevard called...*

❶ **Avinguda Portal de l'Angel:** For much of Barcelona's history, this was one of the main boulevards leading into town. A medieval wall enclosed the city, and there was an entrance here—the "Gate of the Angel"—that gives the street its name. An angel statue atop the gate kept the city safe from plagues and bid voyagers safe journey as they left the security of the city. Imagine the fascinating scene here at the Gate of the Angel, where Barcelona stopped and the wilds began.

Today's street is pretty globalized and sanitized, full of international chain stores. Pause at Carrer de Santa Anna to admire the Art Nouveau awning at (another) El Corte Inglés store.

• *A half-block detour down Carrer de Santa Anna (at #32) leads to a pleasant, flower-fragrant courtyard with the...*

❷ **Church of Santa Anna:** This 12th-century gem was one of those *extra muro* churches, with its marker cross still standing outside. As part of a convent, the church has a fine cloister, an arcaded walkway around a leafy courtyard (viewable through the gate to the left of the church). Climb the modern stairs for views of the bell tower.

BARCELONA

If the church is open, you'll see a bare Romanesque interior and Greek-cross floor plan, topped with an octagonal wooden roof. The recumbent-knight tomb is of Miguel de Boera, renowned admiral of Charles V. The door at the far end of the nave leads to the cloister (church hours vary but usually daily 9:00-13:00 and 18:00-20:00).

• *Continue down Avinguda Portal de l'Angel. At Carrer de Montsió (on the left), side-trip half a block to...*

❸ **Els Quatre Gats ("The Four Cats"):** This restaurant (at #3) is a historic monument, tourist attraction, nightspot, and one of my recommended eateries. It's famous for being the circa-1900 bohemian-artist hangout where Picasso nursed drinks with friends and first publicly hung his art (in 1897, at age 16). The building itself, by prominent architect Josep Puig i Cadafalch, represents Neo-Gothic Modernisme. Stepping inside, you feel the turn-of-the-century vibe. Rich Barcelona elites and would-be avant-garde artists looked to Paris, not Madrid, for cultural inspiration. Consequently, this place was clearly inspired by the Paris scene (especially Le Chat Noir cabaret/café, the hangout of Montmartre intellectuals). Like Le Chat Noir, Els Quatre Gats even published its own artsy magazine for a while. The story of the name? When the proprietor told his friends that he'd stay open 24 hours a day, they said, "No one will come. It'll just be you and four cats" (Catalan slang for "a few crazy people"). While you can have a snack, meal, or drink here, if you just want to look around, ask, *"Solo mirar, por favor?"*

• *Return to Avinguda Portal de l'Angel and continue down the street until you run into a building at a fork in the road, with a...*

❹ **Fountain:** The fountain's blue-and-yellow tilework depicts ladies carrying jugs of water. In the 17th century, this was the last watering stop for horses before leaving town. As recently as 1940, one in nine Barcelonans got their water from fountains like this. It's still used today.

• *Take the left fork, passing by the Royal Art Circle Museum (temporary exhibits). Enter the large square called the...*

❺ **Plaça Nova:** Two bold **Roman towers** flank the main street. These once guarded the entrance gate of the ancient Roman city of Barcino. The big stones that make up the base of the (reconstructed) towers are actually Roman. At the base, find the **modern bronze letters** spelling out "BARCINO." The city's name may have come from Barca, one of Hannibal's generals, who is said to have passed through during Hannibal's roundabout invasion of Italy. At Barcino's peak, the **Roman wall** (see the section stretching to the left of the towers) was 25 feet high and a mile around, with 74 towers. It enclosed an area of 30 acres—population 4,000.

One of the towers has a section of **Roman aqueduct** (a modern reconstruction). These bridges of stone carried fresh water from the distant hillsides into the walled city. Here the water supply split into two channels, one to feed Roman industry, the other for the general populace. The Roman aqueducts would be the best water system Barcelona would have until the 20th century.

Opposite the towers is the modern Catalan College of Architects building with a **frieze designed by Picasso** (1960). In Picasso's distinctive childlike style, it shows branch-waving kings and children celebrating a local festival. Picasso spent his formative years (1895-1904, ages 14-23) in the Barri Gòtic. He had a studio a block east of here (where the big Caixa Catalunya building stands today). He drank with fellow bohemians at Els Quatre Gats (which we just passed) and frequented brothels a few blocks south of here on Carrer d'Avinyo ("Avignon"), which inspired his seminal Cubist painting *Les Demoiselles d'Avignon*. Picasso's Barri Gòtic was a hotbed of trend-setting art, propelling Picasso forward just before he moved to Paris and remade modern art.

• *Now head to the left and take in the mighty facade of the...*

❻ Cathedral of Barcelona (Catedral de Barcelona): This location has been the center of Christian worship since the fourth century, and this particular building dates (mainly) from the 14th century. The facade is a virtual catalog of Gothic motifs: a pointed arch over the entrance, robed statues, tracery in windows, gargoyles, and bell towers with winged angels. The style is French Flamboyant (meaning "flame-like"), and the roofline sports the prickly spires meant to give the impressions of a church flickering with spiritual fires. The facade is typically Gothic...but not medieval. It's a Neo-Gothic work from the 19th century. The area in front of the cathedral is where they dance the *sardana*. Standing in front of the Barcelona cathedral, if you look left, you can see the colorful swooping roof of the Santa Caterina Market (described on page 1297).

The cathedral's interior—with its vast size, peaceful cloister, and many ornate chapels—is worth a visit. For specifics, see the listing on page 1288.

• *The Frederic Marès Museum (see page 1289 for details) is just to the left of the cathedral. But for now, return to the Roman towers. Pass between the towers up Carrer del Bisbe, and take an immediate left, up the ramp to the entrance of the...*

❼ Casa de l'Ardiaca *(Archivo):* It's free to enter this mansion, which was once the archdeacon's house and today functions as the city archives. The elaborately carved doorway is Renaissance. To the right of the doorway is a carved mail slot by 19th-century Modernist architect Lluís Domènech i Montaner. Enter through a small courtyard with a fountain. Notice how the century-old palm

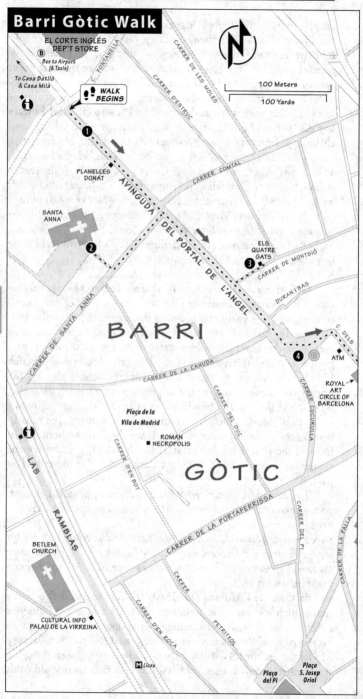

Barri Gòtic Walk

EL CORTE INGLÉS
DEP'T STORE

B Bus to Airport
(& Taxis)

To Casa Batlló
& Casa Milà

C. FONTANELLA

CARRER DE LES MOLES

CARRER D'ESTRUC

WALK
BEGINS

100 Meters

100 Yards

1

PLANELLES
DONAT

CARRER COMTAL

AVINGUDA

SANTA
ANNA

2

DEL PORTAL DE L'ANGEL

ELS
QUATRE
GATS

3

CARRER DE MONTSIÓ

DURAN I BAS

CARRER DE SANTA ANNA

BARRI

C. DELS

4

ATM

CARRER DE LA CANUDA

ROYAL
ART
CIRCLE OF
BARCELONA

CARRER CUCURULLA

Plaça de la
Vila de Madrid

CARRER DEL DUC

ROMAN
NECROPOLIS

GÒTIC

CARRER D'EN BOT

CARRER DE LA PORTAFERRISSA

CARRER DEL PI

CARRER DE LA PALLA

BETLEM
CHURCH

LAS

RAMBLAS

CARRER
DE'EN ROCA

PETRITXOL

CULTURAL INFO
PALAU DE LA VIRREINA

M Liceu

Plaça
del Pi

Plaça
S. Josep
Oriol

BARCELONA

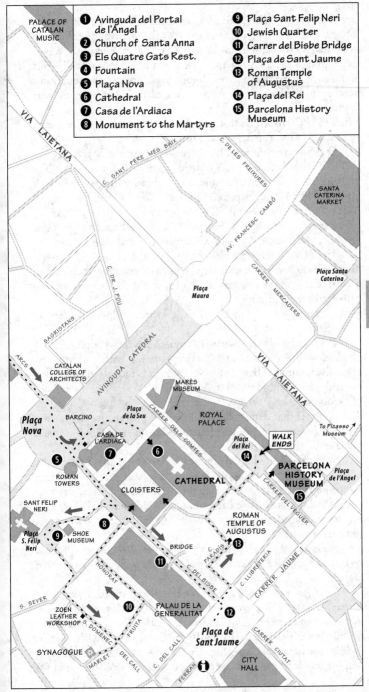

1. Avinguda del Portal de l'Àngel
2. Church of Santa Anna
3. Els Quatre Gats Rest.
4. Fountain
5. Plaça Nova
6. Cathedral
7. Casa de l'Ardiaca
8. Monument to the Martyrs
9. Plaça Sant Felip Neri
10. Jewish Quarter
11. Carrer del Bisbe Bridge
12. Plaça de Sant Jaume
13. Roman Temple of Augustus
14. Plaça del Rei
15. Barcelona History Museum

PALACE OF CATALAN MUSIC

VIA LAIETANA

C. SANT PERE MÉS BAIX

C. DE LES FREIXURES

SANTA CATERINA MARKET

AV. FRANCESC CAMBÓ

CARRER MERCADERS

C. DR. J. POU

Plaça Maura

Plaça Santa Caterina

SAGRISTANS

AVINGUDA CATEDRAL

VIA LAIETANA

ARCS

CATALAN COLLEGE OF ARCHITECTS

BARCINO

Plaça de la Seu

MARÈS MUSEUM

ROYAL PALACE

CARRER DELS COMTES

To Picasso Museum

Plaça Nova

CASA DE L'ARDIACA

Plaça del Rei

WALK ENDS

5

7

6

14

ROMAN TOWERS

CLOISTERS

CATHEDRAL

BARCELONA HISTORY MUSEUM

Plaça de l'Àngel

SANT FELIP NERI

8

15

CARRER DEL VEGUER

Plaça S. Felip Neri

9

SHOE MUSEUM

ROMAN TEMPLE OF AUGUSTUS

S. SEVER

HONORAT

BRIDGE

11

C. PARADIS

13

C. DEL BISBE

C. LLIBRETERIA

CARRER JAUME

ZOEN LEATHER WORKSHOP

10

PALAU DE LA GENERALITAT

FRUITA

S. DOMENEC

12

CARRER CIUTAT

SYNAGOGUE

MARLET

DEL CALL

C. DEL CALL

Plaça de Sant Jaume

FERRAN

CITY HALL

BARCELONA

tree seems to be held captive by urban man. Next, step inside the lobby of the city archives. You can't tour the archives, but there are often temporary exhibits in the lobby. At the left end of the lobby, step through the archway and look down into the stairwell—this is the back side of the ancient Roman wall. Back in the courtyard, head up to the balcony for views of the cathedral steeple and gargoyles.

• *Return to Carrer del Bisbe and turn left. After a few steps you reach a small square with a bronze statue ensemble.*

❽ **Martyrs Statue:** Five Barcelona patriots calmly receive their last rites before being garroted (strangled) for resisting Napoleon's 1809 invasion of Spain. They'd been outraged by French atrocities in Madrid (depicted in Goya's *Third of May* painting in Madrid's Prado Museum). The plaque marking their mortal remains says these martyrs to independence gave their lives *"por Dios, por la Patria, y por el Rey"*—for God, country, and king.

The plaza offers interesting views of the cathedral's towers. The doorway here is the (not-always-open) "back door" entrance to the cathedral (at the cloister), letting you avoid the long lines at the cathedral's main entrance.

• *Exit the square down tiny Carrer de Montjuïc del Bisbe. This leads to the cute...*

❾ **Plaça Sant Felip Neri:** This square serves as the playground of an elementary school and is often bursting with youthful energy. The Church of Sant Felip Neri, which Gaudí attended, is still pocked with bomb damage from the Civil War. As a stronghold of democratic, anti-Franco forces, Barcelona saw a lot of fighting. The shrapnel that damaged this church was meant for the nearby Catalan government building (Palau de la Generalitat, which we'll see later on this walk).

Study the carved reliefs on nearby buildings, paid for by the guilds that powered the local economy. It's clear that the building on the far right must have housed the shoemakers. In fact, just next door is the fun little Shoe Museum (described on page 1294).

• *Exit the square down Carrer de Sant Felip Neri. At the T-intersection, you have a choice:*

You can turn left, returning to the square with the Martyrs Statue, then turn right, walking along Carrer del Bisbe to the bridge (described later).

Or if you're curious about the Jewish chapter of Barcelona's story, turn right at the T-intersection onto Carrer de Sant Sever, then immediately left on Carrer de Sant Domènec del Call. You've entered the...

❿ **Jewish Quarter (El Call):** In Catalan, a Jewish quarter goes by the name El Call—literally "narrow passage," for the tight lanes where medieval Jews were forced to live, under the watchful eye of the nearby cathedral. At its peak, some 4,000 Jews were crammed into just a few alleys.

Walk down Carrer de Sant Domènec del Call, passing the **Zoen leather workshop and showroom,** where everything is made on the spot (on the right, at #15). After passing a charming square, also on the right, take the next lane to the right (Carrer de Marlet). On the right-hand side is the low-profile entrance to what (most likely) was Barcelona's **main synagogue** during the Middle Ages. The structure dates from the third century, but it was destroyed during a brutal pogrom in 1391. The city's remaining Jews were expelled in 1492, and artifacts of their culture—including this synagogue—were forgotten for centuries. In the 1980s, a historian tracked down the synagogue using old tax-collector records. Another clue that this was the main synagogue: In accordance with Jewish traditions, it stubbornly faces east (toward Jerusalem), putting it at an angle at odds with surrounding structures. The sparse interior includes access to two small subterranean rooms with Roman walls topped by a medieval Catalan vault. Look through the glass floor to see dyeing vats used for a later shop on this site (run by former Jews who had forcibly been converted to Christianity).

• *At the synagogue, start back the way you came, continuing straight as the street becomes Carrer de la Fruita. At the T-intersection, turn left, then right, to find your way back to the Martyrs Statue. From here, turn right down Carrer del Bisbe to the...*

❶ **Carrer del Bisbe Bridge:** This Bridge-of-Sighs-like structure connects the Catalan government building on the right with the Catalan president's residence (ceremonial, not actual). Though the bridge looks medieval, it was constructed in the 1920s by Joan Rubió, who also did the carved ornamentation on the buildings.

It's a photographer's dream. Check out the jutting angels on the bridge, the basket-carrying maidens on the president's house, the gargoyle-like faces on the government building. Zoom in even closer. Find monsters, skulls, goddesses, old men with beards, climbing vines, and coats of arms—a Gothic museum in stone.

• *Continue along Carrer del Bisbe to...*

❷ **Plaça de Sant Jaume** (jow-mah): This stately central square of the Barri Gòtic, once the Roman forum, has been the seat of city government for 2,000 years. Today the two top governmental buildings in Catalunya face each other.

For more than six centuries, **Palau de la Generalitat** has housed the autonomous government of Catalunya. It always flies the Catalan flag (red and yellow stripes) next to the obligatory Spanish one. Above the doorway is Catalunya's patron saint—St. Jordi (George), slaying the dragon. From these balconies, the nation's leaders (and soccer heroes) greet the people on momentous days. The square is often the site of demonstrations, from a single aggrieved citizen with a megaphone to riotous thousands.

The **Barcelona City Hall** (Casa de la Ciutat) sports a statue of the king "Jaume el Conqueridor"—not to be confused with Sant Jaume, the plaza's namesake (free, open Sun 10:00-13:30). King Jaume I (1208-1276, also called "the Just") is credited with freeing Barcelona from French control, granting self-government, and setting it on a course to become a major city. He was the driving force behind construction of the Royal Palace (which we'll see shortly).

Locals treasure the independence these two government buildings represent. In the 20th century, Barcelona opposed the dictator Francisco Franco (who ruled from 1939 to 1975), and Franco retaliated. He abolished the regional government and (effectively) outlawed the Catalunyan language and customs. Two years after Franco's death, joyous citizens packed this square to celebrate the return of self-rule.

Look left and right down the main streets branching off the square. Carrer de Ferran (which leads to the Ramblas) is classic Barcelona—lined with ironwork streetlamps and balconies draped with plants.

In ancient Roman days, Plaça de Sant Jaume was the town's forum, or central square, located at the intersection of the two main streets—the *decumanus* (Carrer del Bisbe) and the *cardus* (Carrer de la Llibreteria). The forum's biggest building was a massive temple of Augustus, which we'll see next.

• *Facing the Generalitat, exit the square to the right, heading uphill on tiny Carrer del Paradís. Follow this street as it turns right. When it swings left, pause at #10, the entrance to the...*

⓭ Roman Temple of Augustus: You're standing at the summit of Mont Tàber. A plaque on the wall says it all: "Mont Tàber, 16.9 meters"—elevation 55 feet. The Barri Gòtic's highest spot is also marked with a millstone inlaid in the pavement at the doorstep of #10. It was here, atop this lofty summit, that the ancient Romans founded the town of Barcino around 15 B.C. They built a *castrum* (fort) on the hilltop, protecting the harbor.

Step inside for a peek at the imposing Roman temple (Temple Roma d'August). These four huge columns, from around A.D. 1, are as old as Barcelona itself. They were part of the ancient town's biggest structure, a temple dedicated to the Emperor Augustus, worshipped as a god. These Corinthian columns (with deep fluting and topped with leafy capitals) were the back corner of a 120-foot-long temple that extended from here to the Fòrum (free, good English info; April-Sept Tue-Sun 10:00-20:00; Oct-March Tue-Sat 10:00-14:00 & 16:00-19:00, Sun 10:00-20:00; closed Mon year-round).

• *Continue down Carrer del Paridís one block. When you bump into the back end of the cathedral, take a right, and go downhill a block (down Baixada de Santa Clara) until it emerges into a square called...*

⓮ **Plaça del Rei:** The buildings that enclose this square once housed Spain's kings and queens. The central section (topped by a six-story addition) was the core of the Royal Palace. It has a vast hall on the ground floor that served as the throne room and reception room. From the 13th to the 15th centuries, the Royal Palace housed Catalunya's counts as well as resident Spanish kings. In 1493, a triumphant Christopher Columbus, accompanied by six New World natives (whom he called "Indians") and several pure-gold statues, entered the Royal Palace. King Ferdinand and Queen Isabel rose to welcome him home and honored him with the title "Admiral of the Oceans."

To the right is the palace's church, the Chapel of St. Agatha. It sits atop the foundations of the Roman wall.

To the left is the Viceroy's Palace (for the ruler's right-hand man), which also served as the archives of the Kingdom of Aragon. After Catalunya became part of Spain in the 15th century, the Royal Palace became a small regional residence, and the Viceroy's Palace became the headquarters of the local Inquisition. Today the Viceroy's Palace is once again home to the archives. Step inside the courtyard. It has an impressive Renaissance courtyard, a staircase with coffered wood ceilings, and a temporary exhibit space. Among the archive's treasures (though it's rarely on display) is the 1491 Santa Fe Capitulations, a contract between Columbus and the monarchs about his upcoming voyage.

Ironically, Columbus and the Kingdom of Aragon played a role in Barcelona's decline as an independent kingdom. When Ferdinand of Aragon married Isabel of Castile, Catalunya got swallowed up in greater Spain. Columbus' discovery of new trade routes made Barcelona's port less important, and soon the royals moved elsewhere.

The Barcelona History Museum's entrance is at the near end of Plaça del Rei (see listing on page 1289). It gives visitors the only peek they'll get of the palace interior (and there's disappointingly little to see), but more importantly, provides a fine way to retrace all the history we've seen on this walk—from modern to medieval to the Roman foundations of Barcino.

• *Your walk is over. It's easy to get your bearings by backtracking to either Plaça de Sant Jaume or the cathedral. The Jaume I Metro stop is two blocks away (head downhill and turn left). Or simply wander and enjoy Barcelona at its Gothic best.*

Sights in Barcelona

In the Barri Gòtic, near the Cathedral

For an interesting route from Plaça de Catalunya to the cathedral neighborhood, see my self-guided walk of the Barri Gòtic (described earlier).

▲Cathedral of Barcelona

Although Barcelona's cathedral doesn't rank among Europe's finest (and frankly, barely cracks the Top 20), it's important, easy to visit, and—most of the time—free to see. The cathedral's highlights are its vast nave, rich chapels, tomb of St. Eulàlia, and the oasis-like setting of the cloister. Other sights inside (which you'll pay separately for) are the elaborately carved choir, the elevator up to the view terrace, and the altarpiece museum.

The spacious church is 300 feet long and 130 feet wide. Tall pillars made of stone blocks support the crisscross vaults. Each round keystone where the arches cross features a different saint. Typical of many Spanish churches, there's a choir—an enclosed area of wooden seats in the middle of the nave, creating a more intimate space for worship. The Gothic church also has fine stained glass, ironwork chandeliers, a 16th-century organ (left transept), tombstones in the pavement, and an "ambulatory" floor plan, allowing worshippers to amble around to the chapel of their choice.

Cost and Hours: Generally open to visitors Mon-Fri 8:00-19:30, Sat-Sun 8:00-20:00. Free to enter Mon-Sat before 12:45, Sun before 13:45, and daily after 17:15, but you must pay to enter the cathedral's three minor sights (museum—€2, terrace-€2.50, choir-€2.50). The church is officially "closed" for a few hours each afternoon (Mon-Sat 13:00-17:00, Sun 14:00-17:00), but you can get in by paying for the interior sights. Tel. 933-151-554, www.catedralbcn.org.

Dress Code: The dress code is strictly enforced—no tank tops, shorts, or skirts above the knee.

Getting There: The huge, can't-miss-it cathedral is in the center of the Barri Gòtic, on Plaça de la Seu, Metro: Jaume I.

Getting In: The main, front door is open most of the time. While it can be crowded, the line generally moves fast. Sometimes you can also enter directly into the cloister around back (through door facing the Martyrs Statue on the small square along Carrer del Bisbe).

WCs: A tiny, semi-private WC is in the center of the cloister.

Other Cathedral Sights: The cathedral's extra sights have a small fee and slightly shorter hours than the church itself: **museum—€2**, daily 10:00-19:00; **terrace—€2.50**, Mon-Sat 9:00-18:00, closed Sun; **choir—€2.50**, Mon-Sat 9:00-19:00, closes in the afternoon on Sun. The extra sights can close even earlier on slow days.

▲Barcelona History Museum
(Museu d'Història de Barcelona: Plaça del Rei)

At this main branch of the city history museum (MUHBA for short), you can walk through the history of Barcelona, with a focus on the city's Roman roots.

Cost and Hours: €7; ticket includes English audioguide and other MUHBA branches, including La Casa del Guarda in Park Güell; free all day first Sun of month and other Sun from 15:00—but no audioguide during free times; open Tue-Sat 10:00-19:00, Sun 10:00-20:00, closed Mon; last entry 30 minutes before closing, Plaça del Rei, enter on Vageur street, Metro: Jaume I, tel. 932-562-122.

Visiting the Museum: Though the museum is housed in part of the former Royal Palace complex, you'll see only a bit of that grand space. Instead, the focus is on the exhibits in the cellar. While posted information is only in Catalan and Spanish, the included English audioguide provides informative, if dry, descriptions of the exhibits.

Start by watching the nine-minute introductory video in the small theater (at the end of the first floor); it plays alternately in Catalan, Spanish, and English, but it's worth viewing in any language. Then take an elevator down 65 feet (and 2,000 years—see the date spin back while you descend) to stroll the streets of Roman Barcino.

This was a working-class part of town, so you'll see models of domestic life, sewers, areas used for laundry and dyeing, the remains of a factory that processed fish and created garum (a fish-derived sauce used extensively in ancient Roman cooking), winemaking facilities, and bits of a seventh-century early-Christian church. An exhibit in the 11th-century count's palace shows you Barcelona through its glory days in the Middle Ages.

Finally, head upstairs (or ride the elevator to floor 0) to see a model of the city from the early 16th century. From here, you can also enter **Tinell Hall** (part of the Royal Palace), with its long, graceful, rounded vaults. Nearby, step into the 14th-century **Chapel of St. Agatha,** if it's hosting a temporary exhibit.

Frederic Marès Museum (Museu Frederic Marès)

This museum, with the eclectic collection of local sculptor and packrat Frederic Marès (1893-1991), sprawls around a peaceful courtyard through several old Barri Gòtic buildings. The biggest part of the collection, on the ground and first floors, consists of sculpture—from ancient works to beautiful, evocative Gothic pieces to items from the early 20th century. Even more interesting is the extensive "Collector's Cabinet," consisting of items Marès

Barcelona at a Glance

▲▲▲**Ramblas** Barcelona's colorful, gritty, tourist-filled pedestrian thoroughfare, with the thriving La Boqueria market. **Hours:** Always open (but market closed Sun). See page 1269.

▲▲▲**Picasso Museum** Extensive collection offering insight into the brilliant Spanish artist's early years. **Hours:** Tue-Sun 10:00-19:50, closed Mon. See page 1294.

▲▲▲**Sagrada Família** Gaudí's remarkable, unfinished church—a masterpiece in progress. **Hours:** Daily April-Sept 9:00-20:30, Oct-March 9:00-18:30. See page 1308.

▲▲ **Barri Gòtic** City's Gothic Quarter, with the cathedral, remnants of Barcelona's Roman past, and Picasso's old haunt. **Hours:** Always open. See page 1279.

▲▲ **Palace of Catalan Music** Best Modernista interior in Barcelona. **Hours:** 50-minute English tours daily every hour 10:00-15:00, plus frequent concerts. See page 1296.

▲▲**Casa Milà** Barcelona's quintessential Modernista building and Gaudí creation. **Hours:** Daily March-Oct 9:00-20:00, Nov-Feb 9:00-18:30. See page 1307.

▲▲**Park Güell** Colorful Gaudí-designed park overlooking the city. **Hours:** Daily 10:00-20:00. See page 1316.

▲▲**Catalan Art Museum** World-class showcase of this region's art, including a substantial Romanesque collection. **Hours:** Tue-Sat 10:00-19:00, Sun 10:00-14:30, closed Mon. See page 1323.

▲▲ **CaixaForum** Modernista brick factory now occupied by cutting-edge cultural center featuring excellent temporary art exhibits. **Hours**: Mon-Fri 10:00-20:00, Sat-Sun 10:00-21:00, July-Aug open late on some days—likely Wed until 23:00. See page 1325.

▲**Cathedral of Barcelona** Colossal Gothic cathedral ringed by distinctive chapels. **Hours:** Generally open to visitors Mon-Fri 8:00-19:30, Sat-Sun 8:00-20:00. See page 1288.

▲**Barcelona History Museum** One-stop trip through town history, from Roman times to today. **Hours:** Tue-Sat 10:00-19:00, Sun 10:00-20:00, closed Mon. See page 1289.

▲**Santa Caterina Market** Fine market hall built on the site of an old monastery and updated with a wavy Gaudí-inspired roof. **Hours:** Mon 7:30-14:00, Tue-Wed and Sat 7:30-15:30, Thu-Fri 7:30-20:30, closed Sun. See page 1297.

▲**Church of Santa Maria del Mar** Catalan Gothic church in El Born, built by wealthy medieval shippers. **Hours:** Daily 9:00-13:30 & 16:30-20:00. See page 1297.

▲**Maritime Museum** A sailor's delight, housed in an impressive medieval shipyard (but permanent collection likely closed through 2014). **Hours:** Temporary exhibits daily 10:00-20:00. See page 1299.

▲**Palau Güell** Exquisitely curvy Gaudí interior and fantasy rooftop. **Hours:** April-Sept Tue-Sun 10:00-20:00, Oct-March Tue-Sun 10:00-17:30, closed Mon year-round. See page 1302.

▲**Block of Discord** Noisy block of competing Modernista facades by Gaudí and his rivals. **Hours:** Always viewable. See page 1303.

▲**Casa Batlló** Gaudí-designed home topped with fanciful dragon-inspired roof. **Hours:** Daily 9:00-20:00. See page 1303.

▲**Fundació Joan Miró** World's best collection of works by Catalan modern artist Joan Miró. **Hours:** Tue-Sat 10:00-20:00 (until 19:00 Oct-June), Thu until 21:30, Sun 10:00-14:30, closed Mon year-round. See page 1322.

▲**1929 World Expo Fairgrounds** Expo site at the base of Montjuïc, featuring playful Magic Fountains, the impressive CaixaForum art gallery, cheesy Spanish Village, and a mall converted from a bullring. **Hours:** Grounds always open. See page 1324.

▲**Magic Fountains** Lively fountains near Plaça d'Espanya. **Hours:** Generally May-Sept Thu-Sun 21:00-23:00, no shows Mon-Wed; Oct-April Fri-Sat 19:00-20:30, no shows Sun-Thu. See page 1325.

▲ **Las Arenas** Former bullfighting arena turned modern-day shopping mall, with wonderful view terrace. **Hours:** Daily 10:00-22:00. See page 1326.

BARCELONA

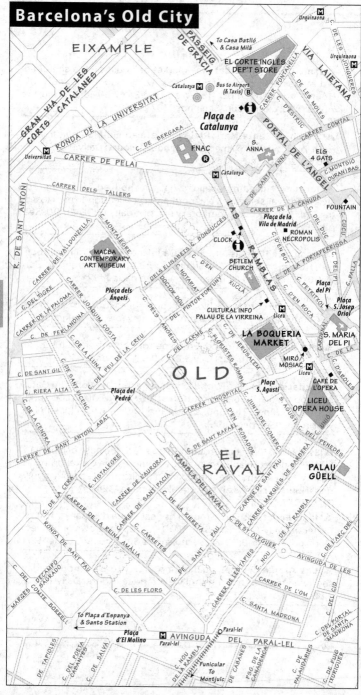

Barcelona's Old City

EIXAMPLE

PASSEIG DE GRACIA

To Casa Batlló & Casa Milà

Urquinaona

VIA LAIETANA

Urquinaona

DE LES JONQUERES

EL CORTE INGLÉS DEP'T STORE

Catalunya

Bus to Airport (& Taxis) B

CARRER FONTANELLA

C. DE LES MOLES

CARRER D'ESTRUC

C. DE LES MAGDALENES

Plaça de Catalunya

PORTAL DE L'ANGEL

CARRER COMTAL

GRAN VIA DE LES CORTS CATALANES

RONDA DE LA UNIVERSITAT

C. DE BERGARA

FNAC

S. ANNA

ELS 4 GATS

C. DE SANTA ANNA

DURAN I BAS

C. MONTSIÓ

Universitat

CARRER DE PELAI

Catalunya

CARRER DE LA CANUDA

FOUNTAIN

CARRER DELS TALLERS

Plaça de la Vila de Madrid

C. DEL DUC

C. CUCU

ROMAN NECROPOLIS

R. DE SANT ANTONI

C. MONTALEGRE

C. DE VALLDONZELLA

MACBA CONTEMPORARY ART MUSEUM

Plaça dels Àngels

CARRER JOAQUIM COSTA

C. DELS ÀNGELS

C. DELS ELISABETS

C. D'EN BONSUCCÉS

CLOCK

LAS RAMBLAS

C. DEL PI

BETLEM CHURCH

C. DE LA PORTAFERRISSA

C. DEL CALL

Plaça del Pi

Plaça S. Josep Oriol

C. DEN BOT

C. PETRITXOL

C. PALLA

C. DEL TIGRE

C. DE LA PALOMA

C. DE FERLANDINA

C. NOTARIAT

DOCTOR DOU

PINTOR FORTUNY

C. DEL CARME

XUCLÀ

CULTURAL INFO PALAU DE LA VIRREINA

Liceu

C. D'EN ROCA

S. MARIA DEL PI

C. DE SANT GIL

C. DEL PEU DE LA CREU

C. JERUSALEM

FLORISTES

RAMBLA

LA BOQUERIA MARKET

MIRÓ MOSAIC

C. DE SANT VICENÇ

C. DE LA LLUNA

Plaça del Pedró

C. DE JESÚS

Liceu

CAFÉ DE L'ÒPERA

C. DE LA CENDRA

C. RIERA ALTA

CARRER L'HOSPITAL

C. JUNTA DEL COMERÇ

Plaça S. Agustí

S. AGUSTÍ

LICEU OPERA HOUSE

O L D

C. DE SANT RAFAEL

C. D'EN ROBADOR

C. DE SANT PAU

C. DEL PENEDÈS

C. DE SANT ANTONI ABAT

CARRER DE SANT RAFAEL

E L R A V A L

CARRER DE BARBERÀ

PALAU GÜELL

C. VISTALEGRE

CARRER DE L'AURORA

RAMBLA DEL RAVAL

C. DE SANT PAGIÀ

C. DE LA RIERETA

CARRER MARQUÈS DE BARBERÀ

DE LA RAMBLA

C. DE L'ARC DEL

C. DE LA CERA

CARRER DE LA REINA AMÀLIA

C. CARRETES

C. SANT PAU

C. DE ST. OLEGUER

RONDA DE SANT PAU

C. NOU

AVINGUDA DE LES

C. DEL CID

C. DEL PORTAL DE SANTA MADRONA

C. DEL DECAMPO SAGRADO

MARQUÈS COMTE BORRELL

C. DE LES FLORS

CARRER DE LES TÀPIES

C. SANTA MADRONA

CARRER DE L'OM

To Plaça d'Espanya & Sants Station

Plaça d'El Molino

AVINGUDA DEL PARAL·LEL

Paral·lel

C. DE PUIG I XURIGUER

C. DE TAPIOLES

C. DEL POETA CABANYES

C. DE SALVÀ

C. NOU DE LA RAMBLA

Funicular To Montjuïc

PASSEIG DE LA CANADENCA

C. DE CABANES

C. DE PALAUDÀRIES

BARCELONA

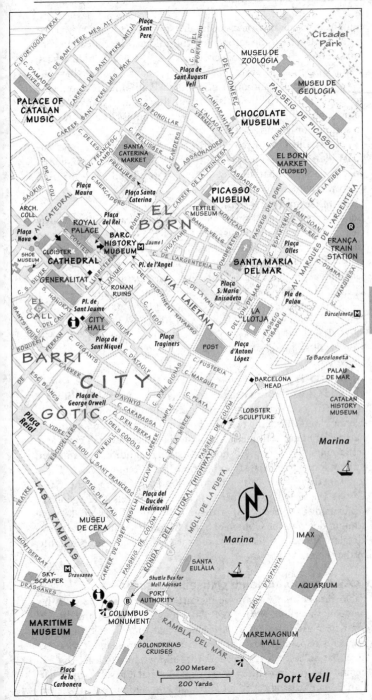

found representative of everyday life in the 19th century. Lovingly displayed on the second and third floors, the collection contains rooms upon rooms of scissors, keys, irons, fans, nutcrackers, stamps, pipes, snuff boxes, opera glasses, pocket watches, bicycles, toy soldiers, dolls, and other bric-a-brac. And in Marès' study are several sculptures by the artist himself. The tranquil courtyard café offers a pleasant break, even when the museum is closed (café open in summer only, until 22:00).

Cost and Hours: €4.20, free Sun from 15:00, 1.5-hour audioguide-€1; open Tue-Sat 10:00-19:00, Sun 11:00-20:00, closed Mon; Plaça de Sant Iu 5-6, Metro: Jaume I, tel. 932-563-500, www.museumares.bcn.cat.

Shoe Museum (Museu del Calçat)
Shoe lovers enjoy this small museum of footwear in glass display cases, watched over by an earnest attendant. You'll see shoes from the 1700s to today: fancy ladies' boots, Tibetan moccasins, big clown shoes, and shoes of minor celebrities such as the president of Catalunya. The huge shoes at the entry are designed to fit the foot of the Columbus Monument at the bottom of the Ramblas.

Cost and Hours: €2.50, Tue-Sun 11:00-14:00, closed Mon, one block beyond outside door of cathedral cloister, behind Plaça de G. Bachs on Plaça Sant Felip Neri, Metro: Jaume I, see page 1286 for directions, tel. 933-014-533.

In El Born
The Old City's El Born neighborhood (also known as "La Ribera") is home to several great sights, including the Picasso Museum. But even without those, the neighborhood is a joy to explore. El Born's narrow lanes are crammed with artsy boutiques, inviting cafés and restaurants, funky one-off shops, rollicking nightlife, and a higher ratio of locals to tourists than most other city-center zones.

Getting There: It's just across Via Laietana from the Barri Gòtic's Plaça de l'Angel (Metro: Jaume I). Carrer de l'Argenteria ("Silversmiths Street") runs diagonally from Plaça de l'Angel straight down to the Church of Santa Maria del Mar. The Palace of Catalan Music is to the north, and the Picasso Museum is roughly in the center.

▲▲▲Picasso Museum (Museu Picasso)
Pablo Picasso may have made his career in Paris, but the years he spent in Barcelona—from ages 14 through 23—were among the most formative of his life. It was here that young Pablo mastered the realistic painting style of his artistic forebears—and it was also here that he first felt the freedom that allowed him to leave that all behind and give in to his creative, experimental urges. When he left Barcelona, Picasso headed for Paris...and revolutionized art forever.

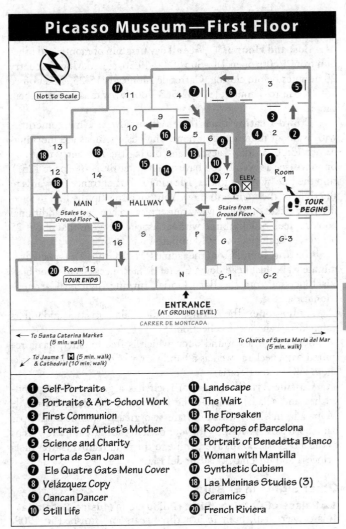

Picasso Museum—First Floor

Not to Scale

17 11 4 7 6 3 5

9 8
10 16 3

5 6 9 4 2 2
13 18 13 9 1

18 13 9 18
15 8 10 Room
12 14 13 7 ELEV. 1

12 11 TOUR
BEGINS

MAIN HALLWAY Stairs from
Stairs to Ground Floor
Ground Floor 19

S P G G-3
16

20 Room 15 N G-1 G-2
TOUR ENDS

ENTRANCE
(AT GROUND LEVEL)
CARRER DE MONTCADA

← To Santa Caterina Market
(5 min. walk)
→ To Church of Santa Maria del Mar
(5 min. walk)

← To Jaume 1 Ⓜ (5 min. walk)
& Cathedral (10 min. walk)

1 Self-Portraits
2 Portraits & Art-School Work
3 First Communion
4 Portrait of Artist's Mother
5 Science and Charity
6 Horta de San Joan
7 Els Quatre Gats Menu Cover
8 Velázquez Copy
9 Cancan Dancer
10 Still Life

11 Landscape
12 The Wait
13 The Forsaken
14 Rooftops of Barcelona
15 Portrait of Benedetta Bianco
16 Woman with Mantilla
17 Synthetic Cubism
18 Las Meninas Studies (3)
19 Ceramics
20 French Riviera

BARCELONA

The pieces in this excellent museum capture that priceless moment just before this bold young thinker changed the world. While you won't find Picasso's famous, later Cubist works here, you will enjoy a representative sweep of his early years, from art-school prodigy to the gloomy hues of his Blue Period to the revitalized cheer of his Rose Period. You'll also see works from his twilight years, including dozens of wild improvisations inspired by Diego Velázquez's seminal *Las Meninas,* as well as a roomful of works that reflect the childlike exuberance of an old man playing like a young kid on the French Riviera. It's undoubtedly the top collection of

Picassos here in his native country and the best anywhere of his early years.

Cost and Hours: €11, free all day first Sun of month and other Sun from 15:00; open Tue-Sun 10:00-19:50, closed Mon, last entry 20 minutes before closing; Carrer de Montcada 15-23, ticket office at #21, Metro: Jaume I, tel. 932-563-000, www.museupicasso.bcn. cat.

Crowd-Beating Tips: There's almost always a line, sometimes with waits of more than an hour. The busiest times are mornings before 13:00, all day Tuesday, and during the free entry times on Sundays (see above). If you have an Articket BCN (see page 1259), skip the line by going to the "Meeting Point" entrance (30 yards to the right of the main entrance). You can also skip the line by buying your ticket online at www.museupicasso.bcn.cat (no additional booking fee). Stuck in line without a ticket? Figure that about 25 people are admitted every 10 minutes.

Getting There: From the Jaume I Metro stop, it's a quick five-minute walk. Just head down Carrer de la Princesa (across the busy Via Laietana from the Barri Gòtic), turning right on Carrer de Montcada.

Audioguide: The 1.5-hour audioguide costs €3 and offers ample detail about the collection.

Services: The ground floor, which is free to enter, has a required bag check, as well as a handy array of other services (bookshop, WC, and cafeteria).

Cuisine Art: The museum itself has a good **café** (€8 sandwiches and salads). Outside the museum, right along Carrer de Montcada in either direction, are two great recommended tapas bars (both closed Mon): With your back to the museum, a few steps to the left is **El Xampanyet,** while to the right (across Carrer de la Princesa and up a block) is **Bar del Pla.**

Other Sights in El Born

▲▲Palace of Catalan Music (Palau de la Música Catalana)

This concert hall, built in just three years and finished in 1908, features an unexceptional exterior but boasts my favorite Modernista interior in town (by Lluís Domènech i Montaner). Its inviting arches lead you into the 2,138-seat hall (accessible only with a tour). A kaleidoscopic skylight features a choir singing around the sun, while playful carvings and mosaics celebrate music and Catalan culture. If you're interested in Modernisme, taking this tour (which starts with a relaxing 12-minute video) is one of the best experiences in town—and helps balance the hard-to-avoid over-focus on Gaudí as "Mr. Modernisme."

Cost and Hours: €15, 50-minute tours in English run daily

every hour 10:00-15:00, tour times may change based on performance schedule, about 6 blocks northeast of cathedral, Carrer
Palau de la Música 4-6, Metro: Urquinaona, tel. 902-442-882,
www.palaumusica.cat.

Advance Reservations Required: You must buy your ticket
in advance to get a spot on an English guided tour (tickets available up to 4 months in advance—ideally buy yours at least 2 days
before, though they're sometimes available the same day or day before—especially Oct-March). You can buy the ticket in person at
the concert hall box office (less than a 10-minute walk from the
cathedral or Picasso Museum, open daily 9:30-15:30); by phone
with your credit card (no extra charge, tel. 902-475-485); or online
at the concert hall website (€1 fee, www.palaumusica.cat).

Concerts: Consider getting a ticket for a concert (300 per year,
€22-49 tickets, see website for details, box office tel. 902-442-882).

▲Santa Caterina Market

This eye-catching market hall was built on the ruins of an old monastery, then renovated in 2006 with a wildly colorful, swooping,
Gaudí-inspired roof and shell built around its original white walls
(a good exhibition at the far corner provides a view of the foundations and English explanations). The much-delayed construction
took so long that locals began calling the site the "Hole of Shame."
Come for the outlandish architecture, but stay for a chance to shop
for a picnic without the tourist logjam of La Boqueria market on
the Ramblas.

Cost and Hours: Free, Mon 7:30-14:00, Tue-Wed and Sat
7:30-15:30, Thu-Fri 7:30-20:30, closed Sun, Avinguda de Francesc
Cambó 16, www.mercatsantacaterina.net.

▲Church of Santa Maria del Mar

This so-called "Cathedral of the Sea" was built entirely with local
funds and labor, in the heart of the wealthy merchant El Born
quarter. Proudly independent, the church features a purely Catalan
Gothic interior that was forcibly uncluttered of its Baroque decor
by Civil War belligerents.

Cost and Hours: Free, daily 9:00-13:30 & 16:30-20:00, Plaça
Santa Maria, Metro: Jaume I, tel. 933-102-390.

Visiting the Church: Before entering, look at the figures on
the front door. These represent the *bastaixos* who hauled the stone
used to build the church all the way from Montjuïc quarries.

Step inside, to the largely unadorned Gothic space. It used
to be more highly decorated with Baroque frills. But during the
Spanish Civil War (1936-1939), the Catholic Church sided with the
conservative forces of Franco against the people. In retaliation, the
working class took their anger out on this church, burning all of its
wood furnishings and decor (carbon still blackens the ceiling).

Today the church remains stripped down—naked in all its Gothic glory. The tree-like columns inspired Gaudí (their influence on the columns inside his Sagrada Família church is obvious). Sixteenth-century sailors left models of their ships at the foot of the altar for Mary's protection. Even today a classic old Catalan ship remains at Mary's feet. As within Barcelona's cathedral, here you can see the characteristic Catalan Gothic buttresses flying inward, defining the chapels that ring the nave. The colorful windows come with modern themes.

Nearby: Around the right side of the church is a poignant memorial to the "Catalan Alamo" of September 11, 1714, when the Spanish crown besieged and conquered Barcelona, slaughtering Catalan insurgents and kicking off more than two centuries of cultural suppression.

Passeig del Born

This long boulevard is the neighborhood center. Formerly a jousting square (as its Roman circus-esque shape indicates), it got its name, "El Born," from an old Catalan word for "tournament" (the name was eventually given to the entire neighborhood). These days, Passeig del Born is a popular springboard for exploring tapas bars, fun restaurants, and nightspots in the narrow streets all around. Wandering around here at night, you'll find piles of inviting and intriguing little restaurants (I've listed my favorites on page 1347). At the far end of Passeig del Born is the vast-but-vacant, steel-frame, 19th-century El Born Market, which served as the city's main produce market hall until 1971, when it was relocated to the suburbs. Plans are under way to convert the market hall into a cultural center and museum.

You'll also find great shopping near this strip—be sure to venture up **Carrer dels Flassaders** (funky shops, to the left as you face the old market hall) and down **Carrer del Rec** (fashionable boutiques, to the right as you face the market).

Chocolate Museum (Museu de la Xocolata)

This museum, only a couple of blocks from the Picasso Museum, is fun for chocolate lovers. Operated by the local confectioners' guild, it tells the story of chocolate from Aztecs to Europeans via the port of Barcelona, where it was first unloaded and processed. But the history lesson is just an excuse to show off a series of remarkably ornate candy sculptures. These works of edible art—which change every year but often include such Spanish themes as Don Quixote or bullfighting—begin as store-window displays for Easter or Christmas. Once the holiday passes, the confectioners bring the sculptures here to be enjoyed.

Cost and Hours: €4.30, Mon-Sat 10:00-19:00, Sun 10:00-15:00, Carrer del Comerç 36, Metro: Jaume I, tel. 932-687-878, www.museuxocolata.cat.

On the Harborfront, at the Bottom of the Ramblas

▲Maritime Museum (Museu Marítim)

Barcelona's medieval shipyard, the best preserved in the entire Mediterranean, is home to an excellent museum. Its permanent collection is closed for renovation, likely through 2014, during which time the museum will host temporary exhibits in various sections.

The building's cavernous halls evoke the 14th-century days when Catalunya was a naval and shipbuilding power, cranking out 30 huge galleys a winter. As in the US today, military and commercial ventures mixed and mingled as Catalunya built its trading empire. When the permanent collection reopens, it'll cover the salty history of ships and navigation from the 13th to the 20th centuries. Riveting for nautical types and interesting for anyone, its modern and beautifully presented exhibits will put you in a seafaring mood. The helpful, included audioguide tells the story well and explains the various seafaring vessels displayed—including an impressively huge and richly decorated royal galley.

Your ticket also includes entrance to the *Santa Eulàlia*, an early 20th-century schooner docked just a short walk from the Columbus Monument.

Cost and Hours: Museum price depends on exhibits, daily 10:00-20:00, last entry 30 minutes before closing; *Santa Eulàlia*—€1 for entry without museum visit, Tue-Fri and Sun 10:00-19:30, Sat 14:00-19:30, closes at 17:30 in Nov-March, closed Mon year-round; breezy café in museum courtyard, Avinguda de la Drassanes, Metro: Drassanes, tel. 933-429-920, www.mmb.cat.

Columbus Monument (Monument a Colóm)

Located where the Ramblas hits the harbor, this 200-foot-tall monument was built for the 1888 world's fair and commemorates Columbus' visit to Barcelona following his first trip to America. The tight four-person elevator takes you to the glassed-in observation area at the top for congested but sweeping views (elevator may be closed when you visit). There is also a small TI inside the base of the monument.

Cost and Hours: €4, daily May-Oct 8:30-20:30, Nov-April 8:00-20:00.

Golondrinas Cruises

At the harbor near the foot of the Columbus Monument, tourist boats called *golondrinas* offer two different unguided trips. As Barcelona's skyline isn't all that striking from the water, these trips are pretty pointless unless you'd just like to go for a boat ride. The shorter version goes around the harbor in 35 minutes (€6.90, daily on the hour 11:30-19:00, every 30 minutes mid-June-mid-Sept, may not run Nov-April, tel. 934-423-106, www.lasgolondrinas.

BARCELONA

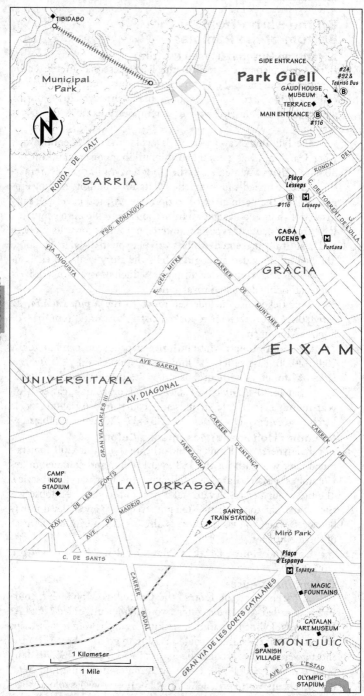

TIBIDABO

Municipal
Park

SIDE ENTRANCE

Park Güell

#24,
#92 &
Tourist Bus

GAUDÍ HOUSE
MUSEUM

TERRACE

MAIN ENTRANCE

#116

RONDA DE DALT

SARRIÀ

PSG. BONANOVA

VIA AUGUSTA

Plaça
Lesseps

#116   Lesseps

RONDA DEL

C. DEL TORRENT DE L'OLLA

CASA
VICENS

Fontana

R. GEN. MITRE

CARRER DE MUNTANER

GRÀCIA

EIXAM

AVE. SARRIÀ

UNIVERSITARIA

AV. DIAGONAL

GRAN VIA CARLES III

TARRAGONA

CARRER D'ENTENÇA

CARRER DEL

CAMP
NOU
STADIUM

TRAV. DE LES CORTS

LA TORRASSA

AVE. DE MADRID

SANTS
TRAIN STATION

Miró Park

Plaça
d'Espanya

C. DE SANTS

CARRER BADAL

Espanya

MAGIC
FOUNTAINS

GRAN VIA DE LES CORTS CATALANES

CATALAN
ART MUSEUM

MONTJUÏC

SPANISH
VILLAGE

AVE. DE L'ESTAD

OLYMPIC
STADIUM

1 Kilometer

1 Mile

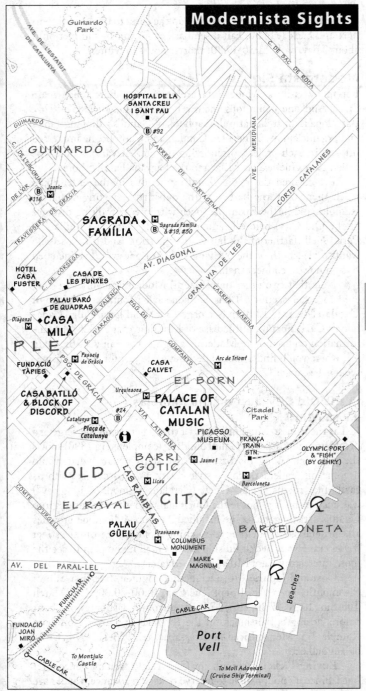

Modernista Sights

BARCELONA

com). The longer 1.5-hour trip goes up the coast to the Fòrum complex and back (€14.50, can disembark at Fòrum in summer only, about 7/day, daily 11:30-19:30, shorter hours in winter).

Modernista Sights

For many visitors, Modernista architecture is Barcelona's main draw. And one name tops them all: Antoni Gaudí (1852-1926). Barcelona is an architectural scrapbook of Gaudí's galloping gables and organic curves. A devoted Catalan and Catholic, he immersed himself in each project, often living on-site. At various times, he called Park Güell, Casa Milà, and the Sagrada Família home.

I've covered the main Gaudí attractions in the order you'd reach them from the harbor to the outskirts—starting along the Ramblas and in the Eixample (both within easy walking distance of the Old City) before heading out to the Sagrada Família and Park Güell (farther afield, but worth the trip). And for those who want to visit both of the outlying sights in one trip, I've included tips on how to connect them.

Note that two other (non-Gaudí) Modernista works are covered in other sections: Lluís Domènech i Montaner's **Palace of Catalan Music** in El Born (see page 1296), and Josep Puig i Cadafalch's **CaixaForum,** at the base of Montjuïc (page 1325). For information on even more Modernista sights, you can visit the main TI, where you'll find a special desk set aside just for Modernisme-seekers (see page 1258).

In the Old City, Just off the Ramblas
▲Palau Güell
Just as the Picasso Museum reveals a young genius on the verge of a breakthrough, this early Gaudí building (completed in 1890) shows the architect taking his first tentative steps toward what would become his trademark curvy style. Dark and masculine, with its castle-like rooms, Palau Güell (Catalans pronounce it "gway") was custom-built to house the Güell clan and gives an insight into Gaudí's artistic genius. The included 24-stop audioguide provides all the details. Despite the eye-catching roof (visible from the street if you crane your neck), I'd skip Palau Güell if you plan to see the more interesting Casa Milà (described later).

Cost and Hours: €10, includes audioguide, free first Sun of the month, open April-Sept Tue-Sun 10:00-20:00, Oct-March Tue-Sun 10:00-17:30, closed Mon year-round, last entry one hour before closing, a half-block off the Ramblas at Carrer Nou de la Rambla 3-5, Metro: Liceu or Drassanes, tel. 933-173-974, www.palauguell.cat.

Buying Tickets: As with any Gaudí sight, you may encounter lines. Since it's not possible to reserve tickets in advance, you'll have to buy them at the ticket window to the left of the entryway, then line up to the right. Each ticket has an entry time, so at busy times you may have to return later, even after buying your ticket.

In the Eixample

The Eixample ("Expansion") was built when a bulging Barcelona burst out of its medieval walls in the mid-19th century. With wide sidewalks, hardy shade trees, chic shops, and plenty of Art Nouveau fun, this carefully planned "new town," just north of the Old City, has a rigid grid plan cropped back at the corners to create space and lightness at each intersection. Conveniently, all of this new construction provided a generation of Modernista architects with a blank canvas for creating boldly experimental designs.

For the best Eixample example, ramble Rambla de Catalunya (unrelated to the more famous Ramblas) and pass along Passeig de Gràcia. While you could simply walk around and see what Modernista masterpieces you stumble upon, most visitors make a beeline to Gaudí's Casa Milà (Metro: Diagonal) and the Block of Discord, where three Modernista greats jockey for your attention (Metro: Passeig de Gràcia). By the way, if you're tempted to snap photos from the middle of the street, be careful—Gaudí died after being struck by a streetcar.

▲Block of Discord

Three colorful Modernista facades compete for your attention along a single block: Casa Batlló (the only one you can really get inside), Casa Amatller, and Casa Lleó Morera. All were built by well-known architects at the end of the 19th century. Because the mansions look as though they are trying to outdo each other in creative twists, locals nicknamed the noisy block the "Block of Discord." It's on Passeig de Gràcia (at the Metro stop of the same name), between Carrer del Consell de Cent and Carrer d'Aragó—three blocks north of Plaça de Catalunya and four blocks south of Casa Milà.

Casa Batlló (#43): First, most famous, and rated ▲, is the green-blue ceramic-speckled facade of Casa Batlló, designed by Antoni Gaudí, with an interior that's open to the public. It has tibia-like pillars and skull-like balconies, inspired by the time-tested natural forms that Gaudí knew made the best structural supports. The tiled roof has a soft-ice-cream-cone turret topped with a cross. The humpback roofline suggests a cresting dragon's back. It's thought that Gaudí based the work on the popular legend of St. Jordi (George) slaying the dragon. But some see instead a Mardi Gras theme, with mask-like balconies, a colorful confetti-like facade, and the ridge of a harlequin's hat up top. The inscrutable Gaudí preferred to leave his designs open to interpretation.

While the highlight is the roof, the interior of this Gaudí

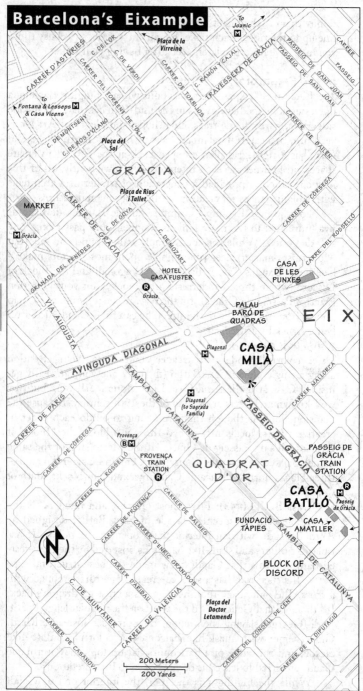

Barcelona's Eixample

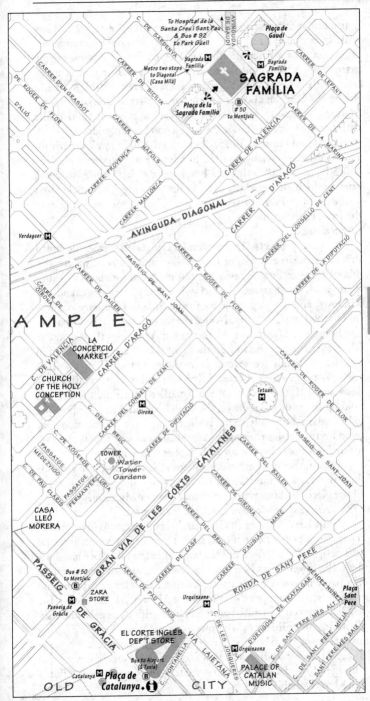

house is also interesting—and even more over-the-top than Casa Milà's (described later). Paid for with textile industry money, the house features a funky mushroom-shaped fireplace nook on the main floor, a blue-and-white-ceramic-slathered atrium, and an attic (with more parabolic arches). There's barely a straight line in the house. You can also get a close-up look at the dragon-inspired rooftop. Because preservation of the place is privately funded, the entrance fee is steep—but it includes a good audioguide.

Cost and Hours: €18.15, daily 9:00-20:00, may close early for special events—closings posted in advance at entrance, tel. 932-160-306, www.casabatllo.cat. Purchase a ticket online to avoid lines—which are especially fierce in the morning. Your eticket isn't a timed reservation (it's good any time), but it will let you skip to the front of the queue.

• *Next door is...*

Casa Amatller (#41): Josep Puig i Cadafalch custom-designed this house for the Amatller family. The facade features a creative mix of three of Spain's historical traditions: Moorish-style pentagram-and-vine designs; Gothic-style tracery, gargoyles, and bay windows; and the step-gable roof from Spain's Habsburg connection to the Low Countries. Notice the many layers of the letter "A": The house itself (with its gable) forms an A, as does the decorative frieze over the bay window on the right side of the facade. Within that frieze, you'll see several more As sprouting from branches (*amatller* means "almond tree"). The reliefs above the smaller windows show off the hobbies of the Amatller clan: Find the cherubs holding the early box camera, the open book, and the amphora jug (which the family collected). Look through the second-floor bay window to see the corkscrew column. If you want, you can pop inside for a closer look at the elaborate entrance hall.

For another dimension of Modernisme, peek into the ground-floor windows of the Bagues Joieria jewelry shop and notice the slinky pieces by Spanish Art Nouveau jeweler Masriera.

• *Head left, to the end of the block. On the corner is...*

Casa Lleó Morera (#35): Here's another paella-like mix of styles, this one by the architect, Lluís Domènech i Montaner, who also designed the Palace of Catalan Music (you'll notice similarities). The lower floors have classical columns and a Greek-temple-like bay window. Farther up are Gothic balconies of rosettes and tracery, while the upper part has faux Moorish stucco work. The whole thing is ornamented with fantastic griffins, angels, and fish. Flanking the third-story windows are figures holding the exciting inventions of the day—the camera, lightbulb, and gramophone—designed to demonstrate just how modern the homeowners were in this age of Modern-isme. Unfortunately, the wonderful interior is closed to the public.

▲▲Casa Milà (La Pedrera)

One of Gaudí's trademark works, this corner house—nicknamed "The Quarry" and located three blocks northwest of the Block of Discord—is an icon of Modernisme. While it's fun to ogle from the outside, it's also worth going inside, as it features the city's purest Gaudí interior. And buying a ticket also gets you access to the delightful rooftop, with its forest of colorfully tiled chimneys (note that the roof may close when it rains).

Cost and Hours: €15, good audioguide-€4, daily March-Oct 9:00-20:00, Nov-Feb 9:00-18:30, last entry 30 minutes before closing, at the corner of Passeig de Gràcia and Provença (visitor entrance at Provença 261-265), Metro: Diagonal, info tel. 902-400-973, www.lapedrera.com.

Crowd-Beating Tips: As lines can be long (up to a 1.5-hour wait to get in), it's best to reserve ahead at www.lapedrera.com or at Catalunya Caixa ATMs (tickets come with an assigned entry time). Articket BCN holders can step right up to the front attendant. If you come without a ticket, the best time to arrive is right when it opens. If the line stretches all the way to the corner, figure about an hour wait.

Free Entrance to Atrium: For a peek at the interior without paying for a ticket, find the door directly on the corner, which leads to the main atrium. Upstairs on the first floor are temporary exhibits (generally free, open daily 10:00-20:00, may be closed between exhibitions).

Nighttime Visits: The building hosts guided after-hour visits dubbed "The Secret Pedrera." On this pricey visit, you'll tour the building with the lights turned down low (€30; late June-early Sept Sun-Wed 21:30-24:00, none on Thu-Sat; March-late June and early Sept-Oct nightly 21:30-24:00; Nov-Feb Wed-Sat 20:00-22:30, none on Sun-Tue; last entry 1.5 hours before closing).

Concerts: On summer weekends, Casa Milà has an evening rooftop concert series, "Summer Nights at La Pedrera," featuring live jazz. In addition to the music, it gives you the chance to see the rooftop illuminated (€25, late June-early Sept Thu-Sat 20:30-23:00, book advance tickets online or by phone, tel. 902-101-212, www.lapedrera.com).

Visiting the House: A visit to Casa Milà covers three sections: the apartment, the attic, and the rooftop. Enter and head upstairs to the apartment. If it's near closing time, continue up to see the attic and rooftop first, to make sure you have enough time to enjoy Gaudí's works and the views.

The typical bourgeois **apartment** is decorated as it might have been when the building was first occupied by middle-class urbanites (a seven-minute video explains Barcelona society at the time).

BARCELONA

Notice Gaudí's clever use of the atrium to maximize daylight in all of the apartments.

The **attic** houses a sprawling multimedia exhibit tracing the history of the architect's career with models, photos, and videos of his work. It's all displayed under distinctive parabola-shaped arches. While evocative of Gaudí's style in themselves, the arches are formed this way partly to support the multilevel roof above. This area was also used for ventilation, helping to keep things cool in summer and warm in winter. Tenants had storage spaces and did their laundry up here.

From the attic, a stairway leads to the undulating, jaw-dropping **rooftop,** where 30 chimneys and ventilation towers play volleyball with the clouds.

Back at the **ground level** of Casa Milà, poke into the dreamily painted original entrance courtyard.

More Modernista Sights in the Eixample

While the buildings listed above are the best Modernista facades in this area, fans of this era may want to seek out a few more examples:

Just around the corner from the Block of Discord, at Carrer d'Aragó 255, the **Fundació Antoni Tàpies,** dedicated to a 20th-century abstract artist from Barcelona, is housed in a Lluís Domènech i Montaner-designed building that sums up the Modernist credo. Constructed of modern brick, iron, and glass, it's decorated with playful motifs and is spacious, functional, and full of light inside. The actual museum collection is pricey and worthwhile only for Tàpies fans.

The **Hotel Casa Fuster** is another fine Modernista building by Lluís Domènech i Montaner (directly across the boulevard called Diagonal from the top of Passeig de Gràcia, at the far end of the small park, Passeig de Gràcia 132).

Nearby are two works by Josep Puig i Cadafalch (a few blocks east from the top of Passeig de Gràcia on Diagonal). **Palau Baró de Quadras** (at #373, on the right) today houses Casa Àsia. Another block and a half down is the distinctively turreted Casa Terrades—better known as **Casa de les Punxes** ("House of Spikes," at #416, on the left).

▲▲▲Sagrada Família (Holy Family Church)

Architect Antoni Gaudí's most famous and awe-inspiring work is this unfinished, super-sized church. With its cake-in-the-rain facade and otherworldly spires, the church is not only an icon of Barcelona and its trademark Modernista style, but also a symbol of this period's greatest practitioner. As an architect, Gaudí's foundations were classics, nature, and religion. The church represents all three.

Gaudí labored on the Sagrada Família for 43 years, from 1883 until his death in 1926. Nearly a century after his death, people

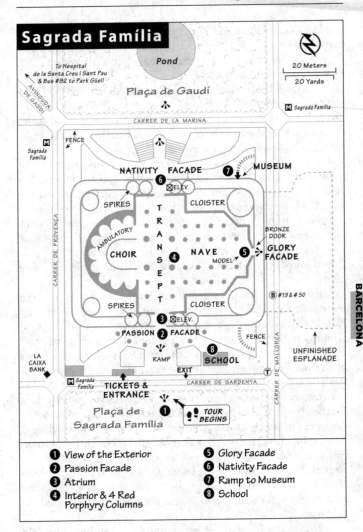

Sagrada Família

To Hospital de la Santa Creu i Sant Pau & Bus #92 to Park Güell

AVINGUDA DE GAUDÍ

Pond

Plaça de Gaudí

20 Meters
20 Yards

M Sagrada Família

CARRER DE LA MARINA

M Sagrada Família

FENCE

NATIVITY FACADE

⑥

⊠ELEV.

⑦ MUSEUM

CARRER DE PROVENÇA

SPIRES

CLOISTER

AMBULATORY

CHOIR

T R A N S E P T

④ NAVE ⑤

MODEL

BRONZE DOOR

GLORY FACADE

B #19 & #50

SPIRES

CLOISTER

③ ⊠ELEV.

PASSION ② FACADE

FENCE

UNFINISHED ESPLANADE

LA CAIXA BANK

RAMP

EXIT

⑧ SCHOOL

M Sagrada Família

TICKETS & ENTRANCE

CARRER DE SARDENYA

T CARRER DE MALLORCA

Plaça de Sagrada Família

① 👣 TOUR BEGINS

① View of the Exterior
② Passion Facade
③ Atrium
④ Interior & 4 Red Porphyry Columns
⑤ Glory Facade
⑥ Nativity Facade
⑦ Ramp to Museum
⑧ School

BARCELONA

continue to toil to bring Gaudí's designs to life. There's something powerful about a community of committed people with a vision, working on a church that won't be finished in their lifetime—as was standard in the Gothic age. The progress of this remarkable building is a testament to the generations of architects, sculptors, stonecutters, fund-raisers, and donors who've been caught up in the audacity of Gaudí's astonishing vision. After paying the steep admission price (becoming a partner in this building project), you will actually feel good. If there's any building on earth I'd like to see, it's the Sagrada Família...finished.

Cost and Hours: €13 (cash only), €16.50 combo-ticket also includes Gaudí House and Museum at Park Güell (see page 1316), daily April-Sept 9:00-20:30, Oct-March 9:00-18:30, last entry 30 minutes before closing, Metro: Sagrada Família, exit toward Plaça de la Sagrada Família, tel. 932-073-031, www.sagradafamilia.cat.

Getting There: The Sagrada Família Metro stop puts you right on the doorstep: Exit toward Plaça de la Sagrada Família. The ticket windows and entrance for individuals (not groups) are on the west side of the church (at the Passion Facade). Inviting parks flank the building, facing the two completed facades.

Crowd-Beating Tips: The ticket windows and entrance for individuals are on the west side of the church, at the Passion Facade. Though the line can seem long (often curving around the block), it generally moves quickly; you can ask for an estimate from the guards at the front of the line. Still, waits can be up to 45 minutes at peak times (most crowded in the morning). To minimize your wait, arrive right at 9:00 (when it opens) or after 16:00. To skip the line, buy advance tickets, take a tour, or hire a private guide.

Advance Tickets: To avoid the ticket-buying line, you can reserve an entry time and buy tickets in advance (€1.30 booking fee). The easiest option is to book online at www.sagradafamilia.cat (English instructions, just type in your information and credit-card number). You can also get tickets from ATMs at many La Caixa bank branches throughout the city—including the branch to the left as you face the ticket windows and Passion Facade (at the corner, just across the street). If tickets are available, you can buy them for the same day, even for immediate entry. However, not every La Caixa ATM sells tickets (use their larger ServiCaixa machines), and the instructions may be in Spanish (though English-only users can figure it out). Start the transaction by selecting "Event Tickets/Entradas Espectáculos" at the top of the screen. If you've pre-purchased tickets, head straight for the "online ticket office" window, to the right of the main ticket line, and show your ticket or eticket to the guard.

Tours: The 50-minute English tours (€4) run June-Oct daily at 11:00, 12:00, and 13:00; Nov-May Mon-Fri at 11:00 and 13:00, Sat-Sun at 11:00, 12:00, and 13:00. Or rent the good 1.5-hour audioguide (€4). Good English information is posted throughout.

Elevators: Two different elevators (€3 each, pay at main ticket office, each ticket comes with an entry time) take you partway up the towers for a great view of the city and a gargoyle's-eye perspective of the loopy church.

The easier option is the **Passion Facade elevator,** which takes you 215 feet up and down. (If you want, you can climb higher, but expect the spiral stairs to be tight, hot, and congested.)

The **Nativity Facade elevator** is more exciting and demanding. You'll get the opportunity to cross the dizzying bridge between the towers, but you'll need to take the stairs all the way down.

Construction Update: Since Gaudí's death in 1926, construction has moved forward in fits and starts, though much progress was made in recent decades, thanks to Barcelona's 1992 Olympics renaissance, the ensuing rediscovery of the genius of Gaudí, and advances in technology. In 2010, the main nave was finished enough to host a consecration Mass by the pope (as a Catholic church, it is used for services, though irregularly). As I stepped inside on my last visit, the brilliance of Gaudí's vision for the interior was apparent.

The main challenges today: Ensure that construction can withstand the vibrations caused by the speedy AVE trains rumbling underfoot, construct the tallest church spire ever built, and find a way to buy out the people who own the condos in front of the planned Glory Facade so that Gaudí's vision of a grand esplanade approaching the church can be realized. The goal, which seems overly optimistic but tantalizing nonetheless, is to finish the church by the 100th anniversary of Gaudí's death, in 2026.

Self-Guided Tour: Start at the ticket entrance (at the Passion Facade) on the western side of the church. The view is best from the park across the street. Before heading to the ticket booth, take in the...

❶ Exterior: Stand and imagine how grand this church will be when completed. The four 330-foot spires topped with crosses are just a fraction of this mega-church. When finished, the church will have 18 spires. Four will stand at each of the three entrances. Rising above those will be four taller towers, dedicated to the four Evangelists. A tower dedicated to Mary will rise still higher—400 feet. And in the very center of the complex will stand the grand 560-foot Jesus tower, topped with a cross that will shine like a spiritual lighthouse, visible even from out at sea.

The Passion Facade that tourists enter today is only a side entrance to the church. The grand main entrance will be around to the right. That means that the nine-story apartment building will eventually have to be torn down to accommodate it. The three facades—Nativity, Passion, and Glory—will chronicle Christ's life from birth to death to resurrection. Inside and out, a goal of the church is to bring the lessons of the Bible to the world. Despite his boldly modern architectural vision, Gaudí was fundamentally traditional and deeply religious. He designed the Sagrada Família to be a bastion of solid Christian values in the midst of what was a humble workers' colony in a fast-changing city.

When Gaudí died, only one section (on the Nativity Facade—the opposite side, not visible from here) had been completed. The rest of the church has been inspired by Gaudí's long-range vision, but designed and executed by others. This artistic freedom was amplified in 1936, when Civil War shelling burned many of Gaudí's blueprints. Supporters of the ongoing work insist that Gaudí, who enjoyed saying, "My client [God] is not in a hurry," knew he wouldn't live to complete the church and recognized that later architects and artists would rely on their own muses for inspiration. Detractors maintain that the church's design is a uniquely, intensely personal one and that it's folly (if not disrespectful) for anyone to try to guess what Gaudí would have intended. Studying the various plans and models in the museum below the church, it's clear that Gaudí's plan evolved dramatically the longer he worked. Is it appropriate to keep implementing a century-old vision that can no longer be modified by its creator? Discuss.

• *Pass through the ticket entrance into the complex, approaching closer to the...*

❷ **Passion Facade:** Judge for yourself how well Gaudí's original vision has been carried out by later artists. The Passion Facade's four spires were designed by Gaudí and completed (quite faithfully) in 1976. But the lower part was only inspired by Gaudí's designs. The stark sculptures were interpreted freely (and controversially) by Josep Maria Subirachs (b. 1927), who completed the work in 2005.

Subirachs tells the story of Christ's torture and execution. The various scenes—Last Supper, betrayal, whipping, and so on—zigzag up from bottom to top, culminating in Christ's crucifixion over the doorway. The style is severe and unadorned, quite different from Gaudí's signature playfulness. But the bone-like archways are closely based on Gaudí's original designs. And Gaudí had made it clear that this facade should be grim and terrifying.

The facade is full of symbolism. A stylized Alpha-and-Omega is over the door (which faces the setting sun). Jesus, hanging on the cross, has hair made of an open book, symbolizing the word of God. To the left of the door, there's a grid of numbers, always adding up to 33—Jesus' age at the time of his death. The distinct face of the man below and just left of Christ is a memorial to Gaudí. Now look high above: The two-ton figure suspended between the towers is the soul of Jesus, ascending to heaven.

• *Enter the church. As you pass through the* ❸ *Atrium, look down at the fine porphyry floor (with scenes of Jesus' entry into Jerusalem), and look right to see one of the* **elevators** *up to the towers. For now, continue into the...*

❹ **Interior:** Typical of even the most traditional Catalan and Spanish churches, the floor plan is in the shape of a Latin cross, 300 feet long and 200 feet wide. Ultimately, the church will encompass 48,000 square feet, accommodating 8,000 worshippers. The nave's roof is 150 feet high. The crisscross arches of the ceiling (the vaults) show off Gaudí's distinctive engineering. The church's roof and flooring were only completed in 2010—just in time for Pope Benedict XVI to arrive and consecrate the church.

Part of Gaudí's religious vision was a love for nature. He said, "Nothing is invented; it's written in nature." Like the trunks of trees, these **columns** (56 in all) blossom with life, complete with branches, leaves, and knot-like capitals. The columns are a variety of colors—brown clay, gray granite, dark-gray basalt. The taller columns are 72 feet tall; the shorter ones are exactly half that.

The angled columns form many **arches.** You'll see both parabolas (u-shaped) and hyperbolas (flatter, elliptical shapes). Gaudí's starting point was the Gothic pointed arch used in medieval churches. But he tweaked it after meticulous study of which arches are best at bearing weight.

Little **windows** let light filter in like the canopy of a rainforest, giving both privacy and an intimate connection with God. The clear glass is temporary and will gradually be replaced by stained glass. As more and more stained glass is installed, splashes of color will breathe even more life into this amazing space. Gaudí envisioned an awe-inspiring canopy with a symphony of colored light to encourage a contemplative mood.

High up at the back half of the church, the U-shaped **choir**—suspended above the nave—can seat 1,000. The singers will eventually be backed by four organs (there's one now).

Work your way up the grand nave, walking through this forest of massive columns. At the center of the church stand four **red porphyry columns,** each marked with an Evangelist's symbol and name in Catalan: angel (Mateu), lion (Marc), bull (Luc), and eagle (Joan). These columns support a ceiling vault that's 200 feet high—and eventually will also support the central steeple, the 560-foot Jesus tower with the shining cross. The steeple will be further supported by four underground pylons, each consisting of 8,000 tons of cement. It will be the tallest church steeple in the world, though still a few feet shorter than the city's highest point at the summit of Montjuïc hill, as Gaudí believed that a creation of man should not attempt to eclipse the creation of God.

Stroll behind the altar through the **ambulatory** to see videos of the 2010 consecration Mass, and look through windows down at the **crypt** (which holds the tomb of Gaudí). Peering down into that surprisingly traditional space, imagine how the church was started as a fairly conventional, 19th-century Neo-Gothic building until Gaudí was given the responsibility to finish it.

• *Head to the far end of the church, to what will eventually be the main entrance. Just inside the door, find the* **bronze model** *of the eventual floor plan of the completed church. Facing the doors, look high up to see*

*Subirachs' statue of one of Barcelona's patron saints, **Jordi**. Go through the doors to imagine what will someday be the...*

❺ Glory Facade: As you exit, study the fine **bronze door,** emblazoned with the Lord's Prayer in Catalan, surrounded by "Give us this day our daily bread" in 50 languages. Once outside, you'll be face-to-face with...drab, doomed apartment blocks. In the 1950s, the mayor of Barcelona, figuring this day would never really come, sold the land destined for the church project. Now the city must buy back these buildings in order to complete Gaudí's vision: that of a grand esplanade leading to this main entry. Four towers will rise up. The facade's sculpture will represent how the soul passes through death, faces the Last Judgment, avoids the pitfalls of Hell, and finds its way to eternal glory with God. Gaudí purposely left the facade's design open for later architects—stay tuned.

• *Re-enter the church, backtrack up the nave, and exit through the right transept. Once outside, back up as far as you can to take in the...*

❻ Nativity Facade: This is the only part of the church essentially finished in Gaudí's lifetime. The four spires decorated with his unmistakably non-linear sculpture mark this facade as part of his original design. Mixing Gothic-style symbolism, images from nature, and Modernista asymmetry, the Nativity Facade is the best example of Gaudí's original vision, and it established the template for future architects.

The theme of this facade, which faces the rising sun, is Christ's birth. A statue above the doorway shows Mary, Joseph, and Baby Jesus in the manger, while curious cows peek in. It's the Holy Family—or "Sagrada Família"—to whom this church is dedicated. Flanking the doorway are the three Magi and adoring shepherds. Other statues show Jesus as a young carpenter and angels playing musical instruments. Higher up on the facade, in the arched niche, Jesus crowns Mary triumphantly.

The facade is all about birth and new life, from the dove-covered Tree of Life on top to the turtles at the base of the columns flanking the entrance. At the bottom of the Tree of Life is a white pelican. Because it was believed that this noble bird would kill itself to feed its young, it was often used in the Middle Ages as a symbol for the self-sacrifice of Jesus. The chameleon gargoyles at the outer corners of the facade (just above door level) represent the changeability of life. It's as playful as the Passion Facade is grim. Gaudí's plans were for this facade to be painted. Cleverly, this attractive facade was built and finished first to bring in financial support for the project.

The four **spires** are dedicated to Apostles, and they repeatedly bear the word "Sanctus," or holy. Their colorful ceramic caps symbolize the miters (formal hats) of bishops. The shorter spires (to the left) symbolize the Eucharist (communion), alternating between a chalice with grapes and a communion host with wheat.

To the left of the facade is one section of the **cloister.** Whereas most medieval churches have their cloisters attached to one side of the building, the Sagrada Família's cloister will wrap around the church, more than 400 yards long.

• *Notice the second **elevator** up to the towers. But for now, head down the ramp to the left of the facade, where you'll find WCs and the entrance to the...*

❼ **Museum:** Housed in what will someday be the church's crypt, the museum displays Gaudí's original **models and drawings,** and chronicles the progress of construction over the last 130 years. Wander among the plaster models used for the church's construction, including a model of the nave so big you walk beneath it. The models make clear the influence of nature. The columns seem light, with branches springing forth and capitals that look like palm trees. You'll notice that the models don't always match the finished product—these are ideas, not blueprints set in stone. The Passion Facade model (near the entrance) shows Gaudí's original vision, with which Subirachs tinkered very freely (see page 1312).

Turn up the main hallway. On the left you can peek into a busy **workshop** still used for making the same kind of plaster models Gaudí used to envision the final product in 3-D. Farther along, a small hallway on the right leads to some original Gaudí architectural **sketches** in a dimly lit room and a worthwhile 20-minute **movie** (generally shown in English at :50 past each hour).

From the end of this hall, you have another opportunity to look down into the crypt and at **Gaudí's tomb.** Gaudí lived on the site for more than a decade and is buried in the Neo-Gothic 19th-century crypt (also viewable from the apse). There's a move afoot to make Gaudí a saint. Perhaps someday his tomb will be a place of pilgrimage.

Back in the main hallway, on the right is the intriguing **"Hanging Model"** for Gaudí's unfinished Church of Colònia Güell (in a suburb of Barcelona), featuring a similar design to the Sagrada Família. The model illustrates how the architect used gravity to calculate the arches that support the church. Wires dangle like suspended chains, forming perfect hyperbolic arches. Attached to these are bags, representing the weight the arches must support. Flip these arches over, and they can bear the heavy weight of the roof. The mirror above the model shows how the right-side-up church is derived from this. Across the hall is a small exhibit commemorating **Pope Benedict XVI**'s 2010 consecration visit.

After passing some original sculptures from the Glory Facade (on the right) and continuing beneath a huge plaster model, turn right to find **three different visions** for this church. Notice how the arches evolved as Gaudí tinkered, from the original, pointy Neo-Gothic arches, to parabolic ones, to the hyperbolic ones he eventually settled on. Also in this hall are replicas of the **pulpit** and **confessional** that Gaudí, the micro-manager, designed for his church. Before exiting at the far end of the hall, scan the photos (including one of the master himself) and timeline illustrating how construction work has progressed from Gaudí's day to now.

• *You'll exit near where you started, at the Passion Facade.*

❽ **School:** The small building outside the Passion Facade was a school Gaudí erected for the children of the workers building the church. Today it includes more exhibits about the design and engineering of the church, along with a classroom and a replica of Gaudí's desk as it was the day he died. Pause for a moment to pay homage to the man who made all this possible. Gaudí—a faithful Catholic whose medieval-style mysticism belied his Modernista architecture career—was certainly driven to greatness by his passion for God.

▲▲Park Güell

Gaudí fans enjoy the artist's magic in this colorful park, located on the outskirts of town. While it takes a bit of effort to get here, Park Güell (Catalans pronounce it "gway") offers a unique look at Gaudí's style in a natural rather than urban context. Designed as an upscale housing development for early-20th-century urbanites, the park is home to some of Barcelona's most famous symbols, including a whimsical staircase guarded by a dragon and a wavy bench with a view—all of it slathered with fragments of vivid tile. It also features a panoramic terrace supported by a forest of columns. Even without its Gaudí connection, Park Güell is simply a fine place to enjoy a break from a busy city, where green space is relatively rare.

Cost and Hours: Park—free, daily 10:00-20:00, tel. 932-130-488; Gaudí House and Museum—€5.50, €16.50 combo-ticket also includes Sagrada Família, daily April-Sept 10:00-20:00, Oct-March 10:00-18:00; La Casa del Guarda—€2, included in Barcelona History Museum ticket (see page 1289), daily April-Sept 10:00-20:00, Oct-March 10:00-18:00, tel. 933-190-222.

Getting There: To reach Park Güell—about 2.5 miles north of Plaça de Catalunya—it's easiest to take a **taxi** from downtown (around €12). Otherwise, the blue Tourist Bus or public **bus** #24 goes from Plaça de Catalunya to the park's side entrance. Or you can ride the Metro to Joanic, exit toward Carrer de l'Escorial, and find the bus stop in front of #20, where you can catch bus #116 to the park's main entrance.

Visiting the Park: This tour assumes you're arriving at the front/main entrance. If you instead arrive at the side entrance, walk straight ahead through the gate to find the terrace with colorful mosaic benches, then walk down to the stairway and front entrance. As you wander the park, imagine living here a century ago—if this gated community had succeeded and was filled with Barcelona's wealthy.

Front Entrance: Entering the park, you walk by Gaudí's wrought-iron gas lamps (1900-1914). His dad was a blacksmith, and he always enjoyed this medium. Two gate houses made of gingerbread flank the entrance. One houses a good bookshop; the other is home to the Gaudí-built La Casa del Guarda (dull exhibit, totally skippable). The Gaudí House and Museum, described later, is better.

Stairway and Columns: Climb the grand stairway, past the famous ceramic dragon fountain. At the top, dip into the "Hall of 100 Columns," designed to house a produce market for the neighborhood's 60 mansions. The fun columns—each different, made from concrete and rebar, topped with colorful ceramic, and studded with broken bottles and bric-a-brac—add to the market's vitality.

As you continue up (on the left-hand staircase), look left, down the playful "pathway of columns" that supports a long arcade. Gaudí drew his inspiration from nature, and this arcade is like a surfer's perfect tube.

Terrace: Once up top, sit on a colorful bench—designed to fit your body ergonomically—and enjoy one of Barcelona's best views. Look for the Sagrada Família church in the distance. Gaudí was an engineer as well. He designed a water-catchment system by which rain hitting this plaza would flow into and through the columns from the market below, and power the park's fountains.

When considering the failure of Park Güell as a community development, also consider that it was an idea a hundred years ahead of its time. Back then, high-society ladies didn't want to live so far from the cultural action. Today, the surrounding neighborhoods are some of the wealthiest in town, and a gated community here would be a big hit.

Gaudí House and Museum: This pink house with a steeple, standing in the middle of the park (near the side entrance), was actually Gaudí's home for 20 years, until his father died (though Gaudí did not design the actual house). His humble artifacts are mostly gone, but the house is now a museum with some quirky Gaudí furniture and a chance to wander through a model home used to sell the others. Though small, it offers a good taste of what could have been.

Montjuïc

Montjuïc (mohn-jew-EEK, "Mount of the Jews"), overlooking Barcelona's hazy port, has always been a show-off. Ages ago it was capped by an impressive castle. When the Spanish enforced their rule, they built the imposing fortress that you'll see the shell of today. The hill has also played an integral role in the construction of Barcelona's great structures—significant parts of the historic city, the cathedral, the Sagrada Família, and much more were all built with stones quarried from Montjuïc.

Montjuïc has also been prominent during the last century. In 1929, it hosted an international fair, from which many of today's sights originated. And in 1992, the Summer Olympics directed the world's attention to this pincushion of attractions once again. While Montjuïc lacks any single knockout, must-see sight, it is home to a variety of very good ones, and most visitors should find one or two attractions here to suit their interests. For the majority of travelers, the most worthwhile sights are the Fundació Joan Miró, Catalan Art Museum, and CaixaForum.

Sightseeing Strategies: I've listed these sights by altitude, from highest to lowest—from the hill-topping castle down to the 1929 World Expo Fairgrounds at the base of Montjuïc (described in the next section). If you're visiting all of my listed sights, ride to the top by bus, funicular, or taxi, then visit them in this order so that most of your walking is downhill. However, if you want to visit only the Catalan Art Museum and/or CaixaForum, you can just take the Metro to Plaça d'Espanya and ride the escalators up (with some stair-climbing as well) to those sights.

Getting to Montjuïc: You have several options. The simplest is to take a **taxi** directly to your destination (about €7 from downtown).

Buses from various points in the city take you up to Montjuïc, including bus #50 (from the corner of Gran Via de les Corts Catalanes and Passeig de Gràcia in the Eixample, or from the Sagrada Família), bus #55 (from Plaça de Catalunya, next to Caja de Madrid building), and the red Tourist Bus. Alternatively, you could ride the Metro to Plaça d'Espanya, then take either bus #50 or #193 up the hill.

A **funicular** takes visitors from the Paral-lel Metro stop up to Montjuïc (covered by Metro ticket, every 10 minutes, 9:00-22:00). To reach the funicular, take the Metro to the Paral-lel stop, then follow signs for *Parc Montjuïc* and the little funicular icon—you can enter the funicular directly without using another ticket (number of minutes until next departure posted at start of entry tunnel). From the top of the funicular, turn left and walk gently downhill two minutes to the Joan Miró museum, six minutes to the Olympic Stadium, or 10 minutes to the Catalan Art Museum. If you're heading all the way up to the castle, you can catch a bus or cable car from the top of the funicular (see castle listing, later).

For a scenic (if very slow) approach to Montjuïc, you could ride the fun circa-1929 Aeri del Port **cable car** *(telefèric)* from the tip of the Barceloneta peninsula (across the harbor, near the beach) to the Miramar viewpoint park in Montjuïc. (Another station, right along the port near the Columbus Monument, is currently closed.) Since the cable car is expensive, loads excruciatingly slowly, and goes between two relatively remote parts of town, it's really not an efficient connection. It's only worthwhile for its sweeping views over town or if you'd like to, say, cap off your Montjuïc day with some beach time near Barceloneta (€10 one-way, €15 round-trip, 3/hour, daily 11:00-19:00, until 20:00 in June-Sept, closed in high wind, tel. 932-252-718).

Getting Around Montjuïc: Up top, it's easy and fun to walk between the sights—especially downhill. You can also connect the sights using the red Tourist Bus or one of the public buses that runs from different points in the city. Each bus has a slightly different route: **Bus #193** does a counterclockwise loop around the hilltop and is the only bus that goes all the way up to the castle; from there, it heads downhill, passing Miramar (cable-car station), the lower castle cable-car station/top of the funicular, Fundació Joan Miró, and Plaça d'Espanya before circling back up past CaixaForum, the Spanish Village, the Catalan Art Museum, and eventually the castle. **Bus #50** goes in both directions—connecting the cable-car/funicular stations, Fundació Joan Miró, the stadium, the Catalan Art Museum, the Spanish Village, CaixaForum, and Plaça d'Espanya—but it doesn't go all the way up to the castle. **Bus #55** connects only Miramar, the funicular/cable-car stations, Fundació Joan Miró, and the Catalan Art Museum.

Castle of Montjuïc

The castle, while just an empty brick-and-concrete shell today, offers great city views from its ramparts...and some poignant history. It was built by the central Spanish government in the 18th century with a Vauban-type star fortress design to keep an eye on Barcelona and stifle citizen revolt. When the 20th-century dictator Franco was in power, the castle was the site of hundreds of political executions. Its military function gone, these days it serves as a park, jogging destination, and host to a popular summer open-air cinema.

Cost and Hours: Free, daily April-Sept 9:00-21:00, Oct-March 9:00-19:00.

Getting There: To spare yourself the hike up to the castle and to see some great views of the city, you can ride bus #193 to the base of the castle, catching it from Plaça d'Espanya, the top of the Montjuïc funicular, or various other points on Montjuïc. Or you can spring for the much pricier **cable car,** which departs from near the upper station of the Montjuïc funicular (€7 one-way, €10 round-trip, daily June-Sept 10:00-21:00, March-May and Oct 10:00-19:00, Nov-Feb 10:00-18:00).

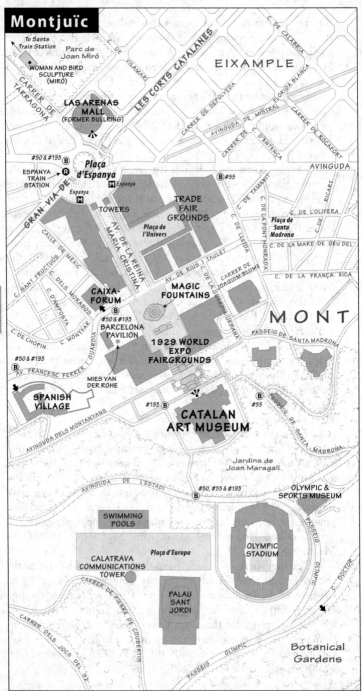

Montjuïc

To Santes Train Station
Parc de Joan Miró
WOMAN AND BIRD SCULPTURE (MIRÓ)
C. DE VILAMARI
C. DE CALABRIA
EIXAMPLE
LES CORTS CATALANES
LAS ARENAS MALL (FORMER BULLRING)
CARRER DE SEPULVEDA
AVINGUDA DE MISTRAL
CARRER DE FLORIDA BLANCA
CARRER DE ROCAFORT
CARRER DE TARRAGONA
CARRER DE D'ENTENCA

#50 & #193
Plaça d'Espanya
AVINGUDA

ESPANYA TRAIN STATION
Espanya
#55
GRAN VIA DE
Espanya
TOWERS
TRADE FAIR GROUNDS
C. DE TAMARIT
C. DE RICART
C. DE L'OLIVERA
Plaça de Santa Madrona
CALLE DE MÉXIC
AV. DE LA REINA MARIA CRISTINA
Plaça de l'Univers
C. DE LLEIDA
C. DE LA FONT HONRADA
C. DE LA MARE DE DÉU DEL

C. SANT FRUCTUÓS
C. DELS MORABOS
C. D'AMPOSTA
CAIXA-FORUM
AV. DE RIUS I TAULET
MAGIC FOUNTAINS
CARRER DE JOAQUIM BLUME
C. DE LA FRANÇA XICA

#50 & #193
BARCELONA PAVILION
C. DE LA MERCÈ URBANA
MONT
PASSEIG DE SANTA MADRONA

C. DE CHOPIN
C. MONTFAR
1929 WORLD EXPO FAIRGROUNDS

#50 & #193
AV. FRANCESC FERRER I GUARDIA
MIES VAN DER ROHE

SPANISH VILLAGE
#193
CATALAN ART MUSEUM
#55
PASSEIG DE SANTA MADRONA

AVINGUDA DELS MONTANYANS

Jardins de Joan Maragall

AVINGUDA DE L'ESTADI
#50, #55 & #193
OLYMPIC & SPORTS MUSEUM

SWIMMING POOLS
Plaça d'Europa
OLYMPIC STADIUM
PASSEIG OLÍMPIC

CALATRAVA COMMUNICATIONS TOWER

CARRER DE PIERRE DE COUBERTIN
PALAU SANT JORDI

CARRER DELS JOCS DEL 92
C. DOCTOR

Botanical Gardens

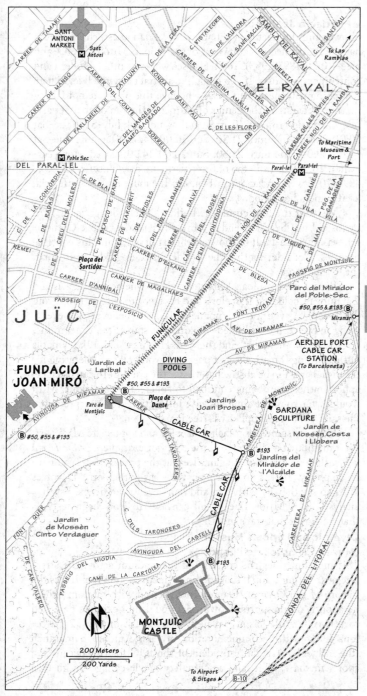

▲Fundació Joan Miró

Showcasing the talents of yet another Catalan artist, this museum has the best collection anywhere of art by Joan Miró (ZHOO-ahn mee-ROH, 1893-1983). You'll also see works by other Modern and contemporary artists. If you don't like abstract art, you'll leave here scratching your head. But those who love this place are not faking it...they understand the genius of Miró and the fun of abstract art.

Cost and Hours: €10, great audioguide-€4; July-Sept Tue-Sat 10:00-20:00, Thu until 21:30, Sun 10:00-14:30; Oct-June Tue-Sat 10:00-19:00, Thu until 21:30, Sun 10:00-14:30; closed Mon year-round, 200 yards from top of funicular, Parc de Montjuïc, tel. 934-439-470, www.fundaciomiro-bcn.org. The museum has a cafeteria, a café, and a bookshop.

Visiting the Museum: The building itself, designed in 1975 by Josep Lluís Sert (a friend of Miró and a student of Le Corbusier), was purpose-built to show off the art of Miró and his contemporaries. Consider renting the wonderful audioguide, well worth the extra charge.

Barcelona-born Joan Miró divided his time between Paris and Catalunya (including Barcelona and his favorite village, Mont-roig del Camp). As you wander, ponder this: Miró believed that everything in the cosmos is linked—colors, sky, stars, love, time, music, dogs, men, women, dirt, and the void. He mixed childlike symbols of these things creatively, as a poet uses words. It's as liberating for the visual artist to be abstract as it is for the poet: Both can use metaphors rather than being confined to concrete explanations. Miró would listen to music and paint. It's interactive, free interpretation. He said, "For me, simplicity is freedom."

Here are some tips to help you enjoy and appreciate Miró's art: First meditate on it, then read the title (for example, *The Smile of a Tear*), then meditate on it again. Repeat the process until you have an epiphany. There's no correct answer—it's pure poetry. Devotees of Miró say they fly with him and don't even need drugs. Psychoanalysts liken Miró's free-for-all canvases to Rorschach tests. Is that a cigar in that star's mouth?

Olympic and Sports Museum (Museu Olímpic i de l'Esport)

This museum rides the coattails of the stadium across the street (see next listing). You'll twist down a timeline-ramp that traces the history of the Olympic Games, interspersed with random exhibits about various sports. Downstairs you'll find exhibits designed to test your athleticism, a play-by-play rehash of the '92 Barcelona Olympiad, a commemoration of Juan Antonio Samaranch (the influential Catalan president of the IOC for two decades), a sports media exhibit, and a schmaltzy movie collage. High-tech but hokey, the museum is worth the time and money only for those nostalgic for the '92 Games.

Cost and Hours: €4.50; April-Sept Tue-Sat 10:00-20:00, Sun 10:00-14:30; Oct-March Tue-Sat 10:00-18:00, Sun 10:00-14:30; closed Mon year-round, Avinguda de l'Estadi 60, tel. 932-925-379, www.fundaciobarcelonaolimpica.es.

Olympic Stadium (Estadi Olímpic)

Aside from the memories of the medals, Barcelona's Olympic Stadium, originally built for the 1929 World Expo, offers little to see today. But if the doors are open, you're welcome to step inside. History panels along the railings overlooking the playing field tell the stadium's dynamic story and show the place in happier times (filled with fans as Bon Jovi, the Rolling Stones, and Madonna pack the place). The stadium was restored for the 1992 Summer Olympics, which were particularly memorable for the USA's basketball Dream Team, and as the first Games after the breakups of Yugoslavia and the Soviet Union (whose athletes took the field as the "Unified Team").

Nearby: Hovering over the stadium is the futuristic **Montjuïc Communications Tower,** designed by prominent Spanish architect Santiago Calatrava and used to transmit Olympic highlights and lowlights around the world.

▲▲Catalan Art Museum
(Museu Nacional d'Art de Catalunya)

The big vision for this wonderful museum is to showcase Catalan art from the 10th century through about the mid-20th century. Often called "the Prado of Romanesque art" (and "MNAC" for short), it holds Europe's best collection of Romanesque frescoes. It also offers a particularly good sweep of modern Catalan art—fitting, given Catalunya's astonishing contribution to the Modern. While some may find it "another boring museum," art aficionados are sure to find something in this diverse collection to tickle their fancy.

Cost and Hours: €10, includes temporary exhibits, ticket valid for two days within one month, free first Sun of month; audioguide-€3.10; open Tue-Sat 10:00-19:00, Sun 10:00-14:30, closed Mon, last entry 30 minutes before closing; in massive National Palace building above Magic Fountains, near Plaça d'Espanya—take escalators up; tel. 936-220-376, www.mnac.cat.

Visiting the Museum: As you enter, pick up a map (helpful for such a big and confusing building). The left wing is Romanesque, and the right wing is Gothic, exquisite Renaissance, and Baroque. Upstairs is more Baroque, plus modern art, photography, coins, and more.

The MNAC's rare, world-class collection of **Romanesque** (Romànic) art came mostly from remote Catalan village churches

BARCELONA

(most of the pieces were moved to the museum in the early 1920s to save them from scavenging art dealers). The Romanesque wing features a remarkable array of 11th- to 13th-century frescoes, painted wooden altar fronts, and ornate statuary. This classic Romanesque art—with flat 2-D scenes, each saint holding his symbol, and Jesus (easy to identify by the cross in his halo)—is impressively displayed on replicas of the original church ceilings and apses.

Across the way, in the **Gothic** wing, fresco murals give way to vivid 14th-century wood-panel paintings of Bible stories. A roomful of paintings (Room 26) by the Catalan master Jaume Huguet (1412-1492) deserves a look, particularly his *Consecration of St. Agustí Vell.*

For a break, glide under the huge **dome,** which once housed an ice-skating rink. This was the prime ceremony room and dance hall for the 1929 World Expo.

From the big ballroom, you can ride the glass elevator upstairs to the **Renaissance and Baroque** section, covering Spain's Golden Age (Zurbarán, heavy religious scenes, Spanish royals with their endearing underbites) and Romanticism (dewy-eyed Catalan landscapes). Down on the ground floor are minor works by major—if not necessarily Catalan—names (Velázquez, El Greco, Tintoretto, Rubens, and so on).

Another museum highlight is the **Modern** section, which takes you on an enjoyable walk from the late 1800s to about 1950. It's kind of a Catalan Musée d'Orsay, offering a big chronological clockwise circle covering Symbolism, Modernisme, *fin de siècle* fun, Art Deco, and more. Find the early 20th-century paintings by Catalan artists Santiago Rusiñol and Ramon Casas, both of whom had a profound impact on a young Picasso (and, through him, on all of modern art). Casas was also one of the financiers of Els Quatre Gats, the hangout of Modernista artists (see page 1345); his fun Toulouse-Lautrec-esque works, including a whimsical self-portrait on a tandem bicycle, are crowd-pleasers. Crossing over to the "Modern 2" section, you'll find furniture (pieces that complement the empty spaces you likely saw in Gaudí's buildings—including a Gaudí wooden sofa), Impressionism, the shimmering landscapes of Joaquim Mir, and several distinctly Picasso portraits of women.

The museum also has a coin collection, seductive sofas scattered about, and the chic Oleum restaurant, with vast city views (and €28 fixed-price lunches).

▲1929 World Expo Fairgrounds

With the World Expo in 1929, Montjuïc morphed into an extravagant center for fairs, museums, and festivals. Except for the factory (now housing the CaixaForum) and the bullring, everything you see here dates from 1929. The expo's theme was to demonstrate how electricity was about more than lightbulbs: Electricity powered the funicular, the glorious expo fountains, the many pavilion displays, and even the flame atop the fountain marking the center of Plaça d'Espanya (and celebrating the electric company that sponsored the show). If Barcelona is known for growing through big events, this certainly is a good example.

Standing at Plaça d'Espanya (or, better yet, on the rooftop terrace of the bullring mall—described later), look through the double-brick-tower gate, down the grand esplanade, and imagine it alive with fountains and lined by proud national pavilions showing off all that was modern in 1929. Today it's home to the Fira de Barcelona convention center. The Neo-Baroque fountain provides a brilliant centerpiece for Plaça d'Espanya.

Getting There: The fairgrounds sprawl at the base of Montjuïc, from the Catalan Art Museum's doorstep to Plaça d'Espanya. The easiest option is to see these sights on your way down from Montjuïc. Otherwise, ride the Metro to Espanya, then use the series of stairs and escalators to climb up through the heart of the fairgrounds (eventually reaching the Catalan Art Museum).

▲Magic Fountains (Font Màgica)

Music, colored lights, and huge amounts of water make an artistic and coordinated splash in the evening at Plaça d'Espanya.

Cost and Hours: Free, 20-minute shows start on the half-hour; almost always May-Sept Thu-Sun 21:00-23:00, no shows Mon-Wed; Oct-April Fri-Sat 19:00-20:30, no shows Sun-Thu; these are first and last show times; from the Espanya Metro stop, walk toward the towering National Palace.

▲▲CaixaForum

The CaixaForum Social and Cultural Center (sponsored by the leading Catalan bank) is housed in one of Barcelona's most important Art Nouveau buildings. In 1912, Josep Puig i Cadafalch (a top architect often overshadowed by Gaudí) designed the Casaramona textile factory, which showed off Modernista design in an industrial rather than a residential context. It functioned as a factory for less than a decade, then later served a long stint as a police station under Franco. Beautifully refurbished, the facility reopened in 2002 as a great center for bringing culture and art to the people of Barcelona for free.

Cost and Hours: Free, Mon-Fri 10:00-20:00, Sat-Sun 10:00-21:00, July-Aug open late on some days—likely Wed until 23:00, Avinguda de Francesc Ferrer i Guàrdia 6-8, tel. 934-768-600, http://obrasocial.lacaixa.es—click on "CaixaForum Barcelona."

Visiting the Center: From the lobby, signs point to *Sala 2, 3, 4,* and *5*; each hosts different (and typically outstanding) temporary exhibitions. Ride the escalator to the first floor, which features a modest but interesting exhibit about the history and renovation of the building, including a model and photos. Then head into the appealing red-brick courtyard, from which you can access the various exhibition halls. (The sight features generally limited English descriptions.)

Take the stairs or elevator up to the Modernista Terrace, boasting a wavy floor, bristling with fanciful brick towers, and offering views over the complex and to Montjuïc. Enjoy the genius of Puig i Cadafalch's Modernista design, which provided state-of-the-art working conditions—natural light, good ventilation, and even two trademark towers filled with water (which could be broken to put out any factory fire). The various buildings (designed to be separate from each other to reduce the risk of fire) were built on terraces to level out the Montjuïc slope. Notice that there's no smokestack. This was one of the first electric-powered factories in town.

Nearby: Architecture pilgrims can head across the street to Ludwig Mies van der Rohe's **Barcelona Pavilion,** designed to host the German exhibits for the expo and to show off the emerging, stripped-down, strictly functional "Modernist" (i.e., decidedly *not* Modernista) style of architecture. This humorless building—sternly staring down the CaixaForum from across the street—is a reminder that even just a couple of decades later, architecture highbrows already considered the over-the-top flourishes of Modernisme passé and overdone, or even embarrassing; Gaudí, Puig i Cadafalch, and company would fall out of fashion until the late 20th century. The pavilion is open to visitors (€4.75, daily 10:00-20:00, Avinguda de Francesc Ferrer i Guàrdia 7, tel. 934-234-016, www.miesbcn.com).

Spanish Village (Poble Espanyol)

This tacky and overpriced five-acre model village (a long hike up from the main World Expo esplanade) was built as part of the expo to show off the cultural and architectural diversity in Spain. Using fake traditional architecture from all over the country, the village was mostly a shell to contain gift shops—and today it still serves the same purpose. Craftspeople do their clichéd thing (mostly in the morning), and friendly shopkeepers offer plenty of tasty samples of traditional and local edibles. This is popular with cruise groups and people who consider Disney World's Epcot Center a history lesson.

Cost and Hours: €9.50, €3 audioguide explains all the buildings, daily 9:00-20:00 or later, closes earlier off-season, www.poble-espanyol.com.

▲Las Arenas (Bullring Mall)

What do you do with a big arena when your society decides to outlaw bullfighting? Make a mall. Catalunya recently made the brutal Spanish sport (or art form, depending on your perspective) illegal. (This was done as much for Catalan national pride as it was out of concern over the barbarity of the very Spanish spectacle.)

The grand Neo-Moorish Modernista *plaça de toros* functioned as an arena for bullfights from around 1900 to 1970, then reopened in 2011 and now hosts everything you'd expect in a modern mall: lots of famous shops, a food-circus basement, a 12-screen cinema complex, a rock-and-roll museum, and a roof terrace with stupendous views of Plaça d'Espanya and Montjuïc (reachable by external glass elevator for €1 or from inside for free).

The **terrace,** with some of the best free views in town, is ringed with eateries. From here you get a bird's-eye perspective of the fairgrounds. In the opposite direction, the park at your feet (called Parc de Joan Miró) includes the giant Miró sculpture *Woman and Bird (Dona i Ocell).* This was one of three works (along with the mosaic on the Ramblas—see page 1276) that the city commissioned Miró to create in order to welcome visitors. Miró's sense of humor is evident—if the sculpture seems phallic, keep in mind that the Catalan word for "bird" is also slang for "penis."

Cost and Hours: Free, daily 10:00-22:00, Gran Via de les Corts Catalanes 373-385, Metro: Espanya, www.arenasdebarcelona.com.

Music
Serious Concerts

Several seriously classy venues host high-end performances. The **Palace of Catalan Music** (Palau de la Música Catalana), with one of the finest Modernista interiors in town (see listing on page 1296), offers a full slate of performances, ranging from symphonic to Catalan folk songs to chamber music to flamenco (€22-49 tickets, Carrer Palau de la Música 4-6, Metro: Urquinaona, box office tel. 902-442-882, www.palaumusica.cat).

The **Liceu Opera House** (Gran Teatre del Liceu), right on the heart of the Ramblas, is a pre-Modernista, sumptuous venue for opera, dance, children's theater, and concerts (tickets from €10, La Rambla 51-59, box office just around the corner at Carrer Sant Pau 1, Metro: Liceu, box office tel. 934-859-913, www.liceubarcelona.cat).

Some of Barcelona's top sights—including **Casa Milà, CaixaForum,** and **Fundació Joan Miró** (all described earlier)—also host good-quality concerts; for details, check their websites.

Touristy Performances of Spanish Clichés

Two famously Spanish types of music—flamenco and Spanish guitar—have little to do with Barcelona or Catalunya, but are performed to keep visitors happy. If you're headed for other parts of Spain where these musical forms are more typical (such as Andalucía for flamenco), you might as well wait until you can experience the real deal. But if this is your best chance to see these types of performances, here are some options.

Flamenco: Tarantos, on Plaça Reial in the heart of the Barri Gòtic, puts on cheap, brief (30 minutes), riveting flamenco performances several times nightly. While flamenco is foreign to Catalunya (locals say that it's like going to see country music in Boston), this is a fun and easy way to enjoy it. Performances are in a touristy little bar/theater with about 50 seats and reliably good-quality performers (€8, nightly at 20:30, 21:30, and 22:30; in July-Aug extra shows at 18:30, 19:30, and 23:30; Plaça Reial 17, tel. 933-191-789, www.masimas.com/en/tarantos). It's right on Plaça Reial, so it's easy to drop by and get tickets.

Spanish Guitar: "Masters of Guitar" concerts are offered nearly nightly at 21:00 in the Barri Gòtic's Church of Santa Maria del Pi (€21 at the door, €3 less if you buy at least 3 hours ahead—look for ticket-sellers in front of church and scattered around town, Plaça del Pi 7; sometimes in Sant Jaume Church instead, Carrer de Ferran 28; tel. 647-514-513, www.maestrosdelaguitarra.com). The same company also does occasional concerts in the Palace of Catalan Music (€25-29).

Sleeping in Barcelona

Book ahead. Barcelona is Spain's most expensive city. Still, it has reasonably priced rooms. Cheap places are more crowded in summer; fancier business-class hotels fill up in winter and offer discounts on weekends and in summer. When considering relative hotel values, in summer and on weekends you can often get modern comfort in business-class hotels for about the same price (€100) as you'll pay for ramshackle charm (and only a few minutes' walk from the Old City action). Most TI branches (including those at Plaça de Catalunya, Plaça de Sant Jaume, and the airport) offer a room-finding service, though it's cheaper to go direct.

While many of my recommendations are on pedestrian streets, night noise can be a problem (especially in cheap places, which have single-pane windows). For a quiet night, ask for "*tranquilo*" rather than "*con vista*."

Business-Class Comfort near Plaça de Catalunya

These hotels have sliding-glass doors leading to plush reception areas, air-conditioning, and perfectly sterile modern bedrooms. Most are on big streets within two blocks of Barcelona's exuberant central square, where the Old City meets the Eixample. As business-class hotels, they have hard-to-pin-down prices that fluctuate wildly. I've listed the average rate you'll pay. But in summer and on weekends, supply often far exceeds the demand, and many of these places cut prices to around €100—always ask for a deal.

Sleep Code

(€1 = about $1.30, country code: 34)
S = Single, **D** = Double/Twin, **T** = Triple, **Q** = Quad, **b** = bathroom, **s** = shower only. Unless otherwise noted, credit cards are accepted, English is spoken, and prices listed generally include the 8 percent IVA tax. Hotel breakfasts can range from simple spreads (either included or cheap) to pricey buffets.

To help you easily sort through these listings, I've divided the accommodations into three categories, based on the price for a standard double room with bath (during high season):

  $$$ **Higher Priced**—Most rooms €150 or more.
   $$ **Moderately Priced**—Most rooms between €100-150.
    $ **Lower Priced**—Most rooms €100 or less.

Prices can change without notice; verify the hotel's current rates online or by email.

Most of these are located between two Metro stops: Catalunya and Universitat; if arriving by Aerobus, note that the bus also stops at both places.

$$$ Hotel Catalonia Plaça Catalunya has four stars, an elegant old entryway with a mod new reception area, splashy public spaces, slick marble and hardwood floors, 140 comfortable but simple rooms, and a garden courtyard with a pool a world away from the big-city noise. It's a bit pricey for the quality of the rooms—you're paying for the posh lobby (Db-€200 but can drop to as low as €100, extra bed-€38, breakfast-€19, air-con, elevator, free Internet access and Wi-Fi, a half-block off Plaça de Catalunya at Carrer de Bergara 11, Metro: Catalunya, tel. 933-015-151, fax 933-173-442, www.hoteles-catalonia.com, catalunya@hoteles-catalonia.es).

$$ Hotel Denit is a small, stylish, 36-room hotel on a pedestrian street two blocks off Plaça de Catalunya. It's chic, minimalist, and fun: Guidebook tips decorate the halls, and the rooms are sized like T-shirts ("small" Sb-€109, "medium" Db-€119, "large" Db-€144, "XL" Db-€164, includes breakfast when you book direct—otherwise pay €6, air-con, elevator, free Wi-Fi, Carrer d'Estruc 24-26, Metro: Catalunya, tel. 935-454-000, fax 935-454-001, www.denit.com, info@denit.com).

$$ Hotel Inglaterra is owned by the same people as Hotel Denit (listed above) but on the other side of Plaça de Catalunya. It has 60 rooms, a more traditional style, a rooftop terrace and swimming pool, and slightly higher prices (Sb-€119, Db-€129, €30 more for bigger "deluxe" rooms, breakfast-€15, air-con, elevator,

Barcelona's Old City Hotels

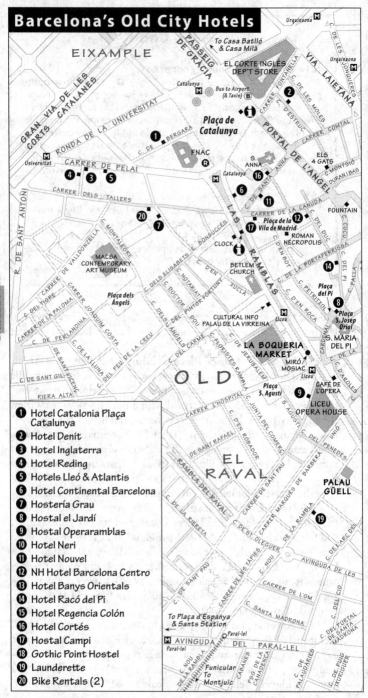

1. Hotel Catalonia Plaça Catalunya
2. Hotel Denit
3. Hotel Inglaterra
4. Hotel Reding
5. Hotels Lleó & Atlantis
6. Hotel Continental Barcelona
7. Hostería Grau
8. Hostal el Jardí
9. Hostal Operaramblas
10. Hotel Neri
11. Hotel Nouvel
12. NH Hotel Barcelona Centro
13. Hotel Banys Orientals
14. Hotel Racó del Pi
15. Hotel Regencia Colón
16. Hotel Cortés
17. Hostal Campi
18. Gothic Point Hostel
19. Launderette
20. Bike Rentals (2)

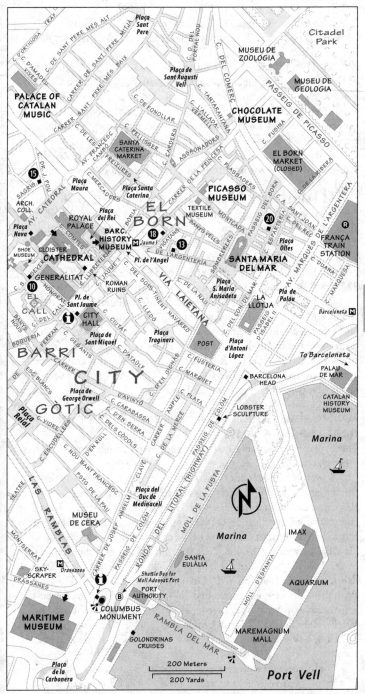

BARCELONA

Plaça Sant Pere

Citadel Park

MUSEU DE ZOOLOGIA

MUSEU DE GEOLOGIA

PALACE OF CATALAN MUSIC

Plaça de Sant Augusti Vell

CHOCOLATE MUSEUM

SANTA CATERINA MARKET

EL BORN MARKET (CLOSED)

15

Plaça Maura

Plaça Santa Caterina

PICASSO MUSEUM

ARCH. COLL.

ROYAL PALACE

Plaça del Rei

TEXTILE MUSEUM

20

Plaça Nova

BARC. HISTORY MUSEUM

EL BORN

FRANÇA TRAIN STATION

SHOE MUSEUM

CLOISTER

18

Jaume I

13

Plaça Olles

CATHEDRAL

SANTA MARIA DEL MAR

GENERALITAT

ROMAN RUINS

VIA LAIETANA

Plaça S. Maria Anisadeta

LA LLOTJA

Pla de Palau

10

EL CALL

Pl. de Sant Jaume

Barceloneta

CITY HALL

Plaça de Sant Miquel

Plaça Traginers

POST

Plaça d'Antoni López

BARRI

CITY

GÒTIC

To Barceloneta

PALAU DE MAR

Plaça de George Orwell

BARCELONA HEAD

CATALAN HISTORY MUSEUM

Plaça Reial

LOBSTER SCULPTURE

Marina

LAS RAMBLAS

Plaça del Duc de Medinaceli

MUSEU DE CERA

Marina

IMAX

SKY-SCRAPER

Drassanes

SANTA EULÀLIA

AQUARIUM

MARITIME MUSEUM

Shuttle Bus for Moll Adossat Port

PORT AUTHORITY

B

COLUMBUS MONUMENT

MAREMAGNUM MALL

Plaça de la Carbonera

GOLONDRINAS CRUISES

RAMBLA DEL MAR

200 Meters

200 Yards

Port Vell

free Internet access and Wi-Fi, Carrer de Pelai 14, Metro: Universitat, tel. 935-051-100, www.hotel-inglaterra.com, recepcion@hotel-inglaterra.com).

$$ Hotel Reding, on a quiet street a 10-minute walk west of the Ramblas and Plaça de Catalunya action, is a slick and sleek place renting 44 mod rooms at a reasonable price (Db-€124—ask about free breakfast with this book but only if you book direct—otherwise pay €14 for breakfast, prices go up during trade fairs, extra bed-€38, air-con, elevator, free Internet access and Wi-Fi, Carrer de Gravina 5-7, Metro: Universitat, tel. 934-121-097, fax 932-683-482, www.hotelreding.com, recepcion@hotelreding.com).

$$ Hotel Lleó (YEH-oh) is well-run, with 92 big, bright, and comfortable rooms; a great breakfast room; and a generous lounge (Db-€130 but flexes way up with demand, can be cheaper in summer, extra bed-about €30, breakfast-€13, air-con, elevator, free Internet access and Wi-Fi, small rooftop pool, Carrer de Pelai 22, midway between Metros: Universitat and Catalunya, tel. 933-181-312, fax 934-122-657, www.hotel-lleo.com, info@hotel-lleo.com).

$$ Hotel Atlantis is solid, with 50 big, nondescript, modern rooms and fair prices for the location (Sb-€92, Db-€120, Tb-€138, check for deals on website, breakfast-€9, air-con, elevator, free Internet access and Wi-Fi, faces busy street—request a quieter room in back, Carrer de Pelai 20, midway between Metros: Universitat and Catalunya, tel. 933-189-012, fax 934-120-914, www.hotelatlantis-bcn.com, inf@hotelatlantis-bcn.com).

Affordable Hotels with "Personality" on or near the Ramblas

These places are generally family-run, with ad-lib furnishings, more character, and lower prices.

$$ Hotel Continental Barcelona, in a building overlooking the top of the Ramblas, offers classic, tiny-view balcony opportunities if you don't mind the noise. Its 39 comfortable but faded rooms come with wildly clashing carpets and wallpaper, and perhaps one too many clever ideas. Choose between your own little Ramblas-view balcony (where you can eat your breakfast) or a quieter back room. J. M.'s (José María's) free breakfast and all-day snack-and-drink bar are a plus (Sb-€95, Db-€105, twin Db-€115, Db with Ramblas balcony-€125, extra bed-€40, mention this book for best prices, includes breakfast, air-con, elevator, free Internet access and Wi-Fi, Ramblas 138, Metro: Catalunya, tel. 933-012-570, fax 933-027-360, www.hotelcontinental.com, barcelona@hotelcontinental.com).

$ Hostería Grau is homey, family-run, and almost alpine. Its 25 cheery, garden-pastel rooms are a few blocks off the Ramblas in the colorful university district. The first two floors have seven-foot-high ceilings, then things get tall again (S-€40, D-€75, Db-€98, extra bed-€18; 2-bedroom family suites: Db-€110, Tb-€130, Qb-€165; slippery prices jump during fairs and big events, ask about discount when you book direct and show this book, breakfast extra, strict cancellation policy, air-con, elevator, free Internet access and Wi-Fi, 200 yards up Carrer dels Tallers from the Ramblas at Ramelleres 27, Metro: Catalunya, tel. 933-018-135, fax 933-176-825, www.hostalgrau.com, reservas@hostalgrau.com, Monica).

$ Hostal el Jardí offers 40 clean, remodeled rooms on a breezy square in the Barri Gòtic. Many of the tight, plain, comfy rooms come with petite balconies (for an extra charge) and enjoy an almost Parisian ambience. It's a good deal only if you value the quaint-square-with-Barri-Gòtic ambience—you're definitely paying for the location. Book well in advance, as this family-run place has an avid following (small basic interior Db-€75, nicer interior Db-€90, outer Db with balcony or twin with window-€95, large outer Db with balcony or square-view terrace-€110, extra bed-€12, breakfast-€6, air-con, elevator, some stairs, free Wi-Fi in lobby, halfway between Ramblas and cathedral at Plaça Sant Josep Oriol 1, Metro: Liceu, tel. 933-015-900, fax 933-425-733, www.eljardi-barcelona.com, reservations@eljardi-barcelona.com).

$ Hostal Operaramblas, with 68 stark rooms 20 yards off the Ramblas, is clean, institutional, modern, and a great value. The street can feel a bit seedy at night, but it's safe, and the hotel is very secure (Sb-€45, Db-€65, no breakfast, air-con only in summer, elevator, pay Internet access, free Wi-Fi in lobby, Carrer de Sant Pau 20, Metro: Liceu, tel. 933-188-201, www.operaramblas.com, info@operaramblas.com).

Places in the Old City

These accommodations are buried in Barcelona's Old City, mostly in the Barri Gòtic. The Catalunya, Liceu, and Jaume I Metro stops flank this tight tangle of lanes; I've noted which stop(s) are best for each.

$$$ Hotel Neri is posh, pretentious, and sophisticated, with 22 rooms spliced into the ancient stones of the Barri Gòtic, overlooking an overlooked square (Plaça Sant Felip Neri) a block from the cathedral. It has big flatscreen TVs, pricey modern art on the bedroom walls, dressed-up people in its gourmet restaurant, and stuffy service (Db-€300, suites-€365-450, generally cheaper on weekdays, breakfast-€22, air-con, elevator, free Wi-Fi, rooftop tanning deck, Carrer de Sant Sever 5, Metro: Liceu or Jaume I, tel. 933-040-655, fax 933-040-337, www.hotelneri.com, info@hotel-neri.com).

$$$ Hotel Nouvel, in an elegant, Victorian-style building on a handy pedestrian street, is less business-oriented and offers more character than the others listed here. It boasts royal lounges and 78 comfy rooms (Sb-€110, Db-€192, online deals can be much much cheaper, ask about discount with this book—you must reserve direct by email, not their website; extra bed-€35, includes breakfast, €20 deposit for TV remote, air-con, elevator, pay Wi-Fi, Carrer de Santa Anna 20, Metro: Catalunya, tel. 933-018-274, fax 933-018-370, www.hotelnouvel.com, info@hotelnouvel.com, Roberto).

$$$ NH Hotel Barcelona Centro, with 156 rooms and tasteful chain-hotel predictability, is professional yet friendly, buried in the Barri Gòtic just three blocks off the Ramblas (Db-€160, rates fluctuate with demand, bigger "superior" rooms on a corner with windows on 2 sides-€25 extra, breakfast-€15, air-con, elevator, pay Internet access, free Wi-Fi in lobby—30-minute limit, Carrer del Duc 15, Metro: Catalunya or Liceu, tel. 932-703-410, fax 934-127-747, www.nh-hotels.com, barcelonacentro@nh-hotels.com).

$$ Hotel Banys Orientals—despite being a big, modern, business-class type place—has a people-to-people ethic and refreshingly straight prices. Its 43 rooms are located in the El Born district on a pedestrianized street between the cathedral and Church of Santa Maria del Mar (Sb-€85, Db-€105, breakfast-€10, air-con, free Wi-Fi, Carrer de l'Argenteria 37, 50 yards from Metro: Jaume I, tel. 932-688-460, www.hotelbanysorientals.com, reservas@hotelbanysorientals.com). They also run the adjacent, recommended El Senyor Parellada restaurant.

$$ Hotel Racó del Pi, part of the H10 hotel chain, is a quality, professional place with generous public spaces and 37 modern, bright, quiet rooms. It's located on a wonderful pedestrian street immersed in the Barri Gòtic (Db-often around €130-145, can be as low as €100, cheaper if you book "nonrefundable" room online, breakfast-€10, air-con, free Internet access and Wi-Fi, around the corner from Plaça del Pi at Carrer del Pi 7, 3-minute walk from Metro: Liceu, tel. 933-426-190, www.h10hotels.com, h10.raco.delpi@h10.es).

$$ Hotel Regencia Colón, in a handy location one block in front of the cathedral, offers 50 slightly older but solid, classy, and well-priced rooms (Db-€110, more on weekends, extra bed-€33, breakfast-€13, air-con, elevator, free Wi-Fi, Carrer dels Sagristans 13-17, Metro: Jaume I, tel. 933-189-858, fax 933-172-822, www.hotelregenciacolon.com, info@hotelregenciacolon.com).

$ Hotel Cortés has 44 rooms on a traffic-free shopping street just off Avinguda Portal de l'Angel (between Plaça de Catalunya and the cathedral). It's a bit sterile and scruffy, but well-priced and wonderfully located. Back rooms overlook an old *extra muro* cloister, while front rooms face the busy pedestrian drag (Sb-€70, Db-€100, includes breakfast, air-con, elevator, free Internet access and

Wi-Fi, Carrer de Santa Anna 25, Metro: Catalunya, tel. 933-179-112, www.hotelcortes.com, reservas@hotelcortes.com).

$ Hostal Campi is big, subdued, and ramshackle, but offers simple class. This easygoing old-school spot rents 24 rooms a few doors off the top of the Ramblas (S-€35, D-€60, Ds-€62, Db-€69, T-€78, Tb-€92, no breakfast, lots of stairs with no elevator, pay Internet access, free Wi-Fi in some rooms, Carrer de la Canuda 4, Metro: Catalunya, tel. & fax 933-013-545, www.hostalcampi.com, reservas@hostalcampi.com, Margarita and Nando).

In the Eixample

For an uptown, boulevard-like neighborhood, sleep in the Eixample, a 10-minute walk from the Ramblas action (see map on page 1336). Most of these places use the Passeig de Gràcia or Catalunya Metro stops. Because these stations are so huge—especially Passeig de Gràcia, which sprawls underground for a few blocks—study the maps posted in the station to establish which exit you want before surfacing.

$$ Hotel Granvía, filling a palatial 1870s mansion, offers Botticelli and chandeliers in the public areas; a large, peaceful sun patio; and 54 spacious rooms—along with deliberate and sometimes quirky service. Its salon is plush and royal, making the hotel worth considering for romantics. To reduce street noise, ask for a quiet interior room or a room overlooking the courtyard in the back of the building (Sb-€75-85, Db-€125-150, Tb-€145-155, does not include 8 percent IVA tax, can be cheaper in slow times, mention Rick Steves to get best available rate, breakfast-€11, air-con, elevator, free Internet access and Wi-Fi, Gran Via de les Corts Catalanes 642, Metro: Catalunya, tel. 933-181-900, fax 933-189-997, www.hotelgranvia.com, hgranvia@nnhotels.com).

$$ Hotel Continental Palacete, with 19 small rooms, fills a 100-year-old chandeliered mansion. With flowery wallpaper and ornately gilded stucco, it's gaudy in the city of Gaudí, but it's also friendly, quiet, and well-located. Guests have unlimited access to the outdoor terrace and the "cruise-inspired" fruit, veggie, and drink buffet (Sb-€105, Db-€140, €35-45 more for bigger and brighter view rooms, ask about discount with this book, extra bed-€55, includes breakfast, air-con, free Internet access and Wi-Fi, 2 blocks north of Plaça de Catalunya at corner of Rambla de Catalunya and Carrer de la Diputació, 30 Rambla de Catalunya, Metro: Passeig de Gràcia, tel. 934-457-657, fax 934-450-050, www.hotelcontinental.com, palacete@hotelcontinental.com).

$ Hotel Ginebra, which may close in 2014, has 12 small rooms in a dated apartment building overlooking the main square. It's minimal, clean, and quiet considering its central location, though rooms facing the square get some noise (Db-€80, extra bed-€15,

BARCELONA

Hotels & Restaurants in Barcelona's Eixample

1. Hotel Granvía
2. Hotel Continental Palacete
3. Hotel Ginebra
4. Hostal Oliva
5. BCN Fashion House B&B
6. Centric Point Hostel
7. Somnio Hostel
8. La Rita Restaurant
9. La Bodegueta
10. Restaurante la Palmera
11. La Flauta
12. Cinc Sentits
13. Tapas 24
14. Quasi Queviures ("Qu Qu")
15. Ciutat Comtal Cerveceria
16. La Tramoia

To Joanic

CARRER DE TORRIJOS
TRAVESSERA DE GRACIA
CARRER DE SANT JOAN
PASSEIG DE SANT JOAN
CARRER DE BAILEN
CARRER DE CORSEGA
CARRER DEL ROSSELLÓ

HOTEL CASA FUSTER
Gràcia

CASA DE LES PUNXES

PALAU BARÓ DE QUADRAS

E I X

C. DE MOZART

VIA AUGUSTA

AVINGUDA DIAGONAL

Diagonal

CASA MILÀ

RAMBLA DE CATALUNYA

Diagonal (To Sagrada Família)

PASSEIG DE GRÀCIA

CARRER DE MALLORCA

CARRER DE PARÍS

CARRER DE CORSEGA

Provença

PROVENÇA TRAIN STATION

QUADRAT D'OR

PASSEIG DE GRÀCIA TRAIN STATION

8

CARRER DEL ROSSELLÓ

CASA BATLLÓ

Passeig de Gràcia

CARRER DE PROVENÇA

CARRER DE BALMES

CARRER D'ENRIC GRANADOS

FUNDACIÓ TÀPIES

CASA AMATLLER

CARRER D'ARIBAU

10

BLOCK OF DISCORD

RAMBLA DE CATALUNYA

6

C. DE MUNTANER

CARRER DE CASANOVA

CARRER DE VALÈNCIA

Plaça del Doctor Letamendi

2

7

12

CARRER DEL CONSELL DE CENT

CARRER DE LA DIPUTACIÓ

200 Meters
200 Yards

11

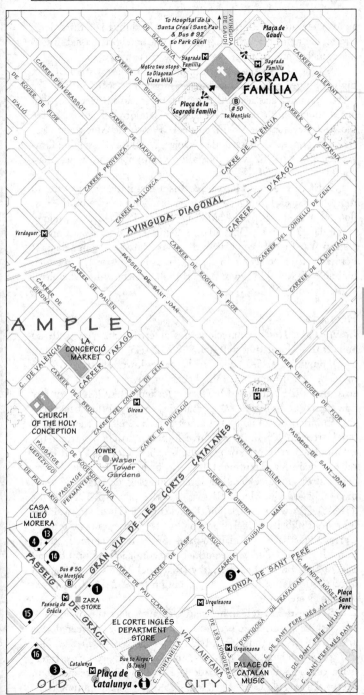

air-con, elevator, free Wi-Fi, Rambla de Catalunya 1/3, third floor, Metro: Catalunya, tel. 933-171-063, www.hotelginebra.net, info@hotelginebra.net, Juan speaks English).

$ Hostal Oliva is a spartan, old-school place with 15 basic, high-ceilinged rooms and no breakfast or public spaces. It's on the fourth floor of a classic old Eixample building in a perfect location, just a couple of blocks above Plaça de Catalunya (S-€40, D-€69, Db-€89, elevator, free Wi-Fi, corner of Passeig de Gràcia and Carrer de la Diputació, Passeig de Gràcia 32, Metro: Passeig de Gràcia, tel. 934-880-162, www.hostaloliva.com, hostaloliva@lasguias.com).

$ BCN Fashion House B&B is a meditative place with 10 rooms, a peaceful lounge, and a leafy backyard terrace on the first floor of a nondescript old building (S-€35-55, D-€55-80, bigger "veranda" D-€70-90, Db-€90-125, 2-night minimum stay, breakfast-€6, Wi-Fi, between Carrer d'Ausiàs Marc and Ronda de Sant Pere at Carrer del Bruc 13, just steps from Metro: Urquinaona, mobile 637-904-044, www.bcnfashionhouse.com, info@bcnfashionhouse.com).

Hostels

Equity Point Hostels: Barcelona has a terrific chain of well-run and centrally located hostels (tel. 932-312-045, www.equity-point.com), providing €25-32 dorm beds (prices lower off-season) in 4- to 14-bed coed rooms with €2 sheets and towels, pay Internet access, free Wi-Fi, included breakfast, lockers (B.Y.O. lock, or buy one there), and plenty of opportunities to meet other backpackers. They're open 24 hours but aren't party hostels, so they enforce quiet after 23:00. There are three locations to choose from: the Eixample, Barri Gòtic, or near the beach. **$ Centric Point Hostel** is a huge place renting 400 cheap beds at what must be the best address in Barcelona (bar, kitchen, Passeig de Gràcia 33—see map on page 1336, Metro: Passeig de Gràcia, tel. 932-151-796, fax 932-461-552, www.centricpointhostel.com). **$ Gothic Point Hostel** rents 130 beds a block from the Picasso Museum (roof terrace, Carrer Vigatans 5—see map on page 1330, Metro: Jaume I, reception tel. 932-687-808, www.gothicpoint.com). **$ Sea Point Hostel** has 70 beds on the beach nearby (Plaça del Mar 4—see map on page 1260, Metro: Barceloneta, reception tel. 932-247-075, www.seapointhostel.com).

$ Somnio Hostel, an innovative smaller place run by a pair of American expats, has 26 beds in 10 rooms. Choose between dorms and private rooms (bunk in 6-bed dorm-€26, S-€44, D-€78, Db-€87; prices include sheets, towels, and lockers; air-con, free Internet access and Wi-Fi, Carrer de la Diputació 251, second floor, Metro: Passeig de Gràcia, tel. 932-725-308, www.somniohostels.

com, info@somniohostels.com). They have a second location that's five blocks farther out.

Apartments

$$ Cross-Pollinate is a reputable online booking agency representing B&Bs and apartments in a handful of European cities, including Barcelona. Choose a place online and submit a reservation; if the place is available, you'll be charged a small deposit and emailed the location and check-in details. Policies vary from owner to owner, but in most cases you'll pay the balance on arrival in cash. Barcelona listings range from a B&B double room near Sagrada Família for €75 per night to a three-bedroom Eixample apartment sleeping eight for €288 per night. Minimum stays vary from one to three nights (US tel. 800-270-1190, www.cross-pollinate.com, info@cross-pollinate.com).

$$ Tournights Barcelona, run by American Frederick and his Spanish wife, rents 55 renovated apartments with kitchens. Most are near the beach in the lively Barceloneta neighborhood; others are in the Barri Gòtic or Eixample (2 people–€105 April-Oct, €85 Nov-March; prices vary with size—see photos and videos on website, €40 cleaning fee, 3-night minimum stay, discount for 7-night stay, 20 percent deposit required to reserve online, pay balance in cash when you arrive, no breakfast, arrange meeting to check in when you reserve, Frederick's mobile 620-585-594, www.tournights.com, info@tournights.com).

Eating in Barcelona

Barcelona, the capital of Catalan cuisine—starring seafood—offers a tremendous variety of colorful eateries, ranging from basic and filling to chic and trendy. Most of my listings are lively spots with a busy tapas scene at the bar, along with restaurant tables for *raciones*. A regional specialty is *pa amb tomàquet* (pah ahm too-MAH-kaht), toasted bread rubbed with a mix of crushed tomato and olive oil.

I've listed mostly practical, characteristic, colorful, and affordable restaurants. My recommendations are grouped by neighborhood—along the Ramblas, in the Barri Gòtic, in El Born (best for foodies), in the Eixample, and in Barceloneta. I also include some budget options scattered throughout the city and a suggested route for finding Catalan sweets. Note that many restaurants close in August (or July), when the owners take a vacation.

Restaurants generally serve lunch from 13:00 to 16:00 and dinner from 20:00 or even later (Spaniards don't start dinner until about 22:00). It's deadly to your Barcelona experience to eat too early—if a place feels touristy, come back later and it may be a thriving local favorite.

Because of their common struggles, Catalans seem to have an affinity for Basque culture, so you'll find a lot of **Basque-style tapas places** here (look for *basca* or *euskal taberna*; *euskal* means "Basque"). Enticing buffets of bite-size tapas invite you to simply take what you want. These places are particularly user-friendly, since you don't have to look at a menu or wait to be served—just grab what looks good, order a drink, and save your toothpicks (they'll count them up at the end to tally your bill). I've listed several such places (including Taverna Basca Irati, Xaloc, and Sagardi Euskal Taberna), though Barcelona has many other similar options. Throughout the city, you'll see signs both for Spanish *tapas* and Catalan *tapes* (same pronunciation and meaning).

Note: Unlike in many Spanish cities, most Barcelona tapas bars do *not* provide a free, small tapa with the purchase of a drink; if you want food, order it separately.

Along the Ramblas

Within a few steps of the Ramblas, you'll find handy lunch places, an inviting market hall, and some good vegetarian options. For locations, see the map on page 1342.

Lunching Simply yet Memorably near the Ramblas

Although these places are enjoyable for a lunch break during your Ramblas sightseeing, many are also open for dinner.

Taverna Basca Irati serves 40 kinds of hot and cold Basque *pintxos* for €1.80 each. These are small open-faced sandwiches—like sushi on bread. Muscle in through the hungry local crowd, get an empty plate from the waiter, and then help yourself. Every few minutes, waiters prance proudly by with a platter of new, still-warm munchies. Grab one as they pass by...it's addictive (you'll be charged by the number of toothpicks left on your plate when you're done). Wash it down with €2-3 glasses of Rioja (full-bodied red wine), Txakolí (sprightly Basque white wine) or *sidra* (apple wine) poured from on high to add oxygen and bring out the flavor (daily 11:00-24:00, a block off the Ramblas, behind arcade at Carrer del Cardenal Casanyes 17, Metro: Liceu, tel. 933-023-084).

Restaurant Elisabets is a rough little neighborhood eatery packed with antique radios; it's popular with locals for its €12 "home-cooked" three-course lunch special. Stop by for lunch, survey what those around you are enjoying, and order what looks best. Apparently, locals put up with the service for the tasty food (Mon-Sat 7:30-23:00, closed Sun and Aug, lunch special served 13:00-16:00, otherwise only €3 tapas, 2 blocks west of Ramblas on far corner of Plaça del Bonsuccés at Carrer d'Elisabets 2, Metro: Catalunya, tel. 933-175-826, run by Pilar).

Café Granja Viader is a quaint time capsule, family-run since 1870. They boast about being the first dairy business to bottle and distribute milk in Spain. This feminine-feeling place—specializing in baked and dairy treats, toasted sandwiches, and light meals—is ideal for a traditional breakfast. Or indulge your sweet tooth: Try a glass of *orxata* (or *horchata*—*chufa*-nut milk, summer only), *llet mallorquina* (Majorca-style milk with cinnamon, lemon, and sugar), *crema catalana* (crème brûlée, their specialty), or *suis* ("Swiss"—hot chocolate with a snowcap of whipped cream). *Mel y mató* is fresh cheese with honey...very Catalan (Tue-Sat 9:00-13:30 & 17:00-20:30, Mon 17:00-20:30 only, closed Sun, a block off the Ramblas behind Betlem Church at Xuclà 4, Metro: Liceu, tel. 933-183-486).

Cafeteria: For a quick, affordable lunch with a view, the ninth-floor cafeteria at **El Corte Inglés** can't be beat (€10 salads and sandwiches, also café with €1.50 coffee and sit-down restaurant with €20 fixed-price meals, Mon-Sat 10:00-22:00, closed Sun, Plaça de Catalunya, Metro: Catalunya, tel. 933-063-800).

Picnics: Shoestring tourists buy groceries at **El Corte Inglés** (described above, supermarket in basement), **Carrefour Market** (Mon-Sat 10:00-22:00, closed Sun, Ramblas 113, Metro: Liceu), and La Boqueria market (closed Sun, described next).

In and near La Boqueria Market

Try eating at La Boqueria market at least once (#91 on the Ramblas). Like all farmers markets in Europe, this place is ringed by colorful, good-value eateries. Lots of stalls sell fun take-away food—especially fruit salads and fresh-squeezed juices—ideal for picnickers. There are several good bars around the market busy with shoppers munching at the counter (breakfast, tapas all day, coffee). The market, and most of the eateries listed here (unless noted), are open Monday through Saturday from 8:00 until 20:00 (though things get very quiet after about 16:00) and are closed on Sunday (nearest Metro: Liceu). For a more complete description of the market itself, see page 1275 of the Ramblas Ramble.

Pinotxo Bar is just to the right as you enter the market. It's a great spot for coffee, breakfast (spinach *tortillas,* or whatever's cooking with toast), or tapas. Fun-loving Juan and his family are La Boqueria fixtures. Grab a stool across the way to sip your drink with people-watching views. Be careful—this place can get expensive.

Kiosko Universal is popular for its great prices on wonderful fish dishes. As you enter the market from the Ramblas, it's all the way to the left in the first alley. If you see people waiting, ask who's last in line *("¿El último?")*. You'll eat immersed in the spirit of the market (€14 fixed-price lunches with different fresh-fish options

BARCELONA

Barcelona's Old City Restaurants

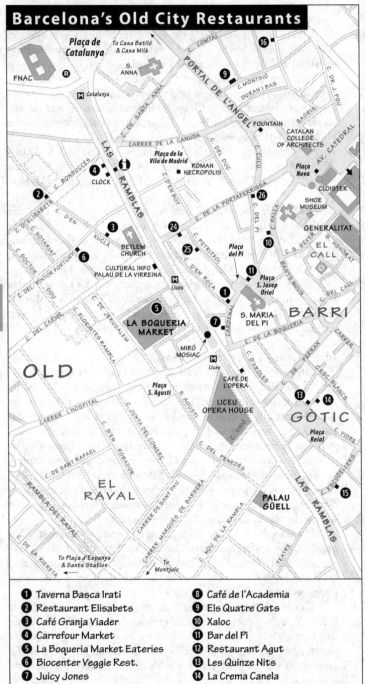

1. Taverna Basca Irati
2. Restaurant Elisabets
3. Café Granja Viader
4. Carrefour Market
5. La Boqueria Market Eateries
6. Biocenter Veggie Rest.
7. Juicy Jones
8. Café de l'Academia
9. Els Quatre Gats
10. Xaloc
11. Bar del Pi
12. Restaurant Agut
13. Les Quinze Nits
14. La Crema Canela

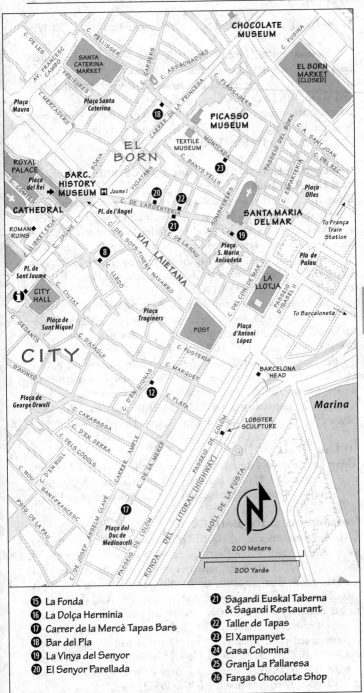

15 La Fonda

16 La Dolça Herminia

17 Carrer de la Mercè Tapas Bars

18 Bar del Pla

19 La Vinya del Senyor

20 El Senyor Parellada

21 Sagardi Euskal Taberna & Sagardi Restaurant

22 Taller de Tapas

23 El Xampanyet

24 Casa Colomina

25 Granja La Pallaresa

26 Fargas Chocolate Shop

12:00-16:00, always packed but better before 12:30, tel. 933-178-286).

Restaurant la Gardunya, at the back of the market, offers tasty meat and seafood meals made with fresh ingredients bought directly from the market (€13.50 fixed-price lunch includes wine and bread, €16.50 three-course dinner specials include wine, €10-20 à la carte dishes, Mon-Sat 13:00-16:00 & 20:00-24:00, closed Sun, mod seating indoors or outside watching the market action, Carrer Jerusalem 18, tel. 933-024-323).

Vegetarian Eateries near Plaça de Catalunya and the Ramblas

Biocenter, a Catalan soup-and-salad restaurant popular with local vegetarians, takes its cooking very seriously and feels a bit more like a real restaurant than most (€8-10 weekday lunch specials include soup or salad and plate of the day, €15 dinner specials, otherwise €7-9 salads and €11-13 main dishes, Mon-Sat 13:00-23:00, Sun 13:00-16:00, 2 blocks off the Ramblas at Carrer del Pintor Fortuny 25, Metro: Liceu, tel. 933-014-583).

Juicy Jones is a tutti-frutti vegan/vegetarian eatery with colorful graffiti decor, a hip veggie menu (served downstairs), groovy laid-back staff, and a stunning array of fresh-squeezed juices served at the bar. Pop in for a quick €2.50 "juice of the day." For lunch you can get the Indian-inspired €6 *thali* plate, the €6.25 plate of the day, or an €8.50 meal including one of the two plates plus soup or salad and dessert (daily 9:00-23:30, also tapas and salads, Carrer del Cardenal Casanyes 7, Metro: Liceu, tel. 933-024-330). There's another location on the other side of the Ramblas (Carrer Hospital 74).

In the Barri Gòtic

These eateries populate Barcelona's atmospheric Gothic Quarter, near the cathedral. Choose between a sit-down meal at a restaurant or a string of tapas bars. For locations, see the map on page 1342.

Restaurants in the Barri Gòtic

Café de l'Academia is a delightful place on a pretty square tucked away in the heart of the Barri Gòtic—but patronized mainly by the neighbors. They serve "honest cuisine" from the market with Catalan roots. The candlelit, air-conditioned interior is rustic yet elegant, with soft jazz, flowers, and modern art. And if you want to eat outdoors on a convivial, mellow square...this is the place. Reservations can be smart (€10-13 first courses, €12-16 second courses, fixed-price lunch for €10 at the bar or €14 at a table, Mon-Fri 13:30-16:00 & 20:30-23:30, closed Sat-Sun, near the City Hall square, off Carrer de Jaume I up Carrer de la Dagueria at Carrer dels Lledó 1, Metro: Jaume I, tel. 933-198-253).

Els Quatre Gats ("The Four Cats") was once the haunt of the Modernista greats—including a teenaged Picasso, who first publicly displayed his art here, and architect Josep Puig i Cadafalch, who designed the building. Inspired by Paris' famous Le Chat Noir café/cabaret, Els Quatre Gats celebrated all that was modern at the turn of the 20th century (for more on the illustrious history of the place, see page 1280 in the "Barri Gòtic Walk"). You can snack or drink at the bar, or go into the back for a sit-down meal. While touristy (less so later), the food and service are good, and the prices aren't as high as you might guess (€17 three-course lunch special Mon-Fri 13:00-16:00, €12-20 plates, daily 10:00-24:00, just steps off Avinguda Portal de l'Angel at Carrer de Montsió 3, Metro: Catalunya, tel. 933-024-140).

Xaloc is *the* place in the old center for nicely presented gourmet tapas. It's a classy, woody, modern dining room with a fun energy, good service, and reasonable prices. The walls are covered with *Ibérica* hamhocks and wine bottles. They focus on homestyle Catalan classics and serve only one quality of ham—and it's tops. A gazpacho, plank of ham, *pa amb tomàquet* (toast with tomato), and nice glass of wine make a terrific light meal (€2-6 tapas, €5-12 main dishes, open daily, a block toward the cathedral from Plaça de Sant Josep Oriol at Carrer de la Palla 13, Metro: Catalunya, tel. 933-011-990).

Bar del Pi is a simple, hardworking bar serving good salads, sandwiches, and tapas. It has just a handful of tables on the most inviting little square in the Barri Gòtic (Tue-Sun 9:00-23:00, closed Mon, on Plaça de Sant Josep Oriol 1, Metro: Liceu, tel. 933-022-123).

Restaurant Agut, around since 1924, features a comfortable, wood-paneled dining room that's modern and sophisticated, but still retains a slight bohemian air. The pictures lining the walls are by Catalan artists who are said to have exchanged their canvases for a meal. The menu includes very tasty traditional Catalan food, with some seasonal specialties (€13 three-course weekday lunch special, €10-14 starters, €13-18 main dishes, Tue-Sat 13:30-16:00 & 21:00-24:00, Sun 13:30-16:00 only, closed Mon, just up from Carrer de la Mercè and the harbor at Carrer d'En Gignàs 16, Metro: Jaume I, tel. 933-151-709).

Andelana Restaurants: A local chain called Andelana has several bright, modern eateries that are wildly popular for their artfully presented Spanish and Mediterranean cuisine, crisp ambience, and unbeatable prices. Because of their three-course €10 lunches and €16-21 dinners (both with wine), all are crowded with locals and in-the-know tourists (à la carte: €7-9 starters, €8-11 main dishes, all open daily 13:00-15:45 & 20:30-23:30, unless otherwise noted; the first three are near Metro: Liceu). Warning: These places are notorious for long lines at the door—arrive 30 minutes before opening, or be prepared to wait. **Les Quinze Nits** has great seating right on atmospheric Plaça Reial (daily 11:00-16:30 & 19:00-23:00, at #6—you'll see the line, tel. 933-173-075). Two others are within a block: **La Crema Canela,** a few steps north of Plaça Reial, feels cozier than the others and is the only one that takes reservations (opens at 20:00 for dinner, Passatge de Madoz 6, tel. 933-182-744). **La Fonda** is a block south of Plaça Reial (opens at 19:30 for dinner, Carrer dels Escudellers 10, tel. 933-017-515). Another location, **La Dolça Herminia,** is near the Palace of Catalan Music in El Born (2 blocks toward Ramblas from Palace of Catalan Music at Carrer de les Magdalenes 27, Metro: Jaume I, tel. 933-170-676); the fifth restaurant in the chain, **La Rita,** is described later, under "Restaurants in the Eixample."

Tapas on Carrer de la Mercè in the Barri Gòtic

This area lets you experience a rare, unvarnished bit of old Barcelona with great *tascas*—colorful local tapas bars. Get small plates (for maximum sampling) by asking for "tapas," not the bigger "*raciones.*" Glasses of *vino tinto* go for about €1. And though trendy uptown restaurants are safer, better-lit, and come with English menus and less grease, these places will stain your journal. The neighborhood's dark, the regulars are rough-edged, and you'll get a glimpse of a crusty Barcelona from before the affluence hit. Nowadays many new, mod restaurants are popping up in this area, but don't be seduced—you came here for something different. Try *pimientos de padrón*—Russian roulette with little green peppers that are lightly fried in oil and salted...only a few are jalapeño-spicy. At the cider bars, it's traditional to order *queso de cabrales* (a very moldy blue cheese) and spicy chorizo (sausage), ideally prepared *al diablo* ("devil-style")—soaked in wine, then flambéed at your table. Several places serve *leche de pantera* (panther milk)—liquor mixed with milk.

From the bottom of the Ramblas (near the Columbus Monument, Metro: Drassanes), hike east along Carrer de Josep Anselm Clavé. Then follow Carrer de la Mercè, the small street that runs along the right side of the church. For a montage of edible memories, wander west to east and consider these spots, stopping wherever looks most inviting. Most of these places close down around 23:00.

Bar Celta (marked *la pulpería,* at #16) has a bit less character than the others, but eases you into the scene with fried fish, octopus, and *patatas bravas,* all with Galician Ribeiro wine. Farther down at the corner (#28), **La Plata** keeps things wonderfully simple, serving extremely cheap plates of sardines (€2.50), little salads, and small glasses of keg wine (less than €1). **Tasca el Corral** (#17) serves mountain favorites from northern Spain by the half-*ración* (see their list), such as *queso de cabrales* and chorizo *al diablo* with *sidra* (hard cider sold by the bottle–€6). **Sidrería Tasca La Socarrena** (#21) offers hard cider from Asturias in €6.50 bottles with *queso de cabrales* and chorizo. At the end of Carrer de la Mercè, **Cervecería Vendimia** slings tasty clams and mussels (hearty *raciones* for €4-6 a plate—they don't do smaller portions, so order sparingly). Sit at the bar and point to what looks good. Their *pulpo* (octopus) is more expensive and is the house specialty. Carrer Ample and Carrer d'En Gignàs, the streets parallel to Carrer de la Mercè inland, have more refined bar-hopping possibilities.

In El Born, near the Picasso Museum

El Born (a.k.a. La Ribera), the hottest neighborhood in town, sparkles with eclectic and trendy as well as subdued and classy little restaurants hidden in the small lanes surrounding the Church of Santa Maria del Mar. While I've listed a few well-established tapas bars that are great for light meals, to really dine, simply wander around for 15 minutes and pick the place that tickles your gastronomic fancy. I think those who say they know what's best in this area are kidding themselves—it's changing too fast, and the choices are too personal. One thing's for sure: There are a lot of talented and hardworking restaurateurs with plenty to offer. Consider starting off your evening with a glass of fine wine at one of the *enotecas* on the square facing the Church of Santa Maria del Mar (such as La Vinya del Senyor). Sit back and admire the pure Catalan Gothic architecture. Most of my listings are either on Carrer de l'Argenteria (stretching from the church to the cathedral area) or on or near Carrer de Montcada (near the Picasso Museum). Many restaurants and shops in this area are, like the Picasso Museum, closed on Mondays. For locations, see the map on page 1342.

Bar del Pla is a local favorite—near the Picasso Museum but far enough away from the tourist crowds. This classic diner/bar, overlooking a tiny crossroads next to Barcelona's oldest church, serves traditional Catalan dishes, *raciones,* and tapas. Prices are the same at the bar or at a table, but eating at the bar puts you in the middle of a great scene (€4-8 tapas, Tue-Sun 12:00-24:00, closed Mon; with your back to the Picasso Museum, head right 2 blocks, past Carrer de la Princesa, to Carrer de Montcada 2; Metro: Jaume I, tel. 932-683-003).

La Vinya del Senyor is recommendable only for its location—with wonderful tables on the square facing the Church of Santa Maria del Mar in the middle of a charming and lively pedestrian zone. Their wine list is extensive—7 cl gives you a few sips, while

14 cl is a standard serving. They also have good cheeses, hams, and tapas (Tue-Sun 12:00-24:00, closed Mon, Plaça de Santa Maria 5, Metro: Jaume I or Barceloneta, tel. 933-103-379).

El Senyor Parellada, filling a former cloister, is an elegant restaurant with a smart, tourist-friendly waitstaff. It serves a fun menu of Mediterranean and Catalan cuisine with a modern twist, all in a classy chandeliers-and-white-tablecloths setting (€10-15 plates, open daily, Carrer de l'Argenteria 37, 100 yards from Metro: Jaume I, tel. 933-105-094).

Sagardi Euskal Taberna offers a wonderful array of Basque goodies—tempting *pintxos* and *montaditos* at €1.80 each—along its huge bar. Ask for a plate and graze (just take whatever looks good). You can sit on the square with your plunder for 20 percent extra. Wash it down with Txakolí, a Basque white wine poured from the spout of a huge wooden barrel into a glass as you watch. When you're done, they'll count your toothpicks to tally your bill (daily 12:00-24:00, Carrer de l'Argenteria 62-64, Metro: Jaume I, tel. 933-199-993).

Sagardi, hiding behind its thriving tapas bar (described above), is a mod, rustic, and minimalist woody restaurant committed to serving Basque T-bone steaks and grilled specialties with only the best ingredients. A big open kitchen with sizzling grills contributes to the ambience. Reservations are smart (€10-20 first courses, €20-25 second courses, plan on €45 for dinner, daily 13:00-16:00 & 20:00-24:00, Carrer de l'Argenteria 62, Metro: Jaume I, tel. 933-199-993).

Taller de Tapas ("Tapas Workshop") is an upscale, trendier tapas bar and restaurant that dishes up well-presented, sophisticated morsels and light meals in a medieval-stone-yet-mod setting. Pay 15 percent more to sit on the square. Elegant, but a bit stuffy, it's favored by local office workers who aren't into the Old World Gothic stuff. Four plates will fill a hungry diner for about €20 (daily 8:30-24:00, Carrer de l'Argenteria 51, Metro: Jaume I, tel. 932-688-559).

El Xampanyet ("The Little Champagne Bar"), a colorful family-run bar with a fun-loving staff (Juan Carlos, his mom, and the man who may be his father), specializes in tapas and anchovies. Don't be put off by the seafood from a tin: Catalans like it this way. A *sortido* (assorted plate) of *carne* (meat) or *pescado* (fish) with *pa amb tomàquet* (bread with crushed-tomato spread) makes for a fun meal. It's filled with tourists during the sightseeing day, but this is a local favorite after dark. The scene is great but—especially during busy times—it's tough without Spanish skills. When I asked about the price, Juan Carlos said, "Who cares? The ATM is just across the street." Plan on spending €20 for a meal with wine (same price at bar or table, Tue-Sat 12:00-15:30 & 19:00-23:00, Sun 12:00-

16:00 only, closed Mon, a half-block beyond the Picasso Museum at Carrer de Montcada 22, Metro: Jaume I, tel. 933-197-003).

In the Eixample

The people-packed boulevards of the Eixample (Passeig de Gràcia and Rambla de Catalunya) are lined with appetizing eateries featuring breezy outdoor seating. Choose between a real restaurant or an upscale tapas bar. For locations, see the map on page 1336.

Restaurants in the Eixample

La Rita is a fresh and dressy little restaurant serving Catalan cuisine near the Block of Discord. Their lunches (three courses with wine for €10, Mon-Fri 13:00-15:45) and dinners (€10 plates, €21 fixed-price dinners, Sun-Thu 20:00-23:00, Fri-Sat from 20:30) are a great value. Like most of its sister Andelana restaurants—described on page 1345—it takes no reservations and its prices attract long lines, so arrive just before the doors open...or wait (near corner of Carrer de Pau Claris and Carrer d'Aragó at d'Aragó 279, a block from Metro: Passeig de Gràcia, tel. 934-872-376).

La Bodegueta is an atmospheric below-street-level bodega serving hearty wines, homemade vermouth, *anchoas* (anchovies), tapas, and *flautas*—sandwiches made with flute-thin baguettes. On a nice day, it's great to eat outside, sitting in the median of the boulevard under shady trees. Its daily €12 lunch special of three courses with wine is served 13:00-16:00. A long block from Gaudí's Casa Milà, this makes a fine sightseeing break (Mon-Sat 8:00-24:00, Sun 19:00-24:00, at intersection with Carrer de Provença, Rambla de Catalunya 100, Metro: Provença, tel. 932-154-894).

Restaurante la Palmera serves a mix of Catalan, Mediterranean, and French cuisine in an elegant room with bottle-lined walls. This untouristy place offers great food, service, and value—for me, a very special meal in Barcelona. They have three zones: the classic main room, a more forgettable adjacent room, and a few outdoor tables. I like the classic room. Reservations are smart (€12-16 plates, creative €20 six-plate *degustation* lunch—also available during dinner Mon-Thu, open Mon-Sat 13:00-15:45 & 20:30-23:15, closed Sun, Carrer d'Enric Granados 57, at the corner with Carrer Mallorca, Metro: Provença, tel. 934-532-338).

La Flauta fills two floors with enthusiastic eaters (I prefer the ground floor). It's fresh and modern, with a fun, no-stress menu featuring €5 small plates, creative €4 *flauta* sandwiches, and a €12.50 three-course lunch deal including a drink. Consider the list of *tapas del día*. Good €2.30 wines by the glass are listed on the blackboard. This is a place to order high on the menu for a satisfying, moderately priced meal (Mon-Sat 13:00-24:00, closed Sun, upbeat and helpful staff recommends the fried vegetables, no

BARCELONA

reservations, just off Carrer de la Diputació at Carrer d'Aribau 23, Metro: Universitat, tel. 933-237-038).

Cinc Sentits ("Five Senses"), with only about 30 seats, is my gourmet recommendation. At this chic, minimalist, but slightly snooty place, all the attention goes to the fine service and beautifully presented dishes. The €59 *essència menu* and the €79 *sensacions menu* are unforgettable extravaganzas. Expect *menus* only—no à la carte. It's run by Catalans who lived in Canada (so there's absolutely no language barrier) and serve avant-garde cuisine inspired by Catalan traditions and ingredients. Reservations are required (Tue-Sat 13:30-15:00 & 20:30-22:30, closed Sun-Mon, near Carrer d'Aragó at Carrer d'Aribau 58, between Metros: Universitat and Provença, tel. 933-239-490, maître d' Amelia).

Tapas Bars in the Eixample

Many trendy and touristic tapas bars in the Eixample offer a cheery welcome and slam out the appetizers. These four are particularly handy to Plaça de Catalunya and the Passeig de Gràcia artery (for all of them, the closest Metro stops are Catalunya and Passeig de Gràcia).

Tapas 24 makes eating fun. This local favorite, with a few street tables, fills a spot a few steps below street level with happy energy, funky decor (white counters and mirrors), and absolutely excellent tapas. The menu has all the typical standbys and quirky inventions (such as the McFoie burger), plus daily specials. Service is friendly, and the owner, Carles Abellan, is one of Barcelona's hot chefs. This is a chance to eat his food at reasonable prices, which are the same whether you dine at the bar, a table, or outside. Figure about €40 for lunch for two with wine (€4-10 tapas, €12-14 plates, Mon-Sat 9:00-24:00, closed Sun, just off Passeig de Gràcia at Carrer de la Diputació 269, tel. 934-880-977).

Quasi Queviures ("**Qu Qu**" for short) offers upscale tapas, sandwiches, or the whole nine yards—classic food served fast from a fun menu with modern decor and a high-energy ambience. It's bright, clean, and not too crowded. Walk through their enticing kitchen to get to the tables in back. Committed to developing a loyal following, they claim, "We fertilize our local customers with daily specialties" (€3-5 tapas, €5 dinner salads, €9-14 plates, prices 17 percent higher on the terrace, daily 8:00-24:00, Sun from 10:30, between Gran Via de les Corts Catalanes and Carrer de la Diputació at Passeig de Gràcia 24, tel. 933-174-512).

Ciutat Comtal Cerveceria brags that it serves the best *montaditos* (€2-4 little open-faced sandwiches) and beers in Barcelona. It's an Eixample favorite, with an elegant bar and tables plus good seating out on the Rambla de Catalunya for all that people-watching action. It's classier than Qu Qu and packed 21:00-23:00, when you'll likely need to put your name on a list and wait. While it has no restaurant-type menu, the list of tapas and *montaditos* is easy, fun, and comes with a great variety (including daily specials). This place is a cut above your normal tapas bar, but with reasonable prices (most tapas around €4-10, daily 8:00-24:00, facing the intersection of Gran Via de les Corts Catalanes and Rambla de Catalunya at Rambla de Catalunya 18, tel. 933-181-997).

La Tramoia, at the opposite corner from Ciutat Comtal Cerveceria, serves piles of €1.70 *montaditos* and tapas at its ground-floor bar and at nice tables inside and out. If Ciutat Comtal Cerveceria is jammed, you're more likely to find a seat here. The brasserie-style restaurant upstairs bustles with happy local eaters enjoying grilled meats (€9-20 plates), but I'd stay downstairs for the €4-9 tapas (daily 12:00-24:00 for tapas, 13:00-16:00 & 17:30-24:00 for meals, also facing the intersection of Gran Via de les Corts Catalanes and Rambla de Catalunya at Rambla de Catalunya 15, tel. 934-123-634).

In Barceloneta

The nearest Metro stop to this former sailors' quarter is Barceloneta. For locations, see the map on page 1260.

Along the Waterfront: Barceloneta's harborfront (Passeig de Joan de Borbó), facing the city, is lined with multiple, interchangeable seafood restaurants and cafés. Locals love to come here for celebrity-spotting. One of many eateries along here is **La Mar Salada,** a traditional seafood restaurant with a slight modern twist. Their à la carte menu includes seafood-and-rice dishes, fresh fish, and homemade desserts. A nice meal will run you about €30-35 per person (€15 fixed-price weekday meal, Wed-Fri and Mon 13:00-16:00 & 20:00-23:00, Sat-Sun 13:00-23:00, closed Tue, indoor and outdoor seating, Passeig de Joan de Borbó 59, tel. 932-212-127).

In the Heart of Barceloneta: **Can Solé,** serving seafood since 1903, is a splurge. Hiding on a nondescript urban lane, this venerable restaurant draws a celebrity crowd, judging by the autographed pictures of the famous and not-so-famous that line the walls. But the place is homey, with sky-blue walls and café curtains, and the charming owner couldn't be more gracious (Tue-Sat 13:30-16:00 & 20:30-23:00, Sun 13:30-16:00 only, closed Mon, Carrer de Sant Carles 4, one block off the harborfront promenade, tel. 932-215-012).

Bakery: **Baluard,** one of Barcelona's most highly regarded artisan bakeries, faces one side of the big market hall in the center of Barceloneta. Line up with the locals to get a loaf of heavenly bread, a pastry, or a slice of pizza (Mon-Sat 8:00-21:00, closed Sun, Carrer del Baluard 38, tel. 932-211-208).

BARCELONA

Budget Meals Around Town

Bright, clean, and inexpensive sandwich shops proudly hold the cultural line against the fast-food invasion that has hamburger-ized the rest of Europe. Catalan sandwiches are made to order with crunchy French bread. Rather than butter, locals prefer *tomàquet* (a spread of crushed tomatoes). You'll see two big local chains (Bocatta and Pans & Company) everywhere, but these serve mass-produced McBaguettes ordered from a multilingual menu. I've had better luck with hole-in-the-wall sandwich shops—virtually as numerous as the chains—where you can see exactly what you're getting. Kebab places are another good, super-cheap standby; you'll see them all over town, offering a quick and tasty meal for about €3-4.

A Short, Sweet Walk

Let me propose this three-stop dessert (or, since these places close well before the traditional Barcelona dinnertime, a late-afternoon snack). Start with a chunk of *torró* or a glass of *orxata*, then munch some *churros con chocolate,* and end with a visit to a fine *xocolateria*—all within a three-minute walk of one another in the Barri Gòtic just off the Ramblas (Metro: Liceu). Start at the corner of Carrer de la Portaferrissa midway down the Ramblas. For the best atmosphere, begin your walk at about 18:00 (note that the last place is closed on Sun). For locations, see the map on page 1342.

Torr at Casa Colomina: Walk down Carrer de la Portaferrissa to #8 (on the right). Casa Colomina, founded in 1908, specializes in homemade *torró* (or *turrón* in Spanish)—a variation of nougat made with almond, honey, and sugar, brought to Spain by the Moors 1,200 years ago. Three different kinds are sold in €8-12 slabs: *blando, duro,* and *yema*—soft, hard, and yolk (€2 prewrapped chunks on the counter). In the summer, the shop also sells ice cream and the refreshing *orxata* (or *horchata,* a drink made from *chufa* nuts—a.k.a. earth almonds or tiger nuts). Order a glass and ask to see and eat a *chufa* nut (Mon-Sat 10:00-20:30, Sun 12:30-20:30, tel. 933-122-511).

Churros con Chocolate at Granja La Pallaresa: Continue down Carrer de la Portaferrissa, taking a right at Carrer Petritxol to this fun-loving *xocolateria*. Elegant, older ladies gather here for the Spanish equivalent of tea time—dipping their greasy *churros* into pudding-thick cups of hot chocolate (€4.50 for five *churros con chocolate*). Or, for a more local treat, try an *ensaimada* (a Mallorca-style croissant with powdered sugar) or the *crema catalana,* like a crème brûlée (Mon-Fri 9:00-13:00 & 16:00-21:00, Sat-Sun 9:00-13:00 & 17:00-21:00, Carrer Petritxol 11, tel. 933-022-036).

Homemade Chocolate at Fargas: For your last stop, head for the ornate Fargas chocolate shop. Continue down Carrer Petritxol to the square, hook left through the two-part square, and then left up Carrer del Pi to the corner of Carrer de la Portaferrissa. Since the 19th century, gentlemen with walking canes have dropped by here for their chocolate fix. Founded in 1827, this is one of the oldest and most traditional chocolate shops in Barcelona. If they're not too busy, ask to see the old chocolate mill *("¿Puedo ver el molino?")* to the right of the counter. (It's still used, but nowadays it's powered by a machine rather than a donkey in the basement.) They sell even tiny quantities (one little morsel) by the weight, so don't be shy. A delicious chunk of the crumbly semi-sweet house specialty costs €0.40 (glass bowl on the counter). The tempting bonbons in the window cost about €1 each (Mon-Sat 9:30-13:30 & 16:00-20:00, closed Sun).

Barcelona Connections

By Train
Sants Station

Barcelona's main station is vast and sprawling, but manageable. In the large lobby area under the upper tracks, you'll find a TI; ATMs; a world of handy shops and eateries; and, in the side concourse, a classy, quiet Sala Club lounge for travelers with first-class reservations (TV, free drinks, study tables, and coffee bar). Sants is the only Barcelona station with luggage storage (small bag-€3.50/day, big bag-€5/day, requires security check, daily 5:30-23:00, follow signs to *consigna*, at far end of hallway from tracks 13-14).

In the vast main hall is a very long wall of ticket windows. Figure out which one you need before you wait in line (all are labeled in English). Generally, windows 1-7 (on the left) are for regional and *media distancia* trains, such as to Sitges; windows 8-21 handle advance tickets for long-distance *(larga distancia)* trains beyond Catalunya; the information windows are 23-26—go here first if you're not sure which window you want; and windows 27-31 sell tickets for long-distance trains leaving today. The information booths by windows 1 and 21 can help you find the right line and can provide some train schedules. Scattered nearby are two types of automated train-ticket vending machines: The red-and-gray machines sell tickets for regional and *media distancia* trains within Catalunya; the purple machines are for national RENFE trains, but these don't sell tickets—you can only use them to print out prereserved tickets (if you have a confirmation code).

Getting Downtown: To reach the center of Barcelona, take a train or the Metro. To ride the subway, follow signs for the Metro (red *M*), and hop on the L3 (green) line, which links to a number of useful points in town, near all of my recommended hotels. To zip downtown even faster (just five minutes), you can take any Rodalies de Catalunya suburban train from track 8 (R1, R3, or R4) to Plaça de Catalunya (departs at least every 10 minutes). Purchase tickets for the trains or Metro at touch-screen machines near the tracks (where you can also buy the cost-saving T10 Card, explained on page 1263).

Train Connections

Unless otherwise noted, all of these trains depart from Sants Station; however, remember that some trains also stop at other stations more convenient to the downtown tourist zone: França Station, Passeig de Gràcia, or Plaça de Catalunya. Figure out if your train stops at these stations (and board there) to save yourself the trip to Sants.

If departing from the downtown Passeig de Gràcia Station, where three Metro lines converge with the rail line, you might find the underground tunnels confusing. You can't access the RENFE station directly from some of the entrances. Use the northern entrances to this station (rather than the southern "Consell de Cent" entrance, which is closest to Plaça de Catalunya).

From Barcelona by Train to Madrid: The AVE train has shaved hours off the journey to Madrid, making it faster than flying (when you consider that you're zipping from downtown to downtown). The train departs at least hourly. The nonstop train is a little more expensive (€130, 2.5 hours) than the slightly slower train that makes a few stops and adds about a half-hour (€110, 3 hours). Regular reserved AVE tickets can be prepurchased (often with a discount) at www.renfe.com and picked up at the station. If you have a railpass, you'll pay only a reservation fee of €23 for first class, which includes a meal (€10 second class, buy at any train station in Spain). Passholders can't reserve online through RENFE but can make the reservation at www.raileurope.com for delivery before leaving the US ($17 in second class, $40 in first class). There's also a slow overnight train to Madrid's Chamartín station (9 hours).

From Barcelona by Train to: Sevilla (11/day, 5.5-6 hours; also 1 night train, 13 hours), **Granada** (1/day, 9.5 hours via AVE and Altaria, transfer in Madrid; also 1 night train daily, 10.5 hours), **Lisbon** (no direct trains, head to Madrid and then catch night train to Lisbon, 17 hours, about €100—or fly).

From Barcelona by Train to France: To connect into France, you'll have to change trains somewhere (except for the one direct, pricey night train to Paris). Spain's tracks meet France's high-speed TGV line at the **Figueres-Vilafant** station (2/day from Barcelona, 1.75 hours). For slower but more frequent connections, you can also change in **Cerbère** (7/day from Barcelona, 2.75 hours). Connections include **Nice** (2/day, 10 hours, change in Figueres-Vilafant and Valence; slower and cheaper connections possible with multiple changes including Cerbère), and **Paris** (2/day, 7.5 hours, change in Figueres-Vilafant, about €140, more connections possible with multiple changes; 1 night train/day, 12.75 hours, about €140 or €50 with railpass, reservation mandatory). Train info: toll tel. 902-320-320, www.renfe.com.

By Bus

Most buses depart from the Nord bus station at Metro: Arc de Triomf, but confirm when researching schedules. Destinations include **Madrid** (nearly hourly, 8 hours, €30—a fraction of the AVE train price, bus info toll tel. 902-260-606, Alsa bus company toll tel. 902-422-242). For bus schedules, see www.barcelonanord.com.

By Plane
El Prat de Llobregat Airport

Barcelona's primary airport is eight miles southwest of town. It has two large terminals: 1 and 2. Air France, Air Europa, American, British Airways, Delta, Iberia, Lufthansa, United, US Airways, Vueling, and others use the newer terminal 1. EasyJet and minor airlines use terminal 2 (which is divided into sections A, B, and C). The terminals are linked by shuttle buses.

Terminal 1 and the bigger sections of terminal 2 (A and B) each have a post office, a pharmacy, a left-luggage office, plenty of good cafeterias in the gate areas, and ATMs (avoid the gimmicky machines before the baggage carousels; instead, use the bank-affiliated ATMs at the far-left end of the arrivals hall as you face the street). TIs are located in terminals 1 and 2B (airport code: BCN, info tel. 913-211-000, www.aena-aeropuertos.es).

Getting Downtown: To reach central Barcelona cheaply and quickly, take either the bus or train (about 30 minutes on either). The **Aerobus** (#A1 and #A2, corresponding with terminals 1 and 2) stops immediately outside the arrivals lobby of both terminals (and in each section of terminal 2). In about 30 minutes, it takes you to downtown, where it makes several stops, including Plaça d'Espanya and Plaça de Catalunya—near many of my recommended hotels (departs every 5 minutes, from airport 6:00-1:00 in the morning, from downtown 5:30-24:15, €5.65 one-way, €9.75 round-trip, buy ticket from machine or from driver, tel. 934-156-020). The line to board the bus can be very long, but—thanks to the high frequency of buses—it moves fast.

The RENFE **train** (on the "R2 Sud" Rodalies line) leaves from terminal 2 and involves more walking. Head down the long orange-roofed overpass between sections A and B to reach the station (2/hour at about :08 and :38 past the hour, 20 minutes to Sants Station, 25 minutes to Passeig de Gràcia Station—near Plaça de Catalunya and many recommended hotels, 30 minutes to França

Station; €3 or covered by T10 Card—described on page 1263—which you can purchase at automated machines at the airport train station). Long-term plans call for the RENFE train and eventually the AVE to be extended to terminal 1, and for the Metro's L9 (orange) line to be extended to both terminals 1 and 2. Stay tuned.

A **taxi** between the airport and downtown costs about €30—about €25 on the meter plus a €3.10 airport supplement and fee of €1 per bag. For good service, add a 10 percent tip.

Girona–Costa Brava Airport

Some budget airlines, including Ryanair, use this airport, located 60 miles north of Barcelona near Girona (airport code: GRO, tel. 972-186-600, www.aena-aeropuertos.es). Ryanair runs a **bus,** operated by Sagalés, to the Barcelona Nord bus station (€15, departs airport about 20-25 minutes after each arriving flight, 1.25 hours, tel. 902-361-550, www.sagales.com). You can also take a Sagalés bus (hourly, 25 minutes, €2.50) or a taxi (€25) to the town of Girona, then catch a train to Barcelona (at least hourly, 1.25 hours, €15-20). A taxi between the Girona airport and Barcelona costs at least €120.

By Cruise Ship

Cruise ships arrive in Barcelona at three different ports (all just southwest of the Old City, beneath Montjuïc). If your trip includes cruising beyond Barcelona, consider my guidebook, *Rick Steves' Mediterranean Cruise Ports.*

Most American cruise lines put in at **Moll Adossat/Muelle Adosado,** a long two miles from the bottom of the Ramblas. This port has four modern, airport-like terminals (lettered A through D); most have a café, shops, and TI kiosk; some have Internet access and other services. Two other terminals are far less commonly used: the **World Trade Center,** just off the southern end of the Ramblas, and **Moll de la Costa,** tucked just beneath Montjuïc (ride the free, private shuttle bus to World Trade Center; from there, it's a short walk or taxi ride to the Columbus Monument).

Getting Downtown: From any of the cruise terminals, it's easy to reach the Ramblas. **Taxis** meet each arriving ship and are waiting as you exit any of the terminal buildings. The short trip into town (i.e., to the bottom of the Ramblas) runs about €10 (the €2.10 cruise-port surcharge is legit). During high season, a ride into town can take longer and cost €10 more. For a one-way journey to other parts of town, expect to pay these fares: to the Picasso Museum or Plaça de Catalunya—€15; to the Sagrada Família—€20; and to the airport—€35-40.

You can also take a **shuttle bus** from Moll Adossat/Muelle Adosado to the Columbus Monument (at the bottom of the Ramblas), then walk or hop on public transportation to various sights. The shuttle bus departs from the parking lot in front of the terminal—follow *Public Bus* signs (*lanzadera*, #T3, a.k.a. Portbús, €3 round-trip, €2 one-way, buses leave every 20-30 minutes, timed to cruise ship arrival, tel. 932-986-000). Pay careful attention to where they drop you off if you want to catch the return bus later.

SWITZERLAND

GIMMELWALD AND THE BERNER OBERLAND

Interlaken • Lauterbrunnen • Gimmelwald • Mürren

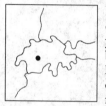

Frolic and hike high above the stress and clouds of the real world. Take a vacation from your busy vacation. Recharge your touristic batteries high in the Alps, where distant avalanches, cowbells, the fluff of a down comforter, the whistle of marmots, and the crunchy footsteps of happy hikers are the dominant sounds. If the weather's good (and your budget's healthy), ride a cable car from the traffic-free village of Gimmelwald to a hearty breakfast at the revolving Piz Gloria restaurant, 10,000 feet up on the Schilthorn. Linger among alpine whitecaps before riding, hiking, or paragliding down 5,000 feet to Mürren and home to Gimmelwald.

Your gateway to the rugged Berner Oberland is the grand old resort town of Interlaken. Near Interlaken is Switzerland's open-air folk museum, Ballenberg, where you can climb through original traditional houses gathered from every corner of this diverse country.

Ah, but the weather's fine and the Alps beckon. Head deep into the heart of the Alps, and ride the cable car to the stop just this side of heaven—Gimmelwald.

Planning Your Time

Rather than tackle a checklist of famous Swiss mountains and resorts, choose one region to savor: the Berner Oberland.

Interlaken is the region's administrative headquarters and transportation hub. Use it for business—banking, post office, laundry, shopping—and as a springboard for alpine thrills.

If the weather's decent, explore the two areas that tower above either side of the Lauterbrunnen Valley, south of Interlaken: On one side is the Jungfrau (and beneath it, the town of Kleine Schei-degg), and on the other is the Schilthorn (overlooking the villages of Gimmelwald and Mürren).

Ideally, spend three nights in the region, with a day exploring each side of the valley. For accommodations without the expense and headache of mountain lifts, consider the valley-floor village of Lauterbrunnen. But for the best overnight options, I'd stay on the scenic ridge high above the valley, in the rustic hamlet of Gimmelwald or the resort town of Mürren. I've also listed a few high-altitude options in the resort of Wengen and several other mountain towns.

For a summary of the wildly scenic activities this region has to offer (from panoramic train rides and lifts to spectacular hikes and mountain biking), see "Activities in the Berner Oberland" on page 1401.

If time is limited, consider a night in Gimmelwald, breakfast at the Schilthorn, an afternoon doing the Männlichen-Wengen hike, and an evening or night train out. What? A nature-lover not spending the night high in the Alps? Alpus interruptus.

Getting Around the Berner Oberland

For more than a century, this region has been the target of nature-worshipping pilgrims. And Swiss engineers and visionaries have made the most exciting alpine perches accessible.

By Lifts and Trains

Part of the fun—and most of the expense—here is riding the many mountain trains and lifts (gondolas and cable cars).

Trains connect Interlaken to Wilderswil, Grindelwald, Lauterbrunnen, Wengen, Kleine Scheidegg, and the Jungfraujoch. Lifts connect Wengen to Männlichen and Grund (near Grindelwald); Grindelwald to First; Lauterbrunnen to Grütschalp (where a train connects to Mürren); and the cable-car station near Stechelberg to Gimmelwald, Mürren, and the Schilthorn.

For an overview of your many options, study the "Alpine Lifts in the Berner Oberland" map on page 1363. Lifts generally go at least twice hourly, from about 7:00 until about 20:00 (sneak preview: www.jungfraubahn.ch or www.schilthorn.ch).

Beyond Interlaken, trains and lifts into the Jungfrau region are only 25 percent covered by Eurail Passes, without using a travel day; with the Swiss Pass, they're free up to Wengen or Mürren (uphill from there, Swiss Pass-holders pay half-price). Ask about discounts for early-morning and late-afternoon trips, youths, seniors, families, groups (assemble a party of 10 and you'll save about 25 percent), and those staying awhile. Generally, round-trips are double the one-way cost, though some high-up trains and lifts are

Berner Oberland

NOTE: THIS BIRD'S-EYE VIEW LOOKS SOUTH

Jungfraujoch 11,300'

Eiger 13,026'
Mönch 13,449'
Jungfrau 13,642'

Schilthorn 9,748'

TUNNEL

BIRG 8,784'

Kleine Scheidegg 6,762'

GIMMEL-WALD 4,593'

GREAT HIKE
WENG.-ALP.
3,025' STECHEL-BERG
MÜRREN 5,381'

GRINDEL-WALD 3,393'
Männlichen 7,317'

LIFT STN.
NICE WALK

GRUND

GRÜTSCHALP 4,879'

To First

WENGEN 4,180'
LAUTERBRUNNEN 2,612'

ISENFLUH

Schynige Platte 6,454'
ZWEILÜTSCHINEN

WILDERSWIL 1,916'

To Luzern
ISELTWALD
EAST STN.

To Bern

BRIENZ
Lake Brienz
Aare River
WEST STN.
SPIEZ
Lake Thun

BALLENBERG OPEN-AIR MUSEUM
INTERLAKEN 1,860'
ST. BEATUS CAVES

10-20 percent cheaper. It's possible to buy your entire package of lifts at once, but then you don't have the flexibility to change with the weather.

Popular Passes: The **Junior Card,** for families traveling with children, is a great deal, and pays for itself in the first hour of trains and lifts (30 SF/one child, 60 SF/two or more children, lets children under 16 travel free with at least one parent, buy at Swiss train stations).

The **Berner Oberland Regional Pass** covers most trains, buses, and lifts in this area (and all the way south to Gstaad and Brig). It doesn't, however, cover the full cost of some popular (and pricey) lifts and trains, such as the Mürren-Schilthorn cable car, and the train from Kleine Scheidegg up to the Jungfraujoch. While it's likely to save you money over individual tickets, consider that it's not much cheaper than a Swiss Pass that covers the whole country (4 days-230 SF, 6 days-290 SF, 8 days-330 SF, discount with Swiss Pass, valid May-Oct, www.regiopass-berneroberland.ch).

The **Jungfraubahnen Pass** is more limited in scope, covering six consecutive days of unlimited transportation in just the Jungfrau region. This pass covers most of the trains, lifts, buses, and

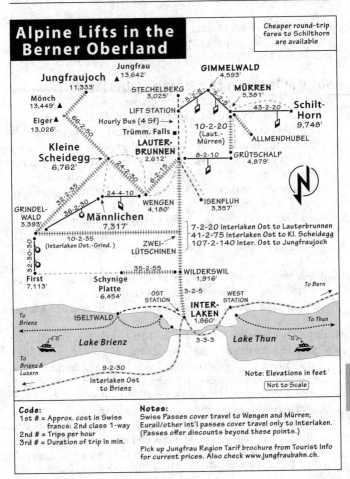

Alpine Lifts in the Berner Oberland

Cheaper round-trip fares to Schilthorn are available

Jungfrau 13,642'

GIMMELWALD 4,593'

Jungfraujoch 11,333'

Jungfraujoch

STECHELBERG 3,025'

MÜRREN 5,381'

Schilt-Horn 9,748'

Mönch 13,449'

LIFT STATION

5-2-5 5-2-5

43-2-20

Eiger 13,026'

Hourly Bus (4 Sf)→

Trümm. Falls ■

10-2-20 (Laut.-Mürren)

ALLMENDHUBEL

Kleine Scheidegg 6,762'

LAUTER-BRUNNEN 2,612'

8-2-10

GRÜTSCHALP 4,879'

66-2-50

24-2-30

6-2-15

N

32-2-35

24-4-10

WENGEN 4,180'

ISENFLUH 3,357'

GRINDEL-WALD 3,393'

36-2-30

Männlichen 7,317'

7-2-20 Interlaken Ost to Lauterbrunnen
41-2-75 Interlaken Ost to Kl. Scheidegg
107-2-140 Inter. Ost to Jungfraujoch

10-2-35 (Interlaken Ost.-Grind.)

ZWEI-LÜTSCHINEN

32-30-30

First 7,113'

Schynige Platte 6,454'

35-2-55

WILDERSWIL 1,916'

OST STATION

3-2-5

WEST STATION

To Bern

To Brienz

ISELTWALD

INTER-LAKEN 1,860'

To Thun

Lake Brienz

3-3-3

Lake Thun

To Brienz & Luzern

9-2-30 Interlaken Ost to Brienz

Note: Elevations in feet

Not to Scale

Code:
1st # = Approx. cost in Swiss francs; 2nd class 1-way
2nd # = Trips per hour
3rd # = Duration of trip in min.

Notes:
Swiss Passes cover travel to Wengen and Mürren;
Eurail/other int'l passes cover travel only to Interlaken.
(Passes offer discounts beyond these points.)

Pick up Jungfrau Region Tarif brochure from Tourist Info for current prices. Also check www.jungfraubahn.ch.

GIMMELWALD

funiculars, with two exceptions: It doesn't cover the cable car that that connects Stechelberg with Gimmelwald, Mürren, Birg, or the Schilthorn (though it does cover the lift/train ride to Mürren via Grütschalp), and you pay half-price for the train between Kleine Scheidegg and the Jungfraujoch (210 SF, 160 SF with Swiss Pass, valid May-Oct, tel. 033-828-7233, www.jungfraubahn.ch).

By Car

Interlaken, Lauterbrunnen, Isenfluh, and Stechelberg are all accessible by car. You can't drive to Gimmelwald, Mürren, Wengen, or Kleine Scheidegg, but don't let that stop you from staying up in the mountains; park the car and zip up on a lift. To catch the lift to Gimmelwald, Mürren, and the Schilthorn, park at the cable-car station near Stechelberg (2 SF/2 hours, 6 SF/day, cash only; see page 1385 for more information). To catch the train to Wengen or Kleine Scheidegg, park at the train station in Lauterbrunnen (2 SF/2 hours, 10 SF/9-24 hours).

Helpful Hints in the Berner Oberland

Weather: Let your plans flex with the weather. If it's good—go! Ask at your hotel or the TI for the latest info. A webcam showing live video from the famous peaks plays just about wherever you go in the area. The weather in villages on or near the valley floor is usually sunnier, and almost always much warmer. For the current weather, you can also check www.swisspanorama. com (entire area), www.jungfraubahn.ch (for Jungfraujoch), or www.schilthorn.ch (for Schilthorn peak).

Closed Days: On Sundays and holidays (including the lesser-known religious holidays), small-town Switzerland is quiet. Hotels are open and lifts and trains run, but many stores are closed.

Off-Season Closures: Note that at higher altitudes many hotels, restaurants, and shops are closed between the skiing and hiking seasons: from late April until late May, and again from mid-October to early December.

Rainy-Day Options: When it rains here, locals joke that they're washing the mountains. If clouds roll in, don't despair. They can roll out just as quickly. With good rain gear and the right choice of trail, you can thoroughly enjoy a hike in the rain, with surprise views popping out all around you as the clouds break. Some good bad-weather options are the North Face Trail, the walk from Mürren or Allmendhubel to Grütschalp, the Sefinen Valley hike, and the Lauterbrunnen Valley walk. Also consider a visit to Trümmelbach Falls or the Lauterbrunnen Valley Folk Museum. All of these options are described in this chapter.

Local Guidebook: For an in-depth look at the area's history, folk life, flora, fauna, and for extensive hiking information, consider Don Chmura's *Exploring the Lauterbrunnen Valley* (sold throughout the valley, 8 SF).

Visitors Cards (*Gästekarten*): The hotels in various towns issue free Visitors Cards that include small discounts on some sights. Though these cards won't save you much, you can ask at your hotel for the details.

Skiing and Snowboarding: The Berner Oberland is a great winter-sports destination, with good snow on its higher runs, incredible variety, relatively reasonable prices, and a sense of character that's missing in many swankier resort areas. You can even swish with the Swiss down the world's longest sledding run (9 miles long, out of Grindelwald, only open when snow's good). Three ski areas cluster around the Lauterbrunnen Valley: Mürren-Schilthorn (best for experts), Kleine Scheidegg-Männlichen (busiest, best variety of runs), and Grindelwald-First (best for beginners and intermediates, but lower elevation can make for iffier snowpack). Lift tickets cost around 70 SF a day, or you can buy the two-day Sportspass Jungfrau, which covers all three areas, for about 130 SF (see www.jungfrauwinter.ch for prices and info).

Interlaken

When the 19th-century Romantics redefined mountains as something more than cold and troublesome obstacles, Interlaken became the original alpine resort. Ever since, tourists have flocked to the Alps "because they're there." Interlaken's glory days are long gone, its elegant old hotels eclipsed by the newer, more swanky alpine resorts. Today, its shops are filled with chocolate bars, Swiss Army knives, and sunburned backpackers.

While European jet-setters are elsewhere, Interlaken is cashing in on a huge interest from India and the Arab world. Indians come to escape their monsoon season—especially in April and May—and to visit places they've seen in their movies. (The Alps often stand in for Kashmir, which is less accessible to film crews.) There's even a restaurant called "Bollywood" atop the Jungfraujoch. People from the hot and dry Arabian Peninsula come here just to photograph their children frolicking in the mist and fog.

Orientation to Interlaken

Efficient Interlaken (pop. 5,500) is a good administrative and shopping center. Take care of business, give the town a quick look, and view the webcam coverage of the weather higher up (at the TI)... then head for the hills.

Tourist Information

The TI, with good information on the region, is located under the 18-story skyscraper on the main street between the two train stations, a 10-minute stroll from either (May-June Mon-Fri 8:00-18:00, Sat 8:00-16:00, closed Sun; July-Aug Mon-Fri 8:00-19:00, Sat 8:00-17:00, Sun 10:00-12:00 & 17:00-19:00; Sept Mon-Fri 8:00-18:00, Sat 9:00-13:00, closed Sun; shorter hours Oct-April, Höheweg 37, tel. 033-826-5300, www.interlaken.ch). The *You Want It All* booklet is an almanac covering everything you need in Interlaken (except for some events, which are covered more thoroughly in the monthly entertainment guide). There's no point in buying a regional map, as good mini-versions of the map are included in various free transportation and hiking brochures.

Arrival in Interlaken

Interlaken has two train stations: Ost (East) and West. All trains coming from western Switzerland stop at both stations. If heading for higher-altitude villages, get off at Ost Station. For hotels in Interlaken, get off at West Station, which has a helpful and friendly information center for in-depth rail questions (Mon-Fri 9:00-12:00 & 13:30-18:20, Sat until 17:00, closed Sun, tel. 058-327-4750, www.bls.ch; ticket windows open daily 6:40-19:00). Ask about discount passes, special fares, railpass discounts, and schedules for the scenic mountain trains. There's an exchange booth next to the ticket windows and a very pricey Internet-access computer. A post office with a cluster of phone booths is a few blocks away.

It's a pleasant 20-minute walk between the West and Ost train stations; an easy, frequent train connection (2-3/hour, 3.40 SF); or a quick trip on the bus (2/hour, 10 minutes, 3.40 SF). From Ost Station, private trains take you deep into the mountainous Jungfrau region (see "Interlaken Connections," on page 1377).

Helpful Hints

Baggage Storage: Both stations have lockers (small locker-4 SF, large-5 SF) as well as left-luggage counters (5 SF, West Station—daily 9:00-12:00 & 13:30-18:00, Ost Station—daily 7:00-18:30).

Laundry: Friendly Helen Schmocker's **Wäscherei** has a change machine, soap, English instructions, and a delightful riverside location (self-service daily 7:00-22:00—wash-6 SF/load, dry-about 5 SF/load; full service Mon-Fri 8:00-12:00 & 13:30-18:00, Sat until 16:00, closed Sun, drop off in the morning and pick up that afternoon—12 SF/load; from the main street take Marktgasse over two bridges to Beatenbergstrasse 5, tel. 033-822-1566).

Bike Rental: You can rent bikes (both regular and electric) at West Station (11.50 SF/2 hours, 25 SF/half-day, 33 SF/day, 5 SF less with Eurail Pass or Swiss Pass, daily 9:00-18:00, www.rentabike.ch).

Flying Wheels, a short walk from Ost Station, is a hip, well-organized, family-friendly outfit that specializes in electric bikes and guided bike tours of the area. Its amiable English-speaking staff can help you pick the right bike and give tips on where to go (electric or hard-core mountain bikes—35 SF/half-day, 50 SF/day; normal mountain bikes—25 SF/half-day, 33 SF/day; 5 SF cheaper with Swiss Pass, no discount with Eurail Pass, tandem electric bikes available, daily 9:00-

19:00, across street from the northeast corner of Höhematte Park at Höheweg 133, tel. 033-511-2161, www.flyingwheels. ch). For info on their tours, see "Adventure Sports," later.

A short walk from West Station, **Eiger Sport** rents bikes for a little less than Flying Wheels (8 SF/hour, 10 SF/2 hours, 15 SF/3 hours, 20 SF/half-day, 30 SF/day, Mon-Fri 8:30-12:00 & 13:30-18:30, Sat 8:30-16:00; from West Station, cross river—it's on the right at Bahnhofstrasse 2, tel. 033-823-2043).

Self-Guided Walk

Welcome to Interlaken

Most visitors use Interlaken as a springboard for high-altitude thrills (and rightly so). But the town itself has history and scenic charm and is worth a short walk. This 45-minute stroll circles from the West train station, down the main drag to the big meadow, past the casino, along the river to the oldest part of town (historically a neighboring town called Unterseen), and back to the station.

• *From the West train station, walk along...*

Bahnhofstrasse: This main drag, which turns into Höheweg as it continues east, cuts straight through the town center from the West train station to the Ost train station. The best Swiss souvenir shopping is along this stretch (finer shops are on the Höheweg stretch, near the fancy hotels). At the roundabout is the handy post office (with free public WCs). At Höheweg 2, the TV in the window of the Schilthornbahn office shows the weather up top.

The 18-story **Metropole Hotel** (a.k.a. the "concrete shame of Interlaken") is by far the town's tallest building. Step right into the main lobby (through the second set of doors) and ride the elevator to the top for a commanding view of the "inter-laken" area, and gaze deep into the Jungfrau region to the scenic south. A meal or drink here costs no more than one back on earth. Consider sipping a drink on its outdoor view terrace (or come back tonight—it's open very late).

• *On your right is...*

Höhematte Park: This "high meadow," or Höhematte (but generally referred to simply as "the park"), marks the beginning of Interlaken's fancy hotel row. Hotels like the Victoria-Jungfrau hearken back to the days when Interlaken was *the* top alpine resort (late 19th century). The first grand hotels were built here to enjoy the views of the Jungfrau in the distance. (Today, the *jung Frau*s getting the most attention are next door, at Hooters.)

The park originated as farmland of the monastery that pre-dated the town (marked today by the steeples of both the Catholic and Protestant churches—neither are of any sightseeing interest). The actual **monastery site** is now home to the courthouse and

GIMMELWALD

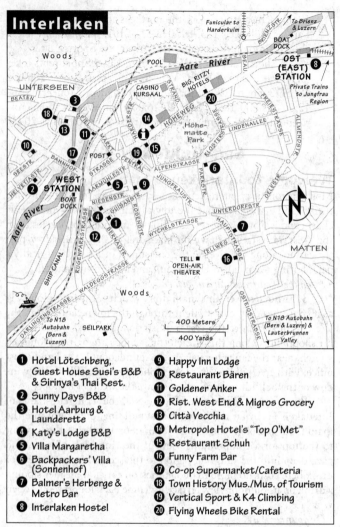

Interlaken

- Woods
- Funicular to Harderkulm
- To Brienz & Luzern
- BOAT DOCK
- Aare River
- POOL
- OST (EAST) STATION
- Private Trains to Jungfrau Region
- UNTERSEEN
- BEATEN
- CASINO KURSAAL
- BIG, RITZY HOTELS
- STRAND
- HÖHEWEG
- Höhematte Park
- HARDERSTR.
- SPIELMATTE
- HELVETIASTR.
- SEESTR.
- BAHNHOF
- POST
- STRASSE
- WEST STATION
- BOAT DOCK
- AARMÜHLESTR.
- CENTRAL
- NIESENSTR.
- GUISANSTR.
- ROSENSTR.
- JUNGFRAUSTR.
- ALPENSTRASSE
- PARKSTR.
- KLOSTERGASSE
- LINDENALLEE
- FREIESTRASSE
- ALLMENDSTR.
- BEAU
- BRIENZSTR.
- ÖLESTR.
- UNTERDORFSTR.
- MATTEN
- KLÜGENPARKSTRASSE
- BERNASTR.
- WYCHELSTRASSE
- HAUPTSTRASSE
- TELLWEG
- TELL OPEN-AIR THEATER
- OSTSIGSTRASSE
- Woods
- SHIP CANAL
- DARLINGENSTRASSE
- WALDEGGSTRASSE
- To N18 Autobahn (Bern & Luzern)
- SEILPARK
- To N18 Autobahn (Bern & Luzern) & Lauterbrunnen Valley
- 400 Meters
- 400 Yards
- Aare River

① Hotel Lötschberg, Guest House Susi's B&B & Sirinya's Thai Rest.
② Sunny Days B&B
③ Hotel Aarburg & Launderette
④ Katy's Lodge B&B
⑤ Villa Margaretha
⑥ Backpackers' Villa (Sonnenhof)
⑦ Balmer's Herberge & Metro Bar
⑧ Interlaken Hostel
⑨ Happy Inn Lodge
⑩ Restaurant Bären
⑪ Goldener Anker
⑫ Rist. West End & Migros Grocery
⑬ Città Vecchia
⑭ Metropole Hotel's "Top O'Met"
⑮ Restaurant Schuh
⑯ Funny Farm Bar
⑰ Co-op Supermarket/Cafeteria
⑱ Town History Mus./Mus. of Tourism
⑲ Vertical Sport & K4 Climbing
⑳ Flying Wheels Bike Rental

GIMMELWALD

county administration building. With the Reformation in 1528, the monastery was shut down, and its land was taken by the state. Later, when the land was being eyed by developers, the town's leading hotels and business families bought it and established that it would never be used for commercial buildings (a very early example of smart town planning). There was talk of building a parking lot under it, but the water table here, between the two lakes, is too high. (That's why the town cemetery is up on the hillside.) Today, this is a fine place to stroll, hang out on the park benches or at Restaurant Schuh, and watch the paragliders gracefully land.

Across the street from the park, right where the path that bisects the park hits Höheweg, turn left onto the grounds of the **Casino Kursaal,** where, at the top of each hour, dwarves ring the toadstools on the flower clock. The Kursaal, originally a kind of 19th-century fat farm, is now both a casino (passport but no tie required to enter) and a convention center.

• *Follow the path left of the Kursaal to the river (huge public swimming pool just over the river). Walk downstream under the train track and cross the pedestrian bridge, stopping in the middle to enjoy the view.*

Aare River: The Aare River is Switzerland's longest. It connects Lake Brienz and Lake Thun (with an 18-foot altitude difference—this short stretch has quite a flow). Then it tumbles out of Lake Thun, heading for Bern and ultimately into the Rhine. Its level is controlled by several sluices. In the distance, a church bell tower marks a different parish and the neighborhood of Unterseen, which shares the town's name, but in German: Like the word *Interlaken, Unterseen* means "between the lakes." Behind the spire is the pointy summit of the Niesen (like so many Swiss peaks, capped with a restaurant and accessible by a lift). Stroll downstream along the far side of the river to the church spire. The delightful riverside walk is lined by fine residences. Notice that your Jungfrau view now includes the Jungfraujoch observation deck (the little brown bump in the ridge just left of the peak).

• *At the next bridge, turn right to the town square lined with 17th-century houses on one side and a modern strip on the other.*

Unterseen: This was a town when Interlaken was only a monastery. The church is not worth touring. A block away to the left, the (generally empty) **Town History Museum/Museum of Tourism** shows off classic posters, fascinating photos of the construction of the Jungfraujoch, and exhibits on folk life, crafts, and winter sports—all well-described in English (5 SF, covered by Swiss Pass, May-mid-Oct Tue-Sun 14:00-17:00, closed Mon and mid-Oct-April, Obere Gasse 26).

Return to Station: From Unterseen, cross the river on Spielmatte, and you're a few minutes' walk from your starting point. On the second bridge, notice the border between the two towns/parishes, marked by their respective heraldic emblems (each with an ibex, a wild mountain goat). A block or so later, on the left, is the Marktplatz. The river originally ran through this square. The town used to be called "Aaremühle" ("Aare mill") for the mill that was here. But in the 19th century, town fathers made a key marketing decision: Since "Aaremühle" was too difficult to pronounce for English tourists who flocked here, they changed the name to "Interlaken." Judging from the throngs of tourists on the main drag, it worked.

GIMMELWALD

Sights near Interlaken

▲▲Swiss Open-Air Folk Museum at Ballenberg

Across Lake Brienz from Interlaken, the Swiss Open-Air Museum of Vernacular Architecture, Country Life, and Crafts in the Berner Oberland is a rich collection of more than 100 traditional and historic buildings brought here from every region of the country. All the houses are carefully furnished, and many feature traditional craftspeople at work. The sprawling 50-acre park, laid out roughly as a huge Swiss map (Italian Swiss in the south, Appenzell in the east, and so on), is a natural preserve providing a wonderful setting for this culture-on-a-lazy-Susan look at Switzerland.

The Thurgau house (#621) has an interesting wattle-and-daub (half-timbered construction) display, and house #331 has a fun bread museum and farmers' shop. There are daily events and demonstrations (near the east entry), hundreds of traditional farm animals (like very furry-legged roosters, near the merry-go-round in the center), and a chocolate shop (under the restaurant on the east side).

An outdoor cafeteria with reasonable prices is inside the west entrance, and fresh bread, sausage, mountain cheese, and other goodies are on sale in several houses. Picnic tables and grills with free firewood are scattered throughout the park.

The little wooden village of Brienzwiler (near the east entrance) is a museum in itself, with a lovely pint-size church.

Cost and Hours: 20 SF, covered by Swiss Pass; RailAway combo-ticket includes transportation to and from Ballenberg—41 SF from West Station, 38 SF from Ost Station, add 15 SF to return by boat instead, ticket available at both Interlaken stations; houses open daily mid-April-Oct 10:00-17:00, grounds and restaurants stay open until 18:00.

Information: Pick up a daily craft demonstration schedule at the entry, and buy the 2-SF map/guide so you'll know where you are. The more expensive picture book is a better souvenir than guide; tel. 033-952-1030, www.ballenberg.ch.

Getting There: From Interlaken, take the train from either station to Brienz (2/hour, 30 minutes, 9.20 SF one-way from West Station or get the RailAway combo-ticket—described earlier). From the Brienz train station, catch a bus to Ballenberg (10 minutes, 4.20 SF one-way). The bus back to Brienz leaves Ballenberg's east entrance on the hour, then picks up at the west entrance at :07 after the hour (after 18:00, buses leave only from the west entrance). Consider returning from Brienz by boat (boat dock next to train station, one-way to Interlaken's Ost Station-28 SF). Parking is free outside both entrances to the park.

Boat Trips

"Interlaken" is literally "between the lakes" of Thun and Brienz. You can explore these lakes on a lazy boat trip, hopping on and off as the schedule allows (free with Swiss Pass or Eurail Pass but uses a travel day, schedules at TI or at travel center in West Station). The boats on Lake Thun (5/day in summer, 2/day spring and fall, 5-hour round-trip, 68 SF) stop at the St. Beatus caves (30 minutes away, described next) and two visit-worthy towns: Spiez and Thun. The boats on Lake Brienz (5/day July-Aug, 2-4/day off-season, 3-hour round-trip, 48 SF) stop at the super-cute village of Iseltwald and at Brienz (near Ballenberg Open-Air Folk Museum; easy bus and train connections back to Interlaken from Brienz).

The **St. Beatus caves** on Lake Thun can be visited with a one-hour guided tour (18 SF, 2/hour, April-mid-Oct daily 9:30-17:00, closed mid-Oct-March, tel. 033-841-1643, www.beatushoehlen. ch). The best excursion plan: Ride bus #21 from Interlaken (1-2/hour, 25 minutes, 5 SF, departs West Station at :17 and :47 past the hour, direction: Thun); tour the caves; take the short, steep hike down to the lake; and return to Interlaken by boat (30 minutes, 13 SF one-way).

Adventure Sports

High-Adrenaline Trips

For the thrill-seeker with money, several companies offer trips such as rafting, canyoning (rappelling down watery gorges), bungee jumping, and paragliding. Costs range from roughly 150 SF to 200 SF—higher for skydiving and hot-air balloon rides. Interlaken's two dominant companies are **Alpin Raft** (tel. 033-823-4100, www.alpinraft.com) and **Outdoor Interlaken** (tel. 033-826-7719, www.outdoor-interlaken.ch). Other companies are generally just booking agents for these two outfits. For an overview of your options, visit www.interlakenadventure.com or study the racks of brochures at most TIs and hotels (everyone's getting a cut of this lucrative industry).

Several years ago, two fatal accidents jolted the adventure-sport business in the Berner Oberland, leading to a more professional respect for the risks involved. Companies have very high standards of safety. Statistically, the most dangerous sport is mountain biking. Enjoying nature up close comes with risks. Adventure sports increase those risks dramatically. Use good judgment.

Indoor Climbing

K44 is a breathtaking indoor climbing facility where you can snack or enjoy a nice cup of hot chocolate while watching hotshots practice their gravity-defying skills.

Cost and Hours: Free entry for viewing, 39 SF for one hour of climbing; open longer hours in bad weather: Mon 16:00-22:00,

Tue-Fri 9:00-22:00, Sat 9:00-20:00, Sun 9:00-18:00; in good weather: Tue-Fri 9:00-18:00, Sat 9:00-16:00, closed Sun-Mon; next to—and run by—**Vertical Sport**, at the back of the park across from Hotel Savoy at Jungfraustrasse 44, tel. 033-821-2821, www.k44.ch.

Rope Courses

Outdoor Interlaken's Seilpark offers five rope courses of varying difficulty and height in a forest, giving you a tree-top adventure through a maze of rope bridges and zip lines.

Cost and Hours: 37 SF, family deals, must weigh between 44 and 264 pounds; June-Aug daily 10:00-18:00; April-May and Sept-Oct Mon-Fri 13:00-18:00, Sat-Sun 10:00-18:00; closed Nov-March; from Interlaken's West Station, it's a 15-minute walk—head right up Rugenparkstrasse and into the park, then look for signs; tel. 033-826-7719, www.outdoor-interlaken.ch.

Bike Tours

Flying Wheels offers bike tours of varying length and difficulty around the area. They also offer an interesting "bike and fly" deal: Ride your electric bike up the hill and paraglide back into Interlaken (around 200 SF). If it rains the day you're booked to go, they'll take you on a bus tour instead to a nearby indoor destination.

Cost and Hours: Interlaken-only tour—60 SF, 3 hours; Lauterbrunnen Valley up to Stechelberg—100-110 SF, 6 hours, includes picnic and Trümmelbach Falls visit; around Lake Brienz—90-100 SF, 6 hours, includes picnic; shorter tours start at 9:45, longer tours at 8:30; for contact info, see page 1366.

Castles

A few impressively well-kept and welcoming old castles in the Interlaken area are worth considering for day trips by boat, bus, or car.

Thun Castle (Schloss Thun)

Built between 1180 and 1190 by the Dukes of Zähringen, the castle houses a five-floor historical museum offering insights into the cultural development of the region over a period of some 4,000 years. From the corner turrets of the castle, you are rewarded with a spectacular view of the city of Thun, the lake, and the Alps.

Cost and Hours: 8 SF, April-Oct daily 10:00-17:00, Nov-Jan Sun only 13:00-16:00, Feb-March daily 13:00-16:00, tel. 033-223-2001, www.schlossthun.ch.

Hünegg Castle (Schloss Hünegg)

Located in Hilterfingen (farther along Lake Thun, toward Interlaken), this castle contains a museum exhibiting furnished rooms from the second half of the 19th century. The castle is situated in a beautiful wooded park.

Cost and Hours: 9 SF, mid-May-mid-Oct Mon-Sat 14:00-

GIMMELWALD

17:00, Sun 11:00-17:00, closed off-season, tel. 033-243-1982, www.schlosshuenegg.ch.

Oberhofen Castle (Schloss Oberhofen)

Also on Lake Thun, this place is ideal for those interested in gardens. Its beautifully landscaped park with exotic trees is a delight. The museum in the castle depicts domestic life in the 16th-19th centuries, including a Turkish smoking room and a medieval chapel.

Cost and Hours: Gardens-free, mid-May-mid-Oct daily 10:00-dusk; museum-10 SF, mid-May-mid-Oct Mon 14:00-17:00, Tue-Sun 11:00-17:00; both closed off-season, 40 minutes from Interlaken on bus #21, tel. 033-243-1235, www.schlossoberhofen.ch.

Nightlife in Interlaken

Youthful Night Scenes

For counterculture with a reggae beat, check out **Funny Farm** (past the recommended Balmer's Herberge hostel, in Matten). The young frat-party dance scene rages at the **Metro Bar** at Balmer's (bomb-shelter disco bar, with cheap drinks and a friendly if loud atmosphere). And if you're into **Hooters,** you won't have a hard time finding it.

Mellower After-Dark Hangouts

To nurse a drink with a view of the park, the outdoor tables at **Restaurant Schuh** are convenient if you don't mind the schlocky music. The **"Top O'Met"** bar and café has great indoor and outdoor view seating with reasonable prices, 18 floors above everything else in town (in the Metropole Hotel skyscraper, open nightly until late, see "Eating in Interlaken," later). **Hotel Oberland** (near the post office) has live alpine music in its restaurant (Tue at 19:00 or 20:00).

Sleeping in Interlaken

I'd sleep in Gimmelwald, or at least Lauterbrunnen (20 minutes by train or car). In ski season, however, prices go down in Interlaken, while they shoot up at most hotels in the mountains. Interlaken is not the Alps. But if you must stay here...

$$$ Hotel Lötschberg, with a sun terrace and 21 rooms, is run with lots of thoughtful touches by English-speaking Susi (Sb-135 SF, Db-178 SF, big Db-198 SF, extra bed-35 SF, family deals, closed Nov-mid-April, elevator, pay Internet access, free Wi-Fi, free laundry machines, free loaner bikes; lounge with microwave, fridge, and free tea and coffee; 3-minute walk from West Station: leaving station, turn right, after Migros at the circle go left to General-Guisan-Strasse 31; tel. 033-822-2545, fax 033-822-2579, www.lotschberg.ch, hotel@lotschberg.ch).

Sleep Code

(1 SF = about $1.10, country code: 41)
S = Single, **D** = Double/Twin, **T** = Triple, **Q** = Quad, **b** = bathroom, **s** = shower only. Unless otherwise noted, credit cards are accepted, English is spoken, and breakfast is included.

To help you sort easily through these listings, I've divided the accommodations into three categories, based on the price for a standard double room with bath during high season:

$$$ **Higher Priced**—Most rooms 150 SF or more.
$$ **Moderately Priced**—Most rooms between 90-150 SF.
$ **Lower Priced**—Most rooms 90 SF or less.

Prices can change without notice; verify the hotel's current rates online or by email. For other updates, see www.ricksteves.com/update.

$$$ Guest House Susi's B&B is Hotel Lötschberg's no-frills, cash-only annex, offering three nicely furnished, cozy rooms and four apartments with kitchenettes (Sb-119 SF, Db-151 SF; apartment-140 SF/2 people, 250 SF/4-5 people; free Wi-Fi, hotel closed Nov-mid-April but apartments available with 5-night stay, same contact info as Hotel Lötschberg, earlier).

$$ Sunny Days B&B is a homey, nine-room place in a quiet residential neighborhood (Sb-108-140 SF, Db-120-158 SF, prices vary with size of room and view, less in winter, 1-night stay-20 SF extra, discount for 4 or more nights, extra bed-about 40 SF, pay Wi-Fi, patio; from West Station: exit left out of station and take first bridge to your left, after crossing two bridges turn left on Helvetiastrasse and go 3 blocks to #29; tel. 033-822-8343, www.sunnydays.ch, mail@sunnydays.ch).

$$ Hotel Aarburg offers nine plain, peaceful rooms over a restaurant in a beautifully located but run-down old building in Unterseen, a 10-minute walk from West Station (Sb-70 SF, Db-140-150 SF, 10 SF more in July-Aug, 2 doors from launderette at Beatenbergstrasse 1, tel. 033-822-2615, hotel-aarburg@quicknet.ch).

$$ Katy's Lodge B&B is a funky old house in a quiet, handy location. It's not cozy, but it rents seven basic rooms at a good price. All the beds are twins—no double beds here (D-90-108 SF, T-114-126 SF, Q-140-160 SF, 6-bed room-160-180 SF, lowest prices in winter, reception open 7:00-12:00 & 14:00-20:00, garden, playground, 3-minute walk from West Station, around the corner from Hotel Lötschberg at Bernastrasse 7, mobile 078-604-6507, www.katys-lodge.ch, katyslodge@hotmail.com).

$$ Backpackers' Villa (Sonnenhof) Interlaken is a creative guest house run by a Methodist church group. Renovated in 2009, it's fun, youthful, and great for families, without the frat-party scene of Balmer's Herberge (listed later). Travelers of any age feel comfortable here (dorm bed in 2- to 7-bed room with free locker, sheets, and towel-37-47 SF, S-69 SF, view S-74 SF, Sb-79 SF, D-98-106 SF, view D-110-114 SF, Db-138 SF, T-135-141 SF, view T-153-159 SF, Tb-165-171 SF, Q-164-172 SF, view Q-180-188 SF, Qb-196-204 SF, view rooms have balconies and WCs, lowest prices in winter, kitchen, garden, movies, small game room, pay Internet access, free Wi-Fi, laundry, free admission to public swimming pool/spa, no curfew, no membership required, open all day, reception open 7:00-23:00, free use of public buses—bus #102 runs from hostel to either of Interlaken's stations, 10-15-minute walk from stations, across the park from the TI at Alpenstrasse 16, tel. 033-826-7171, fax 033-826-7172, www.villa.ch, mail@villa.ch).

$ Villa Margaretha, run by English-speaking Frau Kunz-Joerin, offers the best cheap beds in town. It's like Grandma's big Victorian house on a residential street. Keep your room tidy, and you'll have a friend for life (D-90 SF, T-135 SF, Q-180 SF, the three rooms share one big bathroom, 2-night minimum, apartment for 2-3 people-1,000 SF/week, closed Oct-April, cash only, no breakfast served but dishes and kitchenette available, lots of rules to abide by, go up small street directly in front of West Station to Aarmühlestrasse 13, tel. 033-822-1813, www.villa-margaretha.com, info@villa-margaretha.com).

$ Balmer's Herberge is many people's idea of backpacker heaven. This Interlaken institution comes with movies, table tennis, a launderette, bar, restaurant, tiny grocery, kitchen, bike rental, swapping library, excursions, bus pass, shuttle-bus service (which meets important arriving trains), and friendly, hardworking staff. This hive of youthful fun and activities is home for those who miss their fraternity. It can be a mob scene, especially on summer weekends (bunk in 6- to 12-bed dorm-27 SF, S-45 SF, D-74 SF, T-99 SF, Q-132 SF, these are walk-in prices—booking online costs 1-2 SF more, includes sheets and breakfast, open year-round, emailed reservations recommended at least 5 days in advance for private rooms, free Wi-Fi, pay Internet access, Hauptstrasse 23, in Matten, 15-minute walk from either train station, tel. 033-822-1961, fax 033-823-3261, www.balmers.com, mail@balmers.ch). They also have private rooms in an adjacent guest house (Db-130 SF, Tb-165 SF, Qb-220 SF).

$ Interlaken Hostel, opened in 2012, isn't your cheapest option, but it's convenient (right next to the Ost train station), huge (with 220 beds), thoroughly modern, and full of daylight. It also offers plenty of amenities (bed in 6-bed dorm-39 SF, bed in 4-bed

GIMMELWALD

dorm-43 SF, Sb-121 SF, Db-134-138 SF, includes sheets, all rooms have sinks, restaurant, swimming pool, game room, lockers, Internet access and Wi-Fi, check-in 15:00-24:00, Untere Bönigstrasse 3, tel. 033-826-1090, www.youthhostel.ch/interlaken, interlaken@youthhostel.ch).

$ **Happy Inn Lodge,** above the lively, noisy Brasserie 17 restaurant, has 16 cheap backpacker rooms and two doubles with private baths; come here as a last resort only if you belong to the young-and-scrappy set (bed with bedding in 4- to 8-bed dorm-22-24 SF, S-32-60 SF, D-52-80 SF, Db-84-104 SF, breakfast-8-9 SF, no membership required, no curfew, pay Internet access, free Wi-Fi, bus pass, 5-minute walk from West Station at Rosenstrasse 17, tel. 033-822-3225, fax 033-822-3268, www.brasserie17.ch, info@happyinn.com).

Eating in Interlaken

In Unterseen, the Old Town Across the River

Restaurant Bären, in a classic low-ceilinged building with cozy indoor and fine outdoor seating, is a great value for *Rösti,* fondue, raclette, fish, traditional sausage, and salads (20-30-SF plates including fondue for one, Cordon Bleu is popular; open Tue-Thu 16:30-23:30, Fri-Sun 10:30-23:30 or later—but may close 14:00-17:30 in off-season, closed Mon; from West Station, turn left on Bahnhofstrasse, cross the river, and go several blocks to Seestrasse 2; tel. 033-822-7526).

Goldener Anker is *the* local hangout—with smokers lingering outside, a pool table inside, and a few unsavory types. If you think Interlaken is sterile, you haven't been to the "Golden Anchor." Jeannette serves and René cooks, just as they have for 25 years. This place, with its "melody rock and blues" ambience, sometimes hosts small concerts and has actually launched some of Switzerland's top bands (hearty 15-25-SF salads, fresh vegetables, 3 courses for 15-20 SF, daily from 16:00, Marktgasse 57, tel. 033-822-1672).

Ristorante West End is a reliable Italian place and a local favorite for *cucina casalinga* (20-SF pasta, 25-SF plates, no pizza, Mon-Sat 17:30-22:30, closed Sun, next to West Station and across the street from Migros at Rugenparkstrasse 2, tel. 033-822-1744).

Città Vecchia serves decent Italian with seating indoors or out, on a leafy square (16-22-SF pizzas, 20-28-SF pastas, 30-40-SF plates, daily 10:30-14:00 & 18:00-23:00, closed during the day Tue-Wed Oct-May, on main square in Unterseen at Untere Gasse 5, tel. 033-822-1754, Rinaldo).

GIMMELWALD

On or near Höheweg

Interlaken's main drag, Höheweg, is lined with eateries. Tourists dampen the local ambience, but you have plenty of options.

Sirinya's Thai Restaurant is run by charming Sirinya, who serves great Thai dishes and popular spring rolls at reasonable prices (20-25-SF plates, Tue-Sat 16:00-23:30, Sun 16:00-22:00, closed Mon, at the recommended Hotel Lötschberg, General-Guisan-Strasse 31, tel. 033-821-6535).

Metropole Hotel's "Top O'Met," capping Interlaken's 18-story aesthetic nightmare, is actually a decent café/restaurant serving traditional and modern food at down-to-earth prices. For just 6 SF, you can enjoy a glass of wine and awesome views from an indoor or outdoor table (25-SF lunch deals Mon-Sat include two courses and coffee, 25-35-SF dinner plates, daily 11:30-24:00, no hot food 14:00-18:00 or after 22:00, Höheweg 37, just step into the Metropole Hotel and go up the elevator as far as you can, tel. 033-828-6666).

Supermarkets

Interlaken's two big supermarkets sell picnic supplies and also have reasonable self-service restaurants: **Migros** is across the street from West Station (Mon-Thu 8:00-18:30, Fri 8:00-21:00, Sat 7:30-17:00, closed Sun), while the **Co-op** is across the river from West Station, on your right (same hours as Migros except Mon-Thu until 19:00). The only grocery store open late at night is **Co-op Pronto** (daily 6:00-22:30, 30 yards west of TI on Höheweg).

Interlaken Connections

There are a few long-distance trains from Interlaken—you'll generally transfer in **Bern**. Train info: toll tel. 0900-300-300 or www.rail.ch.

From Interlaken Ost by Train to: Bern (2/hour, 55 minutes, some with change in Spiez), **Spiez** (3/hour, 25 minutes), **Brienz** (2/hour, 20 minutes), **Zürich** and **Zürich Airport** (2/hour, 2-2.5 hours, most with transfer in Bern or Spiez), **Luzern** (2/hour, 2 hours direct, 2.5 hours with 1-2 changes), **Lugano** (hourly, 4.75 hours, 1-2 changes), **Zermatt** (hourly, 2.25 hours, transfer in Spiez and Visp), **Florence** (5/day, 5.5-6 hours, 2-3 changes), **Venice** (6/day, 6-8.5 hours, 2-4 changes), **Nice** (4/day, 8.5-10 hours, 2-4 changes), **Paris** (9/day, 5-6 hours, 1-2 changes).

From Interlaken to the Lauterbrunnen Valley: To reach the heart of the valley, drive or take the train to **Lauterbrunnen** (train leaves hourly from Interlaken's Ost Station, 20 minutes). You cannot drive to Gimmelwald (park at the cable-car station near Stechelberg and ride up on the lift; see page 1385) or to Mürren

GIMMELWALD

or Kleine Scheidegg (park in Lauterbrunnen and take the cable car to Mürren or the train to Kleine Scheidegg). For more details, see "Lauterbrunnen Valley Connections" on page 1384.

Lauterbrunnen

Lauterbrunnen is the valley's commercial center and transportation hub. In addition to its train station and cable car, the one-street town is just big enough to have all the essential services (bank, post office, bike rental, launderette, and so on)—plus several hotels and hostels. It's idyllic, in spite of the busy road that slices it in two. Sitting under sheer cliffs at the base of the valley, with its signature waterfall spurting mightily out from the cliff (floodlit at night), Lauterbrunnen is a fine springboard for Jungfrau and Schilthorn adventures. But for spending the night, I still prefer Gimmelwald or Mürren, perched on the ledge above the valley.

Orientation to Lauterbrunnen

Tourist Information: Stop by the friendly TI to check the weather forecast, find out about guided walks and events, and buy hiking maps or any regional train or lift tickets you need (June-mid-Sept daily 9:00-12:00 & 13:30-18:00, off-season Mon-Fri 9:00-12:00 & 13:30-17:00, closed Sat-Sun, located on the main street a block up from the train station, tel. 033-856-8568, www.mylauterbrunnen. com).

Arrival in Lauterbrunnen: The slick, modern train station has lockers and is across the main street from the cable-car station. Go left as you exit the station to find the TI. Drivers can find parking in the large multistory pay lot behind the station (2 SF/2 hours, 10 SF/9-24 hours, www.jungfraubahn.ch).

Helpful Hints

Medical Help: Dr. Bruno Durrer, who has a clinic (with pharmacy) near the Jungfrau Hotel (look for *Arzt* sign), is good and very busy. He splits his time between seeing patients at his main office here, spending a couple of days a week up in Mürren, and buzzing around the region in helicopters to rescue injured adventure-seekers. He and his associate both speak English (tel. 033-856-2626, answered 24/7).

Money: Several ATMs are along the main street, including one immediately across from the train station.

Internet and Laundry: Two places are within a short walk of each other in the town center: The **Valley Hostel** is auto-

(margin) GIMMELWALD

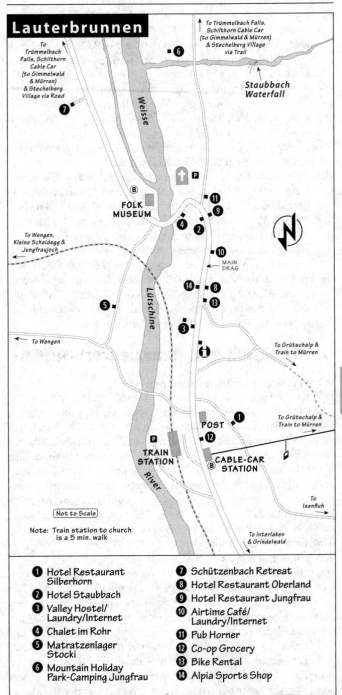

Lauterbrunnen

To Trümmelbach Falls, Schilthorn Cable Car (to Gimmelwald & Mürren) & Stechelberg Village via Road

To Trümmelbach Falls, Schilthorn Cable Car (to Gimmelwald & Mürren) & Stechelberg Village via Trail

Staubbach Waterfall

Weisse

Lütschine

River

FOLK MUSEUM

MAIN DRAG

To Wengen, Kleine Scheidegg & Jungfraujoch

To Wengen

To Grütschalp & Train to Mürren

To Grütschalp & Train to Mürren

POST

TRAIN STATION

CABLE-CAR STATION

To Isenfluh

To Interlaken & Grindelwald

GIMMELWALD

Not to Scale

Note: Train station to church is a 5 min. walk

1. Hotel Restaurant Silberhorn
2. Hotel Staubbach
3. Valley Hostel/ Laundry/Internet
4. Chalet im Rohr
5. Matratzenlager Stocki
6. Mountain Holiday Park-Camping Jungfrau
7. Schützenbach Retreat
8. Hotel Restaurant Oberland
9. Hotel Restaurant Jungfrau
10. Airtime Café/ Laundry/Internet
11. Pub Horner
12. Co-op Grocery
13. Bike Rental
14. Alpia Sports Shop

mated (Internet access-2.50 SF/15 minutes, launderette-5 SF/load, includes soap, May-Oct daily 9:00-22:00, shorter hours Nov-April, don't open dryer door until machine is finished or you'll have to pay another 5 SF to start it again, tel. 033-855-2008); **Airtime** is fully staffed (Internet access-5 minutes free, 2 SF/15 minutes, pay Wi-Fi, self-service laundry-10 SF/load, full-service laundry-25 SF/load, daily 9:00-19:00, closed Nov).

Grocery Store: The **Co-op** is on the main street across from the station (Mon-Sat 9:00-19:00, closed Sun).

Bike Rental: You can rent mountain bikes at **Imboden Bike** on the main street (25 SF/half-day, 35 SF/day; full-suspension—35 SF/half-day, 55 SF/day; daily July-Aug 8:30-20:00, Sept-June 9:00-18:30 except closed for lunch 12:00-13:00 Oct-May, tel. 033-855-2114, www.imboden-bike.ch). They work with the bike-rental shop in Mürren, allowing you to pick up a bike here and drop it off there—or vice versa (8 SF supplement).

Sports Gear: You can rent hiking boots, skis, and snowboards at the **Alpia Sports** shop (daily 8:00-12:30 & 13:30-19:00, shorter hours on weekends and in fall, closed in May, at Hotel Crystal, tel. 033-855-3292, www.alpiasport.ch).

Activities in and near Lauterbrunnen

Hikers' Loop from Lauterbrunnen

If you're staying in Lauterbrunnen, consider this ambitious but great day plan: Ride the cable car to Grütschalp, walk along the ridge to Mürren, take the cable car up to the Schilthorn and back down to Mürren, ride the funicular up to Allmendhubel, hike the North Face Trail to Gimmelwald, take the lift down to the Schilthornbahn station near Stechelberg, catch the PostBus to Trümmelbach Falls, and walk through the valley back into Lauterbrunnen. Make it more or less strenuous or time-consuming by swapping lifts and hikes (all described later in this chapter). Or rent a mountain bike and do a wheeled variation on this (parking your bike in Mürren for the Schilthorn trip).

▲Trümmelbach Falls

If all the waterfalls have you intrigued, sneak a behind-the-scenes look at the valley's most powerful, Trümmelbach Falls. You'll ride an elevator up through the mountain and climb through several caves (wet, with lots of stairs, and—for some—claustrophobic) to see the melt from the Eiger, Mönch, and Jungfrau grinding like God's bandsaw through the mountain at the rate of up to 5,200 gallons a second (that's 20,000 liters—nearly double the beer consumption at Oktoberfest). The upper area is the best; if your legs ache, skip the lower falls and ride down on the elevator.

GIMMELWALD

Cost and Hours: 11 SF, daily July-Aug 8:30-18:00, April-June and Sept-mid-Nov 9:00-17:00, closed mid-Nov-March, tel. 033-855-3232, www.truemmelbach.ch.

Getting There: It's about halfway between Lauterbrunnen and the Schilthornbahn cable-car station; from either, it's a short ride on the PostBus or a 45-minute walk.

▲▲Cloudy-Day Lauterbrunnen Valley Walks

Try the easy trails and pleasant walks along the floor of the Lauterbrunnen Valley. For a smell-the-cows-and-flowers lowland walk—ideal for a cloudy day, weary body, or tight budget—take the PostBus from Lauterbrunnen town to the Schilthornbahn cable-car station near Stechelberg (left of river), and follow the riverside trail back for three basically level miles to Staubbach Falls, near the town church (you can reverse the route, but it's a very gradual uphill to Stechelberg). A trail was cut into the cliff to take visitors up "behind" Staubbach Falls (at the uphill end of Lauterbrunnen town). But, depending on the wind, the trail may be closed short of the actual falls.

You don't ever need to walk along the road. A fine, paved, car-free riverside path goes all the way along the valley (popular with bikers). Detour to Trümmelbach Falls (described earlier) en route (it's a 45-minute walk from the Schilthornbahn station to Trümmelbach Falls, and another 45 minutes to Lauterbrunnen). In this "Valley of Many Waterfalls" (literally), you'll see cone-like mounds piled against the sides of the cliffs, formed by centuries of rocks hurled by tumbling rivers. Look up to see BASE jumpers between Trümmelbach Falls and Lauterbrunnen.

If you're staying in Gimmelwald, try this plan: Take the Schilthornbahn lift down to the station near Stechelberg (5 minutes), then walk 1.5 hours along the river to Lauterbrunnen (side-tripping to Trümmelbach Falls after 45 minutes). To return to Gimmelwald from Lauterbrunnen, take the cable car up to Grütschalp (10 minutes), then either walk to Gimmelwald (1.5 hours) or take the train to Mürren (10 minutes). From Mürren, it's a downhill walk (30 minutes) to Gimmelwald. (This loop trip can be reversed or started at any point along the way—such as Lauterbrunnen or Mürren.)

Hang Out with BASE Jumpers

In recent years, the Lauterbrunnen Valley has become an El Dorado of BASE jumping (parachuting off cliffs), and each season thrill-seekers hike to the top of a cliff, leap off—falling as long as they can (this provides the rush)—and then pull the ripcord to release a tiny parachute, hoping it will break their fall and a gust won't dash them against the walls of the valley. (For a fascinating look at this sport, search for "BASE jumping Lauterbrunnen" at www.youtube.com.)

Some Swiss consider BASE jumpers reckless and don't respect them. But, like other adventure sports, it is getting safer and more accepted. To learn more, talk with the jumpers themselves, who congregate at the **Pub Horner,** at the upper end of town (near the waterfall). This is the grittiest place in Lauterbrunnen, providing cheap beds and meals for BASE jumpers and the only real after-dark scene in town. Locals, jumpers, and stray tourists gather here in the pub each evening (9 rooms, bunks-32 SF, D-86 SF, cheaper apartments, no breakfast, free Wi-Fi and Internet access for customers, dancing nightly from 22:00 upstairs, tel. 033-855-1673, www.hornerpub.ch, mail@hornerpub.ch, run by Gertsch Ferdinand). Their kitchen sells cheap pastas and raclette, and puts out a nightly salad bar (8-14-SF meals, BBQ dinner-15 SF in summer).

Lauterbrunnen Valley Folk Museum (Talmuseum Lauterbrunnen)

This interesting museum shows off the region's folk culture and two centuries of mountaineering from all the towns of this valley. You'll see lots of lace, exhibits on cheese and woodworking, cowbells, and classic old photos.

Cost and Hours: 3 SF, free with Visitors Card given by local hotels, mid-June-mid-Oct Tue and Thu-Sun 14:00-17:30; closed Mon, Wed, and off-season; English handout, just over bridge and below church at the far end of Lauterbrunnen town, tel. 033-855-3586, www.talmuseumlauterbrunnen.ch.

Sleeping in Lauterbrunnen

(2,612 feet, 1 SF = about $1.10, country code: 41)

$$$ Hotel Silberhorn is a big, formal, 32-room, three-star hotel that still manages to feel family-run. It has generous public spaces and a recommended, elegant-for-Lauterbrunnen restaurant just above the quiet lift station across from the train station. Almost every double room comes with a fine view and balcony (Sb-89-109 SF, Db-159-179 SF, bigger "superior" Db-180-209 SF, Internet access, Wi-Fi, tel. 033-856-2210, www.silberhorn.com, info@silberhorn.com).

$$$ Hotel Staubbach, a big, Old World place, is one of the oldest hotels in the valley (1890). The staff is friendly, and the hotel has the casual feel of a national park lodge, with 30 simple and comfortable rooms. It's family-friendly and has a kids' play area. Rooms that face up the valley have incredible views, though you may hear the happy crowd across the meadow at Pub Horner or the church bells chiming on the hour. If the weather's bad, you can watch a DVD of my Switzerland TV show in the lounge (S-100 SF, Sb-120 SF, D-120 SF, Db-150-170 SF, Tb-210-240 SF, Qb-240 SF, closed Nov-mid-April, elevator, free Wi-Fi, 4 blocks up from

GIMMELWALD

station on the left, tel. 033-855-5454, fax 033-855-5484, www.staubbach.com, hotel@staubbach.com, run by American Craig and his Swiss wife, Corinne).

$ Valley Hostel is practical and comfortable, offering 70 inexpensive beds for quieter travelers of all ages, with a pleasant garden and the welcoming Abegglen family: Martha, Alfred, Stefan, and Fränzi (D with bunk beds-66 SF, twin D-66 SF, beds in larger family-friendly rooms-28 SF/person, breakfast-6 SF, rooms have no sinks, free kitchen, Internet access, Wi-Fi, coin-op laundry, reception open 8:00-12:00 & 15:00-22:00, 2 blocks up from train station, tel. & fax 033-855-2008, www.valleyhostel.ch, info@valleyhostel.ch).

$ Chalet im Rohr—a creaky, old, woody firetrap of a place—has oodles of character (and lots of Asian groups, paragliders, and BASE jumpers). It offers 50 beds in big one- to four-bed rooms that share six showers (28 SF/person, no breakfast, cash only, common kitchen, free Wi-Fi, across from church on main drag, tel. & fax 033-855-2182, www.chaletimrohr.ch, bookings@chaletimrohr.ch, Elsbeth von Allmen-Müller).

$ Matratzenlager Stocki is rustic and humble, with the cheapest beds in town (15 SF with sheets in easygoing little 25-bed co-ed dorm with kitchen, closed Nov-Dec, across river from station, tel. 033-855-1754, run by elderly Frau Graf, who often ignores the phone).

$ *Camping:* Two campgrounds just south of town provide beds in dorms and 2- and 4-bed bungalows (rentable sheets, kitchen facilities, cash only, big English-speaking tour groups). **Mountain Holiday Park-Camping Jungfrau,** romantically situated beyond Staubbach Falls, is huge and well-organized by Hans. It also has fancy cabins and mobile homes you can rent by the week (30-35-SF beds, tel. 033-856-2010, www.camping-jungfrau.ch). **Schützenbach Retreat,** on the left just past Lauterbrunnen toward Stechelberg, is a simpler campground (bed in 6- and 12-bed rooms-17 SF, often full with groups, tel. 033-855-1268, www.schuetzenbach.ch).

Eating in Lauterbrunnen

At **Hotel Restaurant Oberland,** Mark (Aussie) and Ursula (Swiss) Nolan take pride in serving tasty, good-value meals from a fun menu. It's a high-energy place with lots of tourists and a huge front porch good for lingering into the evening (17-SF pizzas, 20-25-SF main courses, traditional Swiss dishes, daily 11:30-21:00, tel. 033-855-1241).

Hotel Restaurant Jungfrau, along the main street, offers a wide range of specialties, including fondue and *Rösti*, served by a friendly staff. Their terrace has a great valley view (daily 12:00-14:00 & 18:00-21:00, tel. 033-855-3434, run by Brigitte Melliger).

Hotel Restaurant Silberhorn is the local choice for a fancy meal out. Call to reserve a view table (18-SF salad plate, 23-35-SF main dishes, daily from 18:00, classy indoor and outdoor seating, above the cable-car station, tel. 033-856-2210).

Airtime Café feels like an alpine Starbucks with hot drinks, homemade treats, breakfast, simple lunches, and light early dinners (7.50-SF sandwiches made to order, 6-SF meat pies). Besides food, they offer other services, including laundry, Internet access, Wi-Fi, and an English-language swap library. They can also help you book adventure-sport activities (May-Oct daily 9:00-19:00, shorter hours off-season, closed Nov, tel. 033-855-1515, www.airtime.ch, Daniela and Beni).

Lauterbrunnen Valley Connections

The valley-floor towns of Lauterbrunnen and Stechelberg have connections by mountain train, bus, and cable car to the traffic-free villages, peaks, and hikes high above. Prices and trip durations given are per leg unless otherwise noted.

From Lauterbrunnen by Train to: Interlaken (hourly, 20 minutes, 7.20 SF), **Wengen** (1-2/hour, 15 minutes, 6.40 SF), continues to **Kleine Scheidegg** (hourly, 30 minutes, 30 SF), where you change to a different train to reach the **Jungfraujoch** (2/hour, 50 minutes, 66 SF) or **Grindelwald** (2/hour, 30 minutes, 32 SF).

By Cable Car to: Grütschalp (2/hour, 10 minutes), where you can catch a train to **Mürren** (2/hour, 10 minutes); total trip time 30 minutes, total cost 10.40 SF.

By PostBus to: Schilthornbahn cable-car station (buses depart with the arrival of trains in Lauterbrunnen, 15-minute ride, 4 SF, covered by Swiss Pass), continues to **Stechelberg town.**

By Car to: Schilthornbahn cable-car station (10-minute drive, parking lot: 2 SF/2 hours, 6 SF/day, cash only).

From Schilthornbahn cable-car station near Stechelberg to: Gimmelwald (2/hour, 5 minutes, 5.80 SF), continues to **Mürren** (2/hour, 10 minutes, 10.40 SF) and the **Schilthorn** (2/hour, 20 minutes, 55.20 SF). The cable car runs up from the valley station—and down from Mürren—at :25 and :55 past the hour (5:55-19:55; after 19:55, runs only once an hour until 23:45 Sun-Thu, until 24:55 Fri-Sat). From Gimmelwald to both Mürren and the valley station, the cable car runs at :00 and :30 (6:00-20:00; after 20:00 runs only once an hour).

Gimmelwald

Saved from developers by its "avalanche zone" classification, Gimmelwald was (before modern tourism) one of the poorest places in Switzerland. Its traditional economy was stuck in the hay, and its farmers—unable to make it in their disadvantaged trade—survived only on a trickle of visitors and on Swiss government subsidies (and working the ski lifts in the winter). For some travelers, there's little to see in the village. Others (like me) enjoy a fascinating day sitting on a bench and learning why they say, "If heaven isn't what it's cracked up to be, send me back to Gimmelwald."

Take a walk through the town. The huge, sheer cliff face that dominates your mountain views is the Schwarzmönch ("Black Monk"). The three peaks above (or behind) it are, left to right, Eiger, Mönch, and Jungfrau. While Gimmelwald's population dropped in the last century from 300 to about 120 residents, traditions survive. Most Gimmelwalders have one of two last names: von Allmen or Feuz. They are tough and proud. Raising hay in this rugged terrain is labor-intensive. One family harvests enough to feed only about 15 cows. But they'd have it no other way, and, unlike the absentee-landlord town of Mürren, Gimmelwald is locally owned. (When word got out that urban planners wanted to develop Gimmelwald into a town of 1,000, locals pulled some strings to secure the town's bogus avalanche-zone building code. Today, unlike nearby resort towns, Gimmelwald's population is the same all year.) Those same folks are happy the masses go to touristy and commercialized Grindelwald, just over the Kleine Scheidegg ridge. Don't confuse Gimmelwald and Grindelwald—they couldn't be more different.

Thanks to the leadership of schoolteachers Olle and Maria, and their son Sven, Gimmelwald has a helpful little website (www.gimmelwald.ch), where you can check out photos of the town in different seasons, get directions for 11 of the best hikes out of town, and see all the latest on activities and rooms for rent.

Getting to Gimmelwald

To get from Lauterbrunnen to Gimmelwald, you have two options:

1. Schilthornbahn Cable Car: The faster, easier way—best in bad weather or at the end of a long day with lots of luggage—is to drive. It's 10 minutes from Lauterbrunnen (or 30 minutes from Interlaken) to the Schilthornbahn cable-car station near Stechelberg (parking lot: 2 SF/2 hours, 6 SF/day, cash only).

If you don't have a car, ride the PostBus from Lauterbrunnen to the Schilthornbahn cable-car station (buses depart with the ar-

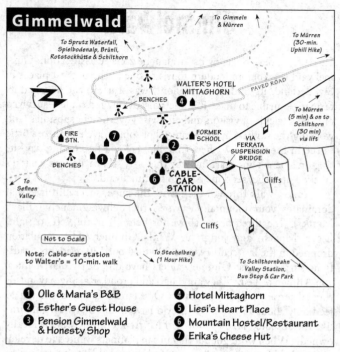

Gimmelwald

To Gimmeln
& Mürren

To Mürren
(30-min.
Uphill Hike)

To Sprutz Waterfall,
Spielbodenalp, Brünli,
Rotstockhütte & Schilthorn

PAVED ROAD

WALTER'S HOTEL
MITTAGHORN

BENCHES

To Mürren
(5 min) & on to
Schilthorn
(30 min)
via lift

FIRE
STN.

FORMER
SCHOOL

VIA
FERRATA
SUSPENSION
BRIDGE

BENCHES

CABLE-
CAR
STATION

Cliffs

To
Sefinen
Valley

Cliffs

Not to Scale

Note: Cable-car station
to Walter's is 10-min. walk

To Stechelberg
(1 Hour Hike)

To Schilthornbahn
Valley Station,
Bus Stop & Car Park

❶ Olle & Maria's B&B
❷ Esther's Guest House
❸ Pension Gimmelwald
   & Honesty Shop
❹ Hotel Mittaghorn
❺ Liesi's Heart Place
❻ Mountain Hostel/Restaurant
❼ Erika's Cheese Hut

GIMMELWALD

rival of trains in Lauterbrunnen, 15-minute ride, 4 SF, www.post-auto.ch).

From Schilthornbahn, the cable car whisks you in five thrilling minutes up to Gimmelwald (2/hour at :25 and :55 past the hour 5:55-19:55; after 19:55, runs only once an hour until 23:45 Sun-Thu, until 24:55 Fri-Sat; 5.80 SF, Gimmelwald is the first stop). Note that the Schilthornbahn cable car is closed for servicing for a week in early May and also from mid-November through early December. If you're here during this time, you'll ride the cargo cable car directly from the valley floor up to Mürren, where a small bus shuttles you down to Gimmelwald.

2. Grütschalp Cable-Car and Mürren Train: This is the more scenic route. Catch the cable car from Lauterbrunnen to Grütschalp. As you glide from Lauterbrunnen upward, notice the bed of the 100-year-old funicular train track that the new cable-car recently replaced. At Grütschalp, a special vintage train will roll you along the incredibly scenic cliffside to Mürren (total trip from Lauterbrunnen to Mürren: 30 minutes, 10.40 SF, www.jungfrau-bahn.ch). From there, either walk to the middle of Mürren and take a left down a moderately steep paved path 30 minutes to Gimmelwald, or walk 10 minutes across Mürren to catch the cable car down to Gimmelwald (5.80 SF).

Self-Guided Walk

Welcome to Gimmelwald

Gimmelwald, though tiny, with one zigzag street, offers a fine look at a traditional Swiss mountain community.

• *Start this quick walking tour at the...*

Cable-Car Station: When the lift came in the 1960s, the village's back end became its front door. Gimmelwald was, and still is, a farm village. Stepping off the cable car and starting up the path, you see a sweet little hut. Set on stilts to keep out mice, the hut was used for storing cheese (the rocks on the rooftop here and throughout the town are not decorative—they keep the shingles on through wild storms). Behind the cheese hut stands the village schoolhouse, long the largest structure in town (in Catholic Swiss towns, the biggest building is the church; in Protestant towns, it's the school). But in 2010, classes ceased. Gimmelwald's students now go to school in Lauterbrunnen, and the building is being used as a chapel when the Protestant pastor makes his monthly visit. Up and across from the station, just beyond the little playground, is the recommended Mountain Hostel and Restaurant.

• *Walk up the lane 50 yards, past the town's Dalí-esque art gallery (Who's showing in the phone booth?), to Gimmelwald's...*

"Times Square": The yellow alpine "street sign" shows where you are, the altitude (1,370 meters, or 4,470 feet), how many hours *(Std.)* and minutes it takes to walk to nearby points, and which tracks are serious hiking paths (marked with red and white, and further indicated along the way with red and white patches of paint on stones). You're surrounded by buildings that were built as duplexes, divided vertically right down the middle to house two separate families. Look for the Honesty Shop at Pension Gimmelwald, which features local crafts and little edibles for sale.

The writing on the post office building is a folksy blessing: "Summer brings green, winter brings snow. The sun greets the day, the stars greet the night. This house will protect you from rain, cold, and wind. May God give us his blessings." Small as Gimmelwald is, it still has daily mail service. The postman comes down from Mürren each day (by golf cart in summer, sled in winter) to deliver mail and pick up letters at the communal mailbox. The date on this building indicates when it was built or rebuilt (1911). Gimmelwald has a strict building code: for instance, shutters can only be painted certain colors.

• *From this tiny intersection, walk away from the cable-car station and follow the town's...*

Main Street: Walk up the road past the gnome greeting committee on the right. Notice the announcement board: one side for tourist news, the other for local news (e.g., deals on chainsaw sharpening, upcoming shooting competitions). Cross the street and peek into the big barn, dated 1995. To the left of the door is a cow-scratcher. Swiss cows have legal rights (e.g., in the winter, they must be taken out for exercise at least three times a week). This big barn is built in a modern style. Traditionally, barns were small (like those on the hillside high above) and closer to the hay. But with trucks and paved roads, hay can be moved more easily, and farm businesses need more cows to be viable. Still, even a well-run big farm hopes just to break even. The industry survives only with government subsidies. As you wander, notice private garden patches. Until recently, most locals grew their own vegetables—often enough to provide most of their family's needs.

• *Go just beyond the next barn. On your right is the...*

Water Fountain/Trough: This is the site of the town's historic water supply—still perfectly drinkable. Village kids love to bathe and wage water wars here when the cows aren't drinking from it. Detour left down a lane about 50 yards (along a wooden fence), passing the lovingly tended pea-patch gardens of the woman with the best green thumb in the village (on your left). Go to the next trough and the oldest building in town, Husmättli, from 1658. (Most of the town's 17th-century buildings are on the road zig-zagging below town.) Study the log-cabin construction. Many are built without nails. The wood was logged up the valley and cut on the water-powered village mill (also below town). Gimmelwald heats with wood, and since the wood needs to age a couple of years to burn well, it's stacked everywhere.

From here (at the water trough), look up at the solar panels on the house of Olle and Maria. A Swiss building code requires that new structures provide 30 percent of their own power, part of a green energy policy. Switzerland is gradually moving away from nuclear power; its last reactor is supposed to close in 2034.

• *Return to the main paved road and continue uphill.*

Twenty yards along, on the left, the first house has a bunch of scythes hanging above the sharpening stone. Farmers pound, rather than grind, the blade to get it razor-sharp for efficient cutting. Feel a blade...carefully.

A few steps farther, notice the cute **cheese hut** on the right. This is Erika's hut, and she loves to sell her alpine cheese to visitors (an arrow points to her house). Its front is an alpine art gallery with nail shoes for flower pots. Nail shoes grip the steep, wet fields—this is critical for safety, especially if you're carrying a sharp scythe. Even today, farmers buy metal tacks and fasten them to boots. The hut is full of strong cheese—up to three years old.

Look up. In the summer, a few goats are kept here (rather than in the high alp) to provide families with fresh milk (about a half-gallon per day per goat). The farmers fence off the fields, letting the goats eat only the grass that's most difficult to harvest.

On the left (at the *B&B* sign) is Olle and Maria's home. Maria runs the **Lilliput shop** (the "smallest shop with the greatest gifts"—handmade delights from the town and region; just ring the bell and meet Maria). She does a booming trade in sugar-coated almonds.

• *Fifty yards farther along is the...*

Alpenrose: At the old schoolhouse, you might see big ceremonial cowbells hanging under the uphill eave. These swing from the necks of cows during the procession from the town to the high Alps (mid-June) and back down (mid-Sept).

• *At the end of town, pause where a lane branches off to the left, leading into the dramatic...*

Sefinen Valley: All the old homes in town are made from wood cut from the left-hand side of this valley (shady side, slow-growing, better timber) and milled at a water-powered sawmill on the valley floor.

• *A few steps ahead, the road switches back at the...*

Gimmelwald Fire Station: The *Föhnwacht Reglement* sheet, posted on the fire-station building, explains rules to keep the village from burning down during the fierce dry wind of the Föhn season. During this time, there's a 24-hour fire watch, and even smoking cigarettes outdoors is forbidden. Mürren was devastated by a Föhn-caused fire in the 1920s. Because villagers in Gimmelwald—mindful of the quality of their volunteer fire department—are particularly careful with fire, the town has not had a terrible fire in its history (a rare feat among alpine villages).

Check out the other posted notices. This year's Swiss Army calendar tells reservists when and where to go (in all four official Swiss languages). Every Swiss male does a 22-week stint in the military, then a few days a year in the reserves until about age 30. The *Schiessübungen* poster details the shooting exercises required this year. In keeping with the William Tell heritage, each Swiss man does shooting practice annually for the military (or spends three days in jail).

• *Take the...*

High Road to Hotel Mittaghorn: The resort town of Mürren hovers in the distance. And high on the left, notice the hay field with terraces. These are from WWII days, when Switzerland, wanting self-sufficiency, required all farmers to grow potatoes. Today, this field is a festival of alpine flowers in season (best at this altitude in May and June).

• *Our walk is over. A peaceful set of benches, just off the lane on the downhill side, lets you savor the view. From Hotel Mittaghorn, you can return to Gimmelwald's "Times Square" via the path with the steps cutting downhill.*

Nightlife in Gimmelwald

These two places provide after-dark entertainment in Gimmelwald. The **Mountain Hostel and Restaurant**, where Petra and her staff serve drinks nightly, is lively with locals and backpackers alike. It's easy to make friends here and share travel experiences. There's a pool table and lots of youthful impromptu fun. **Pension Gimmelwald** (which is next door on the uphill side) offers a mellower scene with an old-time bar, cozy lounge, and view terrace. And from almost anywhere in Gimmelwald, you can watch the sun tuck the mountaintops into bed as the moon rises over the Jungfrau. If that's not enough nightlife, stay in Interlaken.

Sleeping in Gimmelwald

(4,593 feet, 1 SF = about $1.10, country code: 41)

Gimmelwald is my home base in the Berner Oberland. To inhale the Alps and really hold them in, you'll want to sleep high in Gimmelwald, too. Poor and pleasantly stuck in the past, the village has only a few accommodations options—all of them quirky and memorable. Rates include entry to the public swimming pool in nearby Mürren (at the Sportzentrum—see page 1393).

Be warned: You'll meet a lot of my readers in this town. This is a disappointment to some; others enjoy the chance to be part of a fun extended family.

$$ At Olle and Maria's B&B, the Eggimanns rent two rooms—Gimmelwald's most comfortable—in their quirky but alpine-sleek chalet. Having raised three kids of their own here, Maria and Olle offer visitors a rare and intimate peek at this community (D-130 SF, Db with kitchenette-190 SF for 2 or 200 SF for 3 people, optional breakfast-20 SF, 3-night minimum, cash only, guarantee your reservation with PayPal, free Wi-Fi, laundry service; from cable car, continue straight for 200 yards along the town's only road, B&B on left; tel. 033-855-3575, oeggimann@bluewin.ch).

$$ Esther's Guest House, overlooking the village's main intersection, rents seven clean, basic, and comfortable rooms, three of which have private bathrooms and share a generous lounge and kitchen (S-55-75 SF, big D-130 SF, Db-130 SF, big T-150 SF, Tb-180-190 SF, Q-180 SF, Qb-200-210 SF, family room with private bath for up to 5 people-230 SF, cash preferred, breakfast-15 SF, 2-night minimum, pay Internet access, free Wi-Fi, low ceilings, tel. 033-855-5488, fax 033-855-5492, www.esthersguesthouse.ch, info@esthersguesthouse.ch). Esther, a bundle of entrepreneurial energy, also rents two four-person **apartments** with kitchenettes next door (3-night minimum, see website for details).

$$ Pension Gimmelwald is an old, low-ceilinged farmhouse converted into a family-style inn, with 12 simple rooms, a restaurant, and a cozy bar. Its six-bed dorm attracts more mature guests than your usual hostel. Its terrace, overlooking the Mountain Hostel, has gorgeous views across the valley (bed in 6-bed dorm-25 SF, S-60 SF, D-100 SF, T-150 SF, Q-185 SF, less in winter, 10 percent discount for 3 nights with this book, breakfast-12 SF, Wi-Fi, open June-mid-Oct and mid-Dec-mid-April, 2-minute walk up from cable-car station, tel. 033-855-1730, www.pensiongimmelwald.com, tsnewark@yahoo.com, Englishman David).

$$ At Liesi's Heart Place, friendly owner Liesi rents a little suite in her home with a view and terrace (Db-120 SF, Tb-150 SF, Qb-170 SF, minimum 2-night stay, at the town's water fountain find the little house about 100 feet to the left, tel. 033-841-0880, www.liesisheartplace.ch).

$ Hotel Mittaghorn is a classic creaky, thin-walled, alpine-style place with superb views. It's run by Walter Mittler, an elderly Swiss gentleman, with help from trusty Tim. The hotel has three rooms with private showers (first-come, first-served) and four rooms that share a coin-operated shower. Walter's guests-only dinner is the cheapest hot meal in the valley (S-54 SF, D-86 SF, T-129 SF, 6-SF surcharge per person for 1-night stays, cash only, simple but hearty 15-SF dinner at 19:30 by reservation only, free Internet access, open April-Oct, a five-minute climb up the path from the village center, tel. 033-855-1658, www.ricksteves.com/mittaghorn, mittaghorn@gmail.com—email answered May-Sept only). It's necessary to reconfirm by phone the day before your arrival. If no one's there when you arrive, look for a card in the hallway directing you to your room.

$ Mountain Hostel is a beehive of activity, as clean as its guests, cheap, and friendly. The hostel has low ceilings, a self-service kitchen, a mini-grocery, a bar, a free pool table, and healthy plumbing. It's mostly a college-age crowd; families and older travelers will probably feel more comfortable elsewhere. Petra Brunner, who lines the porch with flowers, runs this relaxed hostel with the help of its guests. Read the signs, respect Petra's rules, and leave it tidier than you found it. This is one of those rare spots where a congenial atmosphere spontaneously combusts as the piano plays, and spaghetti becomes communal as it cooks (28 SF/bed in 6- to 15-bed rooms, includes sheets, no breakfast, showers-1 SF, laundry-5 SF, pay Internet access and Wi-Fi, open mid-April-mid-Nov, 20 yards up the trail from lift station, reserve with credit card through website or by phone, tel. 033-855-1704, www.mountainhostel.com, info@mountainhostel.com). The hostel has a full-menu restaurant, described next.

Eating in Gimmelwald

Gimmelwald has two good eating options.

Mountain Hostel Restaurant is open for lunch and dinner and comes with fun, mountain-high energy and a youthful spirit (15-SF plates, popular 17-SF pizzas, daily 12:00-21:00). You can eat inside or with breathtaking views on the terrace.

Pension Gimmelwald Restaurant has a good, simple menu featuring local produce served in a rustic indoor dining room or on a jaw-dropping-view terrace. The atmosphere here is a little more jazz-and-blues mellow (13-22-SF main dishes, daily in summer 12:00-15:00 & 18:00-21:00, bar open until 23:00).

Picnic: Consider packing in a picnic meal from the larger towns. Mürren, a five-minute cable-car ride or a 30-minute hike up the hill, has good restaurants and a grocery (see "Eating in Mürren," later). If you need a few groceries and want to skip the hike to Mürren, you can buy the essentials—noodles, spaghetti sauce, and candy bars—at the Mountain Hostel's reception desk or the little Honesty Shop at Pension Gimmelwald. Farmers post signs to sell their produce. Farmer Erika sells meat, cheese, and eggs—and sometimes bread and milk—from her picturesque hut on the town's main lane (see "Self-Guided Walk," earlier).

Mürren

Pleasant as an alpine resort can be, Mürren is traffic-free and filled with cafés, souvenirs, old-timers with walking sticks, employees enjoying incentive trips, and snap-happy tourists. Its chalets are prefab-rustic. With help from a cliffside train, a funicular, and a cable car, hiking options are endless from Mürren. Sitting on a ledge 2,000 feet above the Lauterbrunnen Valley, surrounded by a fortissimo chorus of mountains, the town has all the comforts of home (for a price) without the pretentiousness of more famous resorts.

Historic Mürren, which dates from 1384, has been overwhelmed by development. Still, it's a peaceful town. There's no full-time doctor, no police officer (they call Lauterbrunnen if there's a problem), and no resident priest or pastor. (The Protestant church—up by the TI—posts a sign showing where the region's roving pastor preaches each Sunday.) There's not even enough business to keep a bakery open year-round (bread is baked down in

Lauterbrunnen and shipped up to the "bakery," which is open in-season only)—a clear indication that this town is either lively or completely dead, depending on the time of year. (Holiday population: 4,000. Permanent residents: 400.) Keep an eye open for the "Milch Express," a tiny cart that delivers fresh milk and eggs to hotels and homes throughout town.

Getting to Mürren

There are two ways to get to Mürren: on the train from Grütschalp (10 minutes, connects by 10-minute cable car to Lauterbrunnen, 30-minute total trip) or on the Schilthornbahn cable car from near Stechelberg (in the valley), which stops at Gimmelwald, Mürren, and continues up to the Schilthorn. The train and cable-car stations (which both have WCs and lockers) are at opposite ends of town.

Orientation to Mürren

Mürren perches high on a ledge, overlooking the Lauterbrunnen Valley. You can walk from one end of town to the other in about 10 minutes.

Tourist Information: Mürren's TI can help you find a room and gives hiking advice (July-mid-Sept daily 8:30-19:00, Thu until 20:00, shorter hours off-season, above the village, follow signs to *Sportzentrum,* tel. 033-856-8686, www.mymuerren.ch).

Helpful Hints

Money: An ATM is by the **Co-op** grocery in the middle of town. You can change money at the TI.

Internet Access: Connect at the **TI** (5 SF/15 minutes), at the **cable-car station** inside an old gondola (5 SF/15 minutes), or at the **Eiger Guesthouse** (4 SF/20 minutes, daily 8:00-23:00, across from the train station).

Laundry: Hotel Bellevue has a slick and modern little self-service launderette in its basement (5 SF/wash, 5 SF/dry, open 24/7).

Bike Rental: You can rent mountain bikes at **Stäger Sport** (25 SF/half-day, 35 SF/day, includes helmet, daily 9:00-18:00, closed late Oct-mid-May, in middle of town, tel. 033-855-2355, www.staegersport.ch). There's a bigger bike-rental place in Lauterbrunnen (Imboden Bike, described on page 1380).

R & R: The slick **Sportzentrum** (sports center) that houses the TI offers a world of indoor activities. The pool is free with the regional Visitors Card given by area hotels (July-mid-Sept daily 8:30-19:00, Thu until 20:00, Sun until 18:00; pool and sauna generally opens at 10:00 Tue-Wed and Fri, otherwise at 13:00; shorter hours off-season, closed May and Nov-mid-

GIMMELWALD

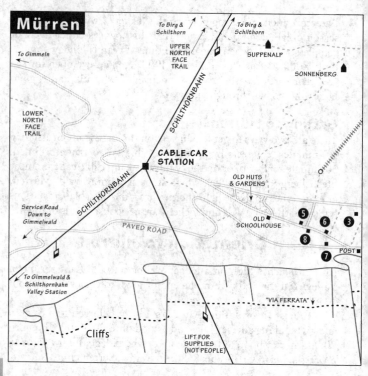

Dec, www.muerren.ch/sportzentrum). In season, they offer squash, mini-golf, table tennis, and a fitness room.

Yoga: Denise offers weekly yoga lessons in summer (off Chalet Fontana, mobile 078-642-3485).

Skiing and Snowboarding: The Mürren-Schilthorn ski area is the Berner Oberland's best place for experts, especially those eager to tackle the famous, nearly 10-mile-long Inferno run. The runs on top, especially the Kanonenrohr, are quite steep and have predictably good snow; lower areas cater to all levels, but can be icier. For rental gear, try the friendly, convenient **Ed Abegglen** shop (best prices, next to recommended Chalet Fontana, tel. 033-855-1245), **Alfred's Sporthaus** (good selection and decent prices, between ski school and Sportzentrum, tel. 033-855-3030), or **Stäger Sport** (one shop in Sportzentrum and another on the lower road near cable-car station, tel. 033-855-2330).

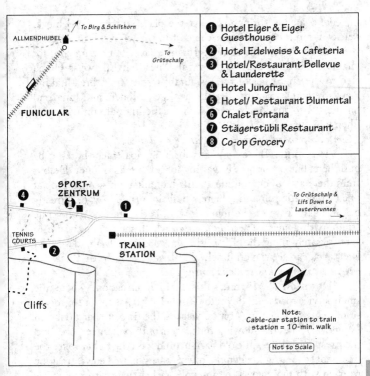

Self-Guided Walk

Welcome to Mürren

Mürren has long been a top ski resort, but a walk across town offers a glimpse into a time before ski lifts. This stroll takes you through town on the main drag, from the train station (where you'll arrive if coming from Lauterbrunnen) to the cable-car station, then back up to the Allmendhubel funicular station.

• Start at the...

Train Station: The first trains pulled into Mürren in 1891. (A circa-1911 car is permanently parked at Grütschalp's station.) A display case inside the station displays an original car from the narrow-gauge, horse-powered line that rolled fancy visitors from here into town. The current station, built in 1964, comes with impressive engineering for heavy cargo. Look out back, where a small truck can be loaded up, attached to the train, and driven away.

• Wander into town along the main road (take the lower, left fork) for a stroll under the...

Alpin Palace Hotel: This towering place was the "Grand Palace Hotel" until it burned in 1928. Today it's closed, and no one knows its future. The small wooden platform on the left—looking like a suicide springboard—is the place where snow-removal trucks dump their loads over the cliff in the winter. Look back at the meadow below the station: This is a favorite grazing spot for chamois (the animals, not the rags). Ahead, at Edelweiss Hotel, step to the far corner of the restaurant terrace for a breathtaking view stretching from the big three (Eiger, Mönch, and Jungfrau) on the left to the lonely cattle farm in the high alp on the right. Then look down.

• *Continue toward an empty lot with a grand view.*

Viewpoints: There are plans for a big apartment-hotel to be built here, but the project is waiting for investment money. Detour from the main street around the cliff-hanging tennis court. Stop at one of the little romantic shelters built into the far wall. Directly below, at the base of the modern wall, is the start of a one-mile "trail" with a steel cable *(via ferrata),* which mountaineers use to venture safely along the cliff all the way to Gimmelwald (described later). You can see the Gimmelwald lift station in the distance.

• *Return to the main street and continue to...*

"Downtown" Mürren: This main intersection (where the small service road leads down to Gimmelwald) has the only grocery store in town (Co-op). A bit farther on, the tiny fire barn (labeled *Feuerwehr*) has a list showing the leaders of the volunteer force and their responsibilities. The old barn behind it on the right evokes the time, not so long ago, when the town's barns housed cows. Imagine Mürren with more cows than people, rather than with more visitors than residents.

About 65 feet beyond the fire barn (across the street from the old schoolhouse—Altes Schulhaus), detour right uphill a few steps into the oldest part of town. Explore the windy little lanes, admiring the ancient woodwork on the houses and the cute little pea patches.

• *Back on the main drag, continue to the far end of Mürren, where you come to the...*

Cable-Car Station: The first cable car (goes directly to the valley floor) is for cargo, garbage, and the (reputedly) longest bungee jump in the world. The other takes hikers and skiers up to the Schilthorn and down to the valley via Gimmelwald.

• *Hiking back into town along the high road, you'll enter...*

Upper Mürren: You'll pass Mürren's two churches, the All-mendhubel funicular station, and the Sportzentrum (with swimming pool and TI).

• *Our walk is finished. Enjoy the town and the views.*

Activities in Mürren

During ski season and the height of summer, the Mürren area offers plenty of activities for those willing to seek them out. In spring and fall, Mürren is pretty dead.

Allmendhubelbahn

A quaint-looking but surprisingly rewarding funicular (from 1912, renovated in 1999) carries nature-lovers from Mürren up to Allmendhubel, a perch offering a Jungfrau view that, though much lower, rivals the Schilthorn. At the station, notice the 1920s bobsled. Consider mixing a mountain lift, grand views, and a hike with your meal by eating at the restaurant on Allmendhubel (good chef, open daily until 18:00).

Allmendhubel is particularly good for families. The entertaining Adventure Trail children's hike—with rough and thrilling kid-friendly alpine rides along the way—starts from here. This is also the departure point for the North Face hike and walks to Grütschalp (see page 1407). While at Allmendhubel, consider its Flower Trail, a 20-minute loop with nice mountain views and (from June through Sept) a chance to see more than 150 different alpine flowers blooming.

Cost and Hours: 7.40 SF one-way, 12 SF round-trip, 6 SF round-trip with Swiss Pass, mid-June–mid-Oct daily 9:00-17:00, runs every 20 minutes, tel. 033-855-2042 or 033-856-2141, www.schilthorn.ch.

Mürren Via Ferrata (Klettersteig Mürren)

Mountaineers and thrill-seekers can test their nerves on this one-mile trail along the cliff running from Mürren to Gimmelwald. A *via ferrata* ("way of iron" in Italian) or *Klettersteig* ("climbing path" in German) is a cliffside trail made of metal steps drilled into the mountainside with a cable running at shoulder length above it. Equipped with a helmet, harness, and two carabiners, you are clipped to the cable the entire way. Experienced mountaineers can rent gear (25 SF from the Gimmelwald hostel or Mürren's Intersport) and do it independently; others should hire a licensed mountain guide. For a peek at what you're getting yourself into, search "*via ferrata* Switzerland Murren" at www.youtube.com.

The journey takes about three hours. While half of the route is easily walked, several hundred yards are literally hanging over a 3,000-foot drop. I did it, and through the most dangerous sections, I was too scared to look down or take pictures. Along with ladders and steps, the trip comes with three thrilling canyon crossings—one by zip line (possible with guide only), another on a single high wire (with steadying wires for each hand), and a final stint on a terrifying suspension bridge (which you can see from the Gimmelwald-Mürren cable-car—look for it just above Gimmelwald).

GIMMELWALD

Cost and Hours: 95 SF, includes gear and donation to the Mürren Via Ferrata Association, guided tours in small groups of 4-8, tel. 033-821-6100, www.klettersteig-muerren.ch.

Nightlife in Mürren

These are all good places for a drink after dinner: **Eiger Guesthouse** (a popular sports bar-type hangout with pool tables, games, and Internet terminals), **Stägerstübli** (where old-timers nurse a drink and gossip), **Hotel Blumental** (with a characteristic cellar—lively when open), and **Hotel Bellevue** (with its elegant alpine-lounge ambience). All of these places are further described under "Sleeping in Mürren" or "Eating in Mürren." In July and August, you can enjoy occasional folkloric evenings (some Wednesdays, at the Sportzentrum—listed earlier, under "Helpful Hints").

Sleeping in Mürren

(5,381 feet, 1 SF = about $1.10, country code: 41)

Prices for accommodations are often higher during the ski season. Many hotels and restaurants close in spring, roughly from Easter to early June, and may also shut down any time between late September and mid-December.

$$$ Hotel Eiger, a four-star hotel dramatically and conveniently situated just across from the tiny train station, is a good bet. Family-run for four generations, Adrian and Susanna Stahli offer all the service you'd expect in a big city hotel (plush lounge, indoor swimming pool, and sauna) while maintaining a creaky, Old World, woody elegance in its 50 rooms. Their family suites, while pricey, include two double rooms and can be a good value for groups of four or five (Db-275-315 SF with grand breakfast, view rooms-about 20 SF extra, discounts for stays of three nights or more, email for best deals, Wi-Fi, tel. 033-856-5454, fax 033-856-5456, www.hoteleiger.com, info@hoteleiger.com). If you opt for their five-course dinner with your reservation, it'll cost you about 50 SF extra per person.

$$$ At Hotel Edelweiss, it's all about the location—convenient and literally hanging on the cliff with devastating views. It's a big, modern building with 30 basic rooms and a busy, recommended restaurant well-run by hard-working Sandra and Daniel Kuster von Allmen (Db-145-180 SF depending on view and balcony, 10 percent discount for 2 nights, Wi-Fi, piano in lounge, tel. 033-856-5600, fax 033-856-5609, www.edelweiss-muerren.ch, edelweiss@muerren.ch).

$$$ Hotel Bellevue has a homey lounge, solid woodsy furniture, a great view terrace, the hunter-themed Jägerstübli restaurant, and 19 great rooms at fair rates—most with balconies and views (Sb-105-145 SF, viewless Db-140 SF, view Db-170-190 SF—150 SF if staying 2 nights or more in June or Sept-Oct, free Internet access and Wi-Fi, closed May and Nov, tel. 033-855-1401, fax 033-855-1490, www.muerren.ch/bellevue, bellevue-crystal@bluewin.ch, Ruth and Othmar Suter). In summer, Othmar offers a morning flowers and wildlife tour of Allmendhubel (10 SF includes funicular ride up, Sun at 9:00, 1.5 hours, meet at Allmendhubel funicular station, tel. 078-604-1401).

$$$ Hotel Jungfrau offers 29 modern and comfortable rooms and an apartment for up to 6 people (Sb-95-120 SF, Db-140-200 SF, lower prices are for viewless rooms, email for best deals, elevator, laundry service-15 SF, Wi-Fi, downhill from TI/Sportzentrum, tel. 033-856-6464, fax 033-856-6465, www.hoteljungfrau.ch, mail@hoteljungfrau.ch, Alan and Véronique).

$$$ Hotel Blumental has 16 older but nicely furnished rooms, a fun game/TV lounge, and a recommended restaurant (Sb-75-80 SF, Db-150-170 SF, 10 percent cheaper in Sept-Oct, higher prices are for July-Aug, outside of July-Aug book direct and ask for a 10 percent Rick Steves discount, pay cable Internet and Wi-Fi, tel. 033-855-1826, fax 033-855-3686, www.muerren.ch/blumental, blumental@muerren.ch; Ralph and Heidi, fourth generation in the von Allmen family). Their modern little chalet out back rents six rooms (Db-140-155 SF, includes breakfast in the hotel).

$$ Eiger Guesthouse offers 12 good budget rooms. This friendly, creaky, easygoing home away from home was renovated in 2009 (S-75 SF, Sb-80-95 SF, D-100-120 SF, Db-130-160 SF, bunk Q-180-200 SF, Qb-200-240 SF, special with this book: D-95 SF with a 2-night minimum year-round—making this a great deal for cheap beds in July-Aug; Wi-Fi, game room, terrace, across from train station, tel. 033-856-5460, fax 033-856-5461, www.eigerguesthouse.com, info@eigerguesthouse.com, Ema and Robert).

$ Chalet Fontana, run by charming Englishwoman Denise Fussell, is a rare budget option in Mürren, with simple, crispy-clean, and comfortable rooms (S-45-55 SF, D-75-85 SF, large D-95 SF, T-130 SF, price varies with size of room, cash only, closed Nov-April, fridge in common kitchen, across street from Stägerstübli restaurant in town center, mobile 078-642-3485, www.chaletfontana.ch, chaletfontana@gmail.com). If no one's home, check at the Ed Abegglen shop next door (tel. 033-855-1245, off-season only). Denise also rents a family apartment with kitchen, bathroom, and breakfast (two bedrooms with 3 beds each, 140 SF/2 people, 160 SF/3 people, 200 SF/4 people, 260 SF/6 people).

GIMMELWALD

Eating in Mürren

Many of these restaurants are in or near my recommended hotels. Outside of summer and ski season, it can be hard to find any place that's open (ask around).

Stägerstübli is everyone's favorite Mürren diner. It's the only real restaurant not associated with a hotel. Located in the town center, this 1902 building was once a tearoom for rich tourists, while locals were limited to the room in the back—which is now the nicer area to eat. Sitting on its terrace, you know just who's out and about in town (18-35-SF lunches and dinners, big portions, lovely lamb, daily 11:30-21:00, closed first week of Sept, Lydia).

Hotel Blumental specializes in typical Swiss cuisine, but also serves fish, international, and vegetarian dishes in a stony and woody dining area. It's one of Mürren's most elegant, romantic settings (18-30-SF specials, 21-31-SF fondue served for one or more, 15-SF pastas, daily from 17:00, tel. 033-855-1826).

Edelweiss cafeteria offers lunches and restaurant dinners with the most cliff-hanging dining in town—the views are incredible (pizzas, hearty salads, sandwiches; daily specials around 20 SF, family-friendly, tel. 033-856-5600).

Hotel Bellevue's restaurant is atmospheric, with three dining zones: a spectacular view terrace, a sophisticated indoor area, and the Jägerstübli—a cozy, well-antlered hunters' room guaranteed to disgust vegetarians. This is a good bet for game, as they buy chamois and deer direct from local hunters (lamb or game-34-44 SF, cheaper options as low as 15 SF, mid-June-Oct daily 11:30-14:00 & 18:00-21:00, closed off-season, tel. 033-855-1401).

Supermarket: The **Co-op** is the only grocery store in town, with good picnic fixings and sandwiches (Mon-Fri 8:00-12:00 & 13:45-18:30, Sat until 17:00, closed Sun). Given restaurant prices, this place is a godsend for those on a tight budget.

Wengen

Wengen—a bigger, fancier Mürren on the east side of the valley—has plenty of grand hotels, restaurants, shops, diversions, and terrific views. This traffic-free resort is an easy train ride above Lauterbrunnen and halfway up to Kleine Scheidegg and Männlichen. From Wengen, you can catch the Männlichen lift up to the ridge and take the rewarding, view-filled, nearly downhill "Männlichen-Kleine Scheidegg" hike, rated ▲▲▲ and described on page 1409.

Wengen's **TI** is two blocks from the station: Go up to the main drag, turn left, and it's on the left. They have info on hiking and sell hiking maps (tel. 033-855-1414, www.mywengen.ch).

The **Co-op grocery**, across the square from the train station, is great for picnic fixings, and is larger than most groceries in the area (Mon-Sat 8:00-18:30, closed Sun).

For an overnight stay, consider **Hotel Falken** (www.hotel-falken.com), **Hotel Berghaus** (www.berghaus-wengen.ch), **Hotel Schönegg** (www.hotel-schoenegg.ch), or the cheaper **Bären Hotel** (www.baeren-wengen.ch).

Activities in the Berner Oberland

Scenic Lifts and Trains

Enjoying at least one of the two high-altitude thrill rides described here is an essential Berner Oberland experience.

▲▲▲The Schilthorn and a 10,000-Foot Breakfast

The Schilthornbahn cable car carries skiers, hikers, and sightseers effortlessly to the 10,000-foot summit of the Schilthorn, where the Piz Gloria cable-car station awaits, with its solar-powered revolving restaurant, shop, and panorama terrace. At the top, you have a spectacular panoramic view of the Eiger, Mönch, and Jungfrau mountains, lined up on the horizon.

Ascending the Schilthorn: You can ride to the Schilthorn and back from several points—the cable-car station near Stechelberg on the valley floor (95 SF), Gimmelwald (85 SF), or Mürren (74 SF). Snare a 25 percent discount for early and late rides (roughly before 9:00 and after 15:30) and in spring and fall (roughly May and Oct). If you have a Swiss Pass (50 percent discount) or Eurail Pass (25 percent off), you might as well go whenever you like, because you can't double up discounts. Lifts go twice hourly, and the ride from Gimmelwald (including two transfers) to the Schilthorn takes 30 minutes. You can park your car at the valley station near Stechelberg (2 SF/2 hours, 6 SF/day, cash only). For more information, including current weather conditions, see www.schilthorn.ch or call 033-826-0007.

As the cable car floats between Gimmelwald and Mürren you'll see the metal bridge that marks the end of the *via ferrata.*

GIMMELWALD

You'll also see fields of wooden tripods, which serve two purposes: They stop avalanches and shelter newly planted trees. Made of wood, they're designed to eventually rot when the tree they protect is strong enough to survive the winter snowpack. From Mürren to Birg, keep an eye on the altitude meter.

At the Top: Head out to the terrace, where information boards identify each peak. The names of the hard-to-miss big three hint at local folklore: The cowled Mönch (monk—note the shape of its peak) fends off the Eiger (ogre) to protect the Jungfrau (maiden—though she hardly seems to need the help). Directional signs point hikers toward some seriously steep downhill climbs. Watch paragliders set up, psych up, and take off, flying 45 minutes with the birds to distant Interlaken. Walk along the ridge out back. This is a great place for a photo of the mountain-climber you. Youth hostelers—not realizing that rocks may hide just under the snow—scream down the ice fields on plastic-bag sleds from the mountaintop. (There's an English-speaking doctor in Lauterbrunnen—see page 1378.)

Inside, Piz Gloria has a free "touristorama" **film** room. The 20-minute video shows the natural wonders of the area, highlights a few activities—including racing down the famous Inferno ski run, briefly shares the story of the Schilthornbahn lift itself, and shows a substantial clip from the 1969 James Bond movie, *On Her Majesty's Secret Service*. That movie used the newly completed station as one of its major film sets.

You can ride up to the Schilthorn and hike down, but it's tough. (Hiking *up* from Gimmelwald or Mürren is easier on your knees...if you don't mind a 5,000-foot altitude gain.) For information on **hikes** from lift stations along the Schilthorn cable-car line, see "Hiking and Biking," later. My favorite "hike" from the Schilthorn is simply along the ridge out back, to get away from the station and be all alone on top of an Alp.

Breakfast at 10,000 Feet: The huge 28-SF "007 Breakfast Buffet" is served 8:00-11:00. The restaurant also serves hot dishes all day at prices that don't rise with the altitude (around 24 SF).

▲▲▲Jungfraujoch

The literal high point of any trip to the Swiss Alps is a train ride through the Eiger to the Jungfraujoch (the saddle between the Mönch and Jungfrau mountains). At 11,300 feet, it's Europe's highest train station. (If you have a heart or lung condition, you may want to check with your doctor before making this ascent.)

Ascending to the Jungfraujoch: Train runs all year to the Jungfraujoch from Lauterbrunnen (166 SF round-trip) and from Kleine Scheidegg (112 SF round-trip). The first trip of the day to the Jungfraujoch is discounted—ask for a Good Morning Ticket and leave the top by 12:30 (first train from Lauterbrunnen—130

SF, leaves about 7:00; from Kleine Scheidegg—90 SF, leaves about 8:00; Nov-April you can get Good Morning rates for the first or second train and return any time that day; confirm all times and prices, 25 percent discount with Swiss Pass and Eurail Pass, rail-pass holders get a better deal than Good Morning Ticket and can't combine discounts). Pick up a leaflet on the lifts at a local TI (www.jungfraubahn.ch). If it's cloudy, skip the trip; for a terse trilingual weather forecast from the Jungfraujoch, call 033-828-7931.

The ride from Kleine Scheidegg takes about an hour (sit on the right side for better views), including two five-minute stops at stations actually halfway up the notorious North Face of the Eiger. You have time to look out windows and marvel at how people could climb the Eiger—and how the Swiss built this train track more than a hundred years ago. The second half of the ride takes you through a tunnel inside the Eiger (some newer train cars run mul-tilingual videos about the history of the train line).

At the Top: Once you reach the top, study the Jungfraujoch chart to see your options (many of them are weather-dependent). There's a restaurant, a history exhibit, an "ice palace" (a cavern with a gallery of ice statues), and a 20-minute video that plays continu-ously. A tunnel leads outside, where you can summer ski (33 SF for gear and lift ticket), sled (free loaner discs with a 5-SF deposit), or hike an hour across the ice to Mönchsjochhütte (a mountain hut with a small restaurant). An elevator leads to the Sphinx obser-vatory for the highest viewing point, from which you can see the Aletsch Glacier—Europe's longest, at nearly 11 miles—stretch to the south. Remember that your body isn't used to such high alti-tudes. Signs posted at the top remind you to take it easy.

You can combine one of the best hikes in the region—from Männlichen to Kleine Scheidegg—with your trip up to the Jung-fraujoch (see page 1409).

Hiking and Biking

This area offers days of possible hikes. Many are a fun combina-tion of trails, mountain trains, and cable-car rides. I've listed them based on which side of the Lauterbrunnen Valley they're on: west (the Gimmelwald/Mürren/Schilthorn side) or east (the Jungfrau side).

On the Gimmelwald (West) Side of the Lauterbrunnen Valley
Hikes from the Schilthorn
Several tough trails lead down from the Schilthorn, but most visi-tors take the cable car round-trip simply for the views (see "Lifts and Trains," earlier). If you're a serious hiker, consider walking all

Gimmelwald Area Hikes

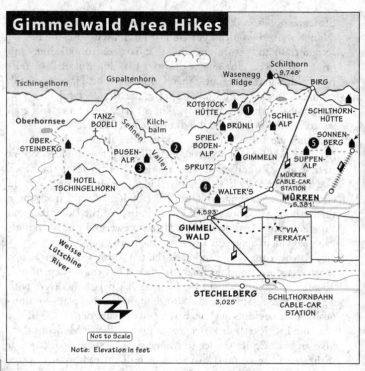

Not to Scale

Note: Elevation in feet

GIMMELWALD

the way down (first hike) or part of the way down (second hike) back into Gimmelwald. Don't attempt to hike down from the Schilthorn unless the trail is clear of snow. Adequate shoes and clothing (weather can change quickly) and good knees are required. You can visit the Sprutz Waterfall on your way to Gimmelwald.

From the Top of the Schilthorn (very difficult)

To hike downhill from the Piz Gloria revolving restaurant at the peak, start at the steps to the right of the cable, which lead along a ridge between a cliff and the bowl. As you pass huge rocks and shale fields, keep an eye out for the painted rocks that mark the scant trail. Eventually, you'll hit the service road (a ski run in the winter), which is steep and not very pleasant. Passing a memorial to a woman killed by lightning in 1865, you come to the small lake called Grauseeli. Leave the gravel road and hike along the lake. From there, follow the trail (with the help of cables when necessary) to scamper along the shale in the direction of Rotstockhütte (to Gimmelwald, see next hike) or Schilttal (the valley leading directly to Mürren; follow *Mürren/Rotstockhütte* sign painted on the rock at the junction).

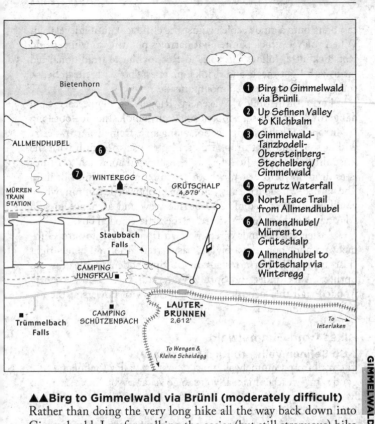

Legend:
1. Birg to Gimmelwald via Brünli
2. Up Sefinen Valley to Kilchbalm
3. Gimmelwald-Tanzbodeli-Obersteinberg-Stechelberg/Gimmelwald
4. Sprutz Waterfall
5. North Face Trail from Allmendhubel
6. Allmendhubel/Mürren to Grütschalp
7. Allmendhubel to Grütschalp via Winteregg

Map labels: Bietenhorn, ALLMENDHUBEL, WINTEREGG, GRÜTSCHALP 4,879', MÜRREN TRAIN STATION, Staubbach Falls, CAMPING JUNGFRAU, CAMPING SCHÜTZENBACH, LAUTERBRUNNEN 2,612', Trümmelbach Falls, To Interlaken, To Wengen & Kleine Scheidegg

▲▲Birg to Gimmelwald via Brünli (moderately difficult)

Rather than doing the very long hike all the way back down into Gimmelwald, I prefer walking the easier (but still strenuous) hike from the intermediate cable-car station at Birg. This is efficiently combined with a visit to the Schilthorn (from Schilthorn summit, ride cable car halfway down, get off at Birg, and hike down from there; buy the round-trip excursion early-bird fare, which is cheaper than the Gimmelwald-Schilthorn-Birg ticket, and decide at Birg whether you want to hike or ride down).

The most interesting trail from Birg to Gimmelwald is the high one via Grauseeli lake and Wasenegg Ridge to Brünli, then down to Spielbodenalp and the Sprutz Waterfall. Warning: This trail is quite steep and slippery in places, and can take four hours. Locals take their kindergartners on this hike, but it can seem dangerous to Americans unused to alpine hikes. Do not attempt this hike in snow, which you might find at this altitude even in the peak of summer. (Get local advice.)

From the Birg lift station, hike toward the Schilthorn, taking your first left down and passing along the left side of the little Grauseeli lake. From the lake, a gravelly trail leads down rough switchbacks (including a stretch where the path narrows and you can hang onto a guide cable against the cliff face) until it levels out. When you see a rock painted with arrows pointing to Mürren and Rotstockhütte, follow the path to Rotstockhütte (traditional old farm with light meals and drinks, mattress loft with cheap beds), traversing the cow-grazed mountainside.

For a thrill, follow Wasenegg Ridge. It's more scary than dangerous if you're sure-footed and can handle the 50-foot-long "tightrope-with-handrail" section along an extremely narrow ledge with a thousand-foot drop. This trail gets you to Brünli with the least altitude drop. (The safer, well-signposted approach to Brünli is to drop down to Rotstockhütte, then climb back up to Brünli.) The barbed-wire fence leads you to the knobby little summit, where you'll enjoy an incredible 360-degree view and a chance to sign your name on the register stored in the little wooden box.

A steep trail winds directly down from Brünli toward Gimmelwald and soon hits a bigger, easier trail. The trail bends right (just before the farm/restaurant at Spielbodenalp), leading to Sprutz. Walk under the Sprutz Waterfall, then follow a steep, wooded trail that deposits you in a meadow of flowers at the top side of Gimmelwald.

Hikes from Gimmelwald

▲Up Sefinen Valley to Kilchbalm (easy)

The trail from Gimmelwald up the Sefinen Valley (Sefinental) is a good rainy-weather hike, as you can go as far as you like. After two hours and a gain of only 800 feet, you hit the end of the trail and Kilchbalm, a dramatic bowl of glacier fields. Snow can make this trail unsafe, even into the summer (ask locally for information), and there's no food or drink along the way.

From the Gimmelwald fire station, walk about 100 yards down the paved Stechelberg road. Leave it on the dirt Sefinental road, which becomes a lane, then a trail. You'll cross a raging river and pass a firing range where locals practice their marksmanship (Fri and Sat evenings; the *danger of fire* sign refers to live bullets). Follow signs to Kilchbalm into a forest, along a river, and finally to the glacier fields.

▲Gimmelwald-Tanzbodeli-Obersteinberg-Stechelberg/ Gimmelwald (more difficult, for good hikers)

This eight-hour, 11-mile hike is extremely rewarding, offering perfect peace, very few people, traditional alpine culture, and spectacular views. (There's no food or drink for five hours, so pack accordingly.) The trail can be a bit confusing, so this is best done with a good, locally purchased map.

About 100 yards below the Gimmelwald firehouse, take the Sefinental dirt road (described in previous listing). As the dirt road switches back after about 30 minutes, take the right turn across the river and start your ascent, following signs to *Obersteinberg*. After 1.5 hours of hard climbing, you have the option of a side-trip to Busenalp. This is fun if the goat-and-cow herder is there, as you can watch traditional cheesemaking in action. (He appreciates a bottle of wine from hikers.) Trail markers are painted onto rocks—watch carefully. After visiting Busenalp, return to the main path.

At the *Obersteinberg 50 Min/Tanzbodeli 20 Min* signpost, head for Tanzbodeli ("Dancing Floor"). This is everyone's favorite alpine perch—great for a little romance or a picnic with breathtaking views of the Obersteinberg valley. From here, you enter a natural reserve, so you're likely to see chamois and other alpine critters. From Tanzbodeli, you return to the main trail (there's no other way out) and continue to Obersteinberg. You'll eventually hit the Mountain Hotel Obersteinberg (see "Sleeping in Obersteinberg," later; American expat Vickie will serve you a meal or drink).

From there, the trail leads to Mountain Hotel Tschingelhorn (see "Sleeping in Obersteinberg," later). About an hour later, you hit a fork in the trail and choose where you'd like your hike to end: back to Gimmelwald (2 hours total) or Stechelberg (near the bottom of the Schilthornbahn cable car, 1.5 hours total).

▲Sprutz Waterfall (moderately difficult)

The forest above Gimmelwald hides a powerful waterfall with a trail snaking behind it, offering a fun gorge experience. While the waterfall itself is not well-signed, it's on the Gimmelwald-Spielbodenalp trail. It's steep, through a forest, and can be very slippery when wet, but the actual crossing under the waterfall is just misty.

The hike up to Sprutz from Gimmelwald isn't worth the trip in itself, but it's handy when combined with the hike down from Birg and Brünli (described earlier) or the North Face Trail (see next listing). As you descend on either of these two hikes, the trail down to Gimmelwald splits at Spielbodenalp—to the right for the forest and the waterfall; to the left for more meadows, the hamlet of Gimmeln, and more gracefully back into Gimmelwald.

Hikes from Mürren/Allmendhubel
▲▲North Face Trail from Allmendhubel (easy and family-friendly)

For a pleasant two-hour hike, head out along this four-mile trail, starting at 6,385 feet and finishing at 5,375 feet (some stretches can be challenging if you're not in shape). To reach the trail, ride the Allmendhubel funicular up from Mürren (much cheaper than Schilthorn, good restaurant at top, see page 1397). From there, follow the well-signed route, which loops counterclockwise around to Mürren (or cut off at Spielbodenalp, near the end, and descend into Gimmelwald via the Sprutz Waterfall). As this trail doesn't technically begin at Allmendhubel, you'll start by following signs

GIMMELWALD

to *Sonnenberg.* Then just follow the blue signs. You'll enjoy great views, flowery meadows, mountain huts, and a dozen information boards along the way, describing the fascinating climbing history of the great peaks around you.

Along the trail, you'll pass four farms (technically "alps," as they are only open in the summer) that serve meals and drinks. Sonnenberg was allowed to break the all-wood building code with concrete for protection against avalanches. Suppenalp is quainter. Lean against the house with a salad, soup, or sandwich and enjoy the view. Just below Suppenalp is a little adventure park with zip lines and other kid-pleasing activities.

Notice how older huts are built into the protected side of rocks and outcroppings, in anticipation of avalanches. Above Suppenalp, Blumental ("Flower Valley") is hopping with marmots. Because hunters are not allowed near lifts, animals have learned that these are safe places to hang out—giving tourists a better chance of spotting them.

The trail leads up and over to a group of huts called Schiltalp (good food, drink, and service, and a romantic farm setting). If the poles under the eaves have bells, the cows are up here. If not, the cows are still at the lower farms. Half the cows in Gimmelwald (about 100) spend their summers here. In July, August, and September, you can watch cheese being made and have a snack or drink. Thirty years ago, each family had its own hut. Labor was cheap and available. Today, it's a communal thing, with several families sharing the expense of a single cow herder. Cow herders are master cheesemakers and have veterinary skills, too.

From Schiltalp, the trail winds gracefully down toward Spielbodenalp. From there you can finish the North Face Trail (continuing down and left through meadows and the hamlet of Gimmeln, then back to Mürren, with more historic signposts), or cut off right (descending steeply through a thick forest and under the dramatic Sprutz Waterfall into Gimmelwald—see Sprutz Waterfall, previous page, for details).

▲Allmendhubel/Mürren to Grütschalp (fairly easy)

For a not-too-tough two-hour walk with great Jungfrau views, ride the funicular from Mürren to Allmendhubel and walk to Grütschalp (a drop of about 1,500 feet), where you can catch the train back to Mürren. An easier version is the lower Bergweg from Allmendhubel to Grütschalp via Winteregg and its cheese farm. For a super-easy family stroll with grand views, walk from Mürren just above the train tracks either to Winteregg (40 minutes, restaurant, playground, train station) or through even better scenery on to Grütschalp (1 hour, train station), then catch the train back to Mürren.

Hikes on the Jungfrau (East) Side of the Lauterbrunnen Valley

▲▲▲Männlichen-Kleine Scheidegg
(easy and with dramatic views)

This is my favorite easy alpine hike (2.5 miles, 1-1.5 hours, 900-foot altitude drop to Kleine Scheidegg). It's entertaining all the way, with glorious mountain views. If you missed the plot, it's the Young Maiden (Jungfrau), being protected from the Ogre (Eiger) by the Monk (Mönch). Trails may be snowbound into June; ask about conditions at the lift stations or at TIs (see "Jungfraujoch" listing on page 1402).

If the weather's good, start off bright and early. From the Lauterbrunnen train station, take the little mountain train up to Wengen. Sit on the right side of the train for great valley and waterfall views. In Wengen, buy a picnic at the Co-op grocery across from the station, walk across town, and catch the lift to Männlichen, located on the top of the ridge high above you. The lift can be open even if the trail is closed; if the weather is questionable, confirm that the Männlichen-Kleine Scheidegg trail is open before ascending. Don't waste time in Wengen if it's sunny—you can linger back here after your hike.

Riding the gondola from Wengen to Männlichen, you'll go over the old lift station (inundated by a 1978 avalanche that buried a good part of Wengen—notice there's no development in the "red zone" above the tennis courts). Farms are built with earthen ramps on the uphill side in anticipation of the next slide. The forest of avalanche fences near the top was built after that 1978 avalanche. As you ascend you can also survey Wengen—the bright red roofs mark new vacation condos, mostly English-owned and used only a few weeks a year.

For a detour that'll give you an easy king- or queen-of-the-mountain feeling, turn left from the top of the Wengen-Männlichen lift station, and hike uphill 10 minutes to the little peak (Männlichen Gipfel, 7,500 feet).

Then go back to the lift station (which has a great kids' area) and enjoy the walk—facing spectacular alpine panorama views—to Kleine Scheidegg for a picnic or restaurant lunch. To start the hike, leave the Wengen-Männlichen lift station to the right. Walk past the second Männlichen lift station (this one leads to Grindelwald, the touristy town in the valley to your left). Ahead of you in the distance, left to right, are the north faces of the Eiger, Mönch, and Jungfrau; in the foreground is the Tschuggen peak, and just behind it, the Lauberhorn. This hike takes you around the left (east) side of this ridge. Simply follow the signs for Kleine Scheidegg, and you'll be there in about an hour—a little more for gawkers, picnickers, and photographers. You might have to tiptoe through streams of

GIMMELWALD

melted snow—or some small snow banks, even well into the summer—but the path is well-marked, well-maintained, and mostly
level all the way to Kleine Scheidegg.

About 35 minutes into the hike, you'll reach a bunch of benches and a shelter with incredible unobstructed views of all three
peaks—the perfect picnic spot. Fifteen minutes later, on the left,
you'll see the first sign of civilization: Restaurant Grindelwaldblick
(the best lunch stop up here, open daily, closed Dec and May, described on page 1412). Hike to the restaurant's fun mountain lookout to survey the Eiger and look down on the Kleine Scheidegg
action. After 10 more minutes, you'll be at the Kleine Scheidegg
train station, with plenty of lesser lunch options (including Restaurant Bahnhof, described on page 1412).

From Kleine Scheidegg, you can catch the train up to "the top
of Europe" (see Jungfraujoch listing, earlier), take the train back
down to Wengen, or hike downhill (gorgeous 30-minute hike to
Wengernalp Station, a little farther to the Allmend stop; 60 more
steep minutes from there into Wengen). The alpine views might
be accompanied by the valley-filling mellow sound of alphorns
and distant avalanches. If the weather turns bad or you run out of
steam, catch the train at any of the stations along the way. After
Wengernalp, the trail to Wengen is steep and, though not dangerous, requires a good set of knees. The boring final descent from
Wengen to Lauterbrunnen is knee-killer steep—catch the train
instead.

▲▲Schynige Platte to First (more difficult)

The best day I've had hiking in the Berner Oberland was when I
made this demanding six-hour ridge walk, with Lake Brienz on
one side and all that Jungfrau beauty on the other. Start at the
Wilderswil train station (just outside Interlaken), and catch the
little train up to Schynige Platte (6,560 feet; 2/hour, 55 minutes,
35 SF). The high point is Faulhorn (8,790 feet, with its famous
mountaintop hotel). Hike to a small mini-gondola called "First"
(7,110 feet), then ride down to Grindelwald and catch a train back
to your starting point, Wilderswil. Or, if you have a regional train
pass (or no car but endless money), take the long, scenic return
trip: From Grindelwald, take the lift up to Männlichen (2/hour,
30 minutes, 36 SF), do the hike to Kleine Scheidegg and down to
Wengen (described earlier), then head down into Lauterbrunnen.

For a shorter (3-hour) ridge walk, consider the well-signposted
Panoramaweg, a loop from Schynige Platte to Daub Peak.

The alpine flower park at Schynige Platte Station offers a delightful stroll through several hundred alpine flowers (free, June-
Sept daily 8:30-18:00, www.alpengarten.ch), including a chance to
see edelweiss growing in the wild.

Lowa, a leading local manufacturer of top-end hiking boots,

has a promotional booth at Schynige Platte Station that provides free loaners to hikers who'd like to give their boots a try. They're already broken in, but bring thick socks (or buy them there).

If hiking here, be mindful of the last lifts (which can be as early as 16:30). Hiking from First (7,113 feet) to Schynige Platte (6,454 feet) gives you a later departure down and less climbing. The TI produces a great Schynige Platte map/guide narrating the train ride up and describing various hiking options from there (available at Wilderswil Station).

Mountain Biking

Mountain biking is popular and accepted, as long as you stay on the clearly marked mountain-bike paths. You can rent bikes in Mürren (Stäger Sport, see page 1393) or in Lauterbrunnen (Imboden Bike, see page 1380). The Lauterbrunnen shop is bigger, has a wider selection of bikes, and is likely to be open when the Mürren one isn't. The two shops work together: For an 8-SF surcharge, you can pick up your bike at one location and leave it at the other. On trains and cable cars, bikes require a separate ticket.

The most popular bike rides include the following:

Lauterbrunnen to Interlaken: This is a gentle downhill ride on a peaceful bike path across the river from the road (don't bike on the road itself). You can return to Lauterbrunnen by train (13 SF total for bike and you). Or rent a bike at either Interlaken station, take the train to Lauterbrunnen, and ride back.

Lauterbrunnen Valley (between Stechelberg and Lauterbrunnen town): This delightful, easy bike path features plenty of diversions along the way (several listed under "Activities in and near Lauterbrunnen" on page 1380).

Mürren to Winteregg to Grütschalp and Back: This fairly level route takes you through high country, with awesome mountain views.

Mürren to Winteregg to Lauterbrunnen: This scenic descent, on a service road with loose gravel, takes you to the Lauterbrunnen Valley floor.

Mürren-Gimmelwald-Sefinen Valley-Stechelberg-Lauterbrunnen-Grütschalp-Mürren: This is the best ride, but it's demanding—with one very difficult stretch where you'll likely walk your bike down a steep gulley for 500 yards. While you'll be on your bike most of the time, to complete the loop take the cable car from Lauterbrunnen up to Grütschalp and then bike back to Mürren.

GIMMELWALD

More in the Berner Oberland

I'd sleep in Gimmelwald, Mürren, or Lauterbrunnen. But you could also consider the following places.

Sleeping and Eating at or near Kleine Scheidegg
(6,762 feet)

This high settlement above the timberline is where you catch the train up to the Jungfraujoch. All of these places serve meals. Confirm prices and availability before ascending. Note that the last train down to Wengen leaves Kleine Scheidegg at 18:30.

$$$ Hotel Bellevue des Alpes, lovingly maintaining a 1930s elegance, is a worthwhile splurge. Since the 1840s, five generations of von Allmens have run this classic old alpine hotel (subsidized by the family income from Trümmelbach Falls). The hallway is like a museum, with old photos (Sb-220-260 SF, Db-370-540 SF, includes breakfast and sumptuous four-course dinner, open only mid-June–mid-Sept, tel. 033-855-1212, fax 033-855-1294, www.scheidegg-hotels.ch, welcome@scheidegg-hotels.ch).

$$ Restaurant Bahnhof invites you to sleep face-to-face with the Eiger (dorm bed-53 SF with breakfast, 73 SF also includes dinner; D-135 SF with breakfast, D-170 SF with breakfast and dinner; in the train station building, tel. 033-828-7828, www.bahnhof-scheidegg.ch, info@bahnhof-scheidegg.ch).

$ Restaurant Grindelwaldblick, a 10-minute hike from the train station, is more charming, romantic, and remote than Restaurant Bahnhof (40 SF/bed in 6- to 20-bed rooms, includes sheets and breakfast, closed Nov and May, tel. 033-855-1374, fax 033-855-4205, www.grindelwaldblick.ch). The restaurant, with a great sun terrace and a cozy interior, sells good three-course lunches (15-25 SF) and 25-SF dinners.

Sleeping in Stechelberg
(3,025 feet)

Stechelberg is the hamlet at the end of the road up the Lauterbrunnen Valley; it's about a mile beyond the Schilthornbahn lift that goes up to Gimmelwald, Mürren, and the Schilthorn (it's a five-minute PostBus ride or a 20-minute trail walk between the lift station and the village). Beyond Stechelberg lies the rugged Rear Lauterbrunnen Valley, the edge of the Jungfrau-Aletsch-Bietschhorn nature reserve—the most glaciated part of the Alps.

$$ Hotel Stechelberg, at road's end, is surrounded by waterfalls and vertical rock, with a garden terrace, a good restaurant, and 16 quiet rooms—half in a creaky old building, half in a concrete, no-character new building (D-90-120 SF, Db-138, Db with balcony-170 SF, T-165 SF, Tb-210 SF, Q-210 SF, bus stops here 1-2/hour, free Wi-Fi, tel. 033-855-2921, fax 033-855-4438, www. hotel-stechelberg.ch, hotel@stechelberg.ch, Marianne and Otto).

$ The **Alpenhof** fills a former "Nature Friends' Hut" with cheap beds. Creaking like a wooden chalet built in 1926 should, and surrounded by a broad lawn, it provides a good, inexpensive base for drivers and families (28 SF/bed in 2- to 6-bed rooms, each group gets a private room, breakfast-12 SF, tel. 033-855-1202, www.alpenhof-stechelberg.ch, alpenhof@stechelberg.ch, Diane and Marc). From the Hotel Stechelberg, go up the paved path, go right at the fork, and cross the river; it's on your left.

Sleeping in Obersteinberg
(5,900 feet)

Here's a wild idea: **$$ Mountain Hotel Obersteinberg** is a working alpine farm with cheese, cows, a mule shuttling up food once a day, and an American (Vickie) who fell in love with a mountain man. It's a 2.5-hour hike from either Stechelberg or Gimmelwald. They rent 12 primitive rooms and a bunch of loft beds. There's no shower, no hot water, and only meager solar-panel electricity. Candles light up the night, and you can take a hot-water bottle to bed if necessary (S-85 SF, D-170 SF, includes linen, sheetless dorm beds-68 SF; these prices include breakfast and dinner, without meals S-37 SF, D-74 SF, dorm beds-20 SF; closed Oct-May, tel. 033-855-2033). The place is filled with locals and Germans on weekends, but it's all yours on weekdays. Why not hike here from Gimmelwald and leave the Alps a day later?

GIMMELWALD

APPENDIX

Embassies and Consulates

Austria: US Embassy, Boltzmanngasse 16, Vienna, tel. 01/313-390, embassy@usembassy.at; consular services at Parkring 12a, daily 8:00-11:30 by appointment only, tel. 01/313-397-535, http://austria.usembassy.gov

Belgium: US Embassy, 27 Boulevard du Régent/Regentlaan, Brussels, tel. 02-811-4300—answered Mon-Thu 8:00-12:30, Fri 13:30-15:30, after-hours emergency call and ask to be connected to the duty officer, passport services by online appointment only, http://belgium.usembassy.gov; US Consulate next door to embassy at 25 Boulevard du Régent/Regentlaan

France: US Embassy, 4 avenue Gabriel, to the left as you face Hôtel Crillon, Paris, Mo: Concorde, tel. 01 43 12 22 22, passport services by appointment, online appointments possible, http://france.usembassy.gov

Germany: US Embassy, Pariser Platz 2, Berlin, tel. 030/83050; consular services at Clayallee 170, Mon-Fri 8:30-12:00 by appointment only, tel. 030/8305-1200—calls answered Mon-Fri 14:00-16:00 only, online appointments possible, http://germany.usembassy.gov

Great Britain: US Embassy, 24 Grosvenor Square, London, Tube: Bond Street, tel. 020/7499-9000; for emergency 36-hour passport service, email LondonEmergencyPPT@state.gov or call general number; http://london.usembassy.gov

Italy: US Embassy, Via Vittorio Veneto 119/A, Rome, 24-hour emergency line—tel. 06-46741, non-emergency—tel. 06-4674-2420 answered Mon-Fri 15:00-17:00, passport services Mon-Fri 8:30-12:00, http://italy.usembassy.gov, uscitizensrome@state.gov;

European Calling Chart

Just smile and dial, using this key:
AC = Area Code, LN = Local Number.

European Country	Calling long distance within ...	Calling from the US or Canada to ...	Calling from a European country to ...
Austria	AC + LN	011 + 43 + AC (without initial zero) + LN	00 + 43 + AC (without initial zero) + LN
Belgium	LN	011 + 32 + LN (without initial zero)	00 + 32 + LN (without initial zero)
Bosnia-Herzegovina	AC + LN	011 + 387 + AC (without initial zero) + LN	00 + 387 + AC (without initial zero) + LN
Britain	AC + LN	011 + 44 + AC (without initial zero) + LN	00 + 44 + AC (without initial zero) + LN
Croatia	AC + LN	011 + 385 + AC (without initial zero) + LN	00 + 385 + AC (without initial zero) + LN
Czech Republic	LN	011 + 420 + LN	00 + 420 + LN
Denmark	LN	011 + 45 + LN	00 + 45 + LN
Estonia	LN	011 + 372 + LN	00 + 372 + LN
Finland	AC + LN	011 + 358 + AC (without initial zero) + LN	999 (or other 900 number) + 358 + AC (without initial zero) + LN
France	LN	011 + 33 + LN (without initial zero)	00 + 33 + LN (without initial zero)
Germany	AC + LN	011 + 49 + AC (without initial zero) + LN	00 + 49 + AC (without initial zero) + LN
Gibraltar	LN	011 + 350 + LN	00 + 350 + LN
Greece	LN	011 + 30 + LN	00 + 30 + LN
Hungary	06 + AC + LN	011 + 36 + AC + LN	00 + 36 + AC + LN
Ireland	AC + LN	011 + 353 + AC (without initial zero) + LN	00 + 353 + AC (without initial zero) + LN
Italy	LN	011 + 39 + LN	00 + 39 + LN

European Country	Calling long distance within ...	Calling from the US or Canada to ...	Calling from a European country to ...
Latvia	LN	011 + 371 + LN	00 + 371 + LN
Montenegro	AC + LN	011 + 382 + AC (without initial zero) + LN	00 + 382 + AC (without initial zero) + LN
Morocco	LN	011 + 212 + LN (without initial zero)	00 + 212 + LN (without initial zero)
Netherlands	AC + LN	011 + 31 + AC (without initial zero) + LN	00 + 31 + AC (without initial zero) + LN
Norway	LN	011 + 47 + LN	00 + 47 + LN
Poland	LN	011 + 48 + LN	00 + 48 + LN
Portugal	LN	011 + 351 + LN	00 + 351 + LN
Russia	8 + AC + LN	011 + 7 + AC + LN	00 + 7 + AC + LN
Slovakia	AC + LN	011 + 421 + AC (without initial zero) + LN	00 + 421 + AC (without initial zero) + LN
Slovenia	AC + LN	011 + 386 + AC (without initial zero) + LN	00 + 386 + AC (without initial zero) + LN
Spain	LN	011 + 34 + LN	00 + 34 + LN
Sweden	AC + LN	011 + 46 + AC (without initial zero) + LN	00 + 46 + AC (without initial zero) + LN
Switzerland	LN	011 + 41 + LN (without initial zero)	00 + 41 + LN (without initial zero)
Turkey	AC (if there's no initial zero, add one) + LN	011 + 90 + AC (without initial zero) + LN	00 + 90 + AC (without initial zero) + LN

- The instructions above apply whether you're calling to or from a European landline or mobile phone.
- If calling from any mobile phone, you can replace the international access code with "+" (press and hold 0 to insert it).
- The international access code is 011 if you're calling from the US or Canada.
- To call the US or Canada from Europe, dial 00, then 1 (country code for US and Canada), then the area code and number. In short, 00 + 1 + AC + LN = Hi, Mom!

US Consulate, Lungarno Vespucci 38, Florence, tel. 055-266-951, http://florence.usconsulate.gov

The Netherlands: US Embassy, Lange Voorhout 102, The Hague, tel. 070/310-2209, visits by appointment only, http://netherlands.usembassy.gov; US Consulate, Museumplein 19, Amsterdam, tel. 020/575-5309 during office hours: Mon-Fri 13:30-16:30, in case of emergency call after-duty officer at tel. 070/310-2209, passport services by online appointment only, http://amsterdam.usconsulate.gov

Spain: US Embassy, Calle Serrano 75, Madrid, tel. 915-872-240, after-hours emergency tel. 915-872-200, http://madrid.usembassy.gov

Switzerland: US Embassy, Sulgeneckstrasse 19, Bern, tel. 031-357-7011 or 031-357-7777, Mon-Fri 9:00-11:30 by appointment only, http://bern.usembassy.gov

Transportation

This section contains basic information on trains, driving, and flights.

By Car or Public Transportation?

If you're debating between public transportation and car rental, consider these factors: Cars are best for three or more people traveling together (especially families with small kids), those packing heavy, and those scouring the countryside. Trains, buses, and boats are best for an ambitious, multi-country itinerary, and especially so for solo travelers, blitz tourists, and city-to-city travelers, and those who don't want to drive in Europe. While a car gives you more freedom and carries your bags for you, trains, buses, and boats zip you effortlessly and scenically from city to city, usually dropping you in the center, often near a tourist-info office. Cars are great in the countryside, but are an expensive headache in places like Rome and Paris.

Public Transportation
Trains

A major mistake Americans make is relating public transportation in Europe to the pathetic public transportation they're used to at home. By rail, you'll have Europe by the tail. While many people simply buy tickets as they go ("point to point"), the various train passes give you the simplicity of ticket-free, nearly unlimited travel, and depending on how many trips you do, often offer a savings over regular point-to-point tickets. Fast, long-distance, international, or overnight trains are more likely to require reservations at some

APPENDIX

POINT-TO-POINT RAIL TICKETS: COST & TIME

This chart shows the cost of second-class train tickets. Connect the dots of your itinerary, add up the cost, compare it with a railpass, and see what is better for your trip.

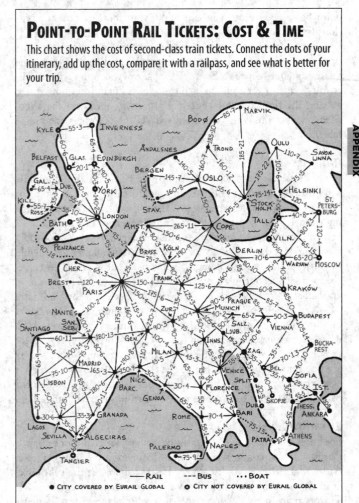

— RAIL   --- BUS   ··· BOAT

● CITY COVERED BY EURAIL GLOBAL   ○ CITY NOT COVERED BY EURAIL GLOBAL

First number between cities = Approximate cost in US dollars for a one-way, second class ticket. **Second number** = Number of hours the trip takes.

Important: These fares and times are for express trains where applicable and are based on European sources. Actual prices may vary due to currency fluctuations, advance purchase, and local promotions. For approximate first-class rail prices, add 50 percent. For shorter routes, see more cost comparison maps at www.ricksteves.com/rail.

point before boarding; you can make your more critical reservations from home.

For a summary of railpass deals and point-to-point ticket options (available in the US and in Europe), check out our free, annually updated *Guide to Eurail Passes* at www.ricksteves.com/rail. If you decide to get a railpass, this guide will help you know you're getting the right one for your trip. To study ahead on the Web, check www.bahn.com (Germany's excellent Europe-wide timetable).

Railpasses

Global Passes offer you nearly unlimited travel on all public railways throughout most of Europe (except Great Britain and some of Eastern Europe). Choose between the consecutive-day pass (ranging from 15 days to three months) or the cheaper flexipass (any 10 or 15 individual days in two months). Travel partners (2-5 people traveling together) save 15 percent with Saver Passes, available in consecutive-day and flexipass versions. Youths under 26 travel cheaper with second-class passes (for the rest of us, this pass is only available for first-class travel). Kids under 12 pay half the adult rate.

Eurail Select Passes give you a selected number of travel days in your choice of three, four, or five adjoining Eurail countries, whether connected by rail or ferry (e.g., a three-country Select Pass could cover Italy, Switzerland, and Germany). Select Passes are fine for a focused trip, but to see the Best of Europe, you'd do best with a Eurail Global pass. These passes also give a 15 percent Saverpass discount to two or more companions traveling together.

Eurail Analysis

For an at-a-glance break-even point, remember that a one-month Eurail Global pass is a good value if, for example, your route is Amsterdam-Rome-Madrid-Paris. Passes pay for themselves quicker in the north, where the cost per mile is higher. Check the Rail Tickets map in this chapter to see if your planned travels merit purchasing a train pass. If it's about even, go with the pass for the convenience of not having to wait in line to buy tickets (on trains that don't require paid reservations) and for the fun and freedom to travel "free." Even if second-class tickets work out a bit cheaper than a first-class pass for travelers over 26, consider the added value of a first-class pass: On a crowded train, your chances of getting a seat are much better if your pass allows you to sit anywhere on the train.

Rail-and-drive passes are popular varieties of many of these passes. Along with a railpass, you get vouchers for a few Hertz or Avis car-rental days. These allow travelers to do long trips by train and enjoy a car where they need the freedom to explore. Great areas for a day of joyriding include Germany's Rhine Valley or Bavaria, France's Provence, and the Alps (for "car hiking"). When comparing prices, remember that each day of car rental comes with about $50 of extra expenses (CDW insurance, gas, parking).

Renting a Car

If you're renting a car, bring your driver's license. In some countries (including Austria, Italy, and Spain), you're required to also

have an International Driving Permit—an official translation of your driver's license (sold at your local AAA office for $15 plus the cost of two passport-type photos; see www.aaa. com). While that's the letter of the law in those countries, I've often rented cars in Europe without having this permit.

As Europe's internal borders fade, your car comes with the paperwork you need to drive wherever you like in Western and most of Eastern Europe (always check when booking). But if you're heading to a country in far-eastern or southeastern Europe that has mandatory border stops, state your travel plans up front to the rental company when making your reservation. Some companies have limits on eastward excursions (for example, you can only take cheaper cars, and you may have to pay extra insurance fees). When you cross these borders, you may be asked to show proof of insurance (called a "green card"). Ask your car-rental company if you need any other documentation for crossing the borders on your itinerary.

For trips of at least three weeks, leasing—which includes taxes and insurance—is the best way to go (for more information, see www.ricksteves.com/driving).

Car Insurance Options

When you rent a car, you are liable for a very high deductible, sometimes equal to the entire value of the car. Limit your financial risk by choosing one of these three options: Buy Collision Damage Waiver (CDW) coverage from the car-rental company, get coverage through your credit card (free, if your card automatically includes zero-deductible coverage), or buy coverage through Travel Guard.

Buying CDW insurance is the easiest but priciest option. Using the coverage that comes with your credit card is cheaper, but can involve more hassle in case of an accident. If you're taking a short trip, the cheapest solution is to buy CDW insurance from Travel Guard (tel. 800-826-4919, www.travelguard.com); it's valid everywhere in Europe except the Republic of Ireland, and some Italian car-rental companies refuse to honor it. Note that various states differ on which products and policies are available to their residents. For more information, see www.ricksteves.com/cdw.

Note that theft insurance (separate from CDW insurance) is mandatory in Italy. The insurance usually costs about $15-20 a day, payable when you pick up the car.

Driving

I use the freeways whenever possible. They're free in the Netherlands and Germany; you'll pay about $5-9 per hour in Italy, France, and Spain; roughly $40 for the toll sticker as you enter Switzerland; and about $11 for a toll sticker in Austria. It costs about $20 a day to park safely in big cities, and there's a $16 "congestion charge" to drive in downtown London.

Be warned that driving is restricted in many Italian city centers. If you drive in an area marked *Zona Traffico Limitato* (ZTL, often shown above a red circle), your license plate can be photographed and a hefty (€100-plus) fine mailed to your home without your ever being stopped by a cop.

Cheap Flights

If you're considering a train ride that's more than five hours long, a flight may save you both time and money. When comparing your options, factor in the time it takes to get to the airport and how early you'll need to arrive to check in.

The best comparison search engine for both international and intra-European flights is www.kayak.com. For inexpensive flights within Europe, try www.skyscanner.com or www.hipmunk.com. If you're not sure who flies to your destination, check its airport's website for a list of carriers. Well-known cheapo airlines include easyJet (www.easyjet.com) and Ryanair (www.ryanair.com).

Be aware of the potential drawbacks of flying on the cheap: nonrefundable and nonchangeable tickets, minimal or nonexistent customer service, treks to airports far outside town, and stingy baggage allowances with steep overage fees. If you're traveling with lots of luggage, a cheap flight can quickly become a bad deal. To avoid unpleasant surprises, read the small print before you book.

Resources

Resources from Rick Steves

Rick Steves' Best of Europe 2014 is one of many books in my series on European travel, which includes country guidebooks, city guidebooks (Rome, Florence, Paris, London, etc.), Snapshot guides (excerpted chapters from my country guides), Pocket Guides (full-color little books on big cities), and my budget-travel skills handbook, *Rick Steves' Europe Through the Back Door*. Most of my titles are available as ebooks. My phrase books—for Italian, French, German, Spanish, and Portuguese—are practical and budget-oriented. My other books include *Europe 101* (a crash course on art and history), *Mediterranean*

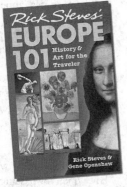

Cruise Ports and *Northern European Cruise Ports* (how to make the most of your time in port), and *Travel as a Political Act* (a travelogue sprinkled with tips for bringing home a global perspective). A more complete list of my titles appears near the end of this book.

Video: My public television series, *Rick Steves' Europe,* covers European destinations in 100 shows. To watch episodes online, visit www.hulu.com; for scripts and local airtimes, see www.ricksteves.com/tv.

Audio: My weekly public radio show, *Travel with Rick Steves,* features interviews with travel experts from around the world. I've

also produced free, self-guided audio tours of the top sights in London, Paris, Florence, Rome, Venice, Amsterdam, Vienna, Salzburg, and the Rhine. All of this audio content is available for free at Rick Steves Audio Europe, an extensive online library organized by destination. Choose whatever interests you, and download it for free via the Rick Steves Audio Europe smartphone app, www.ricksteves.com/audioeurope, iTunes, or Google Play.

Conversions

Numbers and Stumblers

- Europeans write a few of their numbers differently than we do: 1 = 1, 4 = 4, 7 = 7.
- In Europe, dates appear as day/month/year, so Christmas is 25/12/14.
- Except in Great Britain, commas are decimal points, and decimals commas. A dollar and a half is $1,50, one thousand is 1.000, and there are 5.280 feet in a mile.
- When pointing, use your whole hand, palm down.
- When counting with fingers, start with your thumb. If you hold up your first finger to request one item, you'll probably get two.
- What we Americans call the second floor of a building is the first floor in Europe.
- On escalators and moving sidewalks, Europeans keep the left "lane" open for passing. Keep to the right.

Metric Conversions (approximate)

A kilogram is 2.2 pounds, and l liter is about a quart, or almost four to a gallon. A kilometer is six-tenths of a mile. I figure kilometers to miles by cutting them in half and adding back 10 percent of the original (120 km: 60 + 12 = 72 miles, 300 km: 150 + 30 = 180 miles).

1 foot = 0.3 meter	1 square yard = 0.8 square meter
1 yard = 0.9 meter	1 square mile = 2.6 square kilometers
1 mile = 1.6 kilometers	1 ounce = 28 grams
1 centimeter = 0.4 inch	1 quart = 0.95 liter
1 meter = 39.4 inches	1 kilogram = 2.2 pounds
1 kilometer = 0.62 mile	32°F = 0°C

Begin Your Trip at www.ricksteves.com

At our travel website, you'll discover a wealth of free information on European destinations, including fresh monthly news and helpful tips from thousands of fellow travelers. You'll find my latest guidebook updates (www.ricksteves.com/update), a monthly travel e-newsletter (easy and free to sign up), my personal travel blog, and my free Rick Steves Audio Europe smartphone app (if you don't have a smartphone, you can access the same content via podcasts). You can even follow me on Facebook and Twitter.

Our **online Travel Store** offers travel bags and accessories that I've designed specifically to help you travel smarter and lighter. These include my popular carry-on bags (roll-aboard and backpack versions), money belts, totes, toiletries kits, adapters, other accessories, and a wide selection of guidebooks, planning maps, and DVDs.

Choosing the right **railpass** for your trip—amidst hundreds of options—can drive you nutty. We'll help you choose the best pass for your needs and ship it to you for free.

Want to travel with greater efficiency and less stress? We organize **tours** with more than three dozen itineraries and more than 600 departures reaching the best destinations in this book...and beyond. You'll enjoy great guides, a fun bunch of travel partners (with small groups of generally around 24-28), and plenty of room to spread out in a big, comfy bus. You'll find European adventures to fit every vacation length. For all the details, and to get our Tour Catalog and a free Rick Steves Tour Experience DVD (filmed on location during an actual tour), visit www.ricksteves.com or call us at 425/608-4217.

Temperature Conversion: Fahrenheit and Celsius

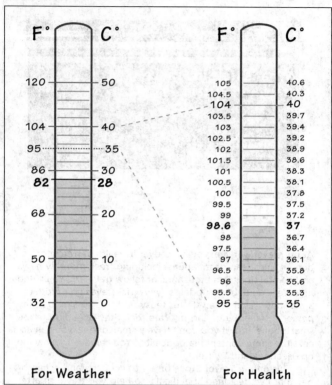

For Weather   For Health

Europe takes its temperature using the Celsius scale, while we opt for Fahrenheit. For a rough conversion from Celsius to Fahrenheit, double the number and add 30. For weather, remember that 28°C is 82°F—perfect. For health, 37°C is just right.

APPENDIX

APPENDIX

Packing Checklist

Whether you're traveling for five days or five weeks, here's what you'll need to bring. Pack light to enjoy the sweet freedom of true mobility. Happy travels!

- ❑ 5 shirts: long- & short-sleeve
- ❑ 1 sweater or lightweight fleece
- ❑ 2 pairs of pants
- ❑ 1 pair of shorts
- ❑ 5 pairs of underwear & socks
- ❑ 1 pair of shoes
- ❑ 1 rainproof jacket with hood
- ❑ Tie or scarf
- ❑ Swimsuit
- ❑ Sleepwear
- ❑ Money belt
- ❑ Money—your mix of:
  - ❑ Debit card
  - ❑ Credit card(s)
  - ❑ Hard cash ($20 bills)
- ❑ Documents plus photo-copies:
  - ❑ Passport
  - ❑ Printout of airline eticket
  - ❑ Driver's license
  - ❑ Student ID, hostel card, etc.
  - ❑ Railpass/train reservations/ car-rental voucher
  - ❑ Insurance details
- ❑ Guidebooks & maps
- ❑ Address list (for sending emails & postcards)
- ❑ Notepad & pen
- ❑ Journal
- ❑ Daypack
- ❑ Toiletries kit:
  - ❑ Toiletries
  - ❑ Medicines & vitamins
  - ❑ First-aid kit
  - ❑ Glasses/contacts/ sunglasses (with prescriptions)
- ❑ Small towel/washcloth
- ❑ Laundry supplies:
  - ❑ Laundry soap
  - ❑ Clothesline
- ❑ Sewing kit

- ❑ Electronics—your choice of:
  - ❑ Camera (& related gear)
  - ❑ Mobile phone
  - ❑ Portable media player (iPod or other)
  - ❑ Laptop/netbook/ tablet
  - ❑ Ebook reader
  - ❑ Headphones or earbuds
  - ❑ Chargers for each of the above
  - ❑ Plug adapter(s)
- ❑ Alarm clock
- ❑ Earplugs
- ❑ Sealable plastic baggies
- ❑ Empty water bottle
- ❑ Postcards & photos from home

If you plan to carry on your luggage, note that all liquids must be in 3.4-ounce or smaller containers and fit within a single quart-size sealable baggie. For details, see www.tsa.gov/travelers.

Hotel Reservation

To: _____   _____
          hotel   *email or fax*

From: _____   _____
          name   *email or fax*

Today's date: _____ / _____ / _____
                  day   *month*   *year*

Dear Hotel _____ ,
Please make this reservation for me:

Name: _____

Total # of people: _____   # of rooms: _____   # of nights: _____

Arriving: _____ / _____ / _____   My time of arrival (24-hr clock): _____
              day *month* *year*   (I will telephone if I will be late)

Departing: _____ / _____ / _____
                day *month* *year*

Room(s): Single___   Double ___   Twin___   Triple ___   Quad___

With: Toilet ___   Shower___   Bath___   Sink only___

Special needs: View___   Quiet___   Cheapest___   Ground Floor___

Please email or fax confirmation of my reservation, along with the type of room reserved and the price. Please also inform me of your cancellation policy. After I hear from you, I will quickly send my credit-card information as a deposit to hold the room. Thank you.

_____
Name

_____
Address

_____
City   *State*   *Zip Code*   *Country*

Before hoteliers can make your reservation, they want to know the information listed above. You can use this form as the basis for your email, or you can photocopy this page, fill in the information, and send it as a fax (also available online at www.ricksteves.com/reservation).

INDEX

MAP INDEX

Audio Europe™

Rick's Free Travel App

Get your FREE **Rick Steves Audio Europe**™ app to enjoy...

- Dozens of self-guided tours of Europe's top museums, sights and historic walks
- Hundreds of tracks filled with cultural insights and sightseeing tips from Rick's radio interviews
- All organized into handy geographic playlists
- For iPhone, iPad, iPod Touch, Android

With Rick whispering in your ear, Europe gets even better.

Find out more at ricksteves.com

Join a Rick Steves tour

Enjoy Europe's warmest welcome... with the flexibility and friendship of a small group getting to know Rick's favorite places and people. It all starts with our free tour catalog and DVD.

Great guides, small groups, no grumps.

▶ Explore Europe

Browse thousands of articles, video clips, photos and radio interviews, plus find a wealth of money-saving tips for planning your dream trip. You'll find up-to-date information on Europe's best destinations, packing smart, getting around, finding rooms, staying healthy, avoiding scams and more.

▶ Travel News

Subscribe to our free Travel News e-newsletter, and get monthly updates from Rick on what's happening in Europe!

▶ Travel Forums

Learn, ask, share—our online community of savvy travelers is a great resource for first-time travelers to Europe, as well as seasoned pros.

Rick Steves' Europe Through the Back Door, Inc

Rick Steves.

www.ricksteves.com

Rick Steves guidebooks are published by Avalon Travel,
a member of the Perseus Books Group.

NOW AVAILABLE:
eBOOKS, DVD & BLU-RAY

TRAVEL CULTURE

Europe 101
European Christmas
Postcards from Europe
Travel as a Political Act

eBOOKS

*Nearly all Rick Steves guides
are available as eBooks. Check
with your favorite bookseller.*

RICK STEVES' EUROPE DVDs

10 New Shows 2011–2012
Austria & the Alps
Eastern Europe
England & Wales
European Christmas
European Travel Skills & Specials
France
Germany, BeNeLux & More
Greece & Turkey
Iran
Ireland & Scotland
Italy's Cities
Italy's Countryside
Scandinavia
Spain
Travel Extras

BLU-RAY

Celtic Charms
Eastern Europe Favorites
European Christmas
Italy Through the Back Door
Mediterranean Mosaic
Surprising Cities of Europe

PHRASE BOOKS & DICTIONARIES

French
French, Italian & German
German
Italian
Portuguese
Spanish

JOURNALS

Rick Steves' Pocket Travel Journal
Rick Steves' Travel Journal

PLANNING MAPS

Britain, Ireland & London
Europe
France & Paris
Germany, Austria & Switzerland
Ireland
Italy
Spain & Portugal

Credits

Contributors
Gene Openshaw

Gene is a writer, composer, and lecturer on art and history. Specializing in writing walking tours of Europe's cultural sights, Gene has co-authored 10 of Rick's books and contributes to Rick's public television series. When not traveling, Gene enjoys composing music, recovering from his 1973 trip to Europe with Rick, and living everyday life with his daughter.

Steve Smith

Steve manages tour planning for Rick Steves' Europe Through the Back Door and co-authors the France guidebooks with Rick. Fluent in French, he's lived in France on several occasions, starting when he was seven, and has traveled there annually since 1986.

Researchers
Mary Bouron

Mary caught the travel bug as a child living in London, and later, as an exchange student in France. Born a Seattleite, Mary now confidently calls herself a Parisian. Deeply in love with a Frenchman, and a mother of two, she occupies her free time hunting for the city's best baguette and digging at the root causes of Franco-American cultural miscommunications.

Amanda Buttinger

Amanda moved to Madrid in 1998, thinking she'd be there a year. Since then she's found many reasons to stay, from learning more Spanish to guiding and travel writing to the best of all—sunny city walks with her dog and her boys.

Ben Cameron

Ben experienced his first taste of European travel when he was three, exploring medieval castles with his parents. Returning after graduation, he was hooked and has spent much of his time since exploring Europe independently and leading tours for Rick Steves. When not living out of his backpack, Ben splits his time between Rome and Seattle.

Brian Cotlove

A native of Seattle, Brian moved to France to immerse himself in the language, but stayed for the food and wine. When he's not doing research for Rick Steves, Brian can be found in Aix-en-Provence with his company, WineInProvence, helping tourists discover the best of Provence's food and wine culture.

Tom Griffin

Tom edits and researches guidebooks for Rick Steves. As a young lad, he acquired an affinity for Dutch and Belgian culture, thanks to Paul Verhoeven movies, Belgian chocolate, and his dad's war stories about the Battle of the Bulge. Tom has lived and worked in London, Paris, and Germany, and now makes his home in Seattle with his wife Julie.

Cameron Hewitt

Cameron writes and edits guidebooks for Rick Steves, specializing in Eastern Europe. For this book, Cameron updated the chapters on London, Florence, and Barcelona. He lives in Seattle with his wife Shawna.

Marijan Krišković

Born and raised in Slovenia and Croatia, Marijan got hooked on *Kaffee und Kuchen* (coffee and dessert) while visiting German relatives. He lives in Ljubljana with his wife, Barbara, and cat, John Travolta III. Whether leading a Rick Steves tour or at home, Marijan is probably drinking *Kaffee* and eating *Kuchen* right now.

Kristen Kusnic Michel

Kristen, a native of Seattle, first came to Europe as an exchange student, studying theater. Years later, she is fluent in French, German, red wine, and dark chocolate. For the last decade, she's been leading tours and researching guidebooks for Rick Steves. She lives in Paris with her husband, Sylvain.

Sarah Murdoch
Sarah has spent most of her adult life split between the US and Italy, ever since studying architecture in Rome during college. She is passionate about history, art, and pistachio gelato. When she isn't researching guidebooks or leading tours, she lives in Seattle with her patient husband Patrick and sons Lucca and Nicola.

Ian Watson
Ian has worked with Rick's guidebooks since 1993, after starting out with Let's Go and Frommer's guides. Originally from upstate New York, Ian speaks several European languages, including German, and makes his home in Reykjavík, Iceland.

Kevin Williams
Kevin has always felt at home in Germany, where he enjoys carnivorous meals, delicious beer, and skilled *Fussball*. When he isn't savoring *Weisswurst* and beer from a stein, he can be found assisting on a Rick Steves tour or answering travel questions at Rick's Travel Center in Edmonds, WA.

Chapter Images

Location	Photographer
Introduction	
Gondolas in Venice	Dominic Bonuccelli
Austria	
Full-page image:	
Vienna—St. Peter's Church	Cameron Hewitt
Vienna—Belvedere Palace Grounds	Cameron Hewitt
Salzburg	Gretchen Strauch
Hallstatt	Gretchen Strauch
Belgium	
Full-page image:	
Bruges Market Square	Cameron Hewitt
Bruges Canal	Dominic Bonuccelli

France
Full-page image:
    Paris—Venus de Milo,
Louvre Museum — Rob Unck
Paris—The Seine — Ben Cameron
Provence—Pont du Gard — Rick Steves
The French Riviera—Nice — Cameron Hewitt

Germany
Full-page image:
    Munich—Marienplatz — Cameron Hewitt
Bavaria—Neuschwanstein Castle — Dominic Bonuccelli
Rothenburg — Ben Cameron
Rhine River — Dominic Bonuccelli
Berlin—Gendarmenmarkt — Cameron Hewitt

Great Britain
Full-page image:
    London's British Museum — Rick Steves
London—Houses of Parliament — Rick Steves

Italy
Full-page image:
    Florence—Michelangelo's David — Rick Steves
Rome—Forum — Ben Cameron
Venice—Gondolier — Dominic Bonuccelli
Florence—Ponte Vecchio — Ben Cameron
The Cinque Terre—Vernazza — Dominic Bonuccelli

Netherlands
Full-page image:
    Amsterdam — Rick Steves
Amsterdam—Canal — Rick Steves
Haarlem—Canal — Gretchen Strauch

Spain
Full-page image:
    Casa Mila, Barcelona — Cameron Hewitt
Barcelona—Catalan Art Museum — Cameron Hewitt

Switzerland
Full-page image:
    Gimmelwald — Dominic Bonuccelli
Gimmelwald — Cameron Hewitt

Avalon Travel
a member of the Perseus Books Group
1700 Fourth Street
Berkeley, CA 94710, USA

For the latest on Rick's lectures, guidebooks, tours, public radio show, and public television series, contact Europe Through the Back Door, Box 2009, Edmonds, WA 98020, 425/771-8303, fax 425/771-0833, www.ricksteves.com, rick@ricksteves.com.

ISBN: 978-1-61238-661-4
ISSN: 1096-7702

Europe Through the Back Door
Managing Editor: Risa Laib
Editors: Jennifer Madison Davis, Glenn Eriksen, Tom Griffin, Cameron Hewitt, Suzanne Kotz, Cathy Lu, John Pierce, Carrie Shepherd, Gretchen Strauch
Maps & Graphics: David C. Hoerlein, Twozdai Hulse, Lauren Mills, Laura VanDeventer, Dawn Tessman Visser

Avalon Travel
Senior Editor and Series Manager: Madhu Prasher
Editor: Jamie Andrade
Associate Editor: Nikki Ioakimedes
Proofreader: Suzie Nasol
Indexer: Stephen Callahan
Cover Design: Kimberly Glyder Design
Maps & Graphics: Kat Bennett, Mike Morgenfeld, Brice Ticen

Front Matter Color Photos: Page i: Reichstag Dome, Berlin © Laura VanDeventer
Front Cover Photo: Saône River Pont St Laurent Mâcon Saône et Loire Bourgogne France © CW Images / Alamy

ABOUT THE AUTHOR

RICK STEVES

Since 1973, Rick Steves has spent 100 days every year exploring Europe. Along with writing and researching a bestselling series of guidebooks, Rick produces a public television series *(Rick Steves' Europe)*, a public radio show *(Travel with Rick Steves)*, and an app and podcast *(Rick Steves Audio Europe)*; writes a nationally syndicated newspaper column; organizes guided tours that take over then thousand travelers to Europe annually; and offers an information-packed website (www.ricksteves.com). With the help of his hardworking staff of 80 at Europe Through the Back Door—in Edmonds, Washington, just north of Seattle—Rick's mission is to make European travel fun, affordable, and culturally enlightening for Americans.

Connect with Rick:

 facebook.com/RickSteves   twitter: @RickSteves